ELEVENTH
EDITION

Dynamic Physical Education

for Elementary School Children

Robert P. Pangrazi
Arizona State University

Victor P. Dauer
Professor Emeritus
Washington State University

ALLYN AND BACON
Boston   London   Toronto   Sydney   Tokyo   Singapore

Editor: Ann Castel Davis
Developmental Editor: Erin Haggerty
Production Editor: Sheryl Glicker Langner
Photo Editor: Anne Vega
Text and Cover Designer: Jill Bonar
Production Manager: Pamela D. Bennett
Illustrations: Steve Botts

Copyright © 1995 by Allyn and Bacon
A Division of Simon & Schuster, Inc.
160 Gould Street
Needham Heights, Massachusetts 02194

Library of Congress Cataloging-in-Publication Data

Pangrazi, Robert P.
    Dynamic physical education for elementary school
children / Robert P. Pangrazi, Victor P. Dauer.—11th ed.
      p. cm.
    Includes bibliographical references and index.
    ISBN 0-02-390691-X
    1. Physical education for children—United States. 2.
Physical education for children—United States—
Curricula. 3. Physical education for children—Study and
teaching—United States. 4. Child development—United
States. I. Dauer, Victor Paul.
II. Title.
GV443.P344   1995
372.86—dc20
                                                        94-316
                                                          CIP

Printed in the United States of America

10 9 8 7 6 5 4   98 97

This book is dedicated with love and respect to my wife, Debbie. She is not only a valued professional colleague, but a special friend.

Robert P. Pangrazi

To my wife, Alice, whose help, inspiration, and encouragement have been of inestimable value in the writing of this book and its revisions.

Victor P. Dauer

Brief Contents

Contents

vii

7

Effective Management and Discipline Techniques 123

8

Children with Disabilities 145

9

Legal Liability and Proper Care of Students 183

16

Rhythmic Movement 355

17

Activities for Developing Manipulative Skills 407

Preface

The latest edition of *Dynamic Physical Education for Elementary School Students (DPE)* continues to change as the field of physical education evolves. The text still offers the broadest and most complete range of activities. Additional activities have been added as new ideas and knowledge have emerged. The dual approach of offering sound instructional methodology and skill development activities has been further strengthened. Management strategies, discipline, safety and liability, planning, and curriculum development have received even greater emphasis.

DPE has been designed for classroom teachers and physical education teachers; it is a text that makes it easy to translate conceptual information into a full implemented program. All activities in the text are listed in progression (order of difficulty). This enables teachers to plan a lesson that incorporates proper sequencing of skills. The accompanying text, *Lesson Plans for Dynamic Physical Education for Elementary School Children*, 11th edition, incorporates the activities listed in *DPE* and organizes them into a sequential set of lesson plans for the academic year. *DPE* and *Lesson Plans* are used in a large number of school districts throughout the world (including the worldwide network of Department of Defense Depen-

dents Schools) to guide basic instruction, which is supplemented by materials and activities that meet local desires and needs.

ELEVENTH EDITION REVISIONS

The text has been rewritten to make it more concise and compact. New approaches and information have been added to keep it abreast of changes in elementary school physical education. The material flows in a systematic and logical manner; continued emphasis is placed on proper teaching techniques while maintaining personal styles of instruction.

Some of the major changes made to the text for this edition follow: Chapter 1 has added new information related to objectives of a physical education program. A new table clearly indicates the broad and specific objectives of physical education programs. New information on the outcomes and benchmarks of physical education as defined by AAHPERD are listed. In addition, developmentally appropriate practices as defined by COPEC have been covered in this chapter. Up-to-date references give students a global and quick overview of physical education in the elementary school.

Chapter 2 has been expanded and updated to include the most recent research related to children. Not only does this chapter cover the growth and development of children, it offers program implications for such patterns of maturity. Current guidelines for exercising children in heat, weight lifting, distance running, and fitness testing safety reflect current research and recommendations.

Chapter 3 offers new information related to motor learning and children. Practical applications of motor learning principles for enhancing skill development in all children are offered. Knowledge of performance and knowledge of results as it applies to novice learners is now covered in detail. In addition, motor development has been given greater coverage to help teachers understand when children are developmentally ready to learn. Intrinsic and extrinsic feedback, random practice, variable practice, and transfer of learning are topics that have been added to this chapter.

Chapters 4 through 7 have been rewritten to make the material more applicable for classroom and physical education teachers. Practical matters such as how to schedule physical education in a school setting, goal structuring, and essential elements of instruction receive in-depth coverage. The application of outcomes-based instruction to physical education is discussed, as it is receiving renewed emphasis in some parts of the country. Cooperative learning and strategies for using it in physical education are included in Chapter 5. A chapter that has received strong support is Chapter 7; using management and discipline techniques. This chapter is important to both beginning and experienced teachers as it offers positive methods for modifying and dealing with a wide range of student behaviors. New discipline strategies have been offered for establishing procedures before the school year begins, establishing respect and rapport during the first weeks of school, and maintaining desired behavior on a continuing basis. Suggestions are offered on how to deal with different scenarios and suggested solutions are included. Learning to manage a class in an activity setting teaches students self-discipline skills while enjoying the benefits of movement.

The discussion of negligence in Chapter 9 has been articulated in terms that are easier for teachers to understand. Understanding the legal ramifications of transporting students to facilities and events is included so teachers know their limits and liability. Guidelines for supervision have been added so teachers know what they need to do to avoid legal problems. The best solution to this concern is to practice proper safety procedures and to follow guidelines for minimizing personal liability; both areas are discussed in detail.

Chapter 10 has been rewritten to include a discussion of process versus product in elementary school physical education. Key points are covered to help teachers understand how their stand on this issue will effect their instructional approach. A new section on grading has been added to help teachers deal with this time-consuming issue. Arguments for and against grading are offered so new teachers can develop a perspective on this procedure. Suggestions for implementing some type of evaluative approach are listed.

The chapter on physical fitness (13) has been expanded to include the explosion of knowledge in this area. The difference between skill-related and health-related fitness is discussed in detail. Criterion-referenced health standards reflect the latest thinking in fitness testing and are explained so teachers can understand this new approach. The new Fitnessgram test is described so teachers are aware of the latest approach to health evaluation. An important issue for teachers is to understand the fitness status of American children. A new, in-depth discussion helps teachers comprehend why it is unreasonable to expect all children to perform similar workloads. Factors such as genetics, trainability, and environmental effects are covered so teachers are sensitive to the dramatic differences in capability of youngsters. New thinking on the issue of activity versus fitness is offered. Finally, actual fitness activities have been added to an already comprehensive list of fitness routines.

Chapters 14 and 15 have been rewritten to help teachers understand how students learn basic skills. Chapter 14 offers movement themes designed to teach movement concepts. Emphasis is placed on learning about the classification and vocabulary of movement. In Chapter 15, fundamental skills are taught, with greater emphasis given to correct technique and mastery. Locomotor, non-locomotor, and manipulative skills are covered with stress points, teaching cues, and suggested activities offered for each of the skills. These chapters assure that students learn about movement and how to move.

The activities and sports chapters (16–31) have been augmented with new ideas and activities. In addition, instructional cues have been added and highlighted to help teachers see what key points of instruction should be covered. This helps assure that students will learn to perform skills in a technically correct manner. The activities in these chapters are written in sequence of easy to most difficult. This is particularly important for classroom teachers who are unsure of the proper progression of skill development. The activities are listed by developmental level so teachers can better select activities that are appropriate for the maturity of students.

A new section has been added to Chapter 32. Many requests were received asking for ideas on integrating subject matter and activity. Specific ideas are given for integrating activity into a wide variety of subjects from art to mathematics.

Quality Control and Field Testing

A tradition that continues in this edition of DPE is to include only activities that have been field tested with children. Dr. Pangrazi continues to teach elementary school children and evaluate new activities based in part on student reception and instructional effectiveness. A number of experts have been involved, ensuring that the content of DPE is accurate and on the cutting edge. Chapter 16, "Rhythmic Movement," was enhanced by Mr. Jerry Poppen, supervisor of physical education for the Tacoma public schools; Mr. Bob Ruff, Wagon Wheel Records; and Ms. Debbie Pangrazi, physical education teacher for the Mesa public schools. Chapter 20 on stunts and tumbling was evaluated by Mr. John Spini, current coach of the Women's Gymnastic Team at Arizona State University. Dr. Carole Casten, University of California, Dominguez Hills, contributed the material for the section on rhythmic gymnastics. Dr. Virginia Atkins Chadwick, Fresno State University, and Dr. Julian Stein, George Mason University, evaluated and contributed to Chapter 8, "Children with Disabilities."

In addition, the authors are indebted to the Mesa School District elementary school physical education specialists in Mesa, Arizona, who have field tested all activities and offered numerous suggestions and ideas for improvement. This stellar group of nearly 70 specialists is led by Dr. Gene Petersen, supervisor. All of these individuals have unselfishly contributed their energies and insights to assure that quality activities and teaching strategies are part of this textbook. The result of this continued field testing is a book filled with activities, strategies, and techniques that *work*.

ORGANIZATION OF THE TEXT

The text is organized to facilitate a logical instructional approach. The opening chapter has been rewritten to include an in-depth discussion of the objectives of physical education, a recent history of elementary school physical education, and important trends and issues that have affected physical education. Following chapters deal with the impact of activity on youngsters and the essentials of movement learning, so that the basis and need for a comprehensive physical education program is clearly established.

Chapters 4 through 7 focus on developing a physical education curriculum, planning for quality instruction, and establishing an effective instructional delivery system. Class management and discipline strategies are offered early in the book so teachers can deal with this area of special concern. Later chapters proffer information needed for teaching children with disabilities, understanding liability, instructional evaluation, and teaching for wellness. With this requisite knowledge at hand, future teachers should be ready to practice instructing children. The remaining chapters are filled with activities that can be used during actual instruction. Not only is the text a guide to teaching, it is a resource of activities that can be used with children of all ages.

SUPPLEMENTARY MATERIALS

The eleventh edition of Lesson Plans for Dynamic Physical Education has been developed concurrently with the text. The plans offer a range of activities and objectives. The lesson plans are presented in three developmental levels, allowing for a greater range of activity and ensuring that presentations are closely aligned to the maturity and experience of students. The plans are filled with activities and instructional objectives to enable teachers to plan and understand *why* various activities are being taught. Offering a framework for planning comprehensive lessons rather than serving to preempt teachers from planning duties is the major reason for utilizing accompanying lesson plans. There is *no* substitute for planning, and this should always be done by the teacher *prior* to the actual presentation of the lesson.

A new edition of the Instructional Resource Materials Package accompanies the text and is available to adopters. Test questions have been expanded and the overhead transparency masters have been revised so they are easier to use. A set of color transparency acetates is a part of the resource materials package.

A complete video program is available to adopters of DPE. Through an exclusive arrangement with the Cable News Network (CNN) a new, specially edited videotape culled from relevant

CNN programs provides an exciting means for enhancing classroom discussion.

Also available is a videotape that illustrates various concepts described in *DPE*. Another video offers two discussions by Dr. Pangrazi, the first a 45-minute discussion on the importance of planning, and the other about the role of physical education in developing healthy children. A fourth videotape covers two sample lessons with children (second and fifth grade) and explains the parts of a lesson and instructional techniques. Computer software for evaluating health-related physical fitness, wellness, and instructional effectiveness of teachers is available.

This package of supplementary materials offers university and college instructors an integrated and comprehensive set of instructional tools. It is available to college instructors who have adopted the *DPE* textbook for use in their classes and may be ordered through Allyn & Bacon sales representatives.

Useful textbooks are the result of cohesive teamwork among the publishing company, reviewers, and the authors. Special thanks go to the following reviewers who helped guide the authors' efforts: Rex B. Brown, Southwest Baptist University; Shan Bumgarner, The Ohio State University; Robert E. Gensemer, Edinboro University of PA; and Steve Moyer, Eastern Michigan University. We are indebted to the professional group at Macmillan for the major contributions they made to this text. Ann Castel Davis, administrative editor, has given ongoing support and encouragement and demonstrated a consistent vision of excellence. Sheryl Langner, production editor, has coordinated development and completion of this text with efficiency and thoughtfulness. The careful and perceptive editing of Robert Marcum, freelance copyeditor, has added to the clarity and conciseness of the text. To these and many other individuals at Macmillan who go unnamed, we give a hearty thank you.

Introduction to Elementary School Physical Education

WHAT IS PHYSICAL EDUCATION?

Physical education is a part of the total educational program that contributes, primarily through movement experiences, to the total growth and development of all children. *Physical education* is defined as education through movement. It should be an instructional program that gives attention to all learning domains—psychomotor, cognitive, and affective. Three outcomes of physical education are unique. The first outcome is the achievement of a personalized physical fitness level. Second is the development of competency in a variety of physical skills to assure that students can function effectively in selected physical activities. The third outcome demands that students acquire requisite knowledge related to motor skill performance and fitness maintenance. Should these outcomes not be accomplished in physical education classes, they will not be realized elsewhere in the curriculum.

THE GENERAL GOAL OF PHYSICAL EDUCATION

The general goal of physical education is to help individuals achieve optimum personal development and contribute to the goals of society. The importance

Learning about flexibility—A fitness outcome

of physical activity in developing a healthy lifestyle must be understood by society and its children. The vitality of a country is directly related to the fitness and energy of its citizens. The concept of dualism, "healthy mind in a healthy body," can be accomplished when citizens understand the importance of a quality physical education program for youngsters. The academic areas of the school curriculum cannot contribute to the fitness and physical skill development of students. If physical education does not produce physically educated students, no other area of the school curriculum can rectify this shortcoming.

OBJECTIVES OF PHYSICAL EDUCATION

Program objectives are the framework of the program; they determine the focus and direction of the physical education program. Accomplishment of objectives must make a significant contribution to the overall goals of school and American society— the development of a well-rounded individual capable of contributing to a democratic society. Quality programs are driven by objectives and move children toward high-level achievement. Two major types of objectives are used to guide physical education programs. *Institutional* objectives determine the direction and focus of the program and give instructors a constant and clear direction for instruction. Institutional objectives determine the content and focus of a physical education program. *Student-centered* objectives provide children with target goals to be accomplished (see pp. 65–66 for examples) and are written after institutional objectives have been determined. This textbook is given

direction by the five major objectives listed in Figure 1.1. The discussion that follows explains each of the objectives in detail.

Motor Skills and Movement Competence

Objective: The physical education program will help children become competent in a variety of motor skills and movements.

All people would like to be skilled and competent in the area of motor performance. The elementary school years are an excellent time to teach motor skills because children have the time and predisposition to learn. The range of skills presented in physical education should be unlimited; youngsters must have the opportunity to encounter and learn all physical skills. Because youngsters vary in genetic endowment and interest, it is important that they have the opportunity to learn about their abilities in all types of skills. The hierarchy of skill development progresses from fundamental motor skills to specialized skills. Components of motor skill development and movement competence follow.

Fundamental Motor Skills

Fundamental skills are those utilitarian skills that children use to enhance the quality of life. This group of skills is sometimes labeled *basic* or *functional.* The designation *fundamental skills* is used in this text because these skills are basic attributes that help children function in the environment. These skills are divided into three categories— locomotor, nonlocomotor, and manipulative.

Locomotor Skills

Locomotor skills are used to move the body from one place to another or to project the body upward, as in jumping and hopping. They also include walking, running, skipping, leaping, sliding, and galloping.

Nonlocomotor Skills

Nonlocomotor skills are performed in place, without appreciable spatial movement. These skills are not as well defined as locomotor skills. They include bending and stretching, pushing and pulling, raising and lowering, twisting and turning, shaking, bouncing, circling, and others.

Manipulative Skills

Manipulative skills are developed when the child handles some kind of object. Most of these skills

I. MOTOR SKILLS AND MOVEMENT COMPETENCE

Fundamental Motor Skills

Locomotor Skills	Nonlocomotor Skills	Manipulative Skills
Walking	Bending	Striking
Running	Twisting	Rolling
Hopping	Turning	Kicking
Skipping	Rocking/Swaying	Catching
Jumping	Balancing	Bouncing
Leaping	Stretching	Trapping
Sliding	Pushing	Throwing
Galloping	Pulling	

Movement Concepts Skills

Body awareness
Space awareness
Qualities of movement
Relationships

Rhythmic Movement Skills

Performance of motor skills in a rhythmic manner

Specialized Motor Skills

Specific skills used in sports, stunts and tumbling, apparatus, and specialized manipulative activities such as rope jumping

II. HEALTH-RELATED PHYSICAL FITNESS AND WELLNESS

Knowledge of health-related fitness components
Ability to do fitness self-testing
Participation in regular fitness activity
Identification of personalized fitness activities
Understanding of wellness components

Figure 1.1 Objectives of physical education

involve the hands and feet, but other parts of the body can also be used. Manipulation of objects leads to better hand-eye and foot-eye coordination, which are particularly important for tracking items in space. Manipulative skills form the basis of many game skills. Propulsion (throwing, striking, kicking) and receipt (catching) of objects are important skills that can be taught by using beanbags and various balls. Rebounding or redirecting an object in flight (such as a volleyball) is another useful manipulative skill. Continuous control of an object, such as a wand or a hoop, is also a manipulative activity.

Movement Concepts Skills

Youngsters need to learn about the classification of movement concepts, which includes body awareness, space awareness, qualities of movement, and relationships. It is not enough to learn only the fundamental skills; youngsters need to perform these skills in a variety of settings. For example, children are asked to run in different fashion, in different directions, at different levels, and along different pathways. They learn to move slowly or quickly or to make a series of strong movements.

III. HUMAN MOVEMENT PRINCIPLES

Know basic kinesiological principles including stability, force, and leverage.

Understand elementary principles of physiology including body composition, training zone, and strength development.

IV. SOCIAL SKILLS AND POSITIVE SELF-CONCEPT

Develop interactive skills including the ability to lead and follow, develop decision making skills, and exchange ideas with other students.

Acquire cooperative skills such as following directions, accepting individual differences, and the ability to be a member of a team.

Exhibit sportsmanship behavior including a sense of fair play, self-discipline, and winning and losing with dignity.

V. LIFETIME PARTICIPATION IN ACTIVITY

Develop competency in a variety of specialized motor skills.

Participate in activities that are suited to personal competencies.

Understand the social and physical benefits of lifetime activity.

Figure 1.1 *continued*

This objective shows children how movement concepts are classified. Movement themes form the foundation of movement experiences necessary for developing specific fundamental skills. Through this process, children develop an increased awareness and understanding of the body as a vehicle for movement, and for the acquisition of a personal vocabulary of movement skills.

Rhythmic Movement Skills

Individuals who excel in movement activities possess a strong sense of rhythmic ability. *Rhythmic movement* involves motion that possesses regularity and a predictable pattern. The aptitude to move rhythmically is basic to skill performance in all areas. A rhythmic program that includes dance,

Developing manipulative skills

Learning body management skills

rope jumping, and rhythmic gymnastics offers a variety of activities to help attain this objective.

Specialized Motor Skills

Specialized skills are used in various sports and other areas of physical education, including apparatus activities, tumbling, dance, and specific games. Specialized skills receive increased emphasis beginning with developmental level II activities. In developing specialized skills, progression is attained through planned instruction and drills. Many of these skills have critical points of technique, and teaching emphasizes correct performance.

Health-Related Physical Fitness and Wellness

Objective: The physical education program will provide children an opportunity to participate in activities designed to develop and maintain health-related physical fitness commensurate with individual needs. Students will also develop an understanding of how to maintain adequate fitness and wellness throughout life.

Physical education programs must provide children with the opportunity to participate in regular physical activity. The focus of the physical fitness component in a lesson must be on the process of activity rather than the product of fitness, i.e., how many, how fast, or how far. Students need the opportunity to offer input about the fitness program and to be able to make activity choices. When students become responsible for participating in regular activity, whether at school or home, physical fitness objectives will be accomplished.

A portion of each class period should be allotted to fitness activities. Physical fitness must be experiential—students must participate in fitness activity to learn what is necessary for fitness enhancement. It is not enough to learn facts about fitness; it must be a participatory experience in the elementary school years. Many people know the facts about fitness but have not learned the habit of participating in regular activity. This is not to say that knowledge is unimportant, but rather that regular participation in activity designed to promote fitness should be the priority in the elementary school years. Positive experiences in fitness activity can help students develop attitudes that ensure they will be active adults. What is gained if students develop high physical fitness levels in the elementary school years but leave school with a strong dislike of physical activity? Establishing the desire in children to maintain fitness and wellness

Motivating children to move

throughout their adult years should be emphasized by elementary school physical education teachers.

Human Movement Principles

Objective: Children will experience a broad variety of movement activities and develop an understanding of movement principles. Youngsters will develop an understanding of their strengths and limitations in the motor performance arena and know how to select activities that assure their safety.

The elementary school years should be the years of opportunity—the opportunity to experience many different types of physical activity. The curriculum should be expansive rather than restrictive. It should allow students to better understand their strengths and limitations and to learn what types of activities they prefer or dislike. Related to this experience is the opportunity to learn basic concepts of movement. Students should leave the elementary school years knowing about stability, force, leverage, and other factors related to efficient movement. Understanding the genetic diversity among people such as in muscle type, cardiorespiratory endurance, and motor coordination is requisite for helping students evaluate their physical capabilities.

A body of knowledge related to human movement and performance has been defined by the National Association for Sport and Physical Education (NASPE) and published in a series of educational materials, titled *Basic Stuff* (1987). This series offers teachers a number of strategies for helping children understand the basic principles of human movement.

Learning to cooperate with others

Related to understanding principles of human movement is knowing how to safely participate in activity. The school has both a legal and a moral obligation to provide a safe environment. Safety must be actively taught, and activities conducted in a safe environment. Instructional procedures in any activity must pay attention to safety factors, and active supervision is necessary to guide children in safe participation.

Social Skills and Positive Self-Concept

Objective: *The physical education environment will help children acquire desirable social standards and ethical concepts. In addition, physical education instruction will offer experiences that help children develop a positive self-concept.*

Physical education classes should offer an environment of effective social living. Children need to internalize and understand the merits of participation, cooperation, competition, and tolerance. Some terms, such as *good citizenship* and *fair play,* help define the desired social atmosphere. The teacher, through listening, empathy, and guidance, helps children differentiate between acceptable and unacceptable ways of expressing feelings. Youngsters should develop an awareness of how they interact with others, and how the quality of

their behavior influences others' response to them. If students do not receive feedback about negative behavior from teachers and peers, they may not perceive behaviors that are strongly resented by others. Teachers need to establish reasonable limits of acceptable behavior and enforce those limits consistently.

It is important for children to learn the value of cooperation. Cooperation precedes the development of competition and should be emphasized in the school setting. If people did not cooperate, competitive games could not be played. The nature of competitive games demands cooperation, fair play, and sportsmanship, and when these are not present, the joy of participation is lost. Cooperative games teach children that all participants are needed. As the nature of competition comes into clearer focus, teachers must help students temper the urge to win at all costs and come to the realization that not all participants can be winners.

The hidden curriculum (Bain, 1975) has a strong impact on development of the self-concept. How the lesson is organized, the types of activities presented, how teachers view students who are less successful, and how children with disabilities are treated send implied messages to students. How teachers and parents respond to children communicates to youngsters that they are loved, capable, and contributing people. On the other hand, teachers and parents can give children negative messages that they are incapable of learning and are incompetent performers. Not only must teachers understand learners, but students should understand themselves, for self-understanding has a powerful influence on human behavior. The self-concept that a child develops is vital to the learning process. It can make learning possible, or it can hinder or block the ability to learn. If children believe that they belong, that they are loved and respected, and that their successes outweigh their failures, they are well on the way to establishing a desirable self-concept. Instruction should focus on a student's strong points rather than weaknesses. Students need to learn how to accept positive feedback from peers, instead of discounting it.

The ability to move with grace, confidence, and ease helps children regard themselves in a favorable light. Achieving self-satisfying levels of skill competency and fitness can also make students feel positive and assured. The self-concept is related to perceived physical skill competence. If students perceive themselves to be competent in an activity setting, they will want to participate in activity outside the school setting. On the other hand, if they are made to feel incompetent, they will avoid activity at all costs in an attempt to maintain their self-esteem.

Lifetime Participation in Activity

Objective: Through physical education, children will learn physical skills that allow them to participate in and enjoy physical activity throughout their adult years.

The basic considerations for lifetime activity are several. First, children must derive enjoyment through activity so they will seek further participation. To this end, children must become proficient in a variety of motor skills. Most adults will not participate in activities unless they have an adequate level of perceived competence. Because learning new motor skills takes a great deal of time and repetition, adulthood often prohibits busy adults from developing a level of skill competence to assure play without embarrassment.

Second, children need a rational basis for play. This can be established through activity orientations that can be transferred to other situations. Such activities should include a variety of games suitable for small groups and sport activities adapted to local situations. Third, children need to learn the social benefits of activity and to experience appropriate

options. Including fitness practice as a part of leisure activity is essential. Jogging and walking should be encouraged, since these are valuable both as personal and as family activities.

The burden of providing a broad orientation to skills, games, and fitness activities falls on the elementary school program. Less required physical education and more choices and options for meeting activity requirements (band, cheer squad, etc.) make it possible to complete high school with few opportunities for learning recreational skills. Preparation in and orientation to many different activities during the elementary school years can provide a background to help students make choices for a lifetime of recreational enjoyment.

THE EVOLUTION OF ELEMENTARY SCHOOL PHYSICAL EDUCATION

A number of concerns, events, and professional organizations have had a significant impact on elementary school physical education programs. Often these programs are created as responses to events that are publicized by the press and other interested parties. The many changes that have occurred in elementary school physical education programming clearly point out how the public's needs and concerns shape the direction of American education.

The German and Swedish Influence

During the nineteenth century, in both Germany and Sweden, physical education systems that centered on body development were established in the schools. Around the middle of the century, German and Swedish immigrants to the United States introduced these concepts of physical education. The German system favored a gymnastic approach and required a good deal of equipment and special teachers. The Swedish system incorporated an exercise program in the activity presentations. The physical education program in many of the schools that adopted this system consisted of a series of structured exercises that children could perform in the classroom. The need for equipment and gymnasiums posed problems for the schools that followed these systems, and many economy-minded citizens questioned the programs. A combination of games and calisthenics evolved and became the first scheduled physical education activity offered in some U.S. schools. The Swedish system was structured and formal and often not suited to the needs of elementary school children.

Fitness and activity are for all children.

The Emphasis on Games and Sports

When about one-third of the American men drafted in World War I were rejected as physically unfit for military service, the result was a new demand for physical education in the schools. State educational authorities legislated minimum weekly time requirements for physical activity in school programs. In many states, these laws established physical education as part of the school curriculum. The laws were, however, quantitative in nature, and little attention was given to program quality.

Training programs designed for soldiers during World War I placed an emphasis on games and sports and proved more effective than strict calisthenics. This shift to the use of games and sports for physical development spawned school programs with similar emphasis. John Dewey, professor of philosophy at Columbia University, had a profound impact on educational theory during the mid twentieth century. When two of Dewey's cardinal aims of education stressed attention to physical activities, the development received impetus. These aims, the promotion of health and the worthy use of leisure time, became school curricular responsibilities. The school was deemed responsible for molding social change, and a high value was placed on games and sports.

Programs stressing sports and games appeared in the secondary schools. The elementary programs became diluted models of these secondary programs, and literally could have been described by answering the question, "What games are we going to play today?" During the Great Depression, equipment was difficult to secure, and

physical education teachers were almost nonexistent. Physical education was relegated to a minor role, and in many cases was eliminated entirely.

During World War II, many new training programs for special groups appeared. Research proved the efficacy of physical fitness development, hospital reconditioning programs, and other innovative approaches. An improvement in the quality of physical education programs might have been expected after the war, but unfortunately, little positive effect trickled down to elementary school programs.

Physical Fitness Testing and The President's Council

A renewed emphasis on fitness occurred in the 1950s, following the publication of comparative studies of fitness levels of U.S. and European children, which were based on the Kraus-Weber tests. A study by Dr. Hans Kraus (1954), comparing strength and flexibility measurements of 4,000 New York–area schoolchildren with a comparable sample of Central European children, had far-reaching results. The press became concerned about the comparative weakness of U.S. children, and as a consequence of this concern, the fitness movement was born. One result of the uproar was the establishment of the President's Council on Physical Fitness and Sports, an agency established to promote physical fitness, not only among schoolchildren, but also among citizens of all ages. Through its many publications, services, and promotions, the President's Council has worked to improve school fitness programs.

Movement Education

Movement education originated in England and was incorporated into American programs. At times, it was a revolt against structured fitness programs, which included calisthenics presented in a formal, command style. Unfortunately, the demanding fitness standards advocated by the President's Council caused some teachers to teach for fitness outcomes rather than present a balanced physical education program that also taught skills and concepts. This created a backlash among some physical educators, who felt that creativity, exploration, and cognition should also be focal points of the profession.

Movement education programs shifted some of the responsibility for learning to children. The methodology featured problem solving and an exploratory approach. Adopting movement education led to the rejection of physical fitness-oriented activities, especially calisthenics, which were labeled as "training" and not education. Controversy arose regarding the application of movement principles to the teaching of specific skills, particularly athletic skills. There was a tendency to apply the exploration methodology to all phases of instruction (i.e., the teaching of specific athletic skills) without examining the effectiveness of such practices. Regardless of the questions raised, movement education has resulted in expanded teaching methodology and increased emphasis on instruction that focuses on the individual child. In addition, movement education has offered an opportunity for diversity of movement through creative instructional methods, and allows students of all ability levels to find success.

Perceptual-Motor Programs

The focus of perceptual-motor programs was corrective in nature and related to remedying learning difficulties attributed to a breakdown in perceptual-motor development. Theorists held that children progressed through growth and developmental stages from head to foot (cephalocaudally) and from the center of the body outward (proximodistally) in an orderly fashion. When disruptions, lags, or omissions occurred in this process, certain underlying perceptual-motor bases failed to develop fully, and impaired the child's ability to function correctly in both the physical and the academic setting.

Perceptual-motor programs grew out of concern for the slow academic learner, sometimes called the slow child or the delayed learner. Some children identified as academically subpar demonstrated motor problems involving movement factors such as coordination, balance and postural control, image of the body and its parts, and relationships involving time and space. Perceptual-motor programs attempted to remediate these shortcomings and gave physical education teachers the hope that their profession would become a necessary part of the academic school curriculum. As researchers examined the effectiveness of such programs, it became apparent that perceptual-motor activities were unable to improve academic achievement. Today, the use of *perceptual-motor* to identify a unique program designed to replace the physical education program has diminished. The legacy of perceptual-motor programs in today's physical education programs is the integration of perceptual-motor principles in skill-learning sequences (i.e., using both sides of the body, practicing balance skills, etc.).

Conceptual Learning

Conceptual understanding (i.e., the application of abstract ideas drawn from experience) plays an important part in physical education. In the process of movement, the child learns to distinguish between near and far, strong and weak, light and heavy, and high and low. Physical education gives children the opportunity to experiment with and establish an understanding of such movement concepts.

NASPE has sponsored the development of the *Basic Stuff* series (1987), a compilation of current knowledge from the subdisciplines of physical education (exercise physiology, kinesiology, motor development, and motor learning). This series consists of nine booklets of information aimed at helping the physical educator incorporate knowledge concepts into the curriculum, grades K–12. This series serves as an excellent reference for teachers and helps delineate knowledge concepts that can be integrated into the physical education curriculum.

Conceptual learning should be an important part of a physical education program, but there must be a balance of both knowledge and physical skill development in the physical education curriculum. Many teachers believe that an academic approach focused on knowledge and cognitive growth instead of physical skill is a more respectable educational endeavor. Others believe that when student knowledge is increased, attitudes and behaviors will also change, causing physical activity to be incorporated into the student's lifestyle. Unfortunately, increasing a person's knowledge does not ensure a change in behavior. Students must also experience and learn physical skills as well as understand the conceptual components.

Value and Attitude Development (Affective Domain Learning)

Since the mid 1960s, many different approaches to values clarification and moral education have emerged. The political views of a number of America's leaders emphasizing law and order have created greater pressure on the schools to teach morals and values. In the annual Gallup Poll reviewing the public's attitudes toward public schools, lack of discipline often heads the list of major problems. Discipline problems also rank as one of the major concerns of teachers.

Values, feelings, beliefs, and judgments are receiving more attention in the schools and in physical education classes in particular. Firm guidelines for moral education have not been forthcoming, and school administrators are often hesitant to enter this domain. Such issues as alcohol and substance abuse, sex education, and AIDS awareness are being presented in the elementary school years to help prevent students from developing problems later in life. Awareness programs are becoming more common in schools and physical educators are often called upon to conduct appropriate district-approved programs.

Federal Mandates

From time to time, concerns of citizens have caused legislation to be passed. Two laws have had a continued, although fluctuating, impact on physical education programs at all levels.

Title IX: Equal Opportunity for the Sexes

Title IX of the Educational Amendments Act of 1972 has had a significant impact on most secondary school physical education programs. Title IX has had a lesser effect on elementary school physical education because the majority of programs at this level have long been coeducational. Title IX rules out any separation of sexes and calls for all offerings to be coeducational. The law is based on the principle that school activities and programs are of equal value for both sexes and that students should not be denied access to participation on the basis of sex. Legal ramifications have forced schools to provide equal access to physical education activi-

ties for both boys and girls. Organizing separate competitions for the sexes is permissible, provided that mixed participation in an activity can be determined to be hazardous. In principle, the law also means that instruction is provided by the most qualified teacher regardless of sex.

Title IX also relates to the elimination of sexism and sex-role typing. Human needs and opportunity must take precedence over the traditional sexual stereotypes of masculinity and femininity. Appreciation of the physical abilities of the opposite sex should be learned at an early age. Segregating children by sex in elementary school physical education classes is thus indefensible.

PL 94–142: Equal Rights for Students with Disabilities

Public Law 94–142 (and its 1990 amendments, PL 101–476) has given hope for a full education to the 3.5 to 4 million youngsters with disabilities in the United States. This federal law mandates that these youngsters have the right to a free and public education, and must be educated in the least restrictive educational environment possible. No longer can such children be assigned to segregated classes or schools unless a separate environment is determined by due process to be in the child's best interest.

The law has resulted in degrees of mainstreaming (full or partial), allowing many children with disabilities to participate in regular physical education classes. The law is commendable and morally sound and often necessitates changing the structure and educational procedures of the school as well as the viewpoints and attitudes of school personnel. Many teachers have neither the educational background, the experience, nor the inclination to handle children with disabilities in addition to children without disabilities. The answer is not to ignore the problem but to provide teachers with the knowledge and attitudes that will allow them to function successfully with children who have disabilities. If disabled children are to function in society when they become adults, they deserve and need the opportunity to participate with able youngsters.

In addition to the mainstreaming of students in normal classes, the law mandates the preparation of a specific learning program for each disabled student, called an individualized educational program (IEP). Establishing the child's due process committee, developing the IEP, and monitoring that program in the best interest of the student is a process of considerable challenge and magnitude. IEPs can be used for able children as well, and aid in making education more personal and individual.

Human Wellness and Healthful Living

Today's educators are centering increased attention on human wellness and healthful living. This focus is pushing physical educators to develop programs that teach more than fitness and skill activities. Wellness is a broader concept than being physically fit. It is a dynamic state of well-being, which implies living fully and deriving the most from life.

Teaching for wellness involves teaching concepts that help students develop an active lifestyle. Understanding of principles of fitness development and knowledge of the benefits of fitness help increase the possibility of students' maintaining lifetime fitness. In addition, students are taught what types of activities are useful for developing various fitness areas, and how to evaluate and prescribe activities for total body fitness. An understanding of mechanical principles underlying various movements accompanies movement patterns and skill-learning activities. Within the instructional framework, basic mechanical principles are related to movement patterns so that children can grasp the underlying basis of efficient movement.

Eating wisely, controlling weight, dealing with tension, understanding body (muscular) movement, getting sufficient rest and sleep, controlling posture, keeping in shape, and dealing with the forthcoming challenges facing youth (such as potential use of alcohol and drugs, and the danger of contracting AIDS or other infectious diseases) are necessary concerns for the physical educator. For example, the problem of weight control merits special attention in the elementary school. Unless lifestyle can be changed at an early age, obese children usually become obese adults. More attention is being devoted to posture and posture problems, and some states have instituted early screening to detect severe scoliosis (lateral curvature of the spine) and the recommendation of appropriate remedial treatment.

Human wellness is an area where physical education can have a lifelong impact on students. It is best handled when classroom teachers and physical education specialists work closely together. The common goal of wellness for all children should help physical education become an integral part of the total school curriculum.

The "Back-to-Basics" Schools

Basic schools were designed as a response to a perceived decline in academic performance. Basic schools stress discipline and cognitive learning, often at the expense of the arts and physical education. To increase academic rigor, the school day is lengthened and physical education and performing arts dropped to allow more time for "the 3 R's." A demand for uninterrupted academic time often makes it impossible to schedule physical education time for youngsters. To combat this trend, physical education programs must demonstrate that they are instructional in nature, of high quality, and make unique contributions to the school curriculum. In 1983, the National Commission on Excellence in Education presented a critical review of the total process of U.S. education in *A Nation at Risk* (Gardner, 1983). In the report, physical education was not included as part of a basic education. Whether the omission was deliberate or happenstance is open to question. In the past, other deliberations and reports have included physical education as a part of basic instruction. Is it possible that the school experiences of commission members in the physical education area were largely of an unorganized fun-and-games approach, and that they perceived little need for such recreation? This illustrates the importance of educating the public about the need for a quality physical education program in the quest to develop well-rounded students.

To conform to the concept of basic education, this text delineates fundamental target objectives expected to be accomplished in physical education at each developmental level. Child-centered outcomes are written in measurable terms so teachers and schools can be held accountable for helping students reach a predetermined level of achievement. Even though accountability is a desirable concept, some abuse can occur when teachers are rewarded based solely on student achievement levels. Some teachers may turn to the use of memorization, drill, and rote learning, and may encourage practice solely in areas in which students will be tested. In physical education, this often means teaching only fitness test activities so that students will score well on a mandated physical fitness test. This approach results in an inferior and narrow program that may satisfy the accountability concerns of the instructor but does little to give students a well-rounded education.

The Health-Related Fitness Resurgence

The fitness emphasis started by Kraus-Weber testing declined during the 1970s and early 1980s. However, due to recent fitness results reported nationally, physical fitness training for elementary school children is receiving renewed stress. A general consensus has developed favoring a health-based definition of physical fitness. While the development of physical skills is still considered an important objective for school physical education, test items that measure abilities such as throwing, jumping (leg power), and running (speed and agility) are not considered to be central components of health-related physical fitness. The current definition of fitness most often recognized by experts (Caspersen, Powell, & Christenson, 1985; Pate, 1988) includes those parts of fitness that relate to good health. Specifically, the essential components of physical fitness are cardiovascular fitness, flexibility, muscular strength/endurance, and body composition. Both the American College of Sports Medicine (1988) and the American Academy of Physical Education (1987) have endorsed health-related definitions of physical fitness.

The document, *Healthy People 2000: National Health Promotion and Disease Objectives* (U.S. Public Health Service, 1990) was released by the government as a strategy to improve the health of all Americans. A majority of the 300 target goals are specifically directed toward improving the health status of American children and youth. The goals focus on decreasing health risks and placing emphasis on preventative approaches to a healthy lifestyle. Several of the objectives in the physical activity and fitness area emphasize increasing the amount of time children age 6 and older participate in light to moderate activity (i.e., activity that promotes cardiorespiratory fitness, strength and endurance, and flexibility). Much of the emphasis on improving the health status of youth can be accomplished through improvement of school programs. Emphasis is placed on offering the health benefits of exercise and activity for all students as contrasted to systems that only reward students who are physically gifted.

The Fitnessgram System (Sterling, 1992) is a health-related fitness test that uses criterion-referenced standards related to health risks (see Chapter 13). The standards for the Fitnessgram System encourage children to score in the healthy fitness zone. If youngsters' scores are below the lower limit of the zone, the result may be an increased risk of hypokinetic disease. Scoring above the upper limit of the zone may cause an increased risk of injury and excessive dieting (trying to maintain a lean look). A fitness battery and awards system for primary- and intermediate-age youngsters has been developed that places emphasis on health-related fitness and regular participation in a variety of activities. This contrasts with other fitness programs that reward only elite performers, resulting in a lack of motivation among less able students.

Organizations Affecting Physical Education

Various professional organizations have had a strong effect on physical education over the past two decades.

The American Alliance for Health, Physical Education, Recreation and Dance (AAHPERD)

The American Alliance for Health, Physical Education, Recreation and Dance, through its section dealing with elementary school physical education, has had a marked influence nationally on elementary programs. AAHPERD delegates direction of elementary programs to the Council on Physical Education for Children (COPEC), a group of professionals with national area representation. COPEC has been active in producing publications and in scheduling conferences, workshops, and convention programs. AAHPERD publications provide national standards and shape program philosophy. Teacher-education institutions are given direction with a publication outlining suggested teacher-preparation guidelines.

A number of recent documents give excellent direction to teachers and future teachers for development of programs and writing outcomes. They have been published in small booklet form and offer practical and useful information. For teachers trying to shape a physical education program, *Guidelines for Elementary School Physical Education* (1988) is helpful. The booklet, developed by the National Association for Sport and Physical Education (NASPE), a member of AAHPERD, is a series of statements by professionals that serve as a guide for personnel who are responsible for developing a quality physical education program. Guidelines are offered for teacher preparation and staff development, the instructional program, evaluation, equipment and facilities, and school-related programs. The purpose of the booklet is to serve as a reference standard for all professionals involved in physical education programming.

The NASPE booklet, *Outcomes of Quality Physical Education Programs* (1992b), is useful for teachers designing and evaluating physical education programs. Twenty major outcomes for a physically educated person are listed under five categories covering the psychomotor, affective, and cognitive learning domains. These outcomes and categories are shown in Figure 1.2. In addition to the outcomes, specific student benchmarks are

A PHYSICALLY EDUCATED PERSON:

HAS learned skills necessary to perform a variety of physical activities

1. . . . moves using concepts of body awareness, space awareness, effort, and relationships.
2. . . . demonstrates competence in a variety of manipulative, locomotor, and non-locomotor skills.
3. . . . demonstrates competence in combinations of manipulative, locomotor, and non-locomotor skills performed individually and with others.
4. . . . demonstrates competence in many different forms of physical activity.
5. . . . demonstrates proficiency in a few forms of physical activity.
6. . . . has learned how to learn new skills.

IS physically fit

7. . . . assesses, achieves, and maintains physical fitness.
8. . . . designs safe, personal fitness programs in accordance with principles of training and conditioning.

DOES participate regularly in physical activity

9. . . . participates in health enhancing physical activity at least three times a week.
10. . . . selects and regularly participates in lifetime physical activities.

KNOWS the implications of and the benefits from involvement in physical activities

11. . . . identifies the benefits, costs, and obligations associated with regular participation in physical activity.
12. . . . recognizes the risk and safety factors associated with regular participation in physical activity.
13. . . . applies concepts and principles to the development of motor skills.
14. . . . understands that wellness involves more than being physically fit.
15. . . . knows the rules, strategies, and appropriate behaviors for selected physical activities.
16. . . . recognizes that participation in physical activity can lead to multi-cultural and international understanding.
17. . . . understands that physical activity provides the opportunity for enjoyment, self-expression and communication.

VALUES physical activity and its contributions to a healthful lifestyle

18. . . . appreciates the relationships with others that result from participation in physical activity.
19. . . . respects the role that regular physical activity plays in the pursuit of life-long health and well-being.
20. . . . cherishes the feelings that result from regular participation in physical activity.

Figure 1.2 Definitions and outcomes of the physical educated person (Reprinted from *Outcomes of Quality Physical Education Programs* with permission of the American Alliance for Health, Physical Education, Recreation and Dance, 1900 Association Drive, Reston, VA 22091. Copyright 1992 by AAHPERD.)

listed for students in kindergarten, second, fourth, sixth, eighth, tenth, and twelfth grade. The benchmarks are examples of types of learning that can be evaluated. They are not meant to be all inclusive, but rather to give teachers a minimal standard of assessment. They also give teachers an indication of when various learning can be evaluated (by grade level). The benchmarks represent reasonable levels of achievement and give direction to a planned systematic approach to evaluation.

A third booklet, *Developmentally Appropriate Physical Education Practices for Children* (1992a)

was developed by COPEC, a subgroup of NASPE. This publication lists a number of components of instructional practices and labels them as appropriate or inappropriate. The booklet is not related to developmental stages of children but gives direction for developing a well-rounded curriculum and using proper teaching methodology. It is a useful source for identifying instructional practices that have resulted in strong criticism of the physical education profession. An example of an inappropriate and accompanying appropriate practice follows (NASPE, 1992, 10–11):

Component: Fitness as punishment

Appropriate practice: Fitness activities are used to help children increase personal physical fitness levels in a supportive, motivating, and progressive manner, thereby promoting positive lifetime fitness attitudes.

Inappropriate practice: Physical fitness activities are used by teachers as punishment for children's misbehavior (e.g., students running laps, or doing push-ups, because they are off task or slow to respond to teacher instruction).

The American Medical Association (AMA)

Strong formal approval and support of physical education programs in the schools have come from the American Medical Association (AMA). The support originated with a statement adopted at the national convention of the AMA in 1960: "Resolved, That the American Medical Association through its various divisions and departments and its constituent and component medical societies do everything feasible to encourage effective instruction in physical education for all students in our schools and colleges."

The 1960 resolution was reaffirmed in 1969, strongly supported by the AMA Committee on Exercise and Physical Fitness, a body that was not in existence at the time of the 1960 resolution. Today, the medical profession continues to support effective school programs and, in particular, good physical development.

The American Academy of Pediatrics (AAP)

The American Academy of Pediatrics (AAP) has published a number of policy statements that support physical activity for children. In addition, the policy statements give direction for the safe implementation of activity that could involve high risk. For example, policy statements have been issued for asthmatic children and activity, for weight training and weight lifting programs, for exercise and climatic heat stress, and for risks in long-distance running.

A recent statement by the AAP (1987) issues strong support for physical education programs. The statement discusses various pressures acting to decrease the emphasis schools are placing on physical education. Included in the policy is a statement of need for teaching health-related physical fitness rather than placing strong emphasis on team sports such as football, baseball, and basketball.

The National Education Association (NEA) and U.S. Public Health Service Endorsements

Two significant groups have added their endorsement to physical education programs. The resolution adopted by the 1981 Representative Assembly of the National Education Association (NEA) reads, "The Association also believes that health and physical education programs should be developed and maintained commensurate with maturation levels of children."

The U.S. Public Health Service has launched an intensive effort to improve the health of Americans, citing the importance of health-related fitness and exercise in preventive care. Although the emphasis on physical fitness and exercise is broad in scope, the schools have been singled out and charged to improve the quality of their physical education programs. The significance of this endorsement lies in the fact that for the first time, the nation's principal health agency has officially recognized physical fitness and exercise as essential elements of preventive health care and as a critical component of physical education programs (U.S. Public Health Service, 1990).

ELEMENTARY SCHOOL PHYSICAL EDUCATION TODAY

Elementary school physical education has been influenced by many trends, organizations, and issues over a long period of time. Sound curricular programs cannot be developed without understanding the historical impact of past events and the current concerns of society. Educational programs are affected by current events. For example, when the Soviet Union launched the Sputnik satellite, Americans became concerned about the quality of mathematics and science instruction in the public schools. In similar fashion, the Kraus-Weber test results caused U.S. citizens to think that our youth were unfit compared with European children, and a renewed emphasis on fitness occurred. Recently, comparison with Japanese youth has helped stimulate the "back-to-basics" school emphasis. Educational programs are generally responsive to the needs of society, and physical education has passed through periods of change due to historical and cultural events. The combination of these various forces, trends, and issues helps shape a physical education program for children that we understand today must be well balanced and must offer something for all children.

Currently, fitness is receiving a great deal of publicity nationally due to studies that have shown American adults and children to be inactive. Fitness must be an easily identified part of each lesson and must focus on the health-related aspects of increased activity. Motor skills have to be taught in a clear, concise manner, so youngsters learn proper movement patterns at an early age. Wellness concepts, intertwined with other material and discussed regularly, can enhance student understanding. Creativity and problem solving are centered around different teaching styles in an attempt to help students work out personal needs and challenges. Today, no single phase of physical education can be ignored at the expense of another. Physical education must be a systematic and comprehensive program that reaches out to children from all walks of life. Only when the needs of all children are met is physical education regarded as an integral part of the total school curriculum.

REFERENCES AND SUGGESTED READINGS

AAHPERD. (1986). *Physical activity and well being.* Waldorf, MD: American Alliance.

AAHPERD. (1990). *Professional preparation of the specialist teaching physical education to children.* Reston, VA: AAHPERD.

American Academy of Pediatrics. (1987). Physical fitness and the schools. *Pediatrics, 80*(3), 449–450.

Bain, L. (1975). The hidden curriculum in physical education. *Quest, 24,* 92–101.

Caspersen, C. J., Powell, K. E., & Christenson, G. M. (1985). Physical activity, exercise and physical fitness: Definitions and distinctions for health-related research. *Public Health Reports, 100,* 126–131.

Dodds, P. (1976). Love and joy in the gymnasium. *Quest, 25,* 109–116.

Fitness and Lifestyle in Canada. (1983, May) *Canada fitness survey.* Ottawa, Canada. (Report funded by Fitness Canada.)

Gardner, David P. (Chair). (1983). A nation at risk: The imperative for educational reform. A report to the nation and the Secretary of Education, U.S. Department of Education. The National Commission on Excellence in Education. *Chronicle of Higher Education, 26*(10), 11–16.

Kraus, H., & Hirschland, R. P. (1954). Minimum muscular fitness tests in school children. *Research Quarterly, 25,* 178–187.

National Association for Sport and Physical Education. (1987). *Basic stuff.* Reston, VA: AAHPERD.

National Association for Sport and Physical Education. (1988). *Guidelines for elementary school physical education.* Reston, VA: AAHPERD.

National Association for Sport and Physical Education. (1992a). *Developmentally appropriate physical education practices for children.* Reston, VA: AAHPERD.

National Association for Sport and Physical Education. (1992b). *Outcomes of quality physical education programs.* Reston, VA: AAHPERD.

Pate, R. R. (1988). The evolving definition of physical fitness. *Quest, 40,* 174–179.

Siedentop, D. (1980). Physical education curriculum: An analysis of the past. *JOPERD, 51*(7), 40–41.

Sterling, C. L. (1992). *Fitnessgram user's manual.* Dallas: Institute for Aerobics Research.

U.S. Department of Education. (1987). *First lessons.* (Document # 065-000-0259-1). Washington, DC: U.S. Government Printing Office.

U.S. Public Health Service. (1990). *Healthy people 2000: National health promotion and disease objectives.* Washington, DC: U.S. Government Printing Office.

Physical Activity and the Growing Child

*T*he purpose of this chapter is to offer an overview of the impact of
physical activity on the growing child. Many of the studies cited in this
chapter offer excellent justification for including physical education in the
total school curriculum. For example, the strong concern about the correla-
tion between heart disease and the lack of activity among children, the
importance of developing skill competency in children so they have the tools
to be active for a lifetime, and the long-term effects of physical activity
become strong arguments for a well-taught, well-organized physical education program.

THE NEED FOR PHYSICAL ACTIVITY

During the past decade, the interest in physical fitness and an increased
awareness of the benefits derived from an active lifestyle have spawned a wide
assortment of health clubs, a vast array of books and magazines concerning
exercise and fitness, a weekly smorgasbord of distance runs and triathalons,
streamlined exercise equipment, and apparel for virtually any type of physical
activity. Unfortunately, most of this interest and lifestyle change has occurred

among middle- and upper-class Americans. Little change in activity patterns has occurred in lower-middle- and lower-class families.

The nation's enthusiasm for physical activity has not trickled down to elementary school youngsters. A statement issued by the American Academy of Pediatrics (1991) reported that children from the ages of 2 to 12 watch about 25 hours of television per week, more time than they spend in school. Only about one-third of our children and youth participate daily in school physical education programs nationwide (Ross, Pate, Corbin, Delpy, & Gold, 1987), and that amount is both declining and insufficient.

The need for activity as an integral part of children's lifestyles is strong. Rather than encourage increased activity among children, schools have focused on physical fitness testing. This excessive concern about the fitness levels of children has resulted in a need to "train children to pass fitness tests" to meet district standards. When fitness results become more important than participation in regular activity, children learn that it is more important to focus on short-term goals (fitness test results) rather than a long-term lifestyle (daily activity). Health goals for the nation for the year 2000 (U.S. Public Health Service, 1990) are primarily based on increasing daily levels of physical activity, not fitness levels. Many of the goals directly target schools, or programs that can take place within the school setting. These goals are stated in terms of activity objectives rather than fitness objectives and emphasis is placed on reducing inactivity and increasing light to moderate physical activity.

Emphasis needs to be placed on developing physical education programs that cause lifestyle changes in physical activity levels so as to improve health-related fitness. (Simons-Morton, Parcel, O'Hara, Blair, & Pate, 1988; Sallis & McKenzie, 1991). Whereas fitness testing has anointed a few gifted children and failed the majority of others, developing programs that change the activity patterns of students will allow all youngsters the opportunity for success and long-term health. Children should be recognized for their willingness to participate rather than their reticence to be tested.

One area of concern in dealing with children's health is heart disease. Common wisdom was that heart disease was of geriatric origin and manifested itself only in older adults. In a study by Glass (1973), 5,000 youngsters in the Iowa public schools were examined over a 2-year period. Of these students, 70 percent had symptoms of coronary heart disease, including 7 percent who had extremely high cholesterol levels, a large percentage with high blood pressure, and at least 12 percent who were obese.

In examining the developmental history of heart disease in humans, Rose (1968) identified the first signs as appearing around age 2. Wilmore and McNamara (1974) examined 95 boys, aged 8 to 12 years, in an effort to determine the extent to which coronary heart disease risk factors derived from an adult population were manifested in a group of young boys. They concluded (p. 531) that "coronary heart disease, once considered to be a geriatric problem, is now recognized as being largely of pediatric origin." Fortunately, an increase in activity can play an important role in combating the onset of such problems.

Other diseases and physical conditions are associated with a lack of activity in young children. One concern is the high incidence of obesity among youngsters. Depending on the source of statistics and the criteria used to define obesity, anywhere from 30 to 60 percent of American children have been identified as obese. The need is clear: Physical education programs must be designed that teach youngsters how to live an active and healthy lifestyle. Chapter 13 discusses the importance of fitness, whether today's children are fit, how to evaluate fitness, and the development of meaningful fitness programs.

THE GROWING CHILD

Growth patterns are generally controlled by genetic makeup at birth. Although unhealthy parents or poor dietary practices can have a negative impact on proper growth and development, the focus of this section is normal maturation common to the majority of youngsters. All youngsters follow a general growth pattern; however, each child's timing is unique. Some children are advanced physically for their chronological age, whereas others are slow maturers. Only when aberration from the norm is excessive should teachers and parents become concerned.

Growth Patterns

Teachers and parents are interested in how fast children are growing. When heights and weights are plotted on a graph from year to year, a distance curve can be developed. These curves (Figure 2.1) give an indication of how tall and heavy children are expected to be during a specific year of life. Another method of examining growth patterns is to look at a velocity curve. The velocity curve is

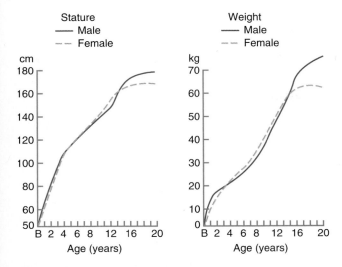

Figure 2.1 Distance curves for height and weight (From Malina, R. 1975. *Growth and development: The first twenty years in man,* 19. Minneapolis: Burgess.)

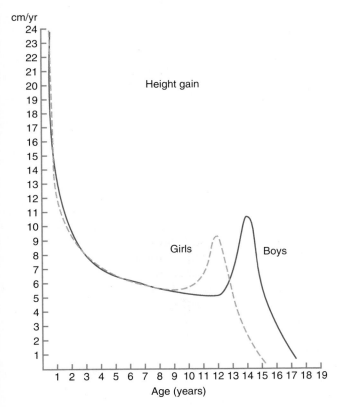

Figure 2.2 Growth velocity curve for height (From Tanner, J. M., Whitehouse, R. H., & Takaishi, M. 1966. *Archives of Diseases in Childhood, 41,* 466.)

useful because it reveals how much a child grows on a year-to-year basis (Figure 2.2). Children go through a rapid period of growth from birth to age 5. From age 6 to the onset of adolescence, growth slows to a steady but increasing pattern. A general rule of thumb in regard to motor learning is that when growth is rapid, the ability to learn new skills decreases. Because the rate of growth slows during the elementary school years, it offers children an excellent opportunity to enhance motor skills.

During adolescence, rapid growth occurs again until adulthood is reached. During the elementary school years, boys are generally taller and heavier. Girls reach the adolescent growth spurt first, and grow taller and heavier during the sixth- and seventh-grade years. Boys quickly catch up, however, and grow larger and stronger. Growth charts based on a larger and more recent sample of children have been developed by the National Center for Health Statistics (Figures 2.3 and 2.4). These tables can be consulted to identify both height and weight percentiles for children aged 2 through 18. The tables offer an opportunity to visualize the marked differences among children in a so-called normal population.

Young children have relatively short legs for their overall height. The trunk is longer in relation to the legs during early childhood. The ratio of leg length (standing height) to trunk length (sitting height) is similar for boys and girls through age 11. The head makes up one-fourth of the child's total length at birth and about one-sixth at age 6. Figure 2.5 illustrates how body proportions change with growth. Maximum growth velocity occurs in the preschool and adolescent years and often diminishes the ability to learn motor skills. During the elementary school years, growth velocity decreases, making it an opportune time to learn motor skills. Because K–2 students have short legs in relation to their upper body, they are often "top heavy" when performing activities such as the curl-up and V-seat. They may fall more easily than adults, because their center of gravity is higher than it will be at maturity. Growth will gradually lower the center of gravity and give children increased stability and balance.

Body Physique

The child's physique can also affect the quality of motor performance. Sheldon, Dupertuis, and McDermott (1954) developed the original scheme for somatotyping, identifying physiques based on the contribution of different components to the body as a whole. The components are termed *endomorphy, mesomorphy,* and *ectomorphy.* Each component is assessed individually from standardized photographs. Rating is done on a 7-point scale, with 1 being the least expression and 7 the most expression of the specific component. The ratings

Figure 2.3 Physical growth percentiles for boys 2 to 18 years. (Adapted from: Hamill, P. V. V., Drizd, T. A., Johnson, C. L., Reed, R. B., Roche, A. F., & Moore, W. M. 1979. Physical growth: National Center for Health Statistics percentiles. *American Journal of Clinical Nutrition,* 32, 607–629. Data from the Fels Research Institute, Wright State University School of Medicine, Yellow Springs, Ohio. Ross Laboratories, Columbus, Ohio.)

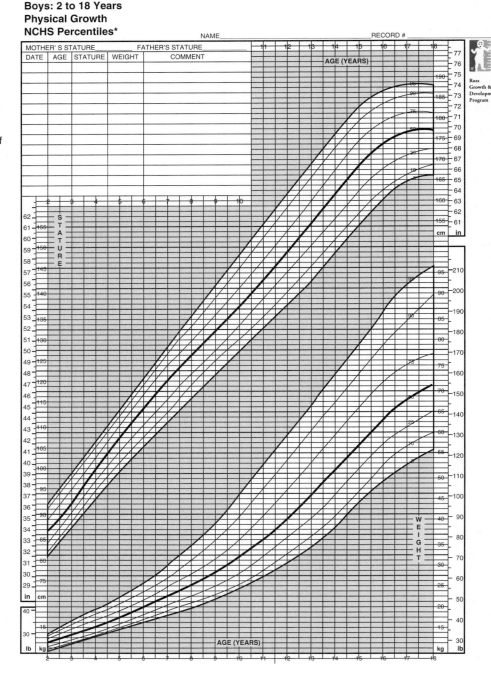

Boys: 2 to 18 Years
Physical Growth
NCHS Percentiles*

of each component give a total score that results in identification of an individual's somatotype. A similar system of classification for children (Petersen, 1967) is available for teachers who are interested in understanding the body physiques of children.

In general, children who possess a mesomorphic body type perform best in activities requiring strength, speed, and agility. The *mesomorph* is characterized as having a predominance of muscle and bone and is often labeled "muscled." These children usually perform well in most team sports, because these activities require strength, speed, and agility. On the other hand, the *ectomorph* is identified as being extremely thin, with a minimum of muscle development, and is characterized as "skinny." These children may be less able in activities requiring strength and power, but do well in aerobic endurance activities such as jogging, cross-country running, and track and field. The

Figure 2.4 Physical growth percentiles for girls 2 to 18 years. (Adapted from: Hamill, P. V. V., Drizd, T. A., Johnson, C. L., Reed, R. B., Roche, A. F., & Moore, W. M. 1979. Physical growth: National Center for Health Statistics percentiles. *American Journal of Clinical Nutrition*, 32, 607–629. Data from the Fels Research Institute, Wright State University School of Medicine, Yellow Springs, Ohio. Ross Laboratories, Columbus, Ohio.)

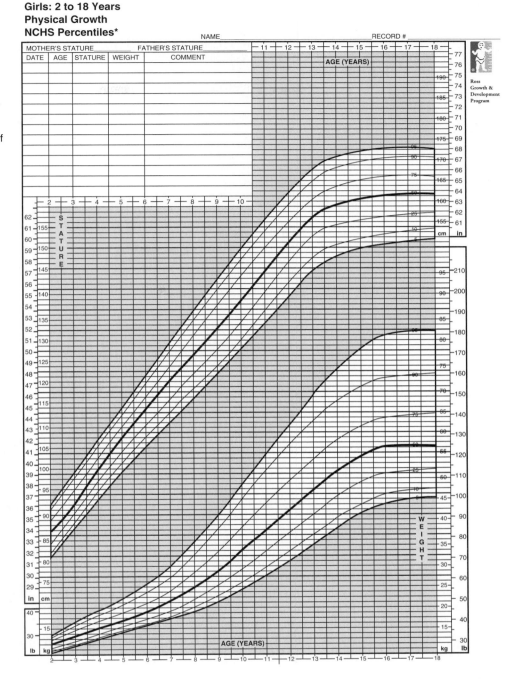

Girls: 2 to 18 Years
Physical Growth
NCHS Percentiles*

third classification is the *endomorph,* who is soft and round, with an excessively protruding abdomen. These children often perform poorly in many areas, including aerobic and anaerobic skill-oriented activities. The obese child is generally at a disadvantage in all phases of physical performance. Somatotype classification illustrates how dramatically children differ in body physique. These obvious differences necessitate that instruction accommodate individual differences.

Skeletal Maturity

The concept of *maturity* is used often by teachers in physical education. Usually, elementary school children are identified as being early, late, or average maturers, with teachers examining the social maturity rather than the physical maturity of the child. Physical maturity, however, has a strong impact on the child's performance in physical education. The most commonly used method to identify

Figure 2.5 Changing body proportions from conception to adulthood. (From Whipple, D. 1966. *Dynamics of development: Euthenic pediatrics,* p. 122. New York: McGraw-Hill.)

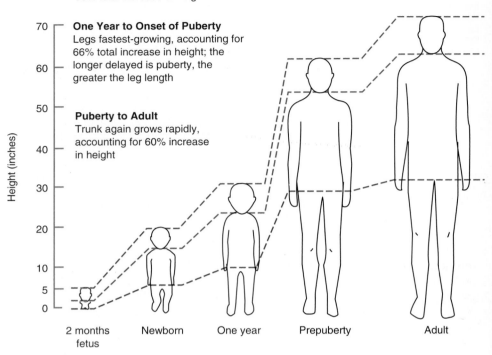

Changing Bodily Proportions

Conception to Birth
Head fastest-growing structure, completing 70% of its total growth

Birth to One Year
Trunk fastest-growing, accounting for 60% total increase in height

One Year to Onset of Puberty
Legs fastest-growing, accounting for 66% total increase in height; the longer delayed is puberty, the greater the leg length

Puberty to Adult
Trunk again grows rapidly, accounting for 60% increase in height

Height (inches)

2 months fetus   Newborn   One year   Prepuberty   Adult

maturity rate is to compare chronological age with skeletal age. Ossification (hardening) of the bones occurs in the center of the bone shaft and at the ends of the long bones (growth plates). The rate of ossification gives an accurate indication of a child's rate of maturation. This rate of maturation or skeletal age, which can be identified by X-raying the wrist bones and comparing the development of the subject's bones with a set of standardized X rays, gives a truer sense of the child's physical maturity (Gruelich & Pyle, 1959; Roche, Chumlea, & Thissen, 1988). Children whose chronological age is ahead of skeletal age are said to be late (or slow) maturers. On the other hand, if skeletal age is ahead of chronological age, these children are labeled early (fast) maturers.

Studies examining skeletal age (Gruelich & Pyle, 1959; Krahenbuhl & Pangrazi, 1983) consistently show that a five- to six-year variation in maturity exists in a typical classroom of youngsters. For example, a class of third graders who are 8 years old chronologically would range in skeletal age from 5 to 11 years. Most teachers would not think of asking a 5-year-old kindergarten child to

perform tasks that 11-year-olds are expected to accomplish. Teachers need to monitor and adjust program activities constantly to allow students to progress at a rate suitable to their level of maturity.

Early-maturing children of both sexes are generally heavier and taller for their age than are average- or late-maturing students. In fact, obese children (endomorphs) are often more mature for their age than are normal-weight children. Early-maturing children also have larger amounts of muscle and bone tissue, due to their larger body size. However, the early maturer also carries a greater percentage of body weight as fat tissue (Malina, 1980). The motor performance of boys is related to skeletal maturity in that a more mature boy usually performs better on motor tasks (Clarke, 1971). For girls, however, motor performance appears not to be related to physiological maturity. In fact, a study by Malina (1978) found that late maturation is commonly associated with exceptional motor performance.

Physical education programs often place importance on learning at the same rate, even though

Children the same age vary in size and maturity.

this practice may be detrimental to the development of students who are developing at a faster or slower rate. Teachers sometimes expect all youngsters to be capable of performing the same activity at the same time, regardless of maturation. Students do not mature at the same rate and are not at similar levels of readiness to learn.

Muscular Development and Strength

In the elementary school years, muscular strength increases linearly with chronological age (Malina, 1980; Beunen, 1989). A similar yearly increase occurs until adolescence, at which time a rapid increase in strength occurs. Strength is related to body size and lean body mass. When differences in strength between the sexes are adjusted for height, there is no difference in lower body strength from age 7 through 17. When the same adjustment between the sexes is made for upper body strength, however, boys have more upper extremity and trunk strength (Malina, 1980). This shows that boys and girls can participate on somewhat even terms in activities demanding leg strength, particularly if their size and mass are similar. On the other hand, in activities demanding arm or trunk strength, boys have a definite advantage, even if they are similar to the girls in height and mass. These considerations should be made when pairing children for competition. Many problems occur when a student is paired with some-

one who is considerably taller and heavier (or more mature) and therefore stronger.

Muscle Fiber Type and Performance

The number of muscle fibers an individual possesses is genetically determined. An increase in muscle size is accomplished by an increase in the size of each muscle fiber. The size of the muscles is determined primarily by the number of fibers and secondarily by the size of the fibers. An individual is therefore somewhat muscularly limited by genetic restrictions.

Skeletal muscle tissue contains fibers that are fast contracting (fast twitch [FT]) and others that are slow contracting (slow twitch [ST]) (Saltin, 1973). The percentage of fast- versus slow-contracting fibers varies from muscle to muscle and among individuals. The percentage of each type of muscle fiber is determined during the first weeks of postnatal life (Dubowitz, 1970). Most individuals are believed to possess a 50:50 split; that is, half of the muscle fibers are FT and half are ST. A small percentage of people have a ratio of 60:40 (in either direction), and researchers have verified that some people possess a more extreme ratio.

What is the significance of variation in the ratio of muscle fiber type? ST fibers have a rich supply of blood and related energy mechanisms. This results in a slowly contracting, fatigue-resistant muscle fiber that is well suited to endurance-type (aerobic) activities. In contrast, FT fibers are capable of bursts of intense activity but are subject to rapid fatigue. These fibers are well suited to activities demanding short-term speed and power (e.g., pull-ups, standing long jump, and shuttle run). ST fibers facilitate performance in the mile run or other endurance-oriented activity.

Surprisingly, elementary-aged children who do best in activities requiring FT fibers also do best in distance running (Krahenbuhl & Pangrazi, 1983). Muscle fiber metabolic specialization does not seem to occur until adolescence, which makes a strong argument for keeping all youngsters involved and interested in varied physical activity throughout the elementary years. A youngster who does poorly in elementary school may do quite well during and after adolescence, when a high percentage of ST fibers will aid in the performance of aerobic activity. On the other hand, the same child may do poorly in a physical education program dominated by team sports that demand quickness and strength. Designing a program that incorporates activities utilizing a range of physical attributes (i.e., endurance, balance, flexibility) is essential.

Strength, Body Size, and Motor Performance

Strength is an important factor in performing motor skills. A study by Rarick and Dobbins (1975) identified and weighted factors that contribute to the motor performance of children. The factor identified as most important was strength or power or both in relation to body size. High levels of strength in relation to body size helped predict which students were most capable of performing motor skills. Deadweight (fat) was the fourth-ranked factor in the study and was weighted negatively. Obese children were less proficient at performing motor skills. Deadweight acts negatively on motor performance by reducing the child's strength in relation to body size. Obese children may be stronger than normal-weight children in absolute terms, but they are less strong when strength is adjusted for body weight. This lack of strength in relationship to body size causes obese children to find a strength-related task (e.g., push-up or curl-up) much more difficult than a similar task would seem to normal-weight children. The need for varied and personalized workloads is important to assure all youngsters the opportunity for success in strength-related activities. Strength is an important part of a balanced fitness program and should be developed to help all youngsters find success in a variety of motor development activities.

Aerobic Capacity

Maximal aerobic power is an individual's maximum ability to use oxygen in the body for metabolic purposes. The oxygen uptake of an individual, all other factors being equal, determines the quality of endurance-oriented performance. Adults interested in increasing endurance-based athletic performance therefore train extensively to increase aerobic power.

Maximal aerobic power is closely related to lean body mass, which explains differences between boys and girls. When maximum oxygen uptake is adjusted per kilogram of body weight, it shows little change for boys (no increase) and a continual decrease for girls (Bar-Or, 1983). This decrease in females is due to an increase in body fat and a decrease in lean body mass. When maximal oxygen uptake is not adjusted for body weight, it increases in similar amounts on a yearly basis for both boys and girls through age 12, even though boys have higher values as early as age 5.

One frequently asked question is whether training will increase the aerobic performance of children. Research results differ. Some researchers have found an increase in aerobic power through training, whereas others report that training has no impact on the aerobic system. A recent study (Payne & Morrow, 1993) analyzed 28 studies dealing with the impact of exercise on aerobic performance in children. The results showed that training caused little, if any, increase in aerobic power in prepubescent children. If there is improvement in running performance in young children, Bar-Or (1983) postulates that it may occur because they become more efficient mechanically or improve in anaerobic metabolism. Another theory is that young children are active enough to make intergroup differences negligible (Corbin & Pangrazi, 1992).

Even though children demonstrate a relatively high oxygen uptake, they do not perform up to this level because they are not economical in running or walking activities. An 8-year-old child running at 180 m per minute is operating at 90 percent of maximal aerobic power, whereas a 16-year-old running at the same rate is operating at only 75 percent of maximum. This explains why young children are less capable than adolescents and adults at competing over long distances, even though they can maintain a slow speed for long distances (Bar-Or, 1983).

Children exercising at a certain workload perceive the activity to be easier than do adults working at a similar level. Youngsters were asked to rate their perceived exertion at different percentages of maximal heart rate (Bar-Or & Ward, 1989) and usually rated the exertion to be less stressful than did adults. Youngsters also demonstrate a rapid recovery rate after strenuous exercise. This implies that teachers should not judge workloads for children based on how they perceive the difficulty of an activity. Second, teachers should use a child's rapid recovery rate to full advantage. Exercise bouts can be interspersed with restful stretching and nonlocomotor movements to maintain the amount of time devoted to exercise. Interval training is a particularly effective training method to use with children.

Body Composition, Obesity, and Physical Activity

Body composition refers to the varying amounts of muscle, bone, and fat within the body. Over half of the fat stored in the body is stored in a layer just below the skin. This is why skinfolds are used to estimate the amount of fat carried within the body. Depending on the criteria used to evaluate the ratio of fat, 25 to 35 percent of youngsters have been identified as being overfat or obese. Obesity restricts children's motor performance. The study of childhood obesity has produced some disturbing findings. Many obese people appear to have a decreased tendency for muscular activity. As weight increases, the impulse for physical exertion decreases further. As children become more obese, they find themselves in a cycle that throws the caloric intake–expenditure out of balance. In many cases, physical activity is a crucial factor in dealing with weight control (see Chapter 8). Comparisons of the diets of obese and normal children showed no substantial differences in caloric consumption. In fact, in some cases, obese children actually consumed less food than did normal-weight children (Corbin & Fletcher, 1968).

The lack of physical activity is common among obese children. In a study of ninth-grade girls (Johnson, Burke, & Mayer, 1956), girls who were obese ate less but also exercised two-thirds less (in total time) than did normal-weight girls. Johnson et al. also examined children in an elementary school in Massachusetts, a study that indicated children gained more weight during the winter, when they were less active. Movies taken of normal-weight and overweight children (Corbin & Fletcher, 1968) demonstrated a great difference in activity level of the two groups, even though diets were quite similar.

Identifying whether obese children are less active due to genetic or environmental factors is difficult. In a study by Rose and Mayer (1968), 4- to 6-month-old babies were divided into groups based on their level of obesity. The most obese children had the fewest limb motions, expending only 20 percent of their total energy on physical activity. In contrast, the leanest babies expended 35 to 40 percent of their energy on physical activity. Griffiths and Payne (1976) selected 4- and 5-year-old children for study based on their parents' level of obesity. At the time of the study, the children were of similar body composition. Children of obese parents were, however, less active and also ate less than did the offspring of leaner parents. If the behavior continues, the children of these obese parents will probably become obese due to lack of activity.

Adults often make the statement, "Don't worry about excessive weight; it will come off when the child reaches adolescence." In fact, the opposite is usually true. Four out of 5 obese children grow into obese adults; however, 28 out of 29 obese teenagers become obese adults (Johnson et al., 1956). Children clearly do not grow out of obesity—they grow into it. Childhood obesity must be challenged at an early age, and this challenge must come from increased movement and activity.

Obesity and Performance

As mentioned, obese children seldom perform physical activities on a par with leaner children (Bar-Or, 1983). In part, this is due to the greater metabolic cost of the obese child's exercise. Obese children require a higher oxygen uptake capacity to perform a given task. Obesity takes a great toll on a child's aerobic power because obese children must perform at a higher percentage of their maximal oxygen uptake. Usually, their maximal uptake values are lower than those of lean children. This gives obese children less reserve capacity and causes them to perceive higher exertion (Bar-Or & Ward, 1989) when performing a task, and to perceive aerobic tasks as demanding and unenjoyable. These reactions contribute to the well-known perception among teachers that "obese children don't like to run." Teachers should bear this in mind when they ask obese children to try to run as far and as fast as normal-weight children. The task is more demanding for the obese child. Teachers need to understand that obese children are working harder than normal-weight children and need adjusted workloads. There is no acceptable premise, physiological or psychological, for asking all children to run the same distance regardless of ability or body type.

Body composition impacts physical performance.

Workloads must be based on time rather than distance. Lean and efficient runners should be expected to move farther than obese youngsters during a stipulated time period. All children *do not and should not* have to do the same amount of exercise. Just as one would not expect kindergarten children to perform the same workload as that of fifth-graders, it is unreasonable to expect obese children to be capable of workloads similar to those of lean, ectomorphic youngsters. *Exercise programs for obese subjects should be designed to increase caloric expenditure rather than improve cardiovascular fitness* (Rowland, 1991). The intensity of the activity should be secondary to the amount of time the student is involved in some type of moderate activity.

CHILDREN IN ORGANIZED SPORT ACTIVITY

Physical educators can play a pivotal role in developing organized sports programs for children because parents and community leaders will look to them to offer expert advice. Too often, these pro-

grams are administered by persons who have little, if any, training and understanding of young, immature children. It is important that teachers step forward and share their knowledge so that programs are based on the developmental characteristics of youngsters. This topic is discussed in detail in Chapter 24.

Maturity and Sports

Maturity plays an important role in dictating which position a child will learn to play in a sport. Will a youngster be a pitcher or a right fielder, play in the line or be a quarterback? Often, these questions are answered for young children by adults, a decision that may not allow youngsters an opportunity to realize their potential. In a study by Hale (1956), skeletally mature athletes were found to be playing in the skilled positions in the Little League World Series. Chronologically, all players were 11 years old, with a skeletal age range similar to that described earlier. The most mature were pitchers and catchers, and the least mature played at less skilled positions. This study points out how skeletally mature children receive more opportunity to throw at an early age (through pitching and catching). These youngsters become better throwers due to the large number of opportunities they receive when throwing in games and practice. In contrast, children who are immature are forced to play right field and receive limited throwing or catching opportunities. Because these less mature children receive much less throwing practice, it is improbable that they will ever have the chance to close the skill gap and develop adequate skill competency.

Another issue related to skill development is allowing youngsters to play all positions in sport activities. If the best athletes are always assigned to skilled positions, it becomes a situation of the rich getting richer and the poor getting poorer. Because all children deserve equal opportunity to learn sport skills, it should be a mandate to teachers that all children play all positions and receive similar amounts of practice time. In addition, reinforcement schedules need to be similar for children regardless of their current skill level. Children participate in activities that offer them reinforcement; it is easy to become discouraged if little encouragement and praise is given to participants trying to learn new skills and positions.

Predicting Athletic Success

The willingness to try new experiences and participate in activities is driven by how people feel about their ability level—their *perceived competence*. Perceived competence becomes more specific as students mature. In other words, very young students think they are good and competent at everything. As they become older (third or fourth grade), they start to realize that other students are better in some areas. If these students are not given the chance to succeed in class, they may develop low perceived competence about their ability to perform physical skills. This "learned helplessness" (Harter, 1978) eventually can result in the student disliking and dropping out of physical education. There is a strong possibility that they will leave school with negative feelings about developing an active lifestyle. Dropping out of physical education commonly occurs at the junior high and high school level or as soon as students have the opportunity to make a choice. Unfortunately, it is quite possible that the process of feeling incompetent began in the elementary school years. Elementary school youngsters are often characterized as gifted (or not gifted) at a young age. This creates a self-fulfilling prophecy, with students identified as gifted receiving more feedback and being expected to reach higher levels of performance. Less able students receive less feedback and expectations remain low.

Even though teachers and parents make early judgments about students, it is difficult to identify outstanding athletes by viewing their performance in the elementary school years. In a study by Clarke (1968), athletes identified as outstanding in elementary school were seldom outstanding in junior high school, and predictions based on elementary school performance were correct only 25 percent of the time. Most people would not risk discouraging a youngster if they knew they were going to be wrong 75 percent of the time. However, youngsters are often labeled at early age, even though three out of four such predictions are incorrect. All children should be treated as if they have the potential to become successful. It is not the purpose of a physical education program to develop athletes, but rather to help *all* students develop physical skills within the limits of their potential. The program should not be presented in such a fashion that it allows the athletically gifted to excel and prosper at the expense of the less talented youngsters.

Starting Them Young: Boon or Curse?

There is no evidence to support the idea that starting a child at a young age assures the child will develop into an outstanding athlete. In fact, many

An early start does not guarantee success.

excellent athletes, particularly in basketball, did not even play the sport until their high school years. One reason that many parents and coaches push to have children start competing in a sport at an early age is that it offers the perception that a better athlete has been developed by the age of 8 or 9. The participating child may seem extremely gifted compared with the nonparticipant, because he has been practicing skills for 4 or 5 years. Naturally, the "early starter" looks advanced compared with a child who has not been in an organized program. In most cases, however, a child who is genetically more gifted quickly catches up to and surpasses the "early superstar" in 1 to 3 years. As Shephard (1984a) states, "Any advantage that is gained from very prolonged training probably lies in the area of skill perfection rather than in a fuller realization of physical potential."

There is concern that children who have been in documented programs will burn out at an early age. A *documented* program is one in which extrinsic rewards are offered. Examples of such rewards are trophies, published league standings, ribbons, and excessive parental involvement. Evidence shows that extrinsic motivation may ultimately decrease intrinsic motivation, particularly in children age 7 years and older. Researchers (Thomas & Tennant, 1978; Whitehead & Corbin, 1991) found that younger children (age 5) perceived a reward as a bonus, thus adding to the joy of performing a throwing motor task. This effect decreased with age, and by the age of 9 the reward was seen as a bribe; intrinsic motivation was undermined. There is no substitute for allowing young children to participate in physical activity for the sheer enjoyment and excitement involved in moving and interacting with peers.

If starting youngsters early may create early burnout, why do parents feel pressured to force their child into a sport program? One explanation is that they constantly compare their children to other children. Parents see other children participating and practicing sport skills in an organized setting. They worry that their child will be unable to "catch up" if they do not get them involved in a similar program immediately. Even though this has not proved to be true, parents need reassurance, and need facts. Physical educators can help parents find programs that minimize pressure and focus on skill development. A key is to find programs that allow the child to participate regardless of ability, and to have fun while playing. Children consider having fun and improving their skills to be more important than winning (Athletic Footwear Association, 1990). Many children drop out of sport activities, but would probably continue to participate if given the opportunity (Petlichkoff, 1992). Unfortunately, some programs become elitist and start eliminating and "cutting" less gifted players. It is difficult to justify this approach at the elementary school level. All children should be given the opportunity to participate if they choose to do so.

Another reason given for starting children at a young age is tied to the commodity that only children have; free time. Parents know they have little time in their lives to learn new skills. They feel their youngsters have an abundance of free time that can be devoted to practice. Unfortunately, if the child shows promise, greater emphasis is placed on increasing practice time since it becomes necessary "to ensure that all this talent is not lost." It is important to remind parents that life includes more than athletic development and that many youngsters have been maimed by an excessive emphasis on sports at the expense of intellectual and social development. Participation in activity should be self-selected. It should be student driven rather than motivated by external factors. Similarly, students should have the opportunity to withdraw from participation in an activity if they choose. Withdrawal should be child controlled rather than externally controlled (Gould, 1987). In other words, participants should not be forced out of the program due to cost, limitation of participants, or injury. On the other hand, if youngsters choose to withdraw, they should be allowed that opportunity without pressure.

PHYSICAL EDUCATION AND INTELLECTUAL DEVELOPMENT

For years, physical educators attempted to demonstrate a relationship between physical education and a child's intellectual potential. If intellectual development or academic achievement could be linked to physical performance, physical education would rank higher as an educational priority. However, according to Shephard (1984a), "Strong proof is lacking." Shephard identifies the many limitations of such investigations, which include (a) studies of special populations such as the mentally challenged or athletes, (b) "halo" effects, because teachers reward star performers with higher marks, (c) self-image gains by athletes due to teacher and peer praise, (d) short duration of training programs, (e) possible side effects from curtailment of academic instruction, and (f) use of retrospective data relating observed academic performance to measures of activity or physical ability.

Perceptual-motor programs received a great deal of emphasis during the late 1960s and 1970s. The programs attempted to link improved motor functioning with increased academic achievement. Physical educators jumped on the bandwagon and begin implementing these programs without clear and convincing research evidence. In many cases, physical education programs were eliminated and replaced by perceptual-motor programs with the hope that the physical education profession could be justified on an academic basis. A comprehensive analysis of over 180 perceptual-motor studies was made by Kavale and Mattson (1983). A summary of their findings indicated that perceptual-motor training has little benefit. Thomas and Thomas (1986) offer a clear and concise summary statement: "Attempts to improve or remediate cognitive function through the use of movement are not theoretically sound, nor does this approach have any empirical support in the research literature."

In any case, physical educators should feel comfortable justifying inclusion of physical education in the total school curriculum on the basis of its unique contributions: motor skill development, and the understanding and maintenance of physical fitness. Since these contributions are unique to physical education and contribute to the physical well-being of youngsters, convincing administrators and parents further that intellectual development is enhanced by physical education should not be necessary. The public will support a physical education program if it aids, nurtures, and shows concern for the physical development of all children.

Even though physical activity does not enhance academic performance, there is a strong need for daily physical education. A study that has created much interest in this area is the Trois Rivieres regional experiment (Shephard, 1984b). The study provided a well-conceived design for increased physical education programming. Even though students received more time for physical education (and less for academics), their academic performance was not decreased. These results appear to counter the objection that more physical education will result in poorer academic performance due to less time spent in the classroom. Administrators need to consider this study, particularly today, when many schools have a back-to-basics emphasis. This emphasis usually means "back to the classroom," without physical activity or the arts. One wonders if this lack of concern for the body, our "home of the brain," is not detrimental to children's total development. The ability to read becomes unimportant if one's health has degenerated. No priority in life is higher than physical well-being.

GUIDELINES FOR EXERCISING CHILDREN SAFELY

Moderation in Exercise

As is usually the case, moderation is the best way to ensure that children grow up enjoying different types of physical activity. Moderate exercise, coupled with opportunities to participate in recreational activity, helps develop a lasting desire to move. Educators are sometimes concerned that a child may be harmed physiologically by too much or too vigorous activity. To date, there is no evidence that a healthy child can be harmed through vigorous exercise. This does not mean that a child is capable of the same unadjusted physical workload as an adult. Evidence does indicate, however, that children can withstand a gradual increase in workload and are capable of workloads comparable to those of adults when the load is adjusted for height and size.

There was concern at one time that the large blood vessels do not grow in proportion to other body parts. This, it was theorized, placed the heart and the circulatory system under stress during strenuous exercise. Research has now established that fatigue causes healthy children to stop exercising long before any danger to health occurs (Shephard, 1984a). In addition, the child's circulatory system is similar in proportion to that of an adult and is not at a disadvantage during exercise.

Exercising in Warm Climates

Teachers must be cautious when exercising youngsters in hot climates. The arrival of summer does not mean that exercise must stop, but certain measures should be used to avoid heat-related illness. Children are not little adults, and they do not adapt to extremes of temperature as effectively as adults do for the following physiological reasons (Bar-Or, 1983; American Academy of Pediatrics, 1991):

1. Children have higher surface area/mass ratios than those of adults. This allows a greater amount of heat to transfer between the environment and the body.

2. When walking or running, children produce more metabolic heat per unit mass than adults produce. Youngsters are not as efficient in executing movement patterns, so they generate more metabolic heat than do adults performing a similar task.

3. Sweating capacity is not as great in children as in adults, resulting in a lowered ability to cool the body.

4. The ability to convey heat by blood from the body core to the skin is reduced in children due to a lower cardiac output at a given oxygen uptake.

These physiological differences are the reasons why children are at a distinct disadvantage compared with adults when exercising in an environment in which the ambient air temperature is higher than the skin temperature.

Individuals do acclimatize to warmer climates. However, children appear to adjust to heat more

Table 2.1 Weather guide: When the humidity and air temperature exceed the corresponding levels, intense activity should be curtailed.

Humidity Level (%)	Air Temperature (°F)
40	90
50	85
60	80
70	75
80	70
90	65
100	60

slowly (up to twice as long) than do adults (Bar-Or, 1983). Often, children do not instinctively drink enough liquids to replenish fluids lost during exercise. The American Academy of Pediatrics Committee on Sports Medicine (1991) offers the following guidelines for exercising children in hot climates:

1. The intensity of activities that last 30 minutes or more should be reduced whenever relative humidity and air temperature are above critical levels. Table 2.1 shows the relationship between humidity and air temperature and when activity should be moderated.

2. At the beginning of a strenuous exercise program or after traveling to a warmer climate, the intensity and duration of exercise should be restrained initially and then increased gradually over a period of 10 to 14 days to acclimatize to the effects of heat.

3. Children should be hydrated 20 to 30 minutes before strenuous activity. During the activity, periodic drinking (e.g., 150 ml of cold tap water every 30 minutes for a child weighing 40 kg) should be enforced. If youngsters are hydrated before going to a 30-minute physical education class, it probably is not necessary to drink until the end of the class period unless conditions are unusually severe.

4. Clothing should be lightweight and limited to one layer of absorbent material to facilitate evaporation of sweat and to expose as much skin as possible. Sweat-saturated garments should be replaced by dry ones. Rubberized sweat suits should never be used to produce weight loss.

The committee identifies children with the following conditions as being at a potentially high risk for heat stress: obesity, febrile (feverish) state, cystic fibrosis, gastrointestinal infection, diabetes insipidus, diabetes mellitus, chronic heart failure, caloric malnutrition, anorexia nervosa, sweating insufficiency syndrome, and mental retardation.

Distance Running and Children

The question often arises as to how much and how far children should be allowed to run, particularly in a competitive or training-for-competition setting. The answer is complex, as parents, teachers, or coaches seldom see the long-term effects. The

Water is mandatory for participation in heat and strenuous activity.

American Academy of Pediatrics Executive Committee (1991) identifies some of the concerns. Lifetime involvement in a sport often depends on the type of early participation and gratification gained. Psychological problems can result from unrealistic goals for distance running by children. A child who participates in distance running primarily for parental gratification may tire of this after a time and quit, or the child may continue, chafing under the parental pressure. In either case, psychological damage may be done, and the child may be discouraged, either immediately or in the long run, from participating in sports. A prepubertal child should be allowed to participate for the enjoyment of running without fear of parental or peer rejection or pressure. A child's sense of accomplishment, satisfaction, and appreciation by peers, parents, and coaches will foster involvement in running and other sports during childhood and in later life.

A strong position taken by the International Athletics Association Federation (IAAF) Medical Committee was reprinted in 1983. In part, it states, "The danger certainly exists that with over-intensive training, separation of the growth plates may occur in the pelvic region, the knee, or the ankle. While this could heal with rest, nevertheless definitive information is lacking whether in years to come harmful effects may result." In view of the above, it is the opinion of the committee that training and competition for long-distance track and road-running events should not be encouraged. Up to the age of 12, it is suggested that not more than 800 m (one-half mile) should be run in competition. An increase in this distance should be introduced gradually—with, for example, a maximum of 3,000 m (nearly 2 miles) in competition for 14-year-olds.

Fitness Testing Considerations

Teachers often test children at the start of the school year in the one-mile run/walk. This practice should be discouraged, since many children may not have ample conditioning to participate safely in the activity. In addition, in many parts of the country, the start of the school year is hot and humid, adding to the stress placed on the cardiovascular system. A recommendation is to test only at the end of the school year after youngsters have had the opportunity to be conditioned. If this is not possible, at least allow youngsters 4 to 6 weeks to condition themselves. Rowland (1990) recommends starting with a one-eighth mile run/walk and gradually building to a mile run/walk over a 4-week period. Another alternative is to use the PACER aerobic fitness test (see p. 274), which can be administered indoors.

Weight Training

Weight training for preadolescent children has generated a great deal of concern among educators. Many worry about safety and stress-related injuries, and others question whether such training can produce significant strength gains. Accepted thinking for some time has been that prepubescents are incapable of making significant strength gains because they lack adequate levels of circulating androgens. Research evidence is continuing to build that contradicts this point of view. A study by Cahill (1986) demonstrated significant increases in strength among 18 prepubescent boys. A study by Servedio et al. (1985) showed significant strength gains in shoulder flexion. Weltman et al. (1986) conducted a 14-week, three times a week program using hydraulic resistance training (circuit training using 10 different stations) in 6- to 11-year-old boys. Results showed an 18 to 37 percent gain in all major muscle groups. It seems that strength can be increased through weight training in prepubescent youngsters. However, the way prepubescent children gain strength differs from how adolescents and adults do (Tanner, 1993). In preadolescent children, it appears that strength gains occur from motor learning rather than muscle hypertrophy. Youngsters develop more efficient motor patterns and recruit more muscle fibers, but show no increase in muscle size (Ozmun, Mikesky, & Surburg, 1991).

Note that the term *weight training* is used here to denote the use of barbells, dumbbells, or machines as resistance. It is in sharp contrast to *weight lifting* or *power lifting,* which is a competitive sport for the purpose of determining maximum lifting ability. There is strong agreement among experts that weight training is acceptable for children, but weight lifting is highly undesirable and may be harmful. In a statement of strength training recommendations, the American Orthopaedic Society for Sports Medicine (AOSSM) (Duda, 1986) states, "(1) competition is prohibited, and (2) no maximum lift should ever be attempted." In addition, AOSSM recommends a physical exam, proper supervision by knowledgeable coaches, and emotional maturity on the part of the participating youngster. Safety and prevention of injury are paramount considerations for those interested in weight training for children. Serious consideration also has to be given as to whether weight training is an appropriate activity for a typical group of children in a physical education class.

When injuries were reported, most occurred due to inadequate supervision, lack of proper technique, or competitive lifting. The majority of weight lifting injuries were caused by the major lifts, the power clean, the clean and jerk, the squat lift, or the dead lift (Tanner, 1993). These lifts often are competitive and performed in an uncontrolled (ballistic) manner; they should not be used with preadolescent children. If knowledge and expertise are limited, weight training programs for children should be avoided. A knowledgeable instructor is required to provide an effective and safe program.

There are no studies that examine the long-term effects of strength training in children. In addition, many experts worry about highly organized training programs that place great emphasis on relative gains in strength. A weight training program should be only one component of a comprehensive fitness program for children. The National Strength and Conditioning Association (NSCA) (1985) recommends that 50 to 80 percent of the prepubescent athlete's training must include a variety of different exercises such as agility exercises (e.g., basketball, volleyball, tennis, tumbling) and endurance training (e.g., distance running, bicycling, swimming).

When a variety of physical activities are experienced in elementary school physical education, there probably is little need for weight training within the school curriculum. However, weight training may have a place on an individual basis with parental approval in a club setting. If a decision is made to develop a weight training program for children, it should be done in a thoughtful and studied manner. Proper supervision and technique are key ingredients in a successful program. Program prescription guidelines recommended by AOSSM and NSCA are as follows:

1. Training is recommended two or three times a week for 20- to 30-minute periods. High repetitions at low resistance appear to be most safe for elementary school–age children.

2. No resistance should be applied until proper form is demonstrated. Six to 15 repetitions equal one set; one to three sets per exercise should be done.

3. Weight or resistance is increased in 1- to 3-pound increments after the prepubescent does 15 repetitions in good form.

4. Maximal lifts should not be performed until youngsters are at least 16 to 17 years old.

REFERENCES AND SUGGESTED READINGS

American Academy of Pediatrics. (1991). *Sports medicine: Health care for young athletes* (2nd ed). Elk Grove Village, IL: American Academy of Pediatrics.

Athletic Footwear Association. (1990). *American youth and sports participation.* North Palm Beach, FL: Athletic Footwear Association.

Bar-Or, O. (1983). *Pediatric sports medicine for the practitioner.* New York: Springer-Verlag.

Bar-Or, O., & Ward, D. S. (1989). Rating of perceived exertion in children. In O. Bar-Or (Ed.), *Advances in pediatric sport sciences. Vol. 3.* Champaign, IL: Human Kinetics.

Beunen, G. (1989). Biological age in pediatric exercise research. In O. Bar-Or (Ed.), *Advances in pediatric sport sciences. Vol. 3.* Champaign, IL: Human Kinetics.

Cahill, R. R. (1986). Prepubescent strength training gains support. *The Physician and Sportsmedicine, 14*(2), 157–161.

Clarke, H. H. (1968). Characteristics of the young athlete: A longitudinal look. *Kinesiology Review, 3,* 33–42.

Clarke, H. H. (1971). *Physical motor tests in the Medford boys' growth study.* Englewood Cliffs, NJ: Prentice-Hall.

Corbin, C. B., & Fletcher, P. (1968). Diet and activity patterns of obese and non-obese elementary school children. *Research Quarterly, 39*(4), 922–928.

Corbin, C. B., & Pangrazi, R. P. (1992). Are American children and youth fit? *Research Quarterly for Exercise and Sport, 63*(2), 96–106

Dubowitz, V. (1970). Differentiation of fiber types in skeletal muscle. In E. J. Briskey, R. G. Cassens, & B. B. Marsh (Eds.), *Physiology and biochemistry of muscle as a food,* Vol. 2. Madison: University of Wisconsin Press.

Duda, M. (1986). Prepubescent strength training gains support. *The Physician and Sportsmedicine, 14*(2), 157–161.

Glass, W. (1973). Coronary heart disease sessions prove vitally interesting. *California AHPER Journal,* (May/June), 7.

Gould, D. (1987). Understanding attrition in children's sport. In *Advances in pediatric sport sciences. Vol. 2. Behavioral issues.* Champaign, IL: Human Kinetics.

Griffiths, M., & Payne, P. R. (1976). Energy expenditure in small children of obese and non-obese parents. *Nature, 260,* 698–700.

Gruelich, W., & Pyle, S. (1959). *Radiographic atlas of skeletal development of the hand and wrist* (2nd ed.). Stanford, CA: Stanford University Press.

Hale, C. (1956). Physiological maturity of Little League baseball players. *Research Quarterly, 27,* 276–284.

Harter, S. (1978). Effectance motivation revisited. *Child Development, 21,* 34–64.

International Athletics Association Federation. (1983). Not kid's stuff. *Sports Medicine Bulletin, 18*(1), 11.

Johnson, M. L., Burke, B. S., & Mayer, J. (1956). The prevalence and incidence of obesity in a cross section of elementary and secondary school children. *American Journal of Clinical Nutrition, 4*(3), 231–236.

Kavale, K., & Mattson, P. D. (1983). "One jumped off the balance beam": A meta-analysis of perceptual-motor training. *Journal of Learning Disabilities, 16,* 165–173.

Krahenbuhl, G. S., & Pangrazi, R. P. (1983). Characteristics associated with running performance in young boys. *Medicine and Science in Sports, 15*(6), 486–490.

Malina, R. M. (1978). Physical growth and maturity characteristics of young athletes. In R. A. Magill, M. H. Ash, & F. L. Smoll (Eds.), *Children and youth in sport: A contemporary anthology.* Champaign, IL: Human Kinetics.

Malina, R. M. (1980). Growth, strength, and physical performance. In G. A. Stull & T. K. Cureton (Eds.), *Encyclopedia of physical education, fitness, and sports.* Salt Lake City, UT: Brighton.

National Strength and Conditioning Association. (1985). Position paper on prepubescent strength training. *National Strength and Conditioning Association Journal, 7*(4), 27–31.

Ozmun, J. C., Mikesky, A. E., & Surburg, P. R. (1991). Neuromuscular adaptations during prepubescent strength training (abstract). *Medicine and Science in Sports and Exercise, 23*(4), S31.

Payne, V. G., & Morrow, Jr., J. R. (1993). Exercise and VO$_2$max in children: A meta-analysis. *Research Quarterly for Exercise and Sport, 64*(3), 305–313.

Pate, R. R., Dowda, M., & Ross, J. G. (1990). Associations between physical activity and physical fitness in American children. *American Journal of Diseases of Children, 144,* 1123–1129.

Petersen, G. (1967). *Atlas for somatotyping children.* The Netherlands: Royal Vangorcum Ltd.

Petlichkoff, L. M. (1992). Youth sport participation and withdrawal: Is it simply a matter of fun? *Pediatric Exercise Science, 4*(2), 105–110.

Rarick, L. G. (Ed.). (1973). *Physical activity, human growth and activity.* New York: Academic.

Rarick, L. G., & Dobbins, D. A. (1975). Basic components in the motor performances of children six to nine years of age. *Medicine and Science in Sports, 7*(2), 105–110.

Roche, A. F., Chumlea, W. C., & Thissen, D. (1988). *Assessing the skeletal maturity of the hand-wrist: Fels method.* Springfield, IL: Thomas.

Rose, H. E., & Mayer, J. (1968). Activity, calorie intake, fat storage and the energy balance of infants. *Pediatrics, 41,* 18–29.

Rose, K. (1968). To keep people in health. *Journal of the American College Health Association, 22,* 80.

Ross, J. G., & Gilbert, G. G. (1985). The national children and youth fitness study: A summary of findings. *Journal of Physical Education, Recreation, and Dance, 56*(1), 45–50.

Ross, J. G., Pate, R. R., Corbin, C. C., Delpy, L. A., & Gold, R. S. (1987). What is going on in the elementary physical education program? *Journal of Physical Education, Recreation, and Dance, 58*(9), 78–84.

Rowland, T. W. (1990). *Exercise and children's health.* Champaign, IL: Human Kinetics.

Rowland, T. W. (1991). Effects of obesity on aerobic fitness in adolescent females. *American Journal of Disease in Children, 145,* 764–768.

Sallis, J. F., & McKenzie, T. L. (1991). Physical education's role in public health. *Research Quarterly of Exercise and Sport, 62,* 124–137.

Saltin, B. (1973). Metabolic fundamentals of exercise. *Medicine and Science of Sports, 5,* 137–146.

Servedio, F. J., Bartels, R. L., Hamlin, R. L., Teske, D., Shaffer, T., & Servedio, A. (1985). The effects of weight training, using Olympic style lifts, on various physiological variables in prepubescent boys. Abstracted. *Medicine and Science in Sports and Exercise, 17,* 288.

Sheldon, W. H., Dupertuis, C. W., & McDermott, E. (1954). *Atlas of men: A guide for somatotyping the adult male at all ages.* New York: Harper & Row.

Shephard, R. J. (1984a). Physical activity and child health. *Sports Medicine 1,* 205–233.

Shephard, R. J. (1984b). Physical activity and ''wellness'' of the child. In R. A. Boileau (Ed.), *Advances in pediatric sport sciences.* Champaign, IL: Human Kinetics.

Simons-Morton, B. B., Parcel, G. S., O'Hara, N. M., Blair, S. N., & Pate, R. R. (1988). Health-related physical fitness in childhood: Status and recommendations. *American Review of Public Health, 9,* 403–425.

Tanner, S. M. (1993). Weighing the risks: Strength training for children and adolescents. *The Physician and Sportsmedicine, 21*(6), 105–116.

Thomas, J. R., & Tennant, L. K. (1978). Effects of rewards on changes in children's motivation for an athletic task. In F. L. Smoll & R. E. Smith (Eds.), *Psychological perspectives in youth sports.* New York: Hemisphere.

Thomas, J. R., & Thomas, K. T. (1986). The relation of movement and cognitive function. In V. Seefeldt (Ed.), *Physical activity and well-being.* Reston, VA: AAHPERD.

U.S. Public Health Service. (1990). *Health people 2000: National health promotion and disease prevention objectives.* Washington, DC: U.S. Government Printing Office.

Weltman, A., Janney, C., Rians, C. B., Strand, K., Berg, B., Tippitt, S., Wise, J., Cahill, B. R., & Katch, F. I. (1986). The effects of hydraulic resistance strength training in pre-pubertal males. *Medicine and Science in Sports and Exercise, 18,* 629–638.

Whitehead, J. R., & Corbin, C. B. (1991). Effects of fitness test type, teacher, and gender on exercise intrinsic motivation and physical self-worth. *Journal of School Health, 61,* 11–16.

Wilmore, J. H., & McNamara, J. J. (1974). Prevalence of coronary disease risk factors in boys, 8 to 12 years of age. *Journal of Pediatrics, 84,* 527–533.

The Basis for Learning Motor Skills

A growing body of knowledge is available to help teachers understand how children develop motor skills. Understanding the nature of movement learning contributes to more efficient teaching. Teaching motor skills is not a difficult process if the guidelines outlined in this chapter are applied. Students can learn many skills through exploration and self-paced practice. However, the advantage of learning skills through instruction in physical education is that the skills can be learned efficiently. With guidance, skills can be properly learned and practiced in a setting where a caring teacher can offer feedback and redirection.

SKILL PERFORMANCE AND INFORMATION PROCESSING

Understanding how skill-related information is processed by learners when learning motor skills is helpful in being a more effective teacher. Figure 3.1 illustrates an information-processing model (Anshel, 1990), and a discussion of each component in the model follows.

Sensory Input: The information that enters the nervous system is sensory input. This information enters through the sense organs such as the eyes and

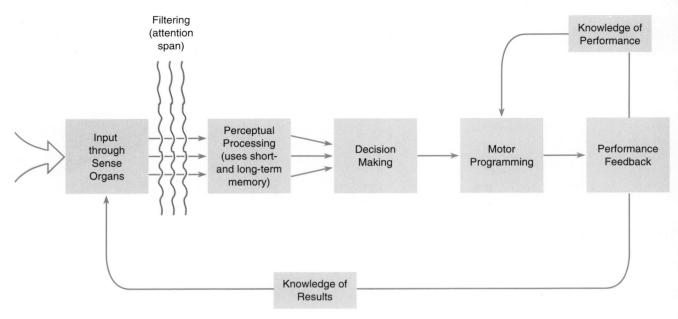

Figure 3.1 Information processing model

the ears. Adults are much more efficient than children at being able to input information. Obviously, the filter (attention span) plays an important part in being able to interpret incoming information. When children are uninterested or bored with an activity, they often exhibit a short attention span, thus making it difficult to accept incoming stimuli.

• *Implications for Teaching Motor Skills.* Youngsters have limited visual scanning ability. Therefore, the environment should be simplified by reducing the need for peripheral vision and offering activities that are easy to view. For example, drills should be done with a partner or in small groups. Increasing the size of groups places much greater demand on the visual awareness of children. The background for the performer should be uncluttered to improve visual acuity. Placing students in a position to practice skills where they won't have to observe other students moving will increase their opportunity for success. If the object to be tracked visually can be slowed down, it will help improve children's opportunity for success. However, if some skills are slowed excessively (usually complex skills), it will change the nature of the skill and reduce the opportunity to learn. For example, it is difficult to slow down striking a ball with a bat; other motor performance factors come into play when the bat is slowed excessively.

To take advantage of students' attention span (filter), teachers should demonstrate as many skills as possible. When students can observe and listen to an explanation, the opportunity to learn is in-

creased. Focus should be placed on teaching one skill or concept at a time, as complex instructions may cause youngsters to become frustrated and filter out further information. Too often, teachers try to be overly verbal and explain more than is necessary. Finally, the environment should be relatively quiet when students are concentrating on learning new skills. Teachers who are constantly talking or fellow students who are making excessive noise destroy the opportunity to maintain attention on the task at hand. Think of physical education as any other academic area; the environment must be conducive to learning if students are to learn.

Perceptual Processing: In this step, the learner attempts to interpret and rehearse the information that has passed through the filter. Two components play major roles in this interpretation process. The first is short-term memory (STM), which is used to rehearse the skill and make immediate decisions about the information. The learner interprets the oncoming data utilizing STM before deciding to store it in the second component, long-term memory (LTM). Data stored in LTM are then recalled whenever they are needed. How to fake out an opponent and how to catch a ground ball are examples of data that can be stored in LTM and retrieved at a later time when the situation demands.

• *Implications for Teaching Motor Skills.* Learning to perceive certain responses is a sophisticated skill that children learn as they mature. For example, youngsters can learn to perceive which way a ball will bounce off the wall; on a more complex level, students can learn to anticipate strategy, how an opponent will react, and when certain shots are going to be used. Since STM has a limited capacity, teachers should remember that young children are not capable of remembering a long list of key points or techniques. To help students remember skill performance points, use verbal cues. For example, when teaching skipping, remind students to "step-hop."

To make effective use of LTM, teachers should try to point out similarities of the current skill with those previously learned. Teachers should remember that LTM is where information is stored to be used at a later time. If the information is stored in an improper sequence, it will be recalled and used improperly. When possible, positive emotion should be tied to the learning experience so that the student couples a positive experience with the skill-learning opportunity.

Decision Making: At this stage, a number of rapid decisions need to be made if the student is to be successful in performing motor skills. Data are gathered for the decision-making process from two sources: STM when there is adequate time to rehearse and interpret the data, and from the perceptual structure when there is almost no time to cognitively process the data.

• *Implications for Teaching Motor Skills.* Primary-grade children have little practice in making quick and accurate decisions. Decision-making opportunities should be simple and not demand excessive speed. To help children have positive experiences, teachers can organize situations that allow students to make decisions without concern for accuracy and speed. For example, low-organized games often demand that students move on a given cue. If students make a mistake or fail to move in the proper direction, the stakes are not high. Decision-making games also involve learning effective strategy and anticipating outcomes. This sense of anticipation is the beginning of learning to make rapid and accurate decisions in a competitive game situation.

Motor Programming: A motor program is a coordinated sequence of subroutines that control movement and do not depend on internal or external feedback. Motor programs are internally directed in the central nervous system and when practiced become overlearned (performed without cognition).

• *Implications for Teaching Motor Skills.* A key issue at this stage of motor learning is repetition and practice of skills. It is important that children

correctly practice the motor skills. Practice alone does not assure that skills will be properly learned; the practice must be correctly performed. When working with closed (fixed) skill patterns, children try to repeat a pattern that brings the greatest amount of success. An example of a closed skill is hitting a ball off a batting tee. However, when working with open (unpredictable) skills, it is important to practice the skill in as many different situations as possible. Striking a pitched ball would be an example of an open skill since the learner cannot predict where the ball will be thrown. (See p. 45 for a discussion of the schema theory of motor learning.) Practicing the skill in many different situations will help students respond successfully even though the context of the skill continually changes.

Feedback: The individual receives two types of feedback about skill performance. When feedback is given to the performer about "how" the skill was performed, it is identified as *knowledge of performance.* Knowledge of performance is delivered by teachers and should focus on form and technique rather than the outcome of the skill. When feedback is given to the performer about the end product of the skill performance, it is referred to as *knowledge of results.* Knowledge of results is based on observing the outcome of the performance and utilizing the results to change and improve the level of performance. For example, when a performer misses a basket, a number of decisions are made as to how to adjust the next shot so it will be more accurate.

• *Implications for Teaching Motor Skills.* Students should be reminded to remember "how it feels" when a successful performance occurs. In addition, allow time for performers to think about what they did correctly or incorrectly and to make adjustments. Knowledge of performance can be increased by giving students feedback about their technique and style. For elementary school youngsters, most emphasis should be placed on learning to perform the skill correctly rather than worrying about the outcome (how many baskets were made, etc.). This demands time and a patient teacher. If knowledge of results is important to the learner, it can be enhanced by designing experiences that give the student measurable feedback, for example, targets for throwing accuracy, distance measurement for striking effectiveness, and counting repetitions of rope jumping. Knowledge of results is most effective when it is positive and is given immediately to the learner.

STAGES IN LEARNING NEW MOTOR SKILLS

Fitts and Posner's (1967) model helps to explain how motor skills are learned. Their model involves three separate but overlapping phases. The first is the introductory or cognitive phase, a relatively shorter period than the two succeeding phases. The second phase is the practice phase, the critical step in ensuring that children develop new skills correctly. The final phase involves consolidation, using the skill automatically in a setting that involves integrating a series of developed skills.

The Introductory Phase

The introductory phase is also known as the verbal-cognitive stage. The student acquires an understanding of the task to be performed and forms a concept of what is to be done. Teachers should demonstrate and verbalize the new skill (i.e., discuss its component parts) so that children can follow the pattern of the task. Much of this should be done in sequenced steps or at slightly reduced speed, depending on the type of challenge. Demonstration can emphasize the critical points of the skill. Films, videotaping, diagrams, and other visual aids will help children develop correct conceptualization of how the skill should be performed. Students should have the opportunity to experiment with different, valid ways of performing a skill, rather than being confined to a single, teacher-selected pattern. For example, when children are learning to toss and catch balloons, they can perform at a slower speed and be successful. Teachers will ask students to watch the balloon, reach out to catch, and move toward the object. A range of performances will result for students learning in this phase.

In this introductory phase, place emphasis on exploration of various skills, using a system of approximation and correction rather than trial and error. Success at this stage is determined when the approximation begins to resemble the movement pattern desired. At this point, little refinement occurs, but the basic form to be practiced is established as the learner begins to adopt a style. This phase of learning usually is short because the cognitive elements of the skill are quickly learned.

Mime can be used to establish basic techniques of a new motor skill. Students can be in mass formation and follow the directions of the leader. Without the implement (e.g., ball, bat, or other object), they can concentrate on the movement and acquire a kinesthetic feeling for the skill.

In this way, many can practice at one time, form can be emphasized, questions answered, and gross errors discovered at an early stage. The mime approach is most effective with the intermediate grades or with youngsters who already have some perception of the skill being taught.

The Practice or Motor Phase

During the practice or motor phase, the learner receives ongoing feedback, eliminates errors, and begins to make necessary adjustments. The task begins to be done with less conscious effort. Timing of the movement is refined during this phase, and execution is polished. Attention begins a gradual shift from the process (performing without concern for the end result) to the product. Emphasis must be placed on learning motor skills through proper development of a reasonable competence level.

Children need repeated trials to learn a skill. Practice by itself, however, does not ensure that learning is occurring unless the practice is purposeful. To be learned, motor patterns must be practiced correctly. During practice sessions, the teacher coaches and helps youngsters attain ad-

Juggling requires repeated practice.

equate levels of skill by analyzing and making corrections. Even more important is that students begin to learn how to analyze their own performance. Changes and modifications to the skill continue as students strive to perform in a consistent manner.

This phase is the one most commonly found in elementary school settings. Students know what it means to catch, skip, or throw, but haven't started to refine the skills. Practicing tossing and catching using a variety of objects and challenges will teach performers to solve the task in different ways.

The Consolidation or Autonomous Phase

The consolidation phase, also termed the autonomous phase, is reached when the child performs easily, without stress, and with little, if any, conscious control. Few elementary school children reach this stage with specialized skills, although they may reach this level with some fundamental skills. The consolidation phase is seldom reached in elementary school physical education because few children have yet to achieve high levels of performance. The focus should be the continued practice of all skills under more challenging conditions. Even overlearned skills need practice.

MOTOR LEARNING PRINCIPLES

The learning process involved in mastering motor skills can be made more productive when teachers understand pertinent tenets from educational doctrine and motor learning research. The applications vary with the stage of learning, the activity presented, and the maturity of the children.

Developmental Patterns

The development of motor skills is an individual matter, and wide variation occurs among children of similar chronological age. However, the sequence of skill development in youngsters is much the same and appears to progress in an orderly fashion. Experts on motor learning have identified three development patterns that typify the growth of primary-grade children.

1. Development in general proceeds from head to foot (cephalocaudal); that is, coordination and management of body parts occur in the upper body before they are observed in the lower. Children can therefore throw before they can kick.

2. Development occurs from inside to outside (proximodistal). For example, children can control their arms before they can control their hands. They can therefore reach for objects before they can grasp them.

3. Development proceeds from the general to the specific. Gross motor movements occur before fine motor coordination and refined movement patterns. As children learn motor skills, nonproductive movement is gradually eliminated. One clear sign of motor learning at any age is learners who are able to eliminate wasteful and tense movement and concentrate on reproduction of a smooth and consistent product.

Readiness

One role of the teacher in teaching skills is to ascertain the time when children are capable and ready to learn, and then to design a learning environment that promotes the most effective development of the skills. A number of factors affect readiness, among them maturity level, previous practice, prerequisite skills, body management skills, and state of physical fitness. Interest in an activity plays a role in readiness, because people do things that interest them. In turn, if they do well at an activity, they become ready to learn more about the activity. People usually want to do well because of the social rewards that accompany success. Teachers should first offer worthwhile experiences that are based on students' existing interests, but they must then go further to establish new student interests and experiences.

Maturity level is defined as the gross physical and neural body management competencies necessary for the child to have a basis for success and to be challenged by the selected movement pattern. For example, children must have the ability to track a moving object before they can become proficient in catching skills. If children lack the capability to perform a task, the activity should be modified in a progressive manner. For example, if children cannot catch a small, rapidly moving object, asking them to play a game involving softball skills will have little value. Instead, they will benefit if the teacher brings out a large, brightly colored, and slower-moving object, such as a beach ball, for practice sessions.

Previous experience and prerequisite skills are usually the result of prior learning experiences. A child who began rope jumping in kindergarten and continued the experience would be ready for advanced activities that would frustrate a beginner of similar age. *Prerequisite skills* refer to the fundamental competencies needed for success in a later unit. As an example, dribbling, trapping, and kicking skills are necessary prerequisites for successful participation in the game of soccer. In addition, physical fitness levels can affect a child's readiness to learn. Children who are strong enough to perform skills, resist fatigue, and sustain the rigors of skill practice are more likely to achieve than are those with an inadequate fitness level.

A learner's *optimum state of readiness* is defined as the level at which the child learns most efficiently and with the least difficulty. Whenever possible, the teacher should identify that optimum state for each child. This state of readiness is often difficult to recognize because students mature at different rates. However, if attempts are not made to analyze each child's progress frequently and if the instruction is beyond the child's level of readiness, frustration and withdrawal may occur.

In the selection of learning activities for children, two decisions face the teacher. First, are students ready for the activity? Second, at what level of difficulty in activity progression and challenge should instruction begin? In an activity unit, the teacher may use a start-and-expand approach. The teacher begins at an entry level where all children can be successful, and expands the activity progression to a point where difficulty in execution is encountered by a majority of the class. It is at this point that the teacher can arrange a learning situation for the development of the new skills. Regardless of the perceived entry level for students, children should be allowed to practice at a level that is within their learning capability.

Stress and Arousal

Arousal is the level of excitement stress produces (Schmidt, 1991). The level of arousal can have a positive or negative impact on motor performance. The key to proper arousal is to find the "just right" amount. Too little arousal and the youngster is uninterested in learning. Too much arousal causes stress and anxiety to become a problem. High arousal will fill a youngster with concern, worry, nervousness, and indecision. This results in a child who is unable to learn, since high anxiety results in a decrease in motor performance. The goal is to arouse youngsters to a level at which they are excited and confident about participation. The more complex the skill, the more easy it is for arousal to disrupt learning. On the other hand, if a skill is simple, such as skipping or running, a greater amount of arousal can be tolerated without causing a reduction in skill performance.

It is important to understand how competition can affect the arousal levels of children. When competition is introduced in the early stages of skill learning, stress and anxiety can reduce a child's ability to learn. On the other hand, if competition is introduced after the skill has been overlearned, it might improve the level of performance. Since most children in elementary school have not overlearned skills, teachers should avoid competitive situations when teaching new skills to children. An example illustrates the point: The teacher's goal is to teach basketball dribbling. The teacher makes the instructional decision to place the youngsters in squads and run a relay where they have to dribble to the opposite end of the gym and return. The first squad finished is the winner. The result: Instead of concentrating on proper dribbling form, students are more concerned about winning the relay. They are overaroused and determined to run as quickly as possible. Dribbling is done poorly (if at all), the balls fly out of control, and the teacher is dismayed by the end result. Unfortunately, the competitive situation overaroused youngsters who had not yet overlearned the dribbling skill.

Feedback

Feedback is important in the teaching process as it reflects what is to be learned, what should be avoided, and how the performance can be modified. *Feedback* is any kind of information about a movement performance. There are basically two types of feedback, intrinsic and extrinsic. *Intrinsic* feedback is internal and inherent to the performance of the skill and travels through the senses such as vision, hearing, touch, and smell. *Extrinsic* feedback is external and comes from an outside source such as a teacher, a videotape, a stopwatch, and so on. Teachers can control extrinsic feedback and decide whether and when to use it. When using feedback, it should be positive (or constructive) and given frequently, should be delivered publicly so all students benefit, and should be contingent on performance or (preferably) effort. A common form of feedback is knowledge of results.

Knowledge of Results

Knowledge of results can be extinsic or intrinsic. Instrinsic feedback occurs when the child watches a successful attempt occur, such as making a basket or striking a ball. Regardless of whether knowledge of results is extrinsic or intrinsic, no learning will take place without some type of feedback. Knowledge of results is a requisite for learning new motor

Students need knowledge of results from teachers.

skills. Teachers cannot affect intrinsic feedback, but they can regulate the extrinsic feedback that offers students insight into skill performance. Knowledge of results is usually verbal information about the performance of a goal, for example, telling players when they succeed at a task. It is often similar to intrinsic feedback because the performer usually knows the results of the performance as well. Knowledge of results is important to the learner because it provides information to the learner about incorrect performance. Learners must have knowledge of their errors so they use the information to adjust the practice trials that follow. This type of feedback need not be negative, but rather should be a statement of fact about some phase of the skill being done incorrectly.

Knowledge of results as discussed here always originates externally from a teacher, peer, or other source. It is a variable that the instructor controls almost exclusively and can use to stimulate effective skill learning. Knowledge of results is critical in the early stages of learning motor skills. As a

student becomes proficient at a skill, performance can be maintained with less need for extrinsic knowledge of results. When performers understand and can perform a skill, they are able to self-analyze their performance and develop their own system of internal feedback. In the case of elementary school students, however, most have not learned skills to a high level of proficiency, thus making knowledge of results a less important type of feedback.

Knowledge of Performance

This type of feedback is similar to knowledge of results in that it is usually verbal, extrinsic in nature, and occurs after the movement. Whereas knowledge of results focuses on the outcome of a skill, knowledge of performance relates to the process of the performance or a part of the skill itself. Teachers using this type of feedback refer to specific aspects of the learner's behavior. Examples might be, "I like the way you kept your chin on your chest," or "That's the way to step toward the target with your left foot." Knowledge of performance is most often used in a teaching setting, particularly with elementary children who are trying to correctly learn new motor patterns.

Knowledge of performance can increase a youngster's motivation by providing feedback about improvement. Many youngsters become easily frustrated because they find it difficult to discern improvement. The teacher's feedback can provide a lift and a rededication to continued practice. Knowledge of performance can be a strong reinforcer, particularly when the instructor mentions something performed correctly. This will motivate youngsters to repeat the same pattern, ultimately resulting in improved performance. The most important aspect of this feedback is that it provides information for future patterns of action.

Feedback about performance should be kept short and concise. The feedback should be content filled and specific. It should tell the youngster exactly what was correct or incorrect (e.g., "That was excellent body rotation"). It should not contain more than one key point or it will confuse the youngster and make concentration on performance difficult. Imagine a youngster who is told: "Step with the left foot, rotate the trunk, lead with the elbow, and snap the wrist on your next throw!" Such excessive feedback will confuse anyone trying to learn a new skill.

If choosing between knowledge of results and knowledge of performance, focus on knowledge of performance. Using knowledge of results to focus on the outcome without concern for the process of skill performance can sometimes lead children to believe that learning to perform a skill correctly is unimportant. A child who manages to get the ball into a basket might believe that the skill performance was performed correctly because of the outcome; even though the technical points of the throw were performed incorrectly. Knowledge of performance should focus on performing the skill correctly with little, if any, emphasis given to the outcome. Remember that the goal of elementary school physical education is to teach skills correctly, with less emphasis placed on outcome of the performance. Later, if youngsters choose to enter the competitive world of athletics, strong emphasis will be placed on product (performance) rather than process (technique).

A final point about knowledge of performance: Allow time for the youngster to internalize the feedback. Often, teachers tell a youngster something and at the same time ask them to "try it again." It is quite possible that the same mistake will be repeated since the youngster did not have time to concentrate on the feedback. It is usually beneficial to offer a student knowledge of performance and move to another youngster. This allows the child a chance to relax, internalize the feedback, and modify future practice attempts.

Concentrate on a positive approach, praising progress and proper performance. Take care to assure that the praise reinforces specific phases of the performance. If a teacher praises simply by saying "Good job" to a child, there is a great deal of latitude for misinterpretation. For example, if the child was performing a forward roll, the teacher may have been praising foot position while the child thought head placement was the focus of the praise. Dwelling on criticism and identifying performances of poor quality encourage peer rejection. Enough equipment should be available so that each child is occupied in a movement task and has no time to ridicule less skilled children. Total student involvement helps reduce stress and anxiety, as it decreases the child's concern that "everybody is watching and waiting for me to fail."

Designing Effective Practice Sessions

Practice is the key to motor learning. For effective motor learning to take place, emphasis must be given to the quality and amount of practice. It is not enough that students receive the opportunity to practice, they must receive the maximum amount of practice in a physical education class and the practice must emphasize quality of movement

(practicing correctly). This section will help teachers design practice sessions that optimize motor learning.

Make Practice Learning Oriented

There are two goals that teachers can focus on when students are practicing. One is performance, where teachers ask that students do the best they can and direct reinforcement to students who perform quality (correct) movements. The other goal is to allow students to learn during practice. Reinforcement is directed toward students who are modifying their skill performance and trying to find the best possible solution. This leads to a product–process conflict. Students who think the teacher is interested in how well they perform will be unwilling to take chances by modifying movements from trial to trial. To make practice learning oriented, teachers should place emphasis on searching for the best pattern and encourage experimentation. Emphasis on high performance will ultimately decrease the student's desire to take risks and learn new ways of performing a skill.

One way for teachers to avoid this conflict is to separate their goals for the practice sessions. If they are interested in allowing students the opportunity to learn, they should tell them, and reinforce those students who are involved in experimentation and error correction. If they want to know how much students have learned, they can clearly tell them that the practice session will be a test. Emphasis is then placed on performing "at your best" and students are rewarded for high performance. A final note here. It will be well to remember that most elementary school children are still learning motor patterns and excessive pressure to perform may stifle their willingness to try (especially less gifted children).

Use Mental Practice Techniques

Mental practice involves focusing on the movement task in a quiet, relaxed environment. In a class setting, this usually means the class is going to have to practice simultaneously to assure quiet. Youngsters should be encouraged to think about the activity and its related sounds, color, and other sensations. They should visualize themselves doing the activity successfully and at regular speed. Images of failure should be avoided (Schmidt, 1991).

Mental practice has the advantage of stimulating children to think about and review the activity they are to perform. Some experience or familiarity with the motor task is requisite before the performer can derive value from mental practice.

Mental practice should be used in combination with regular practice, not in place of it. Before performing the task, students can mentally review the critical factors and sequencing of the act. If students are waiting a turn, they can be encouraged to practice mentally.

Decide on Whole versus Part Practice

There has long been discussion about the teaching of movement skills by the whole method and by the part method. The *whole method* refers to the process of learning the entire skill or activity in one dose. The *part method* involves learning parts of the activity separately, and then combining the parts to form a unified whole. For example, in a rhythmic activity, teachers may teach each section of the dance and then put them together. A simple gymnastics routine may be broken down into its component parts and then put back together for the performance.

The choice of the whole or the part method depends on the complexity and organization of the skill or activity to be learned. *Complexity* refers to the number of serial skills or components there are in a task. *Organization* defines how the parts are related to each other. High organization means that the parts of the skill are strongly related to each other, making it difficult to separate them. An example of a highly organized and complex skill

would be throwing, whereas a low-organized skill might be a folk dance. Generally, if the skill is high in complexity but low in organization, it can be taught in parts. If it is low in complexity but high in organization, it must be taught as a whole. Obviously, there is common ground between the two areas, and the teacher needs to decide whether the activity is simple enough to be taught as a whole or whether it should be broken into parts. A final consideration is the duration of the skill. If the skill is of short duration, such as throwing, batting, or kicking, trying to teach the skill in parts is probably futile. Imagine trying to slow down kicking while trying to teach it part by part. The performer would never develop the proper pattern and timing.

Another criterion for deciding whether to teach a skill by parts is to analyze the relationship of the parts. If each part can be performed independently of the others, the skill probably is conducive to part instruction. Even this is not as simple as it sounds, as the component skill may be dependent on the skill performed before it. For example, in a gymnastics routine, a student may be able to perform the activities separately, but may find difficulty when sequencing them because of not learning how to modify each activity based on the previous one. Regardless, the ultimate goal is to perform the skill as a whole. Teaching a skill in parts is done only when it will optimize the amount of learning in a practice session.

Developing a motor pattern

Determine the Length and Distribution of Practice Sessions

Practice sessions that last a shorter time and involve relatively fewer repetitions usually produce more efficient learning than do longer sessions with more repetitions. This is probably due to both physical and mental fatigue. In physical education settings, the length of the practice period is fixed and decreasing the number of repetitions will hamper learning. The challenge is to try to offer as many repetitions as possible within the practice session. Using varied approaches, challenges, and activities to develop the same skill helps maintain both teacher and student motivational levels. For example, using many different types of beanbag activities will offer novelty to maintain motivation, yet focus on tossing and catching skills.

Another way to gauge the length of practice sessions is by examining the tasks being practiced. If the skill causes physical fatigue, demands intense concentration, or is simple and boring, the practice sessions should be short and frequent with an adequate rest pause between intervals. In some cases, with elementary school–age children, it may be most effective to completely stop practicing the desired skill and play a game until youngsters regain their enthusiasm for learning. On the other hand, practice sessions can be longer and less frequent if the tasks contain several components, are unique and novel, or require a number of complex components.

Practice sessions that occur over a longer time period are usually more effective than many sessions crowded into a shorter period. The combination of practice and review appears to be effective for youngsters. Activities can be taught in a short unit and practiced in review sessions spaced throughout the school year. In the initial stages of skill learning, it is particularly important that practice sessions be distributed in this way. In later stages, when success increases motivational levels, the individual practice sessions can be lengthened.

Use Random Practice Techniques

There are two basic ways to organize the presentation of activities to be taught. The first is *blocked practice,* where all the trials of a task are completed before moving on to the next task. The other method is *random practice,* where the order of task presentations is mixed so that the learner never practices the same task twice in succession. Goode and Magill (1986) showed that random practice is the most effective approach to use when learning skills. Blocked practice gave the best results during the acquisition phase of learning a skill, but students who were learning through random practice demonstrated a much higher level of retention.

The reason random practice results in increased learning is thought to be related to mentally generating solutions. When the same task is practiced over and over, youngsters not only become bored, but don't have to think about how to solve the problem. Since the same motor program is used over and over to complete the task, little effort or thinking is required. In contrast, random practice students never practice the same task back to back. Therefore, they forget the motor program used and have to consciously re-create the solution to be successful. The application of random practice makes sense to teachers of children. Because youngsters become bored quickly when doing the same task over and over, random practice assures this won't occur. Teachers using this approach to practice can feel comfortable about building a variety of tasks into their lessons. Another drawback to blocked practice is that it gives learners false feedback about their performance. Since blocked practice is effective during practice (without lasting effects), learners find rapid improvement occurring due to the opportunity to fine tune each repetition. Unfortunately, when the skill must be applied in a natural setting, the performance level is much lower and less refined and youngsters feel discouraged about their decreased competency.

Is blocked practice ever effective? Blocked practice can be used during the early stages of learning a skill. The rapid improvement will enhance performance quickly and students will be motivated by their progress. It should be explained to older learners why you switch from blocked to random practice to assure learned skills are retained.

Offer Variable Practice Experiences

Motor tasks are grouped into classes of tasks. For example, throwing is a collection of a class of movements. Throwing a ball in a sport setting may require varied parameters, such as different speeds, different trajectories, and varying distances. Even though the throwing tasks are all different, the variations have fundamental similarities. Movements in a class usually involve the same body parts and have similar rhythm, but differ in the parameters of the skill. These differences in parameters form the basis of variable practice.

Variable practice is important to use as it causes an increase in skill performance in a variable setting. To better understand why variable practice is important, it is necessary to understand the schema theory of learning.

Just as practice should be random rather than blocked, variation should be introduced into practice sessions through *variable practice* sessions. This contrasts with constant practice, which focuses on similar experiences within a class of movements. Variable practice offers many different experiences within a movement class. Applied to a teaching situation, this means that teachers ask students to practice within a skill class (throwing, kicking, etc.) with as many different experiences as possible. For example, instead of practicing shooting a number of baskets from the same spot, students should be encouraged to shoot from as many different angles and distances as possible. Even though the movement class is shooting, the variable shooting practice assures that learned skills will be retained.

Schmidt (1975) developed the schema concept, which helps to explain why success occurs when a novel response is dictated. A *novel response* is defined as one that has not been performed in exactly the same manner in previous practice situations. It is almost impossible to practice all the possible responses that might occur in a game situation (i.e., different throwing positions, batting balls thrown at differing speeds and levels, etc.). How can teachers prepare students for the unlimited number of responses they will have to make as they participate in a number of activities? Fortunately, the schema theory offers a solution for teachers.

The *schema theory* implies that a motor skill should be learned under a variety of conditions and should be practiced in as many situations as possible to assure practice variability. Developing a widely based set of experiences upon which a response foundation can be built will allow a youngster to respond to the widest possible range of novel situations. To prepare children for novel responses, practice sessions should contain both a large amount of practice on the skill in a movement class and a variety of situations and parameters in which the skill is performed. One final note: If the skill to be learned involves only one fixed way of performing it (a "closed" skill), such as placekicking a football, variability is much less important. However, most skills are "open," and responses are somewhat unpredictable, thereby making variability in practice the usual mode of operation. Fortunately, in this scenario, the theory coincides with the characteristics of children: They like variety and will practice longer when allowed to try the movement in different settings.

Transfer of Learning

Transfer of learning is the effect that the previous practice or acquisition of movement skills and concepts has on the student's ability to learn new skills. Teachers want students to learn skills and be able to generalize them to the many different situations they will face throughout life. This ability to apply skills learned in practice to game situations is known as *generalization*. Transfer is most obvious and effective when a learner is just beginning to learn a skill. As the skill becomes learned, transfer becomes less important because the skill becomes more specific and has less in common with other similar skills. For example, a volleyball serve and a tennis serve may seem similar to a beginner and could facilitate early learning of the tennis serve. However, as the tennis serve becomes learned, it becomes more distinct and unique. This leads us to the principle of *specificity.* There does not appear to be a general athletic trait that allows one student to excel in all areas. Therefore, when one skill is learned, it does not assure that other skills will be easily learned. Don't use performance in one skill area to predict success in another. Transfer of learning is quite specific. Learning to shoot a basketball will not make a student a better football passer. There does seem to be more transfer from fundamental movement skills (e.g., walking, hopping, jumping) to specific skills using these components than there is between complex skills (e.g., shooting a basket, kicking a soccer ball). As a point of information, negative transfer rarely occurs. Some teachers and coaches believe that participating in one skill will have a negative effect on another, that, say, racquetball play will hurt one's tennis play. Most evidence shows that this is not actually a problem.

Transfer is not automatic, but occurs more readily when the novel skill pattern closely resembles a previously learned skill pattern. A learner may not cognitively recognize the similarity between skill patterns. It is important that teachers make a conscious effort to discuss and apply generalizations about skills and skill applications in similar situations. In addition to transfer among similar tasks, theorists also hold that transfer is more probable if the learner has a good understanding of the movement principles involved in the original task and has learned that task well. Throughout the program, the relevance of pertinent movement principles should be stressed when they are applicable.

The following points should be considered to increase the probability for transfer of learning:

1. Try to identify common skill patterns among activities. For example, throwing a softball and hitting a volleyball might be similar. Serving a tennis ball and throwing are similar, and this could be pointed out in a tennis unit. Transfer occurs most when a well-learned skill can be used in a new setting.

2. Many specialized sport skills form the basis of later games and activities. Provide a variety of situations for students to practice these skills. The use of lead-up games is excellent if they focus and concentrate on specific skills in a gamelike setting. It is important to point out how the skills learned in the lead-up activities could be transferred to the actual sport.

3. When introducing a new skill, identify similarities with previous skills that youngsters have learned. Identify key points of performance among skills; this will help students transfer previously learned movement patterns to the new skill being practiced.

4. Discuss mechanical principles (see the next section of this chapter) that are basic to a class of skills. For example, there are principles that are common to all situations involving propelling objects (i.e., opposition, weight transfer, development of torque, and follow-through). This will help students understand commonalities among skills.

Progression of Skills

Progression is defined as moving the learning process through ordered steps from the least challenging to the more challenging facets of an activity. The ideal starting point is a task that is one step above the student's present ability level, as this will offer challenge and the opportunity for success. Youngsters develop at different rates, however, and any one progression cannot satisfy everyone's requirements.

Motor skills can be ranked in a hierarchy from the simple to the complex. Complex skills are difficult, if not impossible, to attain when the fundamental skills have not been learned. The learning of fundamental motor skills requires considerable time and practice for refinement to take place. Fundamental skills must be overlearned so that they can be performed automatically and without conscious effort. Eventually, this allows the child's thought processes to be directed toward learning

new, complex movements or to thinking about strategy while performing sport activities.

Progression also involves the review of previously learned steps before proceeding to new material; further, the concept includes the development of prerequisite skills before experiencing a more complex activity. When teaching a new skill, it can be simplified by eliminating the locomotor parts in order to concentrate on the fine motor aspects of the skill. For example, a skill performed in place should precede the same skill performed while moving. A basketball dribble is simpler when done in place, and later can be expanded with the addition of locomotor movements. A further progression would be for the dribbler to retain control while moving and being guarded.

Developmental Levels and Progression

To help teachers present skills in proper sequence, the activities in Chapters 16–31 have been listed in progression from simple to complex. This aids the teacher in determining when and in what order activities should be presented to youngsters. *Developmental level I* activities (used most often with kindergarten through second-grade children) are the least complex and form the foundation for more complex skills. The majority of these skills are performed individually or with a partner so as to increase the success of primary-grade children. Examples might be tossing and catching, striking a stationary object, and playing games that simply incorporate fundamental locomotor movements. The number of complex decisions to make while performing the skill is minimized so that youngsters can concentrate on the skill at hand. As youngsters mature and progress into *developmental level II* (usually grades 3–4), the tasks become more difficult and many are performed individually or within small groups. More environmental factors such as different speeds of objects, different sizes of objects, and games requiring locomotor movements and specialized skills (throwing, catching, etc.) are introduced at this level. At *developmental level III* (grades 5–6), students utilize skills in a number of sport and game situations. Simple skills previously learned are sequenced into more complex motor patterns. Cognitive decisions about when to use a skill and how to incorporate strategy into the game are integrated into the learning experiences at this level.

Teachers need to be aware that children learn skills in a natural progression, but not at the same rate. If progression is going to be considered in the skill-learning process, youngsters must be allowed

Performing a developmentally appropriate learning task

to progress at a rate that is best suited for them. This usually means that all children will be learning a category of skills (throwing, striking, etc.) but will progress at different rates and will practice different skills within the category. This premise forms the basis for the current emphasis on a "developmentally appropriate physical education program" (Barrett, Williams, & Whitall, 1992).

MECHANICAL PRINCIPLES INVOLVED IN SKILL PERFORMANCE

The effective performance of movement skills requires an understanding of mechanical principles. In this section we discuss concepts that teachers should understand and help youngsters to apply to skill performance. Intermediate-grade children should begin to analyze their performances (albeit in a somewhat rudimentary fashion) by applying some of these principles.

Stability

Stability reflects balance and equilibrium, which affect the performance of many sport skills. A stable base is necessary when one applies force to a projectile or absorbs force. Instability is useful in some activities, as when a rapid start is desired. (Instability is the basis of the sprinter's start.)

Figure 3.2 Pulling

Children can be introduced to the following concepts:

1. The size of the base of support must be increased to achieve more stability. The base must be widened in the direction in which force is applied or from which force is absorbed.

2. The body's center of gravity must be closer to the base of support (i.e., lower) when stopping quickly or when applying or absorbing force (as in pulling). This lowering is accomplished by bending the knees and hips (Figure 3.2).

3. The center of gravity must be kept over the base of support (within the boundaries of the base) for stability and balance. When the center

THE BASIS FOR LEARNING MOTOR SKILLS ━━━━━━━━━━━ **47**

of gravity passes beyond the boundaries of the base, the person has lost balance. In most activities, the head should be kept up and excessive body lean eliminated. Keeping the body weight centered over the base of support allows for a rapid start in any direction.

4. The use of "free" or non-weight-bearing limbs can be used for counterbalance to aid stability.

Force

Force is essentially a measure of the push or pull that one object or body applies to another. Force is necessary to move objects of various types and size. The larger the object to be moved, the greater the amount of force required to cause the movement. Generating large forces usually requires the involvement of large muscle groups and a greater number of muscles than does the generation of a smaller force.

Torque is the twisting or turning effect that a force produces when it acts eccentrically with respect to a body's axis of rotation. Torque is therefore a rotational movement. An understanding of torque facilitates the understanding of levers.

Concepts that children can use include the following:

1. When resisting or applying force, the bones on either side of the major body joints should form a right angle to each other. This facilitates the development of high levels of torque by the muscles. A muscle is most effective at causing rotation when it pulls at a 90-degree angle.

2. The development of muscle tension is facilitated when the shortening phase is immediately preceded by a stretching phase. Many body movements use a stretch–shorten pattern naturally.

3. To generate greater force, body parts must be activated in a smooth, coordinated manner. For example, in throwing, the hips and trunk are rotated first and are followed in sequence by the upper arm, lower arm, hand, and fingers.

4. More force is generated when the number of muscles used is large. Muscles are capable of generating high levels of force when the contraction speed is low. For example, lifting a very heavy object rapidly is impossible.

5. Force should be absorbed over a large surface area and over as long a period of time as possible. An example of absorbing force over a large surface area is a softball player rolling after a dive through the air to catch a ball. The roll absorbs the force with the hands and the large surface area of the body. Absorbing force over a period of time implies moving, or giving, with the object. Examples are landing in a crash pad after a high jump or "giving" when catching a baseball pitch.

6. The follow-through in striking and throwing activities is necessary for the maximum application of force and the gradual reduction of momentum. An example is the continued swing of the baseball bat after striking the ball. Many errors in skill performance result from lack of follow-through (i.e., stopping the throwing arm after the ball has been released).

Leverage and Motion

Body levers are necessary to amplify force into motion. Levers offer a mechanical advantage so that less effort is needed to accomplish tasks. Motion occurs after force has been applied or when force is absorbed.

A *simple lever* is basically a bar or some other rigid structure that can rotate about a fixed point when force is applied to overcome a resistance. Levers serve one of two functions: (a) They allow a resistance greater than the applied force to be overcome; or (b) they serve to increase the distance or the speed at which a resistance can be moved. In the human body, the individual segments act as levers as they rotate about the joints.

The following are characteristics of levers and the effects they have on movement.

1. The three types of levers in the body are known as first-, second-, and third-class levers (Figure 3.3). Most of the body's levers are third-class levers; they have the point of force (produced by the muscles) between the fulcrum (joint) and the point of resistance (produced by the weight of the object to be moved).

2. Most of the levers in the body are used to gain a mechanical advantage for speed rather than to accomplish heavy tasks. Since the majority of levers are third class, students must learn to work within the body's structural and physical limits.

3. A longer force arm (distance from joint to point of force application) allows greater resistance to be overcome (Figure 3.4). This concept is useful if we are considering how to manipulate an external lever. For example, when we pry open a paint can, we apply force to the screw-

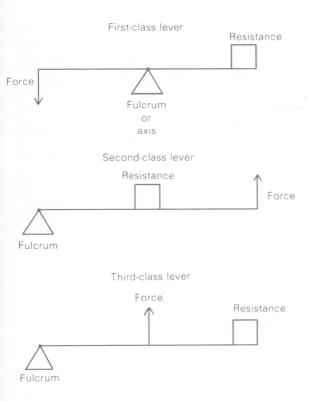

Figure 3.3 Types of levers

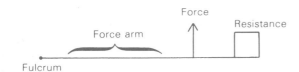

Figure 3.4 Longer force arm

Figure 3.5 Longer resistance arm

driver away from the rim rather than near the paint can. This allows the screwdriver to act as a longer lever.

4. A longer resistance arm (distance from joint to point of resistance) allows greater speed to be generated (Figure 3.5). Rackets and bats are extensions of the arm; that is, they offer longer resistance arms for applying greater speed. The longer the racket or bat, therefore, the greater the speed generated. Unfortunately, however, longer levers are more difficult to rotate. This is why young baseball players are

encouraged to choke up to make the bat easier to swing and control. Even though the lever is shortened, bat velocity (at point of contact with the ball) is probably not much reduced. The important result is that performance improves through more high-quality contacts.

Motion and Direction

Because the majority of skills involved in physical activities are associated with propelling an object, students should understand the basic principles of motion and direction.

Children can be exposed to the following concepts:

1. The angle of release determines how far an object will travel. Theoretically, the optimum angle of release is 45 degrees. The human body has various limitations, however, that cause the optimum angle of projection to be well below 45 degrees. For example, the angle of projection for the shot put is 40 to 41 degrees; for the running long jump, it is 20 to 22 degrees.

2. A ball rebounds from the floor or from the racket at the same angle at which it is hit. However, various factors, such as rotation applied to the ball, the type of ball, and the surface contacted by the ball, can modify the rebound angle.

3. In most throwing situations, the propelled object should be released at a point tangent to the target. During throwing, for example, the arm travels in an arc, and the ball must be released when the hand is in line with the target.

APPLICATION OF MECHANICAL PRINCIPLES

As students are made aware of the existence of mechanical principles, they should start applying them in learning experiences. Some applications are discussed in this section.

Starting and Stopping the Body

The following general principles can be applied to starting and stopping the body in any activity.

Ready Position

In the ready position (Figure 3.6), the feet are spread to shoulder width. For some skills, one foot

Figure 3.6 Ready position

Figure 3.7 Alternative position for a fast start

may be ahead of the other. The knees are bent slightly, the toes are pointed forward, and the weight is carried on the balls of the feet. In this position, the body can be moved equally well in any direction. The back should be reasonably straight, the head up, and the hands ready for action.

Fast Starts

When a fast start in a known direction is desired, the feet are usually spread and pointed in the direction of motion, and the body leans in the direction of the proposed movement (Figure 3.7). The center of gravity is moved forward and lowered somewhat by the body lean and by the increased bend at the knees. This causes a rapid shift of body weight in the direction of movement.

Absorbing Force

When the body is stopped quickly, force must be absorbed. The ankles, knees, and hips should bend to absorb force over as long a period of time as possible.

Falling

Falling is usually an undesirable movement, or at least an unplanned activity. Because it occurs often in sports and in movement activities, however, it must be taught. The force of the fall should be absorbed over as large an area as possible. Rolling helps spread the impact and can be accomplished by tucking the head and doing a forward or judo roll (see Chapter 20). The hands are placed on the ground, with wrists and elbows bent to absorb some of the force of landing.

Propelling Objects

Throwing, striking, kicking, batting, and bowling skills involve applying force to an object. The following principles govern these skills.

Visual Concentration

In object propulsion, the eyes focus on some point, fixed or moving, depending on the skill. When striking an object, the child should watch the ball. In shooting a basket or in bowling, the child should fix his gaze on the target. In kicking, the child should keep her head down and watch the ball. Visual–tactile coordination is required to move the body parts into the pathway of the moving projectile.

Opposition

Opposition refers to the coordinated use of the arms and legs. In walking or running, leg movement is coordinated with arm movement on the opposite side of the body. In right-handed throwing, the forward step should be made with the left foot; that is, a step with the left foot means a forward swing with the right arm.

Weight Transfer

The transfer of weight from the back to the front foot is a critical element in throwing, batting, striking, and bowling skills. Initially, the body weight is on the back foot, with the transfer occurring during execution of the skill. It is important to note that the weight is transferred to the front foot *just prior* to the release of the ball in throwing and bowling skills, and *just prior* to the action of batting or striking. This helps to assure that the body is in opposition.

Development of Torque

Development of torque involves total body coordination. In throwing or batting, the child should start with a forward motion of the hip and rotate the body, thus adding force to the thrown or batted ball.

Many skills require that the entire body be brought into play to perform the skill effectively. A child who throws primarily with the arm should be taught to bring the whole body into the action.

Follow-Through

Follow-through refers to a smooth projection of the already-initiated movement. The principle is vitally important in throwing, striking, batting, and kicking skills. In kicking, the instruction is to kick through the ball, not at it. In batting, the normal swing must be fully completed, not arrested after a hit.

Catching

Catching is an important skill in many activities and should be practiced with different objects, as each presents a different challenge.

Visual Concentration

The child must learn to track the object until it is caught. In addition, hand-eye coordination is critical to assure that the youngster is able to move the hands into the path of the projectile.

Body Position

The body should be positioned directly in line with the incoming object, and the weight should be transferred from the front to the rear foot as the object is caught. This helps spread the force of impact over time. The knees are bent as the catch is made to aid in absorbing the force. The feet are spread to increase body stability.

Giving

The child should reach out for the object and then draw the object softly toward the body as the catch is made. This is known as *giving*. Giving with the arms allows force to be absorbed over a longer period of time and helps prevent the object from rebounding out of the hands. The catch should be made with the pads of the fingers, which are spread and relaxed.

REFERENCES AND SUGGESTED READINGS

AAHPERD. (1987a). *Basic stuff, series I.* Reston, VA: AAHPERD.

AAHPERD. (1987b). *Basic stuff, series II.* Reston, VA: AAHPERD.

Anshel, M. H. (1990). An information processing approach to teaching motor skills. *JOPERD, 61*(5), 70–75.

Barrett, K. R., Williams, K., & Whitall, J. (1992). What does it mean to have a "developmentally appropriate physical education program?" *The Physical Educator, 49*(3), 113–117.

Fitts, P. M., & Posner, M. I. (1967). *Human performance.* Belmont, CA: Brooks/Cole.

Goode, S., & Magill, R. A. (1986). The contextual interference effects in learning three badminton serves. *Research Quarterly for Exercise and Sport, 57,* 308–314.

Haubenstricker, J. L., & Seefeldt, V. D. (1986). Acquisition of motor skills during childhood. In V. D. Seefeldt (Ed.), *Physical activity and well-being.* Reston, VA: AAHPERD.

Keogh, J., & Sugden, D. (1985). *Movement skill development.* New York: Macmillan.

Robertson, M. A., & Halverson, L. E. (1984). *Developing children—Their changing movement: A guide for teachers.* Philadelphia: Lea & Febiger.

Schmidt, R. A. (1975). A schema theory of discrete motor skill learning. *Psychological Review, 82,* 225–260.

Schmidt, R. A. (1977). Schema theory: Implications for movement education. *Motor Skills: Theory into Practice, 2,* 36–48.

Schmidt, R. A. (1991). *Motor learning and performance: From principles to practice.* Champaign, IL: Human Kinetics.

Stallings, L. M. (1982). *Motor learning: From theory to practice.* St. Louis, MO: C. V. Mosby.

Thomas, J. R. (1984). *Motor development during childhood and adolescence.* Minneapolis, MN: Burgess.

Wickstrom, R. L. (1983). *Fundamental motor patterns.* Philadelphia: Lea & Febiger.

Developing a Physical Education Curriculum

A curriculum is developed to give sequence and direction to the learning experiences of students. By necessity, decisions must be made concerning what experiences and activities should be included. Different approaches may be used to select and identify essential activities, but the selective criteria are based ultimately on the philosophical values of those involved in curriculum development. This value base provides the foundation on which the program is developed. Expressed in this foundation is what the writers believe about children, schools, goals, the community, and learning through movement. These philosophical beliefs give weight to the relative importance of various program elements.

Closely allied to the value base is the conceptual framework, which is a set of concepts, beliefs, and basic convictions delineated to guide program development. Out of these grows the curriculum framework. The curriculum is formed through a clear understanding of the basic urges and developmental stages of children. The urges of children in relation to activity provide guidelines for program development. These strong drives, possessed by people of all ages, govern activity participation.

The characteristics and interests of youngsters must also be understood before program objectives are developed. These differ from the basic urges in that they are age specific. Whereas urges are found in all people regardless of age or maturity, characteristics and interests are allied closely to the child's developmental stage. Children undergo considerable development and change from kindergarten through sixth grade, and these characteristics and interests have strong educational implications for curricular planning.

Directed by the philosophical and conceptual framework of the curriculum, writers formulate learning objectives based on the urges, characteristics, and interests of the learners. These objectives guide the selection of content for the curriculum. Simply stated, *curriculum content* is an organized list of learning opportunities designed to achieve expressed objectives for children. The end result for a written curriculum should be a product based on the desires, characteristics, and interests of children. It should reflect sound physical education philosophy and theory, support the objectives of the school system, and conform to the mores and culture of the community.

In building a physical education curriculum, a school or school system can take one of the following approaches:

1. Adopt a program model that is functioning in another locale, one that has been successful in terms of pupil achievement. The value base, conceptual framework, and program design are accepted in toto. Minor program changes are incorporated to fit local school situations and preferences.

2. Adapt a model program. The program selected provides a starting point from which the planners depart to make the program conform to local interests, preferences, and school philosophy. Two or more model programs might be melded into a cohesive unit.

3. Build a new model, coordinating ideas from many sources to form a unified program. This is a difficult challenge, and the group performing the task must have enough breadth of experience and understanding of curriculum development to construct an educationally sound program. As a profession, physical education has suffered from teachers "doing their own thing." In no other area in the total school program are teachers allowed to design and write a curriculum regardless of their experience or knowledge. If the result is a poorly designed curriculum, the credibility of the profession always suffers.

THE ELEMENTARY SCHOOL PHYSICAL EDUCATION CURRICULUM COMMITTEE

The primary mission of a curriculum committee is to establish and maintain a functional, practical, and educationally sound curriculum. A published curriculum must be in the hands of all elementary school teachers and administrators, even those not directly involved in the program. This wide distribution is important so that the values gained in physical education—especially the ideas and practices relevant to human wellness—can be integrated with the values and practices taught in other fields.

Value judgments are a necessary part of the curricular process, for various instructional elements must be interpreted and assigned relative importance. Someone or some group must make these judgments. The school district physical education committee is an effective way to shape a curriculum and share the responsibility for important decisions. Input on formulating or revising the curriculum should come from all concerned sources. The physical education consultant or specialist should head the committee. Committee membership should be open to classroom teacher representatives from primary and intermediate levels, an administrator, parents from the parent-teacher association (PTA), one or more community representatives (from community recreation or a service club, the chamber of commerce, or churches), and possibly selected elementary students. The committee should meet regularly to review and upgrade the curriculum. It is important to schedule a meeting at the end of the school year to consider modifications for the coming year. A report on the year's program operation can also be presented at that meeting.

A public relations plan, both inside and outside the school, should be devised by the committee to cover the new or updated curriculum. The committee should set yearly budget allocations and establish long-range plans for procuring equipment and improving facilities. An evaluation plan should be outlined to determine how well the program has achieved the stated goals, and to secure value judgments about the program from children, teachers, administrators, and parents.

FUNDAMENTAL PRINCIPLES OF CURRICULUM PLANNING

A written curriculum is a program of study that gives direction to an instructional program. It is written with the intent of ensuring that a variety of content will be presented in proper sequence. The intent of a curriculum guide is to ensure all activities are taught so youngsters receive a comprehensive and balanced physical education. The following principles give direction to the curriculum development process and form the foundation upon which a successful program is implemented.

The program is guided by goals and objectives that are appropriate for all youngsters. This implies a balanced curriculum that covers fundamental skills, sport skills, games, rhythms and dance, stunts and tumbling (gymnastics), and individual and dual activities. Emphasis of the program is to develop a broad foundation of motor skills that will develop competency and confidence in all students.

Activities are selected based on their potential to help students reach curriculum objectives. For example, selection should include regular activity of sufficient intensity to promote growth and physical fitness, as well as instructional sequences that lead to a broad range of movement competencies and skills. The elementary years are a time for experimentation, practice, and decision making about *all* activities that exist. This principle implies that activities are selected because they have educational value for all youngsters; not because the teacher likes them or responds to student preferences.

Fitness is an important component of a physical education program. The fitness program should be varied, positive, and educational. Youngsters should develop an understanding of fitness maintenance by participating in a broad and varied program of fitness activities. The fitness program is experiential, that is, students must participate in fitness activities rather than view others doing them. The fitness program should focus on two major areas; fitness activity and fitness concepts. Students should understand that fitness is personal in nature, benefits only active people, and contributes to a healthy lifestyle. Physical fitness testing should be conducted only when necessary and the results should be private and personal.

Physical education programs include activities that enhance cognitive and affective learning. Children should learn more than physical performance of skills. It is important to develop an understanding of skill performance principles. Cognitive learning related to principles and practices of physical fitness and wellness should be emphasized. Many small-group activities in physical education lend themselves to affective development—learning cooperative and social skills. Students should learn the feelings of satisfaction and accomplishment through participation in a physical education program.

The program provides experiences that allow all children to succeed and to feel satisfaction. Attention must be given to minimizing failure and emphasizing success. Learning experiences should be adjusted to the ability level of students. Activities should emphasize self improvement, participation, and cooperation instead of winning and losing. Physical education emphasizes learning, and youngsters should be able to participate without being labled as a winner or loser. Children with special needs must find success in participation.

The program is based on an educational foundation that is consistent with other academic areas in the school. Physical education teachers should have the same working conditions as other teachers in the school setting. Class sizes should be similar to other classrooms (25 to 35 students) and an assigned teaching area (e.g., multipurpose room, etc.) should be available as needed for the physical education program. Enough equipment should be available for maximum activity and participation. This implies one piece of individual equipment for each youngster and ample apparatus to assure small groups. The program should be taught on a daily basis to assure maximum opportunity for learning and retention. Finally, recess is not physical education; recess is *never* a substitute for a quality program.

Activities in the physical education program are presented in an educationally sound sequence. Progression is the soul of learning, and the curriculum should reflect progression vertically (between developmental levels) and horizontally (within each level and within each activity).

Appropriate means of assessing student progress are part of the program. Determining fitness development is important, as is monitoring skill development, cognitive learning, and attitude development toward physical activity. Any assessment conducted should be used to enhance the effectiveness of the program, that is, to individualize instruction, communicate with parents, identify youngsters with special needs, and evaluate the quality of the program. Fitness test scores and individual skill performance should not be criteria for a grade since much of fitness and skill performance is genetically limited (see Chapter 2).

Opportunities are offered in the form of intramurals, sport days, playdays, sport competition, and recreational play. Such programs should give children who are especially interested and skilled an additional opportunity to perform and compete, but should be organized to assure that *all* youngsters can participate without embarrassment. These activities should foster group cooperation and a feeling of importance and contribution for each youngster.

WRITING THE CURRICULUM GUIDE

The curriculum guide should be written in a systematic fashion. The curriculum philosophy and conceptual framework should be established before the selection of activities and movement themes. The steps that follow offer an articulated and sequential approach for designing a meaningful, well-planned guide. The first five steps establish a framework for selecting activities to be used in the curriculum. These steps are often ignored by teachers; instead, they choose to focus on activities and applied material. Unfortunately, this can result in a curriculum with little unified direction. This is similar to building a house or skyscraper without blueprints and prior planning. One result would be a structure that might not fit into the existing environment. In addition, the structure might have too much of one material (such as paint) and not enough of another (perhaps roofing materials). The point is that without planning and direction prior to gathering activities, the finished curriculum is left to chance. It is difficult to justify designing a curriculum without planning when the end result is so important—the education of children.

Step One: Develop a Philosophy for the Program

The initial step in curriculum design is defining a philosophy of physical education. The philosophical statement should define how physical education fits into the total school curriculum and what it should accomplish for each student. What follows in this section is often found in such statements.

Physical education is that portion of the child's overall education that is accomplished through movement. It is education about and involving movement. Physical education must be largely an instructional program if it is to acquire a full partnership in the child's overall education. Only high-quality programs based on developmental goals with demonstrable and accountable outcomes achieve this respect.

Using the overriding educational goal of American schools—to develop an individual who can live effectively in a democracy—one then selects critical contributions that physical education can make to meet this goal. Although physical education stresses psychomotor goals, it also contributes to cognitive and affective learning domains. Physical education programs make unique contributions to child development. Three major and unique contributions of a quality physical education program are as follows.

1. *The development of personal physical fitness habits.* This contribution means more than pushing youngsters through demanding physical exercise. Teachers must teach children the conceptual framework in which personal fitness is developed. This implies teaching the concept of human wellness (i.e., teaching students how to maintain a vibrant and functional lifestyle throughout adulthood).

2. *The development and enhancement of movement competency.* For primary-grade children, movement competency is rooted in developing broad areas of body management and general movement skills. As students mature, instructional progressions lead to increased skill in fundamental movements and to specialized sport skills.

3. *An understanding of movement and movement principles.* Understanding movement includes learning Laban's concepts of movement and understanding both anatomical and mechanical principles that are necessary for critical performance.

A physical education program is of dubious value if it does not accomplish these major outcomes, for these contributions are unique to the physical education area. Only in physical education can students learn how to diagnose, prescribe, and evaluate personal fitness qualities, how to develop lifetime sport skills, and how to analyze movement principles. Youngsters will leave school without these abilities if the physical education program is inadequate, poorly organized, or nonexistent.

Step Two: Build a Conceptual Framework for the Curriculum

The conceptual framework consists of statements that characterize the curriculum. These concepts establish an umbrella for the activities and experiences included in the curriculum. The framework not only directs the activities but also reflects beliefs about education and the learner. Following

Physical education implies movement for all children.

are basic conceptual statements that should consistently guide the formulation of a child-centered, developmental curriculum.

1. *The physical education curriculum must be developmentally appropriate.* Activity selection must be based on the urges and characteristics of youngsters and geared to their developmental level. Children are the center of the curriculum, and experiences must be selected based on their needs. Activities should not be selected because they are favorites of teachers or students, or avoided because the teacher lacks knowledge in an area. A professional looks beyond personal shortcomings—directly into the eyes of the learner.

2. *Students must be viewed as unique in terms of needs and learning capabilities.* All children have the right to reach their potential, and the curriculum must provide an opportunity for such achievement. Children should move at a pace that is challenging, educationally sound, and capable of enhancing their development. Individual differences must dictate the application of the curriculum, so that objectives, activities, and learning experiences meet the needs of individuals rather than the perceived needs of a single, unified group. Because students learn in different ways, alternative teaching methods and styles should be employed. Underlying all teaching approaches is the belief

that students can and do learn independently, and that students must be given the opportunity to make personal decisions about what is important and relevant.

3. *Children must be seen as whole and complete beings.* This means extending the curriculum beyond the development of physical skills and personal fitness. In the cognitive area, associated learnings should accompany the development of physical fitness and skills. In developing physical fitness, for example, children should reach an understanding of why they are doing what they are doing. Skill development should feature not only the how but also the why. In the affective domain, achieving physical success plays a critical role in developing a positive self-concept. Children who achieve motor efficiency and are physically successful are usually better adjusted to school life than are less capable, underdeveloped children. The hidden curriculum, the manner in which the learning environment and the instruction are structured, has a powerful impact on student norms, values, and beliefs.

4. *The program must focus on educating students.* Activities must be directed and conducted in a manner that ensures that the objectives of physical education can be attained. The values of physical education are not gained automatically or by accident. Desired

affective outcomes such as fair play, self-discipline, and peer cooperation do not result simply from participation in physical activities. Physical education must be mainly an instructional program, employing educationally sound teaching strategies.

5. *Movement must be the basis of physical education.* Movement is essential if physical learning and accomplishment are to occur. Program quality can be evaluated in part by the degree of movement each child experiences. Physical education implies activity. Children do not profit from standing in line, waiting for equipment to be arranged, listening to lengthy teacher explanations, or participating in an activity dominated by a few students.

6. *The program must offer students skills for a lifetime of use.* In today's society, the maintenance of physical fitness and wellness is of prime importance. The program must be vigorous and dynamic to develop physiological fitness in students. Fitness, which serves as a foundation for the achievement of most motor skills, should be functional and presented in such a manner that varying workloads are allocated for each student. The emphasis should be on wellness and fitness for life.

Developmental Levels

Activities and units of instruction are organized by developmental levels throughout this text. If instruction is going to be effective and meaningful for students, it must be presented to students in a developmentally appropriate form, one that assures success. Figure 4.1 illustrates the continuum of skill development through which most youngsters progress in a logical manner. Even though this developmental skill continuum is common to all youngsters, there is great variability among individual children as to when they will master certain skills. The reason for placing activities in different developmental levels is to encourage teachers to present activities to children that are appropriate for their maturity and developmental level. When necessary, teachers should incorporate activities from the level that best suits the individual student.

Deciding how to arrange activities for instruction is difficult because schools group children by chronological age and grade rather than develop-

Figure 4.1 Continuum of skill development

Physical Fitness for All Grades

Developmental Sequence

Specialized Skills
Large apparatus, hand apparatus, rhythmics (dance), games and sports, stunts and tumbling, aquatics, fitness activities

Fundamental Skills
Locomotor (walk, run, hop, skip, slide, leap, jump, gallop, stop, dodge, change direction)
Nonlocomotor (bend, twist, reach, lift, raise, lower, turn, curl, stretch, bridge, rock, balance)
Manipulative (throw, catch, volley, kick, bat, strike, bounce, dribble, balance, jump-rope)

Body Management Competence
Control of the body (on floor, across floor, in flight, on apparatus; with emphasis on balance, coordination, laterality, directionality, spatial judgments, identification of body parts, postural efficiency)

Table 4.1 Equating developmental levels to grades and ages

Developmental Level	Grades	Ages
I	K–2	5–7
II	3–4	8–9
III	5–6	10–11

mental level. The majority of classroom teachers are responsible for a graded group of youngsters, and often find it difficult to understand how and when to utilize the developmental levels. Table 4.1 shows how the developmental levels roughly equate with grades and ages. The following section describes characteristics of learners at each level, and identifies skills and competencies typical of children in each of the levels.

Developmental Level I

For the majority of children, activities placed in developmental level I are appropriate for *kindergarten through second-grade* children. Learner characteristics in developmental level I make it necessary to create an enjoyable and instructional learning environment. By stressing joy and rewards through physical activity, positive behaviors are developed that last a lifetime. The majority of activities for younger children are individual in nature and center on learning movement concepts through theme development. Children learn about movement principles, and educational movement themes are used to teach body identification and body management skills.

Developmental Level II

Developmental level II activities are usually appropriate for the majority of *third- and fourth-grade* children. However, as mentioned in Chapter 2, it is common to find youngsters who are performing at level I or level III. In developmental level II activities, refinement of fundamental skills occurs and the ability to perform specialized skills begins to surface. Visual–tactile coordination is enhanced by using manipulative skills. Children should be allowed the opportunity to explore, experiment, and create activities without fear. While not stressing conformity, children need to absorb the how and also the why of activity patterns. Cooperation with peers is important as more emphasis is placed on group and team play. Initial instruction in sport skills begins in developmental level II and a number of lead-up activities are utilized so youngsters can apply newly learned skills in a small-group setting.

Developmental Level III

Developmental level III activities are characterized by more emphasis on specialized skills and sport activities. The majority of activities at this level can be used with *fifth- and sixth-grade* students. Football, basketball, softball, track and field, volleyball, and hockey are added to the sport offerings. Students continue learning and improving sport skills while participating in cooperative sport lead-up games. Less emphasis is placed on movement concept activities and a larger percentage of instructional time is devoted to manipulative activity. Adequate time is set aside for the rhythmic program and for the program area involving apparatus, stunts, and tumbling.

At this level, increased emphasis is placed on physical fitness and developmental activities. Organized and structured fitness routines are offered so that students can begin to make decisions about personal approaches to maintaining fitness levels. Fitness self-testing is incorporated into the program so students can learn how to evaluate and prescribe activities that are personalized for their fitness levels.

Step Three: Examine the Basic Urges of Children

A basic urge is a desire to do or accomplish something. All children have similar feelings, which may be hereditary or environmentally influenced. Basic urges are linked closely to societal influences and can be affected by teachers, parents, and peers. Usually, basic urges are similar among youngsters of all ages and not affected by developmental maturity. These desires provide important direction for writing a physical education curriculum that is child centered.

The Urge for Movement

Children have an insatiable appetite for moving, performing, and being active. They run for the sheer joy of running. For them, activity is the essence of living. The physical education program must satisfy this craving for movement.

The Urge for Success and Approval

Children not only like to achieve; they also want their achievements to be recognized. They wilt under criticism and disapproval, whereas encouragement and friendly support promote maximum growth and development. Failure can lead to frustration, lack of interest, and inefficient learning.

Successes should far outweigh failures, and students should achieve a measure of success during each class meeting.

The Urge for Peer Acceptance and Social Competency

Peer acceptance is a basic human need. Children want others to accept, respect, and like them. The school environment should offer ways to gain peer acceptance. Learning to cooperate with others, being a contributing team member, and sharing accomplishments with friends are important outcomes of the physical education program.

The Urge to Cooperate and Compete

Children enjoy working and playing with other children. They find satisfaction in being a necessary part of a group, and they experience sadness when others reject them. Cooperation must be taught prior to competitive experiences since there can be no competition if people choose not to cooperate and follow the rules. Often, the joy of being part of a group far outweighs the gains from peer competition.

The urge to compete is evident in a child's desire to match physical skill and strength with peers. Children are willing to show this urge when they think they have a chance of winning. If the child has no opportunity to win, then the situation is not competitive and failure is preordained. Equated competition, in which each youngster has a chance to win, should be provided and monitored.

The Urge for Physical Fitness and Attractiveness

Every teacher should understand how eager boys and girls are to be fit and active, and to possess a body that is agile and attractive. Much humiliation is suffered by youngsters who are weak, fat, crippled, or abnormal in any way. Programs should offer opportunity for self-improvement so that youngsters can cope with subpar strength, obesity, lack of physical skill, and inadequate physical fitness. Teachers should monitor reward systems carefully to be sure they acknowledge every child in the class.

The Urge for Adventure

The drive to participate in something different, adventurous, or unusual impels children to participate in interesting new activities. Teachers should space inherently exciting activities throughout the curriculum. This tends to enhance youngsters' levels of anticipation and excitement.

The Urge for Creative Satisfaction

Children like to try different ways of doing things, to experiment with different materials, and to explore what they can do creatively. Finding different ways to express themselves physically satisfies this urge for creative action.

The Urge for Rhythmic Expression

All boys and girls enjoy rhythm. Rhythm implies movement, and children like to move. The program should offer a variety of rhythmic activities that all students can learn well enough to achieve satisfaction. Youngsters should also be shown the natural rhythm involved in all types of activity. Many effective and beautiful sport movements can be done rhythmically (e.g., shooting a lay-up, jumping a rope, running hurdles).

The Urge to Know

Young people are naturally curious. They are interested not only in what they are doing but also in why they are doing it. Knowing why is a great motivator. It takes little time or effort to share with a class why an activity is performed and the contributions it makes to physical development.

Step Four: Identify the Characteristics and Interests of Children

The urges of children represent broad traits that are typical of children regardless of age, sex, or race. In contrast, characteristics and interests are age- and maturity-specific attributes that influence learning objectives. The characteristics and interests chart (Table 4.2) provides critical information for program development and offers direction for appropriate selection and sequencing of curriculum activities. Bear in mind that these are general estimates; youngsters vary a great deal in both physical and psychological maturity.

The information in the characteristics and interests chart is grouped under the three learning domains—psychomotor, cognitive, and affective. This helps assure that activities will be selected based on the needs of the whole child rather than solely the physical domain. Each of these domains is described below.

1. Psychomotor domain. This domain is the primary focus of physical educators. It is based

Rhythmic activity is an important component of physical education.

on learning physical skills. Corbin (1976) developed a taxonomy of objectives in this area. The seven levels in this domain are movement vocabulary, movement of body parts, locomotor movements, moving implements and objects, patterns of movement, moving with others, and movement problem solving. This graduated list progresses in line with the developmental level of learners. Children need to learn the vocabulary of movement before proceeding to simple body part movements. More complex movements are learned to enable youngsters to participate in activities with others and solve personal movement dilemmas.

2. Cognitive domain. This area is often referred to as the knowledge area; however, the cognitive domain was developed by Bloom (1956) and includes more than knowing facts. The six major areas in the cognitive domain are knowledge, comprehension, application, analysis, synthesis, and evaluation. The focus of the cognitive domain in physical education is on knowing rules, health information, safety, and so on, and being able to understand and apply such knowledge. As students mature, they should learn to analyze different activities, develop personalized exercise routines (synthesis), and know how to evaluate their fitness levels.

3. Affective domain. The affective domain (Krathwohl et al., 1964) deals with feelings, attitudes, and values. The major categories of learning in this area are receiving, responding, valuing, organization, and characterization. The affective domain changes more slowly than the psychomotor and cognitive domains. If physical education programs are to have a lasting effect on students, it is important that students have a positive set of values related to this area. How students are treated by teachers and the feelings they develop toward physical education may ultimately be more important than the knowledge and skill developed in physical education programs.

Step Five: Determine Program Objectives

Two types of objectives, institutional and student centered, need to be written when developing the curriculum.

Institutional Objectives

Institutional objectives determine the direction of the program as dictated and desired by the state, district, or individual school. These objectives are general in nature and are used to specify long-term goals of the institution. Institutional objectives dictate the general outcomes that teachers are expected to accomplish and students to learn. Institutional objectives are usually written in the three learning domains: psychomotor, cognitive, and affective. The following are

Table 4.2 Characteristics and interests of children

Characteristics and Interests	Program Guidelines
Developmental Level I	

Psychomotor Domain

Noisy, constantly active, egocentric, exhibitionistic. Imitative and imaginative. Want attention.	Include vigorous games and stunts, games with individual roles (hunting, dramatic activities, story plays), and a few team games or relays.
Large muscles more developed; game skills not developed.	Challenge with varied movement. Develop specialized skills of throwing, catching, and bouncing balls.
Naturally rhythmic.	Use music and rhythm with skills. Provide creative rhythms, folk dances, and singing movement songs.
May become suddenly tired but soon recover.	Use activities of brief duration. Provide short rest periods or intersperse physically demanding activities with less vigorous ones.
Hand-eye coordination developing.	Give opportunity to handle different objects such as balls, beanbags, and hoops.
Perceptual abilities maturing.	Give practice in balance—unilateral, bilateral, and cross-lateral movements.
Pelvic tilt can be pronounced.	Give attention to posture problems. Provide abdominal strengthening activities.

Cognitive Domain

Short attention span.	Change activity often. Give short explanations.
Interested in what the body can do. Curious.	Provide movement experiences. Pay attention to educational movement.
Want to know. Often ask *why* about movement.	Explain reasons for various activities and the basis of movement.
Express individual views and ideas.	Allow children time to be creative. Expect problems when children are lined up and asked to perform the same task.
Begin to understand the idea of teamwork.	Plan situations that require group cooperation. Discuss the importance of such.
Sense of humor expands.	Insert some humor in the teaching process.
Highly creative.	Allow students to try new and different ways of performing activities; sharing ideas with friends encourages creativity.

Affective Domain

No sex differences in interests.	Set up same activities for boys and girls.
Sensitive and individualistic; self-concept very important.	Teach taking turns, sharing, and learning to win, lose, or be caught gracefully.
Accept defeat poorly. Like small-group activity.	Use entire class group sparingly. Break into smaller groups.
Sensitive to feelings of adults. Like to please teacher.	Give frequent praise and encouragement.
Can be reckless.	Stress safe approaches.
Enjoy rough-and-tumble activity.	Include rolling, dropping to the floor, and so on, in both introductory and program activities. Stress simple stunts and tumbling.

Characteristics and Interests	Program Guidelines
Seek personal attention.	Recognize individuals through both verbal and nonverbal means. See that all have a chance to be the center of attention.
Love to climb and explore play environments.	Provide play materials, games, and apparatus for strengthening large muscles (e.g., climbing towers, climbing ropes, jump ropes, miniature Challenge Courses, and turning bars).

Developmental Level II

Psychomotor Domain

Capable of rhythmic movement.	Continue creative rhythms, singing movement songs, and folk dancing.
Improved hand-eye and perceptual-motor coordination.	Give opportunity for manipulating hand apparatus. Provide movement experience and practice in perceptual-motor skills (right and left, unilateral, bilateral, and cross-lateral movements).
More interest in sports.	Begin introductory sports and related skills and simple lead-up activities.
Sport-related skill patterns mature in some cases.	Emphasize practice in these skill areas through simple ball games, stunts, and rhythmic patterns.
Developing interest in fitness.	Introduce some of the specialized fitness activities to 3rd grade.
Reaction time slow.	Avoid highly organized ball games that require and place a premium on quickness and accuracy.

Cognitive Domain

Still active but attention span longer. More interest in group play.	Include active big-muscle program and more group activity. Begin team concept in activity and relays.
Curious to see what they can do. Love to be challenged and will try anything.	Offer challenges involving movement problems and more critical demands in stunts, tumbling, and apparatus work. Emphasize safety and good judgment.
Interest in group activities; ability to plan with others developing.	Offer group activities and simple dances that involve cooperation with a partner or a team.

Affective Domain

Like physical contact and belligerent games.	Include dodging games and other active games, as well as rolling stunts.
Developing more interest in skills. Want to excel.	Organize practice in a variety of throwing, catching, and moving skills, as well as others.
Becoming more conscious socially.	Teach need to abide by rules and play fairly. Teach social customs and courtesy in rhythmic areas.
Like to perform well and to be admired for accomplishments.	Begin to stress quality. Provide opportunity to achieve.
Essentially honest and truthful.	Accept children's word. Give opportunity for trust in game and relay situations.
Do not lose willingly.	Provide opportunity for children to learn to accept defeat gracefully and to win with humility.
Sex difference still of little importance.	Avoid separation of sexes in any activity.

Table 4.2 *continued*

Characteristics and Interests	Program Guidelines

Developmental Level III

Psychomotor Domain

Steady growth. Girls often grow more rapidly than boys.	Continue vigorous program to enhance physical development.
Muscular coordination and skills improving. Interested in learning detailed techniques.	Continue emphasis on teaching skills through drills, lead-up games, and free practice periods. Emphasize correct form.
Differences in physical capacity and skill development.	Offer flexible standards so all find success. In team activities, match teams evenly so individual skill levels are less apparent.
Posture problems may appear.	Include posture correction and special posture instruction; emphasize effect of body carriage on self-concept.
Sixth-grade girls may show signs of maturity; may not wish to participate in all activities.	Have consideration for their problems. Encourage participation on a limited basis, if necessary.
Sixth-grade boys are rougher and stronger.	Keep sexes together for skill development but separate for competition in certain rougher activities.

Cognitive Domain

Want to know rules of games.	Include instruction on rules, regulations, and traditions.
Knowledgeable about and interested in sport and game strategy.	Emphasize strategy, as opposed to merely performing a skill without concern for context.
Question the relevance and importance of various activities.	Explain regularly the reasons for performing activities and learning various skills.
Desire information about the importance of physical fitness and health-related topics.	Include in lesson plans brief explanations of how various activities enhance growth and development.

Affective Domain

Enjoy team and group activity. Competitive urge strong. Much interest in sports and sport-related activities.	Include many team games, relays, and combatives. Offer a variety of sports in season, with emphasis on lead-up games.
Little interest in the opposite sex. Some antagonism may arise.	Offer coeducational activities with emphasis on individual differences of all participants, regardless of sex.
Acceptance of self-responsibility. Strong increase in drive toward independence.	Provide leadership and followership opportunities on a regular basis. Involve students in evaluation procedures.
Intense desire to excel both in skill and in physical capacity.	Stress physical fitness. Include fitness and skill surveys both to motivate and to check progress.
Sportsmanship a concern for both teachers and students.	Establish and enforce fair rules. With enforcement include an explanation of the need for rules and cooperation if games are to exist.
Peer group important. Want to be part of the gang.	Stress group cooperation in play and among teams. Rotate team positions as well as squad makeup.

examples of institutional objectives for a physical education program.

Psychomotor Domain

1. The physical education program will help children become competent in a wide variety of motor skills and movements:
   a. fundamental motor skills, including locomotor, nonlocomotor, and manipulative skills
   b. body management skills
   c. rhythmic movement skills
   d. specialized motor skills

2. The physical education program will provide children an opportunity to participate in activities designed to develop and maintain health-related physical fitness commensurate with individual needs. Students will also learn an active lifestyle and know how to maintain fitness and wellness throughout life.

3. Through physical education, children will learn physical skills that allow them to participate in and enjoy physical activity throughout their adult years.

Cognitive Domain

1. Through a broad program of movement, each child will develop an understanding of movement concepts and the underlying principles of movement involved.

2. Within the physical education program, children will acquire a knowledge of safety skills and habits, and develop an awareness of safety with respect to themselves and others.

Affective Domain

1. The physical education program will provide an environment that will allow children to acquire desirable social standards and ethical concepts.

2. Physical education instruction will help each child develop a desirable self-concept through relevant and positive experiences.

Student-Centered Objectives

After institutional objectives have been determined, student-centered objectives are written. These objectives dictate what specific activities are taught and learned throughout the school year. Student-centered objectives are often written in behavioral terms. Behavioral objectives contain three key characteristics: (a) the desired behavior must be observable; (b) the behavior is measureable; and (c) the criterion for success is measurable. These objectives can be written in all three of the learning domains mentioned above. In physical education they are usually written for the psychomotor domain. The following are examples of behavioral objectives taken from *Lesson Plans for Dynamic Physical Education for Elementary School Children,* by Pangrazi and Dauer:[1]

Psychomotor Domain

1. The student will be able to gallop for 10 seconds.

2. The student will be able to perform grass drills continuously for 90 seconds.

Cognitive Domain

1. The student will be able to identify which bench activities develop arm and shoulder girdle strength.

2. The student will be able to recite the reason exercises should be performed throughout the full range of motion.

Affective Domain

1. The student will demonstrate a positive attitude toward juggling by practicing during free time.

2. The student will demonstrate an understanding of cooperation by playing a team game during free activity.

Behavioral objectives are time consuming to write. Many teachers become bogged down and discouraged due to the fact that the number of objectives that must be written becomes overwhelming. A less complex alternative is to list activities that will be used to reach institutional objectives. For example, a number of activities could be used to develop physical fitness. These activities can be listed under the objective, as shown below.

Physical Fitness: Arm and Shoulder Girdle Strength

1. Exercises
   a. Push-Ups
   b. Reclining Pull-Ups

[1]*Lesson Plans for Dynamic Physical Education for Elementary School Children, 11th edition* (1995), is available from Macmillan. This supplementary text sequences all the activities in this book into lesson plans for developmental levels I, II, and III.

    c. Arm Circles

    d. Crab Kick

    e. Crab Alternate-Leg Extension

    f. Crab Full-Leg Extension

    g. Crab Walk

2. Animal walks

    a. Alligator Crawl

    b. Puppy Dog Run

    c. Cat Walk

    d. Lame Dog Walk

    e. Seal Crawl

    f. Crab Walk

3. Parachute activities

    a. Dorsal Lift

    b. Backward Pull

    c. Flexed Arm Pulls

    d. Elevator

These are just examples of the many types of activities that can be used to develop arm-shoulder girdle strength. Even though this method is not as exacting as behavioral objectives, it does give direction to the curriculum and helps the instructor understand *why* an activity is included in the curriculum. In addition, it makes it easier for the teacher to explain to students why such activities are being used. Students, as well as teachers, need to have a clear understanding of why activities are performed and what value they offer.

Step Six: Consider Restrictive Factors

Restrictive factors are defined as current conditions within the community or school district that limit the scope of the curriculum. Examples of restrictive factors are the amount and type of equipment, budget size, and cultural makeup of the community. Other factors, such as the support of school administrators, also may affect the type of scheduling or amount of required physical education in the school. Many educators start with restrictive factors when developing a curriculum guide. Their thinking is that one should know what can't be done before deciding what can be accomplished. Unfortunately, this approach severely limits the ultimate quality of the curriculum.

Although restrictive factors need to be examined carefully, they should not circumvent and limit curriculum scope and sequence. The curriculum should be a roadmap to excellence. It should be broad in scope and sequence and offer as much

variety and depth as possible. Program objectives should be written prior to reviewing restrictive factors, to assure that the result is a statement to the administration, teachers, and community expressing what elements a quality curriculum contains regardless of district and community shortcomings. It also communicates to school officials what types of equipment, facilities, and schedules are needed to present a quality program. When restrictive factors are considered prior to writing program objectives, the result is a reflection of the status quo and a regurgitation of what is currently being taught in the program. This is a serious problem, because the curriculum guide should communicate to teachers, administrators, parents, and students what a well-conceived program *should* be, rather than reiterate the limitations of the current program. A well-designed curriculum is a goal, direction, and destination for the future; a roadmap to instructional success. Restrictive factors should be considered carefully but not to the degree that they stunt the creativity and scope of the curriculum.

Following are examples of restrictive factors that limit the development of a broad and comprehensive curriculum. Although these factors may be limiting, they can also be handled creatively, to assure an effective curriculum. Think big; develop a comprehensive and ideal curriculum that is as varied, broad, and creative as possible. Seek consistently to expand and develop the curriculum beyond these limiting factors.

School Administrators

The support of school administrators has a significant impact on the curriculum. It is important for physical education teachers to interpret program goals to administrators. Like the general public, many administrators have misconceptions about physical education and its contribution to the overall education of students. Communication between the staff and administration is a key factor if the curriculum is to be expanded and improved on a regular basis. In most cases, administrators will agree with and support physical education if they perceive that program philosophy is built on sound educational principles that can be documented and evaluated.

The Community: People and Climate

The community needs to be considered when implementing a curriculum. Physical educators should become familiar with the types of people prevalent in the community. Occupations, religions, educational levels, cultural values, and physical activity habits are factors that can affect curriculum development. Parents have a strong influence on the activity interests and habits of their children.

The geographical location and the climate of the area are also important factors for consideration. The terrain (mountains, deserts, plains, and so on), combined with the weather conditions particular to each area, has an effect on people's activity interests. Extremely hot or cold climates influence markedly what activities can be arranged in the curriculum and at what time of the year they should be scheduled. The curriculum must include plans and alternatives for rainy climates and for extremely hot or frigid climates.

Facilities and Equipment

The available teaching facilities dictate in part activities that can be offered. Facilities include the on-campus as well as off-campus areas in the neighboring community. Off-campus facilities may include a community swimming pool or park.

Equipment is important for presentation variety and for assuring the maximum practice time for students. It must be available in quality and quantity. In many cases, one piece of equipment per child is necessary if students are to learn at an optimum rate. Equipment can be purchased with school funds or with special funds raised by students through demonstration programs. Some types of equipment can be constructed by school maintenance departments or as industrial arts projects. Yet another possibility is to have the students bring equipment, such as jump ropes, soccer balls, and foam balls, from home.

Laws and Requirements

Laws, regulations, and requirements at the national, state, and local levels may restrict or direct a curriculum. Programs must be developed to conform to these laws. Examples of two national laws affecting physical education programs are Title IX of the Educational Amendments Act of 1972 and Public Law 94–142. The former enforces equal opportunities for both sexes, and the latter mandates equal access to educational services for disabled students. Individual states also may have various laws that affect physical education programming.

Scheduling

The schedule or organizational pattern of the school has an impact on curriculum development. How many times per week the classes meet, the length of the class periods, and who teaches the

Quality programs demand adequate equipment.

classes are factors to consider. Many scheduling alternatives exist: daily, two or three times per week, every other week, and other variations. Regardless of the parameters, most elementary schools put together a scheduling committee consisting of a number of classroom teachers, specialists in other areas such as art and music, and the physical education teacher.

Several factors need to be considered when developing schedules. The length of periods should be near 30 minutes. Some teachers like 40 minutes for upper-grade youngsters; however, such periods can be too long and children may become fatigued. On the other end of the spectrum, periods can be too short. Many schools try to compress periods for primary-grade children to 20 minutes. Most teachers find this to be much too short and are unable to present a balanced and complete lesson. Another question is how many periods a physical education teacher should teach per day. Certainly a physical education teacher should not be expected to have more contact time with students than classroom teachers do. Teaching physical education is demanding and it is unfair to expect physical education specialists to teach all day without some relief. An acceptable workload is eight or nine 30-minute periods per day with at least 5 minutes of passing time between classes so teachers can rearrange the equipment, talk to students, and take care of personal matters. It is difficult to teach with classes scheduled back to back. Not only do teachers need time to prepare for the next lesson, but it keeps classes from overlapping each other and having to wait for the other class to finish. Classes should be scheduled by developmental levels; all developmental level I children should be scheduled in a block, and so on. An effective program is equipment intensive; scheduling by developmental level reduces equipment and teaching preparations.

Budget and Funding

The amount of funding allocated for purchasing new equipment and replacing old supplies has an impact on curriculum growth. This reinforces the need for a broad and varied curriculum guide, because the guide states what equipment and apparatus are necessary to present a comprehensive program. It tells the administration what is needed and documents that the need is based on sound educational objectives. Equipment needs should be listed in order of priority so that budget planners can make decisions about what is needed most and how much it will cost.

Physical educators must seek parity in funding with other school program areas. Students are not expected to learn to read and write without materials and supplies. In similar fashion, they cannot learn physical skills without the necessary equipment and supplies.

Step Seven: Determine Areas of Program Emphasis

A written curriculum gives direction and continuity to the program. The curriculum development process assures that scope, sequence, and balance are considered and planned into the curriculum. Each of these areas must be addressed.

Scope

Scope is generally used to delineate the yearly content of the curriculum. Scope is also referred to as *horizontal articulation*. Planning the scope of the curriculum assures that the content of the program during the academic year will be covered in a systematic and accountable fashion. The scope of the curriculum should include activities that are designed to meet the objectives of the program.

Sequence

The sequence, or *vertical articulation*, of the program defines the skills and activities to be covered on a year-to-year basis. Sequence assures that

there will be an articulation of instruction between grades or developmental levels. Of particular importance is the articulation of program material throughout elementary, junior, and senior high school programs. Sequence also concerns itself with the order in which skills are presented. For example, basic ball skills should be taught before basketball skills. Emphasis on sequence is important if the curriculum is going to be developmental in nature.

Balance

Balance in a curriculum assures that all objectives in the program receive adequate coverage. When reviewing the scope and sequence of the curriculum, checking for balance avoids a skewing toward one particular area. To assure balance, major areas of emphasis are determined based on program objectives. These areas can be allotted a percentage of program time based on the characteristics and interests of students. This determination reveals to administrators, teachers, and parents the direction and emphasis of the program. Table 4.3 illustrates a sample emphasis chart. All areas must have a proportionate share of instructional time, and the percentage of time allotted to each program area should reflect the needs and characteristics of youngsters by their respective developmental levels.

Another way to examine balance is to review the type of organization required for units. For example, units can be categorized by the type of student interaction required, that is, individual, dual (partner), small group, or large group. Team sports require organization in a large group, whereas a movement concepts lesson is individual in nature. Learning to catch could be a partner activity, whereas a lead-up game would require small groups. Curriculums should strive to offer a balance of all types of units to assure children a chance to experience the type of organization they most enjoy. Some children prefer individual activity and others enjoy group activity. Balance can be assured by evenly distributing the types of units being taught throughout the year.

Step Eight: Select Appropriate Activities

The major guideline to follow when selecting activities for the curriculum is: Do the activities contribute to program and institutional objectives? This approach contrasts with selecting activities because they are fun or because the teacher enjoys

Table 4.3 Elementary school physical education program emphasis

Activity	Suggested Yearly Percentage of Time for Each Level
Developmental Level I	
Introductory (warm-up) activities	10
Fitness routines and activities	27
Educational movement	13
Fundamental skills	8
Rhythmic activities	16
Apparatus, stunts, tumbling	9
Low-organized games	17
Swimming and water safety	*
Developmental Level II	
Introductory (warm-up) activities	10
Fitness routines and activities	27
Fundamental skills	5
Rhythmic activities	12
Apparatus, stunts, tumbling, combatives	12
Sport skills and related activities	17
Low-organized games and relays	17
Swimming and water safety	*
Developmental Level III	
Introductory (warm-up) activities	10
Fitness routines and activities	27
Fundamental skills	2
Rhythmic activities	9
Apparatus, stunts, tumbling, combatives	12
Sport skills and related activities	23
Low-organized games and relays	17
Swimming and water safety	*

*Swimming and water safety is a recommended area of instruction for elementary school children. The emphasis on this area depends on the facilities and instruction available. If swimming is included in the school program, the percentage of time allotted to other activities is reduced proportionately.

them. Some teachers fail to include activities in the curriculum if they lack confidence or feel incompetent in teaching them. This severely limits the curriculum, resulting in a program designed by and for the teacher rather than the students. If an activity is appropriate for the curriculum and benefits students, teachers need to develop instructional competency with the activity. Imagine if a math teacher chose not to teach fractions to students because of feelings of incompetence. It is the responsibility of teachers to expand their capabilities and assure that students experience and learn all requisite physical skills.

As many activities as possible should be gathered in the planning stage. The greater the number of activities considered, the more varied and imaginative the final program. Even though it is important to consider the scope, sequence, and balance of the curriculum, emphasis in this step should be placed on selecting activities rather than designing the curriculum. Scope, sequence, and balance are considered carefully in step 10, designing the year-long curriculum plan. At this step, stress should be placed on brainstorming, creating, and innovating without restriction. How can the finished curriculum meet the needs of all children if it is limited at this step?

Step Nine: Organize Selected Activities into Instructional Units

After appropriate and varied activities have been selected, an organizational scheme must be developed. The activities can be placed in instructional activity units or sequences. The activities in these units should be organized along a continuum, from the easiest to the most difficult. As the units are taught and field tested by children, the activity order may be changed. Organizing the activities in a progression (a) helps children meet with success rather than failure at the start of the unit, (b) ensures that safety and liability factors are met, since the activities are presented in proper sequence, and (c) aids teachers in finding a starting point for sound instruction. Initial activities in each unit of instruction should contain activities that all children can perform, and should then move gradually to more challenging activities. One of the best ways to begin a new unit of instruction is to assure that students don't fail. This recommended progression of activities helps students develop a positive feeling about the unit and accomplishes skill review at the same time.

Another valuable technique is to develop a list of pertinent instructional procedures to remind teachers about various points of emphasis. These might include safety hints, notes on how to teach for quality, methods of dispersing equipment, ways to expand the activity for variety, and crucial factors to be emphasized for proper motor skill development. An accompanying lesson plan text by Pangrazi and Dauer (1995) takes all the activities in this textbook and places them into lesson plans by developmental level. The lesson plans contain proper activity progressions, instructional procedures, and learning objectives to help teachers streamline their planning requirements. In addition to the weekly lesson plans, a year-long curriculum plan (see step 10) is offered for each of the three developmental levels.

Step Ten: Develop a Year-Long Curriculum Plan

Table 4.4 is an example of a year-long plan that illustrates the parallel listing of the four parts of the lesson. The suggested percentages in Table 4.3 can be used to determine how many weeks of instruction should be devoted to a specific area. Introductory activities, fitness development, lesson focus, and closing activities should be incorporated into the yearly plan. A plan similar to Table 4.4 ensures that youngsters learn many ways of warming up for activity and approximately 15 different methods of enhancing fitness. In addition, the children are exposed to 20 to 25 lesson focus activities and numerous games.

Organizing the curriculum into weekly activity units is the most common approach found in schools. When using this approach, an activity is extended over an entire week. The weekly plan has three major advantages. First, a teacher needs only one lesson plan for the week, keeping planning duties manageable. The teacher's objective in the lesson is to move children along the path of learning at an optimal rate. To some extent, what cannot be covered one day can wait until the next. Second, less orientation instruction is needed after the first day. Safety factors, instructional techniques, and key points need only a brief review each day, and equipment needs are similar from day to day. Third, progression and learning sequences are evident; both teacher and children can see progress. The teacher can begin a unit with basic skills and progress to a point where instruction and skill practice are again indicated. This procedure provides needed review and adapts the activity to the group. The activity sequence for each day is built on the preceding lesson. If the teacher has difficulty or needs to investigate an approach, there is time be-

tween lessons to clear up questionable issues. Children also can be referred to resource materials to learn more about the activity for the next day or to clarify a point of difficulty from the previous lesson.

An objection raised by some teachers is that a weekly unit program does not have enough variety, causing some children to tire of the same activities presented over a longer period. To remedy this, units should be spaced so that the same type of activity is not presented for more than 2 weeks in succession. If more time is needed for a specific unit, adding another week or two later in the year is a wise strategy. Games can be used to provide a change of pace when the motivational level of the class (and, in turn, the teacher) appears to be waning.

Other combinations of weekly planning have also been used with success. One arrangement offers one type of activity on Monday, Wednesday, and Friday and another type on Tuesday and Thursday. Another approach reserves game activities for Friday of each week, while the first four days are used for presentation of skill-learning material. Both arrangements show elements of progression. A less desirable plan is to have a different program each day of the week. This burdens the teacher with five different lesson plans and allows for little continuity of instruction.

Step Eleven: Evaluate and Modify the Curriculum

Evaluation schedules and suggested techniques for modifying the curriculum should be built into the curricular structure. A number of sources can supply evaluative data: pupils, teachers, consultants, parents, and administrators. The type of data desired can vary. Achievement test scores can supply hard data to compare preassessments and post-assessments with those of other programs. Subjective assessment might include likes and dislikes, value judgments, problem areas, and needed adjustments. The evaluation schedule may select a limited area for assessment, or assessment can be broadened to cover the entire program. Collecting information is only the first step; the information must then be translated into action. Modification of possible program deficiencies should be based on sound educational philosophy. If the program has weak spots, identifying the weaknesses and determining the causes are important steps to take.

A pilot or trial project can be instituted if the new curriculum represents a radical change. One school in the district might be chosen to develop a pilot program. Site selection should offer the program a strong opportunity to succeed, for success

Table 4.4 Suggested yearly plan for developmental level II

Week	Introductory Activity	Fitness Development Activity	Lesson Focus Activity	Game Activity
1	Orientation and class management games			
2	Fundamental movements and stopping	Teacher-leader exercises	Manipulative skills using beanbags	Galloping Lizzie Crows and Cranes
3	Move and Assume Pose	Teacher-leader exercises	Throwing skills, lesson 1	Whistle Mixer Couple Tag Partner Stoop
4	Walk, Trot, and Sprint	Teacher-leader exercises	Soccer related activities, lesson 1	Circle Soccer Soccer Touch Ball Diagonal Soccer Soccer Take-Away
5	Partner Over and Under	Teacher-leader exercises	Soccer related activities, lesson 2	Diagonal Soccer Sideline Soccer Dribblerama Bullseye
6	Run, Stop, and Pivot	Circuit Training	Fundamental skills through playground games	Playground games
7	European Running	Circuit Training	Long-rope jumping skills	Trades Fly Trap
8	Magic Number challenges	Circuit Training	Manipulative skills using playground balls	Fox Hunt Bounce Ball One Step
9	Fastest Tag in the West	Walk, Trot, and Sprint	Throwing skills, lesson 2	In the Prison Snowball Center Target Throw Target Ball Throw
10	Group Tag	Walk, Trot, and Sprint	Jogging skills	Recreational activity
11	Locomotor and manipulative activity	Exercises to music	Rhythmic movement, lesson 1	Whistle March Arches Home Base
12	Movement varieties	Exercises to music	Hockey related activities, lesson 1	Circle Keepaway Star Wars Modified Hockey Circle Straddleball
13	New leader	Astronaut Drills	Hockey related activities, lesson 2	Modified Hockey Lane Hockey
14	Group Over and Under	Astronaut Drills	Individual rope jumping skills	Trades Follow Me Beachball Bat Ball
15	Low-organization games	Continuity Drills	Stunts and tumbling skills, lesson 1	Whistle Mixer Competitive Circle Contests Alaska Baseball
16	Following activity	Continuity Drills	Rhythmic movement, lesson 2	Fox Hunt Steal the Treasure Addition Tag
17	Leapfrog	Aerobic fitness and partner resistance exercises	Fundamental skills using benches	Cageball Kick-Over Squad Tag

Table 4.4 *continued*

Week	Introductory Activity	Fitness Development Activity	Lesson Focus Activity	Game Activity
18	Bridges by Three	Aerobic fitness and partner resistance exercises	Basketball related activities, lesson 1	Birdie in the Cage Dribble Take-Away Captain Ball Basketball Tag
19	Jumping and hopping	Challenge Course	Basketball related activities, lesson 2	Circle Guard and Pass Captain Basketball Around the Key
20	Fleece Ball Fun	Challenge Course	Recreational activities	Recreational activities
21	Ball activities	Challenge Course	Fundamental skills using balance beams	Nonda's Car Lot Fly Trap
22	Moving to music	Aerobic fitness	Stunts and tumbling skills, lesson 2	Partner Stoop Crows and Cranes
23	European Running with variations	Aerobic fitness	Manipulative skills using wands	Home Base Indianapolis 500 Nine Lives
24	Tortoise and Hare	Aerobic fitness	Rhythmic movement, lesson 3	Jump the Shot Beach-Ball Batball Club Guard
25	Bend, Stretch, and Shake	Astronaut Drills	Volleyball related skills	Beachball and Informal Volleyball Shower Service Ball
26	Move and perform task	Astronaut Drills	Manipulative skills using hoops	Hand Hockey Cageball Kickover
27	Tag games	Continuity Drills	Manipulative skills using paddle and balls	Steal the Treasure Addition Tag
28	Combination movement patterns	Continuity Drills	Stunts and tumbling skills, lesson 3	Trades Beachball BatBall
29	European Running with equipment	Exercises to music	Fundamental skills using Tug-of-War ropes	Relays
30	Marking	Exercises to music	Rhythmic movement with equipment, lesson 4	Nonda's Car Lot Box Ball
31	Stretching	Jogging	Track and field related activities, lesson 1	Potato Shuttle Relay
32	Stretching	Jogging	Track and field related activities, lesson 2	Relays
33	Creative routine	Hexagon Hustle	Fundamental skills using parachute activities	Nonda's Car Lot Box Ball
34	Four-Corners Movement	Hexagon Hustle	Manipulative skills using frisbees	Frisbee Keep-Away Frisbee Target Throw Frisbee Golf
35	Long rope routine	Parachute exercises	Softball related activities, lesson 1	Throw It and Run Two-Pitch Softball Hit and Run
36	Squad leader movements	Parachute exercises	Softball related activities, lesson 2	Beat Ball Kick Softball In a Pickle

Week	Introductory Activity	Fitness Development Activity	Lesson Focus Activity	Game Activity
Alternate Lesson Plans				
A	Substitute	Substitute	Football related activities, lesson 1	Football End Ball Five Passes
B	Substitute	Substitute	Football related activities, lesson 2	Football Box Ball Fourth Down
C	Substitute	Substitute	Softball related activities, lesson 3	Beat Ball Kick Softball Two-Pitch Softball
D	Substitute	Substitute	Fundamental skills using balance beams and manipulative equipment	Hand Hockey Nine Lives
E	Substitute	Substitute	Fundamental skills using climbing ropes	Nonda's Car Lot Indianapolis 500
F	Substitute	Substitute	Fundamental skills using magic ropes	Busy Bee Box Ball

depends in large part on the educational climate of the school. In some cases, the experimental program might be implemented with only one class in a school. Enthusiastic, skilled direction is necessary for such projects. Much valuable information can be derived from the pilot process before an entire program is implemented throughout the school system.

Various interest groups may promote new approaches and ideas. These are welcome if the proposals are supported by valid evidence and if the new focus represents progress. Change in itself is not progress; avoid the bandwagon approach.

Probably the most appropriate time to analyze evaluative data is during a curriculum committee meeting late in the school year. The committee can then consider modifications for the coming school year. Times may occur during the year, however, when problems arise that mandate immediate remedial measures.

Figure 4.2 is an example of a curriculum evaluation form that might be used regularly. Questions can be added to be more explicit about a specific curriculum.

1. Are students incorporating physical activity in their lifestyle?
2. Are students participating in other school activities (e.g., intramurals, afterschool sports) and such activities as Little League baseball?
3. Are students acquiring competence in physical skills?
4. Are students developing an understanding of personal fitness and wellness?
5. Are students reaching a desirable level of physical fitness through participation in the program?
6. Do students possess the requisite knowledge required to participate in a variety of sports, games, and exercises?
7. Have students acquired the social and emotional skills necessary for productive participation in school and society?
8. Does the curriculum leave students with a broad understanding of the wealth of physical activities available to them (balance)?
9. Does the curriculum allow students to leave school with a high level of competency in a few activities (depth)?
10. Does the curriculum follow a progressive sequence within the school year as well as between school years (horizontal and vertical curriculum)?

Figure 4.2 Sample curriculum evaluation form

REFERENCES AND SUGGESTED READINGS

Annerino, A. A., Cowell, C. C., & Hazelton, H. W. (1980). *Curriculum theory and design in physical education.* St. Louis, MO: C. V. Mosby.

Barrett, K. R., Williams, K., & Whitall, J. (1992). What does it mean to have a "developmentally appropriate physical education program?" *The Physical Educator, 49*(3), 113–117.

Bloom, B. S. (Ed.). (1956). *Taxonomy of educational objectives, the classification of educational goals, handbook I: The cognitive domain.* New York: David McKay.

Corbin, C. B. (1976). *Becoming physically educated in the elementary school.* Philadelphia: Lea & Febiger.

Gabbard, C., Leblanc, E., & Lowy, S. (1987). *Physical education for children.* Englewood Cliffs, NJ: Prentice-Hall.

Gallahue, D. L. (1987). *Developmental physical education for today's elementary school children.* New York: Macmillan.

Graham, G., Holt/Hale, S. A., & Parker, M. (1993). *Children moving.* Mountain View, CA: Mayfield.

Kirschner, G. (1992). *Physical education for elementary school children* (8th ed.). Dubuque, IA: Wm. C. Brown.

Krathwohl, D. R., Bloom, B. S., & Masia, B. B. (1964). *Taxonomy of educational objectives, handbook II: Affective domain.* New York: David McKay.

Logsdon, B. J., & Barrett, K. R. (1984). Movement—The content of physical education. In B. J. Logsdon, K. R. Barrett, M. R. Broer, M. Ammons, L. E. Halverson, & M. A. Roberson (Eds.), *Physical education for children.* Philadelphia: Lea & Febiger.

Melograno, V. (1985). *Designing the physical education curriculum.* Dubuque, IA: Kendall/Hunt.

Pangrazi, R. P., & Dauer, V. P. (1995). *Lesson plans for dynamic physical education for elementary school children* (11th ed.). New York: Macmillan.

Siedentop, D., Mand, C., & Taggart, A. (1986). *Physical education: Teaching and curriculum strategies for grades 5–12.* Palo Alto, CA: Mayfield.

Willgoose, C. E. (1984). *The curriculum in physical education.* Englewood Cliffs, NJ: Prentice-Hall.

5

Effective Planning for Quality Instruction

*P*lanning is an integral part of effective teaching and helps assure that a sequential and creative lesson is implemented. Regular planning helps teachers retain their creative edge because it keeps them immersed in current ideas, particularly if they choose to read current journals and textbooks. Designing an effective presentation involves understanding and incorporating the essential elements of instruction to help ensure learning occurs. Pre-instructional decisions must be considered to assure how the material will be presented. Examples of preinstructional decisions are selecting teaching styles, effectively using allotted time and teaching space, and arranging students in an instructional formation. Next follows the actual design and implementation of the lesson plan, using a format that is flexible and meaningful to teachers. It has been reported that teachers make up to 200 decisions a minute while teaching. The complexity of teaching is simplified when as many decisions as possible can be made prior to the actual lesson presentation.

ESSENTIAL ELEMENTS OF INSTRUCTION

Increased emphasis has been placed on improving the quality of instruction. For many years, interest and energy were devoted to the enhancement of curriculum content. Curriculum is a critical component of the educational process; however, educators are beginning to accept that if the content is poorly taught, there will be a lack of student progress. The need for high-quality curricular material and instruction has been established.

Hunter (1986) developed essential elements of instruction for classroom teachers. Because many of the principles are effective when teaching any subject, this section modifies the original concepts for physical education instruction. Physical educators sometimes assume that materials designed for classroom teachers cannot be applied to physical education. However, physical educators who modify and use appropriate instructional techniques are usually better supported by classroom teachers.

Designing Student Objectives

Writing educational objectives gives direction and meaning to the physical education curriculum. Objectives should be stated clearly so learners know when they have been reached. Effective learning occurs when youngsters participate actively in selecting and setting objectives and in planning ways to attain them. Teachers can conduct discussions to allow students to help in goal setting. Teaching aids such as movies, filmstrips, videotapes, posters, and speakers can be used to help teachers and students determine desirable objectives.

Learning objectives should be characterized by the following points. First, goals must be *observable*. The teacher and the student must be able to tell when the objective has been reached. If it is not visible, neither party will know when it has been reached. In the physical education setting, this usually poses little problem, as most activities are overt and easy to observe. Second, the objective must *identify the content* to be learned. It must clearly and specifically delineate what the student is expected to learn. When teachers and students clearly understand what is expected, both feel more comfortable about the learning situation. Problems arise when students try to guess what the teacher has in mind. Students have a right to know what is expected of them and what they need to accomplish to reach the goal.

Finally, objectives must *certify* that learning has taken place and that learners know more than they did prior to accomplishing the objective. When objectives are ambiguous or nonexistent, students have no way of judging whether they have improved or have learned anything. The following are examples of objectives that would meet the points listed:

1. The student will demonstrate four ways to perform a forward roll.

2. The student will show an understanding of soccer rules by explaining when a corner kick is awarded.

3. Using a jump rope, the student will be able to perform three consecutive forward crossover moves.

4. The student will demonstrate knowledge and understanding of rhythmic gymnastic routines by diagramming a sample floor routine for balls.

Objectives should be designed for all three learning domains, psychomotor, affective, and cognitive. Psychomotor domain objectives would include learning the various physical skills and developing health-related physical fitness. Objectives designed for the cognitive domain would be aimed at developing knowledge and comprehension of mechanical principles related to skill performance and knowing the precepts related to fitness activities. Affective domain objectives deal with attitudes and behaviors in the physical activity setting, such as learning to cooperate with peers on a team. Many specific objectives in all three domains are listed in *Lesson Plans for Dynamic Physical Education, 11th ed.* by Pangrazi and Dauer (1995).

Goal Structuring

An important part of achieving desired goals is choosing how objectives are structured. Grineski (1993) has identified three different ways to structure goals to facilitate learning. The first is to design individual goals that allow students to work in isolation. For example, in an area such as physical fitness development, each student could design a program of personal activity goals. The achievement of individual goals is meaningful only for the person for whom they were designed. A second method is to structure competitive goals designed to pit individual students or groups of students against each other. A competitive objective is achievable by only one student or group of students. These goals are common in physical education settings where low-organization games and team sport activities allow only a few winners. The third type of goal structuring is cooperative.

Cooperative goals arrange for students to work together to reach desired outcomes. All students within the group are expected to contribute to accomplishing the goal. As an example, assume that a school wants to increase the amount of daily activity students accomplish. The school decides to set a cooperative goal of moving across the United States. A map to record the distance moved by each classroom is displayed in the school. All youngsters are expected to run/walk and contribute their mileage to a collective score for the classroom. The goal is reached when classrooms reach the designated destination.

Grineski (1993) offers recommendations for matching instructional goals to appropriate goal structures.

1. Individual goals are appropriate when goals are designed to promote skill acquisition, development of physical fitness, or other intrapersonal development. This allows maximum time to be devoted to learning and practice, as there is no peer interaction requirement. Individual goal setting may result in increased motivation and self-esteem for those students who reach their goals.

2. Cooperative goal setting is appropriate when the goal is to increase positive social interaction behaviors. Cooperative goals can enhance self-esteem, as they make each member of the group a requisite for success. Because each student is an important part of the group, students often encourage and help members of their group reach the goal.

3. Competitive goal structuring is best used after students have acquired and overlearned motor and cognitive skills. As discussed earlier in the section on stress and arousal (p. 40), competition can reduce learning effectiveness if youngsters think more about winning than correct performance of skills. If students have learned the skills and feel they have a chance to win, competitively structured goals may increase performance.

Task Analysis

An everpresent challenge faced by physical education teachers is the question, "At what skill level do I begin instructing?" Selecting learning tasks at the correct level of difficulty for students is challenging because all classes contain students with a wide variation in skill development and maturation level.

The first step in determining the proper entry level is to formulate a terminal objective (one that is beyond the grasp of the most skillful student in the class). Next, the teacher must outline in proper progression the essential learning tasks that lead up to the terminal objective. At this point, expedient diagnosis for determining entry level takes place. The teacher begins by moving rapidly through the progression of learning steps until a number of students appear to have difficulty performing the activity. This approach serves two purposes: It offers both a quick review of skills and a diagnosis of the ability level of students. For instructional activities where each student has a piece of equipment, students can be instructed to perform two or three activities per instructional episode to speed up the process. When using activities that require sharing a piece of equipment, self-paced instruction can review skills previously learned and determine the correct entry level for students within the group. For example, when teaching activities on the balance beam, a list of movements down the beam can be posted on task charts. Students can move through the progression at their own rate, allowing them the opportunity to determine their correct entry level. Instruction and learning do not begin until the appropriate entry level for a student is established. This requires thorough knowledge of the skill sequence to be utilized for each unit of instruction, beginning with the lowest skill and progressing to the terminal objective.

Anticipatory Set

After objectives and learning strategies have been developed, the instructional process becomes the focal point. The anticipatory set is a simple idea; it is designed to get students to focus on the current instructional concept. For many teachers the most difficult part of the lesson is the opening sequence of instruction. Students enter the gymnasium talking to their friends and seem to be more interested in socializing than learning. Before they are willing to learn, students must be "psychologically warmed up." They must have their thought processes focused on the learning at hand. The anticipatory set should be designed to accomplish this goal.

A key factor in delivering an effective anticipatory set is to tie into students' past experiences or learning. For example, if you were in a basketball unit, you might ask students to think about techniques they would use when shooting. This focus might involve discussing hand placement, eyes on the basket, or keeping the elbows in. In any case, it is a key point and encourages the class to begin thinking about the task at hand.

Another valuable use of anticipatory set is to reveal to the instructor the entry level of students in the class. Students might be asked, "How many of you can explain the rules of floor hockey?" The teacher might also bring a stick and puck to stimulate student interest. The number of students knowing rules of floor hockey would give the teacher an indication as to their previous experience in the activity. This would affect the rate of presentation and the difficulty of the skills covered in the opening lessons. When students learn quickly, it is often because they have had a great deal of previous experience in an activity. Therefore, knowing the entry behavior of students will give the teacher an indication of how fast and effectively learning will take place.

Within the anticipatory set, a teacher may share the learning objective (and its rationale) with students. It is important that students be told exactly what they are expected to learn and why it is important prior to the actual presentation. If learning is going to be effective, students must perceive that they have a need to learn. Very few people will make an effort to learn something if it does not seem to be important in their everyday mode of operation. Learning is enhanced when teachers tell students clearly and concisely *what* and *why* they need to learn. The more convinced students are about the importance of learning something, the more motivated they will be to participate. For example, teachers often talk with students about safety skills and warn them about "what not to do." However, if students do not internalize the danger, cannot perceive the danger, or are just told not to do something, they will almost always fail to heed the warning. It is human nature to balk at doing something when someone demands it. Most individuals respond better to logic and clear explanation related to their personal experiences.

It is not always necessary to use an anticipatory set, although when a teacher chooses not to use one, there should be a good reason for the omission. If students are already set to learn, there is probably little value in using one. On the other hand, at the beginning of a lesson, after an interruption, or when choosing to move to a new objective, using an anticipatory set will be effective.

Some examples of anticipatory sets are as follows:

"On Monday we practiced the skills of passing, dribbling, and shooting lay-ins. Yesterday we put those skills into games of three-on-three. Take a few moments to think about the problems you or others in your game encountered related to dribbling or passing and be ready to discuss them. [Allow time for thought.] Today we are going to use some drills that will improve your passing and dribbling."

"Think of as many activities as you can that require body strength, and be ready when called upon to tell the class. [Allow time for thinking.] This week we are going to learn and practice weight training. It is the most popular strength-development activity in our country."

"What do we call it when we move quickly in different directions? Think of as many activities as you can that require agility, and be ready to tell the class. [Allow time for thinking.] This week we are going to learn the bamboo-pole dance that will improve your agility level."

Input and Modeling

Input involves teaching. It is the process of giving the information to be learned to students. A number of decisions need to be made when presenting content. Information that should be given during input is the definition of the skill, the elements or parts of the skill, and when and why the skill should be used. Some of the more cogent points involved in input follow.

1. Focus instruction on one or two key points. It is difficult for students to remember a series of instructions. During skill performance, it is common practice to tell students everything related to the skill performance, which often leaves them baffled and overwhelmed. Most learners are capable of focusing on only one or two points when performing a skill.

2. Try to restrain from lengthy skill descriptions. Once instructions go beyond 30 to 60 seconds, students become listless and forget much of the material presented. Try to develop a pattern of short, concise presentations, alternated with practice sessions. This offers the instructor many opportunities to refocus class attention on the skill to be practiced and to evaluate the effectiveness of skill-learning sequences.

3. Present the information in its most basic and clearest form. If half the class does not understand the presentation, the teacher has failed, not the students. It is important to check for understanding (see the next section) to assure that the class is comprehending the material.

4. Offer the material through a number of different styles. Some students may learn best through lecture, whereas others must see a visual presentation. It is possible that many will

Effective teachers demonstrate skill techniques.

learn from a peer discussion or through teacher-guided questioning. It is well known that students learn best utilizing different styles. Try to incorporate as many presentation styles as possible during the course of a unit of instruction.

The saying, "What you do speaks louder than what you say," relates closely to modeling behavior. *Modeling* is demonstrating. If teachers are going to ask students to behave in certain ways, it is reasonable to think that they should act in a similar fashion. In physical education, one of the quickest and most effective ways to teach a physical activity is to demonstrate. Effective models should accentuate the critical points of performance. The teacher should verbalize key focal points so that students will know what to observe. Correct modeling involves two parts: *showing* the correct way to do a skill and *labeling* the correct way to do it.

Both teachers and students can model instructional activities. Regardless of who does the modeling, in the early stages of learning it is important

that the demonstration be clear and unambiguous. The aspect to be observed must be identified so that attention is drawn to the correct element of performance. If the teacher is having a student demonstrate, the instructor's narrative description of the activity should accompany the performance. If possible, slow down the performance and try to present it step by step. Many skills can be videotaped and played back in slow motion. The replay can be stopped at critical instances, with students emulating the position. For example, in a throwing unit, the instructor might freeze the frame that illustrates the position of the arm. Students can practice imitating moving the arm into proper position based on the stop-action pose.

The following are examples of using modeling and input in tandem to assure an effective presentation:

Students are in partners spread out about 20 yards apart, with one partner having a football. "When kicking the football, take a short step with your kicking foot, a long step with the other foot, and kick [model]. Again, short step, long step, kick [label]."

"Listen to the first verse of this schottische music. I'll do the part of the schottische step we just learned starting with the second verse [model]. Ready, step, step, step, hop [label]. When I hit the tambourine, begin doing the step."

"Today we are going to work on developing fitness by moving through the Challenge Course. Move through the course as quickly as you can, but do your best at each challenge; quality is more important than speed. Travel through the course like this [model]. Move under the bar, swing on the rope, and so forth [label]. When I say go, start at the obstacle nearest you."

Checking for Understanding

A most essential point of instruction is checking to see if students comprehend the presentation. It is entirely possible that a class may not understand any of the material being presented. In fact, students become very effective at displaying an exterior that says they understand even when they do not. One of the most common habits that teachers develop involves asking periodically, "Does everybody understand?" Even though it appears that the teacher is checking for understanding, this seldom is the case. More often than not, the teacher does not even wait for a response. It takes a brave and confident student to admit to a lack of understanding in front of the class. In fact, many teachers are affronted when a student does venture a question. Therefore, the need for a quick and easy way to check for understanding without causing student embarrassment is important to effective learning.

The following are some suggestions for monitoring whether students are understanding:

1. Use hand signals. Examples might be: "Thumbs up if you understand," or "If you think this demonstration is correct, balance on one foot," or "Raise the number of fingers to signal which student you think did a correct forward roll." If the signals are given quickly and without comment, students will begin to understand that they can signal the teacher quickly and privately without embarrassment. Some teachers have used the method of closing the eyes and signaling if the situation is particularly touchy or embarrassing.

2. Ask questions that can be answered in choral response. Some students may mouth an answer even though they do not know the correct response. Therefore, the indicator for the instructor is the intensity of the group response. A loud response by the class usually indicates that the majority understand.

3. Direct a check to the entire class rather than to a specified student, for example, "Be ready to demonstrate the grapevine step to me." This encourages all members of the class to focus on the activity, knowing that they may be called on to demonstrate. Even though it does not assure that everyone understands, it does increase the odds that more students are thinking about the skill check.

4. Use peer checking methods. Students can pair up and evaluate each other's performance using a teacher-designed instrument. More than one evaluation can be made by different students to help assure the validity of the scoring.

5. Tests and written feedback can be used. Many situations in physical education require cognition of certain concepts. Written tests asking students to diagram and explain the options of an offense or defense could be used. Listing safety precautions for an activity would make the instructor aware of student understanding. Restraint must be used in administering written instruments—a great deal of time that could be devoted to skill practice can be absorbed by written assessment. Use these instruments only when the information cannot be gathered more efficiently with other methods.

In summary, when planning a lesson, be sure to include strategies for input and modeling. If specific activities are not listed on the lesson plan, they probably will be forgotten during the instructional process.

Guided Practice

The reason for offering guided practice is to assure that students are performing the skill correctly. It is a fallacy to assume that practice makes perfect. Correct practice develops correct skill patterns, whereas practicing skills incorrectly will develop imperfection. This leads to the first step in guided practice: moving the class through each step of the skill. During the early phases of guided practice, small amounts of information presented clearly should be the rule. Skills should build on previous skills learned so that the student begins to see the importance of prerequisite learning.

Practice should occur as soon as possible after students have had a chance to do the skill correctly. They should have a chance to get the "feel" of a skill as a whole before they begin to work on the parts. The opportunity to try the complete skill before practicing smaller components enhances the learner's ability to see how the parts fit together. The length of practice sessions should be varied depending on the needs of the youngsters. If it is an initial presentation and possibly the students' first experience with the material, the practice sessions should be massed. Massed practice involves allowing enough time so that students can begin to develop mastery of the material. When reviewing activities in which the basics have been learned, distributed practice sessions can be short and less frequent. All the theory in the world is discounted when students are frustrated in trying to learn a new skill. If frustration sets in, students will need to receive relevant information, guided practice, or a modification in the level of the skill expectation. If this does not work, the practice session may have to be terminated and returned to at a later time.

During guided practice sessions, monitor group responses and offer feedback to ease the pain of learning new activities. Some of the methods described in input and modeling should be used to enhance the learning process. The monitoring process should be overt and regular to assure that students understand and are on task. The feedback should be specific, immediate, and focus on the exact skill being practiced. It is not guided practice if students do not receive regular, meaningful feedback dealing with their performance levels.

Finally, ensure that all students receive the same amount of practice. If anyone should receive less practice, it should be the skilled performer. Too often, drills and lead-up activities result in the least gifted student sitting on the sidelines. This only results in the gifted youngsters improving and the less skilled children falling further behind.

Closure

The purpose of closure is to review the learning that has taken place during the lesson. Closure increases retention and allows students to review what they have learned. The discussion or activity should focus on the learning that has occurred rather than the activities practiced. It is not simply a recall of the activities that were completed, but rather a discussion of the type of skills and knowledge that were learned through practice.

Closure can increase the opportunity for transfer to occur, as the discussion can focus on how the current movement patterns being learned are similar to those practiced earlier. Often, students may not realize that the movement pattern is parallel to one learned earlier unless questions from the teacher encourage students to perceive such relationships. Closure can encourage students to help each other. The discussion of what was learned can alert other students about what they should be learning through practice. A fringe benefit offered the teacher is the opportunity to remind the class to tell their parents and others what they learned. How many times have parents asked, "What did you learn at school today?" only to hear the reply, "Nothing"? In addition, a short closure session can reveal to the instructor which students have learned and which students need additional help.

The following are examples of how closure might be accomplished:

1. Have partners describe two or three key components of skill performance to their partner.

2. Have students demonstrate skills in quick response to verbal cues given by the teacher or a peer.

3. Ask students to participate in a closing activity that requires learned skills be utilized.

4. Perform an activity describing a key point in skill performance that was taught earlier.

PREINSTRUCTIONAL DECISIONS

Preinstructional decisions are basic to the success of the lesson. They are rather mundane, which can cause teachers to avoid planning for them. However, they are every bit as important as planning the content of the lesson. In fact, if this phase of the lesson is not carefully thought out, it may be impossible to present the content. Preinstructional decisions that need to be made prior to the lesson presentation include which teaching style(s) to use, effective use of equipment, how to utilize class time, how to arrange the teaching space, and when to employ various instructional formations.

Choosing Effective Teaching Styles

Competent teachers use more than one style and may even use a number of styles during a single lesson. The choice of teaching style depends on expected student outcomes, on the children's stage of progression, and on the activity. Two reasons for using different styles are to enhance the teaching environment, and to keep both learner and teacher motivated. For a definitive review of teaching styles, see Mosston and Arnsworth (1986). Teachers should make an effort to experiment with different styles of teaching and try to develop the ability to use several approaches. To some degree, each teacher's personality traits and aptitudes determine which teaching styles are most suitable. Figure 5.1 shows a continuum of teaching styles based on the degree of control exercised by the teacher.

Teachers should select a style most likely to enhance student learning. A teaching style should be chosen according to the degree of control the teacher plans to exert over lesson preparation,

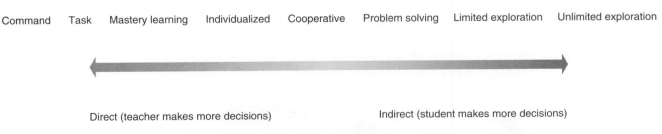

Command   Task   Mastery learning   Individualized   Cooperative   Problem solving   Limited exploration   Unlimited exploration

Direct (teacher makes more decisions)   Indirect (student makes more decisions)

Figure 5.1 Continuum of teaching styles

implementation, and evaluation. If time is short, the command style may be best. On the other hand, if time permits experimentation with alternatives, the limited exploration style might be effective. If children accept responsibility for their own learning, less direct methods can be implemented. The nature of the activity should be considered when choosing a teaching style. For example, an individualized style of teaching is appropriate for a stunts-and-tumbling unit, whereas individual mat activities present an excellent opportunity for the unlimited exploration approach. Cooperative learning is an effective style when teaching games and team sport activities. No single style is superior to another; each has its place and value for a skilled teacher. Regardless of the style used, effective teaching techniques (being prepared, keeping all children active, and teaching with enthusiasm) are vital to successful teaching.

Command Style

The command style is the most direct and teacher-controlled approach. The teacher prepares all facets of the lesson, is wholly responsible for instruction, and monitors the lesson progress by direct methods. Basically, the command style includes explanation, demonstration, and practice. The amount of time devoted to each is determined by the instructor. Evaluation is usually accomplished by the instructor, who has certain preset standards for student performance. Children are guided along almost identical paths toward similar goals.

When the command style is used, instructions should be brief and to the point, with as much practice time as possible following the instruction. Teachers sometimes talk in depth about a skill and include too many details in the introductory remarks, only to find that students usually forget all but the last few points. A demonstration that covers either part or the complete skill activity can shorten the time devoted to explanation.

Most instructors use the command style more than they might imagine, because it is an efficient way to reach teacher-selected goals. In classes where discipline problems are a factor, the command style allows a tighter rein on class management. Teachers invariably are forced to use a command-dominated style with large classes. Another application of command style is for situations where a precise skill or a specific result is the goal. Such circumstances often arise during remediation of low fitness or motor deficiencies. With children who have lower levels of comprehension, the command style is appropriate for accomplishing specific increments of progress. Directions are definite, and children get needed practice in following directions.

Task Style

When using the task style, the instructor is responsible for setting the lesson objectives, selecting the activities, and determining instructional sequences for achieving the objectives. In contrast to the command style, however, students become involved in the pace of the lesson and in the instructional process. The teacher is less focused on how the class is organized or whether all the children are working simultaneously on the same movement patterns. Instead, the teacher focuses on how students are carrying out the defined task. Whereas success in the command style is judged by whether each child reaches the movement goal, in the task style the instructor accepts individual differences in accomplishment. This style may therefore motivate children who cannot achieve at the same level as the majority of the class.

Tasks can be presented verbally or printed on task cards. Students are allowed to accomplish the task at their own pace. They may find a partner to help or may even function as a member of a small group. The format might call for all students to give attention to the same problem or might allow them to work on different problems. Task cards can be useful teaching devices for youngsters capable of reading. Different cards can be made to allow for progression. As a child finishes the task on one card, another card, describing the new task to complete, is issued. Cards for particular areas can be categorized according to the skill level required

Students checking each other (peer checking)

```
┌─────────────────────────────────────────────┐
│                                             │
│        ROPE JUMPING—BEGINNING SKILLS        │
│                                             │
│  Needed: one jump rope                      │
│                                             │
│  1. Check for proper size. The rope ends    │
│     should come up to the armpits when      │
│     the jumper is standing in the rope      │
│     center.                                 │
│                                             │
│  2. Forward turning to the side: Hold the   │
│     rope handles in one hand. Turn the      │
│     rope forward to the side.               │
│                                             │
│  3. Jump and rebound! Without the rope,     │
│     practice the jump and rebound until     │
│     it is in good rhythm.                   │
│                                             │
│  4. Combine jump and rebound with           │
│     turning the rope to the side.           │
│                                             │
│  5. Slow-time jumping: With the hands       │
│     holding the rope in normal rope-        │
│     jumping position and with the rope      │
│     started behind the back, try to perform │
│     regular rope jumping to slow-time       │
│     rhythm.                                 │
│                                             │
│  6. Turn the rope 5 turns without a miss.   │
│                                             │
│  7. Turn the rope 10 turns without a miss.  │
│                                             │
└─────────────────────────────────────────────┘
```

Figure 5.2   Sample task card

by the activity, from beginning (introductory) to intermediate to advanced. A sample task card for skills in rope jumping is shown in Figure 5.2.

Mastery Learning or Outcomes-Based Style

Mastery learning is an instructional strategy requiring that the terminal target skill be broken into progressive subunits, each of which becomes, in progression, the focus of the learner. The key is the division of the final movement capability into progressive teachable units, each of which is to be mastered in order, thus providing an additive effect toward achieving the target competency. The approach is somewhat similar to contract teaching but is more restricted in scope. The continuum of subunits must be mastered at a high level (usually 80 to 90 percent correct) before the student attempts more complicated tasks. The number of subunits depends on the complexity of the skill. If mastery is not achieved, corrective activities are offered so that the student has the opportunity to learn from alternative materials, peer tutoring, or any type of learning activity that meets personal preferences. For an in-depth discussion of mastery learning, see Guskey (1985).

A mastery learning breakdown for the skill of catching is illustrated here. For the sake of brevity, only four subunits are presented.

1. Individually, with a fleece ball, toss with both hands and catch with both hands. Toss with the right and catch with both hands. Toss with the left and catch with both hands.

2. Individually, with a fleece ball, toss the ball from the right hand to the left hand, making a high arc.

3. Individually, with a beanbag, toss the bag around various body parts and catch it. Toss the bag with both hands overhead and catch it behind the back with both hands.

4. Individually, with a beanbag and in an erect position, toss the bag high and catch it as low as you can with both hands. Next, catch with the right and then the left hand as low as possible.

For each step, performance criteria need to be established. In step 1, to reach the mastery level the child may be required to catch four out of five throws in each of the tasks. The final test would be to demonstrate capability in the terminal movement task. Should the child fail the performance criterion for any step, corrective activities are offered and practice is repeated, followed by a second test session. This is the mastery element of the strategy. If a student fails the step a number of times (say, three or four), that step is abandoned, and the child moves to the next subunit.

Mastery learning as a strategy is useful in a number of ways. First, the child moves at an individualized pace and masters preliminaries needed for the target skill. The style is well suited to working with low-skilled and disabled children. It also provides homework for children, enabling them to work during their spare time on areas needing improvement.

The process of the style can be outlined as follows:

1. The target skill or movement competency must be divided into sequenced, progressive units.

2. Prerequisite competency is evaluated.

3. Performance objectives for each of the successive learning units must be established.

4. Informal progress testing can be carried on by the performer to determine readiness for more formal testing by the teacher or a peer.

5. When the child is ready, testing by the teacher determines pass or fail for a particular subunit. A child who passes moves to the next learning unit.

6. Should the child fail, practice continues, incorporating any alternatives or corrective measures provided.

Individualized Style

The individualized style is based on the concept of student-centered learning through an individualized curriculum. This style employs a variety of teaching strategies and allows students to progress at an individual rate. Each student's needs are diagnosed, and a program is prescribed to address those needs. Objectives are stated in behavioral terms. Students are required to learn cognitive factors before moving to psychomotor tasks.

Certain materials and hardware are necessary to establish the proper learning environment for individualized instruction. Equipment is needed for loop films, transparencies, and audiotapes. Reference books, wall charts, and cards for recording student progress are also necessary. Useful equipment includes slide and overhead projectors, cassette tape recorders, screens, and chalkboards. A learning center that includes materials, equipment, and software to direct the learning process can be established. An example of a learning center is shown in Figure 5.3. Clearly, many other arrangements are also possible.

The individualized style of teaching basically follows five steps.

1. Diagnosis. Assessment is made to determine student's present level of cognitive and psychomotor knowledge.
2. Prescription. Each student is given a learning package based on present level of knowledge.
3. Development. The student works on tasks in the learning package until able to perform them successfully. Self-testing goals are offered, and the student decides after testing whether to proceed to the next step.
4. Evaluation. The student goes to the teacher for final evaluation. Both psychomotor and cognitive progress are evaluated at this point.
5. Reinforcement. If a student completes the tasks successfully, the teacher gives positive reinforcement, records the data on the student's progress chart, and prescribes a new learning package based on the student's needs. If the student does not perform the task successfully, the teacher can offer possible alternatives for reaching the objective. The evaluation process gives the teacher an opportunity to counsel each student and to reinforce critical points.

Learning packages form the core of the individualized style. The *learning package* is a student contract that provides the ingredients students need to accomplish. These tasks are listed in a meaningful sequence. The learning package consists of the following parts:

1. The content classification statement describes the task or concept to be learned. This could be a psychomotor task (such as the cartwheel) or a cognitive task (such as learning about how to absorb force).
2. The purpose section explains what the package will do for the learner (e.g., "This contract provides you with activities that will enable you to perform the cartwheel").

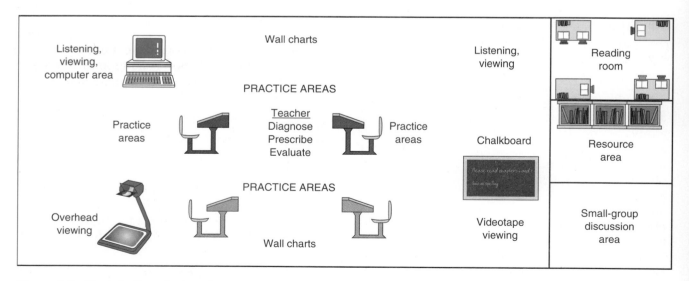

Figure 5.3 Organization of a learning center

3. The learning objectives listed identify what is to be learned, under what conditions the learning will take place, and how the student will perform when learning has occurred.

4. The diagnostic test (pretest) determines the student's knowledge and skill levels. The student is given a cognitive test as well as psychomotor tasks to perform for assessment.

5. The learning activities section offers different ways for the student to learn a skill, concept, or activity. In each contract, different choices should be available. The student can select any of the strategies to enhance learning. Some of the following strategies might be offered: Students can view and analyze transparencies, listen to audiotapes for instruction in cognitive tasks, read various books and manuals (referenced in advance by the instructor) describing the task, view videotapes offering demonstration and explanation of a skill to be performed, or study wall charts that break down the skill into its components. Students can also be directed to ask other students who have successfully completed the activity to help them practice.

6. The self-test phase helps students decide whether they are ready for the final test to be given by the teacher. Students can ask their peers to evaluate whether they are ready for the final test.

7. The final test is an observable measure of the student's achievement. The psychomotor achievements are usually judged by the teacher, while the cognitive learnings are measured by a written exam.

In summary, the individualized style allows the student to control the rate of learning and to receive personalized feedback about progress. The teacher controls the material by designing the packages and by deciding on the size of the learning increments. The student is encouraged to investigate different approaches to learning designated skills through written material, various audiovisual media, and contacts with peers. Experiencing the learning process itself is a valuable acquisition that students can use later to learn new activities or skills.

Cooperative Learning Style

When students are required to compete against each other for a grade or success, they strive for a goal that only a few students can achieve. In competitive situations, students perceive that they can reach their goals only if other students in the

class fail to obtain their goals (Johnson & Johnson, 1987). Cooperative learning grew out of realization that students learn to distrust each other, yet need to work together as adults to accomplish common goals. Cooperative learning involves assigning students to groups so that they can learn to work together to reach common goals. In cooperative activities, individuals seek outcomes that are beneficial to themselves and to the group. An excellent resource about cooperative learning is the text by Johnson, Johnson, and Holubec (1990).

Teachers who want to foster constructive relationships among students will find that cooperative learning can contribute to this outcome. Emphasis is placed on joint rather than individual outcomes and peers are given the opportunity to work with each other regularly. Students should be expected to foster the success of their peers rather than hoping they will fail. This style has the potential to enhance the social and psychological growth of students.

When using this style, learners are assigned a project or goal to complete as a team. Youngsters are grouped heterogeneously (i.e., race, ability, socioeconomic level) so there is diversity within the cooperative unit. Usually, the size of the group is two to five students. They work through the assignment until all group members have understood and completed it. Students must perceive that they cannot achieve the goal alone; that success occurs only when all members of the group reach the goal. The accomplishments of the group are found acceptable if the outcomes are meaningful and cooperation and participation by all group members has occurred.

For teachers, usually the most difficult part of using this style is selecting the project or task that groups are to complete. If the goals can be accomplished without cooperation, use of this style is not indicated. The best tasks demand knowledge and ability of all members of the group, making it clear that "I could not solve this problem alone." It must become clear to the group that all members of the group are needed, even if it is to varying degrees. The following are examples of tasks that might be used in physical education classes:

• Design a fitness routine that requires each member of the group to design one or two exercises for inclusion. The overall routine must show balance (exercise all body parts) and be appropriate for the entire group.

• Ask members of the group to modify a sport or game to make it more inclusive. The goal is to redesign the game so all students can play successfully.

- Each member of the group designs a drill that enhances skill learning and assures that all members of the group improve. The drills must be cohesive and focus on a single skill to be learned (throwing, rope jumping, etc.).

- Assign a group to break a folk dance into various parts so it is easier to learn. Each member of the group is responsible for teaching one of the parts. The group must determine how the parts will be put together (taught) to the rest of the class.

- In a stunts and tumbling unit, students work in a number of small groups to learn basic tumbling activities. Members of the group share their knowledge with each other and analyze each other's performances. When the assigned activities have been learned within the groups, they share their performances with other groups.

Problem-Solving Style

The problem-solving style involves input, reflection, choice, and response. The problem must be structured so that there is no one prescribed answer. When there is just one answer, problem solving becomes guided discovery (a type of limited exploration; see next section).

The problems selected will vary from simple ones for primary-level children to more complex ones for intermediate-level children. A simple problem might be expressed as, "What are the different ways that you can bounce a ball and stay in your personal space?" Emphasis may or may not be placed on a best way. A more complex problem involving deeper thought might be stated as, "What is the most effective way to position and move your feet while guarding an opponent in basketball?" The solution could use an individual, partner, or group approach.

The following steps make up the problem-solving style:

1. Presenting the problem. Students are presented with a problem in the form of a question or statement that provokes thought and reflection. No demonstration or explanation of appropriate responses is given, because solutions should be generated by students.

2. Determining procedures. The student must think about the procedures necessary for arriving at a solution. With younger children, the

problems are simple and this phase is minimal. It is important, however, because the assessment of how to proceed toward a solution has cognitive value. The child may need to define subproblems.

3. Experimenting and exploring. In experimentation, students try different solutions, evaluate them, and make a choice. In exploration, the goal is to seek breadth of activity. Self-direction is important, and the teacher acts in an advisory role—answering questions, helping, commenting, and encouraging, but not providing solutions.

4. Observing, evaluating, and discussing. All children should have the opportunity to offer a solution and to observe what others have discovered. Various kinds of achievement demonstrations can be employed—by individuals, by small groups, by squads, or by part of the class. Discussion should center on justifying a particular solution.

5. Refining and expanding. After observing the solutions that others have selected and evaluating the reasoning behind the chosen solutions, all children should be given the opportunity to rework their movement patterns, incorporating ideas from others.

Children should learn that problems can be solved and that they can find the solutions. To do so, they must be equipped with techniques so that they can proceed under self-direction toward a sound solution. One of the more difficult procedures in the problem-solving style is designing problems to which students do not already know the solution. On the surface, this sounds simple. A student who knows the answer, however, or secures the solution ahead of time, may pass it on to the rest of the class, and the process of solving and exploring is lost. There are few limits to the areas that can be covered in the problem-solving approach. These include concepts, relationships, strategies, and proper use of skills for specific solutions.

Limited Exploration Style

In limited exploration, the teacher is responsible for lesson preparation, subject matter selection, and the general direction of responses. The choice of specific responses is up to the student, since there is no set response for each limitation. In most cases, exploration styles are best suited to teaching broad areas of movement and to developing multiple movement patterns for particular kinds of skills. When learning manipulative movements, for example, a child might show different ways to toss and catch a beanbag in place. The child can react within the limitation of catching while remaining in place. In another example, when children are working with partners to learn ball skills, they can show the different ways to bounce a ball back and forth between them. In this style, an example of fundamental movement teaching would be asking the child to show different ways to jump back and forth over a jump rope on the floor. The method can also be centered on the broader goal of exploring movement elements such as space, time, force, and flow. In this case, the limitation is only that movement elements be explored.

Guided Discovery

This technique is used when there is a predetermined choice or result, of which the teacher is aware, that is to be discovered by students. Suppose that the teacher wants students to acquire the concept of opposition (a right-handed thrower should place the feet in a stride position with the left foot forward). Students are given different foot patterns for experimentation, with the goal of selecting the preferable pattern. They practice right-handed throwing with the following limitations: feet together, feet in a straddle position, feet in a stride position with the left foot forward, and feet in a stride position with the right foot forward. After practicing the four different foot positions, students choose the position that seems best in terms of throwing potential.

Limited exploration is a useful approach for exploring and developing versatility in a particular kind of movement pattern. Progressions in manipulative activities are particularly adaptable to this teaching style. Limited exploration is a flexible style; at any time during a lesson, the style can be used to give children an opportunity to explore a particular situation.

Unlimited (Free) Exploration Style

In unlimited exploration, the only guidance from the teacher is selection of the instructional materials to be used and designation of the area to be explored. Two directives might be: "Today, for the first part of the period, you may select any piece of equipment and see what you can do with it," or "Get a jump rope and try anything with it." No limits, except those dictated by safety, are imposed on children. The teacher may need to forewarn or remind students how to use the equipment safely.

With exploration, the teacher avoids demonstrations and the praising of certain results too early, because these might lead to imitative and noncreative behavior. This does not mean, however, that the teacher is uninvolved. The teacher moves among students—encouraging, clarifying, and answering questions individually. The teacher should concentrate on motivating effort, since the student is responsible for being a self-directed learner. Teachers are wise to offer students the opportunity for self-direction in small doses, with the time being increased as the children become more disciplined. Exploratory opportunities should be offered frequently, for this phase of learning takes advantage of the child's love of movement experimentation and allows the free exercise of natural curiosity. Self-discovery is a necessary and important part of learning, and students should have this concept reinforced by experiencing the joy of creativity.

Use of Equipment

In many situations, equipment will be a limiting factor. Teachers need to know exactly what equipment is available and in working condition. A teacher may roll out the cart of basketballs only to find that half of them are not inflated. Before beginning the lesson, determine how much equipment is available. This will determine the structure of the lesson and how students will need to be grouped. For example, if there are only 16 paddles and balls for a class of 30, some type of sharing or station work will have to be organized.

How much equipment is enough? If it is individual-use equipment, such as rackets, bats, and balls, there should be one piece of equipment for each student. If it is group-oriented equipment, such as gymnastics apparatus, there should be enough to assure waiting lines of no more than four students. Sometimes, teachers settle for less equipment because they teach as they have been taught. An often-observed example finds an instructor teaching volleyball with plenty of available equipment. Rather than have students practice individually (each with a volleyball) against the wall or with a partner, the teacher divides them into two long lines and only uses one or two balls. The majority of equipment remains on the sidelines and most student time is spent waiting in line rather than practicing skills.

If equipment is limited, it obviously becomes necessary to adapt instruction for the time being. Teachers should be careful about accepting limited equipment without expressing concern, because

All students must have a piece of equipment.

many administrators believe that physical educators are always willing to "make do." Communicate with the educational leader on a regular basis, explaining that instruction could be much more effective if necessary equipment were available. Ask parent-teacher groups to conduct fund raisers to help purchase necessary equipment. Math teachers are not expected to teach math without a book for each student, and physical educators should not be expected to teach without adequate equipment. Teachers who settle for less, end up with less.

What are temporary alternatives when equipment is lacking? The most commonly found solution is to teach using the station format. This involves dividing students into small groups where each group has enough equipment. For example, in a softball unit, some students might practice fielding, others batting, others making the double play, and so on. Another approach is to divide the class in half and allow one group to work on one activity while another is involved in an unrelated activity. For example, due to a shortage of paddles and balls, one half of the class is involved in practice while the other half is playing half-court basketball. This approach is less educationally sound and increases the managerial and instructional demands made on the instructor.

Another approach is to use the peer review approach. While one student practices an activity, a peer is involved in offering feedback and evaluation. The two share the equipment and take turns being involved in practice and evaluation. The final approach is to do what is most commonly done— design drills that involve standing in line and waiting for a turn. In most cases, this is the least acceptable from the educational standpoint.

When using equipment, the initial arrangement of the equipment can facilitate a quality lesson.

Usually, the most effective method for distributing individual equipment is to place it around the perimeter of the area. It is the fastest approach and allows students to assume personal responsibility for quickly acquiring a piece of apparatus. Time spent getting a piece of equipment is time that is not available for learning. Large apparatus should be placed in the safest possible manner. This implies arranging it so that all pieces are visible to the teacher from all angles. The initial setup of equipment may depend on the focus of the lesson. For example, the height of the basket may be reduced to emphasize correct shooting form. The height of the volleyball net may be lowered to allow spiking. Nets may be placed at different heights to allow different types of practice. Remember that equipment and apparatus can be modified to best suit the needs of the learner. There is nothing sacred about a 10-foot basket or regulation-sized ball. If modifying the equipment will improve the quality of learning, change it.

Use of Time

Several decisions need to be made prior to instruction. How the time allotted for the total lesson will be utilized is an important consideration discussed previously. The amount of time allowed for fitness and skill development will directly influence what is accomplished in a physical education program. For example, assume a teacher decides to use 10 additional minutes per lesson for fitness development. The end result will be an increase of nearly 30 hours of time devoted to physical fitness during the school year. How time is used greatly affects whether program objectives are met.

Another advantage of programming how lesson time will be used lies in accountability. Assume that evaluation shows that student performance in throwing is subpar. If a stipulated amount of time was not consistently apportioned for the development of throwing skills, it would be difficult to ascertain whether insufficient time was the reason for the lack of progress.

The pace of a lesson is also directly related to time. Skillful teachers know when to terminate practice sessions and move on to new activities. For example, students become bored and begin to display off-task behavior when practice sessions are excessively long. Knowing the right time to refocus their attention on a varied task is important. In most cases, it is better to err on the short side rather than allow them to practice to the point of fatigue and boredom, which could result in class management problems.

Timing the pace of the lesson is difficult since it involves a certain "feel" about the class. A rule of thumb might be to refocus or change the task when five or more students are off task. At this point, the teacher has a few options for extending the length of the practice session.

1. *Refocus the class.* This can be accomplished by asking them to observe another student's performance. Another method is to explain the importance of the skill and how it will help their game-time performance.

2. *Refine or extend the task.* This involves stopping the class and asking them to improve their technique by improving a phase of their performance or to add a more difficult variation. This approach usually redefines the challenge and is a more difficult variation of the skill they were practicing.

3. *Stop and evaluate.* An effective approach is to stop the class and evaluate their performance. Students can work with a partner and check for key points. Emphasis is placed on evaluating and correcting the performance. Practice can resume after a few minutes of evaluation.

Another impact on pacing is whether the lesson is teacher or student directed. When a teacher directs the pace, timing is controlled by the instructor, and students are expected to perform the same task at the same time. Determining whether a presentation should be teacher or student paced depends on the type of skill being taught. If the skill is closed in nature (only one way to perform or respond), teacher pacing appears to be most effective. Teacher pacing can be accompanied by verbal cues and modeling behavior. Teacher pacing is effective in learning skills that are novel or new to the learner because the cues and visual imagery help the learner develop a conception of the pattern to be performed. Student pacing allows learners to progress at their own rate. It is effective when open skills are being learned and a variety of responses are preferred or encouraged.

Use of Space

A common mistake made by teachers is to take a class to a large practice area, tell them a task to accomplish, and fail to define or limit the space where it should be performed. The class spreads out in an area so large that the teacher finds it impossible to communicate and manage the class. The size of the space is dictated by the skills being practiced and the ability of the teacher to control

the class. Delineating a small area for participation will make it easier to control a class. As students become more responsive, the size of the area can be enlarged. Regardless of the size of the space, the practice area must be delineated. An easy way is to set up cones around the perimeter of the area. Chalk lines, evenly spaced equipment, or natural boundaries can also serve to signal restraining lines.

A factor that affects the size of the practice area is the amount of instruction that will be offered. If students are learning a closed skill and need feedback and redirection regularly, it is important that they stay in proximity to the instructor. An effective approach is to establish a smaller area where students move on signal for instruction and then return to the larger area for practice. If this approach is used, care must be taken to prevent wasting time moving between areas.

Available space is often divided into smaller areas to maximize student participation. An example is a volleyball game where only 10 students can play on one available court. In most cases, it would be more effective to divide the area into two courts to facilitate a greater number of students. A related consideration when partitioning space is safety. If the playing areas are too close together, it is possible that players from one area might run into players in the other area. It would be unsafe in a softball setting if a player on one field hit a ball into another play area. In most cases, the safety of students can be ensured by careful planning.

Use of Instructional Formations

The teacher should devise an appropriate formation or arrangement to facilitate learning experiences. Different formations are needed for activities in place (nonlocomotor), activities in which children move (locomotor), and activities in which balls, beanbags, or other objects are thrown, kicked, caught, or otherwise received (manipulative activities). Selecting a formation should focus on assuring maximum activity for all students. When small groups are used, no more than four students should be placed in a squad. This will minimize the amount of time spent standing and waiting for a turn.

Mass or Scattered Formation

Children can be scattered throughout the area in random fashion so that each student has personal space. This formation is useful for in-place activities and when individuals need to move in every direction. In locomotor movement, children should be courteous and avoid collisions. From the beginning, emphasis should be placed on not bumping into, colliding with, or interfering with other children. The scattered formation is basic to such activities as wands, hoops, individual rope jumping, and individual ball skills.

Extended Squad Formation

Extended squad formation is a structured formation based on squad organization. In formal squad formation, members stand about 3 feet apart in a column. In extended formation, the squad column is maintained with more distance (10 to 15 feet) between members. Figure 5.4 shows a regular and an extended squad formation.

Regular Ⓛ X X X X X X

Extended Ⓛ X X X X X X

Figure 5.4 Regular and extended squad formation

Partner Formation

Partner formation is most important in throwing, catching, kicking, and receiving activities. One ball or object is needed for each pair. On the playground, where there is sufficient room, pairs can scatter. Indoors, keeping pairs aligned in somewhat parallel fashion minimizes problems with flying balls (Figure 5.5).

X X X X X X X X
↕ ↕ ↕ ↕ ↕ ↕ ↕ ↕
X X X X X X X X

Figure 5.5 Partner formation

Small Groups

The small-group formation is similar to the partner arrangement but includes a few more children. Children work together on either a fundamental movement problem or ball skills.

Lane or File

Lane, or file, arrangement is the basic relay formation (Figure 5.6). It can be used for locomotor

X X X X
X X X X
X X X X
X X X X
X X X X
X X X X

Figure 5.6 Lane, or file, formation

activity, with those in front moving as prescribed and then taking their place at the rear of the lane.

Squad Formation with Leader

Squad formation with a leader (or lane-plus-one formation) is a useful relay formation, with possible minor application in skill practice. It has utility for throwing and catching skills. Each leader is positioned a short distance in front of the squad (Figure 5.7).

X X X X
X X X X
X X X X
X X X X
X X X X
X X X X

Ⓛ Ⓛ Ⓛ Ⓛ

Figure 5.7 Squad formation with leader

Squad Formation Re-forming at the Other End of the Space

To re-form at the other end of the space from squad formation, the leading child in each squad begins moving across the floor. When that child is about halfway, the next child starts. The squad re-forms at the other end and gets ready for another movement (Figure 5.8).

Squad re-forms on this end

X X X X X
X X X X X ←
X X X X X
X X X X X ←
X X X X X
X X X X X ←
X X X X X
X X X X X ←
X X X X X
X X X X X ←
X X X . X X
X X X X X ←
X X X X X
X X X X X ←

Figure 5.8 Squad formation re-forming at other end of space

Line and Leader

Line-and-leader formation (Figure 5.9) is often used for throwing and catching skills. The leader passes back and forth to each line player in turn. It makes a nice revolving relay.

Figure 5.9 Line-and-leader formation

Semicircle and Leader

Semicircle-and-leader formation (Figure 5.10) is a variation of line and leader.

Figure 5.10 Semicircle-and-leader formation

Circle

Circle formation (Figure 5.11) is useful for ball-handling skills such as passing, kicking, and volleying.

X X
X X
X X
X X

Figure 5.11 Circle formation

Circle and Leader

Circle and leader is another ball-handling formation (Figure 5.12), which can serve as a basis for relays. The leader passes in turn to each member of the circle.

X X
X Ⓛ X
X X
X X

Figure 5.12 Circle-and-leader formation

Double Line

Double-line formation is good for passing and kicking. Figure 5.13 shows a zigzag formation that

Figure 5.13 Double-line formation

is more efficient than positioning the corresponding players in each line opposite each other. The ball is passed from one line to the next.

Regular Shuttle Formation

In shuttle formation (Figure 5.14), the movement of the players is similar to that of a loom shuttle. The formation can be done with as few as three players, but generally more are used. It serves as the basis of passing and dribbling skills in hockey, soccer, and basketball, and of ball-carrying skills in football; it can also serve as a relay formation. Essentially, the player at the head of one line dribbles toward, or passes to, the player at the head of the other line. Each player keeps moving forward and takes a place at the end of the other half of the shuttle.

Figure 5.14 Regular shuttle formation

Shuttle Turn-Back Formation

Shuttle turn-back formation (Figure 5.15) is used for passing, kicking, and volleying. The player at the head of one shuttle line passes to the player at the head of the other. After passing, players go to the back of their half of the shuttle.

Figure 5.15 Shuttle turn-back formation

Special Formations

The following special formations are useful for locomotor movements performed either around the room area or forward and backward. These formations are especially important in teaching fundamental locomotor skills.

Around the Area in Circular Fashion

This formation has children moving about the area in a circular fashion (Figure 5.16). An objection to this arrangement is that it creates competition and generates conformity. Collisions are not likely, however, and the teacher can observe the children more effectively.

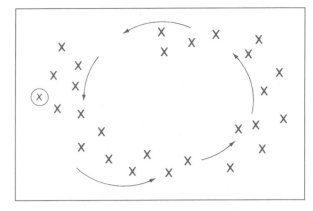

Figure 5.16   Moving around area in circular fashion

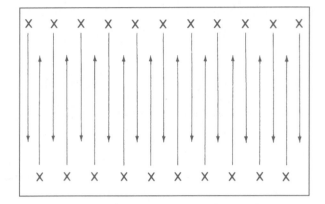

Figure 5.17   Exchanging positions on opposite sides

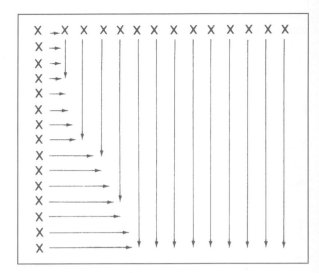

Figure 5.18   Crossing over on adjacent sides

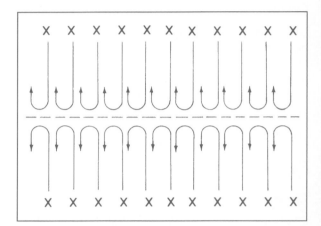

Figure 5.19   Moving to center and back on opposite sides

On Opposite Sides, Exchanging Positions

Children can also start on opposite sides of the gym and exchange positions (Figure 5.17). On signal, they cross to the opposite side of the area, passing through the opposite line without contact.

On Adjacent Sides, Crossing Over

In another arrangement, children form in line on adjacent sides of the gym or area. The two lines of children then take turns crossing to the other side (Figure 5.18).

On Opposite Sides, Moving to the Center and Back

Another formation involves children starting on opposite sides and moving to the center and back. A line can be formed with ropes, wands, or cones to mark the center limit. Children move to the center of the area and then return to place (Figure 5.19).

On Opposite Sides, One Line Moving Across and Back

In a variation of the previous movement, the two sides alternate turns. The line of children from one side crosses to a point near the other line, makes a turn, and then returns to place (Figure 5.20). After the one line has completed the movement, the other group takes a turn.

On Four Sides, Exchanging

The final formation has children starting on four sides and exchanging (Figure 5.21). The children on one pair of opposite sides exchange first, and then the others exchange. They alternate back and forth in this manner.

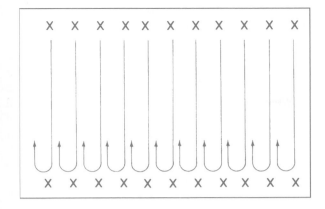

Figure 5.20 One line moving across and back on opposite sides

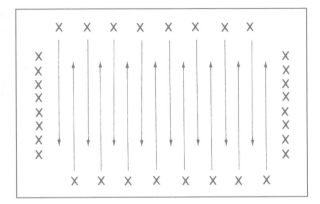

Figure 5.21 Exchanging on four sides

LESSON PLANNING CONSIDERATIONS

The importance of planning a lesson cannot be overemphasized. Instructors have, at times, been criticized for their lack of planning. A cycle of not planning sometimes begins when student teachers observe master teachers doing little, if any, preparation prior to the lesson. The emphasis placed on developing meaningful lesson plans in professional preparation courses seems unnecessary when a master teacher appears successful without the aid of thoughtful planning. The beginning teacher is unable, however, to judge meaningfully the effectiveness of the master teacher because of a lack of perspective and experience. The master teacher has taught the material for many years and has evolved a method of presentation through trial and error. It is possible to present a lesson without planning, but the quality of the lesson can, in almost all cases, be improved through research, preparation, and a well-sequenced plan.

A strong case for planning can be made if a teacher wants to be creative and develop the ability to interact with students. Teachers, regardless of their experience and ability, have many elements to remember while teaching. When presenting a lesson, many situations occur that are impossible to predict: for example, dealing with discipline problems; the need to modify the lesson spontaneously; relating to students by name; and offering praise, feedback, and reinforcement. If the content of the lesson is planned, written, and readily available, the teacher does not have to concentrate solely on the content of the presentation and can place greater emphasis on other, equally important phases of teaching.

The competency of the teacher will determine the depth of the lesson-planning effort. More research and reading will have to be done for an activity in which the teacher has little experience. If the teacher is unfamiliar with a unit and still refuses to plan, the quality of instruction will suffer. In some cases, the scope of a curriculum is limited when teachers are unwilling to prepare and learn new skills and knowledge.

A major reason for planning is to assure that the instructional presentation will result in student learning. If students do not learn, teachers are failing. If the ball is "rolled out" and students are left on their own, little learning, if any, occurs. Allowing students to choose sides and play games without the input of a teacher leaves learning to chance. Considering the following points will help develop an effective lesson plan that facilitates and maximizes student learning.

Optimize Skill Learning

A major objective of physical education is to improve skill performance. Students expect to be physically educated. If they go to a math class, they expect to learn math. In fact, teachers owe students an educational experience rather than a recreational one. A well-developed lesson plan will answer the following questions.

Is there a purpose to the lesson? The lesson should be designed to improve the skill performance of students. What is the purpose of the total program and the lesson plan? If the lesson presentation does not contribute to the fitness and skill development of participants, it probably is difficult to justify. A teacher should know why an activity is taught and how it fits into a developmental scheme designed for optimal student growth.

Is instruction part of the lesson? Instruction should be an observable action. There are many different methods for accomplishing instructional goals, but there must be instruction. Instruction can take many forms, such as working individually with students, evaluating a student's progress on a contingency contract, developing task cards, and conducting group instruction. Regardless of the method used, physical education instruction must occur as a regular and consistent part of the lesson. It is difficult to justify a program that concentrates only on recreational aspects. The recreational approach allows the rich to get richer and the poor to get poorer. For example, if the ball is rolled out for basketball games, the skilled players will handle the ball more and dominate the less skilled players. Under the pressure of competition, unskilled students find it difficult to think about technique and proper performance. Therefore, game situations usually benefit students who have already learned the basic skills.

How does the lesson integrate with past and future instruction? It is important to know the types of experiences that students have participated in prior to the current lesson. Elementary school teachers must be cognizant of objectives that high school teachers have for their students so they can integrate their instruction with these goals. On the other hand, high school teachers must know the types of experiences youngsters receive at the elementary and junior high school levels so they can adjust their learning progressions accordingly. Physical education teachers at all levels must work together to reach common instructional goals.

Another important phase is to ensure progression between lessons in a unit. Skill-development activities should be evenly spread throughout a unit so that instruction is sequential and regular. Offering skill instruction only during the first day or two of a unit makes it difficult for students to develop new motor-skill patterns. Practice opportunities for students learning new skills must be presented in many short sessions throughout the entire unit.

The basic philosophy of the teacher plays a large part in determining whether planning will take place. Does the teacher believe that youngsters must learn on their own and that the total responsibility for learning lies on the students' shoulders? Or does the teacher believe that student and teacher share the burden of learning in an environment where both are determined and dedicated to educational goals? How teachers plan for skill development will strongly influence what students learn. If instructors do not assume the responsibility for assuring that students learn new skills and refine old ones, who will?

Effectively Use Practice and Activity Time

Students can listen to an instructor, read books, and watch gifted athletes and still not improve their motor-skill performance. Without practice sessions emphasizing skill development, participants will demonstrate little improvement in their level of performance. American society has a fetish for buying books that discuss how to improve everything from aerobics to Zen. Many people spend a great deal of money for private lessons and then never practice on their own. Obviously, students will not learn new skills if the lesson does not plan for practice through activity. Of all the elements that go into learning new skills, correct practice is the most critical and necessary. Therefore, plan a lesson that assures necessary instruction and *maximizes* the amount of productive practice time for the learner.

Analyze reasons that students may not receive the maximum amount of activity in a lesson. It may be that there is a limited amount of equipment, and students have to wait to take their turn. Consider how much time can be wasted standing in line waiting for a turn. Contemplate the following example: Students are organized into groups of nine. They are to practice basketball-shooting skills. Unfortunately, there is only one ball available for each group of nine students. Assume that it takes 20 seconds to shoot three shots and recover the ball. That means that each student in the group will have to stand in line nearly 3 minutes before receiving a turn. If the drill continues for 15 minutes, each student will receive only a little more than 1 minute of productive practice. Small wonder that youngsters do not learn skills correctly when such drills are used.

Another factor that may limit practice time is lack of space. This may force the instructor to rotate youngsters in and out of a game instead of organizing two or more games. It is important to use activities that maximize participation and don't eliminate students. Often, the least gifted student is eliminated first and stands on the side waiting for a new game or activity. Students learn little, if anything, standing in line or waiting on the sidelines to return to an activity.

The teacher may be unwilling to allow unguided practice time if there is a possibility that the activity involves high risk. An example might be stunts and tumbling. In this case it might be necessary that students be tightly supervised on an individual basis. However, in most cases, activities taught in a physical education class are not high risk in nature, and a lack of practice time is usually the result of poor planning.

Another point to consider when organizing lessons for maximum practice is the type of environment in which the practice takes place. Whenever possible, drills should provide for private and sensitive practice settings. Students should not be placed in a setting where they will exhibit their mistakes and errors in front of their peers. Not all of this can be prevented, but much can be done to enhance the quality of the setting. For example, students undoubtedly have friends who might accept their errors much more willingly than others. Many drills are best done with such a friend in a one-on-one setting. It might be possible to assign individual homework, or to allow students to work at a personalized pace with the guidance of a contingency contract. Whenever possible, try to ease the burden of learning new skills by reducing the fear of failing in front of peers.

Quality control within practice sessions is important if students are going to be expected to learn skills correctly. Drills in practice sessions must be related to the desired skill outcome. A poorly designed drill can cause skills to be learned incorrectly. For example, assume students are learning to dribble a basketball. To teach dribbling in a different context, students are organized into squads for a dribbling relay that requires that they dribble the length of the floor, make a basket, and return. Odds are high that this drill will result in improper skill development because students will be concentrating on other things beside dribbling. Many of the students will be worrying about making the basket, others will be more concerned about speeding down and back, and others may be preoccupied with failing in front of their peers. Few students will focus on dribbling the ball under control with proper form. The result is a situation in which very little effective and correct dribbling practice takes place.

When developing drills, it is important to eliminate as many distracting factors as possible. What elements will prevent students from correctly practicing the skills? Is this drill designed to offer effective and productive practice, or is it just a way of keeping students busy? What stipulations could be made to assure that students will practice correctly? Does the drill serve as a lead in to actual use in an activity, or is it useful in and for itself? Examine each drill and modify it accordingly when it appears that desired skill outcomes are not being enhanced.

Consider the Developmental Level of Students

Activities and units of instruction throughout this text are organized into developmental levels (page 58). To make instruction effective, it must be presented in a manner consistent with the developmental level of students. Even though students develop in a consistent pattern, there is great variability among individual children as to when they will be capable of mastering certain skills. Placing activities in different developmental levels encourages teachers to present activities that are appropriate to the maturity and developmental level of students. When necessary, teachers should present activities that best suit the individual student regardless of the recommended level.

Deciding on a best way to arrange activities for instruction is difficult because schools group children by chronological age and grade rather than by developmental level. Classroom teachers, responsible for a graded group of youngsters, often find it difficult to understand how and when to utilize the developmental levels. Table 5.1 shows how developmental levels roughly equate with grades and ages.

The planned experience should take into account the past experiences of students to assure that the type of experiences being offered help reach educational outcomes. This means designing drills and activities that are challenging but not threatening. An important key is understanding that an activity is challenging or threatening based on the student's perception, not the instructor's. An activity is challenging when the learner believes it is difficult but achievable. It is threatening when the learner perceives it to be an impossible task. The same drill could be challenging to some students and threatening to others. This is what makes teaching a difficult task—trying to sort out how students perceive various activities.

The planned lesson must allow students to progress at different rates of learning. This does not have to be done at all times, since students can stand a certain amount of failure. On the other

Table 5.1 Equating developmental levels to grades and ages

Developmental Level	Grades	Ages
I	K–2	5–7
II	3–4	8–9
III	5–6	10–11

hand, if they are fed a steady diet of failure, they soon come to believe they *are* failures, leaving little reason for trying. The more opportunities allowed for individual or partner practice, the greater the chance for self-paced learning.

Activities can and should be monitored so teachers can see how students are progressing. A planned activity check, or placheck (see page 206), gives an indication of the number of students on task. In most cases, when students find an activity too difficult, they will avoid it. The percentage of students off task increases quickly, offering the teacher visible feedback. If students complain loudly, the activity should be carefully reviewed. Often, if given the opportunity, students will offer productive and effective modifications.

A strength of pretesting or self-testing at the start of a unit is that it gives the instructor valuable feedback about the experience and capability of the class. It helps teachers avoid the trap of assuming that students know something, only to find that their assumptions were incorrect. A caution must be offered here: It is easy to get wrapped up in evaluation to the point that it consumes a large amount of the time allotted for instruction. A delicate balance must be followed in doing enough diagnostic work for effective teaching without using an inordinate amount of time. Usually, students do not learn during bouts of evaluation, rather they demonstrate what they already know. If the majority of class time is spent on evaluation, both pre- and postevaluation, students will have little opportunity to develop new skills.

A final word on customizing activities to developmental skill levels: Students must succeed a majority of the time if they are going to learn to enjoy an activity during adulthood. An instructor is in the position of being able to force (through punishment or embarrassment) students to do just about anything within the educational setting. If they are forced into activities that result in a great deal of failure, they probably will learn to dislike and avoid the activity for a lifetime. If teachers are concerned with giving students lifetime skills and attitudes, it is important to monitor and adjust their lessons regularly. One of the most serious errors committed by teachers occurs when they lose their sensitivity to the learner's perceptions and feelings.

Teach to Improve Creative Responses

If teachers expect children to be creative, they must introduce originality and personality into the teaching process. Some personalities are better suited to such emphasis and methods than others.

Students performing different movement variations

Through creativity, the child is stimulated to become a self-propelled learner, to develop habits of discovery and reflective thinking, and to increase retention of concepts. When children discover cognitive elements by themselves, the concepts are better retained and more easily retrieved for future use.

Another approach to encouraging creativity is for the teacher to set aside time at the beginning of a movement experience, before instruction, for the child to explore creatively. For example, a child might be given a hoop and told, "Experiment with the different kinds of things you can do with it." Some educators believe strongly in this practice. They hold that direction stifles creativity and that the child should have the opportunity to try, become familiar, and explore the range of movement possibilities before more defined instruction occurs. Opposing this viewpoint are those who believe that only a rudimentary level of learning occurs without direction and that more productive and creative activity is possible when the teacher transmits simple basics before experimentation begins.

The teacher should provide creative opportunity during appropriate segments of the instructional sequence. This can take the form of asking children to add on to a movement progression just presented or to expand it in a new direction. Time for creativity should be designated in the lesson plan, and the lesson plan should be flexible enough to allow for creativity at teachable moments. Allowing an opportunity for creativity after a few progressions have been taught will give breadth to movement responses. Creativity is furthered by the judicious use of movement factors, particularly sequence building and continuity.

The creative process can be stimulated by a show-and-tell demonstration. After a period of exploration, emphasis should be on what types of movement patterns are possible when one creates. Children naturally observe others when they reach a block or are stymied in their thinking. Although concentration should be on developing unique patterns, ideas from others can be a base for devising alternatives.

Creativity is an umbrella that can be superimposed on all activity. Care must be taken, however, to reject the premise that directed teaching is the antithesis of creativity and is disassociated from the creative process. For general movement patterns, choice can be used early in the instructional process. For more specific skills, time for creativity can be offered after the basics of the skills have been acquired. At that point, an exploratory approach can lead to extension and varied use of the learned movement pattern.

Encourage Cognitive Development

Experiences can be enriched by encouraging students to discover ways of improving techniques or remedying problems they are having in skill performance. They can be given opportunities to help each other diagnose and improve techniques. Strategies for game situations can be developed through group discussions and planning. The point here is not to detract from skill learning and performance, but rather to enrich and enhance learning situations so that the student is able to internalize them in a more personalized and meaningful manner. A golden rule does not have to be taught in every lesson, but little will be learned if teachers fail to offer integrated presentations regularly.

Cognitive development can be enhanced by allowing students to help choose the content and implement the lesson. This is not meant to suggest that students will decide what, when, and how learning will take place, but rather that students will become involved in improving the structure of the learning tasks. There are many advantages to involving students in the instructional process, including the following:

1. Students usually will select experiences that are in line with their ability and skill level.

2. Youngsters feel better about an environment in which they have some input. Positive self-concepts are usually the result of a situation where learners help determine their own destiny.

3. When lessons fail because incorrect decisions were made, students must shoulder some of the blame if they offered input. This helps develop decision-making skills that focus on personal responsibility.

Decision making and involvement in the learning process must be learned. People must have the opportunity to make decisions and be placed in a situation where they can realize the impact of their decisions. This means that the opportunity for making incorrect as well as correct decisions must be allowed. There is no decision making involved if only correct decisions are accepted and approved by the teacher. Soon, students begin to choose not to make decisions at all rather than risk making an incorrect choice.

Responsibility is learned. If students are allowed to begin making decisions at a young age, the stakes will be much less than they will be as they grow older. This involves allowing children to make decisions and to choose from alternatives. Allowing students to make choices should be done in a gradual and controlled manner by using some of the following strategies:

1. *Present a limited number of choices.* This allows the teacher to control the ultimate outcome of the situation, but offers students a chance to make a decision about how the outcome will be reached. This may be a wise choice when learners have had little opportunity for decision making in the past. New teachers who have had little experience with their students should allow for student input using this model. An example would be to permit students the choice of practicing either a drive or a pass shot in a hockey unit. The outcome is to practice striking the puck, but students make the choice about which one they want to practice.

2. *Allow students opportunity to modify an activity.* In this setting, the learner is allowed the occasion to modify the difficulty or complexity of the skill being practiced. If used effectively, it will allow learners to adapt the activity to suit their individual skill level. Involving them in this process can actually reduce the burden of the teacher, who no longer has to decide about exceptions and student complaints that "it is too hard to do" or "I'm bored." It becomes the student's responsibility to personalize the task. Options allowed here could be to change the rules, or to change the implement being used. It might mean changing the number of players on a team or using a ball that moves slowly. Some examples are as follows:

    a. using the slower-moving family ball rather than a handball

b. increasing the number of fielders in a softball game

c. lowering the basket in a basketball unit

d. decreasing the length of a distance run or the height of hurdles

3. *Offer tasks that are open ended.* This approach allows children the most latitude for making decisions about the content of the lesson. In this situation, they are told the task and it is their responsibility to decide how it will be reached. In this setting, the teacher decides the educational outcome while the student decides the means that will be used to reach it. As students become adept in using this approach, they will learn to develop alternatives. Examples that might be used at this level are as follows:

a. "Develop a game that requires four passes before a shot at the goal."

b. "Plan a floor exercise routine that contains a forward roll, backward roll, and cartwheel."

c. "Design a long-rope jumping routine that involves four people and two pieces of manipulative equipment."

This problem-solving approach has no predetermined answer. Students do not have to worry about offering the wrong alternative. This technique can be effective in helping students apply principles they have learned previously and to transfer previously learned skills to new situations. Ultimately, the problem is solved through a movement response that has been guided by cognitive involvement.

Develop Affective Skills and Outcomes

The performing arts (physical education, music, and drama) offer a number of opportunities for affective domain development. There are many occasions to learn to share, express feelings, set personal goals, and function independently. Teamwork—learning to be subordinate to a leader, as well as being a leader—can be learned. It is important that teachers realize the importance of teaching the whole person rather than just teaching physical skills. It is sad commentary when one overhears teachers saying, "My job is just to teach skills. I'm not going to get involved in developing attitudes. That's someone else's job." Physical educators have an excellent opportunity to develop positive attitudes and values. The battle may be won but the war lost if teachers produce youngsters with well-developed skills but negative attitudes toward physical activity and participation.

How youngsters feel about a subject will determine their level of motivation to learn. It will also affect the long-range effectiveness of the instruction. It is possible to design experiences that will enhance the development of positive attitudes and values. When developing the lesson plan, review whether the planned experiences result in a positive experience for students. Few people develop positive feelings about an activity when they are embarrassed or fail miserably. Ponder the following situations and the attitudes that could result:

- A teacher asks everyone to run a mile. Overweight students are obviously going to run slower. Many faster students will wait for them to finish—a rather embarrassing situation. Obese students cannot change the outcome of the run even if they wanted to. Failure and belittlement occur every day. Small wonder such students dread coming to class.

- How do students feel when asked to perform in front of the rest of the class even though the teacher knows they are unskilled? The added stress probably results in a poorer than usual response.

- What feelings might a student have when asked to pitch in a softball game, only to find herself unable to throw strikes? Might she do everything possible to avoid having this situation occur in the future?

Students need to know that teachers care about their feelings and want to avoid placing them in embarrassing situations. Sometimes, teachers have the idea that caring for students indicates weakness. This is seldom the case. Teachers can be firm and demanding as long as they are fair and considerate. Knowingly placing students in an embarrassing situation is never justified and will result in negative student attitudes.

It is not the content of the lesson plan that improves positive development of the affective domain. Rather, attitudes and values are formed by students based in part on how they were treated by teachers and peers. Within the affective domain, how instructors teach is more important than what they teach. Students must be acknowledged as human beings with needs and concerns. They should be treated in a courteous and nonderogatory manner. Feelings should be discussed. If teachers fail to sense how students feel, they will not be able to adjust the learning environment in a positive direction. More often than not, the best way to discover how students feel is to ask them. The majority will be honest and tell it as it is. If a teacher can accept student input without taking it personally, the result will be an atmosphere that is conducive to the constructive development of positive attitudes and values.

FORMAT OF THE LESSON PLAN

The physical education lesson for a particular class period should grow out of a unit of instruction or be based on activity progressions. Each lesson should follow a written plan. Written lesson plans vary in form and length, depending on the activity and the background of the teacher. A written plan ensures that thought has been given to the lesson before children enter the activity area. It helps the teacher avoid spur-of-the-moment decisions that might affect the unity and progression of the material. The teacher may modify the lesson, but the written plan keeps the central focus and purpose of the lesson intact.

Progression is more apt to occur in a lesson when the teacher refers to previous lesson plans as a guide. In future years, the teacher can refer back to the collection of weekly lesson plans for suggestions and improvements.

The following is a suggested lesson plan format:

1. introductory activity (3 minutes)
2. fitness development activity (8 minutes)
3. lesson focus (14 to 22 minutes)
   a. review of materials presented previously
   b. new learning experiences
4. closing activity (5 to 7 minutes)

The amount of time varies due to differences in schedules from school to school. The first set of numbers represents the time allotment for a 30-minute lesson, while the second set represents a 40-minute lesson. The numbers can be modified if a lesson of a different length is in effect.

Introductory Activity

Introductory activities are an important part of the lesson format. They have several purposes, including the following:

- Serve as a physiological warm-up, preparing students for physical activity.
- Help students focus on the objectives of the lesson. This can be an ideal time to use an anticipatory set (page 77) or review previously learned skills.
- Be used to review class management skills, e.g., stopping on signal, running under control, and so on.
- Offer students immediate activity upon entry into the activity area. This satisfies the desire of students to move immediately.

Introductory activities can be related to and coordinated with fitness development activities. Since introductory activities are characterized by locomotor movement, they easily interface with any fitness activity. Generally, some type of gross, unstructured movement (usually based on locomotor movements) makes up the introductory activity. An enterprising teacher can employ many different activities and variations effectively as introductory activities. Examples are provided in Chapter 12.

Fitness Development Activity

The second part of the lesson devotes time specifically to fitness development, through the use of activities designed to cultivate the qualities of health-related physical fitness (i.e., strength, endurance, flexibility, and body composition). The lesson plan should include fitness activities, cognitive information to teach, and suggested workloads. Physical fitness activities for inclusion in the physical education lesson are discussed in Chapter 13.

Lesson Focus

The lesson focus presents learning experiences that are designed to help students learn physical skills. The primary purpose of the lesson focus is to assure that skills are taught and practiced in a sequential and success-oriented setting. Before new skills are presented, previously introduced skills should be practiced. After sufficient time is given to review, new learning experiences can be presented. The emphasis is on education so students learn to perform skills correctly and efficiently.

The lesson focus should assure that students have the opportunity to practice newly presented skills. Some teachers move from task to task in an attempt to "keep students busy" rather than allowing time for repetition and refinement. Even though moving to a new task can be motivating, it may result in a lack of learning. Repetition of skills isn't always the most exciting situation; however, it is the only way that quality skills are learned.

Relaxing during the closing activity

Closing Activity

The closing activity is used to bring closure to the lesson by evaluating the day's accomplishments—stressing and reinforcing skills learned, performance techniques, and cognitive concepts. The lesson may be completed with a game that uses skills being developed in the lesson, or the activity may be devoted simply to having fun by finishing up with a game or activity that children enjoy. If a lesson is demanding, relaxation activities can be conducted so that students return to the classroom in a calm state of mind.

In some lessons, the closing activity may be minimal or be deleted entirely. This might be the case when the game or other activity, which is the focus of the lesson, demands as much time as possible. In no case should a game be held over youngsters' heads by suggesting, "We will skip the game if you don't quiet down." This implies that closing activities are not an important component of the lesson, but rather are used to bribe children to behave.

ORGANIZING CONTENT WITHIN THE LESSON PLAN

The lesson plan should contain all the information necessary to provide a high-quality learning experience, including expected outcomes, progressions, means of organization, points to be emphasized, and reminders to the teacher. A well-written lesson plan gives a teacher confidence and pro-

vides unity, completeness, and depth to the movement experiences in the lesson.

Although a lesson plan can cover a single day's lesson, it is more practical to write a plan that covers several days. During any one lesson, the instruction proceeds as far as is educationally feasible and takes up again at that point during the next lesson. The same introductory activity, with modifications, and the same fitness development activities are repeated during the lesson series.

Teachers always have the opportunity to deviate from the lesson plan when, for example, the learning potential can be enhanced by changes in sequence or by the addition of material whose relevance was not evident when the lesson was planned. Teachable moments are legitimate reasons for modifying the plan. A lesson plan format can be developed to allow for the interchange of plans within a school district. If such a format is adopted, a supervisor can then issue lesson plans for the entire district.

A comprehensive lesson plan should contain the following components. See Table 5.2 for an example of a lesson plan on long-rope jumping (Pangrazi & Dauer, 1995).

1. *Supplies and equipment needed.* A list of materials indicating the specific numbers of each item needed should be listed. How the equipment is to be distributed should be included.

2. *Movement experience and content.* This column lists the actual movement and skill experiences that will be taught in the lesson. The activities should be presented in proper devel-

Table 5.2 Sample elementary school physical education lesson plan (Manipulative skills using paddles and balls, developmental level II)

Movement Experience, Content	Organization and Teaching Hints	Expected Student Objectives and Outcomes
Introductory Activity (2–3 minutes): **Tag Games** 1. Addition Tag 2. Squad Tag 3. Couple Tag	*Dynamic Physical Education*, p. 568 Children should know the games so that little instruction is needed. Vary the type of locomotor movement the class can use to chase or flee.	*Psychomotor*—The student will be able to dodge or evade quickly and without falling.
Fitness Development Activity (7–8 minutes): **Continuity Drills** Students alternate jump rope activity with exercises done in two-count fashion. Exercises are done with the teacher saying "Ready." The class answers "One- Two" and performs a repetition of the exercise. Teachers or students can lead. 1. Rope jumping (forward) 30 seconds 2. Double Crab Kick 45 seconds 3. Rope jumping (backward) 30 seconds 4. Knee Touch Curl-Up 45 seconds 5. Jump and slowly turn body 30 seconds 6. Push-Up Challenges 45 seconds 7. Rocker Step 30 seconds 8. Bend and Twist 45 seconds 9. Swing-Step (forward) 30 seconds 10. Side Flex 45 seconds 11. Free jumping 30 seconds 12. Sit and stretch 45 seconds	*Dynamic Physical Education*, p. 303 Use scatter formation. Taped intervals of music and no music can be used to signal rope jumping (with music) and performing exercises (without music). Other exercises can be substituted to add variation to the activity. Allow students to adjust the workload to their fitness level. This implies resting if the rope jumping is too strenuous.	*Psychomotor*—The student will be able to jump rope for 20 seconds without missing. *Affective*—Lack of exercise is one of the key factors in heart disease. Symptoms of heart disease are often found in young people and thus fitness activities may help retard this health problem. Discuss heart disease and the role of exercise.
Lesson Focus (15–20 minutes): **Paddles and Balls** 1. Introduce proper method of holding paddle; forehand and backhand grip. 2. Place ball on paddle and attempt to roll it around the edge of the paddle without allowing it to fall off the paddle. Flip the paddle over and roll ball.	*Dynamic Physical Education*, pp. 423–425 Scatter formation. Ping pong paddles and old tennis balls with holes punched in them work well. Also, the children's hands can be used as paddles and with a fleece ball. This is a limited movement activity, thus break the activity into two	*Cognitive*—The student will be able to name five sports in which paddle skills are used. *Psychomotor*—The student will be able to control the paddle and ball in a variety of situations. *Affective*—One way to improve skills is to experiment with different ways of performing them. Discuss the value of trying new activities

Table 5.2 *continued*

Movement Experience, Content	Organization and Teaching Hints	Expected Student Objectives and Outcomes

3. Balance the ball on the paddle using both right and left hands as well as both grips while trying the following challenges:
  a. Touch the floor with hand.
  b. Move to knees and back to feet.
  c. Sit down and back to feet.
  d. Lie down and get back on feet.
  e. Skip, gallop, or do any other locomotor movement.
  f. Choice activity.
4. Bounce the ball in the air using the paddle.
  a. See how many times it can be bounced without touching the floor.
  b. Bounce it off the paddle into the air and catch it with the other hand.
  c. Increase the height of the bounce.
  d. Kneel, sit down, get into other positions (student choice).
  e. Bounce ball off paddle, do a full turn, and continue bouncing; or balance ball on paddle.
  f. Bounce ball in the air. Switch paddle to the other hand.
5. Dribble the ball with the paddle:
  a. From a kneeling position.
  b. From a sitting position.
  c. From a standing position.
  d. Move in different directions—forward, sideways, in a circle.
  e. Move using different locomotor movements.
  f. Exploratory activity.
6. Alternate bouncing the ball in the air and on the floor.
7. Bounce ball off the paddle into the air and "catch" it with the paddle.
  a. Increase the height of the bounce.
  b. Perform a heel click, full turn, or a similar activity and catch the ball.
	parts separated by some running, rope jumping, or similarly physically demanding activity.
	Concentrate on control of the ball and quality of movement. Take your time going through activities. Use left hands as well as right in developing the paddle skills.
	
	If students have a difficult time controlling the ball, it might be helpful to use fleece balls.
	
	Allow time for student choice.
	
	Change the paddle from hand to hand while the ball is in the air.
		rather than always practicing areas in which we are already skilled.
		Cognitive—The length of a lever determines, in part, the amount of force that can be developed in a striking implement. Understand how paddles are an extension of the arm and increase the force generated for striking.
		Cognitive—Firmness of the grip on a paddle is important when generating force. Force can be lost on impact if the racquet slips.
		Cognitive—The angle of the paddle when the ball is struck will determine the direction that the ball will travel.
		Cognitive—A paddle will give the student a longer lever with which to strike the ball and thus more force can be applied to the ball, which will increase its speed.
		Affective—People practice activities in which they are rewarded and praised. Discuss the importance of praising others and encouraging them to practice.
		Cognitive—A balanced diet is important for good nutrition. Foods should be regularly selected from the following four groups:
		1. Milk and milk protein
		2. Meat and protein
		3. Breads and cereals
		4. Fruits and vegetables
		Discuss the need for a balanced diet when one is involved in strenuous and demanding activity.

Movement Experience, Content	Organization and Teaching Hints	Expected Student Objectives and Outcomes

8. Bounce the ball continuously off the paddle into the air:
  a. Bounce the ball on the side of the paddle.
  b. Alternate sides of the paddle.
9. Place ball on the floor:
  a. Scoop it up with the paddle.
  b. Roll the ball and scoop it up with the paddle.
  c. Start dribbling the ball without touching it with hands.
10. Partner Activities:
  a. Begin partner activities with controlled throwing (feeding) by one partner and the designated stroke return by the other.
  b. Bounce the ball back and forth. How many times can you bounce it back and forth to your partner without missing it?
  c. Increase the distance between partners and the height of the ball.
  d. Catch the ball that is thrown from your partner on your paddle, then return the throw.
  e. Perform stunts while ball is in the air, such as catching ball behind back, under leg, or above head; clap hands, click heels, do full turns, etc.
  f. Use two balls.
  g. Move and keep the balls going; try skipping, hopping, jumping, sliding.
  h. Play Volley Tennis
	Stress the importance of accurate throws.	*Psychomotor*—The student will be able to perform three partner activities.

Game (5–7 minutes)
  Choice:
  1. Steal the Treasure
  2. Addition Tag
	Dynamic Physical Education,
	pp. 570–579	

Note: Supplies and equipment needed: one paddle and ball per child, one individual jump rope per child.

---

opmental sequence. The activities do not have to be described in detail but should offer enough description to be recalled easily.

3. *Organization and teaching hints.* This section provides points for the efficient organization of the class and important learning cues. How equipment is arranged, how students are to be grouped, and proper technique cues represent the type of information placed in this column. In addition, references to other texts for in-depth information can be placed in this section. This section should be filled with teaching cues

that help students learn. Teachers should write down appropriate cue words to help them integrate this instructional vocabulary into their teaching technique.

4. *Expected student objectives and outcomes.* Objectives that students should be expected to reach are listed in this area. The objectives can be written in the three learning domains. The purpose of the objectives should be to give the instructor direction for student learning outcomes.

ANALYZING THE LESSON PLAN

There are different approaches to writing lesson plans, but regardless of the style used, the plan should include the necessary elements for ensuring effective instruction. The following questions can help teachers analyze a lesson plan to assure that it is both comprehensive and effective:

Have you included the following?

1. title, length of lesson, and facility
2. a list of equipment, supplies, and instructional devices
3. objectives of the lesson (Include the three learning domains.)
4. references for further information

Does the instructional process do the following?

1. provide for continuity with previous lessons
2. review past material through lead-up activities
3. communicate to students why the material is important for them to learn
4. build motivational techniques into the presentation

5. provide for students with varying interests and abilities
6. include the special student

Does the lesson plan cover the following points?

1. provide for warm-up, offer students a physical fitness activity, and include an instructional component
2. outline new material clearly and with enough depth
3. progress from simple to complex skill development
4. progress from known activities to the unknown
5. include notations for demonstrations and use of instructional devices
6. include key questions and points that should be covered
7. combine physical education activities with other academic areas when possible
8. provide for the use of a variety of media

Does the lesson plan meet the following criteria?

1. readable and easily used by others
2. usable during the actual instructional process
3. designed for evaluating curriculum effectiveness
4. provide for appropriate evaluation during and after the lesson

In any case, formats used by teachers should cover the areas just listed. This will ensure that the lesson plan format is easily read, augments the instructional process, and provides for students of different abilities.

REFERENCES AND SUGGESTED READINGS

Annerino, A. A., Cowell, C. C., & Hazelton, H. W. (1980). *Curriculum theory and design in physical education.* St. Louis, MO: C. V. Mosby.

Gabbard, C., Leblanc, E., & Lowy, S. (1987). *Physical education for children.* Englewood Cliffs, NJ: Prentice-Hall.

Gallahue, D. L. (1987). *Developmental physical education for today's elementary school children.* New York: Macmillan.

Grineski, S. (1993). Achieving educational goals in physical education—a missing ingredient. *Journal of Physical Education, Recreation and Dance, 64*(6): 32–34.

Guskey, T. R. (1985). *Implementing mastery learning.* Belmont, CA: Wadsworth.

Hunter, M. (1982a). *Motivation theory for teachers.* El Segundo, CA: TIP.

Hunter, M. (1982b). *Reinforcement theory for teachers.* El Segundo, CA: TIP.

Hunter, M. (1982c). *Teach for transfer.* El Segundo, CA: TIP.

Hunter, M. (1986). *Mastery teaching.* El Segundo, CA: TIP.

Johnson, D. W. & Johnson, F. (1987). *Joining together: Group theory and group skills* (3rd ed.). Englewood Cliffs, NJ: Prentice-Hall.

Johnson, D. W., Johnson, R. T., & Holubec, E. J. (1990). *Circles of learning: Coopera-tion in the classroom* (3rd ed.). Edina, MN: Interaction.

Logsdon, B. J. & Barrett, K. R. (1984). Movement—The content of physical education. In B. J. Logsdon et al., *Physical education for children.* Philadelphia: Lea & Febiger.

Melograno, V. (1985). *Designing the physical education curriculum.* Dubuque, IA: Kendall/Hunt.

Mosston, M. & Arnsworth, S. (1993). *Teaching physical education* (4th ed.). New York: Merrill/Macmillan.

Nichols, B. (1986). *Moving and learning: The elementary school physical education experience.* St. Louis, MO: C. V. Mosby.

Pangrazi, R. P. & Dauer, V. P. (1995). *Lesson plans for dynamic physical education for elementary school students* (11th ed.). New York: Macmillan.

Siedentop, D., Mand, C., & Taggart, A. (1986). *Physical education: Teaching and curriculum strategies for grades 5–12.* Palo Alto, CA: Mayfield.

Willgoose, C. E. (1984). *The curriculum in physical education.* Englewood Cliffs, NJ: Prentice-Hall.

Establishing and Maintaining an Environment for Learning

*E*stablishing an effective learning environment demands that teachers communicate effectively with students. Communicating with a learner—indeed, with all learners—is critical for teachers, and communication skills can always be improved. If children are to learn essential information, teachers must communicate in a manner that encourages students to listen.

Quality instructors seem able to create a positive atmosphere for learning. They may not know more about skills and activities than less able teachers, but they often know how to communicate better. Communicating with clarity allows the learner to quickly comprehend instructions. Adapting skills to the developmental level of the learners helps them feel successful and worthy. Meaningful feedback is critical for assuring that students know when they are performing skills correctly or need refinement. This chapter deals with factors that the teacher controls. It is an inward look at the teaching personality and how it affects student desire to learn at an optimum level. How a teacher interacts with students influences how those students will feel about themselves; a positive self-concept will serve students for a lifetime.

COMMUNICATING WITH THE LEARNER

Before communication can take place, securing the children's undivided attention is necessary. Allow five seconds for the class to quiet, then speak with enough volume to reach the group without shouting. Speak in terms consistent with the comprehension level and maturity of the children. Gradually add new words to their vocabulary, but avoid technical terms they do not understand. In working with disadvantaged children, be sure that terms are appropriate and relevant to the group.

When talking with students, assume a physical pose that expresses interest and attention. Kneel at times so that youngsters do not always have to look up. Facial and verbal cues should reinforce your interest and concern. Remember that children want to understand and to be understood. The underlying points will help facilitate the process of communication between student and teacher:

1. *Speak about behavior rather than about the person.* When teachers discuss the person, they often are judgmental. For example, "Can't you do better than that? That was terrible," judges the child as a whole and diminishes the worth of the student. It is much more effective to suggest that "you need to listen when I am talking." This deals with behavior the child can improve and avoids stepping on the child's self-worth. In addition, this approach makes people feel that you are interested in helping rather than belittling them.

2. *Try to understand the child's point of view.* Imagine how you would feel if someone embarrassed you in front of the class. How do you feel when you are inept and trying to learn a new skill? These and other emotions often make listening difficult for youngsters. What conditions are necessary to make it easy for you to accept constructive feedback? It is quite possible that unrestrained feedback may actually stress the youngster and reduce performance. If you are going to suggest ways to improve performance, try to do so on a personal basis and then allow youngsters to practice without scrutiny. To ask students to change and then watch them until they do is intimidating and may cause resentment and excessive pressure.

3. *Understand your feelings about the learner.* At times, teachers send mixed messages to students. They may be unhappy with the student because of another incident, yet unwilling to confront them with the real issue. Instead, they challenge the student with unkind feedback about a skill performance. This was not the teacher's intent but is the result of pent-up feelings over a previous issue. If you feel negative about a student, the student will perceive the unhappiness. Take responsibility for communicating how you feel (albeit negative), but make sure that it is directed at correctable behavior.

4. *Accentuate the positive.* When phrasing the instructional points of a lesson, accent the positive. For example, tell children to "land lightly," rather than saying, "Don't land so hard." An easy way to emphasize the why of an activity is to say, "Do this because. . . ." If there are several different and acceptable ways to perform movement patterns, be explicit. Show students various ways, and discuss with them the reasons behind the different techniques. Children like to know what the correct

Sitting position maximizes eye contact with students.

technique is, even if it is beyond their sphere of accomplishment. Explain only enough, however, to get the activity under way successfully.

5. *Speak precisely.* Limit the use of open-ended directives, and substitute those with precise goals. Instead of saying, "How many times can you . . . ?" or "See how many times you can . . . ," give children a definite target goal. Use directives like "See if you can . . . five times without missing," or "Show me five different ways you can. . . ." Ask children to select a target goal. Using measurable and attainable goals is important when teaching slow learners or special education students.

6. *Focus on correct performance.* Doing an activity in many different ways or doing it many times is a first step in the learning process, not an ultimate goal. Ask children to pick the best way to practice the skill. Youngsters should be told to practice the skill until it is correct and then move on to something else. Youngsters need to learn to assess when they are ready to move on; too often they move forward because they are bored or frustrated.

7. *Optimize speech patterns.* Certain teacher mannerisms may require attention and change. Avoid sermonizing at the least provocation. Excessive reliance on certain words and phrases—"Okay," "All right," and the irritating "and uh"—are unappealing to children. Acquire instead a broad vocabulary of effective phrases for indicating approval and good effort. Also understand that a period of silence can be effective; it allows students time to internalize and digest the information.

8. *Conduct lengthy discussions in a classroom setting.* Whenever possible, lengthy discussions should be held in the classroom for reasons of comfort and student expectations. Students expect to move in the activity area, whereas they have learned to sit and interact cognitively in the classroom. Maximum use of activity time can be made by teaching time-consuming explanations in the classroom before students go to the activity area. Rules can be explained, procedures and responsibilities outlined, and formations illustrated on the chalkboard. Any time discussions in the gymnasium are longer than 30 seconds, youngsters should be asked to sit.

9. *Respect student opinion.* Avoid humiliating a child who gives a wrong answer. Pass over inappropriate answers by directing attention to more appropriate responses. Alternatively, say that the student has offered a good answer, but that the question is not the right one. Ask the student to save the answer and then go back to that student when it is correct for another question. When in-

jecting personal opinion into the question-answer process, label it as such and try not to overemphasize its worth in comparison to student opinion. Do not be stunned, show surprise, or take offense if children comment negatively in response to a query asking for candid opinions about an activity or procedure. When opinions are honest, some are bound to be negative.

DEVELOPING LISTENING SKILLS

Listening skills are often more difficult for teachers to learn than speaking techniques. They have been taught to impart knowledge to students and have practiced speaking for years. Many students have viewed teachers as people who teach you but do not listen. In the majority of cases, poor communication occurs because of a breakdown in listening rather than speaking. There is a lot of truth in the adage, "People were given two ears and one mouth, to make it easy to listen twice as much as they speak."

1. *Be an active listener.* Good listeners convince the speaker they are interested in what the speaker is saying. Much of this is done through nonverbal behavior such as eye contact, nodding the head in agreement, facial expressions, and moving toward the speaker.

2. *Listen to the hidden message of the speaker.* Often, young children are not capable of clearly expressing their feelings. The words expressed

Be an active listener.

may not signal clearly what the child is feeling. For example, a child may say, "I hate P.E." Most children do not hate all phases of physical education; in most cases, something more immediate is the problem. An effective response might be, "You sound angry; are you having a problem you want to discuss?" This makes students feel as though their feelings are of importance to the teacher and allows for an opportunity to clarify concerns. It also prevents the teacher from internalizing student anger (or frustration) and responding in an emotionally charged manner, such as "I don't want to hear that; now get back on task!"

3. *Practice paraphrasing what the student has said.* Paraphrasing is restating what was said to you, including your interpretation of feelings, in your own words. For example, the teacher might respond, "Do I hear you saying that you are frustrated and bored with this activity?" If the paraphrasing is correct, it makes the student feel validated and understood. If the interpretation is incorrect, the student has an opportunity to restate the problem. In addition, it offers the teacher an opportunity to understand clearly how students perceive various situations.

4. *Let students know you value listening.* Teachers who listen to students learn about their feelings. It is important to let students know that you will listen, and then to practice doing it. It is quite possible that good listeners may hear things that are not always positive. For example, students may state honestly which activities they enjoy and which they do not. They may say how they felt when they were criticized. This type of communication can be constructive if it can be accepted by the teacher without taking it personally. It gives the teacher consistent and ongoing evaluation. Even though it may not be valid criticism of the program or procedures, it does offer opportunity for program and instructional improvement. A word of caution: If a teacher finds it difficult to accept such communication, it is probably best to tell students to keep their comments to themselves. Avoiding such interactions is necessary if it affects the confidence of the teacher.

5. *Avoid situations that destroy effective communication.* Certain types of verbal interaction convince students that teachers never listen and are only interested in forcing their feelings on others. Some of the more common examples are as follows:

a. *Preaching or moralizing.* This is often manifested by telling others they "should know better than that!" Obviously, students make mistakes because they are young and are learning. A big part of learning is making mistakes. Expect such mistakes; it will probably facilitate student–teacher relations.

b. *Threatening.* Threats are ultimatums given to students in an attempt to terminate undesirable behavior, even though the teacher knows they will be impossible to carry out. For example, the threat, "If you do not stop that, I'm going to kick you out of class" sounds tough, but is usually impossible to enforce. Teachers are not in a position to expel students, and many students are aware of the teacher's inability to carry out the threat. When students hear enough idle threats, they soon learn to ignore the teacher, and respect gradually wanes. Making only those demands that can be enforced consistently avoids the pitfall of hollow threats.

c. *Ordering and commanding.* If teachers appear bossy, students begin to think they are nothing more than pawns to be moved around the area. Try to develop patterns of communication that ask students to carry out tasks. Courtesy and politeness are requisites for effective teacher–student relationships.

d. *Interrogating.* When there is a problem (e.g., a fight between students), teachers often try to figure out who started the fight rather than dealing with the feelings of the combatants. Very little is gained by trying to solve "who started it." Students will usually shirk the blame and suggest that it was not their fault. A much better solution is to begin the discussion by saying, "You know fighting is not accepted in my class. You must have been very angry to place yourself in this situation." This allows students to talk about their feelings rather than place the blame on the other person. It also tells youngsters that even when they do something wrong, the teacher cares about them.

e. *Refusing to listen.* This technique usually manifests itself by "Let's talk about it some other time." At times, this response is necessary. However, if it is always the situation, students will begin to avoid interaction with the instructor.

f. *Labeling.* In this situation, the teacher tells children, "Stop acting like babies" or "You're behaving like a bunch of first graders." This is not only degrading, but it dehumanizes youngsters. In most cases, labeling is done for the purpose of improving performance. In actuality, it is usually destructive and leaves a person with a negative feeling.

ENHANCING THE CLARITY OF COMMUNICATION

Many words can be spoken, but little is accomplished if students do not understand what has been said. Communication implies more than words; it assumes that understanding has occurred. The following points can enhance the clarity of communication:

1. *Be exciting and dynamic.* It is not necessary to be an outstanding speaker, yet it is important to be interesting and exciting. The chance for effective communication improves if students *want* to listen to a teacher. Use your voice effectively; alter the intensity, raise and lower the pitch, and change the speed of delivery. Use nonverbal behavior to emphasize important points. In addition, keep discussions short and to the point so students can expect any dialogue to be meaningful and helpful rather than a long interruption of practice time.

2. *"Set the table and then bring the food."* If a concept is somewhat difficult to comprehend, set the stage by briefly describing what is to follow and why it is important. This may mean repeating instructions if students are having trouble comprehending. Anticipatory set (see Chapter 5) helps students prepare themselves for forthcoming dialogue. Quite often, learners may miss the first part of the discussion before realizing what the teacher is expressing.

3. *Build on previous knowledge.* Whenever possible, try to tie the discussion to previous skills and knowledge students have mastered. It can be effective to show students how this skill is very similar (or dissimilar) to one learned earlier. Transfer of learning can be optimized if students understand the relationship of the information being presented to their previous experiences.

4. *Present the material in logical sequence.* Skills should be taught in the sequence in which they will be performed. There are exceptions, where a teacher may want to focus on a critical step first and then build around it. For example, in dance, a teacher may teach step patterns and then put them together to complete the dance. However, in most cases the progression should mimic the sequence of performance. Young children usually

assume that the order in which activities are presented is the correct progression. Therefore, the younger the student, the more important it is to present the activity in correct chronological order.

5. *Demonstrate the skill to be learned.* Most children learn more by observing than by listening. This mandates modeling the desired behavior. Most students will learn fastest if they are talked through a visual demonstration. Often, teachers try to verbalize students through all skills and movements rather than demonstrate. Whenever possible, combining instruction with demonstration will improve the efficiency of the communication. The demonstration should include specific pointers that students can focus on while practicing.

6. *Conduct checks on understanding.* Checking for understanding will help teachers monitor the clarity of communication. A most efficient way is to ask a question and have students respond with an observable behavior, for example, "Raise your hand if you do not understand how to land correctly," or "See me if you do not understand how the game is played."

7. *Separate management and instructional episodes.* Much emphasis has been placed on maintaining short episodes of communication and focusing on cues that are easily understood. One more point deserves attention, as it often leads to student confusion: Teachers sometimes combine management activities with instructional activities. For example, during a presentation of a new game, the teacher says: "In this game, we will break into groups of five. Each group will get a ball and form a small circle. On the command go, the game will start. Here is how you play the game. . . ." At this point, a lengthy discussion of game rules and conduct follows. Most students will have forgotten what they were asked to do earlier or will be thinking about whom they want in their group rather than the rules. It is more effective to move the class into the game formation and then discuss the activity. This serves two purposes: it reduces the length of the episode and it makes it easier for the class to conceptualize how the game is played.

Nonverbal Communication

Nonverbal communication often tells students what behavior is acceptable. Nonverbal communication is effective because it is interpreted by students and often is perceived as more meaningful than the words the teacher expresses. Beginning teachers often have a difficult time coordinating their feelings and words with their body

*Using nonverbal communi-
cation*

language. They may be pleased with student performance, yet carry themselves in a less-than-
pleased manner (e.g., a frown on their face and
hands on their hips). A common example is when
teachers want to assert themselves and gain control of a class. They often place their hands in their
pockets, stand in a slouched position, and back
away from the class. This behavior signals anything but assertiveness and gives students mixed
messages.

Many types of nonverbal behavior can be used
to praise a class effectively: the thrust of a finger into
the air to signify "number 1," thumbs up, high fives,
shaking hands, and so on. In contrast to the positive
nonverbal behaviors, the teacher may also deliver
many negative signals, including some of the more
common such as hands on the hips, finger to the
lips, frowning, and staring. In any case, effective use
of nonverbal behavior will increase the validity and
strength of verbal communication.

When using nonverbal communication, consider as far as possible the customs and mores of
different cultures. It is the responsibility of the
teacher to learn how youngsters respond to different types of gestures. For example, Hmong and
Laotian children may be touched on the head only
by parents and close relatives. A teacher who pats
the child on the head for approval is interfering with
the child's spiritual nature. The okay sign, touching
thumb and forefinger, is an indication of approval
in the United States. However, in several Asian
cultures it is a "zero," indicating the child is not

performing properly. In many South American
countries, the okay sign carries a derogatory
sexual connotation. New teachers should ask for
advice when using nonverbal gestures with youngsters from other cultures.

To make nonverbal behavior more convincing,
it is important to view one's behavior and then practice modification. An effective method is to perform
in front of a mirror and attempt to display different
emotions. Another is to work with someone who
does not know you well and display a variety of
behaviors. If this person can identify the emotions
and see them as convincing, you are probably effectively expressing yourself nonverbally.

Videotape recorders are effective tools for self-
analysis. Teachers can self-analyze how they look
when under stress, when disciplining a student,
when praising, and so on. Teachers often exhibit
distracting or unassertive nonverbal behaviors
such as playing with the whistle, slumping, putting
their hands in their pockets, or shuffling their feet.
Just as verbal communication must be practiced
and critiqued, so must nonverbal behavior.

DEMONSTRATING AND MODELING SKILLS

Another form of nonverbal communication is the
use of skill demonstrations. Modeling skills can
illustrate variety or depth of movement, show
something unique or different, point out items of

technique or approach, illustrate different acceptable styles, and show progress. Demonstrations should be directed toward increasing the understanding of skills presented and should encourage students to observe critically and analyze what they have seen. Demonstration should immediately be followed by a period of practice.

Demonstration by the Teacher

Be sure that all the children can see and hear the performance. When explaining technique, the teacher should bring out the reasons behind key performance points. The teacher's demonstration should show proper starting position and be accompanied by verbal instructions from that point to assure a complete, point-by-point demonstration. The terminology should be clear, and techniques demonstrated should be at the children's skill level.

The more complex a skill is, the more demonstration needed. For creative and open-ended movement patterns, demonstrations may not be desirable, because they often lead to imitative behavior, which reduces creativity. In educational movement, a goal is to develop movement variety and versatility; thus, demonstrations should be used infrequently. Instead, children should be given the opportunity to develop individual approaches rather than imitating the style of another. Questions can be raised during the demonstration, but the teacher should not allow the question-and-answer period to take up too much time.

Student Demonstrations

Care must be taken to assure that the students can correctly demonstrate the skill. Rotating demonstration duties among students is not always a sound practice as it may result in embarrassment for students who cannot perform the skill. If they so desire, however, children should have the chance to demonstrate. An effective method is to observe students who are performing the skill during practice and ask them if they would be willing to demonstrate. If they choose to demonstrate, they have made the choice to do so and have to accept responsibility for their performance.

Student demonstration is an effective teaching technique, because it interjects children's ideas into the lesson sequence. As students practice and move, the class can be stopped to let individual children show what they have done. Teacher comments should be positive in nature, not derogatory. If a demonstration is unsatisfactory, the teacher can go on to another child without comment or

Using a student to demonstrate a skill

reprimand, saying only, "Thank you, Janet. Let's see what Carl can do." Or the teacher might simply direct the class to continue practicing.

Multiple Demonstrations

The multiple demonstration can be used to show what has been accomplished after a period of practice or at the end of a unit. A convenient way to organize multiple demonstrations is to have squads demonstrate. The teacher can select one or more squads to perform and then direct the class to return to activity. Another way to arrange such a demonstration is to have half of the class demonstrate while the other half watches.

Teachers Who Cannot Demonstrate

Because of physical limitations, some teachers cannot demonstrate effectively. Few teachers can perform all physical activities well. At times, even a skilled teacher needs to devise substitutions for an instructor demonstration. Through reading, study, analysis of movement, and other devices, teachers can develop an understanding and knowledge of the activities. Even if performing the activity is personally impossible, teachers must be able to verbalize how the activity should be done. In addition, visual aids and media may be used to offer meaningful orientation.

USING INSTRUCTIONAL CUES

Instructional cues are words that quickly and efficiently communicate to the learner proper technique and performance of skills or movement tasks. Children learning new skills need a clear understanding of the critical skill points because motor learning and cognitive understanding of the skill must be developed simultaneously. Often, teachers carefully plan skill and movement activities yet fail to plan for the instructional cues they are going to use during the presentation. This can result in ineffective learning, as students do not clearly understand technique and key points of performance. When using instructional cues, consider the following points.

Develop Precise Cues

Cues are short, descriptive phrases that call to the learner's attention key points of skill technique. If the cue is going to help the learner perform a skill correctly, it must be precise and accurate. It should guide the learner and be part of a comprehensive package of cues that enhance the quality of learning. Different cues should complement each other and make it easy for the learner to sequence a number of new motor patterns. Teachers must study an activity and design cues that will focus student learning on correct performance of skills.

All teachers must instruct activities that they know little about. Few, if any, teachers know everything about all activities. If precise cues are going to be incorporated into instruction, the instructor must do some self-study. Many textbooks and media aids are available as references. These resources will almost always delineate the key points of the skill to be performed. Other avenues to follow are to ask other teachers who have strength in different activities, or to videotape an activity and analyze points of performance where students have the most difficulty. In any case, precise cues are developed through practice and experience. A beginning teacher cannot be expected to possess a vast library of learning cues, but should possess an acceptable level for initial teaching experiences. On the other hand, it is inexcusable to teach without using cues because of an unwillingness to prepare for the skill presentation.

Use Short, Action-Oriented Cues

Cues should be short and to the point. Unfortunately, teachers sometimes make cues much more comprehensive and lengthy than necessary. Sometimes, teachers teach as they were taught in high school. A common model includes telling students everything they need to know at the start of the unit and letting them practice the rest of the time. This assumes the learner has comprehended a long list of instructions and is performing all skills correctly. If this is not the case, the learner will spend the rest of the unit performing skills incorrectly. An incorrect motor pattern practiced for a long period will be most difficult to correct at a later time.

To avoid confusing and overwhelming the learner, choose a small number of cues to be presented during each lesson. The cues should contain key words and should be short. They should encourage the learner to focus on one phase of a skill during practice. For example, if learning to throw, a cue might be, "Begin with your throwing arm farthest from the target." This cue would prevent the student from facing the target, which precludes trunk rotation in later phases of the throw. Other examples of throwing cues might be:

"Step toward the target."

"Keep your eye on the target."

"Shift your weight from the rear to the front foot."

One of the ways to examine the effectiveness of cues is to see if they communicate the skill in total. Have all the critical points of throwing been covered, or is the skill incorrect in certain phases? With most skills, the performance can be broken into three parts: preparation, action, and recovery. Cues should focus on one phase of a skill at a time, as most beginners can best concentrate on only one thing at once. Action-oriented words are most effective with children, particularly if they have an exciting sound. For example, "*Pop* up at the end of the forward roll," "*Twist* the body during the throw," or "*Explode* off the starting line." In other situations, the voice can strongly influence the effectiveness of the cue. For example, if a skill is to be done smoothly and softly, the teacher can speak in a soft tone and ask students to "let the movement *flooooooow*" or to "move *smoooooothly* across the balance beam." Cues will be most effective when the teacher is able to use voice inflections, body language, and action words to signal the desired behavior.

Integrate Cues

Integrate cues to put the parts of a skill together and to give the learner a set of words that focus on the skill as a whole. These cues depend on prior cues used during the presentation of a skill and assume that the learner understands the concepts delineated in earlier phases of instruction. Examples of integrating cues are as follows:

"Step, rotate, throw."

"Run, jump, and forward roll."

"Stride, swing, follow through."

The first cue ("step, rotate, throw") is a set of action words that serve to help the student with timing involved in sequencing the parts of the skill. The second set of words ("run, jump, and forward roll") helps children in primary grades remember the sequence of movement activities to perform. Integrated cues help learners remember the proper sequencing of skills and form mental images of the performance. Depending on the rhythm of the presentation, cues can signal the speed and tempo of the skill performance. In addition, they can serve as specialized language that allows the student and teacher to communicate effectively.

MAINTAINING A PRODUCTIVE CLASS ENVIRONMENT

Teachers need to develop an instructional environment that facilitates student learning. Instructional behaviors can be exhibited by the teacher to ensure that the activity area is safe and productive. Planning for each of these areas will assure students an opportunity to learn skills in a positive and safe setting. Each of the areas discussed here should be considered carefully prior to presentation of the lesson.

Creating a Safe Environment

Teachers should not underestimate the importance of a safe environment. It is possible that a teacher will be removed from the teaching profession if accidents occur due to faulty planning and foresight. Injuries are inevitable in physical education classes, but if they are due to poor planning and preparation, the teacher may be found liable and responsible for such injuries (see Chapter 9). Teachers must foresee the possibility of hazardous situations that could result in student injury. Rules dictating safe and sensible behavior need to be taught and practiced. For example, if students are in a tumbling unit, they need instruction and practice in developing proper methods of absorbing momentum and force. It may be necessary to practice safety procedures such as taking turns, spotting, and following directions.

Another way to assure a safe environment is to offer instructional presentations in proper progression. Injuries can be prevented when students refrain from performing activities for which they are not prepared. A written curriculum expresses to a safety committee or court of law that proper progression and sequencing of activities were used in the lesson presentation. In addition, proper progression of activities gives students confidence because they feel they have the requisite skills to perform adequately.

Safety inspections should be conducted at regular intervals. When apparatus has not been used for awhile, it should be inspected prior to the lesson. This assures that teachers will not have to stop a lesson to fix the equipment, causing unnecessary delays. Equipment such as tumbling mats, beanbags, and benches should be kept clean to prevent the spread of disease.

In spite of the foregoing precautions, accidents do happen. Teachers should not refrain from using activities that have a certain degree of risk, as one of the most important outcomes of a physical education program is to offer students an opportunity to take risks and overcome fear. If students feel that adequate safety precautions have been taken, they will be less hesitant to learn new activities that involve risk.

Observing Student Performance

Observing class performance helps assure that students stay on task and practice activities correctly. A key for any observation approach is to be in a *position* where eye contact can be maintained with all students. Students usually stay on task if they know someone is watching them. Teachers should be unpredictable when positioning themselves throughout the teaching area. If students can predict where the teacher will be, some of them will move to an area away from the teacher. It is common to find students who enjoy being near the teacher and students who like to move as far away as possible. Random movements will assure contact and proximity with all students in the class.

An assumption made by some teachers is that you must move to the same place in the area when giving instructions to students. It is assumed that students will listen only when the teacher is on or near this "instructional spot." Not only is this incorrect, but it can result in some rather negative consequences. Students who choose to exhibit deviant or off-task behavior usually move as far away from the instructor as possible. Since the teacher always instructs from the same place, these students will move farthest from the teacher to a position that is difficult to observe. In addition, it is possible that the teacher may never move near certain students, causing them to believe that the teacher does not care for them. Deliver instruction from the perimeter of the area and vary the location regularly.

Teacher movement coupled with effective observation skills helps keep students on task. Moving into position to observe skill performance will enhance the teacher's ability to improve student learning. For example, if you are observing kicking, it is best to stand to the side rather than behind the student. A judgment that needs to be made when observing performances is how long to stay with a single group of students. Becoming overly involved with one student may cause the rest of the class to move off task. On the other hand, if contacts are short and superficial, it is possible that students won't benefit from the interaction. Probably the best advice is to give a student one or two points on which to concentrate and then move to another student. Follow up later in the lesson to check student progress.

Since the movement of the teacher affects observational effectiveness, it should be regarded as an active part of instruction that should be planned. To facilitate moving throughout the area, divide the instructional area into four (or more) equal areas and make an attempt to move into each area a certain number of times. Instructions and reinforcement should be given from all four quadrants of the area. A student can chart the movement to give the teacher evidence of goal achievement. (See Figure 10.14, page 217, for an example of an observation recording chart.)

Developing a Systematic Observation Plan

There are times when teachers can "look at students but not see." In other words, teachers look at a class, but do not see how students are performing. If teachers do not have a systematic plan designed for observing and monitoring behavior, they find it difficult to recall student behavior. If a teacher wants to keep all students on task, it is important to have a monitoring plan. Such a plan could involve scanning the class from left to right at regular intervals and observing the number of students who are performing the assigned task. When teaching a class of 25 to 35 students, it usually takes 4 to 6 seconds to scan an entire class. If done faster, the teacher usually is not able to internalize the results of the scan. A number of variables can be evaluated through systematic observing: students responding to a start or stop signal (response latency), key points of skill per-

Charting behavior

formance, adherence to safety procedures, and on-task performance.

A plan can be developed to assure student contact. An example of a plan to assure all students receive feedback would be to check off the names of students who were contacted during the lesson. The check-off can be done immediately after the lesson with a class roll sheet, or at a later time if the lesson is videotaped. This plan may reveal to teachers that they do not make regular contact with certain students and do make excessive contact with others. If this behavior continues, students might develop feelings of favoritism or concern that "the teacher does not like me." It is reasonable to assume that not all students can be contacted in a 20- to 30-minute lesson. However, in a 1- to 2-week period, all students have a right to expect some teacher feedback and attention.

Maintaining Class Performance

An important phase of effective instruction is being able to pace the lesson in a manner that keeps students interested, yet not frustrated. Consider the following points to maintain a lesson presentation that results in a high amount of on-task student behavior.

Avoid Overtalking

It is easy to become engrossed in instruction and lose sight of student interest. Most students enter the activity area expecting to be involved in movement. If a teacher immediately sits the class down and talks for 3 to 4 minutes, students may lose interest and motivation. In most cases, instructional episodes should be kept to 30 seconds or less. When episodes are longer, they are filled with more information than students can internalize in one sitting. Most students in elementary school are capable of remembering one or two key points. Beyond this, they forget and move off task.

Teachers can sometimes become angry about misbehavior and spend 2 or 3 minutes talking about the need to be model students. Much of the "sermon" will be general in nature and will reflect the instructor's anger. Lecturing students has little impact. If misbehavior has occurred, speak to it, do something about it, and resume instruction. Often, a whole class is lectured when only a few students were at fault. This forces the majority of students to have to sit and listen to verbalization that has little or no meaning to them. Keep in mind that time spent talking is time spent away from meaningful skill practice. Minimize excessive talking and maximize productive and on-task practice.

Maintain Instructional Focus

Teachers constantly find themselves in a situation where it is easy to become sidetracked. During instructions, a student may try to explain what he did at the park yesterday, express that he has done this activity before, or state that "Johnny is not paying attention." The problem is knowing how to deal with the situation without losing instructional focus. The situation usually demands a quick acknowledgment followed by a continuation of the instructional episode. If you are helping a group of students and others arrive on the scene with something to say, tell the youngsters that you will discuss it in a minute and ask that they return to on-task behavior.

A concern of many teachers is that they may miss important student feedback if they do not listen to everything. This is the type of situation that "tattletale" students thrive on. If they can gain your immediate attention by telling you about other students' misbehaving, they have met *their* immediate need for attention. Acknowledging this type of behavior will only serve to make it occur more often. The best solution is to consider the source of the interruption and the seriousness of the misbehavior being reported. In most cases it is best handled by giving the youngsters a gentle reminder that you are responsible for student misbehavior and would appreciate it if your students would be concerned about staying on task rather than wasting their time speaking to you about the behavior of others.

Maintain Focus on Educational Objectives

It is easy to become derailed when an interesting event occurs in class. Lesson plans are designed to guide the instruction toward desired objectives. If the teacher constantly is "sidetracked" by students to more interesting topics, it is doubtful that predetermined goals will be reached. Effective teachers are able to maintain their momentum toward objectives and still show concern for student ideas. There are times when it is necessary to deviate from planned objectives and take advantage of the "teachable moment." However, this should be the exception, not the rule. Students are well aware that teachers are responsible for guiding the content of the lesson and they expect it.

Plan for Continuity of Instruction

Effective lessons flow in a consistent and well-planned manner. There are many transitions during a lesson: organizing youngsters into groups, changing from one part of the lesson to another, and issuing and putting away equipment. It is important that transitions occur so students perceive them to be an integral part of the instruction. If a transition interrupts the instructional task, students begin to visit and perform other unacceptable behavior. Minimize time spent on transition, as little is learned during this phase of teaching.

Another factor affecting the flow of the lesson is the pace of instruction. How often should a teacher break into practice sessions to clarify a point or to refocus instruction? In most cases there is a natural break in practice episodes when students begin to move off task. This signals that it is time to refocus. If, after an instructional episode, the majority of the class is not performing the task correctly, stop and clarify the situation. On the other hand, if a teacher stops the class frequently without concern for the students' opportunity to practice, the result will be a lesson without flow and continuity. Students become frustrated, feeling that they never receive a long enough period of time to master a task when teachers talk continuously.

Skill instruction demands continuity so that the learner understands the purpose of performing various activities. For example, most instructors break activities into parts, knowing how the skill as a whole is performed. Similarly, students need to know how the various parts of a skill fit together. This should occur within the same lesson. It is expecting too much of learners to ask that they practice parts for 1 or 2 weeks and then put them together as a whole. Always integrate the activity or drill into the ultimate focal point: the accomplishment of an entire skill or activity.

Personalizing Instruction: Showing Concern for Differences

A difficult task for teachers is personalizing instruction to better meet the individual needs of students. Even though the majority of instruction is conducted as a group activity, it is obvious, even to the least experienced teacher, that the ability levels of students vary widely. As students mature, this range of ability increases, multiplying the challenge for teachers. In addition, many students participate in extracurricular activities such as Little League baseball, YBA basketball, and private tutoring in gymnastics. This range of experiences places greater responsibility on the instructor to modify tasks so that all students can find success. The following are methods for personalizing instruction to facilitate learning in spite of developmental differences among youngsters:

1. *Modify the conditions.* Tasks and activities can be modified to allow the child an opportunity for success. For example, move partners closer together if they are learning to catch, use a slower-moving object such as a beach ball or balloon, increase the size of the target, change the size of boundaries or goal areas, allow students to toss and catch individually, or increase the size of the striking implement. An optimum rate of error and success should be the goal of personalized instruction. When students find little success, they exhibit off-task behavior to draw attention away from their subpar performance. This behavior is a clear indicator to the teacher that the error rate is too high and is preventing learning from occurring.

2. *Increase the challenge through self-competition.* When the success rate is too high, students become bored and avoid continued practice. Increase the challenge by adding personal competition to the task. Gifted students can be challenged to see how many times they can perform without missing or to break a personal record, or may be allowed to use the skill in a group competition. Increase the challenge by asking gifted performers to accomplish higher levels of performance, use a faster-moving object, or increase the distance or decrease the size of the goal. Students respond best to challenges; a task is a challenge when it is slightly above the current skill level.

3. *Offer different task challenges.* Students do not all have to be working on the same tasks simultaneously. It is desirable to have a number of tasks of varying complexity so that students of all skills learn to develop personal challenges. Task cards and station teaching allow students the opportunity to learn at an optimum rate. In cases where specialized sport skills are being learned, it is particularly important to offer different tasks. For example, students who have limited upper body strength would find inverted balances to be difficult, if not impossible. Balance activities utilizing the legs could be substituted, allowing all students to work on balance skills through different activity challenges.

4. *Encourage higher levels of performance.* Another solution for personalizing instruction is to refine the performance of skilled individuals. Fine points of technique can be used to offer greater challenge. For example, during throwing instruction, less gifted students may be learning proper footwork, whereas skilled

throwers are working on distance, accuracy, or velocity of throws.

PROVIDING MEANINGFUL INSTRUCTIONAL FEEDBACK

Offering students feedback is an important part of instruction. Used properly, it can enhance a student's self-concept, improve the focus of performance, increase the rate of on-task behavior, and improve student understanding. The following points give direction for improving the quality of feedback used during instruction.

Positive, Corrective, and Negative Feedback

A majority of teachers concentrate on corrective feedback that focuses on rectifying student performance. Usually little outright negative feedback (e.g., "That was a lousy throw") is used by teachers. Instead, corrective feedback is offered, focusing on inaccurate phases of the performance. Some of this type of feedback is expected by students; however, if it is the only feedback offered, youngsters will perceive the teacher as negative. A danger of overusing corrective feedback is that it may result in a climate where students worry about making errors for fear the instructor will embarrass or belittle them. In addition, many youngsters will surmise that no matter what they do correctly, the teacher will never recognize their effort.

A more effective approach is to focus on positive points of student performance. This creates a positive atmosphere where students are more willing to accept a challenge and risk error or failure. Teachers who use positive feedback usually feel better about their students because they look for strengths in performance and use this as a foundation for skill improvement. This is not to suggest that corrective feedback should never be used; in fact, Siedentop (1991) suggests that a 4:1 ratio of positive to corrective feedback is desirable. Because many teachers have been taught in a setting where most feedback was corrective, they often perceive it to be the best way to teach others. Most teachers will find it necessary to consciously increase the amount of positive feedback and decrease the amount of negative feedback shared with students.

Use Meaningful Feedback Statements

Many teachers have developed patterns of interaction that are positive, yet habitual. For example,

Delivering meaningful feedback

statements such as "Nice job," "Way to hustle," "Much better," "Right on," and "Great move" are used over and over. When used indiscriminantly, students soon "tune out" and fail to feel the positive nature of the comments. In addition, since these comments contain little specific information or value content, there is a strong possibility that they may be misinterpreted by the learner. For example, after a student performs a forward roll, the teacher applauds with a "nice job" comment. The teacher reinforced the performance because the student's head was tucked. However, the student thought the teacher was pleased because the legs were bent. This results in the wrong or incorrect behavior being reinforced by the teacher.

Adding specific information or value to the feedback improves desired student behavior. The value content of a feedback statement tells students why it is important to perform a skill in a certain manner. Examples of positive feedback with value content are as follows:

"Good throw. When you look at your target, you are much more accurate."

"Excellent catch. You bent your elbows while catching, which created a soft home for the ball."

"That's the way to stop. When you bend your knees, you always stop under control."

Examples of feedback with specific content are as follows:

"That's the way to tuck your head on the forward roll."

"Wow! Everybody was dribbling the ball with their heads up."

"I'm impressed with the way you kept your arms straight."

These examples focus on verbal behavior; non-verbal behavior by the teacher can also be used, such as showing how the arms were held correctly, the bat was in proper position, and so on. In any case, students clearly understand why their performance was positive and can build on the reinforced behavior.

Distribution of Feedback

Because teachers have a number of students in class, they have to make decisions about the length of feedback episodes as well as the number of students to contact. It is a decision that may depend on the skill being taught. For example, if a skill is learned quickly, it is usually best to move quickly from student to student, assuming there are no major dysfunctions. This fast-moving approach allows the teacher to come into contact with all students a number of times during the lesson. In addition, it helps keep students on task since they know the teacher is moving and "eye-balling" the class regularly.

The drawback to this approach is that little opportunity for in-depth feedback is allowed. If skills are complex and refinement is a goal, it is more effective to take more time with students. This involves watching a student long enough to offer specific and information-loaded feedback. The end result is high-quality feedback to a fewer number of students.

When offering instructional feedback to students, it is usually best to avoid close scrutiny of the student at the completion of the feedback. Many students will become tense if the teacher tells them how to perform the skill correctly and watches to see if they do it exactly as they were instructed. Most students are willing to try new and risky ways of performing if they are allowed to practice without being closely observed by the

teacher or class. Observe carefully, offer feedback, move to another student, and recheck progress at a later time.

Focus of Feedback: Individual or Group?

In elementary school settings, much feedback is group oriented; a common method used is to stop the class and offer feedback to all youngsters. This is an expedient method, but it also allows the most room for misinterpretation. Some students may not understand the feedback, while others may not listen because it does not seem relevant to them. A more effective way is to direct feedback (positive only) to a youngster so the rest of the class can hear it. This allows the feedback to "ripple" through the class, offering instructional feedback for the class and a positive experience for the student identified. In addition, the student can demonstrate the skill and serve as a model for the rest of the class. Care must be taken to avoid giving negative or corrective feedback in this manner. The "ripple" effect with negative feedback can be a debilitating experience for youngsters. All negative or corrective feedback should be administered quietly to the individual so only the teacher and the involved student are privy to the discussion. This avoids resentment that might build due to embarrassment or humiliation in front of peers.

Feedback should focus on the desired task. For example, if students are asked to "give" while catching a ball thrown by a partner, it will cloud the issue if the teacher offers feedback on the quality of the throw being made. If catching is the focus, feedback should be on the technique of catching so students concentrate on catching. An example of feedback in this setting would be, "Watch the way Rachel is reaching out and giving when catching the ball." A final clarification: It is not necessary to have students watch other students accomplish the desired outcome. In fact, watching is effective only if the performer is capable of showing the skill correctly. If this approach is used exclusively, less skilled (or shy) performers will never have an opportunity to receive classwide feedback. It can be just as effective to tell the class how well a student was doing and move on, for example, "Mike always keeps his head up when dribbling."

A final note about feedback: It should be offered to students as soon as possible after a correct performance. If delayed feedback is offered, it should allow opportunity for immediate practice so that students can apply the information. Little is gained and much lost if students are told how to improve but are not allowed a chance to practice before leaving class. Few, if any, students will be able to remember the points given in previous classes. If the end of class is approaching, it is probably best to limit feedback to situations that can be practiced immediately. Write down points to be emphasized at the next class meeting.

REFERENCES AND SUGGESTED READINGS

Anderson, W. G. (1980). *Analysis of teaching physical education.* St. Louis, MO: C. V. Mosby.

Harrison, J. M., & Blakemore, C. L. (1989). *Instructional strategies for secondary school physical education* (2nd ed.). Dubuque, IA: Wm. C. Brown.

Rink, J. E. (1993). *Teaching physical education for learning* (2nd ed.). St. Louis, MO: C. V. Mosby.

Siedentop, D. (1991). *Developing teaching skills in physical education* (3rd ed.). Mountain View, CA: Mayfield.

Templin, T. J., & Olson, J. K. (Eds.). (1983). *Teaching in physical education.* Champaign, IL: Human Kinetics.

Effective Management and Discipline Techniques

S uccessful teachers are always effective at managing student behavior. The skills may vary among teachers in emphasis and focus, but collectively they characterize quality teaching. Effective teachers take guidance from these three assumptions: that teaching is a profession, that students are in school to learn, and that the teacher's challenge is to promote learning. These assumptions imply a responsibility to teach a range of students, both those who accept instruction and those who do not. Teachers must maintain faith that students who have not yet found success will eventually do so. Instructing the majority of children in a class is relatively easy, but making appreciable gains among low-aptitude and indifferent students is the mark of an effective teacher.

CHARACTERISTICS OF A WELL-MANAGED CLASS

A well-managed class results when effective teachers and disciplined students assume the basic responsibility of directing learning toward target goals. Effective teachers vary presentations and select instructional strategies appropriate to the capabilities of students and the nature of activity sequences. How teachers teach, more than the characteristics of a particular teaching style, determines what students learn. Effective class management and organizational skills create a comfortable environment that offers students freedom of choice in harmony with class order and efficient teaching procedures. Management techniques include the mechanics of organizing a class, planning meaningful activities, and enhancing the personal growth of students. Because skillful instructors have the ability to prevent problems before they occur, they spend less time dealing with deviant behavior. In short, teachers who fail to plan, plan to fail.

Teachers need to be aware of the impact their behavior has on students. In many ways, teaching reflects the personality, outlook, ideals, and background of the teacher. A successful teacher provides high-quality learning experiences and communicates a zest for movement that is contagious. Teachers must also be aware of personal habits and attitudes that affect youngsters negatively. Proper dress, a sound fitness level, and the willingness to participate with students are examples of how teacher behavior impacts the profession and the subject. A basic requisite for teachers is to model behavior they desire from students. This means moving quickly if they demand that students hustle. It implies listening carefully to students or performing required fitness activities. Modeling desired behavior has a strong impact on students. The phrase, "Your actions speak much louder than your words," has significant implications for teachers.

Successful teachers communicate to students a belief that youngsters are capable, important, and self-sufficient. Stressing a positive self-concept and offering experiences to promote success are invaluable aids to learning. Teachers must make clear to students what the expectations are for learning and behavior. Well-managed classes function with little wasted time and disruption. They run smoothly and are characterized by routines that students expect and follow. The climate in a productive class setting is work oriented, yet relaxed and pleasant.

PLANNING FOR THE PREVENTION OF BEHAVIOR PROBLEMS

Many class management and discipline problems can be prevented through anticipation and planning. Teachers need to anticipate the types of problems that will occur and must know how to deal with them when they do occur. Figure 7.1 lists some suggestions for preventing behavior problems. Most beginning teachers worry that a situation will occur and they will not know how to deal with it. Anticipating and preparing for problems will give teachers confidence and peace of mind. Starting the school year properly is important. Many experienced teachers will admit that they were not properly prepared to start teaching. Many teachers have had to do a midyear reevaluation of their management and discipline techniques after allowing a number of behaviors to get out of hand.

Preparing Before School Starts

Determine Rules and Procedures for the School Year

For most teachers, rules are fairly standard. Most teachers want students to be respectful to them and to other students. It is not unreasonable to expect students to behave. In fact, if teachers can't manage students, they can't teach them anything.

- Anticipate and explain the rules rather than waiting for them to be broken.
- Talk with students' parents and ask for suggestions for dealing with misbehavior.
- Avoid placing students in situations that give rise to misbehavior, such as pairing up with the "wrong students."
- Be aware of individual students' tolerance for failure. Some students are never willing to fail in front of peers.
- Call attention regularly to desirable behavior.
- Talk with students and try to better understand their feelings. For example, you may find that they feel that you, the teacher, don't like them.
- If feasible, give problem students added responsibility they are capable of handling. For example, make them student helpers or teacher's assistants.
- As a teacher, model behavior you expect students to emulate. For example, ask students to do things politely, and discuss problems in a caring manner.

Figure 7.1 Techniques to prevent problems before they occur

Most school administrators will judge teachers' effectiveness by how well they can manage students. Thus, accept the fact that managing students is a necessary and important part of teaching; in fact, it may be more important (or a requisite) than delivery of content. When writing rules, try to select general categories rather than specific behavior. For example, "respect your neighbor" could mean many things, from not pushing to not swearing at another student. Rules should be posted in the teaching area where all students can easily read them. The following are examples of general rules:

- *Stop, look, and listen.* This implies freezing on signal, looking at the instructor, and listening for instructions.
- *Take care of equipment.* This could include caring for the equipment, distributing and gathering it, and using it properly.
- *Respect the rights of others.* Usually this means not pushing others, leaving their equipment alone, not fighting and arguing.

The number of rules should be minimized. Try not to exceed three to five rules; more than this number makes it difficult for students to remember all the details and makes the teacher appear to be overly strict. Rules should be guidelines to desired behavior rather than negative statements telling students what they can't do. The following list summarizes points to consider when designing rules:

1. Select major categories of behavior rather than a multitude of specific rules.
2. Rules should deal with observable behavior. This makes it easy to determine whether a person is following the rule and does not involve teacher judgment.
3. Rules should be reasonable for the age level of students. In addition, if rules can cut across ages, they can be used throughout the elementary school years.
4. Use no more than three to five rules.
5. State rules briefly and positively. It is impossible to write a rule that covers all situations and conditions. Make the rule brief and broad.

Determine the Consequences of Breaking Rules

When rules are broken, students should realize the consequences of their behavior. Consequences should be listed and posted within the teaching area and discussed with the class. If students are going to make conscious decisions about their behavior, they must know clearly what consequences occur. Rules and consequences should be applied consistently to all students. A primary reason for listing rules and consequences is to avoid punishing students excessively or unfairly. For example, a teacher may like one student more than another, and may therefore inadvertently punish them differently for the same misbehavior. This can quickly lead students to believe that the teacher is unfair. Having agreed on rules and consequences also involves students in developing an environment that, in part, they have designed. When the consequences have been mutually agreed upon, teachers don't have to feel as though they are the "bad person," rather, they are only administering predetermined consequences in an unemotional and concerned manner. Anger and guilt are avoided and both teacher and students can feel better about each other.

Determine Routines for Students

Students feel comfortable when they know what is expected of them. Students expect to follow routines. These routines should be discussed so students understand why the chosen procedures are used. Examples of routines that teachers often use are the following:

1. how students are supposed to enter the teaching area
2. where and how they should meet—in squads sitting, moving and freezing on a spot, in a semicircle, and so on
3. what they should do if equipment is located in the area
4. what signal the teacher uses to freeze a class
5. how they procure and put away equipment
6. how the teacher will group them for instruction

Once these routines are established and practiced, both teacher and students will be able to work together comfortably. Practicing the routines on a regular basis is important if classes are going to work efficiently with the teacher.

Preparing for the First Day of School

There are a number of things that can be done on the first day of teaching to assure that the class takes off on the right foot. The first few days of school require that teachers communicate their expectations in a manner that leaves students with a positive first impression. Students are concerned about developing a positive relationship with the teacher and a meaningful start can leave them confident and excited about the experience. The following points should be covered.

Be a Leader, Not a Friend

Students want a teacher who is knowledgeable, personable, and a leader. They are not looking for a new friend; in fact, most students will feel uncomfortable if they perceive the teacher wants to be "one of them." Let students know that they will learn during the semester and that it is exciting to be teaching them. Don't look to be a part of their personal discussions. There must be a comfortable distance between teacher and students. This is not to say that teachers shouldn't be friendly and caring. It is important to be concerned about students as long as it is expressed in a professional manner. Being a leader means knowing where to direct a class. The teacher is responsible for what will be learned and how it will be presented. Student input is important, but ultimately, it is the teacher's responsibility to lead the class to desired objectives.

Use Activities That Involve the Entire Class

To minimize class management problems, select instructional activities that demand that the entire group be involved in a simultaneous activity. As the teacher develops rapport with the class, different styles of teaching and class organization can be used. This implies that it is usually better to use the command style of teaching in the first few weeks of teaching. This will allow the teacher to view the entire class and see how students respond to the educational setting. Less directed teaching styles and different organizational schemes can be implemented after class management skills have been developed. Station teaching, peer teaching, and other approaches are most effective when the teacher and students have developed a feeling of mutual respect.

Pick Interesting Activities to Teach

In all likelihood, selecting interesting activities implies teaching content that the teacher feels confident in presenting. Teachers should have a curriculum to follow, and it is difficult to justify telling a teacher to only teach activities in which they feel competent. However, during the first week or two of school, most teachers feel stressed by having to learn many names, developing routines, practicing management skills, and teaching content. Selecting instructional content that is easy to present and

that students will enjoy will help generate a positive experience for both students and teacher. After initial routines have been established, instruction should be guided by the curriculum guide rather than personal preferences.

Present Rules and Consequences

Discuss rules and consequences with your class. Explain why such rules are necessary and how consequences will be used. Ask and listen to student input; this is an opportunity for the class to discuss the ramifications of the rules and how they will be enforced. It is possible that students will add new interpretations to the rules and help peers understand how the consequences will be utilized.

Practice Rules Systematically

Rules should stipulate expected behavior within the physical education class setting. If a rule is in place for proper care of equipment, students should have the opportunity to practice how the teacher wants equipment handled. If a rule deals with stopping and listening to the teacher, they should practice such behavior and be reinforced for proper response. Behavior will not always be correct, regardless of rules. It is common to hear teachers tell students, "I told you before not to do that." This assumes that telling students once should result in perfect adherence to the rule. Obviously, this is not the case. Teachers must remember to practice the behavior dictated by rules throughout the school year.

Communicate High Standards

Students perform to teacher's expectations. If a teacher expresses the need for students to perform at a high level, the majority of them will strive to do so. A common expression is, "You get what you ask for." If you ask and expect students to perform to the best of their ability, they probably will do so. On the other hand, if you act like you don't care whether they try, most students will do as little as possible.

Effective Management throughout the School Year

Enforce Rules Consistently

One of the best ways to earn students' respect is to treat them all in a fair and caring manner. Most students are willing to accept the consequences of their misbehavior if they think they will be treated

- The student may be testing the teacher.
- The student may have some type of deficit that causes the behavior problem.
- The student may be looking for reinforcement from the teacher.
- The student may have low self-esteem, which causes the student to misbehave while trying to become the center of attention.
- The student may not understand the directions given.
- The student may be bored and unchallenged by the activities.
- Performing the activities may result in continuous failure, so the student misbehaves to avoid revealing a lack of ability.
- Parents may deal with their children in a manner completely unlike the methods used in physical education.
- The teacher may not like the student, thus forcing the student to be combative and angry.
- Failure in other subjects may carry over to physical education.

Figure 7.2 What is causing misbehavior?

in a manner consistent and equal to how other students were treated. Animosity occurs when students sense that the teacher has favorites. It is common for physical education teachers to favor gifted athletes and students who are physically attractive. Teachers need to be aware of such behavior and to prevent its occurrence when possible. One of the reasons for defining consequences prior to misbehavior is that it helps the teacher administer them equitably. This takes the pressure off the teacher, as it is clearly the student's misbehavior that has triggered the consequences. Once a student chooses to break a rule, the teacher enforces the rule and makes little judgment about the character of the student.

Give Positive Group Feedback

Positive feedback delivered to the class will help develop group morale. A class must see itself as a unit that works together and is rewarded when it meets group goals. Students will work within a group as adults, so learning now about group cooperation and pride in accomplishment will help assure a smoothly running class.

Discipline Individually and Avoid Group Negative Feedback

When negative feedback is delivered, it should be done privately and personally to individual students. Few people want to have negative comments delivered globally for others to hear. All students should not be punished for the behavior of a few misbehaving youngsters. Group negative feedback can have contrary results. Teachers who criticize the group usually lose the respect and admiration of students who were behaving properly.

Give Clear and Specific Instructions

There are situations when students misbehave because they didn't understand the instructions. It is often effective to give students instructions and then proceed with the activity. If some of the students don't perform correctly, it may be that they didn't understand. Clarify the instructions and proceed. This two-tiered approach will usually assure the teacher that directions were clear and ample opportunity was given for all to understand.

Students misbehave for a variety of reasons. Some of these reasons are listed in Figure 7.2. Understanding these reasons and being able to identify them when they occur will help the teacher anticipate and prevent many behavior problems.

CLASS MANAGEMENT SKILLS

Class management skills are a prerequisite to effective instruction. Moving and organizing students quickly and efficiently require comprehension of various techniques coupled with student acceptance of those techniques. If a class is unmanageable, it is unteachable. Teaching management skills should not be viewed as a negative or punishing proposition. Most students and teachers enjoy a learning environment that is organized and efficient and that allows a maximum amount of class time to be devoted to learning skills.

Class management skills should be taught to students in a manner similar to physical skill teaching. All skills need to be learned through practice and repetition until they become second nature. If teachers view class management skills in this light, they will have more empathy for students who do not perform well. Just as students make mistakes when performing physical skills, they will sometimes perform management skills incorrectly. A simple statement to the point, such as, "It appears that you forgot how to freeze quickly. Let's practice," is much more positive than indicting a class for its carelessness and disinterest. Class management skills must be practiced many times with the understanding that student performance will vary.

Deliver Instruction Efficiently

If students are not listening to the teacher when instructions are given, little education occurs. Instructions should be delivered in small doses, focusing on one or two points at a time. The instructions should be specific and as clear as possible and seldom last longer than 30 to 45 seconds. This implies alternating short instructional episodes with periods of activity. This contrasts with the common practice of delivering long and involved technical monologues on skill performance. In a series of spoken items, people usually remember only the first and the last, thus most students will only be able to integrate and concentrate on one or two points during skill practice. Minimizing the amount of content per instructional episode will help eliminate student frustration and allow clear focus on stated goals. This is not to suggest that information should not be delivered to students, but that the "tell it all at the start" style should be replaced by the more effective "input, practice, feedback" model.

Teachers should tell students "when before what." Tell the class when to perform an activity before stating what the activity is. An effective way to implement "when before what" is to signal starting an activity by using keywords, such as *Begin!* or *Start!* or the school nickname. Implement instructions by a statement similar to, "When I say Sun Devils [school nickname], I'd like you to . . ."; for example, "When I say Go! I want you to jog to a beanbag, move to your own space, and practice tossing and catching." Any number of keywords can be used to encourage youngsters to listen to the entire set of instructions. Since the keyword is not given until all directions have been issued, students are not to begin until they hear the selected keyword.

Stop and Start a Class Consistently

The first requisite for being able to teach a class is knowing how to start and stop a class. Learning won't occur if the teacher can't stop the class. Use a consistent signal to stop a class. It does not matter what the signal is, as long as it always means the same thing. Use both an audio signal (such as a whistle blast) and a visual signal (such as raising the hand overhead), as some youngsters may not hear the audio signal if they are engrossed in activity. Whereas a loud audio signal is used to stop a class, a voice command should always be used to start the class. (See the previous discussion on keywords.) Regardless of the signal used to indicate a stop, it is best to select a different signal than the one used to start the class. If children do not respond to the signal to stop, the procedure must be practiced. Asking a class to freeze on signal is effective practice and youngsters should be positively reinforced. Too often teachers reinforce skill performance but fail to reinforce management behavior. If it is not reinforced regularly, it will not be performed well. To evaluate class effectiveness in responding to the stop signal, the teacher can time the latency of the response to the signal (see Chapter 10). If a class takes longer than 5 seconds to freeze and get ready for the next command, stopping and listening should be practiced.

Expect 100 percent cooperation when students are asked to stop. If some students stop and listen to directions and others do not, class morale soon degenerates. Students begin to wonder why they have to stop but other students don't. Scan the class to see if all students are stopped and are ready to respond to the next set of directions. If a teacher settles for less than full attention, students will fulfill those expectations.

Move Students into Groups and Formations Quickly

Physical education instructors constantly move students into small groups and instructional formations. Simple games can be used to accomplish this in an enjoyable and rapid fashion. For example, the game Back to Back (see p. 556) can be used to teach children to quickly find partners. The goal of the game is to get back to back with a partner as fast as possible. Other challenges can be to get foot to foot or shoulder to shoulder or to look into the eyes of a partner. Students without a partner are instructed to go to the center of the teaching area (marked by a cone or spot) immediately and find someone else without a partner. This gives students a designated spot to assume, as opposed to feeling unwanted while running around the area looking for a partner. Emphasis should be placed on rapid selection of the nearest person to

Class in freeze position (stopping the class)

keep children from looking for a favorite friend or telling someone that "he is not wanted" as a partner. If students insist on staying near a friend, tell the class to move throughout the area and find a different partner each time "back to back" is called.

Another effective game for arranging students in groups of a selected size is Whistle Mixer (see p. 580). When the whistle is blown a certain number of times, students form groups corresponding to the number of whistles and sit down to signify that they have the correct number in their group. Students who are left out go to the center of the area, find the needed number of members, and move to an uncrowded area. Once this skill is mastered, students can move quickly into properly sized groups. If students have trouble hearing the whistle blasts, hand signals can also be used to show the size of the groups to be made.

To divide a class into two equal groups, have students get back to back with a partner. One partner sits down while the other remains standing. Those standing are asked to go to one area, after which those sitting are then moved to the desired space. Getting into groups is a skill that needs to be learned and practiced regularly.

Other suggestions for finding partners are to ask students to find a partner wearing the same color, with a birthday during the same month, with a phone number that has two similar numbers in it, and so on. To arrange students in equal-sized groups, place an equal number of different-colored beanbags or hoops on the floor. Students are asked to move throughout the area. On signal, they sit on a beanbag. All students with a red beanbag are in the same group, green beanbags make up another group, and so on.

An effective technique for moving a class into a single-file line or circle is to have students run randomly throughout the area until a signal is given. On the signal to "fall in," while continuing to jog, students move to the perimeter of the area and fall in line behind someone until a circle is formed. This exercise can be done while students are running, jogging, skipping, or walking. As long as students continue to move behind another person, the circle will form automatically. The teacher or a student leader then leads the line into a desired formation or position.

Another method of moving a class into formation is to ask students to get into various formations without talking. They can offer visual signals but cannot ask someone verbally to move. Groups can compete against each other to see which forms the desired formation faster. Teachers can hold up a shape drawn on a large card to signal the desired formation. Young students can learn to visualize various shapes through this technique.

Use Squads to Expedite Class Organization

Some teachers find that squads can help them manage a class effectively. Squads can offer a place for students to meet, can keep certain students from sitting with each other, can group students into pre-arranged teams that are equal in ability, and can help teachers learn students' names. The following are guidelines for using squad formation to maximize teaching effectiveness.

1. Never select squads or groups in a manner that embarrasses a child who might be chosen last. In no case should this be a "slave market" approach, in which the leaders look over the group and visibly pick those whom they favor. A fast way to group youngsters into squads is to use the Whistle Mixer technique, described previously.

2. A designated location should be used for assembling students into squad formation. When the teacher wants students in squads, children move to the predesignated area, with squad leaders in front and the rest of the squad behind.

3. Squads provide opportunities for leadership and followership among peers. Teachers should make maximum use of squad leaders, so that youngsters regard being a leader as a privilege entailing certain responsibilities. Examples of leadership activities are moving squads to a specified location, leading squads through exercises or introductory activities, and appointing squad members to certain positions in sport activities.

4. The composition of squads can be predetermined by the teacher. It may be important to have equal representation of the sexes on each squad. Squad makeup may be determined by ability level so the teacher can quickly organize games with teams of similar ability. Squads can also be used to separate certain students so they don't have the opportunity to disrupt the class. Squad leaders should be changed every 3 weeks, and members should be altered every 9 weeks. Each youngster must have an opportunity to lead.

5. In most cases, an even number of squads should be formed. This allows the class to be broken quickly into halves for games. Having a class of 30 students divided into six squads of five members each places a small number of students on each piece of apparatus and makes for less waiting in line in group activities.

6. Creative teachers make the use of squads an exciting, worthwhile activity, not an approach that restricts movement and creativity. For example, cones can be numbered and placed in different locations around the activity area. When students enter the gym, they are instructed to find their squad number and assemble. The numbers might be written in a different language or hidden in a mathematical equation or story problem. Another enjoyable experience is to spread out task cards in the area that specify how the squads are to arrange themselves. The first squad to follow instructions correctly can be awarded a point or some acknowledgment from the rest of the class. Examples of tasks for the squads might be arranging the members in a circle, sitting with hands on head, or arranging themselves in crab position in a straight line facing northwest. Task cards can be used to specify what children are to do for an introductory activity, or where they should go for the fitness development activity.

7. Allow youngsters to name their squads. This helps them feel part of a select group, and that feeling makes the activity more enjoyable for both teacher and students. Youngsters should be encouraged to develop pride in their squad.

Know Students' Names

Effective class management requires learning the names of students. Praise, feedback, and correction go unheeded when the teacher addresses students as "Hey, you!" The teacher must develop a system to expedite learning names. One approach is to memorize three or four names per class period. The names are written on a note card, and those students are identified at the start and throughout the period. At the end of the period, the teacher again identifies the students. Once the first set of names has been memorized, a new set can be learned. At the start of class when the meeting occurs, those names learned previously can be reviewed and new students identified.

Tell students you are trying to learn their names. Asking students to say their name before performing a skill or answering a question can help you learn students' names. Once learned, you may precede the question or skill performance with the student's name. For example, say, "Mary, it's your turn to jump."

Another effective way to learn names is to take an instant-camera picture of each class in squads and identify students by keying names to the picture. With students in squads, it is easier to identify students, as they will consistently be in the same location. Identify those students whom you know and do not know before the start of the period. Personal goals can be set by calculating the percentage of students whose names are known after each period.

Pre- and Post-teaching Routines

Children enjoy the sense of security that comes from knowing what to do from the time they enter the instructional area until they leave the area. There are a number of procedures that should be conducted in a systematic and routine manner. The following are situations that occur before and after teaching and need to be planned for prior to the lesson.

Nonparticipation

An efficient system should be devised for conveying to the physical education teacher the names of children who are not to participate in the lesson. This decision is best made before children arrive at the lesson area, and is best made by school personnel (nurse or classroom teacher) other than the physical education teacher. This avoids the situation where the physical education teacher encourages students to participate even though they should not do so. A note from the classroom teacher or school nurse, listing the name and health problem of those who are to sit out or to take part in modified activity, can be delivered as children enter the room. The teacher should accept the information at face value. This avoids the time-consuming procedure of questioning students on the sidelines to determine what the problem is and what the solution should be.

Entering the Teaching Area

Nothing is more difficult than trying to start a class that has not entered the teaching area in a quiet orderly fashion. An effective approach is to meet the class at the door before they enter the area. The physical education teacher can then explain how they should enter the area and what they are supposed to do. Another common routine is to have the class enter the area and begin jogging around the area. When told to freeze, the day's activities are described. Another method is to have youngsters enter the area and sit in squads behind their respective cone or floor marker. Instruction starts when all students are in position. Regardless of the method used, students should enter the area under control and know where they are supposed to meet.

Discussing the Lesson Content

Students enter the activity area expecting to move. It is usually effective to take advantage of this desire to move by having them participate in some activity before discussing the content of the lesson. Youngsters are more willing to listen after they participated in vigorous activity. Another related issue is when to deliver instruction. An effective model is to allow students to try the activity before working on points of technique. The theory is that students are more willing to listen to instruction after they have tried an activity and found it difficult to perform correctly. Trying the activity first also gives the teacher an opportunity to assess the ability level of the students.

Closing the Lesson

A regular routine for closing the lesson is important for teachers and students. First, there should be some closure (see p. 81) related to the instructional content. Then there should be a routine for leaving the teaching area. This may be lining up at the door, returning to squads, or kneeling in a semicircle. Using a routine at the end of the lesson will tend to calm and quiet youngsters, which will be appreciated by classroom teachers picking up their class.

Arranging Equipment

Students must learn to pick up equipment and return it where they found it. This minimizes the amount of equipment rearrangement the physical education teacher will have to do. Equipment should be spread around the area before the school day starts and picked up at the end of the day. Student assistance in moving equipment before and after school both is helpful to the teacher and allows the teacher to work closely with students who need special attention.

Discussing Discipline Problems

Youngsters who misbehave during class need to be talked with after class. This is one of the main reasons for scheduling a minimum of 5 minutes passing time between classes. Scheduling classes back to back makes it impossible to talk with students, rearrange equipment, and take care of personal matters. If a student needs to be seen after school for an in-depth discussion, a "meeting appointment" form should be given to the classroom teacher and student. This will remind both parties that the student is to meet with the physical education teacher at the end of the school day.

*Equipment around the pe-
rimeter (using equipment)*

Effective Use of Equipment

When using small equipment such as balls, hoops, and jump ropes, every youngster must have a piece for personal use. When large equipment or apparatus is used, as many stations or groups as possible should be established. For a class of 30, six benches, mats, or jumping boxes should be the minimum amount of equipment available so students have only a short wait in line. One way to avoid standing and waiting for a turn is to use return activities (see p. 460). When using this approach, students are asked to perform a task or tasks on their return to the end of the line.

Demonstrate the proper method of using equipment. Teach youngsters to get a piece of equipment and work with it in an acceptable fashion. Equipment should always be placed in the same (home) position when the class is called to attention. For example, beanbags might be placed on the floor, balls placed between the feet, and jump ropes folded and placed behind the neck. Placing the equipment in home position avoids the problem of youngsters' striking one another with the equipment, dropping it, or practicing activities when they should be listening.

Equipment should be distributed to students as rapidly as possible. When students have to wait for a piece of equipment, time is wasted and behavior problems occur. Often, teachers assign student leaders to get the equipment for a squad. This results in a situation where the leaders are assigned a task, while other students sit and wait (and may become discipline problems). The easiest and fastest method is to have the equipment placed around the perimeter of the area. On signal, youngsters move to a piece of equipment, pick it up, move to their own space and immediately begin practicing an assigned skill (this takes advantage of the natural urge to try the equipment and reinforces those students who procure equipment quickly). The reverse procedure can be used for putting equipment away. This contrasts with the practice of placing the equipment in the middle of the area in a bag and telling students to "run and get a ball." This approach often results in youngsters' being knocked down and bruised. Regardless of the method used, waiting for all students to get a piece of equipment before allowing any student to use it places control in the hands of the slowest and least cooperative student. Avoid this potential problem by starting skill practice; while students are practicing, interact with those students who are slow and less cooperative.

MODIFYING AND MAINTAINING DESIRABLE BEHAVIOR

Teachers find managing student behavior to be a difficult task in teaching. New teachers, especially, often question themselves in terms of their ability to control and manage a classroom of youngsters. A class of children is really a group of individuals, each of whom must be uniquely treated and understood. Some teachers question why instructional discipline is necessary. The most basic of reasons is that it allows children to learn effectively without encroaching on the rights of others. American society is based on freedom hinged to self-discipline. Americans have much personal freedom as long as they do not encroach on the rights

132 CHAPTER 7

- Discuss with students the problem their behavior causes.
- Reinforce proper behavior exhibited by other students.
- Use time out from reinforcement.
- Use a behavior contract.
- Talk with the student and parents about the problem.
- Ask the student to perform activities that are failure proof.
- Substitute one behavior for another: for example, ask a student who doesn't listen carefully to explain to others how to perform an activity, or make that student a leader.
- Use the Premack principle: if you stay on task for 10 minutes, you can have the last 5 minutes for free-time activity.
- Focus reinforcement on something the student does well.
- Use prompts to remind students when they are off task or misbehaving.
- If feasible and the behavior does not disrupt the class, ignore the behavior.

Figure 7.3 Strategies for modifying misbehavior

of others. In similar fashion, children can enjoy freedom as long as their behavior is consistent with educational objectives and does not prevent other students from learning.

The majority of children choose to cooperate and participate in the educational setting. In fact, the learner is largely responsible for allowing the teacher to teach. No one can be taught who chooses not to cooperate. Effective management of behavior means maintaining an environment where all children have the opportunity to learn. It is a teacher's responsibility to fashion a learning environment where all children can learn and feel comfortable. Students who are disruptive and off task infringe on the rights of other students. If a teacher has to spend a great deal of energy working with youngsters who are disorderly, those students who want to learn are short-changed.

The purpose of this section is to help teachers develop an action plan for modifying and maintaining desired behavior. There are three phases to such a program: (a) increasing desired behavior, (b) eliminating undesirable behavior, and (c) maintaining desirable behavior. The focus of a discipline program should be on positive and constructive approaches designed to teach children responsible behavior. Figure 7.3 lists suggested strategies for modifying student behavior.

Increasing Desired Behavior

Behavior that is followed by appropriate positive reinforcement will occur more often in the future. This principle should guide the teacher who wants to be an effective manager of students. The strength of this simple principle is that it focuses on positive, desired educational outcomes. Key points for implementing the principle lie in deciding what to use as reinforcers, selecting those that effectively reinforce individuals, and properly using the reinforcers.

Social Reinforcers

This class of reinforcers is most often used by teachers. The teacher's behavior is used as reinforcement when children perform desired behavior. Most children have been involved in an environment filled with social reinforcers prior to attending school. Parents use praise, physical contact, and facial expressions to acknowledge desired behavior in their children. The following are examples of reinforcers that can be used with students in a physical education setting:

Words of Praise

Great job	Nice going
Exactly right	I really like that job
Perfect arm placement	That's the best one yet
Way to go	Nice hustle

Physical Expressions

Smiling	Winking
Nodding	Clenched fist overhead
Thumbs up	Clapping

Physical Contact

Hand shake	High five

Know what type of social reinforcers students are accustomed to responding to in the school setting. Certain reinforcers may embarrass students or make them feel uncomfortable. For example, some students may not want to be touched even to the point of receiving a "high five." A hug or pat on the back may be taken incorrectly by some students, particularly those of the opposite sex. If unsure, ask the school administrator to define the social reinforcers that are acceptable, and to which students respond positively.

Activity Reinforcers

Various types of activities that are enjoyable for children can be used as reinforcement. An effective way to determine activities that can be used as reinforcers is to observe children. Free time always ranks high among children's preferences. Some examples of activities that might be used to reinforce a class are free time to practice a skill, the opportunity to play a game, extra time in physical education class, the opportunity to help administer equipment, acting as a teacher's aide, being a teacher in a cross-aged tutoring situation, or being a team captain. Students might be given special privileges such as being "student of the day," getting to choose the game to play, or having lunch with the teacher.

Token Reinforcers

Many physical educators feel a need to offer some type of token as a reinforcer. It may be points, gold stars, certificates, or trophies. Physical education is closely related to athletic competition, where awards are often given to winners. This causes some teachers to believe that tokens should be used to motivate children in physical education. The less favorable aspect of giving tokens (ribbons or certificates) is that when they are given only to winners, losers become less likely to be motivated to perform in the future. Some teachers give participation certificates or ribbons to all students; however, this makes the token have little reinforcement value. In addition, there is evidence to show that extrinsic rewards may actually decrease a child's intrinsic desire to participate (Greene & Lepper, 1975; Whitehead & Corbin, 1991). If token reinforcers are used, they work best with primary-grade children. Young children are motivated by the tokens they receive. However, after the age of nine, many students see the tokens as bribery to behave in a certain manner. As a rule of thumb, it is best to use token reinforcers only if it appears that social reinforcers are ineffective.

Selecting Reinforcers

A common question among teachers is, "How do I know what will be reinforcing to my students?" It is impossible to know what will reinforce a student until it is administered. On the other hand, there are a lot of things that most children will respond to (e.g., praise, attention, smiles, games, free time, and privileges). A practical way to identify effective reinforcers is to observe children during free time, analyzing the things they enjoy doing. Another simple solution is to ask them what they would like to do. Most youngsters will tell you that they would like more recess, free time, or other enjoyable activity.

Using Social Reinforcers

Effective use of social reinforcers requires teachers to praise and make positive statements. Some teachers feel uncomfortable when learning to administer positive reinforcement to youngsters because it makes them feel inauthentic. A common complaint of teachers learning how to reinforce is, "I do not feel real and children think I'm a fake." Any change in communication patterns will make teachers uncomfortable. New ways of communicating with a class require a period of adjustment. When teachers are learning new patterns of praise and reinforcement, they often feel as though their behavior is contrived and insincere (fortunately, most students won't know the difference). There is no good alternative because teachers who are unwilling to experience the uneasiness of learning will usually remain unchanged. The assumption that patterns of speech learned as a child are effective in an instructional setting is false. Teachers are made, not born, and find success through hard work and dedication. If practiced regularly, new behavioral patterns will become a natural part of a teacher's repertoire after a period of time.

Praise is effective when it refers to specific behavior exhibited by the youngster. This contrasts with general statements, such as, "Good job" or "You are an excellent performer." General and nonspecific statements do not tell the youngster what was done well. It leaves it to the student to try to identify what the teacher has in mind. If the student's thoughts do not align with the teacher's intent, it is entirely possible that incorrect behavior will be reinforced. To improve the specificity of feedback, describe the behavior to be reinforced rather than judge it. For example, compare the following:

DESCRIBING: "I saw your excellent forward roll, James; you tucked your head just right."

JUDGING: "That's a poor job. I do not see why you cannot do better."

In the first example, the youngster is identified and the specific behavior performed is reinforced. In the second situation, it is impossible to identify what is poor or to whom the feedback is directed. In most cases, if a question can be asked about delivered praise or criticism (e.g., what was good, or why was it a poor performance), the feedback is nonspecific and open to misinterpretation. To increase desired behavior, verbally or physically describe what makes the performance effective, good, or noteworthy. This reinforces the student and communicates to the rest of the class behavior expected by the instructor.

The Premack Principle

The Premack principle (Premack, 1965) is often used unknowingly by teachers to motivate students. This principle states that a highly desirable activity can be used to motivate students to learn an activity they enjoy to a lesser degree. In practice, this principle allows students to participate in a favorite activity if they perform a less enjoyable one. The Premack principle is often referred to as the "Eat your peas before you get dessert" rule. In other words, an activity that children enjoy can be used to motivate youngsters to participate in activities they are reticent to perform. The following are examples of the Premack principle:

"You may shoot baskets [preferred] after you complete the passing drill [less desirable]."

"When everybody is quiet [less desirable], we will begin the game [preferred]."

"Those who raise their hand [less desirable] will be selected to answer the question [preferred]."

Prompting Desired Behavior

Prompts are used to remind students to perform desired behavior. They are used to encourage the development of new patterns of behavior. There are a number of ways to prompt children in the physical education setting. The most common are the following:

1. *Modeling.* The teacher performs the behavior desired to encourage students to respond in similar fashion. For example, the teacher will place equipment being used on the floor when stopping the class to remind the class to do likewise. Modeling is an effective prompt for desired behavior as young students will emulate their teacher.

2. *Verbal cues.* This is a common method of prompting—using words such as "Hustle" and "Keep going." The purpose is to remind students of desired behavior. Usually, they are used to maintain the pace of the lesson, increase the intensity of the performance, or motivate youngsters to stay on task.

3. *Nonverbal cues.* Teachers give many physical cues with body language that communicate concepts such as "Hustle," "Move over here," "Great performance," "Quiet down," and so on. In addition, when teaching skills, physically prompt youngsters by moving them into proper position, helping them through the correct pattern, or placing body parts in proper alignment.

When using prompts, a few points should be considered. Prompts should not be used to the point where students will not perform without them. In fact, the goal is to remove the prompt so that behavior will be self-motivated. This process is called fading and involves gradual removal of the prompt. It is likely that teachers will use prompts at opportune times; however, the major use of prompting is to implement new behavior patterns and increase the occurrence of desired behavior. The weakest (least intrusive) prompt possible should be used to stimulate the behavior. For example, it would be possible to give students a long lecture about the importance of staying on task. However, this approach is time consuming and over reactionary. It is not suited to multiple (repetitive) use and would be ineffective in the long run. Select a cue that is closely identified with the desired skill and that is short and concise.

In addition to these points, assure that the prompt identifies the task being prompted. For example, if the teacher prompts the class to "hustle" and has not tied it to desired behavior, there may be confusion. Some children may think it means to perform the skill as fast as possible; others may see it meaning to stop what they are doing and hustle to the teacher. Tie the prompt to the desired behavior (demonstrate what "hustle" means) in a consistent manner and make sure that students clearly understand the meaning of your prompt.

Shaping Desired Behavior

Shaping techniques can be used to build new and desired behavior. Shaping is used when desired behavior does not exist and uses extinction and reinforcement to shape new behavior. Shaping is slow and inefficient and should be used when prompting is not possible. Two principles are followed when shaping behavior.

Teacher modeling where equipment is placed (prompting desired behavior)

1. *Differential reinforcement is used to increase the incidence of desired behavior.* Reinforce responses that reach a predetermined criterion and ignore those that do not meet the criterion (extinction). An example of this principle involves asking a class to put their equipment down quickly. The teacher decides that students should put the equipment on the floor within 5 seconds. Using differential reinforcement, the teacher will reinforce the students whenever they meet the 5-second criterion and ignore their performance when it takes longer than 5 seconds.

2. *The criterion that must be reached for reinforcement to occur is increased.* The teacher gradually shifts the criterion standard toward the desired goal. For example, if the desired behavior is for the class to become quiet within 5 seconds after a signal has been given, it might be necessary to start with a 12-second interval. Why the longer interval? In all likelihood, it is not reasonable to expect that an inattentive class will quiet down quickly. If a 5-second interval is selected initially, there is a strong possibility that both teacher and students will be frustrated by the lack of success. In addition, this stringent standard of behavior will not be achieved very often, resulting in very few opportunities to praise the class. The result will be a situation where both teacher and youngsters feel they have failed. To avoid this possibility of failure, gradually move toward the desired terminal behavior. In this case, start with 12 seconds until the class performs as desired. Next, shift to a 10-second interval and ask the class to perform to this new standard. The process is gradually repeated until the terminal behavior is reached.

SYSTEMATIC APPROACHES FOR DECREASING UNDESIRABLE BEHAVIOR

Most effective techniques for improving class behavior are designed to guide the student away from behavior that is disrupting the class. Negative consequences can be an effective means for decreasing undesirable behavior. Such consequences are actions that follow misbehavior and teach students that their behavior results in some action. Figure 7.4 outlines a specific plan for altering undesirable student behavior.

Delivering Negative Consequences

When using negative consequences, consider the following points:

- Consequences should be clear and specific. Students should know exactly what will occur if they misbehave.

- Negative consequences have to be enforceable. This means that the teacher must be able to carry out such consequences. For example, keeping a bus student after school may not be possible. "Kicking" a student out of class may

Changing behavior can be done if teachers are willing to experiment and be patient. Teachers want to change behavior quickly and on the spot, and at times make incorrect decisions because they don't have time to think of an effective solution. In-class misbehavior can be temporarily stopped, but may often go unchanged for the future. Realize that change will require long-term action that must be planned ahead of time. The following steps can be used to develop a plan for changing behavior:

- Identify a single behavior that needs to be changed, improved, or strengthened. Don't pick more than one behavior as it will make it much more difficult to monitor change.
- Identify a behavior that will be substituted for the behavior to be changed.
- Determine what positively reinforces the student. Have a discussion with the student to see what is reinforcing.
- Decide whether a negative reinforcer is needed to give momentum to the change process.
- Develop a plan for getting the desired behavior to occur. This will generate a behavior that can be reinforced and used to replace the undesirable behavior.
- Put the plan into effect and set a time frame for evaluation of the plan. Decide what modifications are needed to make the plan more effective. This modification may demand a different set or schedule of reinforcers or negative consequences. If an entirely different plan is needed (because the behavior hasn't decreased or changed) make such changes and proceed.
- Continue evaluating and modifying the plan.

Figure 7.4 A plan for changing behavior

not be possible (or desirable). Make sure that the negative consequence can be used in the school setting and is approved by the appropriate administrator.

- Apply a negative consequence as near to the misbehavior as possible. Just as positive reinforcement should be delivered immediately following the desired behavior, so should negative consequences.
- Negative consequences can be anything the student does not want or need as long as they do not violate the rights or dignity of the student. Just as teachers need to know what reinforces students, they need to know what is a negative experience for students who misbehave.
- Assure yourself that you are using negative consequences to teach youngsters how to behave properly rather than punishing them.

Several approaches can be used to deliver negative consequences. Remember that it is best to use positive reinforcement to increase desired behavior with the hope that it will replace negative behavior. For example, if a skilled youngster is always criticizing less able youngsters, it might be effective to ask that student to help others and serve as a student assistant. The intent would be to teach the youngster to deliver positive and constructive feedback rather than criticism. A good rule of thumb before choosing to use negative consequences is to reinforce the desired behavior

twice. For example, assume a youngster is slow to stop on signal, but the majority of other students are stopping and listening properly. Immediately positively reinforce these correctly behaving students. Practice moving and stopping; stop and reinforce the desired behavior again. Many times the result will be that the misbehaving students will emulate the students who are being reinforced in order to receive similar positive feedback. If not, you may consider using negative consequences. Negative consequences include reprimanding, removal of positive consequences, and time out.

Reprimanding

This is a common approach used to decrease undesirable behavior. If done in a caring and constructive manner, reprimands can serve as effective reminders to behave.

- Identify the unacceptable behavior, state briefly why it is unacceptable, and communicate to students what behavior is desired. For example, "You were talking while I was speaking. It bothers other students, so please listen to me."
- Don't do it in front of other students. Not only does it embarrass students, it can diminish their self-esteem. When students feel belittled, they may lash out and react in a manner more severe than the original behavior.
- Reprimands should speak about behavior, not the person. Ask that the behavior stop rather

than telling the student that "you are always causing problems in this class." General statements related to the personality of the student should be avoided.

- After reprimanding and asking for acceptable behavior, reinforce it when it occurs. Be vigilant in looking for the desired behavior since reinforcing such behavior will cause it to occur more often in the future.

Removal of Positive Consequences

This is a common approach used by parents, so many students are familiar with it. The basic approach is to remove something positive from the student when misbehavior occurs. For example, students give up some of their free time due to misbehavior. They lose points related to a grade. They are not allowed to participate in an activity that is exciting to them. For removal of positive consequences to be effective, teachers must be sure that the students really want to participate in the removal activity. It wouldn't work to keep a student out of a game if the student didn't like the game. A few key principles should be followed when using this technique:

- Make sure the magnitude of the removal fits the crime. In other words, children who commit a minor infraction shouldn't have to miss recess for a week.

- Be consistent in removal among all students and with the same students. Students will think teachers are unfair if they are more severe with one student than another. In addition, a student penalized for a specific misbehavior, should receive the same penalty for a later repetition.

- Make sure students understand the consequences of their misbehavior before the penalties are implemented. This avoids applying penalties in an emotional, unthinking manner. If students know what the consequences will be, they are making the choice to accept the consequences when they choose to misbehave.

- At times, it can be helpful to chart a student's misbehavior to see if the frequency is decreasing. Regardless of the method used, if the behavior is not decreasing or is increasing, change methods until a decrease in frequency occurs.

Time Out

The time-out procedure is an equitable technique for dealing with youngsters in a manner that is consistent with society. Rules are clearly posted and consequences are clear and easy to comprehend. Teachers need to use a consistent approach for dealing with undesirable behavior that occurs randomly on an individual basis. The time-out approach moves youngsters out of the class setting and places them into a predesignated area when they misbehave. Time out means *time out from reinforcement*. It does not imply that the student is a "bad person," but rather that rules have not been followed and there is a need for time out for thinking. When placing students in time out, communicate to children that they are acceptable individuals, but their misbehavior is unacceptable.

Being placed in time out communicates to youngsters that they have disrupted the class and must be removed so that the rest of the class can participate as desired. Children can also use the time-out area as a "cooling-off" spot where they can move voluntarily if they become angry, embarrassed, or frustrated. If youngsters have been placed in the time-out area for fighting or arguing, they should be placed at opposite ends of the area so that the behavior does not escalate. In addition, it can be mandated that they stay in their half (or quadrant) of the teaching area until the next meeting of the class. This will prevent recurring agitation between the two combatants and the possibility of continued animosity.

The implementation of this plan should be discussed with students, so they know exactly what is acceptable and unacceptable behavior and the actions that will be taken if they exhibit undesirable behavior. A list of desired behaviors, as well as consequences for unacceptable behavior, should be posted in the teaching area. Examples of desirable behavior might be listening when the teacher is instructing, keeping one's hands off others, and promptly performing the activities presented by the teacher. In most cases, the list of desired behaviors should number between three and five items. A larger number of behaviors will confuse the class and make it difficult for them to comprehend the focus of the approach.

A key concept to remember is that time out does not serve as a deterrent if the youngster is reinforced. Time-out means receiving *no* reinforcement. If class is a negative experience for students, taking them out of class will be rewarding rather than a negative consequence. Caution must be used in placing students in the time-out area. Too often, sitting a student out results in a reinforcing experience. For example, a student who is sent to the office gets to avoid schoolwork while visiting with friends who come into the office. Notoriety can

Student assigned to time out

be achieved among peers for surviving the office experience and being able to tell others, "I was not scared at all." Sitting on the side of the teaching area and making faces at peers may be a more reinforcing experience than participating in class activities. *Remember! If students don't enjoy being in class, time out will not work.*

As stated, establish a set of consequences and post it in the area. A possible set of consequences for unacceptable behavior follows:

First Misbehavior

The student is warned quietly on a personal basis to avoid embarrassment. At times, students are not aware that they are bothering others and a gentle reminder by the teacher will refocus the youngster.

Second Misbehavior

The student is told to go to a predesignated time-out spot. This might be a chair in the corner of the activity area. The student must stay there until ready to reenter the activity and demonstrate the desired behavior. It is acceptable for the student to go to the area and immediately return to activity since the assumption is that he has agreed to terminate the misbehavior.

Third Misbehavior

The student goes to time out for the remainder of the period. If the misbehavior continues each time the class meets, most schools will use an in-school suspension program. In-school suspension requires the student to leave his class of students, move into another room of students (different grade level), and receive little, if any, reinforcement.

The foregoing steps assume that the teacher will communicate with the student about the misbehavior and the expected behavior. If these consequences are ineffective, the last alternative is to call the parents in for a conference with the principal and teacher. Students and parents must understand that participating in educational endeavors is a privilege and that people who choose to disrupt society ultimately lose their privileges (e.g., incarceration in reform school, prison, etc.).

Behavior Contract

A behavior contract is a written statement specifying certain student behaviors that must occur to earn certain rewards or privileges. The contract is usually signed by the student and teacher, and is drawn up after a private conference to decide on the appropriate behaviors and rewards. This approach allows students to make decisions that will improve their own behavior.

The behavior contract may be a successful strategy for intermediate-grade students with severe behavior problems. Every attempt should be made to find rewards that occur naturally in physical education class (e.g., Frisbee play, jump rope games, aerobics, basketball). If not possible, different types of rewards may have to be used. For example, a student who is interested in music could be allowed to spend some time selecting records to be used for class during the next week. As behavior improves and the student's attitude becomes more positive, rewards should be switched to physical education activities. The contract is gradually phased out over a period of time as the youngster gains control of the behavior and can participate in normal class environments.

Contracts can be written for a small group of students or for an entire class with similar problems, but teachers must be careful about setting up a reward system for too many students. The system can become too complex or time consuming

Figure 7.5 Individual behavior contract

Date:_____

I, _____ , agree to follow the rules as listed below:

1. Listen when the teacher is talking.

2. Do not touch others during class.

If all the rules are followed during physical education class, I will earn 10 minutes of basketball activity for myself and a friend after school on Thursday anytime between 3:00 and 3:45.

Signed: _____ , Student

Signed: _____ , Teacher

GROUP BEHAVIOR CONTRACT

Our squad agrees to follow the rules listed below:

1. Listen when the teacher is talking.

2. Take care of the equipment.

3. Treat others as we would like to be treated.

One point is earned each time the music stops and every member of the squad is following the rules. No points are awarded if one or more members of the squad are not following the rules.
Each point is worth 1 minute of free activity time to be awarded every other Friday.

Signed: Squad Number_____   _____

_____   _____

_____   _____

_____

Figure 7.6 Group behavior contract

to supervise properly. The contract is best used with a limited number of students in several problem situations. Examples of behavior contracts are shown in Figures 7.5 and 7.6. The contract in Figure 7.5 can be used with an individual, a small group, or an entire class of students.

Behavior Games

Behavior games are an effective strategy for changing class behavior in the areas of management, motivation, and discipline. These activities utilize the shaping technique and are useful in changing whole-class behavior (as contrasted to individual student behavior). If a teacher is having problems in any of these areas, a well-conceived behavior game may turn the situation around in a short period. These games can be packaged for a

group of students to compete against each other or against an established criterion. The goal of the game is to use group contingencies to develop behaviors that enhance the learning environment and to eliminate behaviors that detract from the environment. Various forms of behavior games have been used successfully by physical educators (Darst & Whitehead, 1975; McKenzie & Rushall, 1973; Paese, 1982).

The following is an example of a behavior game used successfully with sixth-graders in an effort to improve management behaviors.

1. The class is divided into four to six squads. Each squad has a designated color for identification. Four boundary cones with appropriate colors are arranged to mark a starting area.

2. The rules of the game are as follows:

a. Each squad member has to be ready for activity and in proper position at a designated starting time. *Reward:* 2 points.

b. Each squad member has to move from one activity to another activity within the specified time (10, 20, or 30 seconds) and begin the appropriate behavior. *Reward:* 1 point for each instance.

c. Each point earned is rewarded with 1 minute of free activity time on Friday. Free activity time includes basketball, Frisbee playing, rope jumping, or any other activity popular with students.

d. The squad with the most points for the week earns a bonus of 5 points.

3. The teacher explains the allotted time for each management episode (10, 20, or 30 seconds), and gives a "go" signal. At the end of the allowed time, the teacher signals "stop" and awards points for appropriate behavior.

4. Squads that are successful are praised by the teacher, and the points are recorded on a small card. The unsuccessful squads are not hassled or criticized, just reminded that they did not earn a point.

5. On Fridays, the appropriate squads are awarded the special free-time activities while the other squads continue with the regularly scheduled class activities.

6. The game is slowly phased out (faded) as students begin to manage themselves more quickly.

Research used to evaluate behavior games showed the following results:

1. The use of group contingencies and free-time activities reduced overall class management time.

2. The free-time activities were within the physical education curriculum objectives and served as a break from regular activities.

3. The free-time activities gave the teacher an opportunity to interact with students on a personal level.

4. Students enjoyed the competition and the feeling of success when they behaved appropriately.

5. Students enjoyed the free time with novelty activities.

6. The positive approach of the game seemed to improve the overall teaching–learning atmosphere. Students were more attentive and cooperative.

7. Teachers estimated that more time was available for instruction because of the reduction in management time.

A key point to follow when designing behavior games is to structure them so that any student or squad is able to win the game. Each game need not generate one winner and many losers. All participants should be able to win. Teachers must also be aware that one or two students may find it reinforcing to cause their team to lose the behavior game. They will try to break every game rule to make sure that their team loses consistently. In these cases teachers should have a special team discussion and possibly a vote to eliminate those students from the team and the game. These students are sent to a time-out area or to in-school suspension. They can be asked to sit out for the duration of the behavior game.

Another effective behavior game can be used to help students persist at learning activities in a station-type approach. Often, teachers will set up four to six learning stations for activities. Performance objectives or learning tasks are posted at each station for students to practice. However, it may be that some students are not motivated and do not use their time productively until the teacher rotates to the station where they are working. The teacher may then prod the group, hassling a few students and praising a few others. Overall, the environment is not productive, and the teacher gets tired of hassling unmotivated students. A possible solution to this situation is the following game:

1. Divide the class into four to six squads. Let the students pick a name for their squad.

2. Set up the learning stations with the activities to be practiced. An equal number of squads and learning stations is necessary.

3. Program a cassette tape with popular music. Short gaps of silence should be interspersed throughout the tape.

4. Tell students that if everyone in their squad is properly engaged in practicing the appropriate task, a point will be awarded to the squad at each gap in the music. If one or more persons are not engaged, the point will not be awarded.

5. The points can be exchanged for minutes of time in selected activities such as Frisbee play, juggling, or rope jumping. Fridays can be designated as reward day, when the accumulated time is used.

6. The music can be changed regularly, and the interval between gaps should be changed and slowly increased until the gaps are eliminated.

The music then serves as a discriminative cue for future practice time.

Many teachers have found that students enjoy exercising and practicing skills while listening to music. The music enhances the motivational level and productivity of the environment. Students can be allowed to bring their own music as a special reward for productive behavior. (Teachers should first make sure that the music is not offensive to others due to sexual, ethnic, or religious connotations.)

CRITICISM

Criticism and punishment must be used with much caution and judgment. Criticism is often used by teachers with the belief that it will improve the performance of students. Teachers find scolding and criticism to be their behavior control tools of choice because they give the impression that the results are effective and immediate. Usually, the misbehavior stops and the teacher assumes that the situation has been rectified. Unfortunately, this is not always the case, as will be described. Criticism and punishment lend a negative air to the instructional environment and have a negative impact on both student and teacher. The old saying, "It hurts me more than you," is often the case. The majority of teachers feel uncomfortable when they must criticize or punish students. It makes them feel as though they cannot handle students and that the class is incorrigible. This feeling of incompetence leads to a destructive cycle where students feel negative about the instructor and the instructor negative about the class. In the long run, this is one of the most debilitating effects of criticism and punishment.

As mentioned above, another negative aspect of criticism is that it does not offer a solution. In a study by Thomas, Becker, and Armstrong (1968), a teacher was asked to stop praising a class. Off-task behavior increased from 8.7 percent to nearly 26 percent. When the teacher was asked to increase criticism from 5 times in 20 minutes to 16 times in 20 minutes, more off-task behavior was demonstrated. On some days the percentage of off-task behavior increased to more than 50 percent. The point to be emphasized is that when attention is given to off-task behavior and no praise is offered for on-task accomplishment, the amount of off-task behavior increases dramatically. What happens is that the teacher who primarily criticizes is reinforced by the students (they respond to the request of the criticism), but the students do not change. In fact, the students are reinforced (they receive attention from the teacher) for their off-task behavior. In addition, since their on-task behavior is not praised, it decreases. The net result is exactly the opposite of what is desired.

PUNISHMENT

The question of whether punishment should be used in an educational setting is a difficult one. Punishment can have negative side effects because fear is the primary motivator. Teachers must consider the long-term need for punishment. If the long-term effects of using punishment are more beneficial than not using it, it would be unethical not to use punishment. In other words, if the child is going to be in a worse situation because punishment was not used to deter self-destructive behavior, it would be wrong not to use it. It may be necessary to punish a child for protection from self-inflicted harm (e.g., using certain apparatus without supervision). It may be necessary to punish children so that they learn not to hurt others. Punishment in these situations will cause discomfort to teacher and child in the short run, but may allow the student to participate successfully in society later.

Most situations in the educational setting do not require punishment because they are not as severe as those described above. A major reason for avoiding punishment is that it can have undesirable side effects. When children are punished, they learn to avoid the source of punishment. It forces them to be more covert in their actions. They spend time finding ways to be devious without being caught. Instead of encouraging students to discuss problems with teachers and parents, punishment teaches them to avoid these individuals for fear of being punished. Another side effect is that it teaches children how to be aggressive toward others. Children who have been physically or emotionally punished by parents act in similar fashion to others. The result is a child who is secretive and aggressive with others—certainly a less than desirable trait. Finally, if punishment is used to stop certain behavior, as soon as the punishment stops the behavior will return. Thus, little has been learned; the punishment has just caused short-term change.

If it is necessary to use punishment, remember the following points:

1. *Be consistent and make the "punishment fit the crime."* Students will quickly lose respect for a teacher who treats others with favoritism.

They view the teacher as unfair if punishment is extreme or unfair. Peers will quickly side with the student who is treated unfairly, causing a class morale problem for the instructor.

2. *Offer a warning signal as discussed previously.* This may prevent excessive use of punishment, as students will often behave after receiving a warning. In addition, they will probably view the teacher as caring and fair.

3. *Do not threaten students.* Offer only one warning. Threats have little impact on students and make them feel that the teacher cannot handle the class. One warning gives students the feeling that teachers are not looking to punish them and are fair. Follow through; do not challenge or threaten students and then fail to deal with the behavior.

4. *The punishment should follow the misbehavior as soon as possible.* It is much less effective and more often viewed as unfair when it is delayed.

5. *Punish softly and calmly.* Do not seek revenge or be vindictive. If responsible behavior is expected from students, teachers must reprimand and punish in a responsible manner. Studies (O'Leary & Becker, 1968) have demonstrated that soft reprimands are more effective than loud ones.

A point related to punishment. Try to avoid having negative feelings about a student and internalizing student misbehavior. Teachers who are punitive when handling deviant behavior destroy any chance for a worthwhile relationship. Misbehavior should be handled in a manner that contributes to the development of responsible, confident students who understand that people who function effectively in society must adjust to certain limits. The teacher should try to forget about past bouts of deviant behavior and approach the student in a positive fashion at the start of each class. If this is not done, the students soon become labeled, which makes it much more difficult to make behavioral change. Students may also learn to live up to the teacher's negative expectations.

If punishment is used, make sure that only those youngsters who misbehave are punished. Punishing an entire class for the deviant behavior of a few youngsters is not only unfair but may trigger undesirable side effects. Students become hostile toward those who caused the loss of privileges, and this peer hostility lowers the level of positive social interaction. If the group as a whole is misbehaving, punishing the entire group is appropriate.

EXPULSION: LEGAL CONSIDERATIONS

If serious problems occur, the physical education specialist should discuss the problems with the classroom teacher and principal. Many times, deviant behavior is part of a larger, more severe problem that is troubling a child. A cooperative approach may provide an effective solution. A group meeting involving parents, classroom teacher, principal, counselor, and physical education specialist may open avenues that encourage understanding and increase productive behavior.

Legal concerns involving the student's rights in disciplinary areas are an essential consideration. While minor infractions may be handled routinely, expulsion and other substantial punishments can be imposed on students only after due process. The issue of student rights is complicated, and most school systems have established guidelines and procedures for dealing with students who have been removed from the class or school setting. Youngsters should be removed from class only if they are disruptive to the point of interfering with the learning experiences of other children and all other means of altering behavior have not worked. Sending a child out of class is a last resort and means that both teacher and student have failed.

REFERENCES AND SUGGESTED READINGS

AAHPERD. (1976). *Personalized learning in physical education.* Reston, VA: AAHPERD.

Canter, L., & Canter, M. (1976). *Assertive discipline.* Santa Monica, CA: Canter and Associates.

Canter, L., & Canter, M. (1984). *Assertive discipline elementary resource materials workbook grades K–6.* Santa Monica, CA: Canter and Associates.

Charles, C. M. (1989). *Building classroom discipline* (3rd ed.). New York: Longman.

Cruickshank, D. R. (1980). *Teaching is tough.* Englewood Cliffs, NJ: Prentice-Hall.

Curwin, R. L., & Mendler, A. N. (1988). *Discipline with dignity.* Washington, DC: Association for Supervision and Curriculum Development.

Darst, P. W., & Whitehead, S. (1975). Developing a contingency management system for controlling student behavior. *Pennsylvania JOPER, 46*(3), 11–12.

Glasser, W. (1986). *Control theory in the classroom*. New York: Harper & Row.

Greene, D., & Lepper, M. R. (1975). Turning play into work: Effects of adult surveillance and extrinsic rewards on children's internal motivation. *Journal of Personality and Social Psychology, 31,* 479–486.

McKenzie, T., & Rushall, B. (1973). Effects of various reinforcing contingencies on improving performance in a competitive swimming environment. Unpublished paper. Halifax, Nova Scotia: Dalhousie University.

Nelson, J. (1987). *Positive discipline*. New York: Ballantine.

O'Leary, K. D., & Becker, W. C. (1968). The effects of intensity of a teacher's reprimands on children's behavior. *Journal of School Psychology, 7,* 8–11.

Paese, P. (1982). Effects of interdependent group contingencies in a secondary physical education setting. *Journal of Teaching in Physical Education, 2*(1), 29–37.

Premack, D. (1965). Reinforcement theory. In D. Levine (Ed.), *Nebraska symposium on motivation*. Lincoln: University of Nebraska Press.

Siedentop, D. (1983). *Developing teaching skills in physical education*. Palo Alto, CA: Mayfield.

Thomas, D. R., Becker, W. C., & Armstrong, M. (1968). Production and elimination of disruptive classroom behavior by systematically varying teachers' behavior. *Journal of Applied Behavior Analysis, 1,* 35–45.

Whitehead, J. R., & Corbin, C. B. (1991). Effects of fitness test type, teacher, and gender on exercise intrinsic motivation and physical self-worth. *Journal of School Health, 61,* 11–16.

Wolfgang, C. H., & Glickman, C. D. (1980). *Solving discipline problems*. Boston: Allyn & Bacon.

CHAPTER 7

8

Children with Disabilities

*T*he Education for All Handicapped Children Act (Public Law 94-142) was passed by the Congress of the United States in 1975. The purpose of the law is clear and concise:

> It is the purpose of this act to assure that all handicapped children have available to them . . . a free appropriate public education which emphasizes special education and related services designed to meet their unique needs, to assure that the rights of handicapped children and their parents or guardians are protected, to assist States and localities to provide for the education of all handicapped children, and to assess and assure the effectiveness of efforts to educate handicapped children.[1]

In short, the law requires that all disabled children, ages 3 to 21, receive a free and appropriate education in the least restrictive environment. The law includes youngsters in public and private care facilities and schools. Children with disabilities who can learn in regular classes with the use of supplementary aides and services must be educated with youngsters who are able. Physical

[1]The term *handicapped* is used in PL 94-142 to include youngers who are mentally retarded, hard of hearing, deaf, speech impaired, visually handicapped, seriously emotionally disturbed, orthopedically impaired, other health impaired, deaf-blind, multihandicapped, or specific learning disabled. Currently, *disabled* is the term used to identify youngsters with handicapping conditions. This term is used throughout this chapter.

education is the only specific area mentioned in PL 94–142. The law indicates that the term *special education* "means specially designed instruction, instruction in physical education, home instruction, and instruction in hospitals and institutions."

To comply with PL 94–142, public schools must locate, identify, and evaluate all students who might have a disability. This is the screening process and must be followed by a formal assessment procedure. Assessment must be made and an Individualized Education Program (IEP) developed for each youngster before placement into a special program can be made. The law states who will be responsible for developing the IEP and what the contents of the IEP will include. This is discussed later in the chapter.

The passage of PL 94–142 offered a giant step forward in assuring equality and education for all Americans. The government also assured that funding would be made available to provide quality instruction. The law authorizes a payment to each state of 40 percent of the average per-pupil expenditure in U.S. elementary and secondary schools, multiplied by the number of children who are receiving special education and related services. The federal mandate reveals the concern of the public for comprehensive educational programs for all youngsters regardless of disability.

SCREENING AND ASSESSMENT

An important component of the IEP process is screening and assessment of students. Every state is required by PL 94–142 to develop a plan for locating, identifying, and evaluating all children with disabilities.

Screening

Generally, screening is a process that involves all students in a school setting and is part of the "child find" process. It is often conducted at the start of the school year and is performed districtwide. The physical educator usually conducts the screening tests, which may include commonly used test batteries (e.g., the Fitnessgram). In most situations, screening tests may be administered without parental permission and are used to make initial identification of students who may need special services.

Assessment

Assessment is conducted after screening evaluations have been made. Assessment is usually con-

ducted after "child find" screening by referring identified students to special education directors. Assessment is performed by a team of experts, which may include the physical education specialist. Due process for students and parents is an important requisite when conducting formal assessment procedures. Due process assures parents and children that they will be informed of their rights and that they have the opportunity to challenge educational decisions they feel are unfair or incorrect.

Due Process Guidelines

To assure that due process is offered parents and students, the guidelines discussed here must be followed:

Written Permission

A written notice must be sent to parents stating that their child has been referred for assessment. The notice must explain that the district requests permission to conduct an evaluation to determine if special education services are required for their child. Also included in the permission letter must be the reasons for testing and the tests to be used. Before assessment can begin, the letter must be signed by the parents and returned to the district.

Interpretation of the Assessment

The results of the assessment must be interpreted in a meeting with the parents. Persons who are knowledgeable about the test procedures must be present to answer questions parents may ask. At the meeting, parents must be told whether their child has any disabilities and what services will be provided for the child.

External Evaluation

If parents are not satisfied with the results of the assessment, they may request an evaluation outside the school setting. The district must provide a list of agencies that can perform such assessment. If the results differ from the school district evaluation, the district must pay for the external evaluation. However, if the results are similar, parents must pay for the external testing.

Negotiation and Hearings

If parents and the school district disagree on the results of the assessment, the district is required to try to negotiate the differences. When negotiations fail, an impartial hearing officer listens to both parties and renders an official decision. This is usually the final review; however, both parties do have the right to appeal to the state department of education, which must render a binding and final decision. Civil action through the legal system can be pursued should the district or parents still disagree with this action. However, very few cases ever reach this level of long-term disagreement, and educators should not be hesitant to serve the needs of children with disabilities based on this concern.

Confidentiality

As is the case with other student records, only parents of the child or authorized school personnel can review the student's records. Review by other parties can be done only after written permission has been given by the parents of the child under review.

Procedures for Assuring Assessment Standards

PL 94–142 requires that assessment will be held to certain standards to assure fair and objective results. The following areas are specifically delineated.

Selection of Test Instruments

The test instruments used must be valid examinations that measure what they purport to measure. Thus, when selecting instruments, it must be clear to all parties how the tests were developed and how they will measure correctly the area of possible disability. More than one test procedure must be used to determine the student's status. Both formal and informal assessment techniques should be used to assure that the results measure the student's impairment rather than simply reflect the student's shortcomings.

It is an unfortunate situation that children must be labeled as disabled in order to reap the benefits of a special education program. The stigmatizing effect of labels and the fallibility of various means of testing students is a dilemma that must be faced. Although current pedagogical practices discourage labeling, it is doubletalk, since school districts have to certify the disability (to receive funding) through which the child is classified.

Administration Procedures

Many disabilities interfere with standard test procedures. For example, many students have commu-

nication problems and must be tested in a manner that assures that their motor ability is measured rather than their lack of communication skills. Many students have visual and hearing disabilities that prevent using tests that rely on these faculties.

A probability of misdiagnosis and incorrectly classifying children as mentally retarded can occur with certain ethnic groups, such as native Americans, African Americans, and Spanish-speaking children. These youngsters, often victims of poor and impoverished living, may be only environmentally retarded and in need of cultural enrichment. It is subtle discrimination but must be replaced with understanding that children differ because of culture, poverty, migrancy, and language. Many of the tests are based on white, middle-class standards. Minority children should be carefully assessed to determine the validity of the testing procedure.

Team Evaluation

A number of experts should be used for assessment. Emphasis should be placed on a multidisciplinary team to help assure that all facets of the child will be reviewed and evaluated. Evaluation professionals must be well trained and qualified to administer the various tests. It is the responsibility of the school district to assure that this will occur.

DEVELOPMENT OF THE IEP

PL 94–142 requires that an IEP be developed for each disabled child receiving special education and related services. The IEP must be developed by a committee as stipulated by the law. Included on the committee must be the following members: a local education association representative who is qualified to provide and supervise the administration of special education, the child's parents, the teachers who have direct responsibility for implementing the IEP, and, when appropriate, the student. Other individuals may be included at the discretion of the parents or the school district. This program identifies the child's unique qualities and determines educationally relevant strengths and weaknesses. A plan is then devised based on the diagnosed strengths and weaknesses. Figure 8.1 is an example of a comprehensive IEP form. The IEP must contain the following material:

1. Current status of the child's level of educational performance.

2. A statement of long-term goals and short-term instructional objectives.

Figure 8.1 Example of an individualized educational plan

INDIVIDUALIZED EDUCATION PROGRAM

☐ Initial Placement
☐ Re-evaluation
☐ Change of Placement
☐ Review

A. STUDENT INFORMATION:

Student Name _____ (Last   First   Middle)   Student No. _____   Home School _____

Date of Birth _____   Chronological Age ___ (M___ or F___)   Present Placement/Grade _____

Parent/Guardian Name(s) _____   Receiving School _____

Home Address _____ (Street   City/State   Zip)   Program Recommended _____

Home Phone _____   Work Phone _____   Starting Date _____

Emergency Phone _____   Three (3) Year Re-evaluation   Due Date ___/___/___

Primary Language (Home) _____   (Child) _____   Interpreter Needed: Yes ___ No ___

B. VISION SCREENING RESULTS: Pass ___ Fail ___   **HEARING SCREENING RESULTS:** Pass ___ Fail ___

Date: _____   Comments: _____   Date: _____   Comments: _____

C. REQUIRED OBSERVATION(S): (All categories other than regular teacher)

_____ By: _____   _____ By: _____   _____ By: _____
(Date(s)   Name(s)   Date(s)   Name(s)   Date(s)   Name(s))

D. SUMMARY OF PRESENT LEVELS OF PERFORMANCE:

Educational: _____

Behavioral: _____

E. Additional justification. See comments_____ (Initial)   See addendum_____ (Initial)

F. PLACEMENT RECOMMENDATION INDICATING LEAST RESTRICTIVE ENVIRONMENT:

Related services needed: Yes _____ No _____ (*List below.)

Placement Recommendation	Person Responsible	Amount of Time (Range)	Entry Date On/About	Review Reports On/About	Projected Ending Date	IEP Review Date
Primary:						
*Related Services:						

Transportation Needed? Yes _____ No _____ (If Yes, submit MPS Special Education Transportation Request Form.)

Describe extent student will participate in regular program: _____

Page 1 of _____

3. A statement of special education and related services that will be provided to the youngster. Also, a report as to the extent the youngster will be able to participate in regular educational programs.

4. The dates for initiation of services and anticipated duration of the services.

5. Appropriate objective criteria for determining on an annual basis whether the short-term objectives are being reached.

Developing and sequencing objectives for the student is the first step in formulating the IEP. Short-range and long-range goals should be delineated, and data collection procedures and testing schedules established to monitor the child's progress. Materials and strategies to be used in implementing the IEP should also be established. Finally, methods of evaluation to be used are determined in order to monitor the student's progress and the effectiveness of the program. (Computer assistance is helpful in relieving laborious hand

Student Name _____ Student No. _____

G. PROGRAM PLANNING:

Long-Term Goals:

_____
_____
_____
_____
_____
_____
_____
_____
_____
_____
_____
_____

Short-Term Objectives (Goals):

_____
_____
_____
_____
_____
_____
_____
_____
_____
_____
_____
_____

H. EVALUATION:

Evaluation criteria are described in the Individual Implementation Plan (IIP) which is available in the classroom file.

I. PLACEMENT COMMITTEE:

The following have been consulted or have participated in the placement and IEP decisions:

Names of Members	Position	Present (Initial)	Oral Report	Written Report	Signatures
	Parents/Guardian				
	Parents/Guardian				
	School Administrator				
	Special Ed Administrator				
	School Psychologist				
	Nurse				
	Teacher(s) Receiving				
	Teacher(s) Referring				
	Interpreter				

Dissenting Opinion: Yes _____ No _____ If Yes, see comments _____ See addendum _____ .
                                                                    Initial   *Initial*

J. PARENT (OR GUARDIAN) STATEMENT:

We agree to the placement recommended in this IEP. Yes _____ No _____

We give our permission to have our child counseled by the professional staff, if necessary. Yes _____ No _____

We understand that placement will be on a continuing trial basis and we will be contacted if any placement changes are contemplated. We are aware that such placement does not guarantee success; however, in order to help our child, we accept the responsibility to cooperate in every way with the school program. We acknowledge that we have been notified of and have received a copy of our due process rights pertaining to Special Education placement and have a basic understanding of these rights. We acknowledge that we have received a copy of the completed IEP Form.

_____   _____
Parent or Guardian Signature   Date

COMMENTS: _____
_____
_____
_____
_____
_____
_____
_____
_____
_____

Page 2 of _____

recording.) Movement to a less restrictive environment should be based on achievement of specified competencies that are necessary in the new environment.

The IEP must contain a section determining whether specially designed physical education is needed. If not, the child should be held to the same expectations as the peer group. A child who needs special physical education might have an IEP with specified goals and objectives and might be mainstreamed in regular physical education with goals that do not resemble those of classmates.

Continued and periodic followup of the child is necessary. Effective communication between special and regular teachers is essential, because the child's progress needs careful monitoring. At the completion of the designated time period or school year, a written progress report should be filed along with recommendations for action during the coming year or time period. Here, again, the computer can be of valuable assistance. A program for the summer months is often an excellent prescription to ensure that improvement is maintained. Records should be complete so that information about the youngster's problem and the effects of long-term treatment are always available.

Criteria for Placement of Children

A difficult problem arises in determining what standards will be used for placing children into special programs. Several states have adopted criteria for determining eligibility of children for adapted physical education classes. State guidelines differ, but they should be followed closely if they are in place. These standards are based on the administration of standardized tests for which norms or percentiles have been developed. This procedure helps assure that objective guidelines are used and avoids subjective judgment that may be open to disagreement and controversy. For example, criteria used by the state of Alabama are as follows:

1. Perform below the 30th percentile on standardized tests of
    a. motor development
    b. motor proficiency
    c. fundamental motor skills and patterns
    d. physical fitness
    e. game/sport skills
    f. perceptual motor functioning
    g. posture screening
2. Exhibit a developmental delay of 2 or more years based on appropriate assessment instruments.
3. Function within the severe or profound range as determined by special education eligibility standards.
4. Possess social/emotional or physical capabilities that would render it unlikely for the student to reach his or her physical education goals without significant modification or exclusion from the regular physical education class.

If the student was determined not to be eligible for special education services, it may be beneficial to refer the youngster to programs for able children with special needs (see pp. 164–176). These programs deal with areas that are not delineated by PL 94–142, such as obesity, physical fitness, and motor deficiencies. Unfortunately, many schools do not offer programs for youngsters with these deficiencies, and their needs are not served. Physical educators must show concern for helping youngsters with these problems as obesity and physical fitness are areas of strong concern among parents.

LEAST RESTRICTIVE ENVIRONMENT

PL 94–142 uses the term *least restrictive environment* to determine placement of children with disabilities. The focus should be on placing a child into a setting that offers the most opportunity for educational advancement. It is inappropriate to place a youngster in an environment where success is impossible. On the other hand, it would be debilitating to put a child in a setting that is more restrictive than necessary. Special educators strongly support a physical education program that offers a variety of experiences from participation in regular physical education classes to physical education in a fulltime special school. Figure 8.2 shows a series of options that might be available for physical education.

The least restrictive environment also varies depending on the content of the instructional presentation. For example, for a student in a wheelchair, a soccer or football unit might be very restrictive, whereas in a swimming unit, the environment would not be restrictive. For an emotionally challenged student, the command style of presentation might be the least restrictive environment, while an exploration style of instruction would be more restrictive and would invite failure. Consistent and regular judgments need to be made, as curriculum content and teaching styles vary and change the type of environment the student enters. It is shortsighted to place students into a situation and then forget about them. Evaluation and modification of environments need to be ongoing.

Mainstreaming

Physical educators most often speak in terms of mainstreaming rather than least restrictive environment. *Mainstreaming* involves the practice of placing children with disabilities into classes with able youngsters. Prudent placement in a least restricted educational environment means that the setting must be as normal as possible (normalization), while ensuring that the child can fit in and achieve success in that placement. The placement may be mainstreaming, but it is not confined to this approach. Several categories of placement can be defined relevant to physical education classes.

1. *Full mainstreaming.* Children with disabilities function as fulltime members of a regular classroom group. Within the limitations of their challenge, they participate in physical education with able peers. An example may be auditory-impaired students who with a minimal amount of assistance are able to participate fully.

Figure 8.2 Physical education options, least to most restrictive environments

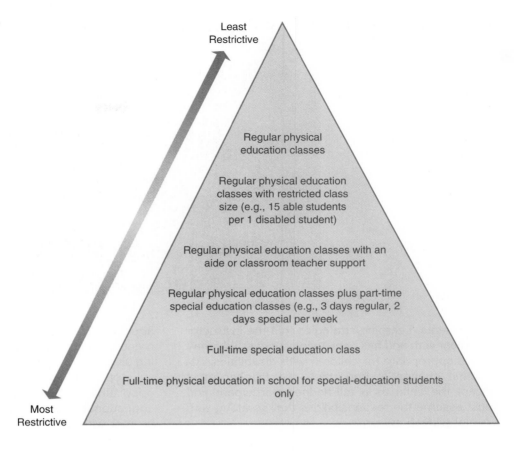

Least Restrictive

Regular physical education classes

Regular physical education classes with restricted class size (e.g., 15 able students per 1 disabled student)

Regular physical education classes with an aide or classroom teacher support

Regular physical education classes plus part-time special education classes (e.g., 3 days regular, 2 days special per week

Full-time special education class

Full-time physical education in school for special-education students only

Most Restrictive

2. *Mainstreaming for physical education only.* Children with disabilities are not members of the regular classroom groups but participate in physical education with regular classes. Students in this setting might be emotionally disabled youngsters who are grouped in the classroom and attend regular physical education classes.

3. *Partial mainstreaming.* Students take part in selected physical education experiences but do not attend on a fulltime basis because they can meet with success in only some of the offerings. Their developmental needs are usually met in special classes.

4. *Special developmental classes.* Students with disabilities are in segregated special education classes.

5. *Reverse mainstreaming.* Able children are brought into a special physical education class to promote intergroup peer relationships.

Segregation can be maintained only if it is in the best interests of the child. The thrust of segregated programs should be to establish a level of skill and social proficiency that will eventually enable the special child to be transferred to a less restricted learning environment. The emphasis on placement in the least restrictive environment in which the child, as an individual, can profit most is the cornerstone of the educational process. Children with disabilities, working on their own, often have been denied opportunities to interact with peers and to become a part of the social and academic classroom network.

Children with disabilities, when mainstreamed, become the responsibility of the physical education specialist. However, they should maintain contact with support personnel such as the special education teacher, school psychologists, and speech therapists. Although the youngsters are the responsibility of the physical education specialist, support personnel should not view the situation as "getting rid of their students," but should rather act as a source of information and support for the teacher in charge.

Guidelines for Successful Mainstreaming Experiences

The concern is not whether to mainstream, but how to mainstream effectively. The physical educator has to teach a number of children with diverse

Successful mainstreaming of disabled youngsters

impairments. Learning strategies that the instructor is familiar with and has been using successfully may not be appropriate for children with disabilities. Attitudinal change is important—the teacher must accept the child as a full-fledged participant and must assume the responsibilities that go along with special education.

An important consideration when planning the IEP is whether the child is ready for mainstreaming. Many children with disabilities have severe developmental lags that become insurmountable factors working against successful integration into normal classes. The child must be physically able to accomplish a portion of the program without much, if any, assistance. Placement should be limited to certain activities in which success can be achieved.

When a child is deemed ready for placement, consultation between the physical education teacher and the special education supervisor is of prime importance. In a setting where emotions and feelings can run high, it is important to ensure regular communication and planning. The reception and acceptance of the special children must not be left to chance. A scheduled plan should be instituted *before* the youngster is mainstreamed. Special and physical education specialists must discuss the needs of the child and develop realistic expected outcomes. It is quite possible that the special education teacher may have to participate in the physical education class to assure a smooth transition. The thrust should center on what the child can do rather than on what cannot be done. Any approach that treats children with disabilities as cripples is dehumanizing. Full information is due the physical education teacher before the child

appears. This procedure should also be implemented when the child moves from one mainstreaming situation to another.

Both able and disabled students must have opportunities to make appropriate progress. The educational needs of children with disabilities must be met without jeopardizing the progress of other students. This does not rule out activity modifications so that those with disabilities can be included. Some adapted equipment may also be necessary.

The teacher is advised to help all students understand the problems related to being disabled. A goal should be to have students understand, accept, and live comfortably with persons with disabilities. They should recognize that students with disabilities are functional and worthwhile individuals who have innate abilities and who can make significant contributions to society. The concept of understanding and appreciating individual differences is one that merits positive development and should concentrate on three aspects:

1. Recognize the similarities among all people: their hopes, rights, aspirations, and goals.

2. Understand human differences and center on the concept that all people are disabled. For some, disabilities are of such nature and severity that they interfere with normal living.

3. Explore ways to deal with those who differ and stress the acceptance of all children as worthwhile individuals. People with disabilities deserve consideration and understanding based on empathy, not sympathy. Overhelp should be avoided.

Children with disabilities should not be permitted to use their challenge as a crutch or as an excuse for substandard work. Youngsters should not be allowed to manipulate people into helping with tasks they are capable of doing. Coping skills need to be developed, because the disabled do encounter teasing, ignorance, and rejection at various times.

Once the mainstreamed child, able students, and teacher have undergone preliminary preparation, consideration can be given to integrating the youngster with a disability into the learning environment. Mainstreaming should allow the child to make commendable educational progress, to achieve in those areas outlined in the IEP, to learn to accept limitations, to observe and model appropriate behavior, to become more socially accepted by others, and in general to become a part of the real world. Some guidelines for successful integration of children with disabilities into physical education follow.

1. In addition to participation in the regular program of activities, meeting the target goals as specified in the IEP is important. This can involve resources beyond the physical education class, including special work and homework.

2. Build ego strength; stress abilities. Eliminate established practices that unwittingly contribute to embarrassment and failure.

3. Foster peer acceptance, which begins when the teacher accepts the child as a functioning, participating member of the class.

4. Concentrate on the child's physical education needs and not on the disability. Give strong attention to fundamental skills and physical fitness qualities.

5. Provide continual monitoring and assess periodically the child's target goals. Anecdotal and periodic recordkeeping are implicit in this guideline.

6. Be constantly aware of the child's feelings and anxiety concerning progress and integration. Provide positive feedback as a basic practice.

7. Modify the regular program to meet the unique capacities, physical needs, and social needs of youngsters with disabilities.

8. Provide individual assistance and keep youngsters active. Peer or paraprofessional help may be needed. On-task time is important.

9. Consult regularly with the special education consultant.

10. Give consideration to more individualization within the program so that youngsters with disabilities are smoothly integrated. The individualized approach must be based on the target goals of the IEP.

11. Strong consideration should be given to the use of computer programs for recording data and generating meaningful reports.

Teacher Behavior and the Mainstreaming Process

The success or failure of the mainstreaming process rests largely on the interaction between the teacher and the child with a disability. There is no foolproof, teacher-proof system. Purposes and derived goals are perhaps more important to children with disabilities than to so-called "normal" peers. Proper levels of organic fitness and skill are vital for healthful living. Such levels enable them to compete with peers. All teachers have to accept responsibility for meeting the needs of children, including those with disabilities that permit some degree of mainstreaming. Teachers need to be able to judge when referral for special assistance or additional services is in order. Physical education specialists must be able to do the following: (a) analyze and diagnose motor behavior of the disabled, (b) provide appropriate experiences for remediation of motor conditions needing attention, and (c) register data as needed on the child's personal record. Classroom teachers who have a minimal background in physical education will need help from a consultant or specialist to accomplish these goals.

Recordkeeping needs to be emphasized. A short period, perhaps the 5 minutes between classes (when not used to meet with students), could be set aside to accomplish the task promptly. The practice by some administrators of running one class on top of another without any time between classes hardly gives the physical education teacher time for recordkeeping. If such a situation is the case, the teacher could use a portable tape recorder for recording evaluative comments during class time.

To work successfully with students with disabilities, teachers must know the characteristics of the specific impairment and how it affects learning. The teacher should also know how to assess motor and fitness needs, and how to structure remediation to meet the demonstrated needs. Referrals should be kept to a minimum. Teachers should have alternative strategies in reserve in case the original method fails. Referral to the special education teacher then becomes a last resort.

Explanations and directions should be couched in terms that all students, including those with mental retardation, can understand. Be sure that the students with disabilities understand what is to be accomplished before the learning experiences begin, especially when working with the hearing impaired. Concentrate on finding activities in which children with disabilities can excel. Try to find some activity through which they can achieve peer regard. In particular, these youngsters should be expected to work to their full capacity. Do not accept a performance that is inferior in terms of the child's abilities.

Avoid placing children with disabilities in situations where success is not likely. Conversely, give them opportunities that make the best use of their talents. Stress the special objectives of the disabled. Obvious increments of improvement toward terminal objectives are excellent motivators for both children and teachers. Let youngsters know that you as a teacher are vitally interested in their progress.

Apply multisensory approaches in teaching the disabled. Visual and auditory modes of learning may not reach slow learners. Manipulate the child through a given movement to communicate the correct "feel." Touch or rub the involved part of the body to provide tactile stimulation. Emphasis should be on helping children perform the skill, not doing it for them.

The presence of children with disabilities in the physical education class requires teachers to become more effective organizers, which ultimately results in an improved program for all. Ideally, all children in the class would have IEPs, so that the teacher could monitor the individual progress of all students.

Teachers should seek sources of information to aid them in dealing effectively with children with disabilities. Books about disabilities and suggested guidelines for dealing with special children are available. Workshops can be organized featuring knowledgeable individuals with successful programs who can help solve specific problems. Larger school systems may organize inservice education for physical education teachers.

UTILIZING MICROCOMPUTER SERVICES

Microcomputers are becoming increasingly available in schools all over the country. The computer is a time-saving device that can take over the

Using a computer to generate an IEP

recordkeeping chores required by the provisions of PL 94–142. Printouts of present and past status reports can be made available on demand. The computer also can provide comparisons with established norms, especially in physical fitness areas, and it can record progress toward the target goals set by the IEP. The advantage of the microcomputer is that it minimizes the time necessary for recording student progress. In addition, computerized graphic compilations facilitate quick comprehension of progress reports. See chapter 10 for a computer program for writing and revising the IEP.

Another significant computer service is related to informational printouts. The due process regulations of PL 94–142 might be one such topic. Information concerning specific disabilities could be made readily available. Guidelines for formulating the IEP are yet another printout possibility. Long- and short-term objectives can be retrieved from a growing data bank.

Relevant information can be made available to students concerning their progress. This serves as excellent motivation and stimulates a systematic approach to the attainment of spotlighted achievements. The same information can also be the basis for reports to parents and other adults who are interested in the child. These reports serve as motivating factors to enhance parental cooperation.

PARENTAL SUPPORT

Having parents on the IEP committee establishes a line of communication between home and school and involves parents. Some kind of home training or homework may be recommended, particularly with younger children. If home training is indicated, two factors are important. First, parents must be committed in terms of time and effort. Their work need not be burdensome but must be done regularly in accordance with the sequenced learning patterns. Second, the school must supply printed and sequenced learning activities for a systematic approach to the homework. Materials should be understandable so that what is to be accomplished is not in doubt. Parents should see obvious progress in their child as assignments unfold.

Older children with disabilities may accept some responsibility for home training, relegating the parent to the role of an interested spectator who provides encouragement. Even if homework is not feasible, parental interest and support are positive factors. The parents can help their youngster realize what skills have been learned and what progress has been made.

RECRUITING AND TRAINING AIDES

The use of aides can be an effective way of increasing the amount of instruction and practice for youngsters who are disabled. Volunteers are usually easy to find among various community organizations, such as parent-teacher, foster grandparents, and community colleges. High school students can serve as volunteers and have been shown to work effectively with elementary school youngsters.

An initial meeting with volunteer aides should explain the type of youngsters they will be working with and what their responsibilities would involve. Aides must receive training to learn how to be most effective in assisting the instructor. Training should include learning how to work effectively with individuals, recording data, and developing special materials and instructional supplies. In addition, the potential aides should receive experience in working with youngsters, to see if they are capable and enjoy such work. Physical education specialists must also learn how to work with aides. In some cases, physical educators often find the task of organizing and supervising aides to be burdensome if they have not learned to supervise and organize experiences.

There are many roles that aides can assume that increase the effectiveness of the instructional situation. Aides may gather and locate equipment and supplies prior to the lesson. They may officiate games and assure that they run smoothly. Seasoned aides enjoy and are capable of offering one-on-one or small-group instruction to youngsters. Aides should not reduce the need for involvement of the physical education instructor—they should only implement instruction strategies that have been organized and developed by the professional educator. In addition, the physical educator must monitor the quality of the presentations made by the aide.

NATIONALLY VALIDATED PROGRAMS

For several years, nationally validated programs of proven practices in special education have been available for adoption. Portions of many of these programs are in or are related to physical education. These programs are funded and endorsed by the U.S. Office of Education. Some deal with screening, assessment, and curriculum for young children with special needs. Others feature management practices associated with special children. A number deal with early recognition and intervention so that the child can be fitted more successfully into the mainstreaming situation. Information pertaining to these programs can be secured from state departments of education or from the U.S. Office of Education. Programs that have been recognized for outstanding contributions and have been identified as demonstration projects are described below.

1. *Project Active.* This program provides direct service delivery to students with psychomotor problems through a competency-based teaching and individualized learning approach. A second component involves inservice training. Materials include a battery of tests and seven program manuals. Conditions addressed are low motor ability, low physical vitality, postural abnormalities, nutritional deficiencies, breathing problems, motor disabilities or limitations, and communication disorders.

2. *Project Unique.* This is a fitness assessment project designed to determine the best tests for measuring fitness in students with sensory (blind or deaf) or orthopedic impairments. Tests include AAHPERD items and others that can be administered in a mainstream setting.

3. *Project I Can.* This project consists of three separate programmatic systems, including preprimary skills; primary skills; and sport, leisure, and

recreation skills. Each system includes an observational assessment approach, illustrative goals, objectives, instructional strategies, and program evaluation materials. Emphasis is placed on an achievement-based curriculum model.

FITNESS AND POSTURE FOR STUDENTS WITH DISABILITIES

The normalization process has directed attention to posture as a factor in peer acceptance. Since many children with disabilities have low physical fitness levels, posture problems often occur in this group. One aim of mainstreaming is to make the special child less visible—hence the need to help disabled children achieve acceptable posture. Values received from an attractive appearance include better acceptance by peers and more employment opportunities later.

Physical fitness is important for children with disabilities. To compete with and gain respect from peers, the goal of fitness, aside from personal values, is a justified thrust of the physical education program. Adequate physical fitness helps the child move through the school day, which may be complicated by a sensory deficit, a mobility problem, or a mental deficiency.

Care must be given to children who have been sheltered without the opportunity to participate in a physical education program. Wheelchair students need special attention given to cardiovascular development by offering activities that stimulate deep breathing. Arm development is important so that youngsters can move in and out of the wheelchair easily.

It is important to evaluate an idiosyncratic gait or an appearance that exudes the impression of deviance. These often are problems for mentally retarded children. Early identification of a problem and inclusion of a posture correction program are important. The physical educator is often best qualified to initiate and supervise this program. Informal screening should include several tasks—walking, sitting, and stair climbing. Height, weight, and body type affect posture. Obesity may need to be considered in amelioration. Once identification is made, a more detailed analysis of the subject's posture can follow. (See p. 179 for a posture check form.) The degree of postural abnormality governs whether referral is indicated. Videotaping can provide baseline data from which to monitor corrections. Achieving acceptable posture is both a short-term (progress) and long-term (achievement) goal to be included in the child's IEP.

The psychosocial aspects of posture should be considered, with attention focused on the establishment of a good self-concept and effective social relations. Behavior management can focus on the motivation for better postural habits in standing, walking, sitting, lifting, and general movement. Proper posture should become a habit.

Exercise and physical conditioning procedures can be selected to help develop antigravity musculature and to provide flexibility training. These must be combined with comprehensive movement training so that the child learns to move as skillfully and gracefully as possible. Referral for severe conditions or for postural conditions that are difficult to correct should involve the support services of a physician or an orthopedic specialist. Braces may be needed, particularly for lateral curvature (scoliosis).

MODIFYING PARTICIPATION

Special education children need additional consideration at times when participating in group activities, particularly when the activity is competitive. Much depends on the physical condition of the child and the type of impairment. Children like to win in a competitive situation, and resentment can be created if a team loss is attributed to the presence of a child with a disability. Equalization is the key. Rules can be changed for everyone so that the disabled child has a chance to contribute to group success. On the other hand, children need to recognize that everyone, including the disabled and the inept, has a right to play.

Be aware of situations that might devalue the child socially. Never use the degrading method of having captains choose from a group of waiting children. Elimination games should be changed so that points are scored instead of players being eliminated. (This is an important consideration for all youngsters.) Determine the most desirable involvement for children with disabilities by analyzing participants' roles in game and sport activities. Assign a role or position that will make the experience as natural or normal as possible.

Offer a variety of individual and dual activities. Disabled youngsters need to build confidence in their skills before they want to participate with others. Individual activities give children a greater amount of practice time without the pressure of failing in front of peers. The aim of these techniques is to make the children with disabilities less visible so that they are not set apart from able classmates. Using youngsters with disabilities as umpires or scorekeepers should be a last resort.

Modifying an activity for successful participation

Overprotectiveness benefits no one and prevents the special student from experiencing challenge and personal accomplishment. The tendency to underestimate abilities of students must be avoided. The following sections offer ideas for modifying activities to facilitate integration of youngsters with disabilities.

Modifications for Youngsters Lacking Strength and Endurance

1. *Lower or enlarge the size of the goal.* In basketball, the goal can be lowered; in soccer the goal might be enlarged.

2. *Modify the tempo of the game.* For example, games might be performed using a brisk walk rather than running. Another way to modify tempo is to stop the game regularly for substitution. Autosubstitutions can be an excellent method for allowing students to determine when they are fatigued. They ask a predetermined substitute to take their place.

3. *Reduce the weight and/or modify the size of the projectile.* A lighter object will move more slowly and inflict less damage upon impact. A larger object will move more slowly and be easier for youngsters to track visually and to catch.

4. *Reduce the distance that a ball must be thrown or served.* Options are to reduce the dimensions of the playing area or add more players to the game. In serving, others can help make the serve playable. For example, in volleyball, other teammates can bat the serve over the net as long as it does not touch the floor.

5. *In games that are played to a certain number of points, reduce the number required for a win.* For example, volleyball games could be played to 7 or 11, depending on the skill and intensity of the players.

6. *Modify striking implements by shortening and reducing their weight.* Rackets are much easier to control when they are shortened. Softball bats are easier to control when the player "chokes up" or selects a lighter bat.

7. *In some games it is possible to slow the ball down by letting some of the air out of it.* This will reduce the speed of rebound and make the ball easier to control in a restricted area. It will also keep the ball from rolling away from players when it is not under control.

8. *Play the games in a different position.* Some games may be played in a sitting or lying position, which is easier and less demanding than standing or running.

9. *Provide matching or substitution.* Match another child on borrowed crutches with a child on braces. Two players can be combined to play one position. A student in a desk chair with wheels can be matched against a child in a wheelchair.

10. *Youngsters can substitute skills for each other.* For example, a child may be able to strike an object but may lack the mobility to run. Permit substitute courtesy runners.

Modifications for Youngsters Lacking Coordination

1. *Increase the size of the goal or target.* Increasing the size of a basketball goal will increase the opportunity for success. Another alternative might be to offer points for hitting the backboard getting near a goal. Since scoring is self-motivating, modification should occur until success is assured.

2. *The lack of coordination will make the youngster more susceptible to injury from a projectile.* Offer protection by using various types of protectors (glasses, chest protectors, face masks, etc.).

3. *When teaching throwing, allow opportunity to throw at maximum velocity without concern for accuracy.* Use small balls that can be grasped easily. Fleece balls and beanbags are easy to hold and release.

4. *When learning to strike an object, begin with one that is held stationary.* The use of a batting tee or tennis ball fastened to a string can offer the child an opportunity for success. In addition, a larger racket or bat can be used and the youngster can choke up on the grip.

5. *If a great deal of time is spent on recovering the projectile, children will receive few practice trials and feel frustrated.* Place them near a backstop or use a goal that rebounds the projectile to the shooter.

6. *When learning to catch, use a soft, lightweight, and slow-moving object.* Beach balls and balloons are excellent for beginning catching skills as they allow the youngster to track their movement visually. In addition, foam rubber balls eliminate the fear of being hurt by a thrown or batted projectile.

Modifications for Youngsters Lacking Balance and Agility

1. *Increase the width of rails, lines, and beam when practicing balance.* Carrying a long pole will help minimize rapid shifts of balance and is a useful leadup activity.

2. *Increase the width of the base of support.* Youngsters should be taught to keep the feet spread at least to shoulder width.

3. *The more body parts in contact with the floor, the easier it is to balance the body.* Beginning balance practice should emphasize controlled movement using as many body parts as possible.

4. *Increase the surface area of the body parts in contact with the floor or beam.* For example, walking flatfooted is easier than walking on tiptoes.

5. *Lower the center of gravity.* This offers more stability and greater balance to the child. Emphasis should be placed on bending the knees and leaning slightly forward.

6. *Assure that surfaces offer good friction.* Floors and shoes should not be slick or children will fall. Carpets or tumbling mats will increase a child's traction.

7. *Some children will require balance assistance.* A barre, cane, or chair can be used to keep the youngster from falling.

8. *Children with balance problems will inevitably fall.* Offer practice in learning how to fall so that children gradually learn how to absorb the force of the fall.

UNDERSTANDING SPECIFIC DISABILITIES

To assist a child with a challenge, an understanding of the disability and what it means to the child is essential. Basic information is provided here, and additional materials may be secured from special education consultants. National associations offer information about various disabilities and suggest ways of helping special children.

Mental Retardation

The capacity of the mentally retarded child does not allow the child to be served by the standard program. Mental retardation is a question of degree, usually measured in terms of intelligence quotient (IQ). Mildly retarded children (with IQs ranging roughly from 50 to 75 or 80) are most often mainstreamed in both physical education and the regular classroom. Children with IQs below 50 usually cannot function in a regular classroom environment; they need special classes. These children are generally not mainstreamed and so are excluded from the following discussion.

Academically, mildly retarded children (also termed *educable mentally retarded*) are slower to understand directions, to follow directions, to complete tasks, and to make progress. Conceptually, they have difficulty pulling facts together and drawing conclusions. Their motivation to stay on task is generally lower. Academic success may have eluded them. These realities must be considered in the physical education setting. Improvement in these areas is a goal to be achieved.

Do retarded children differ physically from other students? In a study comparing 71 educable mentally retarded boys with 71 normal boys, aged 6 to 10 years, the following was noted. Differences between the retarded and the normal in respect to opportunities to be physically active tend to be substantial. Similarly, the motivation to be physically active may be less in the retarded—a reflection of their general motor ineptness. The relatively large proportion of subcutaneous tissue in the retarded is more than suggestive of a physically inactive life resulting in a corresponding low level of motor performance (Dobbins, Garron, & Rarick, 1981).

In another study (Ulrich, 1983), a comparison was made of the developmental levels of 117 disabled and 96 educable mentally retarded children with respect to criterion-referenced testing of 12 fundamental motor skills and 4 physical fitness skills. The investigation supports the findings of the previous study in that the educable mentally retarded students lagged 3.5 years behind normal children in motor skill development, as based on the researcher's selected criterion reference point. The investigator attributes this lag to a lack of opportunity for movement experiences at an early age. The disabled children were from special education classes, not from a mainstreaming situation.

Instructional Procedures

Studies of mildly retarded students support the assumption that they can learn, but do so at a slower rate and not to the depth of normal mentally functioning children. To help the mildly retarded develop their capacities so that they can become participating members of society, the learning process should concentrate on fundamental skills and fitness qualities. Unless this base is established, the retarded child faces considerable difficulty later in learning specialized skills. Minimizing skill and fitness lags can help ease the child into mainstream living.

The fitness approach involves motivation, acquisition of developmental techniques, and application of these to a personalized fitness program. The retarded child reacts well to goal setting, provided that the goals are challenging yet attainable. The pace of learning depends on the degree of retardation. Before children with mental retardation can learn, they need to know what is expected and how it is to be accomplished. Common sense must govern the determination of progress increments. These should be challenging but within the performer's grasp. Often, past experiences have made retarded children the victims of a failure syndrome. The satisfaction of accomplishment must supplant this poor self-image.

Place emphasis on gross motor movement that is progressive in nature. Teach activities that are presented through demonstration rather than verbalization. Many of the skills may have to be accompanied by manual assistance to help children get the "feel" of the skill. To avoid boredom and frustration, practice periods should be short. Allow ample opportunity for youngsters to show off skills they can perform so that they can enjoy the feeling of accomplishment. Shaping behavior by accepting approximation of the skill will encourage

the child to keep trying. Progress arrives in small increments, and teachers must be sensitive to improvement and accomplishment, no matter how small.

Trying should be rewarded. Many youngsters are reticent to try a new activity. Instructions should be repeated a number of times. Safety rules must be followed, as these youngsters may not understand the risk of injury involved.

Epilepsy

Epilepsy is a dysfunction of the electrical impulses emitted by the brain. It is not an organic disease. It can happen at any period of life but generally shows up during early childhood. With proper care and medication, many children overcome this condition and live normal lives.

Epilepsy is a hidden problem. A child with epilepsy looks, acts, and is like other children except for unpredictable seizures. Unfortunately, epilepsy carries an unwarranted social stigma. A child with epilepsy meets with a lack of acceptance, even when adequate explanations are made to those sharing the child's environment. A major seizure can be frightening to others. Revulsion is another possible reaction of observers.

Gaining control of seizures is often a long procedure, involving experimentation with appropriate anticonvulsive medication in proper doses. Fortunately, most epilepsy can be controlled or minimized with proper medication. One factor in control is to be sure that the child is taking the medication as prescribed.

Sometimes a child can recognize signs of seizure onset. If this occurs in a physical education class, the child should have the privilege of moving to the sideline without permission. A seizure may, however, occur without warning. The instructor should know the signs of a seizure and react accordingly. The teacher may be the first (even before the child) to recognize that a seizure is imminent.

Three kinds of seizure are identified. A petit mal seizure involves a brief period (a few seconds) of blackout. No one is aware of the problem, including the child. Sometimes it is labeled inattention and thus is difficult to identify. A psychomotor epileptic seizure is longer lasting (perhaps a few minutes) and is characterized by involuntary movements and twitching. The child acts like a sleepwalker and cannot be stopped or helped. The affected youngster does not respond when addressed and is unaware of the seizure. A grand mal seizure is a total seizure with complete neurological involvement. The child may become unconscious and lose control of the bladder or bowels, resulting in loss of urine, stool, or both. Rigidity and tremors can appear. The seizure must run its course.

Two points are important. First, throughout any seizure or incident, the teacher must preserve a matter-of-fact attitude and try not to exhibit pity. Second, the teacher must educate the other children to understand and empathize with the problem. Stress what the condition is and, later, what it is not. Explain that the behavior during a seizure is a response to an unusual output of electrical discharges from the brain. Everyone needs these discharges to function in normal living, but the person with epilepsy is subject to an unusual amount of the discharges, which results in unusual activity. The condition involves a natural phenomenon that gets out of control.

Children need to understand that the seizure must run its course. When the seizure is over, everyone can resume normal activity, including the involved child, although the child may be disoriented and uncoordinated for a brief period of time. Offer the child the option of resting or returning to activity. Proper emotional climate of the class is established when the teacher maintains an accepting and relaxed attitude.

Information about epilepsy should be a part of the standard health curriculum in the school, rather than a reaction to an epileptic seizure or to the presence of a student who may have seizures. Epilepsy can be discussed as a topic relevant to understanding the central nervous system. Certain risks are involved if the lessons have as their focus the problems of a particular child, because this may heighten the child's feelings of exclusion and place disproportionate attention on what might have been a relatively inconsequential aspect of the student's life. (This caution does not rule out helpful information being given to peers when a seizure has taken place.)

In the event of a grand mal seizure, some routine procedures should be followed. Have available a blanket, a pillow, and towels to clean up any mess that might occur. Make the child comfortable if there is time. Do not try to restrain the child. Put nothing in the mouth. Support the child's head on the pillow, turning it to one side to allow the saliva to drain. Remove from the area any hard or sharp objects that might cause harm. Secure help from a doctor or nurse if the seizure continues more than 3 or 4 minutes or if seizures occur three or more times during a school day. Always notify the school nurse and the parents that a seizure has occurred. Assure the class that the seizure will pass and that the involved child will not be harmed or affected.

Disabled youngsters can find the joy of participation.

Instructional Procedures

Recommendations regarding special modes of conduct and guidelines governing participation in school activities must come from the child's physician, since most epileptic children are under medical supervision. The instructor should stay within these guidelines while avoiding being overprotective.

Today's approach is to bring epilepsy into the open. A concerted effort should be made to educate today's children so that traditional attitudes toward the condition can be altered. Emphasize inclusion of the child rather than exclusion. If there is some doubt about control of the seizures, climbing and elevated activities should be eliminated.

Perhaps tomorrow's adults will possess a better understanding. The child with epilepsy is a normal, functioning person except at the time of a seizure. Epilepsy is not a form of mental illness, and most people with epilepsy are not mentally retarded.

Visual Impairment

Mainstreaming for the visually impaired must be handled carefully and with common sense. The *visually impaired* designation includes those who are partially sighted as well as those who are legally blind. One has only to move about in a dark room to realize the mobility problems faced by a visually impaired child. This disability poses movement problems and puts limits on participation in certain types of physical activity. Total mainstreaming may not be a feasible solution.

There is a need to bring the child into contact with other children, however, and to focus on the child's unique qualities and strengths. Empathy for and acceptance of the visually impaired child are most important. The task of monitoring movement and helping this child should be considered a privilege to be rotated among class members. If participation in the class activity selected is contraindicated, the monitor can help provide an alternate activity.

Instructional Procedures

Visually impaired children have to develop confidence in their ability to move freely and surely within the limits of their disability. Since limited mobility often leads to reduced activity, this inclination can be countered with a specialized physical fitness and movement program in which the lack of sight does not prove insurmountable. The child can take part in group fitness activities with assistance as needed. Exercises should pose few problems. Rope jumping is an excellent activity. Individual movement activities, stunts and tumbling, rhythms and dances (particularly partner dances), and selected apparatus activities can be appropriate. Low balance beams, bench activities, climbing apparatus, and climbing ropes may be within the child's capacity. Manipulative activities, involving tactile senses, are not always appropriate. If the child has some vision, however, brightly colored balls against a contrasting background in good light can permit controlled throwing, tracking, and catching. Through the selection of activities, the sense of balance should be challenged regularly to contribute to sureness of movement. Because vision is limited, other balance controls also need to be developed.

The visually impaired child ordinarily cannot take visual cues from other children or the teacher, so explanations must be precise and clear. Use a whistle or loud verbal cue to signal the class. For some situations, an assigned peer can monitor activity, helping as needed or requested. In running situations, the helper can hold hands with the visually impaired child. Another way to aid the child is with physical guidance until the feel of a movement pattern is established. This should be a last choice, however, occurring only after the child

has had a chance to interpret the verbal instructions and still cannot meet the challenge. Touching a part of the child's body to establish correct sequencing in a movement pattern also can be of help.

Auditory Impairment

Auditory-impaired children are those who are deaf or who must wear hearing aids. In physical education classes, these children are capable of performing most, if not all, activities that able children can perform. Because most instruction is verbal, a deaf child is isolated and often frustrated in a mainstreaming situation unless other means of communication are established. Accomplishing this while keeping the class functioning normally constitutes a problem of considerable magnitude.

Some advocates for the deaf contend that implementing PL 94–142 with its emphasis on mainstreaming is not appropriate for deaf children and thwarts their development. Teaching the deaf is a challenging and specialized process, requiring different communication techniques. Many deaf children have poor or unintelligible speech and inevitably develop a language gap with the hearing world. Sign language, lip reading, and speech training are all important facets of communicative ability for the deaf. Integrating deaf children into the regular physical education class setting is a process that must be handled with common sense. The experience should be satisfying to the deaf child or it is a failure.

Instructional Procedures

Certainly hearing-impaired children can perform physically and at the same level as children with normal hearing when given the opportunity. One successful approach to teaching both hearing-impaired and normal youngsters is to use contract or task card techniques. Written instructions can be read loudly by the teacher or monitor. Pairing children with severe hearing loss with other children can be a frustrating experience for both, but meaningful possibilities also exist. Such a pairing necessitates lip reading, the use of verbal cues, or strong amplification on a hearing aid. Visual cues, featuring a "do as I do" approach, can stimulate certain types of activity.

The deaf child should be near the teacher to increase the opportunities to read lips and receive facial cues. Keep the class physically active. Avoid long delays for explanations or question and answer periods. This becomes a blank time for the

Signing an auditory impaired student

hearing impaired and leads to frustration and aggressive action. For rhythmics, some devices can be of benefit. Keep record player speakers on the floor to provide vibration. Use a metronome or blinking light. For controlling movement patterns, hand signals should be developed for starting, stopping, moving to an area, assembling near the teacher, sitting down, and so on.

Static and dynamic balance problems are prevalent among hearing-impaired children. Focus on activities that challenge balance and insist on proper procedures. Have the child maintain the position or movement for 10 to 15 seconds and recover to the original position, all in good balance.

Orthopedic Disabilities

Orthopedic disabilities in children encompass a range of physical ailments, some of which may involve external support items such as splints, braces, crutches, and wheelchairs. A few post-polio cases may be encountered. Generalizing procedures for such a range of physical abnormalities is difficult. Children with orthopedic problems usually function on an academic level with other children and are regular members of a classroom. As such, they appear with the class for physical education.

Instructional Procedures

Instructional focus must be on what the child can do and on the physical needs that are to be met.

Mobility is a problem for most, and modification is needed if the class activity demands running or agility. Individualized programs are made to order for this group, because the achievement goals can be set within the child's capacity to perform.

Although volleyball and basketball are popular team sports, there will be few leisure opportunities for individuals to participate in due to the difficulty of getting enough participants together for team play. Strong emphasis should be placed on individual and dual sports such as tennis, track and field, road racing, table tennis, badminton, and swimming. This allows the orthopedically impaired individual to play a dual sport with an able or disabled opponent or to participate individually in activities such as road racing and swimming.

For wheelchair children, certain measures are implicit. Special work is needed to develop general musculature to improve conditions for coping with the disability and to prevent muscle atrophy. In particular, wheelchair children need strong arm and shoulder musculature to transfer in and out of the wheelchair without assistance. Flexibility training to prevent and relieve permanent muscle shortening (contracture) should be instituted. Cardiorespiratory training is needed to maintain or improve aerobic capacity, as immobility in the chair decreases activity. From these experiences, the wheelchair child should derive a personal, functioning program of activity that can carry over into daily living.

Time devoted to special health care after class must be considered for children with braces or in

CHAPTER 8

wheelchairs. Children with braces should inspect skin contact areas to look for irritation. If they have perspired, a washcloth and towel will help them freshen up and remove irritants. Wheelchair children can transfer to a sturdy chair that is rigid and stabilized to allow the wheelchair to dry out. Adequate cushioning should be provided for any surface to which an orthopedically impaired person transfers, such as chairs, weight machines, and pool decks, for the prevention of pressure sores and skin abrasions. Schedules can be adjusted so that time for this care is available. Scheduling the class during the last period before lunch or recess or at the end of the day allows this time.

Children with temporary conditions (fractures, sprains, strains) are handled on an individual basis, according to physician recommendations. Remedial work may be indicated.

Emotionally Disturbed Children

PL 94–142 refers to behavior-disordered students as "severely emotionally disturbed." Emotionally disturbed children represent an enigma for mainstreaming. They have been removed from the regular classroom situation because they may cause a disruption and because they need psychological services. Physical education seems to be one area in which they can find success. Each case is different, however, and generalization is difficult.

Instructional Procedures

An important key when working with emotionally disturbed youngsters is to establish a learning environment that is fair and consistent. The child needs to know exactly what is expected and accepted in the instructional setting. In addition, rules must be clearly defined and nonpunitive in nature. Explanation of reasons for rules should be a regular topic of discussion as emotionally disturbed youngsters often feel that someone is making rules that are meant to punish them personally.

Severely emotionally disturbed youngsters are in need of a stable and organized environment that focuses on individual progress. They will become easily frustrated and quit if the activities are too difficult or cause embarrassment. It is important to expect unexpected outbursts, even when instructional procedures have been correct. If the unexpected is anticipated, teachers will not feel as threatened or hurt by the student's behavior. Emphasis should be placed on development of the affective domain. These students need help building a positive self-concept, expressing their feel-

ings appropriately, and learning to accept responsibility for their own behavior.

Emotionally disturbed youngsters need to know their limits of behavior. Set the limits and then enforce them consistently. Youngsters must know who is in charge and what will be accepted. It may take a long period of time to develop confidence in the emotionally disturbed child, and vice versa. During this time it is important that a sense of trust build. Plan on problems and be ready to deal with them before they occur. A teacher who is patient and understanding can have a positive effect on children with this disability. Loving and forgiving teachers are most effective with the emotionally disturbed youngster.

Learning Disabilities

Learning disabilities encompass a range of problems that lack a clear definition. Examples of terms used to describe various learning disabilities are *perceptual handicaps, brain injury, minimal brain dysfunction, dyslexia,* and *developmental aphasia.* This definition used by the federal government is so broad that over 40 percent of schoolaged youngsters can qualify as being learning disabled. More boys than girls (a 2:1 ratio) are identified as learning disabled in today's schools. Additionally, many more elementary than secondary school children are identified. Characteristics of youngsters with learning disabilities might include one or more of the following: hyperactivity, short attention span, perceptual-motor problems, poor self-concept, clumsiness, poor short- or long-term memory, and an unwillingess to persevere when learning motor tasks.

The causes of learning disabilities are poorly understood. Two major theories are currently popular for explaining these problems (Horvath, 1990). The first theory supposes that learning disabilities are organically based, with one of the major causal factors being an injury to the brain. This brain-injured individual is unable to efficiently receive and integrate sensory impulses. The second hypothesis is that learning disabilities are biochemically based. This theory supposes that several biochemical factors such as allergies, mineral and vitamin deficiencies, and glandular disorders cause learning disabilities. It is important that teachers modify the physical education program on an individualized basis for these children, since their disabilities are unique.

Instructional Procedures

Working with learning-disabled youngsters is similar to working with emotionally disturbed children.

The program should be structured and conducted in similar fashion on a day-to-day basis. Youngsters should not be surprised with unexpected changes in the routines. The activity area should be arranged so distractions are kept to a minimum. Equipment should be distributed and collected using a similar routine. This unchanging structure allows the learning-disabled child to explore the environment with confidence. The teaching area should be restricted to the smallest possible size so that student–teacher distance is kept to a minimum. An environment without limits may cause some youngsters to feel threatened or out of control.

Learning-disabled students often find it difficult to learn independently or wait for a turn. Lessons should demand active participation and require students to be on task a large share of the lesson time. It may be necessary to introduce cross-aged tutoring or invite parent volunteers in to work individually with students. Attention based on firmness and concern will help these students learn motor skills and deal with extraneous distractions in their environment. Instructions should be given one at a time. Use short and concise sentences.

Asthma, Cerebral Palsy, Cardiac Problems, and Diabetes

Asthmatic children have restricted breathing capacity. In the past, doctors were quick to excuse asthmatic children from participating in physical education classes. Recent research is showing that physical activity is not contraindicated for children with asthma. A study by Varray, Mercier, Terral, and Prefaut (1991) showed that children with asthma were capable of participating in high intensity exercise without complications. Children who were 11 years old participated in a swimming program and reached an intensity level within 5 percent of their maximal heart rate. These youngsters showed a significant increase in cardiovascular fitness. Parents of the subjects reported a decrease in the intensity of wheezing attacks and were often able to control asthmatic attacks through relaxation and breathing exercises. The researchers concluded that when workloads are individualized for asthmatic children, their cardiovascular fitness can be enhanced through aerobic training. A key to follow when working with children with asthma is to allow each youngster to be the judge of their workload capacity and to stop when rest is needed.

Cerebral palsy, like epilepsy, has strong negative social implications. Peer education and guidance are necessary. The signs of cerebral palsy are quite visible and, in severe cases, result in odd, un-

coordinated movements and a characteristic gait. Medical supervision indicates the limits of the child's activities. Children with cerebral palsy are usually of normal intelligence; their chief problem is control of movement. An important goal is ensuring that they can achieve competency in performing simple movements. The excitability threshold is critical and must not be exceeded. Many need support services for special training in both neural and movement control.

Children with cardiac problems are generally under the guidance of a physician. Limitations and restrictions should be followed to the letter. The child should, however, be encouraged to work to the limits of the prescription.

Occasionally, a diabetic child may be found in a physical education class. Diabetes is an inability to metabolize carbohydrates that results from the body's failure to supply insulin. Insulin is taken either orally or by injection to control serious cases. If the child is overweight, a program of weight reduction and exercise prescription are partial solutions. Diabetics are usually under medical supervision. Knowing that a diabetic child is in the physical education class is important, because the child must be monitored to detect the possibility of hypoglycemia (abnormally low blood sugar level). The condition can be accompanied by trembling, weakness, hunger, incoherence, and even coma or convulsions. The solution is to raise the blood sugar level immediately through oral consumption of simple sugar (e.g., skim milk, orange juice) or some other easily converted carbohydrate. The diabetic usually carries carbohydrates, but a supply should be available to the instructor. Immediate action is needed because low blood sugar level can be dangerous, even leading to loss of life. The diabetic probably has enough control to participate in almost any activity. This is evidenced by the number of diabetic professional athletes who meet the demands of high activity without difficulty.

PROGRAMS FOR CHILDREN WITH SPECIAL NEEDS

The current emphasis on equal education has helped focus attention on children with special needs. Physical education can offer solutions to relevant problems through activity-oriented programs. Instruction has long been aimed at training the physically adept, with little concern or empathy shown for the less gifted. The programs presented in this section are for underachievers in physical fitness, children with weight problems, and children with motor deficiencies.

Underachievers in Physical Fitness

Underachievers in physical fitness, often called low-fitness children, can be helped through prescriptive programs of physical activity tailored to their needs. The program for underachievers also can be used as the activity program for obese children. To a lesser degree, the program for underachievers can be applied to physically challenged children who have deficiencies in fitness that need special attention. Often, these children have experienced little success and have been held in low regard by classmates. Working with such children can be a rewarding experience, because in many cases the results are phenomenal, and the physical well-being and the personalities of such children are, as a consequence, dramatically changed.

The program for the underachiever usually is scheduled for the intermediate grades but can include the lower grades. Children need to accept responsibility for their program and progress. Underachievers should be in the program only if they wish to help themselves. Primary-level children usually do not have the maturity or motivation to accept this personal responsibility.

When the Fitnessgram (Cooper Institute for Aerobic Research, 1992) (see p. 223) is used for screening purposes, an individual is rated as an underachiever if one or more of the results on the test items are below the minimum criterion-referenced standards. The approach to helping underachievers must be systematic. Four documents are suggested.

1. *Letter to parents.* The letter provides an explanation to the parents and contains a return portion on which parents consent to the child's participation in the program. The letter should also deal with the physical examination procedure.

2. *Program description.* A description of the program should accompany the letter to parents. This description spells out all of the necessary program details, including time schedule and means in which the problem will be handled. Some explanation of fitness concepts probably should be included. The description should be complete enough to enable parents to make a rational decision about the child's participation. A formalized brochure or compilation can impress parents that the approach is systematic, well planned, and educationally sound.

3. *Letter to the physician.* The letter to the family physician should be in the form of a physical examination notice specifying the informational items needed. In particular, the letter should request notification of any conditions that need remediation and any findings that might affect the remedial program. The physician should recommend one of three choices: unrestricted participation, participation with stated restrictions, or no participation.

4. *Form for students.* Each student is given a form that describes the basics of physical fitness, outlines the personal program, and provides space to check off activities (Figure 8.3).

In general, if possible, a sound procedure is to have each child in the program examined by a physician. The school should absorb the cost of the examination for those children whose parents have financial problems. A less acceptable alternative is to have parents certify that to their knowledge and according to previous physical examinations, the child has no disabilities that would prevent participation in the program.

The school district should explain to the local medical association or to individual doctors, by letter, the nature of the program and the need for their cooperation. In this way, special arrangements and fees for the examinations might be established, and the physicians would be alerted to the purpose of the program when the children come in for their examination.

After children are selected for the program and parental and medical approvals are secured, each child undergoes a short orientation period. At this time, the candidate is given the Student's Form, which forms the basis of the program. Goals, including subgoals, are set by the supervisor and the child. Some retesting may be needed. Reinforcing the child's commitment is important. The orientation should provide the child with a full explanation of the program and the procedures to follow. The program should operate for a specified period of time, say 12 to 18 weeks. The basic program concept is to have children improve their own fitness, rather than externally forcing improvement.

An alternative means of stimulating the student is the contract approach. The student signs a Physical Fitness Contract (Figure 8.4) that stipulates specifically the fitness assignment. The activities appear in the same format as on the Student's Form.

The program for underachievers is in addition to, not in place of, the regular physical education program. The supervisor meets weekly with the child, either individually or in a very small group, assesses progress, and sets the work load for the coming week. The child is encouraged to work during free time both at school and at home.

STUDENT'S FORM

School District Individual Fitness Program Step Up to Better Fitness

Name ______________________________ Date ______________

School ______________________ Grade ______________ Circle: Boy Girl

This is your program to help you become more physically fit. Please read it carefully, because it can help a great deal, depending on how well you follow directions and work to improve.

What Is Physical Fitness?

Physical fitness means that your body has enough strength, endurance, power, and flexibility to help you do well the things you like so you can get more fun and enjoyment out of living.

What Can Physical Fitness Do for You?

Being physically fit does not have the same value for everyone, but most people agree that physical fitness can help you in these ways:

1. You get more fun out of what you are doing, because you can do things better without becoming easily tired. You can play longer, jump farther, and do other kinds of activities better.
2. You will enjoy your schoolwork more and play better, because you are able to do the same things other boys and girls in your class can do and keep up with them.
3. You are helping yourself toward a better and fuller life. Becoming physically fit can make you look better and can help you grow up to become the kind of person you want to be.
4. If you are interested in playing sports, becoming physically fit is most important.

How Can You Help Yourself to Better Fitness?

First, you must be willing to follow the program outlined for you and to try your best.

Second, you must think of how you can help yourself toward better fitness by improving your eating, sleeping, and other daily living habits. Are you eating the right kinds of food and enough of them? Are you eating a variety of foods, including fruit, vegetables, and milk? Are you in bed and asleep by at least 9:30 if you are in the primary grades, or by 10:00 if you are in grades 4, 5, or 6? Do you play outdoors and are you active generally, or do you just sit and watch TV?

To become physically fit, you have to do more activities and keep at them longer than you did before. Here is what you should do to improve your fitness. Strive to increase gradually the amount of activity you do (as appropriate to the different recommended activities by increasing distance, number of repetitions, or length of activity time, or by selecting a more challenging activity). Remember that the activities you select must be done regularly and correctly to get maximum benefit. In the scoring table, mark down the number of days each week that you did the activity.

Figure 8.3 Student's fitness form

Encouragement should be positive, and it is quite critical that progress be evident to both the child and the parents. The parents' part is one of encouragement and understanding rather than pressuring or forcing the child. Friendly encouragement by the physical education instructor (if different from the supervisor) and by the classroom teacher is of help. These individuals can also provide followup after the program is completed to help the child maintain a proper state of fitness.

A posttest should be administered to evaluate the effectiveness of the program. In addition, the classroom teacher should solicit the reactions of the physical education teacher, the parents, and the child. Parents can allude to observed changes in personality, attitude, or participation on the part of the child.

Children with Weight Problems

Obesity is a common problem in the United States, and the solution is neither simple nor immediate. It is a difficult and sensitive issue. Each case is different, and the approach must fit the subject. Obesity can be defined in terms of percentages. Roughly speaking, a child who is between 10 and

A. General Activity (two items)
Do at least two of the following.

	Weeks											
	1	2	3	4	5	6	7	8	9	10	11	12
1. Jogging—3 or 4 times per week												
2. Rope jumping—daily												
3. Interval running—3 or 4 times per week												
4. Running in place—daily												

B. Increasing Arm Strength (three items)
1. Do either:

Pull-ups—daily												
Flexed-Arm Hang—daily												
2. Do Push-Ups—daily												
3. Do one of the following:												
Crab Walks—daily												
Rope climbing—daily												
Selected isometrics using a wand—daily												

C. Strengthening Abdominal (Tummy) Muscles (one item)
Do one of the following daily:

1. Reverse Curl												
2. Knee Touch Curl-Up												
3. Curl-Up												

D. Body Twisting and Stretching Exercises (two items)
Do two of the following:

1. Bend and Twist												
2. Sitting Stretch												
3. Lower Leg Stretch												
4. Body Twist												
5. Standing Hip Bend												

E. Leisure Activities
Take part in one or more of the following three to four times per week in your leisure time:

_____ Bicycling	_____ Skiing	_____ Walking	_____ Roller-skating
_____ Ice-skating	_____ Soccer	_____ Hiking	_____ YMCA or YWCA activities
_____ Swimming	_____ Basketball	_____ Baseball	_____ Scouting fitness activities

Figure 8.3 *continued*

DESCRIPTION OF ACTIVITIES

A. General Activities

1. **Walking or Jogging:** Set the distance and make it without stopping. Keep as fast a pace as possible, but slow down if needed. Maintain a steady pace.

2. **Rope jumping:** Use fast turning. Use the basic two-foot jump or alternate feet. Set a bout of 50 or 100 turns. Decide on the number of bouts, or set a time limit and jump for that long.

3. **Interval running:** Set a course of either 50 or 100 yards with two markers. Run down to the marker as fast as possible. Turn and walk back to original place. Repeat for one unit. Decide on the number of units before you begin.

4. **Running in place:** Count only the left foot. Fifty counts per bout. Increase the number of bouts gradually.

B. Arm Strength

1. **Pull-ups or a Flexed-Arm Hang:** Set three trials for either. If no Pull-ups can be done, use the Flexed-Arm Hang.

2. **Push-ups:** Use the letdown first, then push up. Let down slowly. Keep the body straight.

3. **Crab Walk:** Go back and forth (round trips) between lines 5 yards apart. Touch one line with a foot and the other line with a hand. Try to keep the seat up.

4. **Rope climbing:** Go up and down several times.

5. **Isometrics:** Use a broom handle or a similar stick. Do sets of three or four isometrics, using different arm positions.

C. Abdominal Exercises

1. **Reverse Curl:** Lie on back with the hands on the floor to the sides of the body. Curl the knees to the chest. The upper body remains on the floor. As abdominal strength increases, the child should lift the buttocks and lower back off the floor.

2. **Knee Touch Curl-Up:** Lie on the back, with feet flat and knees bent, and with hands flat on top of thighs. Leading with the chin, slide the hands forward until the fingers touch the kneecaps and gradually curl the head and shoulders until the shoulder blades are lifted off the floor. Hold for eight counts and return to position.

3. **Curl-Up:** Lie on the back with feet flat, knees bent and arms on the floor at the side of the body with palms down. Lift the head and shoulders to a 45 degree angle and then back in a two-count pattern. The hands should slide forward on the floor 3 to 4 inches.

D. Flexibility Exercises

1. **Bend and Twist:** Stand with the arms crossed, hands on opposite shoulders, knees slightly flexed, and feet shoulder width apart. Bend forward at the waist (count 1). Twist the trunk and touch the right elbow to the left knee (count 2). Twist in the opposite direction and touch the left elbow to the right knee (count 3). Return to the starting position (count 4). Knees can be flexed.

2. **Sitting Stretch:** Sit on the floor with one leg extended forward and the other bent at the knee. The foot is placed in the area of the crotch. The toes of the extended foot are touched with the fingertips of both hands as the chest gradually moves forward.

3. **Lower Leg Stretch:** Stand facing a wall with the feet about shoulder width apart. Place the palms of the hands on the wall at eye level. Slowly walk away from the wall, keeping the body straight, until the stretch is felt in the lower portion of the calf. The feet should remain flat on the floor during the stretch.

4. **Body Twist:** Sit on the floor with the left leg straight. Lift the right leg over the left leg and place it on the floor outside the left knee. Move the left elbow outside the upper right thigh and use it to maintain pressure on the leg. Lean back and support the upper body with the right hand. Rotate the upper body toward the right hand and arm. Reverse the position and stretch the other side of the body.

5. **Standing Hip Bend:** Stand with the knees slightly flexed, one hand on the hip and the other arm overhead. Bend to the side with the hand resting on the hip. The arm overhead should point and move in the direction of the stretch with a slight bend at the elbow. Reverse and stretch the opposite side.

E. Leisure Activities

Count these only if you spend at least 30 minutes doing the activity. You may select different activities to meet the three to four per week count.

Figure 8.3 *continued*

PHYSICAL FITNESS CONTRACT

Name _____ Date _____

School _____ Grade _____ Circle: Boy Girl

I agree to do the following activity program to the best of my ability for _____weeks.

General Activity

1. Rope Jumping. 50 turns, 4 bouts.
2. Running in place. 50 counts on left foot, 4 bouts.

Arm Strength

1. Pull-ups. 3 chins, 3 bouts. Increase number.
2. Push-ups. 5 first week, increase each week.
3. Crab Walks. 6 trips. Increase number.

Abdominal Strength

1. Curl-ups. 10 curl-ups. Increase number.

Flexibility

1. Sitting Stretch. 4 stretches. Increase time and number.
2. Body Twist. 6 sets. Increase number of sets.

Leisure Activities

1. Roller Skating
2. Bicycling
3. Soccer

I agree to participate at least 4 times per week total in these activities.

Signed _____

Figure 8.4   Physical fitness contract

20 percent over the weight designated as appropriate for that child's age and height would be classified as overweight. A child who is 20 percent or more over the ideal is classified as obese. (These percentages vary from one source to another.) The advantage of a percentage definition is that it is meaningful to parents. Skinfold measurement with calipers is a more scientific means of identifying obese individuals. Skinfolds can be converted to a percentage of body fat reading to make the measurement meaningful to parents and children. For research purposes, converting the readings to a percentage is not desirable, but for a student-oriented program, the procedure is acceptable. Basically, the simplest test is the appearance of the child: A child who looks obese, is!

In any solution, the basic factors involved in obesity must be considered. These factors include genetics, emotional stability, hormonal functions, and intake-activity relationships. The overwhelming odds are that a fat child will stay fat. About 85 percent of obese children must fight weight gain for the rest of their lives (Eden, 1975). The assumption that obese children normally grow out of the condition is a fallacy. Some parents rationalize the problem, maintaining that their child "still has some baby fat but will grow out of it later." Unless active measures are taken, the chances of solving the child's problem are small.

Heredity and environment are difficult to separate as causes for obesity, yet weight gain runs in families. If one parent is obese, about half of the children probably will be obese adults. This ratio jumps to 80 percent when both parents are obese (Eden, 1975). One theory supports the importance of finding an early solution for obesity. According to this theory, during childhood the obese child develops more fat cells than a child of normal weight, and the number of fat cells is carried over to adolescence and adulthood. An individual who has more fat cells is more prone to becoming overweight than is a person who has fewer. The obvious implication is that weight-control measures should occur early, before the fat cells increase in number. During adult life, fat cells are thought not to increase in number, but rather to enlarge in size.

Obese children often experience physical activities in ways different from children of normal weight. Success in physical activity is difficult for obese children to attain. When compared with their peers, heavy children are often physically inept. They may be the object of ridicule or the butt of jokes. Their peers sometimes call them names, such as Fatso, Tubby, and Lard Bucket. Children can be hurt deeply and driven even farther from active living, a direction opposite from the one they so desperately need to follow.

Not only does obesity impede the development of motor skills and limit the child's success in physical activities, it also contributes to heart disease, because obese people are generally more inactive than their peers. The most common factor in obesity is an imbalance between caloric intake and energy expenditure. Many obese children fail to involve themselves in enough physical activity to burn up the calories they ingest. Excess calories are then stored in fat cells, and the child is pushed further into obesity.

A practical method for determining obesity uses calipers to measure skinfolds (Figure 8.5). Calipers are relatively inexpensive, and the measurement can be done quickly. The skinfolds over the triceps and calf muscles can be used to estimate the amount of body fat. To measure the skinfolds, the skin on the two sites is held with thumb and forefinger. The calipers are then applied to the skinfold, indicating a reading in millimeters. Three readings should be taken and the median score used. If the sum of the triceps and calf skinfolds is more than 31 mm for boys and 40 mm for girls, the youngsters are considered obese (Lohman, 1987).

Another method is less scientific but offers a reasonable estimate. It is called the pinch test (Figure 8.6). Several skinfold pinches are made with the thumb and forefinger on such areas as the back of the upper arm, the side of the lower chest, the abdomen, and the back just below the shoulder blades. If a skinfold of more than 1 inch can be picked up, the child is considered obese. A skinfold between 0.5 and 1 inch is in the acceptable range.

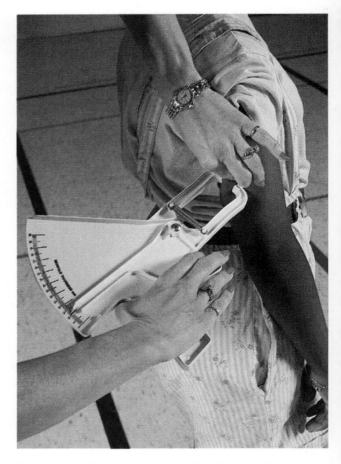

Figure 8.5 Measuring triceps skinfold with calipers

Some children are so obviously obese that measurement is hardly needed.

The solution to an obesity problem involves attention to both diet and activity. Unfortunately, this means that these children must alter their lifestyle, which requires adjustment not only in school life but also in home life. Without a genuine commitment from the child and without the cooperation of the child's parents, a remedial program can have little chance of success. For some children, commitment to the program is a relatively easy step, because they resent being fat and have wanted to do something about their obesity but have not known quite what to do. A protracted time commitment is important, because the remedial program must turn into a program for living or the child will revert to old habits. Getting parents to cooperate can be more difficult, especially if they themselves are obese. The parents may give lip service to cooperation but may in reality do nothing to change the home lifestyle that contributes to the child's obesity.

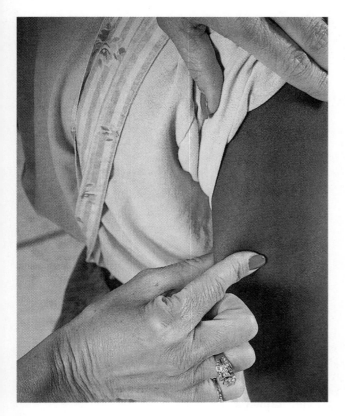

Figure 8.6 Pinch test

Counseling is an important part of the program for fighting obesity and should include both conferences with the child and support through printed instructions. The program of activity for the underachiever in physical fitness (see pp. 165–166) is also excellent for the obese child. Getting the child to follow the activity prescription is vital. This is where the physical educator's emphasis should lie.

Dealing with diet is extremely complex and involves changing the eating habits not only of the obese child but also of parents and siblings. This is complicated by the fact that in some cases, the obese child's diet is not substantially different from that of normal-weight classmates. It is also difficult for a child to change the food received at home, so diet control must be relegated to a minor role in the weight-control program. If the child can be influenced to eat moderately at mealtime and to avoid snacking between meals, much has been accomplished, and the child's diet at school can be monitored.

Treating Obesity: Developing a Success Profile

Any weight-control project should include the entire school and involve the classroom teacher, be-

cause it is necessary to use some class time for conferences with the children in the program. Probably the intermediate level is the most feasible time to deal directly with weight problems, since children at this level become more sensitive to their appearance and their relationships with peers. At the primary level, children usually have little motivation to deal with the problem.

Following is a step-by-step approach to developing a success profile for obese children in the elementary school setting. In many programs, youngsters are selected for treatment because someone feels uneasy about their physical predicament. More meaningful is a selection based on the youngsters' ability to deal successfully with the problem. This approach assumes that certain individuals are better suited to treatment than others. Not treating a child may be the better solution if the treatment outcome is likely to be failure, because failure only reinforces the child's belief that there is little hope, even when teachers want to help. The following approach picks children who show a success profile after initial testing.

Initial Screening of Potential Candidates

1. Explain the program to classroom teachers and emphasize the need for their support.
2. Ask classroom teachers to identify potential candidates.
3. Discuss with the classroom teacher the possibility of success for each candidate.
4. Hold a discussion with each of the students to explain the nature of the problem, the possibility of treatment, and whether the student would like to participate.
5. Select students to be tested based on the comments of the classroom teachers, the students' comments, and the opinion of the physical education specialist.

Evaluation and Selection of Students

This is the critical step in developing a successful program. Students must be selected who are capable of implementing the program objectives. An approach that has worked well is to develop a success profile that is a compilation of selected data on each potential candidate. The following are areas that can be included:

1. *Fitnessgram data.* These include the following:
   a. *Skinfolds.* Children can be selected for inclusion in the program if they fall below the

minimum standard on the Fitnessgram. Some youngsters may be too obese for treatment in a physical education setting. Severe cases require medical attention and counseling beyond the scope of the physical education specialist.

b. *Sit and reach for flexibility.*

c. *Curl-ups to evaluate abdominal strength.*

d. *PACER test to evaluate cardiovascular endurance.*

2. *Height and weight.* These data are collected only for the purpose of communicating with parents about where their child ranks in relation to others (percentile ranking). Standard height and weight charts should be used (see Figures 2.3 and 2.4, pp. 20–21) and are available from Ross Laboratories, Columbus, OH 43216.

3. *Children's Attitude Toward Physical Activity (CATPA) (Simon & Smoll, 1974) evaluation.* This scale gives an indication of the child's feeling about participation in physical activity.

4. *Self-Perception Profile for Children (Harter, 1985).* This instrument offers results that evaluate the perceived competence of children.

All of these factors are weighted in a relative fashion with the exception of the skinfold measurement. It may be wise to avoid including excessively obese children as the possibility of their failure is high. All other factors are weighted, and those children are selected who have a strong sense of perceived competence, the most positive attitude toward physical activity, the highest fitness level, and support from the student, parents, and classroom teacher. The Success Profile Form (Figure 8.7) can be used to analyze the data.

Parental Involvement

1. Meet with the parents of selected students for a conference to explain the program. Topics covered in the meeting should be objectives of the program, operation and organization of the program, data gathered on the success profile, parent responsibilities, and need for followup conferences.

2. Give parents a handout explaining the program and the related responsibilities of the parents and child. This will allow them to discuss the program at home.

3. Parents should leave the meeting with a clear understanding that the program is terminated if either the child or parent fails to perform his or her duties.

4. Give parents a "permission for my child to participate" form and ask them to return it within a stipulated time. This allows the parent and child to discuss whether they really want to participate.

Name _____

Pre _____ Post _____

SUCCESS PROFILE

1. Height and weight

   a. Height _____ inches

   b. Height _____ percentile

   c. Weight _____ pounds

   d. Weight _____ percentile

2. Skinfold measurements

   a. Triceps _____ mm

   b. Calf _____ mm

3. Physical fitness attitude inventory (CATPA)

   a. Score _____

4. Self-perception Profile for Children (Harter, 1985)

   a. Score _____

5. Physical fitness test evaluation

   a. Curl-Ups _____

   b. Sit and Reach _____

   c. PACER _____

6. Parent support _____

7. Classroom teacher support _____

8. Student interest _____

9. PE teacher interest _____

Figure 8.7 Success profile form for analyzing data relevant to weight-control program participation

Implementation of the Program

After the students have been selected, a conference must be arranged with each student. Conferences should be conducted weekly and should not be held during the student's free time, if possible.

1. The conference should last 10 to 20 minutes.
2. A student notebook should be developed, which is the property of the student, who should be able to personalize it and make it something of value. Included in the notebook are the forms that define the student's workload and contain notes and information about exercise, nutrition, and weight control. Included also should be a form for communicating with parents about the child's progress. A parental check-off sheet stating that the youngster completed the weekly fitness assignment is necessary.

Assigning Fitness Activity

The following guidelines should be used when developing activity for obese children:

1. Assigned activity should be aerobic in nature to increase the caloric expenditure.
2. Exercise prescription should be based on the individual's tolerance for exercise. Start at a level that ensures success.
3. Record assigned activity in order to increase the amount of activity gradually and to ensure overload. Computer recording should be considered.
4. If possible, find aerobic activities that the child enjoys. The assignment should not be in lieu of activity already performed. Offer two or three choices for variety.
5. Assignments should be made in terms of minutes per day. Start with 10 minutes and increase 2 minutes per week, until a maximum of 30 to 40 minutes of exercise a day is reached.
6. Suggested activities are walking, skateboarding, roller skating or ice skating, bike riding, hiking, unorganized sport activities, orienteering, jogging, swimming, and rope jumping.

Followup Activities

1. Every third week, parents should receive some type of communication that discusses the youngster's progress. This might be a note, phone call, computer printout, or personal visit.
2. The physical education teacher should visit regularly with the classroom teacher and explain how the youngster is progressing, what treatment is being used, and those areas to be reinforced in the classroom.

The program emphasizes treating systematically those children who have the characteristics to succeed. If students are selected properly, the program success rate can be very high.

Children with Motor Deficiencies

Specialized programs for children with motor deficiencies should be an integral part of the school's overall approach to ameliorating deficiencies, which usually includes other special programs, such as speech and reading programs, psychological services, and behavioral management. Programs for the motor deficient are not a substitute for physical education but are in addition to regular participation in physical education classes.

In addition to the programs for special education children discussed previously (see pp. 156–158), two types of programs can be identified for remedying motor deficiency. The first program category concerns children with academic problems, labeled specific learning disabilities (SLDs). Children with these problems were formerly targets of perceptual-motor training, a term that has lost its usefulness (Reid, 1981). The second type of program concerns children who exhibit motor deficiencies to a degree that does not allow them to participate successfully in movement activities with peers.

Special Learning Disabilities and Motor Deficiencies

A specific learning disability is sometimes called a *specific language disability*. The two terms are interchangeable, and both are referred to as SLDs. Children with SLD have academic performance problems despite an average or above-average IQ. They often exhibit problems such as slow, laborious reading; bizarre and inconsistent spelling; reversing of letters and numbers; clumsy, awkward, and sloppy handwriting; difficulty processing what they hear; hyperactivity and inattentiveness; apparent laziness or behavioral problems; or a discouraged attitude because success is not often achieved.

The learning disabled often suffer from motor deficiencies and exhibit movement and perceptual problems. Formerly, these learning deficiencies and motor problems were postulated to be the result of a lack of sequential development in the perceptual-motor realm. Proponents of this theory believed that if a program of selected movement activities and motor proficiency development (perceptual-motor programs) could be instituted, motor proficiency and academic performance would improve. Unfortunately, research has shown that perceptual-motor programs are usually ineffective in remediating learning difficulties. All movement activities are perceptual-motor in nature. To designate certain activities as "perceptual-motor activities" is confusing and inappropriate. Nevertheless, for two decades educators have used the term to mean activities that enhance balance, laterality, agility, spatial awareness and control, hand-eye coordination, rhythm, and body awareness and image.

In perceptual-motor programs, attention should center on breaking the failure syndrome that some children experience in the school environment. Many children with disabilities accept failure as the natural course because no matter how hard they try, the effort does not seem to be enough. Program goals must be twofold: to give children a taste of success and to improve their motor proficiency so that they can participate successfully with peers and earn peer regard. Children should achieve success in a noncompetitive environment with activities that are a challenge but within their range of achievement. The SLD child can find satisfaction in movement experiences, and these successful experiences can become a means for developing proper body image and self-concept. Other values realized from the remedial program include the following:

1. Improved listening habits and learning to follow directions.
2. Learning to stay on task.
3. Developing pride in achievement and increased interest in school.
4. Increased expectations for accomplishment. The child is singled out for special attention and is expected to do well. Studies show that children do as well as teachers expect them to do.

Clumsiness or Ineptness

An observant teacher can screen for further study those children who exhibit clumsiness and ineptitude in accomplishing movement tasks. The child may be able to walk or run reasonably well but may have trouble in skipping, sliding, or galloping. Simple throwing and catching tasks may meet with little success when target skills are deficient. A child whose sense of spatial relationships is defi-

cient may collide with objects and classmates more frequently than is normal. This child should be assessed with a motor proficiency test.

Motor Proficiency Tests

Assessment of motor ability is the first step in a remedial program. The number of motor ability tests available is amazing, with a conservative estimate showing more than 250 tests (Wade, 1981). Most of these are achievement, as opposed to process-oriented, tests. Achievement tests measure how fast, how far, how many times, or what target score. Process-oriented test items give attention to qualitative changes characterizing movement patterns and relate the movement to a valid developmental sequence norm.

Achievement tests are more easily administered than process-oriented tests, although the latter are considered more valid in terms of motor development. It is much simpler to measure for 10 seconds the balance of a child standing on the preferred leg than to identify what stage the child's throwing pattern assumes in comparison to a scale within the child's age bracket.

One useful test, the Bruininks-Oseretsky Test of Motor Proficiency, is available from Bruininks-Oseretsky Test of Motor Proficiency, American Guidance Service, Inc., Circle Pines, MN 55014. The battery of eight subtests covers gross motor ability, upper limb coordination, and fine motor ability as follows. Four gross motor subtests measure (a) running speed and agility, (b) balance, (c) bilateral coordination, and (d) strength. Upper limb coordination is tested by bouncing and catching balls and by moving and touching body parts. Three fine motor subtests measure response speed, visual-motor control, and upper limb speed and dexterity. The complete battery contains 46 test items distributed among the eight subtests. A short form emphasizes the same eight subtests but consists of only 14 items. The short form takes approximately 20 minutes to administer. The applicable age range is from 4 years 6 months, to 14 years 5 months. Standard scores and percentile ranks are available.

A plus for the Bruininks test is that the importance of strength in performing gross motor skills is recognized. Before a child can acquire skill proficiency, that child must have a necessary reservoir of strength to practice and accomplish the skill. Many of the items in the fine motor section are not physical education items. These involve pencil accuracy tests, sorting and collecting items, and accomplishing small tasks with accuracy. This por-

Balance is a common motor proficiency test.

tion of the test may be more valuable to a classroom teacher than to a physical educator.

The selection of a proper test as an assessment tool is difficult. One must first determine the nature of the motor ineptitude and then must select motor tasks or developmental sequences that give a clue to the degree of ineptitude. Both of these decisions involve subjective judgments, meaning that test results will always differ because human judgment cannot be stabilized.

Remedial Measures for the Motor Deficient

An important goal of any remedial program is to provide training to help motor-deficient children better understand their bodies and become more proficient and effective in executing movement patterns. The critical issue is effective assessment. Without this, the remedial program has little basis. Assessment should identify deficiencies in achievement and in movement patterns. The remedial clinician should be interested in item results (product) and movement patterns (process) through which the overall test results were attained. The approach

to remediation is threefold: (a) give attention to physical fitness qualities, (b) provide broad training in physical education activities, and (c) ameliorate specific deficiencies revealed through assessment procedures.

Physical Fitness

Motor-deficient children tend to be less active than their more skilled peers and usually rank lower in physical fitness qualities. If a child is inactive enough to be classified as an underachiever in physical fitness, the suggestions to help underachievers (pp. 165–166) are appropriate. Otherwise, attention should center on the specific fitness qualities that need development. Basic to the program is developing an understanding of the body—how it functions and how to keep it in proper condition.

Broad Training in Physical Education Experiences

The foundation for the training portion of the program should be fundamental locomotor and manipulative skills taught in a structured, progressive manner. Individual activities done to rhythm, such as rope jumping to music, European Rhythmic Running, rhythmic ball bouncing and dribbling, and selected dance numbers, can supplement these fundamentals. Tumbling, stunts, and apparatus activities offer additional possibilities. These activities should combine sound instructional patterns with emphasis on enjoyment. Teachers should recognize that children enjoy activities in which they find success. The thrust is therefore to get the children to participate successfully in regular, everyday physical education experiences.

Another approach to consider is supplemental instruction (if needed) for current activities in the regular physical education program. This may raise the children's level of skill so that they can compete on an equal basis with peers in the regular physical education class.

Ameliorating Specific Deficiencies

The importance of the assessment process is evident. Specific deficiencies are listed for remediation, with suggestions for appropriate action. If there are many deficiencies, the examiner should establish priority and select critical remediations for early action. The successful correction of one or two items is preferable to a blanket approach to remediation, which may fail.

The method of attack should be a structured, diagnostic teaching approach that follows sound motor learning principles. Repetition and practice, with an on-task approach for the child, should be stressed. When the student has accomplished the target skill level, proficiency can be tested.

Perceptual-Motor Activities

Even though the term *perceptual-motor training* has lost critical meaning, some activity approaches in these programs still have value. For example, *laterality,* which is defined as the ability to control and move corresponding parts of the body independent of or in conjunction with each other, is a major focus in regular physical education programs and has been singled out for special attention in perceptual-motor programs. In this instance, as in others, the distinction between regular physical education and perceptual-motor activities is difficult to perceive.

To enhance laterality, a variety of movement patterns and combinations that include unilateral, bilateral, cross-lateral, and independent movements should be offered. Independent movements entail separate movements of a dissimilar nature of two or more limbs. The object is to offer a broad range of experiences so the child can learn to move with ease and assurance in executing various movements. Angels in the Snow (Figure 8.8) and crawling and creeping patterns are examples of movement sequences that can be employed to enhance laterality. These movements are used infrequently in regular physical education classes because of their corrective nature.

The movement pattern Angels in the Snow received its name from a traditional snow activity in which children lie in the snow on their backs and move their arms in an arc from a position overhead along the ground to their sides, thus outlining angel wings. In the exercise, children lie on the back, with legs together and arms at the sides. On command, designated limbs move, the arms moving along the floor to a position above the head, and the legs moving apart. Commands can single out one limb or two, or a full bilateral action in which both arms

and both legs move. The commands are given as follows: "Right arm, left leg out, (pause) back." The words *out* and *back* are alternated so that the movement pattern is repeated from 6 to 10 times.

The following movements generally comprise the patterns.

1. *Bilateral:* both arms, both legs, both arms and both legs
2. *Unilateral:* right (or left) arm, right (or left) leg, right arm and right leg together, left arm and left leg together
3. *Cross-lateral:* right arm and left leg, left arm and right leg

Angels in the Snow was originally designated as an individual exercise in which the leader pointed to an arm or a leg and said, "Move that arm [or leg]." This, however, proved unsuitable for group work.

Crawling can follow the same basic patterns.

1. *Unilateral:* crawling forward on hands and knees, using the arm and leg on the same side together
2. *Bilateral:* moving forward, reaching out with both hands, and then bringing the feet up to the hands (Bunny Jump)
3. *Cross-lateral:* crawling forward, moving the right arm and left leg at the same time, and vice versa

Unilateral and cross-lateral creeping also can be employed. (Creeping differs from crawling in that the child assumes a prone position in creeping, while she is on hands and knees in crawling. The terms often are used interchangeably, however.) Variations on crawling and creeping patterns are as follows:

1. Move forward, backward, sideward; make quarter turns right and left.
2. Turn the head first toward the leading hand and then opposite to it, coordinating with each step.

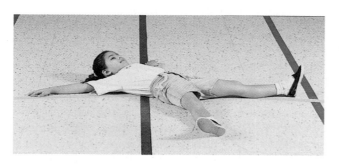

Figure 8.8 Angels in the Snow

POSTURE

The physical education program should include vigorous physical activities that lead to fitness and strengthening of the muscle groups that maintain proper body alignment. Strengthening the abdominal wall and the musculature of the upper back and neck helps maintain proper body alignment. Enough flexibility of the various body segments must be attained so that children are able to move their body with ease and proper postural alignment.

The maintenance of correct posture contributes to physical attractiveness and wellness. *Posture* refers to the habitual or assumed alignment and balance of the body segments while the body is standing, walking, sitting, or lying. Posture is a reflection of the inner self. Appropriate posture radiates a positive self-image, while improper posture (e.g., slouching) may reflect a lack of confidence or fatigue.

The association of posture with physical fitness is justified. The antigravity muscles, those that help support the body against the forces of gravity, must be exercised regularly to accomplish this with ease and without undue fatigue. From a mechanical standpoint, the musculature involved in correct posture must be balanced to hold the bones and joints properly. Faulty alignment can cause undue strain on supporting muscles and ligaments, which leads to early fatigue, muscle strain, and progressive displacement of postural support. In extreme cases, pain may result, and the position and function of vital organs, primarily those located in the abdomen, can be affected adversely.

What Is Correct Posture?

Posture varies with the individual's age, sex, and body type. Very young children often toe out while standing and walking to provide a wider, more stable base. Standing position exhibits an exaggerated lumbar curve and rounded shoulders, which are normal at this developmental stage. By age 6 or 7, however, the lumbar curve is lessening and the prominent abdominal protrusion is beginning to disappear. At this stage, the feet and toes generally point ahead. Less rigid postural standards must be applied in the lower grades. The educational process should assist the child in making the transition from the normal exaggerated curves of young children to proper adult posture in adolescence.

The entire body posture is based on proper positioning of the feet. When the feet are positioned correctly, the rest of the body is more likely to line up properly. If weight is placed improperly on the heels with the knees in a locked position, the pelvis is tilted forward (down), with a compensating increased lumbar curvature and rounded shoulders. Toeing out during walking or standing is undesirable, because it can lead to progressive arch trouble and cause other problems such as less efficient walking and off-balance standing. Another undesirable adaptation occurs in the heel cord, which may curve outward where it joins the heel. Further change occurs as the bony structure of the foot slides toward the inside. This change culmi-

nates in a prominent inside malleolus. (The term *malleolus* refers to a bony protuberance.) The basic components of posture are illustrated in Figures 8.9 and 8.10.

Lateral Deviations in Posture

Consideration to this point has been mostly with the forward-backward plane of body movement, generally assessed from the side. The body also must be in balance in the lateral plane, as viewed from either front or back. The spinal column viewed from the back should show a straight, vertical line that divides the body into two symmetrical halves (Figure 8.11A).

A deviation occurs when this vertical line becomes either a single (C) curve (Figure 8.11B) or a multiple (S) curve (Figure 8.11C). Such deviations are coupled with one or more of the following body adjustments: (a) one shoulder higher than the other, (b) head tilts to one side, (c) hips not level, and (d) weight carried more on one leg than on the other. Marked deviations are noticeable, but moderate deviations are difficult to detect, especially when the body is clothed.

One way in which lateral curvature (scoliosis) can be detected is to have children bend forward and touch their toes. A serious curvature is indicated when the ribs protrude on one side. Early attention to lateral curvature is important because it generally gets worse instead of better with age. By the time youngsters reach high school, the curvature is probably well established and difficult to remedy.

Evaluating Posture

Because elementary school teachers are responsible for detecting and reporting physical problems of children, some program of posture evaluation should be established. Evaluation can be done through observation, both formal and informal, and with measurement devices. A referral system should be established for individuals who exhibit marked posture deviations.

Posture Check Method

For youngsters with posture problems, the application of the posture check can be an educational experience. Two methods of recording are presented: an individual form (Figure 8.12) and a class form (Figure 8.13). Teachers may prefer the single sheet, which includes all of the class, but the individual form is easier for parents and administrators

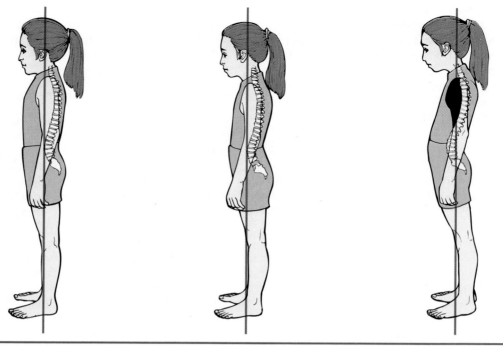

Correct posture	Fair posture	Poor posture
Head up, chin in, head balanced above the shoulders with the tip of the ear directly above the point of the shoulders, eyes ahead Shoulders back and easy, chest up Lower abdomen in and flat Slight and normal curves in the upper and lower back Knees easy Weight balanced with toes pointed forward	Head forward slightly Chest lowered slightly Lower abdomen in but not flat Back curves increased slightly Knees back slightly Weight a little too far back on the heels	Head noticeably forward, eyes generally down Chest flat or depressed Shoulder blades show winged effect Abdomen relaxed and prominent Back curves exaggerated Knees forced back in back-kneed position Pelvis noticeably tilted down Weight improperly distributed

Figure 8.9 Characteristics of correct, fair, and poor posture

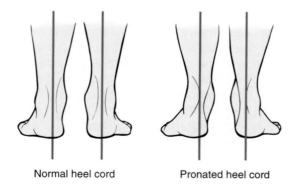

Normal heel cord   Pronated heel cord

Figure 8.10 Normal and pronated heel cord

to interpret. The class form is more adaptable to class analysis and comparisons. Each item is rated 1, 2, or 3 on an ascending scale. By averaging the rating numbers, a mean rating is obtained for each child.

Informal Observation

Formal posture evaluation is an analysis of an assumed posture, which is not necessarily the posture used by children in daily living. To offset this testing effect, posture checks can be made informally when young people are participating in classroom and physical education activities. Teachers should notice how each child walks, stands, or sits when not conscious of an observer. The teacher can make notes and supplement the formal posture check.

Ear–Shoulder Method

In normal posture, the lobe of the ear is directly above the point of the shoulder. Any departure from this relationship indicates a degree of back and shoulder roundness, and can be used as a measure of general posture deviation. When one body area is out of alignment, other body segments

Figure 8.11 Lateral posture

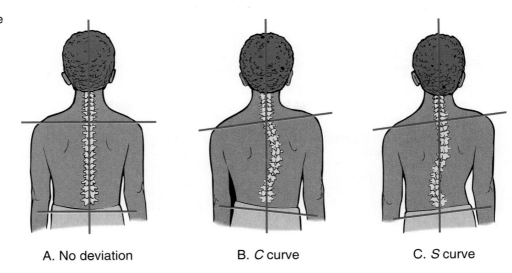

A. No deviation B. *C* curve C. *S* curve

POSTURE CHECK REPORT

Name _____ Grade _____ School _____

Date _____ Check made by _____

Side View

Head
   Erect, chin in _____ Somewhat forward _____ Markedly forward _____

Upper Back
   Shoulders back _____ Slightly rounded _____ Rounded _____

Lower Back
   Slight natural curve _____ Moderately curved _____ Hollowed _____

Abdomen
   Flat _____ Slightly protruded _____ Protruding _____

Knees
   Relaxed _____ Slightly back _____ Hyperextended _____

Feet
   Pointed ahead _____ Pointed out somewhat _____ Pointed out _____

Front and Back View

Shoulders
   Level _____ Slightly uneven _____ Considerably uneven _____

Hips
   Level _____ Slightly uneven _____ Considerably uneven _____

Backs of Ankles and Feet
   Heels and ankles
   straight _____ Turned out somewhat _____ Pronated _____

Remarks

Figure 8.12 Individual posture check form

CLASS POSTURE CHECK

Class _____ School _____

Date _____ Teacher _____

Code

Meets good postural standards	1
Slight but definite deviation	2
Marked deviation	3

Name	Side View						Front and Back View			Remarks
	Head and Neck	Upper Back	Lower Back	Abdomen	Knees	Feet	Level of Shoulders	Level of Hips	Feet and Ankles	
1.										
2.										
3.										

Figure 8.13 Class posture check form

compensate proportionally. For example, if the head is forward, other parts of the body would protrude to counterbalance the poor alignment. If one measures the degree by which the head is forward, then one has an estimate of general posture. Measurement can be made with a wand or pointer and can be expressed in terms of the number of inches the earlobe is positioned from the vertical line above the shoulder point. (In a deviated posture, the earlobe is usually forward, if anything.)

Videotaping and Self-Evaluation

An effective device to employ with children who have obvious posture problems is to videotape and play back pictures of children standing, walking, and in other positions. In this way, they can observe themselves and make their assessments using the posture check report. Roughly the same result can be accomplished with an instant camera.

Referral

The perceptive teacher, observing children in study or play, can screen children who need attention because of poor posture. The child should be referred to the nurse, principal, or an appropriate agency for help. After a program has been established, the teacher can help by encouraging the child to fulfill the prescribed remedial exercises.

Posture and the Instructional Process

Posture is both a practice and a subject. The emphasis should be on hints, reminders, and encouragement during all phases of the program. Even the simplest movements present postural challenges that give opportunities for incidental teaching. Strong postural implications can be derived from exercises when the children understand the why of the movement. Values and advantages of correct posture should be stressed. Emphasis should be placed on helping children accept responsibility for their own posture. Nagging and overzealousness on the part of the teacher or parents can have negative results. The following are examples of cues for correct posture:

Feet: "Feet forward. Weight on entire foot."

Lower back and abdomen: "Tuck the seat under. Flatten the tummy."

Upper body: "Shoulder blades flat. Chest high. Raise chest."

Neck and head: "Stand tall. Head high. Eyes ahead."

Walking: "Feet forward. Eyes ahead. Arms relaxed."

Sitting: "Seat back. Sit erect. Bend forward at the hips when working."

REFERENCES AND SUGGESTED READINGS

Arnheim, D. D., & Sinclair, W. A. (1985). *Physical education for special populations: A developmental, adapted, and remedial approach.* Englewood Cliffs, NJ: Prentice-Hall.

Cooper Institute for Aerobics Research. (1992). *The Prudential Fitnessgram Test Administration Manual.* Dallas: Cooper Institute for Aerobics Research.

Dobbins, D. A., Garron, R., & Rarick, G. L. (1981). The motor performance of educable mentally retarded and intellectually normal boys after covariate control for differences in body size. *Research Quarterly, 52*(1), 6–7.

Eden, A. (1975). How to fat-proof your child. *Reader's Digest, 107* (December), 150–152.

Epstein, L. H., et al. (1984). The modification of activity patterns and energy expenditure in obese young girls. *Behavior Therapy, 15*(1): 101–108.

Fait, H. F., & Dunn, J. M. (1984). *Special physical education: Adapted, individualized approach.* Philadelphia: W. B. Saunders.

Foster, G. D., Wadden, T. A., & Brownell, K. D. (1985). Peer-led program for the treatment and prevention of obesity in the schools. *Journal of Consulting and Clinical Psychology, 53*(4), 538–540.

Harter, S. (1985). *Manual for the self-perception profile for children.* Denver: University of Denver.

Horvath, M. (1990). *Physical education and sport for exceptional students.* Dubuque, IA: Wm. C. Brown.

Kalakian, L. H., & Eichstaedt, C. B. (1982). *Developmental adapted physical education.* Minneapolis, MN: Burgess.

Lohman, T. G. (1987). The use of skinfold to estimate body fatness on children and youth. *Journal of Physical Education, Recreation, and Dance, 58*(9), 98–102.

Miller, A. G., & Sullivan, J. V. (1982). *Teaching physical activities to impaired youth.* New York: Wiley.

Reid, G. (1981). Perceptual-motor training: Has the term lost its utility? *JOPERD, 52*(6), 38–39.

Seaman, J. A., & DePauw, K. P. (1982). *The new adapted physical education.* Palo Alto, CA: Mayfield.

Sherrill, C. (1986). *Adapted physical education and recreation.* Dubuque, IA: Wm. C. Brown.

Simon, J., & Smoll, F. (1974). An instrument for assessing children's attitude toward physical activity. *Research Quarterly, 45*(4), 407–415.

Ulrich, D. A. (1983). A comparison of the qualitative motor performance of normal, educable, and trainable mentally retarded students. In R. L. Eason, T. L. Smith, & F. Caron (Eds.), *Adapted physical activity.* Champaign, IL: Human Kinetics.

Varray, A. L., Mercier, J. G., Terral, C. M., & Prefaut, C. G. (1991). Individualized aerobic and high intensity training for asthmatic children in an exercise readaption program. *Chest, 99,* 579–586.

Wade, M. G. (1981). A plea for process-oriented tests. *Motor Development Academy Newsletter,* (Winter), 1–4.

Legal Liability and Proper Care of Students

S chool district personnel, including teaching and nonteaching members, are obligated to exercise ordinary care for the safety of students. This duty is manifested as the ability to anticipate reasonably foreseeable dangers and the responsibility to take necessary precautions to prevent problems from occurring. Failure to do so may cause the district to be the target of lawsuits.

Compared with other subject matter areas, physical education is particularly vulnerable to accidents and resultant injuries. More than 50 percent of all accidents in the school setting occur on the playground and in the gymnasium. Even though schools cannot be held financially accountable for costs associated with treatment of injuries, they can be forced to pay these expenses if the injured party sues and wins judgment. Legal suits are conducted under respective state statutes. Principles underlying legal action are similar, but certain regulations and procedures vary among states. Teachers should acquire a copy of the legal liability policy in their district. Districts usually have a written definition of situations in which teachers can be held liable.

All students have the right to freedom from injury caused by others or due to participation in a program. Courts have ruled that teachers owe their students a duty of care to protect them from harm. Teachers must offer a standard of care that any reasonable and prudent professional with similar training would apply under the given circumstances. A teacher is required to exercise the teaching skill, discretion, and knowledge that members of the profession in good standing normally possess in similar situations. Lawsuits usually occur when citizens believe that this standard of care was not exercised.

Liability is the responsibility to perform a duty to a particular group. It is an obligation to perform in a particular way that is required by law and enforced by court action. Teachers are bound by contract to carry out their duties in a reasonable and prudent manner. Liability is always a legal matter. It must be proved in a court of law that negligence occurred before one can be held liable.

TORTS

In education, a *tort* is concerned with the teacher–student relationship and is a legal wrong that results in direct or indirect injury to another individual or to property. The following legal definition is from *Black's Law Dictionary* (1990):

> [A tort is] a private or civil wrong or injury, other than breach of contract, for which the court will provide a remedy in the form of an action for damages. Three elements of every tort action are: existence of legal duty from defendant to plaintiff, breach of duty, and damage as proximate result.

As the result of a tort, the court can give a monetary reward for damages that occurred. The court can also give a monetary reward for punitive damages if a breach of duty can be established. Usually, the court rewards the offended individual for damages that occurred due to the negligence of the instructor or other responsible individual. Punitive damages are much less common.

NEGLIGENCE AND LIABILITY

Liability is usually concerned with a breach of duty through negligence. Lawyers examine the situation that gave rise to the injury to establish if liability can be determined. Four major points must be established to determine if a teacher was negligent.

1. *Duty.* The first point considered is that of duty owed to the participants. Did the school or teacher owe students a duty of care that implies conforming to certain standards of conduct? When examining duty or breach of duty, the court looks at reasonable care that a mem-

ber of the profession in good standing would provide. In other words, to determine a reasonable standard, the court uses the conduct of other teachers as a standard for comparison.

2. *Breach of duty.* The teacher must commit a breach of duty by failing to conform to the required duty. After it is established that a duty was required, it must be proved that the teacher did not perform that duty. Two situations are possible: (a) the teacher did something that was not supposed to be done (e.g., put boxing gloves on students to resolve their differences), or (b) the teacher did not do something that should have been done (e.g., failed to teach an activity using proper progressions).

3. *Injury.* An injury must occur if liability is to be established. If no injury or harm occurs, there is no liability. Further, it must be proved that the injured party is entitled to compensatory damages for financial loss or physical discomfort.

4. *Proximate cause.* The failure of the teacher to conform to the required standard must be the proximate cause of the resulting injury. It must be proved that the injury was caused by the teacher's breach of duty. It is not enough to prove simply that a breach of duty occurred. It must simultaneously be shown that the injury was a direct result of the teacher's failure to provide a reasonable standard of care.

Foreseeability

A key to the issue of negligence is foreseeability. Courts expect that a trained professional is able to foresee potentially harmful situations. Was it possible for the teacher to predict and anticipate the danger of the harmful act or situation and to take appropriate measures to prevent it from occurring? If the injured party can prove that the teacher should have foreseen the danger involved in an activity or situation (even in part), the teacher will be found negligent for failing to act in a reasonable and prudent manner.

This points out the necessity of examining all activities, equipment, and facilities for possible hazards and sources of accident. As an example, a common game (unfortunately) in many school settings is bombardment, or dodge ball. During the game, a student is hit in the eye by a ball and loses vision in that eye. Was this a foreseeable accident that could have been prevented? Were the balls being used capable of inflicting severe injury? Were students aware of rules that might have prevented this injury? Were the abilities of the students somewhat equal, or were some capable of throwing with such velocity that injury was predictable? Were all students forced to play the game? These questions would likely be considered in court in an attempt to prove that the teacher should have been able to predict the overly dangerous situation.

TYPES OF NEGLIGENCE

Negligence is defined by the court as conduct that falls below a standard of care established to protect others from unreasonable risk or harm. Several types of negligence can be categorized.

Malfeasance

Malfeasance occurs when the teacher does something improper by committing an act that is unlawful and wrongful, with no legal basis (often referred to as an *act of commission*). Malfeasance can be illustrated by the following incident. A male student misbehaved on numerous occasions. In desperation, the teacher gave the student a choice of punishment—a severe spanking in front of the class or running many laps around the field. The student chose the former and suffered physical and emotional damage. Even though the teacher gave the student a choice whereby he could have avoided the paddling, the teacher is still liable for any physical or emotional harm caused.

Misfeasance

Misfeasance occurs when the teacher follows the proper procedures but does not perform according to the required standard of conduct. Misfeasance is based on performance of the proper action, but not up to the required standard. It is usually the subpar performance of an act that might have been otherwise lawfully done. An example would be the teacher's offering to spot a student during a tumbling routine and then not doing the spotting properly. If the student is injured due to a faulty spot, the teacher can be held liable.

Nonfeasance

Nonfeasance is based on lack of action in carrying out a duty. This is usually an *act of omission:* The teacher knew the proper procedures but failed to follow them. Teachers can be found negligent if they act or fail to act. Understanding and carrying out proper procedures and duties in a manner

befitting members of the profession is essential. In contrast to the misfeasance example, nonfeasance occurs when a teacher knows that it is necessary to spot certain gymnastic routines but fails to do so. Courts expect teachers to behave with more skill and insight than parents (Strickland, Phillip, & Phillips, 1976). Teachers are expected to behave with greater competency because they have been educated to give students a higher standard of professional care than parents.

Contributory Negligence

The situation is different when the injured student is partially or wholly at fault. Students are expected to exercise sensible care and to follow directions or regulations designed to protect them from injury. Improper behavior by the injured party that causes the accident is usually ruled to be *contributory negligence,* because the injured party contributed to the resulting harm. This responsibility is directly related to the maturity, ability, and experience of the child. For example, most states have laws specifying that a child under 7 years of age is incapable of contributory negligence (Baley & Matthews, 1984). To illustrate contributory negligence, assume that a teacher has thoroughly explained safety rules to be followed while hitting softballs. As students begin to practice, one of them runs through a restricted area that is well marked and is hit by a bat. Depending on the age and maturity of the child, the possibility is strong that the student will be held liable for such action.

Comparative or Shared Negligence

Under the doctrine of comparative negligence, the injured party can recover only if found to be less negligent than the defendant (the teacher). Where statutes apply, the amount of recovery is generally reduced in proportion to the injured party's participation in the circumstances leading to the injury.

COMMON DEFENSES AGAINST NEGLIGENCE

Negligence must be proved in a court of law. Many times, teachers are negligent in carrying out their duties, yet the injured party does not take the case to court. If a teacher is sued, some of the following defenses are used in an attempt to show that the teacher's action was not the primary cause of the accident.

Act of God

The act of God defense places the cause of injury on forces beyond the control of the teacher or the school. The defense is made that it was impossible to predict an unsafe condition, but through an act of God, the injury occurred. Typical acts would be a gust of wind that blew over a volleyball standard or a cloudburst of rain that made a surface slick. The act of God defense can be used only in cases in which the injury still would have occurred even though reasonable and prudent action had been taken.

Proximate Cause

This defense attempts to prove that the accident was not caused by the negligence of the teacher. There must be a close relationship between the breach of duty by the teacher and the injury. This is a common defense in cases dealing with proper supervision. The student is participating in an activity supervised by the teacher. When the teacher leaves the playing area to get a cup of coffee, the student is injured. The defense lawyer will try to show that the accident would have occurred regardless of whether or not the teacher was there.

Assumption of Risk

Clearly, physical education is a high-risk activity when compared with most other curriculum areas. The participant assumes the risk of an activity when choosing to be part of that activity. The assumption of risk defense is seldom used by physical education teachers because students are not often allowed to choose to participate or not participate. An instructor for an elective program that allows students to choose desired units of instruction might find this a better defense than one who teaches a totally required program. Athletic and sport club participation is by choice, and players must assume a greater risk in activities such as football and gymnastics.

Contributory Negligence

Contributory negligence is often used by the defense in an attempt to convince the court that the injured party acted in a manner that was abnormal. In other words, the injured individual did not act in a manner that was typical of students of similar age and maturity. The defense attempts to demonstrate that the activity or equipment in question was used for years with no record of accident. A case is made based on the manner of presentation—how students were taught to act in a safe manner—and that the injured student acted outside the parameters of safe conduct. A key point in this defense is whether the activity was suitable for the age and maturity level of the participants.

AREAS OF RESPONSIBILITY

A two-tiered approach for analyzing injuries is useful for determining responsibility. The first tier includes the duties that the administration must assume in support of the program. The second tier defines the duties of the instructor or staff member charged with teaching or supervising students. Each party has a role to fill, but some overlap occurs. The following example illustrates the differences.

A student is hurt while performing a tumbling stunt. A lawsuit ensues charging the teacher with negligence for not following safe procedures. The administration could also be included in the suit, being charged with negligence for hiring an incompetent (not qualified) instructor. The two levels of responsibility should be considered when delegating responsibility because:

1. They identify different functions and responsibilities of the teaching staff and administration.

2. They provide a framework for reducing injuries and improving safety procedures.

3. They provide perspective for following legal precedents.

In the described responsibilities that follow, both administrative and instructional duties are presented.

Supervision

All activities in a school setting must be supervised, including recess, lunch times, and field trips. The responsibilities of the school are critical if supervision is to function properly.

Administration

Two levels are identified in supervision: general and specific. General supervision (e.g., playground duty) refers to broad coverage, when students are not under direct control of a teacher or a designated individual. A plan of supervision should be made, designating the areas to be covered and including where and how the supervisor should rotate. This plan, kept in the principal's office, should cover rules of conduct governing student behavior. Rules should be posted prominently on bulletin boards, especially in classrooms. In addition to the plan, administrators must select qualified personnel, provide necessary training, and monitor the plan properly.

The general supervisor must be concerned primarily with student behavior, focusing on the student's right to a relaxing recreational experience. Supervisors should observe the area, looking for breaches of discipline, particularly when an individual or group "picks on" another youngster. The supervisor needs to look for protruding sprinkler heads, broken glass, and debris on the play area. If it becomes necessary to leave the area, a qualified substitute must be found to prevent the area from going unsupervised.

Staff

General supervision is necessary during recess, before and after school, during lunch hour break, and during certain other sessions where instruction is not offered. The supervisor should know the school's plan for supervision as well as the emergency care procedures to follow in case of an accident. Supervision is a positive act that requires the supervisor to be actively involved and moving throughout the area. The number of supervisors should be determined by the type of activity, the size of the area, and the number and age of the students.

Specific supervision requires that the instructor be with a certain group of students (i.e., a class). An example is spotting students who are performing challenging gymnastic activities. If certain pieces of apparatus require special care and proper use, the teacher should have rules and regulations posted near the apparatus (for upper-grade children). Students should be made aware of the rules and should receive appropriate instruction and guidance in applying the rules. When rules are modified, they should be rewritten in proper form. There is no substitute for documentation when the need to defend policies and approaches arises.

When teaching, arrange and teach the class so that all students are always in view. This implies supervising from the perimeter of the area. Teachers who are at the center of the student group with many students behind them will find it impossible to supervise a class safely and effectively. Equipment and apparatus should not go unsupervised at any time when left accessible to students in the area. An example would be equipment that is left on the playing field between classes. If other students in the area have easy access to the equip-

ment, they may use it in an unsafe manner, and the teacher can be found liable if an injury occurs.

Teachers should not agree to supervise activities in which they are unqualified to anticipate possible hazards. If this situation arises, a written memo should be sent to the department head or principal stating such lack of insight and qualification. Teachers should maintain a copy for their files.

Merriman (1993) offers five recommendations to assure that adequate supervision occurs:

1. The supervisor must be in the immediate vicinity (within sight and hearing).

2. If required to leave, the supervisor must have an adequate replacement in place before departing. Adequate replacements do not include paraprofessionals, student teachers, custodial help, or untrained teachers.

3. Supervision procedures must be preplanned and incorporated into daily lessons.

4. Supervision procedures should include what to observe, listen for, where to stand for the most effective view, and what to do if a problem arises.

5. Supervision requires that age, maturity, and skill ability of participants must always be considered, as must be the inherent risk of the activity.

Instruction

Instructional responsibility rests primarily with the teacher, but administrative personnel have certain defined functions.

Administration

The administration should review and approve the curricular plan. The curriculum should be reviewed regularly to assure that it is current and updated. Activities included in the curriculum should be based on contributions they make to the growth and development of youngsters. It makes little sense in a court of law to say that an activity was included "for the fun of it" or "because students liked it." Instead, make sure activities in the curriculum are included because they meet program objectives.

Administrators are obligated to support the program with adequate finances. The principal and higher administrators should visit the program periodically. Familiarity with program content and operation obviates the possibility that practices were occurring without adequate administrative supervision.

Instructional Staff

With regard to instruction, the teacher has a duty to protect students from unreasonable physical or mental harm. This includes avoiding any acts or omissions that might cause such harm. The teacher is educated, experienced, and skilled in physical education and must be able to foresee situations that could be harmful.

The major area of concern involving instruction is whether the student received adequate instruction before or during activity participation. Adequate instruction means (a) teaching children how to perform activities correctly and use equipment and apparatus properly, and (b) teaching youngsters necessary safety precautions. If instructions are given, they must be correct, understandable, and include proper technique, or the instructor can be held liable. The risk involved in an activity must be communicated to the learner.

The age and maturity level of students play an important role in the selection of activities. Younger students require more care, instructions that are easy to comprehend, and clear restrictions in the name of safety. Some students have a lack of appropriate fear in activities, and the teacher must be aware of this when discussing safety factors. A very young child may have little concern about performing a high-risk activity if an instructor is nearby. This places much responsibility on the instructor to give adequate instruction and supervision.

Careful planning is a necessity. Written curriculum guides and lesson plans should offer a well-prepared approach that can withstand scrutiny and examination by other teachers and administrators. Written lesson plans should include proper sequence and progression of skill. Teachers are on defensible grounds if they can show that the progression of activities was based on presentations designed by experts and was followed carefully during the teaching act. District and state guidelines enforcing instructional sequences and restricted activities should be checked closely.

Proper instruction demands that students not be forced to participate. If a youngster is required to perform an activity unwillingly, the teacher may be open to a lawsuit. In a lawsuit dealing with stunts and tumbling (Appenzeller, 1970), the court held the teacher liable when a student claimed that she was not given adequate instruction in how to perform a stunt called "roll over two." The teacher was held liable because the student claimed she was forced to try the stunt before adequate instruction was offered. Gymnastics and tumbling are areas in which lawsuits are prevalent due to a lack of adequate instruction. Posting the proper sequence of skills and lead-up activities may be useful to ensure that they have been presented properly. Teachers need to tread the line carefully between helpful encouragement and forcing students to try new activities.

For teachers who incorporate punishment as a part of the instructional process, the consequences of its use should be examined carefully before implementation. Physical punishment that brings about permanent or long-lasting damage is certainly indefensible. The punishment used must be in line with the physical maturity and health of the student involved. A teacher's practice of having students perform laps when they have misbehaved might go unchallenged for years. However, what if an asthmatic student or a student with congenital heart disease is asked to run and suffers injury or illness? What if the student is running unsupervised and is injured from a fall or suffers heat exhaustion? In these examples, defending such punitive practices would be difficult. Making students perform physical activity for misbehavior is indefensible under any circumstance. If a child is injured while performing physical punishment, teachers are usually found liable and held responsible for the injury.

The following points can help teachers plan for meaningful and safe instruction:

1. Sequence all activities in units of instruction and develop written lesson plans. Many problems occur when snap judgments are made under the daily pressure and strain of teaching.

2. Scrutinize high-risk activities to assure that all safety procedures have been implemented. If in doubt, discuss the activities with other experienced teachers and administrators.

3. Activities used in the curriculum must be within the developmental limits of the students. Since the range of maturity and development of youngsters in a class is usually wide, activities may be beyond the ability level of some students.

4. If students' grades are based on the number of activities in which they participate, some students may feel forced to try all activities. Teachers should make it clear to students that the choice to participate belongs to them. When they are afraid of getting hurt, they can elect not to perform an activity.

5. Include in written lesson plans necessary safety equipment. The lesson plan should detail how equipment should be arranged, the placement

of mats, and where the instructor will carry out supervision.

6. If a student claims injury or brings a note from parents requesting that the student not participate in physical activity, the teacher must honor the communication. Excuses are almost always given at the start of the period when the teacher is busy with many other duties (e.g., getting equipment ready, taking roll, and opening lockers). It is difficult to make a thoughtful judgment at this time. The school nurse is qualified to make these judgments when they relate to health and should be used in that capacity. If the excuses continue over a long period of time, the teacher or nurse should have a conference with the parents to rectify the situation.

7. Make sure that the activities included in the instructional process are in line with the available equipment and facilities. An example is the amount of space available. If a soccer lead-up activity is brought indoors because of inclement weather, it may no longer be a safe and appropriate activity.

8. If spotting is required for safe completion of activities, it should always be done by the instructor or by trained students. Teaching students how to spot is as important as teaching them physical skills. Safe conduct must be learned.

9. If students are working independently at stations, carefully constructed and written task cards can help eliminate unsafe practices.

10. Have a written emergency care plan posted in the gymnasium. This plan should be approved by health care professionals and should be followed to the letter when an injury occurs.

EQUIPMENT AND FACILITIES

School responsibility for equipment and facilities is required for both noninstructional and class use.

Administration

The principal and the custodian should oversee the fields and playground equipment that are used for recess and outside activities. Students should be instructed to report broken and unsafe equipment, as well as hazards (glass, cans, rocks), to the principal's office. If equipment is faulty, it should be removed from the area. A regular inspection of equipment and facilities, preferably by the physical education specialist, should be instituted, perhaps weekly. If a spe-

cialist is not employed, the inspection will have to be performed by the principal or the custodian. Results of the inspection should be filed with the school district safety committee. Replacement of sawdust, sand, or other shock-absorbing material must be done regularly.

Administrators should develop a written checklist of equipment and apparatus for the purpose of recording scheduled safety inspections. The date of inspection should be noted to show that inspection occurs at regular intervals. If a potentially dangerous situation exists, rules or warnings should be posted so that students and teachers are made aware of the risk before participation is allowed.

Proper installation of equipment is critical. Climbing equipment and other equipment that must be anchored should be installed by a reputable firm that guarantees its work. When examining apparatus, inspection of the installation is important. Maintenance of facilities is also important. Grass should be kept short and the grounds inspected for debris. Holes in the ground should be filled and loose gravel removed. A proper finish that prevents excessive slipping should be used on indoor floors. Shower rooms should have a roughened floor finish applied to prevent falls when the floors are wet.

Equipment and facilities used in the physical education program must allow safe participation in activity. The choice of apparatus and equipment should be based on the growth and developmental levels of the students. For example, allowing elementary school children to use a horizontal ladder that was designed for high school students may result in a fall that causes injury. Hazards found on playing fields need to be repaired and eliminated. The legal concept of an *attractive nuisance* should be understood. This implies that some piece of equipment or apparatus, usually left unsupervised, was so attractive to children that they could not be expected to avoid it. When an injury occurs, even though students may have been using the apparatus incorrectly, the teachers and the school are often held liable because the attractive nuisance should have been removed from the area when unsupervised.

Instructional Staff

Indoor facilities are of primary concern to physical education instructors. While the administration is charged with overall responsibility for facilities and equipment, including periodic inspection, the instructor should make a regular safety inspection of the instructional area. If corrective action is needed, the principal or other designated administrator should be notified *in writing*. Verbal notification is not enough, since it offers little legal protection to the instructor.

Facilities should be used in a safe manner. Often, the side and end lines of playing fields for sports such as football, soccer, and field hockey are placed too close to walls, curbings, or fences. The boundaries should be moved to allow adequate room for deceleration, even though the size of the playing area may be reduced. In the gymnasium, students should not be asked to run to a line that is close to a wall. Another common hazard is baskets positioned too close to the playing area. The poles that support the baskets must be padded.

Proper use of equipment and apparatus is important. Regardless of the state of equipment repair, if it is misused, it may result in an injury. Students must receive instruction in the proper use of equipment and apparatus *before* they are issued to the students and used. All safety instruction should be included in the written lesson plan to ensure that all points are covered.

Equipment should be purchased on the basis of quality and safety as well as potential use. Many lawsuits occur because of unsafe equipment and apparatus. The liability for such equipment may rest with the manufacturer, but this has to be proved, which means that the teacher must state, in writing, the exact specifications of the desired equipment. The process of bidding for lower-priced items may result in the purchase of less safe equipment. If teachers have specified proper equipment in writing, however, the possibility of their being held liable for injury is reduced.

THE SPORTS PROGRAM

A common problem for school administrators with elementary school sports programs is providing qualified coaches. The administration should set minimum requirements for coaches and assure that incompetent individuals are removed from coaching duties. When students are involved in extracurricular activity, teachers (coaches) are responsible for the safe conduct of activities. The following areas often give rise to lawsuits if they are not handled carefully.

Mismatching Opponents

A common error that gives rise to lawsuits is the mismatching of students on the basis of size and ability. Just because the competitors are the same sex and choose to participate does not absolve the instructor

of liability if an injury occurs. The question that courts examine is whether an effort was made to match students according to height, weight, and ability. Courts are less understanding about mismatching in the physical education setting compared with an athletic contest, but mismatching is a factor that should be avoided in any situation.

Waiver Forms

Participants in extracurricular activities should be required to sign a responsibility waiver form. The form should explain the risks involved in voluntary participation and discuss briefly the types of injuries that have occurred in the past during practice and competition. Supervisors should remember that waiver slips do not waive the rights of participants, and that teachers and coaches still can be found liable if injuries occur. The waiver form does communicate clearly, however, the risks involved and may be a strong "assumption of risk" defense.

Medical Examinations

Participants must have a medical examination before participating. Records of the examination should be kept on file and should be identified prominently when physical restrictions or limitations exist. It is common to "red dot" the folders of students who have a history of medical problems. Students must not be allowed to participate unless they purchase medical insurance, and evidence of such coverage should be kept in the folders of athletic participants.

Preseason Conditioning

Preseason conditioning should be undertaken in a systematic and progressive fashion. Starting the season with a mile run for time makes little sense if students have not been preconditioned. Coaches should be aware of guidelines dealing with heat and humidity. For example, in Arizona, guidelines are to avoid strenuous activity when the temperature exceeds 85°F and the humidity exceeds 40 percent (Stone, 1977). When these conditions are exceeded, running is curtailed to 10 minutes and active games to 30 minutes. Drinking water should be available and given to students on demand.

Transportation of Students

Whenever students are transported, teachers are responsible for their safety both en route and during the activity. Transportation liability can be avoided by not providing transportation, but instead requiring participants to meet at the site of the event (Pittman, 1993). If the school must provide transportation, licensed drivers and school-approved vehicles should always be used. Travel plans should include official approval from the appropriate school administrator. One special note: If the driver receives pay or reimbursement for the trip, the possibility of being held liable for injury increases dramatically. To make the matter worse, many insurance policies do not cover drivers who receive compensation for transporting students. If teachers are transporting students and receiving reimbursement, a special insurance rider that provides liability coverage for this situation should be purchased.

SAFETY

The major thrust of safety should be to prevent situations that cause accidents. It is estimated that over 70 percent of injuries that occur in sport and related activities could be prevented through proper safety procedures. On the other hand, some accidents occur despite precautions, and proper emergency procedures should be established to cope with any situation. A comprehensive study of injuries received in sport and related activities was conducted by the U.S. Consumer Product Safety Commission (1992). This study involved a network of computers in 119 hospital emergency rooms that channeled injury data to a central point. The sports and activities that produced the most injuries were, in order, football, touch football, baseball, basketball, gymnastics, and skiing. The facility that produced the most disabling injuries was the swimming pool.

Learning to recognize potential high-risk situations is an important factor in preventing accidents. Teachers must possess a clear understanding of the hazards and potential dangers of an activity before they can establish controls. Instructors must not assume that participants are aware of the dangers and risks involved in various activities. Students must be told of all dangers and risks before participation.

Guidelines for Safety

1. Inservice sessions in safety should be administered by experienced and knowledgeable teachers. Department heads may be responsible for the training, or outside experts can be employed to undertake the responsibility. Giving in-district credit to participating teachers offers strong indication that the district is concerned about using proper safety techniques.

2. Medical records should be reviewed at the start of the school year. Atypical students should be identified and noted within each class listing before the first instructional day. If necessary, the teacher or school nurse can call the doctor of a disabled or activity-restricted student to inquire about the situation and discuss special needs. Physical education teachers should be notified by the classroom teacher or school nurse about youngsters who have special (e.g., epilepsy) or temporary problems (e.g., medication).

3. Throughout the school year, safety orientations should be conducted with students. Discussions should include potentially dangerous situations, class conduct, and rules for proper use of equipment and apparatus. Teachers should urge students to report any conditions that might cause an accident.

4. Safety rules for specific units of instruction should be discussed at the onset of each unit. Rules should be posted and brought to the attention of students regularly. Posters and bulletin boards can promote safety in an enjoyable and stimulating manner.

5. If students are to serve as instructional aides, they should be trained. Aides must understand the techniques of spotting, for example, and must receive proper instruction if they are to be a part of the educational process. Caution must be used when using student aides because teachers are still responsible even if an aide performed a duty incorrectly.

6. Instructional practices need to be monitored for possible hazards. For example, students in competitive situations should be matched by size, maturity, and ability. Proper instruction necessary for safe participation should occur prior to activity. Instructors should receive a competence check to ensure that they are adequately trained to give instruction in various activities. The instructional area should be properly prepared for safe participation; if the area is lacking necessary apparatus and safety devices, instruction should be modified to meet safety standards.

7. An inventory of equipment and apparatus should include a safety checklist. Whenever necessary, equipment in need of repair should be sent to proper agents. If the cost of repair is

Inspecting equipment for safety

greater than 40 percent of the replacement cost, discarding the equipment or apparatus is usually a more economical choice.

8. When an injury occurs, it should be recorded and a report placed in the student's file. An injury should also be filed by type of injury, such as ankle sprain or broken arm. The report should list the activity and the conditions to facilitate analysis at regular intervals. The analysis may show that injuries are occurring regularly during a specific activity or on a certain piece of equipment. This process can give direction for creating a safer environment or for defending the safety record of a sport, activity, or piece of equipment.

9. Teachers need to maintain up-to-date first-aid and CPR certification. Administrators should ensure that teachers meet these standards and should provide training sessions when necessary.

The Safety Committee

Safety should be publicized regularly throughout the school, and a mechanism should exist that allows students, parents, and teachers to voice concerns about unsafe conditions. A safety committee can meet at regular intervals to establish safety policies, rule on requests for allowing high-risk activities, and analyze serious injuries that have occurred in the school district. This committee should develop safety rules that apply district-

wide to all teachers. It may determine that certain activities involve too high a risk for the return in student benefit. Acceptable criteria for sport equipment and apparatus may be established by the committee.

The safety committee should include one or more high-level administrators, physical education teachers, health officers (nurse), parents, and students. Remember that school administrators are usually indicted when lawsuits occur, because they are held responsible for program content and curriculum. Their representation on the safety committee is therefore important. Students on the committee may be aware of possible hazards, and parents may often voice concerns overlooked by teachers.

The Emergency Care Plan

Before any emergency arises, teachers should prepare themselves by learning about special health and physical conditions of students (Gray, 1993). Most schools have a method for identifying students with special health problems. If a student has a problem that may require treatment, a consent-to-treat form should be on file in case the parent or guardian is unavailable. Necessary first-aid materials and supplies should be available in a kit and be readily accessible.

Establishing procedures for emergency care and notification of parents in case of injury is of utmost importance in providing a high standard of care for students. To plan properly for emergency care, all physical education teachers should have first-aid training. *First aid* is the immediate and temporary care given at an emergency before a physician is available. Its purpose is to save life, prevent aggravation of injuries, and alleviate severe suffering. If there is evidence of life-threatening bleeding or if the victim is unconscious or has stopped breathing, the teacher must administer first aid. When already injured persons may be further injured if they are not moved, then moving them is permissible. As a general rule, however, an injured person should not be moved unless absolutely necessary. If there is indication of back or neck injury, the head must be immobilized and should not be moved without the use of a spine board. Remember, the purpose of first aid is to save life. The emergency care plan should consist of the following steps:

1. *Administration of first aid to the injured student is the number one priority.* Treat only life-threatening injuries. The school nurse should be called to the scene of the accident immediately.

Emergency care procedures should indicate whether the student can be moved and in what fashion. It is critical that the individual applying first aid avoid aggravating the injury.

2. *Notify parents as soon as possible when emergency care is required.* Each student's file should list home and emergency telephone numbers where parents can be reached. If possible, the school should have an arrangement with local emergency facilities so that a paramedic unit can be called immediately to the scene of a serious accident.

3. *In most cases, the student should be released to a parent or a designated representative.* Policies for transportation of injured students should be established and documented.

4. *A student accident report should be completed promptly while the details of the accident are clear.* Figure 9.1 is an example of an accident form that covers the necessary details. The teacher and principal should both retain copies and additional copies should be sent to the administrative office.

PERSONAL PROTECTION: MINIMIZING THE EFFECTS OF A LAWSUIT

In spite of proper care, injuries do occur, and lawsuits may be initiated. Two courses of action are necessary to counteract the effects of a suit.

Liability Insurance

Teachers may be protected by school district liability insurance. Usually, however, teachers must purchase their own policy. Most policies provide for legal services to contest a suit and will pay indemnity up to the limits of the policy (liability coverage of $500,000 is most common). Most policies give the insurance company the right to settle out of court. Unfortunately, when this occurs, some may infer that the teacher was guilty even though the circumstances indicate otherwise. Insurance companies usually settle out of court to avoid the excessive legal fees required to try to win the case in court.

Recordkeeping

The second course of action is to keep complete records of accidents. Many lawsuits occur months or even years after the accident, when memory of the situation is fuzzy. Accident reports should be filled out immediately after an injury. The teacher should take care to provide no evidence, oral or written, that others could use in a court of law. Do not attempt to make a diagnosis or to specify the supposed cause of the accident in the report.

If newspaper reporters probe for details, the teacher should avoid describing the accident beyond the basic facts. When discussing the accident with administrators, only the facts recorded on the accident report should be discussed. Remember that school records can be subpoenaed in court proceedings. The point here is not to dissemble, but to be cautious and avoid self-incrimination.

Safety and Liability Checklist

The following checklist can be used to monitor the physical education environment. Any situations that deviate from safe and legally sound practices should be rectified immediately.

Supervision and Instruction

1. Are teachers adequately trained in all of the activities that they are teaching?

2. Do all teachers have evidence of a necessary level of first-aid training?

3. When supervising, do personnel have access to a written plan of areas to be observed and responsibilities to be carried out?

4. Have students been warned of potential dangers and risks, and advised of rules and the reasons for the rules?

5. Are safety rules posted near areas of increased risk?

6. Are lesson plans written? Do they include provisions for proper instruction, sequence of activities, and safety? Are all activities taught listed in the district curriculum guide?

7. When a new activity is introduced, are safety precautions and instructions for correct skill performance always communicated to the class?

8. Are the activities taught in the program based on sound curriculum principles? Could the activities and units of instruction be defended on the basis of their educational contributions?

9. Do the methods of instruction recognize individual differences among students, and are the necessary steps taken to meet the needs of all students, regardless of sex, ability, or disability?

10. Are substitute teachers given clear and comprehensive lesson plans so that they can maintain the scope and sequence of instruction?

STUDENT ACCIDENT REPORT

_____ SCHOOL

In all cases, this form should be filed through the school nurse and signed by the principal of the school. The original will be forwarded to the superintendent's office, where it will be initialed and sent to the head nurse. The second copy will be retained by the principal or the school nurse. The third copy should be given to the physical education teacher if accident is related.

Name of injured _____ Address _____

Phone _____ Grade _____ Home room _____ Age _____

Parents of injured _____

Place of accident _____ Date of accident _____

Hour _____ A.M. P.M. Date reported _____ By whom _____

Parent contract attempted at _____ A.M. P.M. Parent contracted at _____ A.M. P.M.

DESCRIBE ACCIDENT, GIVING SPECIFIC LOCATION AND CONDITION OF PREMISES _____

_____

NATURE OF INJURY _____
(Describe in detail)

CARE GIVEN OR ACTION TAKEN BY NURSE OR OTHERS _____

_____

REASON INJURED PERSON WAS ON PREMISES _____
(Activity at time—i.e., lunch, physical education, etc.)

STAFF MEMBER RESPONSIBLE FOR STUDENT SUPERVISION AT TIME OF ACCIDENT _____

_____

IS STUDENT COVERED BY SCHOOL-SPONSORED ACCIDENT INSURANCE? _____ Yes _____ No

MEDICAL CARE RECOMMENDED _____ Yes _____ No

WHERE TAKEN AFTER ACCIDENT _____
(Specify home, physician, or hospital, giving name and address)

BY WHOM _____ AT WHAT TIME _____ A.M. P.M.

FOLLOW-UP BY NURSE TO BE SENT TO CENTRAL HEALTH OFFICE

REMEDIATIVE MEASURES TAKEN _____
(Attach individual remarks if necessary)

School _____ Principal _____

Date _____ Nurse _____

On the back of this sheet, list all persons familiar with the circumstances of the accident, giving name, address, telephone number, age, and location with respect to the accident.

Figure 9.1 Sample accident report form

11. Is the student evaluation plan based on actual performance and objective data rather than on favoritism or arbitrary and capricious standards?

12. Is appropriate dress required for students? This does not imply uniforms, only dress (including shoes) that ensures the safety of the student.

13. When necessary for safety, are students grouped according to ability level, size, or age?

14. Is the class left unsupervised for teacher visits to the office, lounge, or bathroom? Is one teacher ever asked to supervise two or more classes at the same time?

15. If students are used as teacher aides or to spot others, are they given proper instruction and training?

Equipment and Facilities

1. Is all equipment inspected regularly and are the inspection results recorded on a form and sent to the proper administrators?

2. Is a log maintained recording the regular occurrence of an inspection, the equipment in need of repair, and when repairs were made?

3. Are "attractive nuisances" eliminated from the gymnasium and playing field?

4. Are specific safety rules posted on facilities and near equipment?

5. Are the following inspected periodically?
   a. playing field for presence of glass, rocks, and metal objects
   b. fasteners holding equipment, such as climbing ropes, horizontal bars, or baskets
   c. goals for games, such as football, soccer, and field hockey, to be sure that they are fastened securely
   d. padded areas, such as goal supports

6. Are mats placed under apparatus from which a fall is possible?

7. Are playing fields arranged so participants will not run into each other or be hit by a ball from another game?

8. Are landing pits filled and maintained properly?

Emergency Care

1. Is there a written procedure for emergency care?

2. Is a person properly trained in first aid available immediately following an accident?

3. Are emergency telephone numbers readily accessible?

4. Are telephone numbers of parents available?

5. Is an up-to-date first-aid kit available? Is ice immediately available?

6. Are health folders maintained that list restrictions, allergies, and health problems of students?

7. Are health folders reviewed by instructors on a regular basis?

8. Are students participating in extracurricular activities required to have insurance? Is the policy number recorded?

9. Is there a plan for treating injuries that involves the local paramedics?

10. Are accident reports filed promptly and analyzed regularly?

Transportation of Students

1. Have parents been informed that their students will be transported off campus?

2. Are detailed travel plans approved by the site administrator and kept on file?

3. Are school vehicles used whenever possible?

4. Are drivers properly licensed and vehicles insured?

5. If teachers or parents use their vehicles to transport students, are the students, driver, and car owner covered by an insurance rider purchased by the school district?

REFERENCES AND SUGGESTED READINGS

Appenzeller, H. (1970). *From the gym to the jury*. Charlottesville, VA: Michie Company Law Publishing.

Arnold, D. E. (1983). *Legal considerations in the administration of public school physical education and athletic programs*. Springfield, IL: Charles C. Thomas.

Baley, J. A., & Matthews, D. L. (1984). *Law and liability in athletics, physical education, and recreation*. Boston: Allyn & Bacon.

Black, H. C. (1990). *Black's Law Dictionary* (6th ed.). St. Paul, MN: West.

Blucker, J. A., & Pell, S. W. (1986). Legal and ethical issues. *Journal of Physical Education, Recreation, and Dance, 57,* 19–21.

Dougherty, N. J. (Ed.). (1987). *Principles of safety in physical education and sport.* Reston, VA: AAHPERD.

Gray, G. R. (1993). Providing adequate medical care to program participants. *Journal of Physical Education, Recreation, and Dance, 64*(2), 56–57.

Institute for the Study of Educational Policy, Law Division. (1986). *School athletics and the law.* Seattle: University of Washington Press.

Kaiser, R. A. (1984). *Liability and law in recreation, parks, and sports.* Englewood Cliffs, NJ: Prentice-Hall.

Merriman, J. (1993). Supervision in sport and physical activity. *Journal of Physical Education, Recreation, and Dance, 64*(2), 20–23.

Pittman, A. J. (1993). Safe transportation—A driving concern. *Journal of Physical Education, Recreation, and Dance, 64*(2), 53–55.

Stone, W. J. (1977). Running and running tests for Arizona school children. *Arizona JOHPERD, 21,* 15–17.

Strickland, R., Phillip, J. F., & Phillips, W. R. (1976). *Avoiding teacher malpractice.* New York: Hawthorn.

U.S. Consumer Product Safety Commission. (1992). *Handbook for public playground safety.* Washington, DC: U.S. Government Printing Office.

van der Smissen, B. (1990). *Legal liability and risk management of public and private entities.* Cincinnati, OH: Anderson.

CHAPTER 9

Evaluation of Students and Instruction

*T*he purpose of evaluation is to determine whether progress is being made toward learning objectives established for students. Evaluation should review all phases of education including pupil progress, teacher performance, and program effectiveness. Student evaluation can be formal or informal and can focus on individual or group progress. Teacher evaluation can be used to improve the instructional process or to secure data for measuring teacher effectiveness. Program evaluation is used to examine the total program or selected program areas. Approaches and curriculum that are effective need to be retained and enhanced, and what is deficient needs to be corrected.

EVALUATION OF STUDENTS: PROCESS OR PRODUCT?

Two types of evaluation pertain to students: process evaluation and product evaluation. Process evaluation relates to the performance of general movement patterns with emphasis on correct technique. The form used to execute the movement is the point of focus rather than the outcome of the skill performed. In contrast, product evaluation focuses on performance outcomes in terms of measurable increments of what learners accomplish. For example, if product evaluation is applied to fundamental ball skills, the concern is with how far the ball is thrown or how many times it is caught without a miss. On the other hand, process evaluation focuses on the quality of the throwing pattern and teaching the student proper form.

This leads to several questions: Should physical education focus on a product, with higher education aimed to prepare teachers to teach toward such outcomes? Or, should it focus on the process of skill performance and physical activity and produce teachers capable of reinforcing such objectives? Is the process of skill development and participation in regular physical activity the objective of physical education? Is physical education similar to academic education areas? Should physical education develop a model of instruction and evaluation that compares to math, science, and other disciplines? Physical education has a unique role in the school curriculum. Nowhere else can students receive skill instruction and physical activity. Academics can teach character, knowledge, social skills, and the like, but only physical education can accomplish these unique outcomes. Physical education doesn't have to be like academics; in fact, it is important because it is different. How does physical education differ?

- Physical education doesn't have an absolute and exact product. Knowledge is based on the building block theory, that new learning is based on previously acquired facts. For example, math facts are necessary to perform higher math manipulations. Physical education differs; a basic set of skills are learned and refined throughout the school years. For example, the basic skill of throwing is taught in elementary school and continues to be repeated and refined each year thereafter. After the basic skill is learned, little new is taught about throwing; emphasis is placed on repetition and refinement.

- Perfection (of skill performance) does not occur in physical education. This contrasts with most academic areas that demand accuracy and correctness. New knowledge is based on previously learned information, which is based on a commonly accepted body of information. This contrasts with physical education, where correct performance is impossible to predict and errors are expected. Even the best of athletes miss half of the baskets they shoot or make an out in baseball about 70 percent of the time. Often, physical educators teach as though perfection were a realistic and reason-

able goal. Youngsters may begin to believe that the product or outcome (such as making a basket) is more important than the process of performing the skill correctly. Teachers encourage such thinking by reinforcing skill attempts that are correct while failing to comment on the key points of the skill.

- Skill refinement is not synonymous with performance improvement. Teachers have been taught to evaluate their effectiveness based on how many students reach institutionally based outcomes, such as the number of students who can make a number of baskets or jump a rope a certain number of times. Teachers have been willing to settle for the ruse of achieving skill performance outcomes. Many have even written such outcomes with the intent of getting all students to reach them. Unfortunately, they have attempted to guarantee a product that may not be achievable. For example, when adults hire a professional instructor to improve their golf swing, they do so without guarantees. Creditable golf pros will not guarantee a reduction in golf scores. Rather, they will assure their students that they can improve their swing which, over time, may result in improved scores. They are unable to control the genetic makeup or the psychological willingness of individuals to change and improve. What can be guaranteed is that they will teach with enthusiasm, that they will be knowledgeable, and that they will devote the time necessary to refine a skill. These expectations should be similar for teachers; other expectations may be unreasonable and unachievable.

- The process may be the product of physical education. The *product* in physical education may be the *process* of participation and performance. Teachers help students if they teach them to perform skills correctly and participate in regular activity. This is the product of physical education; graduating students who feel competent and willing to perform skills that assure a lifetime of activity. Leaving students a legacy of knowing how to live an active lifestyle is more important than their knowing that they could make 10 of 15 free throws or hit 20 successful tennis serves.

In addition, students benefit from being taught to value effort more highly than victory. There is something lost for many participants when winning dictates success. Students should be taught that the process of doing one's best is the important issue in activity. It is possible to participate in activity without worrying about winning and losing if teachers will reinforce such behavior. In many areas in the school curriculum, emphasis is placed on cooperative learning. Physical education can benefit by such an approach. Evidence shows that cooperative learning improves self-esteem and attitude toward school and can temper the negative aspects of competition (Johnson, Johnson, & Holubec, 1990). Activity and participation can be enhanced by the joy of working together.

Consider the product-versus-process conflict and how it relates to a teacher's view of the instructional environment. A product-oriented teacher does not show as much concern for how students feel about learning, or about the technique and form used when performing skills. In a game of basketball, for example, the product focused on would be the outcome of the game—winning or losing. The process-oriented teacher, on the other hand, is more concerned that students develop proper patterns of skill performance and positive attitudes toward the activity. The outcome of the game is secondary to the learning experience. A common example of extreme product orientation occurs in an athletic situation, when the coach states, "I don't care if you like me (or practice sessions) or not, as long as we win." Most teachers find themselves somewhere between the two viewpoints and place varying amounts of emphasis on process and product.

Three problems confront the evaluator. The first is to devise a system of recording that is efficient, valid, and not excessively time consuming. The second concerns the number of times a trait needs to be observed or measured before the evaluation can be considered reliable. The third problem pertains to the amount of in-class and out-of-class time needed for effective evaluation. Take the case of the physical education specialist who handles 300 to 600 students each day. How does the specialist evaluate this number of students adequately and record the items properly?

PROCESS EVALUATION

Some motor learning specialists hold that the first concern in the psychomotor domain should be process evaluation: Can the child perform the general motor pattern using the correct technique? Later, concern can be directed toward the product of the pattern. Two means of process evaluation seem to dominate. In the first, stages of motor skill development are identified. The lowest stage is where the child learns the basic motor pattern. The final stage is a mature pattern that occurs when the

child has accomplished the skill technique to a degree of appropriate usefulness for that age level. In between these stages are intermediate steps linking the initial to the mature pattern.

To employ this type of process evaluation, the teacher needs to have accurate knowledge of different learning stages so the child's pattern of development can be observed and categorized. Videotaping is useful for viewing the skill performance a number of times and in slow motion. As an example, normative data might show that a 9-year-old child should be at stage four in throwing development. If a child of this age tests at stage one, a developmental deficiency is indicated.

A second means of process evaluation involves a checklist format. Criteria governing proper technique for the movement pattern are listed, and the child's performance is checked against these points. Limiting coverage to two or three of the critical points of technique is usually best. Ratings for each point can be on a 3-point scale: no conformance, partial conformance, and complete conformance. These could be numbered 0, 1, and 2, respectively, providing a point scale for comparisons. The record sheet can be organized so that the achievement levels are listed, and the evaluator circles the appropriate number. Figure 10.1 is an example of a process evaluation form for some of the fundamental locomotor skills.

PRODUCT EVALUATION

Product evaluation is concerned with how far, how accurate, how many, how much, and how fast. It does not deal with the technique used to perform the skill but measures the performance outcome. Both subjective and objective means of assessment are employed. Four approaches are useful for identifying entry-level behavior and monitoring progress in areas of skill performance and behavioral patterns.

Checklists

Checklists have long been used as a system for reporting progress to students and parents. A class list with skills listed across the top of the sheet is a common method used for recording class progress. It can alert the teacher to youngsters who are in need of special help. If grading is based on the number of activities students master, the checklist can deliver this information. Checklists are usually most effective when skills are listed in the sequence in which they should be learned. In this way, the

Class _____ Grade _____ Date _____

Scoring: 0 = No conformance
1 = Partial conformance
2 = Consistent and
complete conformance

Student's Name	Running			Jumping			Hopping			Skipping		
	Arm Action	Leg Action	Composite	Arm Action	Leg Action	Composite	Arm Action	Leg Action	Composite	Arm Action	Leg Action	Composite

Figure 10.1 Process evaluation checklist for locomotor skills

ROPE-JUMPING CHECKLIST

Student	Jump in Place	Jump, Turn Both Ends	Jump, Pendulum Swing	Slow Time	Fast Time	Alternate-Foot Step	Swing Step Forward	Rocker Step	Spread Legs, Forward	Toe-and-Heel Touch	Shuffle Step	Cross Arms	Cross Arms, Backward	Double Jump
_____														
_____														
_____														
_____														
_____														
_____														

Figure 10.2 Sample skill checklist

teacher can gear the teaching process to diagnosed needs. To avoid disrupting the learning process, teachers can record student progress informally while students are practicing. Figure 10.2 is a sample checklist for rope jumping.

Anecdotal Record Sheets

A record sheet that contains student names and has room for comments about student behavior can be used to assess student progress. Anecdotal records of student progress can be reinforcing to both student and teacher as it is often difficult to remember how much progress has been made over a period of time. With anecdotal records, teachers can inform students of their initial skill level compared with their present performance.

A tape recorder is useful for recording anecdotal information. The teacher may record comments during observation and transcribe them later. This process helps teachers learn the names and behavior patterns of students and leads to an increased understanding of student performance. Observations should be recorded at the start of the unit and compared with observations made at a later date as instruction proceeds. A sample record sheet is illustrated in Figure 10.3.

Student Self-Evaluation

Students in the intermediate grades are capable of self-evaluation. They can be given lists of performance objectives and told to make judgments about their achievement. If more objectivity is desired, students can evaluate each other, or groups of two or three students can evaluate one another. Self-evaluation reduces the amount of teacher evaluation time and allows the teacher more time for instruction. The ability to evaluate oneself and the desire to be evaluated are important outcomes of any effective program.

Standardized Tests

Standardized tests are useful for evaluating measurable outcomes. These types of tests have been administered to large samples of youngsters, and the results are available for comparative purposes. Most of the tests require that exact testing procedures and protocol be followed. The disadvantages of standardized tests are their inflexibility and the need for specialized equipment. The Fitnessgram (Cooper Institute for Aerobic Fitness, 1992) is an example of a standardized test.

The test results, or at least an interpreted summary, should become part of the child's permanent

```
Class  Ms. Massoney          ANECDOTAL RECORD SHEET   Date  2/14/94

Bob: Is making progress on the backward jump. Sent a jump rope home with him for practice


Gene: Seems to be discouraged about rope jumping. Called parents to see
      if there is a problem outside of school.


Linda: Discussed the need for helping others. She is going to be a cross-aged
       tutor for next two weeks, as her performance in batting is excellent.
```

Figure 10.3 Sample anecdotal record sheet

health record and should be included in a periodic progress report to parents. The school report card should contain a section devoted to physical education. Test results for each class and for the school as a whole should be presented in a manner that is easily interpreted by students and parents. Testing is meaningless unless evaluators have a concern for raising the children's performance levels and upgrading the physical education program.

GRADING

A number of issues arise when the topic of grading is reviewed. There is wide variation in physical education grading policies in elementary schools, ranging from no grading to grading with letter grades similar to high school classes. Arguments are made on each side of the issue, to grade or not to grade, and there is no clear-cut answer. If the decision is made to grade, a more difficult question arises: What type of grading approach should be used? For an in-depth review of grading systems and ideas for evaluation, the text by Hastad and Lacy (1994) is recommended.

Arguments against Using a Grading System

- Grades are difficult to interpret between teachers and schools. A grade means one thing to one teacher and another to a different teacher. When moving to a different school, the meaning of the grade does not transfer and teachers at the new school may view the grade differently.

- Physical education does not place emphasis on content and product. Rather, it judges success by improvement on skills. Grades in academic areas reflect achievement and accomplishment; because grades in physical education reflect improvement and effort, they may be interpreted incorrectly.

- Often, physical education classes in elementary schools only meet once or twice a week. Testing for the purpose of assigning a grade is time consuming and takes away from learning opportunities. Physical educators in this setting are trying to squeeze as much learning as possible into a minimal amount of time and grading will dramatically reduce their instructional time.

- Physical education is diverse and broad in nature. Instruction covers all three learning domains, i.e., skill development, attitude formation, and content knowledge. Trying to grade all three of these areas is difficult and demands a great deal of time. In addition, which of these three domains is most important and can any of them be overlooked?

- Grading usually only occurs in areas where standardized instruments have been developed. Fitness testing is the major area in elementary physical education where a variety of standardized tests have been developed. Due the dearth of standardized tests in other areas, excessive attention is given to fitness testing.

- Physical education places emphasis on physical fitness and skill performance. Performance in these areas is strongly controlled by genetics, making it difficult for all children to achieve, even when they "give it their best effort." In addition, when grades are given for physical fitness performance, some youngsters will feel discouraged because they trained and still did not reach standards of high performance (see Chapter 13).

Arguments for Using a Grading System

- Giving grades makes physical education similar to other academic areas in the school curriculum. This gives physical education credibility and gains respect from parents, teachers, and administrators.

- Grades communicate the performance of students to parents. Parents have a right to know how their youngsters perform in physical education. Grades are used by teachers in other areas and are easily understood and interpreted by parents, therefore, they should be used in physical education.

- When grades are not given, academic respect is lost. Physical education already suffers from the misguided perception that physical educators don't teach anything, they just "roll out the ball." Lack of a grading system may make it appear to others that little learning is occurring.

- A grading system gives accountability. When grades are given, administrators and parents often assume that teaching and student accomplishment have occurred.

- A grading system rewards skilled students. Students are rewarded in academic areas for their intelligence and performance and should be similarly rewarded for accomplishment in physical education settings.

Implementing a Grading System

If the decision is made to implement a grading system, more difficult issues follow. There are different ways to grade, and many issues have to be examined before developing a grading approach. The following points should be considered when determining how grades will be assigned.

Improvement or Performance? Grades can be assigned on how youngsters perform in class or whether they improve. Because some youngsters are not gifted athletically, should you give them the opportunity to earn a high grade by showing improvement? If you feel physical education should grade in a manner similar to academics, will you

assign high grades to students who demonstrate the highest level of physical skill?

Negative or Positive? Grades can reward students for what they accomplish. For example, a grade may be earned by accumulating a number of points based on accomplishment of various skills and activities. In addition, additional points could be earned by doing well on knowledge tests and citizenship. The opposing point of view is to take away points when students don't behave or perform well. This approach can be negative, and students may lose their desire to participate in such an experience. The most common negative approach is to subtract points when students do not behave in an acceptable manner. This may cause teachers to focus more on the negative aspects of student performance than on the positive constructs.

Teach for Test Results or for Learning? When teachers decide to grade students, it is important that they consider how the grading system will affect their teaching. Some teachers may feel they have failed if students do not receive high marks. On the other hand, some teachers may feel that a certain number of students should fail. If fitness testing is a part of the grading package, some teachers may spend an excessive amount of time having students train for the test items rather than learning about fitness and discovering the many pathways to fitness. Instruction should be designed to enhance student learning.

Process or Product? This issue was discussed in detail earlier in the chapter. Is the grade based on how well students learn skill patterns (e.g., throwing, kicking, or striking), or on the outcome (e.g., how many strikes are thrown or hits made)? The choice made will determine whether the teacher values correct skill technique or the outcome of the skill performance.

Broad or Narrow Perspective? Should the grade be based on a single factor, such as physical skill performance or written test performance? Should it be based on effort? Should it be based on attitude? Choosing only one or two areas would be grading from a narrow perspective. A broad-based approach would be to include all teaching areas and integrate them into a single grade.

EVALUATING THE INSTRUCTIONAL PROCESS

The instructional process has been evaluated in a variety of ways, including intuition, checklists, rating scales, and observation. Over the years, these methods have proved to be relatively ineffective in assessing the quality of instruction. Intuition relies on the expertise of a supervisor who observes the instructor and recommends changes. The improvement based on such recommendations is difficult to identify, because little or no quantification is offered. Additionally, intuitive recommendations are open to debate because teachers may feel that the supervisor is asking them to accept their changes based on personal feelings or bias. How can goals or target objectives be established and knowledge of when these goals are reached be gained if the outcomes are not discussed in quantifiable terms?

When checklists and rating scales are used, they give the appearance of objective, quantified evaluation (Figures 10.4 to 10.6).Unfortunately, ratings are often unreliable, and become more so as the number of points on the rating scale is increased. Scales and checklists are open to a broad spread of interpretation depending on the experience and capacity of the rater. Most of the evaluation done with checklists and rating scales is subject to the impressions and opinions of the evaluator rather than being based on objective data.

The inherent weakness of checklists necessitates the need for developing a systematic method of observing and quantifying the teaching process. In this section a number of teacher observation methods are described that are systematic in nature and useful for self-evaluation. The methods advocated emphasize the use of systematic observation for self-improvement. If readers desire in-depth information on this subject, the text *Developing Teaching Skills in Physical Education* (Siedentop, 1991) should be consulted as a primary resource. Another relevant text for designing self-evaluation programs is *Analyzing Physical Education and Sport Instruction* by Darst, Zakrajsek, and Mancini (1989). The techniques described in the following section have been designed to facilitate implementation by classroom and physical education teachers in the typical school setting.

IMPROVING INSTRUCTION SYSTEMATICALLY

Information based on the systematic observation of instruction can be gathered in a variety of ways. The first step is to define the area of instruction to be evaluated. The second step is to define the specific behavior to be observed. A description of the observable behavior should be written, to assure consistent and meaningful results. All pro-posed methods in this chapter require little more than pencil, paper, tape recorder, and stopwatch. A videotape recorder adds another dimension, but is not a necessity.

Event Recording

Event recording involves tallying the number of times a predefined event occurs within a specified time period. Event recording identifies the frequency of a specified behavior. The quantity of events is recorded, not the quality of events. For example, teachers might want to know the number of times they interacted with individual students or the number of times a positive statement was made. The defined event could be the number of practice attempts that students receive after a skill has been introduced, or the number of times the teacher asks the class to stop and come to attention. Usually, event recording results are divided by the number of minutes in the evaluation session to give a rate per minute. This allows comparison of lessons of different length.

To minimize the amount of time needed for observation and data analysis, a sampling technique can be used. For example, if the lesson is 30 minutes long, four bouts of recording, each lasting 2 minutes and performed at intervals during the lesson, would reduce the burden of recording and still give representative results. Any observable teacher behavior, student behavior, or behavior between teacher and student can be recorded when the behavior has been defined clearly.

Duration Recording

Where event recording offers insight into the frequency of certain behaviors, duration recording reveals how long the specified behavior endures. Time is the measure used in this type of recording. As with event recording, duration recording does not have to involve an entire lesson. Using representative sampling techniques, generalizations about the entire session can be made based on three or four bouts of observation lasting 3 minutes each.

Data are usually converted to percentages so that comparisons can be made from lesson to lesson. This is done by dividing the length of the entire observation into the amount of time accumulated for a specific behavior. For example, if 20 minutes of observation took place and the student was observed to be in productive activity for 10 of the 20 minutes, the percentage of time spent in activity would be 50 percent. This is expressed as

LESSON OBSERVATION-INSTRUCTOR ASSESSMENT

Rating Scale

   3 Competent, good, high level

   2 Moderate, satisfactory

   1 Needs improvement

   X Not observed or not applicable

Date _____

Instructor _____

Evaluator _____

Grade Level _____

Activities _____

Personal Qualities

   _____ 1. Appearance: neatness, appropriate dress

   _____ 2. Poise, confidence, self-control

   _____ 3. Enthusiasm, energy

   _____ 4. Voice: clarity, force, effectiveness

Comments

Teaching Skills and Classroom Management

   _____ 1. Facilities and equipment prepared

   _____ 2. Supplies: efficient handling

   _____ 3. Effective behavior level and control

   _____ 4. Safety precautions: taught, observed

   _____ 5. Effective use of time: verbal and movement

   _____ 6. Efficient movement of students, use of space

Comments

Communication Skills—Rapport with Students

   _____ 1. Conveys ideas clearly and effectively

   _____ 2. Maintains student interest and enthusiasm

   _____ 3. Uses student ideas and suggestions

   _____ 4. Sensitive to student needs

   _____ 5. Interacts with students

   _____ 6. Provides positive reinforcement, encourages

Comments

The Lesson

   _____ 1. Shows good planning, preparation

   _____ 2. Teaching methods appropriate to content

   _____ 3. Adapts, adjusts to students' abilities

   _____ 4. Appropriate progressions

   _____ 5. Provides for maximum participation

   _____ 6. Accomplishes objectives

   _____ 7. Allows for exploration, creativity

   _____ 8. Provides for critique, evaluation

Comments

General Comments

What were the strong points or commendable aspects of the lesson presentation? What suggestions are made for improving or strengthening the quality of the presentation?

Figure 10.4 Example of a teacher evaluation checklist

EVALUATION FORM

Activity _____ Date _____

Student Teacher _____ Elementary _____ Secondary _____

College Supervisor _____ Cooperating Teacher _____

This evaluation of student teaching serves as a tangible basis for discussion among the cooperating teacher, the college supervisor, and the student. The following symbols will be used: Plus (+) indicates a positive feature of the student teacher's work; minus (−) indicates a need for improvement.

Teaching Competencies

☐ Appearance	☐ Planning and organization
☐ Use of language	☐ Execution of lesson-teaching technique
☐ Voice	☐ Knowledge of subject
☐ Enthusiasm	☐ Demonstration of skills
☐ Poise	☐ Appropriate progression
☐ Creativity	☐ Provisions for individual differences
	☐ Class management-control
	☐ Adaptability, foresight
	☐ Appropriate choice of activity

Comments:

Figure 10.5   Example of a student teacher rating scale

"50 percent of the total time was spent in activity." This approach is best used to identify the duration of certain behaviors, such as practice, managerial, or instructional behaviors.

Interval Recording

Interval recording is most often used to record individual behavior patterns. In interval recording, the intervals should be 6 to 12 seconds in length, with one interval used for observing and the other for recording. For example, if one were using 6-second intervals during a 1-minute session, five intervals would be for observing and five for recording the results. According to Siedentop (1991), at least 90 data points (observe plus record equals 1 point) are necessary to establish the validity of the technique. Using 6-second intervals, it would be possible to generate 100 data points in 20 minutes.

Data generated from this technique are usually converted to a percentage of the data points in which the behavior occurred. If, for example, the behavior occurred in 40 of 100 data points, the figure would be 40 percent. The percentage could then be compared from lesson to lesson. A common way of keeping track of intervals is to wear a headset from a recorder that "beeps" every 6 seconds. The observer can alternate observing and recoding at each signal. This technique is reliable, particularly when intervals are short, and can be used to analyze academic learning time and other types of observable behavior.

Placheck Sampling

Placheck (planned activity check) recording is similar to interval recording in that behavior is observed at different intervals. However, this tech-

	5	4	3	2	1	Comments
Student Teacher _____ Activity _____ Grade _____						
1. Use of language						
2. Quality of voice						
3. Personal appearance						
4. Class management						
5. Presentation and teaching techniques						
6. Professional poise						
7. Enthusiasm, interest						
8. Adaptability, foresight						
9. Adequate activity						
10. Knowledge of subject						
11. Appropriate use of student help						
12. Demonstration (if any)						
13. Progression (if applicable)						
14. General organization						

General evaluation
5–Superior
4–Above average
3–Average
2–Below average
1–Poor

Evaluating Teacher

_____

Date _____

Figure 10.6 Example of a student teacher rating scale

nique is used to observe group behavior. At regular intervals during a lesson, the observer scans the class for 10 seconds. The scan takes place from the left to the right side of the instructional area, and the observer records the number of students who were not performing the predefined behavior. Each student in the class is observed one time only during a scan. The observer does not go back and change the decision, even if the student changes behavior during the 10-second interval.

This technique is often used to identify student effort, on-task behavior, or participation.

Recording the smaller number of students exhibiting a behavior is easiest. For example, if the teacher is interested in identifying the percentage of students on-task, it is probably easier to record the number of students not on-task (hopefully). Intervals should last for 10 seconds and be randomly spaced throughout the lesson. There should be eight to ten observation intervals. Signals to scan the class should be recorded on a tape recorder at random intervals to cue the observer. This technique yields information concerning the behavior of a group.

SELF-IMPROVEMENT THROUGH SYSTEMATIC OBSERVATION

Teachers have different strengths, weaknesses, and concerns for improvement. Approaches used for systematic observation for self-improvement may vary greatly from teacher to teacher. Teachers need to decide which variables to evaluate and then determine the best possible way to record and monitor the data. Evaluating only one behavior when beginning systematic evaluation is usually preferable, since recording more than one variable at a time may be frustrating and confusing. After the teacher determines the behavior to be changed, a plan for evaluation is developed. This means identifying the behavior that affects the desired educational outcome and deciding which method of observation will be most effective. A coding form is then developed to facilitate recording of the data.

Coding sheets should be specific for each situation. Areas on the sheet should provide for recording teacher's name, date, focus and content of the lesson, grade level and competency of the students, duration of the lesson, and a short description of the evaluation procedure. The sheets should be consistent for each type of behavior so the instructor can compare progress throughout the year.

Deciding what behavior to record depends on the instructor's situation. For example, can the data be gathered by students who are not participating? Can another teacher gather the data easily? Can the data be gathered from an audiotape or is a videotape necessary? Is the instructor willing to let others gather the information, or is keeping the data confidential important? These and other considerations determine what areas the teacher is able to evaluate. Most teachers are least threatened by self-evaluation techniques and are willing to change when not pushed by outside authorities. Daily teaching behavior is least affected when outside observers are not present, so self-evaluation techniques are more likely to reveal actual instructional patterns.

Areas that can be evaluated are suggested later in this section, together with appropriate coding forms. These are, however, only examples, and may be modified easily to meet the specific needs of the instructor. Teachers should make self-evaluation an ongoing, integral part of their teaching. They should think continually about ways to improve. Teachers seldom stay the same; either they improve or their performance tapers off.

Improving the Quality of Instruction

Quality instruction results when effective teachers implement a well-planned lesson. Many successful teachers have learned to do this over a period of years through the inefficient method of trial and error. Unfortunately, sheer experience does not guarantee that one will grow into an outstanding teacher. There are many experienced, yet mediocre, teachers. A key for improving teaching ability is coupling experience with meaningful feedback about the teacher's performance.

Teachers often find it difficult to find someone capable of offering evaluative feedback. Principals and curriculum supervisors may be too busy to evaluate teaching regularly, or they may not possess the skills necessary for systematically evaluating teaching behavior. This accentuates the importance of finding ways for self-evaluating teaching as the primary avenue for improvement. Without regular and measurable means of evaluation, improving the quality of teaching becomes next to impossible. Teachers have long been told to talk less, move more, praise more, learn more names, and increase student practice time—all without documented methods of measurement. This section offers methods for evaluating teaching behavior that are observable and therefore measurable. Data can be gathered by the teacher, teaching peers, or selected students.

We emphasize the do-it-yourself approach to evaluation. Feedback that is reviewed in the privacy of one's office is easier to digest and less threatening. Teachers are able to set personal goals and chart their performance privately. When teachers choose to evaluate their teaching procedures, they are making a commitment to change. This attitude is in contrast to the resistance that some teachers feel when principals and supervisors evaluate and dictate change. Instructors often doubt the validity of the latter process and find reasons for not changing.

Instructional Time

The teaching process is educational when teachers choose to instruct. The "roll out the ball and let them play" approach is nothing more than leisure activity in a school setting. Instructors need to be aware of the amount of instruction they offer students. To analyze instructional time, the number of instructional episodes and the length of each episode are recorded. The average length of an instructional episode can be evaluated, as well as the percentage of the lesson that was used for instruction. Generally, episodes should be short and frequent, with an attempt made to limit each episode to 30 seconds or less.

How to Do It

1. Design a form for duration recording.
2. Have a colleague or a nonparticipating student turn on the stopwatch every time the instructor begins an instructional episode; or record the lesson using an audiotape recorder and time the instructional episodes at the end of the day. Establish consistency in identifying the difference between instructional and management episodes.
3. Total the amount of time spent on instruction.
4. Convert the amount of time to a percentage of the total lesson time by dividing the total lesson time into the time spent on instruction. The average length of an instructional episode can

---

INSTRUCTIONAL ANALYSIS

Teacher _____ Observer _____

Class _____ Grade _____ Date and Time _____

Lesson Focus _____ Comments _____

Starting Time _____ End Time _____ Length of Lesson _____

Practice

Instruction

Management

Total time: Pract _____ Inst _____ Mgmt _____ Dead _____

Percent of lesson for: Pract _____ Inst _____ Mgmt _____ Dead _____

No. of episodes: Pract _____ Inst _____ Mgmt _____ Dead _____

Average length of episodes: Pract _____ Inst _____ Mgmt _____ Dead _____

Figure 10.7 Sample form for instructional analysis duration recording

be determined by dividing the amount of instructional time by the number of instructional episodes. Figure 10.7 is an example of a form that could be used.

Class Management Time

Effective teachers are efficient managers of students. Management occurs when students are moved into various formations, when equipment is gathered or put away, and when directions are given relative to these areas. Disciplining a class would be another example of time used for management. As a rule of thumb, if teachers are not giving instructions, they are probably managing students. Figure 10.8 is an example of a form for recording the amount of management time.

The amount of time being used for class management and the length and number of episodes are meaningful data for a teacher to know. The length of each episode can be recorded by an observer. These data are useful for analyzing how much of the lesson time is devoted to management. The instructor may be alerted to inefficient organizational schemes, or may realize that students are not responding quickly to explanations and requests.

How to Do It

1. Design a form to gather the desired data (Figure 10.8).

2. Record the lesson with an audiotape recorder. Time the episodes of management and note the length of each episode on the form.

3. Total the amount of management time and divide it by the length of the period to determine the percentage of management time in the lesson.

4. Total the number of episodes and divide this number into the amount of time devoted to management to find the average length of a management episode.

Practice Time (Time on Task) and Dead Time

To learn physical skills, students must be involved in meaningful physical activity. Physical education pro-

---

MANAGEMENT TIME

Teacher _____   Observer _____

Class _____   Grade _____   Date and Time _____

Lesson Focus _____   Comments _____

Starting Time _____   End Time _____   Length of Lesson _____

Total management time _____

Percent of class time devoted to management _____

Number of episodes _____   Average length of episodes _____

Figure 10.8 Sample form for evaluation of management time

grams have a finite amount of scheduled time per week. Practice time, or time on task, has also been referred to as ALT-PE (Metzler, 1984). This is an acronym for Academic Learning Time in Physical Education. It is the amount of time students spend practicing skills that will result in accomplishment of program objectives. Instructors need to gather data showing the amount of time that students are involved in productive, on-task activity to assure learning can occur. In one well-regarded school district, the authors found that the average amount of activity time per 50-minute period was only 9 to 12 minutes. Certainly one could question whether much learning was taking place in this program.

Duration recording is most meaningful to evaluate practice time. A student or fellow teacher observes the lesson and times when students are involved in practicing skills. Figure 10.9 shows the results of a duration recording for practice time. Teachers should strive to increase the amount of time devoted to skill practice. The amount of practice time could be increased by using more equipment, implementing drills that demand a minimum of standing in line, or streamlining the amount of verbal instructions given.

The amount of dead time in a lesson also can be measured. Dead time occurs when students are off task or are doing something unrelated to practice, management, or instruction. Examples might be standing in line waiting for a turn, doing nothing because instructions were not understood, or playing a game and literally doing nothing other than waiting for the ball to come to them.

How to Do It

1. Design a form for collecting the data (Figure 10.10).

2. Identify a student who will be timed when practicing. This is a critical step. The student chosen should be neither exceptional nor below par and should give a realistic picture of the amount of practice time allotted. If evaluation of dead time is desired, time when that student is not involved in on-task practice, management, or instructional activity. Another way to calculate dead time is to subtract the combined amounts of time used for practice, management, and instruction (assuming all have been timed) from the total length of the lesson.

3. Turn on the stopwatch when the student is involved in practice (or dead) activity. Stop the watch when the student stops (or starts) practicing. Record the amount of practice (or dead) time. Time all practice (or dead) episodes.

4. Total the amount of time devoted to student practice (in minutes) and divide it by the length of the lesson. This is the percentage of practice time in a lesson. Total the amount of dead time and divide it by the length of the lesson to compute the percentage of dead time.

Response Latency

How quickly do students respond when commands or signals are given? This is the essence of identifying response latency. Response latency may occur when instructions are given to begin or stop an activity. An observer records the amount of time that elapses from the moment when a command is given to start or stop activity until the moment when the students actually begin or stop. The amount of elapsed time is the response latency.

The average duration of response latency can be calculated, and the instructor can set a goal for improving this student behavior. A certain amount of response latency should be expected. However, most instructors have a strong feeling about the amount of latency they are willing to tolerate. After

Figure 10.9 Results of a duration recording for practice time

| | Teacher: Debbie Massoney | |
| | School: Whittier Elementary | |
Parts of the lesson	Practicing	Inactive, off task, listening
Introductory activity	1.5 min	0.5 min
Fitness development	6.5 min	1.5 min
Lesson focus	10.0 min	4.0 min
Game	5.0 min	1.0 min
Total	23.0 min	7.0 min

PRACTICE TIME

Teacher _____ Observer _____

Class _____ Grade _____ Date and Time _____

Lesson Focus _____ Comments _____

Starting Time _____ End Time _____ Length of Lesson _____

Total practice time _____

Percent of class time devoted to practice _____

Number of episodes _____ Average length of episodes _____

Figure 10.10 Sample form for collecting data on practice time

more than a 5-second response latency, teachers usually become uneasy and expect the class to stop or start.

How to Do It

1. Develop a form for gathering the data (Figure 10.11).
2. Have a nonparticipating student or colleague time the response latency that occurs when the class is asked to stop (start). The clock should run from the time the command to stop (start) is given until the next command is given or until the class is involved in productive behavior. Starting and stopping latency are two separate behaviors that must be recorded separately.
3. Identify the number of response latency episodes and divide this number into the total amount of time devoted to response latency to calculate the average episode length.

Student Performance

Some classes will have a greater percentage of students performing at optimum level than others. This could signal that the latter classes are poorly motivated, do not understand instructions, or are out of control. In any case, instructors should evaluate the percentage of students who are performing in the desired manner. This can be accomplished by means of the placheck (planned activity check) observation technique, discussed previously (Siedentop, 1991). The placheck can be used to identify a range of behavior. Use of the placheck involves behavior that is "yes or no" in nature. In other words, students either are performing the desired behavior or are doing something else. Examples of areas that might be evaluated are on-task behavior, active behavior, or effort in performing an activity. Once the results are determined, teachers can set goals to increase the percentage of students involved in the desired observable behavior.

How to Do It

1. Design a form for recording the desired data. Figure 10.12 is a sample form for placheck observation. In this case, the same form can be used to identify three different types of student performance.
2. Place 8 to 10 "beeps" at random intervals on a tape recording to signal when to conduct a placheck.
3. Scan the area in a specified and consistent direction from left to right each time the tape-recorded signal is heard. The class is scanned

Teacher _____ Observer _____

Class _____ Grade _____ Date and Time _____

Lesson Focus _____ Comments _____

Starting Time _____ End Time _____ Length of Lesson _____

Starting Response Latency

Stopping Response Latency

Total amount of starting response latency _____

Percent of class time devoted to response latency _____

Number of episodes _____ Average length of episodes _____

Total amount of stopping response latency _____

Percent of class time devoted to response latency _____

Number of episodes _____ Average length of episodes _____

Figure 10.11 Sample form for evaluating response latency

for seven to ten seconds while the observer records the number of students who are engaged in the desired behavior.

4. Convert the data to a percentage by dividing the total number of students into the number of unproductive students and then multiplying the result by 100. Four to six plachecks spaced throughout a class period will yield valid information about class conduct.

Instructional Feedback

Feedback given to students by teachers strongly affects the instructional presentation. Instructors can define and measure feedback used with students and can set meaningful goals for improve-ment. Some people assume that teachers are born, not made. This assumes that it is difficult, if not impossible, to learn to be an effective teacher, and that certain types of people are "naturals." There is no evidence to support such thinking. All teachers must work to develop effective communication skills. Few teachers enter the profession able to communicate with warmth and clarity. The process of changing interaction patterns may create some discomfort and concern, but ultimately it pays dividends. The following areas can be evaluated to give direction for implementing useful change.

Praise and Criticism

When students are involved in activity, teachers should offer feedback related to student performance. This

STUDENT PERFORMANCE

Teacher _____ Observer _____

Class _____ Grade _____ Date and Time _____

Lesson Focus _____ Comments _____

Starting Time _____ End Time _____ Length of Lesson _____

Active/Inactive

On Task/Off Task

Effort/Noneffort

Number of plachecks _____

Total number of students _____

Number of students not on desired behavior _____

Percentage of students not on desired behavior _____

Figure 10.12 Sample form for placheck observation

feedback can be positive and constructive or negative and critical in nature. It is easy to ask a student or peer to record the occurrence of praise and criticism. The results can be tallied and evaluated at the end of the day. The number of instances and the ratio of positive to negative comments are calculated. With this information, the instructor can begin to set goals for increasing the number of comments per minute and modifying the ratio of positive to negative comments.

General versus Specific Feedback

Feedback to students can be general or specific. To illustrate, "Good job," "Way to go," and "Cut that out" are examples of general feedback. General feedback can be positive or negative; it does not specify the behavior being reinforced. In contrast,

specific feedback identifies the student by name and reinforces an actual behavior; it also might be accompanied by a valuing statement. An example would be, "Michelle, that's the way to keep your head tucked! I really like that forward roll!" To evaluate in this area, general and specific feedback instances are tallied. Feedback can be positive or negative, and this distinction can also be made as part of the tallying process.

The use of first names is important in personalizing feedback and directing it to the proper individual. The number of times that first names are used could be totaled. Valuing statements could be evaluated. All of these categories should be divided by the length of the lesson (in minutes) to render a rate per minute. Figure 10.13 is an example of a form that can be used to tally behaviors described in this section.

INSTRUCTIONAL FEEDBACK

Teacher _____ Observer _____

Class _____ Grade _____ Date and Time _____

Lesson Focus _____ Comments _____

Starting Time _____ End Time _____ Length of Lesson _____

Interactions unrelated to skill performance	+								
	−								
General instruction feedback	+								
	−								
Specific positive instructional feedback									
Corrective instructional feedback									
First names									
Nonverbal feedback	+								
	−								

Ratio + to −/nonskill related _____

Ratio + to −/skill related _____

Figure 10.13 Sample form for tallying teaching behaviors

Positive feedback should be specific whenever possible so students know what they performed well. Sometimes, teachers overuse general positive feedback to such a point that it becomes a habitual form of communication (e.g., "Good job," "Nice serve," "Way to go"). Such nonspecific feedback does not identify the desirable behavior and may soon be ignored by students. A negative side effect is that undesirable behavior may also be reinforced when feedback is general.

Corrective Instructional Feedback

Effective teachers move students to higher levels of performance. Part of this process involves giving performers meaningful corrective feedback. Corrective feedback should focus on improving the performance of the participant. Teachers should ignore poor performances if students are already aware of their shortcomings.

Corrective instructional feedback should be specific so performers know what it is that they must correct. An example of corrective instructional feedback would be, "You struck the soccer ball much too high. Try to strike it a little below center." This type of feedback tells the student what was incorrect about the skill attempt and how to perform the skill correctly.

Nonverbal Feedback

Much performance feedback can be given nonverbally. Nonverbal communication is meaningful to students and may be equal to or more effective than verbal forms of communication. Examples of nonverbal feedback that could occur after a desired performance are a pat on the back, a wink, a smile, a nod of the head, the thumbs-up sign, and clapping the hands. Nonverbal feedback can also be negative: a frown, shaking the head in disapproval, walking away from a student, or laughing at a poor performance.

Either a student or another instructor may tally the number of positive and negative nonverbal behaviors exhibited by a teacher. Students are often better at evaluating the instructor in this domain, because they are keenly aware of the meaning of the instructor's nonverbal mannerisms.

How to Do It

1. Design a form to collect the data. Figure 10.13 is an example of such a form.

2. Audiotape a lesson for playback and evaluation at a later time.

3. Record the data to be analyzed. It is usually best to take one category at a time when beginning. For example, analyze the use of first names during the first playback, and then play the tape again to evaluate corrective feedback.

4. Convert the data to a form that can be generalized from lesson to lesson (i.e., rate per minute, rate per lesson, or ratio of positive to negative interactions).

Active Supervision and Student Contact

When instructors are involved in the teaching process, they are actively supervising students. Active supervision means moving among and offering personalized feedback to students. The number of times an instructor becomes personally involved with a student can be counted. This type of feedback differs from total class interaction and demands that the instructor have insight into each student's behavior and concerns.

Allied to this area is the relationship between teacher movement and active supervision. Instructors often establish a particular area in the gymnasium where they feel most comfortable teaching. Before instruction begins, teachers move to this area. This consistent movement pattern may cause students to drift to different areas, depending on their feeling about the activity or the instructor. Students who like the instructor will move closer, whereas students who dislike the teacher or are uneasy about the activity may move as far away as possible. This results in a configuration in which the better performers are near the instructor and the students who may be somewhat less able are farther away and more difficult to observe.

These problems can be avoided by moving throughout the teaching area. Teacher movement can be evaluated by dividing the area into quadrants and tallying the number of times the instructor moves from section to section. A tally is made only if the teacher speaks to a student or the class as a whole. Do not make a tally when the teacher merely passes through a quadrant. The amount of time spent in each quadrant can also be evaluated. Teachers should try to spend similar amounts of time in each area. When students cannot predict where the teacher will be next, they have a greater tendency to remain on task.

Moving related to the use of lesson time can be determined by the amount of time the teacher stays in a quadrant. The length of time a teacher stays in a quadrant can be recorded in a corresponding location on the form. At the end of the lesson, the amount of time the teacher has spent in each quadrant can then be analyzed. Another technique is to code the type of teacher behavior that occurs each time the instructor moves into a new quadrant. For example, an "M" might signify management activity, an "I" instructional activity, and a "P" practice time. This approach would reveal the amount of time the instructor spent in each area and also show where the teacher moves to conduct different types of class activities.

How to Do It

1. Develop a coding form similar to the one in Figure 10.14.

2. Ask a nonparticipating student or a colleague to record the desired data on active supervision. An alternative is to videotape the lesson and evaluate it at a later time.

3. Evaluate the data by calculating the number of moves per lesson, and the number of moves during instruction, management, and practice.

EVALUATION OF THE PHYSICAL EDUCATION PROGRAM

The elementary school physical education program should be evaluated regularly to ensure that it is being developed in the direction of stated program goals. Evaluation instruments can be written to reflect program philosophy of individual districts. Figure 10.15 is a sample instrument that may be adapted, depending on district needs and goals.

This self-evaluation instrument can be used to expose serious program deficiencies and operational difficulties. The results, including program strengths and weaknesses, can be shared with administrators or used by teachers to evaluate a program that they have developed. The instrument can also be used to compare programs or to identify effective programs.

In the sample instrument, evaluative statements are written as a set of standards that, when met, ensure an effective program. Four areas are listed for evaluation: (a) philosophy of the program, (b) instructional procedures, (c) curricular offerings, and (d) facilities, equipment, and supplies. The entire instrument can be used, or any of the four areas can be evaluated individually. Evaluators should read each statement and determine the extent to which there is compliance with the

TEACHER MOVEMENT

Teacher _____ Observer _____

Class _____ Grade _____ Date and Time _____

Lesson Focus _____ Comments _____

Starting Time _____ End Time _____ Length of Lesson _____

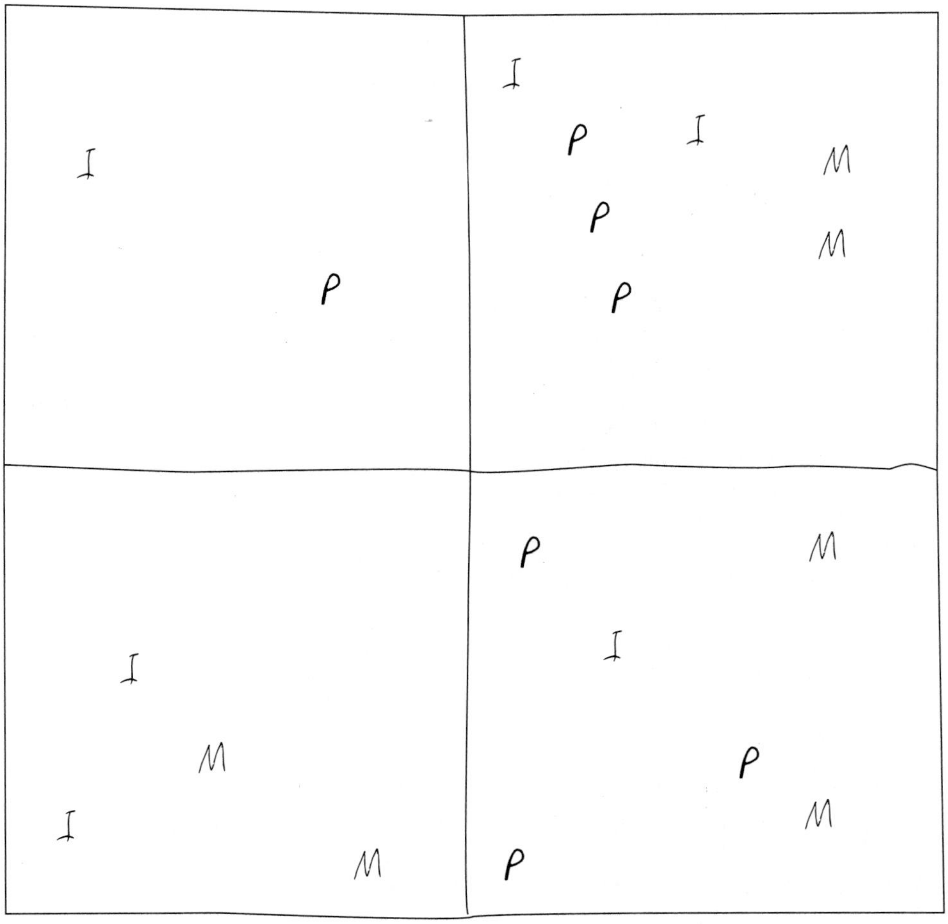

Total number of moves _____

Number of moves (I) _____ (M) _____ (A) _____

Figure 10.14 Form for evaluating teacher movement—student contact

accepted standard and circle the appropriate scale score. Comments can be made at the end of each section. Each statement should be rated and assigned points on the following basis: A rating of 3 represents complete compliance (the program meets the standard fully without deficiencies), 2 represents adequate compliance with room for improvement, 1 represents minimal compliance (improvement is necessary to reach functional compliance), and 0 represents no compliance (the deficiency is serious and a detriment to an effective program).

COMPREHENSIVE PROGRAM EVALUATION

Program Philosophy

1. Physical education is regarded by the administration as an integral part of the total curriculum and is dedicated to the same curricular goal, the fullest possible development of each pupil for living in a democracy.	0	1	2	3
2. The curriculum guide states the program philosophy that is used for direction.	0	1	2	3
3. A written and up-to-date sequential curriculum is available and used by all instructors.	0	1	2	3
4. The course of study includes units of activity appropriate for the grade levels.	0	1	2	3
5. Lesson plans are developed from the course of study and are used as the basis for instruction.	0	1	2	3
6. The physical education program is a developmental program in which youngsters learn through movement sequences that are planned and arranged in sequential fashion.	0	1	2	3
7. A meaningful progression of activities is evident from grade to grade and within each grade.	0	1	2	3
8. Students are classified in physical education classes according to grade level or developmental level.	0	1	2	3
9. Students are scheduled in the physical education program on a regular basis. Music, field trips, and extracurricular activities are not accepted as substitutes for physical education.	0	1	2	3
10. Children are taught the "why" of physical activity in relation to appropriate psychological and physiological principles.	0	1	2	3
11. Youngsters are given physical examinations before entering school (kindergarten) and at the 4th-grade level. The results of the exam are used to determine the extent of participation in physical education.	0	1	2	3
12. Students are excused from physical education on a long-term basis only when they can submit a physician's statement indicating medical concern and the duration of the excuse.	0	1	2	3
13. Appropriate arrangements are made for students with medical, religious, or temporary health excuses.	0	1	2	3
14. A nurse or teachers with suitable first aid training are available in case of accident.	0	1	2	3
15. Grading procedures are consistent with those used in other subject areas.	0	1	2	3
16. The budget specified for equipment and supplies for physical education is adequate.	0	1	2	3
17. Physical education demonstration programs are offered regularly for purposes of public relations and general information.	0	1	2	3
18. The services of an elementary physical education specialist or consultant are available.	0	1	2	3
19. Classroom teachers use effectively the services of the physical education specialist or consultant to supplement and improve physical education instruction.	0	1	2	3
20. When physical education is supplemented by an activity of the classroom teacher, the specialist or consultant provides adequate aid.	0	1	2	3
21. Physical education specialists have a personal, written plan for professional growth and development. This plan might include graduate work, workshops, conferences, conventions, and independent study.	0	1	2	3
22. In-service sessions are organized for improvement of instruction in physical education based on demonstrated need.	0	1	2	3

Figure 10.15 Sample form for evaluating the physical education program

23. Physical education instruction is evaluated regularly by an appropriate supervisor. This information is used to provide immediate feedback for the purpose of improving instruction.　　0　1　2　3

24. A broad intramural program is present with a variety of activities to suit the needs of boys and girls.　　0　1　2　3

25. Any extramural activities are an outgrowth of the instructional program and are limited to the intermediate grades.　　0　1　2　3

Comments:

Instructional Procedures

1. Instructors use sound class management techniques during instruction.　　0　1　2　3
2. Students are allowed to participate in program planning, activity selection, and evaluation.　　0　1　2　3
3. Teachers are familiar with different styles of teaching and use them when the need arises.　　0　1　2　3
4. Leadership opportunities such as demonstrating, officiating, planning, and leading peers are offered to students.　　0　1　2　3
5. Instructors are strong models for students. They possess an appropriate level of fitness and dress properly for physical activity.　　0　1　2　3
6. The minimum amount per class of time allotted for physical education activity is 30 minutes.　　0　1　2　3
7. Each class receives physical education instruction a minimum of three times per week, excluding recess and supervised play.　　0　1　2　3
8. Class sizes are similar to those allotted to classroom teachers, with a maximum of 35 students.　　0　1　2　3
9. Program activities are coeducational in nature.　　0　1　2　3
10. Disciplinary measures in physical education instruction do not include expulsion from class or punishment using physical activity.　　0　1　2　3
11. Youngsters wear appropriate clothing and shoes to physical education so that attire does not restrict activity.　　0　1　2　3
12. Systematic testing is used at regular intervals to evaluate the effectiveness of the program.　　0　1　2　3
13. There is a special program for low-fitness students.　　0　1　2　3
14. There is a special program for obese students.　　0　1　2　3
15. Grading plans (when required) are based on established criteria and indicate the extent to which each student has achieved course objectives.　　0　1　2　3
16. There is an annual review and evaluation of the curriculum for purposes of revision and adjustment.　　0　1　2　3
17. Procedures for dealing with accidents, including administration of first aid, reporting, and follow-up, are in written form.　　0　1　2　3
18. Teachers have knowledge of liability concerns in physical education. Instruction and programming reflect this knowledge through prudent practices.　　0　1　2　3
19. Facilities, equipment, curriculum, and teaching methods are analyzed regularly to reduce the possibility of accidents.　　0　1　2　3

20. Facilities, equipment, and curriculum areas that might be liabilities are reported in writing to appropriate administrators.   0   1   2   3

21. Bulletin boards, charts, pictures, and other visual materials are posted and used in the instructional process.   0   1   2   3

22. Teaching aids such as films, slides, and models are used to enrich and supplement instruction.   0   1   2   3

23. A learning center containing reading materials appropriate to the reading and interest level of youngsters is available for physical education.   0   1   2   3

Comments:

Curricular Offerings

1. The physical education program provides learning experiences to help each child attain the following:

    a. A personalized level of physical fitness and body conditioning   0   1   2   3

    b. Suitable skills in a variety of educational movement patterns on the ground and on appropriate apparatus   0   1   2   3

    c. Manipulative skills leading to the development of specialized skills   0   1   2   3

    d. Specialized skills related to games, rhythms, tumbling, stunts, and sport activities   0   1   2   3

    e. Knowledge of rules, techniques, and strategy related to specialized skills   0   1   2   3

    f. Desirable social standards and ethical behavior   0   1   2   3

    g. Proper safety practices for self and others   0   1   2   3

    h. Competence in activities that can be used during leisure time   0   1   2   3

    i. Knowledge and understanding of concepts leading to human wellness   0   1   2   3

2. Activities are organized and adjusted to suit the maturity and skill levels of youngsters.   0   1   2   3

3. All children are considered important and the program is adjusted to suit the maturity and skill levels of youngsters.   0   1   2   3

4. The program offers something for all children: boys and girls, skilled and unskilled, physically fit and low-fitness youngsters, and special education students.   0   1   2   3

5. Each lesson has a portion of time (7 to 10 minutes) devoted to physical fitness activities.   0   1   2   3

6. The physical education program emphasizes and allocates enough time at the appropriate grade level for each of the following areas:

    a. Educational movement patterns   0   1   2   3

    b. Fundamental skills including locomotor, nonlocomotor, manipulative, and specialized skills   0   1   2   3

    c. Rhythmic activities   0   1   2   3

    d. Stunts, tumbling, and combatives   0   1   2   3

    e. Games and relays   0   1   2   3

    f. Sports and lead-up activities   0   1   2   3

7. The program in the primary grades emphasizes educational movement.   0   1   2   3

8. An up-to-date professional library is available for the physical education specialist and faculty.   0   1   2   3

Figure 10.15 *continued*

9. There is an aquatic program either in the public schools or in the community recreation program (or another agency) so that all children have the opportunity to learn to swim. 0 1 2 3

10. Both indoor and outdoor teaching stations are assigned for physical education instruction. 0 1 2 3

11. The yearly curriculum is planned and written so that a wide variety of activities is offered. 0 1 2 3

12. Units of instruction last no longer than 3 weeks and include skill instruction. 0 1 2 3

Comments:

Facilities, Equipment, and Supplies

1. Facilities include teaching stations that allow all students a minimum of three classes per week. 0 1 2 3

2. Maximum use of facilities for physical education instruction is apparent. 0 1 2 3

3. Outdoor facilities meet the basic acreage standard of 5 acres plus 1 acre for each additional 100 students. 0 1 2 3

4. Outdoor facilities include the following:
   a. Areas where different age groups can play without interference from each other 0 1 2 3
   b. Areas for court games 0 1 2 3
   c. Cement or asphalt spaces marked with a variety of game patterns 0 1 2 3
   d. Backstops and goals for softball, soccer, and basketball 0 1 2 3
   e. Suitable fencing for safety and control 0 1 2 3
   f. Outdoor playground equipment including climbing apparatus, turning bars, and tetherball areas 0 1 2 3

5. The outdoor area is free from rocks, sprinkler heads, and other hazards that might cause injury. 0 1 2 3

6. Indoor facilities meet the following standards:
   a. Clean, sanitary, and free from hazards 0 1 2 3
   b. Well lighted, well ventilated, heated, cooled, and treated for proper acoustics 0 1 2 3
   c. Surfaced with a nonslip finish and include painted game area lines 0 1 2 3

7. There is periodic inspection of all facilities and equipment, both indoor and outdoor, and a written report is sent to the appropriate administrators. 0 1 2 3

8. Storage facilities are adequate for supplies and portable equipment. 0 1 2 3

9. Adequate provision is made for off-season storage of equipment, apparatus, and supplies. 0 1 2 3

10. An office is provided for the physical education instructor; it includes a shower, and is located near the instruction area 0 1 2 3

11. Basic supplies are sufficient in the following areas:*
   a. Manipulative equipment (one piece for each child): fleece balls, small balls, beanbags, wands, hoops, and jump ropes 0 1 2 3
   b. Sport and game balls: softballs, footballs, volleyballs, basketballs, soccer balls, tetherballs, and cageballs in sufficient numbers 0 1 2 3
   c. Sport and game supplies: cones, pinnies, track-and-field standards, jumping pits 0 1 2 3
   d. Testing equipment: measuring tapes, stopwatches, calipers to measure skinfold thickness, and specialized apparatus 0 1 2 3

*For a comprehensive list of equipment needed, see Chapter 33.

12. Sufficient materials are available for a varied rhythmic program: variable-speed record player, records, drums, tambourines, and percussion instruments	0	1	2	3
13. Capital-outlay items for the indoor facility include the following:				
a. Minimum of six tumbling mats (4 by 8 ft or larger)	0	1	2	3
b. Individual mats (32)	0	1	2	3
c. Sufficient climbing apparatus so that at least one half of the class can be active at one time. Apparatus should include wall bars, chinning bars, horizontal bars, climbing ropes on tracks, and ladders.	0	1	2	3
d. Balance beam benches (at least 6)	0	1	2	3
e. Jumping boxes (at least 8)	0	1	2	3
f. Basketball goals, volleyball nets, hockey goals	0	1	2	3

Comments:

Figure 10.15 *continued*

MICROCOMPUTER APPLICATIONS

Computers are today important aids in teaching and evaluating students. Computers are most effective when they are programmed to execute menial and repetitive tasks. They are often used in the evaluation process because evaluative results are quantifiable and can be translated into a meaningful report using a computer program.

The following discussion illustrates possible computer applications in a physical education setting. Using a microcomputer is not a substitute for teacher evaluation or instruction, but can serve as an additional instructional tool. A first step in understanding computer applications is to understand clearly what a computer can and cannot do.

Reporting Fitness Test Results

A payoff for using computer-assisted fitness testing is that the final printed report is usually personalized, easy to interpret, and meaningful to parents. An example of a software program that can be used to generate fitness test printouts for students is the Prudential Fitnessgram system (Cooper Institute for Aerobic Research, 1992). The program prints out a fitness profile (Figure 10.16) for students after their data have been entered. See pages 274–275 for an overview of the Fitnessgram system.

Wellness Reports

Communicating with parents about the health status of their child is important. One way to enhance public relations is not only to share the results of testing with parents but also to tell them what the results mean in terms of their child's health status. The Pangrazi and Pangrazi (1992) Wellness Profile software asks students to enter their wellness data into the computer. The areas evaluated are described in the Wellness Profile (see Figure 11.1, page 229). Once all data are typed in, a printout is generated stating the student's performance, the significance of each area analyzed, and a recommended minimum fitness level. Parents are advised to consult their family physician if the child's scores are below the recommended minimums. This program is available from Macmillan College Publishing Company.

Generating Individualized Education Programs (IEPs)

Developing individualized education programs for a large number of children is time consuming. This software generates an IEP based on data entered by keyboard. Because a large portion of the IEP does not change, this software allows for efficient change and updating. The IEP software is available from EBSCO Curriculum Materials, P.O. Box 1943, Birmingham, AL 35201.

The**Prudential** FITNESSGRAM®

COMMITTED TO HEALTH RELATED FITNESS

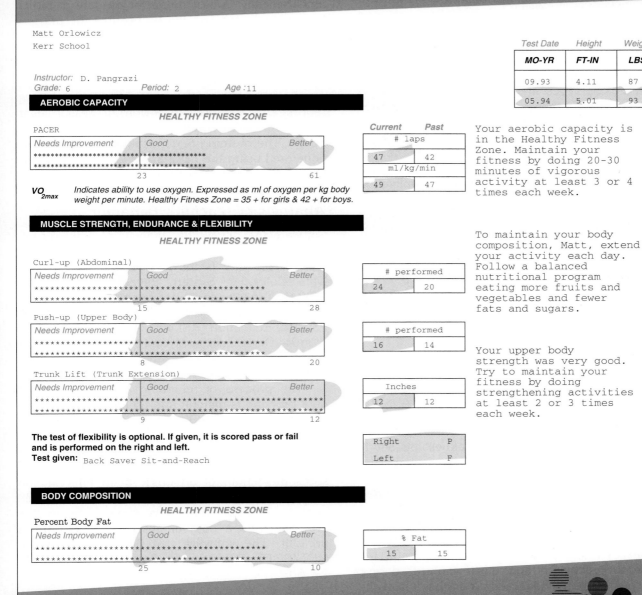

Matt Orlowicz
Kerr School

Instructor: D. Pangrazi
Grade: 6   Period: 2   Age :11

Test Date	Height	Weight
MO-YR	**FT-IN**	**LBS**
09.93	4.11	87
05.94	5.01	93

AEROBIC CAPACITY

HEALTHY FITNESS ZONE

PACER

Needs Improvement	Good	Better

23   61

VO_{2max} Indicates ability to use oxygen. Expressed as ml of oxygen per kg body weight per minute. Healthy Fitness Zone = 35 + for girls & 42 + for boys.

Current	Past
# laps	
47	42
ml/kg/min	
49	47

Your aerobic capacity is in the Healthy Fitness Zone. Maintain your fitness by doing 20-30 minutes of vigorous activity at least 3 or 4 times each week.

MUSCLE STRENGTH, ENDURANCE & FLEXIBILITY

HEALTHY FITNESS ZONE

Curl-up (Abdominal)

Needs Improvement	Good	Better

15   28

# performed	
24	20

To maintain your body composition, Matt, extend your activity each day. Follow a balanced nutritional program eating more fruits and vegetables and fewer fats and sugars.

Push-up (Upper Body)

Needs Improvement	Good	Better

8   20

# performed	
16	14

Your upper body strength was very good. Try to maintain your fitness by doing strengthening activities at least 2 or 3 times each week.

Trunk Lift (Trunk Extension)

Needs Improvement	Good	Better

9   12

Inches	
12	12

The test of flexibility is optional. If given, it is scored pass or fail and is performed on the right and left.
Test given: Back Saver Sit-and-Reach

Right	P
Left	F

BODY COMPOSITION

HEALTHY FITNESS ZONE

Percent Body Fat

Needs Improvement	Good	Better

25   10

% Fat	
15	15

To parent or guardian: *The Prudential FITNESSGRAM is a valuable tool in assessing a young person's fitness level. The area of the bar highlighted in yellow indicates the "healthy fitness zone." All children should strive to maintain levels of fitness within the "healthy fitness zone" or above. By maintaining a healthy fitness level for these areas of fitness your child may have a reduced risk for developing heart disease, obesity or low back pain. Some children may have personal interests that require higher levels of fitness (e.g. athletes).*

Recommended activities for improving fitness are based on each individual's test performance. Ask your child to demonstrate each test item for you. Some teachers may stop the test when performance equals the upper limit of the "healthy fitness zone" rather than requiring a maximal effort.

Developing good exercise habits is important to maintaining lifelong health. You can help your son or daughter develop these habits by encouraging regular participation in physical activity.

© 1992 The Cooper Institute for Aerobics Research

Developed by
The Cooper Institute
for Aerobics Research
Dallas, Texas
Sponsored by
The Prudential
Insurance Company
of America

Figure 10.16 The Prudential Fitnessgram Profile

223

Nutritional Analysis

Many programs currently are available for nutritional analysis. These programs are highly structured and demand that users analyze their diet carefully. In most cases, programs of this nature are probably most useful for individual students who are overweight or malnourished. Information requested includes such personal information as age, weight, height, sex, and amount of physical activity. These data are then used to calculate the individual's caloric, fiber, protein, and lipid needs. The next step is to record the types and amounts of foods eaten daily. A report is then generated that lists calories ingested and expended, the nutrient value for all foods, and the sum total of all nutrients ingested. It is possible to see if a youngster is meeting the recommended dietary allowances (RDA) required.

Another interesting computer application found in some nutritional programs is an accounting of caloric expenditure. The amount of calories expended when performing a specific exercise for a specified amount of time is predicted by the software. An excellent software program for this purpose is *Diet Analysis,* available from Parsons Technology, Inc., One Parsons Drive, P.O. Box 100, Hiawatha, Iowa 52233.

Prescribing Activities

It can be difficult to find activities that will help remedy student shortcomings. An example of a computer program applicable to this area is the Prescriptive Activities program developed by Pangrazi and Pangrazi (1992). Initially, the program asks that the student's area of weakness be identified. Choices are cardiovascular fitness, obesity, flexibility, coordination, and strength in the upper body, lower body, or trunk region. After an area has been identified, the program lists activities to help remediate the area that is deficient. Activities listed by the program offer teachers a variety of remedial options. The program is particularly useful for classroom teachers or specialists who are working with children in individualized programs. It is available from Macmillan College Publishing Company.

Word Processing and Database Packages

A large number of reports can be generated using database and word processing packages. A major use of database software is for entering and storing data, sorting data, and generating a report that makes the data easy to read and analyze for results. For example, with database software, the operator can create a form on the monitor that tells what data to enter and how to enter it. Following the form instructions, a teacher or student can enter test scores and store the data on disk. The data can then be stored (e.g., by best performance, alphabetically by last name, or by date of birth). Any variable entered can be used as the primary sort variable. A printout is then generated and used for instructor analysis or to report student performance.

Word processing software that contains a data-merging feature is now available for generating reports. The advantage of a word processor lies in the easy modification of a report to meet changing needs. The merging feature takes the file of data generated using the database and places the data in the report into proper sequence.

Analysis of Teaching Behavior

Software that allows for analysis of teaching behavior is becoming available. An example of this type of software is the ALT-PE Micro Computer Data Collection System developed by Metzler (1984). If the reader is not cognizant of the technique for measuring Academic Learning Time in Physical Education (ALT-PE), a description can be found in Darst, Zakrajsek, and Mancini (1989). The ALT-PE program analyzes the amount of time engaged in physical education content activity.

The process of recording and analyzing the data by hand is difficult and time consuming. The software program is excellent in that it offers a mode for entering the data directly into the computer and gives a printout as soon as analysis of the lesson is finished. The ALT-PE software measures the length of an observation interval and beeps when it is time to record the data for each interval. When all data have been gathered, the program runs a data analysis and generates a printout. The software can be purchased from METZSOFT, 328 Loudon Road, Blacksburg, VA 24060.

Grading

Software packages are available for generating grade reports. This type of software can generate printouts that show cumulative percentages for all students, for the results of a particular student, or for the class as a whole, and a report containing the students' final percentages and letter grades. Scores for other factors such as attendance and effort can be weighted and entered into the report.

Computer-Assisted Instruction

Computer-assisted instruction can be used with elementary school youngsters in cognitive areas requiring drill and practice. The advantage of this approach is that it offers the student immediate feedback on a correct or incorrect answer. Some type of reinforcement along with feedback can be built into the instructional software.

Areas that can be developed effectively for computer-assisted instruction are quizzes related to various sport strategies, safety rules and regulations, components of and guidelines for developing fitness, and various aspects of school procedure, such as grading and discipline. The cognitive information can be built into crossword puzzles, word searches, fill in the blanks, and true and false questions. When the correct answer is supplied by the student, a reinforcing response is flashed on the screen (e.g., "Exactly right! You must be brilliant."). On the other hand, if an incorrect answer is supplied, the response might be, "Sorry, that is incorrect. Go back and read page 2 of your handout to identify the correct answer."

Computer-assisted instruction is individually applied. It allows students to proceed at a rate that is meaningful to them. Conceivably, students might be released for a short interval from physical education activity to learn to use the computer. Once students can use the computer, teachers' group instruction duties are reduced, allowing them more time to work individually with students.

REFERENCES AND SUGGESTED READINGS

Cooper Institute for Aerobics Research. (1992). *The Prudential Fitnessgram test administration manual.* Dallas: Author.

Darst, P. W., Zakrajsek, D. B., & Mancini, V. H. (1989). *Analyzing physical education and sport instruction* (2nd ed.). Champaign, IL: Human Kinetics.

Hastad, D., & Lacy, A. (1994). *Measurement and evaluation in contemporary physical education* (2nd ed.). Scottsdale, AZ: Gorsuch Scarisbrick.

Metzler, M. W. (1984). *ALT-PE micro computer data collection system.* Blacksburg, VA: METZSOFT.

Johnson, D. W., Johnson, R. T., & Holubec, E. J. (1990). *Circles of learning: Cooperation in the classroom.* Edina, MN: Interaction.

Pangrazi, R. P., & Pangrazi, C. P. (1992). *Fitness and wellness through dynamic physical education.* Tempe, AZ: Pandau Media.

Siedentop, D. (1991). *Developing teaching skills in physical education.* Palo Alto, CA: Mayfield.

Wellness: Developing a Healthy Lifestyle

*I*f a child were asked what the concept of wellness means, a typical answer might be to "feel good." The term means more, however, than just adequate health. It means attainment of a special type of lifestyle driven by nurturing the body and avoiding substances that are destructive to a healthy body. Some adults think that if exercise is done regularly, it is possible to ignore the rest of the factors related to wellness. Physical education should teach that an active lifestyle is not enough; alcohol, drugs, obesity, and poor nutrition can easily negate the benefits of exercise.

Wellness programs, stressing personal wellness planning, are being established in major medical centers. Only recently, however, have schools given attention to the concept. For children, wellness becomes a value issue and a search to understand how the body functions. Motivation is important, because most children have little cultural or educational background for learning the concepts of wellness. Some parents have had minimal exposure to wellness planning, which makes it important that physical educators teach children how to maintain a lifestyle that in turn maintains wellness.

Wellness instruction is subject to individual interpretation by children as a result of their differing backgrounds and experiences. In the educational process, children become listeners and potential consumers. Wellness education in the schools should establish a fundamental basis for effective living. The approach at the elementary school level covers three parts.

First, the physical education program should impart *knowledge* that contributes to the concepts of wellness. A child needs to understand the human body and how it functions. This involves teaching rudimentary anatomy, simple physiology, and relevant movement principles. The information must be relevant to situations that students face.

The second part should develop an *understanding of lifestyles* that contribute to or are destructive to wellness. Wellness is not an entity in itself, but is composed of various lifestyles that form a coordinated whole. Youngsters need to understand and practice healthy lifestyles that help them achieve wellness.

The final step is to provide opportunity for *applying concepts* through a variety of learning experiences. Knowledge is not enough; children must use the knowledge in a context directly related to enhancing wellness. Without this step, the entire process is merely academic practice. The physical education learning environment can help children assimilate the substance of wellness concepts.

TEACHING WELLNESS IN THE PHYSICAL EDUCATION SETTING

Nowhere is it assumed that the achievement of wellness is the concern solely of physical education. Some aspects of wellness, such as development of a personalized level of physical fitness, are emphasized primarily in physical education. Other aspects can be developed cooperatively with classroom teachers. A physical education teacher may justifiably raise the question: How can I develop physical fitness levels, teach skills, and accomplish all the topics listed under wellness? Once again, the question is one of priorities. What is gained if students leave school without a basic wellness understanding? Few schools offer health education programs, which means that if physical educators do not teach wellness, students will not learn about wellness.

There are different approaches used for teaching of wellness in elementary school physical education classes. Physical activity is still the cornerstone of physical education, and the substitution of a knowledge–discussion program at the expense of activity is not recommended. On the other hand, a strong case can be made that activity, without a knowledge base of how and why, will be ineffective in the long run. If classroom time cannot be found for teaching wellness activities, discussions should

be held to a 5-minute limit in physical education classes. Using some of physical education class time for wellness instruction will signal to students that wellness is an important part of the program. Examples of ideas that can be discussed in limited time without disrupting physical education are:

- learning how to take the heart rate
- knowing what activities are aerobic and anaerobic
- muscles that are strengthened by different exercises
- understanding why strength is important in skill performance
- knowing what foods should be avoided
- understanding how weight is maintained through caloric balance of exercise and eating

Each of these topics can be discussed quickly during a closure session at the end of the lesson. The intent of the discussions is to stimulate interaction and rudimentary understanding of basic wellness principles.

Many school districts and parents are demanding that homework be assigned to raise academic standards. Physical education need not be an exception to the rule. Homework can encourage parental participation at home and help parents understand that physical education is more than just activity. In addition, meaningful homework experiences may help teachers in other academic areas view physical education in a more positive light.

Some districts have successfully designed programs that concentrate on wellness for a period of 2 to 4 weeks. Such wellness instruction is spaced out during the school year. During those weeks, physical education classes per se are canceled and moved to a classroom where the physical education specialist conducts wellness sessions. This results in concentrated instruction in a setting (the classroom) that is conducive to cognitive and affective development. Many variations of this approach have been developed to accommodate specific school parameters. At the least, wellness instruction gives children a better understanding of their body and its possibilities, which can mean higher achievement. At best, the wellness approach becomes the pursuit of excellence, inspiring children to make the most of their physical and movement potential.

Wellness Profile

The wellness profile can be an outgrowth of wellness instruction. The profile can be used to identify and assess factors that, if left untreated, could result in later health problems. Typically, schools gather the majority of these data at one time or another but fail to collate the information and make it available to teachers and parents. The wellness profile should be included in the student's permanent record and results sent home to parents so that they are aware of their youngster's health status. The wellness profile is not intended to diagnose disease but to offer basic measurements of health status. If measurements give cause for concern, parents can make a decision to visit the family physician.

The wellness profile in Figure 11.1 illustrates the type of data that can be collected and shared with students and parents. Desirable ranges are offered with a brief explanation of each component measured. A health assessment team that includes school nurses, physical education instructors, and clerical aides can assess a classroom of students in approximately 20 minutes, with the exception of the 1-mile run. Other data that can be included in the wellness profile are results of visual screening, auditory screening, posture checks, and immunization and medical examination records.

INSTRUCTIONAL STRATEGIES FOR TEACHING WELLNESS

Physical education plays a large role in enhancing the fitness and skill levels of students so they have a background that allows them to develop an active lifestyle. Another program goal should also be to help young people make responsible lifestyle decisions. People are faced with many decisions that positively or negatively impact their level of wellness. The ability to make responsible decisions depends on a wide range of factors: an understanding of one's feelings and clarification of personal values, an ability to cope with stress and personal problems, an ability to make decisions, and understanding the impact of various lifestyles on health.

March, 1988

_____
Room

_____
Age of child

To the parent/guardian of: _____
Name of Child

Your child's health status was recently examined as part of the Health Evaluation Program in Mesa Public Schools. Listed below are your child's results and a general interpretation of the scores for a child in this age group. An explanation of the items included in this screening is listed on the next page.

HEALTH COMPONENT	SCORE		ABOVE AVG.	AVG.	BELOW AVG.
Skinfold (sum of tricep and calf)	_____	millimeters	_____	_____	_____
Sit and Reach Test	_____	centimeters	_____	_____	_____
Sit-ups (one minute)	_____	repetitions	_____	_____	_____
Aerobic Field Test (one mile run-walk)	_____	minutes seconds	_____	_____	_____
Height	_____	inches	_____	_____	_____
Weight	_____	pounds	_____	_____	_____
Blood Pressure:			ACCEPTABLE		NEEDS FOLLOW-UP
Systolic	_____	mm/Hg	_____		_____
Diastolic	_____	mm/Hg	_____		_____
Dental/Oral Inspection			_____		_____
Scoliosis Screening			_____		_____

The program is not meant to diagnose disease, but to indicate basic measurements of health. If you are concerned or advised to seek medical attention for your child, please take this form to your doctor or clinic. Please feel free to contact the P.E. teacher or school nurse if you have any questions about the program.

EXPLANATION OF HEALTH COMPONENTS

Skinfold: This measurement relates to the amount of fat a person carries. People who have too much fat are more likely to develop problems such as diabetes (excessive sugar in the blood) and high blood pressure.

Sit and Reach: The sit and reach test measures flexibility of the lower back and hamstring (back of thigh) muscle group. A lack of flexibility often contributes to low back pain.

Sit-ups: Sit-ups measure the strength of the abdominal muscle group. Strength in this area is important for proper posture and to prevent low back pain.

Aerobic Field Test: The aerobic field test consists of running or walking a mile in the least amount of time possible. This test is the best single indicator of cardio-respiratory endurance, which is important in preventing heart disease.

Height and Weight: These are general measurements of a child's growth. It is important that children's growth be observed regularly to assure the body is developing normally.

Blood Pressure: Blood pressure is recorded using two values. The top number (systolic) represents the pressure in the arteries when the heart is pumping blood. The bottom number (diastolic) is the pressure in the arteries when the heart is at rest. High blood pressure increases the risk of heart disease.

Dental/Oral Inspection: An inspection of the gums and teeth is conducted to detect noticeable inflammation, sores, and cavities.

Scoliosis Screening: A visual examination of the spine is done to detect any abnormal curvature. Normal spinal alignment is necessary for optimal heart/lung function and development of muscles.

INTERPRETING THE RESULTS:

Results are in two categories. The first is the raw score, which is the actual performance of your child. The column to the right is derived from a percentile score and allows comparison of your child in relationship to other children of similar age. For example, scores falling between the 75th and 100th percentile are considered above average. Scores between the 25th and 75th percentile are average and scores between 0 and 25th percentile are considered below average. With respect to the skinfold measure, a higher amount of skinfold indicates a higher level of body fat content. Thus an above-average score on skinfold is generally less favorable.

Figure 11.1 Example of a wellness profile

Developing Awareness and Decision-Making Skills

The focus of wellness instruction should be to view the student as a total being. Stability is predicated on all parts fitting together in a smooth and consistent fashion. When a problem occurs, the balance of physiology, thinking, and function tends to be disrupted. Individuals then need to use their knowledge, coping ability, and decision-making skills to restore the equilibrium associated with personal stability. Teachers can try to help students understand their feelings, values, and attitudes, and the impact that these have on coping and decision making.

Coping Skills

Coping is the ability to deal with problems successfully. Learning to cope with life's problems is dependent on and interrelated with knowledge of self, decision-making skills, and the ability to relate to others. Specific skills dealing with coping include the following:

1. *Admit that a problem exists and face it.* Coping with a problem is impossible when the problem is not recognized.

2. *Define the problem and who owns it.* Individuals must identify what needs to be coped with and decide if the problem is theirs or belongs to others.

3. *List alternative solutions to the problem.* A basic step in decision making, problem solving, and coping is to identify what alternatives are open in a given situation.

4. *Predict consequences for oneself and others.* Once alternatives are identified, weighing the potential consequences of each, and then ranking them in order of preference, is an important process.

5. *Identify and consult sources of help.* All possible sources of help available to assist in carrying out alternatives should be considered. To do this, students need to have some knowledge of the available resources or know how to find resources.

6. *Experiment with a solution and evaluate the results.* If the decision did not produce satisfactory results, try another alternative. Evaluation of results also allows people to keep track of their ability to come up with satisfying solutions.

Decision-Making Skills

Youngsters are faced with many life situations in which decisions must be made. Decision making is something that everyone does every day, often without thinking. Because it is a common act, it receives little attention until a person is faced with an important decision that has long-term consequences. Although schools attempt to help students learn how to make personally satisfying decisions, a major portion of teacher time is spent supplying information to students. Although this teacher function is extremely important, it is only one part of the decision-making process. Teachers should ask themselves the question, "If you are going to provide information to others, what do you want them to do with that information?" Opportunities should be provided that help students put the information to use.

Decision making is defined as a process in which a person selects from two or more possible choices. A decision cannot exist unless more than one course of action is available to consider. Decision making enables the individual to reason through life situations, to solve problems, and, to some extent, to direct behavior. There are no right answers for the decision made; rather, the decision is judged by a student's effective use of a process that results in satisfying consequences. This criterion distinguishes decision making from problem solving. Problem solving usually identifies one best or right solution for everyone involved. When making decisions, students should consider each of the following steps.

1. *Gather information.* If meaningful choices are to be made, gathering all available information is important. Information should be gathered from as many sources as possible. Students will generally consider information valid if they see that it comes from many different sources and that it allows them to view both sides of an issue. Too often, teachers present students with information that supports only the instructor's point of view.

2. *Consider the available choices.* The next step is to consider all of the available choices. It does not make sense to consider alternatives that, in reality, have no possibility of being selected. Considering the choices is an important step if students are to realize that they have many different possibilities from which to choose and that what they choose will influence the direction of their life. In the school setting, many choices have been made for students, and they sometimes come to believe that others make all decisions for them and that they, in turn, bear no responsibility for their successes or failures.

3. *Analyze the consequences of choices.* When the various choices are delineated, students must

consider the consequences that accompany each choice. If the consequences are ignored, the choice made may be unwise and detrimental to good health. Making wise decisions about wellness demands that students be aware of the consequences. This means understanding why some people choose to smoke or drink, even when they understand the negative consequences. The most important role of the teacher is to help students identify the positive and negative consequences without moralizing or telling the students how to think.

4. *Make a decision and implement it.* When all the information has been gathered, students must make a decision and integrate it into their lifestyle. These decisions are personal to each student and need not be revealed to others.

Skillful decision makers have more control over their lives because they can reduce the amount of uncertainty in their choices and limit the degree to which chance or their peers determine their future. Two individuals may face a similar decision and make different choices, because each person is different and places differing values on outcomes. The individual makes each decision unique. Learning decision-making skills therefore increases the possibility that students can achieve personal goals.

Decisions also have limits. Each decision is necessarily limited by what a person is capable of doing, by what a person is willing to do, and by the environment in which the decision is made. The environment in which decision-making skills are practiced is important for proper development of these skills. A nonjudgmental atmosphere is usually most appropriate. Since solutions differ for different people, the person making a decision should be free to select from any of the available choices and learn to accept the probable consequences and results of choices made.

LEADING DISCUSSION SESSIONS

The success of discussions depends on how effectively the teacher is able to establish and maintain the integrity and structure of the lesson and the students' psychological freedom. Integrity and structure mean that all students are dealing with the same issue in a thoughtful and responsible way. Psychological freedom means that individual students participate to the degree they want to by (a) commenting when they choose to do so or refraining from comment when they so desire, (b) responding to direct questions or choosing to "pass" for the time being, (c) agreeing or disagreeing with

what others in the group have said, or (d) deciding what data they need, if any, and reaching out to ask for those data. This demands certain teacher behavior to establish a meaningful environment. A brief description of the necessary teaching behaviors follows.

Structuring

The purpose of structuring is to create a climate that is conducive to open communication by all parties. This is accomplished by outlining expectations and role relationships for both teacher and students. Structuring includes any of the following:

1. Establish the lesson climate at the beginning of the lesson by providing an explanation of what the students and teacher will be doing and how they will work together.

2. Maintain the established lesson structure by not allowing students to be pressured to respond and by seeing that no one's ideas are put down.

3. When necessary, add to or modify the lesson structure established at the beginning of the lesson. For example, this might involve changing to small-group sessions rather than continuing a total class discussion.

Focus Setting

The purpose of focus setting is to establish an explicit and common topic or issue for discussion. Since this teaching behavior is used in different circumstances, there are different ways it can be formulated:

1. A topic can be presented, usually in the form of a question, to the group for their discussion.

2. Focus setting can be used to restate the original question during the lesson or to shift to a new discussion topic when students indicate they have finished discussing the original question.

3. Focus setting can bring the discussion back to the original topic when a student unknowingly shifts to a new topic.

4. Focus setting can label a discussion question presented by a student as a new topic to allow discussion of that topic in place of a previous one.

Clarifying

The purpose of clarifying is to invite a student to help the teacher understand the substance or content of

Leading a wellness discussion

the student's comment. Whenever possible, the clarifying should give students an indication of what the teacher does not understand. In addition, the teacher's remarks should be formulated in such a way that the burden of understanding is placed on the teacher, rather than implying that the student is inarticulate, and therefore deficient. Clarifying is used by teachers only when they do not understand. The teacher does not assume the responsibility of clarifying for the students.

Acknowledging

Acknowledging informs a student talking to the teacher that the teacher understands what has been said and that the comments have made a contribution to the discussion. Unlike most teaching behaviors, this one can be implemented nonverbally as well as by verbal means. How acknowledging is worded and when it is used must be considered carefully. To use acknowledging only when the teacher understands and agrees, but to do something else when the teacher understands and disagrees, is a serious misunderstanding of the purpose and function of this teaching behavior.

Acknowledging is intended to be a nonjudgmental way of saying "I understand."

Teacher Silence

Teacher silence is used is to communicate to students through nonverbal means that it is their responsibility to initiate and carry on the discussion. Teacher silence is used only in response to student silence. It protects the students' rights and responsibility to make their own decisions about the topic being discussed. In a sense, this teaching behavior is a nonbehavior.

UNDERSTANDING THE BODY AND HOW IT FUNCTIONS

The material in this section is couched in terms of the knowledge and understandings that elementary school students must develop. The areas presented are rudimentary and illustrate examples of knowledge, concepts, and experiences children must understand to develop a value set that enhances personal wellness. Since most children feel healthy and have little concern about health, this unit should focus on establishing a foundation for developing proper health attitudes for adolescent and adult life.

Students must understand two major categories of wellness concepts. The first is basic knowledge of how the body functions and how it can be maintained through proper care and activity. The second category centers on roadblocks that stand in the path of wellness. Some of these are stress, improper nutrition, obesity, anorexia, substance abuse, and personal safety problems. Basic concepts and suggested learning activities are listed for each area.

The Skeletal System

The skeletal system (Figure 11.2) is the framework of the body and consists of 208 separate bones. The bones act as a system of levers and are linked together by connections (*joints*) that allow movement. The bones are held together at the joints by ligaments and muscles. Ligaments are tough and incapable of stretching. They do not contract the way muscles do and are therefore subject to injury when the bones are moved beyond their natural range.

Joints that are freely movable are called *synovial* joints. Synovial fluid is secreted to lubricate the joint and reduce friction. A thin layer of cartilage also reduces friction at the ends of the bones.

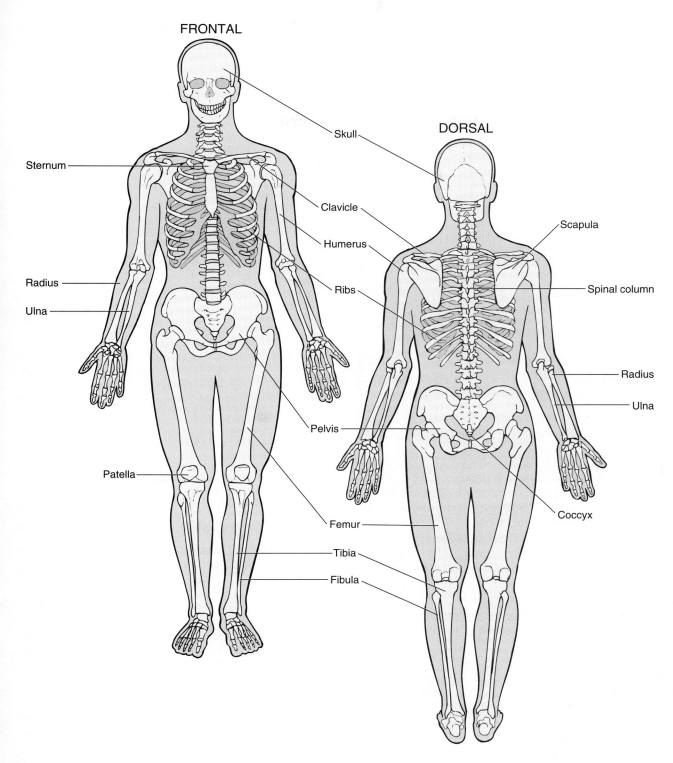

FRONTAL

DORSAL

Skull

Sternum

Clavicle

Humerus

Ribs

Radius

Ulna

Scapula

Spinal column

Radius

Ulna

Pelvis

Patella

Coccyx

Femur

Tibia

Fibula

Figure 11.2 Skeletal system

233

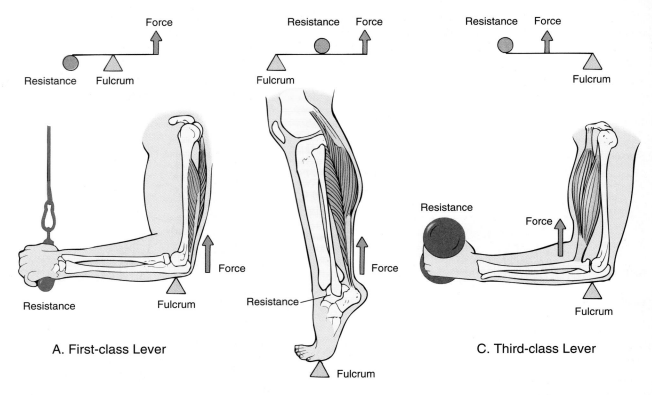

Figure 11.3 Types of levers in human joints

A disk, or meniscus, forms a pad between many of the weight-bearing joints for the purpose of absorbing shock. When a cartilage is damaged, joint dysfunction and pain can occur.

Muscular activity increases the weight-bearing stresses on bones. The bones respond to the added stress by increasing in mineral content and density, increasing in diameter, and reorganizing internal elements to cause an increase in bone strength. The bones serve as a mineral reserve for the body and can become deformed as a result of dietary deficiencies.

The bones and joints establish levers with muscles acting as the force. Three types of lever are identified and classified by the arrangement of the fulcrum, force, and resistance.

The forearm is an example of a first-class lever when it is extended at the elbow joint (fulcrum) by the triceps muscle (Figure 11.3A). A second-class lever exists where the gastrocnemius raises the weight of the body to the toes (Figure 11.3B). Examples of third-class lever actions are the movement of the biceps muscle to flex the forearm at the elbow joint (Figure 11.3C), the sideward movement of the upper arm at the shoulder joint

by the deltoid muscle, and the flexion of the lower leg at the knee joint by the hamstring muscles.

Requisite Knowledge

1. The skeletal system consists of 208 bones and determines the external appearance of the body.

2. Joints are places where two or more bones are fastened together to make a movable connection.

3. Bones are held together by ligaments and muscle tissue. The stronger the muscles surrounding the joint, the more resistant the joint is to injury.

4. Good posture results when the bones are in proper alignment. Alignment depends on the muscular system. When antigravity muscles are weak, greater stress is put on the joints, and poor posture results.

5. The bones and joints establish levers with muscles serving as the force.

6. The attachment of the muscle to the bone determines the mechanical advantage that can be gained at the joint. Generally, the farther

from the joint the muscle attaches, the greater is the force that can be generated.

7. The body has three types of levers. These are classified by the arrangement of the fulcrum, force, and resistance.

Suggested Learning Experiences

1. Identify and locate major bones significant in body movement. The following are suggested:
   a. head-skull
   b. arm-shoulder, girdle-radius, ulna, ribs, humerus, scapula (shoulder blade), clavicle (collarbone)
   c. chest-sternum (breastbone), ribs
   d. back-pelvis-spinal column, pelvis, coccyx
   e. thigh-leg-femur, tibia, fibula, patella (kneecap)

2. Identify the types of movement possible at selected joints. Study the neck, shoulder, elbow, wrist, spinal column, hip, knee, and ankle joints.

3. Catalog the types of levers found in the body. Illustrate the fulcrum, force, and resistance points.

4. Obtain animal bones from a grocery store and analyze their various components. Cartilage, muscle attachments, ligaments, and bone structure can be studied in this way.

5. Obtain outdated X ray films from physicians. These are excellent sources for identifying differences in various bones and joints.

6. Discuss how levers in the body generate force for throwing, striking, and kicking.

7. Vary the size of the base of support and evaluate its effect on stability.

The Muscular System

Muscles (Figure 11.4) apply force to the bones to create movement. Muscles create movement always through contraction, never by pushing. When one set of muscles contracts, another set that pulls in the opposite direction must relax. This set is the *antagonistic muscle group.*

People are born with two distinct types of muscle fiber. These are often called slow-twitch and fast-twitch fibers. Slow-twitch fibers respond well to aerobic activities, whereas fast-twitch fibers are suited to anaerobic activities. This is one of the reasons people perform differently in different physical activities. For example, those born with a high percentage of slow-twitch fibers would be suited to distance running but might do poorly in sprint races.

Strength can be increased when muscles are overloaded. Overload occurs when a person does more than a normal amount of work. In young people, strength can be increased without a change in the muscle size. Exercises should overload as many muscle groups as possible to ensure total body development. Strength is an important factor in the development of motor skills.

Flexibility is the range of motion possible at a given joint. Exercises should apply resistance through the full range of motion to maintain flexibility. Extensor and flexor muscle groups are antagonists to each other, and both groups should be exercised equally.

Requisite Knowledge

1. Muscles can pull and shorten (contract); they never push.

2. Flexors cause a decrease in joint angle, and extensors cause an increase. There should be a balance of development between these antagonistic muscle groups.

3. The fixed portion of a muscle (origin) usually has muscle fibers attached directly to the bone or may be attached by a tendon to the bone. The moving portion of the muscle forms a tendon, which attaches to a bone (insertion).

4. Overload with proper progression is necessary for muscle development. Muscles become strong in both boys and girls through exercise. After adolescence, boys' muscles will increase in size owing to the male hormone testosterone. Girls' muscles do not show the same degree of increase.

5. Muscles are important for proper posture. Good muscle tone makes good posture comfortable and puts a minimum amount of strain on the joints.

6. Different types of training are necessary for aerobic and anaerobic activity.

7. Muscles are composed of many small fibers. When these fibers contract, they do so according to the all-or-none principle—that is, if they contract, they contract completely. Differences in the contraction strength of a muscle are a function of the percentage of muscle fibers recruited and asked to contract.

8. When muscles are fatigued, the muscle fibers will no longer contract.

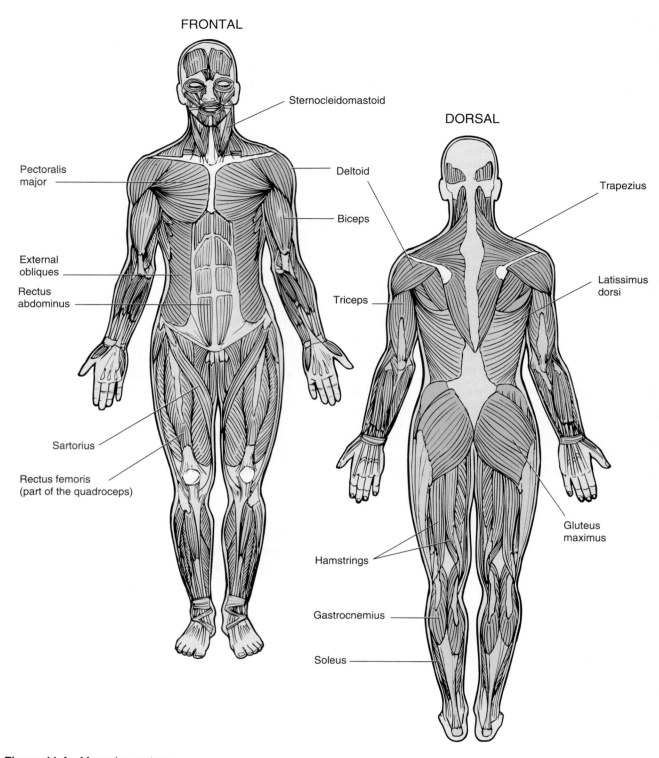

FRONTAL

Sternocleidomastoid

Pectoralis
major

Deltoid

Biceps

External
obliques

Rectus
abdominus

Triceps

Sartorius

Rectus femoris
(part of the quadroceps)

DORSAL

Trapezius

Latissimus
dorsi

Gluteus
maximus

Hamstrings

Gastrocnemius

Soleus

Figure 11.4 Muscular system

236

Suggested Learning Experiences

1. Identify major muscles or muscle groups and their functions at the joint. Muscle groups suggested for elaboration are the following:

   a. head-neck-sternocleidomastoids

   b. arm-shoulder girdle-biceps, triceps, pectorals, deltoid, latissimus dorsi, trapezius

   c. body-abdominals (rectus abdominis and the obliques)

   d. thigh-leg-gluteus, hamstrings, rectus femoris (the quadriceps), gastrocnemius, soleus, sartorius

2. Learn the significance of the suffix -ceps in biceps, triceps, and quadriceps. The suffix refers to the points of origin (heads). The biceps has two points of origin (heads), the triceps has three, and the quadriceps has four.

3. The Achilles and patellar tendons should be identified. How the Achilles tendon got its name makes an interesting story. Achilles's mother dipped Achilles in the River Styx to make him immune from arrows. Unfortunately, she held him by the heel cord, thus preventing that area from coming into contact with the magic water. Achilles was later killed by an arrow that hit his one vulnerable spot, hence the name Achilles tendon.

4. The sartorius muscle is called the tailor's muscle, because years ago, tailors sat cross-legged while sewing, thus causing the muscle to shorten. The tailors then had trouble making ordinary leg movements because of the shortened muscle.

5. Know approximately where each muscle originates and how it causes movement at the joint by attaching to a particular bone or bones. Recognize the muscles being developed by various exercises.

6. Study animal muscle under a microscope. Identify various parts of the muscle.

7. Involve students in a project featuring a "Muscle of the Month." The classroom teacher can cooperate by presenting basic facts about the muscle in classroom work. The physical education teacher can make drawings showing the anatomy of the muscle (origin, insertion, and location) (Figure 11.5) and post these in the gymnasium and classroom. Pay attention to spelling and pronunciation. Over a two-year period, all of the suggested muscle groups can be studied.

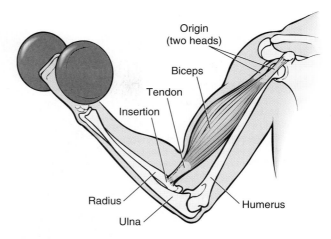

Figure 11.5 Anatomy of a muscle

8. Discuss how antagonistic muscle groups contract and relax alternately to cause movement. Identify which muscles are relaxed and which are contracting when movement occurs.

The Cardiorespiratory System

The cardiorespiratory system consists of the heart, lungs, arteries, capillaries, and veins. The heart is a muscular organ that pumps blood through the circulatory system—arteries, capillaries, and veins, in that order. The heart has its own blood vessels—the coronary arteries—which nourish it to keep it alive, for the heart draws no nourishment from the blood going through the chambers as it pumps. The blood supply to the heart is critical, and a decreased flow can damage the heart muscle. Decreased flow may result from a buildup of fatty deposits or from a blockage, either of which can be serious enough to be regarded as heart disease.

The heart has two chambers, the right and left ventricles (Figure 11.6). The left side of the heart pumps blood carrying nutrients and oxygen to the body through the arteries to the capillaries, where the nutrients and oxygen are exchanged for waste products and carbon dioxide. The waste-carrying blood is returned through the veins to the right side of the heart, from which the blood is routed through the lungs to discharge the carbon dioxide and pick up fresh oxygen. This oxygen-renewed blood returns to the left side of the heart to complete the circuit. Other waste products are discharged through the kidneys.

Each time the heart beats, it pumps both chambers. The beat is called the *pulse*, and its impact travels through the body. The pulse is measured in number of beats per minute: a pulse rate of 75 means that the heart is beating 75 times each

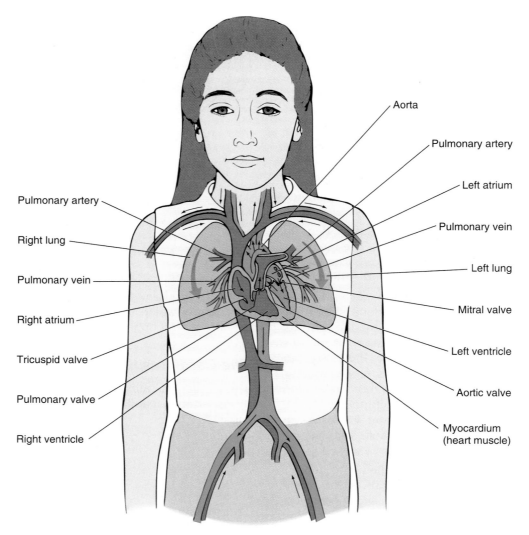

Labels (left side, top to bottom): Pulmonary artery, Right lung, Pulmonary vein, Right atrium, Tricuspid valve, Pulmonary valve, Right ventricle

Labels (right side, top to bottom): Aorta, Pulmonary artery, Left atrium, Pulmonary vein, Left lung, Mitral valve, Left ventricle, Aortic valve, Myocardium (heart muscle)

Figure 11.6 Structure of the heart (After the American Heart Association)

minute. The output of the heart is determined by the pulse rate and by the *stroke volume,* the amount of blood discharged by each beat.

The pulse is measured by placing the two middle fingers of the right hand on the thumb side of the subject's wrist (Figure 11.7) while the subject is seated. Taking the pulse at the wrist is usually preferable to using the carotid artery (along the neck), because pressure on the carotid artery decreases blood flow to the brain. Pulse for baseline data should be taken two or three times to make sure that it is accurate. The pulse is usually taken for 10 or 15 seconds and converted to a per minute rate by using the appropriate multiplier.

The respiratory system includes the entryways (nose and mouth), the trachea (windpipe), the primary bronchi, and the lungs. Figure 11.8 shows

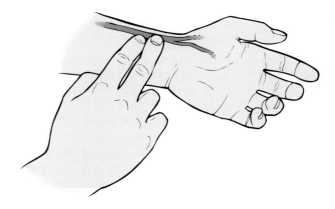

Figure 11.7 Taking the pulse at the wrist

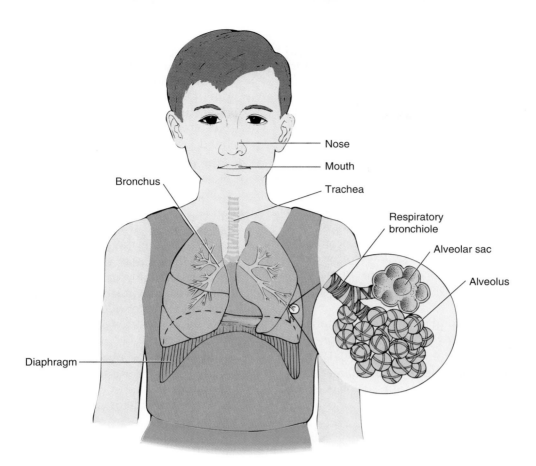

Figure 11.8 Components of the respiratory system

components of the system. Breathing consists of inhaling and exhaling air. Air contains 21 percent oxygen, which is necessary for life. Inspiration is assisted by muscular contraction, and expiration is accomplished by relaxing the muscles. Inspiration occurs when the intercostal muscles and diaphragm contract. This enlarges the chest cavity, and expansion of the lungs causes air to flow in as a result of reduced air pressure. When the muscles are relaxed, the size of the chest cavity is reduced, the pressure on the lungs is increased, and air flows from the lungs. Air can also be expelled forcibly.

The primary function of the lungs is to provide oxygen, carried by the bloodstream, to the cells on demand. The amount of oxygen needed will vary depending on activity level. When an individual exercises strenuously, the rate of respiration increases to bring more oxygen to the tissues. If the amount of oxygen carried to the cells is adequate to maintain the level of activity, the activity is termed *aerobic* (endurance) exercise. Examples are walking, jogging, and bicycling for distance. If, because of high-intensity activity such as sprinting

or climbing stairs, not enough oxygen can be brought to the cells, the body continues to operate for a short time without oxygen. This results in an oxygen debt, which must be repaid later. In this case, the activity is termed *anaerobic* exercise.

After exercise, the respiratory rate gradually returns to normal. The recovery rate is faster if the oxygen debt built up during exercise was a small one. An individual has recovered from an oxygen debt when blood pressure, heart rate, and respiration rate have returned to pre-exercise levels.

Requisite Knowledge

1. The heart is a muscular organ, and its development and maintenance are a function of the demands placed on it through exercise.

2. The heart beats faster when a person exercises.

3. An important factor in establishing cardiorespiratory conditioning is regular exercise. Regular exercise produces a training effect that results in a decreased resting heart rate and an

increased stroke volume (the amount of blood the heart pumps each time it beats) due to hypertrophy of the heart muscle. If the training effect is to occur, the heart rate must be elevated to the training zone (see suggested learning experience 7, following) for 10 to 20 minutes.

4. Through exercise and training, the respiratory system is able to move more oxygen into the body because of an increase in the strength and endurance of the respiratory muscles.

5. The pulse rate varies depending on the level of fitness and other variables. Heart rate among girls usually averages 10 beats per minute more than among boys. As children grow older, their heart rate decreases. Fear, excitement, or a change in body position also affect the resting heart rate.

6. Cardiorespiratory conditioning is important for children. Many circulation and respiratory disorders in adults have a childhood origin.

7. Increased levels of cholesterol and other fats in the blood cause buildup of fatty deposits in the coronary arteries.

8. Some factors (e.g., heredity, sex, race, and age) that affect the cardiorespiratory system are impossible to control. Risk can be minimized, however, by controlling other factors such as smoking, body weight, diet, blood pressure level, and amount of regular exercise.

9. The immediate effects of exercise are to increase the rate of breathing and the volume of air brought into the lungs.

Suggested Learning Experiences

1. Emphasize the risk factors of cardiovascular disease. Use the acronym DANGER.

   *D*on't smoke.

   *A*void foods high in fat and cholesterol.

   *N*ow control high blood pressure and diabetes.

   *G*et regular medical checkups.

   *E*xercise each day.

   *R*educe if overweight.

2. Demonstrate and compare pulse rate in different body positions. Take the baseline pulse rate first (two or three times) with the subject in a sitting position. Take the pulse rate with the subject standing and lying down.

3. Using a single subject, show the relationship between exercise and heart action. Take the resting pulse and record it on the chalkboard.

Have the subject run in place for 1 minute. Take the pulse rate immediately for 10 seconds and record it. Continue taking the pulse at five 2-minute intervals to demonstrate recovery rate. (The pulse rate is approximately doubled after the stipulated exercise.) Discuss why pulse rate increases with exercise and how the heart is strengthened through regular exercise.

4. Take the blood pressure immediately after exercise and again after resting for 3 minutes. Compare the difference.

5. To show how excess weight affects an individual, use two subjects of the same sex who are similar in build. Take the baseline pulse rate for each and record it. Give one subject 15 pounds in added weight (use two 7½-pound weights) and have both subjects travel back and forth ten times across the width of the gym. Immediately take the pulse rates and record them. Compare the rates of the two subjects.

6. Compare pulse rate changes after different kinds of exercise—walking, running, rope jumping, and rope climbing. Standardize the exercise time factor at 1 or 2 minutes.

7. Calculate the heartbeat range that should be maintained to achieve the training effect and to ensure that the individual is not under- or over-exercising. To do this, first determine the estimated maximum heart rate by taking 220 minus the student's age, then multiply the difference by 60 percent and by 80 percent. An example for a child of age 10 follows.

   220 minus 10 = 210

   60 percent of 210 = 126

   80 percent of 210 = 168

   The heart rate range for this student to maintain while exercising is 126 to 168. The pulse rate should be checked during exercise to see whether the training effect is occurring. Charts showing exercising heart rate ranges should be placed on bulletin boards in the gymnasium so that students can quickly translate the results.

8. Compare respiration rates before and after exercise.

9. Compare the volume of air moved before and after strenuous activity. Large plastic garbage bags can be used to collect expired air prior to exercise. After 2 minutes of exercise, expired air can be gathered in another bag. Compare the volume of air collected in the two bags.

10. Allow youngsters to listen to their heartbeats with a stethoscope. Have them exercise for a

Students checking their pulse rate

minute or two and listen to their heartbeats again.

Health-Related Physical Fitness

Physical fitness is defined as the ability to carry out daily tasks with vigor and alertness, without undue fatigue, and with ample energy to enjoy leisure pursuits and to meet unforeseen emergencies. Physical fitness can best be understood in terms of its components, each of which has a distinctive feature and contributes an essential element to the individual. The most important measurable components of physical fitness are muscular strength and endurance, cardiovascular endurance, flexibility, and body composition.

Strength refers to the ability of a muscle or muscle group to exert force. To develop strength, the child's learning experiences should include a regular program of intense activity involving all large-muscle groups. Strength is necessary in skill performance. Without strength, a low standard of performance can be expected, because muscles give out before they can reach their potential. Muscular *endurance* is the ability of the muscles to perform a desired activity without excessive fatigue. It is related to strength in that a stronger person is able to keep up muscular effort longer than a weaker person.

Cardiovascular endurance refers to the ability to maintain total body activity for extended periods of time. People with adequate levels of cardiorespiratory fitness can postpone fatigue and can con-

tinue performing muscular effort. Cardiovascular endurance is based on the movement of oxygen to the muscles at the cellular level so that a constant source of energy is available. Whereas cardiorespiratory endurance is related to general movement (i.e., walking or running), muscular endurance is related to specific activity (i.e., push-ups, throwing, or jumping).

Flexibility is a person's range of movement at the joints. A particularly flexible individual can stretch farther, touch the toes more easily, and bend farther than others. Flexibility allows freedom of movement and the ready adjustment of the body to various movements.

Body composition is the proportion of body fat to lean body mass. Attaining physical fitness is difficult when an individual's body composition contains a high amount of body fat. An understanding of caloric intake and expenditure is important for weight control. It is possible to eat enough to gain weight regardless of the amount of exercise performed.

Requisite Knowledge

1. Physical fitness is acquired only through muscular effort. Activity should be intense, regular, and varied enough to develop all components of physical fitness.

2. The maintenance of physical fitness must be ongoing; gains in fitness levels can be lost in a span of six to eight weeks. Fitness is a lifelong pursuit.

3. Isotonic muscular contractions are the basis of muscular effort, with isometric contractions an important auxiliary.

4. To provide body symmetry, exercises for muscle development should involve similar workloads for extensor and flexor muscle groups. (Flexor muscles decrease the angle of a joint, and extensor muscles cause the return from flexion.)

5. To maintain fitness, a person must have a regular exercise program involving a relatively constant workload. To raise the level of fitness, the workload must be increased progressively.

6. Cardiorespiratory endurance is enhanced by moderate and continued activity, such as jogging, running, or swimming laps, over relatively long periods of time.

7. Exercise, to be beneficial, must be done properly. Certain exercises should be avoided (see pp. 288–289).

8. Flexibility activities should feature static stretching. Muscles are stretched slowly and then held in the maximum position for 15 to 45 seconds. Ballistic stretching, which uses repetitive, forceful movements to stretch a muscle group, is not recommended.

9. Flexibility is specific to a given joint. Students should learn exercises that stretch all joints. General flexibility is the sum total of the flexibility of all joints. Measuring the range of motion at one or two selected joints can, however, give a general indication of overall flexibility.

10. Muscles must be strong enough to accomplish tasks and to keep the joints in line for good posture.

Suggested Learning Experiences

1. Acquire a cardboard or wooden box about 10 inches high with a flat top. Sit on the floor with legs together and flat on the floor so that the soles are placed against the box side. Begin with arms placed behind the back and palms on the floor to support the body in an erect sitting position. Bring both arms forward slowly and bend the body forward, without bouncing, to touch the toes, the box, or beyond the edge of the box. Measure how many inches the student can reach beyond the edge of the box.

2. This experiment requires a large protractor (approximately 2 feet in diameter) and a *goniometer,* an instrument for measuring joint angles. A rough goniometer can be made from two pieces of wood or metal, each piece approximately 2 feet long, 2 inches wide, and ¼ inch thick. In each of the pieces, bore a hole about 1 inch from the end. Connect the two pieces with a bolt and thumbscrew. Now open the goniometer so that the two pieces form a straight line. In measuring the elbow joint, place the bolt at the center of the joint. Raise the forearm as far as possible and bring up one arm of the instrument to match the angle of the flexed movement. Tighten the thumbscrew to maintain the instrument angle. Rubber bands on the limbs can be used to hold the instrument in place. Measure the angle on the homemade goniometer with the protractor to quantify the individual's range of motion.

3. Discuss what a physically fit person is. Is it related to looks? Is it related to athletic ability? If a person is active on a regular basis, is he fit? If a person does well on a fitness test, does that mean she is fit?

4. Allow students to self-test themselves on a fitness test. Use criterion-referenced health standards and discuss how a minimum level of fitness is related to good health.

5. Have students record their activity during a 5-day period. Discuss how the volume of activity will enhance or detract from their fitness levels. Compare the amount of activity they participated in to the amount of television they watched.

6. Identify and discuss the various components of health-related fitness. What are the components of skill-related (athletic) fitness? If students have to choose one or the other, which should be chosen? Why?

7. Rank activities according to their contribution to various components of fitness. Discuss how some activities are excellent for cardiovascular fitness and body composition, some for flexibility, and some benefit muscular strength and endurance.

8. Discuss the acronym FIT and how it relates to fitness development. *F*requency, *I*ntensity, and *T*ime determine fitness workloads. Which of these factors are most important? People who exercise throughout their life are likely to pay attention to which factors?

Physical fitness concepts and fitness activities are discussed further in Chapter 13.

UNDERSTANDING LIFESTYLE ALTERNATIVES

The following areas are important for students to understand. Wellness involves knowing what activities to avoid as well as what to do. When teaching these activities, avoid preaching and indoctrination. Emphasis should be placed instead on showing students the pros and cons of various practices and the consequences of making certain decisions. The ultimate decision and responsibility rest with the student, not the teacher.

The major areas discussed in this section are nutrition and weight control; stress, tension, and relaxation; substance abuse; and personal safety. All are areas in which behavior can be modified to enhance the quality of life. Students' decisions in these areas may affect dramatically how they live and, sometimes, whether they will live.

Nutrition and Weight Control

Proper nutrition is necessary if one is to obtain an optimum level of physical performance from one's body. An area of emphasis in the physical education program should be balanced diet and weight control. Students must understand the reasons for maintaining a balanced diet and the impact of so-called junk foods on the body. All students are concerned about weight control and should understand how excessive caloric intake coupled with reduced exercise result in an accumulation of adipose tissue.

Students should learn about the elements of a balanced diet. A balanced diet draws from each of the basic food groups. Figure 11.9 is the new food guide pyramid developed by the U.S. Department of Agriculture (1992). The pyramid illustrates how the most food should be eaten from the bread, cereal, rice, and pasta group. The smallest number of calories should be ingested from the fats, oils, and sweets group.

Encourage students to moderate the consumption of foods high in cholesterol and fat. Some cholesterol and fat are necessary for proper body function. When too much fat is ingested, however, cholesterol and triglyceride levels in the blood plasma increase. Many studies have shown a relationship between high cholesterol and triglyceride levels and coronary heart disease. (A blood test is needed to determine blood lipid levels.)

Children should be aware of which foods are high in fat and cholesterol. The following are examples of foods high in cholesterol: eggs, cheese,

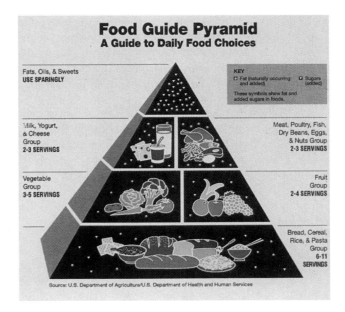

Figure 11.9 Food Guide Pyramid (U.S. Department of Agriculture, Human Nutrition Information Service, August 1992, Leaflet No. 572.) To order a copy of "The Food Guide Pyramid" booklet, send a $1.00 check or money order made out to the Superintendent of Documents to: Consumer Information Center, Department 159-Y, Pueblo, Colorado 81009.

cream, most beef and pork cuts, chocolate milk, shrimp, chocolate candy, cake and cookies, and ice cream.

Depending on the criteria used, anywhere from 30 to 50 percent of elementary school youngsters are overweight, meaning that their body weight is over the accepted limits for their age, sex, and body build. The majority of cases of obesity occur as a consequence of inactivity or overeating, or both. It is therefore important to learn about the caloric content of foods (as well as their nutritional value) in order to monitor the amount of calories ingested. Learning the amount of calories burned by different sports and individual activities is also important. For elementary school children, such levels of awareness may be difficult to achieve. However, students must gain the realization early that when caloric intake exceeds caloric expenditure, fat is stored. Experts agree that obese children do not in general consume more calories than children of normal weight. Rather, they exercise less.

Obesity is a roadblock to wellness. Life insurance companies judge overweight people as poor risks because of their shorter life expectancy. Excessive body fat makes the heart work much harder, increases the chance of having high blood pressure, and lowers the possibility of recovery from a heart attack. In youngsters, it has a detrimental effect on self-image. Students of normal weight find it much easier to perform the physical tasks that are a major source of recognition from peers and adults. Overweight students are often punished more severely for misbehavior and may even receive lower grades for work similar to that of their normal-weight peers.

A systematic program for helping children lose excess body fat is presented in Chapter 8. Body fat must be measured with skin calipers; a scale measures only total body weight. Youngsters involved in weight control programs often gain body weight as measured by a scale, even though they may actually have lost body fat. This weight gain is the replacement of fat mass by lean mass.

Requisite Knowledge

1. The diet should be balanced and contain foods from each of the recommended groups. This ensures that the body is receiving essential nutrients.

2. Caloric expenditure (exercise) and intake (eating) must balance if weight is to be maintained. A weight-reduction program should include a reduction in caloric intake and an increase in daily exercise.

3. Activities vary in the energy they require. Individual needs must be considered when selecting exercise activities.

4. Junk foods add little, if any, nutritional value to the diet and usually are high in calories.

5. Excessive weight makes it difficult to perform physical tasks. This results in less success and in less motivation to be active, thus increasing the tendency toward obesity.

6. Obesity increases the risk of heart disease and related health problems. It is a roadblock to wellness and may decrease the longevity of the individual.

7. Scales are not an accurate indicator of a reduction in body fat. Skin calipers should be used to measure body fat.

Suggested Learning Experiences

1. Post a list of activities and their energy demands on the bulletin board. Discuss the importance of regular activity, especially for students who have a sedentary lifestyle.

2. Use skinfold calipers to measure body fat. The measurements can be compared with criterion-referenced health standards specified in the *Prudential Fitnessgram Test Manual* (Cooper Institute for Aerobic Fitness, 1992) (see p. 274).

3. Analyze the activity level of others in class. Record the exercise time and type of activities participated in daily for one week.

4. Maintain a food diary. Record all the food ingested daily and the amount of calories represented. Compare the amount of calories ingested with the amount of calories expended.

5. Discuss the ways in which society rewards physically fit individuals, and contrast this with the ways in which obese people sometimes are treated in our society and schools.

6. On the bulletin board, post a chart that compares the caloric content of junk foods with that of more acceptable foods.

7. Discuss the fat content of various foods. Examine how foods can be modified to reduce the fat content, i.e., milk can be reduced to 2 percent; 1 percent; and skim. Discuss the benefits of drinking low-fat milk.

8. Discuss the importance of fiber in diet. Identify foods that are high in fiber content.

9. Identify what happens to people when they diet. Discuss the balance of caloric intake versus caloric expenditure.

10. Discuss why people go to fitness centers. What are the reasons people choose to exercise?

11. Teach some exercises that can be done while watching television. Since youngsters watch an average of 3½ hours of television daily, discuss possible alternative behavior.

12. Discuss some of the health problems related to excessive body fat.

A specific program for weight management is found on pages 166–173.

Stress, Tension, and Relaxation

Stress can be defined as a substantial imbalance between environmental demands and the individual's response capability. In situations that induce stress, the failure to meet the environmental demands usually has important consequences. For example, children can be pressured by parents' unrealistically high expectations, by their own desire to be accepted by peers, and by their desire to achieve to meet teacher expectations. Realistic, challenging, and attainable goals tend to eliminate many frustrating situations that could become stressful. Stress management is learning how to respond to situations that might cause tension. Both teacher and child must learn to recognize stressful symptoms before appropriate management techniques can be imposed. The emphasis in this discussion centers on what children should know about stress and what techniques they can learn to adopt to prevent stressful situations.

First, children need to recognize that individuals react differently to stressful situations. Some learn to handle stress productively, so that it actually increases their effectiveness. Some may not sense that a situation is stressful and so may remain calm through a crisis. How an individual perceives a situation usually determines whether it is stressful. Teachers can aid youngsters in achieving a productive and healthy outlook on life that will minimize stress.

A second area of concern deals with the effects of stress on the body. Psychologically, stress can take the form of excitement, fear, or anger. Physical changes are also apparent when a person is under stress. The nervous system may respond to the stress through increased heart rate, increased blood pressure, increased respiration rate, increased muscle tension throughout the body, or decreased digestion (often accompanied by queasiness).

Unrelieved stress has detrimental effects on the body. It increases the risk of heart disease and can lead to insomnia and hypertension. Indigestion is common in stressed individuals, as is constipation. Backaches and general body aches often originate from stress. The inability to relieve stress through productive habits may lead to alcoholism, smoking, and drug abuse, usually among adults.

In the school setting, one antidote to stress is open communication between teacher and children. Teachers must be genuinely interested in helping children solve their problems and must ensure that the children know that they care. Teaching children to respect each other begins with the teacher's showing genuine respect for students. Children need to recognize that how they act influences how other children act toward them. A key for children is to make the most of their abilities: to do their best and allow the consequences to occur as they may. Comparison with others should be avoided. A healthy perspective for competition is a target goal. Place the significance of winning or being the top performer in proper perspective, and concentrate on high personal effort and doing one's best. Children should be made aware of the need for classroom and gymnasium expectations, standards, deadlines, and behavior control, without which schools could not operate effectively. Standards and rules should be realistic and administered fairly and consistently.

Studies have shown that sports and moderate physical activity decrease tension. A side effect of involvement in organized sport activities is that the concentration required provides a diversion from stress and worry. Some experts believe that exercise applies stress to the body in a systematic fashion and thus prepares the body to deal with other stressful situations. One goal of teachers should be to provide students with productive and meaningful ways to relieve tension. Coping skills should be taught to individuals who have characteristics or defects that tend to attract attention. Stress management is learning how, in this situation, to respond to uncomplimentary remarks and teasing. Behavior control should receive attention. A good adage to emphasize is, "Stop to think before you act."

Relaxation is a skill that can be learned. Motor learning promotes patterned movement and inhibits unnecessary muscles from interfering. This results in an ability to relax muscles not specifically required for task performance. Children should learn that relaxation is necessary to achieve top performance in demanding skills, particularly those involving accuracy. A basketball player takes a deep breath, expelling air, to relax before shooting a free throw. Reduction of tension results in conservation of energy and allows the task to be done efficiently and smoothly.

Sometimes, children need to think about whether to try to accomplish a skill at all costs. When performers try too hard at any activity, the result is usually an excess of effort and unnecessary motion. Tenseness produces inefficient motion and can be counterproductive. Relaxation is a release of muscle tension that must be performed consciously. The first step in learning to relax is to recognize stress and tension. At times, children can be given short periods of complete relaxation, generally in a supine position on the floor.

Requisite Knowledge

1. Stress affects all individuals to a certain degree. A certain amount of stress is necessary to stimulate performance.

2. The amount of stress that individuals experience depends on how they perceive the situation. Healthy perceptions are needed to cope effectively with stress.

3. When people have difficulty dealing with stress through productive means, they often attempt to relieve it through unhealthy and potentially dangerous means, such as alcohol, tobacco, and drug use, or inappropriate behaviors.

4. Stress causes changes in body functions. An awareness of these changes is necessary so

Practicing relaxation activities

that students will know when they are under the influence of stress.

5. Stress may increase susceptibility to diseases and can cause psychosomatic illnesses.

6. Exercise is an excellent way to relieve stress and tension.

7. The body works more efficiently if all muscles unrelated to a given task are relaxed.

8. Relaxing antagonistic muscles is possible so that interference is minimized.

9. Relaxation is important in skills demanding concentration and accuracy.

10. Students need to learn to live up to their personal expectations, rather than to the expectations of others.

11. Deep breathing is a natural relaxant. Teach students to take several deep breaths if they feel tense.

Suggested Learning Experiences

1. Select a particular movement. Identify the muscles that are necessary for the movement and those that should be relaxed.

2. Hold an isometric contraction at the elbow joint. With the other hand, feel the contraction in the biceps and triceps. Do the same with other joints and muscles.

3. Tense all muscles and hold for a count of five; relax gently. Repeat as desired.

4. Try shooting a free throw while holding the breath. Inhale and exhale to relax, and then shoot the free throw. Discuss the difference.

5. Discuss overt changes in people when they are under stress. What is meant by "choking" in sports?

6. Discuss the role of perception in tension-building situations. How does it feel to be scared?

7. Discuss situations in physical education class that build stress, for example failing in front of others, not being selected for a team, and being laughed at or yelled at for poor performance.

8. Identify physical activities that seem to relieve tension and stress. Discuss the relationship between involvement in activity and the reduction of stress.

9. Identify and discuss unproductive attempts to relieve stress, such as smoking, drinking, and taking drugs.

Substance Abuse

Substance abuse among elementary school youngsters is common. To make wise decisions in this area, children need to be aware of the impact these substances can have on their lives. Facts should be presented without moralizing or preaching. Making meaningful decisions is difficult for youngsters if most of the information they receive is from peers or moralizing adults. The elementary school years are an opportune time to discuss substance abuse, as many youngsters will soon be making decisions related to use.

Alcohol, tobacco, and drugs are deterrents to wellness and usually are detrimental to total health. These substances need to be discussed with youngsters, because children are in constant contact with them through parents, television, and friends. At regular and opportune intervals, the physical education teacher can supplement presentations made in the classroom.

Alcohol

Alcohol has both short-term and long-term effects. The short-term effects vary as a result of the depressant effect that alcohol has on the central nervous system. People become relaxed, aggressive, and active in differing degrees. Ultimately, lack of coordination and confusion occur if a great deal of alcohol is ingested.

Some long-term effects of excessive alcohol consumption may be liver damage, heart disease, and malnutrition. The greatest concern about long-term drinking is the possibility of becoming an alcoholic. The disease of alcoholism has the following components: the loss of control of alcohol intake, the presence of functional or structural damage (psychological and physical), and the need to have alcohol to maintain an acceptable level of functioning.

Youngsters may drink for any of several reasons—curiosity, a desire to celebrate with parents, peer pressure, to be like adults and appear more mature, to rebel against the adult world, and because their models or admired adults drink. Youngsters usually are ambivalent about alcohol: they know its detrimental effects, yet they see many of their friends and models using it. The problem is difficult, and understandings of moderate use and of abstinence are needed.

Tobacco

Tobacco use is common among youngsters. A long-term habit increases significantly the possibility of heart attack, stroke, and cancer. Chronic bronchitis and emphysema are diseases prevalent among smokers. A recent study revealed that the average life span of long-term smokers is 7 years shorter than that of nonsmokers. Many children live in homes of adult smokers and need to be made aware of the effects of secondary smoke on health.

Children need to understand the impact of smoking on a healthy body. Teachers should dis-cuss the reasons that people choose to smoke or not smoke. In the end, however, as with alcohol, youngsters must make a meaningful and personal choice. Youngsters who choose to smoke do so for reasons similar to those related to drinking.

Drug Abuse

The use of marijuana, cocaine, and other drugs should be discussed with students in a nonthreatening setting. In athletics, discussion can center on the use by some athletes of pep pills, pain relievers, growth hormones, and steroids to improve performance. Excellent materials are available for teachers to help them give meaningful instruction. Substance abuse is so contrary to the concept of physical wellness that physical educators must accept the challenge to increase awareness of the problem.

Requisite Knowledge

1. The earlier one begins to smoke, the greater the risk to functional health.
2. Smoking is done for psychological reasons and makes no contribution to physical development.
3. People choose to smoke and drink for reasons of curiosity, status, and peer pressure.
4. Choosing a lifestyle different from the majority of one's friends takes courage.
5. When decisions about substance use are based on a lack of knowledge, they often are poor decisions. Wise and meaningful decisions can be made only after all alternatives and consequences are understood.
6. Substance abuse is often a misguided attempt to cope with problems and stress. Exercise and activity are more productive and healthy ways of coping.
7. The use of alcohol, tobacco, and drugs prevents people from enjoying certain activities.
8. It is much more important to make decisions based on personal need and direction than to be like everyone else. A positive feeling about oneself is more important than being "part of the crowd."

Suggested Learning Experiences

1. Identify some of the reasons that people choose or choose not to become involved in substance abuse.
2. Discuss the reasons that it is important to be your own person and to make meaningful personal decisions.

3. Develop a bulletin board listing the ways in which the tobacco and alcohol industries attempt to get people to use their products. Reserve a section for advertising (if any) that tries to convince people to abstain or to use moderation.

4. Youngsters often hear about the impairment in physical performance caused by smoking or drinking. Discuss athletes seen smoking or drinking on television and why they perform at high levels in spite of this abuse.

5. Youngsters want to be part of a group at any cost. Discuss how one admires those individuals who had the courage to be different. Examples might be Leonardo da Vinci, Christopher Columbus, Amelia Earhart, Martin Luther King, Jr., or Louis Braille.

6. Discuss how individuals release tension in an attempt to feel good. Discuss productive releases of tension such as recreational pursuits, hobbies, and sports.

7. Develop displays identifying the various effects that alcohol, tobacco, and drugs have on the body. The effects can be discussed briefly at opportune times.

8. Discuss how peer groups can influence lifestyle choices. Discuss ways to make independent choices without losing friends.

9. Discuss that the choice to participate in substance abuse is a personal one. Youngsters are always responsible for personal choices and make such choices when adults aren't around.

Safety and First Aid

Safety and first aid are often included in the physical education program because a higher number of accidents occur in this setting than in any other part of the school curriculum. Safety is an attitude and involves concern for one's welfare and health. An *accident* is an unplanned event or act that may result in injury or death. Often, accidents occur in situations that could have been prevented. The following are some of the most common causes of accidents: (a) lack of knowledge and understanding of risks; (b) lack of skill and competence to perform tasks safely, such as riding a bike or driving a car; (c) false sense of security, which leads people to think that accidents will happen only to others; (d) fatigue or illness, which affect physical and mental performance; (e) drugs and/or alcohol; and (f) strong emotional states such as anger, fear, or worry, which cause people to do things they might not do otherwise.

Traffic accidents are one area where many deaths could be prevented. Wearing seat belts could reduce the number of deaths by half. Drinking alcohol while driving increases the risk of having an accident 20 times over those for a nondrinking driver. Since students are going to be passengers in automobiles, an awareness of the possibility of serious injury should be a part of the wellness program.

Bicycles are another source of numerous accidents. Car drivers have difficulty seeing bicycles, and the resulting accidents frequently are serious. Students need to learn bicycle safety. Often, the physical education setting is the only place where this is discussed. Instruction in bicycling for safety and fitness is usually well received by elementary school children.

Swimming-related accidents are the second leading cause of accidental death among young adults. More than 50 percent of all drownings occur when people unexpectedly find themselves in the water. Physical education programs should see that all students learn to swim and learn safety rules during their school career.

Physical education and sports are sources of injury in the school setting. Proper safety procedures and simple first-aid techniques should be taught. Intermediate-grade students should know how to stop bleeding, treat shock, and administer mouth-to-mouth respiration and cardiopulmonary resuscitation (CPR). Many physical education programs now include a required unit of instruction dealing with these topics. Many lives could be saved if most bystanders knew CPR.

Requisite Knowledge

1. Accidents are unplanned events or acts that may result in injury. Most accidents could be avoided if people were adequately prepared and understood the necessary competencies and risks involved.

2. Wearing seat belts would decrease the number of deaths caused by automobile accidents.

3. Bicycles often are not seen by car drivers. Bicycling safety classes can lower the number of bicycle accidents.

4. Swimming-related accidents are the second leading cause of accidental death among young people. Teaching basic water skills would decrease dramatically the number of deaths.

5. Basic first-aid procedures to prevent further injury to victims are competencies that all students should possess.

Suggested Learning Experiences

1. Discuss the causes of different types of accidents and how many accidents could be avoided.

2. Identify the types of accidents that happen to different age groups and why this is the case.

3. Identify the role of alcohol and drugs in the incidence of accidents. Why are these substances used in recreational settings?

4. Develop a bulletin board that demonstrates how to care for shock victims. Practice carrying out the steps in a mock procedure.

5. Have an Accident Day and let students stage different types of accidents that require treatment such as stoppage of bleeding, artificial respiration, or CPR.

6. Outline the steps to follow in case of a home fire. Discuss how many fires could be prevented.

7. Conduct a bicycle safety fair. Have students design bulletin boards and displays that explain and emphasize bicycle safety.

REFERENCES AND SUGGESTED READINGS

AAHPERD. (1987). *Basic stuff in action, grades K–3*. Reston, VA: AAHPERD.

AAHPERD. (1987). *Basic stuff in action, grades 4–6*. Reston, VA: AAHPERD.

AAHPERD. (1987). *Basic stuff series one: Information books*. Reston, VA: AAHPERD.

Cooper Institute for Aerobics Research. (1992). *The Prudential Fitnessgram test administration manual*. Dallas: Author.

Corbin, C. B., and Lindsey, R. (1990). *Fitness for life* (3rd ed). Glenview, IL: Scott, Foresman.

Hoeger, W. K. (1986). *Lifetime physical fitness and wellness*. Englewood, CO: Morton.

Kuntzleman, C. T. (1977). *Heartbeat*. Spring Arbor, MI: Arbor.

Kuntzleman, C. T. (1978a). *Fitness discovery activities*. Spring Arbor, MI: Arbor.

Kuntzleman, C. T. (1978b). *Values strategies for fitness*. Spring Arbor, MI: Arbor.

Mirkin, G., and Hoffman, M. (1978). *The sportsmedicine book*. Boston: Little, Brown.

Priest, L. (1981). *Teach for fitness: A manual for teaching fitness concepts in K–12 physical education*. Washington, DC: ERIC Clearinghouse on Teacher Education.

Spindt, G. B., Weinberg, H., Hennessy, B., Holyoak, C., & Monti, W. H. (1993). *Moving with Skill*. Dubuque, IA: Kindall/Hunt.

U.S. Department of Agriculture. (1992). *The food guide pyramid*. Pueblo, CO: Superintendent of Documents.

Travis, J. W., and Ryan, S. R. (1981). *Wellness handbook*. Berkeley, CA: Ten Speed.

Introductory Activities

*I*ntroductory activities are presented in the first part of the recommended lesson plan (p. 99). There are many ideas for movement, and teachers are urged to create and develop activities of their own. A characteristic of introductory activities is their vigorous nature. Gross motor movements (generally locomotor activities) are employed. Introductory activities should allow considerable freedom of movement and not be rigidly structured.

Introductory activities are used for the first 2 or 3 minutes of the lesson. There are a number of reasons for using introductory activities, and teachers should select activities based on lesson objectives and student needs. The following are some of the reasons for beginning the lesson with an introductory activity:

1. To warm children up physiologically and prepare them for strenuous fitness activity to follow.

2. To focus youngsters on the objectives of the lesson. This can be an ideal time to establish anticipatory set. Students may move about and review previously learned skills. Teachers can use this time to focus students on learning objectives by telling them the "what and why" of activities in the upcoming lesson focus.

3. To review management skills with a class. Because introductory activities require little instruction, teachers can center on management skills such as stopping, listening, and moving on signal.

4. To offer youngsters immediate activity when entering the gym. This satisfies the need to move and gives the teacher an opportunity to establish a learning attitude (purposive, under control) for the class.

As introductory activities constitute the first activity youngsters receive when entering the gymnasium, they should start moving with moderate intensity and gradually increase to full speed. Introductory activities involve locomotor movements that can be done at a slow pace in the initial stages of warming up. For example, using Rhythmic Running as an introductory activity, children could begin by walking. As they warm up, the movement can be increased to a run. Another example, using Group Over and Under, is to have the students moderately move over, around, and under each other. After all students have had a chance to warm up, the activity can be done at full speed. This accomplishes the goal of physiologically preparing the body for the physical fitness section of the lesson.

EUROPEAN RHYTHMIC RUNNING

Rhythmic Running is used in many European countries to open the daily lesson. The European style is light, rhythmic running to the accompaniment of some type of percussion, usually a drum or tambourine. Skilled runners do not need accompaniment but merely keep time with a leader. Much of the running follows a circular path, but it can be done in scatter formation. To introduce a group of children to Rhythmic Running, have them clap to the beat of the drum. Next, as they clap, have them shuffle their feet in place, keeping time. Following this, have them run in place, omitting the clapping. Finally, the class can run in single-file formation, if desired. The running should be light, bouncy, and rhythmic in time with the beat. When running in single file, youngsters should stay behind the person in front, maintain proper spacing, and lift the knees in a light, prancing step.

A number of movement ideas can be combined with the rhythmic running pattern.

1. On signal (a whistle or a double beat on the drum), runners freeze in place. They resume running when the regular beat begins again.

European running

2. On signal, runners make a full turn in four running steps, lifting the knees high while turning.

3. Children clap hands every fourth beat as they run. Instead of clapping, runners sound a brisk "Hey!" on the fourth beat, raising one arm with a fist at the same time.

4. Children run in squad formation, following the path set by the squad leader.

5. On signal, children run in general space, exercising care not to bump into each other. They return to a circular running formation on the next signal.

6. Students alternate between running with high knee action and regular running.

7. Runners change to a light, soundless run and back to a heavier run. The tone of the drum can control the quality of the movement.

8. Students use Rhythmic Running while handling a parachute.

9. On the command "Center," children run four steps toward the center, turn around (four steps), and run outward four steps to resume the original circular running pattern.

10. On signal, runners go backward, changing the direction of the circle.

11. Students carry a beanbag or a ball. Every fourth step, they toss the item up and catch it while running.

12. A leader moves the class through various formations. A task that is enjoyable and challenging is crossing lines of children while they alternate one child from one line in front of one youngster from another line.

13. The class moves into various shapes on signal. Possible shapes might be a square, rectangle, triangle, or pentagon. The Rhythmic Running

must be continued while the youngsters move into position.

14. When a signal is given, each class member changes position with another student and then resumes the activity. An example might be to change position with the student opposite in the circle.

15. Because the movement is rhythmic, students can practice certain skills, such as a full turn. The turn can be done to a four-count rhythm and should be more deliberate than a quick turning movement that lacks definition.

16. When the drum stops, children scatter and run in random fashion. When the beat resumes, they return to circular formation and proper rhythm.

GROSS MOTOR MOVEMENTS

Most movements of the gross movement type stress locomotor activities, but some include manipulative and nonlocomotor activities. The movements should involve the body as a whole and provide abrupt change from one movement pattern to another. A routine can begin with running and then change to another movement pattern that is either specified by the teacher or determined by youngsters. Signals for change can be supplied with a voice command, whistle, drumbeat, or handclap. Children enjoy being challenged by having to change with the signal. Each part of a routine should be continued long enough for good body challenge and involvement, but not so long that it becomes wearisome.

Running provides much of the basis for gross movement activities, but other activities of a vigorous nature can be employed. The suggested activities are classified roughly according to type and whether they are individual or partner or group oriented.

Individual Running and Changing Movements

Free Running

Students run in any direction, changing direction at will.

Running and Changing Direction

Children run in any direction, changing direction on signal. As a progression, specify the type of angle (e.g., right, obtuse, 45-degree, 180-degree). Alternate right and left turns.

Running and Changing Level

Children run high on their toes and change to a lower level on signal. Require runners to touch the floor sometimes when at the lower level.

Running and Changing the Type of Locomotion

On signal, runners change from running to free choice or to a specified type of locomotion (e.g., walking, jumping, hopping, skipping, sliding, or galloping).

Running and Stopping

Students run in various directions and, on signal, freeze. Stress stopping techniques and an immobilized position.

Move and Perform Athletic Movement

Students move and stop on signal. They then perform an athletic skill move, such as a basketball jump shot, leaping football pass catch, volleyball spike, or soccer kick. Students should place emphasis on correct form and timing. A variation of the activity is for students to move with a partner and throw a pass on signal, punt a ball, or shoot a basket. The partner catches the ball or rebounds the shot.

Run and Assume a Pose

Pupils run and, on signal, assume a statue pose. Allow choice or specify a limitation.

Tortoise and Hare

When the teacher calls out "Tortoise," the children run slowly in general space. On the command "Hare," they change to a rapid, circular run. During the latter, stress good knee lift.

Ponies in the Stable

Each child has a stable, his spot or place on the floor. This can be marked with a beanbag or a hoop. On the initial signal, children gallop lightly (like ponies) in general space. The next signal tells them to trot lightly to their stable and to continue trotting lightly in place.

High Fives

Students move in different directions throughout the area. On signal, they are challenged to run toward a partner, jump, and give a "high five" (slap hands) while moving. Emphasis should be placed on timing so that the "high five" is given at the top of the jump. Combinations of changing the level as well as changing the speed of the movement can be developed.

Adding Fitness Challenges

Running (or other locomotor movements) can be combined with fitness activities. During the signaled stop, exercises such as push-ups and curl-ups can be done.

Move and Perform a Task on Signal

Youngsters move and perform a task on signal. Tasks can be individual or partner activities. Examples are Seat Circles (p. 505), Balances (p. 500), Wring the Dishrag (p. 506), Partner Hopping (p. 520), Twister (p. 520), and Back-to-Back Get-Up (p. 521).

Run, Stop, and Pivot

Students run, stop, and then pivot. This is an excellent activity for game skill development. Youngsters enjoy it especially when they are told to imagine that they are basketball or football players.

Triple S Routine

The triple S's are *speed, style,* and *stop.* Children are in scatter formation throughout the area. On the command "Speed," they run in general space rapidly while avoiding contact with others. On "Style," all run with style (easy, light, loose running) in a large, circular, counterclockwise path. On the command "Stop," all freeze quickly under control. Repeat as necessary.

Agility Run

Pick two lines or markers 5 to 10 yards apart. Students run (or use other locomotor movements) back and forth between the lines for a specified time (10, 15, or 20 seconds). Students can add a personal challenge by seeing how many times they can move back and forth within the given time limit.

Other Individual Movement Combinations

Upright Movement to All Fours

Youngsters begin with a movement in upright position and change to one on all fours.

Secret Movement

The teacher has written a number of movements on cards and selects one. Direction is given by saying, "I want you to show me the secret movement." The children select a movement and continue that movement without change until they are signaled to stop, whereupon the teacher identifies those who performed the movement on the card. The movement is then demonstrated by those who chanced upon it, and all perform it together. If no one comes up with the movement pattern on the card, repeat the activity by asking the children to change their responses.

Airplanes

Children pretend to be airplanes. When told to take off, they zoom with arms out, swooping, turning, and gliding. When they are commanded to land, they drop to the floor in prone position, simulating a plane at rest. To start their engines and take off, they can perform a series of push-ups and move up and down while simulating engine noise.

Combination Movement

Directives for combination movement can establish specified movements or allow some choice. The limitation might be to run, skip, and roll, or to jump, twist, and shake. Another approach is to set a number for the sequence and let the children select the activities. Say, "Put three different kinds of movement together in a smooth pattern."

Countdown

The teacher begins a countdown for blastoff: "Ten, nine, eight, seven, six, five, four, three, two, one—blastoff!" The children are scattered, and each makes an abrupt, jerky movement on each count. On the word *blastoff,* they run in different directions until the stop signal is given.

Magic-Number Challenges

A challenge can be issued like this: "Ten, ten, and ten." Children then put together three movements, doing ten repetitions of each. Or the teacher could say, "Today we are going to play our version of Twenty-One." Twenty-one becomes the magic number that is to be fulfilled with three movements, each of which is done seven times.

Crossing the River

A river can be set up as the space between two parallel lines about 40 feet apart, or it can be the crosswise area in a gymnasium. Each time the children cross the river, they employ a different type of locomotor movement. Children should be

Performing airplanes

encouraged not to repeat a movement. Play is continuous over a minute or so.

Four-Corners Movement

Lay out a square with a cone at each corner. As the student passes each corner, he changes to a different locomotor movement with an agility emphasis. Challenge students with some of the following sport agility movements: backward running, leaps, grapevine step, front crossover, back crossover, high knees, and slide steps. Add variation by changing the qualities of movement (i.e., soft, heavy, slow, fast, etc.). Students can pass to the outside of the area if they are doing a faster-moving movement.

Jumping and Hopping Patterns

Each child has a home spot. The teacher provides jumping and hopping sequences to take children away from and back to their spot. The teacher could say, "Move with three jumps, two hops, and a half turn. Return to place the same way." The teacher should have on hand a number of sequences. Action can extend beyond simply jumping and hopping.

Leading with Body Parts

Students move throughout the area with some body part leading. Try using various body parts, such as elbow, fingers, head, shoulder, knees, and toes. Try the same exercise with different body parts trailing. Try moving and leading with two different body parts. Try with three. Try also with combinations of body parts trailing the body. Children can jog with some body part leading or trailing. On signal, tell them to make a new body part lead or trail the body.

Move, Rock, and Roll

Each youngster procures an individual mat and places it on the floor. Students are challenged to move around, over, and on the mats. When a signal is given, children move to a mat and try different ways of rocking and rolling. Rocking on different parts of the body can be specified, and different body rolls can be suggested. As another challenge, tell the children to do a rock or a roll or both on a mat, get up and run to another mat, and repeat the sequence. Older children enjoy seeing how many mats they can move to within a certain amount of time.

Individual Rhythmic Movements

Musical Relaxation

Musical relaxation can be conducted with a drum or appropriate recorded music. Children run in time to the rhythm. When the rhythm stops, each reclines on the back, closes the eyes, and remains relaxed until the music begins again.

Moving to Rhythm

The possibilities with rhythm are many. Rhythm can guide locomotor movements, with changes in tempo being part of the activity. The intensity of the sound can be translated into light or heavy movements.

Moving to Music

Pieces such as the Bleking song (p. 376) and "Pop Goes the Weasel" (p. 379) can provide a basis for creative movement. These are two-part pieces, so a nonlocomotor movement can be done to the first part and a locomotor movement to the second.

Folk Dance Movement

Use a record or tape recording to stimulate different types of rhythmic movement such as polka, schottische, and two-step. Youngsters can move around the room practicing the steps dictated by the music.

Individual Movements with Manipulation

Individual Rope Jumping

Each child runs with rope in hand. On the signal to change, the child stops and begins to jump rope.

Hoop Activities

Each child runs holding a hoop. When the signal is given to stop, the child either does hula-hooping or lays the hoop on the floor and uses it for hopping and jumping patterns.

Wand Activities

Movements similar to those done with jump ropes and hoops can be performed with wands. After they run and stop, the children do wand stunts.

Milk Carton Fun

Each child has a milk carton stuffed with crumpled newspapers and secured with cellophane tape. The children kick the cartons in different directions for 1 minute.

Ball Activities

Youngsters dribble balls as in basketball or (outside) as in soccer. When a change is signaled, they stop, balance on one leg, and pass the ball under the other leg, around the back, and overhead, keeping both control and balance. Other challenges can be supplied that involve both movement with the ball and manipulative actions performed in place.

Beanbag Touch and Go

Beanbags are spread throughout the area. On signal, youngsters move and touch as many different beanbags as possible with their hands. Different body parts can be specified for children to use for touching. Different colors of beanbags can be selected, and the command might be "Touch as many blue beanbags as possible with your elbow."

Children can also move to and around a beanbag. The type of movement can be varied; for example, they might skip around the yellow beanbags with the left side leading. Change the movement as well as the direction and leading side of the body. Another enjoyable activity for youngsters is to trace out a shape (e.g., triangle, circle, square) as they move from beanbag to beanbag.

Variation: Vanishing Beanbags. Students move around the beanbags as described above. While they are moving, the teacher or a designated student picks up one or two of the bags. On signal, students move to a beanbag and sit on it. The goal is not to be left out. The activity is repeated with all students participating each time.

Long-Rope Routine

Students begin in a loose column composed of four people holding a long jump rope in their right hand at waist level. A series of four signals is given. On the first signal, youngsters jog lightly in a column. On the second signal, the group shifts the rope overhead from the right side to the left side of the body while jogging. At the third signal, the two inside students release the rope and begin jumping as soon as the two students at the end of the rope start turning the rope. On the fourth signal, the turners become jumpers and vice versa. The sequence is repeated a number of times.

Disappearing Hoops

Each child gets a hoop and places it somewhere on the floor. Offer challenges such as "Move through five blue hoops, jump over four yellow hoops, and skip around six green hoops." On signal, the children move to find a hoop and balance inside it. As youngsters are moving, take away two or three hoops. At the signal, some students will not find a hoop. Those left out then offer the class the next movement challenge. Different challenges and stunts inside the hoops can be specified.

Partner and Group Activities

Marking

Each child has a partner who is somewhat equal in ability. Under control, one partner runs, dodges, and tries to lose the other, who must stay within 3 feet of the runner. On signal, both stop. Chasers must be able to touch their partners to say that they have marked them. Partners then change roles.

Following Activity

One partner leads and performs various kinds of movements. The other partner must move in the same fashion. This idea can be extended to squad organization.

Fastest Tag in the West

Every player is a tagger. The object is to tag other players without being tagged. Players who are tagged must sit or kneel and await the next game. (Start new games frequently.) If two or more players tag each other simultaneously, they are both (all) "out."

Medic Tag

Three or four students are designated as "taggers." They try to tag other students; when tagged, a student kneels as if injured. Another student (not one of the taggers) can "rehabilitate" the injured player with a touch, enabling the student to resume play.

Hospital Tag

Every player is a tagger. Any player who is tagged must cover with one hand the body area that was touched. Students may be tagged twice but must be able to hold both tagged spots and keep moving. A student who is tagged three times must freeze. Restart the game when most of the students have been frozen.

Group Over and Under

Half of the children are scattered. Each is in a curled position, face down. The other children leap or jump over the curled children. On signal, reverse the groups quickly. Instead of being curled, the children form arches or bridges, and the moving children go under these. A further extension is to have the children on the floor alternate between curled and bridge positions. If a moving child goes over the curled position, the floor child changes immediately to a bridge. The moving children react accordingly.

Living Obstacles

This activity is similar to Group Over and Under except that the youngsters on the floor are in a bridged position and moving. The children moving over, under, and around must move quickly, as the obstacles are moving. Change positions after a designated amount of time.

Group over and under

Popcorn

Half the class is scattered throughout the area and assume the push-up position. The other half of the class will move and "pop the popcorn." This is done by moving over and under the students who are in push-up position. When a student moves under a student, that youngster lowers to the floor. When a student moves over a student lying on the floor, that student raises to the push-up position. Moving students should exchange places with those on the floor after a designated time.

Pyramid Power

Students move throughout the area. On signal, they find a partner and build a simple pyramid or partner stand. Examples are the hip-shoulder stand, double-crab stand, double-dog stand, and shoulder stand. Students should be cautioned to select a partner of similar size and to stand on the proper points of support.

Bridges by Threes

Three children in a group can set up an interesting movement sequence using bridges. Two of the children make bridges, and the third child goes under both bridges and sets up a bridge. Each child in turn goes under the bridges of the other two. Different kinds of bridges can be specified, and the bridges can be arranged so that a change in direction is made. An over-and-under sequence also provides interest. The child vaults or jumps over the first bridge and then goes under the next bridge before setting up the third bridge.

Rubber Band

Students gather around the teacher in the center of the area. On signal, students move away from the teacher with a designated movement such as run, hop sideways, skip backward, double-lame dog, or grapevine step. On signal, they sprint back to the central point, jump, and give a shout.

New Leader Movements

Squads or small groups run around the area, following a leader. When the change is signaled, the last person goes to the head of the line to lead. Groups of three are ideal for this activity.

Manipulative Activities

Each child has a beanbag. The children move around the area, tossing the bags upward and catching them as they move. On signal, they drop the bags to the floor and jump, hop, or leap over as many bags as possible. On the next signal, they pick up any convenient bag and resume tossing to themselves. Having one fewer beanbag than children adds to the fun. Hoops can also be used in this manner. Children begin by using hoops in rope-jumping style or for hula-hooping. On signal, the hoops are placed on the floor, and the children jump in and out of as many hoops as they can. Next, they pick up a nearby hoop and resume the original movement pattern. The activity also can be done with jump ropes.

Body Part Identification

Enough beanbags for the whole class are scattered on the floor. The children either run between or jump over the beanbags. When a body part is called out, the children place that body part on the nearest beanbag.

Leapfrog

Two, three, or four children can make up this sequence. The children form a straight or curved column, with all except the last child in line taking the leapfrog position. The last child leaps over the other children in turn, and after going over all, assumes the leapfrog position at the head of the column. Lines should be scattered to avoid running into other jumpers.

Drill Sergeant

The drill sergeant leads the squad marching and in line. When desired, the drill sergeant gives these kinds of commands for the movement sequence to be performed: "Walk, jump twice, land, and roll." "Run, jump-turn, and freeze (pose)." "Shake, jump-turn, land, and roll." "Seal Walk, Log Roll, and jump." The squad leader can be given cards with suggested patterns written on them. To add a realistic flavor, the sergeant can call the squad members to attention, give them the directions, and then call, "March!"

CREATIVE AND EXPLORATORY OPPORTUNITIES

Another approach of interest to children is providing creative and exploratory opportunities at the beginning of a lesson. Some examples follow.

1. Put out enough equipment of one type (hoops, balls, wands, beanbags) so that all children have a piece of equipment with which to ex-

plore. This can be open exploration, or the movement can follow the trend of a prior lesson, thus supplying extension to the progression.

2. Have available a number of manipulative items. The children select any item they wish and decide whether to play alone, with a partner, or as a member of a small group.

3. Make available a range of apparatus, such as climbing ropes, climbing apparatus, mats, boxes, balance beams, balance boards, and similar items. Manipulative items also can be a part of the package. The children choose the area in which they want to participate.

TAMBOURINE-DIRECTED ACTIVITIES

The tambourine can signal changes of movement, because it can produce two different kinds of sound: the tinny noise made by vigorous shaking and the percussive sound made by striking the instrument. Movement changes are signaled by changing from one sound to the other.

Shaking Sound

1. The children remain in one spot but shake all over. These should be gross movements.
2. The children shake and gradually drop to the floor.
3. The children scurry in every direction.
4. The children run lightly with tiny steps.

Drum Sound

1. Students make jerky movements to the percussive beat.
2. They jump in place or through space.

3. Youngsters do locomotor movements in keeping with the beat.
4. Responding to three beats, the children collapse on the first beat, roll on the second, and form a shape on the third.

Combinations

To form a combination of movements, select one from each category (shaking or percussive). When the shaking sound is made, the children perform that movement. When the sound is changed to the drum sound, the children react accordingly.

GAMES AND MISCELLANEOUS ACTIVITIES

Selected games are quite suitable for introductory activities, provided that they keep all children active, are simple, and require little teaching. Usually, a familiar game is used so that little organizational time is needed. Some appropriate games are listed.

Addition Tag (p. 570)
Back to Back (p. 556)
Barker's Hoopla (p. 581)
Circle Touch (p. 582)
Couple Tag (p. 574)
Loose Caboose (p. 577)
One, Two, Button My Shoe (p. 565)
Squad Tag (p. 579)
Touchdown (p. 588)
Whistle Mixer (p. 580)

Incorporating Physical Fitness into the Program

*P*hysical education programs in the schools must inoculate youngsters with an activity lifestyle that promotes health and vitality. Sometimes, administrators and school boards feel that physical education is a subject to be taught after all other subjects have received adequate coverage and support. Schools teach children how to achieve academically in order to live a productive life, and few would question the importance of learning to read and write. However, these skills are of little worth when one is near death or suffering from hypokinetic disease. There is no higher priority in life than health. Without it, all other skills lack meaning and utility. Exercise programs for children should be designed to improve the self-confidence of children rather than undermine it. Fitness activities should be individualized and tailored to the needs of each child to assure the experience is successful. The fitness program should be an enjoyable and positive social experience to assure that children develop a positive association with activity.

WHAT IS PHYSICAL FITNESS?

Although it is generally agreed that physical fitness and activity are an important part of the normal growth and development of a child, a general definition regarding the precise nature of physical fitness has not been universally accepted. However, it is becoming increasingly clear that the multidimensional characteristics of physical fitness can be divided into two areas: health-related physical fitness and skill-related physical fitness. This clear differentiation between *physical fitness related to functional health* and *physical performance related primarily to athletic ability* has come about after much discussion and debate. Although these definitions have curricular implications, classifying fitness into two categories should not lessen the importance of either in the total growth and development of youngsters. Understanding the distinctive features of the various components that make up health-related physical fitness and skill-related physical fitness should serve to help educators develop proper fitness objectives and goals for elementary physical education.

Health-Related Physical Fitness

Health-related physical fitness includes those aspects of physiological function that offer protection from diseases resulting from a sedentary lifestyle. It can be improved and/or maintained through regular physical activity. Specific components include cardiovascular fitness, body composition (ratio of leanness to fatness), abdominal strength and endurance, and flexibility. These components are currently measured with test batteries, such as the Fitnessgram System (Cooper Institute for Aerobic Research, 1992). The following are the major components of health-related fitness.

Cardiovascular Fitness

Aerobic fitness plays an important role in living a healthy lifestyle and may be the most important element of fitness. *Cardiovascular endurance* is the ability of the heart, the blood vessels, and the respiratory system to deliver oxygen efficiently over an extended period of time. To develop cardiovascular endurance, activity must be aerobic in nature. Activities that are continuous and rhythmic in nature require that a continuous supply of oxygen be delivered to the muscle cells. During aerobic exercise, oxygen used by the body in a given period of time is called the *maximum oxygen uptake* and is the best indicator of cardiovascular endurance. Activities that stimulate development in this area are paced walking, jogging, biking, rope jumping, aerobics, swimming, and continuous movement sports such as basketball or soccer.

In contrast to aerobic activity is anaerobic exercise, an activity that is so intense the body cannot supply oxygen at the cellular level. The body is limited to performing this type of activity for a short time. Examples of anaerobic activity are sprinting, running up stairs, or all-out effort in any sport.

Body Composition

Body composition is an integral part of health-related fitness. Body composition is the proportion of body fat to lean body mass. After the thickness of selected skinfolds has been measured, the percentage of body fat can be calculated by using formulas that have been developed using other, more accurate methods of measuring body fat. The conversion of skinfold thickness to percent body fat is easier to communicate to parents. Attaining physical fitness is made more difficult when an individual's body composition contains a high amount of body fat. An understanding of caloric intake and expenditure (see Chapter 11) and its impact on body composition should be developed.

Flexibility

Flexibility is the range of movement through which a joint or sequence of joints can move. Inactive individuals lose flexibility, whereas frequent movement helps retain the range of movement. Through stretching activities, the length of muscles, tendons, and ligaments is increased. The ligaments and tendons retain their elasticity through constant use. Flexibility is important to fitness; a lack of flexibility can create health problems for individuals. People who are flexible usually possess sound posture and may have less low-back pain. Many physical activities demand a range of motion to generate maximum force, such as serving a tennis ball, kicking a soccer ball, and so on.

Muscular Strength and Endurance

Strength is the ability of muscles to exert force; a necessary component for efficient learning of motor skills (Rarick & Dobbins, 1975). Most activities that students are involved in do not build strength in areas where it is most needed—the arm-shoulder girdle and the abdominal-trunk region. *Muscular endurance* is the ability to exert force over an extended period. Endurance postpones the onset of fatigue so that activity can be performed for lengthy periods. Most sport activities require muscular endurance, because throwing, kicking, and striking skills have to be performed many times without fatigue.

When muscular strength is a desired training outcome, it is necessary to lift or move near-

Testing flexibility

maximum workloads with minimal repetitions. Strength development is accompanied by muscle *hypertrophy,* an increase in the number of muscle fibers recruited, and an increase in oxygen use capacity. The hypertrophy of muscle fibers occurs primarily in adolescents and adults as the hormone testosterone triggers this growth. Children and females usually do not have high enough levels of the hormone to cause a substantial increase in muscle fiber size.

To develop muscular endurance, a low-resistance, high-repetition workload is suggested. For most athletes, a balance of the two workloads is probably most useful. Usually, muscular strength and endurance workouts should be conducted three days per week, which gives the muscles a chance to recover from the exercise stress.

Skill-Related Physical Fitness

Skill-related fitness includes those physical qualities that enable a person to perform in sport activities. Skill-related fitness is controlled by genetic makeup. Health-related fitness can be improved by all people; however, skill-related fitness is controlled by an individual's genetic endowment. Synonymous with skill fitness is athletic fitness or motor fitness. Whereas health-related fitness is important for good health, skill-related fitness is performance oriented and required for athletic prowess. In addition to the health-related aspects that are important to sport performance, specific components making up skill-related fitness are agility, balance, coordination, power, and speed.

Agility

Agility is the ability of the body to change position rapidly and accurately while moving in space.

Wrestling and football are examples of sports that require agility.

Balance

Balance refers to the body's ability to maintain a state of equilibrium while remaining stationary or moving. Maintaining balance is essential to all sports but is especially important in the performance of gymnastic activities.

Coordination

Coordination is the ability of the body to perform smoothly and successfully more than one motor task at the same time. Needed for football, baseball, tennis, soccer, and other sports that require hand-eye and foot-eye skills, coordination can be developed by practicing over and over the skill to be learned.

Power

Power is the ability to transfer energy explosively into force. To develop power, a person must practice activities that are required to improve strength, but at a faster rate involving sudden bursts of energy. Skills requiring power include high jumping, long jumping, shot putting, throwing, and kicking.

Speed

Speed is the ability of the body to perform movement in a short period of time. Usually associated with running forward, speed is essential for the successful performance of most sports and general locomotor movement skills.

Table 13.1 shows a number of activities that can be used to improve health- and skill-related physical fitness.

Skill-Related Or Health-Related Fitness?

Skill-related fitness components are useful in performing motor tasks related to sport and athletics. The ability to perform well depends on the genetically determined skill of the individual. Asking youngsters to "try harder" only adds to their frustration if they lack native ability and may see their more skilled friends performing well without excessive effort. When skill-related fitness is taught in elementary school, it should be accompanied by an explanation of why some children can perform well with a minimum of effort whereas others, no matter how hard they try, never excel. There are

Table 13.1 Activities that improve physical fitness

Component	Activities
	Health-Related
Cardiovascular fitness	Jogging, cross-country skiing, walking, rope jumping, bicycling, swimming, and aerobic dance.
Body composition	Same as cardiovascular fitness.
Abdominal strength and endurance	Sit-ups, selected animal walks, stretching, and twisting.
Flexibility of lower back	Bending and stretching, sitting stretch, partner stretching, and selected animal walks.
	Skill-Related
Arm and shoulder girdle strength	Pull-ups, rope climbing, and selected animal walks.
Abdominal strength and endurance	Sit-ups, selected animal walks, bending, stretching, and twisting.
Agility	Selected stunts, agility running, and selected sport skills.
Leg power	Treadmill, vertical jumping, running, and long jump.
Speed	Tortoise and Hare, running in place, and selected leg exercises.
Coordination	Locomotor movements, manipulative skill practice, and specialized sport skills.
Balance	Movements on benches or balance beams, balance stunts, and locomotor movements.

many examples that can be used to illustrate the situation, such as individual differences in speed, jumping ability, strength, and physical size.

In contrast, health-related physical fitness takes a different point of view. The focus of health-related fitness is to help youngsters understand how much activity is required for good health. Emphasis is placed on the process of activity and participation rather than the product of high-level performance. Criterion-referenced health standards are incorporated that express the amount of fitness necessary for reduction of health risks. This contrasts with skill-related fitness, which is somewhat influenced by genetic traits and abilities, rewards high performance, and uses normative standards (percentiles).

An important concept emphasized by health-related fitness programs is that of criterion-referenced health standards. In the past, fitness tests have asked students to compare their performance with the performance of other students regardless of the many complicating factors, such as body type, genetic makeup, and age differences. Youngsters have been compared on percentile charts that showed what percentage of the students ranked above and below them. For students who perform poorly, this is a demoralizing process. Newer tests (Cooper Institute for Aerobic Research, 1992) establish minimum levels of performance as an indicator of good health. Perfor-

mance in excess of the minimum is certainly laudable, but not required. This approach educates students to understand that it is critical to maintain a minimum level of fitness through regular activity rather than compare oneself with others solely on the criterion of fitness test performance. In addition, self-improvement becomes the focus of fitness activity rather than improving for the purpose of doing better than someone else.

ARE TODAY'S CHILDREN FIT?

A popular point of view among physical education teachers is that children today are less fit than children were in the past. This opinion is often used as a justification for more physical education time in the schools. Recent research (Corbin & Pangrazi, 1992) suggests that the fitness of today's youngsters has not degenerated and that they do quite well when compared to past students. When data from the last four national surveys of youth fitness conducted by AAHPERD and/or the President's Council on Physical Fitness and Sports were compared, it was found that children and youth today are just as fit as they were in the past. In fact, the only items that were used in all four surveys were pull-ups and the flexed arm hang. Youngsters, both boys and girls, showed an increase in performance when these two items were compared over four decades. The only area where children have shown a minor decrease in fitness is body composition (Gortmaker, Dietz, Sobol, & Wehler, 1987); today's youngsters are slightly fatter than they were 20 years ago.

Why Do Teachers and the Public Believe That Children Are Unfit?

It is quite likely that many physical education teachers want to believe that youngsters are unfit. If it can be demonstrated that youngsters are not fit, a strong case can be made for employing physical education teachers. Unfortunately, physical educators have been teaching for years and the fitness levels of youngsters have not substantially improved (Corbin & Pangrazi, 1992). An explanation for why so many youngsters have been shown to be unfit may be the arbitrary manner in which standards were set and the measurement of fitness through the implementation of a test battery. For years, the only available fitness test for teachers was the *AAHPERD Youth Fitness Test* (1975, 1987), also known as the *President's Council Physical Fitness and Sports Fitness Test*. This test is a skill-related test that offers the Presidential fitness award to youngsters performing at the 85th percentile or better in all test items. Results of the National School Population Fitness Survey (Reiff et al., 1987) funded by the President's Council on Physical Fitness and Sports showed that only one-tenth of 1 percent of boys and three-tenths of 1 percent of girls could pass a battery of six tests at the 85th percentile, the standard used for earning the Presidential fitness award over the years. Why was the standard set at the 85th percentile? The best explanation available is that this compared with academic standards and test developers felt that physical education needed to accomplish at the same level. Since many physical educators and parents felt the 85th percentile standard was unrealistically high, a new award was created—the National fitness award. To earn this award, youngsters must pass the same battery of test items at the 50th percentile or better. Unfortunately, when using a battery of tests, the majority of students will fail at least one item, thus causing them to lose the award and be identified as unfit. Only 15 percent of boys and 19 percent of girls were able to pass the 50th percentile standard. Using a battery of tests to define fitness and setting arbitrary standards are sure ways to fail the majority of children. Even at this lowered standard, over 80 percent of youngsters are failures.

Another reason that people continue to believe that youngsters are unfit is due to changing definitions of fitness. Fitness testing has evolved from skill-related fitness to health-related fitness and its relationship to good health and feelings of well-being. We now know that high performance on fitness test items is not necessary for good health, especially when the performance is based on skill-related items such as the 50-yard dash and the shuttle run. Evidence shows that moderate amounts of health-related physical fitness are enough to contribute to good health (Blair et al., 1989). When health-related fitness test items are compared, today's children perform as well (and better) than those in years past. Modern health standards reveal that the majority of children are indeed fit.

Another contention often made is that today's children are much less active, so they must be much less fit. It is true that children watch much television (American Academy of Pediatrics, 1991). However, whether this equates with inactivity is questionable. Children today are still the most active segment of our society. When daily energy expenditure is examined, it is highest at 6 years of age and gradually reaches a low point at 16–18 years of age (Rowland, 1990). It is interesting to note that adults continue to prod youngsters toward better fitness even though they are the least active age group in our society.

A final consideration is that activity has much less influence on the fitness levels of children than adults. The reason for this is that children are a somewhat "homogenous" group. That is, the majority of them are active. Few are totally inactive, unlike many adults, so the effects of adding activity to children's lifestyle usually doesn't manifest itself in an improved fitness level for the entire group.

Can All Children Meet Standards of Fitness?

It is important to consider whether it is a realistic expectation that all children reach specified standards of fitness. What factors control fitness performance and how much control do youngsters have over their fitness accomplishments? Payne and Morrow (1993) reviewed 28 studies examining training and aerobic performance in children and concluded that improvement is small to moderate in prepubescent children. They state the following:

> The relatively small-to-moderate increase in pre- to post-aerobic improvement and the weak relationship between type of training program and effect size lead to questions concerning traditional practices when dealing with children and their fitness. Are we expecting too much from traditional physical education or fitness programs? Have award structures, designed to

motivate children within these programs or test batteries, been appropriately designed when children appear to elicit only small improvements in aerobic capacity? Clearly, curriculum planners, teachers, fitness directors, exercise physiologists, and physicians need to consider carefully the ramifications of these findings. (p. 312)

A significant amount of fitness test performance is explained by heredity (Bouchard, 1990; Bouchard, Dionne, Simoneau, & Boulay, 1992). Various factors such as environment, nutrition, heredity, and maturation affect fitness performance as reflected in physical fitness test scores. Research clearly shows that heredity and maturation strongly impact fitness scores (Bouchard et al., 1992; Pangrazi & Corbin, 1990). In fact, these factors may have more to do with youth fitness scores than activity level. Lifestyle and environmental factors can also make a difference. For example, nutrition is a lifestyle factor that can influence test scores, and environmental conditions (heat, humidity, and pollution) strongly modify test performances. Fitness performance is only partially determined by activity and training.

Some youngsters have a definite advantage on tests because of the types of muscle fibers they inherit (see Chapter 2). Others inherit a predisposition to perform well on tests. In other words, even in an untrained state, some children score better because of heredity. On the other hand, some youngsters who train will not score as well as others who are untrained because of their genetic predisposition. Beyond heredity lies another factor that predisposes some youngsters to high performance. Recent research has shown that "trainability" is inherited (Bouchard et al., 1992). This implies that some people receive more benefit from training (regular physical activity) than others. As an example, assume that two youngsters perform the same amount of activity throughout a semester. Child A shows dramatic improvement immediately while child B does not. Child A simply responds more favorably to training than child B. Child A inherited a system that is responsive to exercise. Child A not only gets fit and scores well on the test but gets feedback that says, "the activity works—it makes me fit." Child B scores poorly, receives no feedback, and concludes that, "activity doesn't improve my fitness, so why try?" The unfortunate thing is that child B will improve in fitness to a lesser degree than child A and will take longer to show improvement. Child B will probably never achieve the fitness level attained by child A. There are many different examples that could be used to illustrate the many degrees of trainability possessed by different children.

Another factor that impacts fitness performance is physical maturation. All teachers know that some youngsters mature faster than others. Sometimes forgotten is how important maturation is in relationship to performance. If two youngsters are the same age and sex, but one is physiologically older (advanced skeletal maturation), it is likely that the more mature youngster will perform better on tests than the less mature child. Examining fitness norms reveals that children get better on most tests as they grow older. In such cases, fitness test scores for an immature active child could be lower than fitness scores of a more mature, less active youngster. Maturation may override the effects of activity among young children. Age also plays a role in fitness performance (Pangrazi & Corbin, 1988). As little as three months difference in age will help youngsters perform better than younger children regardless of training. Expect older students in the same class with younger children to perform better.

Should teachers assume from this point of view that there is little use in helping students become more active? Certainly not. Whereas heredity plays an important role in fitness and in trainability of fitness, all youngsters benefit from regular fitness activity. It simply takes some children longer to benefit from regular physical activity and to show fitness gains. This means less gifted children will need more encouragement and positive feedback as their improvement will be in smaller increments and of a lesser magnitude.

Do Fitness Test Results Reveal the Activity Levels of Children?

Teachers and parents want to believe that fitness in youngsters is primarily a reflection of the amount of activity children perform on a regular basis. It is true that physical activity generally increases fitness, but the concept that activity builds fitness may lead teachers to the conclusion that youngsters who score high on fitness tests are active and those who don't score well are inactive. Physical activity is an important variable in fitness development for adults, but for children and youth other factors can be of equal or greater importance. Studies have shown that the relationship of physical fitness to physical activity among children is low (Pate, Dowda, & Ross, 1990; Pate & Ross, 1987; Ross, Pate, Caspersen, Damberg, & Svilar, 1987). If teachers make the mistake of assuming that a child is inactive because of scores on a fitness test, problems can result.

It is necessary to understand the problems that may occur when teachers assume that fitness and activity are highly related. Youngsters, particularly in elementary school, are concerned about whether the teacher likes them. They want to behave in ways that please the teacher. If youngsters are encouraged to do regular exercise to improve their fitness scores, many will take this challenge seriously. When fitness tests are given, students will expect to do well on the tests if they have been exercising regularly and, of course, teachers will also expect them to do well. If, however, they receive scores that are lower than expected, they will be disappointed. They will be especially discouraged if the teacher concludes that their low fitness status is a reflection of inactivity. Such a conclusion as, "You are not as fit as you should be compared to other children, therefore you have not been active," could be a destructive and untrue statement. It may cause a loss of self-esteem and a loss of respect between student and teacher. The other side of this issue is assuming that youngsters who make high scores on fitness tests are active. Youngsters who are genetically gifted may be inactive, yet may perform well on fitness tests. If teachers do not teach otherwise, these youngsters could learn that it is possible to be fit and healthy without being active. Neither of these scenarios is accurate and it is the teacher's responsibility to correct such misconceptions.

PHYSICAL ACTIVITY OR FITNESS?

It is apparent that a number of factors impact fitness performance, therefore an important question is, "Should instructors emphasize physical fitness performance or participation in regular activity?" When examining this question, the important thing is to understand several concepts that can help determine an effective instructional approach. Asking the question of "how many, how fast, or how far" places emphasis on the product of fitness. This product orientation places emphasis on the results of fitness testing and performance. To believe that participation in some type of daily activity is important places the focus of instruction on the process of physical activity. A process focus involves activity and participation rather than fitness scores and award systems. Often, exercisers who focus on the product (how fast, how far, how long) of fitness burn out or become discouraged after a short period of time. For example, when

running against the clock, improvement continues to the point where it is impossible to go any faster. This lack of improvement can be discouraging to a product-oriented person. In like fashion, emphasizing product outcomes with children can cause them to become discouraged if they fail to reach goals their peers have reached.

All children have the right to a lifetime of physical activity and health. If schools fail to teach children how to live an active lifestyle, they may not become healthy adults. A study conducted by the U.S. Department of Health and Human Services (Ross & Gilbert, 1985) showed that about half of all American children were not developing adequate exercise knowledge and skill needed to develop a healthy cardiovascular system. The same study showed that only about one-third of America's youth participate in organized physical education programs. A recent statement issued by the American Academy of Pediatrics (1991) reported that children from the ages of 2 to 12 spend about 25 hours a week watching television. Even in school programs, children may be fortunate to spend 1 hour a week in an organized physical education lesson. It is apparent that physical educators must place emphasis on developing activity habits that carry over to out-of-school activities. Patterns of activity cannot be developed solely by the school; it requires that active lifestyles be encouraged at home.

Some professionals question the value of organized fitness activities in the schools. They express the opinion that since physical education classes meet only once or twice a week, actual fitness changes in children may not occur, making it more important to use the time for skill development. This is a mistake. Youngsters are experiential; that is, they learn from participation and develop perceptions based on those experiences. To avoid taking time to teach exercises and other fitness activities is to circumvent teaching important skills that can be integrated into adult lifestyles. Youngsters must learn during their school experiences that daily activity (independently) is an important habit for a healthy lifestyle. Children are taught how to brush their teeth at a tender age in order that their teeth will last a lifetime. In a similar light, how can teachers justify not teaching children to be active for a few minutes each day to assure that one's total health will not decay? Teaching different ways to develop and maintain fitness (even if only one day per week) suggests to students that the school values health and exercise as part of a balanced lifestyle. What better outcome than to teach youngsters to participate in some type of daily activity throughout life?

DEVELOPING POSITIVE ATTITUDES TOWARD ACTIVITY

There are a number of things teachers can do to increase the possibility of students being "turned on" to activity. Fitness activity is neither good nor bad. Rather, how fitness activities are taught determines how youngsters will feel about making fitness a part of their lifestyle. The following strategies can help make activity a positive learning experience.

Individualize Fitness Activities

Students who are expected to participate in fitness activities and find themselves unable to perform exercises are not likely to develop a positive attitude toward physical activity. Fitness experiences should be designed to allow children to determine their personal workloads. Use time as the workload variable and ask children to do the best they can within a time limit. People dislike and fear experiences they perceive to be forced upon them from an external source. Voluntary long-term exercise is more probable when individuals are internally driven to do their best. Fitness experiences that allow children to control the intensity of their workouts offer better opportunity for development of positive attitudes toward activity.

Expose Youngsters to a Variety of Physical Fitness Routines and Exercises

Presenting a variety of fitness opportunities decreases the monotony of doing the same routines week after week and increases the likelihood that students will experience fitness activities that are personally enjoyable. Most youngsters are willing to accept activities they dislike if they know there will be a chance to experience routines they enjoy in the near future. A year-long routine of "calisthenics and running a mile" forces children, regardless of ability and interest, to participate in the same routine whether they like it or not. When youngsters know a new and exciting routine is on the horizon they will accept routines they dislike. Avoiding potential boredom by systematically changing fitness activities is a significant way to help students perceive fitness in a positive way.

Give Students Meaningful Feedback about Their Performance

Teacher feedback contributes to the way children view fitness activities. Immediate, accurate, and specific feedback regarding performance encourages continued participation. Provided in a positive manner, this feedback can stimulate children to extend their participation habits outside the confines of the gymnasium. Reinforce all children, not just those who perform at high levels. All youngsters need feedback and reinforcement even if they are incapable of performing at an elite level.

Teach Physical Skills and Fitness

Physical education programs should concentrate on skill development as well as fitness. Some states mandate fitness testing, which causes some teachers to worry that their students "will not pass." Unfortunately, the skill development portion of physical education is often sacrificed to increase the emphasis on teaching for fitness. Physical education programs must develop two major objectives; fitness and skill development. Skills are the tools that most adults use to attain fitness. The majority of individuals maintain fitness through various skill-based activities such as tennis, badminton, swimming, golf, basketball, aerobics, bicycling, and the like. People have a much greater propensity to participate as adults if they feel competent in an activity. School programs must graduate students with requisite entry skills in a variety of activities.

Be a Good Role Model

Appearance, attitude, and actions speak loudly about teachers and their values regarding fitness. Teachers who display physical vitality, take pride in being active, participate in fitness activities with children, and are physically fit will positively influence youngsters to maintain an active lifestyle. It is unreasonable to expect teachers to complete a fitness routine nine times a day and five days a week. However, teachers must exercise with a class periodically to assure students that they are willing to do what they ask others to do.

Be Concerned about the Attitudes of Children

Attitudes dictate whether youngsters will participate in activity. Too often, adults want to force fitness on children and "make them all fit." This often results in insensitivity to the feelings of participants. Training does not equate to lifetime fitness. When youngsters are trained without concern for their feelings, it is quite possible that the result will be fit children who hate physical activity. Once a negative attitude is developed, it is difficult to change. This does not mean that youngsters should avoid fitness activity. It means that fitness participation must be a positive experience. Youngsters should not all be funneled into one type of fitness activity. For example, running may be detrimental to the health of obese children and lean, uncoordinated students may not enjoy contact activities. Additionally, the fitness experience must be a challenge rather than a threat. A *challenge* is an experience that participants feel they can accomplish. In contrast, a *threat* appears to be an impossible undertaking; one in which there is no use trying. Fitness goals should be kept within the realm of challenge. A final note; whether an activity is a challenge or a threat depends on the perceptions of the learner, not the instructor. Listen carefully to students rather than telling them "they should do it for their own good."

Start Easy and Progress Slowly

Fitness development is a journey, not a destination. No teacher wants students to become fit and then quit being active. A rule of thumb to follow is allow students to start at a level which they can *accomplish*. This usually means self-directed workloads within a specified time frame. Don't force students into heavy workloads too soon. It is impossible to start a fitness program at a level that is too easy. Start with success and gradually increase the workload. This avoids the discouragement of failure and excessive muscle soreness. When students successfully accomplish activities, they should be taught a system of self-talk that looks at their exercise behavior in a positive light. This helps avoid the common practice of self-criticism when students fail to live up to their own or others' standards.

Use Low-Intensity Activity

Activity should be appropriate for the developmental level of the youngster. The amount of activity needed for good health is somewhat dictated by two variables, the intensity of the activity and the duration of the activity. Most children participate in high-volume—low-intensity activity as they exercise sporadically all day. This naturally occurring activity is consistent with the developmental level of children. In contrast, most adults are involved in high-intensity—low-volume activity. The major reason for such activity patterns is available time for exercise. Few adults have time to be active for long periods of time. This contrast of activity styles leads many adults to believe that children need to participate in high-intensity activities to receive health benefits. They view children as unfit because they often refuse to participate in high-intensity fitness activities. This focus on high-intensity activity can lead to children becoming discouraged and burned out at an early age. Youngsters are already the most active segment of society (Rowland, 1990), and it is important to maintain and encourage this trait. If the activity is reinforced, the fitness will follow to the extent that it is possible for each child given heredity and maturation level.

Encourage Lifetime Activity

Teachers want students to exercise throughout their lifetime. Certain activities may be more likely to stimulate exercise outside of school. There is some evidence (Glasser, 1976) that if the following activity conditions are met, exercise will become positively addicting and a necessary part of one's life. These steps imply that many individual activities like walking, jogging, hiking, biking and the like are activities that students might regularly use for fitness during adulthood.

1. The activity must be noncompetitive; the student chooses and wants to do it.
2. It must not require a great deal of mental effort.
3. The activity can be done alone, without a partner or teammates.
4. Students must believe in the value of the exercise for improving health and general welfare.
5. Participants must believe that the activity will become easier and more meaningful if they persist. To become addicting, the activity must be done for at least 6 months.
6. The activity should be accomplished in such a manner that the participant is not self-critical.

THE BROAD PROGRAM OF PHYSICAL FITNESS

There is much more to acquiring physical fitness than just providing physical fitness routines. The components of a broad program are as follows:

1. Teach students to assume responsibility for their personal fitness development. This includes helping students set personal goals that have meaning. It implies an extension of fitness development beyond recess and free time in school, as well as application to the home and community environment.

2. Provide an understanding of how fitness is developed. This means explaining the value of the procedures followed in class sessions so that children understand the purpose of all fitness developmental tasks. In addition, it requires teaching children the basic components of a personal fitness program for life.

   Knowledge of the values of physical fitness, how to apply the principles of exercise, and how fitness can become part of one's lifestyle can positively alter how students view physical activity. Bringing the class together at the end of a lesson to discuss key fitness points presented promotes a clearer understanding of why fitness is important. To share cognitive information, establish a muscle of the week, construct educational bulletin boards to illustrate fitness concepts, or send home handouts explaining principles of fitness development (see Chapter 11).

3. Develop cognition of the importance of fitness for wellness. Students should understand how to perform fitness activities and why these activities should be performed. They need to know the values derived from maintaining a minimal fitness level.

4. Provide basic explanations of rudimentary anatomy and kinesiology. Children should learn the names and locations of major bones and muscle groups, including how they function in relation to selected joint action. Knowledge should relate to fitness actions appropriate to the maturity level of students.

5. Provide a sound fitness development program that is part of each lesson. This is the culmination—the show-me-how procedures that embody the first four program points.

Teachers should examine how the physical education program and accompanying instruction communicate the importance of fitness to children. Too often, the area deleted from physical education instruction is physical fitness. This communicates to children that fitness is the least important aspect of physical education. In fact, values shared with children should develop the comprehension that physical fitness is the foundation of skill performance, personal health, and wellness.

PROMOTING THE PHYSICAL FITNESS PROGRAM

The physical fitness program must be sold to parents and administrators in order to achieve consistent and positive results. How the program is administered and shared with students and parents will determine the amount of goodwill the program creates. The following suggestions should be considered for enriching and promoting the fitness program.

1. Place bulletin boards in the teaching area to explain components of the physical education program to parents and students. Bulletin boards can be used to explain skill techniques, motivational reminders, and fitness activities that will be upcoming in class. Classroom teachers are required to develop bulletin boards for their classes; when physical education teachers design visual aids for the gymnasium, credibility is enhanced.

2. Exploit the use of audiovisual aids. Audiotapes of fitness routines can increase the motivation of youngsters. Exercise videotapes can be an excellent medium for beginning a new fitness activity.

3. Children should understand the values of physical fitness and the physiology of its development and maintenance. Homework dealing with the cognitive aspects of fitness development communicates to parents that their children are gaining knowledge that will serve them for a lifetime.

4. Emphasize self-testing programs that teach children to evaluate their personal fitness levels. In self-evaluation programs, children have a regular opportunity to assess their fitness without concern about others judging them. Fitness is a personal matter for most adults and should be considered a personal matter for youngsters.

5. Cooperation at home is essential. Children are more likely to be involved in fitness activity when their parents exercise regularly. Fitness activities that are sent home for weekend and vacation participation will help parents understand the importance of regular activity. An effective technique is to develop a fitness calendar that lists activities to be performed on various days. A monthly calendar outline can be used to list various fitness activities and sent home to parents.

6. Physical education fitness exhibitions and school demonstrations for parents can feature

a number of fitness routines and activities. Focus should be placed on *all* students participating and enjoying activity. Many parents think youngsters are unfit and not being asked to exercise regularly in school. When parents are able to see their youngsters vigorously exercising, support of the program is usually enhanced.

FITNESS TESTING: GUIDELINES FOR PROPER USE

Fitness testing can be an important part of the physical education program. A number of issues need to be considered before implementing the testing program. The overriding consideration should be to assure that the testing experience is positive and educational. Children should have the opportunity to learn about their personal fitness and how to develop a lifestyle that will help them maintain good health. In addition, no child should ever be turned off by the testing experience; imagine the number of children who were embarrassed when their fitness test results were announced to the class. The following points will help assure a positive and meaningful experience.

The Purposes and Uses of Fitness Tests

Fitness tests are designed to evaluate and educate youngsters about the status of their physical fitness. Obviously fitness tests have limitations, so what becomes important is how the tests are used. Three purposes of fitness tests are to offer personalized, informal self-testing, to establish a personal best fitness performance, and for institutional evaluation of fitness goals. The personalized self-testing program is an effective choice for teachers and students. It can be done in the least amount of time, is educational, and can be done frequently. In addition, little instructional time is lost and children learn how to evaluate their fitness, a skill that will serve them for a lifetime.

The *personalized self-testing program* is an approach that is student centered, concerned with the process of fitness testing, and places less emphasis on performance scores (product). When using this technique, students are asked to find a friend with whom they would like to work. Partners work together to evaluate each other and develop their fitness profiles. The focus is on self-testing. The goal is to teach students the process of fitness testing so they will be able to evaluate their health status during adulthood when teachers are no

Students self-testing each other

longer available. Students are asked to do their best, but the teacher does not interfere in the process. The results are the property of the student and are not posted or shared with other students. The self-testing program is an educational endeavor; it also allows for more frequent evaluation, as it can be done quickly, privately, and informally.

Figure 13.1 is an example of a self-testing form that can be used by students. It allows for two testing trials so they can monitor their progress. In addition, it contains a column to check off whether they met the minimum criterion-referenced health standard for each test item. Students can store the forms or they can be collected by the teacher and returned to the students later for the second test trial. The purpose of recording the data is to help students learn to self-evaluate themselves without the stigma of others having to view or know about it. In addition, students may choose not to be tested on a certain item because they fear embarrassment (i.e., skinfolds) or failure (mile run).

The *personal best testing program* appeals to gifted performers and to students who are motivated by achieving a maximum performance. The objective is to achieve a maximum score in each of the test items. This type of program has been in place for years for most fitness tests. In addition, several awards (Presidential, National, and others) have been issued to high-level performers. This is a formal testing program as compared to the self-testing approach discussed previously. Test items must be performed correctly, following test protocol to the letter. This program requires maximal performance, and may not be motivating to less capable students. It requires a considerable amount of

MY PERSONAL FITNESS RECORD (FITNESSGRAM TEST ITEMS)

Name _____ Age _____ School _____ Grade _____ Room _____

	Trial 1		**Trial 2**	
	Score	HFZ*	Score	HFZ*
Body Composition				
Calf (leg) Skinfold				
Triceps (arm) Skinfold				
Total (leg + arm)				
Cardiovascular Endurance				
PACER				
Abdominal Strength				
Curl-ups				
Upper Body Strength				
Push-ups				

The following items are pass-fail.

Back Strength				
Trunk Lift				
Lower Back Flexibility	L	R	L	R
Sit & Reach				
Upper Back Flexibility	L	R	L	R
Shoulder Stretch				

*HFZ indicates you have scored in the Healthy Fitness Zone. This means that you have achieved or passed the minimum fitness standard required for good health and minimal health risk. Regardless of whether you passed all the tests, you must maintain an active lifestyle for good health. Try to accomplish at least 30 minutes of activity every day.

You do not have to share the results of your personal fitness record. It is for your information and should help you determine your health status. Ask your teacher if you need ideas for increasing your physical activity level.

Figure 13.1 Example of a self-testing form (Fitnessgram test items)

time to complete. Some students are threatened and fear the embarrassment of failing to perform well in front of peers. A way to avoid this situation is to offer time outside of class when students can be tested. This approach is much less threatening, as students can choose to participate in a personal best testing session or decide to avoid such situations. Testing opportunities can be offered after or before school and on a weekend when school is not in session. Some city recreation departments are also willing to offer fitness testing opportunities outside the physical education program.

An *institutional testing program* involves evaluating the fitness levels of students to see if the institution (school) is reaching its desired objectives. Institutional objectives are closely tied to the physical education curriculum. If the curriculum being taught to students is adequate and the goals are reasonable, students should be able to reach institutional goals. A common approach is to establish a percentage of the student body that must meet or exceed criterion-referenced health standards for a fitness test. If the percentage is below established institutional objective standards, it indicates the curriculum should be modified in order to increase the percentage of students meeting the health standards. Because this type of testing impacts teachers and curriculum offerings, it should be done in a formal and standardized manner. A common approach is to train a team of parents to administer tests throughout the system. This ensures accuracy and consistency across all schools in the district. Each test item is reviewed separately, as it is quite possible that objectives are being reached for some but not all of the items. To avoid testing all students every year, many districts evaluate students at regular intervals during their school career, such as at the fifth, eighth, and tenth grades. This minimizes the amount of formal testing youngsters have to endure during their school career.

Fitness Awards

For many years, award systems have been designed to reward those students who demonstrate high levels of performance. The intent of award systems was to motivate youngsters to improve their level of fitness. Unfortunately, performance awards usually only motivate youngsters who feel they have the ability to earn them (Corbin, Lovejoy, & Whitehead, 1988; Corbin, Lovejoy, Steingard, & Emerson, 1990). Many students find it difficult, if not impossible, to earn such awards and end up feeling as though there is no use trying. Since the award focuses on a single episode of fitness accomplishment, the act of participating in daily activity becomes less important and students soon learn that the only thing that counts is performance on the test.

Reward systems that focus on improvement look only at short-term changes. Many fitness award systems only ask students to look at their immediate health status. There is a strong possibility that youngsters who achieve at an acceptable level do so because they are genetically gifted, not because they participate regularly in activity. If gifted students easily pass the test, it may lead them to believe that it is not necessary to exercise regularly. It is important that rewards and awards focus on regular activity—this is the message that students should hear. The goal should be to de-

velop a program that encourages behavior that will last a lifetime. Teachers who focus on long-term behavior talk with students more about their activity level than about their fitness scores.

If used, an award system should incorporate the following points:

1. Awards must be based on achievement of goals that are challenging, yet attainable (Locke & Latham, 1985). Goals that are difficult to attain will not elicit effort from students (Harter, 1978). Students who are least likely to make the effort to earn the award are those with low self-esteem; probably the students who most need to achieve the goals. Effective goals are those that are challenging, yet attainable.

2. If fitness goals do not seem attainable to youngsters, "learned helplessness" will set in (Harter, 1978). This phenomenon occurs when children believe that there is no use trying to reach the goals and that their effort is in vain. "Learned helplessness" often occurs when performance is rewarded, rather than participation or effort. Once again, difficult-to-achieve goals teach youngsters who need to be motivated that there is no use in trying.

3. If an award system is used to motivate children's activity, the system should be faded. Primary-grade children are often motivated by awards; however, by the age of 9 or 10 years, many children start to see the rewards as bribery to do something (Whitehead & Corbin, 1991). Other children may find achievement of the awards to be hopeless and will not be motivated, but discouraged by the rewards being given to others. Gradually removing awards will help students realize that participation is done for intrinsic and personal reasons.

4. An alternative and long-term approach is to develop an award system that recognizes students for regular participation in activity. This places the rewards in reach of all youngsters and helps to establish activity habits that will last a lifetime. In addition, this approach is in unison with *Healthy People 2000* (U.S. Public Health Service, 1988), which lists U.S. objectives for health in process-oriented terms.

Health-Related Physical Fitness Test Batteries

The major reason for using fitness testing is to provide students, teachers, and parents with information about good health. The best-known health-related fitness evaluation program is the Prudential Fitnessgram (1992). It is a comprehensive fitness program (the test is only one part of the total program) that is designed to evaluate health-related fitness. The goals of the program are to promote regular physical activity and to develop behaviors related to daily physical activity.

The Prudential Fitnessgram System

The Prudential Fitnessgram system consists of a flexible test battery, software for reporting results, and an awards system for rewarding participation and/or performance in fitness activities. In addition, an instructor's package filled with information and educational activities for students is available to teachers. The Fitnessgram is a unique and new approach to fitness testing. The flexible test battery allows teachers to select test items as they develop a customized test battery. The software (for Windows, DOS, and Macintosh computers) allows teachers to select the items they want to use. The test printout gives results within a healthy fitness zone as described above.

The Fitnessgram System awards program provides three awards that are available to youngsters. This award system is based primarily on exercise behaviors rather than on students' attempts to demonstrate that they are the "best." The Fitnessgram awards program acknowledges and commends performance; however, it places its highest priority on the development and reinforcement of health-related behaviors that are attainable by all students. Awards that are available are the "Get Fit" and "Fit for Life" incentive programs. These are behavior recognition programs that are used to recognize participants for any of the following activities: completion of exercise logs, achievement of specific and personalized goals, and fulfillment of a contractual agreement (with a responsible adult). A performance recognition award is available, the "I'm Fit" award. The program is used to reward participants for either achievement of health fitness zone on five of six test items or four of five test items, or improvement in performance on at least two test items.

Fitnessgram Test Items

The test items in the Fitnessgram are briefly described. Where more than one item is offered, teachers have the choice of selecting the test they desire to use. A comprehensive test manual, related materials, and software can be ordered from The Prudential Fitnessgram, The Cooper Institute

for Aerobics Research, 12330 Preston Road, Dallas, TX 75230.

Aerobic Capacity

One mile run/walk or the PACER (Progressive Aerobic Cardiovascular Endurance Run). The PACER is an excellent alternative to the mile, as it involves a 20-meter shuttle run and can be performed indoors. The test is progressive and starts out at a level that all youngsters can be successful in and gradually increases in difficulty. The objective of the PACER is to run back and forth across the 20-meter distance within a specified time that gradually gets shorter. The 20-meter distance is not intimidating to youngsters (compared to the mile) and avoids the problem of trying to teach young children to pace themselves rather than running all-out and fatiguing rapidly.

Body Composition

Body composition is evaluated using percent body fat, which is calculated by measuring the triceps and calf skinfolds (Figure 13.2 and Figure 13.3) or Body Mass Index (calculated using height and weight).

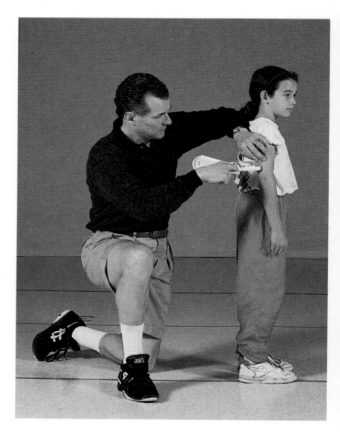

Figure 13.2 Measuring the triceps skinfold

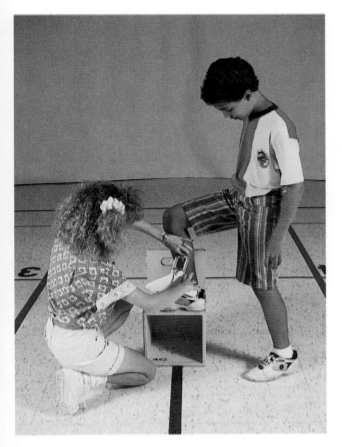

Figure 13.3 Measuring the calf skinfold

Abdominal Strength

Curl-up test. This item uses a cadence (one curl-up every three seconds). The maximum limit is 75. Students lie in a supine position with the knees bent at a 140-degree angle. The hands are placed flat on the mat alongside the hips. The objective is to gradually sit up and move the fingers down the mat a specified distance.

Upper Body Strength

Push-up. This test is done to a cadence (one every 3 seconds) and is an excellent substitute for the pull-up. A successful push-up is counted when the arms are bent to a 90-degree angle. This item allows many more students to experience success as compared to the pull-up and flexed arm hang. Other alternative test items are the modified pull-up, the pull-up, and the flexed arm hang.

Trunk Extensor Strength and Flexibility

Trunk lift. From a face-down position, this test involves lifting the upper body 6 to 12 inches off the floor using the muscles of the back. The posi-

tion must be held until the measurement can be made.

Flexibility

The back-saver sit and reach is similar to the traditional sit and reach test except that it is performed with one leg flexed to avoid encouraging students to hyperextend. Measurement is made on both the right and left legs.

Evaluating the Results of Test Performance

The Fitnessgram uses criterion-referenced *health* standards instead of the more traditional percentile rankings. These standards represent a level of fitness that offers some degree of protection against diseases that result from sedentary living. The Fitnessgram uses an approach that classifies fitness performance into two areas: Needs Improvement and Healthy Fitness Zone (HFZ). All students are encouraged to score in the HFZ, however, there is little advantage to scoring beyond the healthy fitness zone.

Criterion-referenced health standards for aerobic fitness were based on a study by Blair et al. (1989). They reported that a significant decrease in risk of all-cause mortality resulted from getting out of the bottom 20 percent of the population with regard to aerobic activity. The study also reported that risk level continued to decrease as fitness levels increased but not as dramatically as simply getting out of the bottom 20 percent of the population. Aerobic capacity standards for the Fitnessgram HFZ have been established so that the lower end of the HFZ corresponds with achieving a fitness level above the lower 20 percent of the population. The upper end of the HFZ corresponds to a fitness level that includes up to 60 percent of the population.

Criterion-referenced health standards for percent of fat are calculated from equations reported by Slaughter et al. (1988). Detailed information on the development of these equations and other issues related to the measurement and interpretation of body composition information is available in Lohman (1992). Williams et al. (1992) reported that children with body fat levels above 25 percent for boys and 30 to 35 percent for girls are more likely to exhibit elevated cholesterol levels and hypertension. The lower limit of the Fitnessgram HFZ corresponds to these levels of body fat.

Criterion-referenced health standards have not been established for abdominal strength, upper body strength, and flexibility. Instead, criterion-referenced *activity* standards are used for these areas of fitness. The lower limit represents a performance level that youngsters should be able to accomplish if they are reasonably active. Stated another way, these standards reflect a reasonable expectation for students who are sufficiently active. For example, it is difficult to determine whether a lack of upper body strength is important for quality health. Instead, standards have been established that reflect how many push-ups students who are active should be able to perform.

GUIDELINES FOR DEVELOPING PHYSICAL FITNESS

Students should leave a physical education program with the knowledge of basic fitness principles and the ability to apply them to a personal fitness program. To increase a child's present level of physical fitness, that child must perform a higher than normal workload. To ensure that a systematic increase in workload occurs, students should learn to prescribe their workouts using the acronym FIT as a guide, which stands for Frequency, Intensity, and Time. The variables are interrelated, and changing one may require a change in another. In addition to FIT, students should understand the importance of progression, mode of activity, and specificity and types of exercises.

Frequency

Frequency is the number of exercise sessions that an individual will do per week. Three workouts per week is the recommended frequency if benefits are to accrue. In many physical education programs, youngsters meet less, perhaps once or twice a week. Given reduced frequency, some teachers believe that there is little reason to teach physical fitness activities. This is a mistake, because eliminating physical fitness suggests to children that it is unimportant. Another error in this line of reasoning is the assumption that children cannot be taught cognitive material related to physical fitness even when fitness activities are presented only once a week.

Intensity

The heart rate can be used to determine exercise intensity. It gives an indication of whether the workload should be increased or decreased. To monitor heart rate, palpate at the wrist artery, near the joint on the thumb side, using the index and middle fingers. Apply only slight pressure to allow blood flow to continue while taking the pulse.

To count the heart rate, begin within 5 seconds after stopping exercise. The count should be taken for 10 seconds and then multiplied by 6 to give the heart rate per minute. To enhance the level of cardiovascular endurance, the heart rate must be elevated to the training state. Using the following formula, the heartbeat range that should be maintained during exercise can be calculated.

1. Determine the estimated maximum heart rate by taking 220 minus the person's age.
2. Multiply the difference by 60 percent and 80 percent.

The two results provide the heart rate range per minute that should be maintained while exercising. For example, if a child is age 10, subtract 10 from 220, which equals 210. Now multiply 210 by 60 and 80 percent. The result indicates that a heart rate between 126 and 168 beats per minute should be maintained during exercise to reach the training state. Figure 13.4 can be enlarged and posted to help children determine their target heart rate.

Once the training heart rate has been determined, the exercise routine can be undertaken. At the conclusion of the workout, monitor the heart rate. If it is above the beats per minute allowed by the formula, reduce the intensity. On the other hand, if the heart rate is low, increase the intensity of aerobic exercise.

Time

Time is the length of each exercise bout. For developing cardiovascular endurance, the minimum amount of aerobic exercise should be 8 to 10 minutes. Intensity and time are somewhat inversely

---

Are you getting your heart rate into the target zone? Count your pulse for 10 seconds. Look at the chart and see if you are exercising hard enough to exercise your heart!

If your heart rate is between 21 and 30 beats during the 10 seconds you counted it, you are in the training zone. Congratulations!

Remember: You must exercise between 60% and 80% of your maximum heart rate. To determine your maximum heart rate, subtract your age from 220. The result is your maximum heart rate.

Figure 13.4 Heart rate target zone

related when developing effective exercise programs. The greater the intensity, the less time required to receive health benefits. The greater the volume (time) of activity, the less need for intensity. In practice, most youngsters reject the notion of high-intensity activity. They are active individuals who move throughout the day alternating between short bouts of high- and low-intensity activities. In most situations, for children, it is best to monitor the time (duration) of the activity than to try to push for greater intensity. An example is a running activity where the teacher is torn between monitoring the amount of time required to move versus timing the speed (intensity) at which the activity should be performed. Choose the duration of the activity, as it allows children to individualize their workloads. Not all youngsters can run at the same pace, but all can run (or walk) for a certain duration of time. Youngsters should be taught that most adults focus on more intense activities because of limited time. However, if time is available, increasing the volume of activity and reducing the intensity is an effective and often more palatable long-term option.

Progression

Progression is important for maintaining motivation and reducing the chance of injury. Physical fitness activities should be structured so that workloads increase gradually. Teachers can be overenthusiastic about developing fitness in a short amount of time. They need to remember that maintaining fitness is an ongoing process that must be performed for a lifetime. Maintaining the *desire* to exercise is the key issue. Reasonable progression in fitness routines throughout the school year helps ensure that this occurs. Progression involves manipulation of the sequence of exercises and the time factor to prevent some of the negative aspects that often occur with fitness activities. Muscle soreness and the early onset of fatigue due to lack of continuous vigorous activity initially may cause children to balk at high-intensity activity. Since it is common for a child's level of physical fitness to deteriorate during the summer months (if adequate fitness levels have been developed during the school year), fitness routines for the first several weeks of school should be reduced in time and intensity and increased progressively thereafter. If there is a need for a greater workload, the frequency and time factors can be increased accordingly. There is little evidence available outlining a "best" implementation strategy for progression. A general recommendation would be to increase the workload by no more than 10 percent per week. Whatever the case, a conservative approach is best, to foster a positive attitude toward exercise that will last a lifetime.

Mode of Activity

Mode of activity describes the types of activity that are conducive to fitness development. It is important to remember that any activity that can be adapted to comply with FIT standards is appropriate. The most common fitness activities are jogging, walking, swimming, bicycling, cross-country skiing, and aerobics. Specific fitness routines for children are identified in the latter half of this chapter. In addition, the supplementary text, *Lesson Plans for Dynamic Physical Education, 11th ed.* (Pangrazi & Dauer, 1995), lists fitness routines and teaching techniques on a weekly basis. The routines are adjusted for differing age groups and suggest entry-level work loads.

Specificity of Exercise

Specificity refers to developing a particular component of fitness through specifically designed exercises of proper FIT. For example, if the desired outcome is improved abdominal strength, the exercise(s) selected must work the abdominal muscles. The specificity principle means that it is essential to plan carefully fitness routines that will elicit the desired alterations in fitness. Exercises to develop specific components of fitness are described later in the chapter.

The implication of specificity is that exercising a certain part or component of the body develops primarily that part. This emphasizes the importance of a balanced approach to fitness. For example, if one chooses only to jog for fitness, the cardiovascular system will be developed. Flexibility, however, will decrease in the lower back and hamstrings, and abdominal strength will decrease. Muscular power, as revealed by the vertical jump, will decrease also. Developing balanced fitness routines by including flexibility, strength development, and cardiovascular endurance activities is important.

Isotonics, Isometrics, and Isokinetics

The majority of exercises used for routines involve *isotonic* contractions. These are contractions of a muscle through its full range of motion. Walking, jogging, calisthenics, and bicycling are examples of activities that involve isotonic contractions.

Isometric contractions occur without muscle movement. Here the contraction is made against an immovable object, and the muscles do not shorten as they do in isotonic contraction. To receive results, contractions should be an all-out effort held for 8 to 12 seconds. A shortcoming of isometrics is that they build strength only at the angle of contraction. For this reason they should be using different joint angles in an attempt to develop strength throughout the complete range of motion.

Isokinetic contractions are a type of isotonic contraction that requires the use of special machines. Isokinetic contractions are maximum contractions throughout the complete range of motion. Isokinetic devices control the workload mechanically, so that the resistance and rate of movement are maintained regardless of the mechanical advantage that occurs as the contraction is near completion. For strength development, isokinetic exercises appear to be more effective than either isotonic or isometric exercises (Miller & Allen, 1990). However, the requirement of special equipment probably makes this type of exercise impractical for most school settings.

THE YEARLY PLAN

The following is a suggested yearly plan of fitness instruction. It is offered as an example for planning the year's activities. Developing a yearly plan is important to assure that a variety of experiences is offered to learners. It also allows progression to be planned for and assures that youngsters will receive a well-rounded program of instruction. An important point to remember is that physical fitness instruction must be planned in a manner similar to the skill development component of the lesson. For too long, little thought and creativity have been given to fitness. Small wonder that youngsters grow up thinking that physical fitness can be achieved *only* through running laps and calisthenics.

Figure 13.5 is a sample yearly plan that might be used to distribute a variety of fitness activities throughout the school year. When organizing a yearly plan for fitness instruction, consider some of the following points. Units of fitness instruction should vary in length depending on the age of the youngster. Children at developmental level I need to experience a variety of routines in order to maintain a high level of motivation and understand the different faces of fitness. During these years, exposure to many different types of activities is more important than a progressive, demanding fitness routine. The first experiences of fitness in-

struction must be positive and enjoyable. As children mature, units can be extended to 2 weeks. In the upper grades, units of 3 weeks allow for progression and overload to occur within units. In spite of the varying length of units, one principle must be followed: *There are many methods for developing fitness, none of which is best for all children.* Offer a variety of routines and activities so that youngsters learn that fitness is not lockstep and unbending. The yearly plan should offer activities that allow all types of youngsters to find success at one time or another during the school year.

The yearly plan reveals another important criterion to consider when developing a fitness program. The routines become much more structured as youngsters grow older. Most of the activities listed for kindergarten through second-grade children are unstructured and allow for wide variation of performance. For older-grade children, emphasis on proper technique and performance increases. However, this is not to imply that every student must do every activity exactly the same. It is unrealistic to think that an obese youngster will be able to perform at a level similar to a lean child. Allow for variation of performance while emphasizing the importance of "doing your best."

DEVELOPING A FITNESS MODULE

The *fitness module* is that portion of the daily lesson that is exclusively dedicated to the presentation of a variety of fitness activities. The following are suggestions to aid in the successful implementation of the fitness module.

1. Fitness instruction should be preceded by a 2- to 3-minute warm-up period. The introductory activity is useful for this purpose because it allows youngsters the opportunity to "loosen up" and prepare for strenuous activity.

2. The fitness portion of the daily lesson, including warm-up, should not extend beyond 10 to 13 minutes. Some might argue that more time is needed to develop adequate fitness. A higher level of fitness might be developed if more time were devoted to the area. However, the reality of the situation is that most teachers are only allowed a 20- to 30-minute period of instruction. Since skill instruction is part of a balanced physical education program, compromise is necessary to assure that all phases of the program are covered.

3. Activities should be vigorous in nature, exercise all body parts, and cover the major com-

DEVELOPMENTAL LEVEL I

1. Parachute Fitness
2. Movement Challenges
3. Walk, Trot, and Sprint
4. Jump Rope exercises
5. Mini-Challenge Course
6. Circuit Training
7. Movement Challenges
8. Fitness Games and Challenges
9. Parachute Fitness
10. Four-Corners Movement
11. Circuit Training
12. Jump Rope exercises
13. Astronaut Drills
14. Animal Movements and Fitness Challenges
15. Fitness Games and Challenges
16. Parachute Fitness
17. Astronaut Drills
18. Four-Corners Movement
19. Mini-Challenge Course
20. Movement Challenges
21. Astronaut Drills
22. Mini-Challenge Course
23. Walk, Trot, and Sprint
24. Animal Movements and Fitness Challenges
25. Four-Corners Movement
26. Mini-Challenge Course
27. Fitness Games and Challenges
28. Walk, Trot, and Sprint
29. Parachute Fitness
30. Circuit Training
31. Four-Corners Movement
32. Walk, Trot, and Sprint
33. Parachute Fitness
34. Animal Movements and Fitness Challenges

DEVELOPMENTAL LEVEL II

1. Teacher-leader exercises
2. Teacher-leader exercises
3. Teacher-leader exercises
4. Teacher-leader exercises
5. Circuit Training
6. Circuit Training
7. Circuit Training
8. Walk, Trot, and Sprint
9. Walk, Trot, and Sprint
10. Exercises to music
11. Exercises to music
12. Astronaut Drills
13. Astronaut Drills
14. Continuity Drills
15. Continuity Drills
16. Aerobic fitness and partner resistance exercises
17. Aerobic fitness and partner resistance exercises
18. Challenge Course
19. Challenge Course
20. Challenge Course
21. Aerobic fitness
22. Aerobic fitness
23. Aerobic fitness
24. Astronaut Drills
25. Astronaut Drills
26. Continuity Drills
27. Continuity Drills
28. Exercises to music
29. Exercises to music
30. Jogging
31. Jogging
32. Hexagon Hustle
33. Hexagon Hustle
34. Parachute Fitness

Figure 13.5 Yearly plan of fitness activities (Figure continues on page 280)

ponents of fitness. Children are capable performers when workloads are geared to their age, fitness level, and abilities. Exercises must adhere to principles of FIT and be within the capabilities of students.

4. A variety of fitness routines comprising sequential exercises for total body development is the recommended alternative to a yearlong program of regimented calisthenics. A diverse array of routines that appeal to the interest and fitness level of children should replace the traditional approach of doing the same routine day in and day out. The remainder of this chapter describes various fitness activities that can be implemented with children.

5. The fitness routine should be conducted during the first part of the lesson. Relegating fitness to the end of the lesson does little to enhance the image of exercise. Further, by having the exercise phase of the lesson precede skill instruction, the concept, "You get fit to play sport, you do not play sport to get fit," is reinforced.

6. Teachers should assume an active role in fitness instruction. Children respond positively to role

1. Teacher-leader exercises
2. Teacher-leader exercises
3. Hexagon Hustle
4. Hexagon Hustle
5. Hexagon Hustle
6. Circuit Training
7. Circuit Training
8. Circuit Training
9. Jogging
10. Jogging
11. Exercises to music
12. Exercises to music
13. Exercises to music
14. Exercises to music
15. Astronaut Drills
16. Astronaut Drills
17. Astronaut Drills
18. Aerobic fitness and partner resistance exercises
19. Aerobic fitness and partner resistance exercises
20. Parachute Fitness
21. Parachute Fitness
22. Aerobic fitness
23. Aerobic fitness
24. Challenge Course
25. Challenge Course
26. Challenge Course
27. Continuity Drills
28. Continuity Drills
29. Continuity Drills
30. Jogging
31. Jogging
32. Jogging
33. Squad leader exercises with task cards
34. Squad leader exercises with task cards

Figure 13.5 *continued*

modeling. A teacher who actively exercises with children, hustles to assist those youngsters having difficulty performing selected exercises, and is able to make exercise fun begins to instill in children the value of an active lifestyle.

7. Various forms of audio or visual assistance should be used to increase children's motivation. Background music, colorful posters depicting exercises, tambourine or drum assistance to provide rhythmical accompaniment for activity, and other instructional media aids can assist in making vigorous activity more enjoyable.

8. When determining workloads for children, the available alternatives are time or repetitions. It is best to base the workload on time rather than on a specified number of repetitions because youngsters can adjust their workload within personal limits. Having the class perform as many push-ups (or push-up challenges) as possible in a given amount of time (in contrast to requiring that the entire class complete 15 push-ups) will result in more children feeling successful.

9. Teachers can use audiotapes to time fitness activity segments so they are free to move throughout the area and offer individualized instruction. Participation and instruction should be enthusiastic and focus on positive outcomes. If the instructor does not enjoy physical fitness partici-

pation, such an attitude will be apparent to students.

10. Fitness activities should *never* be assigned as punishment. Such a practice teaches students that "push-ups and running are things you do when you misbehave." The opportunity to exercise should be a privilege as well as an enjoyable experience. Think of the money adults spend to exercise. Take a positive approach and offer students a chance to jog with a friend when they do something well. This not only allows them the opportunity to visit with the friend, but to exercise on a positive note. Be an effective salesperson; sell the joy of activity and benefits of physical fitness to youngsters.

FITNESS ACTIVITIES FOR DEVELOPMENTAL LEVEL I

Fitness activities for young children should have the potential to develop components of physical fitness and exercise the various body areas. All the fitness routines that follow are designed to combine strength and flexibility activities with cardiovascular activity. For most routines, strength and flexibility activities are listed. Strength and flexibility activities should be alternated with cardiovascular activities. The introductory activity and fitness development activity should combine to provide broad coverage by including activities for each of these five areas: trunk, abdomen, arm-shoulder girdle, legs and cardiorespiratory system, and flexibility.

Fitness Challenges

Many selected movement challenges can be used to develop fitness routines for children at this level. Nonlocomotor activities should be alternated with locomotor activities to avoid excessively fatiguing youngsters. When youngsters are pushed too hard aerobically, they will express their fatigue in many different manners (i.e., complaining, quitting, misbehaving, or sitting out). Effective fitness instructors are keenly aware of how far to push and when to ease up. Instruction and activities should be sensitive to the capacities of youngsters.

Arm-Shoulder Girdle Development

The following are examples of movement challenges that can be issued to help youngsters develop arm-shoulder girdle strength. All the challenges encourage youngsters to support their body weight with the arms and shoulders.

1. Practice taking the weight completely on your hands.
2. In crab position, keep your feet in place and make your body go in a big circle. Do the same from the push-up position.
3. In crab position, let's see you go forward, backward, and to the side. Turn around, move very slowly, and so on.
4. Successively from standing, supine, and hands-knees positions: Swing one limb (arm or leg) at a time, in different directions and at different levels.
5. Combine two limb movements (arm-arm, leg-leg, or arm-leg combinations) in the same direction and in opposite directions. Vary the levels.
6. Swing the arms or legs back and forth and go into giant circles. In supine position, make giant circles with the feet.
7. In a bent-over position, swing the arms as if swimming. Try a backstroke or a breaststroke. What does a sidestroke look like?
8. Make the arms go like a windmill. Turn the arms in different directions. Accelerate and decelerate.
9. How else can you circle your arms?

Figure 13.6 Push-up positions

10. Pretend that a swarm of bees is around your head. Brush them off and keep them away.

Push-Up Position Challenges

The push-up (Figure 13.6) and crab positions are excellent for developing upper body strength. Allow students to rest with one knee on the floor in the up position rather than lying on the floor. Students should be allowed to select a challenge they feel able to accomplish rather than being forced to fail trying to do push-ups. Many of the directives listed for the push-up position can be used for the crab position. A way to develop a sequence of push-up challenges is to begin with one knee on the floor while practicing a number of challenges. As youngsters develop strength, they can make a controlled descent to the floor from the up position. The following are examples of movement challenges that can be done with one knee down (beginning) or in the regular push-up (more challenging) position.

1. Hold your body off the floor (i.e., push-up position).
2. Wave at a friend. Wave with the other arm. Shake a leg at someone. Do these challenges in the crab position.
3. Lift one foot high. Now the other foot.
4. Bounce both feet up and down. Move the feet out from each other while bouncing.
5. Inch the feet up to the hands and go back again. Inch the feet up to the hands and then inch the hands out to return to the push-up position.
6. Reach up with one hand and touch the other shoulder behind the back.
7. Lift both hands from the floor. Try clapping the hands.

8. Turn over so that the back is to the floor. Now complete the turn to push-up position.

9. Walk on your hands and feet. Try two hands and one foot. Walk in the crab position (tummy toward the ceiling).

10. With one knee on the ground, touch your nose to the floor between your hands. As you get stronger, move your head forward a little and touch your nose to the floor. (The farther the nose touches the floor in front of the hands, the greater the strength demands.)

11. Lower the body an inch at a time until the chest touches the floor. Return to the up position any way possible.

12. Pretend you are a tire going flat. Gradually lower yourself to the floor as if you were a tire going flat.

Trunk Development

Movements that include bending, stretching, swaying, twisting, reaching, and forming shapes are important inclusions. No particular continuity exists, except that a specified approach should move from simple to more complex. A logical approach is to select one or more movements and to use them as the theme for the day. Vary the position the child is to take: standing, lying, kneeling, or sitting. From the selected position, stimulate the child to varied movements based on the theme for the day. Examples of different trunk movements follow.

Bending

1. Bend in different ways.
2. Bend as many parts of the body as you can.
3. Make different shapes by bending two, three, and four parts of the body.
4. Bend the arms and knees in different ways and on different levels.
5. Try different ways of bending the fingers and wrist of one hand with the other. Use some resistance. (Explain resistance.) Add body bends.

Stretching

1. Keep one foot in place and stretch your arms in different directions; move with the free foot. Stretch at different levels.
2. Lie on the floor, stretch one leg different ways in space. Stretch one leg in one direction and the other in another direction.
3. Stretch as slowly as you can and then snap back to original position.

4. Stretch with different arm-leg combinations in several directions.
5. See how much space on the floor you can cover by stretching.
6. Combine bending and stretching movements.

Swaying and Twisting

1. Sway your body back and forth in different directions. Change the position of your arms.
2. Sway your body, bending over.
3. Sway your head from side to side.
4. Select a part of the body and twist it as far as you can in one direction and then in the opposite direction.
5. Twist your body at different levels.
6. Twist two or more parts of your body at the same time.
7. Twist one part of your body while untwisting another.
8. Twist your head to see as far back as you can.
9. Twist like a spring. Like a screwdriver.
10. Stand on one foot and twist your body. Untwist.
11. From a seated position, make different shapes by twisting.

Abdominal Development

The basic position for exercising the abdominal muscles is supine on the floor or on a mat. Challenges should lift the upper and lower portions of the body from the floor, either singly or together. Since developmental level I children are top-heavy, (large head, small body), they will find it difficult to perform most abdominal exercises. Therefore, early abdominal development should begin with young-

Swaying and twisting in different directions (trunk development)

sters lying on the floor and lifting the head. This is followed by starting in a sitting position and gradually lowering (with head tucked) the upper body to the floor. The following are challenges teachers can use to stimulate children to develop abdominal and shoulder girdle strength. In addition, selected abdominal exercises (pp. 293–295) can be modified to provide suitable challenges. The approach should be informal, using directives like "Can you . . . ?" or "Show me how you can. . . ."

1. Lift your head from the floor and look at your toes. Wink your right eye and wiggle your left foot. Reverse.

2. In a supine position, "wave" a leg at a friend. Use the other leg. Use both legs.

3. Lift your knees up slowly, an inch at a time.

4. Pick your heels up about 6 inches off the floor and swing them back and forth. Cross them and twist them.

5. Sit up any way you can and touch both sets of toes with your hands.

6. Sit up any possible way and touch your right toes with your left hand. Do it the other way.

7. In a sitting position, lean the upper body backward without falling. How long can you hold this position?

8. From a sitting position, lower the body slowly to the floor. Vary the positions of the arms (across the tummy, the chest, and above the head).

9. From a supine position, curl up by pulling up on your legs.

10. From a supine position, hold your shoulders off the floor.

11. From a supine position, lift your legs and head off the floor.

Leg and Cardiorespiratory Development

Leg and cardiorespiratory development activities can include a range of movement challenges, either in general space or in place. Youngsters fatigue and recover quickly. Take advantage of this trait by alternating cardiorespiratory activities with arm, trunk, and abdominal exercises.

Running Patterns

Running in different directions
Running in place
Ponies in the Stable (p. 253)
Tortoise and Hare (p. 253)

European Rhythmic Running (pp. 252–253)
Running and stopping
Running and changing direction on signal

Jumping and Hopping Patterns

Jumping in different directions back and forth over a spot
Jumping or hopping in, out, over, and around hoops, individual mats, or jump ropes laid on the floor
Jumping or hopping back and forth over lines, or hopping down the lines

Rope Jumping

Individual rope jumping—allow choice

Combinations

Many combinations of locomotor movements can be suggested, such as run, leap, and roll; or run, jump-turn, and shake. Other combinations can be devised. Following are possible challenges that might be used.

1. Run in place. Do some running steps in place without stopping.

2. Skip or gallop for 30 seconds.

3. Slide all the way around the gymnasium.

4. Alternate hopping or jumping for 30 seconds with 30 seconds of rest.

5 Jump in place while twisting the arms and upper body.

6. Do 10 skips, 10 gallops, and finish with 30 running steps.

7. Hold hands with a friend and do 100 jumps.

8. Jump rope as many times as possible without missing.

9. Hop back and forth over this line from one end of the gym to the other.

10. Try to run as fast as you can. How long can you keep going?

Animal Movements

Animal movements are excellent activities for developing fitness because they develop cardiovascular endurance and strength. They are particularly enjoyable for primary-grade children because they can mimic the sounds and movements of the animals. Most of the animal movements are done with the body weight on all four limbs, which assures development of the arms and shoulders. Children can be challenged to move randomly throughout the area, across the gymnasium, or between cones delineating a specific distance. The distance moved can be lengthened or the amount of time each walk is performed can be increased to assure that overload occurs. To avoid excessive fatigue, alternate the animal movements with stretching activities. The following are examples of animal walks that can be used. Many more can be created simply by asking students to see "if they can move like a specific animal."

Puppy Walk: Move on all fours (not the knees). Keep the head up and move lightly.

Lion Walk: Move on all fours while keeping the back arched. Move deliberately and lift the "paws" to simulate moving without sound.

Elephant Walk: Move heavily throughout the area, swinging the head back and forth like an elephant's trunk.

Seal Walk: Move using the arms to propel the body. Allow the legs to drag along the floor much as a seal would move.

Injured Coyote: Move using only three limbs. Hold the injured limb off the floor. Vary the walk by specifying which limb is injured.

Crab Walk: Move on all fours with the tummy facing the ceiling. Try to keep the back as straight as possible.

Rabbit Jump: Start in a squatting position with the hands on the floor. Reach forward with the hands and support the body weight. Jump both feet toward the hands. Repeat the sequence.

Fitness Games

Fitness games are excellent for cardiovascular endurance and create a high degree of motivation. Emphasis should be placed on *all* students moving. One of the best ways to assure that this occurs is to play games that do not eliminate players. This usually means that players who tag someone are no longer "it" and the person tagged becomes "it." This also makes it difficult for players to tell who is "it," which is desirable since it assures that players cannot stop and stand when the "it" player is a significant distance from them. If various games stipulate a "safe" position, allow that the player can remain in this position for a maximum of 5 seconds. This will assure that activity continues. Because fitness games primarily focus on cardiovascular fitness, alternate the games with strength

and flexibility activities. The following are examples of games that can be played.

Stoop tag: Players cannot be tagged when they stoop.

Back-to-back tag: Players are safe when they stand back to back with another. Other positions can be designated such as toe to toe, knee to knee, and so on.

Train tag: Form groups of three or four and make a train by holding the hips of the other players. Three or four players are designated as "it" and try to hook onto the rear of the train. If "it" is successful, the player at the front of the train becomes the new "it."

Color tag: Players are safe when they stand on a specified color. The "safe" color may be changed by the leader at any time.

Elbow swing tag: Players cannot be tagged as long as they are performing an elbow swing with another player.

Balance tag: Players are safe when they are balanced on one body part.

Push-up tag: Players are safe when they are in push-up position. Other exercise positions, such as bent knee curl-up, V-up, and crab position, can be used.

Group tag: The only time a player is safe is when all are in a group (stipulated by the leader) holding hands. For example, the number might be "4," which means that students must be holding hands in groups of four to be safe.

Miniature Challenge Courses

A miniature Challenge Course (Figure 13.7) can be set up indoors or outdoors. The distance between the start and finish lines depends on the type

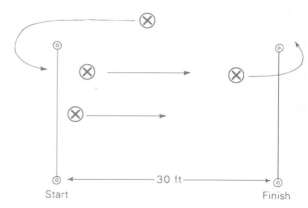

Figure 13.7 Miniature Challenge Course

of activity. To begin, a distance of about 30 feet is suggested, but this can be adjusted. Cones can mark the course boundaries. The course should be wide enough for two children at a time to move down it.

Each child performs the stipulated locomotor movement from the start to the finish line, then turns and jogs back to the start. The movement is continuous. Directions should be given in advance so that no delay occurs. The number of children on each course should be limited to normal squad size or fewer. The following movements can be stipulated:

All types of locomotor movements: running, jumping, hopping, sliding, and so on

Movements on the floor: crawling, Bear Walk, Seal Crawl, and the like

Movements over and under obstacles or through tires or hoops

Sample Routine

1. Crawl under a wand set on two cones.
2. Roll down an inclined mat.
3. Log-roll up an inclined mat.
4. Move up and down on jumping boxes. Climb on the last box, jump and roll.
5. Crawl through hoops or bicycle tires held by individual mats.
6. Walk a balance beam.
7. Pull the body down a bench in prone position.
8. Leap over five carpet squares.
9. Move through a tunnel created by four jumping boxes (or benches) covered with a tumbling mat.
10. Hang on a climbing rope for 10 seconds.
11. Crab walk from one cone to another and back.
12. Run and weave around a series of five cones.

Parachute Fitness Routines

The parachute has been a popular item in elementary physical education for many years. Usually used to promote teamwork, provide maximum participation, stimulate interest, or play games, the parachute has been overlooked as a tool to develop physical fitness. By combining vigorous shaking movements, locomotor circular movement, and selected exercises while holding onto the chute, exciting fitness routines can be developed.

Sample Routine

1. Jog in a circular manner, holding the chute in the left hand.

2. Stop. Grip the chute with two hands and make small and/or big waves.
3. Slide to the right for 16 counts. Repeat to the left for 16 counts.
4. Stop. Lie on back, legs under chute with knees flexed and feet flat on the floor. Pull the chute to the chin until it becomes taut. Perform curl-up exercise while holding onto the chute with both hands.
5. Hold chute with overhand grip and skip (20 to 30 seconds).
6. Stop. Face the center of the chute, spread legs slightly, and flex knees slightly. Pull chute down toward legs. Hold for 5 to 10 seconds. Repeat three to six times.
7. Run in place while holding the chute at different levels. Continue for 20 to 30 seconds.
8. Sit with legs extended under the chute and arms extended forward holding the chute taut. Using only the muscles of the buttocks, move to the center of the chute. Return to original position. Repeat the sequence four to eight times.
9. Set the chute on the ground. Ask children to jog away from the chute; on signal (whistle, drum, etc.) return to chute at same running pace (30 seconds).
10. Facing away from the chute and using an overhand grip, hold the chute above the head with arms extended and pull as hard as possible without losing balance. Hold position for 3 to 5 seconds. Repeat four to six times.
11. Jump up and down as quickly as possible while shaking the chute (15 to 20 seconds).
12. Make a dome by lifting the chute above the head and bringing it to the floor. Holding the edge of the chute down with both hands, do as many push-ups as possible before the center of the chute touches the floor.
13. Hop to the right for 8 counts, then to the left for 8 counts. Repeat three to five times.
14. Face the center and pull hard (tug-of-war) for 5 to 10 seconds. Repeat three to five times.
15. Conclude by making a dome and having everyone move inside the chute and sit on the rim with the back supporting the dome. Rotate trunk to the left for 10 seconds, then to the right for 10 seconds.

Walk, Trot, and Sprint

Four cones can outline a square or rectangular area 30 to 40 yards on a side. (Indoors, the circum-

Performing a parachute fitness routine

ference of the gymnasium is used.) Children are scattered around the perimeter, all facing in the same direction. The signals are given with a whistle. On the first whistle, children begin to walk. On the next whistle, they change to a trot. On the third whistle, they run as rapidly as they can. Finally, on the fourth whistle, they walk again. The cycle is repeated as many times as the capacity of the children indicates. Faster-moving youngsters should pass on the outside of the area.

Another way to signal change is by drumbeat. One drumbeat signals walk, two beats signals trot, and three means run. This allows the teacher to present the three movements in different order. Different locomotor movements such as running, skipping, galloping, and sliding can be used for variation. At regular intervals, students should be stopped so that they can perform various stretching activities and strength development exercises. This will allow short rest periods between bouts of activity. Examples of activities might be one-leg balance, push-ups, curl-ups, touching the toes, and any other challenges.

Jump Rope Exercises

Jump ropes form the basis of a number of exercises and aerobic activities. Each youngster should have a jump rope and space for jumping. Recorded music with taped intervals of silence is an excellent method for alternating periods of rope jumping and exercises. During the periods of silence, youngsters perform an exercise; during the music, children pick up their ropes and begin jumping.

Activity	*Time*
Rope Jumping	30 seconds
Fold the rope, hold over head and sway from side to side. Twist right and left.	20 seconds
Lie on back with the rope held with outstretched arms toward ceiling. Bring up one leg at a time and touch the rope with the toe. Bring up both legs together. Sit up and try to hook the rope over the feet. Release and repeat.	20 seconds
Rope Jumping	20 seconds
Fold the rope and use it for various teacher-led exercises	20 seconds
Place the rope on the floor and perform various locomotor movements around and over the rope. Make different shapes and letters with the rope.	30 seconds
Fold the rope and use it as a tail. Try to keep others from pulling out your tail.	30 seconds
Fold the rope and touch toes. Perform other stretching exercises.	30 seconds
Place the rope on the floor and get into push-up position. Touch the rope with the nose.	20 seconds
Fold the rope, lie on the floor, and place the rope across the chest. Perform a number of curl-ups.	20 seconds
Rope Jumping	30 seconds

Four-Corners Movement

A rectangle is formed by four cones. The student moves around the rectangle. Each time children go around a corner, they change their movement pattern. On long sides, rapid movement such as running, skipping, or sliding should be designated. Moving along short sides, students can hop, jump, or do animal walks. Vary clockwise and counterclockwise directions. On signal, youngsters stop and perform flexibility and strength development challenges.

Using the four-corners ideas as a basis, other combinations can be devised. For example, the pattern in Figure 13.8 requires running along one of the long sides and sliding along the other. One of the short sides has mats and requires three forward rolls, while the other short side requires an animal walk on all fours.

Another variation that stimulates interest in children is to place different equipment around the perimeter of the area. This could be on the inside or outside of the area where youngsters are moving. On signal, youngsters stop and pick up a piece of equipment and manipulate it for a specified time. By interspersing four-corners movement (aerobic movement) with equipment handling (resting), teachers implement interval training. Equipment that can be used might be beanbags, scooters, balance beams, benches, balls, and hoops.

Measurements can vary according to the ages of the children and the movement tasks involved. Outdoors, four rectangles can be laid out. Indoors, at least two should be established. Too much crowding and interference occur when only one rectangle is used for the average-sized class.

Other Fitness Challenges and Routines

Astronaut Drills (p. 304) can be modified for developmental level I. Circuit Training (pp. 300–303) can also be adapted to fit the needs of youngsters

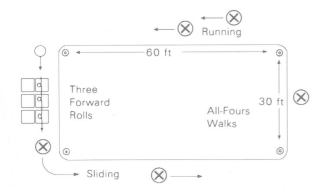

Figure 13.8 Four-corners movement formation

at this level. Stations can include challenging or manipulative activities on an informal basis in addition to exercise routines. Exercises to music (p. 457) can be adapted by combining music and movement challenges (see Chapter 12).

FITNESS ACTIVITIES FOR DEVELOPMENTAL LEVELS II AND III

In contrast to the program of developmental level I activities, the emphasis on fitness at these levels shifts to more structured exercises and routines, with less stress on exploratory movement. Starting off the year with teacher-leader exercises is suggested, as these are the basic exercises used in other routines.

INSTRUCTIONAL PROCEDURES FOR FITNESS ACTIVITIES

1. Students should move into an appropriate formation quickly. Methods for accomplishing this include scattering so that each student has sufficient personal space, going to prearranged places (numbers painted on the floor help), and using extended squad formation. (The squad stays in line but extends spacing between members from front to back, as shown on page 90.)

2. When introducing a new exercise, demonstrate briefly how it is to be done. Explain the purpose of the exercise and its value, including the muscle groups involved. Take children through the exercise by parts (count by count) until it is mastered, and then speed up to normal tempo.

3. Beginning dosages for exercises should start at a level where *all* children will succeed. The best way to assure success is to allow students to adjust the workload to suit their capabilities. Using a specified amount of time per exercise will allow a less gifted child to perform successfully. All children should *not* be expected to perform exactly the same workload. Allow for individual differences by offering dosages in time and asking children to do the best they can within the time constraint.

4. For some exercises, the instructor can allow students to select a modified activity in order to meet success. For example, some students may not be able to perform a push-up. Rather than asking them to continue to fail with this task, ask them to select a different push-up challenge (see page 281). This also is effective with abdominal activities (p. 282).

5. Postural alignment should be maintained. In exercises in which the arms are held in front, to the sides of the body, or overhead, the abdominal wall needs to be tensed and flattened for proper positioning of the pelvis. In most activities, the feet should be pointed forward, the chest should be up, and the head and shoulders in good postural position.

6. Exercises, in themselves, are not sufficient to develop cardiovascular endurance. Additional aerobic activity in the form of jogging, rope jumping, walking, or some other activity is needed to round out fitness development.

HARMFUL PRACTICES AND EXERCISES

The following points contraindicate certain exercise practices and should be considered when offering fitness instruction. For in-depth coverage of contraindicated exercises, see Lindsey and Corbin (1989) or Corbin and Lindsey (1994).

1. The following techniques (Macfarlane, 1993) should be avoided when performing abdominal exercises that lift the head and trunk off the floor:

   • Avoid placing the hands behind the head or high on the neck. This may cause hyperflexion and injury to the discs when the elbows swing forward to help pull the body up.

   • Keep the knees bent. Straight legs cause the hip flexor muscles to be used earlier and more forcefully, making it difficult to maintain proper pelvic tilt.

   • Don't hold the feet on the floor. Having another student secure the feet places more force on the lumbar vertabrae and may lead to lumbar hyperextension.

   • Don't lift the buttocks and lumbar region off the floor. This also causes the hip flexor muscles to contract vigorously.

2. Two types of stretching activity have been used to develop flexibility. Ballistic stretching (strong bouncing movements) formerly was the most common stretching used, but has been discouraged for many years because it was thought to increase delayed onset muscle soreness. The other flexibility activity, static stretching, involves increasing the stretch to the point of discomfort, backing off slightly to where the position can be held comfortably, and maintaining the stretch for an extended time. Static stretching has been advocated because it was thought to reduce muscle soreness and prevent injury. However, a recent study (Smith et al., 1993), has disputed the muscle soreness and tissue damage theory with findings that showed ballistic and static stretching both produced increases in muscle soreness. In fact, the static stretching actually induced significantly more soreness than did ballistic stretching. Until findings show otherwise, it is probably acceptable to use either type of stretching to improve flexibility.

3. If forward flexion is done from a sitting position in an effort to touch the toes, the bend should be from the hips, not from the waist, and should be done with one leg flexed. To conform with this concern, the new Fitnessgram sit and reach test item is now performed with one leg flexed to reduce stress on the lower back.

4. Straight-leg raises from a supine position should be avoided because they may strain the lower back. The problem can be somewhat alleviated by placing the hands under the small of the back, but it is probably best to avoid such exercises.

5. Deep knee bends (full squats) and the duck walk should be avoided. They may cause damage to the knee joints and have little developmental value. Much more beneficial is flexing the knee joint to 90 degrees and returning to a standing position.

6. When doing stretching exercises from a standing position, the knees should not be hyperextended. The knee joint should be relaxed rather than locked. It is often effective to have students do their stretching with bent knees; this will remind them not to hyperextend the joint. In all stretching activities, participants should be allowed to judge their range of motion. Expecting all students to be able to touch their toes is an unrealistic goal. If concerned about touching the toes from this position, do so from a sitting position with one leg flexed.

7. Activities that place stress on the neck should be avoided. Examples of activities in which caution should be used are the Inverted Bicycle, Wrestler's Bridge, and abdominal exercises with the hands behind the head.

8. Avoid the so-called hurdler's stretch. This activity is done in the sitting position with one leg forward and the other leg bent and to the rear. Using this stretch places undue pressure on the knee joint of the bent leg. Substitute a stretch using a similar position with one leg straight

forward and the other leg bent with the foot placed in the crotch area.

9. Avoid stretches that demand excessive back arching. An example: While lying in prone position, the student reaches back and grabs the ankles. By pulling and arching, the exerciser can hyperextend the lower back. This places stress on the discs and stretches the abdominal muscles (not needed by most people).

EXERCISES FOR DEVELOPING FITNESS ROUTINES

Exercises selected fall into the following categories: (a) flexibility, (b) arm-shoulder girdle, (c) abdominal, (d) leg and agility, and (e) trunk-twisting and bending. In any one class session, the exercises should number from 6 to 10. Included in each lesson should be two exercises from the arm-shoulder girdle group and at least one from each of the other categories. Specific exercises should be changed at times, with a minimum of 12 exercises being included in the year's experiences.

Several approaches ensure variety in exercise selection. One system is to select a basic group of exercises. Assume that 12 exercises are selected. These could be divided into two sets of 6 each, with the selection meeting the standards of category coverage previously discussed. Some teachers like to alternate sets day by day. Others prefer to have one set in effect for a week or two before changing.

As a timesaver, teachers can make up sets of exercises on cards, using a different-colored card for each of the categories. In this manner, teachers can be assured of full developmental coverage by having students select a card from each color group, with the stipulation of two from the arm-shoulder girdle group.

Recommended exercises are presented under each of the five categories. Stress points, modifications, variations, and teaching suggestions are presented when appropriate. Teachers can supplement the listed exercises with some of their choice, provided that the exercises are fundamentally sound. A beginning dosage is offered as a starting point for teachers who are meeting a group of youngsters for the first time.

Flexibility Exercises

Many exercises contribute to the development of flexibility. Those included in this section, however, have flexibility as their main goal. The exercises presented here can be done in unison or informally at each student's own pace and capacity.

Bend and Twist

Starting position: Stand with the arms crossed, hands on opposite shoulders, knees slightly flexed, and feet shoulder width apart.

Movement: Bend forward at the waist (count 1). Twist the trunk and touch the right elbow to the left knee (count 2). Twist in the opposite direction and touch the left elbow to the right knee (count 3). Return to the starting position (count 4). Knees can be flexed.

Sitting Stretch

Starting position: Sit on the floor with one leg extended forward and the other bent at the knee. The foot is placed in the area of the crotch. The toes of the extended foot are touched with the fingertips of both hands as the chest gradually moves forward (Figure 13.9).

Movement: Gradually bend forward, taking three counts to bend fully. Recover to sitting position on the fourth count.

Stress point: Bend from the hips.

Partner Rowing

Starting position: Partners sit facing each other, holding hands with palms touching and fingers locked. The legs are spread and extended to touch soles of partner's feet.

Movement: One partner bends forward, with the help of the other pulling backward, to try to bring the chest as close to the floor as possible (Figure 13.10). Reverse direction. Pairs should work individually.

Figure 13.9 Sitting Stretch Position

Figure 13.10 Partner Rowing

Variation: Steam Engine. With both partners in the sitting position, alternate pulling hands back and forth like a pair of steam engine pistons. Do eight sets, right and left combined twists.

Lower Leg Stretch

Starting position: Stand facing a wall with the feet about shoulder width apart. Place the palms of the hands on the wall at eye level (Figure 13.11).

Movement: Slowly walk away from the wall, keeping the body straight, until the stretch is felt in the lower portion of the calf. The feet should remain flat on the floor during the stretch.

Achilles Tendon Stretch

Starting position: Stand facing a wall with the forearms on it. Place the forehead on the back of the hands. Back 2 to 3 feet away from the wall, bend, and move one leg closer to the wall.

Movement: Flex the bent leg with the foot on the floor until the stretch is felt in the Achilles tendon area. The feet should remain flat on the floor as the leg closer to the wall is flexed. Repeat, flexing the other leg.

Body Twist

Starting position: Sit on the floor with the left leg straight. Lift the right leg over the left leg and place it on the floor outside the left knee (Figure 13.12). Move the left elbow outside the upper right thigh and use it to maintain pressure on the leg. Lean back and support the upper body with the right hand.

Movement: Rotate the upper body toward the right hand and arm. Reverse the position and stretch the other side of the body.

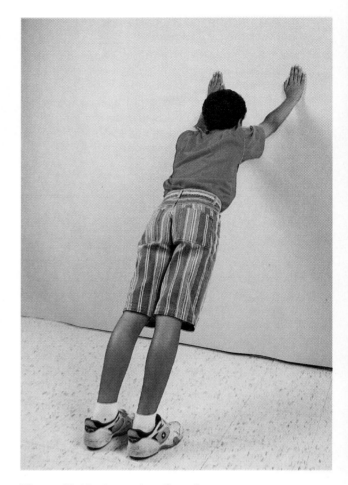

Figure 13.11 Lower Leg Stretch

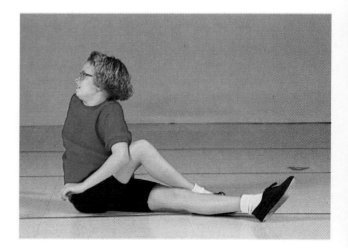

Figure 13.12 Body Twist

Standing Hip Bend

Starting position: Stand with the knees slightly flexed, one hand on the hip and the other arm overhead.

Movement: Bend to the side with the hand resting on the hip. The arm overhead should point and move in the direction of the stretch with a slight bend at the elbow. Reverse and stretch the opposite side.

Arm-Shoulder Girdle Exercises

Arm-shoulder girdle exercises for this age group include both arm-support and free-arm types.

Push-Ups

Starting position: Assume the push-up position (p. 281), with the body straight from head to heels.

Movement: Keeping the body straight, bend the elbows and touch the chest to the ground; then straighten the elbows, raising the body in a straight line.

Stress points: The movement should be in the arms. The head is up, with the eyes looking ahead. The chest should touch the floor lightly, without receiving the weight of the body. The body remains in a straight line throughout, without sagging or humping.

Modification: Many youngsters develop a dislike for push-ups because they are asked to perform them without any modification. Youngsters should be allowed to judge their strength and choose a push-up challenge (p. 281) they feel able to accomplish. Instead of asking an entire class to perform a specified number of push-ups, personalize the workload by allowing each youngster to accomplish as many repetitions as possible of a self-selected push-up challenge in a specified amount of time. This creates a positive experience and feeling about this important exercise.

Teaching suggestion: Controlled movement is a goal; speed is not desirable. Push-ups should be done at will, allowing each child to achieve individually within a specified time limit.

Reclining Pull-Ups

Starting position: One pupil lies in supine position. Partner is astride, with feet alongside the reclining partner's chest. Partners grasp hands with interlocking fingers, with some other suitable grip, or with an interlocked wrist grip.

Movement: The pupil on the floor pulls up with arms until the chest touches the partner's thighs.

Figure 13.13 Reclining Pull-Ups

The body remains straight, with weight resting on the heels (Figure 13.13). Return to position.

Stress points: The supporting student should keep the center of gravity well over the feet by maintaining a lifted chest and proper head position. The lower student should maintain a straight body during the pull-up and move only the arms.

Variation: Raise as directed (count 1), hold the high position isometrically (counts 2 and 3), return to position (count 4).

Triceps Push-Up

Starting position: Assume the inverted push-up position with the arms and body held straight.

Movement: Keeping the body straight, bend the elbows and touch the seat to the ground, then straighten the elbows and raise the body.

Stress points: The fingers should point toward the toes or be turned in slightly. The body should be held firm with movement restricted to the arms.

Arm Circles

Starting position: Stand erect, with feet apart and arms straight out to the side (Figure 13.14).

Movement: Do forward and backward circles with palms facing forward, moving arms simultaneously. The number of circles executed before changing can be varied.

Stress points: Avoid doing arm circles with palms down (particularly backward circles) as it stresses the shoulder joint. Correct posture should be maintained, with the abdominal wall flat and the head and shoulders held back.

Figure 13.14 Arm Circles

Crab Kick

Starting position: Crab position, with the body supported on the hands and feet and the back parallel to the floor. The knees are bent at right angles. On all crab positions, keep the seat up and avoid body sag.

Movement: Kick the right leg up and down (counts 1 and 2) (Figure 13.15). Repeat with the left leg (counts 3 and 4).

Crab Alternate-Leg Extension

Starting position: Assume crab position.

Movement: On count 1, extend the right leg forward so that it rests on the heel. On count 2, extend the left leg forward and bring the right leg back. Continue alternating.

Crab Full-Leg Extension

Starting position: Assume crab position.

Figure 13.15 Crab Kick

Movement: On count 1, extend both legs forward so that the weight rests on the heels. On count 2, bring both feet back to crab position.

Crab Walk

Starting position: Assume crab position.

Movement: Move forward, backward, sideward, and turn in a small circle right and left.

Flying Angel

Starting position: Stand erect, with feet together and arms at sides.

Movement: In a smooth, slow, continuous motion, raise the arms forward with elbows extended and then upward, at the same time rising up on the toes and lifting the chest, with eyes following the hands (Figure 13.16). Lower the arms sideward in a flying motion and return to starting position.

Stress points: The abdominal wall must be kept flat throughout to minimize lower back curvature. The head should be back and well up. The exercise should be done slowly and smoothly, under control.

Variation: Move the arms forward as if doing a breaststroke. The arms are then raised slowly, with hands in front of the chest and elbows out, to full overhead extension. Otherwise, the movement is the same as the Flying Angel.

Figure 13.16 Flying Angel

Abdominal Exercises

For most exercises stressing abdominal development, the child starts from supine position on the floor or on a mat. To involve the abdominal muscles from this position, primary-grade children should first be challenged to lift the head off the floor. This action will tighten the abdominal muscles. Increased challenge can gradually occur by lifting the legs, the upper body, or both at the same time. If the upper body is lifted, the movement should begin with a roll-up (curling) action, moving the head first so that the chin makes contact or near contact with the chest, thus flattening and stabilizing the lower back curve. The bent knee position isolates the abdominal muscles and avoids stressing the lower back region. *When doing abdominal exercises, avoid moving the trunk up to the sitting position (past 45 degrees) since it may cause pain and exacerbate back injury in susceptible individuals* (Macfarlane, 1993). The benefits of abdominal exercise are gained when the trunk is moved from the floor to approximately a 45-degree angle. Beyond 45 degrees, excessive stress may be placed on the back and there is little benefit to the abdominal muscle group.

Many youngsters develop a dislike for abdominal work in the early school years. This often occurs because they are top heavy (large head, small body) and unable to successfully lift their upper body off the floor. To assure success, allow students to choose an abdominal challenge (p. 283) they feel able to accomplish. Instead of asking an entire class to perform a specified number of curl-ups, personalize the workload by allowing youngsters to accomplish as many repetitions as possible in a specified amount of time using a self-selected abdominal challenge. This will help create positive feelings toward abdominal exercises.

Reverse Curl

Starting position: Lie on back with the hands on the floor to the sides of the body.

Movement: Curl the knees to the chest. The upper body remains on the floor. As abdominal strength increases, the child should lift the buttocks and lower back off the floor.

Stress points: Roll the knees to the chest and return the feet to the floor after each repetition. The movement should be controlled, with emphasis on the abdominal contraction.

Variations:

1. Hold the head off the floor and bring the knees to the chin.

2. Instead of returning the feet to the floor after each repetition, move them 1 or 2 inches off the floor. This activity requires greater abdominal strength as there is no resting period (feet on floor).

Pelvis Tilter

Starting position: Lie on the back with feet flat on the floor, knees bent, arms out in wing position, and palms up.

Movement: Flatten the lower back, bringing it closer to the floor by tensing the lower abdominals and lifting up on the pelvis. Hold for 8–12 counts. Tense slowly and release slowly.

Knee Touch Curl-Up

Starting position: Lie on the back, with feet flat and knees bent, and with hands flat on top of thighs.

Movement: Leading with the chin, slide the hands forward until the fingers touch the kneecaps and gradually curl the head and shoulders until the shoulder blades are lifted off the floor (Figure 13.17). Hold for eight counts and return to position. To avoid stress on the lower back, the performer should not curl up to the sitting position.

Curl-Up

Starting position: Lie on the back with feet flat, knees bent and arms on the floor at the side of the body with palms down.

Movement: Lift the head and shoulders (Figure 13.18) to a 45-degree angle and then back in a two-count pattern. The hands should slide forward on the floor 3 to 4 inches. The curl-up can also be done as an eight-count exercise, moving up on one count, holding for six counts, and moving down on the last count.

Figure 13.17 Knee Touch Curl-Up

Figure 13.18 Curl-Up

Stress points: Roll up, with the chin first. Do not lift the hands off the floor.

Curl-Up with Twist

Starting position: Lie on the back with feet flat and knees bent. Arms are folded and placed across the chest with hands on shoulders.

Movement: Do a partial curl-up and twist the chest to the left. Repeat, turning the chest to the right (Figure 13.19).

Variations:

1. Touch the outside of the knee with the elbow.
2. Touch both knees in succession. The sequence is up, touch left, touch right, and down.

Leg Extension

Starting position: Sit on the floor with legs extended and hands on hips.

Movement: With a quick, vigorous action, raise the knees and bring both heels as close to the seat as possible (Figure 13.20). The movement is a drag with the toes touching lightly. Return to position.

Variation: Alternate bringing the knees to the right and left of the head.

Abdominal Cruncher

Starting position: Lie in supine position with feet flat, knees bent, and palms of hands cupped over the ears (not behind the head). An alternate position is to fold the arms across the chest and place the hands on the shoulders.

Figure 13.19 Curl-Up with Twist

Figure 13.20 Leg Extension

Movement: Tuck the chin and curl upward until the shoulder blades leave the floor. Return to the floor with a slow uncurling.

Variation: Lift the feet off the floor and bring the knees to waist level. Try to touch the right elbow to the left knee and vice versa while in the crunch position.

Leg and Agility Exercises

Leg and agility exercises should feature rhythmic, graceful motion with emphasis on control.

Running in Place

Starting position: Stand with arms bent at the elbows.

Movement: Run in place. Begin slowly, counting only the left foot. Speed up somewhat, raising the knees to hip height. Then run at full speed, raising the knees hard. Finally, slow down. The run should be on the toes.

Variations:

1. Tortoise and Hare. Jog slowly in place. On the command "Hare," double the speed. On the command "Tortoise," slow the tempo to original slow jogging pace.

2. March in place, lifting the knees high and swinging the arms up. Turn right and left on command while marching. Turn completely around to the right and then to the left while marching.

3. Fast Stepping. Step in place for 10 seconds as rapidly as possible. Rest for 10 seconds and repeat five or more times.

Jumping Jack

Starting position: Stand at attention.

Movement: On count 1, jump to a straddle position with arms overhead. On count 2, recover to starting position.

Variations:

1. Begin with the feet in a stride position (forward and back). Change feet with the overhead movement.

2. Instead of bringing the feet together when the arms come down, cross the feet each time, alternating the cross.

3. On the completion of each set of eight counts, do a quarter-turn right. (After four sets, the child is facing in the original direction.) Do the same to the left.

4. Modified Jumping Jack. On count 1, jump to a straddle position with arms out to the sides, parallel to the floor, and palms down. On count 2, return to position.

Treadmill

Starting position: Assume push-up position, except that one leg is brought forward so that the knee is under the chest (Figure 13.21).

Movement: Reverse the position of the feet, bringing the extended leg forward. Change back again so that the original foot is forward. Continue rhythmically alternating feet.

Stress points: The head should be kept up. A full exchange of the legs should be made, with the forward knee coming well under the chest each time.

Figure 13.21 Treadmill

Power Jumper

Starting position: Begin in a semicrouched position, with knees flexed and arms extended backward.

Movement: Jump as high as possible and extend the arms upward and overhead.

Variations:

1. Jump and perform different turns (i.e., quarter, half, full).
2. Jump and perform different tasks (i.e., heel click, heel slap, clap hands, catch an imaginary pass, snare a rebound).

Trunk-Twisting and Bending Exercises

Many exercises involve twisting or bending; a few involve both. The twisting or bending should be done throughout the full range of movement. Movements should be large and vigorous.

Trunk Twister

Starting position: Stand with feet shoulder width apart and pointed forward. The hands are cupped and placed loosely over the shoulders, with the elbows out and the chin tucked.

Movement: Bend downward, keeping the knees relaxed. Recover slightly. Bend downward again and simultaneously rotate the trunk to the left and then to the right (Figure 13.22). Return to original position, pulling the head back, with chin in.

Bear Hug

Starting position: Stand with feet comfortably spread and hands on hips.

Movement: Take a long step diagonally right, keeping the left foot anchored in place. Tackle the right leg around the thigh by encircling the thigh with both arms. Squeeze and stretch (Figure 13.23). Return to position. Tackle the left leg. Return to position.

Stress point: The value in flexibility comes from slow, controlled stretching.

Side Flex

Starting position: Lie on one side with lower arm extended overhead. The head rests on the lower arm. The legs are extended fully, one on top of the other.

Movement: Raise the upper arm and leg diagonally (Figure 13.24). Repeat for several counts and change to the other side.

Figure 13.22   Trunk Twister

Figure 13.23   Bear Hug

Variation: Side Flex, Supported. Similar to the regular Side Flex but more demanding. A side-leaning rest position is maintained throughout (Figure 13.25).

Body Circles

Starting position: Stand with feet shoulder width apart, hands on hips, and body bent forward.

Figure 13.24 Side Flex

Figure 13.25 Side Flex, supported

Movement: Make a complete circle with the upper body. A specified number of circles should be made to the right and the same number to the left.

Variations:

1. Circle in one direction until told to stop, then reverse direction.
2. Change to a position in which the hands are on the shoulders and the elbows are kept wide. Otherwise, the exercise is the same. (This is more demanding than the regular Body Circles.)

Windmill

Starting position: Stand with feet shoulder width apart and arms extended sideward with palms down.

Movement: Bend and twist at the trunk, bringing the right hand down to the left toes. Recover to

starting position. Bend and twist again, but bring the left hand to the right toes. Recover to starting position.

Stress point: The arms and legs should be kept straight throughout.

Partner Resistance Exercises

Partner resistance exercises are useful for building strength, but produce little increase in cardiorespiratory endurance. Consequently, they should be used in conjunction with activities that demand considerable endurance, such as Aerobic Fitness Routines, jogging, or Astronaut Drills. Partner resistance exercises can strengthen specific muscle groups and are useful for helping the physically underdeveloped child. The exercises are simple and enjoyable; children can do them as homework with their parents or friends. Children should be made aware of the muscle group developed by each exercise.

Partners should be somewhat matched in size and strength so that they can challenge each other. The exercises are performed throughout the full range of motion at each joint and should take 8 to 12 seconds to complete. The partner providing the resistance counts the duration of the exercise; positions are then reversed. In addition to the partner resistance exercises presented here, similar resistance exercises can be performed with partner tug-of-war ropes, as described in Chapter 17.

Arm Curl-Up

The exerciser keeps the upper arms against the sides with the forearms and palms forward. The partner's fists are put in the exerciser's palms (Figure 13.26). The exerciser attempts to curl the forearms upward to the shoulders. To develop the opposite set of muscles, partners reverse hand positions. Push down in the opposite direction, starting at shoulder level.

Forearm Flex

The exerciser extends the arms and places the hands, palms down, on the partner's shoulders. The exerciser attempts to push the partner into the floor. The partner may slowly stoop lower to allow the exerciser movement through the range of motion. Try with the palms upward.

Fist Pull-Apart

The exerciser places the fists together in front of the body at shoulder level. The exerciser attempts

Figure 13.26 Arm Curl-Up

to pull the hands apart while the partner forces them together with pressure on the elbows. As a variation, with fists apart, the exerciser tries to push them together. The partner applies pressure by grasping the wrists and holding the exerciser's fists apart.

Butterfly

The exerciser starts with arms straight and at the sides. The partner, from the back, attempts to hold the arms down while the exerciser lifts with straight arms to the sides. Try with arms above the head (partner holding) to move them down to the sides.

Camelback

The exerciser is on all fours with head up. The partner sits lightly or pushes on the exerciser's back, while the exerciser attempts to hump the back like a camel.

Back Builder

The exerciser spreads the legs and bends forward at the waist with head up. The partner faces the

exerciser and places clasped hands behind the exerciser's neck. The exerciser attempts to stand upright while the partner pulls downward (Figure 13.27).

Scissors

The exerciser lies on one side, while the partner straddles the exerciser and holds the upper leg down. The exerciser attempts to raise the top leg. Reverse sides and lift the other leg.

Bear Trap

Starting from a supine position on the floor, spread the legs and then attempt to move them together. Resistance is provided by the partner, who tries to keep the legs apart.

Knee Bender

The exerciser lies in prone position with legs straight and arms pointing ahead on the floor. The partner places the hands on the back of the exerciser's ankles. The exerciser attempts to flex the

Figure 13.27 Back Builder

knees while the partner applies pressure (Figure 13.28). Try in the opposite direction, starting with the knee joint at a 90-degree angle.

Push-Up with Resistance

The exerciser is in push-up position with arms bent, so that the body is about halfway up from the floor. The partner straddles or stands alongside the exerciser's head and puts pressure on the top of the shoulders by pushing down (Figure 13.29). The amount of pressure takes judgment by the partner. Too much causes the exerciser to collapse.

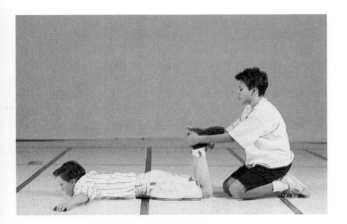

Figure 13.28   Knee Bender

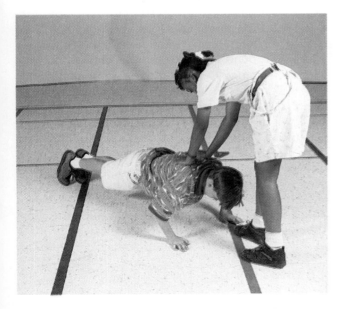

Figure 13.29   Push-up with resistance

DEVELOPING PHYSICAL FITNESS ROUTINES

When planning fitness routines, the instructor should establish variety in activities and include different approaches. This tends to minimize the inherent weaknesses of any single routine. The routines should exercise all major parts of the body. Additionally, when sequencing fitness activities into a routine, try not to overload the same body part with two sequential exercises. For example, if push-ups are being performed, the next exercise should not be crab walking, as it also stresses the arm-shoulder girdle.

Exercise dosage for youngsters should be administered in *time* rather than repetitions. It is unreasonable to expect all youngsters to perform the same number of exercise repetitions. Fitness performance is controlled by a number of factors, including genetics and trainability, making it impossible for all children to do the same workload. When time is used to determine the workload, each child can personalize the amount of activity performed within the time constraints. It is reasonable to expect a gifted youngster to be able to perform more repetitions in a certain amount of time than a less genetically endowed child. An obese youngster may not be able to perform as many push-ups as a leaner peer. Develop positive attitudes toward activity by asking youngsters to do the best they can within the time allotted.

Student Leader Exercises

At times, selected students should lead either single exercises or an entire routine. Careful instruction is needed, and students need prior practice if they are to lead their peers effectively in a stimulating exercise session. Teachers should ask for volunteers and allow students to practice ahead of time. Children should not be forced to lead, because this can result in failure for both the child and the class.

A formation that requires four student leaders can be arranged in the following manner. A student leader stands on each of the four sides of the formation (Figure 13.30). The sequence of leaders is generally clockwise, but it could be otherwise. The first leader, after finishing an exercise, says, "Right face!" The class is now facing the second leader, who repeats the process. Two more exercises and direction changes bring the children back to the original leader. This formation can be adjusted to employ two leaders positioned on

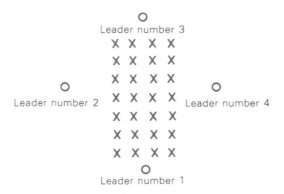

Figure 13.30 Four-leader formation

opposite sides of the formation. The command after the exercise led by the first leader would be "About face!"

Sample Routine

Exercise	Time
Arm Circles	30 seconds
Bend and Twist	30 seconds
Treadmill	25 seconds
Curl-Up	45 seconds
Single-Leg Crab Kick	30 seconds
Knee to Chest Curl	45 seconds
Run in Place	30 seconds
Trunk Twister	45 seconds

Conclude the routine with 2 to 4 minutes of jogging, rope jumping, or other continuous activity.

Squad Leader Exercises

Squad leader exercises provide students with an opportunity to lead exercises in a small group. This approach is an effective method for teaching students how to lead others and to help them learn how a well-balanced fitness routine takes place. A student within each squad is given a task card specifying a sequence of exercises (see following sample routine). After the first student has led the exercise for the desired amount of time, the card is passed to another member of the squad, who becomes the leader. Exercises can be placed in groups on the task card (arm-shoulder girdle, abdominal strength, leg strength, etc.). Each new leader then selects an exercise from a different group of exercises. This will help assure that a balanced fitness routine results.

Sample Routine

Exercises	Time
Push-Up	30 seconds
Sitting Stretch	45 seconds
Jumping Jacks	30 seconds
Leg Extension	45 seconds
Curl-Up	40 seconds
Bear Hug	40 seconds
Stride Jump	45 seconds
Treadmill	45 seconds

Conclude the routine with 2 to 4 minutes of jogging, rope jumping, or other continuous activity.

Exercises to Music

Exercises to music add another dimension to developmental experiences. Many commercial record sets with exercise programs are available, but a most effective approach is to rely on the tape recorder. Most media departments in schools have equipment that will allow music to be mixed with vocal instructions onto audiotape cassettes. (Ask the school media department if the school has a mixer.) This approach gives teachers control over the selection, sequence, and amount of time, and allows the routine to be adapted to the particular needs and characteristics of the group. Starting and stopping exercises can easily be incorporated into the taped sequences.

Taped music is an excellent way to time the length of exercise bouts. For example, if doing Random Moving, students could run/walk as long as the music is playing and stretch when it pauses. If the music is pretaped, it will free teachers from having to keep an eye on a stopwatch. Other exercise modules that work well with music are Circuit Training, Aerobic Fitness Routines, Continuity Exercises, Astronaut Drills, Squad Leader Exercises, and Rope Jumping Exercises.

A way to identify music that will motivate students is to ask them to bring a compact disk or record they own. The music will have to be reviewed to see if it is offensive to any parents or other students. After screening, the music can be recorded. The exercises should then be practiced to the recorded music. When a teacher feels comfortable with narrating the tape, speaking can be mixed with the music.

Circuit Training

Circuit Training incorporates several stations, each with a designated fitness task. The student moves from station to station, generally in a prescribed order, completing the designated fitness task at each station. The exercise tasks constituting the circuit should contribute to the development of all parts of the body. In addition, activities should contribute to the various components of physical fitness (strength, power, endurance, agility, and flexibility).

Instructional Procedures

1. Each station provides an exercise task that the child can learn and perform without the aid of another child. As the child moves from one station to the next, the exercises that directly follow each other should make demands on different parts of the body. In this way, the performance at any one station does not cause local fatigue that could affect the ability to perform the next task.

2. Before the children begin the course, giving them sufficient instruction in the activities is important so that they can perform correctly at each station.

3. The class should be so distributed that some children are starting the circuit at each station. This method keeps the demands on equipment low and the activity high. For example, if there are 30 children for a circuit of six stations, then 5 children start at each spot.

4. A tape recorder can be used effectively to give directions for the circuit. Music, whistle signals, and even verbal directions can be prerecorded. The tape provides a rigid time control and gives a measure of consistency to the circuit. Using tapes also frees a teacher for supervisory duties.

5. The number of stations can vary but probably should be no fewer than six and no more than nine. (Figures 13.31 and 13.32 show a six- and a nine-station course, respectively.) Signs at the different stations can include the name of the activity and any necessary cautions or stress points for execution. When children move between lines as limits (as in the Agility Run), traffic cones or beanbags can be used to mark the designated boundaries.

Timing and Dosage

In general, a fixed time limit at each station seems to be the best plan for Circuit Training at the elementary school level. Children each attempt to do their personal best during the time allotted at a station. Progression can be assured by increasing the amount of time at each station. A suggested progressive timetable is as follows.

Figure 13.31 Sample six-station circuit training course

Six-station course

1 Running in place	2 Curl-ups	3 Arm Circles
6 Crab Walk	5 Trunk Twister	4 Agility Run

Supplies and equipment: Mats for Curl-ups (to hook toes)
Time needed: 4 minutes—based on 30-second activity limit, 10 seconds to move between stations

Nine-station course

1 Rope jumping	2 Push-ups	3 Agility Run	4 Arm Circles
8 Windmill	7 Treadmill	6 Crab Walk	5 Reverse Curl

9 Hula-Hooping (for any relaxing "fun" activity)

Supplies and equipment: Jumping ropes, mats for knee Push-ups (if used), hoops (if used)
Time needed: 6 minutes—based on 30-second activity limit, 10 seconds to move between stations

Figure 13.32 Sample nine-station circuit training course

Time Period	Seconds at Each Station
Introduction (first day)	20
First two weeks	25
Second two weeks	30
After four weeks	35

A 10-second interval should be established to allow children to move from one station to the next. Later, this can be lowered to 5 seconds. Students may start at any station, as designated, but they must follow the established station order.

A second method of timing is to sound only one signal for the change to the next station. With this plan, the child ceases activity at one station, moves to the next, and immediately begins the task at that station without waiting for another signal.

The activity demands of the circuit can be increased by changing the exercises to more strenuous ones. For example, a station could specify knee or bench push-ups and later change to regular push-ups, a more demanding exercise. Another method of increasing intensity is to have each child run a lap around the circuit area between station changes. Cardiovascular endurance can be enhanced by dividing the class into halves. One half exercises on the circuit while the other is running lightly around the area. On signal to change, the runners go to the circuit and the others run.

Another method of organizing a circuit is to list several activities at each station. The circuit can be performed more than once, allowing students to do a different exercise each time they arrive at a station. If the circuit is to be done only once, children can perform their favorite exercise. Exercises at each station should emphasize development of the same body part.

Suggested Activities

A circuit should always include activities for exercising the arm-shoulder girdle and for strengthening the abdominal wall. A variety of activities are suggested and classified in the following section. One activity can be selected from each classification.

General Body Activities

Rope Jumping: Use single-time speed only.

Jumping Jacks (p. 295).

Running in Place: Lift the knees.

Arm-Shoulder Girdle Exercises

Crab Walk (p. 292): Two parallel lines are drawn 6 to 8 feet apart. Start with hands on one line and feet pointing toward the other. Move back and forth between the lines in crab position, touching one line with the heels and the other with the hands.

Crab Kick (p. 292): Start in crab position and alternate with the right and the left foot kicking toward the ceiling.

Leg Exercises

Step-Ups: One bench is needed for every three children at this station. Begin in front of the bench, stepping up on the bench with the left foot and then up with the right foot. Now step down in rhythm, left and then right. The next class period, begin with the right foot to secure comparable development. Be sure that the legs are fully extended and that the body is erect when on top of the bench.

Treadmill (p. 295).

Straddle Bench Jumps: Straddle a bench and alternate jumping to the top of the bench and back to the floor. Since the degree of effort depends on the height of the bench, benches of various heights should be considered. These can be constructed in the form of small, elongated boxes 4 feet long and 10 inches wide, with height ranging from 8 to 10 inches. A 4-foot-long box accommodates two children at a time.

Agility Run—Touch with the Toes: Two lines are established 15 feet apart. Move between the two lines as rapidly as possible, touching one line with the right foot and the other with the left.

Agility Run—Touch with the Hand: Same as above, except touch the lines with alternate hands instead of with the feet.

Arms and Shoulders

Standing Arm Circles (p. 291).

Lying Arm Circles: Lie prone, with arms out to the sides. Alternate forward and backward arm circling, changing after five circles in each direction. The head and shoulders are lifted from the ground during the exercise.

Reverse Curls (p. 293).

Alternate Toe Touching: Begin on the back with arms extended overhead. Alternate by touching the right toes with the left hand and vice versa. Bring the foot and the arm up at the same time and return to the flat position each time.

Flexibility and Back Exercises

Bend and Twist (p. 289).

Windmill (p. 297).

Trunk Twister (p. 296).

Potpourri

Other exercises, stunts, and movements can be used, some in combination. In leg exercises, for example, the task can be designated as 25 running steps in place and then 5 Pogo Stick jumps (p. 504) in place, with the whole task repeated. If the gymnasium is equipped with chinning bars, horizontal ladders, and climbing ropes, circuits can make use of these. Some activities—basketball dribbling, traveling over and under obstacles, tumbling stunts, and manipulative activities—can be included as station tasks to liven things up. Hula-hoop activities are attractive, and gym scooters add a different dimension to many routine movements.

Outdoor Circuits

An outdoor circuit around a 220-yard track or around a comparable area can combine running and station tasks. When a time change is signaled, each participant runs one lap around the area counterclockwise past the station just performed and on to the next station. This is repeated until each station has been completed. Stations should be located inside the track so that there is no interference with the runners. This type of circuit can be used with a jogging trail also, and is sometimes called a *parcourse*. At specified points, different tasks can be performed along the course.

Continuity Drills

Continuity Drills originated in Europe. Continuity exercises, done snappily and with vigor, are enjoyable experiences for youngsters. Children are scattered, each with a jump rope. They alternate between rope jumping and exercises. A specified time period governs the length of the rope-jumping episode, which should be done in fast time (single jumps). At the signal to stop rope jumping, children drop the ropes and immediately take position for the exercise selected. Many of the exercises can use a two-count rhythm. When children are positioned for the exercise, the leader says, "Ready!" The class completes one repetition of the exercise and responds "One, two!" This repeats for each repetition. To increase the enjoyment, the leader can say "P.E.!" and the class will perform the exercise and respond with "is fun!" A number of brief phrases can be used such as "Work hard; keep fit." To enable a successful experience for children, modify the push-up and abdominal challenges (pp. 281–283).

Sample Routine

Exercise	Time
Basic Jumping (Forward Turning)	25 seconds
Single Leg Crab Kick	30 seconds
Basic Jumping (Backward Turning)	25 seconds
Knee Touch Curl-Up	30 seconds
Jump and Slowly Turn Body	25 seconds
Bend and Twist	30 seconds
Hop on One Foot (Forward Turning)	12 seconds
Change Foot (Forward Turning)	12 seconds
Arm Circles	30 seconds
Rocker Step	25 seconds
Side Flex	30 seconds
Free Jumping	25 seconds
Push-Up Challenges	30 seconds
Free Jumping	25 seconds
Sitting Stretch	30 seconds

Hexagon Hustle

A large hexagon is formed using six cones. Students perform the "hustle" by moving around the hexagon, changing their movement patterns every time they reach one of the six points in the hexagon. On signal, the "hustle" stops and selected exercises are performed.

Instructional Procedures

1. To create a safer environment, children should move in the same direction around the hexagon.

2. Laminated posters, with colorful illustrations, should be placed by the cones to inform children of the new movement to be performed.

3. Faster children should be encouraged to pass on the outside of slower children.

4. The direction of the "hustle" should be changed after every exercise segment.

Sample Routine

Exercise	Time
Hustle	30 seconds
Push-Up from Knees	30 seconds
Hustle	30 seconds
Bend and Twist (8 counts)	30 seconds
Hustle	30 seconds

Jumping Jacks (4 counts)	30 seconds
Hustle	30 seconds
Curl-Ups (2 counts)	30 seconds
Hustle	30 seconds
Double-Leg Crab Kick (2 counts)	30 seconds
Hustle	30 seconds
Sitting Stretch (8 counts)	30 seconds
Hustle	30 seconds
Power Jumper	30 seconds
Hustle	30 seconds
Squat Thrust (4 counts)	30 seconds

Conclude the Hexagon Hustle with stretching exercises.

Astronaut Drills

Astronaut Drills are performed in circular or scatter formation. Routines are developed by moving using various locomotor movements, alternated with stopping and performing exercises in place. The following movements and tasks can be incorporated in the routine.

1. Various locomotor movements, such as hopping, jumping, running, sliding, skipping, giant steps, and walking high on the toes.

2. Movement on all fours—forward, backward, or sideward—with respect to the direction of walking. Repeat backward and forward using the Crab Walk.

3. Stunt movements, such as the Seal Walk, Gorilla Walk, and Rabbit Jump.

4. Upper torso movements and exercises that can be done while walking, such as Arm Circles, bending right and left, and body twists.

5. Various exercises are performed when stopped. A balance of arm-shoulder girdle and abdominal exercises should be included.

Astronaut Drills can be adapted successfully to any level. The type of movements selected will determine the strenuousness of the routine. Children who lag can move toward the inner part of the circle, while more active children pass on the outside. Enjoyment comes from being challenged by a variety of movements.

Sample Routine

Exercises or Movements	Time
Jog	15–20 seconds
Double-Leg Crab Kick	30 seconds

Skip	20 seconds
Sitting Stretch	30 seconds
Slide	20 seconds
Jumping Jacks (Variations)	30 seconds
Crab Walk (feet forward)	20 seconds
Curl-Up	30 seconds
Hop to the middle of the circle on the right foot	20 seconds
Hop to the original position on the left foot	
Push-Up	30 seconds
Gallop	20 seconds
Bear Hug	30 seconds
Walk; reach arms to sides and perform arm circles	20 seconds
Pogo Stick	30 seconds
Trot	20 seconds
Squat Thrust	30 seconds

Cool down with 2 to 3 minutes of stretching.

Challenge Courses

Challenge Courses are becoming increasingly popular as a tool for fitness development in the elementary schools. Students should move through the course with proper form rather than run against a time standard. The course should be designed to exercise all parts of the body through a variety of activities. By including running, vaulting, agility tasks, climbing, hanging, crawling, and other activities, teachers can ensure good fitness demands. Equipment such as mats, parallel bars, horizontal ladders, high-jump standards, benches, and vaulting boxes can be used to make effective Challenge Courses. A variety of courses can be designed, depending on the length of the course and the tasks included. Some schools have established permanent courses. A sample indoor course, including a climbing rope, is illustrated in Figure 13.33. The total equipment list for this course is as follows:

Three benches (16 to 18 in. high)

Four tumbling mats (4 by 8 ft.)

Four hoops

One pair of high-jump standards with magic rope

One climbing rope

One jumping box

Five chairs or cones

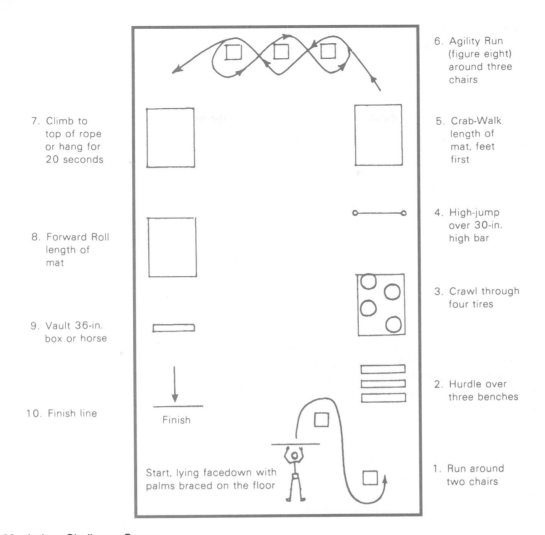

6. Agility Run (figure eight) around three chairs

5. Crab-Walk length of mat, feet first

4. High-jump over 30-in. high bar

3. Crawl through four tires

2. Hurdle over three benches

1. Run around two chairs

7. Climb to top of rope or hang for 20 seconds

8. Forward Roll length of mat

9. Vault 36-in. box or horse

10. Finish line

Finish

Start, lying facedown with palms braced on the floor

Figure 13.33 Indoor Challenge Course

Aerobic Fitness Routines

Aerobics is a popular fitness activity for people of all ages that develops cardiorespiratory fitness as well as strength and flexibility. Music increases effort, duration, and intensity, while reducing the boredom associated with some fitness tasks. Aerobic fitness routines are a mixture of Rhythmic Running, various fundamental movements, dance steps, swinging movements, and stretching challenges.

Aerobic fitness routines generally follow one of two patterns. The first is the leader type, in which students follow the actions of a leader. The second involves choreography based on a piece of music. In the leader type, when the music begins, the leader performs a series of movements and the other students follow. This is the best choice for elementary school students. Teachers may lead, although skilled students can also do an excellent

job. There are few limits to the range of activities a leader can present. The leader may integrate manipulative equipment (e.g., balls, jump ropes, hoops, wands) with the movement activities.

The second method is a formal routine. For elementary school children, routines should be kept uncomplicated. When the music has run through a repetition or phrase, the movement patterns can change. Children can design routines to the music of their choice. For most routines, music should have a tempo of 120 to 140 beats per minute.

Instructional Procedures

1. Use movement increments that are organized by units of 4, 8, or 16 counts. When phrases in the music are repeated, it is often desirable to repeat the previous step.

2. Vary the movements so that stretching and flowing movements are alternated with the more strenuous aerobic activities.

3. Steps should be relatively simple. Students should focus on increasing their fitness levels rather than becoming competent rhythmic performers. Stress continuous movement (moving with the flow) rather than perfection of routines. Running and bouncing steps that children can follow easily are effective and motivating.

4. Routines motivate more children when they are not rigid. Youngsters shouldn't have to worry about being out of step. Both boys and girls should feel comfortable with the activity.

5. Establish cue words to aid youngsters in following routines. Examples are "Bounce," "Step," "Reach," and "Jump."

Basic Steps

The following are examples of basic steps and movements that can be used to develop a variety of routines. The majority are performed to 4 counts, although this can be varied, depending on the skill of the participants and the goals of the teacher.

Running and Walking Steps

1. Do directional runs—forward, backward, diagonal, sideways, and turning.

2. Do rhythmic runs, with a specific movement on the fourth beat. Examples are knee lift, clap, jump, jump-turn, and hop.

3. Run with flair. Run while lifting the knees, kicking up the heels, or slapping the thighs or heels; or run with legs extended as in the goose step.

4. Run with arms in various positions—on the hips, in the air above the head, and straight down.

Movements on the Floor

1. *Side Leg Raises.* Do these with a straight leg while lying on the side of the body.

2. *Alternate Leg Raises.* While on the back, raise one leg to meet the opposite hand. Repeat, using the opposite leg or both legs.

3. *Rhythmic Push-Ups.* Do these in 2- or 4-count movements. A 4 count would be as follows: halfway down (count 1), nose touched to the floor (count 2), halfway up (count 3), and arms fully extended (count 4).

4. *Crab Kicks and Treadmills.* Do these to 4 counts.

Upright Rhythmic Movements

1. *Lunge variations.* Perform a lunge, stepping forward on the right foot while bending at the knee, and extending the arms forward and diagonally upward (counts 1 and 2). Return to starting position by bringing the right foot back and pulling the arms into a jogging position (counts 3 and 4). The lunge can be varied by changing the direction of the move and the depth and speed of the lunge.

2. *Side Bends.* Begin with the feet apart. Reach overhead while bending to the side. This movement is usually done to four beats: bend (count 1), hold (counts 2 and 3), and return (count 4).

3. *Reaches.* Reach upward alternately with the right and left arms. Reaches can be done sideways also and are usually 2-count movements. Fast alternating 1-count movements can be done, too.

4. *Arm and Shoulder Circles.* Make Arm Circles with either one or both arms. Vary the size and speed of the circles. Shoulder shrugs can be done in a similar fashion.

Jumping Jack Variations

1. Jump with arms alternately extended upward and then pulled in toward the chest.

2. Do Side Jumping Jacks with regular arm action while the feet jump from side to side or forward and backward together.

3. Do variations with the feet—forward stride alternating, forward and side stride alternating, kicks or knee lifts added, feet crossed, or heel-toe movements (turning on every fourth or eighth count).

Bounce Steps

1. *Bounce and clap.* This is similar to a slow-time jump-rope step. Clap on every other bounce.

2. *Bounce, turn, and clap.* Turn a quarter or half turn with each jump.

3. *Three bounces and clap.* Bounce three times and bounce and clap on the fourth beat. Turns can be performed.

4. *Bounce and rock side to side.* Transfer the weight from side to side, or forward and backward. Add clapping or arm swinging.

5. *Bounce with body twist.* Hold the arms at shoulder level and twist the lower body back and forth on each bounce.

6. *Bounce with floor patterns.* Bounce and make different floor patterns such as a box, diagonal, or triangle.

7. *Bounce with kick variations.* Perform different kicks such as knee lift and kick; double kicks; knee lift and slap knees; and kick and clap under knees. Combine the kicks with 2- or 4-count turns.

Activities with Manipulative Equipment

1. Use a jump rope. Perform basic steps such as forward and backward, and slow and fast time. Jump on one foot, cross the arms, and while jogging, swing the rope from side to side with the handles in one hand.

2. Use beanbags. Toss and catch while performing various locomotor movements. Use different tosses for a challenge.

3. Use a hula-hoop. Rhythmically swing the hoop around different body parts. Perform different locomotor movements around and over hoops.

4. Try movements with balls. Bounce, toss, and dribble, and add locomotor movements while performing tasks.

Sample Routine

1. March in place, circling the arms in large circles (16 counts).

2. Take side-lunge position, hold, and circle the right arm (8 counts). Reverse, circling with the left arm (8 counts).

3. Bounce forward twice, slapping the thighs. Bounce backward twice, thrusting the arms in the air. Repeat four times (16 counts).

4. Bounce and do a clap turn. Turn a quarter turn on every second bounce. Repeat four times clockwise (8 counts) and four times counter-clockwise (8 counts).

5. Repeat numbers 3 and 4.

6. Do a grapevine step to the right with a clap and hop on the fourth beat. Repeat to the left. Repeat the sequence four times (32 counts).

7. Do a Jumping Jack variation, extending the arms up and out. Repeat four times (32 counts).

8. Bounce and twist (16 counts), with arms in thrust position.

9. Do eight Side Jumping Jacks in a 2-count movement (16 counts).

10. Bounce, bounce, bounce, and clap in a 4-count movement. Repeat four times (16 counts). Turn right and left on each bounce (i.e., right, front, left, front).

11. Do Goose Step Running forward, with a clap on the fourth beat (16 counts). Move backward in the same way. Repeat.

12. Repeat bounce and twist routine (16 counts). Arms are in thrust position.

13. Do Rhythmic Running with a clap on every fourth beat (16 counts).

Aerobic Fitness and Partner Resistance Exercises

Partner resistance exercises combined with Aerobic Fitness Routines make an excellent routine. Partner resistance exercises develop strength but offer little aerobic benefit. Combining them with Aerobic Fitness Routines offers a well-balanced routine. The exercises listed below refer to partner resistance exercises (pp. 297–299). Enough time is allotted so each partner has the opportunity to resist and exercise.

Doing a partner resistance exercise

Sample Routine

Exercise	Time
Aerobic Fitness Routine	20–30 seconds
Arm Curl-Up	45 seconds
Aerobic Fitness Routine	20–30 seconds
Camelback	45 seconds
Aerobic Fitness Routine	20–30 seconds
Fist Pull-Apart	45 seconds
Aerobic Fitness Routine	20–30 seconds
Scissors	45 seconds
Aerobic Fitness Routine	20–30 seconds
Butterfly	45 seconds
Aerobic Fitness Routine	20–30 seconds
Resistance Push-Up	45 seconds
Aerobic Fitness Routine	20–30 seconds
Knee Bender	45 seconds

Sport-Related Fitness Activities

Many sport drills can be modified to place fitness demands on students. An advantage of sport-related fitness activities is that many children are highly motivated by sport activities. This may motivate them to put forth a better fitness effort since they enjoy the activity. Thoughtful preplanning and creative thinking can result in drills that teach sport skills as well as provide fitness benefits. The following are some examples of fitness adaptations of sports skills.

Baseball/Softball

1. *Base running.* Set up several diamonds on a grass field. Space the class evenly around throughout the base paths. On signal, they run to the next base, round the base, take a lead, then run to the next base. Faster runners may pass on the outside.

2. *Most lead-up games.* Children waiting on deck to bat and those in the field perform selected activities (skill or fitness related) while waiting for the batter to hit.

3. *Position responsibility.* Start children at various positions on the field. On command, children are free to move quickly to any other position. Upon reaching that position, the child is to display the movement most frequently practiced at that position (e.g., shortstop fields ball and throws to first base). Continue until all players have moved to each position.

Basketball

1. *Dribbling.* Each child has a basketball or playground ball. Assign one or more people to be "it." On command, everyone begins dribbling the ball and avoids being tagged by those who are "it." If tagged, that child becomes the new "it." A variation would be to begin the game by "its" not having a ball. Their objective would be to steal a ball from classmates.

2. *Dribbling, passing, rebounding, shooting, and defense.* Using the concept of a circuit, assign selected basketball skills to be performed at each station. Be sure that there is ample equipment at each station to keep all youngsters active. Movement from one station to another should be vigorous and may include a stop for exercise.

3. *Game play.* Divide the class into four teams. Two teams take the court and play a game of basketball. The other teams assume a position along respective sidelines, and practice a series of exercises. The playing and exercising teams change positions at the conclusion of the exercise sequence.

Football

1. *Ball carrying.* Divide the class into four to six squads. The first person in line carries the ball while zigzagging through preplaced boundary cones. The remainder of the squad performs a specific exercise. Upon completing the zigzag course, the first person hands off to the next person in line. This hand-off signifies a change in exercise for the remainder of the squad.

2. *Punting.* With partners, one child punts the ball to the other. After the receiver has the ball, the object is to see which child can get to the partner's starting position first. Repeat, with the receiver becoming the punter.

3. *Forward passing.* Divide the children into groups of no more than four. Children practice running pass patterns. Rotate the passing responsibility after every six throws.

Volleyball

1. *Rotating.* Place youngsters in the various court positions. Teach them the rotational sequence. As they reach a new court position, have them complete several repetitions of a specific exercise. On command, rotate to the next position. Select activities that exercise components of fitness to enhance volleyball skill development.

2. *Serving.* Divide the class evenly among available volleyball courts. Starting with an equal number of children and a number of balls on each side of the net, begin practicing the serve. At the conclusion of each successful serve, the children run around the net standard to the other side of the net and retrieve a ball and serve.

3. *Bumping and setting.* Using the concept of the circuit, establish several stations to practice the bump and set. Movement from station to station should be vigorous and may contain a special stop for exercise.

Soccer

1. *Dribbling.* Working with a partner, have one child dribble the ball around the playground with the partner following close behind. On signal, reverse roles.

2. *Passing and trapping.* Working with partners or small groups, devise routines that cause the players to move continuously (e.g., jogging, running in place, performing selected exercises while waiting to trap and pass the soccer ball).

3. *Game play.* Divide the class into teams of three or four players per team. Organize the playground area to accommodate as many soccer fields as necessary to allow all teams to play. Make the fields as large as possible.

Sample Routine

By combining sport skills with the principles of FIT, a variety of fitness routines can be developed. The following routine is an example of sport skills incorporated into an eight-station outdoor circuit.

Station 1, soccer dribble. Using only the feet, dribble the soccer ball to a predetermined point and back as many times as possible in the time provided.

Station 2, basketball chest pass. With a partner, practice the chest pass. To place additional demands on the arm muscles, increase the distance of the pass.

Station 3, football lateral. Moving up and down the field, children practice lateralling the ball to one another.

Station 4, softball batting. Each child has a bat and practices proper swing technique. Be sure to allow ample space between hitters.

Station 5, continuous running long jump. Children take turns practicing the running long jump. After one child completes a jump successfully, the next one begins running down the runway. The activity should be continuous, with station members always moving.

Station 6, soccer inbounds pass. With partners, practice the overhead inbounds pass. Keep the ball overhead and propel the ball forward with a flick of the wrist and proper arm motion.

Station 7, field hockey passing. With partners, pass the field hockey ball back and forth between partners while moving up and down the field.

Station 8, fielding a softball. With partners, practice fielding a thrown ground ball. Make the activity more challenging by throwing the ball so that the partner has to move to field the ball.

Walking and Jogging

Jogging and walking, fitness activity for all ages, can lead to regular activity habits and to a lifelong exercise program. *Jogging* is defined as easy, relaxed running at a pace that can be maintained for long distances without undue fatigue or strain. It is the first level of locomotion above walking. Jogging and walking are unique in that they require no special equipment, can be done almost anywhere, are individual activities, consume relatively little time, and are not geared to a particular time of day. For most people, this type of regular activity is an exercise in personal discipline that can enhance the self-image and raise the confidence level.

Instructional Procedures

1. Youngsters should be allowed to find a friend with whom they want to jog or walk. This will usually be a friend of similar ability level. A way to judge correct pace is to be able to talk with a friend without undue stress. If students are too winded to talk, they are probably running too fast. The selected friend will want to talk and help assure that the experience is positive and within the student's aerobic capacity.

2. Jogging and walking should be done in any direction so children are unable to keep track of the distance covered. Doing laps on a track is one of the surest ways to discourage less able youngsters. They always finish last and are open to chiding by the rest of the class.

3. Jogging and walking should be done for a specified time rather than a specified distance.

Why should all youngsters have to run the same distance? This goes against the philosophy of accompanying individual differences and varying aerobic capacities. Running or walking for a set amount of time will allow the less able child to move without fear of ridicule.

4. Teachers should not be concerned about foot action, since the child selects naturally the means that is most comfortable. Arm movement should be easy and natural, with elbows bent. The head and upper body should be held up and back. The eyes look ahead. The general body position in walking and jogging should be erect but relaxed. Jogging on the toes should be avoided.

5. Jogging and walking should not be a competitive, timed activity. Each youngster should move at a self-determined pace. Racing belongs in the track program. Another reason to avoid speed is that racing keeps youngsters from learning to pace themselves. For developing endurance and gaining health benefits, it is more important to move for a longer time at a slower speed than to run at top speed for a shorter distance.

Continuous Movement Program

The continuous movement program (CMP) can be used to augment physical education classes and help children develop an effective conditioning program. This program is an effective method that classroom teachers can use for developing cardiovascular fitness in a minimal amount of time (Erickson, 1980; Wilcox, 1980). To administer the program, classroom teachers take their classes outside to move in any direction at a self-selected speed. Some youngsters may choose to jog, while others will want to maintain a brisk walking pace. The responsibility of the teacher is to clock the specified time period and encourage youngsters to keep moving.

Continuous movement is a safe physical education activity. The chance of injury or physiological damage occurring is minimal, because youngsters are allowed to monitor and control their workload. Nevertheless, two cautions should be observed. First, children with certain types of handicaps, such as cardiac abnormalities, asthma, and diabetes, should exercise within stipulated medical limitations. Second, progression should be slow (gradually increase the amount of time) and place emphasis on moving rather than how much or how fast students are performing.

Motivational Techniques

The following are some suggestions that help increase a youngster's level of motivation to walk and jog. All of them are designed to improve physical conditioning and increase the amount of knowledge allied to the experience.

1. Set up a number of exercise trails on the playground. Trails should be different lengths so students can increase their workload as their fitness levels improve. Students can keep track of their "mileage" by recording it on a class chart.

2. Walk and jog across the United States by posting a map of the country in the classroom. Each day, the mileage of all the students is added together and the distance plotted on the map. This helps the class work together for a common cause and all can feel as though they are making a meaningful contribution.

3. Set up a large clock (such as a swimming clock) on the playground with a highly visible second hand so students can learn to monitor their heart rate. Encourage them to maintain the heart rate in the target zone for 5 to 10 minutes prior to participation in recess activities. When students are involved in activities that demand longer bouts of activity (e.g., soccer, team handball, tag games), have them stop periodically and monitor their heart rate.

4. Develop a walking and jogging course that utilizes playground equipment for strength development. Most playgrounds have chin-up bars, monkey bars, climbing equipment, and parallel bars. Develop a circuit where youngsters have to jog between each strength development station.

5. Develop an afterschool fitness club. A great deal of time and energy is spent on developing competitive sport programs emphasizing skill-related fitness even though a majority of students do not possess the genetic traits to become outstanding athletes. The attractiveness of a fitness club is that all students regardless of genetic talent can participate in health-related physical fitness activities. The club should focus on fitness and teach a large number of aerobic activities such as bicycling, hiking, power walking, cross-country running, and rope jumping. Students can learn that "you get fit to play sports," which contrasts with the usual pattern of playing sports with the hope (usually unrealized) of developing physical fitness.

6. Using manipulative equipment while walking or jogging is an effective technique for encouraging movement. Examples include playing catch with a football or Frisbee while walking, kicking a soccer ball while running, or running while jumping rope.

Interval Training

Basically all the fitness routines in this chapter take advantage of interval training principles. Interval training can be used effectively with elementary school children, as they fatigue and recover quickly. Interval training involves alternating work and recovery intervals. Intervals of work (large muscle movement dominated by locomotor movements) and recovery (dominated by nonlocomotor activity or walking) are alternated at regular timed intervals.

Interval training can also be done by monitoring the heart rate. The work interval is continued until the heart rate reaches the target zone and is followed by a recovery interval. A common example of interval training is alternating 30 seconds of jogging with 30 seconds of walking. However, with elementary school children, this can be boring. The following are examples of motivating activities that can be alternated with recovery activities.

High Fives: Youngsters run around the area and, on signal, run to a partner, jump, and give a "high five." Various locomotor movements can be used as well as different styles of the "high five."

Over and Under: Students find a partner. One partner makes a bridge on the floor while the other moves over, under, and around the bridge. This continues until a signal is given to "switch," which notifies them to change positions. This automatically assures that one child will be moving (working), while the other is resting. Try different types of bridges and movements to offer variety to the activity.

Rope Jump and Stretch: Each student has a jump rope and is jumping it during the work interval. On signal, the student performs a stretch using the jump rope. An example would be to fold the rope in half and hold it overhead while stretching from side to side and to the toes.

Stick and Stretch: Working with a partner, one partner is "it" and tries to stick like glue to the partner, who attempts to escape. Students should move under control. Upon signal, "it" leads the other person in a stretching (resting) activity. On the next signal, the roles are reversed.

Rubber Band: Students move throughout the area. On signal, they time a move to the center of the area. Upon reaching the center simultaneously, they jump upward and let out a loud "yea!" or similar exhortation and resume running throughout the area. The key to the activity is to synchronize the move to the center. After a number of runs, take a rest and stretch, or walk.

Each of the above activities is used for work intervals. Recovery intervals can be characterized by strength development or stretching activities. Using timed intervals of music is an effective approach for motivating youngsters. For a start, tape 30 seconds of music followed by 30 seconds of silence, taping a series of these alternating music and silent intervals. The music sequence signals youngsters to perform the work interval while the silent interval is time for performing stretching or strength development activities. This frees the teacher to help youngsters and assures that intervals are timed accurately. As youngsters become more fit, the length of the music bouts can be increased by making a new recording. Changing the music on a regular basis keeps children motivated.

Partner Fitness Challenges

Partner challenges are fitness activities that can be used with intermediate-grade youngsters. They can be used to develop aerobic endurance, strength, and flexibility. Another advantage of partner challenges is that they can be performed indoors as a rainy-day activity. It is best if youngsters are paired with someone of similar ability and size. Telling youngsters to pair up with a friend usually helps assure they will select a partner who is caring and understanding. Emphasis should be placed on continuous movement and activity. The following are examples of partner activities that are challenging and enjoyable.

Circle Five

Partner 1 stands stationary in the center of the circle with one palm up. Partner 2 runs in a circle around 1 and "gives a high five" when passing the upturned palm. The size of the circle should be gradually increased. Reverse roles on signal.

Foot Tag

Partners stand facing each other. On signal, they try to touch each other's toes with their feet. Emphasize the importance of a touch, as contrasted to a stamp or kick.

Knee Tag

Partners stand facing each other. On signal, they try to tag the other person's knees. Each time a tag is made, a point is scored. Play for a designated amount of time.

Mini Merry-Go-Round

Partners face each other with the feet nearly touching and the hands grasped in a double wrist grip. Partners slowly lean backward while keeping the feet in place until the arms are straight. Spin around as quickly as possible. It is important that partners be of similar size.

Around and Under

One partner stands with the feet spread shoulder width apart and hands held overhead. The other partner goes between the standing partner's legs, stands up, and slaps the partner's hands. Continue the pattern for a designated time.

Ball Wrestle

Both partners grasp an 8-inch playground ball and try to wrestle it away from each other.

Sitting Wrestle

Partners sit on the floor facing each other with the legs bent, feet flat on the floor, with toes touching and hands grasped. The goal of the activity is to pull the other's buttocks off the floor.

Upset the Alligator

One partner lays face down on the floor. On signal, the other opponent tries to turn the "alligator" over. The alligator tries to avoid being turned over.

Seat Balance Wrestle

Partners sit on the floor facing each other with the knees raised and feet off the floor. If desired, they place the hands under the thighs to help support the legs. Start with the toes touching. Each tries to tip the other person backward using the toes.

Head Wrestle

Partners hold each other's left wrists with their right hands. On signal, they try to touch their partners' heads with their left hands, then switch the handhold and try to touch with the opposite hand.

Pull Apart

One partner stands with the feet spread, arms bent at the elbows in front of the chest, with the fingertips touching. Partner 2 holds the wrists of the other and tries to pull the fingertips apart. Jerking is not allowed; the pull must be smooth and controlled.

Pin Dance

Partners hold hands facing each other with a bowling pin (spot or cone) placed between them. On signal, each tries to cause the other person to touch the pin.

Finger Fencing

Partners face each other with their feet one in front of the other in a straight line. The toes on the front foot of each partner should touch. Partners lock index fingers and attempt to cause the other to move either foot from the beginning position.

REFERENCES AND SUGGESTED READINGS

American Academy of Pediatrics. (1991). *Sports medicine: Health care for young athletes.* Elk Grove Village, IL: AAP.

American Alliance for Health, Physical Education, Recreation. (1976). *AAHPER youth fitness test manual.* Reston, VA: AAHPER.

AAHPERD. (1987). *Youth fitness test manual.* Reston, VA: AAHPERD.

Bar-Or, O. (1983). *Pediatric sports medicine for the practitioner.* New York: Springer-Verlag.

Blair, S. N., Kohl, H. W., Paffenbarger, R. S., Clark, D. G., Cooper, K. H., & Gibbons, L. W. (1989). Physical fitness and all-cause mortality: A prospective study of healthy men and women. *Journal of the American Medical Association, 17,* 2395–2401.

Bouchard, C. (1990). Discussion: Heredity, fitness and health. In C. Bouchard, R. J. Shepard, T. Stephens, J. R. Sutton, & B. D. McPherson. (Eds.), *Exercise, fitness and health* (pp. 147–153). Champaign, IL: Human Kinetics.

Bouchard, C., Dionne, F. T., Simoneau, J., & Boulay, M. (1992). Genetics of aerobic and anaerobic performances. *Exercise and Sport Sciences Reviews, 20,* 27–58.

Chausow, S. A., Riner, W. F., & Boileau, R. A. (1984). Metabolic and cardiovascular responses of children during prolonged physical activity. *Research Quarterly for Exercise and Sport, 55*(1), 1–7.

Cooper Institute for Aerobics Research. (1992). *The Prudential Fitnessgram test administration manual.* Dallas: Cooper Institute for Aerobics Research.

Corbin, C. B., & Lindsey, R. (1993). *Fitness for Life* (3rd ed.). Glenview, IL: Scott, Foresman.

Corbin, C. B., & Lindsey, R. (1994). *Concepts of physical fitness with laboratories* (8th ed.). Dubuque, IA: Wm. C. Brown.

Corbin, C. B., & Pangrazi, R. P. (1992). Are American children and youth fit? *Research Quarterly for Exercise and Sport, 63*(2), 96–106.

Corbin, C. B., Lovejoy, P. Y., & Whitehead, J. R. (1988). Youth physical fitness awards. *Quest, 40,* 200–218.

Corbin, C. B., Lovejoy, P. Y., Steingard, P., & Emerson, R. (1990). Fitness awards: Do they accomplish their intended objectives? *American Journal of Health Promotion, 4,* 345–351.

Erickson, D. M. (1980). The effect of a random running program on cardiorespiratory endurance at the fourth, fifth, and sixth grade levels. Unpublished master's thesis, Department of Health and Physical Education, Arizona State University.

Glasser, W. (1976). *Positive addiction.* New York: Harper & Row.

Gortmaker, S. L., Dietz, W. H., Sobol, A. N., & Wehler, C. A. (1987). Increasing pediatric obesity in the U.S. *American Journal of Diseases in Children, 14,* 535–540.

Harter, S. (1978). Effectance motivation revisited. *Child Development, 21,* 34–64.

Liemohn, W. (1991). Choosing the safe exercise. *Certified News, 2,* 1–3.

Lindsey, R., & Corbin, C. (1989). Questionable exercises—Some safer alternatives. *Journal of Physical Education, Recreation, and Dance, 60*(8), 26–32.

Locke, E. A., & Lathan, G. P. (1985). The application of goal setting to sports. *Journal of Sport Psychology, 7,* 205–222.

Lohman, T. G. (1992). *Advances in body composition.* Champaign, IL: Human Kinetics.

Macek, M., & Vavra, J. (1974). Prolonged exercise in children. *Acta Paediatrica Belgica, 28,* 13–18.

Macfarlane, P. A. (1993). Out with the sit-up, in with the curl-up. *Journal of Physical Education, Recreation, and Dance, 64*(6), 62–66.

Miller, D. K., & Allen, T. K. (1990). *Fitness: A lifetime commitment* (3rd ed.). New York: Macmillan.

Pangrazi, R. P., & Corbin, C. B. (1990). Age as a factor relating to physical fitness test performance. *Research Quarterly for Exercise and Sport, 61*(4), 410–414.

Pangrazi, R. P., & Dauer, V. P. (1995). *Lesson plans for dynamic physical education* (11th ed.). New York: Macmillan.

Pangrazi, R. P., & Hastad, D. N. (1989). *Fitness in the elementary schools* (2nd ed.). Reston, VA: AAHPERD.

Pate, R. R., Dowda, M., & Ross, J. G. (1990). Association between physical activity and physical fitness in American children. *American Journal of Diseases of Children, 144,* 1123–1129.

Pate, R. R., & Ross, J. G. (1987). Factors associated with health-related fitness. *Journal of Physical Education, Recreation, and Dance, 58*(9), 93–96.

Payne, V. G., & Morrow, J. R., Jr. (1993). Exercise and VO_{2max} in children: A meta-analysis. *Research Quarterly for Exercise and Sport, 64*(3), 305–313.

Rarick, L. G., & Dobbins, D. A. (1975). Basic components in the motor performances of children six to nine years of age. *Medicine and Science in Sports, 7*(2), 105–110.

Reiff, G. G., Dixon, W. R., Jacoby, D., Ye, X. Y., Spain, C. G., & Hunsicker, P. A. (1987). *The President's Council on Physical Fitness and Sports 1985 national school population fitness survey.* Washington, DC: U.S. Department of Health and Human Services.

Ross, J. G., & Gilbert, G. G. (1985). The national children and youth fitness study: A summary of findings. *Journal of Physical Education, Recreation, and Dance, 56*(1), 45–50.

Ross, J. G., Pate, R. R., Caspersen, C. J., Damberg, C. L., & Svilar, M. (1987). Home and community in children's exercise habits. *Journal of Physical Education, Recreation, and Dance, 58*(9), 85–92.

Rowland, T. W. (1990). *Exercise and children's health.* Champaign, IL: Human Kinetics.

Slaughter, M. H., Lohman, T. G., Boileau, R. A., Horswill, C. A., Stillman, R. J., Van Loan, M. D., & Benben, D. A. (1988). Skinfold equations for estimation of body fatness in children and youth. *Human Biology, 60,* 709–723.

Smith, L. L., Brunetz, M. H., Chenier, T. C., McCammon, M. R., Hourmard, J. A., Franklin, M. E., & Israel, R. G. (1993). The effects of static and ballistic stretching on delayed onset muscle soreness and creatine kinase. *Research Quarterly for Exercise and Sport, 64*(1), 103–107.

U.S. Public Health Service. (1988). *Healthy People 2000.* Washington, DC: Superintendent of Documents.

Whitehead, J. R., & Corbin, C. B. (1991). Effects of fitness test type, teacher, and gender on exercise intrinsic motivation and physical self-worth. *Journal of School Health, 61,* 11–16.

Wilcox, R. R. (1980). RRP: An approach to cardiorespiratory fitness of primary school children, grades one, two, and three. Unpublished master's thesis, Department of Health and Physical Education, Arizona State University.

Williams, D. P., Going, S. B., Lohman, T. G., Harsha, D. W., Webber, L. S., & Bereson, G. S. (1992). Body fatness and the risk of elevated blood pressure, total cholesterol and serum lipoprotein rations in children and youth. *American Journal of Public Health, 82,* 358–363.

Movement Themes: Teaching Movement Concepts

Physical education places strong emphasis on skill development in the elementary school years. Most experts agree that it is important to learn the fundamental skills in the early years as they are the building blocks for more sophisticated skills. There are two major components of motor skill development; skill technique and movement concepts. Even though these components cannot be separated in skill performance, it is helpful to examine each area separately to learn how to teach in a manner that enhances each of the two components. This chapter deals with movement concepts; learning about the classification and vocabulary of movement. Chapter 15 deals with the second component of motor skill development; learning specific fundamental skill techniques and the proper performance of such skills. The goal for a mature performer is to combine these two major components, with the result being proper skill performance in a variety of settings. Figure 14.1 illustrates the various components of motor skill development.

With primary-grade children (ages 4 to 9), strong emphasis is placed on developing an understanding of movement concepts. Less emphasis is placed on skill technique and proper performance of skills. This is not to say that children are not taught a skill correctly, but that greater emphasis is placed on learning the vocabulary of movement. Primary-grade students learn about the classification of movement concepts, which includes body

Figure 14.1 Components of motor skill development

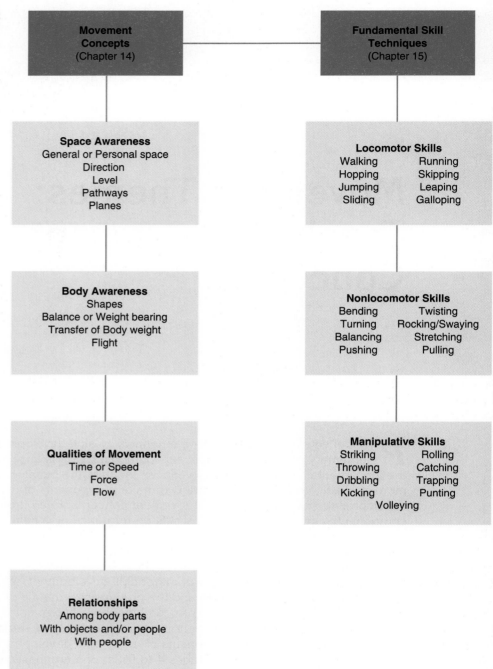

Movement
Concepts
(Chapter 14)

Fundamental Skill
Techniques
(Chapter 15)

Space Awareness
General or Personal space
Direction
Level
Pathways
Planes

Locomotor Skills
Walking	Running
Hopping	Skipping
Jumping	Leaping
Sliding	Galloping

Body Awareness
Shapes
Balance or Weight bearing
Transfer of Body weight
Flight

Nonlocomotor Skills
Bending	Twisting
Turning	Rocking/Swaying
Balancing	Stretching
Pushing	Pulling

Qualities of Movement
Time or Speed
Force
Flow

Manipulative Skills
Striking	Rolling
Throwing	Catching
Dribbling	Trapping
Kicking	Punting
Volleying	

Relationships
Among body parts
With objects and/or people
With people

awareness, space awareness, qualities of movement, and relationships. Children are asked to run in different directions, at different levels, and to take different pathways. They learn to move slowly or quickly or to make a series of strong movements. The objective is to show children how movements are classified and to take advantage of the motivation created by the endless possibilities. Emphasis at this level is placed on the process of moving rather than the product of correct perfor-

mance of a skill. Creativity is rewarded and ingenuity reinforced. Movement themes form the foundation of movement experiences necessary for developing more specific fundamental skills. Through this process, children develop an increased awareness and understanding of the body as a vehicle for movement, and for the acquisition of a personal vocabulary of movement skills.

The second major component of skill development is learning the correct techniques of skill performance and refining skills through practice. These movements are classified as fundamental skills and are covered in detail in Chapter 15. The range of skills is finite in comparison to movement concepts and learning requires repetition until the skills become refined and automatic. Emphasis is placed on this component when children enter the intermediate grades (ages 9–11). Whereas strong emphasis is placed on movement concepts with primary-grade children, the emphasis is decreased with older children because it can be assumed that they have learned the concepts and vocabulary of movement. Thus, more instructional time is placed on skill technique and proper practice at this stage.

Classification of fundamental skills falls into three categories; locomotor, nonlocomotor, and manipulative skills. Fundamental skills are presented in the primary grades and taught with more precision as students reach the intermediate grades. For example, primary-grade children practice movement concepts and locomotor skills when asked to skip in a zigzag pathway. However, the greatest emphasis for primary-grade children is on learning the vocabulary related to the pathway rather than the exact technique of skipping. As children mature, more focus is placed on the skill performance, vocabulary and movement concepts having been learned previously. Related to this point is the need for teachers to remember the concept of developmental age discussed earlier in the text. Children mature and develop at different rates. This change in emphasis from movement concepts to skill technique and performance is guided by the development of students, not the desires of teachers. It implies that children are seldom in the same place at the same time developmentally. Thus, teachers have to be able to know the progression of fundamental skills, how to assess each student's performance, and how to prescribe the proper activities.

An effective way to teach movement concepts is through themes, which can be categorized according to the movement concept classifications of space awareness, body awareness, qualities of movement, and relationships. A space awareness theme might focus on moving in general space and ask children to explore different ways of moving in a specific direction or at a certain level. A theme related to body awareness could incorporate the use of different parts of the body for support or movement. A theme teaching qualities of movement might feature time by asking children to move at a fast or slow pace. A focus on relationships could teach activities in a setting with a partner and manipulative equipment.

CLASSIFICATION OF HUMAN MOVEMENT CONCEPTS

The movement concept categories of body awareness, space awareness, qualities of movement, and relationships give teachers structure and direction for planning experiences to bring out the movement potential of children and develop their movement vocabulary. As youngsters experience movement, they should learn the vocabulary of movement, in order to increase their understanding of the diversity and openness of movement possibilities.

Body Awareness

This category defines *what* the body can perform; the shapes it can make, how it can balance, and the transfer of weight to different body parts. Using the categories to develop challenges can add variety to movement.

1. Shapes the body makes: Many shapes can be formed with the body, such as long or short, wide or narrow, straight or twisted, stretched or curled, symmetrical or asymmetrical.

2. Balance or weight bearing: Balance demands that different parts of the body support the weight or receive the weight. Different numbers of body parts can be involved in the movements and used as body supports.

3. Transfer of body weight: Many skills demand moving the body weight from one body part to another, such as walking, leaping, rolling, and so on.

4. Flight: This category differs from transfer of body weight in that it is explosive movement and involves lifting the body weight from the floor or apparatus for an extended period of time. The amount of time off the floor distinguishes flight from transfer of weight. An example might be running, jumping onto a climbing rope, and hanging.

Space Awareness

Space awareness defines *where* the body can move. The spatial qualities of movement related to moving in different directions and at different levels are the focus. Youngsters need to know how to use space effectively when moving. The following elements determine how space can be modified and utilized in movement experiences.

1. General or personal space: Personal space is the limited area individual children can use

around them, and in most cases is reserved for that individual only. General space is the total space that is used by all youngsters.

2. Direction: This refers to the desired route of movement, whether straight, zigzag, circular, curved, forward, backward, sideward, upward, downward.

3. Level: This defines the relationship of the body to the floor or apparatus, whether low, high, or in between.

4. Pathways: This trait describes the path a movement takes through space. Examples are squares, diamonds, triangles, circles, figure eights, and others.

5. Planes: Planes are somewhat specific pathways defined as circular, vertical, and horizontal. The concept of planes is usually restricted in elementary school to performing simple activities in a specified plane.

Qualities of Movement

These constructs help youngsters understand *how* the body moves. The qualities of movement relate closely to mechanical principles used to move efficiently. In addition, they involve the following characteristics.

1. Time or Speed. This quality deals with the speed and duration of movement. Children learn to move with varying speeds and to control speed throughout a variety of movements. They should learn the relationship between body shape and speed and be able to use body parts to generate speed. The time factor may be varied by utilizing different speeds—moving to a constant rhythm, accelerating, and decelerating.

2. Force. *Force* is the effort or tension generated in movement. Force can be used effectively to aid in executing skills. Youngsters need to understand how to generate, absorb, and direct force. Force qualities may be explored by using words such as *light, heavy, strong, weak, rough,* and *gentle.*

3. Flow. The flow factor establishes how movements are purposefully sequenced to create continuity of movement. Most often this quality is discussed in terms of interrupted (bound) or sustained (free) flow. Interrupted flow would stop at the end of a movement or part of a movement. Sustained flow would involve smoothly linking together different movements or parts of a movement.

Relationships

This element defines *with whom and/or what* the body relates. A *relationship* is defined as the position of the performer to the apparatus or other performers. Examples of relationships would be near–far, above–below, over–under, in front–behind, on–off and together–apart. When done with other people, relationships of leading–following, mirroring–matching, unison–opposites can be explored. Additionally, relationships could also define the body parts of a single performer, such as arms together–apart or symmetrical–asymmetrical.

DESIGNING MOVEMENT THEMES

Four steps are suggested for designing instructional sequences and implementing movement themes. The first two steps are reasonably fixed in the sequence, but the other two can be interchanged or omitted, depending on lesson development. The instructional process can be keyed by the following directions: "Explore," "Discover and expand," "Analyze and select," and "Repeat and extend."

Step One: Set and Define the Problem

The first step defines the problem for students, setting the stage, focus, and limitations. The focus can be within broad or narrow limitations. The *what, where, how* and *with whom or what* need definition.

1. *What are children to do?* An action word must be supplied. Are children to move a certain way, go over and under, explore alternatives, or experiment with some nonlocomotor movement? They may be directed to run, jump, or use some fundamental skill (convergent movement) in a particular way.

2. *Where are children to move?* This is the spatial aspect. What space is to be used—personal or general? What directional factors are to be employed—path or level?

3. *How are children to move?* What are the force factors (light-heavy)? What elements of time are involved (even–uneven, acceleration–deceleration, sudden–sustained)? What are the relationships (over–under–across, in front of–behind)? What body parts are involved for support? For locomotion?

4. *With whom or what are children to move?* With whom are children to work—by themselves,

with a partner, or as a member of a group? Is there a choice involved? With what equipment or on what apparatus are they to perform?

When initiating movement patterns, the challenge can be stated like this: "Let's see you move across the floor, changing direction as you wish, with a quick movement with one foot and a slow movement with the other."

Step Two: Increase the Variety and Depth of Movement

Effective teachers use techniques of observation and analysis so they can modify movement patterns through perceptive guidance. Instruction should encourage youngsters to enhance their movements and increase the variety of responses. Variety provides an important basis for the child's selection of a preferred movement pattern. Securing a variety of responses can be done by using challenges and suggestions. Stimulating effective movement responses from children depends on the phrasing of the problem. Variety can also be achieved by setting limitations and asking youngsters to solve the problem in a different manner. Problems can be presented in the form of questions or statements that elicit and encourage variety, depth, and extent of movement. The use of contrasting terms is also an effective way to help children explore the possible variety of movements. A number of examples follow:

Presenting a Problem

1. Show me how a . . . moves. (Show me how an alligator moves.)
2. Have you seen a . . . ? (Have you seen a kangaroo jump?)
3. What ways can you . . . ? (What ways can you hop over the jump rope?)
4. How would you . . . ? How can you . . . ? (How would you dribble a ball, changing hands frequently?)
5. See how many different ways you can. . . . (See how many different ways you can hang from a ladder.)
6. What can you do with a . . . ? What kinds of things can you . . . ? (What can you do with a hoop?)
7. Can you portray a . . . ? (Can you portray an automobile with a flat tire?)
8. Discover different ways you can. . . . (Discover different ways you can volley a ball against a wall.)

9. Can you . . . ? (Can you keep one foot up while you bounce the ball?)
10. Who can . . . a . . . in such a way that . . . ? (Who can bounce a ball in such a way that it keeps time with the tom-tom?)
11. What does a . . . ? (What does a cat do when it is wet?)
12. Show . . . different ways to. . . . (Show four different ways to move across the floor.)

Securing Variety or Setting Limitations

The following examples are useful for stimulating movement alternatives and/or imposing limitations:

1. Try it again another way. Try to. . . . (Try to jump higher.)
2. See how far (many times, high, close, low). . . . (See how far you can reach with your arms.)
3. Find a way to . . . or find a new way to. . . . (Find a new way to jump over the bench.)
4. Apply . . . to. . . . (Apply a heavy movement to your run.)
5. How else can you . . . ? (How else can you roll your hoop?)
6. Make up a sequence. . . . (Make up a sequence of previous movements, changing smoothly from one movement to the next.)
7. Now try to combine a . . . with. . . . (Now try to combine a locomotor movement with your catching.)
8. Alternate . . . and. . . . (Alternate walking and hopping.)
9. Repeat the last movement, but add. . . . (Repeat the last movement, but add a body twist as you move.)
10. See if you can. . . . (See if you can do the movement with a partner.)
11. Trace (draw) a . . . with. . . . (Trace a circle with your hopping partner.)
12. Find another part of the body to. . . . Find other ways to. . . . (Find another part of the body to take the weight.)
13. Combine the . . . with. . . . (Combine the hopping with a body movement.)
14. In how many different positions can you . . . ? (In how many different positions can you carry your arms while walking the balance beam?)
15. How do you think the . . . would change if . . . ? (How do you think the balance exercise we are doing would change if our eyes were closed?)

16. On signal, ... (On signal, speed up your movements.)

Encouraging Variety Using Contrasting Terms

Another way to increase children's understanding of movement possibilities is to employ terms that stress contrasts. Contrasting terms provide a way for teachers to stimulate variety of movement. Instead of challenging children to move quickly, for example, the teacher can ask the class to contrast a quick movement with a slow movement. The following list includes many common sets of contrasting terms that express relationships between movements or descriptions of ways to move.

Above—below, beneath, under
Across—around, under
Around clockwise—around counterclockwise
Before—after
Between—alongside of
Big—little, small
Close—far
Crooked—straight
Curved—flat, straight
Diagonal—straight
Fast—slow
Forward—back, backward
Front—back, behind
Graceful—awkward
Heavy—light
High—low
In—out
In front of—behind, in back of
Inside—outside
Into—out of
Large—small
Near—far
On—off
On top of—under, underneath
Over—under, through
Reach down—reach up
Right—left
Round—straight
Separate—together
Short—long, tall
Sideways—forward, backward
Smooth—rough
Standing upright—inverted
Sudden—sustained
Swift—slow
Tight—loose
Tiny—big, large
Top—bottom
To the right of—to the left of
Up—down
Upper—lower
Upside down—right side up
Upward—downward
Wide—narrow, thin
Zigzag—straight

Some of the terms may be grouped more logically in sets of three contrasts (e.g., forward–sideways–backward, up–down–in between, over–under–through). Word meanings also can be emphasized according to rank or degree (e.g., near–nearer–nearest, low–lower–lowest).

Step Three: Build Sequences and Combine Movement Patterns

In this step, children select movements that have been practiced and put them together in sequence, focusing on transition (flow) from one movement pattern to another. Youngsters should be challenged to imagine how they can put movements together. In this step, children can select which movements to put in combination or the teacher can specify some limitation on the number of combinations, the types of movements, or the order in which they are sequenced. Achievement demonstrations can be used to stimulate effort, as children enjoy showing what they have put together. These demonstrations

Creating contrasting movements

provide ideas and give other children a rough standard against which they can compare their own movement patterns.

Step Four: Incorporate Cooperative Partner and Small-Group Activity

Cooperative partner and small-group skills are important educational goals. Problems should be realistic and give opportunity for discussion and decision making between partners. The following are examples of partner activities that can be developed:

1. One child is an obstacle, and the partner devises ways of going over, under, and around the positions the "obstacle" takes (Figure 14.2). Additional challenges are provided when one partner holds a piece of equipment such as a wand or hoop to govern movements.

2. One partner supports the weight of the other, either wholly or in part (Figure 14.3), or the two work together to form different kinds of figures or shapes. Bridges can be built.

3. One child does a movement and the other copies or provides a contrasting movement.

4. One child moves and the other attempts to shadow (do the same movements). This must be done slowly, with uninterrupted flow predominating.

5. One child moves and the other provides correction or critique.

6. Partners develop a parallel sequence with both moving together and in the same way.

7. Partners begin 15 to 20 yards apart and come together, using the same selected locomotor movement. They reverse direction and part,

Figure 14.3 Supporting partner's weight

using another selected locomotor movement. Acceleration and deceleration have application here, as well as contrasting terms.

8. One child does a movement. The second child repeats the movement and adds another. The first child repeats both movements and adds a third, and so on. Some limit on the number of movements would need to be set.

9. Children form letters or figures with their bodies on the floor or in erect positions.

Group work in movement activities entails a group of children working together on a movement task. Groups should be small (three to four children) so that each child makes a significant contribution. The task should be definite so efforts are directed toward a common goal. Most of the ways in which children can work with a partner are applicable, with modifications, to small-group work. Designing, inventing, or modifying a game makes an excellent group problem-solving activity. Some examples of movement activities that are feasible for group work follow:

1. Children explore different ways to build a human tower.

2. Groups show different ways to support others wholly or in part.

3. Children practice copying activities. One child sets a movement pattern and the rest copy the actions.

4. Groups make a human merry-go-round.

5. Groups select and make a pyramid.

6. Children do parallel movements as a group.

Figure 14.2 Going under a partner

7. Small groups (five is a good number) do over and under movements. Each child goes over and under the others in turn.

Movement Skills and Concepts Lesson Plans

The accompanying text, *Lesson Plans for Dynamic Physical Education, 11th ed.* (Pangrazi & Dauer, 1995), contains lesson plans for teaching movement skills and concepts. Each of the lesson plans contains four or five parts that present a variety of experiences in movement concepts and skills. This variety of activities offers children a broad spectrum of movement challenges and assures a balance of movement experiences. Each movement lesson plan contains the following sections:

1. *Movement themes.* Two or more movement themes are developed to focus on teaching the concepts of movements. Locomotor and nonlocomotor movements are used as the medium for developing a movement vocabulary. Movement themes focus on a movement quality around which children build patterns and sequences. Exploration of movements is emphasized as children develop body awareness and an understanding of movement concepts.

2. *Fundamental skills.* This section emphasizes a wide variety of experiences for teaching fundamental skills to children. Locomotor skills covered include walking, running, galloping, skipping, sliding, leaping, hopping, and jumping. Nonlocomotor movements covered are bending, rocking, swinging, turning, twisting, stretching, pushing, and pulling. Emphasis is placed on developing proper technique and using the skill in novel situations.

3. *Manipulative skills.* Manipulative skills are practiced in each lesson using a variety of equipment. Skills practiced include throwing, kicking, striking, and catching.

TEACHING MOVEMENT THEMES

Movement themes are used to develop an understanding of movement concepts. Movement themes focus on a movement concept around which children build patterns and sequences. The purpose is to explore and experiment with the theme, gain a thorough understanding of the movement concept,

Using beanbags to develop manipulative skills

and develop skill in the movement area. Children should be allowed considerable latitude in movement patterns. Movement responses, however, should go beyond the challenge of "How many different ways can you . . . ?" Teachers should guide children toward the best response they can produce. Quality must not be neglected in the interest of getting children to respond in different ways.

Movement themes are designed to help youngsters understand the concepts of movement. Some themes involve only a single movement principle or factor, while others involve two or more. An attempt has been made to be specific in exploring the concepts of movement, but in actuality, isolating a particular factor is difficult. For example, in exploring balance, movement possibilities are expanded through the application of body shape, level, and time factors. The themes are classified by the four major concepts of human movement: body awareness, space awareness, qualities of movement, and relationships.

Body Awareness Themes

Body Shapes (Figure 14.4)

"Let's try making shapes and see whether we can name them. Make any shape you wish and hold it. What is the name of your shape, John? [Wide.] Try to make different kinds of wide shapes. Show me other shapes you can make. What is the name of your shape, Susie? [Crooked.] Show me different kinds of shapes that are crooked. Make yourself as crooked as possible."

"Make yourself wide and then narrow. Now tall and then small. How about tall and wide, small and narrow, tall and narrow, and small and wide? Work out other combinations."

"Select three different kinds of shapes and move smoothly from one to another. This time I will clap my hands as a signal to change to a different shape."

"Select four different letters of the alphabet. On the floor, make your body shape successively like these letters. Try with numbers. Make up a movement sequence that spells a word of three letters. Show us a problem in addition or subtraction."

"Use your jump rope and make a shape on the floor. Make a shape with your body alongside the rope."

"Pretend to be as narrow as an arrow or telephone pole. Pretend to be as wide as a house, store, or hippopotamus."

"Squeeze into a tiny shape; now grow slowly into the biggest shape you can imagine. Travel to a different spot on the floor, maintaining the big shape. Quickly assume the tiny shape again."

"Move around the room in groups of three. On signal, form a shape with one standing, one kneeling, and one sitting."

"Pretend you are at a farm. Make a barn with your body."

"Jump upward, making a shape in the air. Land, holding that shape. Begin with a shape, jump upward with a half turn, and land in another shape."

"What body shapes can you assume standing on one foot?"

"Show me what body shapes can be made with your stomach in contact with the floor."

"Look to see where your personal space is in relation to general space. When I say 'Go,' run in general space. On the next signal, return to your space and sit down."

Note: Emphasize the kinds of shapes and reinforce the concept by having the children practice each kind of shape. This exercise can be divided into shapes formed while erect and shapes formed on the floor.

Balancing (Figure 14.5)

"Explore different ways you can balance on different surfaces of your body. Can you balance on three different parts of your body? On two? On one? Put together sequences of three or four balance positions by using different body parts or different numbers of body parts."

"Can you balance on a flat body surface? What is the smallest part of the body you can balance

Figure 14.4 Forming different shapes

Figure 14.5 Balancing on different body parts

on? Support the body on two dissimilar parts. On three dissimilar parts. Support the body on different combinations of body flats and body points."

"Use two parts of the body far away from each other to balance. Shift smoothly to another two parts."

"Who can balance on one foot with the arms stretched overhead? Out to the side?"

"Stand with feet together and eyes closed. Maintain balance while using different arm positions. Balance on one foot for ten counts."

"From a standing position, raise one leg, straighten the leg in front of you, swing the leg to side and back without losing your balance."

"Move from a narrow, unstable base to a wide, stable base."

"Balance on parts of the body forming a tripod." (Explain the term.)

"Show different balance positions with part of the weight supported by the head."

"In a hands and knees position, and later in a crab position, balance on the right arm and right leg, the left arm and left leg, the right arm and left leg, the left arm and right leg."

"Stand on your toes and balance, using different arm positions."

"Place a beanbag on the floor. How many different ways can you balance over it? Try with a hoop. How many different ways can you balance inside the hoop?"

"When I call out a body part or parts, you balance for 5 seconds on that part or part combination." (Use knees, hands, heels, flats, points, and a variety of combinations.)

"Keep your feet together and sway in different directions without losing your balance. Can you balance on one foot with your eyes closed? Bend forward while balancing on one foot? Lift both sets of toes from the floor and balance on your heels? Now sit on the floor. Can you lift your feet and balance on your seat without hand support? Can you balance on your tummy without your feet or hands touching the floor?"

"In a standing position, thrust one leg out sideways and balance on the other foot."

"Make a sequence by balancing on a narrow surface, change to a wide surface, and back again to a different narrow surface."

Note: This theme could also be called *supporting body weight.* Balance positions should be maintained for 3 to 5 seconds before changing.

Bridges (Figure 14.6)

"Show me a bridge made by using your hands and feet. What other kinds of bridges can you make? Can you make a bridge using only three body parts? Only two?"

"Show me a wide bridge. A narrow one. A short bridge. A long one. How about a high bridge? A low one? Can you make a bridge that opens when a boat goes through? Get a partner to be the boat and you be the bridge. If you are the boat, choose three ways of traveling under a bridge. Each time the boat goes under the bridge, change the bridge to another means of support."

"As I touch you, go under a bridge and make another bridge."

"Show how you would make London Bridge fall down."

"With a partner, alternate going under a high bridge and going over a low bridge."

"Can you move one end of the bridge, keeping the other end still?"

"Make a bridge with one side of the body held upward. Change to the other side."

"Show me a twisted bridge. A curved bridge."

"Be an inchworm and start with a long, low bridge. Walk the feet to the hands. Walk the hands forward while the feet are fixed."

"Make a bridge with three points of contact."

"Show me a bridge at a high level. At a low level. In between."

"Work up a sequence of bridge positions, going smoothly from one to the next."

Flight

"Show me three different ways you can go through space. Try again, using different levels. Lead with different parts of your body."

Figure 14.6 Making bridges

"See how high you can go as you move through space. What helps you get height?"

"Practice various combinations for takeoff and landing. See if you can work out five different possibilities for taking off and landing, using one or both feet." (Possibilities are same to same [hop]; one foot to the opposite [leap]; one-foot takeoff, two-foot landing; two-foot takeoff, two-foot landing [jump]; two-foot take-off, one-foot landing.)

"Run and jump or leap through the air with your legs bent. With your legs straight. With one leg bent and the other straight. Try it with your legs spread wide. With your whole body wide. With your whole body long and thin through the air."

"Project yourself upward beginning with the feet together and landing with the feet apart. Run, take off, and land in a forward stride position. Repeat, landing with the other foot forward."

"With a partner, find ways to jump over the partner as she changes shape."

"Using your arms to help you, run and project yourself as high as possible. Practice landing resiliently, with knees bent." (Explain *resiliently*.)

Note: Parallel lines 2 feet apart can represent a creek to be crossed. Other objects, such as small cones, individual mats, and masking tape, are useful.

Moving with the Weight Supported on the Hands and Feet (Figure 14.7)

"Pick a spot away from your personal space and travel to and from that spot on your hands and feet. Try moving with your hands close to your feet. Far away from your feet. Show me bilateral, unilateral, and cross-lateral movements. Build up a sequence."

"Move from your personal space for 8 counts. Do a jump turn (180 degrees) and return to your space using a different movement."

Figure 14.7 Taking the weight on the hands and feet

"Lie on your stomach. Move only using your hands."

"Experiment with different hand–foot positions. Begin with a narrow shape and with hands and feet as close together as possible. Extend your hands from head to toe until they are as far apart as possible. Extend the hands and feet as wide as possible and move. Now try with the hands wide and the feet together. Reverse."

"Practice traveling so that both hands and feet are off the ground at the same time. Go forward, backward, sideward."

"With your body straight and supported on the hands and feet [push-up position], turn the body over smoothly and face the ceiling. The body should remain straight throughout. Turn to the right and left. Recover to your original position."

"What kinds of animal movements can you imitate? Move with springing types of jumps. What shapes can you assume while you move?"

Note: The terms *bilateral, unilateral,* and *cross-lateral* need explanation, including the significance of the prefixes.

Receiving and Transferring Weight

"Support the weight on two different body parts and then transfer the weight smoothly to another pair of parts. Add another pair of unlike parts if you can."

"Take a deep breath, let the air out, relax, and drop to the floor, transferring the weight from a standing position to a position on the floor. Can you reverse the process?"

"Show in walking how the weight transfers from the heel to the ball of the foot with a push-off from the toes. In a standing position, transfer the weight from the toes, to the outside of the foot, to the heel, and back to the toes. Reverse the order."

"Using three different parts, transfer weight from one to another in a sequence."

"Travel with a jump or a leap and then lower yourself gently to your back after landing. Repeat, only lower yourself smoothly to your seat."

"From a standing position, bend forward slowly and transfer the weight partially to both hands. Lift one foot into the air. Return it to the ground gently. Repeat with the other foot. Lift a hand and a foot at the same time and return them smoothly."

"Lower yourself in a controlled manner to take the weight on your tummy. Can you turn over and take the weight on your seat with your hands and feet touching the floor?"

"Move from a supine position to a standing position without using your arms."

"Select a shape. See if you can lower yourself to the ground and return to your original position, retaining the shape."

"Try some jump turns, quarter and half. What is needed to maintain stability as you land?"

"Project yourself into the air and practice receiving your weight in different ways. Try landing without any noise. What do you have to do? See how high you can jump and still land lightly."

"See how many different ways you can transfer weight smoothly from one part of your body to another. Work up a sequence of three or four movements and go smoothly from one to another, returning to your original position."

Stretching and Curling

"In your own space, stretch out and curl. What different ways can you find to do this? Let's go slowly from a stretch to a curl and back to a stretch in a smooth, controlled movement. Curl your upper body and stretch your lower body. Now curl your lower body and stretch your upper body. Work out a smooth sequence between the two combinations."

"Show different curled and stretched positions on body points and on body flats. Go from a curled position on a flat surface to a stretched position supported on body points. Explore how many different ways you can support your body in a curled position."

"Stand in your personal space and stretch your arms at different levels. Lift one leg up and stretch it to the front, side, and back. Repeat with the other leg."

"Stretch with an arm and a leg until it pulls you over."

"In a sitting position, put your legs out in front. Bend your toes forward as far as possible. Bend them backward so that your heels are ahead of your toes. Turn both toes as far as you can inward. Turn them outward."

"Lie on the floor on your back. Stretch one leg at a time in different ways in space."

"Stand. Stretch to reach as far as you can with your hand. Try reaching as far as possible with your toe."

"Show how you can travel on different body parts, sometimes stretched, sometimes curled."

"Jump and stretch as high as possible. Now curl and roll on the floor." Repeat several times.

Taking the Weight on the Hands (Figure 14.8)

Establishing proper hand positioning for taking the weight on the hands (and later for the headstand) is important.

"Put your hands about shoulder width apart, with fingers spread and pointed forward. With knees bent, alternate lifting the feet silently into the air, one foot at a time. Pick a point ahead of your hands (2 feet or so), and watch it with your eyes. Keep from ducking your head between your arms."

"Place both hands on the floor. Kick up like a mule. Can you kick twice before coming down?"

"Take the weight on your hands. Make one foot go past the other while in the air."

"Do as many movements as you can while keeping your hands on the floor."

"See whether you can take the weight on your hands for a brief time. How do you get your body into the air? What is the importance of the center of gravity? What different movements can you make with your feet while your weight is on your hands? See how long you can keep your feet off the ground. Repeat, trying to get your hips above your hands. Now add a twist at the waist to return your feet to the floor at a different spot."

"Try again, but shift the weight to one hand and land both feet at a different spot."

"Begin in a standing position and try to keep your feet over your head for as long as possible.

Figure 14.8 Taking the weight on the hands

Begin with the arms and hands stretched overhead, and repeat. Kick up one leg and then the other.''

Space Awareness Themes (Where the Body Moves)

Moving in General Space

Goals in these movement experiences, in addition to developing movement competence, should also enhance (a) the ability to share space with other children, (b) the ability to move through space without bumping anyone, and (c) the ability to develop consideration for the safety of others.

''Run lightly in the area, changing direction without bumping or touching anyone until I call 'Stop.' Raise your hand if you were able to do this without bumping into anyone.''

''Let's try running zigzag fashion in the area without touching anyone. This time, when I blow the whistle, change direction abruptly and change the type of movement.''

''Run lightly in general space and pretend you are dodging someone. Can you run toward another runner and change direction to dodge?''

''Get a beanbag and drop it to mark your personal space. See how lightly, while under control, you can run throughout the area. When the signal is given, run to your spot, pick up your beanbag, put it on your head, and sit down [or give some other challenge]. Try this skipping.''

''We are going to practice orienteering. [Explain the term.] Point to a spot on the wall, and see whether you can run directly to it in a straight line. You may have to stop and wait for others to pass so as not to bump into anyone, but you cannot change direction. Stay in a straight line. When you get to your spot, pick another spot, and repeat.''

''What happens when general space is decreased? You had no problem running without touching anyone in the large space. Now let's divide the area in half with cones. Run lightly within this area so as not to touch or bump anyone. Now it's going to get more difficult. I'm going to divide the space in half once more, but first let's try walking in the new area. Now, run lightly.'' (Decrease the area as feasible.)

''Get a beanbag and mark your personal space. Run around the beanbag until you hear a 'Bang,' and then explode in a straight direction until I call 'Stop.' Return to your personal space.''

''From your beanbag, take five [or more] jumps [hops, skips, gallops, slides] and stop. Turn to face home, and return with the same number of movements. Take the longest steps you can away from home, and then return home with tiny steps.''

''Show me how well you can move with these combinations in general space: run-jump-roll, skip-spin-collapse. Now you devise a series of any three movements and practice them.''

''Today our magic number is five. Can you move in any direction with five repetitions of a movement? Change direction and pick another movement to do five times. Continue.''

''Blow yourself up like a soap bubble. Can you huff and puff? Think of yourself as a big bubble that is floating around. When I touch you, the bubble breaks, and you collapse to the ground. This time, blow up your bubble and float around. When you are ready, say, 'Pop,' so the bubble bursts.''

''I am going to challenge you on right and left movements. Show me how you can change to the correct direction when I say either 'Right' or 'Left.' Now begin running lightly.''

''This time, see whether you can run rapidly toward another child, stop, and bow to each other. Instead of bowing, shake hands, and say, 'How do you do!' ''

''From your personal space, pick a spot on a wall. See whether you can run to the spot, touch it, and return without bumping anyone. This time, it's more difficult. Pick spots on two different walls, touch these in turn, and return.''

Exploring Personal Space

Personal space is that space that can be reached from a fixed base. Youngsters can take this personal space with them when they are moving in general space. A graphic way to illustrate personal space is to have youngsters take an individual jump rope and double it. From a kneeling position, they swing it in a full arc along the floor. It should not touch another child or rope.

''Show us how big your space is. Keeping one foot in place, outline how much space you can occupy. Sit cross-legged and outline your space. Support your weight on different parts of your body and outline your space.''

''Make yourself as wide [narrow, small, large, low, high] as possible. Try these from different positions—kneeling, balancing on the seat, and others. Show us what kinds of body positions you can assume while you stand on one foot. While you lie on your stomach. On your seat. Try the same with one foot and one hand touching the floor."

"Stand tall in your space. To the beat of a drum, move in increments to a squat position. Reverse."

"Move from a lying position to a standing position without using your arms or hands. Return to lying."

"Can you stay in one place and move your whole self but not your feet? Sway back and forth with your feet together and then with your feet apart. Which is better?"

"Sitting in your personal space, bend your toes forward; now backward. Bend your feet so that the heels move ahead of your toes."

"In a supine position (on your back) move your arms and legs from one position slowly and then move them back quickly to where you started. Explore other positions."

"Keeping one part of your body in place, make as big a circle as you can with the rest of your body."

"Explore different positions while you keep one leg [foot] higher than the rest of your body. Work out a smooth sequence of three different positions."

"Pump yourself up like a balloon, getting bigger and bigger. Hold until I say, 'Bang!' "

"In your personal space, show me how a top spins. Keep your feet together in place. With your arms wide to the sides, twist and make your feet turn."

Note: Children should adjust their personal space so that they do not intrude on the space of others.

Circles and the Body (Figure 14.9)

"Can you form full circles with your hands and arms at different joints—wrist, elbow, and shoulder? Now what circle can you make with your legs and feet? Try this lying on your back. Use other body joints to make circles."

"Travel in general space by skipping [running, hopping, sliding]. Stop on signal and make moving, horizontal [vertical, inclined] circles with an arm. Repeat, but on signal lie down immediately on your back and make the specified circle with one foot."

Figure 14.9 Forming circles

"Show how a swimmer makes circles with the arms when doing the backstroke. Alternate arms and also move them together. Reverse the arm direction to make the crawl stroke. Make vertical circles with one arm and both arms across the body."

"Make a circle with one hand on your tummy and pat yourself on the top of the head with the other hand at the same time. Reverse hands."

"Keep one foot fixed and make a circle with the other foot by turning completely around."

"Select a partner. Match the arm circles the partner makes."

"Can you keep two different circles going at the same time? Make a circle turning one way, and another circle turning the other way. Repeat, using twisting actions of the body parts making the circles."

Note: Carry this far enough to get children to explore most of their body and joint actions.

Planes of Movement

"Show me a variety of movements in a horizontal plane. In a vertical plane. In a diagonal plane. Put together combinations so that you go in sequence from one type of movement to another."

"Here is a challenge. When I call out a plane of movement, respond with one that is correct. Ready?" (Specify the plane of movement.)

"Using a jump rope doubled in one hand, make circles in the different planes. Try the same with a hula hoop."

"Crouch at a low level, spin upward toward the ceiling, then back to the floor. Spin in the other direction."

Note: This theme can be combined with the previous theme, circles and the body.

Levels

"Choose one way of traveling at a high level and another at a low level. Again, move at a high level and stop at a low level. Move at a low level and stop at a high level. Choose one way of traveling at a medium level and add this somewhere in your sequence—beginning, middle, or end."

"Select three different kinds of traveling movement with the arms at a high, medium, and low level. Link these movements together in a smooth sequence."

"Travel around the room raising your arms as high as possible. Travel on your tiptoes. Repeat with your arms as low as possible."

"Run at different levels. Run as high as you can. Run as low as possible. Run at a medium level."

"When I clap my hands, change direction and level."

"Move on all fours with your body at a high level, a medium level, and then as low as possible. Try these movements with your face turned to the ceiling."

"Use a jump rope or a line or board in the floor as your path to follow. Begin at the far end. Show me a slow, low-level movement down and back. What other ways can you go down and back slowly and at a low level? Change to a fast, high-level movement. On what other levels can you move?"

"Combine a low, fast movement down with a high, slow movement on the way back. Explore other combinations. Make different movements by leading with different parts of your body."

Note: Each child has a path outlined by a rope, line, or board with a length of from 8 to 10 feet. This activity can also be organized by means of selected formations (pp. 89–92). The concept of level can be integrated in most movement challenges that emphasize other elements.

Moving in Different Ways

"Discover different ways you can make progress along the floor without using your hands and feet. See whether you can walk with your seat. Let your heels help you."

"What ways can you move sideward or backward? What rolling movements can you make? Look carefully before you move, to make sure you have a clear space."

"Use large movements and travel through general space. Make your body into a straight line and move in straight lines, changing direction abruptly. With your body in a curved shape, move in a curved pathway."

"Each time you change direction, alternate a straight body and a straight path with a curved body shape and a curved path."

"Find ways of moving close to the floor with your legs stretched. Now move with your legs bent, keeping at a low level."

"As you travel forward, move up and down. As you travel backward, sway from side to side."

"Travel, keeping high in the air. Change direction and travel at a low level. Continue to alternate."

"Counting the four limbs [two arms, two legs], travel first on all four, then on three, next on an arm and a leg, and then on one leg. Now reverse the order."

"With your hands fixed on the floor, move your feet in different ways. Cover as much space as possible. With your feet fixed, move your hands around in different ways as far away from the body as you can. Move around general space the way a skater does. The way a person on a pogo stick does. Choose other ways. Change body direction as you move, but keep facing in the original direction."

Qualities of Movement Themes (How the Body Moves)

Time (Speed)

Speed involves the pace of action, which can be slow, fast, or any degree in between. Speed involves acceleration and deceleration; that is, the time factor either can be constant or can employ acceleration or deceleration. Time also can be even or uneven.

"With your arms, do a selected movement slowly and then quickly. Move your feet slowly and then as rapidly as you can. Change your support base and repeat."

"In turn, stretch a part of your body slowly and then return it to place quickly, like a rubber band snapping. Stretch the entire body as wide as possible and snap it back to a narrow shape."

"Travel through the area without touching anyone. Speed up when there is an open area and slow down when it is crowded."

"Choose a way of traveling across the floor quickly and then do the same movement slowly. Do a fast movement in one direction and, on signal, change to a slow movement in another direction."

"Select a magic number between 10 and 20. Do that many slow movements and repeat with fast movements of the same count."

"Choose a partner. With your partner a little bit away from you, begin moving rapidly toward your partner and decelerate as you draw close. Move away by beginning slowly and accelerate until you return to where you started. Repeat. Select the kinds of movement you wish to use together."

"Staying in your own personal space, begin with some kind of movement and accelerate until you are moving as fast as you can. Reverse by beginning with a fast movement and then slow down until you are barely moving. Put together a sequence of two movements by beginning with one and accelerating, then changing to another movement and decelerating. Try doing two different body movements at the same time—one that accelerates and one that decelerates."

Note: Time concepts can be stressed by relating this movement to a car with its accelerator and brakes. Acceleration and deceleration can be combined with many types of movement and challenges. Explain the prefixes of the two words.

Contrasting Movements

Contrasting movements have wide and frequent application in the development of other themes.

"Show me a fast movement. Now a slow one. Show me a smooth movement. Now a rough, jerky movement."

"Find three ways to rise from the floor and three ways to sink to the floor. Choose one way to rise and one way to sink. Try to do this three times very smoothly."

"Make yourself as tall as possible. Now, as short as you can."

"Move with a small and delicate skip. Change to a large skip."

"Show me a wide shape. Now, an opposite one. A crooked shape. Now, its opposite. Show me a high-level movement and its contrast. Can you do a balanced movement? What is its opposite?" (Use light-heavy and other contrasts as well.)

"Pick two contrasting movements. When I clap my hands, do one, and change to the other when I clap again. What are the movements you did?"

Note: Stimulate children to think about and identify opposite movements. One approach is to name one quality and to see whether children can identify the opposite with a movement response. Another is to have children match their choices. Get further suggestions from the children. A list of contrasting terms and their opposites is found on page 320.

Force

"Show me different kinds of sudden movements. Do a sudden movement and repeat it slowly. Put together a series of sudden movements. Put together a series of sustained movements. Mix sudden and sustained movements."

"Pick a partner and do a quick, strong, movement followed by a quick, light movement."

"Take five strong, slow jumps, changing your body for each jump."

"When the drum beat is loud, walk heavily. When the drum beat is soft, walk lightly."

"Reach in different directions with a forceful movement. Crouch down as low as you can and explode upward. Try again, exploding forward. Move as if you were pushing something very heavy. Pretend you are punching a heavy punching bag."

"What kinds of movements can you do that are light movements? Can you make movements light and sustained? Light and sudden? Heavy and sustained? Heavy and sudden? Which is easier? Why?"

"Try making thunder [big noise with hands and feet] and then lightning [same movements without any noise], timing each with five slow counts."

"Can you combine heavy movements in a sequence of sudden and sustained movements?

Can you make one part of your body move lightly and another part heavily?"

Tension and Relaxation

"Make yourself as tense as possible. Now slowly relax. Take a deep breath and hold it tight. Expel the air and relax."

"Hug yourself hard! Now, harder. Follow this with the body relaxed. Shake the hands."

"Reach as high as possible with both hands, relax slowly, and drop to the floor. Tense one part of your body and relax another. Slowly shift the tension to the relaxed part, and vice versa."

"Run forward, stop suddenly in a tensed position, and then relax. Run in a tensed manner, change direction, and then run in a relaxed manner."

"Walk forward with tight, jerky movements. Change direction and walk with loose, floppy movements. Pretend that you are a boxer by using short, tense movements. Now move your arms like a floppy rag doll."

Relationship Themes (To Whom and What the Body Relates)

Moving Over, Under, Around, and Through Things

This theme is flexible and can use any available equipment as obstacles to go over, under, around, and through (Figure 14.10). It can be used effectively in a rotating station system. Equipment can be already arranged, or the children can set it up themselves.

"Using the equipment, explore different ways you can go over, under, around, or through what you have set up. Lead with different parts of the body."

Figure 14.10   Moving over and under

"Three youngsters with jump ropes form a triangle, square, and rectangle, respectively, on the floor. Move in, out, and around the figures."

"Toss your beanbag in the air. When I call out a body part, sit down quickly, and put the beanbag on that part, or on one of the parts named."

Note: Cones, wands, beanbags, blocks, ropes, baseball bats, and chairs are examples of articles that can be used. This is an excellent partner or small-group activity.

Symmetrical and Asymmetrical Movements

"Show me different kinds of symmetrical movements. Now asymmetrical movements. Put together sequences of symmetrical and asymmetrical movements."

"Taking the weight on your hands, show symmetrical and asymmetrical movements of your legs."

"Run and jump high in the air, and place your limbs symmetrically in flight."

Note: The terms need to be explained. Symmetry increases stability because of the counterbalance effect of the two body halves. Asymmetry, with its weight distributed unequally, leads to quick starts and easier sequential flow due to the unequal weight distribution throughout the body.

Relative Location of Body Parts

"We are going to try some special ways of touching. Raise your right hand as high as you can—now down. Raise your left hand as high as you can—now down. Touch your left [or right] shoulder [elbow, knee, hip, ankle] with the right [or left] hand." (Try many combinations.)

"Now, point to a door [window, ceiling, basket] with an elbow [thumb, toe, knee, nose]. Let's see if you can remember right and left. Point your left [or right] elbow to the window." (Try different combinations.)

"When I name a body part, let's see if you can make this the highest part of your body without moving from your place."

"Now, the next task is a little more difficult. Move in a straight line for a short distance and keep the body part named above all the other body parts. What body parts would be difficult to keep above all the others?" (Possibilities are the eyes, both ears, both hips.)

"Touch the highest part of your body with your right hand. Touch the lowest part of your body with your left hand."

"Let's see if you can locate some of the bones in your body. When I name a bone, hold that bone, move and touch a wall, and return to your spot." (These challenges are dependent on bones that the children can identify. The same procedure can be used to identify selected muscles.)

"Now move around the room, traveling any way you wish." (The movement can also be limited.) "The signal to stop will be a word describing a body part. Can you stop and immediately put both hands on that part or parts?" (Or, "On 'Stop,' hide the body part.") "You are to move around the room again. When I call out a body part, find a partner and place the body parts together."

"This time, when I call out a body part, you are to move around the room as you wish, while holding with one hand a named body part. When I call out another name, change the type of movement and hold the part with the other hand as you move. Now I will call out two body parts. Have the parts touch each other."

Leading with Different Parts of the Body (Figure 14.11)

"As you move between your beanbags [lines, markers], explore ways that different parts of

Figure 14.11 Leading with a foot

your body can lead movements. Add different means of locomotion. Work at different levels."

"Have a partner make a bridge and you go under, leading with different parts of the body. Can you find five different ways to go under with different body parts leading? Now try finding five ways to go over or around."

"What body parts are difficult to lead with?"

REFERENCES AND SUGGESTED READINGS

Andrews, G. (1976). *Creative rhythmic movement for children*. Englewood Cliffs, NJ: Prentice-Hall.

Bilbrough, A., & Jones, P. (1966). *Physical education in the primary school*. London: University of London Press Ltd.

Capon, J. (1981). *Successful movement challenges*. Byron, CA: Front Row Experiences.

Gabbard, C., LeBlanc, E., & Lowy, S. (1987). *Physical education for children building the foundation*. Englewood Cliffs, NJ: Prentice-Hall.

Graham, G., Holt/Hale, S. A., & Parker, M. (1993). *Children moving*. Mountain View, CA: Mayfield.

Joyce, M. (1980). *First steps in teaching creative dance to children*. Palo Alto, CA: Mayfield.

Joyce, M. (1984). *Dance technique for children*. Palo Alto, CA: Mayfield.

Logsdon, B. J., Barrett, K. R., Ammons, M., Broer, M. R., Halverson, L. E., McGee, R., & Robertson, M. A. (1984). *Physical education for children: A focus on the teaching process*. Philadelphia: Lea & Febiger.

Laban, R., & Lawrence, F. (1947). *Effort*. London: Union Brothers.

Murray, R. L. (1975). *Dance in elementary education* (3rd ed.). Englewood Cliffs, NJ: Prentice-Hall.

Pangrazi, R. P., & Dauer, V. P. (1995). *Lesson plans for dynamic physical education* (11th ed.). New York: Macmillan.

Teaching Fundamental Skill Techniques

*P*hysical skills are the tools that most adults use to participate in leisure activities. Without a set of physical skills and a positive feeling about their ability to perform in activity settings, most people will relegate themselves to a lifetime of inactivity. Fundamental skills are those skills that form the foundation of human movement. Fundamental skills can be identified by name, such as walking, batting, bouncing, jumping, or pitching. (Most of the fundamental skills can be identified by a name that ends in the suffix -ing.)

Fundamental skills embrace a broad spectrum of skills, from simple to complex. Learning fundamental skills implies that proper technique is involved in skill performance. The more precise the skill, the more critical the need to establish proper technique. Correct technique should prevail over experimentation, even when a child is more comfortable with a known departure from accepted form. A child who is right-handed and steps forward with the right foot while throwing should be taught to shift to a left-footed (opposite side) step to assure the incorrect habit is eliminated. In most cases, changing an incorrectly learned motor pattern is more difficult than initially teaching a pattern correctly.

The learning of fundamental skills requires a more direct approach based on valid progressions and diligent practice. In contrast to learning movement concepts (Chapter 14), emphasis is placed on skill technique rather than creating a variety of movement variations. It is interesting to note that after the skill technique has been learned, a renewed emphasis is placed on practicing the skill under many varying conditions. The schema theory (p. 45) implies that a motor skill should be learned under a variety of conditions and should be practiced in as many situations as possible to assure practice variability. Developing different experiences upon which a response foundation can be built will allow a youngster to respond to the widest possible range of novel situations. Thus, motor skill learning moves through a complete cycle; from general to specific to general.

FUNDAMENTAL SKILLS

Fundamental skills are those utilitarian skills that children need for living and being. This group of skills is sometimes labeled *basic* or *functional*. The designation fundamental skills is used because the skills are necessary for children to function effectively in the environment. These skills set the foundation for adult activity and form the basis of competent movement. All individual, dual, and team sport activities use fundamental and specialized skills of one type or another. If children feel incompetent in performing movement patterns, they may be hesitant to participate in various leisure activities in adulthood. The following skills are grouped for ease of teaching and ease of comprehension by students. Although the skills are presented here individually, they are performed in a seemingly infinite number of combinations, depending on the sport or activity. Fundamental skills are divided into three categories, locomotor, nonlocomotor, and manipulative.

Locomotor Skills

Locomotor skills are used to move the body from one place to another or to project the body upward, as in jumping and hopping. They include walking, running, skipping, leaping, sliding, and galloping. They form the foundation of gross motor coordination and involve large muscle movement.

Nonlocomotor Skills

Nonlocomotor skills are performed without appreciable movement from place to place. These skills are not as well defined as locomotor skills. They include bending and stretching, pushing and pulling, twisting and turning, rocking, swaying, and balancing, among others.

Manipulative Skills

Manipulative skills come into play when children handle some kind of object. Most of these skills involve the hands and feet, but other parts of the body can also be used. The manipulation of objects leads to better hand-eye and foot-eye coordination, which are particularly important for tracking items in space. Manipulative skills form the foundation for many game skills. Propulsion (throwing, batting, kicking) and receipt (catching) of objects are important skills that can be taught by using beanbags and various balls. Rebounding or redirecting an object in flight (such as a volleyball) is another useful manipulative skill. Continuous control of an object, such as a wand or hoop, is also a manipulative activity.

LOCOMOTOR SKILLS

In the descriptions that follow, stress points emphasizing correct technique are listed for each of the locomotor skills. Instructional cues listed are short, concise phrases that teachers can use to remind students how to perform activities correctly. Suggested learning activities fall into two categories. The first, suggested movement patterns, consists of movement-oriented sequences that do not require rhythm. The second category, rhythmic activities, consists of sequences that employ rhythmic background. A drum or appropriate recorded music is effective for reinforcing and expanding rhythmic possibilities.

When teaching locomotor movements, the same methodology used for teaching divergent movement (educational movement) can be employed with modifications made to restrict the variety of responses. Instructors should understand the proper execution of the movement pattern, be able to describe the pattern correctly, teach the factors that affect performance, and provide necessary coaching hints to improve performance.

Walking

When walking, the feet move alternately, with one foot always in contact with the ground or floor. This stepping foot must be placed on the ground before the other foot is lifted. The weight of the body is transferred from the heel to the ball of the foot and then to the toes for push-off. The toes are pointed

Practicing a walking movement pattern

straight ahead and the arms swing freely from the shoulders in opposition to the feet. The body is erect, with the eyes focused straight ahead and slightly below eye level. The legs swing smoothly from the hips, with knees bent enough to clear the feet from the ground. Marching is a precise type of walk, accompanied by lifted knees and swinging arms.

Many different ways of walking should be experienced, but the underlying motive is to have children move gracefully and efficiently in normal walking. Different walking patterns offer an excellent opportunity to stress posture.

Stress Points

1. The toes should be pointed reasonably straight ahead.
2. The arm movement should feel natural. The arms should not swing too far.
3. The head should be kept up and the eyes focused ahead.
4. The stride length should not be excessive. Unnecessary up-and-down motion is to be avoided.

Instructional Cues

1. Head up, eyes forward.
2. Point toes straight ahead.
3. Nice, easy, relaxed arm swing.
4. Walk quietly.

5. Hold tummy in, chest up.
6. Push off from the floor with the toes.

Directives for Suggested Movement Patterns

1. Walk in different directions, changing direction on signal.
2. While walking, bring the knees up and slap with the hands on each step.
3. Walk on the heels, toes, and sides of feet.
4. Gradually lower the body while walking (going downstairs) and raise yourself again slowly (going upstairs).
5. Walk with a smooth, gliding step.
6. Walk with a wide base on the tiptoes, rocking from side to side.
7. Clap the hands alternately in front and behind. Clap the hands under the thighs while walking.
8. Walk slowly, and then increase the speed gradually. Reverse the process.
9. Take long strides. Take tiny steps.
10. On signal, change levels.
11. Walk quickly and quietly. Walk heavily and slowly.
12. Change direction on signal, but keep facing the same way.
13. Walk gaily, angrily, happily. Show other moods.
14. Hold the arms in different positions. Make an arm movement each time you step.
15. Walk in different patterns—circle, square, triangle, figure eight.
16. Walk through heavy mud. On ice or a slick floor. Walk on a rainy day. Walk in heavy snow.
17. Walk like a soldier on parade, a giant, a dwarf, a robot.
18. Duck under trees or railings while walking.
19. Point your toes in different directions—in, forward, and out.
20. Walk with high knees. Stiff knees. One stiff knee. A sore ankle.
21. Walk to a spot, turn in place while stepping, and take off in another direction.
22. Practice changing steps while walking.
23. Walk with a military goose step.
24. Walk and change direction after taking the magic number of steps. (One child picks a magic number.)
25. Tiptoe around the area and through puddles of water.

26. Walk as if you are on a balance beam. Walk across a tight rope.

27. Walk as if you are sneaking up on someone.

28. Walk with funny steps as if you were a clown.

29. Take heel-and-toe steps forward. Without turning around, walk heel-and-toe backwards.

Rhythmic Activities

When using recorded music, youngsters should learn to hear the use of phrases. Children can walk one way during a phrase and then change to another type of walk during the next phrase.

1. Walk forward one phrase (eight counts) and change direction. Continue to change at the end of each phrase.

2. Use high steps during one phrase and low steps during the next.

3. Walk forward for one phrase and sideward during the next. The side step can be a draw step, or it can be of the grapevine type. To do a grapevine step to the left, lead with the left foot, stepping directly to the side. Cross the right foot behind the left, and then in front of the left on the next step with that foot. The pattern is a step left, cross right (behind), step left, cross right (in front), and so on.

4. Find a partner. Face each other and join hands. Pull your partner by walking backward as your partner resists somewhat (eight counts). Reverse roles. Now stand behind your partner and place the palms of your hands on your partner's shoulders. Push your partner by walking forward as your partner resists (eight counts). Reverse roles.

5. Walk slowly, then gradually increase the tempo. Now begin fast and decrease. (Use a drum for this activity.)

6. Walk in various directions while clapping your hands alternately in front and behind. Try clapping the hands under a thigh at each step, or clap the hands above the head in time with the beat.

7. Walk forward four steps, and turn completely around in four steps. Repeat, but turn the other way the next time.

8. While walking, bring the knees up and slap with the hands on each step in time with the beat.

9. On any one phrase, take four fast steps (one count to each step) and two slow steps (two counts to each step).

10. Walk on the heels or toes or with a heavy tramp. Change every four or eight beats.

11. Walk with a smooth, gliding step, or walk silently to the beat.

12. Walk to the music, accenting the first beat of each measure. Now sway your body to the first beat of the measure. (Use a waltz with a strong beat.)

Running

Running (Figure 15.1), in contrast to walking, is moving rapidly so that for a brief moment, both feet are off the ground. Running varies from trotting (a slow run) to sprinting (a fast run for speed). The heels can take some weight in distance running and jogging. Running should be done with a slight body lean. The knees are flexed and lifted while the arms swing back and forth from the shoulders with a bend at the elbows. Additional pointers for sprinting are found in the track, field, and cross-country running unit (Chapter 30).

Running in these sequences should be done lightly on the balls of the feet. It should be a controlled run and not a dash for speed. Children can move throughout the area or run in place.

Stress Points

1. The balls of the feet should be used for sprinting.

2. The faster one desires to run, the higher the knees must be lifted. For fast running, the knees also must be bent more.

3. For distance running, less arm swing is used compared with sprinting for speed. Less body lean is used in distance running, with comfort being the key. The weight is absorbed on the heels and transferred to the toes.

Figure 15.1 Running

Instructional Cues

1. Run on the balls of the feet.
2. Head up, eyes forward.
3. Bend your knees.
4. Relax your upper body.
5. Breathe naturally.
6. Swing the arms forward and backward, not sideways.

Directives for Suggested Movement Patterns

1. Run lightly throughout the area, changing direction as you wish. Avoid bumping anyone. Run zigzag throughout the area.
2. Run and stop on signal. Change direction on signal.
3. Run, turn around with running steps on signal, and continue in a new direction. Alternate turning direction.
4. Pick a spot away from you, run to it, and return without touching or bumping anyone.
5. Run low, gradually increasing the height. Reverse.
6. Run in patterns. Run between and around objects.
7. Run with high knee action. Slap the knees while running.
8. Run with different steps—tiny, long, light, heavy, crisscross, wide, and others.
9. Run with your arms in different positions—circling, overhead, stiff at your sides.
10. Run free, concentrating on good knee lift.
11. Run at different speeds.
12. Touch the ground at times with either hand while running.
13. Run backward, sideward.
14. Run with exaggerated arm movements. Run with a high bounce.
15. Run forward ten steps and backward five steps. Repeat in another direction. (Other tasks can be imposed after the ten steps.)
16. Run forward, then make a jump turn in the air to face in a new direction. Repeat. Be sure to use both right and left turns. Make a full reverse (180-degree) turn.
17. Run the Tortoise and Hare sequence (p. 253) and Ponies in the Stable (p. 253). These are interesting patterns.
18. Run with knees turned outward. Run high on your toes.
19. Show how quietly you can run. Pretend that you are running through high weeds.
20. Run to a wall and back to place. Run and touch two walls.
21. Run lightly twice around your spot. Then explode (run quickly) to another spot.

Rhythmic Activities

Many of the suggested movements for walking are equally applicable to running patterns. Some additional suggestions for running include the following.

1. Walk during a phrase of music and then run for an equal length of time.
2. Run in different directions, changing direction on the sound of a heavy beat (or on a signal).
3. Lift the knees as high as possible while running, keeping time to the beat.
4. Do European Rhythmic Running (pp. 252–253) to supplement the running patterns described previously.

Jumping

Jumping requires taking off with both feet and landing on both feet (Figure 15.2). The arms help with an upswing, and the movement of the body combined with the force of the feet helps lift the weight. A jumper lands lightly on the balls of the feet with the knees bent. Jumping can be done in place or as a locomotor activity to cover ground.

Stress Points

1. The knees and ankles should be bent before takeoff to achieve more force from muscle extension.
2. The landing should be on the balls of the feet, with the knees bent to absorb the impact.
3. The arms should swing forward and upward at takeoff to add momentum to the jump and to gain distance and height.
4. The legs must be bent after takeoff or the feet will touch the ground prematurely.

Instructional Cues

1. Swing your arms forward as fast as possible.
2. Bend your knees.

Figure 15.2 Jumping

3. On your toes.
4. Land lightly with bent knees.
5. Jump up and try to touch the ceiling.

Directives for Suggested Movement Patterns

1. Jump up and down, trying for height. Try small and high jumps. Mix in patterns.
2. Choose a spot on the floor. Jump forward over the spot. Now backward and then sideward.
3. Jump with your body stiff and arms held at your sides. Jump like a pogo stick.
4. Practice jump turns in place—quarter, half, three quarter, and full.
5. Increase and decrease your jumping speed. Increase and decrease the height of the jump.
6. Land with the feet apart and then together. Alternate with one foot forward and one backward.
7. Jump and land quietly. How is this done?
8. Jump, crossing and uncrossing the feet.
9. See how far you can go in two, three, and four consecutive jumps. Run lightly back to place.
10. Pretend that you are a bouncing ball.

11. Clap the hands or slap the thighs while in the air. Try different arm positions.
12. Begin a jump with your hands contacting the floor.
13. Jump in various patterns on the floor.
14. Pretend that you are a basketball center jumping at a jump ball. Jump as high as you can. Jump from a crouched position.
15. Combine a jump for distance with one for height.
16. Jump and click the heels in the air. Can you do two clicks?
17. Jump like a kangaroo. A rabbit. A frog.
18. Combine contrasting jumps: forward and backward. Big and little. Right and left. Light and heavy.
19. Explore different ways a Jumping Jack can be performed.
20. Jump and clap hands in front. Behind you. Overhead.
21. Give three preliminary swings of arms and then jump forward.
22. Jump. While in the air, touch your heels. Touch both knees. Touch both toes in front.
23. One half of the class is on the floor in selected positions. The other half jumps over those on the floor. Exchange position.

Rhythmic Activities

Most of the activities suggested for hopping to rhythm (p. 339) are suitable for jumping. Other suggestions follow.

1. Begin jumping slowly to the drumbeat and then accelerate. Begin jumping fast and decelerate to the beat.
2. Toss a ball upward and jump in time to the bounce. (The ball must be a lively one.)
3. Do varieties of the Jumping Jack. First, move your feet without any arm movement. Now add an arm lift to shoulder height, then lift the arm to a full overhead position. Finally, add body turns and different foot patterns.
4. Take a forward stride position. Change the feet back and forth to the rhythm.

Hopping

Hopping requires propelling the body up and down on the same foot. The body lean, the other foot, and the arms serve to balance the movement.

Children should change to the other foot after a short period. Hopping can be done in place or as a locomotor movement.

Stress Points

1. To increase the height of the hop, the arms must be swung rapidly upward.
2. Hopping should be performed on the ball of the foot.
3. Small hops should be used to start, with a gradual increase in height and distance of the hop.

Instructional Cues

1. Hop with good forward motion.
2. Stay on your toes.
3. Use your arms for balance.
4. Reach for the sky when you hop.
5. Land lightly.

Directives for Suggested Movement Patterns

1. Hop on one foot and then on the other, using numbered sequences such as 1-1, 2-2, 3-3, 4-4, 5-5, 2-1, 1-2, 3-2, 2-3, and so on. The first figure of a series indicates the number of hops on the right foot, and the second specifies the number of hops on the left foot. Combinations should be maintained for 10 to 20 seconds.
2. Hop, increasing height. Reverse.
3. See how much space you can cover in two, three, or four hops.
4. Hop on one foot and do a heel-and-toe pattern with the other. Now change to the other foot. See whether a consistent pattern can be set up.
5. Make a hopping sequence by combining hopping in place with hopping ahead.
6. Hop forward, backward, sideward.
7. Hop in different patterns on the floor.
8. Hop while holding the free foot in different hand positions.
9. Hold the free foot forward or sideward while hopping. Explore other positions.
10. Hop with the body in different positions—with a forward lean, a backward lean, a sideward balance.
11. Hop lightly. Heavily.
12. While hopping, touch the floor with the hands—first one and then both.
13. Hop back and forth over a line, moving down the line as you hop.
14. Trace out numbers or letters by hopping.
15. Turn around while hopping in place.
16. Hop forward and then backward according to a magic number (selected by a student). Repeat in another direction. Now add sideward hopping instead of going backward.
17. Hop softly so that no one can hear you.

Rhythmic Activities

Combining rhythm with hopping patterns is more difficult than walking, running, or skipping to rhythm. The drumbeat is probably the best approach, although some recorded music designed especially for hopping works well. Since hopping on one foot may fatigue students rapidly, the suggested patterns combine other locomotor movements with hopping.

1. Walk four steps, hop three times, rest one count.
2. Walk four steps, then hop four times as you turn in place. Repeat in a new direction.
3. Hop eight times on one foot (eight counts) and then eight times on the other.
4. Hop forward and backward over a line to the rhythm, changing feet each phrase (eight counts).
5. Combine skipping, sliding, or galloping with hopping.
6. Practice the step-hop to music. (The child takes a step followed by a hop on the same foot. This is a two-count movement.)

Sliding

Sliding is done to the side. It is a one-count movement, with the leading foot stepping to the side and the other foot following quickly. Since the same foot always leads, the movement should be practiced in both directions. Sliding is done on the balls of the feet with the weight shifted from the leading foot to the trailing foot. Body bounce during the slide should be minimal.

Stress Points

1. Emphasize the sideways movement. Often, students move forward or backward, which is actually galloping.
2. Both directions should be used, so that each leg has a chance to lead as well as to trail.

Sliding in different directions

3. The slide is a smooth, graceful, and controlled movement.

Instructional Cues

1. Move sideways.
2. Do not bounce.
3. Slide your feet.

Directives for Suggested Movement Patterns

1. Lead in one direction with a definite number of slides, do a half turn in the air, and continue the slide leading with the other leg in the same direction. (A four-plus-four combination is excellent.)
2. Begin with short slides and increase length. Reverse.
3. Slide in a figure-eight pattern.
4. Change levels while sliding. Slide so that the hands can touch the floor with each slide.
5. Slide quietly and smoothly.
6. Pretend to be a basketball defensive player and slide with good basketball position.
7. Slide with a partner.
8. Try sliding individually in a circle.
9. Do three slides and a pause. Change the leading foot and repeat.
10. In circle formation, facing in, the whole class does ten slides one way followed by a pause. Repeat going in the other direction.

Rhythmic Activities

With appropriate music, many of the above movement patterns can be set to rhythm. The use of phrases to signal change of direction or to insert another challenge is recommended.

Galloping

Galloping is similar to sliding, but progress is in a forward direction. One foot leads and the other is brought rapidly up to it. There is more upward motion of the body than in sliding. A way to teach the gallop is to have children hold hands and slide in a circle, either to verbal cues or to a drumbeat. Gradually ask the class to face the direction in which the circle is moving. This takes them naturally from a slide into a gallop. Finally, drop hands and permit free movement in general space.

Stress Points

1. The movement should be smooth and graceful.
2. Each foot should have a chance to lead.

Instructional Cues

1. Keep one foot in front of the other.
2. Now lead with the other foot.
3. Make high gallops.

Directives for Suggested Movement Patterns

1. Do a series of eight gallops with the same foot leading, then change to the other foot. Change after four gallops. Change after two gallops. (Later in the rhythmic program, the gallop is used to teach the polka, so it is important for children to learn to change the leading foot.)
2. Change the size of the gallops.
3. Gallop in a circle with a small group.
4. Pretend to hold reins and use a riding crop.
5. Gallop backward.
6. Gallop like a spirited pony. Like a heavy draft horse.

Rhythmic Activities

Because galloping is essentially a rhythmic movement, many of the patterns described above should be done to rhythm. Using the music phrase to signal changing the lead foot is effective. Check previous sections on locomotor movements for other rhythmic movement suggestions.

Figure 15.3 Leaping

Leaping

Leaping is an elongated step designed to cover distance or move over a low obstacle. It is usually combined with running, since a series of leaps is difficult to maintain alone (Figure 15.3). The suggested movement patterns utilize combinations of running and leaping. Leaping should emphasize graceful flight through space.

Stress Points

1. Height and graceful flight are goals for which to strive.
2. Landing should be light and relaxed.

Instructional Cues

1. Push off and reach.
2. Up and over, land lightly.
3. Use your arms to help you gain height.

Directives for Suggested Movement Patterns

1. Leap in different directions.
2. See how high you can leap.
3. Leap and land softly.
4. Vary your arm position when you leap. Clap your hands as you leap.
5. Leap with the same arm and leg forward. Try the other way.
6. Show a leap in slow motion.
7. Leap and turn backward.
8. Leap over objects or across a specified space.
9. Practice by playing Leap the Brook (p. 563).
10. Leap and move into a balanced position.

Rhythmic Activities

Because the leap is essentially an explosive movement through space, it is difficult to apply rhythm to the movement. Children must gather themselves in preparation for the leap, which makes the movement nonrhythmic in nature.

Skipping

Skipping is a series of step-hops done with alternate feet. To teach children to skip, teach them to do a step and small hop on the same foot. A step and a hop are then performed on the other foot. If children are having trouble skipping, slow down the step-hop sequence and call out "Step, hop." Skipping is done on the balls of the feet with the arms swinging to shoulder height in opposition with the feet.

Another way to teach skipping is to have youngsters hold a large ball (9 inches or more) in front at waist height. A step is taken with one foot followed by raising the other knee to touch the ball. This stimulates the hop. Repeat with the other foot and the opposite knee. Later, the child pretends to hold a ball and continues the pattern.

Stress Points

1. Smoothness and rhythm are goals in skipping. Speed and distance are not.
2. The weight must be transferred from one foot to the other on the hop.
3. The arms swing in opposition to the legs.

Instructional Cues

1. Skip high.
2. Swing your arms.
3. Skip smoothly.
4. On your toes.

Directives for Suggested Movement Patterns

Many of the suggested movement patterns for walking and running can be applied to skipping, particularly those that refer to changing direction, stopping, making different floor patterns, and moving at different speeds and in different size increments. The following should be considered as well.

1. Skip with exaggerated arm action and lifted knees.
2. Skip backward.
3. Clap as you skip.
4. Skip with a side-to-side motion.
5. Skip twice on one side (double skip).

6. Skip as slowly as possible. Skip as fast as possible.

7. Skip so lightly that the movement cannot be heard by your partner.

8. Take as few skips as you can to get to a selected spot.

Rhythmic Activities

Almost all the combinations suggested for walking and running are useful for skipping movements, and many combinations of skipping, walking, and running can be devised. The piece "Pop Goes the Weasel" is excellent music for skipping. On the "Pop," some movement challenge can be specified.

NONLOCOMOTOR SKILLS

Nonlocomotor skills include bending, twisting, turning (in place), moving toward and away from the center of the body, raising and lowering the parts of the body, and other body movements done in place. Body control, flexibility, balance, and a variety of movements that lead to effective body management are important goals.

Bending

Bending is movement at a joint. Emphasis should be on learning where the body bends, why it needs to bend, and how many different bends are combined in various movements (Figure 15.4).

Stress Points

1. Bending as far as possible to increase flexibility and range of movement is a key goal.

2. The bending possibilities of many joints should be explored.

3. Time factors can be introduced in slow and rapid bending.

Instructional Cues

1. Bend as far as possible.

2. Bend one part while holding others steady.

Directives for Suggested Movement Patterns

1. Bend your body down and up.

2. Bend forward and backward, left and right, north and south.

3. Bend as many ways as possible.

4. Bend as many body parts as you can below your waist. Above your waist. Bend with your whole body.

5. Sit down and see whether you can bend differently from the ways you bent in a standing position.

6. Lie down and bend six body parts. Can you bend more than six? Now bend fewer.

Figure 15.4 Bending movements

7. Try to bend one body part quickly while you bend another part slowly.

8. Make a familiar shape by bending two body parts. Add two more parts.

9. Think of a toy that bends; see whether you can bend in a similar fashion.

10. Find a partner and bend together. Have your partner make big bends while you make tiny bends.

11. Show me how you would bend to look funny. To look happy or sad. Bend slowly or quickly.

12. Bend your largest part. Your smallest part.

13. Begin by bending one body part. As you return this part to its original position, bend another part.

14. Bend your fingers. Bend all ten of them.

15. Bend your knees in standing position. In sitting position. In lying position. What other joint must be bent in standing position?

Rocking and Swaying

Rocking occurs when the center of gravity is fluidly and gradually transferred from one body part to another. In rocking, the body is in a rounded position where it touches the floor. The term *swaying* implies a slower movement than rocking and is somewhat more controlled than rocking. In swaying, the base of support is unchanged.

Figure 15.5 Rocking variations

Stress Points

1. Rocking is done best on a body surface that has been rounded. Arm movements and movements of other body parts can facilitate the rocking motion.

2. Rocking should be done smoothly and in a steady rhythm.

3. Rocking can be started with small movements and increased in extent, or vice versa.

4. Rocking and swaying should be done to the full range of movement.

5. Swaying maintains a stable base.

Instructional Cues

1. Rock smoothly.

2. Rock in different directions. At varying speeds.

3. Rock higher (farther).

4. Sway until you almost lose your balance.

Directives for Suggested Movement Patterns

1. Rock in as many different ways as you can (Figure 15.5).

2. Show me how you can rock slowly. Quickly. Smoothly.

3. Sit cross-legged with arms outstretched to the sides, palms facing the floor. Rock from side to side until the hands touch the floor.

4. Lie on your back and rock. Now point your arms and legs toward the ceiling as you rock.

5. Lie on your tummy with arms stretched overhead and rock. Hold your ankles and make giant rocks.

6. Try to rock in a standing position.

7. Rock and twist at the same time.

8. Lie on your back with knees up and rock from side to side.

9. Show me two ways to have a partner rock you.

10. From a standing position, sway back and forth. Right and left. Experiment with different foot positions. Sway slowly and rapidly. What effect does rapid swaying have?

11. Repeat swaying movements from a kneeling position.

12. Start with a small rocking motion and make it progressively bigger.

13. Choose three (or more) ways of rocking and see if you can change smoothly from one to the next.

14. Rock like a cradle. A rocking horse.

15. Sway like a tree in a heavy wind.

Swinging

Swinging involves an action of body parts that resembles a swinging rope or the moving pendulum of a clock. The teacher can put a weight on the end of a string about a yard long and demonstrate swinging motions. Note that most swinging movements are confined to the arms and legs.

Swinging is a rhythmic, smooth motion that is fun to do to waltz music. It is also effective to combine this movement with a step at the beginning of each measure of music. When experimenting with swinging movements, some children carry the swings to such an extreme that they make a full circle. With a musical background, swinging and circular movements can form sequences. Music is important, because it gives children the feeling of the swing.

Stress Points

1. Swinging should be a smooth, rhythmic action.

2. The body parts involved in swinging should be relaxed and loose.

3. The extent of the swing movement should be the same on both sides of the swing.

4. Swinging movements should be as full as possible.

Instructional Cues

1. Loosen up; swing easy.

2. Swing fully; make a full movement.

3. Swing in rhythm.

Directives for Suggested Movement Patterns

1. Explore different ways to swing your arms and legs.

2. Work out swinging patterns with the arms. Combine them with a step pattern, forward and back.

3. Swing the arms back and forth, and go into full circles at times.

4. With a partner, work out different swinging movements (Figure 15.6). Add circles.

5. Develop swinging patterns and combinations. Form sequences with swinging and full-circle movements. (This activity is best done to waltz music with a slow or moderate tempo.)

6. Swing like a clock pendulum. A cow's tail.

Figure 15.6 Partner swinging

Turning

Turning is a movement involving rotation around the long axis of the body. The terms *turning* and *twisting* are sometimes used interchangeably to designate the movements of body parts. Actually, however, turning properly refers to movements of the body as a whole. Most turns are initiated by a twist. In the movement experiences suggested here, action involves movement of the entire body. Movements of body parts are discussed under twisting.

Stress Points

1. Maintaining balance and body control is important.
2. Turning should be tried in both directions, right and left.
3. Turns in standing position can be made by jumping, hopping, or shuffling with the feet.
4. Most turns are made in increments or multiples of quarter turns. Multiples should be practiced.
5. Turns should be practiced in body positions other than standing—seated, on the tummy or the back, and so on.

Instructional Cues

1. Keep your balance.
2. In jump turns, land in a relaxed way with the knees relaxed.
3. Be precise in your movement, whether it is a quarter, half, or full turn.

Directives for Suggested Movement Patterns

1. In standing position, turn your body to the left and right, clockwise and counterclockwise.
2. Turn to face north, east, south, and west. (The teacher should post directions on the wall and might even introduce some in-between directions, northwest, for example.)
3. Stand on one foot and turn around slowly. Now turn around quickly. Now turn with a series of small hops. Try to keep good balance.
4. Show me how you can cross your legs with a turn and sit down. Can you get up again in one movement?
5. Every time you hear the signal, see whether you can turn around once, moving slowly. Can you turn two, three, or four times slowly on signal?
6. Lie on your tummy on the floor and turn your body slowly in an arc. Turn over so that you are on your back. Turn back to your tummy again.
7. Find a friend and see how many different ways you can turn each other. Take turns.
8. Play Follow the Leader with your friend. You make a turn and your partner follows.
9. Begin with a short run, jump into the air, and turn to land facing in a new direction. Practice both right and left turns. Can you make a full reverse (180-degree) turn?
10. Lying on your back, turn and rest on your side. Return. Repeat on the other side.
11. Lying on your back, turn so that you are resting on your stomach. Return. Turn over the opposite way.
12. Find a partner and see how many ways you can rotate each other.
13. Walk in general space and turn completely around on signal.
14. With your hands outstretched to the sides, pretend you are a helicopter.

Twisting

Twisting is the rotation of a selected body part around its own long axis (Figure 15.7). The joints of the following body parts can be used for twisting: spine, neck, shoulders, hips, ankles, and wrists. Twisting differs from turning in that *twisting* involves movement around the body part itself, while *turning* focuses on the space in which the entire body turns. Remember that children are used to

Figure 15.7 Twisting movements

having some of these twisting movements called "turning."

Stress Points

1. Twisting should be extended as far as possible with good control.
2. The body parts on which the twist is based should be stabilized.
3. A twist in one direction should be countered by a reverse twist.
4. Some joints are better for twisting than others. (Explain why this is so.)

Instructional Cues

1. Twist far (fully).
2. Twist the other way.
3. Hold the supporting parts firm.

Directives for Suggested Movement Patterns

1. Glue your feet to the floor. Can you twist your body to the left and to the right? Can you twist your body slowly? Quickly? Can you bend and twist at the same time? How far can you turn your hands back and forth?
2. Twist two or more parts of your body at the same time.
3. Twist one body part in one direction and another in the opposite direction.
4. Try twisting the lower half of your body without twisting the upper half.
5. See what parts you can twist while sitting on the floor.
6. Try to twist one body part around another part. Is it possible to twist together even more parts?
7. Balance on one foot and twist your body. Can you bend and twist at the same time?
8. Show me some different shapes that you can make by twisting your body.
9. Try to twist like a spring. Like a cord on a telephone.
10. Try to move and twist at the same time.
11. With the weight on your feet, twist as far as you can in one direction. Now take the weight on your hands and move your feet.
12. Twist like a pretzel. Like a licorice stick.
13. Twist like you are hitting a home run with a baseball bat.
14. Twist like you are hitting a golf ball.

Stretching

Stretching is a movement that moves body parts away from the body center. Stretching sometimes involves moving a joint through the range of movement. It is important for children to understand that stretching the muscles involves some minor discomfort and controlled movement. The muscle-stretching process is necessary for maintaining and increasing flexibility.

Stress Points

1. Stretching should be extended to the full range of movement.
2. Stretching exploration should involve many body parts.
3. Stretching should be done in many positions.
4. Stretching can be combined with opposite movements, such as curling.
5. Stretching is done slowly and smoothly.
6. Hold full stretching position for 10 seconds.

Instructional Cues

1. Stretch as far as possible. Make it hurt a little.
2. Find other ways to stretch the body part (joint).
3. Keep it smooth. Do not jerk.

Directives for Suggested Movement Patterns

1. Stretch as many body parts as you can.
2. Stretch your arms, legs, and feet in as many different directions as possible.
3. Try to stretch a body part quickly. Slowly. Smoothly.
4. Bend a body part and tell me which muscle or muscles are being stretched.
5. See how many ways you can stretch while sitting on the floor.
6. Lie on the floor and see whether you can stretch two, three, four, or five body parts at once.
7. Try to stretch one body part quickly while you stretch another part slowly.
8. From a kneeling position, see whether you can stretch to a mark on the floor without losing your balance.
9. Stretch your right arm while you curl your left arm.
10. Find a friend and show me how many ways you can help each other stretch.

11. Try to stretch and become as tall as a giraffe. (Name other animals.)

12. Stretch and make a wide bridge. Find a partner to go under, around, and over your bridge.

13. Bend at the waist and touch your toes with your fingers. See whether you can keep your legs straight while you are stretching to touch the toes.

14. Combine stretching with curling. With bending.

15. Stretch the muscles in your chest, back, tummy, ankles, wrists, and fingers.

16. Make a shape with your body. Now stretch the shape so that it is larger.

17. As you move at a low level, curl and stretch your fingers.

18. Find a position in which you can stretch one side of the body.

19. Find a position in which you can stretch both legs far apart in the air. Now make the legs as narrow as possible.

20. Stretch like a rubber band. When I say "Snap!" move the part quickly back to original position.

Pushing

Pushing is a controlled and forceful action performed against an object to move the body away from the object or to move the object in a desired direction by applying force to it (Figure 15.8).

Stress Points

1. A forward stride position should be used to broaden the base of support.

2. The body's center of gravity should be lowered.

3. The line of force is directed toward the object.

Figure 15.8 Pushing

4. The back is kept in reasonable alignment, and the body forces gathered for a forceful push. Do not bend the waist.

5. The push should be controlled and steady.

Instructional Cues

1. Broaden your foot base.

2. Use all your body forces.

3. Push steadily and evenly.

4. Lower yourself for a better push.

Directives for Suggested Movement Patterns

1. Stand near a wall and push it from an erect position, then push with the knees bent and one foot behind the other. In which position can you push with more force?

2. Push an imaginary object that is very light. Now imagine that you are pushing a heavy object.

3. Try to push a partner who is sitting on a jumping box, then try to push a partner who is sitting on a scooter. What changes must you make in your body position?

4. Push an object with your feet without using your arms or hands.

5. Sit down and push a heavy object with your feet. Can you put your back against the object and push it?

6. See how many different ways you can find to push the object.

7. Find a friend and try to push each other over a line in turn.

8. Sit back to back with your partner and see whether you can push each other backward in turn.

9. See if it is possible to lie on the floor and push.

10. Lie on the floor and push your body forward, backward, and sideward.

11. Lie on the floor and push yourself with one foot and one arm.

12. Put a beanbag on the floor and push it with your elbow, shoulder, nose, or other body part.

13. Move in crab position and push a beanbag.

14. Show me how you can push a ball to a friend.

Pulling

Pulling is a controlled and forceful action that moves an object closer to the body or the body closer to an object. If the body moves and an object is being pulled, pulling causes the object to follow the body.

Stress Points

1. For forceful pulling, the base of support must be broadened and the body's center of gravity must be lowered.
2. The vertical axis of the body should provide a line of force away from the object.
3. Pulling should be a controlled movement with a minimum of jerking and tugging.
4. The hand grips must be comfortable if pulling is to be efficient. Gloves or other padding can help.
5. Pulling movements can be isolated in the body, with one part of the body pulling against the other.

Instructional Cues

1. Take a good grip.
2. Get your body in line with the pull. Lower yourself.
3. Widen your base of support.
4. Gather your body forces and pull steadily.

Directives for Suggested Movement Patterns

1. Reach for the ceiling and pull an imaginary object toward you quickly. Slowly and smoothly.
2. Use an individual tug-of-war rope and practice pulling against a partner. Do this with your hands and arms at different levels.
3. From a kneeling position, pull an object.
4. Try to pull with your feet while you sit on the floor.
5. Pretend to pull a heavy object while you are lying on the floor.
6. Clasp your hands together and pull as hard as you can.
7. Try pulling an object while you stand on one foot.
8. Hold hands with a partner, and pull slowly as hard as you can.
9. Have your partner sit down, and then see how slowly you can pull each other. Take turns.
10. With your partner sitting on the floor, see whether you can pull each other to your feet. Take turns.
11. Pull with different body parts.
12. Pull your partner by the feet as your partner sits on a rug square.
13. Reach for the stars with both hands and pull one back to you.
14. Balance on one foot. Try to pull something. What happens?

Pushing and Pulling Combinations

Combinations of pulling and pushing movements should be arranged in sequence. Musical phrases can signal changes from one movement to the other. Balance-beam benches are excellent for practicing pulling and pushing techniques. Individual tug-of-war ropes provide effective pulling experiences. Selected partner resistance exercises (pp. 297–299) are also useful pulling and pushing experiences.

Fleeing, Chasing, and Tagging

Because many physical education games involve fleeing, chasing, and tagging, it becomes an obligation that these skills be taught. Speed and reaction are essential for dodging by the person being chased and the response of the chaser to the movements of the target child.

Stress Points

1. The child fleeing should be in a moderate crouch position with the feet wider than usual. This position enables moving laterally in either direction quickly.
2. The fleeing child should become adept at faking, which means making a preliminary movement in one direction before determining the final path to take.
3. All runners should move on the balls of their feet.
4. The chaser should maneuver the fleeing youngster into a confined area to facilitate tagging.
5. Eyes should be focused on the center of the dodger's body to negate the effectiveness of the fake.
6. The tag should be made between the knees and shoulders in a gentle but firm manner.

Instructional Cues (Chaser)

1. Move on the balls of the feet and maintain a slightly crouched position when approaching the dodger.
2. Focus on the waistline of the dodger.
3. Tag gently but firmly.

Directives for Suggested Movement Patterns

1. Run in general space with the stipulation to run toward other classmates and dodge at the last moment. Avoid contact. (To vary the activity, have students change direction on signal.)

2. In general space, run and stop on signal.

3. In partners, have one person run and the other shadow (follow closely). The runner should change direction often. Change roles.

4. Move into squads, with the leader 10 yards away from and facing the rest of the squad column. All members of the squad take turns running and dodging around a passive captain. Replace the squad captain regularly.

5. Partners mark a small area (12 by 12 feet) with cones. Chase and dodge within this area. Try with two chasers and one dodger.

MANIPULATIVE SKILLS

Manipulative skills are basic to a number of specialized sport skills—catching, throwing, and kicking, among others. These are complex motor patterns, and stages of development have been identified, from initial stages through mature patterns of performance. An example of not learning manipulative skills occurs with throwing where some youngsters never develop mature throwing patterns. Several factors contribute to this situation, such as little emphasis being placed on correct form or children seldom being encouraged to learn properly. If the optimal skill-learning years occur during youth, teaching and encouraging the correct performance of specialized sport skills is necessary for proper development.

Most complex skills should be practiced at near-normal speed. Whereas locomotor skills can be dramatically slowed down to promote learning, doing so with throwing, striking, or kicking will destroy the rhythm of the skills. Analysis of the following skills illustrates developmental stages, which is more important to the learning process than the chronological age of children. Suggested activity challenges for developing throwing, catching, and kicking skills are found in Chapter 17.

Throwing

In throwing, an object is thrust into space and is accelerated through the movement of the arm and the total coordination of the body. Teachers should be aware that young children may need to go through two preliminary tossing stages before entering the stages of throwing.

The first toss is a two-handed underhand throw that involves little foot movement. A large ball, such as a beach ball, is best for teaching this type of throw, which begins with the ball held in front of the body at waist level. The toss is completed by using only the arms, and youngsters often have difficulty maintaining balance when encouraged to throw the ball for any distance.

The second toss is the one-handed underhand throw. In this toss, which resembles pitching a softball, the child begins to develop body torque and is able to shift the weight from the rear to the front foot. This toss requires a smaller object. Beanbags, fleece balls, and small sponge balls work well.

The following skill analysis considers overhand throwing only. Teachers should be concerned that children strive for proper form while throwing, rather than for distance or accuracy. A point to remember is that velocity, not accuracy, is the primary goal for developing patterns characterized by a full range of motion and speed. Throwing for accuracy can be introduced gradually as the pattern matures.

Stage One

Stage one of throwing generally can be observed between the ages of 2 and 3 years. This stage is basically restricted to arm movement from the rear toward the front of the body. The feet remain stationary and positioned at shoulder width, with little or no trunk rotation occurring (Figure 15.9). Most of the movement force originates from flexing the hip, moving the shoulder forward, and extending the elbow.

Stage Two

Stage two of throwing develops between the ages of 3 and 5 years. Some rotary motion is developed as the child attempts to increase the amount of force. This stage is characterized by a lateral fling of the arm, with rotation occurring in the trunk (Figure 15.10). Often, the child takes a step in the direction of the throw, although many children still keep their feet stationary. This throwing style sometimes looks like a discus throw rather than a baseball throw.

Stage Three

Typically, stage three is found among children age 5 to 6 years. The starting position is similar to that of stages one and two in that the body is facing the

Figure 15.9 Throwing form, stage one

Figure 15.10 Throwing form, stage two

target area, the feet are parallel, and the child is erect. In this stage, however, the child steps toward the target with the foot on the same side of the body as the throwing arm. This allows for rotation of the body and shifting of the body weight forward as the step occurs. The arm action is nearer to the overhand style of throwing than is the fling of stage two, and there is also an increase in hip flexion. The throwing pattern of many students never matures beyond this stage.

Stage Four

Stage four is a mature form of throwing and allows the child to apply more force to the object being accelerated. The thrower uses the rule of opposition in this stage, taking a step in the direction of the throw with the leg opposite the throwing arm. This develops maximum body torque. The child addresses the target with the nonthrowing side of the body and strides toward the target to shift body weight. Beginning with the weight on the back leg, the movement sequence is as follows: (a) step toward the target, (b) rotate the upper body, and (c) throw with the arm (Figure 15.11). The cue phrase used is, "Step, turn, and throw." The elbow should lead the way in the arm movement, fol-

Figure 15.11 Throwing pattern, stage four

lowed by forearm extension, and finally a snapping of the wrist. This pattern must be practiced many times to develop total body coordination. Through a combination of sound instruction and practice, the majority of youngsters should be able to develop a mature pattern of throwing by age 8 or 9 years.

Stress Points

1. Stand with the nonthrowing side of the body facing the target. The throwing arm side of the body should be away from the target.

2. Step toward the target with the foot opposite the throwing hand.

3. Rotate the hips as the throwing arm moves forward.

4. Bend the arm at the elbow. The elbow should lead the forward movement of the arm.

5. Body weight remains on the rear foot (away from the target) during early phases of the throw. Just prior to the forward motion of the arm, the weight is shifted from the rear foot to the forward foot (nearer the target).

Teaching Hints

1. Offer a variety of projectiles during throwing practice so that youngsters understand how varying the weight and diameter can regulate throwing distance and speed.

2. When youngsters are learning to throw, they should throw for distance and velocity. Throwing for accuracy will discourage the development of a mature throwing form. Youngsters must be encouraged to "throw as hard as possible." Stress distance and velocity before introducing accuracy.

3. It is ineffective to work on throwing and catching at the same time. If learning to throw is the objective, youngsters will be throwing inaccurately and with velocity. This would make it difficult for a partner to catch the throw. Throwing should be practiced against a wall (velocity) or on a large field (distance).

4. Carpet squares or circles drawn on the floor can be used to teach youngsters proper foot movement (stepping forward).

5. Beanbags and yarnballs are excellent for developing throwing velocity since they do not rebound throughout the area.

Catching

Catching involves using the hands to stop and control a moving object. Catching is more difficult for children to learn than throwing, because the object must be tracked and the body moved into the path of the object at the same time. Another element that makes catching more difficult to master is fear of being hurt by the oncoming object. When teaching the early stages of catching, instructors must be careful to use objects that cannot hurt the receiver. Balloons, fleece balls, and beach balls move slowly, make tracking easier, and do not hurt if they hit a child in the face.

Stage One

In stage one of catching, the child holds the arms in front of the body, with elbows extended and palms up, until the ball makes contact. The child then bends the arms at the elbows (Figure 15.12). The catch is actually more of a trapping movement, since the arms press the ball against the chest. Children often turn their head away or close their eyes because of the fear response. They should be encouraged to watch the object rather than the person who is throwing the object.

Stage Two

In stage two, the child repeats much of the same behavior as in stage one. Rather than waiting for the ball to contact the arms, however, the child makes an anticipatory movement and cradles the ball somewhat.

Stage Three

As the child's catching pattern matures, the catch is prepared for by lifting the arms and bending

Figure 15.12 Catching form, stage one

them slightly. The chest is used as a backstop for the ball. During this stage, the child attempts to make contact with the hands first and then to guide the object to the chest (Figure 15.13).

Stage Four

The fourth and final stage of catching, which should occur at approximately 9 years, is characterized by catching with the hands. The child can be encouraged to catch with the hands by decreasing the size of the ball to be caught. The child, continuing to improve, learns to give with the arms while catching (see p. 51). The legs bend, and the feet are moved in anticipation of the catch.

Stress Points

1. Maintain visual contact with the projectile.
2. Reach for the projectile and absorb its force by bringing the hands into the body. This "giving" makes catching easier by reducing the chance for the object to rebound out of the hands.

Figure 15.13 Catching a large object, stage three

3. The feet should be placed in a stride position rather than a straddle position. A fast-moving object will cause a loss of balance if feet are in the straddle position.
4. Place the body in line with the object rather than reaching to the side of the body to make the catch.

Teaching Hints

1. Remove the fear factor by using projectiles that will not hurt the youngster. It is a normal reaction to dodge an object when one feels it could cause harm. The use of foam balls, yarnballs, beach balls, and balloons will facilitate learning to "keep your eye on the ball."
2. The size of the projectile should get smaller as youngsters improve their catching skills. Larger objects move more slowly and are easier than smaller projectiles to track visually.
3. Prepare youngsters for the catch by asking them to focus on the ball while it is in the thrower's hand. Use a verbal cue such as "Look (focus), ready (for the throw), catch (toss the ball)."
4. Balls and background colors should strongly contrast to facilitate visual perception.
5. If the trajectory of the projectile is raised, it will offer the youngster more opportunity for successful tracking. Beach balls will move slowly throughout a high trajectory, giving children time to focus and move into the path of the oncoming object.
6. Bounce objects off the floor so that youngsters learn to judge the rebound angle of a projectile.

Kicking

Kicking is a striking action executed with the feet. There are different types of kicking. Punting (in which the ball is dropped from the hands and kicked before it touches the ground), and placekicking (kicking the ball in a stationary position on the ground) are two. A third type is soccer kicking, which is probably the most difficult of all kicking skills because the ball is moving before the kick is executed.

Stage One

In stage one, the body is stationary and the kicking foot is flexed as the child prepares for the kick. The kicking motion is carried out with a straight leg and with little or no flexing at the knee. Minimal movement of the arms and trunk occurs as the child concentrates on the ball.

Stage Two

In the second stage of kicking, the child lifts the kicking foot back by flexing at the knee. Usually, the child displays opposition of the limbs. When the kicking leg goes forward, the opposite arm moves forward. In stage two, the child's kicking leg moves farther forward as a follow-through motion than in stage one.

Stage Three

The child runs or walks toward the object to be kicked. There is an increase in the distance that the leg is moved, coupled with a movement of the upper body to counterbalance the leg movement.

Stage Four

The mature stage of kicking involves a preparatory extension of the hip to increase the range of motion. The child runs to the ball and prepares to kick it, taking a small leap to get the kicking foot in position. As the kicking foot is carried forward, the trunk leans backward, and the child takes a small step forward on the support foot to regain balance (Figure 15.14).

Stress Points

1. Youngsters need to step forward with the non-kicking leg. Stand behind and slightly to the side of the ball. Eyes should be kept on the ball (head down) throughout the kick.

2. Practice kicking with both feet.

3. Use objects that will not hurt youngsters. For example, regulation soccer balls hurt young children's feet because they are heavy and hard-covered. Foam balls and beach balls are excellent projectiles that can be used for kicking practice.

Figure 15.14   Kicking a soccer ball, stage four

4. Encourage kickers to move their leg backward in preparation for the kick. Beginners often fail to move the leg backward, making it difficult for them to generate kicking force.

5. Arms should move in opposition to the legs during the kick.

6. After speed and velocity of the kick have been developed, children should begin to focus on altering the force of the kick. Many youngsters learn to kick only with maximum velocity; activities like soccer demand both soft "touch" kicks and kicks of maximum velocity.

Teaching Hints

1. To develop mature kicking form, focus on velocity and distance rather than accuracy. If youngsters are asked to kick accurately, they will poke at the ball rather than develop a full kicking style.

2. Kicking is similar to throwing in that all youngsters should have a ball to kick. Beach balls (for primary grades) and foam balls are excellent as they do not travel a long distance and the youngster can kick and retrieve the ball quickly.

3. Stationary balls are easier to kick than moving balls. This progression should be remembered when teaching beginners to kick.

4. Teach various types of kicks: the toe kick, instep kick, and the side-of-the-foot kick.

Striking

Striking occurs when youngsters hit an object with an implement. The most common forms of striking are hitting a softball with a bat, using a racket for striking in tennis and racquetball, and striking a ball with the hand as in volleyball.

Stage One

In this stage, the feet are stationary and the trunk faces the direction of the tossed ball (or ball on a tee). The elbows are fully flexed and the force is generated by extending the flexed joints in a downward plane. Little body force is generated because there is no trunk rotation and the motion developed is back to front. The total body does not play a role in generation of forces; rather, it comes from the arms and wrists.

Stage Two

In stage two, the upper body begins to generate force. The trunk is turned to the side as the youngster anticipates the ball. The weight shifts from the rear foot to the forward foot prior to contacting the ball. The trunk and hips are rotated into the ball as the swing takes place. The elbows are less flexed and force is generated by extending the flexed joints. Trunk rotation and forward movement are in an oblique plane.

Stage Three

In mature striking skills, the youngster stands sideways to the path of the oncoming object. The weight is shifted to the rear foot and the hips are rotated, followed by a shifting of the weight toward the ball as it approaches the hitter. Striking occurs with the arms extended in a long and horizontal arc. The swing ends with weight on the forward foot. Mature striking is characterized by a swing through the full range of motion and a sequential transfer of weight from the rear to the front plane of the body.

Stress Points

1. Track the ball as soon as possible until it is hit. Even though it is impossible to see the racket hit the ball, it is an excellent teaching hint as it encourages the youngster to track the object as long as possible.

2. Grip the bat with the hands together. If batting right handed, the left hand should be on the bottom (near the small end of the bat).

3. Keep the elbows away from the body. Emphasis should be placed on making a large swing with the elbows extended as the ball is hit.

4. Swing the bat in a horizontal plane. Beginners have a tendency to strike downward in a chopping motion.

Teaching Hints

1. Striking should be done with maximum force and bat velocity when the focus of instruction is on developing a mature striking form.

2. Practice hitting stationary objects before progressing to moving objects. Batting tees and balls suspended on a string are useful for beginners.

3. Use slow-moving objects such as balloons and beach balls in the early stages of striking practice. This helps the child track the moving projectile.

4. As skill in striking increases, the size of the projectile and bat (or racket) can be decreased.

5. Assure that there is good contrast between the ball and the background to enhance visual perception.

6. Use footprints to help children learn to stride (step) into the ball.

REFERENCES AND SUGGESTED READINGS

Gallahue, D. L. (1982). *Understanding motor development in children.* New York: Wiley.

Wickstrom, R. L. (1983). *Fundamental movement patterns.* Philadelphia: Lea & Febiger.

16

Rhythmic Movement

PURPOSE OF ACTIVITIES IN THIS CHAPTER

Activities in this chapter are selected for the purpose of developing rhythmic movements skills. The activities are listed in progression of easy to more complex and by developmental level. The development of social skills and a positive self-concept occur when rhythmic activities are taught in a sensitive and educational manner.

Rhythm is the basis of music and dance. Rhythm in dance is simply expressive movement made with or without music. All body movements tend to be rhythmic—the beating of the heart, swinging a tennis racket, wielding a hammer, throwing a ball. Most movements that take place in physical education class contain elements of rhythm. This chapter deals with movements performed in time to musical accompaniment and movements based on a specific theme as in creative rhythm activities.

Movement to rhythm should begin early in the child's school career and continue throughout. Rhythmic activities are particularly appropriate for younger children. A sizable portion of the developmental level I program should be devoted to such activities. One of the problems in incorporating rhythmic activities in the program is the vast amount of material available, which requires judicious selection to present a broad, progressive program. Another problem is that many teachers are hesitant about the subject area. When teachers prepare properly, they become more comfortable with rhythms and find that these activities are a favorite of children.

Early experiences should center on functional and creative movement forms. The program must go beyond being a collection of movement songs and folk dances, and it must be more than the teacher playing records for the children. Effective planning is necessary to gear the program to meet children's rhythmic needs.

Locomotor skills (pp. 334–342) are inherently rhythmic in execution, and the addition of rhythm can enhance development of these skills. An important component of children's dance is, therefore, fundamental rhythms. Instruction should begin with and capitalize on locomotor skills that the children already possess—walking, running, hopping, and jumping.

Rhythmic activities also provide a vehicle for expressive movement. These activities offer opportunity for broad participation and personal satisfaction for all, since children personalize their responses within the framework of the idea. The youngsters should have a chance to create unique rhythmic responses within action songs and dances.

IMPLEMENTING THE RHYTHMIC MOVEMENT PROGRAM

Rhythmic activities should be scheduled in the same manner as other phases of the program and not regarded as fillers, rainy-day programs, or recreational outlets. The rhythmic program should be balanced and include activities from each of the categories of rhythmic movement. Table 16.1 shows recommended types of rhythmic activities for each developmental level.

Skill Progressions

Another factor in program construction is the progression of basic and specific dance steps. Dances employing the following skills and steps appear in each of the respective developmental level programs.

Developmental Level I: Fundamental locomotor movements. (Skipping and sliding are taught and practiced, but students are not expected to master them.) Combinations of two or more fundamental

Table 16.1 Types of rhythmic activity

Activity	Developmental Level		
	I	II	III
Fundamental rhythms	X	X	S
Creative rhythms	X		
Singing movement songs	X		
Folk dances	X	X	X
Mixers		X	X
Aerobic dancing		X	X
Square dancing			X
Rope jumping to music	S	X	X
Musical games	S	S	S
Rhythmic gymnastics		S	S

Note: X means that the activity is an integral part of the program. S means that the activity is given only minor emphasis.

movements are presented, for example, the bleking step.

Developmental Level II: Fundamental locomotor movements, more combinations of locomotor skills, the step-hop, and the grand right and left. Marching, basic tinikling steps, and introductory square dancing steps are taught as skill improves.

Developmental Level III: The grapevine step, schottische, polka, intermediate tinikling steps, two-step, advanced tinikling step, square dancing, and an understanding of all steps introduced at earlier levels.

Understanding Rhythmic Accompaniment

Music has essential characteristics that children should recognize, understand, and appreciate. These characteristics are also present to varying degrees in other purely percussive accompaniment.

Tempo is the speed of the music. It can be constant or show a gradual increase (acceleration) or decrease (deceleration).

Beat is the underlying rhythm of the music. Some musicians refer to the beat as the pulse of the music. The beat can be even or uneven. Music with a pronounced beat is easier to follow.

Meter refers to the manner in which the beats are put together to form a measure of music. Common meters used in rhythmics are 2/4, 3/4, 4/4, and 6/8.

Certain notes or beats in a rhythmic pattern receive more force than others, and this defines *accent*. Usually, accent is applied to the first beat of a measure and generally is expressed by a more forceful movement in a sequence of movements.

The *intensity* of music can be loud, soft, light, or heavy. *Mood* is related to intensity but carries the concept deeper into human feelings. Music can interpret many moods—happiness, sadness, gaiety, fear, stateliness, and so on.

A *phrase* is a natural grouping of measures. In most cases, a phrase consists of eight underlying beats. Phrases of music are put together into rhythmic *patterns*. Children should learn to recognize when the pattern repeats or changes.

Sources of Rhythmic Accompaniment

Essential to any rhythmic program is accompaniment that encourages desired motor patterns and expressive movement. If children are to move to a rhythm, it must be stimulating, appropriate for the expected responses, and appealing to the learners. Skillful use of a drum or tambourine adds much to rhythmic experiences. The teacher can interject drumbeats into many movement patterns. A major use of the drumbeat is to guide the movement from one pattern to another by signaling tiny increments of change with light beats that control the flow. Some practice is necessary to learn how to beat a drum efficiently. The motion in striking is essentially a wrist action, not an arm movement. An instructor who has problems keeping time can cue on a competent performer to find the correct rhythm.

The tape recorder offers possibilities for rhythmic accompaniment not found in other sources. Voice directions can be superimposed over music; this is useful for establishing an exercise sequence. Tape recorders are especially valuable in providing background for creative rhythms for which changes of music are desirable. When using a tape recorder for square dancing or folk dancing, select a recorder that has a counter. The tape should be labeled with the counter number where each song can be found; otherwise, valuable class time is wasted looking for the starting point for each piece on the tape. A drawback is that most tape recorders cannot vary tempo.

A record player can be started and stopped efficiently and makes locating the beginning of each piece easy. An appropriate record player for physical education should meet the following criteria:

1. provides enough volume to be heard throughout the gymnasium

2. possesses variable speeds: 33, 45, and 78 rpm

3. has a speed control, enabling the record to be played either faster or slower than originally recorded without distortion, a major help when teaching a dance

Each school and teacher should build a collection of records. Record sets created especially for physical education movement patterns and dance are available from a number of sources. Physical education records should be stored in the physical education facility rather than in the school library. Storage should be so arranged that each record has its assigned place and is readily available. Keeping extra copies of the more frequently used records in reserve is an excellent practice, especially in centralized equipment distribution centers for larger school systems. Student operators of the record player need proper instruction so that record damage is minimized.

FUNDAMENTAL RHYTHMS

Fundamental rhythms should be an outgrowth of the movement activities with which the children are already familiar, such as walking (stepping), running, jumping, and hopping. To these acquired skills, rhythm is added. Fundamental rhythms are emphasized in the primary grades and are extended to the intermediate level on a smaller scale. The general purpose of a fundamental rhythms program is to provide a variety of fundamental movement experiences, so the child can learn to move effectively and efficiently and develop a sense of rhythm. Although the creative aspect of fundamental rhythms is important, even more important is first establishing a vocabulary of movement competencies for each child. The skills in a fundamental rhythm program are important as the background for creative dance and also as the basis for the more precise dance skills of folk, social, and square dance, which follow later in school programs. (Fundamental skills are described, together with teaching hints and stress points, in Chapter 15.)

Locomotor Movements

Even rhythm locomotor movements are walking, running, hopping, leaping, jumping, draw steps, and such variations as marching, trotting, stamping, and twirling. Uneven movements are skipping, galloping, and sliding.

Nonlocomotor Movements

Simple nonlocomotor movements are bending, swaying, twisting, swinging, raising, lowering, circling, and rotating various parts of the body. Mimetic movements include striking, lifting, throwing, pushing, pulling, hammering, and other common tasks.

Rhythmic locomotor movements

Manipulative Movements

Manipulative movements involve object handling, such as ball skills. Other objects such as hoops, wands, and even chairs can be used.

Instructional Procedures

1. Success depends on the teacher's initiating and guiding simple patterns. Of prime importance is the class atmosphere, which should be one of enjoyment. Furthermore, the accompaniment must be suitable for the movements to be experienced.

2. The element of creativity should not be stifled in a program of fundamental rhythms. The instruction can be directed toward a specific movement (e.g., walking), and a reasonable range of acceptable performance, which permits individual creativity, can be established.

3. Teachers who feel awkward or insecure about developing rhythmic programs with a strong creative approach will find the fundamental rhythms a good starting point. Combining rhythmic movement with movements students enjoy can be the beginning of a refreshing and stimulating experience for both teacher and child.

4. The approach to fundamental rhythms should be a mixture of direct and indirect teaching. Many of the movements do have standard or preferred techniques. For example, there is a correct way to walk, and children should recognize and learn such fundamentals. Within the framework of good technique, however, a variety of movement experiences can be elicited.

Suggestions for Teaching Fundamental Rhythmic Movements

Children enjoy change and the challenge of reacting to change. They can be encouraged to change the movement pattern or some aspect of it (direction, level, body leads, and so on) at the end of a musical phrase. Changes can be signaled by variations in the drumbeat. A heavy, accented beat, for example, can signal a change in direction or type of movement. Stops and starts, changes to different rhythms, and other innovations are within the scope of this process. The intensity of the drumbeat can call for light or heavy movements or for different levels of movement: high, middle, or low. As an example of how to do this, picture a class of children walking heavily in general space to a heavy, even beat. The teacher sounds one extra-heavy beat, whereupon students change direction abruptly, now moving very lightly on the toes to a light, even beat. This sequence finishes with another heavy beat, which signals children again to change direction and their movement as indicated by the next sequence of beats. The opportunities for movement combinations are many.

The use of different parts of the body, singly and in various combinations, is important in establishing movement variety. Different positions of the arms and legs can vary the ways of moving. Children can perform high on the toes, with toes in or out; on the heels, with stiff knees; kicking high in front or to the rear, with knees brought up high; in a crouched or any number of different positions. The arms can swing at the sides or be held stiff, be held out in front, or held overhead. The arms can move in circles or in different patterns. The body can bend forward, backward, or sideward, and it can twist and turn. By combining different arm, leg, and body positions, the children can assume many interesting position variations. Changes in body level and patterns of movement for outlining circles, squares, triangles, and other shapes also add interest. Ideas and suggestions for using fundamental skills with rhythm are found in Chapter 15.

CREATIVE RHYTHMS

Creativity should be part of all dance and rhythmic activities, with the scope of the activity determining the degree of freedom. Creative rhythms, however, provide a special program area in which creativity is the goal and functional movement is secondary. The emphasis is on the process and not the movement outcomes.

Creativity manifests itself in the opportunity for each child to respond expressively within the scope of the movement idea, which can range from total freedom to stated limits. The child's judgment should be respected, and the teacher should look for original interpretations. Stimulation should be positive in nature, guiding the movement patterns by suggestions, questions, encouragement, and challenges that help children structure their ideas and add variety. Careful guidance is necessary to fan the spark of self-direction, since freedom in itself does not automatically develop creativity.

Instructional Procedures

1. Appropriate music or rhythmic background is important; otherwise, movement can become stilted. An atmosphere of creative freedom must be established. The class should be comfortable and relaxed.

2. In analyzing the setting, the teacher should ask, What is the basic idea? What expressive movements can be expected? What are the guidelines or boundaries of movement? What space are the children to use?

3. Listening is an important element, because children must get the mood or sense of the rhythmic background. Some questions that can be posed to children are, "What does the music make us think of?" and "What does the music tell us to do?" If the movement or interpretation is preselected, little time need be wasted in getting under way. Provide enough music so children can grasp the impact. Have them clap the beat if necessary, and then move into action.

4. Use action-directing statements such as, "Let's pretend we are . . . ," "Let's try being like . . . ," "Try to feel like a . . . ," and "Make believe you are. . . ."

5. In some lessons, the initial focus may be on the selection of appropriate rhythmic background. This is the case when children formulate a creative rhythm of the dramatic type and then seek suitable music for their dance.

6. Children must be given time to develop and try their ideas. This is an open-ended process that has a variety of solutions. Coaching and guidance are important aspects at this stage. Application of time, space, force, flow, and body factors is essential. Teachers should encourage large, free movement of all body parts. Use the entire area and fill in the empty places in general space. Allow time for exploration.

Suggestions for Teaching Creative Rhythms

The following suggestions can be used for development of creative rhythmic activities.

Understanding and Relating to Rhythm

Teachers can bring in the idea of meter (2/4, 3/4, 4/4, and 6/8 time) and have children move in time to the meter. Other movements can illustrate even and uneven time, accents, phrasing, and other elements of rhythmic structure.

Fundamental Motor Rhythms

Creativity can be developed through various locomotor movements. The use of the drum is recommended. A skillful teacher can vary the tempo, signal movement changes, and provide a variety of interesting activities. Some suggested ideas are:

1. On a single loud beat, each student changes direction abruptly, turns around, or jumps or leaps in the air.

2. A quick, heavy, double beat signals children to stop in place without any further movement or to fall to the floor.

3. Various changes in beat and accent pattern can be given, with children instructed to follow the pattern with movement.

Records designed for fundamental movements are excellent teaching aids. The records should have sections featuring separate skills and sections to guide movement combinations. These can be used for both instruction and creative activities. As an example, children who are seated in a circle tap out a rhythm with lummi sticks. After the rhythm is sufficiently established, half of the class moves in general space to the rhythm, which is continued by those who remain seated.

Another instructional option is using a tape recorder. The tape should contain 10 to 12 rhythmic units. Each unit features 15 to 20 seconds of an appropriate rhythm (piano or other recorded music) to which a fundamental movement can be performed. At the end of each unit, a bell is rung or a gong struck. Children move to the rhythm, and at the sound of the bell or gong, they freeze in a pose of their choosing. When the next rhythm begins, the sequence is repeated.

Expressive Movement

Children can express moods and feelings and show reactions to colors and sounds by improvising dances or movements that demonstrate different aspects of force or gestures that depict different feelings. A piece of music is played and is followed by a discussion of its qualities and how it makes the children feel. Children may interpret the music differently. Moods can be described as happy, gay, sad, brave, fearful, cheerful, angry, solemn, silly, stately, sleepy, funny, cautious, bold, or nonchalant.

Identification

There are endless subject sources for identification and interpretation. Children can take on the identity of a familiar character, creature, or object. The following ideas should be useful.

1. Animals—elephants, ducks, seals, chickens, dogs, rabbits, lions, and others

2. People—soldiers, firefighters, sailors, nurses, various kinds of workers, forest rangers, teachers, cowboys and cowgirls, and so on

3. Play objects—seesaws, swings, rowboats, balls, various toys, and many other common articles with which children play

4. Make-believe creatures—giants, dwarfs, gnomes, witches, trolls, dragons, pixies, fairies, and so on

5. Machines—trains, planes, jets, rockets, automobiles, bicycles, motorcycles, tractors, elevators, and the like

6. Circus characters—clowns, various trained animals, trapeze artists, tightrope performers, jugglers, acrobats, and bands

7. Natural phenomena—fluttering leaves, grain, flowers, rain, snow, clouds, wind, tornadoes, hurricanes, volcanoes, and others

Using identification with animals to stimulate creative movement

Dramatization

Dramatization and rhythm are useful vehicles for group activity. Suitable background music or rhythmic accompaniment is a necessary ingredient. Excellent recordings are available, from short numbers lasting a minute or two to more elaborate productions such as those found in the Dance-a-Story series (RCA Victor).

Here are some useful ideas for dramatic rhythms.

1. Building a house, garage, or other building project.
2. Making a snowman, throwing snowballs, going skiing.
3. Flying a kite, going hunting or fishing, going camping.
4. Acting out stories about astronauts, cowboys and cowgirls, firefighters, explorers.
5. Interpreting familiar stories, such as "Sleeping Beauty," "The Three Bears," or "Little Red Riding Hood."
6. Doing household tasks such as chopping wood, picking fruit, mowing the lawn, cleaning the yard, washing dishes, and vacuuming.
7. Celebrating holidays such as Halloween, the Fourth of July, Thanksgiving, or Christmas, or dramatizing the seasons.
8. Playing sports such as football, basketball, baseball, track and field, swimming, tennis, and golf.
9. Divide the class in groups of three or four, and assign each group a sport other than one of the major sports. Have them develop a series of movements dramatizing that sport to the class. Have the remaining groups guess which sport is being presented. Slow-motion movements add to this activity.
10. Plan a trip through a haunted house. A recording by Hap Palmer ("Movin'," Kimbo EA 546) has an excellent sequence about being in a haunted house.
11. Have the children make a motor. One student starts by getting into a position of choice in the middle of the floor and by putting one body part in motion. The motion should be a steady, rhythmic movement. The remaining students, one at a time, attach onto the first person, and each person puts one body part in motion. After all are attached, a machine with many moving parts is the result.
12. Act out the children's favorite parts in popular movies. Having the children perform to the

original sound track brings realism to the performance.
13. Select a favorite poem ("Old Mother Hubbard," "Pat-a-Cake," "The Giant") and design a sequence of activities to fit the meaning of the poem. Stories have excellent appeal.

An example that shows how an idea can be exploited for a lesson on creative rhythm is called "The Wind and the Leaves." One or more children are chosen to be the wind, and the remaining children are the leaves. Two kinds of rhythm are needed; a tambourine can be used. The first rhythm should be high, fast, and shrill, indicating the blowing of the wind. The intensity and tempo should illustrate the speed and force of the wind. The second rhythm should be slow, measured, and light, to represent the leaves fluttering in the still air and finally coming to rest at various positions on the ground. During the first rhythm, children representing the wind act out a heavy gust. While this is going on, the leaves show what it is like to be blown about. During the second rhythm, the wind is still and the leaves flutter to the ground. Other characterizations can be added. For example, street sweepers can come along and sweep up the leaves.

Another lesson strategy is to divide the class into groups and to give each group the task of acting out an idea with percussive accompaniment. Each group puts on a performance for the others. At completion, the other groups guess what the interpretation was. In this game, the interpretations should not be too long.

Creating Dances

A wide range of creative endeavor is possible in making up dances. Efforts can vary from construction of simple routines to formulation of a complete dance to a new or familiar piece of music. Students need to analyze the characteristics of the piece, determine the kinds of movement best suited to the musical elements, and design an appropriate movement routine or dance. This works best with small groups.

FOLK DANCES

A *folk dance* is defined as a traditional dance of a given people. In this concept, a definite pattern or dance routine is usually specified and followed. Folk dancing is one phase of a child's education that can assist in bringing about international understanding. A country's way of life and many other habits are often reflected in its folk music. From these dances, children gain an understanding of why people from certain countries act and live as they do, even though modern times may have changed their lifestyle from that of days gone by. Since folk dances depict the character of a people, these dances were never intended to be changed. However, to promote the joy of folk dance among elementary-level children, some slight modifications, which do not change greatly the inherent nature of the dance, may be instituted. Substituting a double handhold for a closed position, or a basic handhold for a varsouvienne position, are examples of acceptable changes.

Folk dances in developmental level I consist of simple fundamental locomotor movements, either singly or in combination. Dances such as the two-step, polka, and schottische, with more specialized steps, are found at developmental levels II and III. The first consideration when teaching folk dance is to determine whether children know the basic skills required for the dance. If a skill needs to be taught, it can be handled in one of two ways. The first way is to teach the skill separately, before teaching the dance. The second is to teach the dance in its normal sequence, giving specific instruction at the time when the skill appears. The first method is usually best, because children can concentrate solely on learning the skill.

Introducing New Dances

The following instructional sequence can be used for presenting new dances to youngsters:

1. With the children sitting informally or in formation for the dance, briefly discuss the dance and its characteristics.

2. Have the children listen to and analyze the music for accents, phrases, or changes.

3. When presenting a new dance, teach it first to the children individually in scatter formation. When they have learned the dance steps, the youngsters can then learn the necessary formations and groupings such as partners, sets, and so on.

4. Teach the dance at a slowed tempo and gradually increase it to the normal tempo as the children learn the steps.

5. As a general rule, if the dance is short, use the whole teaching approach. If it is a longer dance with several different parts, use the part-whole method and learn one part at a time. For example, have children learn half of a two-part

dance or a third of a three-part dance and then put that part to music. After all the parts are learned, put them together in a complete dance.

6. Add refinements such as partner changes (if the dance is a mixer), points of technique, and other details.

Arranging for Partners

Arranging for partners can be a source of deep hurt or embarrassment for some children. To be acceptable, a method of arranging for partners must avoid the situation in which children are looked over and overlooked. Some suggestions follow.

1. Dancing boy-girl fashion in the traditional mode is not necessary. When starting a dance program with a class that has never danced before or with students who are uncomfortable with each other, allow students to dance with a partner of their choice. If this places boys with boys and girls with girls, allow that arrangement. Partners can be referred to as number 1 and number 2 or colored pinnies can be placed on one of the partners. Instead of giving directions for the girl's part, call it out as "The people in red on the outside of the circle do. . . ." Be careful not to label one group as playing the role of boys or girls. Change partners frequently, and sooner or later the members of both sexes will dance with members of the opposite sex. In this chapter we will use the designations "partner A" and "partner B" for the leading and following positions respectively. Gender references, where they appear, will alternate by example.

2. In a follow-the-leader approach, the teacher puts on some brisk marching music and begins walking among the students, who are scattered in general space. The teacher passes individual students and taps them on the shoulder, and they get in line behind the teacher. Subsequent students go to the end of the line when tagged by the teacher until all students are chosen. This allows the teacher to arrange students as the teacher wishes—boy-girl, or just to separate children who do not work well together.

3. Boys join hands in a circle formation, and each girl steps behind a boy. Reverse the procedure, and have the girls make the circle, or have half of the class wear red pinnies and form the circle.

4. Boys stand in a circle facing counterclockwise, while girls form a circle around them facing

Pinnies can be used to identify partners

clockwise. Both circles move in the direction in which they are facing and stop on signal. The boy takes the girl nearest him as his partner.

5. For square dances, take the first four couples from any of the previous formations to form a set. Continue until all sets are formed.

Records for Folk Dances

Quality recordings can be difficult to find. We have found Wagon Wheel Records to be the most reliable source for a wide variety of records. Records and a catalog of available records can be ordered from the following address:

Wagon Wheel Records
8459 Edmaru Avenue
Whittier, CA 90605

A number of abbreviations for records found in this chapter are listed with each dance. The code for the abbreviations are:

12" LPs

AR and Ed. Act.	Educational Activities
CM	Classroom Materials (Singing Games to Folk Dancing)
HLP	Hoctor Records
Kimbo	Kimbo Educational
MAV	Merit Audio Visual (Young People's Folk Dances)
RPT	Rhythm Production

7" EPs

LS E-	Lloyd Shaw
SD	Squaredance Time

All other record listings are 45 rpm records.

Formations for Folk Dances

Figure 16.1 illustrates the formations that are used with folk dances that follow in this chapter. Each folk dance description begins with a listing of records, skills, and the formation to be used. If teachers are unsure of how the class should be arranged, the figure should be consulted. The formations are grouped into categories of single-circle, double-circle, and other formations.

Dance Positions

In most dance positions, partner A holds a hand or hands palms up and partner B joins the grip with a palms-down position. The following dance positions or partner positions are common to many dances.

Partners Facing Position

In partners facing position, as the name suggests, the partners are facing. Partner A extends hands forward with palms up and elbows slightly bent. Partner B places hands in A's hands.

Side-by-Side Position (Figure 16.2)

In side-by-side position, partner A always has partner B to the right. A offers the right hand, held above the waist, palm up. B places the left hand in A's raised hand.

Closed Position

Closed position is the social dance position. Partners stand facing each other, shoulders parallel, and toes pointed forward. Partner A holds partner B's right hand in A's left hand out to the side, at about shoulder level, with elbows bent. A places the right hand on B's back, just below the left shoulder blade. B's left arm rests on A's upper arm, and B's left hand is on A's right shoulder.

Open Position

To get to open position from closed position, partner A turns to the left and partner B to the right, with their arms remaining in about the same position. Both face in the same direction and are side by side.

SINGLE–CIRCLE FORMATIONS

1. All facing center, no partners
2. All facing counterclockwise

3. By partners, all facing center
4. By partners, with partners facing

DOUBLE–CIRCLE FORMATIONS

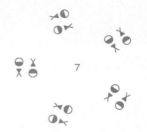

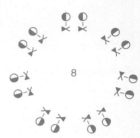

5. Partners facing each other

6. Partners side by side, facing counterclockwise

7. Sets of four, couples facing with girl on partner's right

8. Sets of four, all facing counterclockwise

TRIPLE–CIRCLE FORMATIONS

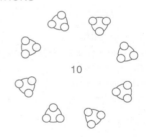

9. Standing side by side

10. In small circles

OTHER FORMATIONS

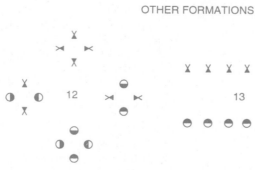

11. Partners in scattered formation

12. Groups of four, partners facing each other

13. Longways set

Couple 1

14

Side couples

Couple 2   Couple 4

Head couples

Couple 3

14. Square dance formation

Figure 16.1 Dance formations

364

Figure 16.2 Side-by-side position

Figure 16.3 Promenade position

Promenade Position (Figure 16.3)

Promenade position is the crossed-arm position in which dancers stand side by side, facing the same direction, with the right hand held by partner's right and the left by partner's left.

Varsouvienne Position

Partners stand side by side and face the same direction. Partner B is slightly in front and to the right of Partner A. A holds B's left hand in his left hand in front and at about shoulder height. B brings the right hand directly back over the right shoulder, and A reaches behind B at shoulder height and grasps that hand with his right.

PROGRESSION OF FOLK DANCES

The dances in this section have been listed in progression beginning with the easiest and progressing to the most difficult dance. Three devel-

opmental levels are listed to give teachers the widest possible latitude in selecting dances that fit the maturity and skill of their youngsters. Table 16.2 lists all dances in alphabetical order by developmental level and lists skills required for the dance. Dances throughout the chapter can be found easily by referring to the page number in the table. This table gives instructors a quick and clear overview of the total dance program.

Regarding level of difficulty, teachers must keep in mind that if a group of students is lacking in rhythmic background, the dances in the progression may be too difficult. A sixth-grade class, for example, lacking in dance skills may need to begin with developmental level II dances. On the other hand, avoid boring a class by starting children on material below their maturity level.

DEVELOPMENTAL LEVEL I DANCES

Dances in this section contain movement songs and folk dances that are introductory in nature and

Table 16.2 Alphabetical listing of folk dances by developmental level

Dance	Skills	Page
Developmental Level I		
Ach Ja	Walking, sliding	371
Bleking	Bleking step, step-hop	376
Bluebird	Walking	368
Bombay Bounce	Hesitation step, side step	375
Carrousel	Draw step, sliding	375
Children's Polka	Step-draw	372
Chimes of Dunkirk (Var. 1)	Turning in a small circle with a partner, changing partners	372
Chimes of Dunkirk (Var. 2)	Turning with a partner, skipping	375
Danish Dance of Greeting	Running or sliding, bowing	370
Did You Ever See a Lassie?	Walking at 3/4 time, creativity	368
Eins Zwei Drei	Walking, sliding	374
Hokey Pokey	Body identification, nonlocomotor movements	369
How D'Ye Do, My Partner?	Bowing, curtsying, skipping	370
Jingle Bells (Var. 1)	Elbow swing, skipping, sliding	378
Jolly Is the Miller	Marching	376
Jump Jim Jo	Jumping, running, draw step	373
Let Your Feet Go Tap, Tap, Tap	Skipping	370
Looby Loo	Skipping or running, body identification	368
Movin' Madness	Keeping time, creativity	368
Muffin Man, The	Jumping, skipping	369
Nixie Polka	Bleking step	377
Pease Porridge Hot	Running, turning in a circle, clapping patterns	373
Seven Jumps	Step-hop, balance, control	371
Shoemaker's Dance	Skipping, heel and toe	373
Shortnin' Bread	Sliding, turning with a partner	372
Skip to My Lou	Skipping, changing partners	370
Turn the Glasses Over	Walking, wring the dishrag	377
Yankee Doodle	Walking, galloping, sliding, bowing	374
Developmental Level II		
Bingo	Walking, right-and-left grand	382
Bird Dance, The (Chicken Dance)	Skipping or walking, elbow swing or star	378
Crested Hen	Step-hop, turning under	386
Csebogar (Csehbogar)	Skipping, sliding, draw step, elbow swing	379
E-Z Mixer	Walking, elbow swing or swing in closed position	385
Grand March	Controlled walking, marching, grand march figures	383
Green Sleeves	Walking, star formation, over and under	384
Gustaf's Skoal	Walking (stately), skipping, turning	387

involve simple formations and uncomplicated changes. The movements are primarily basic loco-motor skills and hand gestures or clapping sequences. There are dances both with and without partners. As the difficulty of the dances increases, patterns become more definite, and more folk dances are included. The movements are still primarily of the simple locomotor type, with additional and varied emphasis on more complicated movement patterns.

Movin' Madness (American)

Records: LS E-9, E-20; MAV 1044, 1041; AR 572

Skills: Keeping time, creativity

Formation: Scattered

Directions: The music is in two parts.

Part I: The tempo is slow, slow, fast-fast-fast. The children do any series of movements of their choice to fit this pattern, repeated four times. The movements should be large, gross motor movements.

Part II: During the second part (chorus) of the music, the children do any locomotor movement in keeping with the tempo. The step-hop or a light run can be used with the tempo of Part II.

Teaching suggestions: Have the youngsters clap the rhythm. They should pay particular attention to the tempo in Part I. The music is Bleking, a dance presented later. The music for "I See You" is also suitable, but note that the movements in Part I are repeated twice instead of four times. The Part II music is suitable for skipping, sliding, or galloping.

Bluebird

Records: Folkcraft 1180

Skill: Walking

Formation: Single circle, with hands joined and held high to form arches. A "bluebird" is placed in the center.

Verse

Bluebird, bluebird, in and out my windows,
Bluebird, bluebird, in and out my windows,
Oh! Johnny (Jenny), I am tired.

Chorus

Take a little boy and tap him on the shoulders,
Take a little boy and tap him on the shoulders,
Oh! Johnny (Jenny), I am tired.

Directions: A bluebird walks around the circle weaving in and out of the arches and stopping behind a student in the circle. The bluebird places hands on the shoulders of the chosen student and taps lightly during the chorus. The dance is repeated with the chosen student leading and the initial bluebird walking behind with the hands on the shoulders. The dance continues until all youngsters are chosen. A long line of students walking is the result.

Did You Ever See a Lassie? (Scottish)

Records: LS E-4; CM-1 1157

Skill: Walking at 3/4 time, creativity

Formation: Single circle, facing halfway left, with hands joined; one child in the center

Verse

Did you ever see a lassie (laddie), a lassie, a lassie?

Did you ever see a lassie go this way and that?

Go this way and that way, and this way and that way?

Did you ever see a lassie go this way and that?

Directions:

Measures	Action
1–8	All walk (one step per measure) to the left in a circle with hands joined. (Walk, 2, 3, 4, 5, 6, 7, 8) The child in the center gets ready to demonstrate some type of movement.
9–16	All stop and copy the movement suggested by the child in the center.

As the verse starts over, the center child selects another to do some action in the center and changes places with her.

Looby Loo (English)

Records: LS E-4; CM 1157; HLP 4026

Skills: Skipping or running, body identification

Formation: Single circle, facing center, hands joined

Chorus

Here we dance looby loo
Here we dance looby light
Here we dance looby loo
All on a Saturday night.

Verses

1. *I put my right hand in,*
   I take my right hand out,
   I give my right hand a shake, shake, shake,
   And turn myself about.
2. *I put my left hand in, . . .*
3. *I put my right foot in, . . .*
4. *I put my left foot in, . . .*
5. *I put my head way in, . . .*
6. *I put my whole self in, . . .*

Directions: The chorus is repeated before each verse. During the chorus, all children skip around the circle to the right. On the verse part of the dance, the children stand still, face the center, and follow the directions of the words. On the words "and turn myself about," they make a complete turn in place and get ready to skip around the circle again. The movements should be definite and vigorous. On the last verse, they jump forward and then backward, shake vigorously, and then turn about.

The dance can be made more fun and more vigorous by changing the tasks in the song. Try these tasks: Right side or hip, left side or hip, big belly, backside.

Hokey Pokey (American)

Records: CAP 6026; MAC 6995; LS E-25

Skills: Body identification, nonlocomotor movements

Formation: Single circle, facing center

Verse

Line 1: *You put your right foot in,*
Line 2: *You put your right foot out,*
Line 3: *You put your right foot in*
Line 4: *And you shake it all about;*
Line 5: *You do the hokey pokey*
Line 6: *And you turn yourself around.*
Line 7: *That's what it's all about.*

Directions: During the first four lines, the children act out the words. During lines 5 and 6, they hold their hands overhead with palms forward and do a kind of hula while turning around in place. During line 7, they stand in place and clap their hands three times.

The basic verse is repeated by substituting, successively, the left foot, right arm, left arm, right elbow, left elbow, head, right hip, left hip, whole self, and backside. The final verse finishes off with the following:

You do the hokey pokey,
You do the hokey pokey,
You do the hokey pokey.
That's what it's all about.

On each of the first two lines, the children raise their arms overhead and perform a bowing motion with the arms and upper body. On line 3, all kneel and bow forward to touch the hands to the floor. During line 4, they slap the floor five times, alternating their hands in time to the words.

Teaching suggestions: Encourage the youngsters to make large and vigorous motions during the hokey pokey portions and during the turn around. This adds to the fun. The records all feature singing calls, but the action sequence of the different records varies. The children should sing lightly as they follow the directions given on the record.

The Muffin Man (American)

Record: LS E-1

Skills: Jumping, skipping

Formation: Single circle, facing center, hands at sides. One child, the Muffin Man, stands in front of another child of the opposite sex.

Verses

1. *Oh, have you seen the Muffin Man,*
   The Muffin Man, the Muffin Man?
   Oh, have you seen the Muffin Man,
   Who lives on _____ Street?
2. *Oh, yes, we've seen the Muffin Man,*
   The Muffin Man, the Muffin Man.
   Oh yes, we've seen the Muffin Man,
   Who lives on _____ Street.

Directions:

Verse 1: The children stand still and clap their hands lightly, with the exception of the Muffin Man and his partner. These two join hands and jump lightly in place while keeping time to the music. On the first beat of each measure, a normal jump is taken, followed by a bounce in place (rebound) on the second beat.

Verse 2: The Muffin Man and his partner then skip around the inside of the circle individually and, near the end of the verse, each stands in front of a child, thus choosing a new partner.

Verse 1 is then repeated, with two sets of partners doing the jumping. During the repetition of verse 2, four children skip around the inside of the circle and choose partners. This procedure continues until all children have been chosen.

The children choose the name of a street to put in the verses.

Skip to My Lou (American)

Records: CM 1159; SD 10021

Skills: Skipping, changing partners

Formation: Scattered with a partner

Verses

1. *Lost my partner, what'll I do . . . (etc.)*
2. *I'll find another one, nice as you . . .*
3. *Go catch a red bird, nice one too . . .*
4. *If you can't find a red bird, take a blue . . .*
5. *If you can't find a blue bird, black bird'll do . . .*

Chorus

Skip, skip, skip to my loo; skip, skip, skip to my loo;

Skip, skip, skip to my loo; skip to my loo my darling.

Directions: During the chorus, partners skip around the area. At the verse, everyone finds a new partner and continues skipping.

Let Your Feet Go Tap, Tap, Tap (German)

Records: LS E-7, E-20

Skill: Skipping

Formation: Double circle, partners facing

Directions:

Verse	Action
Let your feet go tap, tap, tap,	Tap the foot three times. (Tap, 2, 3)
Let your hands go clap, clap, clap,	Clap the hands three times. (Clap, 2, 3)
Let your finger beckon me,	Beckon and bow to partner. (Beckon, bow)
Come, dear partner, dance with me.	Join inside hands and face counterclockwise. (Join hands)

Chorus

Tra, la, la, la, la, la, la, and so on.	All sing and skip counterclockwise. (Skip and sing)

This dance can be done to the tune of "Merrily We Roll Along," with a little adjustment for line 2. If children are having difficulty with skipping, substitute a walking, running, or sliding step.

How D'Ye Do, My Partner? (Swedish)

Records: HLP-4026; LS E-3; MAV 1041

Skills: Bowing, curtsying, skipping

Formation: Double circle, partners facing, partner A on inside

Verse

How d'ye do, my partner?

How d'ye do today?

Will you dance in the circle?

I will show you the way.

Directions:

Measures	Action
1–2	Partners A bow to their partner. (Bow)
3–4	Partners B bow. (Bow)
5–6	A offers the right hand to B, who takes it with the right hand. (Join right hands) Both turn to face counterclockwise. (Face counterclockwise)
7–8	Couples join left hands in promenade position in preparation to skip when the music changes. (Join left hands)
9–16	Partners skip counterclockwise in the circle, slowing down on measure 15. (Skip) On measure 16, Bs stop and As move ahead to secure a new partner. (New partner)

Danish Dance of Greeting (Danish)

Records: HLP-4026; MAV 1041; LS E-6

Skills: Running or sliding, bowing

Formation: Single circle, all face center. Partner A stands to the left of partner B.

Directions:

Measures	Action
1	All clap twice and bow to partner. (Clap, clap, bow)
2	Repeat but turn back to the partner and bow to the neighbor. (Clap, clap, bow)
3	Stamp right, stamp left. (Stamp, stamp)

4	Turn around in four running steps. (Turn, 2, 3, 4)
5–8	Repeat the action of measures 1–4.
9–12	All join hands and run to the left for four measures. (Run, 2, 3, 4, . . . 16)
13–16	Repeat the action of measures 9–12, taking light running steps in the opposite direction. (Run, 2, 3, 4, . . . 16)

Variation: Instead of a running step, use a light slide.

Ach Ja (German)

Records: LS E-2; CM 1158

Skills: Walking, sliding

Formation: Double circle, partners facing counterclockwise, partners A on the inside, inside hands joined

Verse

When my father and my mother take the children
 to the fair,
Ach Ja! Ach Ja!
Oh, they haven't any money, but it's little that
 they care,
Ach Ja! Ach Ja!
Tra la la, tra la la, tra la la la la la la
Tra la la, tra la la, tra la la la la la la
Ach Ja! Ach Ja!

Directions: Explain that "Ach Ja" means "Oh yes."

Measures	Action
1–2	Partners walk eight steps in the line of direction. (Walk, 2, 3, 4, 5, 6, 7, 8)
3	Partners drop hands and bow to each other. (Bow)
4	Each A then bows to the B on the left, who returns the bow. (Bow)
5–8	Measures 1–4 are repeated.
9–10	Partners face each other, join hands, and take four slides in the line of direction. (Slide, 2, 3, 4)
11–12	Four slides are taken clockwise. (Slide, 2, 3, 4)
13	Partners bow to each other. (Bow)

14	A bows to the B on the left, who returns the bow. (Bow) To start the next dance, A moves quickly toward this B, who is the next partner.

Seven Jumps (Danish)

Records: LS E-8; MAV 1043; RM 2

Skills: Step-hop, balance, control

Formation: Single circle, hands joined

Directions: There are seven jumps to the dance. Each jump is preceded by the following action.

Measures	Action
1–8	The circle moves to the right with seven step-hops, one to each measure. On the eighth measure, all jump high in the air and reverse direction. (Step-hop, 2-hop, 3-hop, . . . 7-hop, change direction)
9–16	Circle to the left with seven step-hops. Stop on measure 16 and face the center. (Step-hop, 2-hop, 3-hop, . . . 7-hop, face center)
17	All drop hands, place their hands on hips, and lift the right knee upward with the toes pointed downward. (Knee up)
18	All stamp the right foot to the ground on the signal note, then join hands on the next note. (Stamp)
1–18	Repeat measures 1–18, but do not join hands.
19	Lift the left knee, stamp, and join hands.
1–19	Repeat measures 1–19, but do not join hands.
20	Put the right toe backward and kneel on the right knee. Stand and join hands.
1–20	Repeat measures 1–20; do not join hands.
21	Kneel on the left knee. Stand and join hands.
1–21	Repeat measures 1–21; do not join hands.
22	Put the right elbow to the floor with the cheek on the fist. Stand and join hands.
1–22	Repeat measures 1–22; do not join hands.

23	Put the left elbow to the floor with the cheek on the fist. Stand and join hands.
1–23	Repeat measures 1–23; do not join hands.
24	Put the forehead on the floor. Stand and join hands.
1–16	Repeat measures 1–16.

Teaching suggestion: This dance was performed originally in Denmark by men as a control-elimination competition. Those who made unnecessary movements or mistakes were eliminated. Emphasize control.

Variation: To increase motivation, the dance can be done with a parachute. The dancers hold the parachute taut with one hand during the step-hops. The chute is kept taut with both hands for all jumps except the last, during which the forehead touches the chute on the floor.

Chimes of Dunkirk, Var. 1 (French-Belgian)

Records: LS E-7, E-21; HLP-4026; MAV 1042

Skills: Turning in a small circle with a partner, changing partners

Formation: Double circle, partners facing

Directions:

Measures	Action
1–2	Stamp three times in place, right-left-right. (Stamp, 2, 3)
3–4	Clap hands three times above the head (chimes in the steeple). (Clap, 2, 3)
5–8	Partner A places both hands on partner B's hips; B places both hands on A's shoulders. Taking four steps, they turn around in place. (Turn, 2, 3, 4) On the next four counts, partner B (on the outside) moves one person to the left with four steps. (Change, 2, 3, 4) Repeat the sequence from the beginning.

Teaching suggestion: An alternative to the turn described is to do an elbow turn by linking right elbows.

Shortnin' Bread (American)

Record: Kimbo 7050

Skills: Sliding, turning with a partner

Formation: Scattered with partner

Directions:

Measures	Action
1–2	Clap own hands
3–4	Pat partner's hands
5–6	Clap own hands
7–8	Slap own thighs
9–16	Repeat measures 1–8
17–20	Couples slide to the right holding hands.
21–24	Circle holding hands.
25–32	Repeat measures 17–24 moving to the left.

Children's Polka (German)

Records: HLP-4026; LS E-7; SD 1002

Formation: Single circle of couples, partners facing

Skill: Step-draw

Directions:

Measures	Action
1–2	Take two step-draw steps toward the center of the circle, ending with three steps in place. (Draw, draw, step, 2, 3)
3–4	Take two step-draw steps away from the center, ending with three steps in place. (Draw, draw, step, 2, 3)
5–8	Repeat the pattern of measures 1–4.
9	Slap own knees once with both hands; clap own hands once. (Slap, clap)
10	Clap both hands with partner three times. (Clap, 2, 3)
11–12	Repeat the pattern of measures 9 and 10.
13	Hop, placing one heel forward, and shake the forefinger at partner three times. (Scold, 2, 3)
14	Repeat the "scolding" pattern with the other foot and hand. (Scold, 2, 3)
15–16	Turn once around in place with four running steps and stamp three times in place. (Turn, 2, 3, 4; Stamp, 2, 3)

Shoemaker's Dance (Danish)

Records: HLP-4026; MAV 1042; SD 1001; LS E-5, E-20

Skills: Skipping, heel and toe

Formation: Double circle, partners facing, with partner A's back to the center of the circle

Directions:

Part I Verse

Wind, wind, wind	*Wind, wind, wind*
the bobbin,	*the bobbin,*
Wind, wind, wind	*Wind, wind, wind*
the bobbin,	*the bobbin,*
Pull, pull	*Pull, pull*
Clap, clap, clap.	*Tap, tap, tap.*

Measures	Part I Action
1	With arms bent and at shoulder height, and with hands clenched to form fists, circle one fist over the other in front of the chest. (Wind the thread)
2	Reverse the circular motion and wind the thread in the opposite direction. (Reverse direction)
3	Pull the elbows back vigorously twice. (Pull and tighten the thread)
4	Clap own hands three times. (Clap, 2, 3)
5–7	Repeat the pattern of measures 1–3.
8	Tap own fists together three times to drive the nails. (Tap, 2, 3)

Part II Verse

Heel and toe and away we go,
Heel and toe and away we go,
See my new shoes neatly done,
Away we go to have some fun.

Part II Action

9–16	Partners face counterclockwise, inside hands joined. Skip counterclockwise, ending with a bow. (Skip, 2, 3, . . . 15, bow)

Variation of Part II Action

9	Place the heel of the outside foot forward (counts 1 and), and point the toe of the outside foot in back (2 and).
10	Take three running steps forward, starting with the outside foot and pausing on the last count.

11–12	Repeat the pattern of measures 9–10, starting with the inside foot.
13–16	Repeat the pattern of measures 9–12, entire "heel and toe and run, run, run" pattern dance, four times singing Part II verse.

Jump Jim Jo (American)

Records: LS E-10; MAV 1041

Skills: Jumping, running, draw step

Formation: Double circle, partners facing, both hands joined

Directions:

Measures	Verse
1–2	*Jump, jump, oh jump Jim Jo*
3–4	*Take a little whirl, and around you'll go,*
5–6	*Slide, slide, and point your toe,*
7–8	*You're a jolly little fellow when you jump Jim Jo.*

Measures	Action
1–2	Do two jumps sideward, progressing counterclockwise, followed by three quick jumps in place. (Slow, slow, fast, fast, fast)
3–4	Release hands and turn once around in place with four jumps (two jumps per measure). Finish facing partner and rejoin hands. (Jump, turn, 3, 4)
5	Take two sliding steps sideward, progressing counterclockwise. (Slide, slide)
6	Partners face counterclockwise with inside hands joined and tap three times with the toe of the outside foot. (Tap, tap, tap)
7–8	Take four running steps forward, then face partner, join both hands, and end with three jumps in place. (Run, 2, 3, 4; Jump, 2, 3)

Pease Porridge Hot (English)

Record: LS E-8

Skills: Running, turning in a circle, clapping patterns

Formation: Double circle, partners facing

Verse

Pease porridge hot,
Pease porridge cold,

Pease porridge in a pot,

Nine days old!

Some like it hot,

Some like it cold,

Some like it in a pot,

Nine days old!

Directions: The dance is in two parts. The first is a pat-a-cake rhythm done while the children sing the verse. During the second part, partners dance in a circular movement.

Part I Action

Line 1: Slap the hands to the thighs, clap the hands together, clap the hands to partner's hands. (Thighs, together, partner)

Line 2: Repeat the action of line 1.

Line 3: Slap the hands to the thighs, clap the hands together, clap the right hand against partner's right, clap one's own hands together. (Thighs, together, right, together)

Line 4: Clap the left hand to partner's left, clap one's own hands together, clap both hands against partner's hands. (Left, together, both)

Lines 5–8: Repeat lines 1–4.

Part II Action

Join both hands with partner and run around in a small circle (an elbow swing can be used), turning counterclockwise for the first four lines and ending with the word "old!" (Run)

Reverse direction and run clockwise for the remainder of the verse. (Change direction)

Move one step to the left for a new partner. (New partner)

Variation:

Part I: Children are seated on the floor, facing their partner, with hands braced in back for support. The movements are done with the feet instead of the hands. Instead of clapping the hands to the thighs, knock both heels against the floor. In the partner interaction, the feet do the work of the hands.

Part II: Have children spin on their seat in one direction during the first eight measures and then spin the other way during the next eight. Youngsters must keep their knees up while spinning.

Yankee Doodle (American)

Records: Windsor 7S1; LS E-10

Skills: Walking, galloping, sliding, bowing

Formation: Scattered or open circle facing counterclockwise

Directions:

Measures	Action
1–4	All gallop 8 steps (Gallop, 2, . . . 8)
5–8	All stop, face center, point to cap and bow on word "macaroni." (Stop, point, bow)
9–12	All join hands and take six slides to the right and stamp feet two times on word "dandy." (Slide, 2, 3, . . . 6; Stamp, stamp)
13–16	All slide six times to the left and clap hands two times on the word "candy." (Slide, 2, 3, . . . 6; Clap clap)

Variation: Change the locomotor movements to fit the age and interest of the group. Have the class create new movement patterns.

Eins Zwei Drei (German)

Record: HLP-4026

Skills: Walking, sliding

Formation: Single circle of couples (partner B to partner A's right) facing the center and numbered alternately couple 1, 2, 1, 2

Directions: Explain that "Eins, Zwei, Drei" means "one, two, three" in German.

Measures	Part I Action
1–2	Couples 1 take three steps toward the center of the circle as they clap their hands by brushing them vertically like cymbals. (Forward, 2, 3, pause)
3–4	Couples 1 repeat measures 1–2, walking backward to place. (Back, 2, 3, pause)
5–8	Couples 1 face, join both hands, and take four slides toward the center of the circle and four slides back to place. Partner A starts with the left foot, partner B with the right. (Slide, 2, 3, 4)
9–16	Couples 2 repeat measures 1–8.

	Part II Action
17	Partner A turns and touches the right heel sideward while shaking the right index finger at partner. Partner B does the same with the left heel and left index finger. (Scold, 2, 3)

18	Repeat measure 17 with the corner, reversing footwork and hands. (Scold, 2, 3)
19–20	Repeat measures 17 and 18.
21–24	All join hands and circle left with eight slides. (Slide, 2, 3, . . . 8)
25–32	Repeat measures 17–24, reversing the direction of the slides. (Slide, 2, 3, . . . 8)

Variation: To facilitate learning, practice all steps individually in a scattered formation.

Chimes of Dunkirk, Var. 2 (French-Belgian)

Records: LS E-7, E-21

Skills: Turning with a partner, skipping

Formation: Single circle of couples, partners facing

Directions:

Measures	Action
1–2	Stamp three times in place. (Stamp, 2, 3)
3–4	Clap own hands three times. (Clap, 2, 3)
5–8	Do a two-hand swing with partner. Join both hands with partner and turn once clockwise with eight running or skipping steps. (Swing, 2, 3, . . . 8)
	Chorus Action
1–8	Circle left, singing, "Tra, la, la, la, la, . . ." All join hands and circle left with 16 running or skipping steps, ending with a bow. (Run, 2, 3, . . . 15, bow)

Variations: The dance can also be used as a mixer by partner B's advancing one partner to the left. Also, instead of a two-hand swing with partner, substitute the shoulder-waist position. A places a hand on B's waist, and B places both hands on A's shoulders.

To facilitate forming the circle for the chorus, make a four-step turn instead of an eight-step turn on measures 5–8. This gives the children four counts to get ready for the circle formation and four counts to make the circle.

Bombay Bounce

Record: Any record with a definite and moderately fast beat

Skills: Hesitation step, side step

Formation: Scattered, all facing forward

Part I (16 counts): A hesitation step to the left is performed by taking a short step to the left followed by touching the right foot near the left while the weight remains on the left foot. A hesitation step to the right is similar except it begins with a step to the right. To begin the dance, eight hesitation steps are performed in place with a hand clap on each touch. (Left, touch and clap; right, touch and clap) Repeat 4 times.

Part II (16 counts): Take two side steps to the left, then two to the right. Clap on counts 4 and 8. (Left, close; Left, close and clap; Right, close; Right, close and clap). Repeat the pattern.

Part III (16 counts): Take four side steps left and four side steps right. Clap only on count 8. (Left, close, left, close, left, close, left, close and clap). Repeat to the right.

Part IV (16 counts): Take four steps forward and four steps backward, four steps forward and four steps backward. Clap on counts 4, 8, 12, and 16. (Forward, 2, 3, 4 and clap; Backward, 2, 3, 4 and clap; Forward, 2, 3, 4 and clap; Backward 2, 3, 4 and clap)

Teaching suggestions: Variations are possible (e.g., in Part IV, instead of four steps, use three steps and a kick [swing].)

Carrousel (Swedish)

Records: LS E-13; MAV 1041

Skills: Draw step, sliding

Formation: Double circle, facing center. The inner circle, representing a merry-go-round, joins hands. The outer players, representing the riders, place their hands on the hips of the partner in front.

Verse

Little children, sweet and gay,

Carrousel is running; it will run to evening.

Little ones a nickel, big ones a dime.

Hurry up, get a mate, or you'll surely be too late.

Chorus

Ha, ha, ha, happy are we,

Anderson and Peterson and Henderson and me,

Ha, ha, ha, happy are we,

Anderson and Peterson and Henderson and me.

Directions:

Measures	Verse Action
1–16	Moving to the left, children take 12 slow draw steps and stamp on the last three steps. (Step, together, 2, 3, . . . 12, stamp, stamp, stamp, rest)

Measures	Chorus Action
17–24	Moving left, speed up the draw step until it becomes a slide or gallop. Sing the chorus. (Slide, 2, 3, . . . 8)
25–32	Repeat measures 17–24 while moving to the right. (Slide, 2, 3, . . . 8)

During the chorus, the tempo is increased, and the movement is changed to a slide. Children should take short, light slides to prevent the circle from moving out of control.

Variation: The dance can be done with youngsters holding the perimeter of a parachute.

Jolly Is the Miller (American)

Records: LS E-10; RPT 317

Skill: Marching

Formation: Double circle, partners facing counterclockwise, As on the inside, with inside hands joined. A Miller is in the center of the circle

Directions:

Verse	Action
Jolly is the Miller who lives by the mill; *The wheel goes round with a right good will;* *One hand on the hopper and the other on the sack;* *The right steps forward and the left steps back.*	All sing. Youngsters march counterclockwise, with inside hands joined. During the second line when "the wheel goes round," the dancers turn their outside arm in a circle to form a wheel. Children change partners at the words "right steps forward and the left steps back." The Miller then has a chance to get a partner. The child left without a partner becomes the next Miller.

Bleking (Swedish)

Records: LS E-9, E-20; MAV 1044

Skills: Bleking step, step-hop

Formation: Single circle, partners facing, both hands joined. Partners A face counterclockwise and partners B clockwise.

Directions:

Part I—The Bleking Step: Cue by calling "Slow-slow, fast-fast-fast."

Measures	Action
1	Hop on the left foot and extend the right heel forward with the right leg straight. At the same time, thrust the right hand forward. Hop on the right foot, reversing the arm action and extending the left foot to rest on the heel. (Slow, slow)
2	Repeat the action with three quick changes—left, right, left. (Fast, fast, fast)
3–4	Beginning on the right foot, repeat the movements of measures 1 and 2. (Slow, slow, fast, fast, fast)
5–8	Repeat measures 1–4.

Part II—The Windmills: Partners extend their joined hands sideways at shoulder height.

Measures	Action
9–16	Partners turn in place with a repeated step-hop. At the same time, the arms move up and down like a windmill. The turning is done clockwise, with A starting on the right foot and B on the left. At the completion of the step-hops (16), the partners should be in their original places ready for Part I again. (Step-hop, 2-hop, 3-hop, . . . 16-hop)

Variations:

1. Change from original positions to a double circle, partners facing, As with back to the center. Part I is as described. For Part II, all face counterclockwise, and partners join inside hands. Partners do the basic schottische of "step, step, step, hop" throughout Part II (p. 399).

2. Another excellent variation is to do the dance with partners scattered in general space. Part I is as described. For Part II, the children leave their partners and step-hop in various directions around the dancing area. When the music is about to change back to Part I, performers find a partner wherever they can, and the dance is repeated.

3. Bleking is excellent music for creative dance, with the stipulation that the children maintain

individually the bleking rhythm of "slow-slow, fast-fast-fast" during Part I and do any kind of movement in place that they wish. During Part II, they may do any locomotor or other movement that they choose.

Nixie Polka *(Nigarepolska)* (Swedish)

Records: AR 572; MAV 1041

Skill: Bleking step

Formation: Single circle, all facing center, with one or more children scattered inside the circle

Measures	Part I Action
1–4	With hands joined, all spring lightly onto the left foot and extend the right foot forward, heel to ground, toe up. Next, spring lightly onto the right foot and extend the left foot forward. Repeat this action until four slow bleking steps are completed. (Slow, slow, slow, slow)
5–8	All clap hands once and shout "Hey!" The center child then runs around the inside of the circle, looking for a partner, finally selecting one. They join both hands and run lightly in place until the music is finished. This refrain is repeated, so the children have time to get back to the center of the circle. (Clap, run)

	Part II Action
1–4	The center dancer and partner, with both hands joined, repeat the action of measures 1–4. All dancers in the circle also repeat the action of measures 1–4. (Slow, slow, slow, slow)
5–8	On the first count, all clap hands, shouting "Hey!" The center dancer then about-faces and places both hands on the shoulders of partner, who now becomes the new leader. In this position, both shuffle around the inside of the circle, looking for a third person to dance with. The music is repeated again to allow ample time to return to the center. (Clap, run)

	Part III Action
1–4	The action of measures 1–4 is repeated, with the new dancer facing the circle and the two others facing the new dancer. (Slow, slow, slow, slow)

5–8	On the first count, all clap hands, shouting "Hey!" The two people in the center then about-face. All three now face the center to form a line of three dancers with a new leader, who looks for a fourth dancer. The music is repeated. (Clap, run)

The entire dance is thus repeated, accumulating dancers with each repetition. There should be one center dancer for each dozen dancers in the circle.

Turn the Glasses Over (American-English)

Record: FK 1181

Skills: Walking, wring the dishrag

Formation: Single circle of couples in promenade position. Extra students are in the center.

Directions:

Measures	Verse	Action
1–4	*I've been to Harlem, I've been to Dover,*	The couples walk forward singing the verse. At the words "turn the glasses over," they raise their arms, keeping the hands joined, and turn under the raised arms, making one complete outward "dishrag" turn. Youngsters must anticipate the turn and be prepared to start in time to complete the movement by the end of the phrase.
5–8	*I've traveled this wide world all over,*	
9–12	*Over, over, three times over,*	
13–16	*Drink all the lemonade, and turn the glasses over.*	

Measures	Chorus	Action
1–4	*Sailing east, sailing west,*	Youngsters in the outer circle continue walking while those in the inner circle turn and walk in the opposite direction. An extra player(s) joins one of the circles and continues with the group. At the words "girl in the ocean," youngsters take the nearest person for a new partner. Those without a partner move to the center.
5–8	*Sailing over the ocean,*	
9–12	*You better watch out when the boat begins to rock*	
13–16	*Or you'll lose your girl in the ocean.*	

Jingle Bells, Var. 1 (Dutch)

Record: MAC 2046

Skills: Elbow swing, skipping, sliding

Formation: Double circle, partners facing, with both hands joined

Directions:

Measures	Action
1–2	Partners take eight slides counterclockwise. (Slide, 2, 3, . . . 8)
3–4	Partners turn so they are standing back to back, and take eight more slides in the line of direction. This move is best made by dropping the front hands and swinging the back hands forward until the dancers are standing back to back. They rejoin the hands that are now in back. Make this move with no loss of rhythm. (Slide, 2, 3, . . . 8)
5–6	Repeat the action of measures 1 and 2. To get back to the face-to-face position, let go of the back hands and swing the front hands backward, allowing the bodies to pivot and face again. (Slide, 2, 3, . . . 8)
7–8	Repeat measures 3 and 4. (Slide, 2, 3, . . . 8)
	Chorus Action
1	Clap own hands three times. (Clap own, 2, 3)
2	Clap both hands with partner three times. (Clap both, 2, 3)
3	Clap own hands four times. (Clap own, 2, 3, 4)
4	Clap both hands with partner once. (Clap both)
5–8	Right elbow swing with partner. Partners hook right elbows and swing clockwise with eight skips. (Swing, 2, 3, 4, 5, 6, 7, 8)
9–12	Repeat the clapping sequence of measures 1–4.
13–16	Left elbow swing with partner for eight skips, finishing in the original starting position, ready to repeat the entire dance with the same partner; or do a left elbow swing with partner for four skips, which is once around, then all children in

the inner circle skip forward to the outer dancer ahead and repeat the entire dance from the beginning with a new partner. (Swing, 2, 3, 4, 5, 6, 7, 8)

DEVELOPMENTAL LEVEL II DANCES

Developmental level II activities focus clearly on folk dance. Locomotor skills are still the basis of the movement patterns, but in most of the dances, the patterns are more difficult than those in developmental level I. At this level, each dance always has at least two parts, and may have three or more. Since the movement patterns are longer, the part-whole teaching method is used more often with this age group. These dances are vigorous and fast moving, which makes them exciting for youngsters to perform.

Tinikling and lummi sticks are introduced at this level, which lend challenge and novelty to the progression. Emphasis should be on participation and enjoyment without excessive concern for perfection. Normal progress through the rhythms program will assure that adequate quality will result.

The Bird Dance (Chicken Dance)

Records: AD-831; ESP 001

Skills: Skipping or walking, elbow swing or star

Formation: Circle or scatter formation, partners facing

Directions:

Measures	Part I Action
1	Four snaps—thumb and fingers, hands up
2	Four flaps—arms up and down, elbows bent
3	Four wiggles—hips, knees bent low
4	Four claps
5–16	Repeat action of measures 1–4 three times
	Part II Action
1–8	With a partner, either do a right-hand star with 16 skips or 16 walking steps, or do an elbow swing. (Skip, 2, 3, . . . 15, change hands)
9–16	Repeat with the left hand. On the last four counts of the last swing, everyone changes partners. If dancing in a circle formation, part-

ners B advance forward counter-clockwise to the next partner A. If dancing in a scattered formation, everyone scrambles to find a new partner. (Skip, 2, 3, . . . 12, change partners)

Variations: Perform the dance individually with everyone moving to find a new partner on the skipping sequence. The locomotor movements can be varied to include sliding or galloping.

Csebogar (Hungarian)

Records: LS E-15; MAV 1042

Skills: Skipping, sliding, draw step, elbow swing

Formation: Single circle, partners facing center, hands joined with partners B on the right

Directions:

Part I:

Measures	Action
1–4	Take seven slides to the left. (Slide, 2, 3, 4, 5, 6, 7, change)
5–8	Take seven slides to the right. (Back, 2, 3, 4, 5, 6, 7, stop)
9–12	Take three skips to the center and stamp on the fourth beat. Take three skips backward to place and stamp on the eighth beat. (Forward, 2, 3, stamp; Backward, 2, 3, stamp)
13–16	Hook right elbows with partner and turn around twice in place, skipping. (Swing, 2, 3, 4, 5, 6, 7, 8)

Part II: Partners face each other in a single circle with hands joined.

Measures	Action
17–20	Holding both of partner's hands, take four draw steps (step, close) toward the center of the circle. (Step-close, 2-close, 3-close, 4-close)
21–24	Take four draw steps back to place. (Step-close, 2-close, 3-close, 4-close)
25–26	Go toward the center of the circle with two draw steps. (In-close, 2-close)
27–28	Take two draw steps back to place. (Out-close, 2-close)
29–32	Hook elbows and repeat the elbow swing, finishing with a shout and

facing the center of the circle in the original formation. (Swing, 2, 3, 4, 5, "Csebogar")

Variation: Instead of an elbow swing, partners can use the Hungarian turn. Partners stand side by side, put the right arm around the partner's waist, and lean away from partner. The left arm is held out to the side, with the elbow bent, the hand pointing up, and the palm facing the dancer.

Pop Goes the Weasel (American)

Records: MAV 1041; LS E-15, E-21

Skills: Walking, skipping, turning under

Formation: Double circle of sets of four; couples facing with partner B on partner A's right. Couples facing clockwise are number 1 couples; couples facing counterclockwise are number 2 couples.

Directions:

Measures	Action
1–4	Join hands in a circle of four and circle left, once around, with eight skipping or sliding steps. (Circle, 2, 3, 4, 5, 6, 7, 8)
5–6	Take two steps forward, raising the joined hands, and two steps backward, lowering the hands. (Forward, 2; Back, 2)
7–8	"Ones" pop the "Twos" under (i.e., couples number 1 raise their joined hands to form an arch and pass the number 2 couples under). All walk ahead to meet a new couple. (Forward, and pop through)

Repeat as desired.

Variations:

1. Dancers are in sets of three, all facing counterclockwise. Each forms a triangle with one child in front and the other two with joined hands forming the base. The front dancer reaches back and holds the outside hands of the other two dancers. The groups of three are in a large circle formation.

Measures	Action
1–2	Sets of three dancers skip forward four times. (Forward, 2, 3, 4)
3–4	Sets of three skip backward four times. (Backward, 2, 3, 4)
5–6	Sets of three skip forward four times. (Forward, 2, 3, 4)
7–8	On "Pop goes the weasel," the two back dancers raise their joined

hands, and the front dancer backs up underneath to the next set. This set, in the meantime, has "popped" its front dancer back to the set behind it. (Raise and pop under)

2. "Pop Goes the Weasel" is excellent for stimulating creative movement. The music actually consists of a verse and a chorus part. During the verse part, the children can slide, gallop, or skip until the "Pop" line, at which time they make a half or full turn in the air. During the chorus, they can do jerky nonlocomotor movements. Other options include ball routines, in which the children dribble in time to the music during the verse and pass the ball around various parts of the body during the chorus. Another variation involves ropes. The children carry a jump rope while skipping, sliding, or galloping. During the chorus, they jump in time to the music, and on the word "Pop," they try to do a double jump.

Teddy Bear Mixer (American)

Record: LS E-11

Skills: Walking, pausing, partner change

Formation: Double circle of couples facing counterclockwise, partner B on right side of partner A, inside hands joined. Walking step is used throughout.

Directions:

Measures	Action
1–2	Starting with partner A's left foot (B's right), walk three steps in the line of direction and pause. (Walk, 2, 3, pause)
3–4	Starting with A's right foot (B's left), walk backwards three steps in the reverse line of direction and pause. (Back, 2, 3, pause)
5–6	Starting on the left foot, As move three steps toward the center of the circle and pause. Starting on the right foot, Bs move away from the center of the circle three steps and pause. At the completion of the third step, a handclap may be used during the pause. (Separate, 2, 3, pause)
7–8	Starting on A's right foot (B's left), both move toward each other, rejoining inside hands. (Together, 2, 3, pause)
9–10	Repeat measures 1 and 2. (Walk, 2, 3, pause)
11–12	Repeat measures 3 and 4. (Back, 2, 3, pause)
13–14	Repeat measures 5 and 6. (Separate, 2, 3, pause)
15–16	Starting with A's right foot (B's left), both move together diagonally, with A moving forward to the B ahead to acquire a new partner for the next repetition. (Diagonally, 2, 3, pause)

Wild Turkey Mixer

Record: GR 15008

Skills: Walking, elbow swing, partner change

Formation: Trios abreast facing counterclockwise around the circle

Directions:

Measures	Action
1–8	In lines of three, with the right and left person holding the near hand of the center person, all walk 16 steps forward. (Walk, 2, 3, . . . 16)
9–12	The center person (Wild Turkey) turns the right-hand person once around with the right elbow. (Turn, 2, 3, 4, 5, 6, 7, 8)
13–16	The Wild Turkey turns the left-hand person with the left elbow, and then moves forward to repeat the dance with the two new people ahead. (Turn, 2, 3, 4; Forward, 2, 3, 4)

The same dance can be adapted to other pieces of music. With a faster tempo, the elbow swings are done with a skip instead of a walk.

La Raspa (Mexican)

Records: EZ 716; LS E-8; MAV 1043

Skills: Bleking step, running, elbow swing

Formation: Partners facing, couples scattered around the room

Directions: La raspa means "the rasp" or "the file," and the dance movements are supposed to represent a rasp or file in action. Directions are the same for both partners.

Part I: To begin, the partners face each other, partner B with hands at sides and partner A with hands behind the back.

Measures	Action
1–4	Beginning right, take one bleking step (p. 376). (Slow, slow, fast, fast, fast)
5–8	Turn slightly counterclockwise away from partner (right shoulder to right shoulder) and, beginning with a jump on the left foot, repeat measures 1–4. (Slow, slow, fast, fast, fast)
9–12	Repeat action of measures 1–4, facing opposite direction (left shoulder to left shoulder). (Slow, slow, fast, fast, fast)
13–16	Repeat action of measures 1–4, facing partner. (Slow, slow, fast, fast, fast)

Part II: Partners hook right elbows; left elbows are bent and left hands are pointed toward the ceiling.

Measures	Action
1–4	Do a right elbow swing, using eight running or skipping steps. Release and clap the hands on the eighth count. (Swing, 2, 3, 4, 5, 6, 7, clap)
5–8	Do a left elbow swing, using eight running or skipping steps. Release and clap the hands on the eighth count. (Swing, 2, 3, 4, 5, 6, 7, clap)
9–16	Repeat the actions of measures 1–8.

Variations:

1. Face partner (all should be in a single-circle formation for this version) and do a grand right and left around the circle. Repeat Part I with a new partner.

2. All face center or face a partner and do the Bleking or raspa step. On each pause, clap own hands twice.

Patty Cake (Heel and Toe) Polka (International)

Records: MAC 5003; LS E-24; Windsor 4624

Skills: Heel and toe polka step, sliding, elbow swing, skipping

Formation: Double circle, partners facing, A in the inner circle with back to the center. Both hands are joined with partner. A's left and B's right foot are free.

Directions:

Measures	Part I Action
1–2	Heel-toe twice with A's left and B's right foot. (Heel, toe, heel, toe)
3–4	Take four slides sideward to A's left, progressing counterclockwise. Do not transfer the weight on the last count. Finish with A's right and B's left foot free. (Slide, 2, 3, 4)
5–8	Repeat the pattern of measures 1–4, starting with A's right and B's left foot, progressing clockwise. Finish with the partners separated and facing. (Heel, toe, heel, toe; slide, 2, 3, 4)

Measures	Part II Action
9	Clap right hands with partner three times. (Right, 2, 3)
10	Clap left hands with partner three times. (Left, 2, 3)
11	Clap both hands with partner three times. (Both, 2, 3)
12	Slap own knees three times. (Knees, 2, 3)
13–14	Right elbow swing with partner. Partners hook right elbows and swing once around with four walking steps, finishing with A's back to center. (Swing, 2, 3, 4)
15–16	Progress left to a new partner with four walking steps. (Left, 2, 3, 4)

Repeat the entire dance with the new partner.

Polly Wolly Doodle (American)

Record: MAV 1041

Skills: Sliding, turning, walking

Formation: Double circle of dancers, partners facing with both hands joined, partner A with back to the center of the circle

Measures	Part I
1–4	*Oh, I went down south for to see my Sal,*
5–8	*Sing polly wolly doodle all the day.*
9–12	*My Sally am a spunky gal*
13–16	*Sing polly wolly doodle all the day.*

Verse

1–4	*Oh, my Sal she am a maiden fair,*
5–8	*Sing polly wolly doodle all the day,*
9–12	*With laughing eyes and curly hair,*
13–16	*Sing polly wolly doodle all the day.*

Part II

1–4	*Fare thee well, fare thee well,*
5–8	*Fare thee well, my fairy fay,*
9–12	*For I'm going to Louisiana for to see my Susyanna,*
13–16	*Sing polly wolly doodle all the day.*

Directions:

Measures	**Part I Action**
1–4	All slide four steps—As to left, Bs to right, counterclockwise. (Slide, 2, 3, 4)
5–8	Drop hands and all turn solo circle, As to left, Bs to right, with five stamps in this rhythm: 1-2-1, 2, 3. (Stamp on the word "polly," stamp on the other foot on the word "doodle," and take three quick stamps on the word "day.") (Turn, 2, stamp, 2, 3)
9–16	Repeat measures 1–8, but in the opposite direction, As moving to right and Bs to left. (Slide, 2, 3, 4; Turn, 2, stamp 2, 3)

	Part II Action
1–4	Both bow to each other, As with hands on hips, Bs with hands at sides. (As bow; Bs bow)
5–8	With four walking steps (or skipping steps), both move backward, away from each other. (Back, 2, 3, 4)
9–12	Both move diagonally forward to own left to meet a new partner. (Diagonal, 2, 3, 4)
13–16	With the new partner, elbow swing in place using a skipping step. (Swing, 2, 3, 4) Repeat the dance from the beginning with the new partner.

Bingo (American)

Records: LS E-13, E-21; CM 1159; MAV 1043

Skills: Walking, right-and-left grand

Formation: Double circle, partners side by side and facing counterclockwise, partners A on the inside and inside hands joined

Note: Bingo is a favorite of young people. The singing must be brisk and loud. The dance is in three parts.

Directions:

Part I: Partners walk counterclockwise around the circle, singing the following refrain. (Walk, 2, 3, . . . 15, face center)

A big white dog sat on the back porch and Bingo was his name.

A big white dog sat on the back porch and Bingo was his name.

Part II: All join hands to form a single circle, partner B on partner A's right. They sing (spelling out) with these actions.

Song	Action
B-I-N-G-O,	All take four steps into the center.
B-I-N-G-O,	All take four steps backward.
B-I-N-G-O,	All take four steps forward again.
And Bingo was his name	Take four steps backward, drop hands, and face partner.

Part III: Shake right hands with the partner, calling out *B* on the first heavy note. All walk forward, passing their partner, to meet the oncoming person with a left handshake, calling out *I* on the next chord. Continue to the third person with a right handshake, sounding out the *N.* Pass on to the fourth person, giving a left handshake and a *G.* Instead of a handshake with the fifth person, face each other, raise the arms high above the head, shake all over, and sound out a long, drawn-out *O.* The fifth person becomes the new partner, and the dance is repeated.

Variations:

1. A real desperado by the name of Ringo actually had quite a reputation as a gunman, and his name can be used in the dance. The wording of the verses is then changed as follows.

There was a fast gunman in the West and Ringo was his name!

There was a fast gunman in the West and Ringo was his name!

R-I-N-G-O (Repeat three times.)

And Ringo was his name.

2. The dance can be adapted to the use of a parachute. At the end of Part II (the end of the line "And Bingo was his name") partners A face the chute and hold it with both hands, lifting it to shoulder level. Partners B drop their hands from the parachute and get ready to move clockwise. On each of the letters *B-I-N-G-O,* they move inside the first A, outside the next, and so on, for five changes. They then take a new place as indicated and get ready to repeat the dance. The next sequence can have partners B remaining in place, holding the chute, while partners A move counterclockwise.

Grand March (American)

Record: LS E-16; or any good march or square dance record

Skills: Controlled walking, marching, grand march figures

Formation: Partners B are on the left side of the room, facing the end, and partners A are on the right side, facing the same end. This is the foot of the hall. The teacher or caller stands at the other end of the room, the head of the hall. An alternative formation is to put half of the class on each side of the room and to designate each half with different colored pinnies.

Directions:

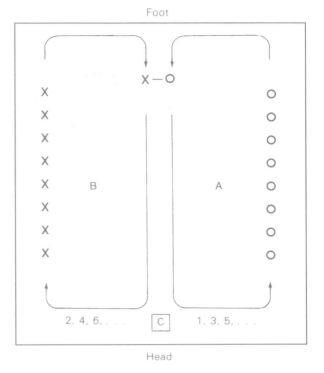

Figure 16.4 Formation and action for grand march

Call	Action
Down the center by twos.	The lines march forward to the foot of the hall, turn the corner, meet at the center of the foot of the hall, and march in couples toward the caller (Figure 16.4), with inside hands joined. The Bs' line should be on the proper side so that, when the couples come down the center, A is on B's left. Odd couples are numbered 1, 3, 5, and so on. Even couples are numbered 2, 4, 6, and so on.
Twos left and right.	The odd couples go left and the even couples go right around the room and meet at the foot of the hall.
Down the center by fours.	The couples walk down the center, four abreast.
Separate by twos.	When they approach the caller, odd couples go left and even couples right. They meet again at the foot of the hall.
Form arches.	Instead of coming down the center, odd couples form arches and even couples tunnel under. Each continues around the sides of the hall to meet at the head.
Other couples arch.	Even couples arch, and odd couples tunnel under. Each continues around the sides of the room to the foot.
Over and under.	The first odd couple arches over the first even couple, then ducks under the second even couple's arch. Each couple goes over the first couple and under the next. Continue around to the head of the hall.
Pass right through.	As the lines come toward each other, they mesh and pass through each other in the following fashion: All drop handholds. Each B walks between the A and B

	of the opposite couple and continues walking to the foot of the hall.	
Down the center by fours.	Go down the center four abreast.	
Fours left and right.	The first four go left around the room, and the second four go right. The fours meet at the foot of the hall.	
Down the center by eights.	Go eight abreast down the center.	
Grapevine.	All persons in each line join hands and keep them joined. The leader takes either end of the first line and starts around the room with the line trailing. The other lines hook on to form one long line.	
Wind it up.	The leader winds up the group in a spiral formation, like a clock spring. She makes the circles smaller and smaller until she is in the center.	
Reverse (un-wind).	The leader turns and faces in the opposite direction and walks between the lines of winding dancers. She unwinds the line and leads it around the room.	
Everybody swing.	After the line is unwound, everybody does a square dance swing.	

Teaching suggestions: The leaders (couples 1 and 2) should maintain an even, steady pace and not hurry, or the march becomes a race. When one set of couples forms arches (as in movements 5 and 6) for the other set of couples to tunnel under, the arches should be made with the inside arms, and the couples should continue marching while they form the arches.

Green Sleeves (English)

Records: LS E-11; MAV 1042; RPT 107

Skills: Walking, star formation, over and under

Formation: Double circle with couples in sets of four, facing counterclockwise. Two couples form a set and are numbered 1 and 2. Inside hands of each couple are joined.

Directions:

Measures	Call	Action
1–8	Walk	Walk forward 16 steps.
9–12	Right-hand star	Each member of couple 1 turns individually to face the couple behind. All join right hands and circle clockwise (star) for eight steps.
13–16	Left-hand star	Reverse direction and form a left-hand star. This should bring couple 1 back to place facing in the original direction.
17–20	Over and under	Couple 2 arches and couple 1 backs under four steps while couple 2 moves forward four steps. Couple 1 then arches and couple 2 backs under (four steps for each).
21–24	Over and under	Repeat the action of measures 17–20.

Jingle Bells, Var. 2 (Dutch)

Record: MAC 2046

Skills: Skipping, promenade position, sliding, elbow swing

Formation: Circle of couples facing counterclockwise, partner B on partner A's right. Promenade position, hands crossed in front, right hands joined over left, right foot free.

Directions:

Measures	Part I Action
1–2	Take four skips forward and four skips backward, starting with the right foot free. (Forward, 2, 3, 4; Back, 2, 3, 4)
3–4	Repeat the pattern of measures 1 and 2. (Forward 2, 3, 4; Back, 2, 3, 4)
5	Do four slides to the right, away from the center of the circle. (Out, 2, 3, 4)
6	Now do four slides left, toward the center. (In, 2, 3, 4)

7–8	Execute eight skips, making one turn counterclockwise, with partner A pivoting backward and partner B moving forward. Finish in a double circle, partners facing, with A's back to the center. (Skip, 2, 3, 4, 5, 6, 7, 8)

Part II Action

1	Clap own hands three times. (Clap, 2, 3)
2	Clap both hands with partner three times. (Both, 2, 3)
3	Clap own hands four times. (Clap, 2, 3, 4)
4	Clap both hands with partner once. (Both)
5–8	Right elbow swing with partner. Partners hook right elbows and swing clockwise for eight skips. (Swing, 2, 3, 4, 5, 6, 7, 8)
9–12	Repeat clapping pattern of measures 1–4.
13–16	Left elbow swing with partner using eight skips and finishing in the original starting position to repeat the entire dance with the same partner; or left elbow swing with partner once around, then all of the children in the inner circle skip forward to the outer dancer ahead and repeat the entire dance with a new partner. (Swing, 2, 3, 4, 5, 6, 7, 8)

E-Z Mixer

Record: GR 2204

Skills: Walking, elbow swing or swing in closed position

Formation: Circle formation with couples in promenade position, inside hands joined, facing counterclockwise.

Directions:

Measures	Action
1–2	With partner B on the right, walk forward four steps. (Forward, 2, 3, 4) Back out to face center in a single circle. (Circle, 2, 3, 4)
3–4	Partners B walk to the center. (In, 2, 3, 4) Back out of the center. (Out, 2, 3, 4)

5–6	Partners A take four steps to the center, turning one half left face on the fourth step. (In, 2, 3, turn left face) They take four steps toward the corner. (Out, 2, 3, 4)
7–8	As swing the corner B twice around, opening up to face counterclockwise, back in starting position, to begin the dance again. (Swing, 2, 3, open)

Any piece of music with a moderate 4/4 rhythm is appropriate for this basic mixer.

Ve David (Israeli)

Records: CM 1161; HLP 4028

Skills: Walking, pivoting, buzz-step turn

Formation: Double circle, couples facing counterclockwise, partner B on partner A's right. Inside hands joined, right foot free.

Directions:

Measures	Part I Action
1–2	All walk forward and form a ring. Take four walking steps forward, starting with the right foot and progressing counterclockwise, then back out, taking four walking steps to form a single circle, facing center, with all hands joined. (Walk, 2, 3, 4; Single, circle, 3, 4)
3–4	All forward and back. Four steps forward to center and four steps backward, starting with the right foot. (Forward, 2, 3, 4; Back, 2, 3, 4)

	Part II Action
1–2	Bs forward and back; As clap. Partners B, starting with the right foot, walk four steps forward to the center and four steps backward to place while Partners A clap. (Bs in, 2, 3, 4; Out 2, 3, 4)

	Part III Action
1–2	Partners A forward, circle to the right, and progress to a new partner; all clap. As, clapping hands, walk four steps forward to the center, starting with the right foot. They turn right about on the last "and" count and walk forward

four steps, passing their original partner and progressing ahead to the next. (As in, 2, 3, 4; Turn to new partner)

3–4   Swing the new partner. The A and the new partner B swing clockwise with right shoulders adjacent, right arms around each other across in front, and left arms raised—pivoting with right foot for an eight count "buzz-step" swing. (Swing, 2, 3, 4, 5, 6, 7, 8)

Repeat the entire dance.

Irish Washerwoman (Irish)

Records: LS E-11, E-22; MAV 1043
Skills: Walking, elbow swing, promenade
Formation: Single circle, couples facing center, partner B to the right, hands joined
Directions: Dancers follow the call.

Call	Action
All join hands and go to the middle.	Beginning left, take four steps to the center. (Center, 2, 3, 4)
And with your big foot keep time to the fiddle.	Stamp four times in place (Stamp, 2, 3, 4)
And when you get back, remember my call.	Take four steps backward to place (Back, 2, 3, 4)
Swing your corner and promenade all.	Swing the corner and promenade in the line of direction. (Swing, 2, 3, promenade)

Dancers keep promenading until they hear the call again to repeat the pattern.

Oh, Susanna (American)

Records: LS E-14, E-23; MAV 1043; RPT 317
Skills: Walking, promenade position, grand right and left
Formation: Single circle, all facing center, partner B on the right
Directions:

Measures	Part I Action
1–4	Partners B walk forward four steps and back four, as partners A clap hands. (Forward, 2, 3, 4; Back, 2, 3, 4)
5–8	Reverse, with As walking forward and back, and Bs clapping time. (Forward, 2, 3, 4; Back, 2, 3, 4)

	Part II Action
1–8	Partners face each other, and all do a grand right and left by grasping the partner's right hand, then passing to the next person with a left-hand hold. Continue until reaching the seventh person, who becomes the new partner. (Face, 2, 3, 4, 5, 6, 7, 8)

	Chorus
1–16	All join hands in promenade position with the new partner and walk counterclockwise around the circle for two full choruses singing: "Oh Susanna, oh don't you cry for me, For I come from Alabama with my banjo on my knee." (Promenade, 2, 3, . . . 16)

Repeat the dance from the beginning, each time with a new partner. For variety in the chorus, skip instead of walk, or walk during the first chorus and swing one's partner in place during the second chorus.

Crested Hen (Danish)

Records: HLP 4027; MAV 1042
Skills: Step-hop, turning under
Formation: Sets of three. One child is designated the center child.
Directions:
Part I:

Measures	Action
1–4	Dancers in each set form a circle. Starting with a stamp with the left foot, each set circles to the left, using step-hops. (Stamp and, 2 and, 3 and, 4 and, 5 and, 6 and, 7 and, stop)
5–8	The figure is repeated. Dancers reverse direction, beginning again with a stamp with the left foot and following with step-hops. The change of direction should be vigorous and definite, with the left foot crossing over the right. At the end of the sequence, two dancers release each other's hands to break

the circle and stand on either side of the center person, forming a line of three while retaining joined hands with the center dancer. (Stamp and, 2 and, 3 and, 4 and, 5 and, 6 and, 7 and, line)

Part II: During this part, the dancers use the step-hop continuously while making the pattern figures.

Measures	Action
9–10	The dancer on the right moves forward in an arc to the left and dances under the arch formed by the other two. (Under and, 2 and, 3 and, 4 and)
11–12	After the right dancer has gone through, the two forming the arch turn under (dishrag), to form once again a line of three. (Turn and, 2 and, 3 and, 4 and)
13–16	The dancer on the left then repeats the pattern, moving forward in an arc under the arch formed by the other two, who turn under to unravel the line. (Under and, 2 and, 3 and, 4 and; Turn and, 2 and, 3 and, circle)

As soon as Part II is completed, dancers again join hands in a small circle. The entire dance is repeated. Another of the three can be designated the center dancer.

Troika (Russian)

Records: WT 10010; CM 1160

Skills: Running step, turning under

Formation: Trios face counterclockwise. Start with hands joined in a line of three. The body weight is on the left foot; the right foot is free.

Directions:

Measures	Part I Action
1	Take four running steps diagonally forward right, starting with the right foot. (Forward, 2, 3, 4)
2	Take four running steps diagonally forward left, starting with the right foot. (Diagonal, 2, 3, 4)
3–4	Take eight running steps in a forward direction, starting with the right foot. (Forward, 2, 3, 4, 5, 6, 7, 8)

5–6	The center dancer and the left-hand partner raise joined hands to form an arch and run in place. Meanwhile, the right-hand partner moves counterclockwise around the center dancer with eight running steps, goes under the arch, and back to place. The center dancer unwinds by turning under the arch. (Under, 2, 3, 4; Turn, 2, 3, 4)
7–8	Repeat the pattern of measures 5 and 6, with the left-hand partner running under the arch formed by the center dancer and the right-hand partner. (Under, 2, 3, 4; Turn, 2, 3, circle)

Part II Action

9–11	The trio joins hands and circles left with 12 running steps. (Run, 2, 3, 4, 5, 6, 7, 8, 9, 10, 11, 12)
12	Three stamps in place (counts 1–3), pause (count 4). (Stamp, 2, 3, pause)
13–15	The trio circles right with 12 running steps, opening out at the end to reform in lines of three facing counterclockwise. (Run, 2, 3, 4, 5, 6, 7, 8, open, 10, 11, 12)
16	The center dancer releases each partner's hand and runs under the opposite arch of joined hands to advance to a new pair ahead. Right- and left-hand partners run in place while waiting for a new center dancer to join them in a new trio. (Stamp, 2, line, pause)

Teaching suggestions: Practice the running steps in groups of three. Then introduce turning under the arch and finish by practicing the running circle with accent stamps.

Gustaf's Skoal (Swedish)

Records: HLP 4027; LS E-11, E-22; MAV 1044; RPT 107

Skills: Walking (stately), skipping, turning

Formation: The formation is similar to a square dance set of four couples, each facing center. Partner A is to the left of partner B. Couples join inside hands; the outside hand is on the hip. Two of the couples facing each other are designated the head couples. The other two couples, also facing each other, are the side couples.

Directions: The dance is in two parts. During Part I, the music is slow and stately. The dancers perform with great dignity. The music for Part II is light and represents fun.

Measures	Part I Action
1–2	The head couples, inside hands joined, walk forward three steps and bow to the opposite couple. (Forward, 2, 3, bow)
3–4	The head couples take three steps backward to place and bow to each other. (The side couples hold their places during this action.) (Back, 2, 3, bow)
5–8	The side couples repeat action of measures 1–4 while the head couples hold their places. (Forward, 2, 3, bow; Back, 2, 3, bow)
9–16	The dancers repeat measures 1–8.

Measures	Part II Action
17–22	The side couples raise joined hands to form an arch. Head couples skip forward four steps, release partners' hands, join inside hands with opposite person, and skip under the nearest arch with new partner. After going under the arch, they drop hands and head back home to their original partner. (Head couples: Skip, 2, 3, 4; Under, 2, 3, 4; Around, 2, 3, 4)
23–24	All couples join both hands with partners and swing once around with four skipping steps. (Swing, 2, 3, 4)
25–30	Head couples form arches while side couples repeat the action of measures 17–22. (Side couples: Skip, 2, 3, 4; Under, 2, 3, 4; Around, 2, 3, 4)
31–32	All couples then repeat the movements in measures 23–24. (Swing, 2, 3, 4)

Variation: During the first action sequence of Part I (in which the dancers take three steps and bow), a shout of "Skoal" and raising the right fist high above the head as a salute can be substituted for the bow. The word *skoal* is a toast. (Note that the dancers' hands are not joined.)

Lummi Sticks

Records: KIM 2000, 2014, 2015; HLP Lummi Sticks

Skills: Rhythmic tapping, flipping, and catching of sticks

Formation: Couples scattered throughout the area

Lummi sticks are smaller versions of wands; they are 12 to 15 inches long. Some believe that lummi sticks were a part of the culture of the Lummi Indians in northwest Washington. Others give credit to South Pacific cultures for the origin of the sticks. The actual origin remains obscure.

The chant (Figure 16.5) sets the basis for the movements and should be learned first, so it becomes automatic. Most lummi stick activities are done by partners, although some can be done individually. Each child sits cross-legged, facing a partner at a distance of 18 to 20 inches. Children adjust this distance as the activities demand. The sticks are held in the thumb and fingers (not the fist) at about the bottom third of the stick.

Routines are based on sets of six movements; each movement is completed in one count. Many different routines are possible. Only the basic ones are presented here. The following one-count movements are used to make up routines.

Vertical tap: Tap both sticks upright on the floor.

Figure 16.5 "The Lummi Stick Chant"

Partner tap: Tap partner's stick (right stick to right stick, or left to left).

End tap: Tilt the sticks forward or sideward and tap the ends on the floor.

Cross-tap: Cross hands and tap the upper ends to the floor.

Side tap: Tap the upper ends to the side.

Flip: Toss the stick in air, giving it a half turn, and catch other end.

Tap together: Hold the sticks parallel and tap them together.

Toss right (or left): Toss the right-hand stick to partner's right hand, at the same time receiving partner's right-hand stick.

Pass: Lay the stick on the floor and pick up partner's stick.

Toss right and left: Toss quickly right to right and left to left, all in the time of one count.

A number of routines, incorporating the movements described, are presented here in sequence of difficulty. Each routine is to be done four times to complete the 24 beats of the chant.

1. Vertical tap, tap together, partner tap right, vertical tap, tap together, partner tap left.

2. Vertical tap, tap together, pass right stick, vertical tap, tap together, pass left stick.

3. Vertical tap, tap together, toss right stick, vertical tap, tap together, toss left stick.

4. Repeat numbers 1, 2, and 3, but substitute an end tap and flip for the vertical tap and tap together. Perform the stated third movement (e.g., end tap, flip, partner tap right, end tap, flip, partner tap left).

5. Vertical tap, tap together, toss right and left quickly, end tap, flip, toss right and left quickly.

6. Cross-tap, cross-flip, vertical tap (uncross arms), cross-tap, cross-flip, vertical tap (uncross arms).

7. Right flip side—left flip in front, vertical tap in place, partner tap right. Left flip side—right flip in front, vertical tap in place, partner tap left.

8. End tap in front, flip, vertical tap, tap together, toss right, toss left.

9. Vertical tap, tap together, right stick to partner's left hand, toss own left stick to own right hand. Repeat. This is the circle throw.

10. Same as in number 9, but reverse the circle.

The activity can be done by four children with a change in the timing. One set of partners begins at the start, and the other two start on the third beat.

All sing together. In this way, the sticks are flying alternately.

Tinikling (Philippine Islands)

Records: KIM 8095, 9015; MAV 1047

Skills: Tinikling steps

Formation: Sets of fours scattered around the room. Each set has two strikers and two dancers (Figure 16.6).

Note: The dance represents a rice bird as it steps, with its long legs, from one rice paddy to another. The dance is popular in many countries in Southeast Asia, where different versions have arisen.

Directions: Two 8-foot bamboo poles and two crossbars on which the poles rest are needed for the dance. A striker kneels at each end of the poles; both strikers hold the end of a pole in each hand. The music is in waltz meter, 3/4 time, with an accent on the first beat. The strikers slide and strike the poles together on count 1. On the other two beats of the waltz measure, the poles are opened about 15 inches apart, lifted an inch or so, and tapped twice on the crossbars in time to counts 2 and 3. The rhythm "close, tap, tap" is continued throughout the dance, each sequence constituting a measure.

Basically, the dance requires that a step be done outside the poles on the close (count 1) and that two steps be done inside the poles (counts 2 and 3) when the poles are tapped on the crossbars. Many step combinations have been devised.

The basic tinikling step should be practiced until it is mastered. The step is done singly, although two dancers are performing. Each dancer takes a position at an opposite end and on the opposite side so that the dancer's right side is to the bamboo poles.

Count 1: Step slightly forward with the left foot.

Count 2: Step with the right foot between the poles.

Count 3: Step with the left foot between the poles.

Count 4: Step with the right outside to dancer's own right.

Count 5: Step with the left between the poles.

Count 6: Step with the right between the poles.

Count 7: Step with the left outside to the original position.

The initial step (count 1) is used only to get the dance under way. The last step (count 7) to original

Figure 16.6 Tinikling set

position is actually the beginning of a new series (7, 8, 9–10, 11, 12).

Some tinikling dances and records guide the dancers with a different type of rhythm (tap, tap, close), necessitating adjustment of the steps and patterns in these descriptions.

Tinikling steps also can be adjusted to 4/4 rhythm (close, close, tap, tap), which requires the poles to be closed on two counts and open on the other two. The basic foot pattern is two steps outside the poles and two inside. For the sake of conformity, we present all routines in the original 3/4 time (close, tap, tap). If other rhythms are used, adjust accordingly.

Dancers can go from side to side, or can return to the side from which they entered. The dance can be done singly, with the two dancers moving in opposite directions from side to side, or the dancers can enter from and leave toward the same side. Dancers can do the same step patterns or do different movements. They can dance as partners, moving side by side with inside hands joined, or facing each other with both hands joined.

Teaching suggestions: Steps should be practiced first with stationary poles or with lines drawn on the floor. Jump ropes can be used as stationary objects over which to practice. Students handling the poles should concentrate on watching each other

rather than the dancer to avoid becoming confused by the dancer's feet.

To gain a sense of the movement pattern for 3/4 time, slap both thighs with the hands on the "close," and clap the hands twice for movements inside the poles. For 4/4 time, slap the right thigh with the right hand, then the left thigh with the left hand, followed by two claps. This routine should be done to music, with the poles closing and opening as indicated. Getting the feel of the rhythm is important.

Other Tinikling Steps and Routines

Straddle step: Dancers do a straddle jump outside the poles on count 1 and execute two movements inside the poles on counts 2 and 3. Let the dancers explore the different combinations. Jump turns are possible.

Jump step: Dancers begin the side jump with their side toward the poles. They can execute the jump from either side.

Measure 1:

Count 1: Jump lightly in place.

Counts 2 and 3: Jump twice between the poles.

Measure 2:

Count 1: Jump lightly in place (other side).

Counts 2 and 3: Jump twice between the poles.

The feet should be kept close together to fit between the poles. Dancers can exit to the same side from which they entered, or can alternate sides. Another way to enter and exit is by facing the poles and jumping forward and backward rather than sideward. When jumping sideward, one foot can be kept ahead of the other in a stride position. This position can be reversed on the second jump inside the poles.

Rocker step: For the rocker step, dancers face the poles and begin with either foot. As they step in and out (forward and backward), they make a rocking motion with the body.

Crossover step: The crossover step is similar to the basic tinikling step, except that the dancer begins with the right foot (forward step) and steps inside the poles with the left foot, using a cross-foot step. Each time, the dancer must step in or out using a cross-step.

Circling poles: For circling the poles, dancers position themselves as in the basic tinikling step (Figure 16.7) and execute the following movements:

Measure 1:

Count 1: Step slightly forward with the left foot.

Count 2: Step with the right foot between the poles.

Count 3: Step with the left foot between the poles.

Measure 2:

Count 1: Step with the right foot outside the poles to the right.

Counts 2 and 3: With light running steps, make a half circle to a position for the return movement.

Measures 3 and 4: Dancers return to their original position using the same movements as in measures 1 and 2.

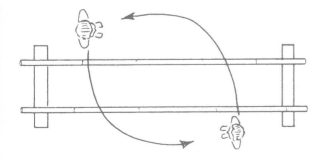

Figure 16.7 Circling poles for tinikling

Fast tinikling trot: The fast tinikling trot is similar to circling the poles, except that the step goes twice as fast and thus requires only two sets of three counts. Instead of having the side of the body to the poles, as in the basic tinikling step, the dancers face the poles. The following steps are taken:

Measure 1:

Count 1: Shift the weight to the left foot and raise the right foot.

Count 2: Step with the right foot between the poles.

Count 3: Step with the left foot outside the poles and begin turning to the left.

Measure 2:

Count 1: Step with the right foot outside the poles, completing the left turn to face the poles again.

Count 2: Step with the left foot inside the poles.

Count 3: Step outside with the right foot.

The next step is done with the left foot to begin a new cycle. The movement is a light trot with quick turns. Note that the step outside the poles on count 3 in each measure is made with the poles apart.

Cross-step: To do the cross-step, the dancer begins with the basic tinikling position, and uses the following sequence:

Measure 1:

Count 1: Cross-step across both poles with the left foot, hopping on the right side.

Counts 2 and 3: Hop twice on the right foot between the poles.

Measure 2:

Count 1: Hop on the left foot outside the poles to the left.

Counts 2 and 3: Hop twice again on the right foot between the poles.

Line of poles: Three or more sets of poles are about 6 feet apart. The object is to dance down the sets, make a circling movement (as in Circling Poles), and return down the line in the opposite direction (Figure 16.8). The dancer keeps his right side toward the poles throughout.

During measure 1 (three counts), the dancer does a basic tinikling step, finishing on the right side of the first set of poles. During measure 2 (three counts), he uses three light running steps to position himself for the tinikling step at the next set

Figure 16.8 Movement through line of poles for tinikling

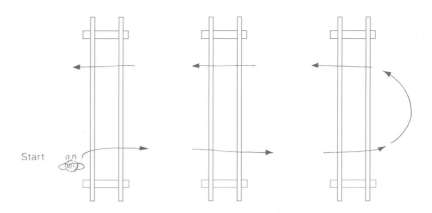

Start

of poles. When he gets to the end, he circles with three steps to get in position for the return journey.

Square formation: Four sets of poles can be placed in a square formation for an interesting dance sequence (Figure 16.9). Four dancers are positioned as shown. The movements are as follows: During measure 1, each dancer does a tinikling step, crossing to the outside of the square. On measure 2, the dancers circle to position for a return tinikling step. During measure 3, the dancers do a tinikling step, returning to the inside of the square. On measure 4, they rotate counterclockwise to the next set of poles with three running steps.

The basic tinikling step must be mastered if children are to enjoy the activity. Tell them to look ahead (not at the poles), so they learn by thinking and doing and not by gauging the pole distances visually.

Four pole set: This arrangement features two longer crossbars, on which two sets of poles rest, leaving a small space between the poles when the sets are open. Four clappers control the poles. Two

dancers begin by each straddling a set of poles on opposite ends, so the dancers face each other. Changes in foot pattern should be made every 16 measures, which for most records is a full pattern of music. The following steps and routines are suggested.

1. Straddle, jump, jump, exiting on measure 16 to the left.

2. Do the basic tinikling step, exiting on the left foot.

3. Do the basic tinikling step, first on one's own set of poles and then on the other set of poles. As the dancer comes out of the first set of poles with the right foot, she makes a half turn to do the tinikling step through the other poles. On the return, she makes another half turn in the middle to face and return to her original position. Repeat the sequence twice.

4. Do the same routine as in number 3, but move diagonally, passing the oncoming dancer with right shoulder to right shoulder, in effect changing places. (Do not use half turns.) Turn around in six steps and return to position. Repeat.

5. Jump to a straddle position with one foot in each of the pole openings. On "close," jump to the space between the sets. On measure 16, the dancer jumps out to the left on both feet.

6. Two-footed step: Jump twice with both feet inside the first set of poles, to the space between, twice inside the second set, and out. Return. Repeat twice.

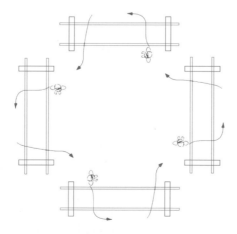

Figure 16.9 Square formation for tinikling

DEVELOPMENTAL LEVEL III DANCES

At this level, children should be adept dancers, especially if they have participated in rhythmic activities for several years. If students do not have a well-developed dance background, it is recommended that they first learn dances from developmental levels I and II. Developmental level III dances include dance patterns that must be performed with skill and finesse. At this level, patterns become longer, requiring more concentration and memorization. The schottische, polka, and two-step make their first appearance in these dances. The progression ranges from a dance that is performed in a circle and introduces square dance moves, to dances that feature the two-step, polka step, and schottische.

Hora (Hava Nagila) (Israeli)

Records: WT 10001; MAV 1043; RPT 106

Skills: Stepping sideward, step-swing

Formation: Single circle, facing center, hands joined. The circle can be partial.

Note: The hora is regarded as the national dance of Israel. It is a simple dance that expresses joy. The traditional hora is done in circle formation, with the arms extended sideward and the hands on the neighbors' shoulders. It is easiest to introduce the dance step individually. Once the step is learned, youngsters can join hands and practice the circle formation counterclockwise or clockwise. The clockwise version is presented here.

There are an old and a new hora, as done in Israel. The new hora is more energetic, with the dancers springing high in the air and whirling around with shouts of ecstasy. The hora can be done to many tunes, but the melody of "Hava Nagila" is the favorite.

Directions—Old Hora:

Measures	Action
1–3	Step left on the left foot. Cross the right foot in back of the left, with the weight on the right. Step left on the left foot and hop on it, swinging the right foot forward. Step-hop on the right foot and swing the left foot forward. The same step is repeated over and over. (Side, behind, side, swing; Side, swing)

The circle may move to the right also, in which case the same step is used, but the dancers begin with the right foot.

Directions—New Hora:

Measures	Action
1–3	Face left and run two steps. Jump in place. Hop on the left foot, swinging the right foot forward.

Take three quick steps in place. Continue in the same manner, moving to the left. (Run, run, jump, hop-swing, step, step, step)

The hora often begins with the dancers swaying in place from left to right as the music builds. Gradually, the dance increases in pace and intensity. Shouts accompany the dance as the participants call to each other across the circle. The words *Hava Nagila* mean "Come, let us be happy!"

Virginia Reel (American)

Records: MAC 7345; LS E-12, E-23

Skills: Skipping, arm turn, do-si-do, sliding (sashay), reeling

Formation: Six couples in a longways set of two lines facing. Partners on one end of the set are designated the head couple.

Directions:

Measures	Call	Action
1–4	All go forward and back.	Take three steps forward, curtsy or bow. Take three steps back and close.
5–8	Right hands around.	Move forward to partner, turn once in place using a right forearm grasp and return to position.
9–12	Left hands around.	Repeat measures 5–8 with a left forearm grasp.
13–16	Both hands around.	Partners join both hands, turn once in a clockwise direction, and move backward to place.
17–20	Do-si-do your partner.	Partners pass each other right shoulder to right shoulder and then back to back and move backward to place.
21–24	All go forward and back.	Repeat the action of measures 1-4.
25–32	Head couple sashay.	The head couple, with hands joined, takes eight slides down to the foot of the set and eight slides back to place.
33–64	Head couple reel.	The head couple begins the reel with linked right elbows and turns one and one-half times to face the next couple in line. Each member in the head couple then links left elbows with the person

		facing and turns once in place. The head couple meets again in the center and turns once with a right elbow swing. The next dancers down the line are turned with a left elbow swing and then the head couple returns to the center for another right elbow turn. The head couple thus progresses down the line, turning each dancer in order. After the head couple has turned the last dancers, they meet with a right elbow swing, turn halfway around, and sashay (slide) back to the head of the set
65–96	Everybody march.	All couples face toward the head of the set with the head couple in front. The person on the right turns to the right while the person on the left turns to the left and goes behind the line followed by the other dancers. When the head couple reaches the foot of the set, they join hands and make an arch, under which all other couples pass. The head couple is now at the foot of the set and the dance is repeated with a new head couple.

The dance is repeated until each couple has had a chance to be the head couple.

Teaching suggestions: Versions of this dance vary. Some allow time at the beginning for a do-si-do after the both hands around (measures 13–16) while others do not. Check the music for phrasing before presenting the dance to the class.

Technically, the dance is written for eight couples in each set. For the head couple to reel all couples in the set, they must not miss one beat of the music or they will be behind the phrasing for the reel section. When introducing the dance to a class for the first time, having only six couples in each set is helpful. Then, if a couple gets behind the music for the reeling section, they still can stay in time to the music and finish before the "casting off" section begins.

Teaching the Two-Step

Children can be taught the forward two-step simply by moving forward on the cue "Step, close, step," starting on the left foot and alternating thereafter. The close-step is made by bringing the toe of the closing foot to a point even with the instep of the other foot. All steps are almost slides, a kind of shuffle step.

The two-step just described is nothing more than a slow gallop, alternating the lead foot. One way to help students learn the step-close-step pattern is to put them in a single circle and have them gallop forward. They should all start on the left foot and move forward eight slow gallops. Stop the class and have them put their right foot forward and repeat the gallops. Continue this pattern, and have the students make the change from galloping with their left foot forward to galloping with their right foot forward without stopping. When they make this transition, they should bring the right foot forward in a walking step—the weight being on the left foot. Reverse the procedure when moving the left foot forward. The movement should be very smooth. When the students master this pattern, repeat the sequence, but do four gallops with each foot forward. After this pattern is mastered, repeat the pattern with two gallops on each foot. When students can do this, they are performing the forward two-step.

Next, arrange the children by couples in a circle formation, partners A on the inside, all facing counterclockwise. Repeat the instruction, with both partners beginning on the left foot. Practice the two-step with a partner, with partner A beginning on the left foot and partner B starting on the right. In the next progression, the children move face to face and back to back.

Teaching the Polka Step

The polka and the two-step are much alike. They both have a step-close-step pattern. The two-step is simply step-close-step, but the polka is step-close-step-hop. Technically, the polka is usually described as hop-step-close-step (or hop-step-together-step). However, the first description is probably more helpful when working with beginning students.

The polka step can be broken down into four movements: (1) step forward left, (2) close the right foot to the left, bringing the toe up and even with the left instep, (3) step forward left, and (4) hop on the left foot. The series begins with the weight on the right foot.

Several methods can be used to teach the polka:

1. *Step-by-step rhythm approach.* Analyzing the dance slowly, have the class walk through the steps together in even rhythm. The cue is "Step, close, step, hop." Accelerate the tempo to normal polka time and add the music.

2. *Gallop approach.* A method preferred by many elementary instructors is the gallop approach. (Review the previous section on teaching the two-step, which uses the gallop.) The approach is the same, but add the polka hop and speed up the tempo. When moving the right foot forward, a hop must be taken on the left foot. When moving the left foot forward, the hop is on the right foot.

3. *Two-step approach.* Beginning with the left foot, two-step with the music, moving forward in the line of direction in a single circle. Accelerate the tempo gradually to a fast two-step and take smaller steps. Without stopping, change to a polka rhythm by following each two-step with a hop. Use a polka record for the two-step, but slow it down considerably to start.

4. *Partner approach.* After the polka step has been learned individually by one of the three methods, the step can be practiced with partners in a double-circle formation, partners A on the inside and all facing counterclockwise, with inside hands joined. Partners A begin with the left foot and partners B with the right.

Klumpakojis (Swedish)

Record: MAV 1042

Skills: Walking, stars, polka step

Formation: Couples in a circle, side by side, all facing counterclockwise, with partner B to the right

Directions:

Measures	Part I Action
1–4	With inside hands joined, free hand on hip, all walk briskly around the circle for eight steps counterclockwise. (Walk, 2, 3, 4, 5, 6, 7, turn)
5–8	Turn individually to the left, reverse direction, change hands, and walk eight steps clockwise. (Walk, 2, 3, 4, 5, 6, 7, turn)

	Part II Action
9–12	Face partner and make a star by joining right hands (making certain that the right elbow is bent). The left hand is on the hip. With partner, walk around clockwise for eight walking steps. Change hands and repeat the eight steps, reversing direction. (Star, 2, 3, 4, 5, 6, 7, 8; Reverse, 2, 3, 4, 5, 6, 7, 8)

	Part III Action
13–16	Listen to the musical phrase, then stamp three times on the last two counts. Listen to the phrase again, then clap own hands three times. (Listen, listen, stamp, 2, 3; Listen, listen, clap, 2, 3)
17–20	Shake the right finger in a scolding motion at partner. (Scold, 2, 3) Shake the left finger. (Scold, 2, 3)
21–24	Turn solo to the left, clapping partner's right hand once during the turn. Use two walking steps to make the turn, and finish facing partner. (Turn, 2, stamp, 2, 3)
25–32	Repeat the action of measures 13–24.

	Part IV Action
33–40	With inside hands joined, do 16 polka steps (or two-steps) forward, moving counterclockwise. (Later, as the dance is learned, change to the promenade position.) On polka steps 15 and 16, partner A moves forward to take a new partner B while handing the original partner B to the A in back. New couple joins inside hands. (Step, close, step, hop; Step, close, step, hop; Repeat for a total of 16 polka steps)

Alley Cat (American)

Records: AT 13113; RM 3

Skills: Grapevine step, touch step, knee lifts

Formation: None, although all should face the same direction during instruction

Directions:

Measures	Action
1–2	Do a grapevine left and kick: Step sideward left, step right behind left, step left again, and kick. Repeat to the right. (Left, behind, left, kick; Right, behind, right, kick)

3–4	Touch the left toe backward, bring the left foot to the right, touch the left toe backward again, bring the left foot to the right, taking the weight. Repeat, beginning with the right toe. (Left and, left and; Right and, right and)
5–6	Raise the left knee up in front of the right knee and repeat. Raise the right knee up twice, similarly. (Left and, left and; Right and, right and)
7–8	Raise the left knee and then the right knee. Clap the hands once and make a jump quarter turn to the left. (Left and, right and, clap and, jump)

After the routine is repeated three times, the dancer should be facing in the original direction.

Ten Pretty Girls (American)

Record: EZ 5003

Skills: Walking, grapevine

Formation: Circle of groups of any number, with arms linked or hands joined, all facing counter-clockwise

Directions:

Measures	Action
1–2	Starting with the weight on the right foot, touch the left foot in front, swing the left foot to the left and touch, swing the left foot behind the right foot and put the weight on the left foot, step to the right, close the left foot to the right. (Front, side, back-side, together)
3–4	Repeat, starting with the weight on the left foot and moving to the right. (Front, side, back-side, together)
5–6	Take four walking or strutting steps forward, starting on the left foot. (Walk, 2, 3, 4)
7–8	Swing the left foot forward with a kicking motion; swing the left foot backward with a kicking motion; stamp left, right, left, in place. (Swing, swing, stamp, stamp, stamp)

Repeat the entire dance 11 times, starting each time with the alternate foot. The dance can be used as a mixer when performed in a circle by groups of three. On measures 7–8, have the middle person move forward to the next group during the three stamps.

Comin' Round The Mountain (American)

Record: AR 32

Skills: Touch step, step-hop, back-side-together step

Formation: Triple circle of three abreast facing counterclockwise

Directions:

Measures	Action
1–4	Touch left toe on the floor to the front, then to the side. Step the left foot behind the right so the legs are crossed; step the right foot one step to the right; then close the left foot to the right. The rhythm of steps is slow, slow, fast-fast-fast. (Front, side, back, side, together)
5–8	Touch the right toe on the floor to the front, then to the outside. Step the right foot behind the left so the legs are crossed; step the left foot one step to the left; then close the right foot to the left. (Front, side, back, side, together)
9–16	Repeat measures 1–8.
17–20	Moving forward, take a step-hop on the left foot and one on the right foot followed by four walking steps. (Step, hop, step, hop; Walk, 2, 3, 4)
21–32	Repeat measures 17–20 three additional times.

Limbo Rock

Records: WT 10034; RM 2

Skills: Touch step, swivel step, jump clap step

Formation: Single circle or scattered

Directions:

Measures	Part I Action
1–2	Touch left foot in. Touch left foot out. Three steps in place. (In, out, left, right, left)
3–4	Repeat measures 1 and 2 beginning with opposite foot. (In, out, right, left, right)
5–8	Repeat measures 1–4.

Part II Action

9–10	Swivel toes right, swivel heels right. Repeat and straighten feet. (Swivel, 2, 3, straighten)
11–12	Repeat beats 1 and 2 beginning with swivel toes left.
13–14	Jump in, clap; jump out, clap. (Jump, clap, jump, clap)
15–16	Repeat measures 13 and 14.

Variation: An easier version involves walking eight steps right during measures 9–16.

Jessie Polka (American)

Records: MAC 5001; CM 1160

Skills: Step and touch, two-step, or polka step

Formation: Circle, couples facing counterclockwise with inside arms around each other's waist

Directions:

Measures	Part I Action
1	Beginning left, touch the heel in front, then step left in place. (Left heel, together)
2	Touch the right toe behind. Then touch the right toe in place, or swing it forward, keeping the weight on the left foot. (Right toe, touch)
3	Touch the right heel in front, then step right in place. (Right heel, together)
4	Touch the left heel to the left side, sweep the left foot across in front of the right. Keep the weight on the right. (Left heel, crossover)

Measures	Part II Action
5–8	Take four two-steps or polka steps forward in the line of direction. (Step, close, step; Step, close, step; Step, close, step; Step, close, step)

Variation: The dance may be done as a mixer by having partner B turn out to the right on the last two two-steps and come back to the A behind her. Partners A continue to move forward on the last two two-steps, to make it easier to meet the B coming toward them. Another variation is to perform this activity as a line dance. Youngsters place the hands on the waist or shoulders of the dancer in front of them.

Jiffy Mixer

Records: KIM 1146; Windsor 4684

Skills: Heel-and-toe step, chug step

Formation: Double circle, partners facing.

Directions: The Windsor record has an introduction. Directions are for partners A; B's actions are opposite.

Measures	Introduction—use with Windsor record only
1–4	Wait, wait, balance apart (push away on the left foot and touch the right). Balance together (forward on the right and touch the left).

	Action
1–4	Strike the left heel diagonally out and return to touch the toe near the right foot. Repeat. Do a side step left with a touch. (Heel, toe; Heel, toe; Side, close; Side, touch)
5–8	Repeat while moving in the opposite direction, beginning with the right foot. (Heel, toe; Heel, toe; Side, close; Side, touch)
9–12	Take four chug steps backward clapping on the up beat. (Chug, clap, chug, clap, chug, clap, chug, clap)
13–16	Starting with the left foot, take four slow, swaggering steps diagonally to the right, progressing to a new partner. (Walk, 2, 3, 4)

The chug step is done by jumping and dragging both feet backward. The body is bent slightly forward.

Teaching suggestion: The dance can be introduced by having all join hands in a single circle, facing inward. There are no partners and no progressions to new partners.

Hot Time in the Old Town Tonight (*Old Town Stomp*) (American)

Record: AR-32

Skills: Directional walking, two-step

Formation: Single circle facing center or a series of lines facing forward

Directions:

Measures	Part I Action
1–4	Starting with the left foot, walk backward four steps ending with the feet together. Move forward

ending with the feet together.
(Back, 2, 3, 4; Forward, 2, 3, 4)

5–6	Place the left heel forward followed by a step on the left beside the right. Repeat beginning with the right heel. (Heel, together, heel, together)
7–8	Bend the knees; straighten the knees; and follow with two claps. (Down, up, clap, clap)
9–16	Repeat measures 1–8.

Part II Action

17–18	Move sideways left with a two-step followed by a stamp with the right foot alongside the left foot. (Left, close, left, stamp)
19–20	Repeat to the right and end with the weight on the left foot. (Right, close, right, stamp)
21–22	Step sideways on the left and stamp the right foot alongside the left foot. Repeat in the opposite direction. (Left, stamp, right, stamp)
23–24	Take four steps in place. (Left, right, left, right)
25–32	Repeat measures 1–8.

Inside-Out Mixer

Record: Any record with a pronounced beat suitable for walking at a moderate speed

Skills: Walking, wring the dishrag, change partners

Formation: Triple circle (three children standing side by side), facing counterclockwise, with inside hands joined. A pinney can be worn by the center person for identification.

Directions:

Measures	Action
1–4	Take eight walking steps forward. (Forward, 2, 3, 4, 5, 6, 7, 8)
5–8	Form a small circle and circle left in eight steps back to place. (Circle, 2, 3, 4, 5, 6, 7, 8)
9–12	The center person walks forward under the raised arms opposite, pulling the other two under to turn the circle inside out. (Inside-out, 2, 3, 4, 5, 6, 7, 8)
13–16	The trio circles left in eight steps, returning to place. When almost back to place, drop hands. The

center person walks forward counterclockwise, and the other two walk clockwise (the way they are facing) to the nearest trio for a change of partners. (Circle, 2, 3, 4, mix, 6, 7, 8)

D'Hammerschmiedsgselln (Bavarian)

Records: LS E-19; CM 1238

Skills: Clapping routine, step-hops

Formation: Circle of four

Directions: Translated, the title of the dance means "The Journey Blacksmith."

Measures	Chorus Action
1–16	First opposites do a clapping pattern beginning on the first count of measure 1, while the other pair does a clapping pattern beginning on the first count of measure 2. The six-count pattern is performed as follows: With both hands, slap own thighs (count 1), slap own chest (count 2), clap own hands (count 3), clap right hands (count 4), clap left hands (count 5), and clap opposite's hands (count 6). (Thighs, chest, together, right, left, both) Repeat the six-count pattern seven additional times.

Part I

17–24	Join hands and circle left with eight step-hops. (Step-hop, 2-hop, . . . 8-hop)
25–32	Circle right in the same manner. (Step-hop, 2-hop, . . . 8-hop)
33–48	Repeat the chorus action.

Part II—Star

49–56	Right-hand star with eight step-hops. (Step-hop, 2-hop, . . . 8-hop)
57–64	Left-hand star in the same manner. (Step-hop, 2-hop, . . . 8-hop)
65–80	Repeat the chorus action.

Part III—Big Circle

| 81–88 | Circles of four open to form one large circle, and circle left with eight step-hops. (Step-hop, 2-hop, . . . 8-hop) |
| 89–96 | Reverse direction, continuing with eight step-hops. (Step-hop, 2-hop, . . . 8-hop) |

Variation: As a mixer, try the following sequence.

Measures	Action
1–16	Use the chorus clapping pattern described.
17–24	As in Part I or II, circle left, or do a right-hand star with step-hops (or simple walking steps).
25–32	Do eight step-hops with the corner in general space or in any comfortable position, progressing anywhere.

Repeat the entire sequence with a new foursome.

Teaching the Schottische Step

The schottische is actually a light run, but when students are learning, it should be practiced as a walking step. (This is also true in polka instruction.) Lively music will quicken the step later. The cue is "Step, step, step, hop; step, step, step, hop; step-hop, step-hop, step-hop, step-hop." A full pattern of the schottische, then, is three steps and a hop, repeated once, followed by four step-hops. Partner A starts on the left foot and partner B on the right. The step can be learned first in scattered formation, then a single circle, and practiced later by couples in a double circle. An effective way to introduce the schottische is with the "Horse and Buggy Schottische."

Horse and Buggy Schottische (American)

Records: MAC 5003; LS E-14; RPT 108

Skill: Schottische step

Formation: Couples in sets of four in a double circle, facing counterclockwise. Couples join inside hands and give outside hands to the other couple (Figure 16.10).

Directions:

Measures	Action
1–2	Moving forward, perform two schottische steps. (Step, step, step, hop; Step, step, step, hop)
3–4	Progress in line of direction performing four step-hops. (Step-hop, 2-hop, 3-hop, 4-hop)

During the four step-hops, one of three movement patterns can be done.

1. The lead couple drops inside hands and step-hops around the outside of the back couple,

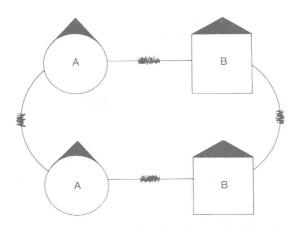

Figure 16.10 Horse and Buggy Schottische formation

who move forward during the step-hops. The lead couple then joins hands behind the other couple, and the positions are reversed.

2. The lead couple continues to hold hands and move backward under the upraised hands of the back couple, who untwist by turning away from each other.

3. Alternate 1 and 2.

Kalvelis (Little Blacksmith) (Lithuanian)

Records: HLP 4028; RPT 108

Skills: Polka step, swing, clapping pattern, grand right and left

Formation: Single circle of couples facing center, partner B on partner A's right, all hands joined in a single circle with the right foot free

Directions:

Measures	Part I Action
1–8	Circle right with seven polka steps, ending with three stamps. (Circle and, 2 and, 3 and, 4 and, 5 and, 6 and, 7 and, stamp, stamp, stamp)
9–16	Circle left with seven polka steps, ending with three stamps. (Circle and, 2 and, 3 and, 4 and, 5 and, 6 and, 7 and, stamp, stamp, stamp)

	Chorus
1–2	Clap own hands four times, alternating, left hand onto own right, then right hand onto own left. (Clap, 2, 3, 4)
3–4	Right elbow swing with four skips. (Swing, 2, 3, 4)
5–6	Repeat the clapping pattern of measures 1 and 2. (Clap, 2, 3, 4)

| 7–8 | Left elbow swing with four skips. (Swing, 2, 3, 4) |

| 9–16 | Repeat the pattern of measures 1–8. |

Part II Action

| 1–8 | Partners B dance three polka steps forward toward the center, ending with three stamps. They then turn to face their partner and return to place with three polka steps forward, ending with three stamps, facing center again. (Step-close-step-hop; Step-close-step-hop; Step-close-step-hop; Stamp, stamp, stamp) |

| 9–16 | Partners A repeat the pattern of measures 1–8, but dance more vigorously, stamping on the first beat of each measure. (Step-close-step-hop; Step-close-step-hop; Step-close-step-hop; Stamp, stamp, stamp) |

Chorus

| 1–16 | As described above. |

Part III Action

| 1–16 | Grand right and left around the circle with 16 polka steps, meeting a new partner on the last measure. (Step-close-step-hop; Repeat 16 times) |

Chorus

| 1–16 | As described, but with a new partner. |

Cotton-Eyed Joe (American)

Records: Belco 257; MAV 1045

Skills: Heel-toe, two-step

Formation: Double circle of couples with partner B on the right, holding inside hands and facing counterclockwise. Varsouvienne position can also be used.

Directions:

Measures	Action
1–2	Starting with the left foot, cross the left foot in front of the right foot, kick the left foot forward. (Cross, kick)
3–4	Take one two-step backward. (Left, close, left)
5–6	Cross the right foot in front of the left foot; kick the right foot forward. (Cross, kick)
7–8	Do one two-step backward. (Right, close, right)
9–16	Repeat measures 1–8.
17–32	Perform eight two-steps counter-clockwise beginning with the left foot. (Step, close, step; Repeat eight times)

Variation: During measures 17–32, the last four two-steps may be done in a circle.

Jugglehead Mixer (American)

Records: Any music with a definite and steady beat

Skills: Two-step, elbow turn (forearm grasp)

Formation: Double circle facing counterclockwise in promenade position

Directions: Actions described are for the inside partner; directions are opposite for the partner on the outside of the circle.

Measures	Call	Action
1–4	Two-step left and two-step right, walk-2-3-4.	Do a two-step left and two-step right and take four walking steps forward.
5–8	Two-step left and two-step right, walk-2-3-4.	Repeat measures 1–4.
9–10	Turn your partner with the right.	Inside partner takes the outside partner's right hand and walks around to face the person behind.
11–12	Now your corner with your left.	Inside partner turns the person behind with the left hand.
13–14	Turn your partner all the way around.	Inside partner turns partner with the right hand going all the way around.
15–16	And pick up the forward lady.	Inside partner steps up one place to the outside person ahead, who becomes the new partner.

Teton Mountain Stomp (American)

Records: Windsor 4615; CM 1243

Skills: Walking, banjo position, sidecar position, two-step

Formation: Single circle of partners in closed dance position, partners A facing counterclockwise, partners B facing clockwise

Directions:

Measures	Action
1–4	Step to the left toward the center of the circle on the left foot, close right foot to the left, step again to the left on the left foot, stomp right foot beside the left but leave the weight on the left foot. Repeat this action, but start on the right foot and move away from the center. (Side, close; Side, stomp; Side, close; Side, stomp)
5–8	Step to the left toward the center on the left foot; stomp the right foot beside the left. Step to the right away from the center on the right foot, and stomp the left foot beside the right. In "banjo" position (modified closed position with right hips adjacent), partner A takes four walking steps forward while partner B takes four steps backward, starting on the right foot. (Side, stomp, side, stomp; Walk, 2, 3, 4)
9–12	Partners change to sidecar position (modified closed position with left hips adjacent) by each making a one half turn to the right in place, A remaining on the inside and B on the outside. A walks backward while B walks four steps forward. Partners change back to banjo position with right hips adjacent by each making a left-face one half turn; then they immediately release from each other. A walks forward four steps to meet the second B approaching, while B walks forward four steps to meet the second A approaching. (Change, 2, 3, 4; New partner, 2, 3, 4)
13–16	New partners join inside hands and do four two-steps forward, beginning with A's right foot and B's left. (Step, close, step; Repeat four times)

Variation: If the dancers are skillful enough, use the following action for measures 13–16: New partners take the closed dance position and do four turning two-steps, starting on A's left (B's right) and make one complete right-face turn while progressing in the line of direction.

Alunelul (Romanian)

Records: WT 10005; CM 1162

Skills: Step behind step, grapevine step, stomping

Formation: Single circle, hands on shoulders to both sides, arms straight ("T" position)

Directions: The Romanians are famous for rugged dances. This dance is called "Little Hazelnut." The stomping action represents the breaking of the hazelnuts. The title is pronounced "ah-loo-NAY-loo."

Measures	Part I Action
1–2	Sidestep right, step left behind right, sidestep right, step left behind right, sidestep right, stomp left foot twice. (Side, back, side, back, side, stomp, stomp)
3–4	Beginning with the left foot, repeat the action but with reverse footwork. (Side, back, side, back, side, stomp, stomp)
5–8	Repeat the action of measures 1–4.

Measures	Part II Action
9–10	Sidestep right, left behind right, sidestep right, stomp. (Side, back, side, stomp)
11–12	Sidestep left, right behind left, sidestep left, stomp. (Side, back, side, stomp)
13–16	Repeat the action of measures 9–12.

Measures	Part III Action
17–18	In place, step right, stomp left; step left, stomp right; step right, stomp left twice. (Side, stomp, side, stomp, side, stomp, stomp)
19–20	In place, step left, stomp right; step right, stomp left; step left, stomp right twice. (Side, stomp, side, stomp, side, stomp, stomp)
21–24	Repeat action of measures 17–20.

Teaching suggestions: The stamps should be made close to the supporting foot. In teaching the dance, scatter the dancers in general space so they can move individually.

Korobushka (Russian)

Records: HLP 4028; CM 1162; WT 10005

Skills: Schottische step, balance step, cross-out-together step, walking step

Formation: Double circle, partner A's back to the center, with partners facing and both hands joined. A's left and B's right foot are free.

Directions:

Measures	Part I Action
1–2	Take one schottische step away from the center (partner A moving forward, partner B backward) starting with A's left and B's right foot. (Out, 2, 3, hop)
3–4	Repeat the pattern of measures 1 and 2, reversing direction and footwork. (In, 2, 3, hop)
5–6	Repeat the pattern of measures 1 and 2, ending on the last count with a jump on both feet in place. (Out, 2, 3, jump)
7–8	Hop on the left foot, touching the right toes across in front of the left foot (count 1). Hop on the left foot, touching the right toes diagonally forward to the right (count 2). Jump on both feet in place, clicking the heels together (count 1), pause, and release the hands (count 2). (Across, apart, together)

Measures	Part II Action
9–10	Facing partner and beginning with the right foot, take one schottische step right, moving sideways away from partner. (Side, back, side, hop)
11–12	Facing and beginning with the left foot, take one schottische step left, returning to partner. (Side, back, side, hop)
13–14	Joining right hands with partner, balance forward and back: Step forward on the right foot (count 1), pause (count 2), rock back on the left foot in place (count 3), pause (count 4). (Forward, hop, back, hop)
15–16	Take four walking steps forward, starting with the right foot, and change places with partner. (Walk, 2, 3, 4)
17–24	Repeat the pattern of measures 9–16, returning to place.

Variation: To use the dance as a mixer, during measures 19 and 20, move left to the person just before partner and continue with this new partner.

Teaching suggestion: Practice the schottische steps in different directions prior to introducing the dance as a whole.

Oh Johnny (American)

Record: MAC 2042

Skills: Shuffle step, swing, allemande left, do-si-do, promenade

Formation: Single circle of couples facing inward with partner B on the right

Directions: A shuffle step is used throughout this dance.

Call	Action
You all join hands and you circle the ring.	All join hands and circle for eight steps.
Stop where you are, give your partner a swing.	All stop and swing with partner.
Swing that little girl behind you.	As turn to their left and swing the corner B.
Now swing your own if she hasn't flown.	Swing with partner again.
And allemande left with the corner girl.	As turn to their left and do an allemande left with their corner.
And you do-si-do with your own.	As turn to their right and do a do-si-do with their partner.
Then you all promenade with the sweet corner maid singing, "Oh Johnny, Oh Johnny, Oh!"	As promenade with the corner B, who becomes the new partner for the next repetition.

Teaching hint: To simplify the dance, begin in scattered formation and teach each call with students changing from partner to corner using any nearby person. Since this is a fast-moving dance, the music should be slowed down until students can successfully complete the dance.

Doudlebska Polka (Czechoslovakian)

Records: LS E-16, E-19

Skills: Polka step, walking, clapping pattern

Formation: Either one large circle or several smaller circles scattered around the floor. The following description is for one large circle.

Directions:

Measures	Part I Action
1–16	Partners assume the varsouvienne position and do 16 polka steps around the circle, one couple following another. (Polka, 2, 3, . . . 16)

	Part II Action
17–32	Partner A puts the right arm around partner B's waist as they stand side by side, while B puts the left hand on A's right shoulder. A puts the left hand on the shoulder of the A in front. This closes the circle. Partners A move sideward to the center to catch up with the A ahead. In this position, all march forward counterclockwise and sing loudly, "La, la, la," and so forth. This takes 32 walking steps. (Walk, 2, 3, . . . 32)

	Part III Action
33–48	Partners A face the center, and partners B drop behind their partner. Bs turn to face the other way, clockwise, and polka around the circle (around the As) with their hands on hips. At the same time, As, who face center, clap a rhythm as follows: Clap hands twice, then extend both hands, palms outward, toward the neighbor on each side, and clap hands once with the neighbor. Repeat this pattern over and over. For variation, As may slap a thigh occasionally, or duck down, or cross their arms when clapping the neighbor's hand. (As: Clap, clap, out; Repeat 16 times) (Bs: Polka, 2, 3, . . . 16)

At the end of Part III, partners A turn around, take whichever partner B is behind them, and resume the dance from the beginning. If some children are without a partner, they move to the center and thus find a partner.

Extra children can enter the dance during the clapping part for partners A, and some can join the ring to polka around the outside. Those left without a partner wait for the next turn. When the group is large, several circles can be made, and it is perfectly proper for unpartnered children to steal into another circle. The polka in this case is done anywhere around the room. During the march, make circles of any number of people.

INTRODUCTORY SQUARE DANCE

Introductory square dance should be just that—introductory. In no case should the goal be finished, accomplished square dancing. The emphasis should be on enjoyment and learning the basics within the maturity capabilities of elementary school children. This can involve, however, considerable skill and polish. Square dancing is a broad and colorful activity with numerous figures, patterns, and dances. The large quantity of materials (introductory, intermediate, and advanced) poses a selection problem given the limited amount of program time that can be allocated to the activity.

Square dance fun begins with an effective caller, and calling takes practice. In a few instances, youngsters can develop into satisfactory callers. One solution is to select records that have square dance music and calls on one side and music only on the other side. Directions are usually supplied with the records. Singing calls should be used that can be done by one individual, by a group, or by the entire class. Singing calls are fun to dance to, because youngsters know what is coming next.

Square dance instruction should begin modestly in the fourth grade, with the impetus increasing in the fifth and sixth grades. This does not rule out the use of square dance–related figures in folk dances taught earlier. Square dance as a specialized dance activity requires the application of appropriate methodology. Some teaching suggestions follow.

1. In early figure practice or patter calls, pairing off by sex is not important. Let boys dance with boys and girls with girls if necessary. Avoid labeling one position for boys and one for girls.

In a couple, one partner becomes the left partner and the other the right. The goal is, however, to have boys dance with girls, and vice versa. In the following section, calls will be given in their traditional forms, and gender references, where they appear, will correspond with the traditional calls.

2. The shuffle step should be used, rather than the skipping or running step that beginners usually tend to use. The shuffle step makes a smoother and more graceful dance, has better carryover to other dancing, and conserves energy. It is a quick walk, almost a half glide, in time to the music and is done by reaching out with the toes in a gliding motion. The body should be in good posture position and should not bounce up and down on each step.

3. Teach the children to listen to the call. Equally important is that they know what the call means. They should have fun, but they must be quiet enough to hear the call.

4. It is important to follow the caller's directions and not to move too soon. The children should be ready for the call and then move at the proper time.

5. Generally, the caller explains the figures, has the children walk through the patterns, and then calls the figures.

6. The teacher should remember that there are many different ways to do different turns, swings, hand positions, and so on, and as many opinions on how these should be done. Settle on good principles and stick with them.

7. When a set becomes confused, each couple should return to their home position and try to pick up from that point. Otherwise, the choice is to wait until the dance is over or a new sequence has started.

8. Change partners at different times during the dancing. Have each partner A move one place to the right and take a new partner, or have all of the As (or Bs) keep their positions and have their partners change to another set.

The Movement Approach to Square Dance

Many square dance terms can be taught using a movement approach. The students are scattered in general space. A piece of country and western music with a strong beat is played. Anytime students hear the call, they perform the same task with the person nearest to them. Note that there are no boy or girl roles. The two-handed swing is to be used instead of the regular buzz-step swing.

Two calls are basic. "Hit the lonesome trail" directs students to promenade individually in general space in diverse directions. This call can be inserted at any time to move the students in new directions. The other basic call is "Stop where you are and keep time to the music." Students stop and beat time to the music with light claps. Other calls can be selected from the following list.

1. *Right (or left) arm round.* With a forearm grasp, turn your partner once around and return to place.

2. *Honor your partner, honor your corner.* Bow to one person, then bow to another.

3. *Do-si-do your partner, do-si-do your corner.* Pass around one person, right shoulder to right shoulder, and back to place. Repeat with another person.

4. *Right- (or left-) hand star.* Place indicated hands (palm to palm with fingers pointed upward) about shoulder height with elbow somewhat bent. The next call will indicate how far to turn the star.

5. *Two-hand swing.* Partners grasp both hands, lean away from each other, and circle clockwise once around.

6. *Go forward and back.* Move forward with three steps and a touch toward another person, who is moving similarly toward you. Move back to place with three steps and a touch.

The next teaching strategy is to divide the class into groups of four. Use a call such as, "Circle up, four hands round." Groups of four circle clockwise. There usually will be extras. If there are three extras, one person can pretend to have a partner. Rotate the extras in and out.

Circle fours until all groups are formed. With the call, "Break and swing," the fours separate into pairs within the foursome. Position the pairs so they face each other. Use the terms "left partner" and "right partner" instead of boy and girl. If convenient, when there are mixed pairs put the girl on the right.

The following figures can be practiced in fours.

1. *Circle to the left (or right).* Join hands and circle once around as indicated.

2. *Form a right- (or left-) hand star.* Hold right hands at about shoulder height and turn clockwise. A left-hand star reverses the direction.

3. *Swing your opposite and swing your partner.* Left partners walk toward their right partner

opposite and swing. They walk back to their own partner and swing. The call can be reversed.

4. *Birdie in the cage and three hands round.* One child (the birdie) goes to the center, while the other three join hands and circle left once around.

5. *The birdie hops out and the crow hops in.* The birdie joins the circle and another child goes in the center.

6. *Go into the middle and come back out; go into the middle and give a little shout.* This is done from a circle-right or circle-left formation. The dancers face center and come together. Repeat again, but with a light shout.

7. *Round and round in a single file; round and round in frontier style.* Circle left (or right), drop hands and move into a single file.

8. *Dive for the oyster—dig for the clam.* Usually after circling left once around, one couple goes partially under the raised joined hands of the other couple. The other couple repeats the same maneuver. Stepping should be: In, 2, 3, touch; out, 2, 3, touch.

The caller can use the "Hit the lonesome trail" call at any time to break up the makeup of the fours, and then reorganize later with different combinations of students.

Square Dance Formation

Each couple is numbered around the set in a counterclockwise direction. It is important that the couples know their position. The couple with their backs to the music is generally couple 1, or the head couple. The couple to the right of them is number 2, and so on. While the head couple is number 1, the term *head couples* includes both couples 1 and 3; couples 2 and 4 are the *side couples*.

With respect to any one left-hand partner (gent), the following terms are used in traditional calls (adjust references to sex as necessary):

Partner: The other (right-hand) dancer of the couple

Corner or corner lady: The right-hand partner on the left

Right-hand lady: The right-hand partner in the couple to the right

Opposite or opposite lady: The right-hand partner directly across the set

Other terms that are used include these:

Home: The couple's original or starting position

Active or leading couple: The couple leading or visiting the other couples for different figures

Once the square dance formation has been introduced, the figures and patter calls discussed previously should be practiced in the full formation of four couples. Although there is some repetition of material already presented in the movement approach section, the following figures merit discussion with the square dance formation as the background.

American Square Dance Figures

Some common square dance figures are the following:

1. *Honor your partner.* Partners bow to each other.

2. *Honor your corner.* Left-hand dancer bows to corner, who returns the bow.

3. *Shuffle step.* A light walking step on the ball of the foot. The body is upright and movement is in time with the music.

4. *Do-si-do your partner (or corner).* Partners face and pass each other right shoulder to right shoulder, move around each other back to back, and return to the original position facing their partner.

5. *Promenade.* The couple walks side by side, right hand joined to right hand and left to left in a crossed-arm promenade position. They walk around the square once and return to home position.

6. *Circle right (or left).* All eight dancers join hands and circle. The caller can add "Into the center with a great big yell." The circle can be broken with a swing at home place.

7. *Right-and-left grand.* All face their partner, join right hands, walk past the partner, and join left hands with the next person in the ring, and so on down the line. This causes left-hand partners to go in one direction (counterclockwise) around the circle and right-hand partners to go in the other direction, alternately touching right and left hands until partners meet again. Right-and-left grand starts with your partner and ends with your partner, at which time another call is needed.

8. *Allemande left.* Left-hand dancer faces corner, grasps corner with a left-forearm grip, walks around corner, and returns to partner.

9. *Arm swing.* Left-hand dancer turns partner with a right-arm swing, using a forearm grasp.

10. *Swing your partner (or corner)*. Partners stand side by side with right hip against right hip. The dancers are almost in social dance position, except that the left-hand partner's right arm is more around to the side than back at the shoulder blade. The dancers walk around each other with a slight lean away from each other until they reach their starting position.

11. *Do paso*. Starting position is a circle of two or more couples. Partners face, take a left forearm grasp, and turn each other counterclockwise until facing the corner. Turn corner with right forearm grasp until facing partner. Take partner with the left hand; left-hand partner turns the other with a courtesy turn.

12. *All around your left-hand lady, seesaw your pretty little taw*. Corners move one time around each other in a loop pattern, left-hand dancer starting behind the corner, on around corner and back to place, right-hand dancer starting in front of corner and around back to place. Repeat with partner to complete the other half of the loop.

13. *Ladies chain*. From a position with two couples facing each other, the girls cross over to the opposite boy, touching right hands as they pass each other. When they reach the opposite boy, they join left hands with him. At the same time, each boy places his right arm around the girl's waist and turns her once around to face the other couple. On "Chain right back," the girls cross back to their partner in a similar figure.

14. *Right-and-left through (and back)*. Two couples face each other. Dancers join right hands and pull past opposite, passing right shoulder to right shoulder. Couples have backs to each other. Courtesy turn to face again and repeat to original place.

Selecting Square Dances and Records

In past years, the types of square dances suggested for elementary students were traditional square dances using a patter call. Today, square dancing is a popular form of adult recreation. The singing call and use of modern music has helped in adult popularity, but more important is the difference in traditional calls versus modern calls. In traditional square dancing everyone knew what call was coming next. In modern square dancing nobody knows what the next call will be and nobody wants to know.

Two popular series of albums with different developmental levels and proper progression are the *Wagon Wheel Fundamentals of Square Dancing, Levels 1, 2, & 3* and *Square Dance Party for the New Dancer, No. 1 & No. 2*. Both series feature the calling of Bob Ruff. They can be ordered from the following source:

Wagon Wheel Records and Books
8459 Edmaru Avenue
Whittier, CA 90605

CULMINATING EVENTS FOR THE RHYTHMS UNIT

Country-Western Day

After all grade levels have reached a specified performance level in square dancing, a country-western day can be sponsored by the school. Teachers and students should be encouraged to wear country-western-style clothing all day, and then during the last hour of the school day, the student body can have a square dance. It is important to include activities that everyone, from third-grade students to sixth graders, can do together. The movement approach presented previously can help achieve this goal.

May Festival

In the spring when the rhythm program is drawing to a close, it is exciting to feature in a May festival all of the dances learned. To have this activity include everyone, each class or grade level should make a dance presentation. The announcer should describe the history and background of each dance (consult specialty dance books for a description of the various dances), and the festival should end with the entire school performing the Maypole Dance.

Activities for Developing Manipulative Skills

PURPOSE OF ACTIVITIES IN THIS CHAPTER
Activities in this chapter are designed to develop *manipulative skills*. These include striking, rolling, kicking, catching, dribbling, bouncing, trapping, volleying, and throwing. Development of *sport skills* results from practicing and learning advanced activities in this chapter. Rhythmic gymnastic activities combine *rhythmic and manipulative skills* using a particular piece of manipulative equipment while moving to accompaniment.

Manipulative activities are characterized by the use of some type of implement, usually with the hands but possibly with the feet or other body parts. Manipulative activities invite application of educational movement methodology, adding an important dimension to movement experiences. Manipulative activities develop both hand-eye and foot-eye coordination as well as dexterity.

Activities with balloons, hoops, wands, beanbags, balls of various types, tug-of-war ropes, lummi sticks, Frisbees, and scoops round out a basic program. Activities with jump ropes are important in the program because they offer multiple possibilities: manipulative activity, rhythmic activity, and fundamental movement. Because of the complexity and interrelatedness of the activities, a separate chapter (Chapter 18) is devoted to activities with jump ropes.

Balloons, beanbags, and yarn balls provide early throwing and catching activities for younger children. A soft object reduces the fear younger children have of being hurt while catching an object. After the introductory skills are mastered, other types of balls and more demanding skills can be brought in. Since early competency in handling objects provides a basis for later, more specialized skills, the basic principles of skill performance (pp. 35–37) have strong application, particularly as related to throwing and catching skills.

The start-and-expand approach is sound for teaching manipulative activities. Start children with a challenge that allows all to achieve success, and then expand the skills and experiences from that base. Concern for progression usually dictates that most activities begin with the individual approach and move later to partner activity.

PROGRESSION AND MOVEMENT THEMES

Activities within each unit in this chapter are presented in progression and take the form of movement themes or movement tasks and challenges. Movement themes, as opposed to simply listing a series of activities in progression, help teachers instruct toward desired objectives. For example, the first movement theme in beanbag activities is titled "Tossing to Self in Place." Suggestions for the development of this theme follow. Teachers can take either of two approaches. They can develop one or two themes in depth, exhausting all of the possibilities, or they can select a few activities from a number of themes, moving from one to the other with more dispatch. In the latter case, when the lesson is repeated the following day, the teacher can use the same themes but pose different challenges.

Opportunity for creative expression should be offered on a planned basis. This offers youngsters a chance to practice their favorite skills, work on learning new skills, or invent different ways of performing. The lesson plan should allow time for creative activity in the progressions.

Reinforcing Skills with Creative Games

Skills can be reinforced and enhanced through creative games. Children can be given a brief outline of a game situation on which they can structure a game applying the skills just learned. Specification of the game situation can range from open choice to creativity within guidelines. In either case, the focus is on using the skills just learned. As an example, the teacher might tell youngsters to create a game embodying a certain skill in which they are to select the equipment needed, outline the game space, specify number of participants, and set the rules, including scoring. More specifically, the teacher might outline certain conditions, such as use of two hoops and two bowling pins, space limitations of two lines 20 to 30 feet apart, and competing sides of two against two. Within those parameters, students would then create a game.

Creative games can be oriented toward individuals, partners, or small groups. Groups should be kept small, or individual input becomes minimal. Different kinds of equipment can be specified (e.g., mats, wands, goals, benches). After a period of time, different games can be demonstrated. While the creative process certainly has excellent value, the focus on the skill to be practiced must not be lost.

ACTIVITIES WITH BEACH BALLS AND BALLOONS

Balloons provide interesting movement experiences and emphasize hand-eye coordination. Success can be achieved with balloons when students are not ready for faster-moving ball skills. Keeping a balloon afloat is within the capability of young children and special education students. Beach balls are larger, move slowly, and are more predictable in movement. Both objects are harmless and allow youngsters to learn to catch without fear of being hurt by the projectile. Emphasis should be placed on proper footwork. Since these objects move slowly, there is ample time for students to learn proper footwork, i.e., preparing for a volley, catching, and striking.

Balloons are inexpensive and readily available. Extras are needed, since there is always breakage. The balloons should be of good quality and spherical in shape. At times, however, oddly shaped balloons can provide a change of pace. Balloons should be inflated only moderately, because high inflation increases the chance of breakage. Beach balls should be inflated with a ball pump. When they are no longer needed for instruction, they can be deflated and stored.

Instructional Procedures

1. Use the following instructional cues when teaching balloon and beach ball skills:

a. catch and control with the fingertips.

b. keep your eyes on the object.

c. move your body into the path of the oncoming object.

d. reach, catch, and move the object to the body (giving).

2. After blowing up each balloon, twist the neck and fix it with a twist tie of the type used to close plastic bags. This permits the balloon to be deflated easily and reused. Tying a knot in the neck makes deflating difficult.

3. Beach balls should not be overinflated. They will last longer and be easier to control if they are a bit underinflated. Sixteen- to 20-inch diameter beach balls are best for most youngsters and can also be used with older students for lead-up games in volleyball and soccer.

Recommended Activities

1. Begin with free exploration, having children play under control with their balloon (Figure 17.1). The objective is to have the children gain a sense of the balloon's flight.

Figure 17.1 Batting balloons from different body positions

2. Introduce specific hand, finger, and arm contacts. Include using alternate hands; contacting at different levels (low, high, in between); jumping and making high contact; using different hand contacts (palm, back, side, and different fist positions); using different finger combinations (two fingers, index finger, thumb only, others); and using arms, elbows, and shoulders.

3. Expand the activity to use other body parts. Establish contact sequences with three or four body parts. Use various levels and body shapes. Make some visual cards with names of body parts. Students must take their eye off the balloon to see the named body part. This is an excellent challenge to help young children learn to track a moving object.

4. Bat from various body positions—kneeling, sitting, lying.

5. Use an object to control the balloon (e.g., a lummi stick, a ball, a stocking paddle).

6. Restrict movement. Keep one foot in place. Keep one or both feet within a hoop or on a mat or carpet square.

7. Work with a partner by alternating turns, batting the beach ball back and forth, employing follow-the-leader patterns, and so on.

8. Introduce some aspects of volleyball technique, including the overhand pass, the underhand pass, and the dig pass. Begin with a volleyball serve. Make this informal and on a "let's pretend" basis. Check the volleyball unit (Chapter 31) for technique suggestions.

9. Propel a balloon upward. Pick up a hoop from the floor, pass it around the balloon, replace the hoop on the floor, and keep the balloon from touching the ground.

10. Have four to six children seated on the floor in a small circle. Each circle gets two balloons to be kept in the air. Children's seats are "glued" to the floor. Once a balloon hits the floor, it is out of play. Play for a specified time (30 to 60 seconds). Increase the challenge by using beach balls.

ACTIVITIES WITH BEANBAGS

Activities with beanbags provide valuable learning experiences for elementary school children at all levels. All parts of the body can be brought into play. For tossing and catching, though, the beanbag encourages manipulation with the hands; playground balls lead to arm and body catching. Bean-bag activities can be used with older youngsters provided that the activities are selected carefully to challenge students. The more challenging partner activities—juggling, different and unique methods of propulsion, and the split-vision drill (p. 412)—are examples of suitable activities.

Instructional Procedures

1. Use the following instructional cues when teaching beanbag activities:
   a. Stress a soft receipt of the beanbag by giving with the hands, arms, and legs. "Giving" involves the hands going out toward the incoming beanbag and bringing it in for a soft landing.
   b. Keep your eyes on the beanbag when catching.
   c. When tossing and catching, toss slightly above eye level.

2. Make sure that beanbags are at least 6 inches square. This size balances well and can be controlled on various parts of the body, thus offering greater challenge to intermediate-level children.

3. Throwing and catching skills involve many intricate elements. Emphasize the principles of opposition, eye focus, weight transfer, and follow-through. It is important that children track the object being caught and focus on the target when throwing.

4. Stress laterality and directionality when teaching throwing and catching skills. Children should be taught to throw, catch, and balance beanbags with both the left and right sides of their body. They should learn to catch and throw at different levels.

5. Children should throw at chest height to a partner, unless a different type of throw is specified. Teach all types of return: low, medium, high, left, and right.

6. In partner work, keep distances between partners reasonable, especially in introductory phases. Fifteen feet or so seems to be a reasonable starting distance.

7. In partner work, emphasize skillful and varied throwing, catching, and handling of the beanbag. Throwing too hard or out of range, to cause the partner to miss, should be avoided.

Most activities are classified as individual or partner activities. A few activities are for groups of three or more.

Individual Activities

Tossing to Self in Place

1. Toss with both hands, with right hand only, and with left hand only. Catch the same way. Catch with the back of the hands.

2. Toss the beanbag progressively higher. Reverse.

3. Hold the beanbag in one hand and make large arm circles (imitating a windmill). Release the bag so that it flies upward, and then catch it.

4. Toss from side to side, right to left (reverse), front to back (reverse), and around various body parts in different combinations.

5. Toss upward and catch with hands behind the back. Toss upward from behind the body and catch in front. Toss upward and catch on the back, on the knees, on the toes, and on other body parts.

6. Hold the bag at arm's length in front of the body, with palms up. Withdraw hands quickly from under the bag, and catch it from on top in a palms-down stroke before it falls to the floor.

7. Toss upward and catch as high as possible. As low as possible. Work out a sequence of high, low, and in between.

8. Toss upward and catch with the body off the floor. Try tossing as well as catching with the body off the ground.

9. Toss in various fashions while seated and while lying.

10. Toss two beanbags upward and catch a bag in each hand.

Adding Stunts in Place

1. Toss overhead to the rear, turn around, and catch. Toss, do a full turn, and catch.

2. Toss, clap the hands, and catch. Clap the hands more than once. Clap the hands around different body parts.

3. Toss, do pretend activities (e.g., comb hair, wash face, brush teeth, shine shoes), and catch.

4. Toss, touch different body parts with both hands, and catch. Touch two different body parts, calling out the name of the parts. Touch two body parts, clap hands, and catch.

5. Toss, kneel on one knee, and catch. Try this going to a sitting or lying position. Reverse the position order, coming from a lying or sitting position to a standing position to catch.

6. Toss, touch the floor, and catch. Explore with other challenges. Use heel clicks or balance positions.

7. Bend forward, reach between the legs, and toss the bag onto the back or shoulders.

8. Reach one hand over the shoulder, drop the beanbag, and catch it with the other hand behind the back. Reverse the hands. Drop the beanbag from one hand behind the back and catch it with the other hand between the legs. Put the beanbag on the head, lean back, and catch it with both hands behind the back. Catch it with one hand.

Locomotor Movements

1. Toss to self, moving to another spot to catch. Toss forward, run, and catch. Move from side to side. Toss overhead to the rear, run back, and catch.

2. Add various stunts and challenges described previously. Vary with different locomotor movements.

Balancing the Beanbag on Various Body Parts

1. Balance the beanbag on the head. Move around, keeping the beanbag in place. Sit down, lie down, turn around, and so on.

2. Balance the beanbag on other parts of the body and move around. Balance on top of the instep, between the knees, on the shoulders, on the elbows, under the chin. Use more than one beanbag.

Propelling with Various Body Parts

1. Toss to self from various parts of the body: the elbow, the instep, the knees, the shoulders, between the feet, between the heels.

2. Sit and toss the bag from the feet to the hands. Practice tossing in a supine position. From a supine position, pick up the bag between the toes and place it behind the head, using a full curl position. Go back and pick it up, returning it to place.

Juggling

1. Begin with two bags and juggle them in the air. (See pp. 417–421 for instructions on juggling.)

2. Juggle three bags.

Other Activities

1. From a wide straddle position, push the beanbag between the legs as far back as possible. Jump in place with a half turn and repeat.

2. Take the same position as above. Push the bag back as far as possible between the legs, bending the knees. Without moving the legs, turn to the right and pick up the bag. Repeat to the left.

3. Stand with feet apart and hold the beanbag with both hands. Reach as high as possible (with both hands), bend backward, and drop the bag. Reach between the legs, and pick up the bag.

4. On all fours, put the bag in the small of the back. Wiggle and force the bag off the back without moving the hands or knees from place.

5. In crab position, place the beanbag on the stomach, and try to shake it off. Put it on the back and do a Mule Kick (p. 508).

6. Push the beanbag across the floor with different body parts, such as the nose, shoulder, or knee.

7. Each student drops a beanbag on the floor. See how many different ways students can move over, around, and between the beanbags. As an example, jump three bags, crab-walk around two others, and cartwheel over one more.

8. Spread the legs about shoulder width. Bend over and throw the beanbag between the legs and onto the back. Next, throw the beanbag all the way over the head, and catch it.

Partner Activities

Tossing Back and Forth

1. Begin with various kinds of two-handed throws: underhand, overhead, side, and over the shoulder. Change to one-handed tossing and throwing.

2. Throw at different levels, at different targets, right and left.

3. Throw under the leg, around the body. Center as in football. Try imitating the shot put and the discus throw. Try the softball (full arc) throw.

4. Have partners sit cross-legged about 10 feet apart. Throw and catch in various styles.

5. Use follow activities, in which one partner leads with a throw and the other follows with the same kind of throw.

6. Jump, turn in the air, and pass to partner.

7. Toss to partner from unexpected positions and from around and under different body parts.

8. Stand back to back and pass the bag around both partners from hand to hand as quickly as

Propelling two beanbags back and forth

possible. Also try moving the bag around and through various body parts.

9. Toss in various directions to make partner move and catch.

10. Run around partner in a circle, tossing the bag back and forth.

11. Propel two beanbags back and forth. Each partner has a bag, and the bags go in opposite directions at the same time. Try having one partner toss both bags at once in the same direction, using various types of throws. Try to keep three bags going at once.

Propelling Back and Forth with Different Body Parts

1. Toss the bag to partner with foot or toes, from on top of the feet, and from between the feet, with elbow, shoulder, head, and any other body part. Use a sitting position.

2. With back to partner, take a bunny-jump position. With the bag held between the feet, kick the bag back to partner. Try kicking with both feet from a standing position.

3. Partners lie supine on the floor with heads pointing toward each other, about 6 inches apart. One partner has a beanbag between the feet and deposits it in between their heads. The other partner picks up the bag with the feet (reaching over the head) and places it on the floor by the feet after returning to a lying position. With both partners in backward curl position, try to transfer the bag directly from one partner to the other with the feet.

Group Activities and Games

Split-Vision Drill

A split-vision drill from basketball can be adapted to beanbags. An active player faces two partners about 15 feet away. They are standing side by side, a short distance apart. Two beanbags, one in the hands of the active player and the other with one of the partners, are needed for the drill. The active player tosses to the open partner and at the same time receives the bag from the other partner. The two bags move back and forth between the active player and the other two, alternately (Figure 17.2). After a period of time, change positions.

Target Games

Wastebaskets, hoops, circles drawn on the floor, and other objects can be used as targets for beanbag tossing. Target boards with holes cut out are available from commercial sources. Holes can be triangles, circles, squares, and rectangles, thus stressing form concepts.

Beanbag Quoits

The game is played in the same way as horseshoes. A court is drawn with two spots on the floor about 20 feet apart. Spots can be made with masking tape and should be 1 inch in diameter. Each competitor has two bags, a different color for each player. Tosses are made from behind one spot to the other spot. The object is to get one or both bags closer to the mark than the opponents do. If a bag completely blocks out the spot, as viewed from directly overhead, the player scores 3 points. Otherwise, the bag nearest the spot scores 1 point. Games are played to 11, 15, or 21 points. In each round, the player winning the previous point tosses first.

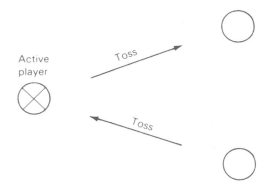

Figure 17.2 Split-vision drill for beanbags

Other Games

Children enjoy playing One Step (p. 578). Teacher Ball (p. 569) is also readily adaptable to beanbags.

ACTIVITIES WITH BALLS

Included in this section are the ball skills in which the child handles balls without the aid of other equipment such as a bat or paddle. Ball skills are mostly of two types: (a) hand-eye skills, including throwing, catching, bouncing, dribbling (as in basketball), batting (as in volleyball), and rolling (as in bowling); and (b) foot-eye skills, including kicking, trapping, and dribbling (as in soccer).

Types of Balls

For younger children, sponge rubber, yarn, and fleece balls are all excellent for introductory throwing and catching, because they help overcome the fear factor. (See Chapter 33 for instructions on how to make balls from yarn.) The innovative teacher can probably develop other suitable objects, such as crumpled-up newspaper balls wrapped with cellophane tape, papier-mache balls, stitched rolls of socks, and stuffed balloons.

The whiffle ball, a hollow plastic ball with holes cut in the surface, is also useful. Scoops, either commercial or home constructed, provide an extension of whiffle ball activities. Another type of ball that has value is a soft softball, a much softer version of the regular softball. It is suitable for catching and throwing but does not hold up well if batted.

The inflated rubber playground ball (8½-inch size) should be the ball used for most ball-handling experiences. Balls should be inflated moderately so that they bounce well, but not overinflated, which makes them difficult to catch. Overinflation can also distort the ball's spherical shape.

Balls that last longer and have more utility for youngsters are the 8½-inch foam balls. The foam balls are easier to catch and pass and will not hurt if youngsters are accidentally hit by one. There are many different types of foam used to make these balls and it is important to make sure that the balls are dense and that they have adequate bounce. Many of the cheaper styles are extremely light and will not bounce. An even better (but more expensive) alternative are the foam "tough-skin" balls. These are foam balls that are covered with a tough plastic coating. This skin causes the balls to bounce better and to resist damage to the soft foam. In the long run, these "tough-skin" balls may be the most economical as they will not leak or develop punctures like the standard playground ball.

Some attention should be given to the color of the balls. In a study comparing blue, yellow, and white balls against a black background and a white background, "blue and yellow balls produced significantly higher catching scores than did a white ball" (Morris, 1976). However, no data were provided for the common playground balls of red color.

Types of Organization

Instruction with younger children should begin with individual work and progress to partner and group activities. After the children have acquired some skill, a lesson can include both individual and partner activities. In propelling the ball back and forth between partners, the children can progress from rolling the ball, to throwing with one bounce, to throwing on the fly. Be sure that a disparity in skill level between partners does not cause a problem for either.

Distance between partners should be short at first and should be lengthened gradually. The concept of targets is introduced by directing the children to throw the ball to specified points. Later, a change from a stationary target to a moving target maintains progression. Relays are useful for reinforcing learning, but the skills should be learned reasonably well before application in a relay.

Group work should be confined to small groups (of three to six), so that each child can be active, and should include activities not possible in individual or partner activity.

Instructional Procedures

1. Use the following instructional cues when teaching ball skills.
   a. Keep your eyes on the ball.
   b. Catch and dribble the ball with the pads of the fingers.
   c. Use opposition and weight transfer (pp. 50–51) when passing the ball.
2. In catching, soft receipt of the ball is achieved by "giving" with the hands and arms. The hands should reach out somewhat to receive the ball and then cushion the impact by bringing the ball in toward the body in a relaxed way.

3. To catch a throw above the waist, the hands should be positioned so that the thumbs are together. To receive a throw below the waist, the little fingers should be kept toward each other and the thumbs kept out.

4. In throwing to a partner, unless otherwise specified, the throw should reach the partner at about chest height. At times, different target points should be specified—high, low, right, left, at the knee, and so on.

5. A lesson should begin with basic skills within the reach of all and progress to more challenging activities.

6. Laterality is an important consideration. Right and left members of the body should be given practice in turn.

7. Split-vision should be incorporated in bouncing and dribbling. Children should learn to look forward, rather than at the ball, when bouncing and dribbling. A split-vision drill (p. 412) is of value for throwing.

8. Tactile senses can be enhanced by having children dribble or bounce the ball with eyes closed.

9. Rhythmic accompaniment, particularly for bouncing and dribbling activities, adds another dimension to ball skills.

10. Enough balls should be available so that each child has one.

11. The problem of uncontrolled balls can be solved by telling children to ignore stray balls, as someone is sure to be coming after them.

Activities with balls are presented with an 8½-inch ball in mind. Some modification is needed if the balls used are smaller or are of the type that does not bounce.

Individual Activities

Each child has a ball and practices alone. In the first group of individual activities, the child remains in the same spot. Next, the child rebounds the ball against a wall. (The wall should be reasonably free of projections and irregular surfaces so that the ball can return directly to the student.) In the third group of activities, the child performs alone while on the move.

Controlled Rolling and Handling in Place

1. In a wide straddle position (other possible positions are seated with legs crossed or outstretched, and push-up position), place the ball

Rolling the ball in a figure 8 pattern

on the floor, and roll it with constant finger guidance between and around the legs.

2. Roll the ball in a figure-eight path in and out of the legs.

3. Reach as far to the left as possible with the ball and roll it in front of you to the other side. Catch it as far to the right of the body as possible.

4. Turn in place and roll the ball around with one hand in a large circle.

5. Roll the ball around while lying on top of it. Roll the ball around the floor while on all fours, guiding it with the nose and forehead.

6. With the back moderately bent, release the ball behind the head, let it roll down the back, and catch it with both hands.

7. Make different kinds of bridges over the ball while using the ball as partial support for the bridge.

8. Starting with one arm above the head, roll the ball down that arm, behind the back, and down the other arm, and then catch it.

Bouncing and Catching in Place

1. Beginning with two hands, bounce and catch the ball. Bounce a given number of times. Bounce at different levels. Bounce one-handed in a variety of ways. Bounce under the legs. Close the eyes and bounce and catch.

2. Bounce, perform various stunts (e.g., a heel click, body turn, or handclap), and catch.

3. Bounce the ball around, under, and over the body.

4. Practice various kinds of bounces, catching all with the eyes closed.

5. Bounce the ball with various body parts, such as the head, elbow, or knee.

6. Bounce the ball, using consecutive body parts (e.g., the elbow and then the knee), and catch.

Tossing and Catching in Place

1. Toss and catch, increasing height gradually. Toss from side to side. Toss underneath the legs, around the body, and from behind. Add challenges while tossing and catching. Clap the hands one or more times, make body turns (quarter, half, or full), touch the floor, click the heels, sit down, lie down, and so on.

2. To enhance body part identification, toss and perform some of the following challenges: Touch the back with both hands, touch the back with both hands by reaching over both shoulders, touch both elbows, touch both knees with crossed hands, touch both heels with a heel slap, and touch the toes. Be sure to catch the ball after completing each challenge. The teacher or a leader can quickly call out the body part, and the class must respond with a toss, touch, and catch.

3. Toss upward and catch the descending ball as high as possible. As low as possible. Work out other levels and create combinations. Catch with crossed arms.

4. From a seated position, toss the ball to self from various directions. Lie down and do the same. Toss with the feet.

5. Practice catching by looking away after the ball is tossed upward. Experiment with different ways of catching with the eyes closed.

Batting to Self in Place

1. Bat the ball as in volleyball by using the fist, an open hand, or the side of the hand.

2. Bat and let the ball bounce. Catch in different fashions.

3. Rebound the ball upward, using different parts of the body. Let it bounce. Practice serving to self.

4. Bat and rebound the ball so that it does not touch the ground. Change position while doing this.

5. Bat the ball, perform a stunt, and bat again.

Foot Skills in Place

1. Put the toes on top of the ball. Roll the ball in different directions, keeping the other foot in place but retaining control.

2. Use a two-foot pickup, front and back. This is done by putting the ball between the feet and hoisting it to the hands.

3. From a seated position with legs extended, toss the ball with the feet to the hands.

4. Try doing a full curl with the ball between the feet, retaining control until the ball is again placed on the floor. Try bringing the ball between the feet to a point directly over the body. With the arms outstretched for support, lower the feet with the ball to the right and left.

5. In a supine position, hold the ball on the floor above the head. Do a curl-up, bring the ball forward, touch the toes with it, and return to supine position.

6. Drop the ball, and immediately trap it against the floor with one foot. Try to bounce the ball with one foot.

Dribbling Skills in Place

1. Dribble the ball first with both hands and then with the right and the left. (Emphasize that the dribble is a push with good wrist action. Children should not bat the ball downward.) Use various number combinations with the right and left hands. Dribble under the legs in turn and back around the body. Kneel and dribble. Go from standing to lying, maintaining a dribble. Return to standing position. Dribble the ball at different levels and at various tempos.

2. Dribble without looking at the ball. Dribble and change hands without stopping the dribble. Dribble with the eyes closed. Dribble the way the Harlem Globetrotters do.

Throwing against a Wall (Catching on the First Bounce)

1. Throw the ball against the wall, and catch the return after one bounce. Practice various kinds of throws: two-handed, one-handed, overhead, side, baseball, chest pass.

2. Throw at a target mounted on the wall.

Throwing against a Wall (Catching on the Fly)

Repeat the throws used in the previous activity, but catch the return on the fly. It may be necessary to move closer and to have the ball contact the wall higher.

Batting against a Wall (Handball Skills)

1. Drop the ball, and bat it after it bounces. Keep the ball going as in handball.
2. Serve the ball against the wall as in volleyball. Experiment with different ways to serve.

Kicking against a Wall and Trapping (Foot-Eye Skills)

1. Practice different ways to control kicking against the wall and stopping (trapping) the ball on the return. Try using the foot to keep returning the ball against the wall on the bounce.
2. Put some targets on the wall and kick the ball at a target. See how many points are scored after ten kicks.

Rolling on the Move

1. Roll the ball, run alongside it, and guide it with the hands in different directions.
2. Roll the ball forward, then run and catch up with it.

Tossing and Catching on the Move

1. Toss the ball upward and forward. Run forward and catch it after one bounce. Toss the ball upward in various directions (forward, sideward, backward), run under it, turn, and catch it on the fly.
2. Add various stunts and challenges, such as touching the floor, clicking the heels, or turning around.

Batting on the Move

With first the right and then the left hand, bat the ball upward in different directions, and catch it on the first bounce or on the fly.

Practicing Foot Skills on the Move

Dribble the ball (soccer style) forward and in other directions. Dribble around an imaginary point. Make various patterns while dribbling, such as a circle, square, triangle, or figure eight.

Dribbling on the Move

1. Dribble (basketball style) forward using one hand, and dribble back to place with the other. Change direction on a signal. Dribble in various directions, describing different pathways. Dribble around cones, milk cartons, or chairs.
2. Place a hoop on the floor. Dribble inside the hoop until a signal is sounded, then dribble to another hoop and continue the dribble inside that hoop. Avoid dribbling on the hoop itself.

Practicing Locomotor Movements While Holding the Ball

1. Hold the ball between the legs and perform various locomotor movements.
2. Try holding the ball in various positions with different body parts.

Partner Activities

Rolling in Place

Roll the ball back and forth to partner. Begin with two-handed rolls and proceed to one-handed rolls. When partner rolls the ball, pick it up with the toes and snap it up into the hands.

Throwing and Catching in Place

1. Toss the ball to partner with one bounce, using various kinds of tosses. Practice various kinds of throws and passes to partner.

Holding the ball between the legs and moving

2. Throw to specific levels and points: high, low, right, left, at the knee, and so on. Try various throws: from under the leg, around the body, backward tosses, and centering as in football.

3. Throw and catch over a volleyball net.

4. Work in a threesome, with one person holding a hoop between the two partners playing catch. Throw the ball through the hoop held at various levels. Try throwing through a moving hoop.

Batting in Place (Volleyball Skills)

1. Toss the ball upward to self and bat it two-handed to partner, who catches and returns it in the same manner. Serve as in volleyball to partner. Partner makes a return serve. Toss the ball to partner, who makes a volleyball return. Keep distances short and keep the ball under control. Try to keep the ball going back and forth as in volleyball.

2. Bat the ball back and forth on one bounce. Bat it back and forth over a line, wand, jump rope, or bench.

Kicking in Place

1. Practice different ways of controlled kicking between partners and different ways of stopping the ball (trapping).

2. Practice a controlled punt, preceding the kick with a step on the nonkicking foot. Place the ball between the feet and propel it forward or backward to partner.

3. Practice foot pickups. One partner rolls the ball, and the other hoists it to self with extended toes.

Throwing from Various Positions in Place

Practice different throws from a kneeling, sitting, or lying position. (Allow the children to be creative in selecting positions.)

Two-Ball Activities in Place

Using two balls, pass back and forth, with balls going in opposite directions.

Follow Activities in Place

Throw or propel the ball in any manner desired. Partner returns the ball in the same fashion.

Throwing and Catching against a Wall

Alternate throwing and catching against a wall. Alternate returning the ball after a bounce, as in handball.

Throwing on the Move

1. One child remains in place and tosses to the other child, who is moving. The moving child can trace different patterns, such as back and forth between two spots or in a circle around the stationary child. (Spatial judgments must be good to anticipate where the moving child should be to receive the ball. Moderate distances should be maintained between children.)

2. Practice different kinds of throws and passes as both children move in different patterns. (Considerable space is needed for this type of work.) Practice foot skills of dribbling and passing.

3. Partners hold the ball between their bodies without using the hands or arms. Experiment with different ways to move together.

4. Carrying a ball, run in different directions while partner follows. On signal, toss the ball upward so that the child following can catch it. Now change places and repeat the activity.

JUGGLING

Juggling is a novel task that is exciting to elementary school youngsters. It is a challenging task that demands practice and repetition to learn. An excellent medium for teaching beginners is sheer, lightweight scarves that are 18 to 24 inches square. These move slowly, allowing children to track them visually. Juggling with scarves teaches children correct patterns of object movement; however, it does not transfer easily to juggling with faster-moving objects such as fleece balls, tennis balls, rings, and hoops. Therefore, two distinct sections for juggling are offered: a section dealing with learning to juggle with scarves and a second discussion explaining juggling with balls. Juggling with scarves will bring success to a majority of the class. Youngsters who have mastered the scarves can move to balls and other objects.

Juggling lessons should allow opportunity for children to move, at will, between scarves and faster-moving objects. This will allow them to find an acceptable balance between success and frustration. Much practice is necessary to learn to juggle, and there will be a lot of misses during the acquisition of this skill. Since youngsters tire quickly if they are not having success, it may be desirable to play a game and then return to juggling practice.

Juggling with Scarves

Scarves are held by the fingertips near the center. To throw the scarf, it should be lifted and pulled into the air above eye level. Scarves are caught by clawing, a downward motion of the hand, and grabbing the scarf from above as it is falling. Scarf juggling should teach proper habits (e.g., tossing the scarves straight up in line with the body rather than forward or backward). Many instructors remind children to imagine that they are in a phone booth or large refrigerator box—to emphasize tossing and catching without moving.

Cascading

Cascading is the easiest pattern for juggling three objects. The following sequence can be used to learn this basic technique.

1. *One scarf.* Hold the scarf in the center. Quickly move the arm across the chest and toss the scarf with the palm out. Reach out with the other hand and catch the scarf in a straight-down motion (clawing). Toss the scarf with this hand using the motion and claw it with the opposite hand. Continue the tossing and clawing sequence over and over. The scarf should move in a figure-eight pattern as shown in Figure 17.3.

2. *Two scarves—two hands.* Hold a scarf with the fingertips in each hand. Toss the first one across the body as described in step 1. When it reaches its peak, look at it, and toss the second scarf across the body in the opposite direction. The first scarf thrown is caught (clawed) by the hand throwing the second scarf and vice versa (Figure 17.4). Verbal cues such as "Toss, claw, toss, claw" are helpful.

3. *Two scarves—one hand.* This sequence is a requisite if youngsters are going to juggle three scarves. Start with both scarves in one hand (hold them as described below in three-scarf cascading). The important skill to learn is to toss the first scarf, then the second scarf, and then catch the first and the second. Verbal cues to use are toss, toss, catch, catch. If youngsters cannot toss two scarves before catching one, they will not be able to master juggling with three scarves. Practice tossing skills with both hands.

4. *Three-scarf cascading.* A scarf is held in each hand by the fingertips as described in step 2. The third scarf is held with the ring and little

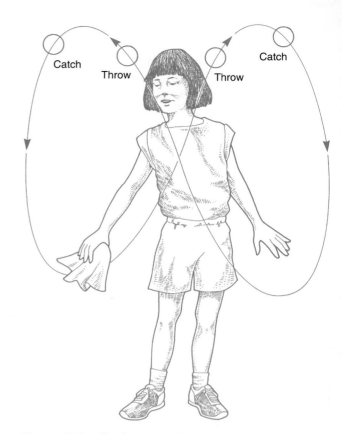

Figure 17.3 Clawing a scarf

Figure 17.4 Tossing and clawing with two scarves

fingers against the palm of one hand. The first scarf to be thrown will be from the hand that is holding two scarves. Toss this scarf from the fingertips across the chest as learned earlier. When scarf one reaches its peak, scarf two from the other hand is thrown across the body. As this hand starts to come down, it catches scarf one. When scarf two reaches its peak, scarf three is thrown in the same path as that of scarf one. To complete the cycle, as the hand comes down from throwing scarf three, it catches scarf two. The cycle is started over by throwing scarf one with the opposite hand. Figure 17.5 illustrates the figure-eight motion that is used in cascading. Tosses are always alternated between left and right hands with a smooth, even rhythm.

Reverse Cascading

Reverse cascading involves tossing the scarves from waist level to the outside of the body and allowing the scarves to drop down the midline of the body (Figure 17.6).

1. *One scarf.* Begin by holding the scarf as described previously. The throw goes away from the midline of the body over the top, releasing the scarf so that it falls down the center of the body. Catch it with the opposite hand and toss it in similar fashion on the opposite side of the body.

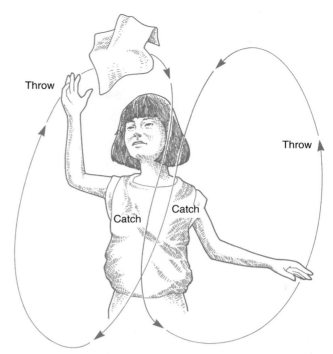

Figure 17.6   Reverse cascading

2. *Two scarves.* Begin with a scarf in each hand. Toss the first as described in step 1. When it begins its descent, toss the second scarf. Catch the first scarf, then the second, and repeat the pattern in a toss, toss, catch, catch manner.

3. *Reverse cascading with three scarves.* Think of a large funnel fixed at eye level directly in front of the juggler. The goal is to drop all scarves through this funnel so that they drop straight down the center of the body. Begin with three scarves as described previously for three-scarf cascading. Toss the first scarf from the hand holding two scarves.

Column Juggling

Column juggling is so named because the scarves move straight up and down as though they were inside a large pipe or column and do not cross the body. To perform three-scarf column juggling, begin with two scarves in one hand and one in the other hand. Begin with a scarf from the hand that has two scarves, and toss it straight up the midline of the body overhead. When this scarf reaches its peak, toss the other two scarves upward along the sides of the body (Figure 17.7). Catch the first scarf with either hand and toss it upward again. Catch the other two scarves and toss them upward continuing the pattern.

Figure 17.5   Three-scarf cascading

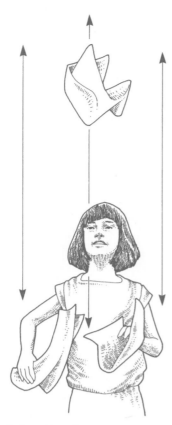

Figure 17.7 Column juggling

Showering

Showering is more difficult than cascading because of the rapid movement of the hands. There is less time allowed for catching and tossing. The scarves move in a circle following each other. It should be practiced in both directions for maximum challenge.

Start with two scarves in the right hand and one in the left. Begin by throwing the first two scarves from the right hand. Toss the scarves in a large circle away from the midline of the body and overhead as high as possible. As soon as the second scarf is released, toss the scarf across to the left hand and throw it in the same path with the right hand (Figure 17.8). All scarves are caught with the left hand and passed to the right hand.

Juggling Challenges

1. While cascading, toss a scarf under one leg.
2. While cascading, toss a scarf from behind the back.
3. Instead of catching one of the scarves, blow it upward with a strong breath of air.

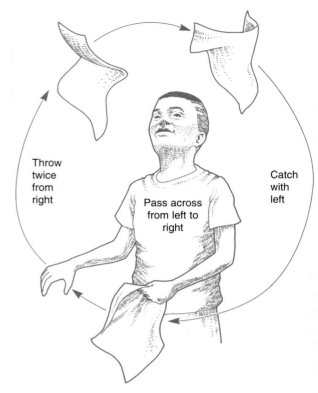

Figure 17.8 Showering with scarves

4. Begin cascading by tossing the first scarf into the air with a foot. Lay the scarf across the foot and kick it into the air.
5. Try juggling three scarves with one hand. Do not worry about establishing a pattern, just catch the lowest scarf each time. Try both regular and reverse cascading as well as column juggling.
6. While doing column juggling, toss up one scarf, hold the other two, and make a full turn. Resume juggling.
7. Juggle three scarves while standing alongside a partner with inside arms around each other. This is actually easy to do, because it is regular three-scarf cascading.
8. Try juggling more than three scarves (up to six) with a partner.

Juggling with Balls

Two balls can be juggled with one hand, and three balls can be juggled with two hands. Juggling can be done in a crisscross fashion, which is called *cascading,* or it can be done in a circular fashion, called *showering.* Cascading is considered the easier of the two styles and should be the first one attempted.

Instructional Procedures

1. Juggling requires accurate, consistent tossing, and this should be the first emphasis. The tosses should be thrown to the same height on both sides of the body, about 2 to 2½ feet upward and across the body, since the ball is tossed from one hand to the other. Practice tossing the ball parallel to the body; the most common problem in juggling is that the balls are tossed forward and the juggler has to move forward to catch them.

2. The fingers, not the palms, should be used in tossing and catching. Stress relaxed wrist action.

3. The student should look upward to watch the balls at the peak of their flight, rather than watching the hands. Focus on where the ball peaks, not the hands.

4. The balls should be caught about waist height and released a little above this level.

5. Two balls must be carried in the starting hand, and the art of releasing only one must be mastered.

6. Progression should be working successively with first one ball, then two balls, and finally three balls (Figure 17.9).

Recommended Progression for Cascading

1. Using one ball and one hand only, toss the ball upward (2 to 2½ feet), and catch it with the same hand. Begin with the dominant hand, and later practice with the other. Toss quickly, with wrist action. Then handle the ball alternately with right and left hands, tossing from one hand to the other.

2. Now, with one ball in each hand, alternate tossing a ball upward and catching it in the same hand so that one ball is always in the air. Begin again with a ball in each hand. Toss across the body to the other hand. To keep the

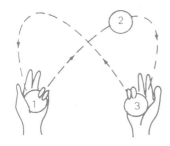

Figure 17.9   Cascading with three balls

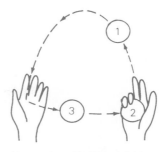

Figure 17.10   Showering with three balls

balls from colliding, toss under the incoming ball. After some expertise has been acquired, alternate the two kinds of tosses by doing a set number (four to six) of each before shifting to the other.

3. Hold two balls in the starting hand and one in the other. Toss one of the balls in the starting hand, toss the ball from the other hand, and then toss the third ball.

Recommended Progression for Showering

1. The showering motion is usually counterclockwise. Hold one ball in each hand. Begin by tossing with the right hand on an inward path and then immediately toss the other ball from the left directly across the body to the right hand. Continue this until the action is smooth.

2. Now, hold two balls in the right hand and one in the left. Toss the first ball from the right hand on an inward path and immediately toss the second on the same path. At about the same time, toss the ball from the left hand directly across the body to the right hand (Figure 17.10).

3. A few children may be able to change from cascading to showering and vice versa. This is a skill of considerable challenge.

ACTIVITIES WITH SCOOPS AND BALLS

Scoops can be purchased (Figure 17.11) or made with bleach bottles or similar containers (see Chapter 33). They are excellent for practicing catching and tossing skills using an implement rather than the hands. The following activities are recommended.

Individual Activities

1. Put the ball on the floor and pick it up with the scoop. Toss the ball upward and catch it with

Figure 17.11 Catching a whiffle ball with a scoop

the scoop. Throw the ball against a wall and catch it in the scoop. Put the ball in the scoop, throw it in the air, and catch it. Throw the ball against a wall with the scoop and catch it with the scoop.

2. Throw the ball, switch the scoop to the opposite hand, and catch in the scoop. Toss the ball upward from the scoop, perform a stunt, such as a heel click or a body turn, and catch the ball in the scoop.

3. Toss the ball upward and catch it as low as possible. As high as possible. Toss it a little higher each time, and catch it in the scoop. Tell students to toss the ball so that they have to stretch to catch it. (Most activity should begin with a toss from the free hand and later employ a toss from the scoop.)

Partner Activities

1. One partner rolls the ball on the floor, and the other catches it in the scoop. Partners throw the ball back and forth and catch it in the scoop. Play One Step (p. 578) while playing catch to add some challenge to the activity.

2. One partner tosses the ball from the scoop and the other partner catches. Throw the ball from the scoop at different levels and catch it at different levels. Throw and catch from various positions, such as sitting, back to back, prone, and kneeling.

3. Work with more than one partner, with more than one ball, and with a scoop in each hand.

Games and Relays

Many games and relays can be played using scoops. Modified lacrosse can be played using the scoops and a whiffle ball. Set up a lesson in which children devise games for themselves that use the scoop and a ball.

BOWLING ACTIVITIES

Younger children should practice informal rolling. As they mature, the emphasis should change from informal rolling to bowling skills. Bowling skills begin with a two-handed roll and progress to one-handed rolls using both the right and left hand. Various targets can be used, including bowling pins, milk cartons, small cones, blocks, and even people.

The 8½-inch foam or playground ball is excellent for teaching bowling skills. Volleyballs and soccer balls also can be used. Stress moderate speed in the motion of the ball. The ball should roll off the tips of the fingers with good follow-through action.

The four-step approach is the accepted form for ten-pin bowling, and its basis can be set in class work. The technique, in brief form, for a right-handed bowler follows:

Starting position: Stand with the feet together and the ball held comfortably in both hands in front of the body.

Step one: Step forward with the right foot, pushing the ball forward with both hands and a little to the right.

Step two: Step with the left foot, allowing the ball to swing down alongside the leg on its way into the backswing.

Step three: Step with the right foot. The ball reaches the height of the backswing with this step.

Step four: Step with the left foot and bowl the ball forward.

For instructional cues, the teacher can call out the following sequence for the four steps: "Out," "Down," "Back," and "Roll."

Bowling activities are organized mostly as partner or group work. When targets are being used, having two children on the target end is desirable. One child resets the target, while the other recovers the ball. The following are partner activities unless otherwise noted. A fine game for rounding off the activities is Bowling One Step (p. 578).

Recommended Activities

1. Employ a wide straddle stance, and begin with two-handed rolls from between the legs.

2. Roll the ball first with the right and then with the left hand. The receiver can employ the foot pickup, done by hoisting the ball to the hands with the extended toes.

3. Practice putting different kinds of spin (English) on the ball. (For a right-handed bowler, a curve to the left is called a *hook* ball, and a curve to the right is a *backup* ball.)

4. Get into groups of three (Figure 17.12) and employ human straddle targets. Using a stick 2 feet long, make marks on the floor for the target child, who is in the middle between the two bowlers. The target child stands so that the inside edges of the shoes are on the marks, thus standardizing the target spread. (Targets must keep their legs straight and motionless during the bowling. Otherwise, they can make or avoid contact with the ball and upset the scoring system.) Start from a moderate distance (15 to 20 feet) at first, and adjust as proficiency increases. Scoring can be 2 points for a ball that goes through the legs without touching and 1 point for a ball that goes through but touches the leg.

5. Use milk cartons or bowling pins as targets. Begin with one and progress to two or three. (Plastic bowling pins are available. Other targets might be a wastebasket lying on its side—the ball is rolled into it—or a 3-lb. coffee can for a smaller ball.)

ACTIVITIES WITH PADDLES AND BALLS

The present popularity of racquet sports makes it imperative that the schools give attention to racquet skills. For primary-level children, the nylon-stocking paddle (see Chapter 33 for its construction)

Figure 17.12 Bowling through a human straddle target

can be used to introduce the racquet sports. Much of this early activity is devoted to informal, exploratory play. Different types of objects can be batted: table tennis balls, newspaper balls, shuttlecocks, and tennis balls. The use of plastic or wooden paddles (see Chapter 33) and appropriate balls can be used to establish a basis for future play in racquetball, table tennis, squash, and regular tennis. These activities, particularly paddle tennis, take considerable space, so emphasis must be placed on controlled stroking rather than wild swinging.

Instructional Procedures for Wooden or Plastic Paddles

1. Use the following instructional cues:
   a. Hold the wrist reasonably stiff.
   b. Use a smooth arm action.
   c. Stroke through the ball and follow through.
   d. Watch the ball strike the paddle.
2. All paddles should have leather wrist thongs. The hand goes through the leather loop before grasping the paddle. No play should be permitted without this safety precaution.
3. Proper grip must be emphasized, and seeing that children maintain this is a constant battle. The easiest method to teach the proper grip is to have the student hold the paddle perpendicular to the floor and shake hands with it (Figure 17.13). Young people tend to revert to the inefficient hammer grip, so named because it is similar to the grip used on a hammer.
4. Accuracy and control should be the primary goals. The children should not be concerned with force or distance.

Figure 17.13   Handshake grip

5. Early activities can be attempted with both the right and the left hand, but the dominant hand should be developed in critical skills.
6. During a lesson, related information about racquet sports may be quite relevant.
7. Practice in racquet work should move from individual to partner work as quickly as is feasible, because partner work is basic to racquet sports.
8. For the forehand stroke, the body is turned sideways; for a right-handed player, the left side points in the direction of the hit.
9. For the backhand stroke, the thumb is placed against the handle of the racquet for added support and force, and the body is turned sideways so the shoulder on the side of the racquet hand points in the direction of the stroke.
10. During either type of stroke, a step is made with the foot that is forward with respect to the direction of the stroke.
11. A volley is made with a sort of punch stroke. The hitter faces in the direction of the hit, and the racquet is pushed forward rather than being stroked. To practice volleys, students need a firm surface from which the ball can rebound.

Individual Activities

1. Place a ball on the paddle and attempt to keep it from falling off. As skill increases, attempt to roll the ball around the edges of the paddle.
2. Using the paddle, rebound the ball upward. Bounce it on the paddle without letting it touch the floor. Bounce it off the paddle upward, and catch it with the other hand. Increase the height of the bounce.
3. Dribble the ball with the paddle, first while stationary and then while moving. Change the paddle from hand to hand while the ball is bouncing off the floor.
4. Alternate bouncing the ball in the air and on the floor.
5. Bounce the ball off the paddle upward and catch it with the paddle. This requires giving with the paddle to create a soft home for the ball.
6. Put the ball on the floor and scoop it up with the paddle. Start dribbling on the ball without touching it with the hands. Put a reverse spin on the ball and scoop it up into the air.

7. Bounce the ball off the paddle into the air and turn the paddle to the other side as you bounce the ball.

8. Bat the ball into the air and perform the following stunts while the ball is in the air: Touch the floor, do a heel click (single and double), clap the hands, turn completely around. Do various combinations of these activities.

Partner Activities

Beginning partner activity should involve feeding (controlled throwing) by one partner and the designated stroke return by the other. In this way, the child can concentrate on the stroke without worrying about the competitive aspects of the activity.

1. Return partner's feed with a forehand stroke. Return backhand. Switch roles.

2. Stroke back and forth with partner, first forehand and then backhand.

3. Play back and forth over a net. The "net" can be a jump rope lying on the floor crosswise to the field of play, a wand supported on blocks or cones, or a bench. (See Chapter 33 for a diagram of a home-constructed net.)

4. Volley partner's feed. Volley back and forth with partner. (In the volley, the ball does not touch the floor.)

5. Play doubles. Partners on each side alternate turns returning the ball.

6. Volley using a whiffle ball. (A whiffle ball moves slowly and allows children time to position their feet properly.) Play with a partner. Allow the ball to bounce before returning it. Perform stunts while the ball is in the air.

7. Dribble the ball with your paddle and try to pull a flag from an opponent's pocket without losing control of the ball.

8. While moving with a partner, keep the ball in the air by alternating bounces.

9. Develop a cooperative score by developing a routine with five individual tasks in sequence.

ACTIVITIES WITH FRISBEES (FLYING DISKS)

Frisbee activities are popular with children of all ages, but younger children may need considerable guidance to develop skills. The following are the basic skills that should be taught before a variety of activities are presented.

Throwing the Disk

Backhand Throw

The backhand grip (Figure 17.14) is used most often. The thumb is on top of the disk, the index finger along the rim, and the other fingers underneath. To throw the Frisbee with the right hand, stand in a sideways position with the right foot toward the target. Step toward the target and throw the Frisbee in a sideways motion across the body, snapping the wrist and trying to keep the disk flat on release.

Underhand Throw

The underhand throw uses the same grip as in the backhand throw, but the thrower faces the target and holds the disk at the side of the body. Step forward with the leg opposite the throwing arm while bringing the Frisbee forward. When the throwing arm is out in the front of the body, release the Frisbee. The trick to this throw is learning to release the disk so that it is parallel to the ground.

Figure 17.14 Gripping the Frisbee for a backhand throw

Catching the Disk

Thumb-Down Catch

The thumb-down catch is used for catching when the disk is received at waist level or above. The thumb is pointing toward the ground. The Frisbee should be tracked from the thrower's hand. This clues the catcher about any tilt on the disk that may cause it to curve.

Thumb-Up Catch

The thumb-up catch is used when the Frisbee is received below waist level. The thumb points up, and the fingers are spread.

Trick Catches

The disk can be caught in different positions. The two most popular trick-catch positions are behind the back and between the legs. In the behind-the-back catch, the thumb-up technique is used, and the disk is caught with the arm that is farthest away from the thrower. For the between-the-legs catch, the thumb-up catch is also used, and one leg can be lifted to facilitate the catch.

Instructional Procedures

1. Use the following instructional cues:
   a. Release the disk parallel to the ground. If it is tilted, a curved throw results.
   b. Step toward the target and follow through on release of the disk.
   c. Snap open the wrist and make the Frisbee spin.
2. If space is limited, all Frisbees should be thrown in the same direction. Students can line up on either side of the area and throw across to each other.
3. Each child should have a disk so that practice time can be maximized. However, most activities are best practiced by pairs of students using one disk.
4. Youngsters can develop both sides of the body by learning to throw and catch the disk with either hand. The teacher should design the activities so that youngsters get both right-hand and left-hand practice.
5. Since a Frisbee is somewhat different from the other implements that children usually throw, devote some time to teaching form and style in throwing and catching. Avoid drills that reward speed in throwing and catching.

Recommended Activities

1. Throw the Frisbee at different levels to a partner.
2. Catch the Frisbee, using various catching styles and hand positions.
3. Throw a curve by tilting the disk. Try curving it to the left, the right, and upward. Throw a slow curve and then a fast slider.
4. Throw a bounce pass to partner. Throw a low, fast bounce. Throw a high, slow bounce.
5. As the catcher, do various stunts after the disk has left partner's hand. Examples are a full turn, heel click, handclap, or touching the ground.
6. Throw the disk with the nondominant hand. Try to throw for accuracy first, and then strive for distance.
7. Make the disk respond like a boomerang. Throw into the wind at a steep angle and see whether it comes back to you.
8. Throw the Frisbee into the air, run, and catch it. Try to increase the throwing distance and still make the catch before the disk touches the ground.
9. Have partner hold a hoop as a target. See how many times you can throw the Frisbee through the hoop. Play a game of One Step in which you move back a step each time you throw the disk through the hoop. When you make two misses in a row, your partner gets a chance to try.
10. Place a series of hoops on the ground. Different colored hoops can signify different point values. Have a contest with your partner to see who can earn more points in five throws.
11. Play catch while both partners are moving. Try to throw the disk so that your partner does not have to break stride to catch it.
12. Throw for distance. Try to throw farther than your partner by using a series of four throws.
13. Throw for both distance and accuracy. Using a series of four or more throws, try to reach a goal that is a specified distance away. Many different objects can be used as goals, such as basket standards, fence posts, and trees. (This could be the start of playing Frisbee Golf, which is becoming a popular recreational sport.)
14. Set a time limit of 30 seconds. Within this time, see how many successful throws and catches can be made. A certain distance apart must be set for all pairs, and missed catches do not count as throws.

15. Working in groups of three, try to keep the disk away from the person in the middle. The children can establish their own rules as to when someone else must move to the middle.

16. In groups of three, with one person in the middle, try to throw the Frisbee through the middle person's legs. A point is scored each time the disk is thrown through the legs without touching. Legs must be spread to shoulder width.

ACTIVITIES WITH WANDS

Wands have been used in physical education programs for many years, but only recently have a wide variety of interesting and challenging activities been developed. Wands can be made from ¾-inch maple dowels or from a variety of broom and mop handles. If two lengths are chosen, make them 36 and 42 inches. If only one size is to be used, a length of 1 meter is recommended. Wands are more interesting when they are painted with imaginative designs, a chore that can be a class project. Wands are noisy when they hit the floor. Putting rubber crutch tips on the ends of a wand alleviates most of the noise and makes it easier to pick up. The tips should be put on with mucilage.

The year's supply of wands should include five or six extras beyond the number of children. There will be some breakage. Wands serve the physical education program in four ways: challenge activities, stunts, exercises, and combative activities. Challenge activities, stunts, and exercises are presented here, and combatives are presented in Chapter 21.

Instructional Procedures

1. Because wands are noisy when dropped, the children should hold their wands with both hands or put them on the floor during instruction.

2. Many wand activities require great flexibility, which means that not all children are able to do them. Girls usually perform better than boys at flexibility stunts.

3. An adequate amount of space is needed for each individual, because wand stunts demand room.

4. Wands are not to be used as fencing foils. Children may easily be injured using wands improperly. Teach children proper use of wands. Emphasize the need to use care when handling wands to avoid injury to self and others. Do not allow *any* improper use of wands (or other potentially dangerous equipment).

Recommended Activities

Wands can be used for challenge activities that offer a relatively unstructured approach. The following are some of the many possible challenges.

1. Can you reach down and pick up your wand without bending your knees?

2. Try to balance your wand on different body parts. Watch the top of the wand to get cues on how to retain the balance.

3. Can you hold your stick against the wall and move over and under it?

4. Let's see whether you can hold the stick at both ends and move through the gap.

5. Can you spin the wand and keep it going like a windmill?

6. Let's see how many different ways you can move over and around your wand when it is on the floor.

7. Put one end of the wand on the floor and hold the other end. How many times can you run around your wand without getting dizzy?

8. Place one end of the wand against a wall. Holding the other end and keeping the wand against the wall, duck underneath. Place the wand lower and lower on the wall and go under.

9. Place the wand between your feet and hop around as though you are on a pogo stick.

10. Throw your wand into the air and catch it.

11. Hold the wand vertically near the middle. Can you release your grip and catch the wand before it falls to the floor?

12. Have a partner hold a wand horizontally above the floor. Jump, leap, and hop over the wand. Gradually raise the height of the wand.

13. Put your wand on the floor and try making different kinds of bridges over it.

14. Place the wand on the floor. Curl alongside it, just touching it. Curl at one end of the wand.

15. Balance the wand vertically on the floor. Release the wand and try to complete different stunts—clapping the hands, doing a heel click, touching different body parts—before the wand falls to the floor.

16. Put the wand on the floor and see how many ways you can push it, using different body parts.

Individual Wand Stunts

Wand Catch

Stand a wand on one end and hold it in place with the fingers on the tip. Loop the foot quickly over the stick, letting go of the wand briefly but catching it with the fingers before it falls. Do this right and left for a complete set. Try to catch the wand with just the index finger.

Thread the Needle (V-Seat)

Maintaining a V-seat position, with the wand held in front of the body with both hands, bend the knees between the arms and pass the wand over them and return, without touching the wand to the legs. Try with the ankles crossed.

Thread the Needle (Standing)

Holding the wand in both hands, step through the space, one leg at a time, and return without touching. Step through again, but this time bring the wand up behind the back, over the head, and down in front. Reverse. Try from side to side with the stick held front and back.

Grapevine

Holding the wand near the ends, step with the right foot around the right arm and over the wand inward, toward the body (Figure 17.15). Pass the wand backward over the head and right shoulder (Figure 17.16), and continue sliding the wand down the body until you are standing erect with the wand between the legs. Reverse the process back to original position. Try with the left foot leading.

Back Scratcher

Hold the wand with an underhand grip (palms up), arms crossed in front of the body (Figure 17.17). Bend the elbows so that the wand can go over and behind the head. Attempt to pass the wand down the length of the body from the back of the shoulders to the heels. Do not release the grip on the wand. The wand is worked down behind the back while the arms stay in front of the body.

Wand Whirl

Stand the wand upright in front of the body. Turn around quickly and grasp the wand before it falls. Do the movement both right and left. Try making two full turns and still catching the wand before it falls.

Figure 17.15 Beginning the Grapevine

Twist Under

Grasp the upright wand with the right hand. Twist around under the right arm without letting go of the wand, taking it off the floor, or touching the knee to the floor. Repeat, using the left arm.

Jump Wand

Holding the wand in front with the fingertips of both hands, jump over it. Jumping back is not recommended, because the wand can hit the heels and cause an awkward fall. (A rope or a towel can be substituted for the wand if children are having difficulty.)

Balancing the Wand

Balance the wand vertically with one hand. Experiment with different hand and finger positions. Walk forward, backward, and sideward. Sit down, lie down, and move into other positions while keeping the wand balanced. Keep the eyes on the top of the wand. Balance the wand horizontally on the hands, arms, feet, and thighs. Balance it across the back of the neck. In crab position, balance it across the tummy.

Figure 17.16 Grapevine, second stage (head ducks under, and wand is pressed down the back)

Figure 17.17 Back Scratcher (wand has been passed overhead and is now being forced down the back)

The Sprinter

Get into a sprinter's position, with the wand on the floor, between the feet, and perpendicular to the direction of the sprint. Change the feet rapidly, alternating over the wand. Try moving both feet together forward and backward over the wand.

Crab Leap

Place the wand on the floor. Get into crab position and attempt to move the feet back and forth over the wand without touching it. Try this with alternating feet.

Long Reach

Stand with legs extended and feet spread about 12 inches apart. Hold a wand in the left hand, and use

it like a third limb. With a piece of chalk in the right hand, reach forward as far as possible and make a mark. Use the wand as a support and see whether the mark can be bettered.

Wand Bridge

On a mat, start in a straddle stance with legs straight. Hold a wand near one end, with the other end above the head and pointed toward the ceiling. Bend backward, place the wand on the mat behind you, and walk the hands down the wand. Return to standing position.

Wand Twirl

Children in the class who have baton-twirling experience can show the class some points of technique.

Partner Wand Stunts

Partner Catch

Partners face each other a short distance (5 feet) apart, each holding a wand in the right hand. On signal, each throws the wand to the partner with the right hand and catches the incoming wand with the left. Distances can be increased somewhat.

Partner Change

Partners face each other a short distance (5 feet) apart. Each has a wand standing upright, held on top by the right hand. On signal, each runs to the other's wand and tries to catch it before it falls. This can also be done in the same way as the Wand Whirl, with each whirling to the other's wand. Try with a small group of five or six. On signal, all move to the next wand.

Turn the Dishrag

Partners face each other and grasp a wand. When ready, they perform a dishrag turn (p. 506).

Jump the Wand

One partner moves the wand back and forth along the floor, while the other partner jumps over it. To add challenge, partners should change the tempo of movement and raise the level of the wand.

Wand Reaction

One partner holds the wand horizontally. The other partner places one hand directly above the wand, palm down. When the first partner drops the wand, the second partner tries to catch it before it strikes the floor.

Cooperative Movements

Holding a wand between them, partners stand toe to toe and circle either way with light foot movements. Together, partners squat down and stand up. Sit down and come up. Kneel and hold the wand overhead as they face each other. Bend sideways and touch the wand to the floor.

Isometric Exercises with Wands

The isometric exercises with wands presented here are mainly grip exercises. A variety of grips should be employed. With the wand horizontal, use either the overhand or underhand grip. With the wand in vertical position, grip with the thumbs pointed up, down, or toward each other. Repeat each exercise

with a different grip. Exercises can also be repeated with the wand in different positions: in front of the body (either horizontal or vertical), overhead, or behind the back. Hold each exercise for 8 to 12 seconds.

Pull the Wand Apart

Place the hands 6 inches apart near the center of the wand. With a tight grip to prevent slippage and with arms extended, pull the hands apart. Change grip and position.

Push the Wand Together

Hold the wand as previously, except push the hands together.

Wand Twist

Hold the wand with both hands about 6 inches apart. Twist the hands in opposite directions.

Bicycle

Holding the wand horizontally throughout and using an overhand grip, extend the wand outward and downward. Bring it upward near the body, completing a circular movement. On the downward movement, push the wand together, and on the upward movement, pull the wand apart.

Arm Spreader

Hold the wand overhead with hands spread wide. Attempt to compress the stick. Reverse force, and attempt to pull the stick apart.

Dead Lift

Partially squat and place the wand under the thighs. Place the hands between the legs and try to lift. Try also with hands on the outside of the legs.

Abdominal Tightener

From a standing position, place the wand behind the buttocks. With hands on the ends of the wand, pull forward and resist with the abdominal muscles.

Stretching Exercises with Wands

Wands are useful for stretching, bending, and twisting movements.

Side Bender

Grip the wand and extend the arms overhead with feet apart. Bend sideways as far as possible, maintaining straight arms and legs. Recover, and bend to the other side.

Body Twist

Place the wand behind the neck, with arms draped over the wand from behind. Rotate the upper body first to the right as far as possible and then to the left. The feet and hips should remain in position. The twist is at the waist.

Body Twist to Knee

Assume body twist position. Bend the trunk forward and twist so that the right end of the wand touches the left knee (Figure 17.18). Recover, and touch the left end to the right knee.

Shoulder Stretcher

Grip the wand at the ends in a regular grip. Extend the arms overhead and rotate the wand, arms, and shoulders backward until the stick touches the back of the legs. The arms should be kept straight.

Figure 17.18   Body Twist to Knee

Those who find the stretch too easy should move their hands closer to the center of the wand.

Toe Touch

Grip the wand with the hands about shoulder width apart. Bend forward, reaching down as far as possible without bending the knees. The movement should be slow and controlled. Try the same activity from a sitting position.

Over the Toes

Sit down, flex the knees, place the wand over the toes, and rest it against the middle of the arch. Grip the stick with the fingers at the outside edge of the feet. Slowly extend the legs forward, pushing against the stick and trying for a full extension of the legs.

ACTIVITIES WITH HOOPS

Most hoops manufactured in the United States are plastic, but Europeans sometimes use wooden ones. The plastic variety is less durable but more versatile. Extra hoops are needed because some breakage will occur. The standard hoop is 42 inches in diameter, but it is desirable to have smaller hoops (36 inches) for primary-grade children.

Instructional Procedures

1. Hoops produce noisy activity. The teacher may find it helpful to have the children lay their hoops on the floor when they are to listen.

2. Hoops can be a creative medium for children. Allow them free time to explore their own ideas.

3. Give the children an adequate amount of space in which to perform, for hoops require much movement.

4. In activities that require children to jump through hoops, instruct the holder to grasp the hoop lightly, so as not to cause an awkward fall if a performer hits it.

5. Hoops can serve as a "home" for various activities. For instance, the children might leave their hoops to gallop in all directions and then return quickly to the hoop on command.

6. Hoops are good targets. A hoop can be made to stand by placing an individual mat over its base (p. 475).

7. When teaching the reverse spin with hoops, have the students throw the hoop up, in place,

rather than forward along the floor. After they learn the upward throw, they can progress to the forward throw for distance.

Recommended Activities

Hoops as Floor Targets

Each child has a hoop, which is placed on the floor. A number of movement challenges can give direction to the activity.

1. Show what different patterns you can make by jumping or hopping in and out of the hoop.

2. Do a Bunny Jump and a Frog Jump into the center and out the other side.

3. Show what ways you can cross from one side of the hoop to the other by taking the weight on your hands inside the hoop.

4. What kinds of animal walks can you do around your hoop?

5. On all fours, show the kinds of movements you can do, with your feet inside the hoop and your hands outside. With your hands inside the hoop and your feet outside. With one foot and one hand inside, and one foot and one hand outside.

6. (Set a time limit of 15 to 30 seconds.) See how many times you can jump in and out of your hoop during this time. Now try hopping.

7. Balance on and walk around the hoop. Try to keep your feet from touching the floor.

8. Curl your body inside the hoop. Bridge over your hoop. Stretch across your hoop. See how many different ways you can move around the hoop.

9. Pick up your hoop and see how many different machines you can invent. Let your hoop be the steering wheel of a car. What could it be on a train or a boat?

10. Jump in and out of the hoop, using the alphabet. Jump in on the vowels and out on the consonants. Use odd and even numbers in the same way. Vary the locomotor movements.

11. Get into the hoop by using two different body parts. Move out by using three parts. Vary the number of body parts used.

12. Get organized in squads or comparable groups, and divide the hoops. Arrange the hoops in various formations, and try different locomotor movements, animal walks, and other ways of maneuvering through the maze. (After the chil-

dren have gained some experience, this can become a follow-the-leader activity.)

Hoop Handling

1. Spin the hoop like a top. See how long you can make it spin. Spin it again, and see how many times you can run around it before it falls to the floor.

2. Hula-hoop using various body parts such as the waist, legs, arms, and fingers. While hula-hooping on the arms, try to change the hoop from one arm to the other. Lie on the back with one or both legs pointed toward the ceiling and explore different ways the legs can twirl the hula hoop. Hula-hoop with two or more hoops.

3. Jump or hop through a hoop held by a partner. Further challenge can be added by varying the height and angle of the hoop.

4. Roll the hoop and run alongside it. Change direction when a command is given.

5. Hula-hoop on one arm. Throw the hoop in the air and catch it on the other arm.

6. Hold the hoop and swing it like a pendulum. Jump and hop in and out of the hoop.

7. Use the hoop like a jump rope. Jump forward, backward, and sideward. Do a crossover with the hands.

8. Roll the hoop with a reverse spin to make it return to you. The key to the reverse spin is to pull down (toward the floor) on the hoop as it is released. Roll the hoop with a reverse spin, jump over it, and catch it as it returns. Roll the hoop with a reverse spin, and as it returns, hoist it with the foot and catch it. Roll the hoop with a reverse spin, kick it up with the toe, and go through the hoop. Roll the hoop with a reverse spin, run around it, and catch it. Roll the hoop with a reverse spin, pick it up, and begin hooping on the arm—all in one motion.

9. Play catch with a partner. Play catch with two or more hoops.

10. Hula-hoop and attempt to change hoops with a partner.

11. Have one partner roll the hoop with a reverse spin and the other attempt to crawl through the hoop. (This is done most easily just after the hoop reverses direction and begins to return to the spinner. Some children can go in and out of the hoop twice.)

12. Tell partners to spin the hoops like tops and see who can keep theirs spinning longer.

Games with Hoops

Cooperative Musical Hoops

Hoops, one per student, are placed on the floor. Players are given a locomotor movement to do. On signal, they cease the movement, find a hoop, and sit cross-legged in the center of it. Music can be used, with the children moving to the music and seeking a hoop when the music stops. Hoops can be removed by the teacher challenging students to share hoops with each other. This can continue until all students are in three or four hoops.

Around the Hoop

The class is divided into groups of three, with children in each group numbered 1, 2, and 3. Each threesome sits back to back inside a hoop. Their heels may need to be outside the hoop. The leader calls out a direction (right or left) and names one of the numbers. The child with that number immediately gets up, runs in the stipulated direction around the hoop, then runs back to place and sits down. The winner is the first group sitting in good position after the child returns to place.

Hula-Hoop Circle

Four to six children hold hands in a circle, facing in, with a hoop dangling on one pair of joined hands. They move the hoop around the circle and back to the starting point. This requires all bodies to go through the hoop. Hands can help the hoop move, but grips cannot be released.

Hula-Hoop Relay

Relay teams of four to six players, each with a hoop, are placed in line or circle formation. The hoop must be held upright with the bottom of the hoop touching the floor. On signal, designated starters drop their hoops and move through the hoops held by squad members. The sequence repeats until every player has moved through the hoops.

Bumper Car Tag

The class is divided into partners. The partners stand inside a hoop held at waist level. Three or more sets of partners are declared to be it. The object is to tag other partners, who are also moving inside a "bumper car." The game can also be played with three players in a hoop. This is challenging, as players will want to move in different directions.

Hoop Addition Relay

Divide the class into relay teams of four. On signal, the first person moves to the end marker, returns, and takes the next person to the marker and so on, until all four players are in the hoop. Players must sit down in the hoop when the relay is completed.

ACTIVITIES WITH PARTNER TUG-OF-WAR ROPES

A partner tug-of-war rope is about 6 feet long with a loop on each end. (See Chapter 33 for instructions on making partner tug-of-war ropes.) Tug-of-war ropes help in the development of strength, because contestants must use maximum or near-maximum strength in the contests. These strength demands may continue over a short period of time. Because considerable effort is demanded in some cases, force concepts are concomitant learnings. An in-depth discussion of instructional procedures and formations for conducting combative activities is found in Chapter 21.

Instructional Procedures

1. Contests should be between opponents of comparable ability. Each child should have a chance to win.

2. Plan a system of rotation so that children meet different opponents.

3. Caution students to not let go of the rope. If the grip is slipping, they should inform the other student, renew the grip, and start over.

4. Individual ropes are excellent for partner resistance activities. A few of these activities should be practiced each time the children use the ropes.

5. Make the starting routine clear so that each contestant understands. Make definite rules about what constitutes a win and how long a contest must endure to be called a tie.

6. A line on the floor perpendicular to the direction of the rope makes a satisfactory goal for determining a win. One child pulls the other forward until the second child is over the line. If the distance seems too short, two parallel lines can be drawn 8 to 10 feet apart, with the object now being to pull the opponent out of the area between the lines. Another criterion for a win could be for children to pick up objects placed behind them.

Partner Activities

Children should try the following ways of pulling. The tug-of-war rope offers good possibilities in movement exploration. Let students try to devise ways other than those mentioned by which they can pull against each other.

1. Pull with the right hand only, the left hand only, both hands.

2. Grasp with the right hand, with the body supported on three points (the left hand and the feet). Change hands.

3. Pull with backs toward each other, with the rope between the legs, holding with one hand only.

4. Opponents get down on all fours, with feet toward each other. Hook the loops around one foot of each opponent. For each contestant, the force is provided by both hands and the foot that remains on the floor.

5. Opponents get into crab position and pull the rope by hooking a foot through the loop (Figure 17.19).

6. Opponents face each other and stand on one foot only. Contestants try to pull each other off balance without losing their own balance. If the raised foot touches the floor, the other person is declared the winner.

7. Contestants stand with opposite sides toward each other. They hold a tug-of-war rope with opposite hands and move apart until the rope is taut. The goal is to make the other person move the feet by pulling and giving on the rope. The legs must be kept straight, and only the arms can be used in the contest.

8. Students stand 10 feet away from the rope, which is on the floor. On signal, they run to the rope, pick it up, and have a tug-of-war. Contestants can start from different positions, such as push-up, curl-up, or Crab.

9. Instead of opponents pulling each other across a line, each tries to pull the other toward a peg or bowling pin placed behind them so that they can pick up the objects.

10. Two individual ropes are tied together at the center so that four loops are available for pulling. Four cones form a square, and four children compete to see who can pick up a cone first.

11. Two children pull against two others. The rope loops should be made big enough so that both can secure handholds on each end. They can use right hands only or left hands only.

12. For *Frozen Tug-of-War,* two children take hold of a rope, each with both hands on a loop. The children are positioned close enough together so that there is some slack in the rope. A third child grasps the rope to make a 6-inch bend at the center, and the contestants then pull the rope taut so that there is no slack (Figure 17.20). On the signal "Go," the third child drops the loop, and the opponents try to pull each other off balance. The feet are "frozen" to the floor; if the position of either foot is moved, that player loses.

13. *Hawaiian Tug-of-War* is an exciting game activity for youngsters. Two parallel lines are drawn about 20 feet apart. The game is between two people, but as many pairs as are in a class can play. A partner tug-of-war rope is laid on the floor at right angles to, and midway between, the two parallel lines. The players position themselves so that each is standing about 1 foot from one of the loops of the rope. They are in position to pick up the rope and pull against each other on signal. The object of the game is

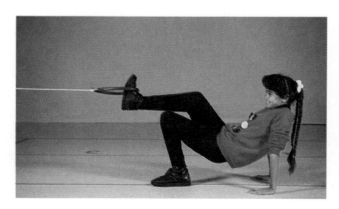

Figure 17.19 Pulling in Crab Position

Figure 17.20 Frozen Tug-of-War

434

to pull the other child far enough to be able to touch the line behind. The magic word is "Hula." This is the signal to pick up the rope and begin to pull. Children must not reach down and pick up the rope until "Hula" is called. The teacher can use other commands, such as "Go" and "Begin," to deceive the children.

14. Group contests are possible. (See Figure 33.18, p. 761 for a diagram of rope arrangements suitable for groups.)

Partner Resistance Activities

Children should follow exercise principles, exerting sufficient force (near maximum), maintaining resistance through the full range of motion for 8 to 10 seconds, and stabilizing the base so that the selected part of the body can be exercised. The force is a controlled pull, not a tug. The partner should not be compelled to move out of position. Much of the exercise centers on the hands and arms, but other parts of the body come into play as braces. Partners work together, both in the same position.

As in other activities, grip can be varied. The upper grip (palms away from performer) and the lower grip (palms toward performer) are usually used. Occasionally, a mixed grip, with one hand in upper position and one hand in lower position, can be used. Laterality must be kept in mind so that the right and left sides of the body receive equal treatment.

Partners Standing with Sides toward Each Other

1. Use a lower grip. Do a flexed-arm pull, with elbows at right angles.
2. Use an upper grip. Extend the arm from the side at a 45-degree angle. Pull toward the side.
3. Use a lower grip. Extend the arm completely overhead. Pull overhead.
4. Loop the rope around one ankle. Stand with feet apart. Pull with the closer foot.

Partners Standing, Facing Each Other

1. Use a lower grip. Do a flexed-arm pull, with one and then both hands.
2. Use an upper grip. Extend the arms at the side or down. Pull toward the rear.
3. Use an upper grip. Pull both hands straight toward chest.
4. Use an upper grip. Extend the arms above head. Pull backward.

Figure 17.21 Partner resistance activity in sitting position

Partners Sitting, Facing Each Other

1. Repeat the activities described for standing position (Figure 17.21).
2. Hook the rope with both feet. Pull.

Partners Prone, Facing Each Other

1. Use an upper grip. Pull directly toward the chest.
2. Use a lower grip. Do a flexed-arm pull.

Partners Prone, Feet toward Each Other

1. Hook the rope around one ankle. With knee joint at a right angle, pull.
2. Try with both feet together.

Pulling Resistance Activities

Using mostly the standing positions, work out resistance exercises such as the following: One child pulls and makes progress with eight steps. The other child then pulls the first back for eight counts. The addition of music makes this an interesting activity. The child being pulled must provide enough resistance to make the puller work reasonably hard.

MANIPULATIVE ACTIVITIES WITH FOOTSIES

The program of manipulative activities can be expanded with any number of objects that may have limited or local popularity. Footsies are one such object. (Directions for constructing a footsie can be found in Chapter 33.) Some activities involving footsies are the following:

1. Turn the footsie with the right foot and then with the left foot, clockwise and counterclockwise.

2. Travel forward, backward, and sideward while twirling the footsie.

3. Turn around in place in the same direction as the footsie. Now turn the opposite way.

4. Bounce a ball while twirling. Toss the ball and catch it. Play catch with a partner.

FOOTBAG ACTIVITIES

A footbag is an official object used in footbag skills and games. The construction varies with the manufacturer, although most footbags are constructed of leather and are stitched internally for durability. Normal size is about 2 inches in diameter, and the weight is a little over 1 ounce. The object of the activities is to keep the bag in the air by means of foot contact.

The kicking motion used for footbag activities is new to most participants because of the lift, which is performed by lifting the foot upward, not away from the body. The lifting motion enables the footbag flight to be directed upward for controlled consecutive kicks and passes. The ball is soft and flexible, with no bounce. It must be designed specifically as a footbag.

Several points contribute to successful footbag work. The basic athletic stance (ready position) is used with the feet at approximately shoulder width and pointed straight ahead. Knees are bent slightly, with the weight lowered.

There should be equal use of both feet for lifting and kicking. The support (nonkicking) foot is important for maintaining balance and keeping the body in a crouched position. Eye focus on the footbag is essential. Kicking speed should be slow; most beginners tend to kick too quickly. The kicking speed should be about that of the descending footbag. "Slow" and "low" are the key words in kicking.

The arms and upper body are used for balance and control. For the outside and back kicks, an outstretched arm, opposite to the kicking foot and in line with it, aids in maintaining balance. The near arm is carried behind the body so as not to restrict the player's vision. For inside kicks, the arms are relaxed and in balanced position.

To begin, start with a hand toss to self or with a courtesy toss from another player. A restriction is made that touching the footbag with any part of the body above the waist is a foul and interrupts any sequence of kicks. Three basic kicks are recommended.

1. *Inside kick*. This kick is used when the footbag falls low and directly in front of both shoulders. Use the inside of the foot for contact by turning the instep and the ankle upward to create a flat striking surface. Curling the toes under aids in creating a flat striking surface. Contact with the footbag is made at about knee level.

2. *Outside kick*. This kick is used when the footbag falls outside of either shoulder. The outside of the foot is used by turning the ankle and knee in to create a flat striking surface. With the kicking foot now parallel to the playing surface, use a smooth lifting motion, striking the footbag at approximately knee level. Pointing the toes up aids in creating a flat surface.

3. *Back kick*. This kick is somewhat similar to the outside kick and serves when the footbag goes directly overhead or is approaching the upper body directly. The hips and body must rotate parallel to the flight direction to enable the footbag to pass while still maintaining constant eye contact. Lean forward in the direction of the footbag's flight and allow it to pass by before executing the kick.

Play can take different forms.

1. *Individual play*. Individuals attempt to see how many consecutive times they can keep the footbag in play. One point is scored for each kick.

2. *Partner play*. Partners alternate kicking the footbag. Score 1 point for each alternate successful kick.

3. *Group play*. A circle of four or five individuals is the basic formation. Rules governing consecutive kicks are (a) all members of the circle must have kicked the footbag for a consecutive run to count, and (b) return kicks are prohibited; that is, kickers may not receive return kicks from the person to whom they kicked the footbag.

Footbag play is an enjoyable activity, but the skills are not easily learned. Persistence and patience are needed. There will be many misses before students slowly gain control. Many physical education suppliers carry footbags, but if sources are needed and information is desired, write to: World Footbag Association, 1317 Washington Avenue, Suite 7, Golden, CO 80401.

RHYTHMIC GYMNASTICS

Rhythmic gymnastics became popular in the United States during the 1970s, and was then accepted as an official sport competition in the 1984 Olympic Games. The activities are broad in scope and merit far more explanation than can be presented in this context. Essentially, activities in rhythmic gymnastics are routines done to music by a performer using a particular type of manipulative equipment. The routine can be either individual, partner, or team competition. Equipment used are balls, jump ropes, hoops, ribbons, and clubs. Wands, flags, and scarves are sometimes included, but not in national or international competition. The elements of competition will not be discussed in this presentation.

Many movement qualities, such as balance, poise, grace, flow of body movement, coordination, rhythm, and kinesthetic sense, grow out of serious participation in rhythmic gymnastics. Fitness qualities of agility, flexibility, and proper posture are also developed. Furthermore, skill in handling the various pieces of manipulative equipment is enhanced, because these skills must be mastered before they can be organized into a routine set to music.

Participants, after initial practice in skill development, should work with music. In competitive situations the music is restricted to one instrument. In the school setting the music should be instrumental, light, lively, and enjoyable to the gymnast. Most record companies dealing in music for physical education stock specialized records for gymnastic movement, with different selections specified for various pieces of equipment. Most records contain directions for suggested routines. There is no substitute, however, for teacher ingenuity in helping children expand and create their routines.

This is an excellent unit for developing group routines where a class works together. Routines are most impressive and can be used for physical education demonstrations, back-to-school presentations, and at halftimes of athletic events. The routines are impressive and do not require a high level of skill. All youngsters are capable of participating and will enjoy the opportunity to be involved in a "team" event.

Organizing the Program

The activities presented here focus on balls, jump ropes, hoops, and ribbons, all of which ordinarily are covered in the elementary program. The club is one of the most difficult of the hand apparatus to use and is therefore not an item for instruction in elementary school programs.

The goal of rhythmic gymnastics is continuous body movement with the selected piece of equipment. Composition goals are originality, variety of movement, use of the performing area, performance presentation, and smoothness of transition. Harmony of movement with the music, the appa-ratus, and execution factors are also important. The length of an individual competitive routine is 1 minute to 1 minute and 30 seconds, but performing time should be shortened for youngsters. Group routines last 2 to 3 minutes and may involve one or two types of equipment. The primary goal is the personal satisfaction that students receive from participating in the program. Offering students an introduction to these activities is more important than the competitive aspect.

Probably the most practical way to include rhythmic gymnastics in the curriculum is a dual approach. The basic skills are taught to all children in physical education classes, allowing opportunity for expression through the composition of creative routines. More refined work can take place through the intramural program or a sport club. Students can choose on an elective basis to participate in competition. Instructors often lack background in these activities. This problem may be solved by bringing in dance instructors from private clubs to introduce the activities.

Developing Routines

Routines for the elementary level should be uncomplicated and based on learned skills. Aesthetics, although important as skill develops, should be of secondary emphasis. Ballet, jazz, and modern dance movements, along with basic dance steps, are normal conclusions in high-level competition.

In developing routines to music, children need to remember that most music is based on units of 8 or 16 counts. Movements are performed in the sagittal, frontal, and horizontal planes. This is the terminology used when developing routines and should be learned by youngsters. The *sagittal* plane is an imaginary division of the body into right and left halves. Movements "in the sagittal" are performed parallel to this plane on either side of the body. The *horizontal* plane involves movements that are parallel to the floor. The *frontal* plane divides the body into front and rear halves. Movements in this plane are performed parallel to this plane either in front of or in back of the body.

An effective way to form a routine is to teach the beginning of a routine and then let youngsters create the remainder. For example, perform the following movements using ribbons. End each series with the hands in front of the waist.

Sagittal forward circles on the right side (6 counts)

Sagittal forward circles on the left side (6 counts)

Elevator (p. 502) (4 counts)

In this fashion the routine could consist of a number of 16-count units, each of which is concluded with the Elevator (4 counts). Students could develop additional units. For any one piece of apparatus, certain skill areas can be specified. It is then up to the participant to include these at some point in the routine.

Rhythmic Gymnastic Ball Skills

The ball should be of sufficient size that it cannot be grasped by the hand but must rest in the hand and be controlled by balance. For elementary school children, use either a 6-inch or an 8½-inch ball. Balls should be moderately inflated.

In handling the ball, the fingers should be closed and slightly bent, with the ball resting in the palm. In throwing, the ball can roll from the fingertips. After catching, the ball returns immediately to the palm.

The following ball skills are representative of activities that can be combined to develop a routine:

1. Rolling. In a sitting position, try the following activities: Roll under the legs and around the back; around the body; down the legs; down the arms; down the legs, lift legs and toss the ball off the toes into the air and catch.

2. Bouncing. Combine basketball dribbling drills with graceful body movements; execute locomotor dance-type movements while bouncing.

3. Toss and catch the ball employing different body positions.

4. Add locomotor movements to tosses and catches.

5. Perform body waves with the ball.

6. Throw and/or bounce the ball in a variety of ways.

7. Execute swinging movements (also circular movements). Swinging movements are more difficult than they first appear. The ball must be retained in the palm while the movements are performed.

8. Try different balancing movements. These are spirals, curls, and other balances that are inherent to rhythmic gymnastics.

9. Allow opportunity for student exploration combining a number of these activities.

Figure 17.22 is an example of a simple routine using balls. The numbers refer to the floor area in the figure where each activity should be performed.

1. Bounce the ball in place.
2. Bounce the ball while moving forward slowly.

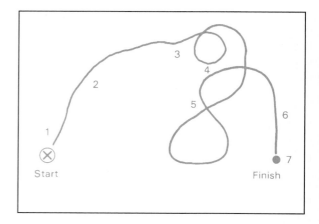

Figure 17.22 Floor pattern for routine using balls

3. Run forward while making swing tosses from side to side.

4. Bounce the ball and make a full turn.

5. Run in a figure-eight pattern.

6. Toss the ball up and catch it with one hand.

7. Finish with a toss and catch behind the back.

Rhythmic Gymnastic Rope Routines

As with ball routines, jump rope routines can be categorized in a number of areas. Most important is that the participant be able to do the basic jumps with consummate skill. Ropes can be used full length, folded in half, or folded in fourths. Knotting the end of the rope makes it easier to handle. Proper length is determined by standing on the center of the rope with one foot and extending the rope ends to the outstretched hands at shoulder level. Handles are not appropriate. Most rope jumping is done with the hands far apart. The rope should not touch the floor, but should pass slightly above it. The jumping techniques used for rhythmic gymnastics obviously differ from those taught in the physical education class. The following are examples of movements that can be performed using jump ropes.

1. Try single and double jumps forward and backward.

2. Circle the rope on each side of the body holding both ends of the rope.

3. Make figure-eight swings: Holding both ends of the rope; holding the center of the rope and swinging the ends.

4. Swing the rope in pendulum fashion and jump it.

5. Run or skip over a turning rope. Try forward and backward.

6. Do a schottische step over a turning rope.

7. Holding the ends and center of the rope, kneel and horizontally circle the rope close to the floor. Stand and circle the rope overhead.

8. Perform a body wrap with the rope. (Hold one end on the hip, wrap the rope around the body with the other hand.)

9. Upon completion of a jump over a backward-turning rope, toss the rope with both ends into the air and catch.

10. Run while holding both ends of the rope in one hand and circling the rope sagittally backward at the side of the body. Toss the rope and catch it while running.

11. While performing a dance step, toss and catch the rope.

12. Hold both ends of the rope and swing it around the body like a cape.

13. Perform leaps while circling the rope sagittally at one side of the body.

14. Try different balance movements. Balance movements add variety and permit the performer to catch his breath. These involve held body positions, with the rope underneath the foot or hooked around a foot.

15. Hold the rope around the foot and make shapes with the body and foot-rope connection.

16. Explore and combine a number of the activities described.

Rhythmic Gymnastic Hoop Movements

The basic hoop stunts and challenges (pp. 431–433) should first be mastered. The same hoop used in physical education classes is suitable for these routines. The hoop may be held, tossed, or caught in one or both hands and with a variety of different grips. Hoops may turn forward or backward. Some suggested rhythmic movements with hoops follow.

1. Swinging movements. A variety of swinging movements are possible. The swinging movement should be very large. Good alignment between body and hoop is important. Hoops can be swung in a frontal, sagittal, or horizontal plane. The movements can be done in place or involve locomotion. Examples are the following:

   a. across the body

   b. with body lean

Rhythmic gymnastic movements using hoops

   c. around the body, changing hands

   d. across the body, changing hands

   e. overhead, changing hands, and swinging downward

   f. swinging in a figure-eight pattern

2. Spinning movements. This movement entails turning the hoop, usually with both hands but sometimes with one. The hoop also can be spun on the ground. Examples are the following:

   a. Spin in front of the body.

   b. Spin on the floor.

   c. Spin and kick one leg over the hoop. Add a full body turn after the kickover.

3. Circling movements. These are the movements most characteristic of hoop activities. Hoops can be twirled by the hand, wrist, arm, leg, or body (hula-hooping). Changes are made from one hand or wrist to the other. Examples of possible activities are the following:

   a. Extend the arm in front of the body. Circle on the hand between the thumb and first finger in the frontal plane.

   b. Circle the hoop while swaying from side to side.

   c. Circle the hoop horizontally overhead.

   d. Hold both sides of the hoop and circle it in front of the body.

   e. Circle the hoop around different parts of the body.

4. Tossing and catching movements. The hoop can be tossed high in the air with one or both hands. The catch should be one-handed, between the thumb and index finger. Most tosses

grow out of swinging or circling movements. Examples are the following:

   a. Try with one- and two-handed catches.

   b. Toss the hoop in different directions.

   c. Toss overhead from hand to hand.

   d. Circle the hoop on the hand, toss into the air, and catch.

5. Rolling movements. The hoop can be rolled on the floor—either forward or reverse (return) rolling—or can be rolled on the body in diverse ways. If rolled along the floor, various jumps can be executed over the rolling hoop. The hoop can be rolled along one arm to the other, on the front or the back of the body. Specific rolling activities are the following:

   a. Roll the hoop and run alongside it.

   b. Roll the hoop and move through it.

   c. Roll the hoop and jump over it.

6. Jumping movements. The hoop, turned forward or backward, can be used in a manner similar to a jump rope.

Rhythmic Gymnastic Ribbon Movements

Ribbon movements are spectacular and make effective demonstrations. Official ribbon length is around 21 feet with the first 3 feet doubled, but for practical purposes, shorter lengths are used at the elementary school level.

Ribbons can be made easily in a variety of colors. A rhythmic flow of movement is desired, featuring circular, oval, spiral, and wavelike shapes. A light flowing movement is the goal, with total body involvement. The dowel or wand to which the ribbon is attached should be an extension of the hand and arm. Laterality is also a consideration. The following are basic ribbon movements.

1. Swinging movements. The entire body should coordinate with these large, swinging motions:

   a. Swing the ribbon forward and backward in the sagittal plane.

   b. Swing the ribbon across and in front of the body in the frontal plane.

   c. Swing the ribbon overhead from side to side.

   d. Swing the ribbon upward and catch the end of it.

   e. While holding both ends of the ribbon, swing it upward, around, and over the body.

2. Circling movements. Large circles should involve the whole arm; smaller circles involve the wrist. Circles are made in different planes: frontal, sagittal, and horizontal.

   a. Circle the ribbon at different levels.

   b. Circle the ribbon horizontally, vertically, or diagonally.

   c. Circle the ribbon in front of the body, around the body, and behind the body.

   d. Run while circling the ribbon overhead; leap as the ribbon is circled downward and under the legs.

   e. Add dance steps and turns while circling the ribbon.

3. Figure-eight movements. Figure eights are also made in the three planes. The two halves of the figure eight should be the same size and on the same plane level. The figure can be made with long arm movements or with movements of the lower arm or wrist. While performing a figure eight, hop through the loop when the ribbon passes the side of the body.

4. Zigzag movements. Zigzag movements can be made in the air or on the floor. These are done with continuous up-and-down hand movements, using primarily wrist action. The following are suggested:

   a. Execute the zigzag in the air in front, around, and behind the body.

   b. Run backward while zigzagging the ribbon in front of the body. Perform at different levels.

   c. Run forward while zigzagging behind the body at different levels.

5. Spiral movements. The circles in the spiral can be of the same size or of an increasing or decreasing progression. Spirals can be made from left to right or the reverse.

   a. Execute spirals around, in front of, or beside the body while performing locomotor dance steps.

   b. Execute spirals while performing forward and backward rolls.

6. Throwing and catching movements. These skills are usually combined with swinging, circling, or figure-eight movements. The ribbon is tossed with one hand and is caught with the same hand or with the other hand. Throwing and catching is a difficult maneuver.

7. Exchanges. During group routines, the ribbon is handed or tossed to a partner.

REFERENCES AND SUGGESTED READINGS

Finnigan, D. (1987). *The complete juggler.* New York: Random House.

Morris, G. S. (1976). Effects ball and background color have upon the catching performance of elementary school children. *Research Quarterly, 47,* 409–415.

Schmidt, A. M. (1976). *Modern rhythmic gymnastics.* Palo Alto, CA: Mayfield.

Jump Rope Activities: Developing Specialized Motor Skills

PURPOSE OF ACTIVITIES IN THIS CHAPTER
Jump rope activities develop specialized motor skills, particularly visual-tactile coordination. Rope jumping can also be used to enhance aerobic fitness. Activities in this chapter progress from individual movements guided by rope patterns, to long-rope jumping with turners, to individual rope-jumping challenges.

Rope jumping is an excellent activity for conditioning all parts of the body. It increases coordination, rhythm, and timing, while offering a wide range of challenges. Rope jumping is regarded as an excellent medium for fitness development. It can be designed to suit the activity needs of all individuals regardless of age or condition. Workloads can easily be measured and modified by changing the amount of time jumped or the number of turns. It is a useful activity to teach children, because it offers carryover value for activity in later life.

Rope jumping can be taught during any part of the school year and can be used as a fitness or lesson focus activity. Activities begin with moving over a rope placed on the floor to complex and challenging activities based on rope jumping. As a point of interest, some educators refer to rope jumping as rope skipping. The term *rope jumping* should be used instead, because jumping is the predominant skill in this activity.

Rope jumping has increased in popularity during the past decade, with the Jump Rope for Heart program offering national leadership. The program is sponsored by the American Alliance for Health, Physical Education, Recreation, and Dance as a fund-raising activity for the American Heart Association (Jump Rope for Heart materials can be obtained by contacting your local affiliate of the American Heart Association or by calling AAHPERD Special Events Office at 703-476-3489. This nationwide movement has spawned school teams, exhibitions, and competition in the form of state and national tournaments. It is a creative medium with an incredible number of variations possible. Rope-jumping skills presented in this chapter are those deemed suitable for inclusion in an elementary school physical education program. Not included are highly advanced and complex activities that are often used in competitive settings. The difficulty of advanced activities makes them less suitable for bringing success to all youngsters in physical education programs. For more information about advanced activities, review the references at the end of the chapter.

Rope jumping is a learned skill, so it is difficult to allocate the various activities to grade levels. Rope-jumping activities in this chapter have been grouped into three categories: (a) movements guided by rope patterns, (b) long-rope jumping, and (c) individual rope jumping.

MOVEMENTS GUIDED BY ROPE PATTERNS

Ropes can be placed on the floor in various fashions to serve as stimuli for different locomotor and nonlocomotor movements. The activities should stress creative responses within the limits of the challenge. The educational movement factors of space, time, force, and flow can be interwoven in the activity. The key is teacher ingenuity in providing direction for the movement patterns. The child can move as an individual, with a partner, or as a member of a small group. Generally, a rope is placed in a straight line or in a circle. Geometric figures can be formed, however, and numbers or letters of the alphabet featured. The discussions are organized around these patterns.

Rope Forming a Straight Line

When the rope is placed in a straight line, one approach is for children to begin at one end and to perform activities as they move down the line. Much of the movement can be based on hopping or jumping. The children then return, back up the line, to the starting point. Movement suggestions follow.

1. Jog around the rope forward and backward. Try other locomotor skills such as hopping, jumping, skipping, and sliding. Crab Walk down and back. Use various animal walks such as Bear Walk or Lame Dog Walk.

2. Hop back and forth across the rope, moving down the line. Return, using the other foot.

3. Jump lightly back and forth down the line. Return.

4. Hop slowly, under control, down the line. Hop rapidly back.

5. Jump so that the rope is between the feet each time, alternately crossing and uncrossing the feet.

6. Move on all fours, leading with different body parts.

7. Do Crouch Jumps back and forth across the rope. Vary with three points and then two points of contact.

8. Jump as high as possible going down the line and as low as possible coming back.

9. Hop with a narrow shape down and a different shape back.

10. Walk the rope like a tightrope.

11. Begin with a bridge and move the bridge down the line. Return with a different bridge.

12. Lie across the rope, holding one end. Roll down the line, causing the rope to roll around the body. Unroll the rope back to position.

13. Do a movement with the rhythm slow-slow, fast-fast-fast, going down the line, and repeat coming back.

14. "Pull" yourself down the line and "push" yourself back.

For the following movements, the child is positioned close to the center of the line and simply moves back and forth across it without materially changing the relative position.

1. Hop back and forth across the line. Jump back and forth.

2. Go over with a high movement. Come back with a low one.

3. Do a Bunny Jump across and back. A Frog Jump. A Crouch Jump.

4. Lead with different parts of the body back and forth. Propel with different parts.

5. Get into a moderately crouched position over the rope. Jump the feet back and forth over the rope.

6. Take a Sprinter's Position with the rope between the feet. Alternate the feet back and forth over the rope.

7. Jump back and forth lightly on the tiptoes.

8. Go back and forth, employing different shapes.

9. With toes touching the rope, drop the body forward across the rope, taking the weight on both hands. Walk the hands forward, out to the limit.

10. Pretend that the rope is a river. Show different kinds of bridges that you can make over the river.

11. Stand straddling the rope. Jump up, perform a Heel Click (or two), and return to original position.

Rope Forming a Circle

With the rope in a circle, children can do movements around the outside clockwise and counter-clockwise—walking, skipping, hopping, sliding (facing toward and away from the circle), jumping, running, and galloping. The following activities can be done with hoops also.

1. Hop in and out of the circle, moving around. Jump.

2. Jump directly in and then across. Jump backward.

3. Jump in, collapse, and jump out, without touching the rope.

4. Begin in the center of the circle. Jump forward, backward, and sideward, each time returning to the center.

5. Place the feet in the circle and walk the hands all around the outside of the circle. Place the hands inside and the feet outside. Face the floor, the ceiling, and to the side.

6. Inside the circle, make a small shape. Make a large shape so that you are touching all sides of the circle.

7. Try different balance stunts inside the circle. Close your eyes and balance.

8. Make a bridge over the circle. How many types of bridges can you make?

9. Do a Pogo Stick Jump in and out of the rope circle.

10. Do a Tightrope Walk clockwise and counter-clockwise.

11. Jump and click the heels, landing inside the circle. Repeat, going out.

12. Do jump turns inside the circle without touching the rope: quarter turns, half turns, and full turns.

13. Jump in with a Bunny Jump. Jump out. Try with a Frog Jump.

14. Take the weight on the hands inside the circle so that the feet land on the other side. Try a Cartwheel.

Rope Forming Various Figures

Have the rope form different figures, such as geometric shapes, letters, and numbers. In addition to the following challenges, many of the previous ones can be applied here, too.

1. With the rope and your body, form a triangle, a square, a rectangle, a diamond shape, and a figure eight.

2. With the rope and your body, form a two-letter word. Form other words.

3. Get a second rope and make your own patterns for hopping and jumping.

4. Toss the rope in the air and let it fall to the floor. Try to shape your body into the same figure that the rope made on the floor.

Partner Activity

Partner activity with ropes is excellent. Partners can work with one or two ropes, and can do matching, following, or contrasting movements. Add-On is an interesting game: One partner does an activity and the other adds on an activity to form a sequence. Using the suggested rope forms (multiple ropes) in Figure 18.1, one partner makes

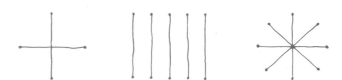

Figure 18.1 Suggested rope forms

a series of movements. The other partner has to try to duplicate the movements.

Group Activity

Group activity with jump ropes also has good possibilities. Each child brings a rope to the group. Patterns for hopping, jumping, and other locomotor movements can be arranged with the ropes. An achievement demonstration after a period of practice allows each group to show the patterns that they have arranged and the movements that can be done in the patterns. A further extension is to leave the patterns where they are and to rotate the groups to different locations.

LONG-ROPE JUMPING

Long-rope jumping is an excellent activity for beginning jumpers. Youngsters can concentrate on jumping the rope without learning the skill of turning. Many activities with two or more long ropes add a great deal of variety to long-rope jumping and can make it challenging for the most skilled jumpers. Long jump ropes should be 9 to 14 feet in length, with 12 to 14 feet the most commonly used. The exact length depends on the age and skill of the children; the longer the rope, the more difficult it is to turn. For primary-grade children, individual jump ropes can be used to teach beginning skills as they are shorter, making it easier for young children to turn. Another alternative is to fasten one end of the rope with a snap to an eye bolt fixed on a post or to the side of a wall. This eases the task of turning and allows more children to be actively jumping.

Chants are suggested for many of the jumping sequences. Rope-jumping chants represent a cultural heritage. In many cases, children have their own favorites. Traditionally, many chants used girls' names, because rope jumping was considered a feminine activity. Today, however, this has changed, and both sexes participate in rope-jumping activities with equal vigor and success. Several of the chants included have been modified to reflect this change.

Instructional Procedures

1. Four or five children is an appropriate group size for practicing long-rope skills. Two members of the group turn the rope while the others practice jumping. A plan for rotating turners is important so that all children receive similar amounts of practice jumping.

2. Turning the rope is a difficult skill for young children. It must be practiced regularly until children can maintain an even, steady rhythm. Effective turning is one key to successful jumping. If turning is not rhythmic, skilled jumpers will have problems. Youngsters must be taught: Learn to turn first, then learn to jump.

3. When learning to turn the rope, incorporate the following points:
   a. Keep the elbow close to the body and concentrate on turning the rope with the forearm.
   b. The thumb should stay up during the turning motion of the hands. This will emphasize turning with the forearm.
   c. Hold the rope in front of the body at waist level. Keep the body perpendicular to the rope.

4. To practice turning, youngsters are motivated by turning the rope under a lively bouncing ball. Turners stand ready, and a third child tosses a ball upward so that it will remain in one spot while bouncing. Turners adjust the speed of the turning as the bounces become smaller and more rapid. A count can be kept of the number of successful turns before the ball ceases bouncing.

5. Children of all ages can perform long-rope jumping. To check the readiness of the children, see if they are capable of jumping in place with both feet leaving the ground simultaneously. They should be able to jump at least 2 to 3 inches off the ground, be well balanced, and land lightly with reasonably straight knees.

6. Children should understand the terms used to describe entry into the long jump rope. *Front door* means entering from the side where the rope is turning forward and toward the jumper after it reaches its peak. *Back door* means entering from the side where the rope is turning backward and away from the jumper. To enter front door, the jumper follows the rope in and jumps when it completes the turn. To enter back door, the jumper waits until the rope reaches its peak and moves in as the rope moves downward. Learning to enter at an angle is usually easier, but any path that is comfortable is acceptable.

7. Introducing and teaching youngsters long-rope jumping skills can be accomplished with the following steps:
   a. Use a shorter long rope (8 to 12 foot). Lay the rope on the floor and have youngsters jump back and forth across the rope. Em-

phasis should be on small, continuous jumps and learning to jump back and forth continuously without stopping. Jumps should not be high, just enough to clear the rope.

b. Turners slowly move the rope back and forth along the floor while the jumper moves over the rope each time it moves near. The speed of the rope moving along the floor should be increased gradually. The jumper should be encouraged to jump up and down with as little forward-backward-sideways movement as possible. If necessary, use white shoe polish to mark an "X" on the floor and encourage the child to stay on target.

c. The jumper stands near the center of the rope. The rope is now moved in pendulum fashion back and forth while the jumper clears the rope each time it hits the floor. Typically, this activity is called Blue Bells.

d. The jumper starts by facing the center of the stationary rope. Use three pendulum swings followed by a full turn of the rope rotating from the jumper's back to the front. Continue jumping until a miss occurs. Verbal cueing helps most beginners find success; each time the rope hits the floor, say "Jump." If youngsters are having difficulty, have them stand behind a turner and jump (sans rope) each time the rope hits the floor.

e. When jumpers have difficulty with the rhythm, they can practice off to one side without actually jumping over the rope. A drumbeat can reinforce the rhythm with alternating heavy (jump) and light (rebound) beats.

f. Teach front-door and back-door entry, making sure that the jumper enters at an angle rather than perpendicular to the rope.

8. Instructional cues to teach long-rope jumping skills are:
   a. Turn the rope with the forearm.
   b. Lock the wrist and keep the thumb up while turning.
   c. Stand perpendicular to the rope.
   d. Barely touch the floor with the turning rope.
   e. Don't cross the midline of the body with the forearm while turning the rope.
   f. Jump on the balls of the feet.
   g. To enter, stand near the turner and move to the center of the rope.

Introductory Skills

Some introductory skills and routines follow.

1. Holders hold the rope in a stationary position 6 inches above the ground. Jumpers jump over, back and forth. Raise the rope a little each time. Be sure to hold the rope loosely in the hands. This is called Building a House.

2. Ocean Wave is another stationary jumping activity. Turners make waves in the rope by moving the arms up and down. Jumpers try to time it so that they jump over a low part of the wave.

3. Holders stoop down and wiggle the rope back and forth on the floor. Jumpers try to jump over the rope and not touch it as it moves. This activity is called Snake in the Grass.

4. The jumper stands in the center between the turners, who carefully turn the rope in a complete arc over the jumper's head. As the rope completes the turn, the jumper jumps over it and exits immediately in the direction in which the rope is turned.

5. Children run through the turning rope (front door) without jumping, following the rope through.

6. While the rope is being turned, the jumper runs in (front door), jumps once, and runs out immediately.

7. Children can play school and go through the following sequence, trying to pass to the sixth grade. To pass kindergarten, run through the turning rope. To pass first grade, run in, take one jump, and run out. For the second through sixth grades, increase the number of jumps by one for each grade. A jumper who misses becomes a turner.

8. When children can jump a number of times consecutively, add motivation by using some of the chants that follow.

Intermediate Skills, Routines, and Chants

Intermediate routines require the jumper to be able to go in front door, jump, and exit front door, and to do the same sequence back door. Enough practice in the simple jumping skills and exits should be held so that confidence is fortified; students then can turn to more intricate routines. Entries and exits should be varied in the following routines.

1. Jumpers run in, jump a specified number of times, and exit.

2. Children can add chants that dictate the number of jumps, which are followed by an exit. Here are some examples.

Tick tock, tick tock,

What's the time by the clock?

It's one, two, [up to midnight].

I like coffee, I like tea,

How many people can jump like me?

One, two, three, [up to a certain number].

Hippity hop to the butcher shop,

How many times before I stop?

One, two, three, [and so on].

Bulldog, poodle, bow wow wow,

How many doggies have we now?

One, two, three, [and so on].

Michael, Michael (student's name) at the gate,

Eating cherries from a plate.

How many cherries did he (she) eat?

One, two, three, [and so on].

3. Children can label their first jump "kindergarten" and exit at any "grade." To graduate from high school, the exit would be at the 12th grade. Each grade should be sounded crisply in succession.

4. Kangaroo (or White Horse) gets its name from the jump required for back-door entry, in which the jumper resembles a kangaroo or a leaping horse. The jumper calls out "Kangaroo!" takes the entry jump through the back door, and exits. Next time, the same jumper calls out "Kangaroo one!" and adds a jump. Successive jumps are called and added until a designated number is reached.

5. An interesting challenge is to turn the rope over a line parallel to it and have the jumper jump back and forth over the line. The jumper can vary foot position: feet together, feet apart, stride forward and back.

6. Jumpers can vary the pattern with turns. Make four quarter turns until facing the original direction. Reverse the direction of the turns.

7. Youngsters can add stunts as directed by selected chants.

Teddy Bear, Teddy Bear, turn around.

Teddy Bear, Teddy Bear, touch the ground.

Teddy Bear, Teddy Bear, show your shoe.

Teddy Bear, Teddy Bear, you better skidoo.

Teddy Bear, Teddy Bear, go upstairs.

Teddy Bear, Teddy Bear, say your prayers.

Teddy Bear, Teddy Bear, turn out the light.

Teddy Bear, Teddy Bear, say good night.

Daddy, daddy (mommy, mommy), I am sick.

Get the doctor quick, quick, quick.

Daddy, daddy, turn around.

Daddy, daddy, touch the ground.

Daddy, daddy, are you through?

Daddy, daddy, spell your name.

8. In Hot Pepper, turners turn the rope faster and faster, while the jumper tries to keep up with the increased speed. The following chants are good for Hot Pepper.

Charlie, Charlie (student's name), set the table.

Bring the plates if you are able.

Don't forget the salt and

Red hot pepper!

(On the words "Red hot pepper," the rope is turned as fast as possible until the jumper misses.)

Pease porridge hot, pease porridge cold,

Pease porridge in a pot, nine days old.

Some like it hot, hot, hot!

Ice cream, ginger ale, soda water, pop.

You get ready 'cause we're gonna turn hot!

9. In Calling In, the first player enters the rope and calls in a second player by name. Both jump three times holding hands, and then the first runs out. The second player then calls in a third player by name. Both jump three times holding hands, and the second player exits. Players should be in an informal line, since the fun comes from not knowing when one is to enter.

10. Children can enter and exit according to the call in the following chants.

In the shade and under a tree,

I'd like _____ to come in with me.

She's (he's) too fast and I'm too slow.

He stays in and I must go.

Calling in and calling out,

I call (student's name) in and I'm getting out.

House for rent,

Inquire within.

When I move out,

Let (student's name) move in.

11. In High Water, the rope is turned so that it becomes gradually higher and higher off the ground.

    At the beach, at the sea,

    The waves come almost to the knee.

    Higher, higher, [and so forth].

12. In Stopping the Rope, the jumper (a) stops and lets the rope hit the feet, (b) stops the rope by straddling it, (c) stops with the legs crossed and the rope between the feet, or (d) stops the rope by stamping on it. The following chant works well, with accompanying action as indicated.

    Junior, Junior, climb the tree.

    Junior, Junior, slap your knee.

    Junior, Junior, throw a kiss.

    Junior, Junior, time to miss.

13. Two, three, or four children can jump at a time. After some skill has been achieved, children in combination can run in, jump a specified number of times, and run out, keeping hands joined all the time.

14. Two, three, or four children can start as a small moving circle. They run in and jump in a circle, keeping the circle moving in one direction. They run out as a circle.

15. The jumper takes in a ball or other object. Bounce the ball while jumping. Try balancing a beanbag on a body part while jumping.

16. A partner stands ready with a ball and tosses it back and forth to the jumper.

17. For Chase the Rabbit, four or five jumpers are in single file with a leader, the Rabbit, at the head. The Rabbit jumps in any manner she wishes, and all of the others must match the movements. Anyone who misses must go to the end of the line. A Rabbit who misses or stops the rope, she goes to the end of the line, and the next child becomes the new Rabbit. Set a limit on how long a Rabbit can stay at the head of the line.

18. In On Four Cylinders, the challenge is to do activities in a series of fours—four of one kind of jump, four of another, and so on. The number of series can be specified, and the children may choose what they wish to include. (Tell the children that their "engines are running on four cylinders.")

19. In Begging, a jumper runs in and works his way up the rope toward one of the turners. As he jumps, he says, "Father, Father, give me a dollar." The turner replies, "Go see your mother." The jumper works his way toward the other turner and says, "Mother, Mother, give me a dollar." The turner replies, "Go to your father." This continues until a miss occurs or until one of the turners says in reply, "Get out" or "Get lost," at which time the jumper exits.

20. In Setting the Table, a jumper enters and starts jumping. A partner stands ready with at least four beanbags. While the following verse is recited, the partner tosses in the beanbags one at a time, and the jumper catches and places them in a row on the side (with the upward swing of the rope) and then exits.

    Debbie, Debbie (student's name), set the table [toss in one bag],

    Bring the plates if you are able [toss in another bag],

    Don't forget the bread and butter [toss in the other two bags].

21. Partners can go in and perform a number of stunts, such as Wring the Dishrag (p. 506), Partner Hopping (p. 520), or Bouncing Ball (p. 505). Examine the partner stunts for other selections.

22. Children can enter and begin with a hop (one foot), then make a jump (two feet), add a hand touch next (two feet, one hand), and then jump with both hands and feet (two feet, two hands). Selected movements on hands and feet, such as Rabbit Jumps or push-ups, can be executed.

23. For jumping with the eyes closed, single or multiple jumpers enter and begin jumping to this chant.

    Peanuts, popcorn, soda pop,

    How many jumps before you stop?

    Close your eyes and you will see

    How many jumps that this will be!

    The eyes remain closed during the jumping, which continues to a target number or a miss.

24. One or both holders can go inside and jump, turning with their outside hands. First attempts should begin with a pendulum swing and proceed to a full turn.

DOUBLE DUTCH (TWO-ROPE) JUMPING

Double Dutch rope jumping is popular on playgrounds and in gymnasiums across the country. This type of jumping requires two rope turners using two long ropes that are turned in opposite directions. Turning two ropes simultaneously requires practice, and time must be allotted for this. Handling two ropes is tiring, so turners should be rotated frequently.

Instructional Procedures

1. Arm positions and turning motions are similar to turning a single long rope. In short, keep the upper arm stationary, rotate at the elbow with locked wrist, and keep the thumb up. Avoid crossing the midline of the body, and establish an even cadence. Rotate the hands inward toward the midline of the body (right forearm counterclockwise and left forearm clockwise). Students should concentrate on the sound of the ropes hitting the floor so that they make an even and rhythmic beat.

2. Double Dutch turning takes considerable practice. Take time to teach it as a skill that is necessary for successful jumping experiences.

3. When entering, stand beside a turner and run into the ropes when the back rope (farther from the jumper) touches the floor. Turners should be taught to say "Go" each time the back rope touches the floor.

4. Concentrate on jumping in the center of the ropes facing a turner. Use white shoe polish to mark a jumping target.

5. Exit the ropes by facing and jumping toward one turner and exiting immediately after jumping. The exit should be made as close to the turner's shoulder as possible.

6. Practice many of the skills listed in the long-rope jumping section (pp. 446–449). Many of the chants and stunts provide challenge and variety to the unit.

Double Dutch Skills

1. Basic jump on both feet. Land on the balls of the feet, keeping ankles and knees together with hands across the stomach.

2. Turnaround. Circle left or right using the basic jump. Begin circling slowly at first and then increase speed. To increase the challenge, try the turnaround on one foot.

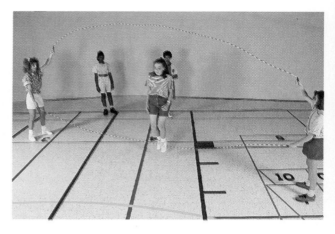

Double Dutch rope jumping

3. Straddle Jump. Jump to the straddle position and return to closed position. Try a Straddle Cross Jump by crossing the legs on return to the closed position. The straddle jumps should be performed facing away from the turners.

4. Scissors Jump. Jump to a stride position with the left foot forward and the right foot back about 8 inches apart. Each jump requires reversing the position of the feet.

5. Jogging Step. Run in place with a jogging step. Increase the challenge by circling while jogging.

6. Hot Peppers. Use the Jogging Step and gradually increase the speed of the ropes.

7. Half turn. Perform a half turn with each jump. Remember to lead the turn with the head and shoulders.

8. Ball tossing. Toss and catch a beanbag or playground ball while jumping.

9. Individual rope jumping. Enter double dutch with an individual rope and jump. Face the turner and decrease the length of the individual jump rope.

10. The following activities are interesting variations for reviving motivation:

   a. Double Irish. Two ropes are turned in the reverse directions used in Double Dutch. The left hand turns counterclockwise and the right hand clockwise. Entry is made when the near rope hits the floor. Jumpers should time their entry by following the near rope on its downward swing.

   b. Egg Beater. Two long ropes are turned at right angles simultaneously by four turners (Figure 18.2). Entry is made at the quadrant where both ropes are turning front

Figure 18.2 Egg Beater

doors. The number of ropes being turned can be increased to three or four. This activity is easier than jumping Double Dutch since the jumping action is similar to single-rope jumping. It is an excellent activity for building confidence in jumping more than one long rope.

Formation Jumping

For formation jumping, four to six long ropes with turners can be placed in various patterns, with tasks specified for each rope. Ropes can be turned in the same direction, or the turning directions can be mixed. Several formations are illustrated in Figure 18.3.

INDIVIDUAL ROPE JUMPING

Individual rope jumping should place emphasis on establishing basic turning skills and letting children create personal routines. Individual rope jumping is particularly valuable as part of the conditioning process for certain sports. It lends itself to prescribed doses based on number of turns, length of

participation, speed of the turning rope, and various steps. Since rope jumping is of a rhythmic nature, the addition of music is a natural progression. Music adds much to the activity and enables the jumper to create and organize routines to be performed to the musical pieces. The most effective approach is probably a combination of experiences with and without music.

There are a number of types of jump ropes on the market, all of which are satisfactory, depending on the likes and dislikes of the instructor. The most popular appear to be the solid plastic speed (often called licorice) ropes and the beaded or segmented ropes. The speed rope is excellent for rapid turning and doing tricks. It does not maintain momentum as well as the segmented ropes, which can be important for beginners. Sash cord is economical but doesn't wear well on blacktop or cement. In addition, without handles, it is a second-rate jump rope.

Instructional Procedures

1. The length of the rope is dependent on the height of the jumper. It should be long enough so that the ends reach to the armpits (Figure

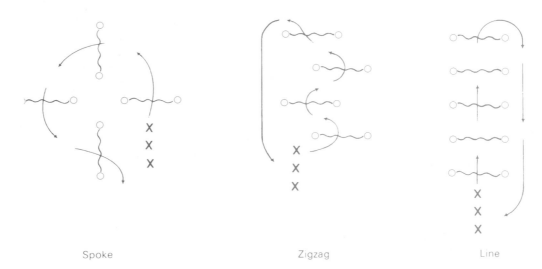

Spoke   Zigzag   Line

Figure 18.3 Formations for jumping rope

18.4) or slightly higher when the child stands on its center. Preschool children generally use 6-foot ropes, and the primary-level group needs mostly 7-foot ropes, with a few 6- and 8-foot lengths. Grades three through six need a mixture of 7-, 8-, and 9-foot ropes. A 9- or 10-foot rope serves well for tall students and most instructors. Ropes or handles can be color-coded for length.

Two types of ropes are available; the beaded (plastic segment) and the plastic (licorice) rope. The beaded ropes are heavier and seem easier to turn for beginning jumpers. The drawback to the beaded ropes is that they hurt when they hit another student. Also, if the segments are made round, the rope will roll easily on the floor and cause children to fall when they step on it. The plastic licorice ropes are lighter and give less wind resistance. For experienced jumpers more speed and control can be gained with this type of rope. An ideal situation would be to have a set of each type.

2. Posture is an important consideration in rope jumping. The body should be in good alignment, with the head up and the eyes looking straight ahead. The jump is made with the body in an erect position. A slight straightening of the knees provides the lift for the jump, which should be of minimal height (about 1 inch). The wrists supply the force to turn the rope, with the elbows kept close to the body and extended at a 90-degree angle. A pumping action and lifting of the arms is unnecessary. The landing should be made on the balls of the feet, with the knees bent slightly to

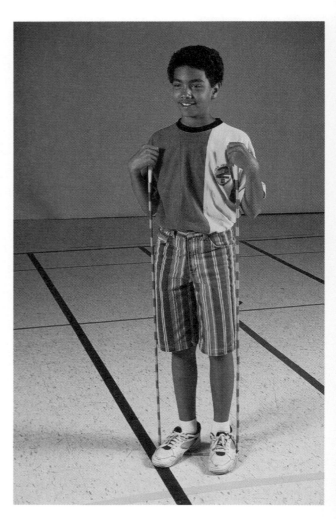

Figure 18.4 Correct jump rope length

cushion the shock. Usually, the feet, ankles, and legs are kept together, except when a specific step calls for a different position.

3. The rope should be held by the index finger and thumb on each side with the hands making a small circle. The elbows should be held near the sides to avoid making large arm circles with the rope.

4. Introducing and teaching youngsters individual rope jumping skills can be accomplished with the following steps:

   a. Students should first jump without the rope until they learn the correct rhythm and footwork. For slow time, this would be a jump and then a rebound step. Children can pretend that they are turning the rope. Remember that rope jumping involves learning two separate skills: jumping a rope and turning a rope. Youngsters who have a problem need to practice the parts separately before they are put together as a whole.

   b. Turn the rope over the head of the jumper and catch it with the toes.

   c. The jumper holds the rope stationary in front of the body. Jump forward and backward over the rope. To increase the challenge, swing the rope slightly. Gradually increase the swing until a full turn of the rope is made.

   d. Hold the rope to one side with both hands, swing the rope forward and jump each time the rope hits the floor. If swinging the rope is a problem, practice without jumping first.

5. Music can be added when jumpers have learned the first stages of jumping. Music provides a challenge for continued jumping.

6. In the primary-level group, some children cannot jump, but by the third grade, all children who have had some experience should be able to jump. Children who cannot jump may be helped by the pendulum swing of the long rope, or another student jumping with the child inside an individual rope. Cues such as "Jump" or "Ready-jump" should be used.

7. Most steps can be done with either rhythm: slow time or fast time. In slow-time rhythm, the performer jumps over the rope, rebounds, and then executes the second step (or repeats the original step) on the second jump. The rebound is simply a hop in place as the rope passes over the head. Better jumpers bend the knees only slightly, without actually leaving the floor on rebound. The object of the rebound is to carry the rhythm between steps. The rope is rotating slowly, passing under the feet on every other beat, and the feet also move slowly, since there is rebound between each jump.

In fast-time rhythm, the rope rotates in time with the music, one turn per beat (120 to 180 turns per minute, depending on the tune's tempo), and the performer executes a step only when the rope is passing under the feet.

8. To collect ropes at the completion of a rope-jumping activity, have two or three children act as monitors. They put both arms out to the front or to the side at shoulder level. The other children then drape the ropes over their arms (Figure 18.5). The monitors return the ropes to the correct storage area.

9. Instructional cues to use for improving jumping technique are as follows:

   a. Keep the arms at the side of the body while turning. (Many children lift the arms to shoulder level trying to move the rope overhead. This makes it impossible for the youngster to jump over the elevated rope.)

   b. Turn the rope by making small circles with the wrists.

   c. Jump on the balls of the feet.

   d. Bend the knees slightly to absorb the force of the jump.

   e. Make a small jump over the rope.

Basic Steps

The basic steps presented here can be done in slow or fast time. After youngsters have mastered the first six steps in slow time, fast time can be intro-

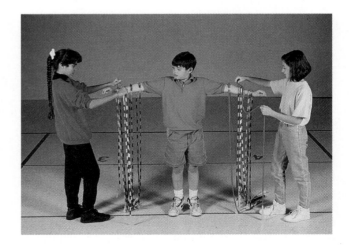

Figure 18.5 Collecting the ropes

duced. The Alternate-Foot Basic Step and Spread Legs Forward and Backward are two steps that work well for introducing fast-time jumping.

Side Swing

Swing the rope, held with both hands to one side of the body. Switch and swing the rope on the other side of the body.

Double Side Swing and Jump

Swing the rope once on each side of the body. Follow the second swing with a jump over the rope. The sequence should be swing, swing, jump.

Two-Foot Basic Step

In the Two-Foot Basic Step, jump over the rope with feet together as it passes under the feet, then take a preparatory rebound while the rope is over the head.

Alternate-Foot Basic Step

In the Alternate-Foot Basic Step, as the rope passes under the feet, the weight is shifted alternately from one foot to the other, raising the unweighted foot in a running position.

Bird Jumps

Jump with the toes pointed in (pigeon walk) and with the toes pointed out (duck walk). Alternate toes in and toes out.

Swing-Step Forward

The Swing-Step Forward is the same as the Alternate-Foot Basic Step, except that the free leg swings forward. The knee is kept loose and the foot swings naturally.

Swing-Step Sideward

The Swing-Step Sideward is the same as the Swing-Step Forward, except that the free leg is swung to the side. The knee should be kept stiff. The sideward swing is about 12 inches.

Rocker Step

In executing the Rocker Step, one leg is always forward in a walking-stride position. As the rope passes under the feet, the weight is shifted from the back foot to the forward foot. The rebound is taken on the forward foot while the rope is above the head. On the next turn of the rope, the weight is shifted from the forward foot to the back foot, repeating the rebound on the back foot.

Spread Legs Forward and Backward

For Spread Legs Forward and Backward, start in a stride position (as in the Rocker) with weight equally distributed on both feet. As the rope passes under the feet, jump into the air and reverse the position of the feet.

Straddle Jump

Alternate a regular jump with a straddle jump. The straddle jump is performed with the feet spread to shoulder width.

Cross Legs Sideward

In Cross Legs Sideward, as the rope passes under the feet, spread the legs in a straddle position (sideward) to take the rebound. As the rope passes under the feet on the next turn, jump into the air and cross the feet with the right foot forward. Then repeat with the left foot forward and continue this alternation.

Toe-Touch Forward

To do the Toe-Touch Forward, swing the right foot forward as the rope passes under the feet and touch the right toes on the next count. Then alternate, landing on the right foot and touching the left toes forward.

Toe-Touch Backward

The Toe-Touch Backward is similar to the Swing-Step Sideward, except that the toes of the free foot touch to the back at the end of the swing.

Shuffle Step

The Shuffle Step involves pushing off with the right foot and sidestepping to the left as the rope passes under the feet. Land with the weight on the left foot and touch the right toes beside the left heel. Repeat the step in the opposite direction.

Skier

The Skier is a double-foot jump similar to a technique used by skiers. A chalked or painted line is needed. The jumper stands on both feet to one side of the line. Jumping is done sideways back and forth over the line. Children should try it in a forward and backward direction also.

Heel-Toe

In the Heel-Toe, as the rope passes under the feet, jump with the weight landing on the right foot while touching the left heel forward. On the next turn of the rope, jump, land on the same foot, and touch the left toes beside the right heel. This pattern is repeated with the opposite foot bearing the weight.

Leg Fling

On the first jump, bring the right leg up so that it is parallel to the floor with the knee bent. On the second jump, kick the same leg out and up as high as possible. Try with the other leg.

Heel Click

Do two or three Swing-Steps Sideward, in slow time, in preparation for the Heel Click. When the right foot swings sideward, instead of a hop or rebound when the rope is above the head, raise the left foot to click the heel of the right foot. Repeat on the left side.

Step-Tap

In the Step-Tap, as the rope passes under the feet, push off with the right foot and land on the left. While the rope is turning above the head, brush the sole of the right foot forward and then backward. As the rope passes under the feet for the second turn, push off with the left foot, land on the right, and repeat.

Skipping

Do a step-hop (skip) over the rope. Start slowly and gradually increase the speed of the rope.

Schottische Step

The schottische step can be done to double-time rhythm, or it can be done with a varied rhythm. The pattern is step, step, step, hop (repeat), followed by four step-hops. In varied rhythm, three quick turns in fast time are made for the first three steps and then double-time rhythm prevails. The step should be practiced first in place and then in general space. Schottische music should be introduced.

Bleking Step

The bleking step has the pattern slow-slow, fast-fast-fast. The rope should turn to conform to this pattern. The step begins with a hop on the left foot with the right heel forward, followed by a hop on the right with the left heel forward. This action is repeated with three quick changes: right, left, right. The whole pattern is then repeated, beginning with a hop on the right foot with the left heel extended. If done to the music for the bleking dance (p. 376), four bleking steps of slow-slow, fast-fast-fast are done. The second part of the music (the chorus) allows the children to organize a routine of their own. They must listen for changes in the music.

Crossing Arms

Once the basic steps are mastered, crossing the arms while turning the rope provides an interesting variation. Crossing the arms during forward turning is easier than crossing behind the back during backward turning. During crossing, the hands exchange places. This means that for forward crossing, the elbows are close to each other. This is not possible during backward crossing. Crossing and uncrossing can be done at predetermined points after a stipulated number of turns. Crossing can be accomplished during any of the routines.

Double Turning

The double turn of the rope is also interesting. The jumper does a few basic steps in preparation for the double turn. As the rope approaches the feet, the child gives an extremely hard flip of the rope from the wrists, jumps from 6 to 8 inches in height, and allows the rope to pass under the feet twice before landing. The jumper must bend forward at the waist somewhat, which increases the speed of the turn. A substantial challenge for advanced rope jumpers is to see how many consecutive double-turn jumps they can do.

Shifting from Forward to Backward Jumping

To switch from forward to backward jumping without stopping the rope, any of the following techniques can be used.

1. As the rope starts downward in forward jumping, rather than allowing it to pass under the feet, the performer swings both arms to the left (or right) and makes a half turn of the body in that direction (i.e., facing the rope). On the next downward swing, the jumper spreads the arms and starts turning in the opposite direc-

tion. This method also works for shifting from backward to forward jumping.

2. When the rope is directly above the head, the performer extends both arms, causing the rope to hesitate momentarily, at the same time making a half-turn in either direction and continuing to skip with the rope turning in the opposite direction.

3. From a crossed-arm position, as the rope is going above the performer's head, the jumper may uncross the arms and turn simultaneously. This starts the rope turning and the performer jumping in the opposite direction.

Sideways Skipping

In sideways skipping, the rope is turned laterally with one hand held high and the other extended downward. The rope is swung around the body sideways. To accomplish this, the jumper starts with the right hand held high overhead and the left hand extended down the center of the body. Swing the rope to the left, at the same time raising the left leg sideways. Usually the speed is slow time, with the rebound taken on each leg in turn. Later, better jumpers may progress to fast-time speed. The rope passes under the left leg, and the jumper then is straddling the rope as it moves around his body behind him. Take the weight on the left foot, raising the right foot sideways. A rebound step on the left as the rope moves to the front brings the jumper back to the original position.

Combination Possibilities

Numerous combinations of steps and rope tricks are possible in rope jumping. Some ideas are:

1. Changes in the speed of the turn—slow time and fast time—can be made. Children should be able to shift from one speed to another, particularly when the music changes.

2. Developing expertise in various foot patterns and steps is important. Children should practice changing from one foot pattern to another.

3. The crossed-hands position should be tried both forward and backward. Many of the basic steps can be combined with crossed-hands position to add challenge.

4. Moving from a forward to a backward turn and returning should be practiced. Perform the turn while doing a number of different basic steps.

5. Double turns combined with basic steps look impressive and are challenging. A few children may be able to do a triple turn.

6. Children should try to move forward, backward, and sideward, employing a variety of the basic steps.

7. Backward jumping is exciting as it is a different skill than forward jumping. Most basic steps can be done backward or modified for the backward turn.

8. Speedy turns (Hot Peppers) can be practiced. Have children see how fast they can turn the rope for 15 or 30 seconds.

Individual Rope Jumping with Partners

Many interesting combinations are possible when one child turns the individual rope and one or more children jump it. For those routines in which the directions call for a child to run into a jumping pattern, it may be more effective to begin with the child already in position, before proceeding to the run-in stage.

1. The first child turns the rope and the other stands in front, ready to enter.

    a. Run in and face partner, and both jump (Figure 18.6).

Figure 18.6 Rope jumping with a partner

b. Run in and turn back to partner, and both jump.

c. Decide which steps are to be done; then run in and match steps.

d. Repeat with the rope turning backward.

e. Run in with a ball and bounce it during the jumping.

2. Partners stand side by side, clasp inside hands, and turn the rope with outside hands.

   a. Face the same direction and turn the rope.

   b. Face opposite directions, clasp left hands, and turn the rope.

   c. Face opposite directions, clasp right hands, and turn the rope.

   d. Repeat routines with inside knees raised.

   e. Repeat routines with elbows locked. Try other arm positions.

3. The first child turns the rope while the second is to the rear ready to run in. The second child runs in and grasps the first child's waist or shoulders, and they jump together (engine and caboose).

4. The children stand back to back, holding a single rope in the right hand.

   a. Turn in one direction—forward for one and backward for the other.

   b. Reverse direction.

   c. Change to left hands, and repeat.

5. Three children jump. One turns the rope forward; one runs in, in front; and one runs in behind. All three jump. Try with the rope turning backward.

6. Two jumpers, each with a rope, face each other and turn both ropes together, forward for one and backward for the other, jumping over both ropes at once. Turn the ropes alternately, jumping each rope in turn.

7. The partner turning jumps in a usual individual rope pattern. The other is positioned to the side. The turning partner hands over one end of the rope, and the other maintains the turning rhythm and then hands the rope back.

   a. Try from the other side.

   b. Turn the rope backward.

8. Using a single rope held in the right hand, partners face each other and turn the rope in slow time. With the rope overhead, one partner makes a turn to the left (turning in) and jumps inside the rope, exiting by turning either way. See if both can turn inside.

Movement Sequences to Music

The opportunities for creative movement sequences performed to music are unlimited. Music must have a definite beat and a bouncy quality. Pieces with a two-part format, usually labeled the verse and the chorus, are excellent. The change from the verse to the chorus signals changes in rope-jumping pattern. Many of the records listed in Chapter 16 can be used quite successfully for rope jumping to music. Schottisches, marches, and polkas provide good background. Popular rock music can be used to motivate youngsters if it has a strong and even rhythm. In addition, special records for rope jumping are available from commercial sources. Suggested records include:

> The Muffin Man (pp. 369–370)
> Looby Loo (p. 368–369)
> Bleking (p. 376)
> Pop Goes the Weasel (pp. 379–380)
> Schottische (p. 399)
> Polka (p. 372)

Devising Sequences to Music

Devising jumping sequences is a good opportunity for children to create their own routines to selected records. Simple changes from slow time to fast time can introduce this activity. Later, different steps can be incorporated, crossing and uncrossing arms can be included, and then the turning direction can be varied. Partner rope-jumping stunts can also be adapted to music. Suggestions for incorporating different steps in the sequences follow.

1. "Pop Goes the Weasel" has a definite verse and chorus change. The children can switch from slow-time jumping to fast-time jumping on the chorus.

2. Bleking offers an interesting change in rope speed. The rhythm is slow-slow, fast-fast-fast (four times). The rope should be turned in keeping with the beat. Later, the bleking step can be added.

3. Using schottische music, children can do the schottische step in place twice and four moving step-hops in different directions during the chorus.

4. To "Little Brown Jug," a four-part routine can be done to four rounds of the music.

   First verse: Two-Foot Basic Step (slow time)
   Chorus: Two-Foot Basic Step (fast time)
   Second verse: Alternate-Foot Basic Step (slow time)

Chorus: Alternate-Foot Basic Step (fast time)

Third verse: Swing-Step Forward (slow time)

Chorus: Swing-Step Forward (fast time)

Fourth verse: Swing-Step Sideward (slow time)

Chorus: Swing-Step Sideward (fast time)

Assessment of Individual Rope Jumping

Individual rope-jumping stunts, because of their specificity and individuality, can be adapted easily to learning packages and contract teaching. Skill assessment can be based on the accomplishment of a stated maneuver in so many turns of the rope.

The assessment can be organized progressively, or can be grouped by beginning, intermediate, and advanced tests. An example of a beginning test follows. All test items are done first in slow time and then in fast time.

1. *Two-Foot Basic Step:* 10 turns
2. *Alternate-Foot Basic Step:* 10 turns
3. *Turning rope backward:* 10 turns
4. *Alternate crossing arms:* 10 turns
5. *Running forward:* 20 turns

Intermediate and advanced tests can be organized similarly.

REFERENCES AND SUGGESTED READINGS

American Alliance for Health, Physical Education, Recreation, and Dance. (1992). *Jump rope for heart.* Reston VA: AAHPERD. (Jump Rope for Heart materials can be obtained by contacting your local affiliate of the American Heart Association or by calling AAHPERD Special Events Office at 703-476-3489.)

American Heart Association. (1984a). *Jump for the health of it: Basic skills.* Dallas, TX: American Heart Association.

American Heart Association. (1984b). *Jump for the health of it: Intermediate single and double dutch skills.* Dallas, TX: American Heart Association.

Melson, B., & Worrell, V. (1986). *Rope skipping for fun and fitness.* Wichita, KS: Woodlawn.

Poppen, J. D. (1989). *Action packet on jumping rope.* Puyallup, WA: Action Productions.

Sutherland, M., & Carnes, C. (1987). *Awesome jump rope activities book.* Carmichael, CA: Education Co.

Apparatus Activities: Developing Body Management Skills

PURPOSE OF ACTIVITIES IN THIS CHAPTER
Apparatus activities are designed to develop body management skills. Performing on apparatus requires strength, agility, balance, flexibility, and body control. Body management skills are specialized because they are performed on apparatus.

Children have an innate desire for the physical expression that apparatus allows them. Part of the fundamental makeup of children is the desire to run, jump, throw, swing, and climb. Apparatus plays a large role in the child's overall physical development. Exercising on overhead and climbing apparatus benefits the arm and shoulder girdle. Children learn to manage their bodies free of ground support. The flexibility and stretching effects from apparatus activities have value in the maintenance of posture.

Equipment placed on the floor provides important extensions of educational movements. Individual responses should be stressed. Further variety in apparatus activities can be achieved by the addition of hand apparatus such as beanbags, balls, wands, hoops, blocks, and other items. Individual or partner manipulative activities performed on apparatus add another dimension to movement possibilities. Combinations of pieces of apparatus offer more challenges to children than single pieces. For example, jumping boxes used with balance beams and individual mats allow a wider variety of activity than boxes used alone.

Many apparatus activities involve a three-part sequence: (a) mounting, or getting on, the apparatus, (b) doing a skill or meeting a challenge, and (c) dismounting. Some attention should be given to the dismount. It should be a controlled movement, with the landing performed in bent-knee position and the weight balanced over the balls of the feet. Children should land under control and hold the position momentarily. Many challenges, such as shapes through the air, turns, and stunts following the landing, can be structured into dismounts.

Teachers should establish traffic rules stipulating when children start their turn. Return routes to the starting point can be established, too. At some point in all apparatus activity sequences, teachers should provide an opportunity for creativity by telling children to develop something different than was presented in the sequences.

RETURN ACTIVITIES

The use of return activities increases the movement potential of apparatus. Return activity has the children perform some kind of movement task on the way back to their place in line. This technique avoids having children stand in line after they have finished their task on the apparatus. To increase the challenge of the return activity, a marker can be placed some distance in front of the apparatus. Before their apparatus routine, students must perform the return activity on the way to the marker, after the apparatus routine, on their way from the marker, and to the end of the line.

The return activity is usually a change from the instructional emphasis. The teacher's concentration is centered on the lesson activities, so the return movements should demand little supervision. Choice and exploration characterize return activities. Return activity in combination with bench activity might have children performing on the benches, accomplishing dismounts, and doing a Forward Roll on the way back to place. Three children are active: one is performing, another is dismounting, and the third is rolling. Another popular return activity makes use of a magic number. Instructions for the return are given in this way. "Today, our magic number for return activity is five." Children can solve the magic number prob-

lem by doing, for example, three jumps and two hops or four Push-Ups and one Frog Jump.

SAFE USE OF APPARATUS

Children should be instructed in the proper setup, storage, and safe use of apparatus and mats. Guidelines can be established with the following points in mind. Children should handle apparatus only with a teacher's guidance.

1. Placement of tumbling mats for shock absorption is critical. Tumbling mats should be positioned for safety in dismounting and where falls are possible. Tumbling mats should be placed directly under all climbing ropes.

2. Apparatus should be carried, not dragged, across the floor. For particular pieces that need cooperation among the children, designate the number of children and the means of carrying. Children should be taught how to lift and carry the apparatus properly. Proper setup and storage of apparatus should be discussed and practiced by students.

3. Activity on apparatus should occur only when it is directed by teachers. Youngsters should be instructed to avoid all apparatus in the area that has been prearranged for later use.

4. Since improper use of apparatus can result in injury, instruction should precede apparatus activity. Signs emphasizing proper use of apparatus can be placed on cones near individual pieces of equipment.

ACTIVITIES WITH CLIMBING ROPES

Climbing ropes offer high-level developmental possibilities for the upper trunk and arms as well as training in coordination of different body parts (Figure 19.1). Adequate grip and arm strength are prerequisites for climbing. Becoming accustomed to the rope and gaining confidence are important early goals.

Instructional Procedures

1. Mats should be placed under all ropes.
2. The hand-over-hand method should be used for climbing and the hand-under-hand method for descending.
3. Caution the children not to slide; sliding can cause rope burns on the hands and legs.

Figure 19.1 Rope climbing on an eight-rope set

Preliminary Activities

Progression is important in rope climbing, and the fundamental skill progressions should be followed.

Supported Pull-Ups

In supported Pull-Up activities, a part of the body remains in contact with the floor. The Pull-Up is hand-over-hand and the return is hand-under-hand.

1. Kneel directly under the rope. Pull up to the tiptoes and return to kneeling position.
2. Start in a sitting position under the rope. Pull up; the legs are supported on the heels. Return to sitting position.
3. Start in a standing position. Grasp the rope, rock back on the heels, and lower the body to the floor. Keep a straight body. Return to standing position.

Hangs

In a hang, the body is pulled up in one motion and held up for a length of time (5, 10, or 20 seconds). Progression is important.

1. From a seated position, reach up as high as possible and pull the body from the floor, except for the heels. Hold.
2. Same as the previous stunt, but pull the body completely free of the floor. Hold.
3. From a standing position, jump up, grasp the rope, and hang. This should be a Bent-Arm Hang with the hands about even with the mouth. Hold.
4. Repeat the previous stunt, but add leg movements—one or both knees up, bicycling movement, Half Lever (one or both legs up, parallel to the floor), Full Lever (feet up to the face).

Pull-Ups

In the Pull-Up, the body is raised and lowered repeatedly. The initial challenge should be to accomplish one Pull-Up in the defined position. The number of repetitions should be increased with care. All of the activities described for hangs are adaptable to Pull-Ups. The chin should touch the hands on each Pull-Up.

Inverted Hang

For the Inverted Hang, both hands reach up high. The rope is kept to one side. The performer jumps to a bent-arm position, and at the same time brings

4. A climber who becomes tired should stop and rest. Proper rest stops should be taught as part of the climbing procedure.
5. Children also should be taught to leave enough margin for a safe descent. No children should go higher than their strength allows.
6. Spotters should be used initially for activities in which the body is inverted.
7. Rosin in powdered form and magnesium chalk aid in gripping. It is particularly important that they be used when the rope becomes slippery.
8. Children swinging on the ropes should be instructed to make sure that other children are out of the way.
9. Marks to limit the climb can be put on the rope with adhesive tape. A height of 8 to 10 feet above the floor is reasonable until a child demonstrates proficiency.
10. If the ceiling is higher than 15 or 16 feet, a wooden stop (circle) positioned on the rope to limit climbing beyond that height is suggested.

the knees up to the nose to invert the body, which is now in a curled position. In a continuation of the motion, the feet are brought up higher than the hands, and the legs are locked around the rope. The body should now be straight and upside down. In the learning phase, teachers should spot.

Swinging and Jumping

For swinging and jumping, a bench, box, or stool can serve as a takeoff point. To take off, the child reaches high and jumps to a bent-arm position. Landing should be with bent knees.

1. Swing and jump. Add half turns and full turns.
2. Swing and return to the perch. Add single- and double-knee bends.
3. Jump for distance, over a high-jump bar or through a hoop.
4. Swing and pick up a bowling pin and return to the perch.
5. Carry objects (e.g., beanbags, balls, deck tennis rings). A partner, standing to the side away from the takeoff bench, can put articles to be carried back on the takeoff perch by placing each article between the knees or feet.
6. Not using a takeoff device, run toward a swinging rope, grasp it, and gain momentum for swinging.

Climbing the Rope

Scissors Grip

For the Scissors Grip, approach the rope and reach as high as possible, standing with the right leg forward of the left. Raise the back leg, bend at the knee, and place the rope inside the knee and outside the foot. Cross the forward leg over the back leg, and straighten the legs with the toes pointed down (Figure 19.2). This should give a secure hold. The teacher can check the position.

To climb using the Scissors Grip, raise the knees up close to the chest, the rope sliding between them, while supporting the body with the hand grip. Lock the rope between the legs and climb up, using the hand-over-hand method and stretching as high as the hands can reach. Bring the knees up to the chest and repeat the process until you have climbed halfway. Later, strive for a higher climb.

Leg-Around Rest

To do the Leg-Around Rest, wrap the left leg completely around the rope, keeping the rope between

Figure 19.2 Scissors Grip

the thighs. The bottom of the rope then crosses over the instep of the left foot from the outside. The right foot stands on the rope as it crosses over the instep, providing pressure to prevent slippage. To provide additional pressure, release the hands and wrap the arms around the rope, leaning away from the rope at the same time.

To climb using the Leg-Around Rest, proceed as in climbing with the Scissors Grip, but loosen the grip each time and re-form higher up on the rope.

Descending the Rope

There are four methods to descend the rope. The only differences are in the use of the leg locks, as the hand-under-hand is used for all descents.

Scissors Grip

From an extended scissors grip position, lock the legs and lower the body with the hands until the knees are against the chest. Hold with the hands, and lower the legs to a new position.

Leg-Around Rest

From the leg-around rest position, lower the body until the knees are against the chest. Lift the top foot, and let the feet slide to a lower position (Figure 19.3). Secure with the top foot and repeat.

Instep Squeeze

Squeeze the rope between the insteps by keeping the heels together. Lower the body while the rope slides against the instep.

Stirrup Descent

Have the rope on the outside of the right foot and carry it over the instep of the left. Pressure from the left foot holds the position. To get into position, let the rope trail along the right leg, reach under, and hook it with the left instep. When the pressure from the left leg is reduced, the rope slides smoothly while the descent is made with the hands.

Figure 19.3 Leg-Around Rest

Other Climbing Activities

Climbing for Time

To climb for time, a stopwatch and a definite mark on the rope are needed. The height of the mark depends on the children's skill and capacity. Each child should have three trials (not in succession, however), with the best time recorded. Children should start from a standing position with hands reaching as high as desired. The descent should not be included in the timing, because too much emphasis on speed in descent may incite the children to drop or may promote rope burns.

Climbing Without Using the Feet

The strenuous activity of climbing without using the feet should be attempted only by the more skilled. During early sessions, the mark should not be set too high. Climbers start from a sitting position. The activity can be timed.

Organizing a Tarzan Club

The teacher can put a marker at the top limit of the rope. Each child who climbs to and touches the marker becomes a member of the Tarzan Club. A Super-Tarzan Club can be formed for those who can climb to the marker without using their feet. The climber must start from a sitting position on the floor.

Stunts Using Two Ropes

Two ropes hanging close together are needed for the following activities.

Straight-Arm Hang

To do the Straight-Arm Hang, jump up, grasp one rope with each hand, and hang with the arms straight.

Bent-Arm Hang

Perform as for the Straight-Arm Hang, but bend the arms at the elbows.

Arm Hangs with Different Leg Positions

1. Do single- and double-knee lifts.
2. Do a Half Lever. Bring the legs up parallel to the floor and point the toes.
3. Do a Full Lever. Bring the feet up to the face and keep the knees straight.
4. Do a Bicycle. Pedal as on a bicycle.

Pull-Ups

The Pull-Up is the same as on a single rope, except that each hand grasps a rope.

Inverted Hangs

1. Hang with the feet wrapped around the ropes.
2. Hang with the feet against the inside of the ropes.
3. Hang with the toes pointed and the feet not touching the ropes (Figure 19.4).

Skin the Cat

From a bent-arm position, kick the feet overhead and continue the roll until the feet touch the mat. Return to the starting position. A more difficult stunt is to start from a higher position so that the feet do not touch the mat. Reverse to original position.

Climbing

1. Climb up one rope, transfer to another, and descend.
2. Climb halfway up one rope, cross over to another rope, and continue to climb to the top.

Figure 19.4 Spotting an inverted hang on two ropes
(Holding the performer's hands ensures confidence and safety.)

3. Climb both ropes together without using the legs. This is difficult and requires the climber to slide one hand at a time up the ropes without completely releasing the grip.
4. Climb as on a single rope, with hands on one rope and feet on the other rope.

Activity Sequences

Rope-climbing activities are conducive to forming sequences through which the child can progress. The following sequence represents the kind of progressive challenges that can be met.

1. Jump and hang (10 seconds).
2. Pull up and hold (10 seconds).
3. Scissors climb to blue mark (10 feet).
4. Scissors climb to top (15 feet).
5. Demonstrate Leg-Around Rest (10 feet).
6. Do an Inverted Hang, with body straight (5 seconds).

Teachers can structure three achievement levels from the activities included in this chapter. Each level could be given a characteristic name and organized as a task card or a contract project.

ACTIVITIES WITH HORIZONTAL LADDERS

Horizontal ladders are manufactured in a variety of models. The most usable ladder is one that can be stored against the wall out of the way. If the ladder can be inclined, the movement possibilities are extended. Horizontal ladders provide a good lead-up activity for rope climbing, because their rigidity makes them easier to climb. Grip strength and arm-shoulder girdle development are enhanced by the suspension of body weight. This development can help improve posture.

Instructional Procedures

1. The opposed-thumb grip, in which the thumb goes around the bar, is important. In most activities, the back of the hands should face the child. (This is the upper grip.) The grip should be varied occasionally, making use of the lower grip (palms toward the face) and the mixed grip (one hand facing one way and one the other).
2. Whenever the child is doing an Inverted Hang, spotters should be present.

3. Speed is not a goal of climbing activity. In fact, the longer the child hangs from the ladder, the more beneficial the activity is. There is value in simply hanging.

4. In activities involving movement across the ladder, all children should travel in the same direction.

5. Mats must be placed under the apparatus when it is in use.

6. Children should be instructed in the dismount. They should land in a bent-leg position, on the balls of the feet.

Activities with Horizontal Ladders

Hangs

Hangs should be performed with the opposed-thumb grip and usually with straight arms. Encourage children to hang in a bent-arm position, however, to involve more muscles in the upper arm. The following variations of the Hang are suggested.

1. Keep the legs straight and point the toes toward the ground.

2. Lift the knees as high as possible toward the chest.

3. Lift the knees and pedal a bicycle.

4. Bring the legs up parallel to the ground, with the knees straight and the toes pointed.

5. Touch the toes of one or both feet to a rung or to the side of the ladder.

6. Bring the feet up and over one rung and hook the toes under a second rung. Release the hand grip and hang in an inverted position.

7. Stand on a box if necessary to get into position for a Flexed-Arm Hang. Hang as long as possible with the chin even with the hands.

8. Swing the body back and forth.

9. Swing back and forth and jump as far as possible. Vary with turns.

10. Hang from the ladder, first with one hand and then with the other.

Traveling Activities

Throughout the suggested traveling activities, have the children use different body shapes.

1. Travel the length of the ladder, using the rungs. Start by traveling one rung at a time, and then skip one or more rungs to add challenge.

2. Travel the length of the ladder, using both side rails. Now use one rail only to travel the ladder.

3. Hang with both hands on the side rails. Progress the length of the ladder by jumping both hands forward at once.

4. Hang with both hands on the same rung. Progress by jumping both hands forward simultaneously.

5. Travel underneath the ladder in monkey fashion, with both hands and feet on the rungs. Try with the feet on the side rails.

6. Travel the length of the ladder carrying a beanbag, a ball, or any similar object.

7. Travel the length of the ladder sideways and backward.

8. Travel the length of the ladder, doing a half turn each time a move is made to a new rung.

9. Get a partner. The children start at opposite ends of the ladder, and they pass each other along the way.

ACTIVITIES ON THE EXERCISE BAR (LOW HORIZONTAL BAR)

Horizontal bars should be installed on the playground in a series of at least three at different heights. Indoor bars can be freestanding and have adjustable heights. Care must be taken that they are secured properly. The primary program should be limited to hangs, travels, and simple stunts. To perform many of the more complicated stunts on the bar, sufficient arm strength is necessary to pull the body up and over the bar. Some of the youngsters in the third grade will begin to have this capacity, but the emphasis in the primary grades should be on the more limited program. In the intermediate program, attention should turn to gymnastic stunts. The advanced skills are, however, difficult and the teacher should not be discouraged by the children's apparent lack of progress.

Instructional Procedures

1. Only one child should be on a bar at one time.

2. The bar should not be used when it is wet.

3. The basic grip is the opposed-thumb grip, facing away.

Activity Sequences

Hangs

To hang from the bar, point the feet, one or both knees up, in a Half or Full Lever (p. 461). Bring the toes up to touch the bar inside the hands. Outside the hands. Use different body shapes.

Swings

Swing back and forth, release the grip, and propel the body forward. Land in a standing position.

Moving along the Bar

Begin at one side and move hand against hand to the other end of the bar. Move with crossed hands. Travel with different body shapes.

Sloth Travel

Face the end of the bar, standing underneath. Grasp the bar with both hands and hook the legs over the bar at the knees like a sloth. In this position, move along the bar to the other end. Return by reversing the movement.

Arm and Leg Hang

Grasp the bar with an upper grip. Bring one of the legs up between the arms and hook the knee over the bar.

Double-Leg Hang

Perform as in the preceding stunt, but bring both legs between the hands and hook the knees over the bar. Release the hands and hang in the inverted position. If the hands touch or are near the ground, a dismount can be made by releasing the legs and dropping to a crouched position on the ground.

Skin the Cat

Bring both knees up between the arms as in the previous stunt, but continue the direction of the knees until the body is turned over backward. Release the grip and drop to the ground.

Skin the Cat Return

Perform as in the preceding stunt, but do not release the hands. Bring the legs back through the hands to original position.

Front Support

Grasp the bar with an upper grip, and jump to a straight-arm support on the bar. Jump down.

Front Support Push-Off

Mount the bar in the same way as for a Front Support. In returning to the ground, push off

straight with the arms and jump as far back as possible.

Tummy Balance

Jump to the bar as in the preceding stunt. Position the body so that you can balance on the tummy with hands released.

Sitting Balance

Jump to the bar as for a Front Support. Work the legs across the bar so that a sitting balance can be maintained. If you lose your balance backward, grasp the bar quickly and bend the knees.

Tumble Over

Jump to a front-support position. Change the grip to a lower grip. Bend forward and roll over to a standing position under the bar.

Single-Knee Swing

Using the upper grip, swing one leg forward to hang by the knee. Using the free leg to gain momentum, swing back and forth.

Side Arc

Sit on the bar with one leg on each side, both hands gripping the bar in front of the body. Lock the legs and fall sideways. Try to make a complete circle back to position. Good momentum is needed.

Single-Leg Rise

Using the position of the Single-Knee Swing, on the backswing and upswing, rise to the top of the bar. The down leg must be kept straight. Swing forward (down) first, and on the backswing, push down hard with straight arms. A spotter can assist by pushing down on the straight leg with one hand and lifting on the back with the other.

Knee Circles

Sit on top of the bar, with one leg over and one under the bar. Lock the feet. With the hands in an upper grip, shift the weight backward so that the body describes a circle under the bar and returns to place. Try this with a forward circle, with hands in a lower grip. Note that considerable initial momentum must be developed for the circle to be completed.

ACTIVITIES ON THE BALANCE BEAM

Balance-beam activities contribute to control in both static and dynamic balance situations (Figure 19.5). The balance-beam side of a balance beam bench is ideal for such activities, with its 2-inch-wide and 12-foot-long beam. Balance-beam benches can be purchased from the Robert Widen Company, P.O. Box 2075, Prescott, AZ 86302 (800-862-0761). Balance beams come in many other sizes, however, and can be constructed from common lumber materials (see Chapter 33). Some teachers prefer a wider beam for kindergarten and first-grade children and, in particular, for special education children. Students should graduate to the narrower beam as soon as the activities on the wider beam no longer seem to challenge them.

Other ideas for balance equipment are also interesting. A pole with ends shaped to fit the supports can be substituted for the flat balance beam. The pole is more challenging. Another idea is constructing a beam that begins with a 2-inch width and narrows to a 1-inch width at the other end. Beams of varying widths (from 1 to 4 inches) can also be used. Children progress from the wider to the narrower beams. A variety of widths is preferable for children with disabilities.

Instructional Procedures

1. Children should move with controlled, deliberate movements. Speed is not a goal. The teacher should advise performers to recover their balance before taking another step or making another movement.

Figure 19.5 Walking on a balance beam bench

2. In keeping with the principle of control, children should step slowly on the beam, pause momentarily in good balance at the end of the activity, and dismount with a small, controlled jump from the end of the beam when the routine is completed.

3. Mats can be placed at the end of the bench to cushion the dismount and to allow for rolls and stunts after the dismount.

4. Visual fixation is important. Children should look straight ahead rather than down at the feet. Eye targets can be marked on or attached to walls to assist in visual fixation. This fixation allows balance controls other than vision to function more effectively. From time to time, movements can be done with the eyes closed, entirely eliminating visual control of balance.

5. Children should be told to step off the beam when they lose their balance, rather than teetering and falling off awkwardly. Allow the performer to step back on the beam and to continue the routine.

6. Success in a balance-beam activity can be based on two levels. The lower level allows the performer to step off the beam once during the routine. The higher level demands that the student remain on the beam throughout. For both levels, the children should pause in good balance at the end of the beam before dismounting.

7. Both laterality and directionality are important. Right and left feet should be given reasonably equal treatment. For example, if a performer does steps leading with the right foot, the next effort should be made leading with the left foot. Directions right and left should be given equal weight. A child naturally uses the dominant side and direction but must be encouraged to perform with both sides.

8. The child next in line should begin when the performer ahead is about three-quarters of the distance across the beam.

9. Return activities (see p. 460) are a consideration for enhancing the breadth of activity.

10. A child or the teacher can assist the performer. The assistant holds the hand palm up, ready to help the performer if and when help is needed.

Activity Sequences

Activities for the balance beam are presented as a progression of movement themes. The teacher can develop fully all of the activities and possibilities within a theme before proceeding to the next theme, or can take a few activities from each theme and cover more territory.

Activities on Parallel Beams

Activities on two parallel beams are presented first as lead-up practice for the single-beam tasks. The beams should be placed about 10 to 30 inches apart. The parallel-beam activities can be done alone or with a partner when more security is desired.

1. With a partner, join inside hands and walk forward, backward, and sideward. Walk sideward, using a grapevine step. Hold a beanbag in the free hand.
2. Without a partner, perform various animal walks, such as the Crab Walk, Bear Walk, Measuring Worm, and Elephant Walk.
3. With one foot on each beam, walk forward, backward, and sideward.
4. Step to the opposite beam with each step taken.
5. Progress the length of the beams with hands on one beam and feet on the other.
6. Progress to the middle of the beams and perform various turns and stunts, such as picking up a beanbag, moving through a hoop, and stepping over a wand.

Movements across the Full Length of a Single Beam

1. Perform various locomotor tasks, such as walking, follow steps, heel-and-toe steps, side steps, tiptoe steps, the grapevine step (step behind, step across), and so on.
2. Follow different directions—forward, backward, sideward.
3. Use different arm and hand positions—on the hips, on the head, behind the back, out to the sides, pointing to the ceiling, folded across the chest.
4. Move across the beam assuming different shapes.
5. Balance an object (beanbag or eraser) on various body parts—on the head, on the back of the hands, on the shoulders. Try balancing two or three objects at once.

Half-and-Half Movements

Half-and-half movements repeat the movements, arm positions, and balancing stunts described pre-

viously, except that the performer goes halfway across the beam using a selected movement and then changes to another type of movement on the second half of the beam.

Challenge Tasks or Stunts

For challenge tasks, the performer moves halfway across the beam with a selected movement, performs a particular challenge or stunt at the center, and finishes the movements on the second half of the beam. Examples of challenges or stunts that can be performed at the center of the beam are the following:

1. Balances: Forward Balance (p. 500), Backward Balance (p. 501), Stork Stand (p. 500), Seat Balance (p. 515).
2. Stunts: Leg Dip (p. 515), Finger Touch (p. 516).
3. Challenges: Make a full turn, pick up a beanbag at the center, pick up some paper at the center with the teeth, do a Push-Up.

More Difficult Movements across the Beam

1. Hop the length of the beam—forward, sideward, and backward.
2. Do the Cat Walk (p. 495), Rabbit Jump (p. 495), Lame Dog Walk (p. 496), Seal Crawl (p. 507), or Crab Walk (p. 496).
3. Do various locomotor movements with the eyes closed.
4. Walk to the center of the beam and do a Side-Leaning Rest. Try on the other side as well.
5. Walk to the center and do a complete body turn on one foot only.

Activities with Wands and Hoops

1. Carry a wand or hoop. Step over the wand or through the hoop in various fashions.
2. Step over or go under wands or hoops held by partner.
3. Twirl a hula-hoop on the arms or around the body while moving across the beam.
4. Balance a wand on various body parts while moving across the beam.
5. Balance a wand in one hand and twirl a hoop on the other hand and proceed across the beam.

Manipulative Activities with Self

1. Using one or two beanbags, toss to self in various fashions—over the head, around the body, under the legs.

2. Using a ball, toss to self. Circle the ball around the body, under the legs.

3. Bounce a ball on the floor. On the beam. Dribble on the floor.

4. Roll a ball along the beam.

Manipulative Activities with a Partner

With a partner standing beyond the far end of the beam, throw a beanbag or ball back and forth. Have partner toss for a volleyball return. Bat the ball (as in a volleyball serve) to partner.

Stunts with a Partner

1. Do a Wheelbarrow (p. 522) with the supporting performer keeping the feet on the floor.

2. Partners start on opposite ends of the beam and move toward each other with the same kind of movement, do a balance pose together in the center, and return to their respective end of the beam.

3. Partners start on opposite ends of the beam and attempt to pass each other without losing their balance and without touching the floor. Find different ways to pass.

ACTIVITIES ON BENCHES

The balance-beam bench is effective in developing strength and balance. Bench activities are challenging to children and offer a variety of movement possibilities.

Instructional Procedures

1. All activities on the benches should be broken down into three distinct parts: the approach to and mounting of the bench, the actual activity on the bench, and the dismount from the bench.

2. Mats should be placed at the ends of the benches to facilitate the dismount and various rolls and stunts executed after the dismount.

3. Benches can be positioned horizontally or inclined. They can also be combined with other equipment for variation and greater challenge.

4. Four to five children is the maximum number that should be assigned to one bench.

5. The child next in turn should begin when the performer ahead is about three-quarters of the way across the bench.

6. Return activities (p. 460) add to the activity potential.

7. Speed is not a goal in bench activities. Movements should be done deliberately and carefully, with attention given to body control and body management.

8. Attention also should be paid to laterality and directionality. For example, if a child hops on the right foot, the next effort should be made on the left foot. In jump turns, both right and left movements should be used.

Activity Sequences

Animal Walks

Perform various animal walks on the bench, such as the Seal Crawl (p. 507), Cat Walk (p. 495), Lame Dog Walk (p. 496), and Rabbit Jump (p. 495).

Locomotor Movements

Perform various locomotor movements along the length of the bench, such as stepping on and off the side of the bench, jumping on and off the side of the bench, hopping on and off the side of the bench, skipping on the bench, and galloping on the bench.

Pulls

Pull the body along the bench, using different combinations of body parts. Use the arms only, the legs only, the right leg and the left arm, or the left leg and the right arm. Pull along the bench, using the following positions.

1. prone position (headfirst and feetfirst) (Figure 19.6)

2. supine position (headfirst and feetfirst) (Figure 19.7)

3. side position (headfirst and feetfirst)

Various leg positions (such as legs up in a half-lever position, knees bent, and so on) should be used in performing pulls and pushes. Those body parts not being used to pull can be used to carry a piece of manipulative equipment, such as a beanbag, ball, or wand. Employ different body

Figure 19.6 Prone movements, headfirst

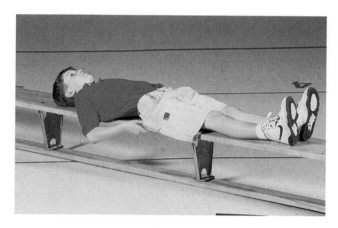

Figure 19.7 Supine movements, feetfirst

shapes. Try the Submarine (one foot in the air like a periscope).

Pushes

Push the body along the bench, using different parts of the body as discussed for pulls. Push the body, using the following positions.

1. prone position (headfirst and feetfirst)
2. supine position (headfirst and feetfirst)
3. side position (headfirst and feetfirst)

Movements along the Side of the Bench

Proceed alongside the bench in the following positions with the hands on the bench and the feet on the floor as far from the bench as possible.

1. prone position
2. supine position
3. turn-over (Proceed along the bench, changing from prone to supine position.)

Repeat these positions with the feet on the bench and the hands on the floor as far from the bench as possible.

Scooter Movements

Sit on the bench and proceed along it without using the hands in the following ways.

1. Do a Scooter. Proceed with the feet leading the body. Try to pull the body along with the feet.
2. Do a Reverse Scooter. Proceed as for the Scooter but with the legs trailing and pushing the body along the bench.
3. Do a Seat Walk. Proceed forward by walking on the buttocks. Use the legs as little as possible.

Crouch Jumps

Place both hands on the bench and jump back and forth over it. Progress the length of the bench by moving the hands forward a few inches after each jump.

1. Do a regular Crouch Jump (Figure 19.8). Use both hands and both feet. Jump as high as possible.
2. Do a Straddle Jump. Straddle the bench with the legs, take the weight on the hands, and jump with the legs as high as possible.

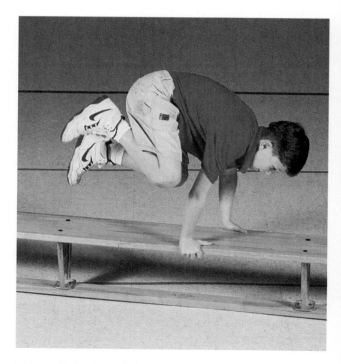

Figure 19.8 Crouch jumping

3. Use one hand and two feet. Do a Crouch Jump, but eliminate the use of one hand.

4. Use one hand and one foot. Perform the Crouch Jump, using only one hand and one foot.

5. Stand to one side, facing the bench, with both hands on it. With stiff arms, try to send the seat as high as possible into the air. Add the Mule Kick (p. 508) before coming down.

Basic Tumbling Stunts

Basic tumbling stunts can be incorporated into bench activities: the Back Roller (p. 497), Backward Curl (p. 498), Forward Roll (p. 497) (Figure 19.9), Backward Roll (p. 498), and Cartwheel (p. 512).

Dismounts

All bench activities in which the child moves from one end of the bench to the other should end with a dismount. The following dismounts are suggested. Many other stunts can be used.

1. Single jump (forward or backward) (Figure 19.10).

2. Jump with turns (half turn, three quarter turn, or full turn).

3. Jackknife. Jump, kick the legs up, and touch the toes with the fingertips. Keep the feet together.

4. Jackknife Split. Same as the Jackknife, but spread the legs as far as possible.

5. Jump to a Forward Roll.

6. Backward jump to a Backward Roll.

7. Side jump to a Side Roll (p. 497).

8. Judo Roll.

9. Jump with combinations of the stunts noted in this list.

Additional Experiences on Benches

1. The range of activities can be extended with the addition of balls, beanbags, hoops, and wands. Wands and hoops can be used as obstacles to go over, under, around, or through. Basic balance and manipulative skills can be incorporated into the activity with balls and beanbags.

2. Two can perform at one time, each child near an opposite end of the bench, doing different balance positions on the bench.

Figure 19.9 Preparing to do a Forward Roll on the bench

Figure 19.10 Dismounting from a bench

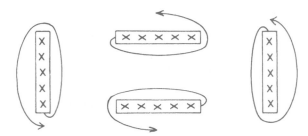

Figure 19.11 Rectangular bench activities

3. Children like to go over and under a row of benches arranged in a kind of obstacle course. Some of the benches can be supported by jumping boxes, making them excellent for vaulting activities.

4. A bench can be supported by two jumping boxes and used as a vaulting box. Each bench is long enough to accommodate three children. They can jump off it, Mule Kick on it, and vault over it.

5. Four benches can be placed in a large rectangle (Figure 19.11), with a squad standing at attention on top of each bench. On signal, each squad gets off its bench, runs around the outside of the other three benches, and then runs back to its own bench. The first squad back and at attention on the bench is the winner.

6. Benches can be placed in a square formation, with children moving around the square and doing a different movement on each bench.

7. One end of the bench can be placed on a jumping box or on another bench. Children receive jumping practice by running up the incline and striving for jump height at the end of the bench.

8. Benches are appropriate for some partner activities. Partners can start on each end and

pass through or around each other, reversing original positions. Wheelbarrow Walks are also suitable.

9. Another enjoyable activity is arranging the benches in a course as illustrated in Figure 19.12. A student is chosen to lead the squad or class through the Challenge Course. A different activity must be performed at each bench.

ACTIVITIES WITH JUMPING BOXES

Jumping boxes can be constructed or purchased. They provide opportunities for children to jump from a height and propel the body through space. Activities with jumping boxes are generally confined to the primary grades. Boxes can be of varying heights; 8 inches and 16 inches are suggested. A rubber floor pad can be placed under the box to protect the floor and to prevent sliding. Plans for constructing boxes are given in Chapter 33.

Instructional Procedures

1. Attention should be given to landing in proper form. Lightness, bent-knee action, balance, and body control should be stressed.

2. Mats should be used to cushion the landing.

3. The exploratory and creative approach is important; there are few standard stunts in jumping box activities.

4. No more than four or five children should be assigned to each series of boxes.

5. Additional challenges can be incorporated by the use of hoops, wands, balls, and the like. Rolling stunts after the dismount extend the movement possibilities.

6. Return activities work well with boxes.

Figure 19.12 Challenge Course using benches

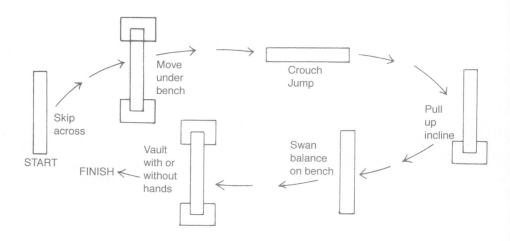

7. Children should strive for height and learn to relax as they go through space.

Activity Sequences

The activities that follow can be augmented easily. Let the children help expand the activity.

Various Approaches to the Boxes

The approach to the boxes can be varied by performing movements such as these.

1. fundamental locomotor movements: Run, gallop, skip, and hop
2. animal walks: Bear Walk, Crab Walk, and so on
3. moving over and under various obstacles: jumping over a bench, moving through a hoop held upright by a mat, doing a Backward Roll on the mat
4. rope jumping to the box: students try to continue jumping while mounting and dismounting the box

Mounting the Box

Many different combinations can be used to get onto the box.

1. Practice stepping onto the box (mounting) by taking the full weight on the stepping foot and holding it for a few seconds. This develops a sense of balance and tends to stabilize the support foot.
2. Mount the box, using locomotor movements such as a step, jump, leap, or hop. Perform various turns—quarter, half, three-quarter, and full—while jumping onto the box.
3. Use a Crouch Jump to get onto the box.
4. Back up to the box and mount it without looking at it.
5. Mount the box while a partner tosses you a beanbag.
6. Make various targets on top of the box with a piece of chalk, and try to land on the spot when mounting.

Dismounting the Box

The following dismounts can be used to develop body control.

1. Jump off with a quarter turn, half turn, or full turn.
2. Jump off with different body shapes: stretching, curling up in a ball, jackknifing.
3. Jump over a wand or through a hoop.
4. Jump off, and do a Forward Roll or a Backward Roll.
5. Change the foregoing dismounts by substituting a hop or a leap in place of the jump.
6. Increase the height and distance of the dismount.
7. Dismount in various directions, such as forward (Figure 19.13), backward, sideward, northward, and southward.
8. Jump off, using a jackknife or wide straddle dismount.
9. Perform a balance stunt on the box and then dismount.

After the class has learned the basic movements used with jumping boxes, continuous squad motion can be incorporated. The squad captain is responsible for leading the group through different approaches, mounts, and dismounts. The same activity cannot be used twice in succession.

Addition of Equipment

Various pieces of equipment enhance box activities. Some suggestions follow.

1. Toss beanbags up while dismounting, or try to keep one on your head while mounting or dismounting the box.
2. Try to dribble a playground ball while performing the box routine.
3. Jump through a stationary hoop, held by a partner, while dismounting, or use the hoop as a jump rope and see how many times you can jump through it while dismounting.
4. Jump over or go under a wand.

Figure 19.13 Jump dismounting

Box Combinations

Boxes can be arranged in a straight line and in other patterns. Children do a different movement over each box as though running a Challenge Course.

ACTIVITIES WITH MAGIC ROPES

Magic rope activities originated in Germany. Each rope is similar to a long rubber band. Magic ropes can be made by knitting wide rubber bands together, or they can be constructed from ordinary ¾-inch elastic tape available in most clothing stores. Children place their hands through loops on each end and grasp the rope. Ropes should be long enough to stretch to between 30 and 40 feet (see Chapter 33). A major advantage of the magic rope is its flexibility; children have no fear of hitting it or tripping on it while performing. Ropes should be stretched tight, with little slack.

Instructional Procedures

1. Two or more children are rope holders while the others are jumping. The teacher should develop some type of rotation plan so that all children participate as holders.

2. Many variations can be achieved with the magic ropes by changing the height or by raising and lowering opposite ends of the ropes.

3. The jumping activities are strenuous and should be alternated with activities that involve crawling under the ropes.

4. The class should concentrate on not touching the rope. The magic rope can help develop body perception in space if the rope is regarded as an obstacle to be avoided.

5. Better use can be made of the rope by using an angled approach, which involves starting at one end of the rope and progressing to the other end by using jumping and hopping activities. In comparison, the straight-on approach allows the child to jump the rope only once.

6. A total of 8 to 12 ropes is needed for a class, 2 for each squad. Squads are excellent groups for this activity, because the leader can control the rotation of the rope holders.

7. The child next in turn begins when the child ahead is almost to the end of the rope.

Activity Sequences

Activities with Single Ropes

Start the ropes at a 6-inch height and raise them progressively to add challenge.

1. Jump over the rope (Figure 19.14).
2. Hop over the rope.
3. Jump and perform various body turns while jumping.
4. Make different body shapes and change body size while jumping.
5. Crawl or slide under the rope.
6. Crouch-jump over the rope.
7. Hold the rope overhead and have others jump up and touch it with their foreheads.
8. Gradually lower the rope, and do the limbo under it without touching the floor with the hands.
9. Jump over the rope backward without looking at it.
10. Perform a Scissors Jump over the rope.

Activities with Double Ropes

Vary the height and spread of the ropes.

1. Do these activities with the ropes parallel to each other.

Figure 19.14 Jumping over a single magic rope

Figure 19.15 Hopping in and out of two magic ropes

a. Jump in one side and out the other.

b. Hop in one side and out the other (Figure 19.15).

c. Crouch-jump in and out.

d. Perform various animal walks in and out of the ropes.

e. Do a long jump over both of the ropes.

f. Perform a stunt while jumping in between the two ropes. Possible stunts are the Heel Click, body turn, handclap, and Straddle Jump.

g. Jump or leap over one rope and land on the other rope.

2. With the ropes crossed at right angles to each other, do these activities.

a. Perform various movements from one area to the next.

b. Jump into one area and crawl out of that area into another.

3. With one rope above the other to effect a barbed-wire fence, do these activities. Vary the height and distance apart of the ropes. This adds much excitement to the activity because the children are challenged not to touch the ropes.

a. Step through the ropes without touching.

b. Crouch-jump through.

Miscellaneous Activities with Magic Ropes

These miscellaneous activities are useful, too. The class should be given time to create their own ideas with the ropes and other pieces of equipment.

1. Perform the various activities with a beanbag balanced on the head. Perform while bouncing a ball.

2. Use four or more ropes to create various floor patterns.

3. Use a follow-the-leader plan to add variety to the activity.

4. Create a Challenge Course with many ropes for a relay.

ACTIVITIES WITH INDIVIDUAL MATS

Individual mats have an English origin and are the basis for many exploratory and creative movements. Essentially, the mat serves as a base of operation or as an obstacle to go over or around. Mats vary in size, with the most popular being 24 by 48 inches. Standard thickness is 0.75 inch, but this also varies. The mat should have rubber backing to prevent slipping. Rubber-backed indoor-outdoor carpeting makes excellent mats.

Instructional Procedures

1. Educational movement techniques are very important in mat work.

2. Body management and basic skills of locomotor and nonlocomotor movement should be emphasized.

3. Mats should be far enough apart to allow free movement around them.

4. Each child should have a mat.

Activity Sequences

Rigid adherence to the sequence presented below is not necessary. The activities are quite flexible and require only fundamental skills.

Command Movements

In command movements, children change movement on command. The commands used are the following:

Stretch: Stretch your body out in all directions as wide as possible.

Figure 19.16 Curl activities on individual mats

Curl: Curl into a tight little ball (Figure 19.16).

Balance: Form some kind of balanced position.

Bridge: Make a bridge over the mat.

Reach: Keeping the toes of one foot on the mat, reach out as far as possible across the floor in a chosen direction.

Rock: Rock on any part of the body.

Roll: Do some kind of roll on the mat.

Twist: Make a shape with a part of the body twisted.

Prone: Lie prone on the mat.

Melt: Sink down slowly into a little puddle of water on the mat.

Shake: Shake all over, or shake whatever parts of the body are designated.

Fall: Fall to the mat.

Collapse: The movement is similar to a fall but follows nicely after a bridge.

Sequencing can be established in several ways. The children can emphasize flow factors by moving at will from one movement to another, or changes can be made on a verbal signal or on the beat of a drum. The magic-number concept can be used, too.

Another means of exploration is selecting one of the movement challenges—say, Stretch—and changing from one type of stretch position to another. If Balance is selected, the movement sequence can begin with a balance on six body parts; then the number can be reduced by one on each signal until the child is balancing on one body part. Different kinds of shapes can be explored.

Movements on and off the Mat

Children do different locomotor movements on and off the mat in different directions. Turns and shapes can be added. Levels are another good challenge.

1. Take the weight on the hands as you go across the mat.

2. Lead with different body parts as you go on and off the mat. Move on and off the mat with a specified number of body parts (one, two, three, four, five) used for landing.

3. Jump backward, forward, sideward. Make up a rhythmic sequence. Move around the area, jumping from mat to mat.

Movements over the Mat

Movements over the mat are similar to the preceding movements, but the child goes completely over the mat each time.

Movements around the Mat

Locomotor movements around the mat are done both clockwise and counterclockwise.

1. Do movements around the mat, keeping the hands on the mat. Now do movements around, keeping the feet on the mat.

2. Change to one foot and one hand on the mat. Vary with the Crab position.

3. Work out combinations of stunt movements and locomotor activities, going around the mats. Reverse direction often.

4. Move throughout the area, running between the mats, and on signal jump over a specified number of mats.

Activities Using Mats as a Base

1. Stretch and reach in different directions to show how big the space is.

Movements on and off the mats

2. Do combination movements away from and back to the mat. For example, do two jumps and two hops or six steps and two jumps.

3. Use the magic-number concept.

4. See how many letters you can make. Find a partner, put your mats together, and make your bodies into different letters and numbers.

Mat Games

Each child is seated on a mat. On signal, each rises and jumps over as many different mats as possible. On the next signal, each child takes a seat on the nearest mat. The last child to be seated can pay a penalty. The game can also be played by eliminating one or two mats so that one or two children are left without a home base. The teacher can stand on a mat or turn over mats to put them out of the game. To control roughness, the rule should be that the first child to touch a mat gets to sit on it.

A variation of this game is to have each child touch at least ten mats and then sit cross-legged on the eleventh, or a child can be required to alternate touching a mat and jumping over the next mat until a total of ten is reached. "See how many mats you can cartwheel or jump over in 10 seconds." Change the challenge and try again.

Developmental Challenges

1. Experiment with Curl-Ups (partial or full). (This can be done informally and on a challenge basis.)

2. From a sitting position on the mat, pick up the short sides of the mat and raise the feet and upper body off the floor. Try variations of the V-Up (p. 530).

Manipulative Activities

Keeping one foot on the mat, maintain control of a balloon in the air, either with a hand, a nylon-stocking paddle, or a lummi stick. Try the same activity with a stocking paddle and a paper ball. The number of touches, or strokes, can be counted. Try with both feet on the mat.

ACTIVITIES WITH PARACHUTES

Parachute play can be enjoyed by children of all ages. Activities must be selected carefully for younger children, since some of the skills presented would be difficult for them. One parachute is generally sufficient for a class of 30 children. Parachutes come in different sizes, but those with diameters ranging from 24 to 32 feet are suitable for a regular class. The size with most utility is the 28-foot parachute. Each parachute has an opening near the top to allow trapped air to escape and to keep the parachute shaped properly. Most parachutes are constructed of nylon. A parachute should stretch tight and not sag in the middle when it is pulled on by children spaced around it. One that does not do so has limited usefulness.

Values of Parachute Play

Parachutes provide an interesting means of accomplishing physical fitness goals: good development of strength, agility, coordination, and endurance. Strength development is focused especially on the arms, hands, and shoulder girdle. At times, however, strength demands are made on the entire body. A variety of movement possibilities, some of which are rhythmic, can be employed in parachute play. Locomotor skills can be practiced while manipulating the parachute. Rhythmic beats of the tom-tom or appropriate music can guide locomotor movements. Parachute play provides many excellent cooperative group learning experiences.

Grips

The grips used in handling the parachute are comparable to those employed in hanging activities on an apparatus. Grips can be with one or two hands, overhand (palms facing away), underhand (palms facing toward), or mixed (one hand underhand and the other overhand). The grips should be varied.

Instructional Procedures

1. Certain terms peculiar to parachute activity must be explained carefully. Terms such as *inflate, deflate, float, dome,* and *mushroom* need to be clarified when they are introduced.

2. For preliminary explanations, the parachute can be stretched out on the ground in its circular pattern, with the children seated just far enough away so that they cannot touch the parachute during instructions. When the children hold the parachute during later explanations, they should retain their hold lightly, letting the center of the parachute drop to the ground. Children must be taught to exercise control and not to manipulate the parachute while explanations are in progress.

3. The teacher explains the activity, demonstrating as needed. If there are no questions, the

activity is initiated with a command such as "Ready—begin!"

4. Squads can be used to form the parachute circle, with each squad occupying a quarter of the chute's circumference. Squads are useful for competitive units in game activity.

5. The teacher must watch for fatigue, particularly with younger children.

Activities are presented according to type, with variations and suggestions for supplementary activities included. Unless otherwise specified, activities begin and halt on signal. Pupils' suggestions can broaden the scope of activity.

Exercise Activities

Exercises should be done vigorously and with enough repetitions to challenge the children. In addition to the exercises presented, others can be adapted to parachute play.

Toe Toucher

Sit with feet extended under the parachute and hold the chute taut with a two-hand grip, drawing it up to the chin. Bend forward and touch the grip to the toes. Return parachute to stretched position.

Curl-Up

Extend the body under the parachute in curl-up position, so that the chute comes up to the chin when held taut. Do Curl-Ups, returning each time to the stretched chute position.

Dorsal Lift

Lie prone, with head toward the parachute and feet pointed back, away from it. Grip the chute and slide toward the feet until there is some tension on it. Raise the chute off the ground with a vigorous lift of the arms, until head and chest rise off the ground. Return.

V-Sit

Lie supine, with head toward the chute. Do V-Ups by raising the upper and lower parts of the body simultaneously into a V-shaped position. The knees should be kept straight.

Backward Pull

Face the parachute and pull back, away from its center. Pulls can be made from a sitting, kneeling, or standing position.

Other Pulls

With arm flexed, do Side Pulls with either arm. Other variations of pulling can be devised.

Hip Walk and Scooter

Begin with the parachute taut. Move forward with the Scooter (p. 517) or Hip Walk (p. 517). Move back to place with the same movement until the chute is taut again.

Elevator

Begin with the chute taut and at ground level. On the command "Elevator up," lift the chute overhead while keeping it stretched tight. On the command "Elevator down," lower the chute to starting position. Lowering and raising can be done quickly or in increments. Levels can also bring in body part identification, with children holding the chute even with their head, nose, chin, shoulders, chest, waist, thighs, knees, ankles, and toes.

Running in Place

Run in place while holding the chute at different levels.

Isometrics

Hold the chute taut at shoulder level and try to stretch it for 10 seconds. Many other isometric exercises can be performed with the parachute to develop all body parts.

Dome Activities

To make a dome, children begin with the parachute on the floor, holding with two hands and kneeling on one knee. To trap air under the chute, children stand up quickly, thrusting their arms above the head (Figure 19.17), and then return to starting position (Figure 19.18). Some or all of the children can change to the inside of the chute on the down movement. Domes can also be made while moving in a circle.

Students under the Chute

Tasks for under the chute can be specified, such as turning a certain number of turns with a jump rope, throwing and catching a beanbag, or bouncing a ball a number of times. The needed objects should be under the chute before the dome is made.

Figure 19.17 Making a dome

Number Exchange

Children are numbered from one to four. The teacher calls a number as the dome is made, and those with the number called must change position to be under the dome before the chute comes down. Locomotor movements can be varied.

Punching Bag

Children make a dome and stand on the edges. They then punch at the chute while slowly and gently walking the edges of the chute toward the center.

Blooming Flower

Children make a dome and kneel with both knees on the edge of the chute. Youngsters hold hands around the chute and lean in and out to represent a blooming flower opening.

Lights Out

While making a dome, the children take two steps toward the center and sit inside the chute. The chute can be held with the hands at the side or by sitting on it.

Mushroom Activities

To form a mushroom, students begin with the chute on the ground, kneeling on one knee and holding with two hands. They stand up quickly, thrusting the arms overhead. Keeping the arms overhead, each walks forward three or four steps toward the center. The arms are held overhead until the chute is deflated.

Mushroom Release

All children release at the peak of inflation and either run out from under the chute or move to the center and sit down, with the chute descending on top of them.

Mushroom Run

Children make a mushroom. As soon as they move into the center, they release holds and run once around the inside of the chute, counterclockwise, back to place.

Figure 19.18 Holding the air inside a dome

Activities with Other Equipment

Ball Circle

Place a basketball or a cageball on the raised chute. Make the ball roll around the chute in a large circle, controlling it by raising or lowering the chute. Try the same with two balls. A beach ball is also excellent.

Popcorn

Place a number of beanbags (from six to ten) on the chute. Shake the chute to make them rise like corn popping (Figure 19.19).

Cageball Elevator

A 2-foot cageball is placed on the chute. On signal, the class elevates the chute and allows it to make a mushroom. Just before the chute with the ball on it reaches its apex, youngsters snap the chute to the floor. Done correctly, the cageball should be elevated to the ceiling.

Team Ball

Divide the class in half, each team defending half of the chute. Using from two to six balls of any variety, try to bounce the balls off the opponents' side, scoring 1 point for each ball.

Poison Snake

Divide into teams. Place from 6 to 10 jump ropes on the chute. Shake the chute and try to make the ropes hit players on the other side. For each rope that touches one team member, that team has a point scored against it. The team with the lower score is the winner.

Circular Dribble

Each child has a ball suitable for dribbling. The object is to run in circular fashion counterclockwise, holding onto the chute with the left hand and dribbling with the right hand, retaining control of the ball. As an equalizer for left-handers, try the dribbling clockwise. The dribble should be started first, and then, on signal, children start to run. A child who loses a ball must recover it and try to hook on at his original place.

Hole in One

Use four or more plastic whiffle balls the size of golf balls. The balls should be of two different colors.

Figure 19.19 Popping popcorn

The class is divided into two teams on opposite sides of the chute. The object is to shake the other team's balls into the hole in the center of the chute.

Other Activities

Merry-Go-Round Movements

Merry-go-round movements, in which children rotate the chute while keeping the center hole over the same spot, offer many opportunities for locomotor movements, either free or to the beat of a tom-tom. European Rhythmic Running is particularly appropriate. Also appropriate are fundamental movements, such as walking, running, hopping, skipping, galloping, sliding, draw steps, and grapevine steps. The parachute can be held at different levels. Holds can be one- or two-handed.

Shaking the Rug and Making Waves

Shaking the Rug involves rapid movements of the parachute, either light or heavy. Making Waves involves large movements to send billows of cloth up and down. Waves can be small, medium, or high. Different types of waves can be made by

having children alternate their up-and-down motions, or by having the class work in small groups around the chute. These small groups take turns showing what they can do. For a more demanding activity, children can perform locomotor movements while they shake the rug.

Chute Crawl

Half of the class, either standing or kneeling, stretches the chute at waist level parallel to the ground. The remaining children crawl under the chute to the opposite side from their starting position.

Kite Run

The class holds the chute on one side with one hand. The leader points in the direction they are to run while holding the chute aloft like a kite.

Running Number Game

The children around the chute count off by fours; then they run lightly, holding the chute in one hand. The teacher calls out one of the numbers. Children with that number immediately release their grip on

Parachute tug-o-war

the chute and run forward to the next place vacated. They must put on a burst of speed to move ahead.

Routines to Music

Like other routines, parachute activities can be adapted to music. A sequence should be based on eight counts, with the routine composed of an appropriate number of sequences.

Tug-of-War

For team Tug-of-War, divide the class in halves. On signal, teams pull against each other and try to reach a line located behind them. Another approach that is often more enjoyable for primary-age children is an individual tug, in which all children pull in any direction they desire.

Action Songs and Dances

A number of action songs, games, and dances can be performed while children hold onto a parachute. The following are suggested: Carrousel (p. 375), Bingo (p. 382), and Seven Jumps (p. 371).

ACTIVITIES WITH GYM SCOOTERS

Gym scooters make excellent devices for developmental activity when used properly. The minimum number is one scooter for two children, unless the scooters are used for relays only. In that case, four or six scooters will suffice for an average-sized class. Two rules are important in the use of scooters. First, children are not to stand on scooters as they would on skateboards. Second, scooters, with or without passengers, must not be used as missiles.

Children can work individually or in pairs. A child working alone can do many different combinations by varying the method of propulsion and the method of supporting the body. Children can propel the scooter with their feet, their hands, or both. The body position can be kneeling, sitting, prone, supine, or even sideways. The body weight can be wholly or partially supported on the scooter. The variation of space factors, particularly direction, adds interest.

When children work in pairs, one child rides and the other pushes or pulls. The rider's weight may be wholly supported by the scooter or partially supported by the scooter and partially supported by the partner. Educational movement methodology is applicable to scooter work, but care should be exercised so that the scooter activities are developmental and not just a free play session. Scooters are excellent for relays, and many games can be adapted for their use.

Stunts and Tumbling: Developing Body Management Skills without Apparatus

---

PURPOSE OF ACTIVITIES IN THIS CHAPTER
Stunts and tumbling activities develop body management skills without the need for equipment and apparatus. Flexibility, agility, balance, strength, and body control are outcomes that are enhanced through participation in stunts and tumbling. Specialized motor skills such as body rolling, balance skills, inverted balances, and tumbling skills are learned through these activities.

Gymnastic activities are an important part of every child's overall experience in physical education and can make a significant contribution to the goals of physical education. Through the stunts and tumbling program, such personal characteristics as dedication and perseverance can be furthered, for stunts are seldom mastered quickly. Since much of the work is individual, children face challenges and have the opportunity to develop resourcefulness, self-confidence, and courage. When a challenging stunt is mastered, satisfaction, pride of achievement, and a sense of accomplishment contribute to improved self-esteem. Social interplay is provided through various partner and group stunts requiring cooperative effort. The social attributes of tolerance, helpfulness, courtesy, and appreciation for the ability of others grow out of the lessons when the methodology is educationally sound.

Important physical values can emerge from an instructionally sound gymnastics program. Body management opportunities are presented, and coordination, flexibility, and agility are enhanced. The opportunity to practice control of balance is present in many activities. The raw physical demands of holding positions and executing stunts contribute to the development of strength and power in diverse parts of the body. Many stunts demand support, wholly or in part, by the arms, thus providing needed development of the often weak musculature of the arm-shoulder girdle. Gymnastics activities also contribute to overall physical fitness.

PROGRESSION AND DEVELOPMENTAL LEVEL PLACEMENT

Progression is the soul of learning experiences in the stunts and tumbling program. In this book, activities are listed in progression within the three developmental levels. To avoid safety problems, it is essential that the order of these activities be reasonably maintained. Adherence to developmental level is secondary to this principle. If children come with little or no experience in these activities, the teacher should start them on activities specified at a developmental level.

The activities in this chapter are divided into six basic groups: (1) animal movements, (2) tumbling and inverted balances, (3) balance stunts, (4) individual stunts, (5) partner and group stunts, and (6) partner support activities. This arrangement allows the teacher to pick activities from each group for a well-balanced lesson. Too often, teachers concentrate on tumbling activities, causing some children to become bored and fatigued. In addition, for those children who do not like tumbling activities; choosing activities from all the categories will help increase motivation. At the heart of a gymnastic program are the standard tumbling activities, such as rolls, stands, springs, and related stunts. In performing the activities, emphasis should be placed on exposure and overcoming fear. Perfect technique is less important than developing positive approach behaviors. The suggested progression of the basic activities is presented in the following list.

Developmental Level I

Rolling Log
Side Roll

Forward Roll (Tuck Position)
Back Roller
Forward Roll (Straddle Position)
Backward Curl
Backward Roll (Handclasp Position)
Climb-Up
Three-Point Tip-Up
Mountain Climber—Handstand Lead-Up Activity
Switcheroo—Handstand Lead-Up Activity

Developmental Level II

Forward Roll (Pike Position)
Backward Roll (Inclined)
Backward Roll (Regular)
Frog Handstand (Tip-Up)
Half Teeter-Totter—Handstand Lead-Up Activity
Cartwheel
Forward Roll to a Walkout
Forward Roll Combinations
Backward Roll Combinations
Headstand Practice and Variations
Teeter-Totter—Handstand Lead-Up Activity
Handstand

Developmental Level III

Forward and Backward Roll Combinations
Back Extension
Headstand Variations
Handstand Against a Wall
Freestanding Handstand
Cartwheel and Round-Off
Judo Roll
Forward and Backward Roll Combinations
Developing Gymnastic Routines
Straddle Press to Headstand
Headspring
Walking on the Hands
Walk-Over

The developmental level I program relies on simple stunts with a gradual introduction to tumbling stunts classified as lead-ups or preliminaries to more advanced stunts. Stunts requiring exceptional body control, critical balancing, or substantial strength should be left for higher levels of development. The developmental level II and III programs are built on activities and progressions developed earlier. Emphasis is placed on learning more standard gymnastic activities. While most stunts at developmental level I can be performed with a certain degree of choice, at developmental levels II and III more conformance to correct technique is desirable. In general, the upper developmental level activities place higher demands on strength, control, form, agility, balance, and flexibility.

Most activities at developmental level I can be done—at least in some fashion—by most students, but certain activities at levels II and III may be too challenging for some students. The teacher should arrange lessons that include stunts that everyone can do, stunts that are moderately challenging, and stunts that are quite challenging.

INSTRUCTIONAL METHODOLOGY FOR STUNTS AND TUMBLING

Warm-Up and Flexibility Activity

Normal introductory activity and fitness development activity usually supply sufficient warm-up for the stunts and tumbling lesson. If additional stretching seems warranted, take a wide straddle position with the feet about 3 feet apart and the toes pointed ahead. With arms out to the sides, bend, twist, and generally stretch in all directions. Next, touch the floor with the hands to the front, sides, and back, with some bending of the knees.

Extra flexibility is required in the wrists, ankles, and neck. The following activities, which focus on these areas, can be used prior to participating in the gymnastic activities.

Wrists

1. Extend one arm forward. With the other hand, push the extended hand down, thus stretching the top of the wrist and forearm muscles. Hold the position for eight counts. Next, pull the hand backward and hold for eight counts to stretch the wrist flexor muscles.

2. Clasp the fingers of both hands in front of the chest. Make circles with both hands and stretch the wrists.

Ankles and Quadriceps

1. Kneel and sit on both feet. Smoothly and gently lean backward over the feet, using the arms to support the body.

Warming up the neck muscles

2. In a sitting position, cross one leg over the other. Use the hands to help rotate each foot through its full range of motion. Reverse legs and repeat.

Neck

1. In a sitting position, slowly circle the head in both directions through the full range of motion.

2. In the same position, hold the chin against the chest for eight counts. Repeat with the head looking backward as far as possible. Look to each side and hold for eight counts.

Lower Back and Shoulders

Begin in a supine position. Place the hands back over the head on the mat so that the fingers point toward the toes. Bridge up by extending the arms and legs. While in the bridge position, slowly rock back and forth.

Effective Class Management

A commonly heard criticism of stunts and tumbling lessons is that children must wait in line for turns on the mat. Waiting must be controlled so that everyone is reasonably active. How children are arranged depends on the activities selected and whether mats are required. The following list will help establish priorities.

1. Whenever possible, all children should be active and performing. When mats are not required for the activities, there is little problem. Individual mats can be used for many of the simple balances and rolling stunts, particularly at developmental

level I. When larger mats are required, teachers must be more ingenious. Ideally, each group of three students should have a mat. When return activities are used in conjunction with groups as small as three, there is little standing around. Small groups also work well when spotting and other types of cooperation are needed.

2. When the number of mats is limited, children can perform across the mats sideways. On a 6-foot-long mat, two children can tumble sideways. An 8-foot-long mat can be used by three performers at the same time. With this arrangement, the focus is on single rolls, but an occasional series of rolls lengthwise on the mat is not ruled out. The ends of the mats can be used for various stands, as long as children do not fall toward each other.

3. Station teaching can be considered if equipment is limited. Careful planning is necessary to ensure that the experience stresses progress and diligence. All stations can involve tumbling and inverted balance experiences, or only a few tumbling and inverted balance stations can be included, with other stations featuring less demanding activities. The arrangement might include Forward and Backward Rolls at the first station, Headstands at the second, Cartwheels at the third, and partner stunts at the fourth. Wall charts listing the activities in progression provide excellent guidance. A chart illustrated with stick figures can be made as a class project.

Formations for Teaching

Some formations that organize the class for gymnastic activities follow.

1. *Squad formation.* Mats are placed in a line, with squads lined up behind the mats. Each child takes a turn and then goes to the end of the squad line, with the others moving up. An alternative method is for each child to perform and then return to a seated position.

2. *Semicircular formation.* Students are placed in a semicircular arrangement. This formation directs attention toward the teacher, who stands in the center.

3. *U-shaped formation.* The mats are placed in the shape of a large U. This formation allows good control for the teacher, and children are able to see what their classmates are doing.

   Demonstration mat. One mat is placed in a central position and is used exclusively for demonstrations. Little movement is necessary for children to be able to see the demonstrations.

Description and Demonstration of New Gymnastic Activities

To enhance student learning when presenting an activity, the following sequence may be helpful.

1. *Significance of the name.* Most stunts have a characteristic name, and this should be given attention by the teacher. If the stunt is of an imitative type, the animal or character represented should be described and discussed.

2. *Description of the activity.* Stunts can be approached in terms of three parts: starting position, execution, and finishing position. Most stunts have a defined starting position. To perform properly, the child should understand what position to assume as the first step. Next, key movements for proper execution of the activity should be stressed. Such factors as how far to travel, how long to balance, and how many times a movement should be done must be clarified. In some gymnastic activities, a definite finishing position or action is part of the stunt. In balancing stunts it is important that the child return to a standing (or some other) position without losing balance and without moving the feet.

3. *Demonstration of the activity.* Three levels of demonstration are recognized: (a) minimal demonstration in the form of the starting position, (b) slow, step-by-step demonstration of the entire stunt, with an explanation of what is involved, and (c) execution of the stunt as the students would normally do it. The teacher should keep in mind that children need to analyze and solve problems. Too much demonstration defeats this goal. Explanation and demonstration should cover only one or two points. Try not to demonstrate too far in advance, but rather show only those points necessary to get the activity under way. Add further details and refinements as the instruction progresses. Demonstrations have a place later in the instruction sequence also. These later demonstrations can use students to show the successful execution of activities that others are having difficulty performing. Demonstrations at the end of a unit can show what has been achieved. Each squad or group can demonstrate its achievements in turn.

Opportunities for Practice and Improvement

The character of each stunt determines the amount of practice needed and the number of times the stunt should be performed. Teachers should analyze a stunt thoroughly enough so that they can verbalize the small points necessary for proper performance. A reasonable standard of performance should be maintained. Instruction should make clear to students what is involved in satisfactory performance so they know whether they performed within the bounds of correct performance.

Practice and repetition are essential in establishing effective movement patterns. Often, a teacher leaves an activity too soon for progress to have occurred. The following system is suggested. When explanations and demonstrations are completed, each child should have the opportunity to practice the stunt. When each child in the group has had the desired turns at an activity, the group remains in formation, waiting for the next instruction. If this system is to function properly, groups must be about the same size and must move at about the same speed. A teacher can ascertain at a glance whether the class is ready for the next instruction.

An alternative method is to allow the class to practice the activity a desired number of times. On the command or whistle to "freeze," the class stops whatever they are doing without returning to formation. Directions are then given for the next activity, and the class resumes practicing. This method decreases the amount of management time spent waiting for each squad to finish and return to formation.

SAFETY CONSIDERATIONS

Safety is a foremost consideration in the gymnastic program. The inherent hazards of an activity and how to avoid them must be included in the instructional procedures.

Spotting

The purpose of spotting is twofold. First and most important is the performer's safety and the prevention of injury. Of secondary importance is the guiding of the performer through the stunt to help develop proper body awareness. When spotting for safety, the goals are to assist the performer, help support the body weight, and prevent a hazardous fall. A particularly difficult problem is working with the obese children in tumbling activities.

Two major questions usually arise related to spotting. Should teachers be expected to spot youngsters? Can other students spot their peers? The answer is grounded in the expertise and experience of the teacher. Many teachers have little, if any, gymnastics background. This makes spotting correctly a difficult task. In addition, obese youngsters may actually weigh more than the teacher, making spotting next to impossible. If this is the case, it is probably best to avoid activities that involve spotting. The issue of peer spotting is also a sensitive one. In many situations, it is difficult to get all students to take spotting responsibilities seriously. Additionally, if many students are spotting in the class, how does the teacher assure quality control? If an accident would occur while a student was spotting, who would be liable? Undoubtedly, legal authorities would try to show that the teacher was not supervising the spotting carefully and that students are too young and irresponsible to fulfill the duties of correct spotting.

The bottom line is that each teacher will have to decide whether to teach activities that require spotting. If a teacher lacks confidence in this area or lacks adequate knowledge about proper presentation of the activities, it is probably best to avoid tumbling and inverted balance activities. Since tumbling and inverted balance activities make up only about 20 percent of the activities in this chapter, there are many other stunts and balance activities that can be offered to teach youngsters body management skills. Above all, youngsters should not be forced to participate in tumbling and inverted balance activities. Specific spotting techniques are offered in this chapter with activities that demand spotting.

Other Safety Considerations

Pockets should be emptied, and jewelry, glasses, watches, and other articles of this nature removed. A special depository for these articles should be provided, or they can be left in the classroom. Teachers must guard against fatigue and strain in young children. The children should be encouraged but not forced to try stunts. Care should be taken not to use peer pressure to stimulate participation.

ADDITIONAL METHODOLOGY CONSIDERATIONS

Instructional Procedures

1. Although mats are not necessary for some stunts, it is wise to include stunts requiring mats in every lesson. Children like to perform on mats, and rolling stunts using mats are vital to the gymnastic program.

2. Many partner stunts work well only when partners are about the same size. If the stunt

requires partner support, the support child should be strong enough to hold the weight of the other.

3. No two children are alike. Respect individual differences, and allow for different levels of success.

4. Relating new activities to those learned previously is important. An effective approach is to review the lead-up stunt for an activity.

5. Horseplay and ridicule have no place in a stunts and tumbling program. Children should have fun, but not at the expense of the performance of less talented classmates.

6. Proper gym shoes are a help, but children can tumble in bare feet (not socks) if necessary.

7. When a stunt calls for a position to be held for a number of counts, use a standard counting system (e.g., "One thousand one, one thousand two, . . ." or "Monkey one, monkey two, . . .").

8. At times, the teacher can have children work in pairs, with one child performing and the second providing a critique.

9. In using manipulative equipment (wands, hoops, and the like) with stunts, having one item for each child is best. If this is not possible, a minimum of two pieces is needed for each group, so the child next in line does not have to wait for the return of the required object. One person, generally the leader of the group, should be designated to secure and return hand apparatus.

10. Shifting of mats should not be necessary during the course of instruction. In arranging a gymnastic routine for a day's lesson, the mat stunts should be grouped. The tumbling mats should be bordered with Velcro so that, once fastened, they stay fastened together.

11. Soft background music can occasionally contribute to a pleasant atmosphere, but it should be low enough in volume so as not to interfere with the instruction.

12. The beat of a drum or tom-tom can direct controlled movements. Children should change position in small increments as guided by the beat. In Lowering the Boom (p. 503), for example, children can lower themselves a little each time the drum sounds.

Start-and-Expand Technique

The start-and-expand technique should be applied to stunts when feasible. Consider someone teaching a simple Heel Click (p. 503). The instructor begins by saying, "Let's see all of you jump high in the air and click your heels together before you come down." (This is the start.) "Now, to do the stunt properly, you should jump into the air, click your heels, and land with your feet apart with a nice bent-knee action to absorb the shock." (This is the expansion.) Further expansion could be adding a quarter or half turn before landing, clapping the hands overhead while clicking the heels, or clicking the heels twice before landing. In general, the start is made simple, so that all children can experience a measure of success. The instruction then expands to other elements of the stunt, with variations and movement factors added and refined as indicated.

Basic Mechanical Principles

Certain mechanical principles should be established as the foundation of an effective gymnastic program. If children can build on these basic principles, instruction is facilitated. (Consult Chapter 3 if more in-depth coverage is desired.)

1. Momentum needs to be developed and applied, particularly for rolls. Tucking, starting from a higher point, and preliminary raising of the arms are examples of ways to increase momentum.

2. The center of weight must be positioned over the center of support in balance stunts, particularly in the inverted stands.

3. In certain stunts, such as the Headspring, the hips should be projected upward and forward to raise the center of gravity for better execution.

4. In stunts in which the body is wholly or partially supported by the hands, proper positioning of the hands is essential for effective performance. The hands should be approximately shoulder width apart, and the fingers should be spread and pointed forward.

Stunt Check-Off System

Some teachers like to establish a check-off system to keep track of student progress. Two systems are suggested. The first simply checks those stunts that the student has completed. The second differentiates between a stunt done well and one meeting the minimum requirements. In the latter system, the teacher can make a diagonal line (/) for a stunt meeting minimum requirements and a cross over that line (an X) for a stunt well done.

Basic Gymnastic Positions

Students should be able to recognize and demonstrate those basic positions that are unique to gymnastics. Emphasis at the elementary level should be placed on a clear understanding of how the positions are performed, rather than on pure technique.

Tuck Position

The tuck position is performed with the legs bent and the chin tucked to the chest. Students can be cued to "curl up like a ball." There are three different tuck positions, and students should know all of them: the Sitting Tuck (Figure 20.1), the Standing Tuck, and the Lying Tuck.

Pike Position

The pike position is performed by bending forward at the hips and keeping the legs straight. The three basic pike positions are the Sitting Pike (Figure 20.2), the Standing Pike, and the Lying Pike.

Straddle Position

The straddle position is accomplished by bending forward at the hips and spreading the legs apart to the sides as far as possible. The legs should be kept straight. Variations of the straddle position are the Sitting Piked Straddle (Figure 20.3), the Standing Piked Straddle, and the Lying Piked Straddle.

Front-Support Position

This position is similar to the push-up position. The body is straight with the head up (Figure 20.4).

Figure 20.2   Pike position

Figure 20.3   Straddle position

Figure 20.1   Tuck position

Figure 20.4   Front-support position

Back-Support Position

The back-support position is an inverted push-up position. The body is kept as straight as possible (Figure 20.5).

Gymnastic Dance Positions

Attitude

An attitude is a position in which the body weight is supported on one leg while the other leg is lifted

Figure 20.5 Back-support position

Figure 20.6 Attitude

and bent at the knee. The arm on the side of the lifted leg is usually bent over the head, and the other arm is extended at the side (Figure 20.6).

Lunge Position

In lunge position, the nonsupporting rear leg is straight while the forward, supporting leg is bent at the hip and knee. Most of the weight is placed on the forward leg. The arms are extended, and the head is up with the eyes forward (Figure 20.7).

Plié

A plié is the bending of the knees. Both knees are bent, the arms are extended at right angles to the sides, and the seat is tucked to maintain a flat abdominal wall. The plié teaches children how to absorb the force of the landing. There are different plié positions, but the basic purpose of the plié in gymnastic instruction is to teach landing with grace and control.

Relevé

The relevé is an extension movement from the plié position. The movement goes from the plié (knees

Figure 20.7 Lunge position

bent) position to the extended position. Extension should be complete through all of the joints, stretching upward from the balls of the feet.

Arabesque

In the arabesque position, the weight is supported on one leg while the other leg is extended to the rear. The extended leg is kept straight with the toe pointed, and the chest is kept erect (Figure 20.8). The Back Extension and the Cartwheel are often brought to completion with an Arabesque.

Jumps

Three jump variations are used commonly in gymnastic dance. They are the Tuck Jump, the Pike Jump, and the Straddle Jump. These jumps are simply a jump with the prescribed position added. The arms are raised in a lifting motion to increase the height of the jump and to enhance balance. The impact of the landing is absorbed at the ankles and knee joints.

Figure 20.8 Arabesque

Chassé

The Chassé is a slide. This basic locomotor movement involves one leg chasing the other out of position. It is done close to the floor with a light spring in the step.

STUNTS AND TUMBLING ACTIVITIES

The stunts and tumbling activities are organized in order of difficulty into three developmental levels. Table 20.1 lists all the activities in each of the levels and offers a page reference for rapid access to descriptions of each activity. A brief discussion of each of the developmental levels follows.

DEVELOPMENTAL LEVEL I ACTIVITIES

Developmental level I consists primarily of imitative walks and movements, plus selected balance stunts and rolls. The Forward Roll is practiced, but its refinement is left to later levels. The Back Roller is practiced as a prelude to the Backward Roll.

Emphasis should be placed on the creative aspects of the activities as well as with performance standards. Children at this level tend to do stunts in different ways because of their different interpretations of what is required. Directional concepts and a basic understanding of common movement terminology should have a prominent place in the instruction. The "why" of an activity should be explained to children.

Animal Movements

Alligator Crawl

Lie facedown on the floor with elbows bent. Move along the floor in alligator fashion, keeping the hands close to the body and the feet pointed out (Figure 20.9). First, use unilateral movements—that is, right arm and leg moving together—then change to cross-lateral movements.

Kangaroo Jump

Carry the arms close to the chest with the palms facing forward. Place a beanbag or ball between the knees. Move in different directions by taking small jumps without dropping the object.

Puppy Dog Run

Place the hands on the floor, bending the arms and legs slightly. Walk and run like a happy puppy.

Table 20.1 Stunts and tumbling activities

Animal Movements		Tumbling and Inverted Balances		Balance Stunts		Individual Stunts		Partner and Group Stunts	
				Developmental Level I					
Alligator Crawl	491	Rolling Log	496	One-Leg Balance	500	Directional Walk	502	Bouncing Ball	505
Kangaroo Jump	491	Side Roll	497	Double-Knee Balance	500	Line Walking	502	Seesaw	505
Puppy Dog Run	491	Forward Roll	497	Head Touch	500	Fluttering Leaf	502	Wring the Dishrag	506
Cat Walk	495	Back Roller	497	Head Balance	500	Elevator	502	Partner Toe Toucher	506
Monkey Run	495	Forward Roll— Straddle Position	497	One-Leg Balance Stunts	500	Cross-Legged Stand	502	Double Top	507
Bear Walk	495	Backward Curl	498	Kimbo Stand	500	Walking in Place	502	Roly Poly	507
Gorilla Walk	495	Backward Roll— Handclasp Position	498	Knee-Lift Stand	500	Jump Turns	502		
Rabbit Jump	495	Climb-Up	499	Stork Stand	500	Rubber Band	503		
Elephant Walk	495	Three Point Tip-up	499	Balance Touch	500	Pumping Up the Balloon	503		
Siamese Twin Walk	496	Mountain Climber	499	Single-Leg Balance	500	Rising Sun	503		
Tightrope Walk	496	Switcheroo	499	Forward Balance	500	Heel Click	503		
Mountain Climber	496			Backward Balance	501	Lowering the Boom	503		
Lame Dog Walk	496			Side Balance	501	Turn-Over	503		
Crab Walk	496			Hand-and-Knee Balance	501	Thread the Needle	503		
				Single-Knee Balance	502	Heel Slap	503		
						Pogo Stick	504		
						Top	504		
						Turk Stand	504		
						Push-Up	504		
						Crazy Walk	505		
						Seat Circle	505		

Developmental Level II

Animal Movements		Tumbling and Inverted Balances		Balance Stunts		Individual Stunts		Partner and Group Stunts		Partner Support Stunts	
Cricket Walk	507	Forward Roll to a Walkout	509	One-Leg Balance Reverse	514	Reach-Under	516	Partner Hopping	520	Double Bear	524
Frog Jump	507	Backward Roll	509	Tummy Balance	514	Stiff Person Bend	516	Partner Twister	520	Table	524
Seal Crawl	507	Backward Roll—Inclined	510	Leg Dip	515	Coffee Grinder	517	Partner Pull-Up	521	Statue	524
Reverse Seal Crawl	507	Headstand	510	Balance Jump	515	Scooter	517	Back-to-Back Get-Up	521	Lighthouse	525
Elbow Crawl	508	Climb-Up	510	Seat Balance	515	Hip Walk	517	Rowboat	521	Hip-Shoulder Stand	525
Measuring Worm	508	Kick-Up	511	Face-to-Knee Touch	515	Long Bridge	517	Leapfrog	521		
Mule Kick	508	Frog Handstand (Tip-Up)	511	Finger Touch	516	Heelstand	517	Wheelbarrow	522		
Walrus Walk	508	Half Teeter-Totter	512			Wicket Walk	518	Wheelbarrow Lifting	523		
Double-Lame Dog	508	Cartwheel	512			Knee Jump to Standing	518	Camel Lift and Walk	523		
Turtle	508	Forward Roll—Pike Position	512			Knee Drop	518	Dump the Wheelbarrow	523		
Walrus Slap	508	Forward Roll Combinations	512			Forward Drop	518	Dromedary Walk	523		
Reverse Walrus Slap	509	Backward Roll Combinations	512			Dead Body Fall	519	Centipede	523		
		Headstand Variations	513			Stoop and Stretch	519	Double Wheelbarrow	523		
		Teeter-Totter	513			Tanglefoot	519				
		Handstand	513			Egg Roll	519				
						Toe Touch Nose	520				
						Toe Tug Walk	520				

Table 20.1 *continued*

Developmental Level III

Tumbling and Inverted Balances		Balance Stunts		Individual Stunts		Partner and Group Stunts		Partner Support Stunts	
Forward and Backward Roll Combinations	526	V-Up	530	Wall Walk-Up	532	Double Scooter	534	Back Layout	538
Back Extension	526	Push-Up Variations	530	Skier's Sit	532	Double Roll	534	Front Sit	538
Headstand Variations	526	Flip-Flop	530	Rocking Horse	532	Tandem Bicycle	535	Flying Dutchman	539
Handstand Against a Wall	527	Long Reach	531	Heel Click (Side)	532	Circle High Jump	535	Knee-and-Shoulder Balance	539
Freestanding Handstand	527	Toe Jump	531	Walk-Through	533	Stick Carries	535	Press	540
Cartwheel and Round-Off	527	Handstand Stunts	531	Jump-Through	533	Two-Way Wheelbarrow	536	All-Fours Support	540
Judo Roll	527	Front Seat Support	531	Circular Rope Jump	533	Partner Rising Sun	536	Angel	540
Advanced Forward and Backward Roll Combinations	528	Elbow Balance	531	Bouncer	533	Triple Roll	537	Side Stand	541
Gymnastics Routines	528			Pretzel	533	Quintuplet Roll	537	Pyramids	541
Straddle Press to Headstand	528			Jackknife	533	Dead Person Lift	537		
Handstand Variations	529			Heel-and-Toe Spring	534	Injured Person Carry	537		
Headspring	529			Single-Leg Circle (Pinwheel)	534	Merry-Go-Round	537		
Walking on the Hands	529								
Walk-Over	530								

Figure 20.9 Alligator Crawl

Look straight ahead. Keeping the head up, in good position, strengthens the neck muscles (Figure 20.10). Go sideward, backward, and so on. Turn around in place.

Variations:

1. *Cat Walk.* Use the same position to imitate a cat. Walk softly. Stretch at times like a cat. Be smooth and deliberate.
2. *Monkey Run.* Turn the hands and feet so that the fingers and toes point in (toward each other).

Bear Walk

Bend forward and touch the ground with both hands. Travel forward slowly by moving the hand and foot on the same side together (i.e., first the right hand and foot, then the left hand and foot) (Figure 20.11). Make deliberate movements.

Figure 20.10 Puppy Dog Run

Figure 20.11 Bear Walk

Variation: Lift the free foot and arm high while the support is on the other side.

Gorilla Walk

Bend the knees and carry the trunk forward. Let the arms hang at the sides. Touch the fingers to the ground while walking.

Variation: Stop and beat on the chest like a gorilla. Bounce up and down on all fours with hands and feet touching the floor simultaneously.

Rabbit Jump

Crouch with knees apart and hands placed on the floor. Move forward by reaching out with both hands and then bringing both feet up to the hands. The eyes look ahead.

The teacher should emphasize that this is a jump rather than a hop because both feet move at once. Note that the jump is a bilateral movement.

Variations:

1. Try with knees together and arms on the outside. Try alternating with knees together and apart on successive jumps. Go over a low hurdle or through a hoop.
2. Experiment with taking considerable weight on the hands before the feet move forward. To do this, raise the seat higher in the air when the hands move forward.

Elephant Walk

Bend well forward, clasping the hands together to form a trunk. The end of the trunk should swing close to the ground. Walk in a slow, deliberate, dignified manner, keeping the legs straight and swinging the trunk from side to side (Figure 20.12). Stop and throw water over the back with the trunk. Recite the following verse while walking, and move the trunk appropriately.

The elephant's walk is steady and slow,
His trunk like a pendulum swings to and fro.
But when there are children with peanuts around
He swings it up and he swings it down.

Figure 20.12 Elephant Walk

Variation: With a partner, decide who will be the mahout (the elephant keeper) and who will be the elephant. The mahout walks to the side and a little in front of the elephant, with one hand touching the elephant's shoulder. Lead the elephant around during the first two lines of the poem, and then during the last two lines release the touch, walk to a spot in front of the elephant, and toss the elephant a peanut when the trunk is swept up. Return to the elephant's side and repeat the action.

Siamese Twin Walk

Stand back to back with a partner. Lock elbows (Figure 20.13). Walk forward, backward, and sideward in unison.

Tightrope Walk

Select a line, board, or chalked line on the floor as the high wire. Pretend to be on the high wire and do various tasks with exaggerated loss and control of balance. Add tasks such as jumping rope, juggling balls, and riding a bicycle. Pretend to hold a parasol or a balancing pole while performing.

Children should give good play to the imagination. The teacher can set the stage by discussing what a circus performer on the high wire might do.

Lame Dog Walk

Walk on both hands and one foot. Hold the other foot in the air as if injured. Walk a distance and

Figure 20.13 Siamese Twin Walk

change feet. The eyes should look forward. Move backward also and in other combinations. Try to move with an injured front leg.

Crab Walk

Squat down and reach back, putting both hands on the floor without sitting down. With head, neck, and body level, walk forward, backward, and sideward (Figure 20.14).

Children have a tendency to lower the hips. The teacher should emphasize that the body is kept in a straight line.

Variations:

1. As each step is taken with one hand, slap the chest or seat with the other.

2. Move the hand and foot on the same side simultaneously.

3. Try balancing on one leg and the opposite hand for 5 seconds.

Tumbling and Inverted Balances

Rolling Log

Lie on the back with arms stretched overhead (Figure 20.15). Roll sideways the length of the

Figure 20.14   Crab Walk

Figure 20.15   Rolling Log

mat. The next time, roll with the hands pointed toward the other side of the mat. To roll in a straight line, keep the feet slightly apart.

Variation: Alternately curl and stretch while rolling.

Side Roll

Start on the hands and knees, with one side toward the direction of the roll. Drop the shoulder, tuck both the elbow and the knee under, and roll over completely, returning to the hands-and-knees position. Momentum is needed to return to the origi-

nal position. Practice rolling back and forth from one hand-and-knee position to another.

Forward Roll

Stand facing forward, with the feet apart. Squat and place the hands on the mat, shoulder width apart, with elbows against the insides of the thighs. Tuck the chin to the chest and make a rounded back. A push-off with the hands and feet provides the force for the roll (Figure 20.16). Carry the weight on the hands, with the elbows bearing the weight of the thighs. If the elbows are kept against the thighs and the weight is assumed there, the force of the roll is transferred easily to the rounded back. Try to roll forward to the feet. Later, try with the knees together and no weight on the elbows.

Spotting: The spotter should kneel alongside the child and place one hand on the back of the child's head and the other under the thigh (Figure 20.17). As the child moves through the roll, give an upward lift on the back of the neck to assure the neck does not absorb the weight of the body. This technique should be used for all forward roll variations.

Back Roller

Begin in a crouched position with knees together and hands resting lightly on the floor. Roll backward, securing momentum by bringing the knees to the chest and clasping them with the arms (Figure 20.18). Roll back and forth rhythmically. On the backward movement, go well back on the neck and head. Try to roll forward to original position. If you have difficulty rolling back to original position, cross the legs and roll to a crossed-leg standing position. (This stunt is a lead-up to the Backward Roll.)

Forward Roll (Straddle Position)

Start with the legs spread in the straddle position. Bend forward at the hips, tuck the head, place the

Figure 20.16   Forward Roll

Figure 20.17 Spotting the Forward Roll (One hand is on the back of the head and one is under the thigh.)

Figure 20.18 Back Roller

hands on the mat, and roll forward. A strong push with the hands at the end of the roll is necessary to return to the standing position.

Forward Roll Practice

Review the Forward Roll (tucked), with spotting and assistance as necessary. Work on coming out of the roll to the feet. Grasping the knees at the end of the roll will help.

Variations:

1. Roll to the feet with ankles crossed.
2. Try to roll with knees together.

Backward Curl

Approach this activity in three stages. For the first stage, begin in a sitting position, with the knees drawn up to the chest and the chin tucked. The hands are clasped and placed behind the head with the elbows held out as far as possible. Gently roll backward until the weight is on the elbows (Figure 20.19). Roll back to starting position.

In stage two, perform the same action as before, but place the hands alongside the head on the mat while rolling back. The fingers are pointed in the direction of the roll, with palms down on the mat. (A good cue is, "Point your thumbs toward your ears and keep your elbows close to your body.")

For stage three, perform the same action as in stage two, but start in a crouched position on the feet with the back facing the direction of the roll. Momentum is secured by sitting down quickly and bringing the knees to the chest. This, like the Back Roller, is a lead-up to the Backward Roll. Teach children to push against the floor to take pressure off the back of the neck.

Backward Roll (Handclasp Position)

Clasp the fingers behind the neck, with elbows held out to the sides (Figure 20.20). From a crouched position, sit down rapidly, bringing the knees to the chest for a tuck to secure momentum. Roll completely over backward, taking much of the weight

Figure 20.19 Backward Curl (handclasp position)

Figure 20.20 Handclasp Position

Figure 20.21 Backward Roll

on the forearms (Figure 20.21). With this method, the neck is protected.

Spotting: Spotting is not necessary for this lead-up activity. Youngsters can have early success in learning the backward roll by using this approach. Children should be reminded to keep their elbows back and out to the sides to ensure maximum support and minimal neck pressure. This is a lead-up activity to the regular backward roll. If youngsters cannot roll over, allow them to practice rocking back and forth with the elbows out. In *no* case should force be applied to the hips by another individual in an attempt to force the child over.

Climb-Up

Begin on a mat in a kneeling position, with hands placed about shoulder width apart and the fingers spread and pointed forward. Place the head forward of the hands, so that the head and hands form a triangle on the mat. Walk the body weight forward so that most of it rests on the hands and head. Climb the knees to the top of the elbows. (This stunt is a lead-up to the Headstand.)

Spotting: In the Climb-Up as well as in the Three-Point Tip-Up, overweight or weak children may need spotting. This is done by placing one hand on

the child's shoulder and the other on the back of the thigh.

Variation: Raise the knees off the elbows.

Three-Point Tip-Up

Squat down on the mat, placing the hands flat with fingers pointing forward. The elbows should be inside and pressed against the inner part of the lower thighs. Lean forward, slowly transferring the body weight to the bent elbows and hands until the forehead touches the mat (Figure 20.22). Return to starting position.

The Three-Point Tip-Up ends in the same general position as the Climb-Up, but with the elbows on the inside of the thighs. Some children may have better success by turning the fingers in slightly, thus causing the elbows to point outward more and offering better support at the thigh contact point. This stunt is a lead-up to the Headstand and the Handstand done at later levels.

Spotting: Same as the Climb-Up.

Variation: Tuck the head and do a Forward Roll as an alternative finishing act.

Mountain Climber

This activity is similar to the exercise known as the Treadmill. The weight is taken on the hands with one foot forward and one foot extended back, similar to a sprinter's start. When ready, the performer switches foot position with both feet moving simultaneously. This activity is a lead-up to the Handstand and teaches children to support the body weight briefly with the arms.

Switcheroo

This Handstand lead-up activity begins in the front lunge position with the arms overhead. In one continuous movement, bend forward at the hips, place the hands on the mat, and invert the legs over the head. Scissor the legs in the air, and then reverse the position of the feet on the mat. Repeat in a smooth and continuous motion.

Figure 20.22 Three-Point Tip-Up

Balance Stunts

One-Leg Balance

Lift one leg from the floor. Later, bring the knee up. The arms should be free at first and then assume specified positions: folded across the chest, on the hips, on the head, or behind the back.

Double-Knee Balance

Kneel on both knees, with the feet pointed to the rear. Lift the feet from the ground and balance on the knees. Vary the position of the arms. Experiment with different arm positions.

Head Touch

On a mat, kneel on both knees, with feet pointed backward and arms outstretched backward for balance. Lean forward slowly and touch the forehead to the mat. Recover to position (Figure 20.23). Vary the arm position.

Head Balance

Place a beanbag, block, or book on the head (Figure 20.24). Walk, stoop, turn around, sit down, get up, and so on. The object should be balanced so that the upper body is in good posture. Keep the hands out to the sides for balance. Later, vary the position of the arms—folded across the chest or placed behind the back or down the sides. Link together a series of movements.

One-Leg Balance Stunts

Each of the following stands should be done with different arm positions, starting with the arms out to the sides and then folded across the chest. Have children devise other arm positions.

Each stunt can be held first for 3 seconds and then for 5 seconds. Later, the eyes can be closed during the count. The child should recover to original position without loss of balance or excessive movement. Stunts should be repeated, using the other leg.

Figure 20.23 Head Touch

Figure 20.24 Head Balance

1. *Kimbo Stand.* With the left foot kept flat on the ground, cross the right leg over the left to a position in which the right foot is pointed partially down and the toe is touching the ground.
2. *Knee-Lift Stand.* From a standing position, lift one knee up so that the thigh is parallel to the ground and the toe is pointed down. Hold. Return to starting position.
3. *Stork Stand.* From a standing position, shift all of the weight to one foot. Place the other foot so that the sole is against the inside of the knee and thigh of the standing leg (Figure 20.25). Hold. Recover to standing position.

Balance Touch

Place an object (eraser, block, or beanbag) a yard away from a line. Balancing on one foot, reach out with the other foot, touch the object (no weight should be placed on it) (Figure 20.26), and recover to the starting position. Reach sideward, backward.

Variation: Try placing the object at various distances. On a gymnasium floor, count the number of boards to establish the distance for the touch.

Single-Leg Balances

1. *Forward Balance.* Extend one leg backward until it is parallel to the floor. Keeping the eyes

Figure 20.25 Stork Stand

Figure 20.26 Balance Touch

forward and the arms out to the sides, bend forward, balancing on the other leg (Figure 20.27). Hold for 5 seconds without moving. Reverse legs. (This is also called a Forward Scale.)

2. *Backward Balance.* With knee straight, extend one leg forward, with toes pointed. Keep the

Figure 20.27 Forward Balance

arms out to the sides for balance. Lean back as far as possible. The bend should be far enough back so that the eyes are looking at the ceiling.

3. *Side Balance.* Stand on the left foot with enough side bend to the left so that the right (top) side of the body is parallel to the floor. Put the right arm alongside the head and in line with the rest of the body. Reverse, using the right leg for support. (Support may be needed momentarily to get into position.)

Hand-and-Knee Balance

Get down on all fours, taking the weight on the hands, knees, and feet, with toes pointed backward. Lift one hand and the opposite knee (Figure 20.28). Keep the free foot and hand from touching during the hold. Reverse hand and knee positions.

Figure 20.28 Hand-and-Knee Balance

STUNTS AND TUMBLING: DEVELOPING BODY MANAGEMENT SKILLS WITHOUT APPARATUS ━━━━ **501**

Single-Knee Balance

Perform the same action as in the previous stunt, but balance on one knee (and leg), with both arms outstretched to the sides (Figure 20.29). Use the other knee.

Individual Stunts

Directional Walk

For a left movement, begin in standing position. Do all of the following simultaneously: Take a step to the left, raise the left arm and point left, turn the head to the left, and state crisply "Left." Close with the right foot back to standing position. Take several steps left and then reverse.

The Directional Walk is designed to aid in establishing right-left concepts. Definite and forceful simultaneous movements of the arm, head (turn), and leg (step) coupled with a crisp enunciation of the direction are the ingredients of this stunt.

Line Walking

Use a line on the floor, a chalked line, or a board. Walk forward and backward on the line as follows. First, take regular steps. Next, try follow steps—the front foot moving forward and the back foot moving up. The same foot always leads. Then do heel-and-toe steps, bringing the back toe up against the front heel on each step. Finally, hop along the line on one foot. Change to the other foot. The eyes should be focused ahead.

Fluttering Leaf

Keeping the feet in place and the body relaxed, flutter to the ground slowly, just as a leaf would do

Figure 20.29 Single-Knee Balance

in autumn. Swing the arms back and forth loosely to accentuate the fluttering.

Elevator

With the arms out level at the sides, pretend to be an elevator going down. Lower the body a little at a time by bending the knees, but keep the upper body erect and the eyes forward. Return to position. Add a body twist to the downward movement. (A drum can be used.)

Cross-Legged Stand

Sit with the legs crossed and the body bent partially forward. Respond appropriately to these six commands.

"Touch the right foot with the right hand."

"Touch the left foot with the right hand."

"Touch the right foot with the left hand."

"Touch the left foot with the left hand."

"Touch both feet with the hands."

"Touch the feet with crossed hands."

The commands should be given in varied sequences. The child must interpret that his right foot is on the left side, and vice versa. If this seems too difficult, have children start with the feet in normal position (uncrossed).

Variation: Do the stunt with a partner, one child giving the commands and the other responding as directed.

Walking in Place

Pretend to walk vigorously by using the same movements as in walking but without making any progress. This is done by sliding the feet back and forth. Exaggerated arm movement should be made. (Children can gain or lose a little ground. Two children can walk alongside each other, with first one and then the other going ahead.)

Jump Turns

Do jump turns (use quarter turns and half turns) right and left, as directed. The arms should be kept outstretched to the sides. Land lightly without a second movement.

Jump turns reinforce directional concepts. Number concepts can also be developed with jump turns. The teacher calls out the number as a preparatory command and then says, "Move." Number signals are: "One" for a left quarter turn, "Two" for a right quarter turn, "Three" for a left half turn, and "Four" for a right half turn. Give children a moment after the number is called and before the "Move" command.

Rubber Band

Get down in a squat position with the hands and arms clasped around the knees. On the command "Stretch, stretch, stretch," stretch as tall and as wide as possible. On the command "Snap," snap back to original position.

Variation: Pumping Up the Balloon. One child, the pumper, is in front of the other children, who are the balloons. The pumper pretends to use a bicycle pump to inflate the balloons. The balloons get larger and larger until the pumper shouts, "Bang," whereupon the balloons collapse to the floor. The pumper should give a "shoosh" sound every time a pumping motion is made.

Rising Sun

Lie on the back. Using the arms for balance only, rise to a standing position.

Variation: Fold the arms over the chest. Experiment with different positions of the feet. The feet can be crossed, spread wide, both to one side, and so on.

Heel Click

Stand with the feet slightly apart, jump up, and click the heels, coming down with the feet apart (Figure 20.30). Try with a quarter turn right and left.

Variations:

1. Clap the hands overhead as the heels are clicked.
2. Join hands with one or more children. Count, "One, two, THREE," jumping on the third count.

Figure 20.30 Heel Click

3. Begin with a cross-step to the side, then click the heels. Try both right and left.
4. Try to click the heels twice before landing. Land with the feet apart.

Lowering the Boom

Start in push-up (front-leaning rest) position. Lower the body slowly to the floor. The movement should be controlled so that the body remains rigid.

Variations:

1. Pause halfway down.
2. Go down in stages, inch by inch. (Be sure that children understand the concept of an inch as a measure of distance.)
3. Go down slowly to the accompaniment of noise simulating air escaping from a punctured tire. Try representing a blowout, initiated by an appropriate noise.
4. Go down in stages by alternating lowering movements of the right and left arms.
5. Vary the stunt with different hand-base positions, such as fingers pointed in, thumbs touching, and others.

Turn-Over

From a front-leaning rest position, turn over so that the back is to the floor. The body should not touch the floor. Continue the turn until the original position is reassumed. Reverse the direction. Turn back and forth several times. The body should be kept as rigid as possible throughout the turn.

Thread the Needle

Touch the fingertips together in front of the body. Step through with one foot at a time while keeping the tips in contact (Figure 20.31). Step back to the original position. Next, lock the fingers in front of the body, and repeat the stunt. Finally, step through the clasped hands without touching the hands.

Heel Slap

From an erect position with hands at the sides, jump upward and slap both heels with the hands (Figure 20.32).

Variation: Use a one-two-three rhythm with small preliminary jumps on the first and second counts. Make a quarter or half turn in the air. During a jump, slap the heels twice before landing.

Figure 20.31 Thread the Needle

Figure 20.32 Heel Slap

Pogo Stick

Pretend to be on a pogo stick by keeping a stiff body and jumping on the toes. Hold the hands in front as if grasping the stick (Figure 20.33). Progress in various directions. (The teacher should stress upward propelling action by the ankles and toes, with the body kept stiff, particularly at the knee joints.)

Figure 20.33 Pogo Stick

Top

From a standing position with arms at the sides, try jumping and turning to face the opposite direction, turning three-quarters of the way around, or making a full turn to face the original direction. Land in good balance with hands near the sides. No movement of the feet should occur after landing. Turn both right and left. (Number concepts can be stressed in having children do half turns, three-quarter turns, and full turns.)

Variation: Fold the arms across the chest.

Turk Stand

Stand with feet apart and arms folded in front. Pivot on the balls of both feet, and face the opposite direction. The legs are now crossed. Sit down in this position. Reverse the process. Get up without using the hands for aid, and uncross the legs with a pivot to face in the original direction. Little change should occur in foot position (Figure 20.34).

Push-Up

From a front-leaning rest position, lower the body and push up, back to original position. Be sure that

Figure 20.34 Turk Stand

the only movement is in the arms, with the body kept rigid. (Because the Push-Up is used in many exercises and testing programs, it is important for children to learn proper execution early.)

Variation: Stop halfway down and halfway up. Go up and down by inches.

Crazy Walk

Progress forward in an erect position by bringing one foot behind and around the other to gain a little ground each time (Figure 20.35). (The teacher can set a specified distance and see which children cover the distance in the fewest steps.)

Figure 20.35 Crazy Walk

Variation: Reverse the movements and go backward. This means bringing the foot in front and around to gain distance in back.

Seat Circle

Sit on the floor, with knees bent and hands braced behind. Lift the feet off the floor and push with the hands, so that the body spins in a circle with the seat as a pivot (Figure 20.36). Spin right and left.

Variation: Place a beanbag between the knees or on the toes and spin without dropping it.

Partner and Group Stunts

Bouncing Ball

Toss a lively utility ball into the air and watch how it bounces lower and lower until it finally comes to rest on the floor. From a bent-knee position with the upper body erect, imitate the ball by beginning with a high bounce and gradually lowering the height of the jump to simulate the ball coming to rest. Children should push off from the floor with the hands to gain additional height and should absorb part of the body weight with their hands as well. Toss a real ball into the air and move with the ball.

Variations: Try this with a partner, one partner serving as the bouncer and the other as the ball (Figure 20.37). Reverse positions. Try having one partner dribble the ball in various positions.

Seesaw

Face and join hands with a partner. Move the seesaw up and down, one child stooping while the

Figure 20.36 Seat Circle

Figure 20.37   Bouncing Ball

Figure 20.38   Wring the Dishrag

other rises. Recite the words to this version of "Seesaw, Margery Daw."

Seesaw, Margery Daw,
Maw and Paw, like a saw,
Seesaw, Margery Daw.

Variation: Jump upward at the end of the rise each time.

Wring the Dishrag

Face and join hands with a partner. Raise one pair of arms (right for one and left for the other) and turn under, continuing a full turn until back to original position (Figure 20.38). Take care not to bump heads. Reverse.

Variation: Try the stunt at a lower level, using a crouched position.

Partner Toe Toucher

Partners lie on their backs with heads near each other and feet in opposite directions. Join arms with partner using a hand-wrist grip, and bring the legs up so that the toes touch partner's toes. Keep high on the shoulders and touch the feet high

Figure 20.39   Partner Toe Toucher

(Figure 20.39). Strive to attain the high shoulder position, as this is the point of most difficulty. (Partners should be of about the same height.)

Variation: One child carries a beanbag, a ball, or some other article between the feet, and transfers the object to the partner, who lowers it to the floor.

Figure 20.40 Double Top

Double Top

Face partner and join hands. Experiment to see which type of grip works best. With straight arms, lean away from each other and at the same time move the toes close to partner's (Figure 20.40). Spin around slowly in either direction, taking tiny steps. Increase speed.

Variations:

1. Use a stooped position.
2. Instead of holding hands, hold a wand and increase the body lean backward. Try the stunt standing right side to right side.

Roly Poly

Review the Rolling Log. Four or five children lie facedown on the floor, side by side. The last child does a Rolling Log over the others and then takes a place at the end. Continue until all have rolled twice.

DEVELOPMENTAL LEVEL II ACTIVITIES

In developmental level II, more emphasis is placed on form and quality of performance than at the previous level. Stunts such as the Frog Handstand,

Mule Kick, Teeter-Totter, and Handstand give children experience in taking the weight totally on the hands. Partner support stunts are introduced. Flops or falls are another addition.

Animal Movements

Cricket Walk

Squat. Spread the knees. Put the arms between the knees and grasp the outside of the ankles with the hands. Walk forward or backward. Chirp like a cricket. Turn around right and left. See what happens when both feet are moved at once!

Frog Jump

From a squatting position, with hands on the floor slightly in front of the feet, jump forward a short distance, landing on the hands and feet simultaneously (Figure 20.41). Note the difference between this stunt and the Rabbit Jump. Emphasis eventually should be on both height and distance. The hands and arms absorb part of the landing impact to prevent excessive strain on the knees.

Seal Crawl

Start in the front-leaning rest position, the weight supported on straightened arms and toes. Keeping the body straight, walk forward, using the hands for propelling force and dragging the feet (Figure 20.42). Keep the body straight and the head up.

Variations:

1. Crawl forward a short distance and then roll over on the back, clapping the hands like a seal, with appropriate seal barks.
2. Crawl with the fingers pointed in different directions, out and in.
3. *Reverse Seal Crawl.* Turn over and attempt the crawl, dragging the heels.

Figure 20.41 Frog Jump

Figure 20.42   Seal Crawl

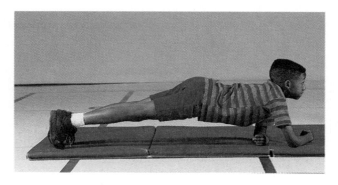

Figure 20.43   Elbow Crawl

4. *Elbow Crawl.* Assume the original position but with weight on the elbows. Crawl forward on the elbows (Figure 20.43).
5. Use the crossed-arm position for a more challenging stunt.

Measuring Worm

From a front-leaning rest position, keeping the knees stiff, inch the feet up as close as possible to the hands. Regain position by inching forward with the hands. Keep the knees straight, with the necessary bending occurring at the hips (Figure 20.44).

Figure 20.44   Measuring Worm

Mule Kick

Stoop down and place the hands on the floor in front of the feet. The arms are the front legs of the mule. Kick out with the legs while the weight is supported momentarily on the arms (Figure 20.45). Taking the weight on the hands is important. The stunt can be learned in two stages. First, practice taking the weight momentarily on the hands. Next, add the kick.

Variation: Make two kicks before the feet return to the ground.

Walrus Walk

Begin in a front-leaning rest position, with fingers pointed outward. Make progress by moving both hands forward at the same time (Figure 20.46). Try to clap the hands with each step. (Before doing this stunt, review the similar Seal Crawl [p. 507] and its variations.)

Variation: Move sideways so that the upper part of the body describes an arc while the feet hold position.

Double-Lame Dog

Support the body on one hand and one leg (Figure 20.47). Move forward in this position, maintaining balance. The distance should be short (5 to 10 feet), as this stunt is strenuous. Different leg-arm combinations should be employed such as cross-lateral movements (right arm with left leg and left arm with right leg).

Variation: Keep the free arm on the hip.

Turtle

Hold the body in a wide push-up position with the feet apart and the hands widely spread (Figure 20.48). From this position, move in various directions, keeping the plane of the body always about the same distance from the floor. Movements of the hands and feet should occur in small increments only.

Walrus Slap

From the front-leaning rest position, push the body up in the air quickly by force of the arms, clap the hands together, and recover to position. Before doing this stunt, review the Seal Crawl (p. 507) and the Walrus Walk (above).

Figure 20.45 Mule Kick

Figure 20.46 Walrus Walk

Figure 20.48 Turtle

should be attempted only by the more skilled. Work on a mat.

Tumbling and Inverted Balances

Forward Roll to a Walkout

Perform the Forward Roll as described previously, except walk out to a standing position. The key to the Walkout is to develop enough momentum to allow a return to the feet. The leg that first absorbs the weight is bent while the other leg is kept straight.

Spotting: Same as the Forward Roll; see p. 497.

Backward Roll (Regular)

In the same squat position as for the Forward Roll, but with the back to the direction of the roll, push off quickly with the hands, sit down, and start rolling over onto the back. The knees are brought to the chest, so that the body is tucked and momentum is increased. Quickly bring the hands up over the shoulders, with palms up and fingers pointed backward. Continue rolling backward with knees close to the chest. The hands touch the mat

Figure 20.47 Double-Lame Dog

Variations:

1. Try clapping the hands more than once.
2. Move forward while clapping the hands.
3. *Reverse Walrus Slap.* Turn over and do a Walrus Walk while facing the ceiling. Clapping the hands is quite difficult in this position and

at about the same time as the head. It is necessary at this point to push hard with the hands to release pressure on the neck. Continue to roll over and to push off the mat until the roll is completed (Figure 20.49). Emphasize proper hand position by telling children to point their thumbs toward their ears and spread their fingers for better push-off control.

Spotting: In spotting, care must be taken never to push a child from the hip, thus forcing the roll. This puts undue pressure on the back of the neck. The proper way to aid the child who has difficulty with the stunt is as follows: The spotter stands in a straddle position, with the near foot alongside the spot where the performer's hands and head will make contact with the mat (Figure 20.50). The

Figure 20.49 Regular Backward Roll

Figure 20.50 Spotting the Backward Roll (The lift is at the hips of the roller. The performer should be lifted, not forced, over.)

other foot is one stride in the direction of the roll. The critical point is for the spotter to lift the hips just as the head and hands of the performer make contact with the mat. This is accomplished by taking the back hand and reaching across to the far hip of the performer, getting under the other hip with the near hand. The lift is applied on the front of the hips just below the beltline. The object is to relieve the pressure on the neck.

Rather than spotting the youngster who is having trouble doing the Backward Roll, it may be wise to substitute the Handclasp Backward Roll (p. 498) and practice on an inclined mat (see the following activity).

Backward Roll (Inclined)

If possible, the Handclasp Backward Roll should be practiced on an inclined mat. The gentle incline allows the youngster to learn to develop momentum in a nonthreatening manner. An inclined mat can be made by leaving one mat folded and laying a crash pad or another mat over it.

Headstand

Two approaches are suggested for the Headstand. The first is to relate the Headstand to the Climb-Up, and the second is to go directly into a Headstand, using a kick-up to achieve the inverted position. With either method, maintaining the triangle position of the hands and the head is essential.

In the final inverted position, the feet should be together, with legs straight and toes pointed. The weight is evenly distributed among the three points—the two hands and the forward part of the head. The body should be aligned as straight as possible.

The safest way to come down from the inverted position is to return to the mat in the direction that was used in going up. Recovery is helped by bending at both the waist and the knees. The child should be instructed, in the case of overbalancing, to tuck the head under and go into a Forward Roll. Both methods of recovery from the inverted position should be included in the instructional sequences early in the presentation.

Headstand Climb-Up

Take the inverted position of the Climb-Up (p. 499) and move the feet slowly upward to the headstand position (Figure 20.51), steadied by a spotter only as needed.

Spotting: The spotter is stationed directly in front of the performer and steadies as needed. The

Figure 20.51 Headstand based on the Climb-Up

spotter can first apply support to the hips and then transfer to the ankles as the climb-up position is lengthened into a Headstand. If unable to control the performer, the spotter must be alert to moving out of the way when the performer goes into a Forward Roll to come out of the inverted position.

Headstand Kick-Up

Keeping the weight on the forward part of the head and maintaining the triangle base, walk the feet forward until the hips are high over the body, somewhat similar to the Climb-Up position. Keep one foot on the mat, with the knee of that leg bent, and the other leg extended somewhat backward. Kick the back leg up to the inverted position, following quickly with a push by the other leg, thus bringing the two legs together in the inverted position (Figure 20.52). The timing is a quick one-two movement.

The teacher should emphasize the importance of the triangle formed by the hands and the head and the importance of having the weight centered on the forward part of the head. Most problems that occur during performance of the Headstand come from an incorrect head–hand relationship. The correct positioning has the head placed the length of the performer's forearm from the knees and the hands placed at the knees. A useful technique to aid children in finding the proper triangle is to mark the three spots on the mat with chalk. (More lasting spots can be made with paint.)

Spotting: When learning, youngsters can attempt the stunt with a spotter on each side. Each spotter kneels, placing the near hand under the shoulder of the performer. The performer then walks the weight above the head and kicks up to position. The spotter on each side supports by grasping a leg (Figure 20.53).

It is not desirable to let children stay too long in the inverted position or to hold contests to see who can remain in the Headstand longest. Most of the responsibility for getting into the inverted position should rest with the performer. Spotters may help some, but they should avoid wrestling the performer up. The goal of the kick-up method is to establish a pattern that can be used in other inverted stunts.

Frog Handstand (Tip-Up)

Squat down on the mat, placing the hands flat, with fingers pointing forward and elbows inside and pressed against the inner part of the knees. Lean forward, using the leverage of the elbows against the knees, and balance on the hands (Figure 20.54). Hold for 5 seconds. Return to position. The head does not touch the mat at any time. The hands may be turned in slightly if this makes better

Figure 20.52 Headstand based on the Kick-Up

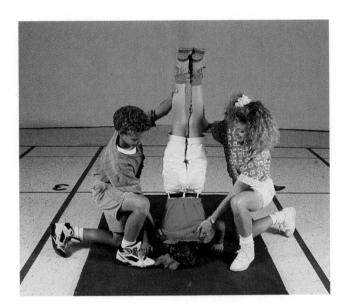

Figure 20.53 Spotting the Headstand

STUNTS AND TUMBLING: DEVELOPING BODY MANAGEMENT SKILLS WITHOUT APPARATUS ━━━━━ **511**

Figure 20.54 Frog Handstand

contact between the elbows and the insides of the thighs. (This stunt follows from the Three-Point Tip-Up.)

Half Teeter-Totter

This is continued lead-up activity for the Handstand. Begin in the lunge position and shift the weight to the hands. Kick the legs up in the air to a 135-degree angle, then return to the feet. This activity is similar to the Switcheroo, except that the feet are kicked higher without switching foot position.

Cartwheel

Start with the body in an erect position, arms outspread and legs shoulder width apart. Bend the body to the right and place the right hand on the floor. Follow this, in sequence, by the left hand, the left foot, and the right foot (Figure 20.55). Perform with a steady rhythm. Each body part should touch the floor at evenly spaced intervals. The body should be straight and extended when in the in-

Figure 20.55 Cartwheel

verted position. The entire body must be in the same plane throughout the stunt, and the feet must pass directly overhead.

Children who have difficulty with the Cartwheel should be instructed to concentrate on taking the weight of the body on the hands in succession. They need to get the feel of the weight support and later can concentrate on getting the body into proper position. After the class has had some practice in doing Cartwheels, a running approach with a skip can be added before takeoff.

Spotting: In spotting, the spotter stands behind and moves with the performer. To assist, the spotter assumes a crossed-arm position and grasps the performer at the waist. The spotter's arms uncross as the performer wheels.

Forward Roll (Pike Position)

Begin the piked Forward Roll in a standing pike position. Keep the legs straight and bend forward at the hips. Place the hands on the mat, bend the elbows, and lower the head to the mat. Keep the legs straight until nearing the end of the roll. Bend at the knees to facilitate returning to the feet.

Forward Roll Combinations

Review the Forward Roll, with increased emphasis on proper form. Combinations such as the following can be introduced.

1. Do a Forward Roll preceded by a short run.
2. Do two Forward Rolls in succession.
3. Do a Leapfrog (p. 521) plus a Forward Roll.
4. Do a Forward Roll to a vertical jump in the air, and repeat.
5. Do a Rabbit Jump plus a Forward Roll.
6. Hold the toes while doing a Forward Roll.

Backward Roll Combinations

Review the Backward Roll. Continue emphasis on the Push-Off with the hands. Combinations to be taught are these:

1. Do a Backward Roll to a standing position. A strong push by the hands is necessary to provide enough momentum to land on the feet.
2. Do two Backward Rolls in succession.
3. Do a Crab Walk into a Backward Roll.
4. Add a jump in the air at the completion of a Backward Roll.

Headstand Practice and Variations

Continue work on the Headstand. Try the following variations. (Spot as needed.)

Variations:

1. Clap the hands and recover. The weight must be shifted momentarily to the head for the clap. (Some children will be able to clap the hands twice before recovery.)

2. Use different leg positions (Figure 20.56)—legs split sideward, legs split forward and backward, and knees bent.

3. Holding a utility ball or a beanbag between the legs, go into the Headstand, retaining control of the ball.

Teeter-Totter

The Teeter-Totter is the final lead-up activity for the Handstand. It is performed in a manner similar to the Half Teeter-Totter, except that the feet are held together for a moment in the handstand position before returning to the standing position.

Handstand

Start in the lunge position. Do a Teeter-Totter to the inverted position. The body, which is extended in a line from the shoulders through the feet, should be kept straight with the head down. It is helpful to teach the correct position first in a standing position with the arms overhead and the ears between the arms.

Spotting: The Handstand can be done with double or single spotting. In double spotting, the spotters are stationed on both sides of the performer. Each spotter should have a firm grip with one hand beneath the performer's shoulder. The other hand can assist the lift by upward pressure on the thigh (Figure 20.57). The performer walks the hips forward until they are over the hands and then kicks up with one foot, pushing off with the other and raising that leg to join the first in the inverted position (Figure 20.58). The rhythm is a one-two count.

In single spotting, the spotter takes a stride position, with the forward knee bent somewhat (Figure 20.59). The performer's weight is transferred over the hands, and the body goes into the handstand position with a one-two kick-up. The spotter catches the legs and holds the performer in an inverted position (Figure 20.60).

Figure 20.56 Headstand Variation

Figure 20.57 Double spotting for the Handstand, first stage (Note the hand support under the shoulders.)

Figure 20.58 Double spotting for the Handstand, second stage

Figure 20.60 Single spotting for the Handstand, second stage (Note knee pressure against performer's shoulder.)

Figure 20.59 Single spotting for the Handstand, first stage (The performer's shoulder is against the spotter's leg.)

Balance Stunts

One-Leg Balance Reverse

Assume a forward balance position (p. 500). In a quick movement, to give momentum, swing the free leg down and change to the same forward balance position facing in the opposite direction (a 180-degree turn) (Figure 20.61). No unnecessary movement of the supporting foot should be made after the turn is completed. The swinging foot should not touch the floor.

Tummy Balance

Lie prone on the floor with arms outstretched forward or to the sides, with palms down. Raise the arms, head, chest, and legs from the floor and

Figure 20.61 One-Leg Balance Reverse

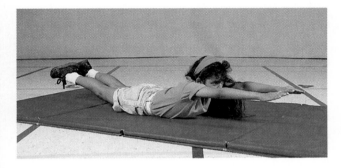

Figure 20.62 Tummy Balance

Figure 20.63 Balance Jump, starting position

Figure 20.64 Balance Jump

balance on the tummy (Figure 20.62). The knees should be kept straight.

Leg Dip

Extend both hands and one leg forward, balancing on the other leg. Lower the body to sit on the heel and return without losing the balance or touching the floor with any part of the body. Try with the other foot. (Another child can assist from the back by applying upward pressure to the elbows.)

Balance Jump

With hands and arms out to the sides and body parallel to the ground, extend one leg back and balance the weight on the other leg (Figure 20.63). Quickly change balance to the other foot, maintaining the initial position but with the feet exchanged (Figure 20.64). Keep the body parallel to the ground during the change of legs. Try with arms outstretched forward. Working in pairs might be helpful. One student critiques the other's performance to make sure that the arms and body are straight and parallel to the floor.

Seat Balance

Sit on the floor, holding the ankles in front, with elbows inside the knees. The feet are flat on the floor, and the knees are bent at approximately a right angle. Raise the legs (toes pointed) so that the knees are straight (Figure 20.65), and balance on the seat for 5 seconds.

Face-to-Knee Touch

Begin in a standing position with feet together. Placing the hands on the hips, balance on one foot, with the other leg extended backward. Bend the trunk forward and touch the knee of the supporting leg with the forehead (Figure 20.66). Recover to original position.

Teachers can have children begin by keeping the arms away from the sides for balance and then stipulate the hands-on-hips position later. In the learning stages, assistance can be given from behind by supporting the leg extended backward, or the child can place one hand against a wall.

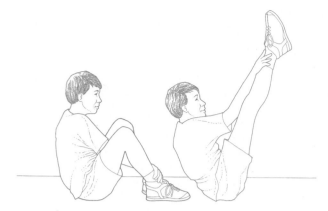

Figure 20.65 Seat Balance

Figure 20.66 Face-to-Knee Touch

Finger Touch

Put the right hand behind the back with the index finger straight and pointed down. Grasp the right wrist with the left hand. From an erect position with the feet about 6 inches apart, squat down and touch the floor with the index finger (Figure 20.67). Regain the erect position without losing balance. Reverse hands. (In the learning stages, the teacher

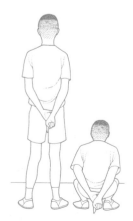

Figure 20.67 Finger Touch

can use a book or the corner of a mat to decrease the distance and make the touch easier.)

Individual Stunts

Reach-Under

Take a position with the feet pointed ahead (spaced about 2 feet apart) and toes against a line or a floor board. Place a beanbag two boards in front of, and midway between, the feet. Without changing the position of the feet, reach one hand behind and between the legs to pick up the beanbag. Now pick up with the other hand. Repeat, moving the beanbag a board farther away each time.

Variation: Allow the heels to lift off the floor. Use the other hand.

Stiff Person Bend

Place the feet about shoulder width apart and pointed forward. Place a beanbag a few inches behind the right heel. Grasp the left toes with the left hand, thumb on top. Without bending the knees, reach the right hand outside the right leg

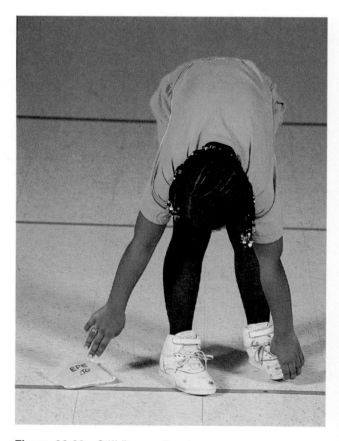

Figure 20.68 Stiff Person Bend

and pick up the beanbag without releasing the hold on the left toes. Gradually increase the distance of the reach. Reverse sides (Figure 20.68).

Coffee Grinder

Put one hand on the floor and extend the body to the floor on that side in a side-leaning rest position. Walk around the hand, making a complete circle and keeping the body straight (Figure 20.69). The stunt should be done slowly, with controlled movements. The body should remain straight throughout the circle movement.

Figure 20.69   Coffee Grinder

Scooter

Sit on the floor with legs extended, arms folded in front of the chest, and chin held high. To scoot, pull the seat toward the heels, using heel pressure and lifting the seat slightly (Figure 20.70). Extend the legs forward again and repeat the process. (This is an excellent activity for abdominal development.)

Hip Walk

Sit in the same position as for the Scooter, but with arms in thrust position and hands making a partial fist. Progress forward by alternate leg-seat movements. The arm-leg coordination is unilateral.

Long Bridge

Begin in a crouched position with hands on the floor and knees between the arms. Push the hands forward a little at a time until an extended push-up position is reached (Figure 20.71). Return to original position. (The teacher should challenge children to extend as far forward as they can and still retain the support.)

Variations:

1. Begin with a forward movement and then change to a sideward movement, establishing as wide a spread as possible.
2. Work from a crossed-hands position.

Heelstand

Begin in a full-squat position with the arms dangling at the sides. Jump upward to full leg extension with the weight on both heels and fling the arms out diagonally. Hold momentarily, then return

Figure 20.70   Scooter

Figure 20.71   Long Bridge

Figure 20.72 Heelstand

to position (Figure 20.72). Several movements can be done rhythmically in succession.

Wicket Walk

Bend over and touch the floor with the weight evenly distributed on the hands and feet, thus forming a wicket. Walk the wicket forward, backward, and sideward. Keep the arms and legs as nearly vertical as possible (Figure 20.73). Be sure that the knees are reasonably straight, for the stunt loses much of its flexibility value if the knees are bent too much. A common error in the execution of this stunt is to keep the hands positioned too far

Figure 20.73 Wicket Walk

forward of the feet. (The stunt gets its name from the child's position, which resembles a wicket in a croquet game.)

Knee Jump to Standing

Kneel, with seat touching the heels and toes pointing backward (shoelaces against the floor). Jump to a standing position with a vigorous upward swing of the arms (Figure 20.74). It is easier to jump from a smooth floor than from a mat, because the toes slide more readily on the floor.

Variation: Jump to a standing position, doing a quarter turn in the air in one quick motion. Try a half turn.

Individual Drops or Falls

Drops, or falls, can challenge children to achieve good body control. Mats should be used. The impact of a forward fall is absorbed by the hands and arms. During the fall, the body should maintain a straight-line position. Make sure that little change in body angles occurs, particularly at the knees and waist.

Knee Drop

Kneel on a mat, with the body upright. Raise the feet up, off the floor, and fall forward, breaking the fall with the hands and arms (Figure 20.75).

Forward Drop

From a forward balance position (p. 500) on one leg with the other leg extended backward and the arms extended forward and up, lean forward slowly, bringing the arms toward the floor. Continue to drop forward slowly until overbalanced, then let the hands and arms break the fall (Figure 20.76). The head is up and the extended leg is raised high,

Figure 20.74 Knee Jump to Standing

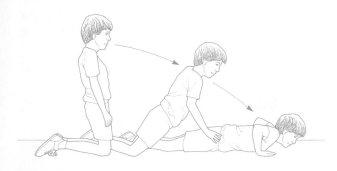

Figure 20.75 Knee Drop

Figure 20.76 Forward Drop

with knee joints kept reasonably straight. Repeat, changing position of the legs.

Dead Body Fall

Fall forward from an erect position to a down push-up position (Figure 20.77). A slight bend at the waist is permissible, but the knees should be kept straight, and there should be no forward movement of the feet.

Stoop and Stretch

Hold a beanbag with both hands. Stand with heels against a line and feet about shoulder width apart.

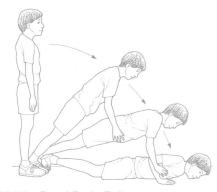

Figure 20.77 Dead Body Fall

Keeping the knees straight, reach between the legs with the beanbag and place it as far back as possible. Reach back and pick it up with both hands.

Variations:

1. Bend at the knees, using more of a squatting position during the reach.
2. Use a piece of chalk instead of a beanbag. Reach back and make a mark on the floor. Try writing a number or drawing a small circle or some other figure.

Tanglefoot

Stand with heels together and toes pointed out. Bend the trunk forward and extend both arms down between the knees and around behind the ankles. Bring the hands around the outside of the ankles from behind and touch the fingers to each other (Figure 20.78). Hold for a 5-second count.

Variation: Instead of touching, clasp the fingers in front of the ankles. Hold this position in good balance for 5 seconds without releasing the handclasp.

Egg Roll

In a sitting position, assume the same clasped-hands position as for Tanglefoot. Roll sideways

Figure 20.78 Tanglefoot

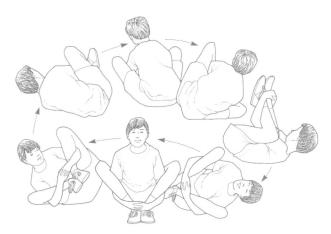

Figure 20.79 Egg Roll

over one shoulder, then to the back, then to the other shoulder, and finally back up to the sitting position (Figure 20.79). The movements are repeated in turn to make a full circle back to place. The secret is a vigorous sideward movement to secure initial momentum. If mats are used, two should be placed side by side to cover the extent of the roll. (Some children can do this stunt better from a crossed-ankle position.)

Toe Touch Nose

From a sitting position on the floor, touch the toes of either foot to the nose with the help of both hands. Do first one foot and then the other. More flexible youngsters will be able to place the foot on top of the head or even behind the neck. Although this is a flexibility exercise, caution should be used; the leg can be forced too far.

Variation: Perform from a standing position. Touch the toes to the nose and return the foot to original position without losing balance. Try the standing version with eyes closed.

Toe Tug Walk

Bend over and grasp the toes with thumbs on top (Figure 20.80). Keep the knees bent slightly and the eyes forward. Walk forward without losing the grip on the toes. Walk backward and sideward to provide more challenge. Walk in various geometric patterns, such as a circle, triangle, or square. (This stunt can be introduced in an easier version by having children grasp the ankles, thumbs on the insides, and perform the desired movements.)

Variation: Try doing the walk with the right hand grasping the left foot, and vice versa.

Figure 20.80 Toe Tug Walk

Partner and Group Stunts

Partner Hopping

Partners coordinate hopping movements for short distances and in different directions and turns. Three combinations are suggested.

1. Stand facing each other. Extend the right leg forward to be grasped at the ankle by partner's left hand. Hold right hands and hop on the left leg (Figure 20.81).
2. Stand back to back. Lift the leg backward, bending the knee, and have partner grasp the ankle. Hop as before.
3. Stand side by side with inside arms around each other's waist. Lift the inside foot from the floor and make progress by hopping on the outside foot.

If either partner begins to fall, the other should release the leg immediately. Reverse foot positions.

Partner Twister

Partners face and grasp right hands as if shaking hands. One partner swings the left leg over the

Figure 20.81 Partner Hopping

Figure 20.82 Partner Twister

head of the other and turns around, taking a straddle position over partner's arm (Figure 20.82). The other swings the right leg over the first partner, who has bent over, and the partners are now back to back. First partner continues with the right leg and faces in the original direction. Second partner swings the left leg over the partner's back to return to the original face-to-face position. Partners need to duck to avoid being kicked by each other's feet as the legs are swung over.

Variation: The stunt can be introduced by grasping a wand instead of holding hands.

Partner Pull-Up

Partners sit facing each other in a bent-knee position, with heels on the floor and toes touching. Pulling cooperatively, they come to a standing position (Figure 20.83).

Variation: Try with feet flat on the floor.

Back-to-Back Get-Up

Partners sit back to back and lock arms. From this position, they try to stand by pushing against each other's back (Figure 20.84). Sit down again. If the feet are sliding, do the stunt on a mat.

Variations:

1. Try with three or four children.
2. Try from a halfway-down position, and move like a spider.

Rowboat

Partners sit on the floor or on a mat, facing each other with legs apart and feet touching. Both grasp a wand with both hands. Pretend to row a boat. Seek a wide range of movement in the forward-backward rowing motion. (The stunt can be done without a wand by having children grasp hands.)

Leapfrog

One student forms a back. A leaper takes a running start, lays hands flat on the back at the shoulders, and vaults over the low student. Backs are formed at various heights (Figure 20.85). To form a low back, crouch down on the knees, curling into a tight ball with the head tucked well down. To form a medium back, reach down the outside of the legs from a standing position and grasp the ankles. The feet should be reasonably spread and the knees straight. The position must be stable in order to absorb the shock of the leaper. To form a high back, stand stiff-legged, bend over, and brace arms against the knees. The feet should be spread, the head down, and the body braced to absorb the vault.

Leapfrog is a traditional physical education activity, but the movement is actually a jump-and-vault pattern. The takeoff must be made with both feet. At the height of the jump, the chest and head must be held erect to avoid a forward fall. The teacher should emphasize a forceful jump to achieve height, coordinated with light hand pressure to vault over the back. Landing should be done lightly and under good control, with a bent-knee action.

Figure 20.83 Partner
Pull-Up

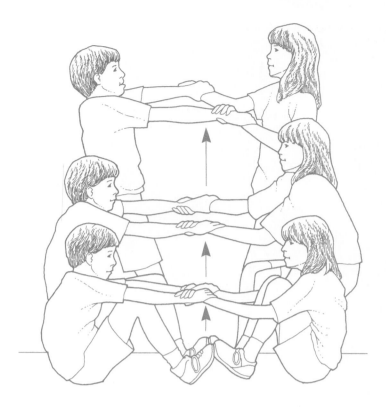

Figure 20.84 Back-to-Back Get-Up

Figure 20.85 High, medium, and low Leapfrog positions

Variations:

1. Work in pairs. Alternate leaping and forming the back while progressing around the room.

2. Have more than one back for a series of jumps.

3. Using the medium back, vault from the side rather than from the front. The vaulter's legs must be well spread, and the back must keep the head well tucked down.

4. Following the Leapfrog, do a Forward Roll on a mat.

Wheelbarrow

One partner gets down on the hands with feet extended to the rear and legs apart. The other partner (the pusher) grasps partner's legs about halfway between the ankles and the knees. The wheelbarrow walks forward on the hands, supported by the pusher (Figure 20.86). Movements should be under good control.

Children have a tendency to grasp the legs too near the feet. The pusher must not push too fast. The wheelbarrow should have the head up and look forward. Fingers should be pointed forward and well spread, with the pads of the fingers supporting much of the weight. The pusher should carry the legs low and keep the arms extended.

Figure 20.86 Wheelbarrow

Wheelbarrow Lifting

Partners assume the wheelbarrow position. The pusher lifts partner's legs as high as possible without changing the hand position. The pusher should be able to lift the legs enough so that the lower child's body is at an angle of about 45 degrees to the floor.

Variation: The pusher brings the legs up to the level described, changes the handgrip to a pushing one, and continues to raise the lower child toward a handstand position. The lower child keeps arms and body straight.

Camel Lift and Walk

In the wheelbarrow position, the wheelbarrow raises the seat as high as possible, forming a camel. Camels can lower themselves or walk in the raised position.

Dump the Wheelbarrow

Get into the wheelbarrow position. Walk the wheelbarrow over to a mat. The lower child ducks the head (chin to waist), raises the seat (bending at the

waist), and exits from the stunt with a Forward Roll. The pusher gives a little push and a lift of the feet to help supply momentum.

Dromedary Walk

One child (the support) gets down on the hands and knees. The other child sits on the support, facing the rear, and fixes the legs around the support's chest. The top child leans forward, to grasp the back of the support's ankles. The top child's arms are reasonably extended (Figure 20.87). The support takes the weight off the knees and walks forward with the top child's help.

Centipede

One child, the stronger and larger individual, gets down on the hands and knees. The other child faces the same direction, places the hands about 2 feet in front of the support's, then places the legs and body on top of the support. The knees should be spread apart and the heels locked together. The centipede walks with the top child using hands only and the supporting child using both hands and feet. The support should gather the legs well under while walking and not be on the knees.

Variation: More than two can do this stunt (Figure 20.88). After getting into position, the players should keep step by calling "Right" and "Left" out loud.

Double Wheelbarrow

Two children assume the same position as for the Centipede, except that the under child has the legs extended to the rear and the feet apart. A third child stands between the legs of the under child, reaches down, and picks up the legs of the lower

Figure 20.87 Dromedary Walk

Figure 20.88   Centipede

Figure 20.89   Double Wheelbarrow

child (Figure 20.89). The Double Wheelbarrow moves forward with right and left arms moving together.

An easy way to get into position for this activity is to form the front of the wheelbarrow first and then to pick up the legs of the second child. This stunt usually is done by three children but can be done by more.

Partner Support Stunts

Several considerations are important in the conducting of partner support stunts at this level. The lower child (the support) should keep the body as level as possible. This means widening the hand base so that the shoulders are more nearly level with the hips. The support performer must be strong enough to handle the support chores. Spotters are needed, particularly when the top position involves a final erect or inverted pose. The top child should avoid stepping on the small of the lower child's back. In the Lighthouse and the Hip-Shoulder Stand, the top performer can remove the shoes, making the standing position more comfortable for the support. When holding the final pose, the top child should fix the gaze forward and relax as much as possible while maintaining the position.

Double Bear

The bottom child gets down on the hands and knees. The top child assumes the same position directly above the support, with hands on the shoulders and knees on the hips of the support (Figure 20.90). Touch up the final position by holding heads up and backs straight.

Table

The bottom performer assumes a crab position. The top performer straddles this base, facing the rear, and positions the hands on the base's shoulders, fingers pointing toward the ground. The top child then places the feet on top of base's knees, forming one crab position on top of another (Figure 20.91). As a final touch, the heads are positioned so that the eyes look up toward the ceiling, and the seats are lifted so that the backs are straight.

Statue

The first child gets down in crab position. The second child straddles either foot, facing the child in crab position. With the help of a third person, the second child mounts each knee of the base child so

Figure 20.90 Double Bear

Figure 20.91 Table

Figure 20.92 Statue

that the statue is standing erect (Figure 20.92). Hold the position for a few seconds. Partners should be facing each other. The top child should not mount with back toward the base child. (Spot-

ters are important and must not be eliminated until the stunt is mastered.)

Lighthouse

The support gets down on the hands and knees. The top child completes the figure by standing on the support's shoulders and facing in the same direction. The lighthouse stands erect with hands out to the sides (Figure 20.93).

Variation: The support turns around in a small circle, while the partner keeps the standing balance.

Hip-Shoulder Stand

The support is on the hands and knees, with hands positioned out somewhat so that the back is level. The top child faces to the side and steps up, first with one foot on support's hips and then with the other on the shoulders (Figure 20.94).

A spotter should stand on the opposite side and aid in the mounting. Care must be taken to avoid stepping on the small of the support's back.

Figure 20.93 Lighthouse

Figure 20.94 Hip-Shoulder Stand

DEVELOPMENTAL LEVEL III ACTIVITIES

Children at this level should be skillful in both the Forward and the Backward Roll. Routines involving these rolls can be expanded. The Judo Roll, Cartwheel with Round-Off, and Double Roll continue the mat-type activities. Improvement in the Headstand is expected. Such stunts as the Headspring, Front Seat Support, Elbow Balance, Straddle Press to Headstand, and Walk-Over provide sufficient breadth for even the most skilled. It is unrealistic to expect all children to accomplish the entire list of stunts at this level.

Particular attention should be paid to the gymnastic-type stunts. Although there is still opportunity at this level for exploration and individual expression, more emphasis is placed on execution, conformity, and form.

Tumbling and Inverted Balances

Forward and Backward Roll Combinations

Combinations from developmental level II should be reviewed. The following routines can be added.

1. Begin with a Forward Roll, coming to a standing position with feet crossed. Pivot the body to uncross the feet and to bring the back in the line of direction for a Backward Roll (Figure 20.95).
2. Hold the toes, heels, ankles, or a wand while rolling. Use different arm positions, such as out to the sides or folded across the chest. Use a wide straddle position for both the Forward Roll and the Backward Roll.

Back Extension

Carry the Backward Roll to the point where the feet are above and over the head. Push off vigorously with the hands, shoot the feet into the air, and land on the feet.

Headstand Variations

Review the various aspects of the Headstand, using the single-spotter technique as needed. Vary with different leg positions. Add the two-foot recovery. After the stand has been held, recover by bending at the waist and knees, pushing off with the hands, and landing on the feet back in the original position.

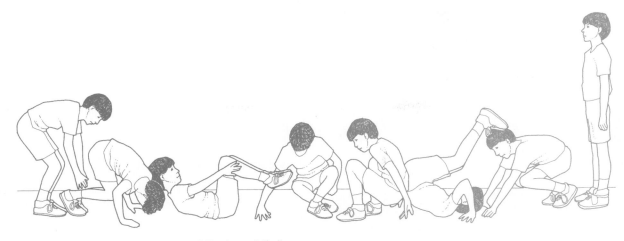

Figure 20.95 Alternating Forward and Backward Rolls

Handstand against a Wall

Using a wall as support, do a Handstand. The arms must be kept straight, with the head between the arms (Figure 20.96). Some performers like to bend the knees so that the soles of the feet are against the wall.

A critical point in the Handstand against a Wall is to position the hands the correct distance from the wall. It is better to be too close than too far. Being too far can cause the performer to collapse before the feet gain the support of the wall. A mat should be used in the preliminary stages.

Freestanding Handstand

Perform a Handstand without support. Students must learn to turn the body when a fall is imminent, so that they land on the feet. (Spotters can be used to prevent an awkward fall.) Move the hands to help control the balance.

Cartwheel and Round-Off

Practice the Cartwheel, adding a light run with a skip for a takeoff. To change to a Round-Off, place the hands somewhat closer together during the early Cartwheel action. Bring the feet together and make a quarter turn to land on both feet, with the body facing the starting point. The Round-Off can be followed by a Backward Roll.

Judo Roll

For a left Judo Roll, stand facing the mat with the feet well apart and the left arm extended at shoulder height. Bring the arm down and throw the left shoulder toward the mat in a rolling motion, with the roll made on the shoulder and the upper part of

Figure 20.96 Handstand against a Wall

STUNTS AND TUMBLING: DEVELOPING BODY MANAGEMENT SKILLS WITHOUT APPARATUS ━━━ **527**

Figure 20.97 Judo Roll

the back (Figure 20.97). Reverse for a right Judo Roll. Both right and left Judo Rolls should be practiced. Later, a short run and a double-foot takeoff should precede the roll. The Judo Roll is a basic safety device to prevent injury from tripping and falling. Rolling and taking the fall lessen the chances of injury. The Judo Roll is essentially a Forward Roll with the head turned to one side. The point of impact is the back of one shoulder and the finish is a return to the standing position.

Variations:

1. Roll to the feet and to a ready position.
2. Place a beanbag about 3 feet in front of your-self and go beyond the bag to start the roll.

Advanced Forward and Backward Roll Combinations

Put together different combinations of Forward Rolls and Backward Rolls. The emphasis should be on choice, exploration, and self-discovery. Variations can involve different approaches, execution acts, and finishes. Try the following variations of the Forward Roll.

1. Roll while holding the toes, heels, ankles, or a wand.
2. As above, but cross the hands.
3. Roll with hands on the knees or with a ball between the knees.
4. Roll with arms at the sides, folded across the chest, or on the back of the thighs.
5. Press forward from a front-leaning rest position and go into the roll.

Try the following suggestions with the Backward Roll.

1. Begin with a Stiff-Legged Sitdown and go into the roll.
2. Push off into a Back Extension (p. 526), landing on the feet.

3. Roll to a finish on one foot only.
4. Roll with hands clasped behind the neck.
5. Roll with a ball between the knees.
6. Walk backward using a Crab Walk and then roll.

In addition to these, combine Forward Rolls with Backward Rolls in various ways.

Developing Gymnastic Routines

The teacher can put together in sequence various stunts and other movements. The problems might be structured like the following.

1. Specify the number and kind of stunts and movements to be done and the sequence to be followed. For example, tell the child to do a balance stunt, a locomotor movement, and a rolling stunt.
2. Arrange the mats in some prescribed order so that they become the key to the movement problems. Two or three might be placed in succession, three or four in a U shape, or four in a hollow-square formation. There should be some space between mats, depending on the conditions stated in the problem. The problem could be presented like this: "On the first mat, do a Forward Roll variation and then a movement to the next mat on all fours. On the second mat, do some kind of balance stunt, and then proceed to the next mat with a jumping or hopping movement. On the third mat, you have a choice of activity." The problem can also be stated in more general terms, and children can do a different stunt or variation on each mat and a different movement between mats.
3. Have partners work out a series of stunts. The paired children should be of equal size and strength, so that they can alternate as the support. If children are of different sizes, the larger child can provide support for the smaller, and a third child may act as a spotter to take care of safety factors. After children have practiced for a period of time, each partnership can demonstrate the routines they have developed.

Straddle Press to Headstand

Begin by placing the hands and head in the Triangular Headstand position. The feet are in a wide straddle position and the hips are up. Raise the hips slowly by pressing to a point over the base of support. Slowly raise the legs to a straddle position and finish with the legs brought together in regular Headstand position. All movement is done as a slow, controlled action. (This is a more difficult stunt than the regular Headstand.)

Handstand Variations

The first two stages of the Handstand, done with double spotting and then single spotting with knee support (pp. 513), should be reviewed. Progression can then follow this order.

1. Single spotting, without knee support
2. Handstand against a Wall
3. Freestanding Handstand
4. Walking on the Hands
5. Stunts against a wall

Spotting: For single spotting without knee support, the performer and the spotter face each other 4 or 5 feet apart. The performer lifts both arms and the left leg upward as a preliminary move, with the weight shifted to the right leg. The lifted arms and forward leg come down forcefully to the ground, with the weight shifted in succession to the left leg and then to the arms. The right leg is kicked backward and upward for initial momentum and is followed quickly by the left leg. The downward thrust of the arms, coupled with the upward thrust of the legs, inverts the body to the handstand position. The placement of the hands should be about 2 feet in front of the spotter, who reaches forward and catches the performer between the knees and the ankles (Figure 20.98).

Headspring

With forehead and hands on the mat and knees bent, lean forward until almost overbalanced. As the weight begins to overbalance, raise the feet sharply and snap forward, pushing with the hands. As the feet begin to touch the ground, snap the body to a bent-knee position (Figure 20.99). Keep control of balance and rise to a standing position.

Spotting: Two spotters should be used, one on each side of the performer. Each spotter places one hand under the performer's back and the other hand under a shoulder. The spotters should give the performer a lift under the shoulders to help in snapping to the standing position.

Some instructors like to introduce this stunt by performing it over a rolled-up mat, which provides more height for the turn. A slight run may be needed to get the proper momentum.

Figure 20.98 Single spotting for the Handstand

Figure 20.99 Headspring

Walking on the Hands

Walk on the hands in a forward direction, bending the knees slightly, if desired, for balance. (Walking can be done first with a spotter supporting, but this support should be minimal.)

Variation: Walk on the hands, using a partner. The performer does a Handstand and the partner catches the feet. The performer then walks the hands forward until they are on the partner's feet. The two walk cooperatively.

Walk-Over

Do preliminary movements as if for the Handstand. Let the legs continue beyond the handstand position and contact the floor with a one-two rhythm. The body must be well arched as the leading foot touches the floor. Push off with the hands and walk out.

Spotting: The spotter gives support under the small of the back.

Balance Stunts

V-Up

Lie on the back, with arms overhead and extended. Keeping the knees straight and the feet pointed, bring the legs and the upper body up at the same time to form a V shape. The entire weight is balanced on the seat (Figure 20.100). Hold the position for 5 seconds.

This exercise, like the Curl-Up, is excellent for development of the abdominal muscles. It is quite similar to the Seat Balance except for the starting position.

Variation: Place the hands on the floor in back for support. (This makes the stunt easier for those having trouble.)

Push-Up Variations

Begin the development of Push-Up variations by reviewing proper Push-Up techniques. The only movement is in the arms. The body should come close to, but not touch, the floor. Explore the following variations.

Figure 20.100 V-Up

Monkey Push-Up

Point the fingers toward each other. Next, bring the hands close enough for the fingertips to touch.

Circle-O Push-Up

Form a circle with each thumb and forefinger.

Fingertip Push-Up

Get up high on the fingertips.

Different Finger Combinations

Do a Push-Up using the thumb and three or two fingers only.

Extended Push-Up

Extend the position of the hands progressively forward or to the sides.

Crossed Push-Up

Cross the arms. Cross the legs. Cross both.

One-Legged Push-Up

Lift one leg from the floor.

One-Handed Push-Up

Use only one hand, with the other outstretched or on the hip.

Exploratory Approach

See what other types of Push-Ups or combinations can be created.

Flip-Flop

From a push-up position, propel the body upward with the hands and feet, doing a Turn-Over (Figure 20.101). Flip back. The stunt should be done on a mat. (Review the Turn-Over [p. 503] before having students try this stunt.)

Figure 20.101 Flip-Flop

Long Reach

Place a beanbag about 3 feet in front of a line. Keeping the toes behind the line, lean forward on one hand and reach out with the other hand to touch the beanbag (Figure 20.102). Recover in one clean, quick movement to the original position, lifting the supporting hand off the floor. Increase the distance of the bag from the line.

Toe Jump

Hold the left toes with the right hand (Figure 20.103). Jump the right foot through without losing the grip on the toes. Try with the other foot.

Figure 20.102   Long Reach

Figure 20.103   Toe Jump

(Teachers should not be discouraged if only a few can do this stunt; it is quite difficult.)

Handstand Stunts

Try these challenging activities from the handstand position against a wall.

1. Turn the body in a complete circle, maintaining foot contact with the wall throughout.

2. Shift the support to one hand and hold for a moment.

3. Do an Inverted Push-Up, lowering the body by bending the elbows and then returning to handstand position by straightening the elbows.

Front Seat Support

Sit on the floor, with the legs together and forward. Place the hands flat on the floor, somewhat between the hips and the knees, with fingers pointed forward. Push down so the hips come off the floor, with the weight supported on the hands and heels. Next, lift the heels and support the entire weight of the body on the hands for 3 to 5 seconds. (Someone can help the performer get into position by giving slight support under the heels.)

Elbow Balance

Balance the body facedown horizontally on two hands, with elbows supporting the body in the hip area. To get into position, support the arched body with the toes and forehead. Work the forearms underneath the body for support, with fingers spread and pointed to the back. Try to support the body completely on the hands for 3 seconds, with elbows providing the leverage under the body (Figure 20.104). (Slight support under the toes can be provided.)

The Elbow Balance presents a considerable challenge. The teacher should take time to discuss the location of the center of gravity. The elbow support point should divide the upper and lower body mass.

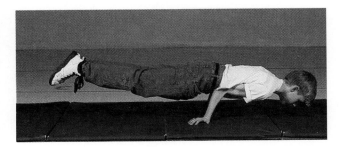

Figure 20.104   Elbow Balance

Individual Stunts

Wall Walk-Up

From a push-up position with feet against a wall, walk up the wall backward to a handstand position (Figure 20.105). Walk down again.

Skier's Sit

Assume a sitting position against a wall with the thighs parallel to the floor and the knee joints at right angles. (The position is the same as if sitting in a chair, but, of course, there is no chair.) The hands are placed on the thighs with the feet flat on the floor and the lower legs straight up and down (Figure 20.106). Try to sit for 30 seconds, 45 seconds, and 1 minute.

The Skier's Sit is an isometric type of activity and is excellent for developing the knee extensor muscles. It is done by skiers to develop the muscles used in skiing.

Variation: Support the body with crossed legs. A more difficult stunt is to support the body on one leg, with the other leg extended forward.

Rocking Horse

Lie facedown on a mat with arms extended overhead, palms down. With back arched, rock back and forth (Figure 20.107). (Some children may need to have someone start them rocking.)

Variation: Reach back and grasp the insteps with the hands. (The body arch is more difficult to maintain in this position.) Also try rocking from a side position.

Heel Click (Side)

Balance on one foot, with the other out to the side. Hop on the supporting foot, click the heels, and return to balance. Try with the other foot.

The child should recover to the one-foot balance position without excessive foot movement. The teacher should insist on good balance.

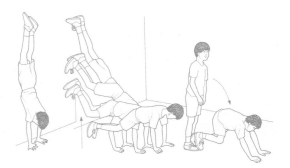

Figure 20.105   Wall Walk-Up

Figure 20.106   Skier's Sit

Figure 20.107   Rocking Horse

Variations:

1. Take a short step with the right foot leading. Follow with a cross-step with the left and then a hop on the left foot. During the hop, click the heels together. To hop on the right foot, reverse these directions.

2. Jump as high as possible before clicking the heels.

3. Combine right and left clicks.

Walk-Through

From a front-leaning rest position, walk the feet through the hands, using tiny steps, until the body is fully extended with the back to the floor (Figure 20.108). Reverse the body to original position. The hands stay in contact with the floor throughout.

Jump-Through

Starting in a front-leaning rest position, jump the feet through the arms in one motion. Reverse with another jump and return to original position. The hands must push off sharply from the floor, so the body is high enough off the floor to allow the legs to jump under. (The child may find it easier to swing a little to the side with one leg, going under the lifted hand, as indicated in Figure 20.109.)

Circular Rope Jump

Crouch down in a three-quarter knee bend, holding a folded jump rope in one hand. Swing the rope under the feet in a circular fashion, jumping it each time (Figure 20.110). Reverse the direction of the rope. Work from both right and left sides with either a counterclockwise or clockwise turn of the rope.

Variations:

1. Perform the rope jump with a partner.
2. Jump using different foot patterns (e.g., one foot or alternate feet) and using slow and fast time.
3. Establish standards for declaring a class champion in different areas. Some categories could be maximum number of turns in 30 seconds, most unique routine, and most jumps without a miss.

Figure 20.108 Walk-Through

Figure 20.109 Jump-Through

Figure 20.110 Circular Rope Jump

Bouncer

Start in a push-up position. Bounce up and down with the hands and feet leaving the ground at the same time. Try clapping while doing this. Move in various directions. Turn around.

Pretzel

Touch the back of the head with the toes by raising the head and trunk and bringing the feet to the back of the head. Try first to bring the toes close enough to the head so the head-to-toe distance can be measured by another child with a handspan (the distance between the thumb and little finger when spread) (Figure 20.111). If this distance is met, then try touching one or both feet to the back of the head.

Jackknife

Stand erect with hands out level to the front and a little to the side. Jump up and bring the feet up quickly to touch the hands. Vary by starting with a short run. Be sure the feet come up to the hands, rather than the hands moving down to the feet (Figure 20.112). Do several Jackknives in succession.

Figure 20.111 Pretzel

Figure 20.112 Jackknife

The takeoff must be with both feet, and good height must be achieved.

Heel-and-Toe Spring

Place the heels against a line. Jump backward over the line while bent over and grasping the toes. (Lean forward slightly to allow for impetus and then jump backward over the line.) Try jumping forward to original position. To be successful, the child should retain the grasp on the toes. The teacher can introduce the stunt by first having children grasp their ankles when making the jumps. This is less difficult.

Single-Leg Circle (Pinwheel)

Assume a squatting position, with both hands on the floor, left knee between the arms and right leg extended to the side. Swing the right leg forward and under the lifted right arm, under the left leg and arm, and back to starting position (Figure 20.113). Several circles should be made in succession. Reverse position and try with the left leg.

Partner and Group Stunts

Double Scooter

Two children about the same size face each other, sitting on each other's feet (Figure 20.114). With arms joined, scoot forward or backward with cooperative movements. When one child moves the seat, the other child should help by lifting with the feet. Progress is made by alternately flexing and extending the knees and hips. (Review the Scooter [p. 517] before doing this stunt.)

Double Roll

One child lies on a mat with his feet in the direction of the roll. The other takes a position with feet on either side of the first child's head. The first child reaches back and grasps the other's ankles with thumbs on the inside and then raises his own feet, so that the other child can similarly grasp his ankles. The second child propels her hunched

Figure 20.113 Single-Leg Circle

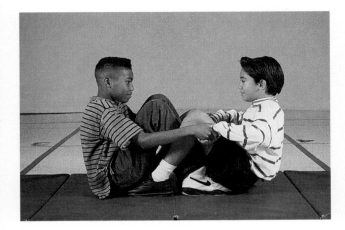

Figure 20.114 Double Scooter

body forward, while the first sits up and takes the position originally held by the other (Figure 20.115). Positions are then reversed and the roll continues.

Be sure that the top child hunches well and ducks the head to cushion the roll on the back of the neck and shoulders. Also, when the top child propels herself forward, bent arms should momentarily take the weight. It is important that the underneath child keep his knees bent.

Tandem Bicycle

One child forms a bicycle position, with back against a wall and knees bent, as if sitting. The feet should be placed under the body. The second child backs up and sits down lightly on the first child's knees. Other children may be added in the same fashion, their hands around the waist of the player immediately in front for support (Figure 20.116). Forward progress is made by moving the feet on the same side together.

Circle High Jump

Stand in circles of three, each circle having children of somewhat equal height. Join hands. One child tries to jump over the opposite pair of joined hands (Figure 20.117). To be completely success-

Figure 20.116 Tandem Bicycle

ful, each circle must have each child jump forward in turn over the opposite pair of joined hands. (Jumping backward is not recommended.) To reach good height, an upward lift is necessary. Try two small preliminary jumps before exploding into the jump over the joined hands.

Variation: Precede the jump with a short run by the group. A signal can be sounded so that all know when the jump is to occur during the run.

Stick Carries

Children of similar weight stand in groups of three, each group having a sturdy broom handle about 4 feet long. Using movement exploration techniques, two of the children carry the third with the broom handle (Figure 20.118). The child who is carried may be partially or wholly supported by the

Figure 20.115 Double Roll

Figure 20.117 Circle High Jump

handle. Exchange positions. (It is better to use special sticks for this purpose because ordinary wands may break.)

Two-Way Wheelbarrow

One child holds two wheelbarrows, but with one in front and one behind. The child secures the front wheelbarrow first in a normal wheelbarrow position. The back wheelbarrow assumes position by placing the ankles over the already established hand position of the holder (Figure 20.119). (Review the various wheelbarrow activities [pp. 522–524] before doing this stunt.)

Partner Rising Sun

Partners lie facedown on the floor, with heads together and feet in opposite directions. They hold a volleyball or a basketball (or a ball of similar size) between their heads (Figure 20.120). Working together, they stand up and return to position while retaining control of the ball. Do not touch the ball with the hands.

A slightly deflated ball works best. Some caution is necessary to prevent bumping heads if the ball is suddenly squeezed out.

Figure 20.119 Two-Way Wheelbarrow

Figure 20.118 Stick Carry

Figure 20.120 Partner Rising Sun

Triple Roll

Three children get down on their hands and knees on a mat, with heads all in the same direction to one of the sides. The performers are about 4 feet apart. Each is numbered—1, 2, or 3—with the number 1 child in the center. Number 2 is on the right and number 3 is on the left. Number 1 starts rolling toward and under number 2, who projects upward and over number 2. Number 2 is then in the center and rolls toward number 3, who projects upward and over number 2. Number 3, in the center, rolls toward and under number 1, who, after clearing number 3, is back in the center. Each performer in the center thus rolls toward and under the outside performer (Figure 20.121). (Review the Side Roll [p. 497] before doing this stunt.)

Children should be taught that as soon as they roll to the outside, they must get ready to go over the oncoming child from the center. There is no time for delay. The upward projection of the body to allow the rolling child to go under is important.

Quintuplet Roll

Five children can make up a roll series. They are numbered 1 through 5, as shown in Figure 20.122. Numbers 3 and 5 begin by going over numbers 2 and 4, respectively, who roll under. Number 1 goes over number 3 as soon as possible. Each then continues to go alternately over and under.

Figure 20.121   Triple Roll

Figure 20.122   Quintuplet Roll

Dead Person Lift

One child lies on her back, with body stiff and arms at the sides. Two helpers stand, one on each side of the "dead" person, with hands at the back of the neck and fingers touching. Working together, they lift the child, who remains rigid, to a standing position (Figure 20.123). From this position, the child is released and falls forward in a Dead Body Fall.

Injured Person Carry

The "injured" child lies on the back. Six children, three on each side, kneel down to do the carry. The lifters work their hands, palms upward, under the person to form a human stretcher, then lift up (Figure 20.124). (The "injured" child must maintain a stiff position.) They walk a short distance and set the person down carefully.

Merry-Go-Round

From 8 to 12 children are needed. Half of the children form a circle with joined hands, using a

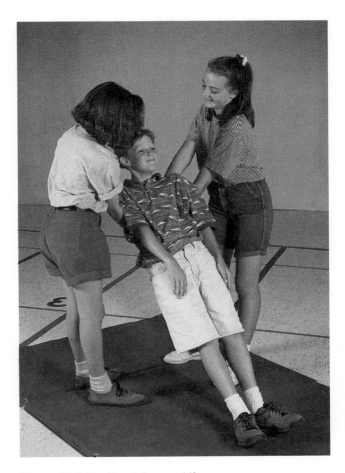

Figure 20.123   Dead Person Lift

Figure 20.124 Injured Person Carry

Figure 20.125 Merry-Go-Round

wrist grip. The remaining children drape themselves (each over a pair of joined hands) to become riders. The riders stretch out their bodies, faces up, toward the center of the circle, with the weight on the heels. Each rider then leans back on a pair of joined hands and connects hands, behind the circle of standing children, with the riders on either side. There are two sets of joined hands—the first circle, or merry-go-round, and the riders (Figure 20.125). The movement of the Merry-Go-Round is counterclockwise. The circle children, who provide the support, use sidesteps. The riders keep pace, taking small steps with their heels.

Partner Support Stunts

The basic instructions for partner support stunts (p. 524) should be reviewed.

Back Layout

The under, or support, partner lies on the back, with arms outstretched and palms down for support. The legs are raised, and the feet are positioned as if pushing up the ceiling. The support bends the knees and the partner lies back, resting the small of the back on support's soles. The top partner balances in a layout position with arms out to the sides for bal-

Figure 20.126 Back Layout

ance and body in a slight curve. The bottom partner reaches up and gives support to the top child's arms to provide stability (Figure 20.126). (A spotter can help position the top partner.)

Front Sit

The support gets down in the same position as for the Back Layout. The top partner straddles the support so that the support and the top partner are looking at each other. The top partner backs up to

Figure 20.127 Front Sit

Figure 20.128 Flying Dutchman

Figure 20.129 Knee-and-Shoulder Balance

sit on support's feet. As the support raises the top partner into a seated position, the top partner extends the legs forward so that the support can reach up and grasp them to stabilize the seated position (Figure 20.127). (Spotting should be done from behind.)

Flying Dutchman

The support takes a position as for the Back Layout. The top child takes a position facing the support, grasping support's hands and at the same time bending over support's feet. The support then raises the top partner from the floor by extending the knees. The top child arches the back and can then release the grip and put the arms out level to the sides in a flying position (Figure 20.128). A little experimentation determines the best place for the foot support. (Spotting should be available for getting into position and for safety.)

Knee-and-Shoulder Balance

The support partner is lying supine, knees well up and feet flat on the floor. Support puts the hands out, ready to brace the shoulders of the top child.

The top child takes a position in front of the support's knees, placing the hands on them. The top performer leans forward so that the shoulders are supported by the hands of the bottom partner, and kicks up (Figure 20.129).

Spotters are needed on both sides of the pair. If the top child begins to fall, the support partner should maintain the support under the shoulders so that the top child will land on the feet. Key points for the top partner are to keep the arms straight and the head up, and to look directly into the support partner's eyes.

Press

The bottom partner lies on the back, with knees bent and feet flat on the floor. The top partner takes a straddle position over the bottom partner, facing the support's feet. Performers then join hands with each other. The top partner sits on the joined hands, supported by the bottom partner, and rests the legs across the bottom partner's knees (Figure 20.130). Both performers should keep the elbows quite straight. Hold for a specified time.

All-Fours Support

The bottom performer lies on the back with legs apart and knees up. The hands are positioned close to the shoulders with palms up. The top performer stands on the partner's palms and leans forward, placing the hands on the support performer's knees. The support raises the top performer by lifting with the arms. The top performer is then in an all-fours position, with feet supported by the bottom performer's extended arms and hands supported by the bottom performer's knees (Figure 20.131).

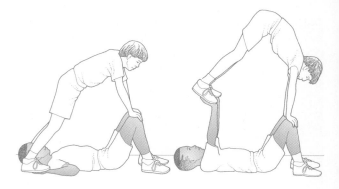

Figure 20.131 All-Fours Support

Angel

The top performer stands in front of the support partner. Both face the same direction. The support squats down, placing the head between the legs of the top performer. Support rises, so that the top partner is sitting on support's shoulders. The top performer then proceeds to take a position on support's knees. Support must lean well back for

Figure 20.130 Press

Figure 20.132 Angel

balance, removing the head from between the top performer's legs. The top performer stands erect on support's knees, with arms held level out to the side. The bottom performer takes hold of the top's thighs and leans back to place the pose in balance (Figure 20.132). Hold for 5 seconds. (Children need to experiment to determine the best way to achieve the final position.)

Side Stand

The support partner gets down on the hands and knees to form a rigid base. The top performer stands to the side, bends over the support's back, and hooks the hands, palms up, well underneath the support's chest and waist. The top child leans across, steadying with the hands, and kicks up to an inverted stand (Figure 20.133). (Spotters are needed on the far side.)

Variation: The top performer, instead of hooking hands underneath, grasps the bottom performer's arm and leg.

Pyramids

Making pyramids is a pleasurable activity for children and uses skills learned in the stunts and tumbling program. Emphasis in this section is on smaller pyramid groups. Pyramids provide an opportunity for creativity, since a variety of figures can be made. Stunts using only one performer or pair should be practiced as a preliminary to pyramid building with three students. The examples presented in Figure 20.134 A-F on the following page are composed of three performers; groups larger than this are not recommended as it increases the potential for accidents.

Figure 20.133 Side Stand

Figure 20.134 Pyramid formations

Combative Activities

PURPOSE OF ACTIVITIES IN THIS CHAPTER
Combative activities primarily focus on nonlocomotor and locomotor skills. In addition, combatives present an opportunity to teach social skills such as cooperation, competition, and sportsmanship.

Combatives offer students an opportunity to match strength and wits with others. When teaching combatives, teachers should be sensitive to the feelings of participants, as the appeal of such activities is not universal among all children. Children who are quick and strong perform well in combatives. However, youngsters who are less aggressive may not enjoy extensive participation in such activities. Proper perspective is important when using combative activities. The goal is to give students an opportunity to test themselves. Little is gained by trying to determine a class champion or placing youngsters in situations where they continually lose. Teachers should use a specific combative once or twice and then move to another activity.

Combatives should be restricted to use with children in developmental levels II and III. They are most often presented to add variety to stunts and tumbling instruction. Tumbling activities are not aerobically demanding, and combatives can provide a change of pace and renewed excitement. On the other hand, excessive use of combatives may be too exhausting or frustrating for children.

If desired, activities with partner tug-of-war ropes (Chapter 17) can be utilized as combative experiences at each level. Teachers can combine them with the combative activities suggested in this chapter.

INSTRUCTIONAL PROCEDURES

1. Safety factors must be emphasized. Youngsters should be matched for size; a common method is to ask students to pair up with someone who is similar in height. The length of bouts should be short—usually 5–10 seconds of contesting is adequate. Children should freeze immediately when the whistle is blown. In tug-of-war contests, no one should let go suddenly to avoid sending other children sprawling backward.

2. Instructions for the contest should be as explicit as necessary. Starting positions should be defined so that both contestants begin in an equal and neutral position. What constitutes a win and the number of trials permitted should be defined.

3. Fair play should be stressed. Children should be encouraged to find strategies and maneuvers to gain success, but always within the framework of the rules.

4. Contests can be started on signal by the teacher, or children can be allowed to start contests on their own. If children are not self-disciplined, it is best for the instructor to start and stop all contests.

5. To add variety, contests should be done with the right side (arm or leg), the left side, and both sides. Body position can be varied. Children can stand, crouch, sit, or lie for the same contest.

6. Develop a system of rotation, so that youngsters have more than one opponent. Rotating assures that one child will not continually dominate another.

SUGGESTED ACTIVITIES

Hand Wrestle

Starting Position: Contestants place right foot against right foot and grasp right hands in a hand-shake grip. The left foot is planted firmly to the rear for support.

Action: Try to force the other, by hand and arm pressure, to move either foot. Any movement by either foot means a loss.

Variations:

1. Stand left foot against left foot and contest with left hands.

2. Stand balanced on the right foot and clasp right hands. A player loses if the right foot is moved or if the back foot touches the ground. Try with the left foot and left hand. The foot off the ground can be held with the free hand.

Finger Fencing

Starting Position: Contestants stand on the right foot and hold the left foot with the left hand.

Action: Hook index fingers of the right hands and try to push the opponent off balance. Change feet and hands. Any movement of the supporting foot means a loss.

Touch Knees

Starting Position: Contestants stand on both feet and face each other.

Finger fencing

Action: Touch one of the opponent's knees without letting the opponent touch yours. Five touches determine the victor.

Variations:

1. Grasp left hands and try to touch the knees with the right hand. The first one to touch wins that bout.
2. Either with hands free or with left hands grasped, try to step lightly on the other's toes.

Grab the Flag

Starting Position: Opponents are on their knees, facing each other on a tumbling mat. Each has a flag tucked in the belt near the middle of the back.

Action: Remain on the knees at all times. Try to grab the flag from the other.

Variation: Try this as a group contest in which contestants pull flags until a champion is established.

Rooster Fight

Starting Position: Players stoop down and clasp hands behind the knees.

Action: Try to upset the other player or cause the handhold to be released.

Variations:

1. Squat down and hold the heels with the hands. A player loses when she is upset or when her hands come loose from her heels.
2. Try this as a group contest. Children stand around the edges of an area large enough to contain the group. On signal, they come forward and compete team against team or as individuals. A child who is pushed out of the area is eliminated. The last one left is the winner.

Palm Push

Starting Position: Contestants face each other, standing 12 inches apart. They place the palms of their hands together and must keep them together throughout the contest.

Action: Try to push the opponent off balance.

Variation: Use a wand instead of pushing the palms together.

Bulldozer

Starting Position: Opponents are on their hands and feet (not knees), facing each other, with right shoulders touching.

Action: Try to push (not bump) each other backward. Pushing across the mat or across a restraining line determines the winner. Change shoulders and repeat.

Breakdown

Starting Position: Opponents are in a front-leaning rest (push-up) position, facing each other.

Action: Using one hand, try to break down the other's position by pushing or dislodging his support while maintaining your own position.

Variation: Try the contest with each contestant in wheelbarrow position with the legs held by a partner.

Elbow Wrestle

Starting Position: Contestants lie on the floor or sit at a table and face each other. Their right hands are clasped, with right elbows bent and resting on the surface, and right forearms pressed against each other.

Action: Force the other's arm down while keeping the elbows together. Raising the elbow from the original position is a loss.

Variation: Change to a position using the left arm.

Leg Wrestle

Starting Position: Opponents lie on their backs on the floor or on a mat, with heads in opposite directions, trunks close, and near arms locked at the elbow.

Action: Three counts are given. On each of the first two counts, lift the leg nearer to the opponent to a vertical position. On the third count, hook legs with the opponent near the foot. Try to roll the opponent over backward.

Variation: Use the right and left legs in turn.

Catch-and-Pull Tug-of-War

Starting Position: Two teams face each other across a line.

Action: Try to catch hold of and pull any opponent across the line. A player pulled across the line waits in back of the opposing team until time is called. The team capturing the most players wins.

Teaching Suggestion: Pulling by catching hold of clothing or hair is not permitted. The penalty is disqualification. Players may cross the line to pull if they are securely held by a teammate or by a chain of players.

Variation: Have those pulled across the line join the other team. This keeps all children in the game.

Stick Twist

Starting Position: Contestants face each other with their feet approximately 12 inches apart. They hold a wand above their heads with both hands, the arms completely extended.

Action: On signal, try to bring the wand down slowly without changing the grip. The object is to maintain the original grip and not to let the wand twist in the hands. The wand does not have to be forced down, but rather should be moved down by mutual agreement. It can be moved down completely only if one player allows it to slip.

Toe Touch

Starting Position: Contestants form a large circle.

Action: On signal, try to step lightly on the opponent's toes (those on the left and right side) while not allowing the opponent to step on your toes. Keep score by counting the number of touches made.

Variation: Try in push-up position. The goal is to touch the opponent's hand.

Crab Contest

Starting Position: Both contestants are in crab position with seats held high.

Action: On signal, try, by jostling and pushing, to force the other's seat to touch the mat.

Variation: Place a beanbag on the tummy. Try to knock the opponent's beanbag to the floor.

Shoulder Shove

Starting Position: Each contestant raises the left leg, holding the ankle with the right hand and holding the right elbow with the left hand.

Action: Try to bump the other person off balance with the left shoulder so that one hand releases its position.

Teaching Suggestion: The teacher or a referee should call a loss when the left hand releases the right elbow, because this is difficult for the opponent to see. Dropping the hold on the ankle is definite and visible.

Variations:

1. Stand on one foot and fold the arms. Try to knock the other player off balance so that the uplifted foot touches the ground.

2. Using a 6- or 8-foot circle, try to force the opponent out of the circle.

3. Use a kangaroo theme. Carry a volleyball between the legs at the knees. Try to maintain control of the ball while shoving the opponent with the shoulder.

Wand Wrestle

Starting Position: Players face each other, grasping a wand between them. The grips must be fair, with each child having an outside hand.

Action: By twisting and applying pressure on the wand, try to get the opponent to relinquish her grip.

Variations:

1. *Basketball Wrestle.* Use a basketball instead of a wand. Each should have the same grasp advantage at the start.

2. Squat down while maintaining a grip on the wand. Attempt to take away the wand or to upset the opponent.

Partner Pull-Up

Starting Position: Two students sit on the floor and face each other, with knees straight and soles of the feet against the opponent's. Each bends forward, and they grasp a wand between them.

Action: Pull the other player forward to cause him to release the grip. Only straight pulling is allowed.

Teaching Suggestion: To provide a straight pull, one player should have both hands on the inside and the other both hands on the outside, rather than having alternate grip positions.

Wand Lift

Starting Position: Two contestants stand facing each other and hold a 3-foot-long stick or wand between them. Each holds one end of the stick with the right hand, using an underhand grip. Each places the left hand, in an overhand grip, next to and touching the opponent's right-hand grip. The elbows are bent at approximately a right angle.

Action: Press down with the left hand and lift with the right to bring the stick up to a vertical position. The body can be braced for action, but body motion should be minimal. This contest is meant to be a test of pure strength.

Variation: Try with a left-hand lift.

Sitting Elbow Wrestle

Starting Position: Contestants sit on a mat, back to back, with elbows locked. The legs are spread wide.

Action: Pull to the left in an attempt to tip the opponent.

Variations:

1. Reverse direction.
2. Position the legs so the knees are bent and the soles of the feet are flat on the mat.

Power Pull

Starting Position: One contestant stands with fingers touching in front of and close to chest. The other person stands facing the opponent and grasps opponent's wrists.

Action: On signal, the contestant holding the wrists attempts to pull the opponent's fingers apart. A straight pull (no jerking) is the action.

Rope Tug-of-War

Starting Position: Two equal teams face each other on opposite ends of a rope. A piece of tape marks the center of the rope. Two parallel lines are drawn about 10 feet apart. At the start, the center marker on the rope is midway between the lines.

Action: Try to pull the center marker over your team's near line.

Teaching Suggestion: The rope should be long enough to accommodate the children without crowding. It should be at least ¾ inch in diameter. Children should never wrap the rope around the hands, arms, or body in any manner.

Variation: Use different positions for pulling—with the rope overhead (teams have their backs toward each other), with one hand on the ground, or from a seated position (with feet braced on the floor).

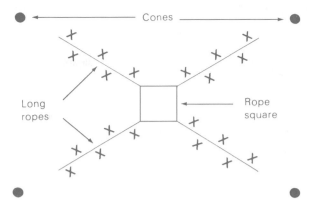

Figure 21.1 Formation for Four-Team Tug-of-War

Four-Team Tug-of-War

Starting Position: Four teams line up as shown in Figure 21.1. A special rope is needed, the size and extent of which depend on the number of children. A cone, a bowling pin, or a beanbag is placed an equal distance behind each team.

Action: Pull, on signal, in the direction of your team's cone. A team wins when the player on the end of the rope can knock over the cone, or pick up the club or beanbag, without losing contact with the rope.

Teaching Suggestion: An automobile tire can be substituted for the center rope square. Simply tie four tug-of-war ropes to the tire.

Variation: Try this as a three-team contest, with the center figure a rope triangle.

Games: Teaching Group Interaction, Sportsmanship, and Cooperation

---

PURPOSE OF ACTIVITIES IN THIS CHAPTER

Games are excellent activities for developing social skills. Students can be taught to display appropriate interactive skills such as leading, following, and making decisions. Cooperative skills that include following directions, accepting individual differences, and participating in a teamwork situation are necessary for reaching common goals. Game situations offer many scenarios for teaching sportsmanship behavior.

As an integral part of the physical education program, games need to be scrutinized carefully and evaluated in terms of what they offer children. Games that involve few children, allow some children to dominate, and offer little in the way of skill development are being eliminated from the repertoire of traditional activities. Children can create and modify games to meet their needs. Through these experiences, intermediate-level children learn about game components and how to change different components in a meaningful way.

Teachers should view games as a valuable contribution to the child's total development. Through games, children can experience success and accomplishment. In addition, social objectives accomplished through a game encounter are the development of social skills, acceptance of rule parameters, and a better understanding of oneself in a competitive and co-operative situation. Games are a laboratory where children can apply newly learned skills in a meaningful way. Many games help develop large-muscle groups and enhance the child's ability to run, dodge, start, and stop under control while sharing space with others. Cognitive development is also enhanced as children learn to understand and follow rules. By applying strategy in games, children learn the importance of alertness and the mental aspect of participation.

EVALUATING GAMES

Teachers can evaluate games by looking at the skills required, the number of participants, and the complexity, length, and progression. As teachers become adept at game evaluation, they can use this skill to select new games and modify games previously learned to ensure that the activities are suited to the maturity and skill levels of children.

The game should first be evaluated in terms of skills that are required to participate successfully. If children have not learned a skill required to play a game, they will almost certainly not be able to learn and apply that skill in a game setting. For example, children may be able to throw with proper form, but they may not be able to throw accurately in a game setting. They may be able to hit a stationary object but not a moving target.

Children must learn to cooperate with teammates and to compete against peers. The greater the number of teammates and competitors, the more difficult the game becomes. Cooperating with teammates is just as difficult as competing in a meaningful fashion. Teachers should use a progression of games, moving from partner activities to small-group games to team games. Many games are actually more effective when played in small groups, because the participants handle objects more often and have more chances to be a leader.

The number of rules and the degree of strategy required in games are important considerations. Primary-level children typically have difficulty playing a game that has many rules and they probably will not enjoy such an activity. If extensive strategy is required, students must be able to use overlearned physical skills so that they can apply their concentration to the mental aspect of the game. Most elementary school children are not able to concentrate on skill performance and strat-

egy simultaneously. Complex games require team members to play specific roles, and some of these roles (e.g., goalkeeper or line positions) may not appeal to many youngsters. In contrast, many of the more popular games are spontaneous in nature and demand little concentration on strategy.

Children should receive positive feedback from the game experience. Many games must be played for a period of time before the outcome is determined. The younger children are, the less willing they are to wait for the outcome; feedback must be immediate. Children become bored, and tire of playing long games. Fatigue is also a factor in the interest level of children, and the teacher must watch carefully for signs of it.

Games require a combination of skills. A game in which children must sequence many skills may result in failure or frustration for many. Lead-up games are developed for the express purpose of limiting the number of skills needed for successful participation. The instructor should evaluate the number of skills required and build a progression of games that gradually increases the use of skill combinations.

CREATING OR MODIFYING GAMES

Games can be modified and new variations created by the teacher or the students or by both together. For example, a teacher may observe that a specific game is not meeting the desired objectives and may decide to modify or change the game to facilitate skill development. In another situation, the teacher may stop the class and ask them to think of a way to make the game better. Alternatives can be implemented and the newly created activity tested to see whether it is indeed more effective. With intermediate-level students, the teacher can offer some parameters for developing a game and then allow children to work as a group to implement the activity. Ground rules can be established to facilitate group dynamics. The teacher can suggest voting on a rule change or can specify a maximum number of changes allowed per period.

If students and teachers are to make meaningful modifications, they must understand how to analyze a game. The most recognized elements that structure games are desired outcomes, skills, equipment, rules or restrictions, number of players, and scheme of organization. Morris and Stiehl (1989) provide an approach to game analysis. Readers are referred to this text if they are interested in game modification. Instructors should remember that youngsters need to learn how and what to modify and that they need to practice the process. Some suggestions to start youngsters thinking include the following:

1. Change the distance to be run by decreasing or increasing it. For example, in Star Wars, go around once instead of twice.

2. Change the means of locomotion. Use hopping, walking, skipping, or galloping instead of running.

3. Play the game with one or more partners. The partners can move and act as if they were a single child.

4. Change the method of tagging in simple tag games. Call out "Reverse" to signal that the chaser is to become the tagger and vice versa.

5. Make goals or restricted areas larger or smaller. In Over the Wall, the restraining area should be made larger or smaller or its shape can be changed.

6. Vary the boundaries of the game. They can be made larger or smaller, as dictated by the number of players.

7. Change the formation in which the game is played. For example, Circle Kickball could be played in a square or triangular shape.

8. Change the requirements necessary for scoring. In Hand Hockey, students might be required to make four passes before a shot is taken.

9. Increase the number of players, taggers, or runners. The amount of equipment used can also be increased. For example, in Nine Lives, the more fleece balls used, the more practice the youngsters get in throwing at a moving target.

10. Change the rules or penalties of the game. For example, players might be allowed a maximum of three dribbles or might be allowed to hold the ball for no more than 3 seconds.

Many of the games in this chapter have been modified by students and teachers. These variations are presented with the description of each game.

COOPERATION AND COMPETITION

Most games require cooperation and competition. *Cooperation* involves two or more children working together to achieve a common goal. *Competition* is characterized by opponents working against each other as each tries to reach a goal or reward. An in-depth look at competition is offered in Chapter 24. The teacher should strive to emphasize cooperation rather than competition and to develop a spirit of working together, a concern for teammates, and an appreciation of the collective skills of the group.

Achieving a balance between offense and defense in games is important. In tag and capture games, there should be an opportunity to remain safe as well as a strong challenge to be at risk and elude capture. Teachers should evaluate the game components continually and modify them in the interest of retaining an enjoyable environment. Teams should be somewhat equal so that all participants have an opportunity to find success. There is no motivation when there is no opportunity to win. Emphasizing cooperation reinforces for children the need to play with all classmates regardless of ability level. Teachers should rotate students regularly so that children have the chance to play with all of their classmates and to play on equal teams. Rotation plans should, of course, include youngsters with disabilities.

SAFETY

Safety is a primary consideration in game situations. The play area should be checked for dangerous objects and hazards. Tables, chairs, equipment, and apparatus can become dangerous when a high-speed game is under way. Children should learn to move in a controlled fashion and to use the entire playing area to avoid collisions. They must be taught to stop playing immediately when a signal is given. This is an important prerequisite for later sports experiences.

When playing games that involve a goal line or running to a line, a *safety zone* should be established. Instead of using a wall or line near the wall as the goal, safety lines should be drawn 10 feet from the wall to allow for deceleration. Cones or spots can be used to mark the deceleration zone.

INSTRUCTIONAL PROCEDURES

1. The instructor must study the game before attempting to teach it. Safety hazards should be identified, difficult concepts anticipated, and the game adapted to the class and the situation. Physical preparations should be completed prior to teaching. Boundaries should be

established and equipment made ready for distribution.

2. When presenting a new game to a class, the teacher should put the youngsters in the formation that they are going to use. They can then sit and be comfortable while listening to instructions. Directions should be as brief as possible, and children should try the game quickly. A useful rule of thumb is to offer minimal instruction to get the game under way and then gradually to implement the more subtle rules. Try the game first, and then answer any questions that the students may have. This ensures that they have some perception of the game and how it is to proceed.

3. Having a trial period during the first stages of learning a game is important. This avoids the possibility of children feeling resentful about losing a point or being caught because they did not understand the activity.

4. Social learning should be enhanced through game experiences. Allow children to call infractions or penalties on each other and on themselves. Youngsters must learn to accept calls made by officials as an integral part of any game situation. When disagreements occur, the teacher should adopt the role of arbitrator, rather than taking one side or the other. Children thus learn negotiation skills and eventually should resolve many differences among themselves rather than having the teacher decide each issue.

5. In the early phases of a game, instruction should continue. The teacher can look for opportunities to stop the game briefly and offer instruction or correction. Coaching hints for improving performance are also a part of the game environment.

6. Games are enjoyable when they are novel. Often, it is effective to stop the game at the height of interest. Children will then look forward to playing it the next time. In addition, a wide variety of games should be offered to stimulate interest.

7. The instructor must make sure that all children have a chance to participate in those games that require taking turns. A good policy for games in which numbers are called is to write the numbers down on a card. Caution must be used in games that eliminate children. If children must be eliminated, it should be for one or two turns only, and they should then be allowed back in the game. Another solution is to have

play continue until a few youngsters are eliminated. Then the rest of the players can be declared winners.

8. The teacher should have a rotation plan that allows all children to play an equal amount of time. The object is to avoid the situation in which winners stay on the court and losers sit out, receiving much less practice than the better players.

9. If identifying teams is difficult, use pinnies, crepe paper armbands, colored shoulder loops, or flag football belts.

SELECTION OF GAMES

The games in this chapter were selected because they require low organization and offer activity for all children. Games should be analyzed to identify the skills that children must practice before playing. Drills and skill practice become more meaningful when children comprehend that the skill will be used in a game situation.

The games have been sorted by difficulty and placed into three developmental levels. Table 22.1 lists each of the games alphabetically by developmental level. Also listed in Table 22.1 are the skills required for successful play and the page in the text where the description of the game is listed. Games in developmental level I do not require a high degree of specialized sport skill. Most use basic locomotor skills and offer an environment in which children can practice and participate successfully. These games can be modified easily to allow all children to have enjoyable experiences.

Specialized sport skills are required in many of the games in developmental levels II and III. Ball-handling and movement skills, with emphasis on agility, are important for success in many of these games. Teachers should offer opportunities for children to practice requisite game skills prior to being placed in a competitive situation.

Sport Lead-Up Games

Games in developmental levels II and III fall into two categories: sport lead-up games and low-organization games. This chapter includes low-organization games only; however, sport lead-up games can also be integrated into the games program. Sport lead-up games limit the number of skills required for successful participation in order to help children experience success in a sport setting. For example, Five Passes is a game designed

Table 22.1 Alphabetical listing of games by developmental level

Games	Skills	Page
Developmental Level I Games		
Animal Tag	Imagery, running, dodging	556
Aviator	Running, locomotor movements, stopping	556
Back to Back	Fundamental locomotor movements	556
Ball Passing	Object handling	558
Blindfolded Duck	Fundamental locomotor movements	558
Bottle Bat Ball	Batting, retrieving balls	558
Bottle Kick Ball	Kicking, trapping	559
Cat and Mice	Running, dodging	559
Change Sides	Body management	559
Charlie over the Water	Skipping, running, stopping, bowling (rolling)	560
Circle Stoop	Moving to rhythm	560
Circle Straddle Ball	Ball rolling, catching	560
Colors	Color or other perceptual concepts, running	561
Corner Spry	Light, silent walking	561
Firefighter	Running	561
Flowers and Wind	Running	561
Forest Ranger	Running	562
Freeze	Locomotor movements to rhythm	562
Hill Dill	Running, dodging	562
Hot Potatoes	Object handling	562
Jack Frost and Jane Thaw	Running, dodging, holding position	563
Leap the Brook	Leaping, jumping, hopping, turning	563
Marching Ponies	Marching, running	563
May I Chase You?	Running, dodging	563
Midnight (Lame Wolf)	Running, dodging	564
Mix and Match	Fundamental locomotor movements	564
Mousetrap	Skipping, running, dodging	564
Musical Ball Pass	Passing and handling	565
One, Two, Button My Shoe	Running	565
Popcorn	Curling, stretching, jumping	565
Red Light	Fundamental locomotor movements, stopping	566
Right Angle	Rhythmic movement, body management	566
Rollee Pollee	Ball rolling, dodging	566
Scarecrow and the Crows, The	Dodging, running	567
Sneak Attack	Marching, running	567
Soap Bubbles	Body management	567
Squirrel in the Trees	Fundamental locomotor movements	567
Statues	Body management, applying force, balance	568
Stop Ball	Tossing, catching	568

Table 22.1 *continued*

Games	Skills	Page
Developmental Level I Games		

Tag Games (Simple)
    Back-to-Back
    Bowing
    Frozen
    Locomotor
    Nose-and-Toe
    Skunk
    Stoop
    Stork
    Turtle
	Fundamental locomotor movements, dodging	568

Teacher Ball (Leader Ball)	Throwing, catching	569
Tommy Tucker's Land	Dodging, running	569
Twins (Triplets)	Body management	569
Where's My Partner?	Fundamental locomotor movements	569
Developmental Level II Games		
Addition Tag	Running, dodging	570
Alaska Baseball	Kicking, batting, running, ball handling	570
Arches	Moving rhythmically	571
Bat Ball	Batting, running, catching, throwing	571
Beach Ball Bat Ball	Batting, tactile handling	571
Bounce Ball	Throwing, ball rolling	572
Box Ball	Running, ball handling	572
Busy Bee	Fundamental locomotor movements	572
Cageball Kick-Over	Kicking	573
Club Guard	Throwing	573

Competitive Circle Contests
    Circle Club Guard
    Touch Ball
	Throwing, catching	573

Couple Tag	Running, dodging	574
Crows and Cranes	Running, dodging	574
Fly Trap	Fundamental locomotor movements	575
Follow Me	All locomotor movements, stopping	575
Fox Hunt	Running, dodging	575
Galloping Lizzie	Throwing, dodging, running	576
Hand Hockey	Striking, volleying	576
Home Base	Reaction time, locomotor movements, body management	576
Indianapolis 500	Running, tagging	577
Jump the Shot	Rope jumping	577
Loose Caboose	Running, dodging	577
Nine Lives	Throwing, dodging	577
Nonda's Car Lot	Running, dodging	578

to develop passing skills. Children do not have to perform other skills (i.e., dribbling, shooting) required by the regulation sport to achieve success. Table 22.2 lists all sport-related lead-up games presented in Chapters 25 to 31. If a teacher is teaching soccer skills and wants to finish the lesson with a lead-up game, this chart can be consulted to find an appropriate application. Many of the lead-up games are excellent choices for skill development, particularly with developmental level III youngsters.

DEVELOPMENTAL LEVEL I

Games in the early part of developmental level I feature individual games and creative play. Little emphasis is placed on team play or on games that have a scoring system. The games are simple, easily taught, and not demanding of skills. Dramatic elements are present in many of the games, while others help establish number concepts and symbol recognition. As children mature, they enjoy participation in running, tag, and ball games. Few team activities are included and the ball games require the skills of throwing and catching.

Animal Tag

Supplies: None
Skills: Imagery, running, dodging
Formation:

Two parallel lines are drawn about 40 feet apart. Children are divided into two groups, each of which takes a position on one of the lines. Children in one group get together with their leader and decide what animal they wish to imitate. Having selected the animal, they move over to within 5 feet or so of the other line. There they imitate the animal, and the other group tries to guess the animal correctly. If the guess is correct, they chase the first group back to its line, trying to tag as many as possible. Those caught must go over to the other team. The second group then selects an animal, and the roles are reversed. If the guessing

team cannot guess the animal, however, the performing team gets another try. To avoid confusion, children must raise their hands to take turns at naming the animal. Otherwise, many false chases will occur. If children have trouble guessing, the leader of the performing team can give the initial of the animal.

Aviator

Supplies: None
Skills: Running, locomotor movements, stopping
Formation:

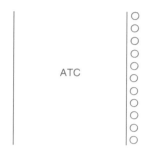

Players are parked (in push-up position) at one end of the playing area. The air traffic controller (ATC) is in front of the players and calls out, "Aviators aviators, take off!" Youngsters take off and move like airplanes to the opposite side of the area. The first person to move to the other side and land the plane (get into push-up position facing the ATC) is declared the new ATC.

If the ATC yells out some type of stormy weather, all planes must return to the starting line and resume the parked position. Examples of stormy weather commands are lightning, thunder, hurricane, and tornado. Each ATC is allowed to give stormy weather warnings once.

Back to Back

Supplies: None
Skills: Fundamental locomotor movements
Formation: Scattered

The number of children must be uneven. (If not, the teacher can play.) On signal, each child stands back to back with another child. One child will be without a partner. This child claps the hands for the next signal, and all children change partners, with the extra player from the previous game seeking a partner.

Variation: Considerably more activity can be achieved by putting in an extra command. After children are in partner formation back to back, the

Table 22.2 Lead-up games from sport Chapters 25 to 31*

Table 22.2 *continued*

Softball (Chapter 29)	
Developmental Level III	*Page*
Slow-Pitch Softball	700
Babe Ruth Ball	700
Hurry Baseball (One Pitch)	700
Three-Team Softball	701

Volleyball (Chapter 31)	
Developmental Level II	
Beach Ball Volleyball	724
Informal Volleyball	725
Shower Service Ball	725

Volleyball (Chapter 31)	
Developmental Level III	*Page*
Keep It Up	726
Mini-Volleyball	726
Rotation Mini-Volleyball	726
Regulation Volleyball	726
Three-and-Over Volleyball	727
Rotation Volleyball	727
Four-Square Volleyball	727
Wheelchair Volleyball	728

*Many of these games are used as culminating activities with sport lesson plans.

teacher says, "Everybody run [skip, hop, jump, slide]!" Other commands, such as "Walk like an elephant," can also be given. Children move around in the prescribed manner. When the signal is sounded, they immediately find a new partner and stand back to back.

Ball Passing

Supplies: Five or six different kinds of balls for each circle

Skill: Object handling

Formation: Circles with 15 or fewer in each circle

The class is divided into two or more circles, with no more than 15 children in any one circle. Each circle consists of two or more squads, but squad members need not stand together.

The teacher starts a ball around the circle; it is passed from player to player in the same direction. The teacher introduces more balls until five or six are moving around the circle at the same time and in the same direction. If a child drops a ball, he must retrieve it, and a point is scored against his squad. After a period of time, a whistle is blown, and the points against each squad are totaled. The squad with the lowest score wins. Beanbags, large blocks, or softballs can be substituted for balls.

Blindfolded Duck

Supplies: A wand, broomstick, cane, or yardstick

Skills: Fundamental locomotor movements

Formation:

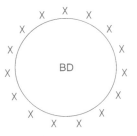

One child, designated the duck (Daisy if a girl, Donald if a boy), stands blindfolded in the center of a circle and holds a wand or similar article. She taps on the floor and tells children to hop (or perform some other locomotor movement). Children in the circle act accordingly, all moving in the same direction. Daisy then taps the wand twice on the floor, which signals all children to stop. Daisy moves forward with her wand, still blindfolded, to find a child in the circle. She asks, "Who are you?" The child responds, "Quack, quack." Daisy tries to identify this person. If the guess is correct, the identified child becomes the new duck. If the guess is wrong, Daisy must take another turn. After two unsuccessful turns, another child is chosen to be the duck.

Bottle Bat Ball

Supplies: A plastic bottle bat, whiffle ball, batting tee (optional), home plate, base marker

Skills: Batting, retrieving balls

Formation: Scattered

A home plate is needed, and a batting tee can be used. Foul lines should be marked wide enough so as not to be restrictive.

Batters get three pitches (or swings) to hit a fair ball, or they are out. The pitches are easy (as in slow-pitch softball), so that the batter has a good chance to hit the ball. The batter hits the ball and runs around the base marker and back to home. If the ball is returned to the pitcher's mound before the batter reaches home, the batter is out. (A marker should designate the pitcher's mound.) Otherwise, the batter has a home run and bats again. One fielder other than the pitcher is needed, but another can be used. The running distance to first base is critical. It can remain fixed or can be made progressively (one step) longer, until it reaches such a point that the fielders are heavily favored.

Teaching Suggestion: The game should make use of a plastic bottle bat and fun (whiffle) ball. A rotation system should be established when an out is made.

Variation: A batting tee can be used.

Bottle Kick Ball

Supplies: Plastic gallon jugs (bleach or milk containers) and 8-inch foam balls

Skills: Kicking, trapping

Formation:

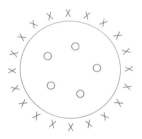

Players form a large circle around 10 to 12 plastic gallon jugs (bowling pins) standing in the middle of the circle. Students kick the balls and try to knock over the bottles.

Variation: Use as many foam balls as necessary to keep all children active. If the group is large, make more than one circle of players.

Cat and Mice

Supplies: None

Skills: Running, dodging

Formation:

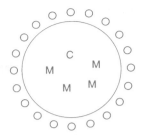

Children form a large circle. One child is the cat and four others are the mice. The cat and mice cannot leave the circle. On signal, the cat chases the mice inside the circle. As they are caught, the mice join the circle. The last mouse caught becomes the cat for the next round.

Teaching Suggestions: The teacher should start at one point in the circle and go around the circle selecting mice so that each child gets a chance to be in the center.

Sometimes, one child has difficulty catching the last mouse or any of the mice. If this is the case, children forming the circle can take a step toward the center, thus constricting the running area. The teacher should cut off any prolonged chase sequence.

Change Sides

Supplies: None

Skill: Body management

Formation:

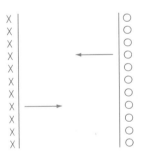

Two parallel lines are established 30 feet apart. Half of the children are on each line. On signal, all cross to the other line, face the center, and stand at attention. The first group to do this correctly wins a point. Children must be cautioned to use care when passing through the opposite group. They should be spaced well along each line; this allows room for them to move through each group. The locomotor movements should be varied. The teacher may say, "Ready—walk!" Skipping, hopping, long steps, sliding, and other forms of locomotion can be specified. The position to be assumed at the finish can be varied also.

Teaching Suggestion: Because success depends on getting across first, the teacher should watch for shortcutting of the rules and talk this problem over with the children.

Variation: The competition can be by squads, with two squads on each line.

Charlie over the Water

Supplies: A volleyball or playground ball

Skills: Skipping, running, stopping, bowling (rolling)

Formation: Scattered

The children are in circle formation with hands joined. One child, Charlie (or Sally, if a girl), is in the center of the circle, holding a ball. The children skip around the circle to the following chant.

Charlie over the water,

Charlie over the sea,

Charlie caught a bluebird,

But he can't catch me!

On the word *me,* Charlie tosses the ball in the air and children drop hands and scatter. When Charlie catches it, he shouts "Stop!" All of the children stop immediately and must not move their feet. Charlie rolls the ball in an attempt to hit one of the children. If he hits a child, that child becomes the new Charlie. If he misses, he must remain Charlie, and the game is repeated. If he misses twice, however, he picks another child for the center.

Circle Stoop

Supplies: Music or tom-tom

Skills: Moving to rhythm

Formation:

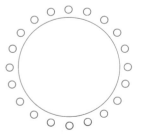

Children are in a single circle, facing counterclockwise. A march or similar music, or a tom-tom beat, can be used. The children march with good

posture until the music stops. As soon as children no longer hear the music or the tom-tom beat, they stoop and touch both hands to the ground without losing balance. The last child to touch both hands to the ground and those children who lost balance pay a penalty by going into the mush pot (the center of the circle) and waiting out the next round of the game. The children must march in good posture, and anyone stooping, even partially, before the music stops should be penalized. The duration of the music should be varied, and children should not be able to observe the stopping process if a record player is used.

Variations:

1. Using suitable music, have children employ different locomotor movements, such as skipping, hopping, or galloping.

2. Vary the stopping position. Instead of stooping, use positions such as the push-up, Crab, or Lame Dog, or balancing on one foot or touching with one hand and one foot. Such variations add to the interest and fun.

Circle Straddle Ball

Supplies: Two or more 8-inch foam balls

Skills: Ball rolling, catching

Formation: Circles of 10–15 students

Children are in circle formation, facing in. Each stands in a wide straddle stance with the side of the foot against the neighbor's. The hands are on the knees. Two balls are used. The object of the game is to roll one of the balls between the legs of another player before that player can get hands down to stop the ball. Each time a ball goes between the legs of an individual, a point is scored. The players having the fewest points scored against them are the winners. Keep the circles small so students have more opportunities to handle the ball.

Teaching Suggestion: The teacher should be sure that children catch and roll the ball, rather than batting it. Children must keep their hands on their knees until a ball is rolled at them. After some practice, the following variation can be played.

Variation: One child is in the center with a ball and is it. The other children are in the same formation as before. One ball is used. The center player tries to roll the ball through the legs of any child, masking intent by using feints and changes of direction. Any child allowing the ball to go through becomes it.

Colors

Supplies: Colored paper (construction paper) cut in circles, squares, or triangles for markers

Skills: Color or other perceptual concepts, running

Formation:

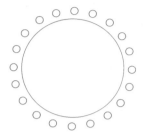

Five or six different-colored markers should be used, with a number of children having the same color. Children are standing or seated in a circle with a marker in front of each child.

The teacher calls out a color, and everyone having that color runs counterclockwise around the circle and back to place. The first one seated upright and motionless is declared the winner. Different kinds of locomotor movement can be specified, such as skipping, galloping, walking, and so on. After a period of play, the children leave the markers on the floor and move one place to the left.

Variation: Shapes (e.g., circles, triangles, squares, rectangles, stars, and diamonds) can be used instead of colors, as can numbers or other articles or categories, such as animals, birds, or fish. This game has value in teaching identification and recognition.

Corner Spry

Supplies: Blindfold

Skills: Light, silent walking

Formation:

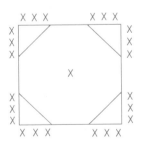

One person is blindfolded and stands in the center of the square. The other players are scattered in the corner areas. On signal they travel as quietly as possible from corner area to corner area.

The blindfolded person, when ready (less than 20 seconds), calls out "Corner Spry!" All players finish their trips to the corner nearest them. The blindfolded person then picks (by pointing) a corner, trying to select the one with the most players. A new player is then selected to be blindfolded.

Variation: The corners can be numbered 1, 2, 3, 4. The leader then calls out the corner number. The leader can also start class movement by naming the locomotor movement to be used.

Firefighter

Supplies: None

Skill: Running

Formation:

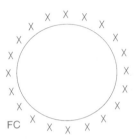

A fire chief runs around the outside of a circle of children and taps a number of them on the back, saying "Firefighter" each time. After making the round of the circle, the chief goes to the center. When the chief says "Fire," the firefighters run counterclockwise around the circle and back to place. The one who returns first and is able to stand in place motionless is declared the winner and the new chief.

The chief can use other words to fool children, but they run only on the word *Fire*. This merely provides some fun, since there is no penalty for a false start. The circle children can sound the siren as the firefighters run.

Flowers and Wind

Supplies: None

Skill: Running

Formation:

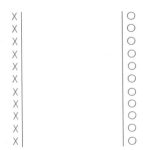

Two parallel lines long enough to accommodate the children are drawn about 30 feet apart. Children are divided into two groups. One is the wind and the other the flowers. Each of the teams takes a position on one of the lines and faces the other team. The flowers secretly select the name of a common flower. When ready, they walk over to the other line and stand about 3 feet away from the wind. The players on the wind team begin to call out flower names—trying to guess the flower chosen. When the flower has been guessed, the flowers run to their goal line, chased by the players of the other team. Any player caught must join the other side. The roles are reversed and the game is repeated. If one side has trouble guessing, a clue can be given to the color or size of the flower or the first letter of its name.

Forest Ranger

Supplies: None

Skill: Running

Formation:

Half of the children form a circle and face the center. These are the trees. The other half of the children are forest rangers and stand behind the trees. An extra child, the forest lookout, is in the center. The forest lookout starts the game by calling, "Fire in the forest. Run, run, run!" Immediately, the forest rangers run around the outside of the circle to the right. After a few moments, the lookout steps in front of one of the trees. This is the signal for each of the rangers to step in front of a tree. One player is left out, who then becomes the new forest lookout. The trees become rangers and the rangers become trees. Each time the game is played, the circle must be moved out somewhat, because the formation narrows when the rangers step in front of the trees.

Freeze

Supplies: Music or tom-tom

Skills: Locomotor movements to rhythm

Formation: Scattered

Children are scattered about the room. When the music starts, they move throughout the area, guided by the music. They walk, run, jump, or use other locomotor movements, depending on the selected music or beat. When the music is stopped, they freeze and do not move. Any child caught moving after the cessation of the rhythm pays a penalty. A tom-tom or a piano is a fine accompaniment for this game, because the rhythmic beat can be varied easily and the rhythm can be stopped at any time.

This is an excellent game for practicing management skills. The game reinforces freezing on a stop signal.

Variations:

1. Specify the level at which children must freeze.
2. Have children fall to the ground or balance or go into a different position, such as the push-up, Crab, Lame Dog, or some other defined position.

Hill Dill

Supplies: None

Skills: Running, dodging

Formation:

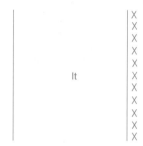

Two parallel lines are established 50 feet apart. One player is chosen to be it and stands in the center between the lines. The other children stand on one of the parallel lines. The center player calls,

Hill Dill! Come over the hill,
Or else I'll catch you standing still!

Children run across the open space to the other line, while the one in the center tries to tag them. Anyone caught helps the tagger in the center. The first child caught is it for the next game. Once children cross over to the other line, they must await the next call.

Hot Potatoes

Supplies: One to three balls or beanbags for each group

Skill: Object handling

Formation: Circles with 8–12 players

Children are seated in small circles (8 to 12 per circle) so that objects can be passed from one to another around the circle. Balls or beanbags or both are passed around the circle. The teacher or a selected student looks away from the class and randomly shouts, "stop!" The point of the game is to avoid getting stuck with an object. If this happens, the player(s) with an object must get up and move to the next circle. The teacher should begin the game with one object and gradually add objects if the class is capable.

Variation: The passing direction can be reversed on signal.

Jack Frost and Jane Thaw

Supplies: A white streamer for Jack Frost, a streamer of another color for Jane Thaw

Skills: Running, dodging, holding position

Formation: Scattered

Children are scattered and move to avoid being frozen (tagged) by Jack Frost, who carries a white streamer in one hand. Frozen children must remain immobile until touched (thawed) by Jane Thaw, identified by a streamer of a different color. Freezing occurs instantly, but thawing is a more gradual process. Two Jack Frosts can help keep the action moving.

Leap the Brook

Supplies: None

Skills: Leaping, jumping, hopping, turning

Formation:

A brook is marked off on the floor for a distance of about 30 feet. For the first 10 feet, it is 3 feet wide; for the next 10 feet, it is 4 feet wide; for the last 10 feet, it is 5 feet wide. Children form a single file and jump over the narrowest part of the brook. They should be encouraged to do this several times, using different styles of jumping and leaping. After they have satisfactorily negotiated the narrow part, they move to the next width, and so on.

Teaching Suggestion: The teacher should stress landing lightly on the balls of the feet in a bent-knee position. Good form should be stressed throughout the game. The selection of the distances is arbitrary, and the distances can be changed if they seem unsuitable for any particular group of children.

Variations: Children can use different means of crossing the brook—leaping, jumping, hopping. They also can vary the kinds of turns to be made—right or left; or quarter, half, three-quarter, or full. They should use different body shapes, different arm positions, and so on.

Marching Ponies

Supplies: None

Skills: Marching, running

Formation:

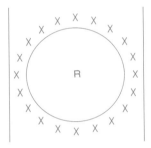

One child, the ringmaster, crouches in the center of a circle of ponies formed by the other children. Two goal lines on opposite sides of the circle are established as safe areas. The ponies march around the circle in step, counting as they do so. At a predetermined number (whispered to the ringmaster by the teacher), the ringmaster jumps up and attempts to tag the others before they can reach the safety lines. Anyone tagged joins the ringmaster in the center and helps catch the other children the next time. The game should be reorganized after six to eight children have been caught. Those left in the circle are declared the winners.

Variation: Other characterizations, such as lumbering elephants, jumping kangaroos, and the like, can be tried. A child who suggests a unique movement could be allowed to be the ringmaster.

May I Chase You?

Supplies: None

Skills: Running, dodging

Formation:

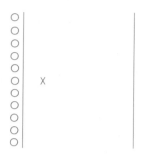

The class stands behind a line long enough to accommodate all. The runner stands about 5 feet in front of the line. One child in the line asks, "May I chase you?" The runner replies, "Yes, if you are wearing . . . ," naming a color, an article of clothing, or a combination of the two. All who qualify immediately chase the runner until she is tagged. The tagger becomes the new runner. Children can think of other ways to identify those who may run.

Midnight

Supplies: None
Skills: Running, dodging
Formation:

```
X|
X|
X|
X|
X|   Mr. Fox
X|     O
X|
X|
X|
X|
X|
```

A safety line is established about 40 feet from a den in which one player, the fox, is standing. The others stand behind the safety line and move forward slowly, asking, "Please, Mr. Fox, what time is it?" The fox answers in various fashions, such as "Bedtime," "Pretty late," "Three-thirty." The fox continues to draw the players toward him. At some point, he answers the question by saying "Midnight," and then chases the others back to the safety line. Any player who is caught joins the fox in the den and helps to catch others. No player in the den may leave, however, until the fox calls out "Midnight."

Variation: Lame Wolf. The wolf is lame and advances in a series of three running steps and a hop. Other children taunt, "Lame Wolf, can't catch me!" or "Lame Wolf, tame wolf, can't catch me!" The

wolf may give chase at any time. Children who are caught join the wolf and must also move as if lame.

Mix and Match

Supplies: None
Skills: Fundamental locomotor movements
Formation:

```
X    X    X  |  O    O   O
  X    X     |   O    O  O
X    X       |  O
  X    X     |   O    O
X            |  O    O
    X        |       O
  X    X     |   O    O   O
X   X        |  O   O
X       X    |       O    O
  X    X     |   O    O
X    X    X  |  O   O    O
```

A line is established through the middle of the area. Half of the children are on one side and half are on the other. There must be an odd person, the teacher or another child. The teacher gives a signal for children to move as directed on their side of the line. They can be told to run, hop, skip, or whatever. At another signal, children run to the dividing line, and each reaches across to join hands with a child from the opposite group. The goal is to not be left out. Children may reach over but may not cross the line. The person left out is moved to the opposite side so that players left out come from alternating sides of the area.

Variation: The game also can be done with music or a drumbeat, with the players rushing to the centerline to find partners when the rhythm stops.

Mousetrap

Supplies: None
Skills: Skipping, running, dodging
Formation:

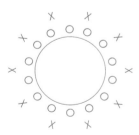

Half of the children form a circle with hands joined and face the center. This is the trap. The other children are on the outside of the circle. These are the mice. Three signals are given for the game. These can be word cues or other signals. On the first signal, the mice skip around, outside the circle, playing happily. On the second signal, the trap is opened. (The circle players raise their joined hands to form arches.) The mice run in and out of the trap. On the third signal, the trap snaps shut. (The arms come down.) All mice caught inside join the circle.

The game is repeated until all or most of the mice are caught. The players then exchange places, and the game begins anew. A child should not run in and out of the trap through adjacent openings.

Variation: This game is excellent with a parachute. The chute drops down and traps the mice.

Musical Ball Pass

Supplies: Playground ball per group, music
Skills: Passing and handling
Formation:

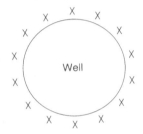

Players stand in circle formation facing the center. One ball is given to a player and is passed to the circle players when the music starts. When the music stops, the player with the ball (or the last player to touch the ball) goes into the "well" in the center of the circle. The player in the well stays there until another player is caught with the ball.

Variation: More than one ball may be used, depending on the skill of the class.

One, Two, Button My Shoe

Supplies: None
Skill: Running
Formation:

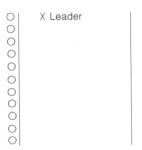

Two parallel lines are drawn about 50 feet apart. One child is the leader and stands to one side. The rest of the children are behind one of the lines. The leader says "Ready." The following dialogue takes place between the leader and the children.

CHILDREN: One, two.

LEADER: Button my shoe.

CHILDREN: Three, four.

LEADER: Close the door.

CHILDREN: Five, six.

LEADER: Pick up sticks.

CHILDREN: Seven, eight.

LEADER: Run, or you'll be late!

As children carry on the conversation with the leader, they toe the line, ready to run. When the leader says the word *late,* children run to the other line and return. The first child across the original line is the winner and becomes the new leader. The leader can give the last response ("Run, or you'll be late!") in any timing she wishes—pausing or dragging out the words. No child is to leave before the word *late* is uttered.

Popcorn

Supplies: None
Skills: Curling, stretching, jumping
Formation:

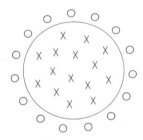

The teacher should give a short preliminary explanation of how popcorn pops in response to the heat applied. Half of the children are designated as popcorn; they crouch down in the center of the circle formed by the rest of the children. The circle children, also crouching, represent the heat. One of them is designated the leader, and his actions serve as a guide to the other children. The circle children gradually rise to a standing position, extend their arms overhead, and shake them vigorously to indicate the intensifying heat. In the meantime, the popcorn in the center starts to pop. This should begin at a slow pace and increase in speed and height as the heat is applied. In the final stages, children are popping up rapidly. After a time, the groups change places and the action is repeated.

Red Light

Supplies: None

Skills: Fundamental locomotor movements, stopping

Formation:

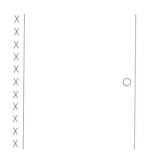

A goal line is established at one end of the area. The object of the game is to move across the area successfully without getting caught. One player is the leader and stands on the goal line. The leader turns away from the players, claps hands five times, and turns around on the fifth clap. In the meantime, the players move toward the goal line, timing their movements to end on the fifth clap. If the leader catches any movement by any person, that person is required to return to the starting line and begin anew. After the leader turns away, she can turn back immediately to catch any movement. Once she begins clapping, however, five claps must be completed before she turns around. The first child to reach the goal line successfully without being caught in an illegal movement is the winner and becomes the leader for the next game.

Variations:

1. An excellent variation of the game is to have the leader face the oncoming players. She calls out "Green light" for them to move and "Red light" for them to stop. When the leader calls other colors, the players should not move.

2. Different types of locomotion can be explored. The leader names the type of movement (e.g., hop, crawl, skip) before turning her back to the group.

3. The leader can specify how those caught must go back to place—walk, hop, skip, slide, crawl.

Teaching Suggestion: In the original game of Red Light, the leader counts rapidly, "One, two, three,

four, five, six, seven, eight, nine, ten—red light," instead of clapping five times. This has proved impractical in most gymnasiums, however, because children moving forward cannot hear the counting. Clapping, which provides both a visual and an auditory signal, is preferable.

Right Angle

Supplies: Music

Skills: Rhythmic movement, body management

Formation: Scattered

A tom-tom can be used to provide the rhythm for this activity. Some of the basic rhythm records also have suitable music. Children change direction at right angles on each heavy beat or change of music. The object of the game is to make the right-angle change on signal and not to bump into other players.

Rollee Pollee

Supplies: Many 8-inch foam balls

Skills: Ball rolling, dodging

Formation:

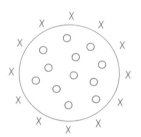

Half of the children form a circle; the other half are in the center. Balls are given to the circle players. The circle players roll the balls at the feet and shoes of the center players, trying to hit them. The center players move around to avoid the balls. A center player who is hit leaves the center and joins the circle.

After a period of time or when all of the children have been hit, the teams trade places. If a specified time limit is used, the team having the fewer players hit wins, or the team that puts out all of the opponents in the shorter time wins.

Teaching Suggestion: The instructor can have the children practice rolling a ball first. Balls that stop in the center are dead and must be taken back to the circle before being put into play again. The preferable procedure is to have the player who recovers a ball roll it to a teammate rather than return to place with the ball.

The Scarecrow and the Crows

Supplies: None

Skills: Dodging, running

Formation:

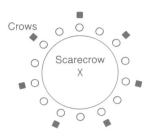

Children form a large circle representing the garden, which one child, designated the scarecrow, guards. From six to eight crows scatter on the outside of the circle, and the scarecrow assumes a characteristic pose inside the circle. The circle children raise their joined hands and let the crows run through, into the garden, where they pretend to eat. The scarecrow tries to tag the crows. The circle children help the crows by raising their joined hands and allowing them to leave the circle, but they try to hinder the scarecrow. If the scarecrow runs out of the circle, all the crows immediately run into the garden and start to nibble at the vegetables, while the circle children hinder the scarecrow's reentry.

When the scarecrow has caught one or two crows, a new group of children is selected. If, after a reasonable period of time, the scarecrow has failed to catch any crows, a change should be made.

Sneak Attack

Supplies: None

Skills: Running

Formation:

Two parallel lines are drawn about 60 feet apart. Children are divided into two teams. One team takes a position on one of the lines, with their backs to the area. These are the chasers. The other team is on the other line, facing the area. This is the sneak team. The sneak team moves forward on signal, moving toward the chasers. When they get reasonably close, a whistle or some other signal is given, and the sneak team turns and runs back to their line, chased by the other team. Anyone caught before reaching the line changes to the chase team. The game is repeated, with the roles exchanged.

Soap Bubbles

Supplies: Cones to delineate space, music

Skills: Body management

Formation: Scattered

Each player is a soap bubble floating throughout the area. The teacher calls out the locomotor movement youngsters use to move in the area. The entire area is used to start the game. As the game progresses, the size of the area is decreased by moving the cones. Bubbles freeze on signal. Music can be used to stimulate movement.

The object of the game is not to touch or collide with another bubble. When this occurs, both bubbles burst and sink to the floor and make themselves as small as possible. The space is made smaller until those who have not been touched are declared the winners. Those players who are broken bubbles may move to the unrestricted area and move. This is an excellent game for teaching the concept of moving in general space without touching anyone.

Squirrel in the Trees

Supplies: None

Skills: Fundamental locomotor movements

Formation:

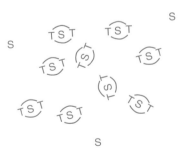

A number of trees are formed by two players facing each other and holding hands or putting hands on each other's shoulders. A squirrel is in the center of each tree, and one or two extra squirrels are outside. A signal to change is given. All squirrels move out of their tree to another tree, and the extra players try to find a free tree. Only one squirrel is allowed in a tree.

Teaching Suggestion: As a system of rotation, when each squirrel moves into a tree, he can change places with one of the players forming the tree. The rotation is important, because it ensures that all children eventually are active.

Statues

Supplies: None

Skills: Body management, applying force, balance

Formation: Scattered in pairs

Children are scattered in pairs around the area. One partner is the swinger and the other the statue. The teacher voices a directive, such as "Pretty," "Funny," "Happy," "Angry," or "Ugly." The swinger takes the statue by one or both hands, swings it around in a small circle two or three times (the teacher should specify), and releases it. The statue then takes a pose in keeping with the directive, and the swinger sits down on the floor.

The teacher or a committee of children can determine which children are the best statues. The statue must hold the position without moving or be disqualified. After the winners are announced, the partners reverse positions. Children should be cautioned that the purpose of the swinging is to position the statues and that it must be controlled.

Variation: In the original game, the swinging is done until the directive is called. The swinger then immediately releases the statue, who takes the pose as called. This gives little time for the statue to react. Better and more creative statues are possible if the directive is given earlier.

Stop Ball

Supplies: A ball

Skills: Tossing, catching

Formation:

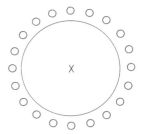

One child, with hands over the eyes, stands in the center of a circle of children. A ball is tossed clockwise or counterclockwise from child to child around the circle. Failing to catch the ball or making a bad toss incurs a penalty. That child must take one long step back and stay out of the game for one turn.

At a time of her own selection, the center player calls, "Stop." The player caught with the ball steps back and stays out for one turn. The center player should be allowed three or four turns and then be changed.

Tag Games (Simple)

Supplies: None

Skills: Fundamental locomotor movements, dodging

Formation: Scattered

Tag is played in many ways. Children are scattered about the area. One child is it and chases the others, trying to tag one of them. When a tag is made, he says, "You're it." The new it chases other children.

Variations:

1. Touching a specified type of object (e.g., wood, iron) or the floor or an object of a specified color can make a runner safe.

2. Children can be safe by doing a particular action or by striking a certain pose.
   a. *Stoop Tag.* Players touch both hands to the ground.
   b. *Stork Tag.* Players stand on one foot. (The other cannot touch.)
   c. *Turtle Tag.* Players get on their backs, feet pointed toward the ceiling.
   d. *Bowing Tag.* Players make an obeisance with forehead to the ground.
   e. *Nose-and-Toe Tag.* Players touch the nose to the toe.
   f. *Back-to-Back Tag.* Players stand back to back with any other child.
   g. *Skunk Tag.* Players reach an arm under one knee and hold the nose.

3. *Locomotor Tag.* The child who is it specifies how the others should move—skipping, hopping, jumping. The tagger must use the same kind of movement.

4. *Frozen Tag.* Two children are it. The rest are scattered over the area. When caught, they are "frozen" and must keep both feet in place. Any

free player can tag a frozen player and thus release her. The goal of the tagger is to freeze all players. Frozen players can be required to hop in place until released.

Teacher Ball (Leader Ball)

Supplies: A volleyball or rubber playground ball

Skills: Throwing, catching

Formation:

One child is the teacher or leader and stands about 10 feet in front of three other students, who are lined up facing the teacher. The object of the game is to move up to the teacher's spot by avoiding making bad throws or missing catches. The teacher throws to each child in turn, beginning with the child on the left, who must catch and return the ball. Any child making a throwing or catching error goes to the end of the line, on the teacher's right. Those in the line move up, filling the vacated space.

A teacher who makes a mistake must go to the end of the line and the child at the head of the line becomes the new teacher. The teacher scores a point by remaining in position for three rounds (three throws to each child). After scoring a point, the teacher takes a position at the end of the line and another child becomes the teacher.

Teaching Suggestion: This game should be used only after children have a minimal competency in throwing and catching skills. It can be a part of the skill-teaching program.

Variation: The teacher can suggest specific methods of throwing and catching, such as "Catch with the right hand only" or "Catch with one hand and don't let the ball touch your body."

Tommy Tucker's Land

Supplies: About ten beanbags for each game

Skills: Dodging, running

Formation:

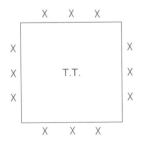

One child, Tommy Tucker (or Tammi Tucker, if a girl), stands in the center of a 15-foot square, within which the beanbags are scattered. Tommy is guarding his land and the treasure. The other children chant,

I'm on Tommy Tucker's land,
Picking up gold and silver.

Children attempt to pick up as much of the treasure as they can while avoiding being tagged by Tommy. Any child who is tagged must return the treasure and retire from the game. The game is over when only one child is left or when all of the beanbags have been successfully filched. The teacher may wish to call a halt to the game earlier if a stalemate is reached. In this case, the child with the most treasure becomes the new Tommy.

Variation: This game can be played with a restraining line instead of a square, but there must be boundaries that limit movement.

Twins (Triplets)

Supplies: None

Skills: Body management, running

Formation: Scattered with partner

Youngsters find a space in the area. Each youngster has a partner (twin). The teacher gives commands such as "Take three hops and two leaps" or "Walk backward four steps and three skips." When the pairs are separated, the teacher says, "Find your twin!" Players find their twin and stand frozen back to back. The goal is to not be the last pair to find each other and assume the frozen position.

Students need to move away from each other during the movements. One alternative is to find a new twin each time. Another variation is to separate twins in opposite ends of the playing area.

Variation: The game becomes more challenging when played in groups of three (triplets). When using this variation, new partners should be selected each time.

Where's My Partner?

Supplies: None

Skills: Fundamental locomotor movements

Formation:

Children are in a double circle by couples, with partners facing. The inside circle has one more player than the outside. When the signal is given, the circles skip (or walk, run, hop, or gallop) to the right. This means that they are skipping in opposite directions. On the command "Halt," the circles face each other to find partners. The player left without a partner is in the mush pot (the center area of the circle). When play starts again, this child enters either circle. The circles should be reversed after a time.

Variation: The game can also be played with music or a drumbeat. When the music stops, the players seek partners.

DEVELOPMENTAL LEVEL II

Compared with the games in developmental level I, the games program undergoes a definite change. Chase and tag games become more complex and demand more maneuvering. Introductory lead-up games make an appearance. The interests of children turn to games that have a sport slant, and kicking, throwing, catching, batting, and other sport skills are beginning to mature.

Addition Tag

Supplies: None

Skills: Running, dodging

Formation:

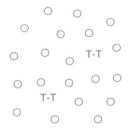

Two couples are it, and each stands with inside hands joined. These are the taggers. The other children run individually. The couples move around the playground, trying to tag with the free hands. The first person tagged joins the couple, making a trio. The three then chase until they catch a fourth. Once a fourth person is caught, the four divide and form two couples, adding another set of taggers to the game. This continues until all children are tagged.

Teaching Suggestions: Some limitation of area should be established to enable the couples to catch the runners; otherwise, the game moves slowly and is fatiguing. The game moves faster if started with two couples. A tag is legal only when the couple or group of three keeps their hands joined. The game can be used as an introductory activity, as all children are active.

Alaska Baseball

Supplies: A volleyball or soccer ball

Skills: Kicking, batting, running, ball handling

Formation:

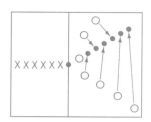

The players are organized in two teams, one of which is at bat while the other is in the field. A straight line provides the only out-of-bounds line, and the team at bat is behind this line at about the middle. The other team is scattered around the fair territory.

One player propels the ball, either batting a volleyball or kicking a stationary soccer ball. Her teammates are in a close file behind her. As soon as the batter sends the ball into the playing area, she starts to run around her own team. Each time the runner passes the head of the file, the team gives a loud count.

There are no outs. The first fielder to get the ball stands still and starts to pass the ball back overhead to the nearest teammate, who moves directly behind to receive it. The remainder of the team in the field must run to the ball and form a file behind it. The ball is passed back overhead, with each player handling the ball. When the last field player in line has a firm grip on it, she shouts "Stop." At this signal, a count is made of the number of times the batter ran around her own team. To score more sharply, half rounds should be counted.

Five batters or half of the team should bat; then the teams should change places. This is better than allowing an entire team to bat before changing to the field, because players in the field tire from many consecutive runs.

Variation: Regular bases can be set up, and the batter can run the bases. Scoring can be in terms of a home run made or not; or the batter can continue around the bases, getting a point for each base.

Arches

Supplies: Music

Skills: Moving rhythmically

Formation:

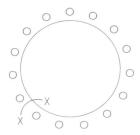

The game is similar to London Bridge. An arch is placed in the playing area. (To form an arch, two players stand facing one another with hands joined and arms raised.) When the music starts, the other players move in a circle, passing under the arch. Suddenly, the music stops, and the arch is brought down by dropping the hands. All players caught in an arch immediately pair off to form other arches, keeping in a general circle formation. If a caught player does not have a partner, he waits in the center of the circle until one is available. The last players caught (or left) form arches for the next game.

The arches should be warned not to bring down their hands and arms too forcefully so that children passing under are not pummeled.

Variation: Different types of music can be used, and children can move according to the pattern of the music.

Bat Ball

Supplies: An 8-inch foam ball

Skills: Batting, running, catching, throwing

Formation:

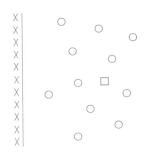

A serving line is drawn across one end of the field, and a 3-by-3-foot base is established about 50 feet from the serving line. Children are divided into two teams. One team is scattered over the

playing area. The other team is behind the serving line, with one player at bat. The batter puts the ball into play by batting it with a hand into the playing area. To be counted as a fair ball, the ball must land in the playing area or be touched by a member of the fielding team. As soon as the ball is hit, the batter runs to the base and back across the serving line. In the meantime, the fielding team fields the ball and attempts to hit the runner below the shoulders with it.

Fielders may not run with the ball. It must be passed from fielder to fielder until thrown at the batter. A pass may not be returned to the fielder from whom it was received. Violation of any of these rules constitutes a foul.

A run is scored each time the batter hits a fair ball, touches the base, and gets back to the serving line without being hit. A run is also scored if the fielding team commits a foul.

The batter is out when the ball is caught on the fly. Two consecutive foul balls also put the batter out. The batter is out when hit by a thrown ball in the field of play. Sides change when three outs are made.

Variation: *Shotgun Ball.* The entire batting team runs each time there is a fair ball. The defensive team tries to hit as many of the runners as possible. Instead of touching the base, the runners round it from either direction and return to the serving line. Each safe runner scores a run. More outs (six to ten) should be allowed before the teams change sides.

Beach Ball Bat Ball

Supplies: Four to six beach balls

Skills: Batting, tactile handling

Formation:

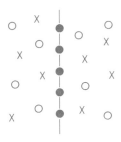

Two games are played across the gymnasium area. The teams are scattered throughout the area without restriction as to where they may move. To begin the game, the balls are placed on the center-line dividing the court area. Four to six beach balls are in play at the same time. A score occurs when the beach ball is batted over the end line. Once the ball moves across the end line it is dead. Players concentrate on the remaining balls in play.

If a ball is on the floor, it is picked up and batted into play. At no time may a ball be carried. After all four balls are scored, the game ends. A new game is started after teams switch goals.

Bounce Ball

Supplies: Volleyballs or rubber playground balls of about the same size

Skills: Throwing, ball rolling

Formation:

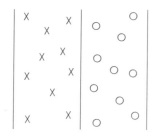

The court is divided into halves (30 by 40 feet each). Children form two teams. Each team occupies one half of the court and is given a number of balls. One or two players from each team should be assigned to retrieve balls behind their own end lines. The object of the game is to bounce or roll the ball over the opponents' end line. A ball thrown across the line on a fly does not count.

Two scorers are needed, one at each end line. Players can move wherever they wish in their own area but cannot cross the centerline. After the starting signal, the balls are thrown back and forth at will.

Variation: A row of benches is placed across the center line. Throws must go over the benches and bounce in the other team's area to score.

Box Ball

Supplies: A sturdy box, 2 feet square and about 12 inches deep; four volleyballs (or similar balls)

Skills: Running, ball handling

Formation:

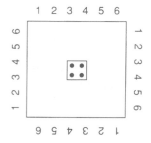

The class is divided into four even teams, with 6 to 10 players per team. Each team occupies one side of a hollow square at an equal distance from the center. Players face inward and number off consecutively from right to left.

A box containing four balls is put in the center. The instructor calls a number, and the player from each team who has that number runs forward to the box, takes a ball, and runs to the head of her line, taking the place of player 1. In the meantime, the players in the line have moved to the left just enough to fill in the space left by the runner. On reaching the head of the line, the runner passes the ball to the next person and so on down the line to the end child. The last child runs forward and returns the ball to the box. The first team to return the ball to the box scores a point.

The runner must not pass the ball down the line until she is in place at the head of the line. The ball must be caught and passed by each child. Failure to conform to these rules results in team disqualification. Runners stay at the head of the line, retaining their original number. Keeping the lines in consecutive number sequence is not important.

Busy Bee

Supplies: None

Skills: Fundamental locomotor movements

Formation:

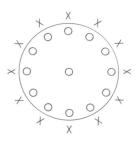

Half of the children form a large circle, facing in, and are designated the stationary players. The other children seek partners from this group, and stand in front of the stationary players. An extra child in the center is the busy bee. The bee calls out directions such as "Back to back," "Face to face," "Shake hands," "Kneel on one knee [or both]," and "Hop on one foot." The other children follow these directions.

The center child then calls out, "Busy bee." Stationary players stand still, and their partners seek other partners while the center player also tries to get a partner. The child without a partner becomes the new busy bee.

Teaching Suggestions: Children should be instructed to think about the different movements that they might have the class do if they become the busy bee. In changing partners, children must select a partner other than the stationary player next to them. After a period of time, the active and stationary players are rotated. Different methods of locomotion should also be used when children change partners.

Variations:

1. All children who have not repeated any partner during a specified number of exchanges (say, ten) and who have not been caught as the busy bee are declared winners.

2. Instead of standing back to back, children lock elbows and sit down as in the Back-to-Back Get-Up (p. 521). After they sit down and are declared safe, they can get up, and the game proceeds as described.

Cageball Kick-Over

Supplies: A cageball, 18-, 24-, or 30-inch size
Skill: Kicking
Formation:

```
O |   | X
O |   | X
O |   | X
O |   | X
O |   | X
O |   | X
O |   | X
O |   | X
O |   | X
O |   | X
O |   | X
```

Players are divided into two teams and sit facing each other, with legs outstretched and soles of the feet about 3 to 6 feet apart. While maintaining the sitting position, each player supports his weight on the hands, which are placed slightly to the rear.

The teacher rolls the cageball between the two teams. The object of the game is to kick the ball over the other team, thereby scoring a point. After a point is scored, the teacher rolls the ball into play again. A good system of rotation is to have the player on the left side of the line take a place on the right side after a point is scored, thus moving all the players one position to the left. When the ball is kicked out at either end, no score results, and the ball is put into play again by the teacher.

Variation: Children can be allowed to use their hands to stop the ball from going over them.

Club Guard

Supplies: A juggling club or bowling pin and foam rubber ball
Skill: Throwing
Formation:

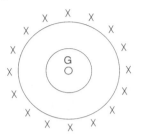

A circle about 15 feet in diameter is drawn. Inside the circle at the center, an 18-inch circle is drawn. The club is put in the center of the small circle. One child guards the club. The other children stand outside the large circle, which is the restraining line for them.

The circle players throw the ball at the club and try to knock it down. The guard tries to block the throws with the legs and body. She must, however, stay out of the small inner circle. The outer circle players pass the ball around rapidly so that one of the players can get an opening to throw, as the guard needs to maneuver to protect the club. Whoever knocks down the club becomes the new guard. If the guard steps into the inner circle, she loses the place to whoever has the ball at that time.

Teaching Suggestion: A small circle cut from plywood (or a hula hoop or similar object) makes a definite inner circle so that determining whether the guard steps inside is easier. The outer circle should also be definite.

Variation: More than one club can be in the center.

Competitive Circle Contests

Supplies: Volleyballs or 8-inch foam rubber balls, two bowling pins
Skills: Throwing, catching
Formation: Two circles with the same number of students in each

Two teams arranged in independent circles compete against each other. The circles should be of the same size; lines can be drawn on the floor to ensure this. The players of each team are numbered consecutively so that each player in one circle corresponds to a player in the other circle. The numbered players, in sequence, go to the center of the opponents' circle to compete for their team in either of the following activities.

1. *Circle Club Guard.* The center player guards a bowling pin. The circle that knocks down the club first wins a point. The ball should be rolled at the club.

2. *Touch Ball.* The circle players pass the ball from one to another while the center player tries to touch it. The center player who touches the ball first wins a point for the respective team. In case neither player is able to touch the ball in a reasonable period of time, the action should be cut off without awarding a point.

After all players have competed, the team with the most points wins. For Circle Club Guard, there must be three passes to different people before the ball can be thrown at the center. Establishing circle lines may be necessary to regulate throwing distance.

Couple Tag

Supplies: None

Skills: Running, dodging

Formation:

It couple

Two goal lines are established about 50 feet apart. Children run in pairs, with inside hands joined. All pairs, except one, line up on one of the goal lines. The pair in the center is it. They call "Come," and the children, keeping hands joined, run to the other goal line. The pair in the center, also retaining joined hands, tries to tag any other pair. As soon as a couple is caught, they help the center couple. The game continues until all are caught. The last couple caught is it for the next game.

Variation: Triplet Tag. The game can be played with sets of threes. Tagging is done with any pair of joined hands. If a triplet breaks joined hands, it is considered caught.

Crows and Cranes

Supplies: None

Skills: Running, dodging

Formation:

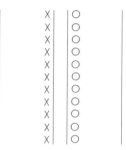

Two goal lines are drawn about 50 feet apart. Children are divided into two groups—the crows and the cranes. The groups face each other at the center of the area, about 5 feet apart. The leader calls out either "Crows" or "Cranes," using a *cr-r-r-r-r* sound at the start of either word to mask the result. If "Crows" is the call, the crows chase the cranes to the goal line. If "Cranes" is the call, then the cranes chase. Any child caught goes over to the other side. The team that has the most players when the game ends is the winner.

Variations:

1. Instead of facing each other, children stand back to back, about a foot apart, in the center.

2. The game can be played with the two sides designated as red and blue. A piece of plywood painted red on one side and blue on the other can be thrown into the air between the teams, instead of having someone give calls. If red comes up, the red team chases, and vice versa.

3. *Blue, black, and baloney.* On the command "Blue" or "Black," the game proceeds as described. On the command "Baloney," no one is to move. The caller should draw out the *bl-l-l-l* sound before ending with one of the three commands.

4. Another variation of the game is to have a leader tell a story using as many words beginning with *cr-* as possible. Words that can be incorporated into a story might be *crazy, crunch, crust, crown, crude, crowd, crouch, cross, croak, critter.* Each time one of these words is spoken, the beginning of the word is lengthened with a drawn out *cr-r-r-r* sound. No one may move on any of the words except *crows* or *cranes.*

Fly Trap

Supplies: None

Skills: Fundamental locomotor movements

Formation:

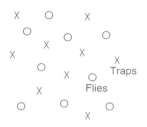

Half of the class is scattered around the playing area, sitting on the floor in cross-legged fashion. These children form the trap. The other children are the flies, and they buzz around the seated children. When a whistle is blown, the flies must freeze where they are. If any of the trappers can touch a fly, that fly sits down at that spot and becomes a trapper. The trappers must keep their seats glued to the floor.

The game continues until all of the flies are caught. Some realism is given to the game if the flies make buzzing sounds and move their arms as wings.

Teaching Suggestion: Some experience with the game enables the teacher to determine how far apart to place the seated children. After all (or most) of the flies have been caught, the groups trade places. The method of locomotion should be changed occasionally also.

Follow Me

Supplies: A marker for each child (squares of cardboard or plywood can be used; individual mats or beanbags work well)

Skills: All locomotor movements, stopping

Formation:

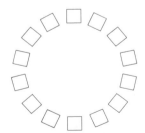

Children are arranged in a rough circle, each standing or sitting with one foot on a marker. An extra player is the guide. He moves around the circle, pointing at different players and asking them to follow. Each player chosen falls in behind the guide. The guide then takes the group on a tour, and the members of the group perform just as the guide does. The guide may hop, skip, do stunts, or execute other movements, and children following must do likewise. At the signal "Home," all run for places with a marker. One child is left without a marker. This child chooses another guide.

Teaching Suggestions: Making the last child the new leader is not a good idea, because this causes some children to lag and try to be last. Another way to overcome the tendency to lag is to make the first one back the guide. The teacher can also use a special marker; the first one to this marker becomes the new leader. A penalty can be imposed on the one who does not find a marker.

Fox Hunt

Supplies: None

Skills: Running, dodging

Formation:

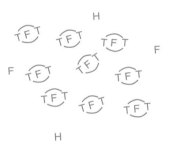

Two players form trees by facing each other and holding hands. The third member of the group is a fox and stands between the hands of the trees. Three players are identified as foxes without trees and three players are designated as hounds. The hounds try to tag foxes who are not in trees. The extra foxes may move to a tree and displace the fox who is standing in the tree. In addition, the foxes in trees may leave the safety of their trees at any time. If the hound tags a fox, their roles are reversed immediately, the fox becoming the hound.

The game should be stopped at regular intervals to allow the players who are trees to change places with the foxes and hounds. Different locomotor movements can be specified to add variety to the game.

Galloping Lizzie

Supplies: A beanbag or fleece ball

Skills: Throwing, dodging, running

Formation: Scattered

One player is it and has a beanbag or fleece ball. The other players are scattered around the playground. The player with the bag or ball runs after the others and attempts to hit another player below the shoulders with the object. The person hit becomes it, and the game continues. The tagger must throw the bag or ball, not merely touch another person with it.

Variation: A pair of children is it, with one of the players handling the bag or ball. A specific kind of toss can be called for (e.g., overhand, underhand, left-handed).

Hand Hockey

Supplies: 8-inch gray foam balls

Skills: Striking, volleying

Formation:

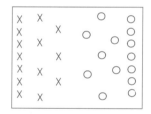

The players are on two teams. Half of the players on each team are guards and are stationed on the goal line as defenders. The other half are active players and are scattered throughout the playing area in front of their goal line.

The object of the game is to bat or push the ball with either hand so that it crosses the goal line that the other team is defending. Players may move the ball as in hockey but may not throw, hoist, or kick it. The defensive goal line players are limited to one step into the playing field when playing the ball.

The ball is put into play by being rolled into the center of the field. After a goal has been scored or after a specified period, guards become active players, and vice versa. An out-of-bounds ball goes to the opposite team and is put into play by being rolled from the sidelines into the playing area. If the ball becomes entrapped among players, play is stopped, and the ball is put into play again by a roll from the referee.

Players must play the ball and not resort to rough tactics. A player who is called for unnecessary roughness or for illegally handling the ball must go to the sidelines (as in hockey) and remain in the penalty area until the players change positions. Players should scatter and attempt to pass to each other rather than bunch around the ball.

Once youngsters learn the game, introduce more than one ball to increase the amount of activity.

Variation: *Scooter Hockey.* The active center players from each team are on gym scooters. The position that each child takes on the gym scooter can be specified or can be a free choice. Possible positions are kneeling, sitting, or balancing on the tummy. A hard surface is needed. This game version is usually played indoors on a basketball court.

Home Base

Supplies: Cones to delineate the area, four pinnies

Skills: Reaction time, locomotor movements, body management

Formation:

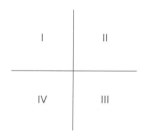

The area is divided into four quadrants with cones or floor lines. Each quadrant is the home base for one of the squads. The captain of the squad wears a pinnie for easy identification. The teams begin in a straight line sitting on the floor. The teacher calls out a locomotor movement that the players use to move throughout the area. When the teacher calls "Home base," the students return to their quadrant and return to the starting position behind their captain. The first team to return to proper position (sitting in a straight line) is awarded 2 points. Second place receives 1 point.

Teaching Suggestion: Avoid calling "Home base" until the students have left the area of their quadrant. A number of different formations can be specified which students must assume upon return to their home base.

Indianapolis 500

Supplies: None
Skills: Running, tagging
Formation:

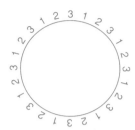

Children start in a large circle and are numbered off in threes or fours. A race starter says "Start your engines," and then calls out a number. Those children with the corresponding number run clockwise around the circle and try to tag players in front of them. If the leader yells "Pit stop," all runners have to stop and return to their original position. If "Accident" is called by the leader, all runners must change direction and proceed counterclockwise. Change the starter often.

Jump the Shot

Supplies: A jump-the-shot rope
Skill: Rope jumping
Formation:

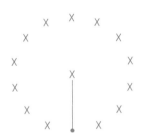

The players stand in circle formation. One player with a long rope stands in the center. A soft object is tied to the free end of the rope to give it some weight. An old, deflated ball or beanbag makes a good weight (tie the rope to it and use duct tape to keep it from becoming untied). The center player turns the rope under the feet of the circle players, who must jump over it. A player who touches the rope with the feet must move up to the next group.

Variations:

1. Change the center player after one or two misses. The center player should be cautioned to keep the rope along the ground. The rope

speed can be varied. A good way to turn the rope is to sit cross-legged and turn it over the head. Different tasks can be performed such as hopping, jumping and turning, or jumping and clapping.

2. Squads line up in spoke formation. Each member does a specified number of jumps (from three to five) and then exits. The next squad member in line must come in immediately without missing a turn of the rope. A player scores a point for the squad by coming in on time, jumping the prescribed number of turns, and exiting successfully. The squad with the most points wins.

3. Couples line up in the same formation. They join inside hands and stand side by side when jumping.

Loose Caboose

Supplies: None
Skills: Running, dodging
Formation:

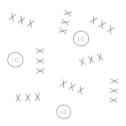

One child is designated as the loose caboose and tries to hook onto a train. Trains are formed by three or four children standing in column formation with each child placing the hands on the waist of the child immediately in front. The trains, by twisting and turning, endeavor to keep the caboose from hooking onto the back. Should the caboose manage to hook on, the front child in the train becomes the new caboose. Each train should attempt to keep together. If the number of children is 20 or more, there should be three or more cabooses.

Nine Lives

Supplies: Fleece balls
Skills: Throwing, dodging
Formation: Scattered

Any number of fleece balls can be used—the more the better. At a signal, players get a ball and hit as many people below waist level as possible. When a player counts that she has been hit nine times, she leaves the game and stands out of bounds until she has counted to 25. A player may run anywhere with a ball or to get a ball, but may possess only one ball at a time. Players must not be hit in the head. This puts the thrower out.

Teaching Suggestion: Children often cheat about the number of times they have been hit. A few words about fair play may be necessary, but a high degree of activity is the important game element.

Variations:

1. For a ball caught on the fly, a designated number of hits may be taken away.
2. Either left- or right-hand throwing can be specified.

Nonda's Car Lot

Supplies: None

Skills: Running, dodging

Formation:

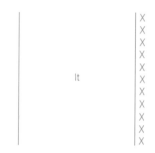

One player is it and stands in the center of the area between two lines established about 50 feet apart. The class selects four brands of cars (e.g., Honda, Corvette, Toyota, Cadillac). Each student then selects a car from the four but does not tell anyone what it is.

The tagger calls out a car name. All students who selected that name attempt to run to the other line without getting tagged. The tagger calls out the cars until all students have run. When a child (car) gets tagged, he must sit down at the spot of the tag. He cannot move but may tag other students who run too near. When the one who is it calls out "Car lot," all of the cars must go. The game is played until all students have been tagged.

One Step

Supplies: A ball or beanbag for each pair of children

Skills: Throwing, catching

Formation:

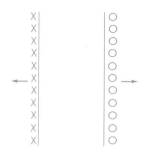

Two children stand facing each other about 3 feet apart. One has a ball or a beanbag. The object of the game is to throw or toss the item in the stipulated manner so that the partner can catch it without moving the feet on or from the ground. When the throw is completed successfully, the thrower takes one step backward and waits for the throw from her partner. Children can try to increase their distance to an established line, or the two children who move the greatest distance apart can be declared the winners. Variables to provide interest and challenge are type of throw, type of catch, and kind of step. Throwing can be underhand, overhand, two-handed, under one leg, around the back, and so on. Catching can be two-handed, left-handed, right-handed, to the side, and so on. The step can be a giant step, a tiny step, a hop, a jump, or a similar movement.

When either child misses, moves the feet, or fails to follow directions, the partners move forward and start over. A double line of children facing each other makes a satisfactory formation.

Variation: Bowling One Step. In groups of squad size or smaller, each of the players in turn gets a chance to roll the ball at a bowling pin. A minimal distance (5 to 10 feet) is established, so that most bowlers can hit the pin on the first try. The player takes a step backward each time the pin is knocked down, and keeps rolling until he misses. The winner is the child who has moved the farthest from the pin. Instead of backward steps, stipulated distances (5, 10, 15, and 20 feet) can be used.

Partner Stoop

Supplies: Music

Skills: Marching rhythmically

Formation:

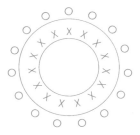

The game follows the same basic principle of stooping as in Circle Stoop, but is played with partners. The group forms a double circle, with partners facing counterclockwise, one partner is on the inside and one is on the outside. When the music begins, all march in the line of direction. After a short period of marching, a signal (whistle) is sounded, and the inside circle reverses direction and marches the other way—clockwise. The partners are thus separated. When the music stops, the outer circle stands still, and the partners making up the inner circle walk to rejoin their respective outer circle partners. As soon as children reach their partner, they join inside hands and stoop without losing balance. The last couple to stoop and those who have lost balance go to the center of the circle and wait out the next round.

Insist that players walk when joining their partner. This avoids the problem of stampeding and colliding with others.

Squad Tag

Supplies: Pinnies or markers for one squad, stopwatch

Skills: Running, dodging

Formation:

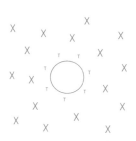

An entire squad acts as taggers. The object is to see which squad can tag the remaining class members in the shorter time. The tagging squad should be marked. They stand in a football huddle formation in the center of the area. Their heads are down, and their hands are joined in the huddle. The remainder of the class is scattered as they wish throughout the area. On signal, the tagging squad scatters and tags the other class members. A class member who is tagged stops in place and remains there. Time is recorded when the last person is tagged. Each squad gets a turn at tagging.

Teaching Suggestion: Children should be cautioned to move under control, because there is much chasing and dodging in different directions. Definite boundaries are needed.

Steal the Treasure

Supplies: A bowling pin
Skill: Dodging
Formation:

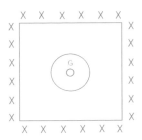

A playing area 20 feet square is outlined, with a small circle in the center. A bowling pin placed in the circle is the treasure. A guard is set to protect the treasure. Players then enter the square and try to steal the treasure without getting caught. The guard tries to tag them. Anyone tagged must retire and wait for the next game. The player who gets the treasure is the next guard.

Teaching Suggestion: If getting the treasure seems too easy, the child can be required to carry the treasure to the boundary of the square without being tagged.

Variation: *Bear and Keeper.* Instead of a treasure, a bear (seated cross-legged on the ground) is protected by a keeper. Anyone who touches the bear without being tagged becomes the new keeper, with the old keeper becoming the bear.

Trades

Supplies: None
Skills: Imagery, running, dodging

Formation:

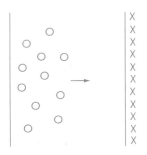

The class is divided into two teams of equal number, each of which has a goal line. One team, the chasers, remains behind its goal line. The other team, the runners, approaches from its goal line, marching to the following dialogue:

RUNNERS: Here we come.

CHASERS: Where from?

RUNNERS: New Orleans.

CHASERS: What's your trade?

RUNNERS: Lemonade.

CHASERS: Show us some.

Runners move up close to the other team's goal line and proceed to act out an occupation or a specific task that they have chosen previously. The opponents try to guess what the pantomime represents. On a correct guess, the running team must run back to its goal line chased by the others. Any runner tagged must join the chasers. The game is repeated with roles reversed. The team ending with the greater number of players is the winner.

Teaching Suggestion: If a team has trouble guessing the pantomime, the other team should provide hints. Teams also should be encouraged to have a number of activities selected so that little time is consumed in choosing the next activity to be pantomimed.

Trees

Supplies: None

Skills: Running, dodging

Formation:

Two parallel lines are drawn 60 feet apart. All players, except the one who is it, are on one side of the area. On the signal "Trees," the players run to the other side of the court. The tagger tries to tag as many as possible. Any player tagged becomes a tree, stopping where tagged and keeping both feet in place. A tree cannot move the feet but can tag any runners who come close enough. The child who is it continues to chase the players as they cross on signal until all but one are caught. This player becomes it for the next game.

To speed up the action, two or more taggers may be chosen. Children cross from side to side only on the signal "Trees."

Whistle March

Supplies: Music

Skill: Moving rhythmically

Formation: Scattered

A record with a brisk march is needed. Children are scattered around the room, individually walking in various directions and keeping time to the music. A whistle is blown a number of times. At this signal, lines are formed of that precise number of children, no more and no fewer. To form the lines, children stand side by side with locked elbows. As soon as a line of the proper number is formed, it begins to march to the music counterclockwise around the room. Any children left over go to the center of the room and remain there until the next signal. On the next whistle signal (a single blast), the lines break up, and all walk individually around the room in various directions.

When forming a new line, make a rule that children may not form the same combinations as in the previous line.

Whistle Mixer

Supplies: A whistle

Skills: All basic locomotor movements

Formation: Scattered

Children are scattered throughout the area. To begin, they walk around in any direction they wish. The teacher blows a whistle a number of times in succession with short, sharp blasts. Children then form small circles with the number in the circles equal to the number of whistle blasts. If there are four blasts, children form circles of four—no more, no less. The goal is not to be left out or caught in a circle with the incorrect number of students. Children should be encouraged to move to the center of the area and raise their hands to facilitate finding others without a group.

After the circles are formed, the teacher calls "Walk," and the game continues. In walking, children should move in different directions.

Variation: A fine version of this game is done with the aid of a tom-tom. Different beats indicate different locomotor movements—skipping, galloping, slow walking, normal walking, running. The whistle is still used to set the number for each circle.

Wolfe's Beanbag Exchange

Supplies: One beanbag per child

Skills: Running, dodging, tossing, catching

Formation: Scattered

Five or six children are identified as taggers. The remaining children start scattered throughout the area, each with a beanbag in hand. The taggers chase the players with beanbags. When a tag is made, the tagged player must freeze, keeping her feet still and beanbag in hand. To unfreeze a player, a nonfrozen player can exchange his beanbag for a beanbag held by a frozen player. If two frozen players are within tossing distance, they can thaw each other by exchanging their beanbags through the air using a toss and catch. *Both* tosses have to be caught or the beanbags must be retrieved and tried again.

Variation: After students have learned the game, tell the taggers that they may interfere with the tossing of beanbags between two frozen players by batting them to the floor. This forces the toss to be tried again and the players remain frozen until successful catches are made by both players.

DEVELOPMENTAL LEVEL III

Games at this level become more complex and organized. A great deal more cooperation is needed to make the activities enjoyable. In addition, an opportunity to use strategy exists, thus encouraging cognitive development.

Barker's Hoopla

Supplies: Hoops, beanbags

Skill: Running

Formation:

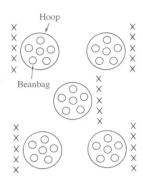

Five hoops are arranged with one in each corner and the other in the center of the playing area. Any distance between hoops can be used, but 25 to 30 feet is a challenging distance. Five to six beanbags are placed in each hoop. The class is divided into five equal teams, one group near each hoop. This is their home base. The object of the game is to steal beanbags from other hoops and return them to the hoop that is home base for each respective team.

The following rules are in effect:

1. A player can take only one beanbag at a time. That beanbag must be taken to the player's home base before she can return for another one.

2. Beanbags cannot be thrown or tossed to the home base, but must be placed on the floor in the hoop before being released.

3. No player can protect the home base or its beanbags with any defensive maneuver.

4. Beanbags may be taken from any hoop.

5. When the stop signal is given, every player must freeze immediately and release any beanbags in possession. Any follow-through of activities to get a final score is penalized.

The team with the most beanbags in their home-base hoop is declared the winner.

Bomb the Pins

Supplies: 8 to 12 bowling pins per team, 10 to 12 foam rubber balls

Skill: Throwing

Formation:

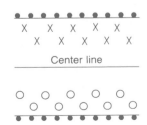

A line is drawn across the center of the floor from wall to wall. This divides the floor into two courts, each of which is occupied by one team. Another line is drawn 25 feet from the centerline in each court. This is the line where each team spaces its bowling pins. Each team has at least five balls.

The object of the game is to knock over the other team's pins—not to throw at opponents. Players throw the balls back and forth, but the players cannot cross the centerline. Whenever a pin is knocked over by a ball or player (accidentally or not), that pin is removed. The team with the most pins standing at the end of the game is declared the winner. Out-of-bounds balls can be recovered but must be thrown from inside the court.

Variations: Pins can be reset instead of removed. Two scorers, one for each pin line, are needed. Rolling the balls is an excellent modification.

Cageball Target Throw

Supplies: A cageball (18- to 30-inch), 12 to 15 smaller balls of various sizes

Skill: Throwing

Formation:

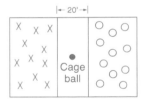

An area about 20 feet wide is marked across the center of the playing area, with a cageball in the center. The object of the game is to throw the smaller balls against the cageball, thus forcing it across the line in front of the other team. Players may come up to the line to throw, but they may not throw while inside the cageball area. A player may enter the area, however, to recover a ball. No one is to touch the cageball at any time, nor may the cageball be pushed by a ball in the hands of a player.

Teaching Suggestion: If the cageball seems to roll too easily, it should be deflated slightly. The throwing balls can be of almost any size—soccer balls, volleyballs, playground balls, or whatever.

Variation: Two rovers, one from each team, can occupy the center area to retrieve balls. These players cannot block throws or prevent a ball from

hitting the target. They are there for the sole purpose of retrieving balls for their team.

Chain Tag

Supplies: None

Skills: Running, dodging

Formation:

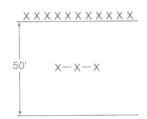

Two parallel lines are established about 50 feet apart. The center is occupied by three players who form a chain with joined hands. The players with free hands on either end of the chain do the tagging. All other players line up on one of the parallel lines.

The players in the center call "Come," and children cross from one line to the other. The chain tries to tag the runners. Anyone caught joins the chain. When the chain becomes too long, it should be divided into several smaller chains.

Variation: *Catch of Fish.* The chain catches children by surrounding them like a fishing net. The runners cannot run under or through the links of the net.

Circle Touch

Supplies: Yarnballs

Skills: Dodging, body management

Formation:

One child plays against three others, who form a small circle with joined hands. The object of the game is for the lone child to touch a designated child (on the shoulders) in the circle with a yarn-ball. The other two children in the circle, by dodging and maneuvering, attempt to keep the tagger away from the third member of the circle. The circle players may maneuver and circle in any direction but must not release hand grips. The tagger, in attempting to touch the protected circle player, must go around the outside of the circle. He is not permitted to go underneath or through the joined hands of the circle players.

Teaching Suggestion: The teacher should watch for roughness by the two in the circle protecting the third. To avoid roughness, the game should be played in short, 20-second bouts and then rotate in a new tagger.

Variation: A piece of cloth, a handkerchief, or a flag is tucked into the belt in back of the protected child. The fourth child, the tagger, tries to pull the flag from the belt.

Fast Pass

Supplies: One 8-inch foam rubber ball, pinnies
Skills: Passing, catching, moving to an open area
Formation: Scattered

One team begins with the ball. The object is to complete five consecutive passes without the ball touching the floor. The team without the ball attempts to intercept the ball or recover an incomplete pass. Each time a pass is completed, the team shouts the number of consecutive passes completed it represents. Each time a ball touches the floor or is intercepted, the count starts over.

Players may not contact each other. Emphasis should be placed on spreading out and using the entire court area. If players do not spread out, the area can be broken into quadrants and players restricted to one quadrant.

Flag Chase

Supplies: Flags, stopwatch
Skills: Running, dodging
Formation: Scattered

One team wears flags positioned in the back of the belt. The flag team scatters throughout the area. On signal, the object is for the chasing team to capture as many flags as possible in a designated amount of time. The flags are brought to the teacher or placed in a box. Players cannot use their hands to ward off a chaser. Roles are reversed. The team pulling the most flags is declared the winner.

Galactic Empire and Rebels

Supplies: None
Skills: Chasing, fleeing, dodging
Court markings:

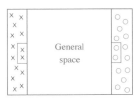

This game can be played indoors or outdoors in a square that is approximately 100 feet on each side. Each team's spaceport is behind the end line, where the single space fighters are stationed, waiting to issue against the enemy. To begin, one or more space fighters from either team move from their spaceport to entice enemy fliers for possible capture. A flyer leaving the spaceport may capture only opposing flyers who previously have left their respective spaceport. This is the basic rule of the game. A flyer may go back to her spaceport and be eligible immediately to issue again to capture an opponent who was already in general space. The technique of the game is to entice enemy flyers close to the spaceport so that fellow flyers can issue and capture (tag) an opposing flyer.

As an illustration of how the game proceeds: Rebel flyer 1 moves into general space to entice Empire flyer 1 so that he can be captured. Rebel flyer 1 turns back and heads for her spaceport, chased by Empire flyer 1. Rebel flyer 2 now leaves her spaceport and tags Empire flyer 1 before the Empire flyer can tag Rebel flyer 1. The Empire flyer is now a prisoner.

A player captured by an opposing flyer is taken to the tagger's prison—both captor and captive are given free passage to the prison. In prison, the captives form a chain gang, holding hands and extending the prisoners' line toward their own spaceport. The last captive is always at the end of the prisoners' line with one foot in the prison. Captives can be released if a teammate can get to them without being tagged. The released prisoner (only the end one) is escorted back to her own spaceport and both players are given free passage.

The game becomes one of capturing opposing flyers and securing the release of captured teammates. Flyers stepping over the sideline automatically become prisoners. One or two players in the spaceport should be assigned to guard the prison.

Set a time limit of 10 minutes, and declare the team with the most prisoners the winner.

Jolly Ball

Supplies: A cageball 24 inches or larger (or a 36- to 48-inch pushball)

Skill: Kicking

Formation:

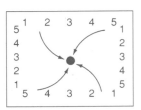

Four teams are organized, each of which forms one side of a hollow square. Children sit down, facing in, with hands braced behind them (crab position). The members of each team are numbered consecutively. Children wait until their number is called. Four active players (one from each team) move in crab position and try to kick the cageball over any one of the three opposing teams. The sideline players can also kick the ball. Ordinarily, the hands are not used, but this could be allowed in the learning stages of the game.

A point is scored against a team that allows the ball to go over its line. A ball that goes out at the corner between teams is dead and must be replayed. When a point is scored, the active children retire to their teams and another number is called. The team with the fewest points wins the game. This game is quite strenuous for the active players, so they should be rotated after a reasonable length of time when there is no score.

Variation: Two children from each team can be active at once.

Jump-the-Shot Variations

Supplies: A jump-the-shot rope

Skill: Rope jumping

Formation:

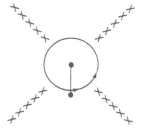

Before the following variations are tried, the jump-the-shot routines and variations listed previously (p. 577) should be reviewed.

1. Two or more squads are in file formation facing the rope turner. Each player runs clockwise (against the turn of the rope), jumping the rope as often as necessary to return to the squad.

2. Each player runs counterclockwise and tries to run around the circle before the rope can catch up with him. If this happens, he must jump to allow the rope to go under him. The best time for a player to start his run is just after the rope has passed.

3. Players can try some of the stunts in which the hands and feet are on the ground, to see whether they can have the rope pass under them. The Rabbit Jump, push-up position, Lame Dog, and others are possibilities.

Octopus

Supplies: None

Skills: Maneuvering, problem solving

Formation: Groups of six to nine, holding hands, tangled

Octopus is a game that gets its name from the many hands joined together in the activity. Children stand shoulder to shoulder in a tight circle. Everyone thrusts the hands forward and reaches through the group of hands to grasp the hands across the circle. Players must make sure that they do not hold both hands of the same player. Players also may not hold the hand of an adjacent player. The object is to untangle the mess created by the joined hands by going under, over, or through fellow players. No one is permitted to release a hand grip during the unraveling. What is the end result? Perhaps one large circle or two smaller connected circles.

Teaching Suggestion: If, after a period of time, the knotted hands do not seem to unravel, call a halt and administer first aid. The teacher and group can decide where the difficulty is and allow a change in position of those hands until the knot is dissolved. This should not be used as a competitive game because the difficulty of the knots cannot be equalized.

One-Base Tagball

Supplies: A base (or standard), a volleyball (8-inch foamball for younger children)

Skills: Running, dodging, throwing

Formation:

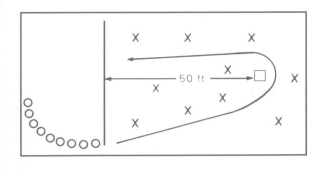

A home line is drawn at one end of the playing space. A base or standard is placed about 50 feet in front of the home line. Two teams are formed. One team is scattered around the fielding area, the boundaries of which are determined by the number of children. The other team is lined up in single file behind the home line.

The object of the game is for the fielding team to tag the runners with the ball. Two runners at a time try to round the base and head back for the home line without being tagged. The game is continuous, meaning that as soon as a running team player is tagged or crosses the home line, another player starts immediately.

The fielding team may run with the ball and pass it from player to player, trying to tag one of the runners. The running team scores a point for each player who runs successfully around the base and back to the home line.

At the start of the game, the running team has two players ready at the right side of the home line. The others on the team are in line, waiting for a turn. The teacher throws the ball anywhere in the field, and the first two runners start toward the base. They must run around the base from the right side. After all of the players have run, the teams exchange places. The team scoring the most points wins.

Teaching Suggestions: To facilitate tagging a runner, players on the fielding team should make passes to a person close to the runner. They must be alert, because two children at a time are running. The next player on the running team must watch carefully in order to start the instant one of the two preceding runners is back safely behind the line or has been hit.

Over the Wall

Supplies: None
Skills: Running, dodging

Formation:

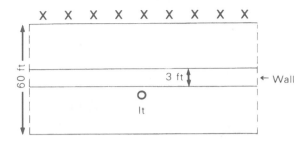

Two parallel goal lines are drawn about 60 feet apart. Two additional parallel lines about 3 feet apart are laid out parallel to the goal lines in the middle of the game area. This is the wall. One player is it and stands on, or behind, the wall. All of the other players are behind one of the goal lines. The tagger calls "Over the wall." All of the players must then run across the wall to the other goal line. The child who is it tries to tag any player she can. Anyone caught helps catch the others. Players also are considered caught when they step on the wall. They must clear it with a leap or a jump and cannot step on it anywhere, including on the lines. After crossing over to the other side safely, players must wait for the next call. The game can be made more difficult by increasing the width of the wall. The taggers can step on or run through the wall at will.

Pacman

Supplies: Markers in the shape of Pacman
Skills: Fleeing, reaction time
Formation:

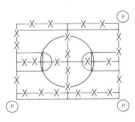

Three students are it and carry the Pacman marker. The remainder of the class is scattered throughout the area, standing on a floor line. Movement can only be made on a line.

Begin the game by placing the three taggers at the corners of the perimeter lines. Play is continuous; a player who is tagged takes the marker and becomes a new tagger. If a player leaves a line to escape being tagged, that player must secure a marker and become an additional tagger.

Pin Knockout

Supplies: Many playground balls, 12 bowling pins

Skills: Rolling, dodging

Formation:

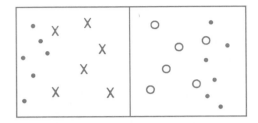

Two teams of equal number play the game. Each team is given many playground balls and six bowling pins. A court 30 by 60 feet or larger with a centerline is needed. The size of the court depends on the number of children in the game. The object of the game is to knock down all of the opponents' bowling pins. The balls are used for rolling at the opposing team's pins. Each team stays in its half of the court.

A player is eliminated if any of the following occurs:

1. He is touched by any ball at any time, regardless of the situation (other than picking up a ball).

2. She steps over the centerline to roll or retrieve a ball. (Any opposing team member hit as a result of such a roll is not eliminated.)

3. He attempts to block a rolling ball with a ball in his hands and the ball touches him in any manner.

A foul is called when a player holds a ball longer than 10 seconds without rolling at the opposing team. Play stops and the ball is given to the opposing team.

The bowling pins are put anywhere in the team's area. Players may guard the pins, but must not touch them. When a pin is down, even though it might have been knocked over unintentionally by a member of the defending team, it is removed immediately from the game. The game is over when all pins on one side have been knocked down.

Right Face, Left Face (Maze Tag)

Supplies: None

Skills: Running, dodging

Formation:

Children stand in rows that are aligned both from front to rear and from side to side. A runner and a chaser are chosen. Children all face the same way and join hands with the players on each side. The chaser tries to tag the runner, who runs between the rows with the restriction that she cannot break through or under the arms. The teacher can help the runner by calling "Right face" or "Left face" at the proper time. On command, the children drop hands, face the new direction, and grasp hands with those who are then on each side, thus making new passages available. When the runner is caught or when children become tired, a new runner and chaser are chosen.

Variations:

1. Directions (north, south, east, west) can be used instead of the facing commands.

2. *Streets and Alleys.* The teacher calls, "Streets," and the children face in one direction. The call "Alleys" causes them to face at right angles.

3. The command "Air raid" can be given, and children drop to their knees and make themselves into small balls, tucking their heads and seats down.

4. Having one runner and two chasers speeds up the action.

Scooter Kickball

Supplies: A cageball, gym scooters for active players

Skill: Striking with various body parts

Formation:

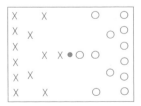

Each team is divided into active players (on scooters) and goal defenders. The active players are seated on the scooters, and the goal defenders are seated on the goal line, with feet extended. The object of the game is to kick the cageball over the goal line defended by the opposite team. The players are positioned as shown above.

The game starts with a face-off of two opposing players on scooters at the center of the court. The face-off is also used after a goal is scored. The active players on scooters propel the ball mainly with their feet. Touching the ball with the hands is a foul and results in a free kick by the opposition at the spot of the foul. A player also may use the head and body to stop and propel the ball.

The players defending the goal are seated on the goal line. They may not use their hands either, but use of the feet, body, and head is permitted. (If scoring seems too easy, then the defenders can be allowed to use their hands.) Defenders should be restricted to the seated position at the goal line; they are not permitted to enter the field of play to propel or stop the ball.

Teaching Suggestions: If the sidelines are close to the walls of the gymnasium, out-of-bounds balls need not be called because the ball can rebound from the wall. The number of scooters determines the number of active players. The game works well if half of the players from each team are in the center on scooters and the other half are goal defenders. After a goal or after a stipulated time period, active players and goal defenders exchange places.

Some consideration should be made for glasses; otherwise they might be broken. Any active player who falls off a scooter should be required to sit again on the scooter before becoming eligible to propel the ball.

Variation: If there are enough scooters for everyone, the game can be played with rules similar to soccer. A more restricted goal (perhaps half of the end line) can be marked with standards. A goalie defends this area. All other players are active and can move to any spot on the floor. The floor space should be large enough to allow some freedom of play. Putting too many active players in a relatively small space causes jamming.

Star Wars

Supplies: Four bowling pins
Skill: Running

Formation:

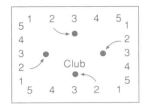

A hollow square, about 10 yards on each side, is formed by four teams, each of which occupies one side, facing in. The teams should be even in number, and the members of each team should count off consecutively from right to left. This means that one person on each team has the same number as one child on each of the other three teams. Children are seated cross-legged.

A number is called by the teacher. The four children with the number run to the right, all the way around the square, and through their own vacated space toward the center of the square. Near the center, in front of each team, stands a bowling pin. The first child to put the bowling pin down on the floor is the winner. The pins should be at an equal distance in front of the teams and far enough away from each other to avoid collisions in the center.

Scoring is kept by the words *Star Wars.* The player who puts the pin down first gets to write two letters of the name. The player who is second gets to write one letter. The lettering can be done in a space in front of each team, where the name would be reasonably protected from the runners. The first team to complete the name is the winner.

Teaching Suggestion: In number games of this type, the numbers are not called in order. The teacher should keep a tally to make sure that every number is called.

Variation: Instead of being seated, each child can take a prone position, as if ready to do a push-up. The teacher gives a preliminary command, such as "Ready," and each child comes up to a push-up position. The teacher then calls the number. Children with other numbers return to the prone position. Each child does a push-up every time a number is called.

Sunday

Supplies: None
Skills: Running, dodging

Formation:

```
X          |              | O
X          |              | O
X          |              | O
X          |              | O
X          |     It       | O
X          |              | O
X          |              | O
X          |              | O
X          |              | O
X          |              | O
```

Two parallel lines are drawn about 50 feet apart. One player is it and stands in the center of the area between the two lines. All of the other children are on one of the two lines. The object is to cross to the other line without being tagged and without making a false start.

All line players stand with their front foot on the line. The line players must run across the line immediately when the tagger calls "Sunday." Anyone who does not run immediately is considered caught. The tagger can call other days of the week to confuse the runners. No player may make a start if another day of the week is called. The tagger must be careful to pronounce "Monday" in such a way that it cannot be confused with "Sunday." If confusion does occur, "Monday" can be eliminated from the signals for the false start.

Teaching Suggestion: "Making a start" must be defined clearly. To begin, it can be defined as a player moving either foot. Later, when children get better at the game, a forward movement of the body can constitute a start.

Touchdown

Supplies: A small object that can be concealed in the hand

Skills: Running, dodging

Formation:

Two parallel lines about 60 feet apart are needed. Two teams face each other, each standing on one of the parallel lines. One team goes into a huddle, and the members decide which player is to carry an object to the opponents' goal line. The team moves out of the huddle and takes a position like a football team. On the charge signal "Hike," the players run toward the opponents' goal line, each player holding the hands closed as if carrying the object. On the charge signal, the opponents also run forward and tag the players. On being tagged, a player must stop immediately and open both hands to show whether or not he has the object.

If the player carrying the object reaches the goal line without being tagged, she calls "Touchdown" and scores 6 points. The scoring team retains possession of the object and gets another try. If the player carrying the object is tagged in the center area, the object is given to the other team. They go into a huddle and try to run it across the field to score.

Triplet Stoop

Supplies: Music

Skill: Moving rhythmically

Formation:

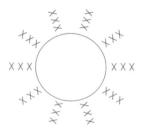

The game is played in groups of three with the three youngsters holding hands and marching abreast, counterclockwise. On signal, the outside player of the three continues marching in the same direction. The middle player of the three stops and stands still. The inside player reverses direction and marches clockwise. When the music stops, the groups of three attempt to reunite at the spot where the middle player stopped. The last three to join hands and stoop are put into the center for the next round.

Whistle Ball

Supplies: A ball for each group of six to eight players

Skills: Passing, catching

Formation: Circles of six to eight

Eight or fewer children stand in circle formation. A ball is passed rapidly back and forth among them in any order. The object is to be the player who stays in the game the longest. A child sits down in place who makes any of the following errors:

1. He has the ball when the whistle blows. (The teacher should set a predetermined time period, at the end of which a whistle is blown. The time period can be varied from 5 to 20 seconds.)

2. She makes a bad throw or fails to catch a good throw.

3. He returns the ball directly to the person from whom it was received.

Teaching Suggestion: One way to control the time periods is to appoint a child as timer and to give her a list of the time periods, a whistle, and a stopwatch. The timer should be cautioned not to give any advance indication of when the stop signal will be blown. An automatic timer enhances the game. When the game gets down to two or three players, declare them the winners and begin anew.

Miscellaneous Playground Games

The following games are useful only for small groups, but children do enjoy playing them on the playground.

Suggested Games

Four Square

Frisbee Golf (disk golf)

Team Handball

Tetherball

Two Square

Volley Tennis

Four Square (Developmental Levels II and III)

Supplies: 8-inch playground ball or volleyball

Skill: Batting a ball

Court markings:

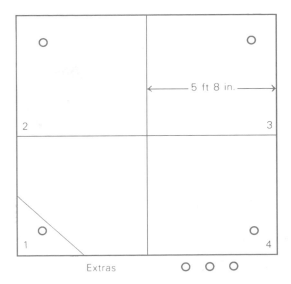

Lines are drawn as shown above. The squares should be numbered 1, 2, 3, and 4. A service line is drawn diagonally across the far corner of square 1. The player in this square always serves and must stay behind the line when serving.

The ball is served by dropping and serving it underhanded from the bounce. If the serve hits a line, the server is out. The server can hit the ball after it has bounced once in his square. The receiver directs it to any other square with an underhand hit. Play continues until one player fails to return the ball or commits a fault. Any of the following constitutes a fault:

1. hitting the ball sidearm or overhand

2. landing a ball on a line between the squares (A ball landing on an outer boundary is considered good.)

3. stepping into another square to play the ball

4. catching or carrying a return volley

5. allowing the ball to touch any part of the body except the hands

When a player misses or commits a fault, she goes to the end of the waiting line and all players move up. The player at the head of the waiting line moves into square 4.

Variations:

1. A 2-foot circle can be drawn at the center of the area. Hitting the ball into the circle constitutes a fault.

2. The game can be changed by varying the method of propelling the ball. The server sets the method. The ball can be hit with a partially closed fist, the back of the hand, or the elbow. A foot or knee also can be used to return the ball. The server calls "Fisties," "Elbows," "Footsies," or "Kneesies" to set the pattern.

3. *Chain Spelling.* The server names a word, and each player returning the ball must add the next letter in the sequence.

4. Hula-Hoops can be used so that all students can play at one time.

5. Cooperative scoring can be used with Level I students to see how many consecutive hits they can make without missing.

Frisbee Golf

Supplies: One Frisbee per person, hoops for hole markers, cones

Skills: Frisbee throwing for accuracy

Suggested golf course design:

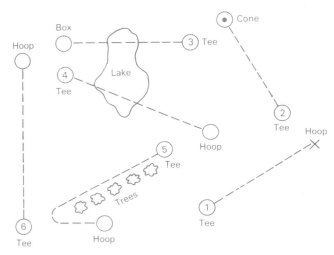

Frisbee Golf or disk golf is a favorite game of many students. Boundary cones with numbers can be used for tees, and holes can be boxes, hula hoops, trees, tires, garbage cans, or any other available equipment on the school grounds. Draw a course on a map for students and start them at different holes to decrease the time spent waiting to tee off. Regulation golf rules apply. The students can jog between throws for increased activity.

Disk golf is played like regular golf. One stroke is counted for each time the disk is thrown and when a penalty is incurred. The object is to acquire the lowest score. The following rules dictate play:

Tee-throws: Tee-throws must be completed within or behind the designated tee area.

Lie: The lie is the spot on or directly underneath the spot where the previous throw landed.

Throwing order: The player whose disk is the farthest from the hole throws first. The player with the least number of throws on the previous hole tees off first.

Fairway throws: Fairway throws must be made with the foot closest to the hole on the lie. A run-up is allowed.

Dog leg: A dog leg is one or more designated trees or poles in the fairway that must be passed on the outside when approaching the hole. There is a two-stroke penalty for missing a dog leg.

Putt throw: A putt throw is any throw within 10 feet of the hole. A player may not move past the point of the lie in making the putt throw. Falling or jumping putts are not allowed.

Unplayable lies: Any disk that comes to rest 6 feet or more above the ground is unplayable. The next throw must be played from a new lie directly underneath the unplayable lie (one-stroke penalty).

Out-of-bounds: A throw that lands out-of-bounds must be played from the point where the disk went out (one-stroke penalty).

Course courtesy: Do not throw until the players ahead are out of range.

Completion of hole: A disk that comes to rest in the hole (box or hoop) or strikes the designated hole (tree or pole) constitutes successful completion of that hole.

Team Handball

Supplies: Team handball, foam rubber ball, or volleyball; cones; pinnies

Skills: Running, dribbling, passing, throwing, catching

Court markings:

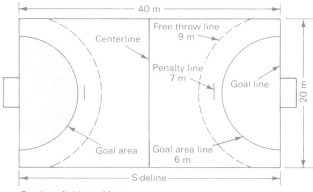

Outdoor field markings

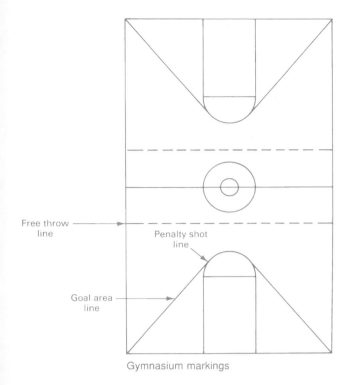

Free throw
line

Penalty shot
line

Goal area
line

Gymnasium markings

The court is marked with a 6-meter goal area, a 7-meter penalty line, and a 9-meter free-throw line. The goal is 2 by 3 meters. The goal area inside the 6-meter line is only for the goalie. Other players are not allowed in this area. The 7-meter line is used for a major penalty shot, and the 9-meter line is used for a minor penalty shot. A regulation court is 20 by 40 meters. Boundary cones, tape on the wall, rope through a chain-link fence, soccer goals, or field hockey goals can be substituted for actual team handball goals. For indoor play, a basketball court can be modified for team handball by running a line from the corners of the court to top of the key.

The object of the game is to move a small soccer ball down the field by passing and dribbling and then to throw the ball into a goal area that is 3 meters wide and 2 meters high. In regulation play, each team has six court players and one goalie. The six court players cover the entire court. A player is allowed three steps before and after dribbling the ball. There is no limit on the number of dribbles. Dribbling is, however, discouraged because passing is more effective. A double dribble is a violation. A player can hold the ball for 3 seconds only before passing, dribbling, or shooting. Players cannot kick the ball in any way, except the goalie.

One point is awarded for a goal. Violations and penalties are similar to basketball. A free throw is taken from the point of the violation, and defense must remain 3 meters away while protecting the

goal. A penalty throw is awarded from the 7-meter line for a major violation. A major violation occurs when an offensive player who is inside the 9-meter line in a good shooting position is fouled. During a penalty throw, all players must be behind the 9-meter line. For more in-depth coverage of rules, a rulebook can be secured from the United States Team Handball Federation, 1750 E. Boulder, Colorado Springs, CO 80909.

The offensive team starts the game with a throw-on from the center line. A throw-on also initiates play after each goal. All six offensive players line up at the centerline, and a teammate throws the ball to a teammate. The defense is in position, using either a zone or person-to-person defense. Offensive strategy is similar to basketball with picks, screens, rolls, and movement to open up shots on the goal. With a zone defense, short, quick passes are made in an overloaded portion of the zone.

The defensive strategy is similar to basketball, with person-to-person and zone defense being popular. Beginning players should start with the person-to-person defense and learn how to stay with an offensive player. The back players in the zone are back against the goal line, while the front players are just inside the 9-meter line. The zone rotates with the ball as passes are made around the court.

Teaching Suggestions: Learning stations can be set up for passing, shooting, goal tending, dribbling, and defensive work. Performance objectives are useful for structuring practice time at each station. Students can play with nerf balls, playground balls, and volleyballs to get more practice attempts and to help beginning goalies perfect their skills. Group drills from basketball are applicable to team handball defense, offense, passing, and dribbling. Various instructional devices can be included for targets in passing, timing for dribbling through cones, or narrowing the goal area for shots to the corners. Penalty shots should be practiced. Competitive-type drills are enjoyable and motivating for most students.

Variation: Sideline Team Handball. This game can be played when space is limited and too many students are in a class. Extra team members spread out along each sideline. These sideline players can receive passes from teammates and can help pass the ball down the court. Sideline members can only pass the ball, however, and the 3-second rule applies to them. One sideline can be one team, and the other sideline the other team. A challenging variation might have different team members on each sideline. This distribution forces the active players to sharpen their passing skills.

Tetherball (Developmental Levels II and III)

Supplies: A tetherball assembly (pole, rope, and ball)

Skill: Batting a ball

Court markings:

The first server is picked by lot. One player stands on each side of the pole. The server puts the ball into play by tossing it into the air and hitting in the direction he chooses. The opponent must not strike the ball on the first swing around the pole. On its second swing around the pole, she hits the ball back in the opposite direction. As the ball is hit back and forth, each player tries to hit it so that the rope winds completely around the pole in the direction in which he is hitting the ball. The game is won by the player who succeeds in doing this or whose opponent forfeits the game by making a foul. A foul is any of the following:

1. hitting the ball with any part of the body other than the hands or forearms
2. catching or holding the ball during play
3. touching the pole
4. hitting the rope with the forearms or hands
5. throwing the ball

6. winding the ball around the pole below the 5-foot mark

After the opening game, the winner of the preceding game serves. Winning four games wins the set.

Two Square (Developmental Levels II and III)

Supplies: A playground ball or volleyball

Skill: Batting a ball

The basic rules and lines are the same as for Four Square, except that only two squares are used. If there are players waiting for a turn, the active player who misses or fouls can be eliminated as in Four Square. If only two players wish to play, score can be kept. The ball must be served from behind the baseline.

Volley Tennis

Supplies: A volleyball

Skills: Most volleyball skills

Formation: Scattered

The game can be played as a combination of volleyball and tennis. The net is put on the ground, as in tennis, and the ball is put into play with a serve. It may bounce once or can be passed directly to a teammate. The ball must be hit three times before going over the net. Spiking is common because of the low net. A point is scored when it cannot be returned over the net to the opposing team.

REFERENCES AND SUGGESTED READINGS

Morris, G. S. D., & Stiel, J. (1989). *Changing kids' games,* Champaign, IL: Human, Kinetics.

Relays

PURPOSE OF ACTIVITIES IN THIS CHAPTER
Relays teach cooperative skills because all students must follow specific rules to reach common goals. Relays are *not* useful for teaching motor skills as they focus on competition rather than proper skill performance. All relays in this chapter require a fundamental skill, i.e., running, jumping, and so on. Because these skills have been overlearned by Level II and III students, relays in this chapter can be completed successfully by all students.

Relays can help children learn to cooperate because they demand that team-mates follow rules and directions. The use of relays is appropriate if they feature skills that children have overlearned. Youngsters do not learn new motor skills in relay activity, and teachers should avoid using them with such a goal in mind. Instead, skills that children have already learned should be used as the basis for movement in a relay. This implies restricting relays to types that emphasize learned locomotor skills. Teachers mistakenly think that practicing a skill in a relay is an effective way to learn. The truth of the matter is that youngsters concentrate on the outcome of the relay rather than correctly performing the skill.

Instructors sometimes use relays to solve motivational problems, because relays do motivate some children. However, teachers should remember that some youngsters will dislike having to perform competitively in front of others. Few skills are learned in a relay because the emphasis is on winning rather than learning. Another inherent problem with relays is that the majority of children are inactive—standing in line waiting for their turn. For these reasons, relays should be used sparingly and only at opportune times.

INSTRUCTIONAL PROCEDURES

1. Teams should be restricted to four or five players. Too many on a team increases the amount of time spent waiting for a turn.

2. If teams have uneven numbers, some players on the smaller teams can run twice. All children on teams with fewer members must take a turn running twice; otherwise, the more skilled runners may always run and create an unfair advantage.

3. Teams should be changed regularly so that all youngsters have a chance to be on a winning team. Teachers should reserve the right to change team makeup as well as the order in which the students are placed on individual teams.

4. Placing less skilled players in the first or last position of the relay team will force these students to perform in front of the class and reveal to others that they are inferior. To avoid this situation, place less skilled students in the middle of the team. Discretion can be used when moving players to avoid labeling them as unskilled performers.

5. Infractions of the rules should be discussed. Relays are a social learning experience. Children are in a situation where they must conform to rules if the experience is going to be enjoyable for all students. This is an effective time to discuss how cooperation precedes competition; it is impossible to compete if players choose not to cooperate.

6. The finishing order must be determined properly. In giving instructions, teachers should be definite about the start, the turning point, and the finishing act.

7. A deceleration area should be delineated by a marker to prevent running into a wall. This turn-around and end area can be marked by

cones, bowling pins, jump standards, or beanbags. With cones and bowling pins, knocking over the marker is a disqualification unless the runner resets it before proceeding.

8. Too much emphasis on winning makes the skilled resent losing and intimidates those of lesser ability. The idea of winning at any cost must be discussed and discouraged.

9. A trial run should always be made so that each team understands the procedures. If a new relay does not seem to have been started properly, stop the activity and review the instructions. Practice the relay first before embarking on a serious competitive run.

10. Traffic rules should be clear. In most cases, the way to the right governs. When runners go around the turning point, they do it from the right (counterclockwise), returning past the finish line on the right side. Some procedures to ensure a fair tagging off of the next runner should be instituted. Runners should not leave the restraining line before being tagged. Exchanging a baton or a beanbag can help ensure fair play.

RELAYS FOR DEVELOPMENTAL LEVELS II AND III

Most of the relays presented here can be used successfully with children at developmental levels II and III. The relays incorporate already learned motor skills and are arranged roughly according to increasing difficulty. If youngsters have not learned the skill required for the relay, the relay should not be utilized until proper learning occurs.

Beanbag Relays

Beanbag relays make a good starting point for younger children, because beanbags can be handled more easily than balls.

Beanbag Pass Relay

Players are in a line, standing side by side. The player on the right starts the beanbag, which is passed from one player to the next down the line. When it gets to the end of the line, the relay is over. The teacher should be sure that each player handles the bag. Children should rotate positions in line.

In the next stage, a revolving relay can be developed in which each member of the team rotates from the right of the squad to the left. When each child has had an opportunity to be the lead member of the group, the relay is finished. This relay can be varied with an underleg pass. The child passes the beanbag underneath one leg to the next player.

Circle Beanbag Pass Relay

Players stand in a circle, facing out, but close enough so that the beanbag can be handed from player to player. One circuit begins and ends with the same player. The underleg pass can be used in this formation also.

Carry-and-Fetch Relay

Players are in closed squad formation, with a hoop or circle positioned up to 30 feet in front of each team. The first runner on each team has a beanbag. On the command "Go," this player carries the beanbag forward and puts it inside the hoop, then returns and tags off the next runner. The second runner goes forward, picks up the beanbag, and hands it off to the third runner. One runner carries the beanbag forward and the next runner fetches it back. Different locomotor movements can be specified.

Beanbag Circle Change Relay

Players are in lane formation. Two hoops or circles are about 15 and 30 feet in front of each team. A beanbag is in the far hoop (Figure 23.1). The first runner runs forward, picks up the beanbag, and moves it to the inner hoop. The next player picks it up and takes it back to the other hoop. The beanbag must rest inside the hoop.

The Farmer and the Crow Relay

Runners are in lane formation. A line is drawn about 20 feet in front of the teams. The first runner of each team is the farmer, the second runner the crow, and so on. The farmer has five beanbags. On the signal "Go," the farmer hops forward and drops the five beanbags in a reasonably spaced fashion, with the last beanbag placed beyond the drawn line. The farmer then runs back and tags the next player, the crow. The crow runs to the farthest

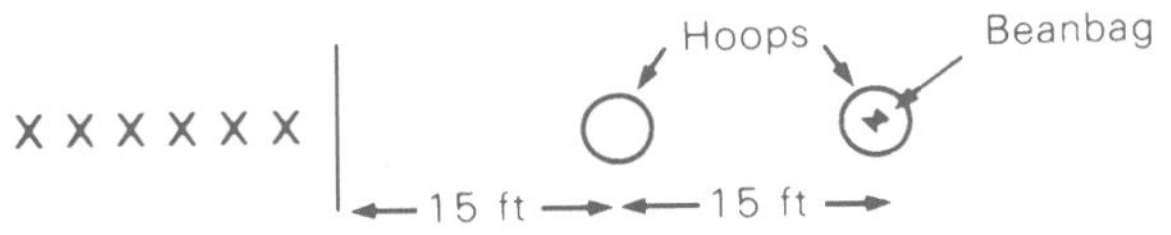

Figure 23.1 Formation for Beanbag Circle Change Relay

beanbag, begins hopping, picking up the beanbags. The crow hands the five beanbags to the third runner, another farmer, who puts the objects out again.

Whenever players have a beanbag, they hop; when they have no beanbags, they run. The last beanbag should be placed beyond the far line, because this determines how far each player has to move. The relay can be done with only hopping allowed.

Lane Relays without Equipment

In lane relays, each runner runs in turn. The race is over when the last runner finishes. Lane relays are usually regular relays. Different types of movements can be used to challenge the runners.

1. Locomotor movements: Walking, running, skipping, hopping, galloping, sliding, jumping
2. Stunt and animal movements: Puppy Dog Run (p. 491), Seal Crawl (p. 507), Bear Walk (p. 495), Rabbit Jump (p. 495), Frog Jump (p. 507), Crab Walk (p. 496)
3. Restricted movements: Heel-and-toe walk, sore toe walk (hold the left foot with the right hand), walking on the heels, Crazy Walk (p. 505), Toe Tug Walk (p. 520)

Partner relays are also challenging and fun.

1. Children run (walk, skip, gallop, hop) with partners (inside hands joined) just as a single runner would.
2. Children face each other with hands joined (as partners), slide one way to a turning point, and slide back to the starting point—leading with the other side.
3. *Wheelbarrow Relay.* One person walks on her hands while the partner holds her by the lower legs, wheeling her down to a mark. Positions are switched for the return. Distances should not be too long.

Lane Relays with Equipment

The use of equipment can be added to basic lane relays.

1. *All Up, All Down Relay.* Three bowling pins are set in a small circle about 20 feet in front of each team. The first player runs forward and sets up the pins one at a time, using only one hand. The pins must stand. The next player puts them down again, and so on.

2. A short line (24 inch) is drawn about 20 feet in front of each team. A bowling pin stands on one side of the line. Each player must run forward and stand the pin on the other side of the line, using one hand only.

3. Two adjacent circles are drawn about 20 feet in front of each team. Three bowling pins stand in one of the circles. A player runs forward and moves the pins, one at a time, standing each pin in the other circle. The next player moves the pins back, one at a time, to the original circle, and so forth.

4. *Roll-and-Set Relay.* Each team has a mat and a bowling pin. The mat is placed lengthwise in front of the team (40 to 60 feet away), and the pin is between the team and the mat. The first player runs toward the mat, picking up the pin. Carrying the pin in one hand, he does a Forward Roll, sets the pin beyond the far edge of the mat, and runs back and tags off the next player. This player runs to the pin, picks it up, does a Forward Roll on the way back, and sets the pin in the original spot. The players alternate in this fashion until all have run. The pin must stand each time, or the player must return and make it stand.

Three-Spot Relay

Three parallel lines are drawn in front of the teams to provide three spots for each team (Figure 23.2). Each player is given three tasks to perform, one at each spot. She then runs back and tags off the next player, who repeats the performance. Suggestions for the tasks are:

1. Lie prone.

2. Lie supine.

3. Do an obeisance (i.e., touch the forehead to the floor).

4. Do a nose-and-toe (i.e., touch the toe to the nose from a sitting position).

5. Do a specified number of hops, jumps, push-ups, or curl-ups.

6. Perform a designated stunt, such as the Coffee Grinder or Knee Dip.

7. Jump rope for a specified number of turns.

Figure 23.2 Formation for Three-Spot Relay

The runner must perform according to the directions at each spot, completing the performance before moving to the next spot. Other task ideas can be used. The winning team selects the requirements for the next race.

Gym Scooter Relays

Each team has a gym scooter. Scooters lend themselves to a variety of movements, both with individuals and with partners. Scooters should not, however, be used as skateboards. Some suggestions for individual movements are:

1. Sit on the scooter and propel with the hands or feet.

2. Kneel and propel with the hands.

3. Lie facedown and move in alligator or swimming fashion.

Partner activity can feature any of several approaches. Partners can operate as a single unit, doing the task and passing the scooter to the next pair, or one partner can push or pull the other to the turning point, where they exchange roles and return to the starting line. A third approach is for the pusher to become the rider on the next turn. Some partner actions follow.

1. Rider kneels, and partner pushes or pulls.

2. Rider sits in a Seat Balance, and partner pushes or pulls on the rider's feet.

3. Rider does a Tummy Balance, and partner pushes on his feet.

A wheelbarrow race also can be done with the down person supporting the hands on the scooter.

Potato Relay

A small box about a foot square is placed 5 feet in front of each lane. Four 12-inch circles are drawn at 5-foot intervals beyond the box (Figure 23.3). This makes the last circle 25 feet from the starting point. Four blocks or beanbags are needed for each team.

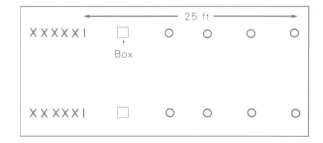

Figure 23.3 Formation for Potato Relay

To start, the blocks are placed in the box in front of each team. The first runner goes to the box, takes a single block, and puts it into one of the circles. She repeats this performance until there is a block in each circle; then she tags off the second runner. This runner brings the blocks back to the box, one at a time, and tags off the third runner, who returns the blocks to the circles, and so on.

Using a box to receive the blocks makes a definite target. When the blocks are taken to the circles, some rules must be made regarding placement. The blocks should be considered placed only when they are inside or touching a line. Blocks outside need to be replaced before the runner can continue. Paper plates or pie plates can be used instead of circles drawn on the floor.

Variation: The race can also be done with bowling pins. Instead of being placed in a box, they are in a large circle at the start.

Sack Race

Sack races have long been a popular picnic event and hold strong attraction for children. Each team has a sack, and the runners must progress with their feet inside the sack. Either lane or shuttle formation can be employed. In lane formation, the sacked runner goes around a marker, returns to the team, and gives the sack to the next participant. Another way to run the race is to have the runner move to a marker while in the sack, get out of the sack, and run back to the head of the line. In shuttle formation, the first runner moves in the sack across the area and gives the sack to the next runner.

Sturdy grain sacks made of burlap hold up well. Large plastic bags can be used, but they are more breakable, especially on rough surfaces.

Lane Relays with Balls

A number of interesting lane relays (some regular and some revolving) feature ball-handling skills. The balls should be handled crisply and cleanly. A mishandled ball must reenter the race at the point of error.

Bounce Ball Relay

A circle is drawn 10 to 15 feet in front of each team. The first player runs to the circle, bounces the ball once, runs back to the team, and gives the ball to the second player, who repeats the routine. Each player has a turn, and the team whose last child carries the ball over the finish line first wins.

To vary the relay, players can bounce the ball more than once.

Kangaroo Relay

The first player in each lane holds a ball between the knees. He jumps forward, retaining control of the ball, rounds the turning point, jumps back to the head of the file, and hands the ball to the next player. If a player loses the ball from between the knees, she must stop and replace it. Slightly deflated balls are easier to retain.

Basketball or Soccer Ball Dribbling Relays

See Chapters 25 and 28 for some suggested basketball and soccer ball dribbling relays.

Bowling Relay

The player at the head of each team has a ball. A line is drawn 15 to 20 feet in front of each team. The first player runs to the line, turns, and rolls the ball back to the second player. The second player must wait behind the starting line to catch the ball and then repeats the pattern. The race is over when the last player has received the ball and carries it over the forward line.

Crossover Relay

The Crossover Relay is similar to the Bowling Relay, except that the ball is thrown instead of rolled.

Obstacle Relays

Obstacle relays involve some kind of task that the runners must do.

Over-and-Under Relay

A magic rope is stretched about 18 inches above the floor to serve as the turning point. Each runner jumps over the rope and starts back immediately by going under the rope.

Figure-Eight Relay

Three or four cones are spaced evenly in front of each team. Players weave in and out in figure-eight fashion.

Bench Relays

Several interesting races can be run using benches. A balance-beam bench or an ordinary bench stands in front of each of two teams in lane formation. The following races are suggested.

1. Run forward, jump over the bench, jump back again, return, and tag off.

2. Run to the bench, pass a beanbag underneath it, run around the bench, pick up the beanbag, and return to the team. Give the beanbag to the next player.

3. Place a beanbag about 3 feet in front of the bench. The first player runs forward, picks up the beanbag, and jumps over the bench while carrying the bag. The child then drops the bag on the far side of the bench, jumps back over the bench, returns to the line, and tags off. The next runner jumps over the bench, picks up the bag, jumps back over the bench with it, and places it on the floor near original position. The pattern is alternately carrying the bag over and bringing it back to the near side.

Iceberg Relay

Teams are in lane formation, with each team having two rubber marking spots. The marks represent icebergs, and the task is to use the spots as stepping stones. Players race two at a time. One player is the stepper, and one moves the marking spots. The stepper may not touch the floor (fall in the ocean). The handler moves the marking spots to the turning point and then exchanges places with the stepper for the return trip. An alternative is to have the handler convey the stepper back to the starting point, give the marking spots to the next player at the head of the line, and then become the new stepper.

Variation: The race can also be run in shuttle formation. Because the partners go both ways during the race, the stepper and the marking spot handler exchange places halfway.

Jack Rabbit Relay (Jump Stick Relay)

Each runner carries a broomstick or wand, 1 meter in length, with both hands. A turning point is established about 30 feet in front of each lane. The race starts with the first player in line running forward around the turning point and back to the head of the line (Figure 23.4). In the meantime, the next

Figure 23.4   Formation for Jack Rabbit Relay

player takes a short step to the right and gets ready to help with the stick. The runner with the stick returns on the left side and shifts the stick to the left hand. The second player reaches out with the right hand and takes the other end of the stick. The two then pass the stick under the others in the line, who must jump up to let it go through. When the stick has passed under all players, the original player releases the grip and remains at the end of the line. The second runner runs around the turning point and returns, and the next player in line helps with the stick, becoming the next runner when the stick has gone under all of the jumpers. Each player repeats until all have run.

To end the race properly takes a little doing. The simplest way is to call the race complete when the last runner crosses the line with the wand. Another way is to have the last runner, helped by the original first runner who by now has rotated to the front of the line, carry the wand under the team. The last runner releases the wand, and the first runner returns the wand to the head of the line.

Teaching Suggestion: If children are unfamiliar with the relay, practice is needed. When they carry the stick back, under the jumpers, they should hold it close to the ground.

Hula-Hoop Relay

Each team consists of a file of five or six children who join hands. The leader, in front, holds a hoop in the free hand. The object is to pass the hoop down the line so that all bodies go through it, until the last person holds the hoop. The last person takes the hoop to the head of the line, and the process is repeated until the original leader is again at the head. Children may manipulate the hoop with their hands as long as they keep their hands joined. They should lock little fingers if necessary. All team members must pass through the hoop, including the last person.

The hoop can be moved around a circle of children with hands joined. The hoop starts on a pair of joined hands. When it has gone around the circle, over all of the bodies, and returned to the same spot, the race is over.

Revolving Team Ball Relays

Arch Ball Relay

Each team is in lane formation. Each player, using both hands, passes a ball overhead to the next person, and so on to the back player. The last player, on receiving the ball, runs to the head of the column, and the activity is repeated. The race is over when the original front player comes back to his spot at the head of the line. Each player must clearly handle the ball.

Right and Left Relay

The action is the same as for Arch Ball, except that the ball is handed to the person behind with a side turn. The first turn is to the right, and the next person turns to the left.

Straddle Ball Relay

Players are in lane formation. Each player takes a wide straddle stance, forming an alley with the legs. The ball is rolled down the alley to the back person, who runs to the front with it and repeats the activity. Players may handle the ball to help it down the alley, but it is not required that each person do so.

Over and Under Relay

Players take a straddle position in lane formation. The first player hands the ball overhead with both hands to the player behind, who in turn hands the ball between her legs to the next player. The ball goes over and under down the line.

Pass and Squat Relay

One player (number 1) with a ball stands behind a line 10 feet in front of his teammates, who are in lane formation (Figure 23.5). Number 1 passes the ball to number 2, who returns the ball to number 1. As soon as he has returned the ball to number 1, number 2 squats down so that the throw can be made to number 3, and so on, down the file. When the last person in line receives the ball, she does not return it but carries it forward, straddling the members of her team, including number 1, who has taken a place at the head of the file. The player carrying the ball forward then acts as the passer. The race is over when the original number 1 player receives the ball in the back position and straddles the players to return to his original position.

Some care must be taken that the front player in the file is behind the team line as the passing starts. After the straddling, repositioning the file is necessary. Each player should form a compact ball during the straddling activity. This is an interesting

relay, but some practice is needed for it to function properly.

Circle Pass Relays

Circle Pass relays involve ball handling in a circular formation.

Simple Circle Relay

Each team forms a separate circle of the same size. At first, the circle should be small enough so that players can hand the ball to each other. The leader of each group starts the ball around the circle by handing it to the player on her right. As soon as the ball gets back to the leader, the entire team sits down. The first team to be seated in good formation wins.

Later, the circle can be enlarged so that the ball must be passed from player to player. More than one circuit of the circle can be specified. The leader can hold the ball aloft to signal completion.

Circle-and-Leader Relay

A circle 15 to 20 feet in diameter is formed. One player is in the center with a ball. The ball is passed in succession to each of the players. The race is over when the ball is returned to the center player by the last circle player. Different passes can be specified.

Corner Fly Relay

The players are in a line or semicircle facing the leader (Figure 23.6), who has a ball. The ball is passed to and received from each player, beginning with the player on the left. When the last player receives the ball, he calls out "Corner fly" and takes the position of the leader. The leader takes a position in the line to the left. In the meantime, all players adjust positions to fill the spot vacated by the new leader. The relay continues, with each player becoming the leader in turn.

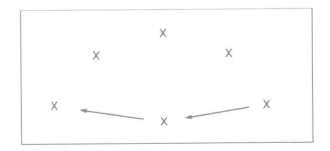

Figure 23.6 Formation for Corner Fly Relay

Figure 23.5 Formation for Pass and Squat Relay

When the original leader returns to the spot in front of the team, the relay is over.

A marker can be placed behind the leader so that the last player in line, when she receives the ball, runs around the marker to the leader's spot. This gives a little more time for the team to shift places and get ready for the new leader.

If a team is one person short of the number of players on the other teams, two consecutive passes could be made by the leader to the first person. Alternatively, the initial leader might take two turns (first and last), which means that another person comes forward after the second turn to provide the finish.

Tadpole Relay

One team forms a circle, facing in, and has a ball. Another team is in lane formation about 10 feet behind the circle (Figure 23.7). The object of the game is to see how many times the ball can be passed completely around the circle while the other team completes a relay. Each player from the team in lane formation runs in turn around the outside of the circle and tags off the next runner until all have run. In the meantime, the ball is being passed around the circle on the inside. Each time the ball makes a complete circuit, the circle players count the number loudly. After the relay is completed and the count established, the teams trade places and the relay is repeated. The team making the higher number of circuits by passing is the winner. The relay gets its name from the shape of the formation, which resembles a tadpole.

Variation: Different types of passes and different methods of locomotion provide variation.

Miscellaneous Relays

The following relays are interesting.

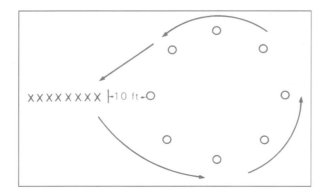

Figure 23.7 Formation for Tadpole Relay

Pass the Buck Relay

Players are facing sideways, with teams about 5 feet apart. All players of a team are linked by joined hands. The leader is on the right of each team. On signal, the leader "passes the buck" to the next player by squeezing his hand. This player in turn passes the squeeze to the next, and so on down the line. The end player, when she receives the buck, runs across the front of the team and becomes the new leader. She starts the squeeze, and it is passed down the line. Each player in turn comes to the front of the line, with the original leader finally returning to the head position.

Rescue Relay

Lane formation is used, with the first runner behind a line about 30 feet in front of the team (Figure 23.8). The first runner runs back to the team, takes the first player in line by the hand, and "rescues" him by leading him back to the 30-foot line. The player who has just been rescued then runs back to the team and gets the next player, and so on, until the last player has been conducted to the line.

Around-the-Bases Relay

Four bases are laid out as in a baseball diamond. Two teams, lined up at opposite bases on the inside of the diamond (Figure 23.9), compete at the same time. The lead-off player for each team makes one complete circuit of the bases and is followed by each player in turn.

Variations: The same type of relay can be run indoors by using chairs or bowling pins at the four corners. Further variations can require children to run more than one lap or circuit on a turn.

Modified Relays

In modified relays, players are numbered and run as individuals. These are not relays in the true sense of the term.

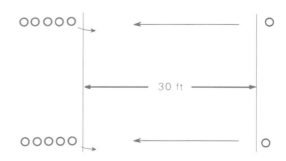

Figure 23.8 Formation for Rescue Relay

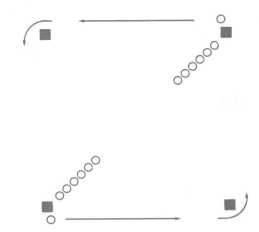

Figure 23.9 Formation for Around-the-Bases Relay

Attention Relay

The players on each team are facing forward in lane formation with team members about arms' distance apart. The distance between the teams should be about 10 feet. Two turning points are established for each team—one 10 feet in front of the team and the other 10 feet behind (Figure 23.10). Players are numbered consecutively from front to rear. The teacher calls, "Attention." All come to the attention position. The teacher calls out a number. (The route of player number 2 is shown in Figure 23.10.) The player on each team holding that number steps to the right, runs around the front and the back markers, and returns to place. The rest of the team runs in place. The first team to have all members at attention, including the returned runner, wins a point.

The numbers should not be called in consecutive order, but all numbers should be called. There must be enough distance between teams so that runners do not collide.

Variations:

1. Different means of locomotion can be used.

2. The teams can be organized by pairs, and two can run at one time, holding inside hands.

3. *Under the Arch.* The leader calls two consecutive numbers, say, numbers 3 and 4. Immediately, numbers 3 and 4 on each team face each other and form an arch by raising both hands. The players in front of the arch (numbers 1 and

2) run forward around the front marker, around the back marker, and then back to place, passing under the arch. The players behind the arch run under the arch first, around the front marker, around the back marker, and back to place. When all have returned to place, the arch players drop hands and resume position. The first team to be at attention is the winner. The running is always forward at the start. Each player follows the person ahead, keeping in numbered order. Each goes around the front marker, around the back marker, and back to place after passing under the arch.

4. Each team stands on a bench. With the teams standing at attention, a number is called, and that team member jumps down from the bench, runs completely around it, and runs back to place on top of the bench.

Circular Attention Relay

Two teams form a circle, with players facing counterclockwise and each team occupying half of the circle. The players of each team are numbered consecutively (Figure 23.11). The teacher calls the group to attention and then calls a number. Children with that number (one on each team) immediately run counterclockwise around the circle and back to place, and stand at attention. The first to get back to place scores a point for the team. All numbers should be called.

Variation: Circle Leapfrog. All players crouch on their knees, facing counterclockwise, with the forehead supported in cupped hands on the floor. When a number is called, the runner straddles or leapfrogs all children around the circle, returns to place, and resumes the original position. Scoring is the same as in Circular Attention.

Figure 23.10 Formation for Attention Relay

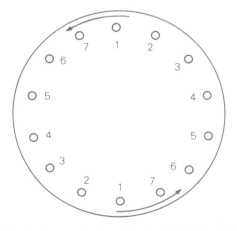

Figure 23.11 Formation for Circular Attention Relay

Supine Relay

Players lie supine on the floor, in a circle, with their heads toward the center of the circle and hands joined. The members of each team are numbered consecutively. When a number is called, the player with that number runs around or over the players on her team, and then returns to her place, assuming the supine position with hands rejoined. The first player back scores a point for the team. The game can continue to a definite score or until all numbers are called.

Variations: The following are exciting for children.

1. Human Hurdle. Each team forms a small circle and sits with backs to the center. The action is the same as for the Supine Relay.

2. Cyclone. This is a team race, with the team getting back to original place first declared the winner. At the signal, the first player gets up and starts around the group. Immediately after the first player passes him, the second player follows. The third player follows as soon as the first two have passed. The remaining players follow in the same manner. When the first player gets back to place, she takes her original seated position. Each player in turn goes around until she is back to her original place. The last player cannot move until all the other players have gone by. When she gets back to place, the race is over.

Implementing a
Sports Program

Sports are a part of the American scene, and little justification is needed for their inclusion in the elementary school program. The sports program has long been a major part of the elementary curriculum. Today's sports program must provide challenges for all: boys, girls, skilled, unskilled, and youngsters with disabilities. Few school administrators will tolerate heavy emphasis on the development of a few youngsters who promise to become high school varsity players while excluding less gifted children. The need for a rational, educationally sound approach is apparent. The program must meet the needs and interests of children and be geared to their development. When presented correctly, sport activities can help children develop many physical, educational, personal, and social values.

Sports selected for inclusion in the program are basketball, football, hockey, soccer, softball, track and field, and volleyball. The activities have been modified to make participation a learning experience. The broad goal of the sports program is to create interest and provide background for immediate and future participation. Instructional sequences should be organized so children develop a reasonable level of skill, have the opportunity to compete in lead-up and modified sports, and acquire necessary cognitive elements.

A balanced sports program has a dual approach. Class instruction provides opportunities for all to learn the basics of sport. Intramurals emerge from this base and provide additional instruction, practice, and opportunities for competition.

ORGANIZING THE SPORTS PROGRAM

This section contains organizational and instructional elements common to sports selected for the program. Specifics concerning each sport are found in the separate sport chapters (Chapters 25 through 31).

Safety

Physical conditioning is an important prerequisite to competitive play. Fatigue must be controlled and attention given to matters of physical and mental stress. Safety instruction is essential, because each sport has particular hazards.

Facilities and Equipment

Proper equipment and supplies are a primary consideration. Preparation of facilities, particularly outdoors, must be anticipated. Fields should be laid out and lined. Additional information about the requirements for specific sports can be found in the respective sport chapter. An adequate quantity of equipment should be available so that standing and waiting for turns occurs seldom. In many cases, official balls are not needed, and substitutes can be used.

Organizing Teams for Equal Competition

The squad, with a designated leader, is an effective unit for instructional purposes, particularly for rotating (or station) instruction. Small-group organization within squads allows maximum activity. Most introductory phases of instruction should make use of groups of four or fewer children. Homogeneous and heterogeneous groups have both advantages and disadvantages. Having skilled and unskilled players together when the activity demands a great deal of progression and ability is often a disadvantage. In a relay involving basket shooting, for example, a team might never win because of the poor performance of one player. Such a problem is solved by letting good players play on a team together and compete against another team of good shooters. This arrangement makes competition

more meaningful. The other side of the coin is that in many situations, playing with athletes who are more skilled improves the performance and success of less skilled players. Heterogeneous grouping might increase the opportunities for youngsters to help each other reach team or group goals. One guideline is to avoid keeping the same teams for too long. Frequent rotation of team members gives students the opportunity to play with all peers and at the same time counteracts the problem of frequent losing because of the deficiencies of one or two students.

Choosing teams can be done in any of the following ways.

1. Names can be drawn out of a hat, or the children can pick colored tags out of a hat. Youngsters with tags of the same color become teammates.

2. Youngsters can be placed on teams by skill level, which has been predetermined by teacher observation or skill testing. Depending on the situation, teachers could group children heterogeneously or homogeneously.

3. Four to six leaders can be selected by the teacher or elected by their classmates. They choose teams in a private session outside the classroom.

4. Depending on ability levels, the class can be arranged by height or weight and separated into teams. This is particularly useful in activities in which heavier and stronger children have an advantage.

Lead-Up Games

Lead-up games emphasize one or two skills and serve as a learning laboratory for the sport they precede. Each lead-up game should be analyzed for the skills involved. Lead-up games that increase the amount of activity *each* child receives during play should receive high priority for use. The following points should be kept in mind when lead-up games are used.

1. Lead-up games should not replace drills. Drills are used when students have not learned specific skills, whereas lead-up games are used to practice skills that have been learned.

2. Drills usually maximize the amount of practice time that each student receives in a given period. Whereas regulation sports require the use of all necessary skills, lead-up games limit the number of skills that are used in a competitive situation. The amount of time that each

student practices a skill will vary, depending on skill level and aggressiveness. Skills are best learned when the pressure of competition is decreased.

3. Lead-up games should involve all players and use as much equipment as possible. The more youngsters participate, the more opportunity they have to develop a positive attitude toward the sport involved. If a game cannot (or should not) be played with the entire class, a number of games should be organized and played simultaneously to maximize participation.

4. Lead-up games should be modified so that a newly learned technique is practiced. For example, if students have practiced ways of dodging an opponent in soccer, the game can be modified by adding a restriction that one opponent must be dodged before a pass can be made.

Skills Practice Through Creative Games

Creative games designed by children are an excellent supplement to the practice of sport skills. Creative games are not regarded as substitutes for lead-up games, but they do offer a quick and convenient practice situation. A creative game may be one that children design without restriction or with limiting factors specified by the teacher. Games can be organized on an individual, partner, or team basis, as specified by the teacher or students.

Modifying Activities

Most sport activities need modification to enable elementary school children to derive enjoyment and achieve success. Changing selected elements can increase the probability of successful participation. The most important reason for modifying an activity is to allow children to use and learn proper movement patterns. For example, many children learn to throw a basketball at a 10-foot-high basket rather than learning to shoot properly. Patterns learned and practiced for a period of 2 or 3 years are difficult, if not impossible, to alter. Lowering the basket and reducing the size and weight of the ball help children learn proper form. The following ideas may increase learning.

1. Decrease the number of players on a side, particularly in soccer and football games.

2. Shorten the field or court.

3. Shorten the playing time.

4. Lower nets and baskets.

5. Make scoring easier by increasing the size of goals, removing goalies, or substituting a different kind of scoring.

6. Change to more appropriate equipment, such as softer softballs, a beach ball in place of a volleyball, or junior-size footballs and basketballs.

7. Use zones to guarantee more position play.

8. Change rules to increase successful play. For instance, move up the serving distance or allow an assist on the serve in volleyball.

Officiating

If children are to officiate, some instructional time must be devoted to teaching them how. Rules should be clarified and posted, and simple officiating techniques covered. Impartial enforcement teaches respect for rules.

Instructional Procedures

1. The principles of motor learning (Chapter 3) have a direct bearing on the acquisition of sport skills and should be incorporated in instruction and coaching during practice. The how and why of an activity are inseparable in sport instruction. If children are asked to perform a skill in a certain manner, they should know why.

2. Each player should practice all skills, and the pattern of practice should reflect this. Rotation during lead-up games ensures that children receive experience at all positions and that play is not dominated by a few skilled individuals.

3. Instruction should include critical points of the skill. Noting similarities to other skills establishes basic concepts and aids transfer. Individual coaching during practice is a vital part of instruction. Students should be encouraged to concentrate on correct execution, and the instructor should circulate among students to see that this occurs.

4. Students should be encouraged to participate, to evaluate, and to make adjustments to movement patterns during skill practice. They must be given many opportunities to try various aspects of the skill and make individual decisions. Small groups permit experimentation without undue peer or performance pressure.

5. Relays that function as skill drills should be avoided because students in their haste to win often revert to sloppy performance.

6. An athlete from a local high school can be introduced to motivate students, provide technical help, and answer questions. Another motivational device is to arrange a trip to a ball game. Special arrangements can be made for groups, with help provided for those children who cannot afford tickets.

YOUTH SPORTS PHILOSOPHY

Youth sports give rise to the many problems of dealing with competitive situations. The precedent set by professional, college, and even high school sports programs often fosters a philosophy of winning at all costs at the elementary school level. A coaching manual, *Youth Sports Guide for Coaches and Parents* (Thomas, 1977), contains a "Bill of Rights for Young Athletes" (Figure 24.1) and offers insight into the many facets of a youth sports program.

The following points are useful for examining competitive situations.

1. *Competitive situations can be rewarding for those students capable of winning regularly.* Highly skilled children usually enjoy competition, because they have a chance of finding success. The teacher should be guided by the feelings of low-achieving youngsters in evaluating the effect of competition on the children.

2. *When children compete, the teacher should emphasize enjoyment of the activity by everyone.* In unfortunate cases, children receive the teacher's attention and approval only when they win. This places a heavy premium on winning.

3. *There is evidence* (Greene & Lepper, 1975; Corbin, Lovejoy, & Whitehead, 1988; Whitehead & Corbin, 1991) *to show that extrinsic rewards, such as ribbons or trophies, actually decrease a child's motivation to participate in an activity.* When the extrinsic motivation is removed, the child may no longer want to participate simply for fun. In some cases, this response may generalize to all physical activity. Emphasis should be placed on the joy of participation rather than on the importance of receiving a reward. If rewards are given, however, they should be based on achievement rather than on mere participation.

4. *All children should have a chance to succeed.* This might be accomplished by careful grouping, by pairing children with others of similar ability, and by making comparisons based on improvement and effort rather than on sheer ability. For example, competitive situations might be varied by matching individuals against others of somewhat equal ability, thus keeping the goals of competition within the student's level of achievement. Another useful form of competition is autocompetition, in which the students compete against themselves and try to improve on their past performances.

5. *The practice of starting children as young as possible in a sport pursuit so that they supposedly will develop into better athletes is questionable.* No evidence supports the contention that starting youngsters at an early age accom-

---

BILL OF RIGHTS FOR YOUNG ATHLETES

1. Right of opportunity to participate in sports regardless of ability level.
2. Right to participate at a level that is commensurate with each child's developmental level.
3. Right to have qualified adult leadership.
4. Right to participate in safe and healthy environments.
5. Right of each child to share in the leadership and decision making of their sport participation.
6. Right to play as a child and not as an adult.
7. Right to proper preparation for participation in the sport.
8. Right to an equal opportunity to strive for success.
9. Right to be treated with dignity by all involved.
10. Right to have fun through sport.

Figure 24.1 Bill of Rights for Young Athletes (From Thomas, J. R. [ed.]. 1977. *Youth sports guide for coaches and parents.* Washington, DC: Manufacturer's Life Insurance Company and the National Association for Sport and Physical Education.)

plishes this goal. The youngster who has started early may reach a psychological or physical peak at a younger age and may give the appearance of being much better than youngsters of a similar age who have not started early. This does not mean that a better athlete has been developed but merely that the youngster has peaked earlier (Shephard, 1984). Indeed, some educators believe that early starters burn out early. The strongest argument for starting children at an early age is that they have more free time available for practice. However, children also need time for their total development—social, academic, and physical—and youth sport practice often becomes the only important activity in the child's life.

6. *Studies have shown that skeletally mature children tend to play skilled positions in youth sports* (Hale, 1956). This creates a situation in which the skilled become more skilled and the unskilled remain unskilled. The gap between skilled and unskilled becomes greater, and the unskilled student feels incompetent and drops out of the activity. Such tendencies must be guarded against.

INTRAMURAL PROGRAMS

An *intramural* program is an organized activity for students that is an extension of the physical education program. Student attendance and participation are voluntary, and the program is limited to the boundaries of a specific school. The intramural program can be a laboratory for using skills and knowledge gained in the physical education program. In terms of supervisory personnel, equipment, and facilities, the intramural program should be funded by the school district. In some cases, fees are required if the activity involves private facilities, such as for bowling, skating, and horseback riding.

When a broad variety of activities is offered in the intramural program, physical education teachers can delegate more class time to instruction, because the opportunity to play the sport can occur in the intramural setting. The intramural program can also be a social meeting ground for students. Youngsters have the opportunity to participate in an activity that they may enjoy and use throughout a lifetime.

Who participates in an intramural program? Hopefully, every student in the school setting. The program should offer some activity of interest to all students and should provide appropriate competitive experiences for students of all sizes, shapes, and skill levels. All students should have ample opportunity to find success and enjoyment in the setting, regardless of their physical stature or ability level.

An intramural program offers students an opportunity to develop interest and competence in a wide range of recreational activities. The program also gives students an opportunity to develop and maintain a reasonable level of fitness. Evidence has shown that if people do not develop competence and confidence during their school years in their ability to participate in recreational activities, they seldom participate in later life. In the intramural program, students learn to compete and cooperate in an environment that has little at stake in terms of winning and losing. The program can be a setting for developing friendships that last a lifetime.

The intramural program can also be a place to learn leadership and followership skills. Students learn to compromise and assert themselves. Through these programs, students, parents, and teachers often become closer friends. Finally, the program offers students a place to spend some of their out-of-school time in a supervised setting rather than "hanging out" with nothing to do. Few programs for youth offer so many benefits at such a low cost to society. The intramural program for the elementary school should grow out of and be an extension of the physical education program. The term *intramural* literally means "within the walls" and describes a program conducted within the confines of the school and its grounds. Its purpose is to provide a recreational and competitive program to serve all children, including those with disabilities.

A few administrators believe misguidedly that an extramural competitive sports program meets the needs of the majority of students, and for some educators this becomes an excuse not to operate an intramural program. Unfortunately, heavy emphasis on interschool sports often monopolizes the available facilities and leaves little time for intramurals. The problem of extramural emphasis can be further compounded by some parents of skilled children who bask in the reflected glory of their prodigy's participation.

The first requirement for a functioning intramural program is a commitment by the school community, based on recognition of the program's potential value for children. For an intramural program to be an extension of the physical education program, a close relationship between the two must exist. The physical education program concentrates on skill learning with minimal concern for the amount of playing time. In the intramural program, in contrast, playing time is the central focus.

Suggested Operating Procedures

The following are considerations in setting up an elementary intramural program.

1. All available times should be used. Afterschool hours are most common, but the hour before school, the noon hour, and Saturdays merit consideration. Some evening participation is a possibility.

2. The program should be open to all interested students. Teams should be composed of enough children to ensure successful play but should not be so large that some members become spectators. Usually one or two (no more) beyond the required team number is a good standard. A minimum playing time for each team member should be set, with the goal being to have players share the playing time equally. Free substitution should be the rule. Rotating positions can help prevent domination by the more skilled participants.

3. Rules should be modified according to facilities, equipment, and level of skill. Elimination games or single elimination tournaments should be avoided and participation stressed.

4. During competition, each team should be designated clearly by pinnies, armbands, or other means. Modest team shirts are acceptable, but elaborate and costly uniforms should be banned.

5. All youngsters should receive equal opportunity to participate and should have equal access to quality equipment, programming, and facilities.

6. Safety awareness and procedures should be emphasized to participants.

7. A bulletin board with pertinent information is important. Rules of play governing each activity can be posted, and individual and team rosters listed. Tourney information and progress should be displayed. A place to pick up intramural information should be at or near the bulletin board.

Motivating Students to Participate

There are many methods for promoting intramural programs and encouraging participation. Regardless of the method used, to have the program work, students must see the benefits of participating. The program must exude a spirit and be an "in thing"

to do. Some of the following suggestions have been used with success in varying situations and can be modified to meet the needs of a particular school.

Intramural bulletin board: Bulletin boards, located throughout the school, display schedules, standings, and future activities. Pictures of champions can also be posted and labeled.

Patches: Winners are awarded arm patches with a school designation, the year, and the activity. Some successful programs have awarded patches for participating in a certain number of activities regardless of winning or losing.

T-shirts: This is similar to the awarding of patches, except that T-shirts are given to winners or participants. The school can hold a T-shirt day on which teachers and participants wear their shirts to school.

Point total chart: Points are given for winning first, second, third, or fourth place in an activity, or points can be awarded simply for participation in an activity. The points may be awarded to homeroom teams or on an individual basis. The point total chart keeps a running tally throughout the year.

Newspaper reports: These articles are written by students and are placed in the school or local newspaper. They motivate best when they explicitly name a number of students.

Field trips: Field trips are awarded to all participants at the end of the activity. For instance, at the end of the basketball tournament, all participants might attend a college or professional game together.

Two schools of thought are involved when promoting intramural programs. One awards notoriety and trophies to winners, while the other offers awards and equal publicity to all participants. A case can be made for both approaches. A final consideration might lie in the fact that winners receive a great deal of reinforcement, but others of lesser accomplishment may need additional positive strokes, which makes equal publicity for all students important in the implementation of a successful program.

Officials

Critical to the success of any athletic endeavor is the quality of officiating. The intramural program should be officiated by students. It is unrealistic to think that teachers will be willing to work ball games. Many students who do not play competitively are willing to officiate and enjoy being an integral part of an event. Recruiting students from nearby junior high schools to officiate can often be a rewarding experience.

Fifth- and sixth-grade students can be recruited and paired with older students so that they can work confidently with experienced officials. They should be trained in rules and game mechanics prior to a tournament and should be allowed to practice with as little pressure as possible. The word of the officials is absolute and students must learn to accept the judgment without complaint. If a disagreement arises, it is filed and resolved through the instructor in charge of the intramural program. Officials can be given points for the number of games they work; they can also be awarded patches, T-shirts, and trophies for their accomplishments in a fashion similar to participants. Without some recognition, students have little motivation for carrying out the thankless obligations of officiating.

Equating Competition

All participants should know that they have an opportunity to succeed in the intramural setting. Students seldom continue to participate if they foresee a constant diet of losing or other negative experiences. Grouping by ability has both advantages and disadvantages. It can be awkward to have skilled and unskilled players together when the activity demands a great deal of progression and skill performance. In those cases, having similarly skilled students play together and compete against teams of similar ability is probably the better arrangement. On the other hand, placing less skilled players with skilled participants may improve the performance level of the unskilled students and enhance their confidence. It also provides opportunities for skilled persons to aid the less skilled.

When grouping teams, the following two methods can be utilized. First, homerooms can compete against homerooms. This is the most heterogeneous method of grouping. Students of varying skill levels will then play on the same team. If students have been randomly assigned to homerooms, this may be a feasible method to use for grouping, since all homerooms should be approximately equal in ability. A second method is to use divisions of competition. Depending on the activity, students can be grouped by ability, size, or age. Homerooms could sponsor two or more teams of different ability that would play in different leagues. The advantage of homeroom sponsorship lies in

the camaraderie developed among students and the possibility of enhancing the classroom relationships. Probably the best solution is to equalize the competition regardless of homeroom assignments or other segregating factors. Choosing teams that are somewhat equal can be done in the following ways:

1. Leaders are elected by the students. The leaders then choose teams in a private session held away from the rest of the participants.
2. Students are arranged by height or weight. The names of students within a certain range are put into one box, and the names of students with a different range of heights are put into another. Teams are then selected by drawing the names of an equal number of students of similar size for each team.

Whatever method is used to form teams, the supervisor should be sensitive to maintaining a balance of competition and preventing embarrassing situations. Teams should never be selected in such a fashion that the poorest player is chosen last. The intramural experience should be positive and all students should look forward to the experience. If the program is to succeed, participants are needed and should be treated as important and meaningful people.

Intramural Programming

A variety of programming possibilities exist, ranging from highly structured to informally organized activities, even to activities pursued simply for pure enjoyment. A number of categories, with suggested activities, follow.

Team Sports

The team sports selected should be those in which prior skill training has been offered. Modification of rules is essential so that a high degree of activity is possible. For example, in basketball, one might play three on three in half-court play. In soccer, the rules might call for 5- or 7-person teams, rather than for 11-person teams. In softball, play might feature Tee-Ball or Two-Pitch. Volleyball activities might stress Beach Ball Volleyball. Low-organization team games such as Alaska Baseball and the like are a good idea.

Track and Field

Track and field activities can be individual or team oriented. Entry in each event should be limited. Modified cross-country racing is excellent. The concept of a track and field day can be broadened to include nonstandard events such as the softball throw, the triple standing long jump, Frisbee throwing, the football target or distance throw, and the predicted time jog.

PLAYDAYS

A *playday* is a festival setting in which children from one or several schools meet to take part in physical education activities. The emphasis is on social values rather than on competition. Competition has a role, but playdays that attempt to glorify champions are undesirable. The real purpose of a playday is to have everyone be on a team and to have a team for everyone.

A playday may be held within a particular school, but the more usual situation is for a playday to be held between schools. It can occur during the school day, after school, or on a Saturday. The program may consist of sport activities, or it may include simple games, relays, and contests. Stunts, individual athletic events, and even rhythms are the bases of activities in some meets. The programs vary according to the size of the participating schools and the grade level of the children.

The children should have a large part in the planning. This experience gives them an opportunity to act as hosts or as guests in a social situation. The program may emphasize activities that have previously been practiced or rehearsed, or it can include new and unique events that broaden the scope of the physical education experience.

TOURNAMENTS

Depending on the teacher's preference, the level of the students, the time available, and the limitations of facilities and equipment, tournaments can be an enjoyable culmination of a sport unit. Various types of tournament drawings can be used with success.

Round-Robin Tournament

The round-robin drawing is a good choice when there is a fair amount of time. In round-robin play, every team or individual plays every other team or individual once. Final standings are based on win-loss percentages. To determine the amount of time required for completion of the tournament, the following formula can be used:

$$\frac{TI(TI - 1)}{2}$$

where TI is the number of teams or individuals. For example, if there are five teams in a volleyball unit, 5(5 − 1)/2 = 10 games to be scheduled.

To arrange a tournament for an odd number of teams, each team should be assigned a number. (Number the teams down the right column and up the left column.) All numbers rotate, and the last number each time draws a bye. An example using seven teams follows.

Round 1	Round 2	Round 3	Round 4
7-Bye	6-Bye	5-Bye	4-Bye
6–1	5–7	4–6	3–5
5–2	4–1	3–7	2–6
4–3	3–2	2–1	1–7

Round 5	Round 6	Round 7
3–Bye	2–Bye	1–Bye
2–4	1–3	7–2
1–5	7–4	6–3
7–6	6–5	5–4

To arrange a tournament for an even number of teams, the plan is similar, except that the position of team 1 remains stationary, and the other teams revolve around it until the combinations are completed. An example of an eight-team tournament follows.

Round 1	Round 2	Round 3	Round 4
1–2	1–8	1–7	1–6
8–3	7–2	6–8	5–7
7–4	6–3	5–2	4–8
6–5	5–4	4–3	3–2

Round 5	Round 6	Round 7
1–5	1–4	1–3
4–6	3–5	2–4
3–7	2–6	8–5
2–8	8–7	7–6

Ladder Tournament

A ladder format can be used for an ongoing tournament that is administered either formally by the teacher or informally by students. Competition occurs by challenge and is minimally supervised. Arrangements vary, but usually a participant may challenge only opponents who are two steps above the challenger's present ranking. A challenger who wins changes places with the loser. The teacher can establish an initial ranking, or positions can be drawn from a hat. A shuffleboard tournament could be handled by a ladder ranking (Figure 24.2).

Figure 24.2 Ladder ranking

Figure 24.4 Simple elimination tournament for six teams

Pyramid Tournament

A pyramid tournament is similar to a ladder tournament but has more challenge and variety because the choice of opponents is wider (Figure 24.3). In the pyramid tournament, a player may challenge any opponent one level above the challenger's present ranking. Another variation is that a player must challenge someone on the same level and beat that person before challenging a player at a higher level.

Elimination Tournament

An elimination tournament is not the best format for elementary school youngsters, because teams that lose early have to sit out and observe. In many cases, these are the teams that need more participation and success, rather than less. An example of a simple elimination tournament for six teams is illustrated in Figure 24.4.

CLUBS AND SPECIAL-INTEREST GROUPS

Clubs and special-interest groups have not been exploited enough. Club work can provide extra opportunity for sport practice and can cater to special interests: archery, backpacking, swimming, gymnastics, rhythmics (dancing), baton twirling, cycling, tennis, skiing, skating, bowling, golf, and wrestling, among others. Competent leadership is vital and may have to be sought outside of the school family.

Club activities satisfy the urge for adventure, for something different and new. These activities also provide the highly skilled with an opportunity for effective participation.

Clubs can be organized within a school, but the most effective special-interest groups usually are organized in larger systems. One of the district schools can be specified as the location of a weekly interest group meeting, supervised by qualified personnel. Parents must assume responsibility for getting interested children in the district to the school and back home.

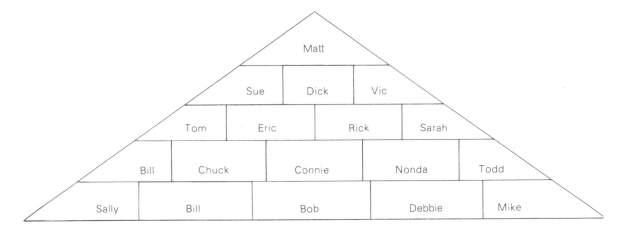

Figure 24.3 Pyramid tournament

REFERENCES AND SUGGESTED READINGS

Calgary Board of Education. (1980). *Intramurals in the elementary school.* Calgary, Canada: Calgary Board of Education.

Colgate, J. A. (1978). *Administration of intramural and recreational activities.* New York: Wiley.

Corbin, C. B., Lovejoy, P. Y., & Whitehead, J. R. (1988). *Youth physical fitness awards.* Quest, *40,* 200–218.

Foley, J. (1980). *Questions parents should ask about youth sports programs.* East Lansing, MI: Youth Sports Institute.

Greene, D., & Lepper, M. R. (1975). Turning play into work: Effects of adult surveillance and extrinsic rewards on children's internal motivation. *Journal of Personality and Social Psychology, 31,* 479–486.

Hale, C. (1956). Physiological maturity of Little League baseball players. *Research Quarterly, 27,* 276–284.

Howell, R. D. (1980). *Pre-season checklist for youth sport coaches.* East Lansing, MI: Youth Sports Institute.

Lewis, G., & Appenzeller, H. (Eds.). (1981). *Youth sport, a search for direction.* Greensboro, NC: Sport Studies Foundation.

Martens, R., Christina, R. W., Harvey, J. S., Jr., & Sharkey, B. J. (1981). *Coaching young athletes.* Champaign, IL: Human Kinetics.

Micheli, L. J. (1990). Sportswise: An essential guide for young athletes, parents, and coaches. Boston: Houghton Mifflin.

Orlick, T., & Botterill, C. (1975). *Every kid can win.* Chicago: Nelson-Hall.

Seefeldt, V., Smoll, F. L., Smith, R. E., & Gould, D. (1981). *A winning philosophy for youth sports programs.* East Lansing, MI: Youth Sports Institute.

Shephard, R. J. (1984). Physical activity and child health. *Sports Medicine, 1,* 205–233.

Thomas, J. R. (Ed.). (1977). *Youth sports guide for coaches and parents.* Washington, DC: Manufacturer's Life Insurance Company and the National Association for Sport and Physical Education.

Tutko, T., & Bruns, W. (1976). *Winning is everything and other American myths.* New York: Macmillan.

Whitehead, J. R., & Corbin, C. B. (1991). Effects of fitness test type, teacher, and gender on exercise intrinsic motivation and physical self-worth. *Journal of School Health, 61,* 11–16.

Basketball

*B*asketball is an activity enjoyed by many American boys and girls. The reinforcement offered when a basket is made renders it an attractive game, and this, when coupled with the impact that basketball has on the participants' cardiorespiratory system, makes it a strong contributor to the total curriculum.

Basketball instruction in the elementary school should focus on developing skills and competence so that students will choose to participate later in life. Often, elementary basketball programs have sought to develop future high school stars with little concern for less talented youngsters. The emphasis should be on lead-up games that allow all students to experience success and enjoyment. A range of fundamental activities should be offered.

With the emphasis on instruction and skill development in the physical education setting, little time is available for regulation basketball during school hours. More skilled and interested students should be given additional opportunities through intramural programs, recreational leagues (e.g., the Youth Basketball Association), or an educationally sound interschool competitive league.

Ball-handling skills should be developed slowly and are an outgrowth of fundamental skills learned in the primary grades. Primary-grade children learn the elements of catching, bouncing, passing, and dribbling using many types of objects. As they progress through the intermediate grades, shooting, offensive and defensive play, and comprehension of rules are added to this base.

Modifying the equipment used by elementary school children is important. Smaller balls and lower baskets help develop technically correct patterns, increase the success of the participants, and maintain motivation. It is impossible for youngsters to practice the ball control drills if the ball is too large for their hands.

INSTRUCTIONAL EMPHASIS AND SEQUENCE

Table 25.1 shows the sequence of basketball activities divided into two developmental levels. In most cases, youngsters are not ready to participate in the activities in this chapter until the age of 8.

Developmental Level II

Little emphasis is placed on regulation basketball at this level. Concentration should be on the fundamental skills of passing, catching, shooting, and dribbling. Lead-up games such as Birdie in the Cage, Circle Guard and Pass, and Basketball Tag allow participants to learn skills in a setting that offers enjoyment and success. Movement of players is somewhat limited, which increases the opportunity for a positive experience.

As children mature at this level, a goal should be to develop a range of skills, including passing, catching, dribbling, and shooting. The lay-up shot and the one-hand push shot should receive instructional attention. Captain Ball adds elements of simple defense, jump balls, and accurate passing.

Developmental Level III

A number of lead-up activities are introduced at this level. Shooting games, such as Twenty-One and Freeze Out, become favorites. Sideline Basketball and Captain Basketball offer meaningful competition. Continued practice on fundamental skills is necessary to ensure a good base of motor development. Drills to enhance skill performance are used, and rules for regulation basketball are presented.

Skilled youngsters should be encouraged to refine their skills. Officiating should be taught so that youngsters learn to appreciate the importance and difficulty of refereeing. Players should also be able to conduct some games through self-officiating.

Table 25.1 Suggested basketball program

Developmental Level II	Developmental Level III
Skills	
Passing	
Chest pass	All passes to moving targets
Baseball pass	Two-hand overhead pass
One-hand push pass	Long passes
Bounce pass	Three-player weave
Underhand pass	
Two-hand overhead pass	
Catching	
Above the waist	While moving
Below the waist	
Dribbling	
Standing and moving	Figure eight
Down and back	Pivoting
Right and left hands	Individual dribbling skills
Shooting	
One-hand (set) push shot	Free throw shot
Lay-up, right and left	Jump shot
Defending and stopping	
Pivoting	Parallel stop
Feinting	Stride stop
Knowledge	
Dribbling	Held ball
Violations	Personal fouls
Traveling	Holding
Out-of-bounds	Hacking
Double dribbling	Charging
	Blocking
	Pushing
	Conducting the game
	Officiating

Table 25.1 *continued*

Developmental Level II	Developmental Level III
Activities	
Circle Guard and Pass	Captain Basketball
Basketball Tag	Quadrant Basketball
Dribblerama	Sideline Basketball
Birdie in the Cage	Twenty-One
Captain Ball	Lane Basketball
Around the Key	Freeze Out
Five Passes	Flag Dribble
	One-Goal Basketball
	Basketball Snatch Ball
	Three-on-Three
	Basketrama
Skill Tests	
Dribble	Figure-eight dribble
	Wall pass test
	Baskets per minute
	Free throws

BASKETBALL SKILLS

Skills needed in basketball at the elementary level can be divided into the following categories: passing, catching, dribbling, shooting, defending, stopping, and pivoting. Feinting should be taught as part of the passing, dribbling, and offensive maneuvers.

Passing

Certain factors are common to all passes regardless of which pass is used. For firm control, the ball should be handled with the thumb and finger pads, not with the palms of the hands. The passer should step forward in the direction of the receiver. Passes should be made with a quick arm extension and a snap of the wrists, with thumbs and fingers providing momentum. After the pass is released, the palms should be facing the floor. Passers should avoid telegraphing the direction of the pass. They should learn to use peripheral vision and keep their eyes moving from place to place to develop an awareness of their teammates' positions. At the same time, they should anticipate the spot toward which a teammate will be moving to receive the pass.

The following are instructional cues that can be used to help students focus on proper performance of passing.

1. Fingers spread with thumbs behind the ball.
2. Elbows in; extend through the ball.
3. Step forward, extend arms, and rotate hands slightly inward.
4. Throw at chest level to the receiver.
5. For bounce passes, bounce the ball past the halfway point nearer the receiver.

Chest (or Two-Hand) Pass

For the chest, or two-hand, pass, one foot is ahead of the other, with the knees flexed slightly. The ball is released at chest level, with the fingers spread on each side of the ball (Figure 25.1). The elbows remain close to the body, and the ball is released by extending the arms and snapping the wrists as one foot moves toward the receiver (Figure 25.2).

Figure 25.1 Ready for a chest push pass

Figure 25.2 Chest push pass

Baseball (or One-Hand) Pass

For the baseball, or one-hand, pass, the passer imitates the action of a baseball catcher throwing the ball to second base. The body weight shifts from the back to the front foot. Sidearm motion should be avoided, because it puts an improper spin on the ball. Figure 25.3 shows a left-hander throwing the pass.

One-Hand Push Pass

For a one-hand push pass, the passer holds the ball with both hands but supports the ball more with the left than with the right, which is a little back of the ball. The ball is pushed forward, with a quick wrist snap, by the right hand.

Figure 25.3 Baseball pass

Bounce Passes

Any of the preceding passes can be adapted to a bounce pass. The object is to get the pass to the receiver on the first bounce, with the ball coming to the receiver's outstretched hands at about waist height. Some experimentation determines the distance. The ball should be bounced a little more than halfway between the two players to make it come efficiently to the receiver.

Underhand Pass

For a two-hand underhand pass, the ball should be held to one side in both hands, with the foot on the opposite side toward the receiver. The ball is "shoveled" toward the receiver and a step is made with the leading foot (Figure 25.4). The one-hand underhand pass is made like an underhand toss in baseball.

Two-Hand Overhead Pass

The two-hand overhead pass is effective against a shorter opponent. The passer is in a short stride position, with the ball held overhead (Figure 25.5). The momentum of the pass comes from a forceful wrist and finger snap. The pass should take a slightly downward path.

Catching

Receiving the ball is a most important fundamental skill. Many turnovers involve failure to handle a pass properly. The receiver should move toward the pass with the fingers spread and relaxed, reaching for the ball with elbows bent and wrists relaxed. The hands should give as the ball comes in.

Instructional cues for catching include the following:

1. Move to the ball.
2. Spread the fingers and catch with the fingertips.

Figure 25.4 Underhand pass

Figure 25.6 Dribbling

little arm motion. Younger children tend to slap at the ball rather than push it. The dribbling hand should be alternated, and practice in changing hands is essential.

Instructional cues for dribbling include the following:

1. Push the ball to the floor. Don't slap it.
2. Push the ball forward when moving.
3. Eyes forward and head up.

Shooting

Shooting is an intricate skill, and students need to develop consistent and proper technique rather than be satisfied when the ball happens to drop into the basket.

1. Good body position is important. Both the toes and the shoulders should face the basket. The weight should be evenly distributed on both feet. In preliminary phases, the ball should be held between shoulder and eye level.
2. A comfortable grip, with fingers well spread and the ball resting on the pads of the fingers, is essential. One should be able to see daylight between the palm of the hand and the ball. For one-hand shots, the shooting elbow is directly below the ball.
3. As soon as the decision is made to shoot, the eye is fixed on the target (the rim or the backboard) for the rest of the shot.
4. As the shot starts, the wrist is cocked.
5. The follow-through imparts a slight backspin to the ball. The arms are fully extended, the wrist is completely flexed, and the hand drops down toward the floor. The arc should be 45 degrees or a little higher.

Figure 25.5 Releasing the two-handed overhead pass

3. Reach for the ball.
4. Give with the ball (absorb the force of the ball by reaching and bringing the ball to the chest).

Dribbling

Dribbling is used to advance the ball, break for a basket, or maneuver out of a difficult situation. The dribbler's knees and trunk should be slightly flexed (Figure 25.6), with hands and eyes forward. Peripheral vision is important. The dribbler should look beyond the ball and see it in the lower part of the visual area. The ball is propelled by the fingertips with the hand cupped and relaxed. There is

The following instructional cues aid skill development:

1. Use the pads of the finger. Keep the fingers spread.
2. Keep the shooting elbow near the body.
3. Extend through the ball.
4. Bend the knees and use the legs.
5. Release the ball off the fingertips.

One-Hand (set) Push Shot

The one-hand push shot is usually a jump shot at short distances and a set shot at longer distances. The ball is held at shoulder-eye level with both hands; the body is erect, and the knees are flexed slightly in preparation for a jump. For a jump shot, the shooter executes a vertical jump, leaving the floor slightly (Figure 25.7). (In a set shot, the shooter rises on the toes.) The supporting (nonshooting) hand remains in contact with the ball until the top of the jump is reached. The shooting hand then takes over with fingertip control, and the ball rolls off the center three fingers. The hand and wrist follow through. Visual concentration on the target is maintained throughout. Proper technique should be emphasized rather than accuracy.

Lay-Up Shot

The lay-up is a short shot taken when going in toward the basket either after receiving a pass or at the end of a dribble. In a shot from the right side, the takeoff is with the left foot, and vice versa. The ball is carried with both hands early in the shot and then shifted to one hand for the final push. The ball, guided by the fingertips, should be laid against the backboard with a minimum of spin.

Figure 25.7   One-handed push shot

Free-Throw Shot

Free-throw shooting can be performed successfully with different types of shots. The one-hand foul shot is most popular. Complete concentration, relaxation, and a rhythmic, consistent delivery are needed. Some players find it helpful to bounce the ball several times before shooting. Others like to take a deep breath and exhale completely just before shooting. The mechanics of the shot do not differ materially from those of any shot at a comparable distance. Smoothness and consistency are most important.

Jump Shot

The jump shot has the same upper-body mechanics as the one-hand push shot already described. The primary difference is the height of the jump. The jump should be straight up, rather than at a forward or backward angle. The ball should be released at the height of the jump (Figure 25.8). Since the legs cannot be used to increase the force applied to the ball, the jump shot is difficult for the majority of elementary school youngsters. It may be best to avoid teaching the shot to youngsters who lack enough strength to shoot the ball correctly and resort to throwing it. If the jump shot is presented, the basket should be at the lowest level available and a junior-sized basketball used to develop proper shooting habits.

Another way to practice proper form with the jump shot is to use gray foam balls. They are light and can be shot easily by children. Concentrate on proper form rather than making baskets. Reinforce students who use good technique.

Defending

Defending involves a characteristic stance. The defender, with knees bent slightly and feet comfortably spread (Figure 25.9), faces the opponent at a distance of about 3 feet. The weight should be distributed evenly on both feet to allow for movement in any direction. Sideward movement is done with a sliding motion. The defender should wave one hand to distract the opponent and to block passes and shots. A defensive player needs to learn to move quickly and not be caught flatfooted.

Instructional cues for proper defending are as follows:

1. Keep the knees bent.
2. Keep the hands up.
3. Don't cross the feet when moving.

Figure 25.8 One-handed jump shot

Figure 25.9 The defensive position

Figure 25.10 Stopping

Stopping

To stop quickly, the weight of the body is dropped to lower the center of gravity and the feet are applied as brakes (Figure 25.10). In the **parallel stop**, the body turns sideward and both feet brake simultaneously. The **stride stop** comes from a forward movement and is done in a one-two count. On the first count, one foot hits the ground with a braking action; the other foot is planted firmly ahead on the second count. The knees are bent, and the center of gravity is lowered. From a stride stop, the player can move into a pivot by picking up the front foot and carrying it to the rear and, at the same time, fading to the rear.

Pivoting

Pivoting is a maneuver that protects the ball by keeping the body between the ball and the defensive player. The ball is held firmly in both hands, with elbows out to protect it. One foot, the pivot foot, must always be in contact with the floor. Turning on that foot is permitted, but it must not be

BASKETBALL

Figure 25.11 Pivoting

dragged away from the pivot spot. The lead foot may, however, step in any direction (Figure 25.11).

If a player has received the ball in a stationary position or during a jump in which both feet hit the ground simultaneously, either foot may become the pivot foot. If a player stops after a dribble on a one-two count, the pivot foot is the foot that made contact on the first count.

Feinting

Feinting (faking) masks the intent of a maneuver or pass and is essential to basketball. Feinting is a deceptive motion in one direction when the intent is to move in another direction. It can be done with the eyes, the head, a foot, or the whole body. In passing, feinting means faking a pass in one manner or direction and then passing in another.

INSTRUCTIONAL PROCEDURES

1. Many basketball skills do not require the use of basketballs. Other balls, such as volleyballs or rubber balls, can be used successfully.

2. Many skills can be practiced individually or in pairs with playground balls. This allows all children to develop at their own pace, regardless of skill level. Dribbling, passing, and catching skills receive more practice when many balls are used.

3. Baskets should be lowered to 7, 8, or 9 feet, depending on the size of the youngsters. If the facility is also used for community purposes, adjustable baskets—preferably power driven—are the key. Baskets of 5- or 6-foot height are good for children in wheelchairs. This height

also allows for experimentation by younger children. These lower baskets can be mounted directly on a wall and set up and removed as needed. No backboard is necessary. When the baskets are mounted to one side, disabled children can shoot baskets even though they may not be able to participate in other basketball activities.

4. The program should concentrate on skills and include many drills. Basketball offers endless possibilities, and using many drills gives variety and breadth to the instructional program. Each child should have an opportunity to practice all skills. This is not possible when a considerable portion of class time is devoted to playing regulation basketball on a full-length court.

BASIC BASKETBALL RULES

The game of basketball played at the elementary school level is similar to the official game played in the junior and senior high schools, but is modified to assure the opportunity for success and for proper skill development. A team is made up of five players, including two guards, one center, and two forwards. The game is divided into four quarters, each 6 minutes in length. The game is under the control of a referee and an umpire, both of whom have an equal right to call violations and fouls. They work on opposite sides of the floor and are assisted by a timer and a scorer. The following rules apply to the game for elementary school children.

Putting the Ball into Play

Each quarter is started with a jump ball at the center circle. Throughout the game, the jump ball is used when the ball is tied up between two players or when it is uncertain which team caused the ball to go out-of-bounds. After each successful basket or free throw, the ball is put into play at the end of the court under the basket by the team against whom the score was made.

Violations

The penalty for a violation is to award the ball to the opponents near the out-of-bounds point. The following are violations.

1. Traveling, that is, taking more than one step with the ball without passing, dribbling, or shooting (sometimes called walking or steps).

2. Stepping out-of-bounds with the ball or causing the ball to go out-of-bounds.

3. Taking more than 10 seconds to cross the centerline from the back to the front court. (Once in the forward court, the ball may not be returned to the back court by the team in control.)

4. Double dribbling, which is taking a second series of dribbles without another player's having handled the ball; palming (not clearly batting) the ball; or dribbling the ball with both hands at once.

5. Stepping on or over a restraining line during a jump ball or free throw.

6. Kicking the ball intentionally.

7. Remaining more than 3 seconds in the area under the offensive basket, which is bounded by the two sides of the free-throw lane, the free-throw line, and the end of the court.

8. To equalize scoring opportunities, a time limit (30 seconds) may be established during which the offensive team must score or give up the ball.

Fouls

Personal fouls are holding, pushing, hacking (striking), tripping, charging, blocking, and unnecessary roughness. When a foul is called, the person who was fouled receives one free throw. If fouled in the act of shooting and the basket was missed, the child receives two shots. If, despite the foul, the basket was made, the score counts and one free throw is awarded. A player who has five personal fouls is out of the game and must go to the sidelines.

Scoring

A basket from the field scores 2 points and a free throw 1 point. In most cases, the 3-point goal is not a consideration due to the distance of the shot. If desired, teachers could create a 3-point line to simulate the game played by older students. The team that is ahead at the end of the game is declared the winner. If the score is tied, an overtime period of 2 minutes is played. If the score is still tied after this period, the next team to score (1 or 2 points) is declared the winner.

Substitutes

Substitutes must report to the official scorer and await a signal from the referee or umpire before entering the game. The scorer will sound the signal at a time when the ball is not in play so that the official on the floor can signal for the player to enter the game.

BASKETBALL DRILLS

Drills should emulate actual games situations. Youngsters should understand that practice is ineffective unless it is purposeful and correct. When utilizing drills, instructors should use the technique suggestions for the skill being practiced and apply movement principles (pp. 49–51). The drills presented here cover both single skills and combinations of skills.

Ball-Handling Drills

These drills are practiced continuously for about 30 seconds. The ball is handled with the pads of the fingers. The drills are listed in order of difficulty.

Around the Body Drills

1. *Around the waist.* Hold the ball in the right hand, circle it behind the back, and transfer to the left hand. The left hand carries it to the front of the body for a transfer to the right hand. Start with the left hand and move the ball in the opposite direction.

2. *Around the head.* With shoulders back, send the ball around the head in much the same manner described above. Perform in both directions.

3. *Triple play.* Begin by circling around the head; move to waist level and follow by knee level circles. Move the ball in the opposite direction.

Figure Eight

1. Begin in a squatting position with the ball in the right hand. Move the ball around the leg to the right and bounce the ball between the legs to the left hand. Circle the ball around the left leg, through the legs to the right hand.

2. Bounce the ball through the legs front to back followed by the figure-eight motion.

Speed Drill

Feet are placed shoulder width apart. The ball is held between the legs with one hand in front and the other behind the back in contact with the ball. In a quick motion, flip the ball slightly upward and reverse the hand positions. Using a quick exchange of the hands, make a series of rapid exchanges. The ball will appear to be suspended between the legs (Figure 25.12).

Double Circle Drill

Beginning with the ball in the right hand, go around both legs, with an assist from the left hand. When the ball returns to the right hand, move the left foot away from the right foot. With the ball moving in the same direction, circle the right leg. Move the leg back to the starting position and circle both legs followed by moving the legs apart and circling the left leg (Figure 25.13). In short, circle both legs, circle the right leg, circle both legs, circle the left leg. Try moving the ball in the opposite direction.

Two-Hand Control Drill

Start from a semicrouched position with the feet shoulder width apart. The ball is held with both hands between the legs in front of the body (Figure 25.14). Let go of the ball, move the hands behind the body, and catch it before it hits the floor. It may be helpful to give the ball a slight upward flip to facilitate the catch. Reverse the action moving the hands to the front of the body. Perform continuously.

Figure 25.14 Two-hand control drill

Changing Hands Control Drill

Begin with the ball in the right hand; move it around the back of the right leg and catch with both hands. The right hand should be in front and the left hand behind. Drop the ball and quickly change position of the hands on the ball after it has bounced once (Figure 25.15). Immediately after the catch, bring the ball to the front of the body with the left hand and switch the ball to the right hand. Repeat continuously. Try moving the ball in the opposite direction.

Individual Dribbling Drills

Hoop Dribbling Drill

Each youngster has a ball and hula hoop. Place the hoop on the floor and practice dribbling the ball inside the hoop while walking outside the hoop. Dribble counterclockwise using the left hand and clockwise using the right hand. Repeat with the dribbler inside the hoop and the ball dribbled outside the hoop.

Random Dribbling

Each child has a ball. Dribbling is done in place, varied by using left and right hands. Develop a sequence of body positions (i.e., standing, kneel-

Figure 25.12 Speed drill

Figure 25.13 Double circle drill

CHAPTER 25

Figure 25.15 Changing hands control drill

ing, lying on the side, on two feet and one hand). Encourage players to develop a sequence by dribbling a certain number of times in each selected position. Dribble with each hand.

One-Hand Control Drill

Begin with the right hand holding the ball. Make a half circle around the right leg to the back. Bounce the ball between the legs (back to front) and catch it with the right hand and move it around the body again (Figure 25.16). After continuing for a short time, switch to the left hand.

Figure-Eight Dribbling Drill (Speed)

Start with the right or left hand. Dribble outside the respective leg, between the feet, and continue in front with the opposite hand in figure-eight fashion. Begin slowly and gradually increase the speed of the dribble.

Figure-Eight Dribbling Drill (One Bounce)

Assume a semicrouched position with the feet shoulder width apart. Start with the ball in the right hand and bounce it from the front of the body between the legs. Catch it with the left hand behind the legs (Figure 25.17). Bring the ball to the front of the body with the left hand and start the sequence over with that hand.

Figure 25.17 Figure-eight dribbling drill (one bounce)

Figure-Eight Dribbling Drill (Two Bounces)

Begin in the same position as described in the preceding drill. Using the right hand, take one dribble outside the right leg (angled toward the back) and a second dribble between the legs to the left hand in front of the body (Figure 25.18). Repeat, starting with the left hand.

Group Dribbling Drills

Dribbling can be practiced as a single skill or in combination with others.

File Dribbling

In file dribbling, players dribble forward around an obstacle (such as a bowling pin, a cone, or a chair) and back to the line, where the next player repeats

Figure 25.16 One-hand control drill

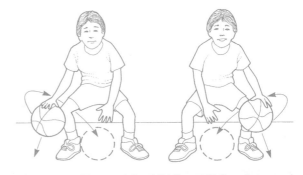

Figure 25.18 Figure-eight dribbling drill (two bounces)

Figure 25.19 File dribbling

(Figure 25.19). A variation has each player dribbling down with one hand and back with the other.

Shuttle Dribbling

Shuttle dribbling begins at the head of a file. The head player dribbles across to another file and hands the ball off to the player at the head of the second file. The first player then takes a place at the end of that file (Figure 25.20). The player receiving the ball dribbles back to the first file. A number of shuttles can be arranged for dribbling crossways over a basketball court.

Obstacle, or Figure-Eight, Dribbling

For obstacle, or figure-eight, dribbling, three or more obstacles are positioned about 5 feet apart. The first player at the head of each file dribbles in and around each obstacle, changing hands so that the hand opposite the obstacle is the one always used (Figure 25.21).

Dribbling and Pivoting Drills

In dribbling and pivoting drills, the emphasis is on stopping and pivoting.

File Drill

For the file drill, each player in turn dribbles forward to a designated line, stops, pivots, faces the file, passes back to the next player, and runs to a place at the end of the line (Figure 25.22). The next player repeats the pattern.

Figure 25.20 Shuttle dribbling

Figure 25.21 Obstacle, or figure-eight, dribbling

Figure 25.22 File drill

Figure 25.23 Dribble-and-pivot drill

Dribble-and-Pivot Drill

For the dribble-and-pivot drill, players are scattered by pairs around the floor (Figure 25.23). One ball is required for each pair. On the first whistle, the front player of the pair dribbles in any direction and fashion on the court. On the second whistle, she stops and pivots back and forth. On the third whistle, she dribbles back and passes to the partner, who immediately dribbles forward, repeating the routine.

Passing Drills

In passing practice, regular use should be made of the various movement formations (Chapter 5), including two-line, circle, circle-and-leader, line-and-leader, shuttle turn-back, and regular shuttle formations. A number of other drills should be considered.

Slide Circle Drill

In the slide circle drill, a circle of four to six players slides around a person in the center. The center person passes to and receives from the sliding players. After the ball has gone around the circle twice, another player takes the center position.

Circle-Star Drill

With only five players, a circle-star drill is particularly effective. Players pass to every other player, and the path of the ball forms a star (Figure 25.24). The star drill works well as a relay. Any odd number of players will cause the ball to go to all participants, assuring that all receive equal practice.

Triangle Drill

Four to eight players can participate in the triangle drill. The ball begins at the head of a line and is passed forward to a player away from the line. This player then passes to a teammate out at a corner, who then passes back to the head of the line (Figure 25.25). Each player passes and then moves to the spot to which he passed the ball, thus making a continual change of positions.

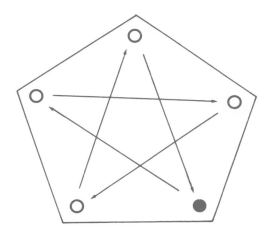

Figure 25.24 Circle-star drill formation

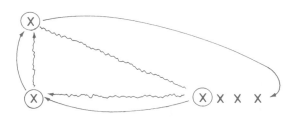

Figure 25.25 Triangle drill formation

Squad Split-Vision Drill

This drill requires two basketballs. The center player holds one ball, while player 1 (see Figure 25.26) has the other. The center player passes the ball to player 2, while receiving the other ball from player 1. The center player now passes to player 3 and receives the other ball from player 2 until the

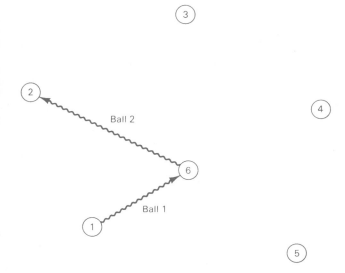

Figure 25.26 Squad split-vision drill

balls move completely around the semicircle. To rotate to a new center player, the center player becomes player 1 while player 6 (with the ball) moves to the center spot. All players adjust one space to the right.

Three-Lane Rush

This is a lead-up to the three-player weave, which is difficult for elementary school youngsters to learn. Youngsters are in three lines across one end of the area. The first three players move parallel down the court while passing the ball back and forth to each other. A lay-up shot can be taken as players near the basket.

Three-Player Weave

This drill requires practice and should be learned at slow speed. Walking students through the drill can sometimes help. If it is too difficult for a class, it should be avoided. The player in the center always starts the drill. She passes to another player coming across in front and then goes behind that player. Just as soon as she goes behind and around the player, she heads diagonally across the floor until she receives the ball again. The pass from the center player can start to either side.

Shooting Drills

Shooting drills may involve just shooting or a combination of shooting and other skills.

Simple Shooting Drill

In one simple shooting drill, players form files of no more than four people, and take turns shooting a long and a short shot or some other prescribed series of shots.

File-and-Leader Drill

For a file-and-leader drill, the first player in each file has a ball and is the shooter. He passes the ball to the leader, who returns the ball to the spot that the shooter has selected for the shot (Figure 25.27).

Dribble-and-Shoot Drill

For the dribble-and-shoot drill, two files are established on one end of the floor. One file has a ball. The first player dribbles in and shoots a lay-up. A member of the other file recovers the ball and passes it to the next player (Figure 25.28). As each person in turn either shoots or retrieves, she goes

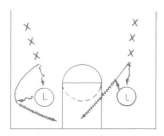

Figure 25.27   File-and-leader drill

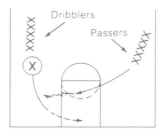

Figure 25.28   Dribble-and-shoot drill

to the rear of the other file. After some proficiency in the drill has been developed, two balls can be used, allowing for more shooting opportunities.

Set-Shot Drill

In the set-shot drill, players are scattered around a basket in a semicircle, with a leader in charge (Figure 25.29). Players should be close enough to the basket so that they can shoot accurately. The leader passes to each in turn to take a shot. The leader chases the ball after the shot. A bit of competition can be injected by allowing a successful shooter to take one step back for the next shot, or a player can shoot until he misses.

Lay-Up Drill

The lay-up drill is a favorite. One line passes to the other line for lay-up shots (Figure 25.30). Shooters come in from the right side first (this is easier), then from the left, and finally from the center. Each player goes to the end of the other line.

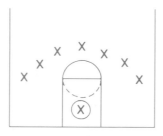

Figure 25.29   Set-shot drill formation

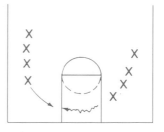

Figure 25.30   Lay-up drill

Figure 25.31   Jump-shot drill

Jump-Shot Drill

The jump-shot drill is similar to the lay-up drill, except that the incoming shooter receives the ball, stops, and takes a jump shot. The line of shooters should move back so that there is room for forward movement to the shooting spot. As soon as the passer releases the ball to the shooter, he moves to the end of the shooter's line. The shooter goes to the passer's line after shooting (Figure 25.31).

One extension of this drill is to allow a second jump shot when the shooter makes the first. In this case, the incoming passer passes to the shooter taking a second shot as well as to the next shooter. Another extension, which creates a gamelike situation, is having both the shooter and the incoming passer follow up the shot when the basket has not been made. As soon as the follow-up shot is made or there are three misses by the followers, the passer passes the ball to the new shooter. The avenues by which the shooters approach should be varied, so that children practice shooting from different spots.

Offensive and Defensive Drills

Group Defensive Drill

For the group defensive drill, the entire class is scattered on a basketball floor, facing one of the sides (Figure 25.32). The instructor or the student leader stands on the side, near the center. The drill can be done in a number of ways.

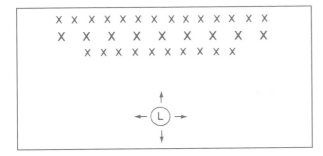

Figure 25.32 Group defensive drill

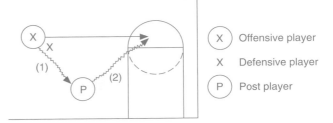

Figure 25.33 Offensive-defensive drill with post

1. The leader points in one direction (forward, backward, or to one side) and gives the command "Move." When the students have moved a short distance, the leader commands, "Stop." Players keep good defensive position throughout.

2. Commands can be changed so that movement is continuous. Commands are "Right," "Left," "Forward," "Backward," and "Stop." The leader must watch that movement is not so far in any one direction that it causes players to run into obstructions. Commands can be given in order, and pointing can accompany commands.

3. The leader is a dribbler with a ball, who moves forward, backward, or to either side, with the defensive players reacting accordingly.

It is important to stress good defensive position and movement. Movement from side to side should be a slide. Movement forward and backward is a two-step, with one foot always leading.

Offensive-Defensive Drill with a Post

The offensive-defensive drill with a post consists of an offensive player, a defensive player, and another player who acts as a passing post. The post player generally remains stationary and receives the ball from and passes to the offensive player. The player on offense tries to maneuver around or past the defensive player to secure a good shot (Figure 25.33). Plays can be confined to one side of an offensive basket area, thus allowing two drills to go on at the same time on one end of the basketball floor. If there are side baskets, many drills can be operated at the same time. After a basket has been attempted, a rotation of players, including any waiting player, is made.

The defensive player's job is to cover well enough to prevent shots in front of her. Some matching of ability must occur or the drill is nonproductive.

BASKETBALL ACTIVITIES

Developmental Level II

Circle Guard and Pass

Playing Area: Any smooth surface with circle markings

Players: Eight to ten per team

Supplies: A basketball or playground ball

Skills: Passing, catching, guarding

The offensive team moves into formation around a large (30-foot diameter) circle. One of the offensive players moves to the center. The defensive team is in position around a smaller (20-foot) circle inside the larger circle. On signal, the offensive team tries to pass the ball to the center player. They may pass the ball around the circle to each other before making an attempt to the center. The defensive team must bat the ball away but cannot catch it. After a stipulated time (1 minute), offensive and defensive teams trade positions. If score is kept, 2 points are awarded for each successful pass.

Variation: More than one ball can be used and different types of passes can be stipulated. The defensive team also can earn points for each time they touch the ball.

Basketball Tag

Playing Area: Gymnasium or playground area, 30 by 50 feet

Players: Eight to ten per team

Supplies: A foam rubber basketball, pinnies

Skills: Catching, passing, dribbling, guarding

Two versions of this game can be played. The simpler version is to designate three to five students to be it and wear a pinny. The rest of the class passes the ball and tries to tag one of the students who is it with the ball. If desired, more than one ball can be used.

A more difficult version of the game allows tagging. A player from each team is designated to be it and wears a pinnie. The object of the game is to tag the other team's target player with the ball. The player who is it may move only by walking. Players can move the ball by dribbling or by passing the ball to teammates. The player who is it tries to avoid moving near the ball, while others try to pass, dribble, and move near the roving it. The team without the ball plays defense and tries to intercept the ball.

Variation: More than one ball can be used and more than one player per team can be identified as it.

Dribblerama

Playing Area: Any smooth surface

Players: Entire class

Supplies: One basketball for each player

Skills: Dribbling and protecting the ball

The playing area is a large circle or square, clearly outlined. All players dribble within the area. The game is played on two levels.

Level 1: Each player dribbles throughout the area, controlling the ball so that it does not touch another ball. If a touch occurs, both players go outside the area and dribble counterclockwise around the area. Once youngsters have completed dribbling one lap around the path, they can reenter the game.

Level 2: While dribbling and controlling the ball, each player attempts to cause another player to lose control of the ball. When control is lost, that player takes the ball and dribbles around the perimeter of the area. Play continues until only two or three players who have not lost control of their ball are left. These are declared the winners. Bring all players back into the game and repeat.

Birdie in the Cage

Playing Area: Any smooth surface with circle marking

Players: 8 to 15 per team

Supplies: A soccer ball, basketball, or volleyball

Skills: Passing, catching, intercepting

Players are in circle formation with one child in the middle. The object of the game is for the center player to try to touch the ball. The ball is passed from player to player in the circle, and the center player attempts to touch the ball on one of these passes. The player who threw the ball that was touched takes the place in the center. In case of a bad pass resulting in the ball's leaving the circle area, the player who caused the error can change to the center of the ring.

Teaching Suggestions: The ball should move rapidly. Passing to a neighboring player is not allowed. If touching the ball proves difficult, a second center may join the first. Play can be limited to a specific type of pass (bounce, two-hand, push).

Variation: As few as three children can play, with two children passing the ball back and forth between them while a third tries to touch it. An excellent version of this game calls for four players, with three forming a triangle and positioning themselves about 15 feet apart.

Captain Ball

Playing Area: Playground or gymnasium area, about 30 by 40 feet

Players: Seven on each team

Supplies: A basketball, pinnies, eight hoops

Skills: Passing, catching, guarding

Two games can be played crosswise on a basketball court. A centerline is needed (Figure 25.34); otherwise, the normal out-of-bounds lines can be used. Hoops can provide the circles for the forwards and the captains. Captain Ball is a very popular game that is played with many variations. In this version, a team is composed of a captain, three forwards, and three guards. The guards throw the ball to their captain. The captain and the three forwards are each assigned to respective circles and must always keep one foot inside the circle. Guarding these four circle players are three guards.

The game is started by a jump at the centerline by two guards from opposing teams. The guards can rove in their half of the court but must not enter

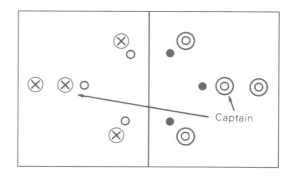

Figure 25.34 Formation for Captain Ball

the circles of the opposing players. The ball is put into play after each score in much the same manner as in regular basketball. The team scored on puts the ball into play by a guard throwing the ball in bounds from the side of the court.

As soon as a guard gets the ball, he throws it to one of the forwards, who must maneuver to be open. The forward then tries to throw it to the other forwards or in, to the captain. Two points are scored when all three forwards handle the ball and then it is passed to the captain. One point is scored when the ball is passed to the captain but has not been handled by all three forwards.

Stepping over the centerline is a foul. It is also a foul if a guard steps into a circle or makes personal contact with a circle player. The penalty for a foul is a free throw.

For a free throw, the ball is given to an unguarded forward, who has 5 seconds to get the ball successfully to the guarded captain. If the throw is successful, one point is scored. If it is not successful, the ball is in play. Successive fouls rotate free throws among the forwards.

As in basketball, when the ball goes out of bounds, it is awarded to the team that did not cause it to go out. If a forward or a captain catches a ball with both feet out of their circle, the ball is taken out of bounds by the opposing guard. For violations such as traveling or kicking the ball, the ball is awarded to an opposing guard out of bounds. No score may be made from a ball that is thrown in directly from out of bounds.

Teaching Suggestions: Some instruction is necessary for children to absorb the basic strategy of the game. An effective offensive formation seems to be one in which the guards are spaced along the centerline (Figure 25.35—only the offensive team is diagrammed). By passing the ball back and forth among the guards, the forwards have more oppor-tunity to be open, since the passing makes the guards shift position.

The guards may dribble, but this should be held to a minimum and used for advancing the ball only when necessary. Otherwise, dribbling accomplishes little.

The forwards and the captain should learn to shift back and forth to become open for passes. Considerable latitude is available, as they need keep only one foot in the hoop. Short and accurate passing uses both high and bounce passes. Circle players may jump for the ball but must come down with one foot in the circle.

Variations:

1. Four guards can be used, but scoring is then more difficult.
2. A five-circle formation can be used, forming a five spot like that on a die. Nine players are needed on each team: four forwards, four guards, and one captain.
3. A platform 6 to 8 inches high and 20 inches square can elevate the captain to make reception of the ball easier.

Around the Key

Playing Area: One end of a basketball floor
Players: Three to eight
Supplies: A basketball
Skill: Shooting

Spots are arranged for shooting as indicated in Figure 25.36. A player begins at the first spot and continues until a miss. When a miss occurs, the player can stop and wait for the next opportunity

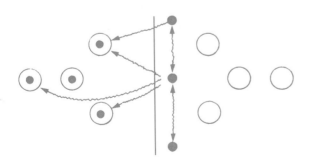

Figure 25.35 An effective offensive formation in Captain Ball

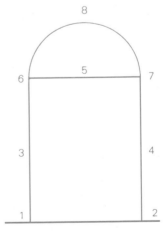

Figure 25.36 Shooting positions for Around the Key

and begin from the point where the miss occurred, or can "risk it" and try another shot immediately from the point where the first try was missed. If the shot is made, the player continues. If the shot is missed, the player must start over on the next turn. The winner is the player who completes the key first or who makes the most progress.

Variations:

1. Each child shoots from each spot until a basket is made. A limit of three shots from any one spot should be set. The child finishing the round of eight spots with the lowest number of shots taken is the winner.

2. The order of the spots can be changed. A player can start on one side of the key and continue back along the line, around the free-throw circle, and back down the other side of the key.

Five Passes

Playing Area: Half of a basketball floor

Players: Four or five on each team

Supplies: A basketball, pinnies

Skills: Passing, guarding

Two teams play. The object of the game is to complete five consecutive passes, which scores a point. On one basketball floor, two games can proceed at the same time, one in each half.

The game is started with a jump ball at the free-throw line. The teams observe regular basketball rules in ball handling and with regard to traveling and fouling. Five consecutive passes must be made by a team, who count out loud as the passes are completed.

The ball must not be passed back to the person from whom it was received. No dribbling is allowed. If for any reason the ball is fumbled and recovered or improperly passed, a new count is started. After a successful score, the ball can be thrown up again in a center jump at the free-throw line. A foul draws a free throw, which can score a point. Teams should be well marked to avoid confusion.

Variations:

1. After each successful point (five passes), the team is awarded a free throw, which can score an additional point.

2. After a team has scored a point, the ball can be given to the other team out of bounds to start play again.

3. Passes must be made so that all players handle the ball.

Developmental Level III

Captain Basketball

Playing Area: A basketball court with centerline

Players: Six or eight on each team

Supplies: A basketball, pinnies

Skills: All basketball skills except shooting

A captain's area is laid out by drawing a line between the two foul restraining lines 4 feet out from the end line. The captain must keep one foot in this area. Captain Basketball is closer to the game of basketball than Captain Ball is. The circle restrictions of Captain Ball limit movements of the forwards. Captain Basketball brings in more natural passing and guarding situations, and the game is played in much the same way as basketball.

A team normally is composed of three forwards, one captain, and four guards. The captain must keep one foot in his area under the basket. The game is started with a jump ball, after which the players advance the ball as in basketball. No player may cross the centerline, however. The guards must therefore bring the ball up to the centerline and throw it to one of their forwards. The forwards maneuver and attempt to pass successfully to the captain. A throw by one of the forwards to the captain scores 2 points; a free throw scores 1 point.

Fouls are the same as in basketball. In addition, stepping over the centerline or a guard stepping into the captain's area draws a foul.

In the case of a foul, the ball is given to a forward at the free-throw line. She is unguarded and has 5 seconds to pass successfully to the captain, who is guarded by one player. The ball is in play if the free throw is unsuccessful.

Teaching Suggestions: A folding tumbling mat can be used to designate the captain's area at each end of the court. Use of a mat tends to discourage intrusion by guards into the captain's area.

While players are required to remain in their own half of the court, they should be taught to move freely within that area. Short, quick passes should be stressed, because long passes are not effective. This is also good practice for proper guarding techniques.

Quadrant Basketball

Playing Area: Basketball court divided into four equal areas

Players: Eight per team, two placed in each area

Supplies: Basketball, pinnies

Skills: Passing, catching, dribbling, guarding, shooting

The court is divided by its length and width into four equal areas with markers. Play can be started with a jump ball or by giving it to one team. Two offensive and two defensive players are placed in each quadrant. Players may not leave the quadrant during the course of play. Normal rules of basketball are used with the exception of limiting the number of dribbles to three. This game forces youngsters to remain spaced throughout the area.

Teaching Suggestion: Rotate players to different quadrants so that they have the opportunity to play offense and defense.

Variation: Limit the number of passes that may be made consecutively in one quadrant to encourage passing to other areas. In addition, limiting the amount of time a player may hold the ball to 5 seconds will encourage passing.

Sideline Basketball

Playing Area: Basketball court

Players: Entire class

Supplies: A basketball, pinnies

Skills: All basketball skills

The class is divided into two teams, each lined up along one side of the court, facing the other. The game is played by three or four active players from each team. The remainder of the players, who stand on the sideline, can catch and pass the ball to the active players. Sideline players may not shoot, nor may they enter the playing floor. They must keep one foot completely out of bounds at all times.

The active players play regular basketball, except that they may pass and receive the ball from sideline players. The game starts with the active players occupying their own half of the court. The ball is taken out of bounds under its own basket by the team that was scored upon. Play continues until a period of time (1 or 2 minutes) elapses. The active players then take places on the left side of their line and three new active players come out from the right. All other players move down three places in the line.

No official out of bounds on the sides is called. The players on that side of the floor simply recover the ball and put it into play by a pass to an active player without delay. Out of bounds on the ends is the same as in regular basketball. If one of the sideline players enters the court and touches the ball, it is a violation, and the ball is awarded out of

bounds on the other side to a sideline player of the other team. Free throws are awarded when a player is fouled. Sideline players may not pass to each other but must pass back to an active player. Sideline players should be well spaced along the side.

Twenty-One

Playing Area: One end of a basketball court

Players: Three to eight in each game

Supplies: A basketball

Skills: Shooting

Players are in file formation by teams. Each child is permitted a long shot (from a specified distance) and a follow-up shot. The long shot, if made, counts 2 points and the short shot counts 1 point. The follow-up shot must be made from the spot where the ball was recovered from the first shot. The normal one-two-step rhythm is permitted on the short shot from the place where the ball was recovered.

The first player scoring a total of 21 points is the winner. If the ball misses the backboard and basket altogether on the first shot, the second shot must be taken from the corner.

Variations:

1. A simpler game allows dribbling before the second shot.

2. Players can continue to shoot as long as every shot is made. This means that if he makes both the long and the short shot, a player goes back to the original position for a third shot. All shots made count, and the shooter continues until a miss.

3. The game works well as a team competition, with each player contributing to the team score.

4. Various combinations and types of shots may be used.

Lane Basketball

Playing Area: Basketball court divided into six lanes

Players: Five per team

Supplies: Basketball, pinnies, cones to mark zones

Skills: All basketball skills

The court is divided into six lanes as shown in Figure 25.37. Players must stay in their lane and cannot cross the midcourt line. Regular basketball rules prevail with the exception that players cannot

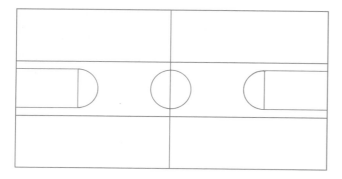

Figure 25.37 Court markings for Lane Basketball

dribble more than four times. Play is started with a jump ball. At regular intervals, youngsters should rotate to the next lane to assure they get to play all positions.

A number of rule changes can be implemented to change the focus of the game. For example, three passes may be required before shooting may occur. Youngsters could be allowed to move the entire length of the floor within their lane.

Freeze Out

Playing Area: One end of the basketball court

Players: Four to eight

Supplies: A basketball

Skill: Shooting under pressure

There are many types of freeze-out shooting games. This version is an interesting shooting game that culminates quickly and allows players back into the game quite soon.

Each player can have three misses before being out. After the first miss, the player gets an O; after the second, a U; and after the third, a T. This spells OUT and puts the player out. The last player remaining is the winner.

The players start in file formation. The first player shoots a basket from any spot desired. If the basket is missed, there is no penalty and the next player shoots. If the basket is made, the following player must make a basket from the same spot or it is scored as a miss. Players keep track of their own misses. Players should remember that if the player ahead of them makes a basket, they must do likewise or have a miss scored against them. If the player ahead of them misses, they may shoot from any spot they choose without penalty.

Flag Dribble

Playing Area: One end of a basketball floor or a hard-surfaced area outside with boundaries

Players: 4 to 15

Supplies: A basketball and a flag for each player

Skill: Dribbling

To play this game, children must have reasonable skill in dribbling. The object is to eliminate the other players while avoiding being eliminated. Players are eliminated if they lose control of the ball, if their flag is pulled, or if they go out of bounds. Keeping control of the ball by dribbling is interpreted to mean continuous dribbling without missing a bounce. A double dribble (both hands) is regarded as a loss of control.

The game starts with players scattered around the area near the sidelines. Each has a ball, and all have flags tucked in the back of their belts. Extra players wait outside the area. On signal, all players begin to dribble in the area. While keeping control of the dribble and staying in bounds, they attempt to pull a flag from any other player's back. They can also knock aside any other player's ball to eliminate that player. As soon as the game is down to one player, that player is declared the winner. Sometimes two players lose control of their basketball at about the same time. In this case, both are eliminated. Sometimes, two players are left and the game results in a stalemate. In this case, both are declared winners and the game starts over.

Variations:

1. If using flags is impractical, the game can be played without this feature. The objective then becomes to knock aside or deflect the other basketballs while retaining control of one's own ball.

2. Flag Dribble can be played by teams or squads. In this case, each squad or team should be clearly marked.

One-Goal Basketball

Playing Area: An area with one basketball goal

Players: Two or four on each team

Supplies: A basketball, pinnies (optional)

Skills: All basketball skills

If a gymnasium has four basketball goals, many children can be kept active with this game. If only two goals are available, a system of rotation can be worked out. The game is played by two teams according to the regular rules of basketball but with the following exceptions.

1. The game begins with a jump at the free-throw mark, with the centers facing the sidelines.

2. When a defensive player recovers the ball, either from the backboard or on an interception, the ball must be taken out beyond the foul-line circle before offensive play is started and an attempt at a goal is made.

3. After a basket is made, the ball is taken in the same fashion away from the basket to the center of the floor, where the other team starts offensive play.

4. Regular free-throw shooting can be observed after a foul, or some use can be made of the rule whereby the offended team takes the ball out-of-bounds.

5. An offensive player who is tied up in a jump ball loses the ball to the other team.

Fouls are something of a problem, because they are called on individuals by themselves. An official can be used, however.

Variations:

1. A system of rotation can be instituted whereby the team that scores a basket holds the floor and the losing team retires in favor of a waiting team. For more experienced players, a score of 3 or more points can be required to eliminate the opponents.

2. *One-on-One.* This variation differs from One-Goal Basketball primarily in the number of players. Only two play. Otherwise, the rules are generally the same. The honor system should be stressed since officials usually are not present and players call fouls on themselves. There is more personal contact in this game than in One-Goal Basketball. The game has value because of its backyard recreational possibilities. It is popular because it has been featured on television broadcasts of professional basketball players.

Basketball Snatch Ball

Playing Area: Basketball court
Players: 6 to 15 on each team
Supplies: Two basketballs, two hoops
Skills: Passing, dribbling, shooting

Each of two teams occupies one side of a basketball floor. The players on each team are numbered consecutively and must stand in the numbered order. The two balls are placed inside two hoops, one on each side of the centerline. When the teacher calls a number, the players from each team whose number was called run to the ball, dribble it to the basket on their own right, and

try to make the basket. As soon as a successful basket is made, the player dribbles back and places the ball on its spot within its hoop. The first player to return the ball after making a basket scores a point for that team. The teacher should use some system to keep track of the numbers so that all children have a turn. Numbers can be called in any order.

Teaching Suggestion: In returning the ball, emphasis should be placed on legal dribbling or passing. In the hurry to get back, illegal traveling sometimes occurs.

Variations:

1. Players can run by pairs, with either a pair of players assigned the same number or the teacher calling two numbers. Three passes must be made before the shot is taken and before the ball is replaced inside the hoop.

2. Three players can run at a time, with the stipulation that the player who picks up the ball from the hoop must be the one who takes the first shot. All players must handle the ball on the way down and on the way back.

3. To make a more challenging spot for the return, use a deck tennis ring. This demands more critical control than placing the ball in a hoop. In either case, the ball must rest within the designated area to score.

4. A more demanding task calls for a single player to pass the ball to successive teammates on the way down and on the way back. Teammates scatter themselves along the sideline after the number has been called.

Three-on-Three

Playing Area: Half of a basketball court
Players: Three to five teams of three players each
Supplies: A basketball
Skills: All basketball skills

An offensive team of three stands just forward of the centerline, facing the basket. The center player has a basketball. Another team of three is on defense and awaits the offensive team in the area near the foul line. The remaining teams, waiting for their turn, stand beyond the end line.

Regular basketball rules are used. At a signal, the offensive team advances to score. A scrimmage is over when the offensive team scores or when the ball is recovered by the defense. In either case, the defensive team moves to the center of the floor and becomes the offensive unit. A waiting team comes out on the floor and gets ready for defense. The old offensive team goes to the rear of the line of waiting players. Each of the teams should keep its own score. Two games can be carried on at the same time, one in each half of the court.

Variations:

1. If the offensive team scores, it remains on the floor, and the defensive team drops off in favor of the next team. If the defense recovers the ball, the offensive team rotates off the floor.

2. If a team has a foul (by one of the players), that team rotates off the floor in favor of the next team.

3. A team wins when it scores 3 points. The contest becomes a regular scrimmage in which the offensive team becomes the defensive team upon recovering the ball. When a team scores 3 points, the other team is rotated off the floor. Rules for One-Goal Basketball prevail.

4. The game can be played with four against four.

Basketrama

Playing Area: Area around one basket

Players: Usually two

Supplies: A basketball for each player

Skill: Shooting under pressure

On signal, two players, each with a basketball, begin to shoot individually as rapidly as possible, taking any kinds of shots they wish, until one scores 10 baskets and becomes the winner. Each player must handle her own basketball and must not impede or interfere with the other's ball. Naturally, the balls do collide at times, but deliberate interference by knocking the other ball out of the way or kicking it means disqualification.

Balls should be marked so that there is no argument as to ownership. This can be done by using different types of basketballs or by marking with chalk or tape. Each player can count out loud each basket he makes, or another student can keep score for each contestant.

Variations:

1. The game can be played with more than two players, but this can cause confusion and mix-ups of the respective basketballs.

2. The scoring method can be varied. A time limit can be set, and the player's score is the number of baskets she makes during the set time. Another method is to time the player to see how many seconds it takes her to make 10 baskets.

BASKETBALL SKILL TESTS

Tests in basketball cover dribbling, passing, shooting, and making free throws. For each of the first four tests presented here, a stopwatch is needed.

Straight Dribble

A marker is placed 15 yards down the floor from the starting point. The dribbler must dribble around the marker and back to the starting position, where he finishes by crossing the starting line. The marker must remain standing or disqualification results. The teacher should allow two or three trials and take the best time.

Figure-Eight Dribble

Four obstacles (bowling pins, bases, or cones) are placed 5 feet apart in a straight line beginning 5 feet from the starting line. The player must dribble in and out of the markers in the path of a figure eight, finishing at the point where she started. The teacher can allow two or three trials and take the best time.

Wall Pass Test

A player stands 5 feet from a smooth wall. He is given 30 seconds to make as many catches as he can from throws or passes against the wall. The two-hand or chest pass is generally used. Balls must be caught on the fly to count. Another student should do the counting. Only one trial is allowed. A board or mat provides a definite restraining line.

Baskets Made in Thirty Seconds

A player stands near the basket in any position she wishes. On signal, she shoots and continues shooting for a period of 30 seconds. Her score is the number of baskets she makes during the time period. Another student should do the counting. Only one trial is allowed.

Free Throws

Score is kept of the number of free throws made out of ten attempts. The player should get three or four warm-up trials and announce when he is ready. Score should be kept by another student with pencil and paper. An X is marked for a basket made, and an O for a miss.

Football

The shape of the football makes throwing and catching more difficult than with a round ball. Specialized skills are needed, which means that the teacher must spend more time on football skills if children are to enjoy participating. Touch and Flag Football are modifications of the game of American football. A ball carrier usually is considered down in Touch Football when touched by one hand. Some rules do call for a two-handed touch, however. In Flag Football, a player wears one or two flags, which the opponents must seize to down the ball carrier, hence the name Flag Football. Flag Football has advantages over Touch Football in that there is more twisting and dodging, which makes the game more interesting and challenging. In addition, in Flag Football, argument over whether the ball carrier was downed is less likely.

INSTRUCTIONAL EMPHASIS AND SEQUENCE

Table 26.1 shows the sequence of football activities divided into two developmental levels. Regular and junior-sized footballs are difficult to throw and catch. The ends of the football are hard and can hurt children who haven't mastered catching skills. For this reason, the use of foam footballs is encouraged. A

Table 26.1 Suggested football program

Developmental Level II	Developmental Level III
Skills	
Forward pass	Stance
Centering	Pass receiving
Catching	Punting
	Blocking
	Carrying the ball
	Running and dodging
	Handing off the ball
	Lateral pass
Knowledge	
Football rules	Plays and formations
Activities	
Football End Ball	Kick-Over
Five Passes	Fourth Down
Speed Football	Football Box Ball
	Flag Football
	Pass Ball
Skill Tests	
Passing for distance	Kicking for distance
Centering	Passing for distance
	Passing for accuracy

number of companies manufacture the balls in a size that is suitable for youngsters. Youngsters will show a greater tendency to participate when they know the projectile is harmless.

Developmental Level II

Passing, centering, and catching receive the majority of focus at this level. Most of the instructional time should be spent on skills. The lead-up games of Five Passes and Football End Ball make use of the skills listed.

Developmental Level III

At this level, emphasis shifts to passing skills, with moving receivers in football drills. Punting and kicking games are introduced. More specialized skills, such as blocking, carrying the ball, exchanging the ball, and football agility skills, provide lead-up work for the game of Flag Football.

FOOTBALL SKILLS

Forward Pass

Skillful forward passing is needed in Flag Football and in the lead-up games; passing is a potent weapon. The ball should be gripped lightly behind the middle with the fingers on the lace. The thumbs and fingers should be relaxed (Figure 26.1).

In throwing, the opposing foot should point in the direction of the pass, with the body turned sideways. In preparation for the pass, the ball is raised up and held over the shoulders. The ball is delivered directly forward with an overhand movement of the arm and with the index finger pointing toward the line of flight. A left-hander is used in Figure 26.2.

Figure 26.1 Preparing to pass

Figure 26.2 Passing (left-handed thrower)

The following instructional cues will help students improve their throwing technique:

1. Turn the nonthrowing side toward the direction of the throw.
2. Grasp the ball with the pads of the fingers.
3. Throw the ball with an overhand motion.
4. Step toward the pass receiver.
5. Follow through with the arm after releasing the ball.

Lateral Pass

Lateral passing is a simple underhand toss of the ball to a teammate (Figure 26.3). The ball must be tossed sideward or backward to qualify as a lateral. It should be tossed with an easy motion, and no attempt should be made to make it spiral like a forward pass.

Catching

In catching, the receiver should keep both eyes on the ball and catch it in the hands with a slight give (Figure 26.4). As soon as the ball is caught, it should be tucked into the carrying position. The little fingers are together for most catches.

The following instructional cues will help students focus on catching technique:

1. Keep eyes on the ball.
2. Thumbs together for a high pass (above shoulder level).
3. Thumbs apart for a low pass (below shoulder level).

Figure 26.3 Lateraling the ball

4. Reach for the ball, give, and bring the ball to the body.

Handing Off the Ball

Children enjoy working plays where the ball is exchanged from one player to another, as for a reverse. In a reverse, the object is to start the play in one direction and then give the ball to another player heading in the opposite direction. The ball can be handed backward or forward. The player with the ball always makes the exchange with the inside hand, the one near the receiving player. The ball is held with both hands until the receiver is about 6 feet away. The ball then is shifted to the hand on that side, with the elbow bent partially away from the body. The receiver comes toward

Figure 26.4 Catching a pass

Figure 26.5 Handing off the ball

the exchange player with the near arm bent and carried in front of the chest, the palm down. The other arm is carried about waist height, with the palm up (Figure 26.5). As the ball is handed off (not tossed), the receiver clamps down on the ball to secure it. As quickly as possible, the receiver then changes to a normal carrying position.

A fake reverse, sometimes called a bootleg, is made when the ball carrier pretends to make the exchange but keeps the ball instead and hides it momentarily behind one leg.

Carrying the Ball

The ball should be carried with the arm on the outside and the end of the ball tucked into the notch formed by the elbow and arm. The fingers add support for the carry (Figure 26.6).

Centering

Centering involves transferring the ball, on a signal, to the quarterback. In elementary school, the shotgun formation is most often used. This requires snapping the ball a few yards backward to the quarterback. A direct snap involves placing the hands under the buttocks of the center. The ball is then lifted, rotated a quarter turn, and snapped into the hands of the quarterback.

The centering player takes a position with the feet well spread and toes pointed straight ahead. Knees are bent and close enough to the ball to reach it with a slight stretch. The right hand takes about the same grip as is used in passing. The other hand is on the side near the back of the ball and merely acts as a guide (Figure 26.7). On signal from the quarterback, the center extends the

Figure 26.6 Carrying the ball securely

arms backward through the legs and centers the ball to the quarterback.

Instructional cues for centering include the following:

1. Keep legs spread and toes straight ahead.
2. Reach forward for the ball.
3. Snap the ball with the dominant hand.
4. Guide the ball with the nondominant hand.

Stance

The three-point stance is the offensive stance most generally used in Flag Football. The feet are about shoulder width apart and the toes point straight ahead, with the toes of one foot even with the heel of the other. The hand on the side of the foot that is back is used for support; the knuckles rest on the ground. The player should look straight ahead and always take the same stance (Figure 26.8).

Figure 26.7 Centering (note the hand and finger positions)

Figure 26.8 Offensive three-point stance

Some players prefer the parallel stance, in which the feet, instead of being in the heel-and-toe position, are lined up evenly. In this case, either hand can be placed down for support. Some defensive players like to use a four-point stance, as shown. Both hands are in contact with the ground (Figure 26.9).

Figure 26.9 Defensive four-point stance

The following instructional cues will help students learn proper stance:

1. Bend the knees; keep the back parallel to the ground.
2. Keep the majority of the weight on the legs.
3. Don't lean forward or backward.

Blocking

In blocking for Flag Football, the blocker must maintain balance and not fall to the knees. The elbows are out and the hands are held near the chest. The block should be more of an obstruction than a takeout and should be set with the shoulder against the opponent's shoulder or upper body (Figure 26.10). Making contact from the rear in

Figure 26.10 Blocking position

any direction not only is a penalty but also could cause serious injury.

Instructional cues for blocking technique are the following:

1. Keep feet spread and knees bent.
2. Keep head up.
3. Stay in front of the defensive player.
4. Move your feet; stay on the balls of the feet.

Punting

The kicker stands with the kicking foot slightly forward. The fingers are extended in the direction of the center. The eyes should be on the ball from the time it is centered until it is kicked, and the kicker should actually see the foot kick the ball. After receiving the ball, the kicker takes a short step with the kicking foot and then a second step with the other foot. The kicking leg is swung forward and, at impact, the leg is straightened to provide maximum force. The toes are pointed, and the long axis of the ball makes contact on the top of the instep. The leg should follow through well after the kick (Figure 26.11). Emphasis should be placed on dropping the ball properly. Beginners have a tendency to throw it in the air, making the punt more difficult.

Instructional cues for teaching punting are the following:

1. Drop the football; don't toss it upward.
2. Keep the eyes focused on the ball.
3. Kick upward and through the ball.
4. Contact the ball on the outer side of the instep.

INSTRUCTIONAL PROCEDURES

1. All children need the opportunity to practice all skills, and a system of rotation should be set up to ensure this.

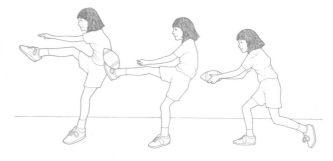

Figure 26.11 Punting

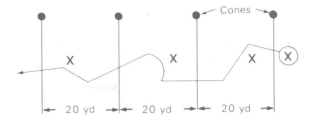

Figure 26.12 Ball carrying drill

ORGANIZING FOR INSTRUCTION

The differences between sexes should be allowed for in football activities. The instruction may follow one of two patterns. Skills are taught together but the sexes are separated for other phases, or the skills and simple selected lead-up games may have coeducational participation. Blocking and scrimmage play are not suitable for mixed participation. When boys are participating in Flag Football, Fourth Down, or Pass Ball, girls might do likewise in another area. Noncontact games such as Football Endball, Five Passes, or Football Box Ball may have mixed participation. (Gender references will alternate by example in the following drill descriptions.)

Passing and catching skills can be practiced informally. More room is needed for kicking skills. Ball exchange drills work well with three or four children. Informal work gives children a chance to experiment and explore without pressure.

FOOTBALL DRILLS

Ball Carrying

Formation: Scattered

Players: Four to six

Supplies: A football, a flag for each player, cones to mark the zones

The ball carrier stands on the goal line ready to run. Three defensive players wait at 20-yard intervals, each one stationed on a zone line of a regular Flag Football field, facing the ball carrier (Figure 26.12). Each defender is assigned to the zone that she is facing and must down the ball carrier by pulling a flag while the carrier is still in the zone. The ball carrier runs and dodges, trying to get by

each defender in turn without having her flag pulled. If the flag is pulled, the runner continues, and the last defender uses a two-handed touch to down the ball carrier. After the runner has completed the run, she goes to the end of the defender's line and rotates to a defending position.

Ball Exchange

Formation: Shuttle, with the halves about 15 yards apart

Players: Four to ten

Supplies: A football

The two halves of the shuttle face each other across the 15-yard distance. A player at the head of one of the files has a ball and carries it over to the other file, where he makes an exchange with the player at the front of that file (Figure 26.13). The ball is carried back and forth between the shuttle files. The receiving player should not start until the ball carrier is almost up to him. A player, after handing the ball to the front player of the other file, continues around and joins that file.

Combination

Formation: Regular offensive formation with passer, center, end, and ball chaser

Players: Four to eight

Supplies: A football

Passing, centering, and receiving skills are combined in one drill. Each player, after her turn, rotates to the next spot. A minimum of four players is needed. The center player centers the ball to the passer; the passer passes the ball to the end; the end receives the pass; and the ball chaser retrieves the ball if missed by the end, or takes a pass from the end (if she caught the ball) and carries the ball

Figure 26.13 Ball exchange drill

to the center spot, which is her next assignment (Figure 26.14).

The rotation follows the path of the ball. This means that the rotation system moves from center to passer to end to ball chaser to center. Extra players should be stationed behind the passer for their turns.

One-on-One Defensive Drill

Formation: Center, passer, end, defender

Players: Eight to ten

Supplies: A football

The one-on-one defensive drill is as old as football itself. A defensive player stands about 8 yards back, waiting for an approaching end. The passer tries to complete the pass to the end while the defender tries to break up the pass or intercept the ball. One defender should practice against all the players and then rotate (Figure 26.15). The passer must be able to pass well or this drill has little value.

Variation: The drill can be played with two ends and two defenders. The passer throws to the end who appears to be most unguarded.

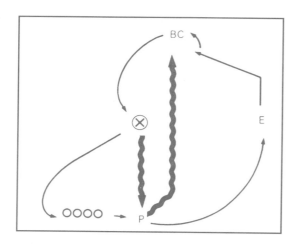

Figure 26.14 Combination drill

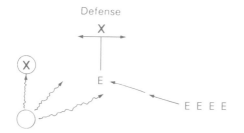

Figure 26.15 One-on-one defensive drill

Punt Return

Formation: Center, kicker, two lines of ends, receivers

Players: 10 to 20

Supplies: A football, a flag for each player

The object of the drill is for the receiver to catch a punted ball and return it to the line of scrimmage while two ends attempt to pull a flag or make a tag. Two ends are ready to run downfield. The center snaps the ball to the kicker, who punts the ball downfield to the punt receiver. The ends cannot cross the line of scrimmage until the ball has been kicked. Each end makes two trips downfield as a "tackler" before rotating to the punt-receiving position.

Teaching Suggestions: An effective punter is necessary for this drill. Only children with the degree of skill required to punt far enough downfield should be permitted to kick. It is also important for the ends to wait until the ball is kicked, or they will be downfield too soon for the receiver to have a fair chance of making a return run.

Stance

Formation: Squads in extended file formation

Players: Six to eight in each file

Supplies: None

The first person in each file performs and when finished with his chores, goes to the end of his file. On the command "Ready," the first person in each file assumes a football stance. The teacher can correct and make observations. On the command "Hike," the players charge forward for about 5 yards (Figure 26.16). The new player at the head of each line gets ready.

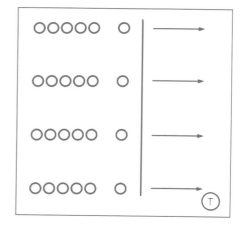

Figure 26.16 Stance drill

FOOTBALL ACTIVITIES

Developmental Level II

Football End Ball

Playing Area: A court 20 by 40 feet

Players: 9 to 12 on each team

Supplies: Footballs

Skills: Passing, catching

The court is divided in half by a centerline. End zones are marked 3 feet wide, completely across the court at each end. Players on each team are divided into three groups: forwards, guards, and ends. The object is for a forward to throw successfully to one of the end-zone players. The players from each team are positioned as diagrammed in Figure 26.17. End-zone players take positions in one of the end zones. Their forwards and guards then occupy the half of the court farthest from this end zone. The forwards are near the centerline, and the guards are back near the end zone of their half of the court.

The ball is put into play with a center jump between the two tallest opposing forwards. When a team gets the ball, the forwards try to throw over the heads of the opposing team to an end-zone player. To score, the ball must be caught by an end-zone player, who must have both of her feet inside the zone. No moving with the ball is permitted by any player. After each score, play is resumed by a jump ball at the centerline.

A penalty results in loss of the ball to the other team. Penalties are assessed for the following.

1. Holding a ball for more than 5 seconds
2. Stepping over the end line or stepping over the centerline into the opponent's territory
3. Pushing or holding another player

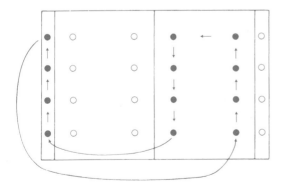

Figure 26.17 Player positions for Football End Ball

In case of an out-of-bounds ball, the ball belongs to the team that did not cause it to go out. The nearest player retrieves the ball at the sideline and returns it to a player of the proper team.

Teaching Suggestions: Fast, accurate passing is to be encouraged. Players in the end zones must practice jumping high to catch the ball while still landing with both feet inside the end-zone area.

A system of rotation is desirable. Each time a score is made, players on that team can rotate one person (see Figure 26.17).

To outline the end zones, some instructors use folding mats (4 by 7 feet or 4 by 8 feet). Three or four mats forming each end zone make a definite area and eliminate the problem of defensive players (guards) stepping into the end zone.

Five Passes (Football)

Playing Area: Football field or other defined area

Players: Six to ten on each team

Supplies: A football, pinnies or other identification

Skills: Passing, catching

Players scatter on the field. The object of the game is for one team to make five consecutive passes to five different players without losing control of the ball. This scores 1 point. The defense may play the ball only and may not make personal contact with opposing players. No player can take more than three steps when in possession of the ball. More than three steps is called traveling, and the ball is awarded to the other team.

The ball is given to the opponents at the nearest out-of-bounds line for traveling, minor contact fouls, after a point has been scored, and for causing the ball to go out of bounds. No penalty is assigned when the ball hits the ground. It remains in play, but the five-pass sequence is interrupted and must start again. Jump balls are called when the ball is tied up or when there is a pileup. The official should call out the pass sequence.

Speed Football

Playing Area: Football field 30 by 60 yards divided into three equal sections

Players: Entire class divided into two teams

Supplies: Football, flag for each player

Skills: Passing, catching, running with ball

The ball can be kicked off or started at the 20-yard line. The object is to move the ball across the opponent's goal by running or passing. If the ball drops to the ground or a player's flag is pulled when carrying the ball, it is a turnover and the ball is set into play at that spot. Interceptions are turnovers and the intercepting team moves on offense. Teams must make at least four complete passes before they are eligible to move across the opponent's goal line. No blocking is allowed.

Variation: Playing more than one game at a time on smaller fields will allow more students to be actively involved in the game. This is also an enjoyable game when played with Frisbees.

Developmental Level III

Kick-Over

Playing Area: Football field with a 10-yard end zone

Players: Six to ten on each team

Supplies: A football

Skills: Kicking, catching

Teams are scattered on opposite ends of the field. The object is to punt the ball over the other team's goal line. If the ball is caught in the end zone, no score results. A ball kicked into the end zone and not caught scores a goal. If the ball is kicked beyond the end zone on the fly, a score is made regardless of whether the ball is caught.

Play is started by one team with a punt from a point 20 to 30 feet in front of its own goal line. On a punt, if the ball is not caught, the team must kick from the spot of recovery. If the ball is caught, three long strides are allowed to advance the ball for a kick.

Teaching Suggestion: The player kicking next should move quickly to the area from which the ball is to be kicked. Players should be numbered and should kick in rotation. If the players do not kick in rotation, one or two aggressive players will dominate the game.

Variation: Scoring can be made only by a drop-kick across the goal line.

Fourth Down

Playing Area: Half of a football field or equivalent space

Players: Six to eight on each team

Supplies: A football, pinnies

Skills: Most football skills, except kicking and blocking

Every play is a fourth down, which means that the play must score or the team loses the ball. No kicking is permitted, but players may pass at any time from any spot and in any direction. There can be a series of passes on any play, either from behind or beyond the line of scrimmage.

The teams line up in an offensive football formation. To start the game, the ball is placed into the center of the field, and the team that wins the coin toss has the chance to put the ball into play. The ball is put into play by centering. The back receiving the ball runs or passes to any of his teammates. The one receiving the ball has the same privilege. No blocking is permitted. After each touchdown, the ball is brought to the center of the field, and the team against which the score was made puts the ball into play.

To down a runner or pass receiver, a two-handed touch above the waist is made. The back first receiving the ball from the center has immunity from tagging, provided that he does not try to run. All defensive players must stay 10 feet away unless he runs. The referee should wait for a reasonable length of time for the back to pass or run. If the ball is still held beyond that time, the referee should call out, "Ten seconds." The back must then throw or run within 10 seconds or be rushed by the defense.

The defensive players scatter to cover the receivers. They can use a one-on-one defense, with each player covering an offensive player, or a zone defense.

Because the team with the ball loses possession after each play, the following rules are used to determine where the ball should be placed when the other team takes possession.

1. If a ball carrier is tagged with two hands above the waist, the ball goes to the other team at that spot.

2. If an incomplete pass is made from behind the line of scrimmage, the ball is given to the other team at the spot where the ball was put into play.

3. Should an incomplete pass be made by a player beyond the line of scrimmage, the ball is brought to the spot from which it was thrown.

Teaching Suggestion: The team in possession should be encouraged to pass as soon as is practical, because children tire from running around to become free for a pass. The defensive team can score by intercepting a pass. Since passes can be made at any time, on interception the player should look down the field for a pass to a teammate.

Variation: The game can be called Third Down, with the offensive team having two chances to score.

Football Box Ball

Playing Area: Football field 50 yards long

Players: 8 to 16 on each team

Supplies: A football, pinnies

Skills: Passing, catching

Five yards beyond each goal is a 6-by-6-foot square, which is the box. The teams should be marked so that they can be distinguished. The game is similar to End Ball in that the teams try to make a successful pass to the captain in the box.

To begin the play, players are onside, which means that they are on opposite ends of the field. One team, losing the toss, kicks off from its own 10-yard line to the other team. The game then becomes a kind of keep-away, with either team trying to secure or retain possession of the ball until a successful pass can be made to the captain in the box. The captain must catch the ball on the fly and still keep both feet in the box. This scores a touchdown.

A player may run sideward or backward when in possession of the ball. Players may not run forward but are allowed momentum (two steps) if receiving or intercepting a ball. The penalty for illegal forward movement while in possession of the ball is loss of the ball to the opponents, who take it out of bounds.

The captain is allowed only three attempts to score or one goal. If either occurs, another player is rotated into the box. On any incomplete pass or failed attempt to get the ball to the captain, the team loses the ball. If a touchdown is made, the team brings the ball back to its 10-yard line and kicks off to the other team. If the touchdown attempt is not successful, the ball is given out of bounds on the end line to the other team.

Any out-of-bounds ball is put into play by the team that did not cause the ball to go out of bounds. No team can score from a throw-in from out of bounds.

In case of a tie ball, a jump ball is called at the spot. The players face off as in a jump ball in basketball.

Players must play the ball and not the individual. For unnecessary roughness, the player is sidelined until a pass is thrown to the other team's captain. The ball is awarded to the offended team out of bounds.

On the kickoff, all players must be onside, that is, behind the ball when it is kicked. If the kicking team is called offside, the ball is awarded to the other team out of bounds at the centerline. After the kickoff, players may move to any part of the field. On the kickoff, the ball must travel 10 yards before it can be recovered by either team. A kickoff outside or over the end line is treated as any other out-of-bounds ball.

A ball hitting the ground remains in play as long as it is in bounds. Players may not bat or kick a free ball. The penalty is loss of the ball to the other team out of bounds. Falling on the ball also means loss of the ball to the other team.

Teaching Suggestion: A 4-by-7-foot or a 4-by-8-foot folding tumbling mat can be used to define the box where the captain must stand to catch the ball for a score.

Flag Football

Playing Area: Field 30 by 60 yards

Players: Six to nine on a team

Supplies: A football, two flags per player (about 3 inches wide and 24 inches long), pinnies

Skills: All football skills

The field is divided into three zones by lines marked off at 20-yard intervals. There also should be two end zones, from 5 to 10 yards in width, defining the area behind the goal in which passes may be caught. Flag Football is played with two flags on each player. The flag is a length of cloth that is hung from the side at the waist of each player. To down (stop) a player with the ball, one of the flags must be pulled.

Flag Football should rarely, if ever, be played with 11 players on a side. This results in a crowded field and leaves little room to maneuver. If six or seven are on a team, four players are required to be on the line of scrimmage. For eight or nine players, five offensive players must be on the line.

The game consists of two halves. A total of 25 plays makes up each half. All plays count in the 25, except the try for the point after a touchdown and a kickoff out of bounds.

The game is started with a kickoff. The team winning the coin toss has the option of selecting the goal it wishes to defend or choosing to kick or receive. The loser of the toss takes the option not exercised by the first team. The kickoff is from the goal line, and all players on the kicking team must be onside. The kick must cross the first zone line or it does not count as a play. A kick that is kicked out of bounds (and is not touched by the receiving team) must be kicked again. A second consecutive kick out of bounds gives the ball to the receiving team in the center of the field. The kickoff may not be recovered by the kicking team unless caught and then fumbled by the receivers.

A team has four downs to move the ball into the next zone or they lose the ball. If the ball is legally advanced into the last zone, then the team has four downs to score. A ball on the line between zones is considered in the more forward zone.

Time-outs are permitted only for injuries or when called by the officials. Unlimited substitutions are permitted. Each must report to the official.

The team in possession of the ball usually huddles to make up the play. After any play, the team has 30 seconds to put the ball into play after the referee gives the signal.

Blocking is done with the arms close to the body. Blocking must be done from the front or side, and blockers must stay on their feet.

A player is down if one of her flags has been pulled. The ball carrier must make an attempt to avoid the defensive player and is not permitted to run over or through the defensive player. The tackler must play the flags and not the ball carrier. Good officiating is needed, because defensive players may attempt to hold or grasp the ball carrier until they are able to remove one of her flags.

All forward passes must be thrown from behind the line of scrimmage. All players on the field are eligible to receive and intercept passes.

All fumbles are dead at the spot of the fumble. The first player who touches the ball on the ground is ruled to have recovered the fumble. When the ball is centered to a back, she must gain definite possession of it before a fumble can be called. She is allowed to pick up a bad pass from the center when she does not have possession of the ball.

All punts must be announced. Neither team can cross the line of scrimmage until the ball is kicked. Kick receivers may run or use a lateral pass. They cannot make a forward pass after receiving a kick.

A pass caught in an end zone scores a touchdown. The player must have control of the ball in the end zone. A ball caught beyond the end zone is out of bounds and is considered an incomplete pass.

A touchdown scores 6 points, a completed pass or run after touchdown scores 1 point, and a safety scores 2 points. A point after touchdown is made from a distance of 3 feet from the goal line. One play (pass or run) is allowed for the extra point. Any ball kicked over the goal line is ruled a touchback and is brought out to the 20-yard line to be put into play by the receiving team. A pass intercepted behind the goal line can be a touchback if the player does not run it out, even if she is tagged behind her own goal line.

A penalty of 5 yards is assessed for the following:

1. Being offside
2. Delay of game (too long in huddle)
3. Failure of substitute to report
4. Passing from a spot not behind line of scrimmage (This also results in loss of down.)
5. Stiff-arming by the ball carrier, or not avoiding a defensive player
6. Failure to announce intention to punt
7. Shortening the flag in the belt, or playing without flags in proper position
8. Faking the ball by the center, who must center the pass on the first motion

The following infractions are assessed a 15-yard loss:

1. Holding, illegal tackling
2. Illegal blocking
3. Unsportsmanlike conduct (This also can result in disqualification.)

Teaching Suggestions: Specifying 25 plays per half eliminates the need for timing and lessens arguments about a team's taking too much time in the huddle. Using the zone system makes the first-down yardage point definite and eliminates the need for a chain to mark off the 10 yards needed for a first down.

Pass Ball

Playing Area: Field 30 by 60 yards

Players: Six to nine on a team

Supplies: A football, flags (optional), pinnies

Skills: All football skills, especially passing and catching

Pass Ball is a more open game than Flag Football. The game is similar to Flag Football with these differences.

1. The ball may be passed at any time. It can be thrown at any time beyond the line of scrimmage, immediately after an interception, during a kickoff, or during a received kick.
2. Four downs are given to score a touchdown.
3. A two-handed touch on the back is used instead of pulling a flag. Flags can be used, however.
4. If the ball is thrown from behind the line of scrimmage and results in an incomplete pass, the ball is down at the previous spot on the line

of scrimmage. If the pass originates otherwise and is incomplete, the ball is placed at the spot from which this pass was thrown.

5. Because the ball can be passed at any time, no downfield blocking is permitted. A player may screen the ball carrier but cannot make a block. Screening is defined as running between the ball carrier and the defense.

FOOTBALL SKILL TESTS

Tests for football skills cover centering, passing, and kicking (punting).

Centering

Each player is given five trials to center at a target. The target should be stationed 6 yards behind the center. Some suggestions for targets follow.

1. An old tire can be suspended so that the bottom of the tire is about 2 feet above the ground. For centering the ball through the tire, 2 points are scored. For hitting the tire but not going through it, 1 point is scored. The possible total is 10 points.

2. A baseball pitching target from the softball program can be used. Scoring is the same as with the tire target.

3. A 2-by-3-foot piece of plywood is held by a player at the target line in front of his body, with the upper edge even with the shoulders. The target is held stationary and is not to be moved during the centering. For hitting the target, 1 point is scored. The possible total is 5 points.

Passing for Accuracy

To test accuracy in passing, each player is given five throws from a minimum distance of 15 yards at a tire suspended at about shoulder height. (To make the tire fairly stable, it can be suspended from goal posts or from volleyball standards.) As skill increases, increase the distance.

For throwing through the tire, 2 points are scored. For hitting the tire but not passing through, 1 point is scored. The possible total is 10 points.

Passing for Distance

Each player is allotted three passes to determine how far she can throw a football. The longest throw is measured to the nearest foot. Reserve the test for a relatively calm day, because the wind can be quite a factor (for or against the player) in this test.

The passes should be made on a field marked off in 5-yard intervals. Use markers made from tongue depressors to indicate the first pass distance. If a later throw is longer, the marker should be moved to that point. When individual markers are used, the members of a squad can complete the passing turns before measuring.

Kicking for Distance

Punting, place kicking, and drop kicking can be measured for distance by using techniques similar to those described for passing for distance.

FLAG FOOTBALL FORMATIONS

A variety of offensive formations are shown in Figures 26.18 and 26.19, including the T-formation. The T-formation has limited use in Flag Football, because the passer (the quarterback) is handicapped by being too close to the center. Emphasis should be on using a variety of formations and on spread formations, with flankers and ends positioned out beyond normal placement.

Balanced (tight ends):

E O X O E

Unbalanced right (tight ends):

E X O O E

Line over right (tight end):

X E O O E

Right end out (can be one or both):

E O X O (5 yards) E

Right end wide (can be one or both):

E O X O (15 yards) E

Right end wide, left end out (can be reversed):

E (5 yards) O X O (15 yards) E

Spread (3 to 5 yards between each line position):

E O X O E

Figure 26.18 Offensive line formations

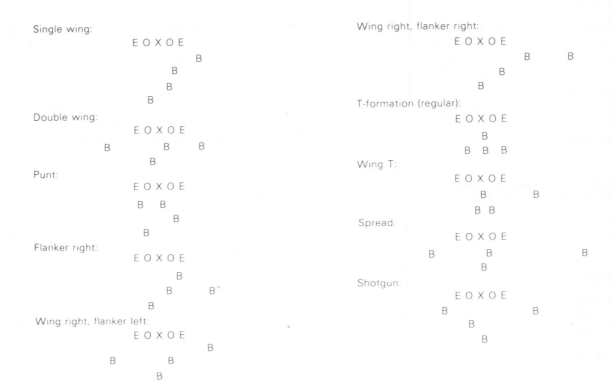

Figure 26.19 Offensive backfield formations

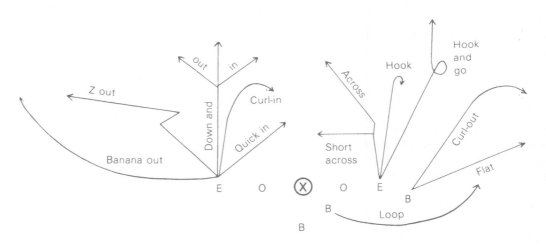

Figure 26.20 Pass patterns

The following formations are based on a nine-player team, with four in the backfield and five on the line. The formations will vary if the number on each team is decreased. Presenting a variety of formations to players makes the game more interesting. Backfield formations can be right or left (Figure 26.19).

Offensive Line Formations

Only formations to the right are presented in Figure 26.18. The center is indicated by an X, backs by B, ends by E, and line positions by O.

Offensive Backfield Formations

The formations diagrammed in Figure 26.19 can be combined with any of the offensive line forma-

tions. For purposes of clarity, however, the illustrations for all formations show a balanced line with tight ends.

Pass Patterns

The pass patterns illustrated in Figure 26.20 (see previous page) may be run by the individual pass catcher, whether he occupies a line position or is a back. They are particularly valuable in practice, when the pass receiver informs the passer of his pattern.

Hockey

Hockey is a fast-moving game that can be adapted for use in the elementary school. Hockey at the elementary level is a lead-up to ice hockey as well as to field hockey. With a plastic puck or yarn ball, hockey can be played indoors. Outdoors, a plastic whiffle ball is used (Figure 27.1). Play can be mixed, with boys and girls playing on an equal basis. Shin guards are not needed in elementary school hockey.

Success at hockey demands much running and team play. Children should develop good fundamental skills and learn position play rather than the disorganized "everyone chase the puck" style of hockey often played in schools.

INSTRUCTIONAL EMPHASIS AND SEQUENCE

Table 27.1 shows the sequence of hockey activities divided into two developmental levels. The actual presentation of activities is dictated by the maturity and past experience of participants.

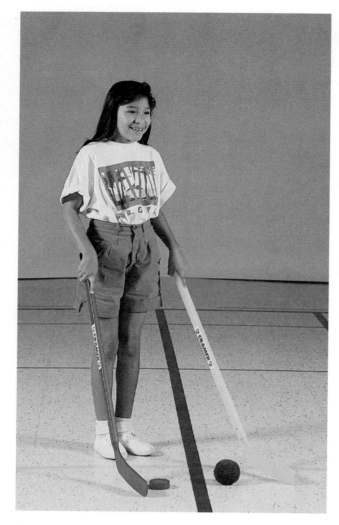

Figure 27.1 Hockey equipment

Developmental Level II

At this level, little strategy is introduced. Drills are used to develop the fundamental skills. Learning to dribble loosely, fielding the ball, and making short passes should receive the most attention.

Developmental Level III

At developmental level III, skill development continues, with more emphasis on ball control and passing accuracy. Lead-up games that use the skills involved in regulation hockey are played. The drills presented are designed to foster team play. The use of lead-up games introduces strategy and field positioning. The rules of regulation hockey are introduced, and the actual game is played. Skills should be reviewed and practiced through the use of selected drills and lead-up games.

Table 27.1 Suggested hockey program

Developmental Level II	Developmental Level III
Skills	
Gripping and carrying the stick	Controlled dribble
Loose dribble	Side field
Passing	Tackle
Front field	Dodging
Goalkeeping	Face-off
	Driving
	Jab shot
Knowledge	
Hockey rules	Ball handling and passing
	The game of hockey
	Team play and strategy
Activities	
Circle Keep-Away	Goalkeeper Hockey
Star Wars Hockey	Sideline Hockey
Lane Hockey	Regulation Elementary
Modified Hockey	Hockey
Skill Tests	
Passing for accuracy	Dribbling for speed
Fielding	Driving for distance

HOCKEY SKILLS

Gripping and Carrying the Stick

The hockey stick should be held with both hands and carried as low to the ground as possible. The basic grip puts the left hand at the top of the stick and the right hand 6 to 12 inches below the left (Figure 27.2). The player should learn to carry the stick to the right of the body, with the blade close to the ground, while running. To ensure accuracy as well as safety, the stick must not be swung above waist height.

Dribbling

Dribbling is used to move and control the ball without the aid of teammates. Players should be taught to look for a pass first and then dribble if there is no immediate opportunity to make a pass.

Figure 27.2 Gripping and carrying

The following instructional cues offer points of emphasis for skill performance.

1. Control the puck. It should always be within reach of the stick.
2. Move under control.
3. Hold the stick firmly.
4. Keep the head up.
5. Keep the elbows away from the body.

Loose Dribble

The loose dribble is an elementary form of moving the ball under control. It demands less skill than controlled dribbling. In loose dribbling, the ball is pushed 10 to 15 feet in front of the player. The player then runs to the ball and gives it another push, repeating the sequence. This type of dribble is used in open-field play when there is little chance that an opponent will intercept the ball. The loose dribble also allows skilled players to run at maximum speed. The ball must be pushed with the flat side of the blade and kept in front of the body.

Controlled Dribble

The controlled dribble consists of a series of short taps in the direction in which the player chooses to

move. The hands should be spread 10 to 14 inches apart to gain greater control of the stick. As the player becomes more skilled, the hands can be moved closer together. The stick is turned so that the blade faces the ball. The grip should not be changed, but rather, the hands should be rotated until the back of the left hand and the palm of the right hand face the ball (Figure 27.3). The ball can then be tapped just far enough in front of the player to keep it away from the feet but not more than one full stride away from the stick. The emphasis should be on controlling the ball during heavy traffic so that opposing players cannot easily intercept it.

Passing

The most commonly used passes in floor hockey are the forehand pass and the quick hit. The quick hit should be taught simultaneously with dribbling skills. Emphasis should be on accuracy rather than swinging wildly. The following instructional cues can be used to help youngsters concentrate on correct technique.

1. Approach the puck with the side facing the direction of the pass.
2. Keep the head down and eyes on the puck.
3. Keep the stick below waist level at all times.
4. Transfer weight from the rear to the front foot.
5. Drive the stick through the puck.

Figure 27.3 Starting the dribble

Figure 27.4 Driving

6. Keep the stick on the floor until the puck is struck.

Forehand Pass

The forehand pass is a short pass that usually occurs from the dribble. It should be taught before driving, because the quick hit requires accuracy rather than distance. The player spreads the feet with toes pointed slightly forward when striking. Approach the ball with the stick held low and bring the stick straight back, in line with the intended direction of the hit. The hands should be the same distance apart as in the carrying position, and the stick should be lifted no higher than waist level. The player's right hand guides the stick down and through the ball. The head should be kept down with the eyes on the ball. A short follow-through occurs after contact.

Driving

Driving (Figure 27.4) is used to hit the ball moderate to long distances and to shoot at the goal. It differs from other passes in that the hands are brought together more toward the end of the stick. This gives the leverage necessary to apply greater force to the ball and results in more speed and greater distance. The swing and hit are similar to the quick hit. Stick control should be stressed so that wild swinging does not occur.

Fielding

The term *fielding* refers to stopping the ball and controlling it. Fielding the ball in hockey is as important as catching the ball in basketball. As a skill, it requires much practice. Emphasize the following instructional cues:

1. Field with a "soft stick." This means holding the stick with relaxed hands.

2. Allow the puck to hit the stick and then "give" to make a soft reception.

3. Keep the hands apart on the stick.

Front Field

For the front field, the student must keep an eye on the ball, move to a point in line with its path, and extend the flat side of the blade forward to meet the ball (Figure 27.5). The faster the ball approaches, the more she must learn to give with the stick to absorb the momentum of the ball. The player should field the ball in front of the body and not permit it to get too close.

Side Field

A ball approaching from the left or right side is more difficult to field than one approaching from the front. When the ball is approaching from the player's left, he must allow the ball to travel in front of his body before fielding it. If the ball is approaching from the right, it must be intercepted before it crosses in front of his body (Figure 27.6). The player's feet should be pointed in the direction in which he plans to move after controlling the ball. Regardless of the direction of the ball, the side of the blade must always be used to field it.

Figure 27.5 Front field position

654 ———————————————

Figure 27.6 Side field position

Tackling

The tackle is a means of taking the ball away from an opponent. The tackler moves toward the opponent with the stick held low. The tackle is timed so that the blade of the stick is placed against the ball when the ball is off the opponent's stick (Figure 27.7). The tackler then quickly dribbles or passes in the direction of the goal. Throwing the stick or striking carelessly at the ball should be discouraged. Players need to remember that a successful tackle is not always possible.

Jab Shot

The jab shot is used only when a tackle is not possible. It is a one-handed, poking shot that attempts to knock the ball away from an opponent.

Figure 27.7 Tackling

Dodging

Dodging is a means of evading a tackler and maintaining control of the ball. The player dribbles the ball directly at the opponent. At the last instant, the ball is pushed to one side of the tackler, depending on the direction the player is planning to dodge. If the ball is pushed to the left, the player should move around the right side of the opponent to regain control of the ball, and vice versa. Selecting the proper instant to push the ball is the key to successful dodging. Dodging should not be attempted if a pass would be more effective.

Face-Off

The face-off is used at the start of the game, after a goal, or when the ball is stopped from further play by opposing players. The face-off is taken by two players, each facing a sideline, with their right sides facing the goal that their team is defending. Each player hits the ground on her side of the ball and the opponent's stick over the ball, alternately, three times. After the third hit the ball is played, and each player attempts to control the ball or to pass it to a teammate. The right hand can be moved down the stick to facilitate a quick, powerful movement. An alternate means of starting action is for a referee to drop the ball between the players' sticks.

Goalkeeping

The goalie may kick the ball, stop it with any part of the body, or allow it to rebound off the body or hand. He may not, however, hold the ball or throw it toward the other end of the playing area. The goalkeeper is positioned in front of the goal line and moves between the goal posts. When a ball is hit toward the goal, the goalie should attempt to move in front of the ball and to keep his feet together. This allows the body to block the ball should the stick miss it. After the block, the ball is passed immediately to a teammate.

INSTRUCTIONAL PROCEDURES

1. For many children, hockey is a new experience. Few have played the game and many may never have seen a game. Showing a film of a hockey game as an introduction may be helpful.

2. Since few children have had the opportunity to develop skills elsewhere, it is necessary to teach the basic skills in a sequential manner

and to allow ample time in practice sessions for development.

3. Hockey is a rough game when children are not taught the proper methods of stick handling. They need to be reminded often to use caution and good judgment when handling hockey sticks.

4. Ample equipment increases individual practice time and facilitates skill development. A stick and a ball or puck for each child are desirable.

5. If hockey is played on a gym floor, a plastic puck or yarn ball should be used. If played on a carpeted area or outdoors, a whiffle ball is used. An 8-foot folding mat set on end makes a satisfactory goal.

6. Hockey is a team game that is more enjoyable for all when the players pass to open teammates. Excessive control of the ball by one person should be discouraged.

7. An individual who is restricted to limited activity can be designated as a goalie. This is an opportunity for children with disabilities to participate and receive reinforcement from peers. An asthmatic child, for example, might serve as a goalkeeper.

8. Fatigue may be a problem, for hockey is a running game that demands agility and endurance. Children should be in reasonably good physical condition to participate. Rotation and rest periods help prevent fatigue.

HOCKEY DRILLS

Dribbling Drills

1. Successful hockey play demands good footwork and proper stick handling. To develop these skills, all players can spread out on the field, carrying the stick in proper position, in a group mimetic drill. On command, players move forward, backward, and to either side. Quick reactions and good footwork are the focus.

2. Each player with a ball practices dribbling individually. Dribbling should be practiced first at controlled speeds and then at faster speeds as skill develops.

3. Players can practice in pairs, with partners standing about 20 feet apart. One player dribbles the ball toward a partner, goes around the partner, and returns to the starting spot (Figure 27.8). The ball is then passed to the

Figure 27.8 Dribbling drill

partner, who moves in a similar manner. A shuttle type of formation can be used with three players.

Passing and Fielding Drills

1. In pairs, about 20 feet apart, players pass the ball quickly back and forth. Emphasis should be on passing immediately after fielding the ball. The cue phrase might be "Field, pass."

2. One player passes the ball to a partner, who fields the ball, dribbles twice, and passes back to the other. Passes should be fielded from various angles and from the right and left sides.

3. The shuttle turn-back formation, in which two files of four or five players face each other, can be used. The first person in the file passes to the first person in the other file, who in turn fields the ball and returns the pass. Each player, when finished, goes to the end of the file.

4. The downfield drill is useful for polishing passing and fielding skills while moving. Three files of players start at one end of the field. One player from each file proceeds downfield, passing to and fielding from the others until the other end of the field is reached. A goal shot can be made at this point. The players should remain close together for short passes until a high level of skill is reached.

5. Driving for distance and accuracy can be practiced with a partner.

Dodging and Tackling Drills

1. Players are spread out on the field, each with a ball. On command, they dribble left, right, forward, and backward. On the command "Dodge," the players dodge an imaginary tackler. Players should concentrate on ball control and dodging in all directions.

2. Three players form the drill configuration as diagrammed in Figure 27.9. Player 1 has the ball in front, approaches the cone (which represents a defensive player), dodges around the cone, and passes to player 2, who repeats the dodging maneuver in the opposite direction. Player 2 passes to player 3, and the drill continues in that manner.

Figure 27.9 Shuttle-type drill

3. Players work in pairs. One partner dribbles toward the other, who attempts to make a tackle. If the tackle is successful, roles are reversed. This drill should be practiced at moderate speeds in the early stages of skill development.

4. A three-on-three drill affords practice in many skill areas. Three players are on offense and three are on defense. The offense can concentrate on passing, dribbling, and dodging, while the defense concentrates on tackling. A point is given to the offense when they reach the opposite side of the field. The defensive team becomes the offensive team after a score.

HOCKEY ACTIVITIES

Developmental Level II

Circle Keep-Away

Playing Area: A 20- to 25-foot circle

Players: Eight to ten

Supplies: One stick per person, a puck or ball

Skills: Passing, fielding

Players are spaced evenly around the circle, with one player in the center. The object of the game is to keep the player in the center from touching the puck. The puck is passed back and forth, with emphasis on accurate passing and fielding. If the player in the center touches the puck, the player who last passed the puck takes the place of the center player. A change of players also can be made after a passing or fielding error.

Star Wars Hockey

Playing Area: Playground or gymnasium

Players: Four teams of equal size

Supplies: One stick per player, four pucks or balls

Skill: Dribbling

Each team forms one side of a square formation. The game is similar to Star Wars (p. 587), with the following exceptions:

1. Four pucks (or balls) are used. When a number is called, each player with that number goes to

a puck and dribbles it out of the square through the spot previously occupied, around the square counterclockwise, and back to the original spot. Circles 12 inches in diameter are drawn on the floor to provide a definite place to which the puck must be returned. If the game is played outdoors, hoops can mark the spot to which the puck must be returned.

2. No player is permitted to use anything other than the stick in making the circuit and returning the puck to the inside of the hoop. The penalty for infractions is disqualification.

Lane Hockey

Playing Area: Hockey field or gymnasium, 60 by 100 feet

Players: Nine per team

Supplies: Hockey stick per player, puck, two goals

Skills: All hockey skills

The field is divided into eight lanes as illustrated in Figure 27.10. A defensive and an offensive player are placed in each of the eight lanes. A goalkeeper for each team is also positioned in front of the goal area. Players may not leave their lane during play. A shot on goal may not be taken until a minimum of two passes have been completed. This rule encourages looking for teammates and passing to someone in a better position before a shot on goal is taken.

Players should be encouraged to maintain their spacing during play. The purpose of the lanes is to force them to play a zone rather than rushing to the puck. Rules used for regulation hockey (p. 659) enforce situations not described here. A free hit (unguarded) is awarded a team if a foul occurs. Players should be rotated after a goal is scored or at regular time intervals.

Figure 27.10 Field markings for Lane Hockey

Variation: Increase the number of lanes to five or six. This involves a larger number of players. On a large playing area, the lanes may be broken into thirds rather than halves. Increase the number of passes that should be made prior to a shot on goal.

Modified Hockey

Playing Area: Hockey field or gymnasium

Players: 7 to 11 on each team

Supplies: One stick per person, a puck or ball

Skills: Dribbling, passing, dodging, tackling, face-off

The teams may take any position on the field as long as they remain inside the boundaries. The object of the game is to hit the puck through the opponent's goal. No goalies are used. At the start of the game and after each score, play begins with a face-off. Each goal is worth one point.

Teaching Suggestion: The distance between goal lines is flexible but should be on the long side. If making goals is too easy or too difficult, the width of the goals can be adjusted accordingly.

Developmental Level III

Goalkeeper Hockey

Playing Area: A square about 40 by 40 feet

Players: Two teams of equal size

Supplies: One stick per player, a puck or ball

Skills: Passing, fielding, goalkeeping

Each team occupies two adjacent sides of the square (Figure 27.11). Team members are numbered consecutively from left to right. Two or three numbers are called by the instructor. These players enter the playing area and attempt to capture the ball, which is placed in the center of the square, and to pass it through the opposing team. A point is scored when the ball goes through the oppo-

nent's side. Sideline players should concentrate on goalkeeping skills. When a score is made, the active players return to their positions, and new players are called.

Teaching Suggestions: The teacher needs to keep track of the numbers called so that all players have an equal opportunity to play. Different combinations can be called.

Sideline Hockey

Playing Area: Hockey field or gymnasium area, 60 by 100 feet

Players: 6 to 12 players on each team

Supplies: One hockey stick per player, a puck or ball, two 4-by-8-foot folding tumbling mats

Skills: Most hockey skills, except goaltending

Each team is divided into two groups. They are positioned as indicated in Figure 27.12, which shows eight players on each team. Half of each team is on the court; these are the active players. The others stand on the sidelines. No goalkeeper is used. A face-off at the center starts the game and puts the ball into play after each score. Each team on the field, aided by the sideline players, attempts to score a goal. The sideline players help keep the ball in bounds and can pass it onto the court to the active players. Sideline players may pass only to an active player and not to each other.

Any out-of-bounds play on a sideline belongs to the team guarding that sideline and is put into play with a pass. An out-of-bounds shot over the end line that does not score a goal is put into play by the team defending the goal. The group of players on the field changes places with the sideline players on their team as soon as a goal is scored or after a specified time period.

Illegal touching, sideline violations, and other minor fouls result in loss of the ball to the opposition. Roughing fouls and illegal striking should

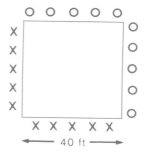

Figure 27.11 Team positions for Goalkeeper Hockey

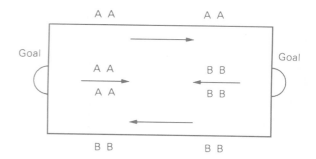

Figure 27.12 Team positions for Sideline Hockey

result in banishment to the sideline for the remainder of the competitive period.

Teaching Suggestions: Some attention must be given to team play and passing strategies rather than having all players simply charge the ball. Teams should use the sideline players by passing to them and receiving passes from them in return. Teams can be rotated so that the same two teams do not face each other continually.

Regulation Elementary Hockey

Playing Area: Hockey field or gymnasium area, approximately 40 to 50 feet by 75 to 90 feet

Players: Six on each team

Supplies: One stick per player, a puck or ball

Skills: All hockey skills

In a small gymnasium, the walls can serve as the boundaries. In a large gymnasium or on an outdoor field, the playing area should be delineated with traffic cones. The area should be divided in half, with a 12-foot restraining circle centered on the midline. This is where play begins at the start of the periods, after goals, or after foul shots. The official goal is 2 feet high by 6 feet wide, with a restraining area 4 by 8 feet around the goal to protect the goalie (Figure 27.13). Each team has a goalkeeper, who stops shots with her hands, feet, or stick; a center, who is the only player allowed to move full court and who leads offensive play (the center has her stick striped with black tape); two guards, who cannot go beyond the centerline into the offensive area and who are responsible for keeping the puck out of their defensive half of the field; and two forwards, who work with the center on offensive play and who cannot go back over the centerline into the defensive area.

A game consists of three periods of 8 minutes each, with a 3-minute rest between periods. Play is started with a face-off by the centers at midcourt. Other players cannot enter the restraining circle until the ball has been hit by the centers. The clock starts when the puck is put into play and runs continuously until a goal is scored or a foul is called. Substitutions can be made only when the clock is stopped. If the ball goes out of bounds, it is put back into play by the team that did not hit it last.

Whenever the ball passes through the goal on the ground, 1 point is scored. If, however, the ball crosses the goal line while in the air, it must strike against the mat or back wall to count for a score. Under no circumstances can a goal be scored on a foul. The puck can deflect off a player or equipment to score, but it cannot be kicked into the goal.

The goalkeeper may use her hands to clear the puck away from the goal, but she may not hold it or throw it toward the other end of the playing area. She is charged with a foul for holding the puck. The goalkeeper may be pulled from the goal area but cannot go beyond the centerline. No other player may enter the restraining area without being charged with a foul.

The following are fouls and are penalized by loss of the puck at the spot of the foul.

1. Illegally touching the puck with the hands
2. Swinging the stick above waist height (called sticking)
3. Guards or forwards moving across the centerline
4. Player other than the goalie entering the restraining area
5. Goalie throwing the puck
6. Holding, stepping on, or lying on the puck

Defenders must be 5 yards back when the puck is put into play after a foul. If the spot where the foul occurred is closer than 5 yards to the goal, only the goalkeeper may defend. The puck is then put into play 5 yards directly out from the goal.

Personal fouls include any action or rough play that endangers other players. A player committing a personal foul must retire to the sidelines for 2 minutes. The following are personal fouls.

1. Hacking or striking with a stick
2. Tripping with either the foot or the stick
3. Pushing, blocking

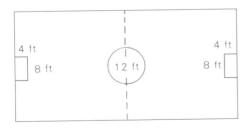

Figure 27.13 Regulation elementary hockey playing field

HOCKEY SKILL TESTS

Passing for Accuracy

In passing for accuracy, the player has five attempts to pass the puck or ball into a 3-by-3-foot target. The target can be drawn or taped on the wall, or a 3-foot square of cardboard can be used. The player must pass from a distance of 30 feet. He can approach the 30-foot restraining line in whatever fashion he chooses. Two points are awarded for each successful pass.

Dribbling for Speed

To test dribbling for speed, three cones are placed in line 8 feet apart. The first cone is 16 feet from the starting line. The player dribbles around the cones in a figure-eight fashion to finish at the original starting line. A stopwatch is used for timing, and the score is recorded to the nearest tenth of a second. Two trials are given, and the faster trial is recorded as the score.

Fielding

Three players are designated as passers and pass from different angles to a person being tested in fielding. The ball must be definitely stopped and controlled. The instructor can judge whether the pass was a good opportunity for the player to field. Six passes, two from each angle, are given, and one point is awarded for each successful field.

Driving for Distance

Driving for distance should be tested outdoors only. A restraining line can be used as a starting point. Each player is given five trials, and the longest two attempts are recorded as the player's score. Distance is measured to the nearest foot. Players can be lined up in four or five squads behind the restraining line. At any one time, one-third of the class can measure distances and return the balls. After players have taken their five trials, they can exchange places with someone who is measuring or returning balls. The test should be done on grass, because solid ground permits the ball to roll unimpeded.

Soccer

Soccer is a game of "educated" feet. If players are to improve their playing ability, organized practice that emphasizes handling the ball as often as possible and being in possession of the ball for as long as possible is essential for each child. Maneuvering the ball with the feet must become second nature, and this is accomplished by frequent opportunities on offense to kick, control, dribble, volley, and shoot and frequent opportunities on defense to mark, guard, tackle, and recover the ball.

Teachers should avoid the tendency to place children in soccer playing without the needed skills. Success in soccer depends on how well individual skills are coordinated in team play. Effective soccer stresses position play, in contrast to a group of children dashing around the ball like bees around a honey pot.

MODIFICATIONS OF SOCCER FOR ELEMENTARY SCHOOL CHILDREN

The 11-person game is not suitable for elementary school children and should be played only as a matter of orientation. The predominant game should be Mini-Soccer, with six or seven players on a side. Two games can be played crosswise on a regulation soccer field. With the exception of a penalty area and the out-of-bounds lines, the field does not have to be marked.

The official regulation soccer goal, 24 feet wide and 8 feet high, is too large for elementary play. The size should be such that teams have a reasonable chance of scoring as well as preventing a score. The suggested size is from 18 to 21 feet in width and 6 to 7 feet in height. The size can be further scaled down as determined by the character of the game. If a line of players makes up the goal, the ball should be required to pass below either waist or shoulder height to count as a score.

The soccer ball is oversized and heavy for some beginning soccer players. Many youngsters will avoid contact with the ball for fear of getting hurt. There are a number of manufacturers producing junior-sized soccer balls that move and rebound in a manner identical to regulation balls. "Nerf" or dense foam balls that are covered with a tough plastic skin to simulate the appearance of a soccer ball negate the fear of being hurt, and allow youngsters to head the ball properly.

INSTRUCTIONAL EMPHASIS AND SEQUENCE

Table 28.1 shows the sequence of soccer activities divided into two developmental levels. Depending on the amount of experience children have received through community sports programs, the actual sequence may differ in certain areas and communities.

Developmental Level II

The two basic skills in soccer are (a) controlling or stopping the ball with the foot so that the ball is in a position to be kicked and (b) passing the ball with the foot to another player or to a target. Activities at this level should stress games and drills that facilitate practice and involvement of these fundamental skills. To maximize involvement, one ball for every two players should be available.

Developmental Level III

The two basic skills continue to be important throughout the learning of the game and are developed further at this level. To enhance control of the ball, dribbling skills are introduced and students are taught to control the ball with other parts of the body, such as the thigh and chest. Passing should continue to receive major emphasis so that small-

Table 28.1 Suggested soccer program

Developmental Level II	Developmental Level III
Skills	
Dribbling	Dribbling
Inside-of-the-foot pass	Outside-of-the-foot pass
Long pass	Ball control (trapping)
Foot trap	Passing
Passing	Tackling
Goalkeeping	Kicking goals
Defensive maneuvers	Kickoff (placekicking)
	Punting
	Volleying
	Heading
Knowledge	
Soccer rules	Ball control and passing
	The game of soccer
	Team play and strategy
Activities	
Circle Kickball	Manyball Soccer
Soccer Touch Ball	Addition Soccer
Diagonal Soccer	Over the Top
Dribblerama	Lane Soccer
Bull's-Eye	Line Soccer
Pin Kickball	Mini-Soccer
Sideline Soccer	Six-Spot Keepaway
	Regulation Soccer
Skill Tests	
Controlled passing	Figure-eight dribbling
Kicking for accuracy	Controlling (three types)
Placekicking	Punting for distance
	Penalty kicking

side games or Mini-Soccer, with two to five players per team, can be introduced. The basic goalkeeping skills of catching low and high balls are taught. Further development of the basic skills is recommended, along with the introduction of shooting, tackling, heading, jockeying, and the concept of two-touch soccer for more advanced players. Fundamentals of team and positional play should be introduced, along with the rules of the regular game. The 7-player game is a much better substitute for the 11-on-a-side game, as it increases player involvement. A unit of study focusing on soccer as an international game is of value because few American children realize how important this game is in other countries.

SOCCER SKILLS

Offensive skills that should be taught in the elementary grades are passing, kicking, controlling, dribbling, volleying (including heading), and shooting. *Shooting* is defined as taking a shot at the goal with the intent to score. Defensive skills include marking, guarding, jockeying, tackling, and recovering the ball.

Dribbling

Dribbling is moving the ball with a series of taps or pushes to cover ground and still retain control. It allows a player to change direction quickly and to avoid opponents. The best contact point is the inside of the foot, but the outside of the foot will be used at faster running speeds. The ball should be kept close to the player to maintain control. The following instructional cues can be used to emphasize proper form:

1. Keep the head up in order to see the field.
2. Move on the balls of the feet.
3. Contact the ball with the inside, outside, or instep of the foot.
4. Keep the ball near the body so it can be controlled. (Don't kick it too far in front of the body.)
5. Dribble the ball with a controlled tap.

Passing

Balance and timing provide the key to accurate passing. The basic purposes of passing are to advance the ball to a teammate and to shoot on goal. Occasionally, a pass is used to send the ball downfield so that a team has a chance to regroup, with their opponents having an equal chance to recover the ball.

The following are instructional cues to enhance accurate passing:

1. Place the nonkicking foot alongside the ball.
2. Head down and eyes focused on the ball during contact.
3. Spread the arms for balance.
4. Follow through with the kicking leg in the intended direction of the ball.

5. Make contact with the outside or inside of the foot rather than with the toe.
6. Practice kicking with both the left and right foot.

Inside-of-the-Foot Pass (Push Pass)

The inside-of-the-foot pass is used for accurate passing over distances of up to 15 yards. Because of the technique used, this pass is sometimes referred to as the push pass. The nonkicking foot is placed well up, alongside the ball. As the kicking foot is drawn back, the toe is turned out. During the kick, the toe remains turned out so that the inside of the foot is perpendicular to the line of flight. The sole is kept parallel to the ground. At contact, the knee of the kicking leg should be well forward, over the ball, and both knees should be slightly bent (Figure 28.1).

Outside-of-the-Foot Pass (Flick Pass)

The nonkicking foot is placed more to the side of the ball than for the inside-of-the-foot kick, and the approach of the kicking leg is from directly behind

Figure 28.1 Preparing for an inside-foot kick

the ball. The kicking foot is fully extended and contact with the ball is on the outside of the foot between laces and sole-line. This pass can be used effectively while running, without breaking stride, or for flicking the ball to the side.

The Long Pass (Shoelace Kick)

The long pass is the power pass in soccer. It is used for kicking for distance or for power to kick it past a goalie. Beginners often use the toes instead of the top of the foot (shoelace) area, which can result in injury or an inaccurate kick. The ball is approached at an angle to the line of flight in a full running stride. The nonkicking foot is placed alongside the ball, with the kicking leg cocked in the backswing. Just before contact, the ankle of the kicking foot is fixed with the toes pointed down. As with all passes, the head is kept down with the eyes focused on the ball. Contact is made with the top of the foot on the shoelaces. The passer gives the lower leg a good forward snap at the knee. A normal follow-through in the intended direction of the pass completes the action. To lift the ball, contact is made below the midline of the ball, close to the ground, with the body leaning slightly backward. The nonkicking leg is placed to the side and slightly behind the ball so that the kicking foot makes contact just on the start of the upswing of the leg. The lofted pass is made over the opposition.

Ball Control (Trapping)

Learning to receive a ball and how to place it into the ideal position for making a pass or shot is vital. In fact, one of the best measures of skilled players is how quickly they can bring the ball under control with either the feet, legs, or torso. Advanced players are able to achieve this in one smooth movement, with one touch of the ball. The second touch occurs when the pass is made.

For efficient control, a large surface should be presented to the ball. On contact, the surface should be momentarily withdrawn to produce a spongelike or shock-absorbing action, which decelerates the ball and allows it to drop in an ideal position about a yard in front of the body. The pass or shot can then be made. The following instructional cues will help students develop ball control skills:

1. Move in line with the path of the ball.
2. Reach to meet the ball and give with the contact.
3. Stay on the balls of the feet.
4. Keep the eyes on the ball.

Inside-of-the-Foot Trap

This is the most common method of control, and is used when the ball is either rolling along the ground or bouncing up to knee height. The full surface of the foot, from heel to toe, should be presented perpendicular to the ball (Figure 28.2).

Chest and Thigh Traps

The inside of the thigh and the chest also are used to deflect the ball downward when it is bouncing high. The chest trap requires that the chest be lined up squarely with the direction from which the ball is traveling (Figure 28.3). On contact, the chest and waist are drawn back, causing a forward body lean. This will cause the ball to drop directly to the ground in front of the player. The thigh trap demands that the player turn her body sideways to the flight of the ball. The ball is contacted with the inside of the thigh. Upon contact with the ball, the thigh is relaxed and drawn backwards. This absorbs the force of the ball and causes it to drop to the ground ready to be played.

Figure 28.2 Controlling with the inside of the foot

Figure 28.3 Chest trap

Sole-of-the-Foot Trap

This method of control, sometimes called trapping the ball, is used occasionally to stop the ball. With beginners, it is not as successful a method as the inside-of-the-foot control, because the ball can roll easily under the foot. The sole is also used to roll the ball from side to side in dribbling and to adjust for a better passing position.

Heading

Heading is a special kind of volleying in which the direction of flight of the ball is changed through an impact with the head (Figure 28.4). In heading, the neck muscles can be used to aid in the blow. The eye must be kept on the ball until the moment of impact. The point of contact is the top of the forehead at the hairline. In preparation for contacting the ball with the head, the player should stand in stride position, with knees relaxed and trunk bent backward at the hips. At the moment of contact, the trunk moves forward abruptly, driving the forehead at the ball. Heading can be achieved in midair, and is especially useful in beating other players to the ball. This can be done by a running one-footed takeoff or a standing two-footed jump.

Defensive Maneuvers

Tackling is a move by a player to take possession of the ball away from an opponent who is dribbling. The most common tackle is the front block, which

Figure 28.4 Heading

involves contacting the ball with the inside of the foot just as the opponent touches it. The tackler presents a firm instep to the ball, with weight behind it. The stronger the contact with the ball, the greater the chance of controlling it. Body contact should be avoided, as this may constitute a foul. Other tackles may be made when running alongside the player with the ball.

How much tackling to teach in elementary school programs is a question of concern. In most cases, it is probably best to teach tackling skills that involve the defensive player remaining upright. Methods like the hook slide and split slide are of little value in elementary school instructional programs.

Jockeying

Knowing when to and when not to make a tackle is one of the most difficult skills to learn. A failed tackle may mean that an attacker breaks through with a free shot on goal. Often, defenders should jockey until defensive support arrives. This means backing off while staying close enough to pressure the advancing player. The defender should stay on the toes, watch the ball rather than the opponent's feet, and keep within 1 to 2 yards of the ball.

Throw-Ins

The throw-in is the only time the ball can be handled by field players with their hands. The throw-in is guided by rules that must be followed closely or the result is a turnover to the other team. The rules are as follows:

1. Both hands must be on the ball.
2. The ball must be released from over the thrower's head.
3. The thrower must face the field.
4. The thrower may not step onto the field until the throw is released.
5. Both feet must remain in contact with the ground until the ball is released.
6. The thrower cannot play the ball until it has been touched by another player on the field.

The throw-in from out of bounds (see Figure 28.21) may be executed from a standing or running position. Beginning players should learn the throw without a running start. The feet often are placed one behind the other, with the rear toe trailing along the ground. Delivery of the ball should be from behind the head, using both arms equally. Release should be from in front of the forehead with arms outstretched. Instructional cues to help students perform correctly are "drag your back foot" and "follow through with both hands pointing toward the target."

Shooting

Scoring is the purpose of the game, and shooting skills should be practiced both while stationary and while on the run. As with passing, the inside, outside, and top of the foot can be used.

Goalkeeping

Goalkeeping involves stopping shots by catching, stopping, or otherwise deflecting the ball. Goalkeepers should become adept at catching low rolling balls, diving on rolling balls, catching airborne balls at waist level and below (Figure 28.5), and catching airborne balls at waist height and above.

Youngsters should practice catching low rolling balls in much the same manner as a baseball outfielder does. The goalie gets down on one knee, with her body behind the ball to act as a backstop, and catches the ball with both hands, fingers pointing toward the ground.

Figure 28.5 Goalie catching a ball below waist level

If the goalie must dive for the ball, he should throw his body behind it and cradle it with his hands. A goalie should always try to get his body behind the ball.

When catching a ball below the waist, the thumbs should point outward and the arms reach for the ball, with body and arms giving and bringing the ball into the abdomen. For balls above waist level, the thumbs should be turned inward, arms reaching to meet the ball and giving to guide it to the midsection.

Drills for goalies should offer opportunities to catch the different shots described. All students should receive goaltending practice.

Punting

Used by the goalkeeper only, the punt can be stationary or can be done on the run. The ball is held in both hands at waist height in front of the body and directly over the kicking leg. For the stationary punt, the kicking foot is forward. A short step is taken with the kicking foot, followed by a full step on the other foot. With the knee bent and the toe extended, the kicking foot swings forward and upward. As contact is made with the ball at the instep, the knee straightens, and additional power is secured from the other leg through a coordinated rising on the toes or a hop (Figure 28.6).

Figure 28.6 Punt

The goalkeeper has an advantage who can develop a strong placekick. Distance and accuracy are important in setting up the next attack. Over shorter distances, throwing both underhand and overhand are sometimes more accurate than kicking. A straight arm should be used for rolling or throwing the ball to players.

INSTRUCTIONAL PROCEDURES

1. Soccer skills must be developed if children are to participate successfully in the sport. Controlling the ball and passing should predominate in practices. Drills and activities should be organized to maximize the involvement of all children. One ball is needed for every two children.

2. Many combination drills featuring both offense and defense should be included. Enjoyment is the key to continued learning. Drills and lead-up activities can be used to make the skills challenging, but all activities should be appropriate to the developmental level of players.

3. Small-group games (between two and five players) should be used frequently to ensure maximum activity. The number of team members can be increased as skill improves.

4. Lead-up games should encourage the use of the skills practiced in drills. For example, if long passing is the skill of the day, lead-up games requiring and rewarding long passing should be played. In the early stages of learning soccer, it may be best not to allow tackling.

5. Using cones or chalk, a grid system of 10-yard squares can be marked on a playing field. The grid can be useful when organizing drills, activities, and small-sized games. The number of squares needed depends on the size of the class, but at least one square for every three students is recommended. Possible layouts are shown in Figure 28.7. Squares can be used as confines for tackling, keeping possession, and passing diagonally or sideways. Drill and game areas can be defined easily, so that a number of small-sized games can be played simultaneously.

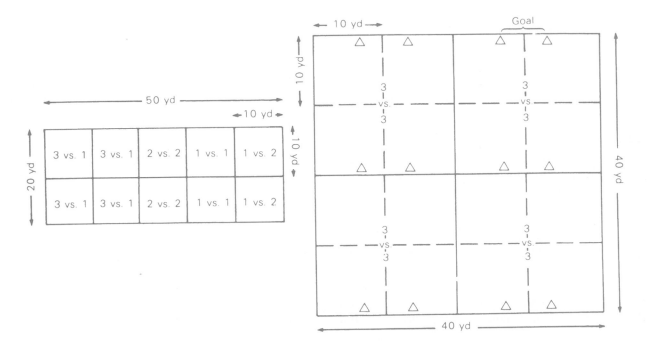

Figure 28.7 Examples of grid layouts and usage

6. Balls smaller than the regular soccer ball should be used. Molded rubber balls or partially deflated 8½-inch rubber playground balls can be used, provided their quality is good enough to withstand the kicking. A better alternative for novices is the dense foam rubber training ball. It withstands heavy usage and does not hurt youngsters on impact. The key to soccer practice is to have plenty of balls available. Rubber balls mean more fun, because they can be kicked far, controlled easily, and even headed without discomfort. Junior-sized soccer balls (No. 4) are also excellent but are more expensive.

7. Soccer, with its attack and defense, can be a rough game. Rough play such as pushing, shoving, kicking, and tripping must be controlled. Rules need to be strictly enforced. Attention to proper heading, volleying, and kicking techniques helps eliminate injuries that result from contact with the ball. Players need to watch for kicked balls, which may strike them in the face or head unexpectedly. Glasses should be removed when possible, and shin guards are recommended in very competitive situations.

8. Soccer is a vigorous game, and the teacher should use methods of rotation to help players rest. Children can rotate in and out of the goalkeeper position (generally, the least demanding position). Stretching should be emphasized before and after each session to minimize injuries.

9. Scoring can be modified in keeping with the players' capabilities. To score must be a challenge—neither too easy nor too difficult. To avoid arguments in situations in which the ball is to be kicked through a line of children, the height of the kick should be limited to shoulder level or below. This emphasizes an important soccer principle: control of the ball on the ground. Cones, jump standards, and similar devices can be used to mark goal outlines. Formal soccer goals are not necessary for the elementary school program.

SOCCER DRILLS

In soccer drills, two approaches should be recognized. The first is the practice of technique with no opposition from any defense. The second is the skill approach, which involves both offensive and defensive players and perhaps a target. In drills using the skill approach, the goal is to outmaneuver the opponent. Some drills begin with the technique approach and then move to the skill approach.

Individual practice can be carried on early, particularly with dribbling techniques, but most work should be with combinations of two or three students and small groups.

Communication becomes a problem when children are scattered over a playing area. One solution is a central demonstration location. On signal, children leave the soccer balls at their respective areas and come to the demonstration point for instructions.

The type of surface has a marked effect on the quality of soccer practice. Grass is the most desirable practice surface, but some schools have only hard-top surfaces. In this case, balls should be deflated slightly to approximate how they travel on grass. If space is to be restricted, the areas can be outlined by cones, beanbags, jugs, or boundary boards. Ten-yard lines on a football field make convenient grid lines to outline practice areas.

Individual Work

Dribbling practice is well suited to individual work. Activity can begin by having youngsters dribble in various directions and encouraging them to make right and left turns. As a variation, children can react to signals: One whistle means turn left, two means turn right, and three means reverse direction. Ten cones or so can be scattered around the area. Players dribble around one cone clockwise and then around another cone counterclockwise.

Heading can be practiced by players tossing the ball to themselves and heading it. This is followed by a short period of dribbling and then repeated. The teacher can signal to remind youngsters to pick up the soccer ball and begin heading again.

A child can drop a ball and learn to smother it with a foot. Another gambit is to toss the ball in the air and let it bounce, followed by a kick to oneself with an instep kick so the ball can be caught. Yet another trick is to toss the ball high and use the instep kick to control the ball.

Rebounding to oneself continuously, although not actually used in the game of soccer, is an excellent way to learn ball control. (This is sometimes called foot juggling.) Begin by dropping the ball so that it bounces at waist height, and then follow this pattern:

1. Rebound the ball with alternating feet, letting it bounce between contacts.

2. Play the ball twice with one foot, let it bounce, and then play it twice with the other foot.

3. Toss the ball so that it can be handled with the thigh and then catch. Add successive rebounds with the thigh.

4. Play ball with the foot, thigh, head, thigh, foot, and catch.

Other combinations can be devised. The teacher needs to move slowly with these skills, for some children will find them difficult.

The foot pickup can be learned in two ways. The first is to put the ball between the feet, jump up, and hoist the ball so that it can be caught. The second is the toe pickup. Put the toe on top of the ball. Pull the toe back and down, so that the ball spins up the instep from which it can be hoisted to the hands.

Another bit of individual work is toe changing on top of the ball. Put the ball of the foot on top of the ball. On signal, change feet. This movement can also be done using the Bleking step (see p. 376). During the first part of the music, the rhythm is slow, slow, fast, fast, fast. During the second part of the music, players dribble in diverse directions. Repeat.

Drills for Two Players

Many introductory drills can be practiced by paired players. Students are scattered in twos, with space needs determined by the type of drill. The pairs can sometimes be arranged in two lines so that both students react to the same challenges.

One of the best ways to organize partner drills is to use grid lines, mentioned earlier, placed 10, 20, or 30 yards apart. The distance between the grids depends on the skill to be practiced. Partners position themselves opposite each other so that two lines of players are formed, which gives the teacher a clear view of the class in action (Figure 28.8). This approach is recommended for introducing all new skills, such as passing with both sides of the foot, ball control, and heading. Skill combinations can be used, such as throw-ins by one partner and control-and-pass by the other. Within the grids, partners can work on passing, dribbling in a confined space, keepaway, and one-on-one games.

The following are examples of drills that can be used in partner formation.

1. *Dribbling, marking, and ball recovery.* Pairs are scattered, with one player in each pair having a soccer ball. That player dribbles in various directions, and the second player attempts to stay close to the first (marking). As skill development occurs, the defensive player can attempt to recover the ball from the dribbler. If successful, roles are reversed.

2. *Dribbling.* One player of the pair has a ball and dribbles in different directions. On signal, she passes to her partner, who repeats the dribbling, continuing until another signal is given.

3. *Dribbling, moving, and passing.* Two lines of paired children face each other across a 40-to-60-foot distance, as illustrated in the diagram (Figure 28.9). Each child in one of the lines has a ball and works with a partner directly across from him. A player with a ball from line A moves forward according to the challenges listed below. When he moves near his partner, he passes to him, and the partner (line B) repeats the same maneuver back to

Figure 28.8 Class organized along grid lines

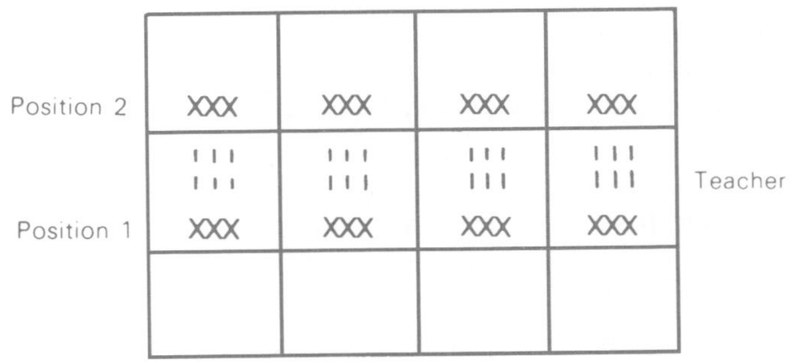

Figure 28.9 Dribbling, moving, and passing

40–60 ft

line A. Repeating the maneuver immediately results in both players returning to their starting place.

a. Dribble across to partner. Dribble using the outside of either foot.

b. Gallop across, handling the ball with the front foot only. On return, lead with the other foot.

c. Skip across, dribbling at the same time.

d. Slide across, handling the ball with the back foot. On return, lead with the other foot.

e. Hop across, using the lifted foot to handle the ball. Be sure to change feet halfway across.

f. Dribble the ball to a point halfway across. Stop the ball with the sole of the foot and leave it there. Continue to the other line. In the meantime, the partner from line B moves forward to dribble the ball back to line A.

g. Player A dribbles to the center and passes to player B. Player A now returns to line A. Player B repeats and returns to line B.

4. *Heading, volleying, and controlling.* Pairs of players are scattered. One player in each pair has a ball and acts as a feeder, tossing the ball for various receptive skills-heading, different volleys, and controlling balls in flight. Controlled tossing is essential to this drill.

Drills for Three Players

With one ball for three players, many of the possibilities suggested for pair practice are still possible. An advantage of drills for three players is that fewer balls are needed.

1. *Passing and controlling.* The trio of players set up a triangle with players about 10 yards apart. Controlled passing and practice in ball control should occur.

2. *Heading, volleying, controlling.* One player acts as a feeder, tossing to the other two players, who practice heading, volleying, and controlling air flight balls.

3. *Dribbling and passing.* A shuttle-type drill can be structured as shown in Figure 28.10. Players keep going back and forth continuously. Player 1 has the ball and dribbles to player 2, who dribbles the ball back to player 3, who in turn dribbles to player 1. Players can dribble the entire distance or dribble a portion of the

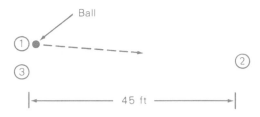

Figure 28.10 Shuttle-type dribbling drill

distance and then pass the ball to the end player. Obstacles can be set up to challenge players to dribble through or around each obstacle.

4. *Dribbling and stopping the ball.* Three dribblers are in line, each with a ball. The leader moves in various directions, followed by the other two players. On signal, each player controls her ball. The leader circles around to the back ball, and the other two move one ball forward. The dribbling continues for another stop. A third stop puts the players back in their original positions.

5. *Passing.* Players stand in three corners of a 10-yard square. After a player passes, he must move to the empty corner of the square, which is sometimes a diagonal movement (Figure 28.11).

6. *Passing and defense.* One player is the feeder and rolls the ball to either player. As soon as she rolls the ball, she attempts to block or tackle the player receiving the ball to prevent a pass to the third player, who, if the pass is completed, attempts to pass back (Figure 28.12).

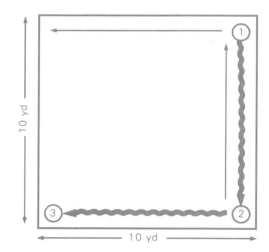

Figure 28.11 Passing drill

Note: The following symbols are used in soccer game formation diagrams: X Defensive player O Offensive player ➡ Player moving without the ball ┅▶ Player dribbling ➡ Pass, kick, or shot on goal

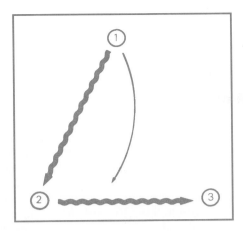

Figure 28.12 Passing and defense drill

Drills for Four or More Players

Drills for four or more players should be organized so that a rotation gives all players an equal opportunity to practice skills.

1. *Dribbling.* Four players are in line as diagrammed in Figure 28.13. Each player in front has a ball. Both front players dribble to the center, where they exchange balls and continue dribbling to the other side. The next players perform similarly. A variation is to have the two players meet at the center, exchange balls, and dribble back to their starting point. Action should be continuous.

2. *Passing, guarding, and tackling.* Four players occupy the four corners of a square respectively (Figure 28.14). One player has a ball. Practice begins with one player rolling the ball to the player in the opposite corner, who, in turn, passes to either of the other two players. There should be two attempts each round so that kicks are possible both ways. The next progression calls for the player who rolled the ball to move forward rapidly to block the pass to either side. Several tries should occur before another player takes over the rolling duties.

3. *Shooting, goalkeeping, and defense.* A shooting drill against defense can be run with four players and a 15-foot goal set off with cones or other markers (Figure 28.15). One player has the ball. He advances and attempts to maneuver around a second player so that he can

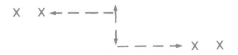

Figure 28.13 Dribble exchange drill

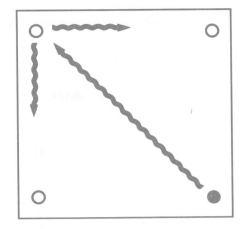

Figure 28.14 Passing, guarding, and tackling drill

Figure 28.15 Shooting, goalkeeping, and defense

shoot past the goalkeeper guarding a goal. A fourth player acts as the retriever. Rotate positions.

4. *Dribbling.* Four or five players, each with a ball, form a line. A "coach" stands about 15 yards in front of the line. Each player, in turn, dribbles up to the coach, who indicates with a thumb in which direction the player should dribble past. The coach should give the direction at the last possible moment.

5. *Passing, controlling, and defense.* Four players stand in the four corners of a square, 10 yards on a side. Two defensive players are inside the square. The corner players stay in place within the square and attempt to pass the ball among themselves, while the two defenders attempt to recover the ball (Figure 28.16). After a period of time, another two players take over as defenders.

6. *Shooting.* For two-way goal practice, two to six players are divided, half on each side of the goal. The width of the goal can vary, depending on the skill of the players. Two types of shooting should be practiced: (a) kicking a stationary ball from 10 to 20 yards out and (b) preceding a kick with a dribble. In the second type, a restraining line 12 to 15 yards out is needed. This line can be marked by cones, as illustrated (Figure 28.17). Use at least four balls for this two-way drill. After a period of

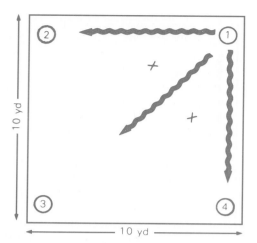

Figure 28.16 Passing, controlling, and defense

Figure 28.18 Shooting and goalkeeping

kicking, the groups should change sides. Ball chasers are the players at the end of each line.

7. *Shooting and goalkeeping.* Scoring can also be practiced with a goalkeeper (Figure 28.18). Practice should be done with a stationary ball from 12 yards out (penalty distance) and with kicks preceded by a dribble. The goalie and the chaser should remain for one complete round and then rotate. Having a second ball to play with saves time because play can continue while the chaser is recovering the previous ball.

8. *Kicking and trapping.* This is an excellent squad drill. Approximately eight players form a circle 15 yards in diameter. Two balls are passed back and forth independently. Passes should be kept low, using primarily the side-of-the-foot kick. Using three balls can be tried also.

9. *Passing and shooting.* The drill can be done with four to six players. Two balls are needed. A passer is stationed about 15 yards from the goal, and a retriever is behind the goal. The shooters are in line, 20 yards from the goal and to the right. The first shooter passes to the passer, and then runs forward. The passer returns the ball to the shooter. The shooter tries to time her run forward so that she successfully shoots the pass through the goal. Both the passer and the retriever should stay in position for several rounds of shooting and then rotate to become shooters. The first pass can be from a stationary ball. Later, however, the kicker can be allowed to dribble forward a short distance before making the first pass. Reverse the field and practice from the left, shooting with the nondominant leg (Figure 28.19).

10. *Tackling and ball handling.* A defender is restricted to tackling in the area between two parallel lines, which are 1 yard apart. The field is 20 by 40 yards (Figure 28.20). Four to six players can practice this drill. Player 1 advances the ball by dribbling and attempts to maneuver past the defender. After he has evaded the defender, he passes to player 2 and takes his place at the other side of the field.

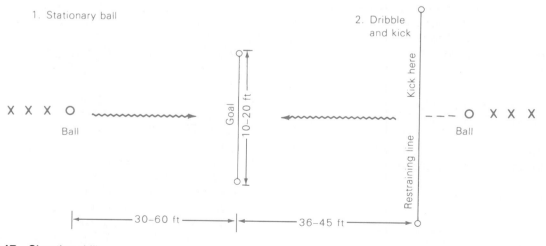

Figure 28.17 Shooting drill

X Retriever

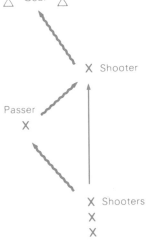
△ Goal △

X Shooter

Passer
X

X Shooters
X
X

Figure 28.19 Passing and shooting

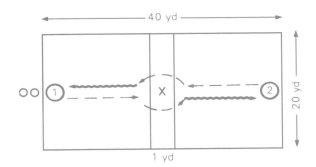

Figure 28.20 Tackling and ball-handling drill

Player 2 repeats the routine, passing the ball off to the next player in the line. If the ball goes out of control or is stopped by the defender, it is rolled to the player whose turn is next. Play is continuous, with the defender maintaining his position for several rounds.

BASIC SOCCER RULES FOR LEAD-UP GAMES

The ball may not be played deliberately with the hands or arms, but incidental or unintentional handling of the ball should be disregarded in the early stages. Eventually, a violation leads to a direct free kick in which the ball is placed on the ground with the opposition a specified distance away (10 yards on a full-sized field). A goal can be scored directly from this type of kick.

The goalkeeper is allowed to handle the ball within her area by catching, batting, or deflecting with the hands. If the goalie has caught the ball, she may not be charged by the opponents. While the goalie is holding the ball, official rules limit her to four steps. In elementary school play, the teacher should insist on the goalkeeper's getting rid of the ball immediately by throwing or kicking. This removes the temptation to rough up the goalie. In some lead-up games, a number of students may have the same ball-handling privileges as the goalie. The rules need to be clear, and ball handling should be done within a specified area.

All serious fouls, such as tripping, kicking a player, holding, or pushing, result in a direct free kick. If a defender commits one of these fouls or a handball in his own penalty area, a *penalty kick* is awarded. Only the goalkeeper may defend against this kick, which is shot from 12 yards out. All other players must be outside the penalty area until the ball is kicked. In lead-up games, consideration should be given to penalty fouls committed in a limited area near the goal by the defensive team. A kick can be awarded or an automatic goal can be scored for the attacking team.

The ball is out of play and the whistle blown when the ball crosses any of the boundaries, when a goal is scored, or when a foul is called. The team that last touched the ball or caused it to go out of bounds on the side of the field loses possession. The ball is put into play with an overhead throw-in using both hands (Figure 28.21).

If the attacking team causes the ball to go over the end line, the defending team is awarded a kick from any point chosen near the end line of that half of the field. If the defense last touched the ball going over the end line, then the attacking team is awarded a *corner kick*. The ball is taken to the corner on the side where the ball went over the end line, and a direct free kick is executed. A goal may be scored from this kick.

The game is normally started by a kickoff with both teams onside. In lead-up games, the ball can be dropped for a free ball. In some games, the teacher may find it advisable simply to award the ball for a free kick in the backcourt to the team not making the score.

Lead-up games can continue for a set length of time (by halves) or until a predetermined score is attained. In a regular soccer game, the play is timed.

When the ball is ensnarled among a number of players or when someone has fallen, a quick whistle is needed. The ball can be put into play by dropping it between players of the opposing teams.

Figure 28.21 Throwing in, from out of bounds

Even though implementation of the offside rule is of little value in elementary school play, children should understand the rule and the reasons for it. Its purpose is to prevent the "cheap" goal (i.e., a player on offense waits near the goal to take a pass behind the defenders and to score easily against the goalkeeper). Although the concept of *offsides* involves a number of details, it essentially means that a player on offense who is ahead of the ball must have two defensive players between her and the goal when the ball is kicked forward. One of these players is, of course, the goalie. The offside rule does not apply when the player receives the ball directly from an attempted goal kick, from an opponent, on a throw-in or corner kick, or when the player is in her own half.

Players should not raise their feet high or show the soles or cleats when other players are in the vicinity. This constitutes dangerous play, and an *indirect free kick* is awarded.

SOCCER ACTIVITIES

Developmental Level II

Circle Kickball

Playing Area: Playground or gymnasium

Players: 10 to 20

Supplies: Two soccer balls or 8-inch foam rubber balls

Skills: Kicking, controlling

Players are in circle formation. Using the side of the foot, players kick the balls back and forth inside the circle. The object is to kick a ball out of the circle beneath the shoulder level of the circle players. A point is scored against each of the players where a ball leaves the circle between them. If, however, a lost ball is clearly the fault of a single player, then the point is scored against that player only. Any player who kicks a ball higher than the shoulders of the circle players has a point scored against him. Players with the fewest points scored against them win. Players must watch carefully as two balls are in action at one time. A player cannot be penalized if he leaves the circle to recover a ball and the second ball goes through the vacated spot.

Soccer Touch Ball

Playing Area: Playground or gymnasium

Players: Eight to ten

Supplies: A soccer ball

Skills: Kicking, controlling

Players are spaced around a circle 10 yards in diameter with two players in the center. The object of the game is to keep the players in the center from touching the ball. The ball is passed back and forth as in soccer. If a center player touches the ball with a foot, the person who kicked the ball goes to the center. If a circle player commits an error (i.e., misses a ball), the person responsible changes places with a center player. A rule that no player may contain or hold the ball longer than 3 seconds tends to keep the game moving.

Diagonal Soccer

Playing Area: A square about 60 by 60 feet

Players: 20 to 30

Supplies: A soccer or foam rubber ball, pinnies (optional)

Skills: Kicking, passing, dribbling, some controlling, defending, blocking shots

Two corners are marked off with cones 5 feet from the corners on both the sides, outlining triangular dead areas. Each team lines up as illustrated in Figure 28.22 and protects two adjacent sides of the square. The dead area on the opposite corner marks the opposing team's goal lines. To begin competition, three players from each team move into the playing area in their own half of the space. These are the active players. During play, they may roam anywhere in the square. The other players act as line guards.

The object of the game is for active players to kick the ball through the opposing team's line (beneath shoulder height) to score. When a score is made, active players rotate to the sidelines and new players take their place. Players on the sidelines may block the ball with their bodies but cannot use their hands. The team against whom the point was scored starts the ball for the next point. Only active players may score. Scoring is much the same as in Circle Kickball in that a point is awarded for the opponents when any of the following occur:

1. A team allows the ball to go through its line below the shoulders.

2. A team touches the ball illegally.

3. A team kicks the ball over the other team above shoulder height.

Variations:

1. If the class is large, a bigger area and more active players can be used.

2. If scoring seems too easy, the line defenders can use their hands to stop the ball.

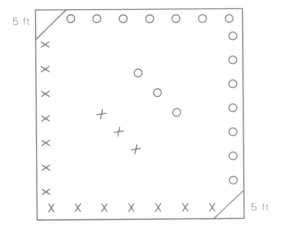

Figure 28.22 Formation for diagonal soccer

Dribblerama

Playing Area: Playground
Players: 10 to 20
Supplies: One soccer ball for each player
Skills: Dribbling, protecting the ball

The playing area is a large circle or square, clearly outlined. All players dribble within the area. The game is played on two levels.

Level 1: Each player dribbles throughout the area, controlling the ball so that it does not touch another ball. If a touch occurs, both players go outside the area and dribble counterclockwise around the area. Once youngsters have completed dribbling one lap of the counterclockwise path, they may reenter the game.

Level 2: While dribbling and controlling the ball, each player attempts to kick any other ball out of the area. When a ball is kicked out, the player owning that ball takes it outside and dribbles around the area. Play continues until only two or three players who have not lost control of their ball are left. These are declared the winners. Bring all players back into the game and repeat.

Bull's-Eye

Playing Area: Playground
Players: Six to ten
Supplies: One soccer ball per player
Skills: Dribbling, protecting the ball

The playing area is a large outlined area—circle, square, or rectangle. One player holds a ball in her hands, which serves as the bull's-eye. The other players dribble within the area. The player with the bull's-eye attempts to throw her ball (basketball push shot) at any other ball. The ball that is hit now becomes the new bull's-eye. The old bull's-eye becomes one of the dribblers. A new bull's-eye cannot hit back immediately at the old bull's-eye. A dribbler should protect the ball with her body. If the group is large, have two bull's-eyes. No score is kept and no one is eliminated.

Pin Kickball

Playing Area: Playground or gymnasium
Players: Seven to ten on each team
Supplies: Six or more pins (cones or bowling pins), two soccer balls
Skills: Kicking, controlling

Two teams start about 20 yards apart, facing each other. At least six pins are placed between the two lines of players. One ball is given to each team at the start of the kicking (Figure 28.23). Kicks should be made from the line behind which the team is standing. Players should trap and concentrate on accuracy. Each pin knocked down scores a point for that team.

Teaching Suggestions: This is a flexible game; the number of pins, balls, and players can be varied easily. The type of kick can be specified, or it can be left up to the player to choose.

Domination of the game by one or two players can be controlled somewhat by having those who have just scored go to either end of the line. More soccer balls can be added when the game seems slow. As accuracy improves, the distance between the teams can be increased. Players on each end of the lines are the ball chasers. After all of the pins have been knocked down, they are reset, and the game resumes.

Sideline Soccer

Playing Area: Rectangle about 60 by 100 feet

Players: 10 to 12 on each team

Supplies: A soccer ball, four cones, pinnies (optional)

Skills: Most soccer skills, competitive play

The teams line up on the sidelines of the rectangle. Three or four active players from each team are called from the end of the team line (Figure 28.24). These players remain active until a point is scored; then they rotate to the other end of the line.

The object is to kick the ball between cones that define the scoring area. The active players on each team compete against each other, aided by their teammates on the sidelines.

To start play, a referee drops the ball between two opposing players at the center of the field. To

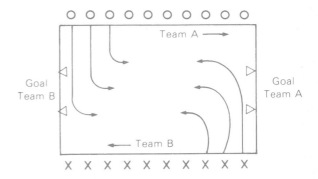

Figure 28.24 Formation for Sideline Soccer

score, the ball must be kicked last by an active player and must go through the goal at or below shoulder height. A goal counts one point. Sideline players may pass to an active teammate, but a sideline kick cannot score a goal.

Regular rules generally prevail, with special attention to the restrictions of no pushing, holding, tripping, or other rough play. Rough play is a foul and causes a point to be awarded to the other team. For an out-of-bounds ball, the team on the side of the field where the ball went out-of-bounds is awarded a free kick near that spot. No score can result from a free kick. Violation of the touch rule also results in a free kick.

Teaching Suggestions: A system of rotation in which active players move to the opposite end of the sideline and new players come forth is necessary. More active players can be added when the class is large, and the distance between goals can be increased. A number of passes to sideline players can be mandated before a shot on goal can be taken. After some expertise is acquired, the cones should be moved in to narrow the goal area. If the ball goes over the end line but not through the goal area, the ball is put into play by a defender with a kick.

Developmental Level III

Manyball Soccer

Playing Area: Soccer field

Players: Entire class

Supplies: Six foam or soccer balls, cones, pinnies

Skills: All soccer skills

Players are divided into two teams and begin in their defensive half of the field. Players are free to roam the entire field with the exception of the goalie boxes, which are delineated with cones.

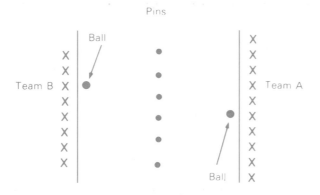

Figure 28.23 Formation for Pin Kickball

Only the goalie is allowed in the goalie box. Goalies are the only players who can touch the ball with their hands. The goalie tries to keep the balls from going between the cones. The goalie can return the ball to play by punting or throwing.

The object is to kick one of the six balls through the goal. If a ball goes through the goal, the player who scored retrieves the ball (not the goalie) and returns it to the midline for play. All balls are in play simultaneously except when being returned after a goal. Basic soccer rules (pp. 679–681) are used to control the game.

Variation: Use more than one goalie.

Addition Soccer

Playing Area: Playground

Players: 10 to 15

Supplies: One soccer ball per player, except for the person who is designated as defender

Skills: Dribbling, ball control

One player is designated to defend against the other players. The remainder of the players dribble throughout the area, trying to keep the defender from touching any ball with his foot. The first ball that he touches makes the owner of that ball the ball collector at the ball control station.

The defender now tries to touch any other ball with his foot. When the ball is touched, that player rolls the ball to the ball control station and joins hands with the defender to become his partner. They operate as a twosome and must keep hands joined as they chase to touch other balls. When another ball is touched, that player takes the ball to the control station and waits until yet another ball is touched to provide him with a partner. The new twosome now become defenders too, adding their efforts to those of the first twosome. Play continues until all balls are in the ball control station and all players have been caught.

If partners break joined hands in touching a ball, the tag is voided. The last one caught becomes the defender for the next match. The game is similar to Addition Tag (p. 570).

Over the Top

Playing Area: Playground

Players: Two teams of five to seven

Supplies: Each player on offense has a ball

Skills: Dribbling, ball control, guarding, tackling

One team is on offense and one on defense, placed according to Figure 28.25. Defensive play-

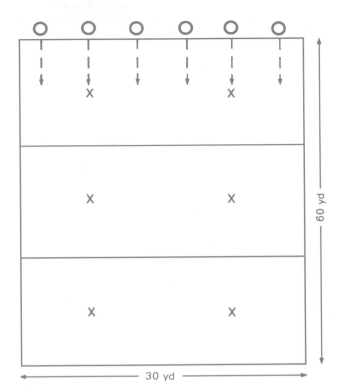

Figure 28.25 Over the Top

ers must stay in their respective areas. On signal, all offensive players begin to dribble through the three areas. A player is eliminated if her ball is recovered by a defensive player or goes out of bounds. The offensive team scores 1 point for each ball that is dribbled across the far end line. Reverse roles and give the other team a chance to score. Field markings need to be definite to keep the defensive players in their respective zones. Some teachers like to put neutral zones between the active zones.

Lane Soccer

Playing Area: Soccer field

Players: Nine per team

Supplies: Soccer ball, pinnies

Skills: All soccer skills

The field is divided into four lanes (eight equal sections) as illustrated in Figure 28.26. A defensive and an offensive player are placed in each of the eight areas. A goalkeeper guards the goal per regulation soccer goals. At least two passes must be made before a shot on goal can be taken. Basic soccer rules (pp. 679–681) guide play. The goalie is the only player who can handle the ball with the hands. A free kick is given to a player who has

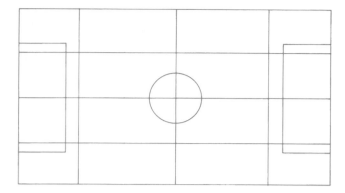

Figure 28.26 Field markings for Lane Soccer

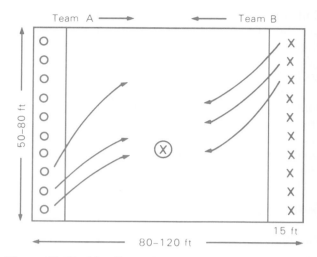

Figure 28.27 Line Soccer

been fouled by an opponent. Failing to stay within a lane also results in a free kick. Players must be rotated after a goal is scored or a specified amount of time has elapsed. This rotation will enable all students to play four positions; defense, midfield defense, midfield offense, and offense.

Teaching Suggestion: The number of lanes can be varied depending on the number of players and the size of the field. Students can be allowed to choose their opponent for their lane. Usually, they will choose an opponent of equal ability.

Line Soccer

Playing Area: Soccer field

Players: Eight to ten players on each team

Supplies: A soccer ball, four cones, pinnies

Skills: Most soccer skills, competitive play

Two goal lines are drawn 80 to 120 feet apart. A restraining line is drawn 15 feet in front of and parallel to each goal line. Field width can vary from 50 to 80 feet. Each team stands on one goal line, which it defends. The referee stands in the center of the field and holds a ball (Figure 28.27). At the whistle, three players (more if the teams are large) run from the right side of each line to the center of the field and become active players. The referee drops the ball to the ground, and the players try to kick it through the other team defending the goal line. The players in the field may advance by kicking only.

A score is made when an active player kicks the ball through the opposing team and over the end line (provided that the kick was made from outside the restraining line). Cones should be put on field corners to define the goal line. A system of player rotation should be set up.

Line players act as goalies and are permitted to catch the ball. Once caught, however, the ball must

be laid down immediately and either rolled or kicked. It cannot be punted or drop-kicked.

One point is scored when the ball is kicked over the opponent's goal line below shoulder level. One point is also scored in case of a personal foul involving pushing, kicking, tripping, and the like.

For illegal touching by the active players, a direct free kick from a point 12 yards in front of the penalized team's goal line is given. All active players on the defending team must stand to one side until the ball is kicked. Only goalies defend.

A time limit of 2 minutes is set for any group of active players. If no goal is scored during this time, play is halted and the players are changed.

An out-of-bounds ball is awarded to the opponents of the team last touching it. The regular soccer throw-in from out of bounds should be used. If the ball goes over the shoulders of the defenders at the end line, any end-line player may retrieve the ball and put it into play with a throw or kick.

Teaching Suggestion: Line Soccer should be played with the regular soccer rules when possible.

Variations:

1. If there is enough space, the teams can count off by threes. They need not keep any particular order at the end lines but simply come out as active players when their number is called. By using numbers, the teacher can pit different groups against each other.

2. Instead of giving a score for a personal foul, a penalty kick can be awarded. The ball is kicked from 12 yards out, and only three defenders are permitted on the line.

Mini-Soccer

Playing Area: Any large area 100 by 150 feet, with goals

Players: Seven on each team

Supplies: A soccer ball, pinnies or colors to mark teams, four cones for the corners

Skills: All soccer skills

Each end of the field has a 21-foot-wide goal marked by jumping standards. A 12-yard semicircle on each end outlines the penalty area. The center of the semicircle is at the center of the goal (Figure 28.28).

The game follows the general rules of soccer, with one goalie for each side. One new feature, the corner kick, needs to be introduced. This kick is used when the ball, last touched by the defense, goes over the end line but not through the goal. The ball is taken to the nearest corner for a direct free kick, and a goal can be scored from the kick. In a similar situation, if the attacking team last touched the ball, the goalkeeper kick is awarded. The goalie puts the ball down and placekicks it forward.

The players are designated as center forward, outside right, outside left, right halfback, left halfback, fullback, and goalie. Players should rotate positions. The forwards play in the front half of the field, and the guards in the back half. Neither position, however, is restricted to these areas entirely, and all may cross the centerline without penalty.

A foul by the defense within its penalty area (semicircle) results in a penalty kick, taken from a point 12 yards distant, directly in front of the goal. Only the goalie is allowed to defend. The ball is in play, with others waiting outside the penalty area.

Teaching Suggestion: Position play should be emphasized. The lines of three should be encouraged to spread out and hold reasonable position.

Variation: The number of players can vary, with some games using as few as three on a side in a more restricted area. If teams have more than seven players, the seven-player game should be maintained but with frequent substitutions.

Six-Spot Keepaway

Playing Area: Playground, gymnasium

Players: Two teams, six on each side

Supplies: One soccer ball, stopwatch

Skills: Passing, ball control, guarding

There is a total of six offensive players. Five are arranged in a pentagon formation, with one player in the center (Figure 28.29). The pentagon is about 20 yards across. For the offense, play is divided into two periods of 1 minute each. Three defenders from the other team attempt to interrupt the passing of the offensive team from one to another. A player may not pass the ball back to the person from whom it was received. The game begins with the ball in possession of the center player.

The object of the game is, for 1 minute (i.e., the first period), to make as many good passes as possible against three defenders. During the other period, the remaining three defenders rotate into the game. They may move as they wish. Offensive players should stay reasonably in position. Change offense and defense and repeat.

Regulation Soccer

Playing Area: Soccer field (Figure 28.30)

Players: 11 on each team

Supplies: A soccer ball, pinnies

Skills: All soccer skills

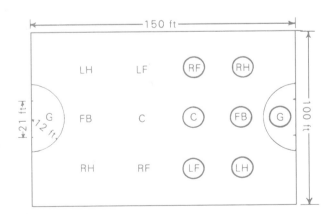

Figure 28.28 Formation for Mini-Soccer

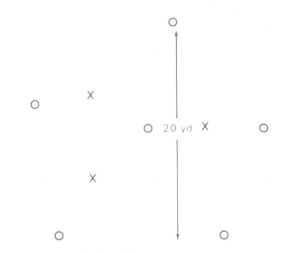

Figure 28.29 Six Spot Keepaway

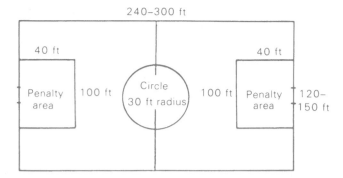

Figure 28.30 Regulation soccer field

A team usually consists of three forwards, three midfield players, four backline defenders, and one goalkeeper. Forwards are the main line of attack. They need to develop good control, dribbling, and shooting skills, and they must have a strong desire to score. They should be encouraged to shoot frequently. Midfield players tend to be the powerhouse of the team. They need good passing and tackling skills as well as a high level of cardiovascular fitness. Defenders should work well together and know when to tackle. They should play safely by clearing the ball away from their own penalty area, and not risk dribbling or passing toward their own goal unless it is absolutely safe to do so. Goalkeepers must be quick and agile, be good decision makers, and have ball-handling skills.

On the toss of the coin, the winning team gets its choice of kicking off or selecting which goal to defend. The loser exercises the option not selected by the winner.

On the kickoff, the ball must travel forward about 1 yard, and the kicker cannot touch it again until another player has kicked it. The defensive team must be 10 yards away from the kicker. After each score, the team not winning the point gets to kick off. Both teams must be onside at the kickoff. The defensive team must stay onside and out of the center circle until the ball is kicked. Regular soccer rules call for scoring by counting the number of goals made.

Elementary school children usually play 6-minute quarters. There should be a rest period of 1 minute between quarters and 10 minutes between halves.

When the ball goes out of bounds on the sideline, it is put into play with a throw-in from the spot where it crossed the line. No goal may be scored, nor may the thrower play the ball a second time until it has been touched by another player. All opponents are to be 10 yards back at the time of the throw.

If the ball is caused to go out of bounds on the end line by the attacking team, a goal kick is awarded. The ball is placed in the goal area and kicked beyond the penalty area by a defending player, who may not touch the ball twice in succession. If the ball is touched by a player before it goes out of the penalty area, it is not yet in play and should be kicked again.

If the defensive team causes the ball to go out of bounds over the end line, a corner kick is awarded. The ball is placed 1 yard from the corner of the field and kicked into the field of play by an attacking player. The 10-yard restriction also applies to defensive players.

If the ball is touched by two opponents at the same time and caused to go out of bounds, a drop ball is called. The referee drops the ball between two opposing players, who cannot kick it until it touches the ground. A drop ball also is called when the ball is trapped among downed players.

If a player is closer to the opponent's goal line than to the ball at a time when the ball is played in a forward direction, it is an offside infraction. Exceptions exist, and a player is not offside when he is in his half of the playing field, when two opponents are nearer their goal line than the attacking player at the moment when the ball is played, or when the ball is received directly from a corner kick, a throw-in, or a goal kick.

Personal fouls involving unnecessary roughness are penalized. Tripping, striking, charging, holding, pushing, and jumping an opponent intentionally are forbidden.

It is a foul for any player, except the goalkeeper, to handle the ball with the hands or arms. The goalkeeper is allowed only four steps and must then get rid of the ball. After the ball has left his possession, the goalkeeper may not pick it up again until another player has touched it. Players are not allowed to screen or obstruct opponents, unless they are in control of the ball.

Penalties are as follows:

1. A direct kick is awarded for all personal fouls and handballs. A goal can be scored from a direct free kick. Examples of infringements are pushing, tripping, kicking a player, and holding.

2. A penalty kick is awarded if direct free-kick infringements are committed by a defender in his own penalty area.

3. An indirect free kick is awarded for offsides, obstruction, dangerous play such as high kicking, a goalkeeper's taking more than four steps or repossessing the ball before another player

has touched it, and playing the ball twice after a dead-ball situation. The ball must be touched by a second player before a goal can be scored. The referee should signal if the kick is indirect by pointing one arm upward vertically.

Teaching Suggestions: Players should be encouraged to use the space on the field to the best advantage. When a team is in possession of the ball, players should attempt to find a position from which they can pass either behind the player with the ball to give support, or toward the goal to be in a better position to shoot. When a team is forced into defense, the defenders should get "goalside" of attackers (between the attackers and their own goal) to prevent them from gaining an advantage.

From an early stage, players should be taught to give information to each other during the game, especially when they have possession of the ball. Valuable help can be given by shouting instructions such as "Man on," "You have time," or "Player behind," and also by calling for the ball when in a good position to receive a pass.

SOCCER SKILL TESTS

The tests for soccer skills cover various kinds of kicks, dribbling, and controlling. An excellent use of the skill tests is to set up self-testing stations. Signs will tell students how to test themselves. If desired, the teacher can formally test at one of the stations. Students rotate from station to station after a designated amount of time.

Passing against a Wall

Players pass the ball from behind a line between 5 and 10 yards away from a wall. The student should be encouraged to control the ball before kicking. The score is the number of passes made from behind the line in 1 or 2 minutes. This is an excellent test of general ball control and short passing skill.

Figure-Eight Dribbling

For a figure-eight dribbling test, three obstacles or markers are arranged in a line, 4 yards apart, with the first marker positioned 4 yards from the starting line. The finish line is 4 yards wide. A stopwatch is used, and the timing is done to the nearest tenth of a second.

Each player gets three trials, with the fastest trial taken as the score. On each trial, the player dribbles over the figure-eight course and finishes by kicking or dribbling the ball over the 4-yard finish line, at which time the watch is stopped. The test is best done on a grass surface, but if a hard surface must be used, the ball should be deflated somewhat so that it can be controlled.

Controlling

For the controlling test, the formation is a file plus one. A thrower stands 15 to 20 feet in front of the file and rolls or bounces the ball to the player at the head of the file. Three trials each are given for the sole-of-the-foot control, the foot control, and body control. The ball must be definitely stopped and controlled. A score of 9 points, one for each successful control, is possible.

The thrower should adopt one type of throw for all controls and for all players. If the scorer judges that the roll was not a good opportunity, the trial is taken over. Five trials can be allowed.

Placekicking and Punting for Distance and Accuracy

To test punting for distance, a football field or any other field marked in gridiron fashion at 5- or 10-yard intervals is needed. One soccer ball is required, but when three are used, considerable time is saved. A measuring tape (25 or 50 feet) plus individual markers complete the supply list.

Each player is given three kicks from behind a restraining line. One child marks the kick for distance, while one or two others act as ball chasers. After three kicks, the player's marker is left at the spot of the longest kick. This is determined by marking the point at which the ball first touched after the kick. Measurement is taken to the nearest foot.

Every student in the squad or small group should kick before the measurements are taken. The punt must be from a standing, not a running, start. If a child crosses the line during the kick, it counts as a trial and no measurement is taken.

Placekicking for distance is tested in the same way as punting for distance, with two exceptions. The ball is kicked from a stationary position. It must be laid on a flat surface and not elevated by dirt, grass, or other means. The child is given credit for the entire distance of the kick, including the roll. The kicking should be done on a grassy surface, because the ball will roll indefinitely on a smooth, hard surface. If the surface presents a problem, the test can be limited to the distance the ball has traveled in flight.

Penalty Kicking and Short Passing Accuracy

In the penalty-kicking test, the kicker faces a target area from a point 12 yards out, where the ball has been placed. The target area is formed by a rope stretched tight 6 feet above the ground. Four ropes, at distances 5 feet apart, are dropped from the stretched rope. This outlines three target areas 6 feet high and 5 feet wide. The center target area scores 1 point and the side areas 2 points (Figure 28.31). (This reflects the principle that a penalty kick should be directed away from a goalkeeper toward either corner of the goal.) Each child is allotted five kicks at the target. A score of 10 points is possible.

The same target is used for kicking for accuracy, but the center area scores 2 points and the

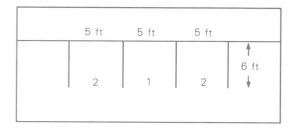

Figure 28.31 Penalty-kicking target area

side areas 1 point each. A balk line is drawn about 20 feet from the target. The child is back another 20 feet for the start. The player dribbles the ball forward and must kick the ball as it is moving and before it crosses the balk line. Five trials are given and a score of 10 points is possible.

Softball

*T*he main emphasis in softball should be on instruction and lead-up games. Children have adequate opportunity during recess, at the noon hour, and at other times to play the regulation game. In many physical education classes, too much softball participation is of the "choose sides and let 'em go" variety. Youngsters enjoy softball, and a good program should make use of this drive.

INSTRUCTIONAL EMPHASIS AND SEQUENCE

Table 29.1 shows the sequence of softball activities divided into two developmental levels. Youngsters can practice many of the skills of softball, but may not be ready to participate in the activities in this chapter until the age of 8.

Developmental Level II

The fundamental skills of batting, throwing, and catching are emphasized at this level. Batting must receive attention, for softball is little fun unless children can hit. Proper form and technique in all three fundamental skills should be part of the instruction, with attention paid not only to the how but also to the

Table 29.1 Suggested softball program

Developmental Level II	Developmental Level III	Developmental Level II	Developmental Level III
Skills			
Throwing		*Pitching*	
Gripping the ball	Throw-in from outfield	Simple underhand	Target pitching
Overhand throw	Sidearm throw	Application of pitching rule	Slow pitches
Underhand toss			
Around the bases		**Knowledge, Rules**	
Catching and Fielding		Strike zone	Pitching rule
Catching thrown balls	Catching flies from fungo bat	Foul and fair ball	Position
Catching fly balls		Safe and out	Illegal pitches
Grounders	Infield practice	Foul tip	Infield fly
Fielding grounders in infield		Bunt rule	Keeping score
Sure stop for outfield		When batter safe or out	Base running
			Situation quiz
Batting		**Activities**	
Simple skills	Different positions at plate	Throw-It-and-Run Softball	Five Hundred
Tee batting	Bunting	Two-Pitch Softball	Batter Ball
Fungo hitting		Hit and Run	Home Run
		Kick Softball	Tee Ball
Fielding Positions		In a Pickle	Scrub (Work-Up)
Infield practice	Backing up other players	Beat Ball	Slow-Pitch Softball
How to catch	Double play		Babe Ruth Ball
			Hurry Baseball (One-Pitch)
Base Running			Three-Team Softball
To first base and turn	Fast start off base	**Skill Tests**	
Circling the bases	Tagging up on fly ball	Throwing for distance	Pitching
	Sacrifice	Throwing for accuracy	Circling the bases
			Fielding grounders

why. A wide range in skill levels should be expected. Lead-up games are simple, but they provide an introduction to the basic rules of the game. As youngsters mature, specific skills for pitching, infield play, base running, and batting make up the instructional material. Proper pitching technique is important to the budding softball player.

Developmental Level III

Youngsters at this level should develop the background to play the game of regulation softball. Instructional material is aimed at this goal. Tee Ball provides a good opportunity for developing all softball skills except pitching and catching. Home

Run and the ever-popular Scrub (Work-Up) provide a variety of experiences, while Batter Ball stresses hitting skills.

Experiences with batting, throwing, catching, and infield play continue. New pitching techniques, situation play, and double-play work are added. Slow-Pitch Softball provides lots of action. Babe Ruth Ball emphasizes selective hitting.

SOFTBALL SKILLS

Children can find many ways to execute softball skills effectively by trial and error and through instruction. Care must be taken not to attempt to mold every child into a prescribed form, but to work toward making the most of each child's movement patterns.

Gripping the Ball

The standard softball grip, difficult for elementary school children, calls for the thumb to be on one side, the index and middle fingers on top, and the other fingers supporting along the other side (Figure 29.1). Younger children with small hands will find it best to use a full-hand grip, in which the thumb and fingers are spaced rather evenly (Figure 29.2). Regardless of the grip used, the pads of the fingers should control the ball.

Throwing (Right-Handed)

Softball requires accurate throwing. Players must practice proper throwing technique if they are going to be able to perform well in softball. Of all the team sports, softball is probably the most difficult for youngsters because of the fine motor coordination required. The following instructional cues can be used to help students develop proper throwing technique:

1. Place the throwing arm side of the body away from the target.
2. Step toward the target with the foot opposite the throwing hand.
3. Rotate the hips as the throwing arm moves forward.
4. Bend and raise the arm at the elbow. Lead with the elbow.
5. Prior to the forward motion of the arm, shift the weight from the rear foot to the forward foot (nearest the target).

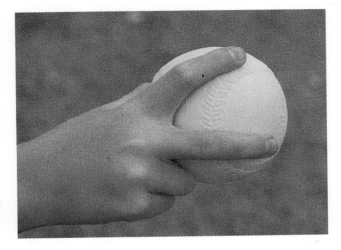

Figure 29.1 Gripping the ball, two-finger grip

Figure 29.2 Gripping the ball, full grip (The little finger supports on the side.)

Overhand Throw

In preparation for throwing, the child secures a firm grip on the ball, raises the throwing arm to shoulder height, and brings the elbow back. For the overhand throw, the hand with the ball is then brought back over the head so that it is well behind the shoulder at about shoulder height. The left side of the body is turned in the direction of the throw, and the left arm is raised in front of the body. The weight is on the back (right) foot, with the left foot advanced and the toe touching the ground. The arm comes forward with the elbow leading, and the ball is thrown with a downward snap of the wrist (Figure 29.3). The body weight is brought forward into the throw, shifting to the front foot. There should be good follow-through so that the palm of the throwing hand faces the ground at completion of the throw. The eye should be on the target throughout, and the arm should be kept free and loose during the throw.

Sidearm Throw

The sidearm throw is much the same as the overhand throw, except that the entire motion is kept near a horizontal plane. The sidearm throw is used for shorter, quicker throws than the overhand and

Figure 29.4 Pitching

Figure 29.3 Throwing overhand

employs a quick, whiplike action. On a long throw, the sidearm throw curves more than the overhand, because a side-spinning action is usually imparted to the ball on release. There is generally some body lean toward the side of the throwing arm.

Underhand Throw

For the underhand throw, the throwing hand and arm are brought back, with palm facing forward, in a pendulum swing. The elbow is bent slightly. The weight is mostly on the back foot. The arm comes forward, almost in a bowling motion, and the ball is tossed. The weight shifts to the front foot during the toss. The flight of the ball should remain low and arrive at about waist height.

Pitching

Official rules call for the pitcher to have both feet in contact with the pitcher's rubber, but few elementary schools possess a rubber. Instead, the pitcher can stand with both feet about even, facing the batter, and holding the ball momentarily in front with both hands. The pitcher takes one hand from the ball, extends the right arm forward, and brings it back in a pendulum swing, positioning the ball well behind the body. A normal stride taken toward the batter with the left foot begins the throwing sequence for a right-handed pitcher. The arm is brought forward with an underhanded slingshot motion, and the weight is transferred to the leading foot. Only one step is permitted. The follow-through motion is important (Figure 29.4).

The windmill is an alternate pitching motion in which the arm describes a full arc overhead, moving behind the body and then forward toward the batter. The arm goes into full extension on the downward swing in the back, gathering momentum

as the forward motion begins. The pitch is otherwise the same as the normal motion. The windmill is generally a difficult style for youngsters to master. Instructional cues for pitching are as follows:

1. Face the plate.
2. Keep your eyes on the target.
3. Swing the pitching arm backward and step forward.
4. Keep the pitching arm extended.

Fielding

Infielders should assume the ready position—a semicrouch, with legs spread shoulder width apart, knees bent slightly, and hands on or in front of the knees (Figure 29.5). As the ball is delivered, the

Figure 29.5 Ready position for the infielder

weight is shifted to the balls of the feet. The out-fielder's position is a slightly more erect semi-crouch. Instructional cues for fielding are the following:

1. Move into line with the path of the ball.
2. Give when catching the ball.
3. Use the glove to absorb the force of the ball.
4. For grounders, keep the head down and watch the ball move into the glove.

Fly Balls

There are two ways to catch a fly ball. For a low ball, the fielder keeps the fingers together and forms a basket with the hands (Figure 29.6). For a higher ball, the thumbs are together, and the ball is caught in front of the chin (Figure 29.7). The fielder should give with the hands, and care must be taken with a spinning ball to squeeze the hands sufficiently to stop the spinning. The eye is on the ball continually until it hits the glove or hands. The

Figure 29.7   Catching a high fly ball

knees are flexed slightly when receiving and aid in giving when the ball is caught.

Grounders

To field a grounder, the fielder should move as quickly as possible into the path of the ball (Figure 29.8) and then move forward and play the ball on a good hop. The eyes must be kept on the ball, following it into the hands or glove. The feet are spread, the seat is kept down, and the hands are

Figure 29.6   Catching a low fly ball

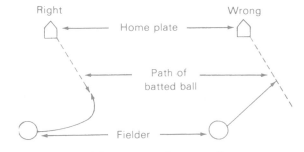

Figure 29.8   Fielding a grounder correctly

Figure 29.9   Fielding a grounder

Figure 29.10   Sure stop

carried low and in front (Figure 29.9). The weight is on the balls of the feet or on the toes, and the knees are bent to lower the body. As the ball is caught, the fielder straightens up, takes a step in the direction of the throw, and makes the throw.

Sure Stop for Outfield Balls

To keep the ball from going through the hands and thus allowing extra bases, the outfielder can use the body as a barrier. The fielder turns half right and lowers one knee to the ground at the point toward which the ball is traveling (Figure 29.10). The hands catch the rolling ball, but if it is missed, the body will generally stop the ball.

First-Base Positioning

When a ball is hit to the infield, the first-base player moves to the base until the foot is touching it. The player then judges the path of the ball, stepping toward it with one foot and stretching forward. The other foot remains in contact with the base (Figure 29.11).

Figure 29.11   First-base player stretching for a catch

Catcher's Position

The catcher assumes a crouched position with the feet about shoulder width apart and the left foot slightly ahead of the right. The catcher should use a glove and wear a mask. A body protector is desirable. The catcher is positioned just beyond the range of the swing of the bat (Figure 29.12).

Batting (Right-Handed)

The batter stands with the left side of the body toward the pitcher. The feet are spread and the weight is on both feet. The body should be facing the plate. The bat is held with the trademark up, and the left hand grasps the bat lower than the right. The bat is held over the right shoulder, pointing both back and up. The elbows are away from the body (Figure 29.13). The swing begins with a hip roll and a short step forward in the direction of the pitcher. The bat is then swung level with the ground at the height of the pitch. The eyes are kept on the ball until it is hit. After the hit, there must be good follow-through.

The batter should avoid the following: lifting the front foot high off the ground, stepping back with

Figure 29.13 Batter's position

the rear foot, dropping the rear shoulder, chopping down on the ball, golfing, dropping the elbows, or crouching or bending forward. Failure to keep the eyes on the ball is a serious error. Youngsters should get experience with the choke grip (Figure 29.14), the long grip (Figure 29.15), and the middle grip (Figure 29.16). Beginning batters can start with the choke grip. In any case, the grip should not be too tight. The following are instructional cues for batting:

1. Keep the hands together.
2. Swing the bat horizontally.
3. Swing through the ball.
4. Hold the bat off the shoulder.
5. Watch the ball hit the bat.

Bunting (Right-Handed)

To bunt, the batter turns to face the pitcher, the right foot alongside home plate. As the pitcher releases the ball, the upper hand is run about

Figure 29.12 Catcher's position

Figure 29.14 Choke grip

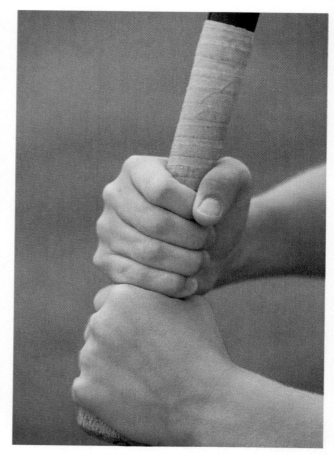

Figure 29.15 Long grip

halfway up the bat. The bunter holds the bat loosely in front of the body and parallel to the ground to meet the ball (Figure 29.17). The ball can be directed down the first- or third-base line.

The surprise, or drag, bunt is done without squaring around to face the pitcher. The batter holds the bat in a choke grip. When the pitcher lets go of the ball, the batter runs the right hand up the bat and directs the ball down either foul line, keeping it as close as possible to the line in fair territory.

Base Running

A batter who hits the ball should run hard and purposefully toward first base, no matter what kind of hit it is. The runner should run past the bag, tagging it in the process, and should step on the foul-line side of the base to avoid a collision with the first-base player.

Because a runner on base must hold the base position until the pitcher releases the ball, securing a fast start away from the base is essential. With either toe in contact with the base, the runner assumes a body lean, the weight on the ball of the leading foot and the eyes on the pitcher. After the pitch is made, the runner takes a few steps away from the base in the direction of the next base.

INSTRUCTIONAL PROCEDURES

1. Safety is of the utmost importance. The following precautions should be observed.

   a. Throwing the bat is a constant danger. The members of the batting team should stand on the side opposite the batter. For a right-handed batter, the batting team members should be on the first-base side, and vice versa.

   b. The following techniques help keep the batter from throwing the bat.
      (1) Have the batter touch the bat to the ground before dropping it.
      (2) Call the batter out if the bat is thrown.
      (3) Have the batter carry the bat to first base.
      (4) Have the batter change ends of the bat before dropping it.

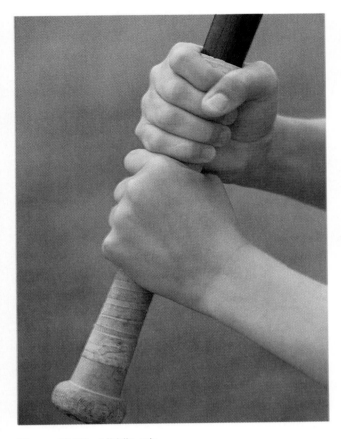

Figure 29.16 Middle grip

Figure 29.17 Regular bunt position

(5) Have the batter place the bat in a 3-foot circle before running.

c. Sliding can lead to both bodily injury and destruction of clothing. No sliding should be permitted. Runners should be called out when they slide into base.

d. A catcher who stands close behind the plate while catching must wear a mask. A body protector is also recommended.

e. Colliding while running for the ball can be held to a minimum if players call for the ball and do not trespass on another player's area.

f. When changing fields at the beginning of an inning, the batting team stays on the first-base side of the infield. The fielding team goes to bat via the third-base side of the infield.

g. Soft softballs should be used, particularly in the early stages of development. Fleece balls are excellent for introductory fielding skills. Many youngsters fear batted balls, which necessitates using balls that will not hurt them.

h. All bats should be taped. Broken or cracked bats should not be used, even when taped.

2. Batting skills must be stressed. There is no more ego-shattering experience for a youngster than to stand at the plate and demonstrate an ineptness that draws scorn and ridicule from peers. Make sure that youngsters know the correct stance and proper mechanics of batting. Improved hitting will come with practice.

3. The spoiler of many softball games is the pitcher-batter duel. If this becomes prolonged, the other players become justifiably bored from standing around. Having a member of the batting team pitch is one way to eliminate the problem.

4. Players should rotate positions often. A good rule in physical education classes is that everyone, including the pitcher, should rotate to another position at the start of a new inning.

5. The distance between the bases greatly affects the game. The distance should be lessened or increased according to the game and the capacities of players.

6. Umpires can be appointed, or the team at bat can umpire. A convenient rule to follow is that the person who made the last out of the previous inning will be the umpire for the next inning. All students should receive instruction in umpiring. It is poor teaching to expect a child to umpire properly without proper instruction.

7. Players should be encouraged to recognize and give approval and support to those who are less skillful. Because there will be many differences in ability, the opportunity is present for a lesson in tolerance. It is important not to let an error become a tragedy to a child.

8. Each player should run out a hit, no matter how hopeless it seems.

9. Each lead-up game should be analyzed for its purpose. The needed skills should be practiced before inclusion in the game.

10. Children must recognize that the perfection of softball skills comes only through good practice.

11. Respect for officials and acceptance of the umpire's judgment must be taught. The disreputable practice of baiting the umpire should not be a part of the child's softball experiences.

12. Care of equipment is the responsibility of all. The bat trademark should be kept up when the ball is contacted, and the bat should be used to bat softballs only. Hitting rocks and sticks with the bat damages it and lessens its effectiveness and life expectancy. The bat should be carried, not thrown, from one person to another.

ORGANIZING FOR INSTRUCTION

It is essential that students develop skills in softball and acquire knowledge about the various phases of the game. The amount of field space and the equipment available determine the instructional organization. To cover the many phases of the game, a multiple-activity or station pattern is best. The approach should use the following guidelines.

1. Children should have many opportunities to practice the different skills. Even with rotation, there should be as many small groups as possible. Throwing and fielding grounders can be practiced between two children, for example.

2. The basis of the rotational system can be the squad, with responsibility centered on the captain for the conduct of the practice at different stations.

3. The Little League problem cannot be ignored. These "stars" generally have skill levels higher than those of others in the class. Their skills can be used in various phases of instruction, provided that sufficient direction for these efforts is given.

4. Activities and procedures to be stressed at each station should be carefully planned and communicated to all participants. Prior meetings with captains and other helpers are valuable. Appropriate softball rules should be covered.

5. Complete rotation of stations is not necessary at each class session. During a class session, teams may practice at one station for part of the time and then use the remainder of the time to participate in an appropriate lead-up game.

6. There must be directions for each station, and individuals also must assume responsibility for cooperating during the planned activities and for making the most of the skill development opportunities.

7. The use of the rotational station system does not rule out activities involving the class as a whole. Mimetic drills (i.e., drills without equipment) are valuable for establishing fundamental movement patterns for most skills. Students can practice such techniques as batting, pitching, throwing, and fielding without worrying about results. Correct technique should be emphasized. Discussions of rules and various demonstrations for the entire class are fruitful.

8. Station teaching provides an excellent opportunity for visiting high school students to provide assistance. In many school systems, high school students visit elementary schools on a regular basis for observation and educational experiences, some of which admittedly are sterile. Here is an opportunity to make good, meaningful use of these visitors.

9. The teacher's role in the rotational system is to circulate from one station to another to provide encouragement, correction, coaching, and motivation for learning.

10. A motivational factor can be introduced through comparisons of the rotational system with varsity or major league practices. This gives the activity an adult flavor.

11. Selection can be made from the list of lead-up games, particularly for activities that are suitable for squads or smaller groups.

BASIC SOFTBALL RULES

Most sporting goods establishments have copies of the official rules for softball. Although an official rule guide should be used by students when they are studying rules, a general idea of the basic rules of the game can be obtained from the following discussion. The official diamond has 60-foot baselines and a pitching distance of 46 feet. In elementary school it is recommended that youngsters use a diamond with baselines no longer than 45 feet and a pitching distance of 35 feet or less. The nine players on a softball team are the catcher, pitcher, first-, second-, and third-base players, shortstop, and left, center, and right fielders. The right fielder is the outfielder nearest first base.

Batting Order

Players may bat in any order, although having them bat according to their positions in the field is at times convenient in class. Once the batting order has been established, it may not be changed, even if the player changes to another position in the field.

Pitching

The pitcher must face the batter with both feet on the pitching rubber and with the ball held in front with both hands. The pitcher is allowed one step toward the batter and must deliver the ball while taking that step. The ball must be pitched underhanded. The pitcher cannot fake a pitch or make any motion toward the plate without delivering the ball. It is illegal to roll or bounce the ball to the batter. No quick return is allowed before the batter is ready. To be called a *strike,* a pitch must be over the plate and between the knees and shoulders of the batter. A *ball* is a pitch that does not go through this area.

Batting

The bat must be a softball bat. The batter cannot cross to the other side of the plate when the pitcher is ready to pitch. If a player bats out of turn, she is out. A bunt that goes foul on the third strike is an out. A pitched ball that touches or hits the batter entitles the batter to first base, provided she does not strike or bunt at the ball.

Striking Out

A batter is out who misses the ball on the third strike. This is called striking out.

Batter Safe

The batter who reaches first base before the fielding team can field the ball and throw it to first is safe.

Fair Ball

A fair ball is any batted ball that settles on fair territory between home and first base and home and third base. A ball that rolls over a base or through the field into fair territory is a fair ball. Fly balls (including line drives) that drop into fair territory beyond the infield are fair balls. Foul lines are in fair territory.

Foul Ball

A foul ball is a batted ball that settles outside the foul lines between home and first or between home and third. A fly ball that drops into foul territory beyond the bases is a foul.

Fly Ball

Any fly ball (foul or fair), if caught, is an out. A foul fly, however, must rise over the head of the batter or it is ruled a foul tip. A foul tip caught on the third strike, then, puts the batter out.

Base Running

In base running, no leadoff is permitted. On penalty of being called out, the runner must stay on base until the ball leaves the pitcher's hand. On an overthrow when the ball goes into foul territory and out of play, runners advance one base beyond the base to which they were headed at the time of the overthrow. On an overthrow at second base by the catcher with the ball rolling into center field, the runners may advance as far as they can. The runner may try to avoid being tagged on a baseline but is limited to a 3-foot distance on each side of a direct line from base to base. A runner hit by a batted ball while off the base is out. The batter, however, is entitled to first base. Base runners must touch all bases. If a runner fails to touch a base, it is an *appeal play,* which means that the fielding team must call the oversight to the attention of the umpire before he will rule on the play.

Runners may overrun first base without penalty. On all other bases, the runner must maintain contact with the base or be tagged out. To score, the runner must make contact with home plate.

Scoring

A run is scored when the base runner makes the circuit of the bases (i.e., first, second, third, and home) before the batting team has three outs. If the third out is a force out, no run is scored, even if the runner crossed home plate before the out was actually made.

The situation needing the most clarification occurs when a runner is on base with one out and the batter hits a fly ball that is caught, making the second out. The runner is forced to return to the base previously occupied before the ball reaches that base, or she, too, is out. If she makes the third out as a result of her failure to return to the base in time, no run is scored.

SOFTBALL DRILLS

Softball drills lend themselves to a station setup. For a regular class of 30 students, four squads with 7 or 8 students each is suggested. Activities at each station can emphasize a single skill or a combination of skills. Situational drills can also be incorporated. Children should realize that constant repetition is necessary to develop, maintain, and sharpen softball skills.

The multitude of softball skills to be practiced allows for many different combinations and organizations. The following are examples of combinations and organizations that can be used in station teaching.

1. Batting can be organized in many ways. One key to an effective program is to ensure that each child has many opportunities to hit the ball successfully. Sufficient area is needed.

   a. Use a batting tee. For each station, two tees are needed, with a bat and at least two balls for each tee. Three to five children are assigned to each tee. There should be a batter, a catcher to handle incoming balls, and fielders. When only three children are in a unit, the catcher should be eliminated. Each batter is allowed a certain number of swings before rotating to the field. The

catcher becomes the next batter, and a fielder moves up to catcher.

   b. Organize informal hitting practice. A batter, a pitcher, and fielders are needed. Two batting groups should be organized at each station. A catcher is optional.

   c. Practice hitting a foam rubber ball thrown underhanded. The larger ball is easier to hit.

   d. Practice bunting with groups of three: a pitcher, batter, and fielder.

2. To practice throwing and catching, do the following drills.

   a. Throw back and forth, practicing various throws.

   b. Throw ground balls back and forth for fielding practice.

   c. One player acts as a first-base player, throwing grounders to the other infielders and receiving the put-out throw.

   d. Throw flies back and forth.

   e. Hit flies, with two or three fielders catching.

   f. Establish four bases and throw from base to base.

3. Proper pitching and catching form should be used for pitching practice.

   a. Pitch to another player over a plate.

   b. Call balls and strikes. One player is the pitcher, the second is the catcher, and the third is the umpire. A fourth player can be a stationary batter to provide a more realistic pitching target.

   c. Pitch toward pitching targets—either a wooden target (see p. 702) or a similar area outlined on a wall.

4. For infield drill, children are placed in the normal infield positions: behind the plate; at first, second, and third base; and at shortstop. One child acts as the batter and gives directions. The play should begin with practice in throwing around the bases either way. After this, the batter can roll the ball to the different infielders, beginning at third base and continuing in turn around the infield, with each player throwing to first to retire an imaginary runner. Various play situations can be developed. A batter who is skillful enough can hit the ball to infielders instead of rolling it, thus making the drill more realistic. Using a second softball saves time when the ball is thrown or batted past an infielder, because players do not have to wait

for the ball to be retrieved before proceeding with the next play. After the ball has been thrown to first base, other throws around the infield can take place. The drill can also be done with only a partial infield.

5. Various situations can be arranged for practicing base running.

   a. Bunt and run to first. A pitcher, a batter, an infielder, and a first-base player are needed. The pitcher serves the ball up for a bunt, and the batter, after bunting, takes off for first base. A fielding play can be made on the runner.

   b. Bunt and run to second base. The batter bunts the ball and runs to first base and then on to second, making a proper turn at first.

6. *Play Pepper.* (This is one of the older skill games in baseball.) A line of three or four players is about 10 yards in front of and facing a batter. The players toss the ball to the batter, who attempts to hit controlled grounders back to them (Figure 29.18). The batter stays at bat for a period of time and then rotates to the field.

7. Some of the game-type activities, such as Batter Ball, In a Pickle, Five Hundred, and Scrub, can be scheduled at stations. Stations might be organized as follows. (Numbers and letters refer to the drills just listed. Page number refers to activities not yet discussed.)

   Station 1: Batting (see 1a)

   Station 2: Throwing, fielding grounders (see 2c)

   Station 3: Base running—In a Pickle (see p. 697)

   Station 4: Bunting and base running (see 5a)

   Another example of station arrangement is the following.

   Station 1: Batting and fielding—Pepper (see 6)

   Station 2: Pitching and umpiring (see 3b)

   Station 3: Infield practice (see 4)

   Station 4: Batting (see 1b)

   Stations might also be arranged as follows.

   Station 1: Fly ball hitting, fielding, throwing (see 2e)

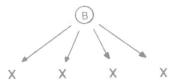

Figure 29.18 Play Pepper

Station 2: Bunting and fielding (see 1d)

Station 3: Pitching to targets (see 3c)

Station 4: Batting (see 1a and 1b)

SOFTBALL ACTIVITIES

Developmental Level II

Throw-It-and-Run Softball

Playing Area: Softball diamond reduced in size

Players: 7 to 11 (usually 9) on each team

Supplies: A softball or similar ball

Skills: Throwing, catching, fielding, base running

Throw-It-and-Run Softball is played like regular softball with the following exception. With one team in the field at regular positions, the pitcher throws the ball to the batter, who, instead of batting the ball, catches it and immediately throws it into the field. The ball is then treated as a batted ball, and regular softball rules prevail. No stealing is permitted, however, and runners must hold bases until the batter throws the ball. A foul ball is an out.

Variations:

1. *Under-Leg Throw.* Instead of throwing directly, the batter can turn to the right, lift the left leg, and throw the ball under the leg into the playing field.

2. *Beat-Ball Throw.* The fielders, instead of playing regular softball rules, throw the ball directly home to the catcher. The batter, in the meantime, runs around the bases. A point is scored for each base the batter touches before the catcher receives the ball. A ball caught on the fly would mean no score. Similarly, a foul ball would not score points but would count as a turn at bat.

Two-Pitch Softball

Playing Area: Softball diamond

Players: 7 to 11 on each team

Supplies: A softball, a bat

Skills: Most softball skills, except regular pitching

Two-Pitch Softball is played like regular softball with the following changes.

1. A member of the team at bat pitches. A system of rotation should be set up so that every child takes a turn as pitcher.

2. The batter has only two pitches in which to hit the ball, and must hit a fair ball on one of these pitches or is out. The batter can foul the first ball, but if the second is fouled, the batter is out. There is no need to call balls or strikes.

3. The pitcher does not field the ball. A member of the team in the field acts as the fielding pitcher.

4. If the batter hits the ball, regular softball rules are followed. No stealing is permitted, however.

Teaching Suggestion: Since the pitcher is responsible for pitching a ball that can be hit, the pitching distance can be shortened to give the batter ample opportunity to hit the ball. The instructor can act as the pitcher.

Variation: Three Strikes: In this game, the batter is allowed three pitches (strikes) to hit the ball. Otherwise, the game proceeds as in Two-Pitch Softball.

Hit and Run

Playing Area: Softball field or gymnasium

Players: 6 to 15 players on each team

Supplies: A volleyball or soccer ball or playground ball, home plate, base markers

Skills: Catching, throwing, running, dodging

One team is at bat, and the other is scattered in the field. Boundaries must be established, but the area does not have to be shaped like a baseball diamond. The batter stands at home plate with the ball. In front of the batter, 12 feet away, is a short line over which the ball must be hit to be in play. In the center of the field, about 40 feet away, is the base marker.

The batter bats the ball with the hands or fists so that it crosses the short line and lands inside the area, then attempts to run down the field, around the base marker, and back to home plate without being hit by the ball (Figure 29.19). The members of the other team field the ball and throw it at the runner. The fielder may not run or walk with the ball but may throw to a teammate who is closer to the runner.

A run is scored each time a batter runs around the marker and back to home plate without getting hit by the ball. A run also is scored if a foul is called on the fielding team for walking or running with the ball.

The batter is out in any of the following circumstances.

1. A fly ball is caught.

2. The batter is hit below the shoulders with the ball.

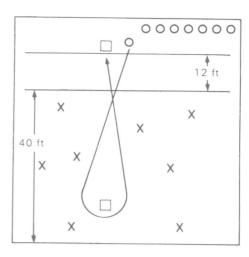

Figure 29.19 Hit and Run

3. The ball is not hit beyond the short line.

4. The team touches home plate with the ball before the runner returns. (This out is used only when the runner stops in the field and does not continue.)

The game can be played in innings of three outs each, or a change of team positions can be made after all members of one team have batted.

Teaching Suggestion: The distance the batter runs around the base marker may have to be shortened or lengthened, depending on players's ability.

Variation: Five Passes: The batter is out when a fly ball is caught or when the ball is passed among five different players of the team in the field, with the last pass to a player at home plate beating the runner to the plate. The passes must not touch the ground.

Kick Softball

Playing Area: Regular softball field with a home base 3 feet square

Players: 7 to 11 on each team

Supplies: A soccer ball or another ball to be kicked

Skills: Kicking a rolling ball, throwing, catching, running bases

The batter stands in the kicking area, a 3-foot-square home plate. The batter kicks the ball rolled on the ground by the pitcher. The ball should be rolled at moderate speed. An umpire calls balls and strikes. A strike is a ball that rolls over the 3-foot square. A ball rolls outside this area. Strikeouts and walks are called the same as in regular softball.

The number of foul balls allowed should be limited. No base stealing is permitted. Otherwise, the game is played like softball.

Variations:

1. The batter kicks a stationary ball. This saves time, as there is no pitching.
2. *Punch Ball.* The batter can hit a volleyball as in a volleyball serve or punch a ball pitched by the pitcher.

In a Pickle

Playing Area: Any flat surface with 60 square feet of room

Players: Three or more

Supplies: A softball, two bases 45 to 55 feet apart

Skills: Throwing, catching, running down a base runner, tagging

A base runner who gets caught between two bases and is in danger of being run down and tagged is "in a pickle." To begin, both fielders are on bases, one with a ball. The runner is positioned in the base path 10 to 15 feet away from the fielder with the ball. The two fielders throw the ball back and forth in an attempt to run down and tag the runner between the bases. A runner who escapes and secures a base gets to try again. Otherwise, a system of rotation is established, including any sideline (waiting) players. No sliding is permitted.

Beat Ball

Playing Area: Softball diamond, bases approximately 30 feet apart

Players: Two teams of 5 to 12

Supplies: Soft softball, bat, batting tee (optional)

Skills: All softball skills

One team is at bat and the other team in the field. The object of the game is to hit the ball and run around the bases before the fielding team can catch the ball, throw it to first base, and then throw it to the catcher at home plate. If the ball beats the hitter home or a fly ball is caught, it is an out. If the hitter beats the ball to home plate, a run is scored. All players on a team bat once before switching positions with the fielding team. The ball must be hit into fair territory before the hitter can run. Only three pitches are allowed each hitter.

Variations:

1. Depending on the maturity of the players, a batting tee may be used. The hitter can be

allowed the option of using the batting tee or hitting a pitched ball.
2. The pitcher can be selected from the batting team. This assures that an attempt will be made to make pitches that can be hit.
3. The distance can be varied so that hitters have a fair opportunity to score. If hitters score too easily, another base can be added.

Developmental Level III

Five Hundred

Playing Area: Field big enough for fungo hitting

Players: 3 to 12 (or more)

Supplies: A softball, a bat

Skills: Fungo batting, catching flies, fielding grounders

There are many versions of the old game of Five Hundred. A batter stands on one side of the field and bats the ball to a number of fielders, who are scattered. The fielders attempt to become the batter by reaching a score of 500. Fielders earn 200 points for catching a ball on the fly, 100 points for catching a ball on the first bounce, and 50 points for fielding a grounder cleanly. Whenever a change of batters is made, all fielders lose their points and must start over.

Variations:

1. The fielder's points must total exactly 500.
2. Points are subtracted from the fielder's score if a ball is mishandled. If a fly ball is dropped, for example, 200 points are lost.

Batter Ball

Playing Area: Softball diamond

Players: 8 to 12 on each team

Supplies: A softball, a bat, a mask

Skills: Slow pitching, hitting, fielding, catching flies

Batter Ball involves batting and fielding but no base running. It is much like batting practice but adds the element of competition. A line is drawn directly from first to third base. This is the balk line over which a batted ball must travel to be fielded. Another line is drawn from a point on the foul line 3 feet behind third base to a point 5 feet behind second base and in line with home plate. Another line connects this point with a point on the other baseline 3 feet behind first base. The shaded area in the diagram is the infield (Figure 29.20).

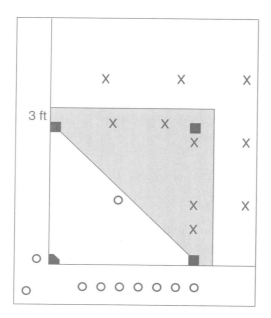

Figure 29.20 Field for Batter Ball

Each batter is given three pitches by a member of his own team to hit the ball into fair territory across the balk line. The pitcher may stop any ground ball before it crosses the balk line. The batter then gets another turn at bat.

Scoring is as follows:

1. A successful grounder scores 1 point. A grounder is successful when an infielder fails to handle it cleanly within the infield area. Only one player may field the ball. If the ball is fielded properly, the batter is out.

2. A line drive in the infield area is worth 1 point if not caught. It can be handled for an out on any bounce. Any line drive caught on the fly is also an out.

3. A fly ball in the infield area scores 1 point if not caught. For an out, the ball must be caught legally by the first person touching it.

4. A two-bagger scores 2 points. Any fly ball, line drive or not, that lands fairly in the outfield area without being caught scores 2 points. If it is caught, the batter is out.

5. A home run scores 3 points. Any fly ball driven over the head of the farthest outfielder in that area scores a home run.

Three outs can constitute an inning, or all batters can be allowed one turn at bat and then the team changes to the field. A new set of infielders should be in place for each inning. The old set goes to the outfield. Pitchers should be limited to one inning. They also take a turn at bat.

Teaching Suggestion: Many games of this type require special fields, either rectangular or narrowly angled. This game was selected because it uses the regular softball field with the added lines. The lines can be drawn with a stick or can be marked using regular marking methods.

The pitcher has to decide whether to stop the ball. If the ball goes beyond the restraining line, it is in play even if the pitcher touched it.

Variations: Batter Ball can be modified for use as a station in rotational teaching, with the emphasis on individual batting and squad organization. One member of the squad would be at bat and would get a definite number of chances (e.g., five) to score. She keeps her own point total. The other squad members occupy the necessary game positions.

Home Run

Playing Area: Softball diamond (only first base is used)

Players: Four to ten

Supplies: A softball, a bat

Skills: Most softball skills, modified base running

The crucial players are a batter, a catcher, a pitcher, and one fielder. Any other players are fielders; some can take positions in the infield. The batter hits a regular pitch and on a fair ball must run to first base and back home before the ball can be returned to the catcher.

The batter is out whenever any of the following occurs:

1. A fly ball (fair or foul) is caught.

2. The batter strikes out.

3. On a fair ball, the ball beats the batter back to home plate.

Teaching Suggestions: To keep skillful players from staying too long at bat, a rule can be made that, after a certain number of home runs, the batter automatically must take a place in the field. A rotation (work-up) system should be established. The batter should go to right field, move to center, and then go to left field. The rotation continues through third base, shortstop, second base, first base, pitcher, and catcher. The catcher is the next batter. Naturally, the number of positions depends on the number of players in the game. If there are enough players, an additional batter can be waiting to take a turn.

The game can be played with only three youngsters, eliminating the catcher. With only one fielder, the pitcher covers home plate. The first-base distance should be far enough away to be a challenge but close enough so that a well-hit ball scores a home run. The distance depends on the number playing and the capacities of players.

Variations:

1. This game can be played like softball—allowing the batter to stop at first base if another batter is up.

2. A fly ball caught by a fielder puts that player directly to bat. The batter then takes a place at the end of the rotation, and the other players rotate up to the position of the fielder who caught the ball. This rule has one drawback. It may cause children to scramble and fight for fly balls, which is not desirable in softball. The ball belongs to the player in whose territory it falls.

3. *Triangle Ball.* First and third bases are brought in toward each other, thus narrowing the playing field. Second base is not used. The game gets its name from the triangle formed by home plate and the two bases. The batter must circle first and third bases and return home before the ball reaches home plate. This game can also be played with as few as three players, with the pitcher covering home plate.

Tee Ball

Playing Area: Softball field

Players: 7 to 11 on each team

Supplies: A softball, a bat, a batting tee

Skills: Most softball skills (except pitching and stealing bases), hitting a ball from a tee

This game is an excellent variation of softball and is played under softball rules with the following exceptions.

1. Instead of hitting a pitched ball, the batter hits the ball from a tee. The catcher places the ball on the tee. After the batter hits the ball, the play is the same as in regular softball. With no pitching, there is no stealing. A runner stays on the base until the ball is hit by the batter.

2. A fielder occupies the position normally held by the pitcher. The primary duty of this fielder is to field bunts and ground balls and to back up the infielders on throws.

Teams can play regular innings for three outs or change to the field after each player has had a turn at bat.

Teaching Suggestions: A tee can be purchased or made from a radiator hose. An improvised batting

Figure 29.21   Improvised batting tee

tee is shown in Figure 29.21. (For another type of tee, see page 758.) If the tee is not adjustable, three different sizes should be available. The batter should take a position far enough behind the tee so that, in stepping forward to swing, the ball will be slightly in front of the midpoint of the swing.

Tee Ball has many advantages. There are no strikeouts, every child hits the ball, there is no dueling between pitcher and batter, and fielding opportunities abound.

Scrub (Work-Up)

Playing Area: Softball field

Players: 7 to 15

Supplies: A softball, a bat

Skills: Most softball skills

The predominant feature of Scrub is the rotation of the players. The game is played with regular softball rules, with individuals more or less playing for themselves. There are at least two batters, generally three. A catcher, pitcher, and first-base player are essential. The remaining players assume the other positions. A batter who is out goes to a position in right field. All other players move up one position, with the catcher becoming the batter. The first-base player becomes the pitcher, the pitcher moves to catcher, and all others move up one place.

Variation: If a fly ball is caught, the fielder and batter exchange positions.

Slow-Pitch Softball

Playing Area: Softball diamond

Players: Ten on each team

Supplies: A softball, a bat

Skills: Most softball skills

The major difference between regular softball and Slow-Pitch Softball is in the pitching, but there are other modifications to the game as well. With slower pitching, there is more hitting and thus more action on the bases and in the field. Outfielders are an important part of the game, because many long drives are hit. Rule changes from the game of official softball are as follows.

1. The pitch must be a slow pitch. Any other pitch is illegal and is called a ball. The pitch must be slow, with an arc of 1 foot. It must not rise over 10 feet from the ground, however. Its legality depends on the umpire's call.

2. There are ten players instead of nine. The extra one, called the *roving fielder,* plays in the outfield and handles line drives hit just over the infielders.

3. The batter must take a full swing at the ball and is out if he chops at the ball or bunts.

4. If the batter is hit by a pitched ball, she is not entitled to first base. The pitch is merely called a ball. Otherwise, balls and strikes are called as in softball.

5. The runner must hold base until the pitch has reached or passed home plate. No stealing is permitted.

Teaching Suggestion: Shortening the pitching distance somewhat may be desirable. Much of the success of the game depends on the pitcher's ability to get the ball over the plate.

Babe Ruth Ball

Playing Area: Softball diamond

Players: Five

Supplies: A bat, a ball, four cones or other markers

Skills: Batting, pitching, fielding

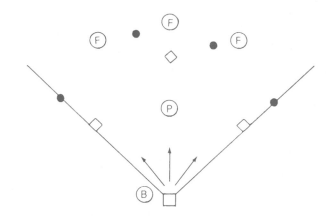

Figure 29.22 Babe Ruth Ball

The three outfield zones—left, center, and right field—are separated by four cones. It is helpful if foul lines have been drawn, but cones can define them (Figure 29.22). The batter calls the field to which he intends to hit. The pitcher throws controlled pitches so that the batter can hit easily. The batter remains in position as long as he hits to the designated field. Field choices must be rotated. The batter gets only one swing to make a successful hit. He may allow a ball to go by, but if he swings, it counts as a try. There is no base running. Players rotate.

Teaching Suggestions: Children play this game informally on sandlots with a variety of rules. Some possibilities to consider are these: What happens when a fly ball is caught? What limitations should be made on hitting easy grounders? Let the players decide about these points and others not covered by the stated rules.

Hurry Baseball (One-Pitch Softball)

Playing Area: Softball diamond

Players: 8 to 12 on each team

Supplies: A softball, a bat

Skills: Slow pitching, most softball skills except stealing bases and bunting

Hurry Baseball demands rapid changes from batting to fielding, and vice versa. The game is like regular softball, with the following exceptions.

1. The pitcher is from the team at bat and must not interfere with, or touch, a batted ball on penalty of the batter's being called out.

2. The team coming to bat does not wait for the fielding team to get set. Because it has its own pitcher, the pitcher gets the ball to the batter just as quickly as the batter can grab a bat and

get ready. The fielding team has to hustle to get out to their places.

3. Only one pitch is allowed to a batter. The batter must hit a fair ball or she is out. The pitch is made from about two-thirds of the normal pitching distance.

4. No stealing is permitted.

5. No bunting is permitted.

The batter must take a full swing. The game provides much activity in the fast place changes that must be made after the third out. Teams in the field learn to put the next hitter as catcher, so that she can bat immediately when the third out is made. Batters must bat in order. Scoring follows regular softball rules.

Three-Team Softball

Playing Area: Softball diamond

Players: 12 to 15

Supplies: A mask, a ball, a bat

Skills: All softball skills

Three-Team Softball works well with 12 players, a number considered too few to divide into two effective fielding teams. The players are instead divided into three teams. The rules of softball apply, with the following exceptions.

1. One team is at bat, one team covers the infield (including the catcher), and the third team provides the outfielders and the pitcher.

2. The team at bat must bat in a definite order. This means that because of the small number of batters on each side, instances can occur when the person due to bat is on base. To take a turn at bat, the runner must be replaced by a player not on base.

3. After three outs, the teams rotate, with the outfield moving to the infield, the infield taking a turn at bat, and the batters going to the outfield.

4. An inning is over when all three teams have batted.

5. The pitcher should be limited to pitching one inning only. A player may repeat as pitcher only after all members of that team have had a chance to pitch.

SOFTBALL SKILL TESTS

Throwing for Accuracy

To test accuracy in throwing, a target with three concentric circles of 54, 36, and 18 inches is drawn on a wall. Scoring is 1, 2, and 3 points, respectively, for the circles. Five trials are allowed, for a possible score of 15. Balls hitting a line score the higher number.

Instead of the suggested target, a tire can be hung. Scoring allows 2 points for a throw through the tire and 1 point for simply hitting the tire. A maximum of 10 points is possible with this system.

Throwing for Distance

In the test of throwing for distance, each child is allowed three throws, and the longest throw on the fly is recorded.

Fielding Grounders

A file of players is stationed behind a restraining line. A thrower is about 30 feet in front of this line. Each player in turn attempts to field five ground balls. The score is the number of balls fielded cleanly. It is recognized that inconsistencies will occur in the throw and bounce of the ground balls served up for fielding. If the opportunity was obviously not a fair one, the child should get another chance.

Circling the Bases

Runners are timed as they circle the bases. A diamond with four bases is needed, plus a stopwatch for timing. Two runners can run at one time by starting from opposite corners of the diamond. Two watches are needed with this system. The batter can bunt a pitched ball and run around the bases. The timing starts with the bunt and finishes when the batter touches home plate.

Pitching

Pitching is one of the easier skills to test in softball and is certainly one of the most popular with children. Two basic methods are used for testing. In the first, each child takes a certain number of pitches at a target. Scoring is on the basis of the number of strikes that can be thrown. In the second, each child pitches regularly, as if to a batter, with balls and strikes being counted. Batters are either struck out or walked. The test score is the number of batters the child is able to strike out from a given number at bat. This is expressed as a percentage.

In either method, a target is needed. It should be 19 inches wide and 42 inches high. It can be outlined temporarily on a wall with chalk or paint.

The lower portion of the target should be about 18 inches above the ground or floor. If the target is constructed from plywood or wood, some means of support or of hanging the target will be needed. The boundaries of the target should be counted as good. The pitching distance should be normal (35 feet), and regular pitching rules should be observed.

Old Woody is the name of a pitching target in the form of a stand that can be moved from school to school. The target size is shown in Figure 29.23. A sturdy frame holds the target and allows it to be used in almost any spot.

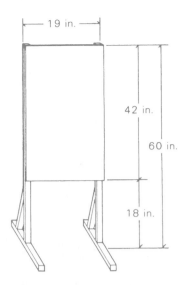

Figure 29.23 Old Woody pitching target

Track, Field, and Cross-Country Running

*T*he elementary program in track and field should consist of short sprints (40 to 100 yards), running and standing long jumps, high jumps, hop-step-and-jumps, and relays. Jogging and distance running should be encouraged throughout the program. The primary emphasis should be on practice and personal accomplishment, but modified competition in cross-country running is quite acceptable. Hurdling can be included when the equipment is available.

Children should experience the differences between walking, sprinting, running, striding (for pace), and jogging. Sprinting techniques are particularly important, with instruction centering on correct form for starting, accelerating, and sprinting. Speed and quickness are important attributes that govern the degree of success in many play and sport activities. Rules for the different events should be explained. Since few elementary schools have a permanent track, laying out and lining the track (see p. 711) each year can be a valuable educational experience.

INSTRUCTIONAL EMPHASIS AND SEQUENCE

Table 30.1 divides track and field activities into two developmental levels. The activities are listed in progression. Since many track and field skills involve locomotor movements, youngsters of all ages can enjoy and participate in these activities.

Developmental Levels I and II

Running and jumping are skills that are easily mastered by children, allowing them to be introduced in developmental level I. Early experiences at this level should stress running short distances, learning different starting positions, and participating in the two types of long jump. Some running for distance is included and cross-country meets are introduced. Relays offer exciting experiences and involve a large number of youngsters in a quasi-team activity.

Developmental Level III

More serious efforts to achieve proper form begin at this level. The scissors style can be introduced in high jumping, and experimentation with other styles can be encouraged. Students should begin to use check marks with the running long jump. Running for distance and cross-country activities are emphasized.

Hurdling using modified hurdles is an exciting event. In the high jump, critical points of the Straddle Roll and the Western Roll are explained. Developing pace in distance running without strong elements of competition is important. Re-

Table 30.1 Suggested track, field, and cross-country program

Developmental Levels I and II	Developmental Level III
Track and Cross-Country Skills	
40-to-60-yd sprints	50-to-100-yd sprints
Standing start	Distance running
Sprinter's start	Relays
Jogging and cross-country running	Hurdling
	Baton passing
Field Skills	
Standing long jump	High jump
Long jump	Hop-step-and-jump

laxed, flowing running is the goal. The hop-step-and-jump extends the range of jumping activities. Relays and baton passing are given increased coverage at this level. Sprinting instruction should emphasize the start, acceleration, and drive for the finish line.

TRACK AND FIELD SKILLS

Starting

Standing Start

The standing start should be practiced, for this type of start has a variety of uses in physical education activities. Many children find it more comfortable than the sprinter's start. As soon as is practical, however, children should accept the sprinter's start for track work. In the standing start, the feet should be in a comfortable half-stride position. An extremely long stride is to be avoided. The body leans forward so that the center of gravity is forward. The weight is on the toes, and the knees are flexed slightly. The arms can be down or hanging slightly back (Figure 30.1).

Norwegian Start

The Norwegians use the standing start in a novel way. On the command "On your mark," the runner takes a position at the starting line with the right foot forward. On "Get set," the left hand is placed on the right knee and the right hand is carried back for a thrust (Figure 30.2). On "Go," the right hand comes forward, coupled with a drive by the right foot. The advantage claimed for this start is that it forces a body to lean and makes use of the forward thrust of the arm coordinated with the step off on the opposite foot.

Sprinter's Start

There are several kinds of sprinter's starts, but teachers are advised to concentrate on a single one. The "On your mark" position places the toe of the front foot from 4 to 12 inches behind the starting line. The thumb and first finger are just behind the line, with other fingers adding support. The knee of the rear leg is placed just opposite the front foot or ankle (Figure 30.3).

For the "Get set" position, the seat is raised so that it is nearly parallel to the ground. The knee of the rear leg is raised off the ground, and the shoulders are moved forward over the hands. The weight is evenly distributed over the hands and feet

Figure 30.1 Standing start

Figure 30.2 Norwegian start

(Figure 30.4). The head is not raised, as the runner should be looking at a spot a few feet in front of the starting line.

On the ''Go'' signal, the runner pushes off sharply with both feet, with the front leg straightening as the back leg comes forward for a step. The body should rise gradually rather than pop up suddenly. The instructor should watch for a stumbling action on the first few steps. This results from too much weight resting on the hands in the ''Get set'' position.

Running

Sprinting

In proper sprinting form, the body leans forward, with the arms swinging in opposition to the legs. The arms are bent at the elbows and swing from the shoulders in a forward and backward plane, not across the body (Figure 30.5). Forceful arm action aids sprinting. The knees are lifted sharply forward and upward and are brought down with a vigorous

motion, followed by a forceful push from the toes. Sprinting is a driving and striding motion, as opposed to the inefficient pulling action displayed by some runners.

Distance Running

In distance running, as compared with sprinting, the body is more erect and the motion of the arms is less pronounced. Pace is an important consideration. Runners should try to concentrate on the qualities of lightness, ease, relaxation, and looseness. Good striding action, a slight body lean, and good head position are also important. Runners should be encouraged to strike the ground with the heel first and then push off with the toes (Figure 30.6).

Relays

Two types of relay are generally included in a program of track and field for children. Instruction in baton passing should be incorporated into relay

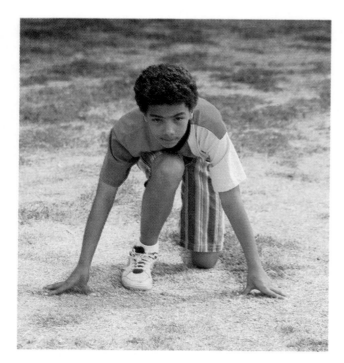

Figure 30.3 Sprinter's start—"On your mark"

Figure 30.4 Sprinter's start—"Get set!"

activity. Running on the track is always done in a counterclockwise direction.

Circular (Pursuit) Relays

Circular relays make use of the regular circular track. The baton exchange technique is important, and practice is needed. On a 220-yard or 200-

Figure 30.5 Proper sprinting form

Figure 30.6 Proper running form

meter track, relays can be organized in a number of ways, depending on how many runners are spaced for one lap. Four runners can do a lap, each running one quarter of the way; two can do a lap, each running one half of the distance; or each runner can complete a whole lap. In these races, each member of the relay team runs the same distance. Relays can also be organized so that members run different distances.

Shuttle Relays

Because children are running toward each other, one great difficulty in running shuttle relays is control of the exchange. In the excitement, the next runner may leave too early, and the tag or exchange is then made ahead of the restraining line. A high-jump standard or cone can be used to prevent early exchanges. The next runner awaits the tag with an arm around the standard or a hand on a cone.

Baton Passing

There are two methods of baton passing commonly used. The first method is the right hand to left hand method and is used in longer distance relays. It is the best choice for elementary school children as it is easy and offers a consistent method for passes. This pass allows the receiver to face the inside of the track while waiting to receive the baton in the left hand. The oncoming runner holds the baton in the right hand like a candle when passing it to a teammate. The receiver reaches back with the left hand, fingers pointing down and thumb to the inside, and begins to run as the runner advances to within 3 to 5 yards. The receiver grasps the baton and shifts it from the left to the right hand while moving. If the baton is dropped, it must be picked up, or the team is disqualified. An alternative way to receive the baton is to reach back with the hand facing up; however, the fingers-down method is considered more suitable for sprint relays.

The second style of passing, the alternating handoff, is usually used in the 400- and 800-meter relays. The first exchange is right to left, the second exchange is left to right, and the third exchange is right to left. This method prevents the runner from having to switch the baton from hand to hand while sprinting. This method is used in high-level competition in short distances, but probably is less useful with elementary-age youngsters.

Receivers can look over their shoulders to see the oncoming runner or can look forward in the direction of the run. Looking backward is called a *visual pass* and is slower than passing while looking forward (called a *blind pass*). However, there is a greater chance for error when the receiver is not looking backward and at the baton during the pass. The visual pass is recommended for elementary school children.

Horizontal Jumping Events

In both the standing and the running long jump, the measurement is made from the takeoff board or line to the nearest point on the ground touched by the jumper. It is therefore important for children not to fall or step backward after making the jump.

Standing Long Jump

In the standing long jump, the child toes the line with feet flat on the ground and fairly close together. The arms are brought forward in a preliminary swing and are then swung down and back (Figure 30.7). The jump is made with both feet as the arms are swung forcibly forward to assist in lifting the body upward and forward. In the air, the knees should be brought upward and forward, with the arms held forward to sustain balance.

Long Jump

For the running long jump, a short run is needed. The run should be timed so that the toes of the jumping foot contact the board in a natural stride.

Figure 30.7 Standing long jump (Note position of the hands and arms.)

The jumper takes off from one foot and strives for height. The landing is made on both feet after the knees have been brought forward. The landing should be in a forward direction, not sideward.

More efficient jumping is achieved when a checkpoint is used. The checkpoint can be established about halfway down the run. Competitors can help each other mark checkpoints. Each jumper should know how many steps back from the takeoff board the checkpoint is located. On the run for the jump, the student hits the mark with the appropriate foot (right or left) so as to reach the board with the correct foot in a normal stride for the jump.

The jumper should arrive at the checkpoint at full speed. The last four strides taken before the board should be relaxed in readiness for the takeoff. The last stride can be shortened somewhat (Figure 30.8).

A fair jump takes off behind the scratch line. A foul (scratch) jump is called if the jumper steps beyond the scratch line or runs into or through the pit. Each contestant is given a certain number of trials (jumps). A scratch jump counts as a trial. Measurement is from the scratch line to the nearest point of touch.

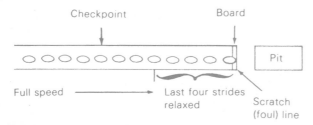

Figure 30.8 Long jump

Hop-Step-and-Jump

The hop-step-and-jump event is increasing in popularity, particularly because it is now included in Olympic competition. A takeoff board and a jumping pit are needed. The distance from the takeoff board to the pit should be one that even less skilled jumpers can make. The event begins with a run similar to that for the running long jump. The takeoff is with one foot, and the jumper must land on the same foot to complete the hop. He then takes a step followed by a jump. The event finishes like the long jump, with a landing on both feet (Figure 30.9). The pattern can be changed to begin with the left foot. A checkpoint should be used, as for the running long jump.

The jumper must not step over the takeoff board in the first hop, under penalty of fouling. Distance is measured from the front of the takeoff board to the closest place where the body touches. This is usually a mark made by one of the heels, but it could be a mark made by an arm or another part of the body if the jumper landed poorly and fell backward.

High Jumping

High-jump techniques are developed by practice. The bar should be at a height that offers challenge but allows concentration on technique rather than on height. Too much emphasis on competition for height quickly eliminates the poorer jumpers, who need the experience most. The practice of keeping the entire class together on a single high-jump facility is poor methodology. This arrangement determines who are the best jumpers in class but does little else.

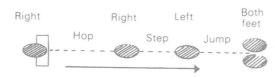

Figure 30.9 Hop-step-and-jump

Scissors Jump

For the Scissors Jump, the high-jump bar is approached from a slight angle. The takeoff is by the leg that is farther from the bar. The near leg is lifted and goes over, followed quickly in a looping movement by the rear leg. A good upward kick with the front leg, together with an upward thrust of the arms, is needed. The knees should be straightened at the highest point of the jump. The landing is made on the lead foot followed by the rear foot.

Straddle Roll

For the Straddle Roll (Figure 30.10), the approach is made from the left side at an angle of no more than 45 degrees. There are four basic parts to the jump with respect to coaching. Each jumper should seek to develop his own style.

1. Gather. The last three steps must be fast and vigorous, with the body leaning back a bit. The takeoff is on the left foot.

2. Kick. The right leg is kicked vigorously as the jumping foot is planted.

3. Arm movement. An abrupt lift with both arms is made, with the left arm reaching over the bar and the right moving straight up. This puts the jumper in a straddle position while going over.

4. Back leg clearance. Clearance is accomplished by straightening the body, rolling the hips to the right (over the bar), or dropping the right shoulder.

Good pit protection is needed. A crash pad should be used to absorb the force of the landing.

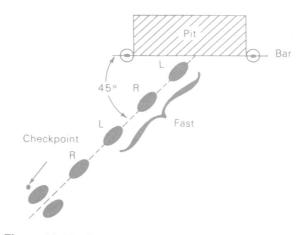

Figure 30.10 Straddle Roll

Start X |25 ft|25 ft|25 ft|25 ft|25 ft|25 ft|30 ft| Finish
←——————— 180 ft ———————→

Figure 30.11 Hurdling course

Western Roll

For the Western Roll, the approach, gather, and kick are the same as for the Straddle Roll, but instead of being facedown, the jumper clears the bar by lying parallel to it on her side. The left arm is pointed down at the legs just at crossing and then is lowered. The head is turned toward the pit after clearance, and the landing is made on both hands and the left (takeoff) foot.

Hurdling

Hurdling is an interesting activity, but it poses equipment problems. Hurdles can be formed from electrical conduit pipe. (See page 759 for a diagram.) Wands supported on blocks or cones can also be used as hurdles. Hurdles should begin at about 12 inches in height and increase to 18 inches. They should be placed about 25 feet apart. Using six hurdles, a 60-yard (180-foot) course can be established as diagrammed in Figure 30.11.

A single or double course can be set up for practice. If there is competition, it should be on a personal best time basis. If regular hurdles are available, practice on lower temporary hurdles should precede work on regular hurdles. A hurdles course or practice area can be set up in a location other than on the track. In this way, the hurdles can be left in place for more concentrated use.

Several key points govern good hurdling technique. The runner should adjust his stepping pattern so that the takeoff foot is planted 3 to 5 feet from the hurdle. The lead foot is extended straight forward over the hurdle; the rear (trailing) leg is bent, with the knee to the side. The lead foot reaches for the ground, quickly followed by the trailing leg. The hurdler should avoid floating over the hurdle. Body lean is necessary.

A hurdler may lead with the same foot over consecutive hurdles or may alternate the leading foot. Some hurdlers like to thrust both arms forward instead of a single arm. A consistent step pattern should be developed.

INSTRUCTIONAL PROCEDURES

1. Spiked running shoes are not permitted. They create a safety problem and also give an unfair advantage to those children whose parents can afford them. Many light gym or running shoes are available. Running in bare feet is not recommended.

2. Form should be stressed at all times, but it should be appropriate to the individual. The child should realize that good results are due to good form and diligent practice. Each child should be encouraged to develop good technique within her own style. Observation of any event at a track meet bears out the fact that many individual styles are successful.

3. The program should offer something for all—boys and girls, the highly skilled and the less skilled, and those with physical problems. Children with weight problems need particular attention. They must be stimulated and encouraged, since their participation will be minimal if little attention is paid to them. Special goals can be set for overweight children, and special events and goals can also be established for children with handicaps.

4. The amount of activity, particularly distance work, should be increased progressively. A period of conditioning should precede any competition or all-out performance, such as the 1600-meter run-walk test. If this procedure is followed, children will show few adverse effects.

5. Warm-up activity should precede track and field work and should include jogging as well as bending and stretching exercises.

6. Pits for the long jump and the high jump must be maintained properly. They should be filled with fresh sand of a coarse variety. For high jumping, commercial impact landing pads are necessary though expensive. If they are not available, high jumping should be restricted to the scissors style, with stacked tumbling mats used for the landing area.

7. The metal high-jump crossbar is economical in the long run, although it will bend. Sometimes bamboo poles can be procured from rug and carpet establishments. A satisfactory crossbar also can be made of nylon cord with a weight on each end to keep it taut while still allowing it to be displaced. In Europe, small leather bags with shot are used as weights to keep the ropes level. Magic ropes (rubberized stretch ropes) can be adapted for low-level jumping practice.

8. The use of a track starter signal is recommended. The clapboard track starter approximates the sound of the usual starter's gun and

does not have the drawback of requiring expensive ammunition. (See page 766 for a diagram showing how to construct this starting device.)

9. The goal of the program should be to allow students to develop at their own rate. The instructional sessions should be strenuous enough to ensure some overload but not so strenuous that students become discouraged or physically ill. The instructor needs to be perceptive enough to determine whether students are working too hard or too little. Special attention must be given to those who appear disinterested, dejected, emotionally upset, or withdrawn.

ORGANIZING FOR INSTRUCTION

Track, field, and cross-country running differ from other areas of the elementary school program in that considerable preparation must be made before the classes begin.

1. A track or a cross-country course must be laid out when there are no permanent courses. This can be done with marking lime. Lanes for sprinting are of value but are not an absolute requirement.

2. A hurdling area should be similarly outlined in an appropriate location.

3. Separate pits should be placed for the running long jump, the high jump, and the hop-step-and-jump. These should be spaced well apart to minimize interference.

4. High-jump equipment should be checked. Standards with pins, crossbars (or cord substitutes), and cushioned landing pads are needed.

5. Takeoff boards for the long jump and hop-step-and-jump should be in place. Jumping without the use of a takeoff board is not a satisfying experience. Pits should be filled with fresh building sand of a coarse variety.

6. Accessory materials should be gathered, including batons, starter clapboards, watches, hurdles, and yarn for the finish line.

7. The value of starting blocks is debatable. Doubtless, they add interest to the program, but their use and adjustment are sometimes difficult for the elementary school student to master.

The organization of students is as important as the organization of equipment. Height and weight are factors affecting the degree of physical performance in track, field, and cross-country activities.

More efficient instruction is possible when children are grouped by height and weight. They also can be arranged by sex. The following groups may serve as a basis for instruction: (1) heavier and taller boys, (2) shorter and lighter boys, (3) heavier and taller girls, and (4) shorter and lighter girls. A simple way to form groups is to rank boys and girls separately according to the following formula, which yields a standard number: Score = 10 × age (to the nearest half-year) + weight (in pounds).

After the boys have been ranked, the upper 50 percent are assigned to group 1 and the remainder to group 2. A similar division is made with the girls. Some decisions regarding borderline cases must be made.

Some track and field skills can be practiced with a single-activity organization. Starting skills can be practiced with perhaps one-fourth of the children at one time. Four groups can practice baton-passing skills at one time. Striding for distance can be practiced with each group running as a unit.

The predominant plan of organization should be one of multiple activity. Four stations can make use of the selected group organization, but more stations are desirable. If eight stations are used, two stations can be assigned to each group. Stations can be selected from the following skill areas: (1) starting and sprinting, (2) baton passing, (3) standing and running long jump, (4) hop-step-and-jump, (5) high jump, (6) hurdles, (7) striding for distance and pace judgment, and (8) the Potato Shuttle Race. (See the following section.)

It is generally not sound to have children practice at all stations in any one class session. The entire circuit can be completed during additional sessions. Putting written directions at each station is helpful. The directions can state what is to be accomplished as well as offering points of technique.

In later instruction, students can select the skills that they desire to practice. With guidance, the choice system could embrace the entire program, with children determining at each session those areas on which they would like to concentrate. This choice approach can be related to individualized or contract instruction.

TRACK AND FIELD DRILLS AND ACTIVITIES

Potato Shuttle Race

The Potato Shuttle Race is an adaptation of an old American custom during frontier harvest celebrations. For each competitor, a number of potatoes were placed in a line at various distances. The winner was the one who brought in his potatoes first, one at a time. He won a sack of potatoes for the best effort.

The modern version of this race uses blocks instead of potatoes, and each runner runs the following course. A box is placed 15 feet in front of the starting line, with four blocks in individual circles, which are the same distance (15 feet) apart (Figure 30.12). The runner begins behind the starting line and brings the blocks, one at a time, back to the box. She can bring the blocks back in any order desired, but all blocks must be put inside the box. The box should be 12 by 12 inches, with a depth of 3 to 6 inches. Blocks must be placed or dropped, not thrown, into the box.

The most practical way to organize competition in this race is to time each individual and then award places on the basis of elapsed time, for the race is physically challenging. The competitors must understand that each person is running individually and that they should strive for their best time, regardless of position or place of finish in the race.

Timers can act as judges to see that the blocks are not thrown into the box. A block that lands outside the box must be placed inside before the student goes after another. Blocks should be about 2 inches square, but this can vary.

The race can be run as a relay. The first runner brings all of the blocks in, one at a time, and then tags off the second member of the team, who returns the blocks, one at a time, to the respective spots. The third relay member brings the blocks in again, and the fourth puts them out again. For this race, it is necessary to have pie tins, floor tiles (9 by 9 inches), or some other items in addition to the box so that when the blocks are put out by the second and fourth runners, it can be determined definitely that they rest in the proper spot. A block must be on its spot in the proper fashion before the runner delivers the next one.

Running for Pace

Children should have some experience in running for moderate distances to acquire an understanding of pace. The running should be loose and relaxed. Distances up to 1600 meters may be part

of the work. To check his time, each runner needs a partner. Someone with a stopwatch loudly counts the elapsed time second by second, and the partner notes the runner's time as he crosses the finish line.

Allowing children to estimate their pace and time can be motivating. On a circular track, at a set distance, let each runner stipulate a target time and see how close she can come to it.

Interval Training

Children should know the technique of interval training, which consists of running at a set speed for a specified distance and then walking back to the starting point. On the 1/8-mile track, children can run for 110 yards and then walk to the starting point, repeating this procedure a number of times. They can also run the entire 220 yards, take a timed rest, and then repeat. Breathing should return to near normal before the next 220-yard interval is attempted.

SUGGESTED TRACK FACILITY

The presence of a track facility is a boon to any program. Few elementary schools have the funds or space for a quarter-mile track. A shorter track facility that can be installed permanently with curbs or temporarily with marking lime is suggested. Discarded fire hoses can be used to mark curbs and can be installed each spring with spikes.

The short facility is 1/8 mile (220 yards) in length and has a straightaway of 66 yards, which is ample for the 60-yard dash (Figure 30.13). It allows flexibility in relays, since relay legs of 55, 110, and 220 yards are possible. In keeping with international practice, a 200-meter track may be preferable (Figure 30.14). Running on a track is always done in a counterclockwise direction.

Start Box

X ⟵ 15 ft ⟶ □ ⟵ 15 ft ⟶ ○ ⟵ 15 ft ⟶ ○ ⟵ 15 ft ⟶ ○ ⟵ 15 ft ⟶ ○

Figure 30.12 Potato Shuttle Race

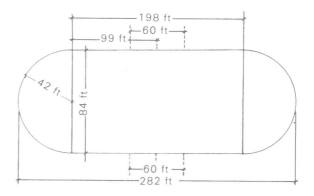

Figure 30.13 One-eighth-mile (220-yd) track

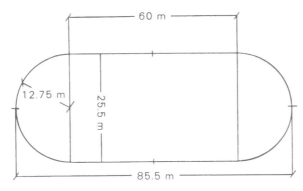

Figure 30.14 200-m track

CONDUCTING TRACK AND FIELD DAYS

Track and field days can range in organization from competition within a single classroom to competition between selected classes, from an all-school playday meet to a meet between neighboring schools or an areawide or all-city meet. In informal meets within a class or between a few classes, all children should participate in one or more events. Each student can be limited to two individual events plus one relay event, with no substitutions permitted. An additional condition could be imposed that competitors for individual events enter only one track event and one field event.

For larger meets, two means of qualification are suggested.

1. Qualifying times and performance standards can be set at the start of the season. Any student meeting or bettering these times or performances is qualified to compete.

2. In an all-school meet, first- and second-place winners in each class competition qualify for entry. For a district or all-city meet, first- and second-place winners from each all-school meet become eligible.

Generally, competition is organized for each event by sex and grade or age. This does not preclude mixed teams competing against mixed teams in relays. Height and weight classifications can be used to equalize competition.

Planning the Meet

The order of events should be determined by the type of competition. Relays are usually last on the program. If preliminary heats are necessary, these are run off first. Color-coded cards should be given to the heat qualifiers. This helps get them into the correct final race.

The local track coach can give advice about details of organizing the meet. Helpers can be secured from among school patrons, secondary students, teacher-training students, and service clubs. Adequate and properly instructed help is essential. A list of key officials and their duties follows.

1. *Meet director.* The meet director should be positioned at a convenient point near the finish line, with a table on which all official papers are kept.

2. *Announcer.* The announcer can be in charge of the public address system. Much of the success of the meet depends on the announcer's abilities.

3. *Clerk of the course.* The clerk of the course has charge of all entries and places the competitors in their proper starting slots.

4. *Starter.* The starter works closely with the clerk of the course.

5. *Head and finish judges.* There should be one finish judge for each place awarded, plus one extra. The first competitor "out of the money" is identified in case there is a disqualification. The head judge can cast the deciding vote if there is doubt about the first- and second-place winners.

6. *Timers.* Three timers should time first place, although fewer can be used. Another timer, if available, can time second place. Timers report their times to the head timer, who determines the correct winning time. Accurate timing is important if records are a factor.

7. *Messenger.* A messenger takes the entry card from the clerk of the course to the finish judge, who records the correct finish places and the winner's time after the race is completed. The messenger then takes the final record of the race to the meet director's table.

8. *Field judges and officials.* Each field event should be managed by a sufficient crew, headed by a designated individual. Each crew head should be given a clipboard with the rules of the particular event fully explained.

9. *Marshals.* Several marshals should be appointed to keep general order. They are responsible for keeping noncompetitors from interfering with the events. Competitors can be kept under better control if each unit has an

assigned place, either in the infield or in the stands.

Only the assigned officials and competitors should be present at the scenes of competition.

In smaller meets, first, second, and third places are usually awarded, with scoring on a 5-, 3-, and 1-point basis, respectively. Relays, because of multiple participation, should count double in the place point score. For larger meets, more places can be awarded, and the individual point scores can be adjusted.

Ribbons can be awarded to winners but need not be elaborate. The name of the meet should be printed on the ribbon, with the individual event and the place designated. Blue ribbons are given for first place, red for second, and white for third. They are usually awarded after each event. Awarding ribbons at the conclusion of a large interschool meet is anticlimactic, since many spectators will have left.

An opening ceremony, including a salute to the flag, is desirable for larger meets. Competitors from each unit can be introduced as a group, with announcements and instructions emphasized or clarified at this time. Holding the event on a school morning or afternoon gives status to the affair and allows all children to participate.

It is helpful if the competitors wear numbers. Safety pins, rather than straight pins, should be used to keep the numbers in place. Numbers can be made at the individual schools prior to the meet when well-defined instructions pertaining to the materials, colors, and sizes have been given.

Organizing the Competition

The overriding goal of elementary school competition is to have many children take part and experience a measure of success. The determination of individual champions and of meet winners is lower in priority. Track and field competition can take many forms.

In informal competition, competitors are assigned to different races and compete only in those races. There are no heats as such, nor is there advancement to a final race. Races are chosen so that individuals on the same team usually do not run against each other. Points may or may not be given toward an overall meet score. The informal meet is more like a playday and can include nontrack events also, such as the softball throw, the football kick, and the Frisbee throw.

Track and field competition can be focused on individuals or teams. In individual competition, there is no team scoring and only individuals are declared winners. When team competition is incorporated, both individual winners and team winners are determined. Points scored by individual winners, such as 5 points for first place, or 3 points for second place, are credited to respective teams. The team with the highest score wins. Different team winners can be determined for different grades and/or levels.

Relay competition is a carnival in which a number of relays make up the program. Performances can be combined for several individuals if field events are to be included. Few, if any, uncombined scores are taken into consideration. A number of relays should be part of track and field days under any plan. Relays increase student participation. Mixed relays are a possibility.

CROSS-COUNTRY RUNNING

Many youngsters are motivated by running laps around a track. Others soon tire of these circular efforts, however, and can be motivated by cross-country running. Students can run marked or unmarked courses for enjoyment of the competition. Emphasis is on improving one's personal time rather than on winning. This enables all students to have personalized goals and an ongoing incentive for running.

Cross-country courses can be marked with a chalk line and cones so that runners follow the course as outlined. Checkpoints every 220 yards offer runners a convenient reference point so that they can gauge accurately how far they have run. Three courses of differing lengths and difficulty can be laid out. The beginning course can be 1 mile in length, the intermediate 1.25 mile, and the advanced 1.5 mile. Including sandy or hilly areas in the course increases the challenge. When students run cross country, they can select the course that challenges them appropriately.

It is important for students to learn the concept of *pace* when running long distances. One technique for teaching students how to pace themselves is to place cones at similar intervals and to challenge students to run from cone to cone at a specified rate. A student or the instructor can call out the time at each cone, and students can adjust their running to the desired pace. Another method is to break down long-distance runs into smaller segments and times, which enables youngsters to get a feel for how fast they must run the shorter distances to attain a certain cumulative time over the longer distance. Table 30.2 gives times for the 40- and 100-yard dashes.

Table 30.2 Times for 40- and 100-yard dashes

To run a mile in:	Runner has to run 40-yd dash 44 times—each dash run in:	Runner has to run 100-yd dash 17.6 times—each dash run in:
3:44 minutes (world record time)	5.18 seconds	12.95 seconds
5:00 minutes	6.81 seconds	17.04 seconds
6:00 minutes	8.18 seconds	20.45 seconds
7:00 minutes	9.55 seconds	23.87 seconds
8:00 minutes	10.90 seconds	27.25 seconds
10:00 minutes	13.62 seconds	34.08 seconds

CROSS-COUNTRY MEETS

Cross-country meets provide a culminating activity for youngsters involved in distance running. The attractiveness of cross-country competition lies in the fact that it is a team activity and all members of the team are crucial to its success. Youngsters should learn how to score a meet. Probably the easiest way to keep team scores is to assign seven (depending on class size) members to each team. Points are assigned to finishers based on their placement in the race. For example, the first-place runner receives 1 point, the tenth-place runner 10 points, and so on. The points for all team members are totaled, and the team with the lowest score is declared the winner.

Teams can be equalized by having youngsters run the course ahead of the meet and recording their times. Teams can then be organized by the teacher so that members are somewhat matched. As a guideline, Table 30.3 offers suggested competitive divisions and distances to be run. Divisions 5 and 6 are classed as open divisions, which any child in the elementary school may enter, even if below the age of 12. Ages are defined by birthdays; that is, a child is classified as being a certain age until the next birthday.

A primary concern is that children gauge their running pace so that they are able to finish the race. Improvement of previous times should be the focus of the activity, with place at the finish of the race a secondary goal. The timekeeper can voice the time as each runner finishes to help children evaluate their performance.

A funnel made of cones at the finish line prevents tying times (Figure 30.15). As runners go through the funnel, the meet judges and helpers can hand each one a marker with the place of finish on it. This simplifies scoring at the end of the meet. Each team captain can total the scores and report the result.

Cross-country runners should learn to cool down on completion of a race. Youngsters have a tendency to fall down rather than to move. They should jog gently until they are somewhat rested. Since runners do not all finish at the same time, it is sometimes helpful to have some recreational activities set out near the track so that the youngsters can stay involved in activity.

Table 30.3 Suggested divisions for cross-country meets

Division	Age	Sex	Distance (in miles)
1	8–9	M	1
2	8–9	F	1
3	10–11	M	1.25
4	10–11	F	1.25
5	12–13	M	1.5
6	12–13	F	1.5

Figure 30.15 Funneling runners at the finish line

Volleyball

Volleyball can be started in the elementary grades, with instruction serving as a basis for later high school participation. To play successfully on the elementary level, a skill foundation must be established. This requires sufficient practice of serving and passing skills and development of hand-eye and body coordination for effective ball control. Attention to proper technique is essential.

Informal practice should begin in the primary grades with activities that mimic volleyball skills—passing, serving, and rebounding of all types. Setting and spiking are questionable activities for the regular class lesson plans. Even more mature youngsters have difficulty employing these more advanced techniques successfully. Blocking can receive some attention when it occurs in normal play.

INSTRUCTIONAL EMPHASIS AND SEQUENCE

Indoor facilities sometimes are a problem with volleyball. In some gymnasiums, the lack of court space means playing with 12 to 15 children on a side in a single game. This arrangement usually results in little activity for the majority of participants. A few skilled players on each side dominate the game. The usual basketball court should be divided into two volleyball courts on which players play crosswise. Nets should be lowered to 6 feet and raised 6 to 12 inches as children mature. Attachments on the walls should reflect these varied net heights. Furthermore, the nets should be attached firmly so that both the upper and lower net cords are tight. A loosely hanging net does not allow for ball recovery from the net. Walls may not be suitable for rebounding activities.

The number of volleyballs also can be a problem. When children practice individually with a ball, the number of balls can be supplemented with beach balls and foam balls of comparable size. Few schools have 30 to 35 volleyballs available. When possible, all volleyballs should be properly inflated. In larger school systems, the problem of volleyball supply can be solved by having a rotating schedule of volleyball activities from school to school. Few practice activities require a net, so outdoor participation is possible.

The skills of the overhand serve, the setup, the spike, and blocking should be introduced only when a competitive situation exists, as in intramurals or an interschool program, in which the emphasis shifts to winning. Normally, in physical education classes, the program dwells on keeping the ball in play, thereby increasing activity, skill development, and enjoyment. As a matter of game orientation, however, students should know about the setup, the spike, and blocking techniques.

In the primary grades, children should have had ball-handling experiences related to volleyball skills. Rebounding and controlling balloons is an excellent related experience, particularly for younger children. Included in ball-handling experiences with beach balls or foam rubber training balls should be exploratory work in batting with the hands and other body parts. This preliminary experience in visual tracking is advantageous for volleyball. Table 31.1 shows the sequence of volleyball activities divided into two developmental levels. In most cases, youngsters are not ready to participate in the activities in this chapter until the age of 8.

Developmental Level II

Experiences at this level should be based on the use of the beach ball and should culminate in the game of Beach Ball Volleyball. A beach ball is larger and more easily handled than a volleyball and allows a level of success not possible with a smaller ball. Simple returns and underhand serves should be practiced with beach balls. The game of Informal Volleyball and Shower Service Ball should

Table 31.1 Suggested volleyball program

Developmental Level II	Developmental Level III
Skills	
Underhand serve	Overhand pass
Simple returns	Forearm pass
	Overhand serve
	Setup*
	Spike*
	Blocking*
Knowledge	
Simple rules	Basic game rules
Rotation	Game strategy
Activities	
Beach Ball Volleyball	Keep It Up
Informal Volleyball	Mini-Volleyball
Shower Service Ball	Rotation Mini-Volleyball
	Regulation Volleyball
	Three-and-Over Volleyball
	Rotation Volleyball
	Four-Square Volleyball
Skills	
Simplified serving	Serving for accuracy
	Wall volleying

*Skilled players only.

be played with a volleyball trainer ball, which moves slower and is easier to handle.

Developmental Level III

Beach balls and foam balls can be used at this level of instruction, but a shift to volleyball trainer balls should be made when the maturity of the youngsters dictates. Foam rubber and training volleyballs (8½-inch) are excellent substitutes for volleyballs (Figure 31.1). They do not hurt youngsters, move slowly, and afford an opportunity for successful play. Students should begin to exhibit basic technique in handling high and low passes. Only the most skilled students are able to learn the overhand serve, setup, spike, and blocking. The majority of instruction should focus on the underhand serve and the overhand and forearm passes. An introduction to elementary strategy should be part of the instructional approach.

Figure 31.1 Different balls for volleyball

VOLLEYBALL SKILLS

Serving

The serve is used to start play. The underhand serve is easiest for elementary school children to learn even though the overhand (floater) serve is the most effective. Few youngsters will be capable of mastering the overhand serve. The following instructional cues focus on correct performance of the serve:

1. Use opposition. Place the opposite foot of the serving hand forward.
2. Transfer the weight to the forward foot.
3. Keep the eyes on the ball.
4. Decide prior to the serve where it should be placed.
5. Follow through; don't punch at the ball.

Underhand Serve

Directions are for a right-handed serve. The player stands facing the net with the left foot slightly forward and the weight on the right (rear) foot. The ball is held in the left hand with the left arm across and a little in front of the body. The ball is lined up with a straightforward swing of the right hand. The left-hand fingers are spread, and the ball rests on the pads of these fingers. On the serving motion, the server steps forward with the left foot, transferring the weight to the front foot, and at the same time brings the right arm back in a preparatory motion. The right hand now swings forward and contacts the ball just below center. The ball can be hit with an open hand or with the fist (facing forward or sideward). An effective follow-through with the arm ensures a smooth serve (Figure 31.2). Children should explore the best way to strike the ball, with the flat of the hand or the fist. Each player can select the method that is personally most effective.

Overhand Serve

This serve is seldom mastered by elementary school youngsters. It can be presented as an option for students who have mastered the underhand serve. For the right-handed serve, stand with the left foot in front and the left side of the body turned somewhat toward the net. The weight is on both feet. The server must master two difficult skills: how to toss the ball and how to contact the ball. The ball is held in the left hand directly in front of the face. The ball must be tossed straight up and should come down in front of the right shoulder. As the ball is tossed, the weight shifts to the back foot. The height of the toss is a matter of choice, but from 3 to 5 feet is suggested. As the ball drops, the striking arm comes forward, contacting the ball a foot or so above the shoulder. The weight is shifted to the forward foot, which can take a short step forward. The contact is made with the open palm or with the fist. An effective serve is one that has no spin—a floater.

Passing (or Returning)

The overhand pass is probably the most used skill in elementary school volleyball. Using beach balls and trainer volleyballs will allow youngsters time to move into the path of the volleyball instead of reaching for the ball. Proper footwork is critical to the success of volleyball; using proper balls will

Figure 31.2 Underhand serve

help assure that youngsters learn correctly. Instructional cues of passing include the following:

1. Move into the path of the ball; don't reach for it.
2. Bend the knees prior to making contact.
3. Contact the ball with the fingertips (overhand pass).
4. Extend the knees upon contact with the ball.
5. Follow through after striking the ball.

Overhand Pass

The overhand pass, or return, must be mastered if there is to be interesting, competitive play. If the ball is served and not returned well or often, the game is dull. To execute an overhand pass, the player moves underneath the ball and controls it with the fingertips. Feet should be in an easy, comfortable position, with knees bent. The cup of the fingers is made so that the thumbs and forefingers are close together and the other fingers are spread. The hands are held forehead high, with elbows out and level with the floor. The player, when in receiving position, looks ready to shout upward through cupped hands (Figure 31.3).

The player contacts the ball at above eye level and propels it with the force of spread fingers, not with the palms. At the moment of contact, the legs are straightened and the hands and arms follow through. If the ball is a pass to a teammate, it should be high enough to allow for control. If the pass is a return to the other side, it can be projected forward with more force.

Forearm Pass (Underhand Pass)

The forearm pass takes the place of the old underhand pass, in which the ball was contacted with the palms of the hands. The body must be in good position to ensure a proper volley. The player must move rapidly to the spot where the ball is descending to prepare for the pass. Body position is important. The trunk leans forward and the back is straight, with a 90-degree angle between the thighs and the body. The legs are bent, and the body is in a partially crouched position, with the feet shoulder width apart (Figure 31.4). The hands are clasped together so that the forearms are parallel. The clasp should be relaxed, with the type of handclasp a matter of choice. In one method, the thumbs are kept parallel and together, and the fingers of one hand make a partially cupped fist, with the fingers of the other hand overlapping the fist. In another method, both hands are cupped and turned out a little, so that the thumbs are apart. In either case,

Figure 31.3 Completing an overhand pass

the wrists are turned downward and the elbow joints are reasonably locked. The forearms are held at the proper angle to rebound the ball, with contact made with the fists or forearms between the knees as the receiver crouches.

Dig Pass

The dig pass is an emergency return when neither the overhand nor the forearm pass is possible. It is a stiffened rebound from one arm, contact being made with the cupped fist (Figure 31.5), the heel of the hand, or the inside or outside of the forearm. The dig pass should not be employed as a standard return.

Advanced Volleyball Skills

The setup, the spike, and blocking are skills that are difficult for the majority of youngsters to master. Volleyball lead-up games do not require the use

Figure 31.4   Forearm (underhand) pass position

of these skills. Because the majority of children will not be able to master these skills, it is best to introduce them on an individual basis.

Setup

The term *setup* applies to a pass that sets the ball for a possible spike. The object is to raise the ball with a soft, easy pass to a position 1 or 2 feet above the net and about 1 foot away from it. The setup is generally the second pass in a series of three. An overhand pass is used for the setup. It is important for the back line player, who has to tap to the setter, to make an accurate and easily handled pass.

Spike

The spike is the most effective play in volleyball, and when properly done is extremely difficult to return. Its success depends a great deal on the ability of a teammate to set up properly. At the elementary school level, spiking should be done by jumping high in the air and striking the ball above the net, driving it into the opponent's court. Experienced players may back up for a short run, but

Figure 31.5   Dig pass

the jump must be made straight up so that the player does not touch the net and the striking hand does not go over the net.

Blocking

Blocking involves one or more members of the defensive (receiving) team forming a screen of arms and hands near the net to block a spike. At the elementary school level, blocking is usually done by a single individual, and little attention is given to multiple blocking. To block a ball, a player jumps high with arms outstretched overhead, palms facing the net, and fingers spread. The jump must be timed with that of the spiker, and the blocker must avoid touching the net. The ball is not struck but rather rebounds from the blocker's stiffened hands and arms. Students should know about blocking even if it is used infrequently in elementary play.

INSTRUCTIONAL PROCEDURES

1. Most volleyball-type games begin with a serve, so it becomes critical that this be successful. Regular volleyball rules call for one chance to serve the ball over the net without touching the

net. Three modifications can achieve more successful serving. The first is to serve from the center of the playing area instead of the back line. A second is to allow another serve if the first is not good. The third is to allow an assist by a team member to get the ball over the net.

2. To save time, instruct players to roll the ball back to the server. Other players should let the ball roll to its destination without interception.

3. Effective instruction is possible only when the balls can be rebounded from the hands and arms without pain. A heavy or underinflated ball takes much of the enjoyment out of the game.

4. The predominant instructional pattern should be individual or partner work. For individual work, each child needs a ball.

5. An 8½-inch foam rubber training ball has much the same feel as a volleyball but does not cause pain. The foam balls should be used early in skill practice. A new ball, the volleyball trainer, most closely resembles a volleyball but is larger in diameter and lighter in weight. Either ball helps keep children from developing a fear of the fast-moving object.

6. The use of the fist to hit balls on normal returns causes poor control and interrupts play. Except for dig passes, both hands should be used to return the ball. Teachers should rule hitting with the fist a loss of a point if the practice persists.

7. Rotation should be introduced early and used in lead-up games. Two rotation plans are illustrated in Figure 31.6.

ORGANIZING FOR INSTRUCTION

Practice sessions can be categorized as individual play, partner work, or group work. These tasks can be prefaced by "Can you . . ." or "Let's see if you can. . . ." A skill to learn early is a toss to oneself to initiate a practice routine. This occurs when the practice directions call for a pass from one individual to oneself or to another.

Individual Play

1. For wall rebounding, stand 6 feet away from a wall. Throw the ball against the wall and pass it to the wall. The player then catches and begins again. Allow two passes against the wall before a catch is made. A further extension is to pass

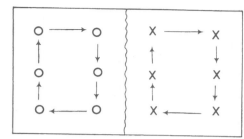

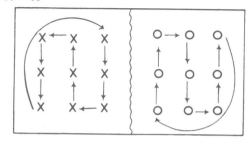

Figure 31.6 Rotation plans

the ball against the wall as many times as possible without making a mistake.

2. From a spot 6 feet from the wall, throw the ball against the wall and alternate an overhand pass with a forearm pass. The player then catches the ball.

3. In another wall-rebounding exercise, the player throws the ball to one side (right or left) and then moves to the side to pass the ball to the wall. Catch the rebound.

4. The player passes the ball directly overhead and catches it. Try making two passes before catching the ball. Later, alternate an overhand pass with a forearm pass and catch the ball. A further extension of the drill is to keep the ball going five or six times with one kind of pass or with alternate passes. This is a basic drill and should be mastered before proceeding to others.

5. The player passes the ball 10 feet high and 10 feet forward, moves rapidly under the ball, and catches it. Later, make additional passes without the catch.

6. The player passes the ball 15 feet overhead, makes a full turn, and passes the ball again. Vary with other stunts such as touching the floor, making a half turn, clapping the hands at two different spots, and others. Allow choice in selecting the stunt.

7. Two lines 3 feet apart are needed. The player stands in front of one line, makes a backward

pass overhead, moves to the other line, and repeats the procedure.

8. The player passes 3 feet or so to one side, moves under the ball, and passes it back to the original spot. The next pass should be to the other side.

9. The player passes the ball directly overhead. On the return, jump as high as possible to make a second pass. Continue.

10. The player stands with one foot in a hoop. Pass the ball overhead and attempt to continue passing while keeping that foot in the hoop. Try with both feet in the hoop.

11. The player stands about 15 feet away from a basketball goal, either in front or to the side. Pass toward the goal in an attempt to make a basket. Score 3 points if the basket is made, 2 points for no basket but for hitting the rim, and 1 point for hitting the backboard only. A further challenge would be for the player to make a pass to himself first and a second pass toward the goal.

Partner Work (Passing)

1. Players are about 10 feet apart. Player A tosses the ball (controlled toss) to player B, who passes the ball back to A, who catches the ball. Continue for several exchanges and then change throwers. Another option is for player B to make a pass straight overhead, catch the ball, and then toss to player A. Yet another variation is to have one player toss the ball slightly to the side. Player B then makes a pass to player A. Player A can make the toss in such a fashion that player B must use a forearm return.

2. Two players are about 15 feet apart. Player A passes to herself first and then makes a second pass to player B, who catches the ball and repeats. This can be followed with a return by player B.

3. Players A and B try to keep the ball in the air continuously.

4. Players are about 15 feet apart. Player A remains stationary and passes in such a fashion that player B must move from side to side. An option is to have player B move forward and backward.

5. Players are about 10 feet apart. Both have hoops and attempt to keep one foot in the hoop while passing. Try keeping both feet in the hoop.

6. Two players pass back and forth, making contact with the ball while off the ground.

7. Players are about 15 feet apart. Player B is seated. Player A attempts to pass to player B. A second method is for both players to stand. Player A passes to player B and then sits down quickly. Player B attempts to pass the ball back to player A, who catches it in the seated position.

8. Player A passes to player B and does a complete turnaround. Player B passes back to player A and also does a full turn. Other stunts can be used.

9. Player A is stationed near a basketball goal, with player B in the lane. Player A passes to player B in the lane, who attempts a pass to the basket. Count 3 points for a basket, 2 points for a miss that hits the rim, and 1 point for hitting the backboard only. Any pass from player A that lands outside the center lane is void, and another chance is given.

10. Partners stand on opposite sides of a volleyball net. The object is to keep the ball in the air. The drill can be done by as many as six players.

11. One player stands on a chair in front of the net and holds a ball in such a fashion that spikers can knock the ball over the net. The next progression is to toss the ball about 2 feet above the net for spiking practice.

12. If the net is stretched properly, recovery can be practiced. One player throws the ball against the net, and the active player recovers with a forearm pass.

Partner Work (Serving and Passing)

1. Partners are about 20 feet apart. Partner A serves to partner B, who catches the ball and returns the serve to partner A.

2. Partner A serves to partner B, who makes a pass back to partner A. Change responsibilities.

3. *Service One-Step.* Partners begin about 10 feet apart. Partner A serves to partner B, who returns the serve with partner A catching. If there is no error and if neither receiver moved the feet to catch, both players take one step back. This is repeated each time no error or foot movement by the receivers occur. If an error occurs or if appreciable foot movement is evident, the players revert to the original distance of 10 feet and start over.

4. A player stands at the top of the key on a basketball court. The object is to serve the ball into the basket. Scoring can be as in other

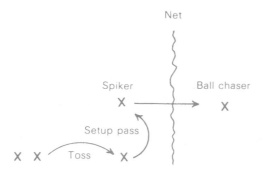

Figure 31.7 Setup and spiking drill

basket-making drills: 3 points for a basket, 2 points for hitting the rim, and 1 point for hitting the backboard but not the rim. Partner retrieves the ball.

Group Work

1. A leader stands in front of not more than four other players, who are arranged in a semi-circle. The leader tosses to each player in sequence around the circle and they return the ball. After a round or two, another player comes forward to replace the leader.

2. For blocking, six players are positioned alongside the net, each with a ball. The players take turns on the other side of the net, practicing blocking skills. Each spiker tosses the ball to himself for spiking. A defensive player moves along the line to block consecutively a total of six spikes. The next step is to have two players move along the line to practice blocking by pairs.

3. Setup and spiking can be practiced according to the drill shown in Figure 31.7. A back player tosses the ball to the setup player, who passes the ball properly for a spike. The entire group or just the spikers can rotate.

4. Two groups of children stand on opposite sides of a net. Eight to ten balls must be available to make this a worthwhile experience. Players serve back of the baseline and recover balls coming from the other team. The action should be informal and continuous.

BASIC VOLLEYBALL RULES

Officially, six players make up a team, but any number from six to nine make a suitable team in the elementary school program.

To begin, captains toss a coin for the order of choices. The winner can choose to serve or to select a court. The opposing captain takes the option that the winner of the toss did not select. At the completion of any game, teams change courts, and the losing side serves.

To be in the proper position to serve, a player must have both feet behind the right one third of the end line and must not step on the end line during the serve. The server covers the right back position. Only the serving team scores. The server retains the serve, scoring consecutive points, until that side loses a point and is put out. Members of each team take turns serving, the sequence being determined by the plan of rotation.

Official rules allow the server only one serve to get the ball completely over the net and into the opponent's court. Even if the ball touches the net (a net ball) and goes into the correct court, the serve is lost. The lines bounding the court are considered to be in bounds; that is, balls landing on the lines are counted as good. Any ball that touches or is touched by a player is considered to be in bounds, even if the player who touched the ball was clearly outside the boundaries at the time. The ball must be returned over the net by the third volley, which means that the team has a maximum of three volleys to make a good return.

The following major violations cause the loss of the point or serve:

1. Touching the net during play.
2. Not clearly batting the ball—sometimes called palming or carrying the ball.
3. Reaching over the net during play.
4. Stepping over the centerline. (Contact with the line is not a violation.)

A ball going into the net may be recovered and played, provided that no player touches the net. The first team to reach a score of 15 points wins the game if the team is at least 2 points ahead. If not, play continues until one team secures a 2-point lead. Only players in the front line may spike, but all players may block. No player may volley the ball twice in succession.

VOLLEYBALL ACTIVITIES

Developmental Level II

Beach Ball Volleyball

Playing Area: Volleyball court
Players: Six to nine on each team

Supplies: A beach ball 12 to 16 inches in diameter

Skills: Most passing skills, modified serving

The players of each team are in two lines on their respective sides of the net. Serving is done, as in regulation volleyball, by the player on the right side of the back line. The distance is shortened, however, because serving a beach ball successfully from the normal volleyball serving distance is difficult. The player serves from the normal playing position on the court in the right back position. Scoring is as in regulation volleyball. Play continues until the ball touches the floor.

A team loses a point to the other team when it fails to return the ball over the net by the third volley or when it returns the ball over the net but the ball hits the floor out of bounds without being touched by the opposing team. The server continues serving as long as that team scores. Rotation is as in regulation volleyball.

Teaching Suggestion: The server must be positioned as close to the net as possible while still remaining in the right back position on the court. Successful serving is an important component of an enjoyable game.

Variations:

1. In a simplified version of Beach Ball Volleyball, the ball is put into play by one player in the front line, who throws the ball into the air and then passes it over the net. Play continues until the ball touches the floor, but the ball may be volleyed any number of times before crossing the net. When either team has scored 5 points, the front and back lines of the respective teams change. When the score reaches 10 for the leading team, the lines change back. Game is 15.

2. Any player in the back line may catch the ball as it comes initially from the opposing team and may immediately make a little toss and pass the ball to a teammate. The player who catches the ball and bats it cannot send it across the net before a teammate has touched it.

Informal Volleyball

Playing Area: Volleyball court, 6-foot net

Players: Six to eight on a team

Supplies: A trainer volleyball

Skills: Passing

This game is similar to regulation volleyball, but there is no serving. Each play begins with a student on one side tossing to herself and passing the ball high over the net. Points are scored for every play, as there is no "side out." As soon as a point is scored, the nearest player takes the ball and immediately puts it into play. Otherwise, basic volleyball rules govern the game. Rotation occurs as soon as a team has scored 5 points, with the front and back lines changing place. Action is fast, and the game moves rapidly, as every play scores a point for one team or the other.

Shower Service Ball

Playing Area: Volleyball court

Players: 6 to 12 on each team

Supplies: Four to six trainer volleyballs

Skills: Serving, catching

A line parallel to the net is drawn through the middle of each court to define the serving area. Players are scattered in no particular formation (Figure 31.8). The game involves the skills of serving and catching. To start the game, two or three volleyballs are given to each team and are handled by players in the serving area.

Balls may be served at any time and in any order by a server, who must be in the back half of the court. Any ball served across the net is to be caught by any player near the ball. The person catching or retrieving a ball moves quickly to the serving area and serves. A point is scored for a team whenever a served ball hits the floor in the other court or is dropped by a receiver. Two scorers are needed, one for each side.

Teaching Suggestion: As children improve, all serves should be made from behind the baseline.

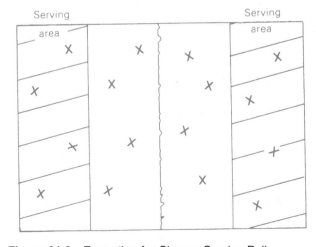

Figure 31.8   Formation for Shower Service Ball

Developmental Level III

Keep It Up

Playing Area: Playground or gymnasium

Players: Five to eight on each team

Supplies: A trainer volleyball for each team

Skills: Overhand, forearm, and dig passes

Each team forms a small circle of not more than eight players. The object of the game is to see which team can make the greater number of volleys in a specified time or which team can keep the ball in the air for the greater number of consecutive volleys without error.

On the signal "Go," the game is started with a volley by one of the players. The following rules are in force.

1. Balls are volleyed back and forth with no specific order of turns, except that the ball cannot be returned to the player from whom it came.

2. A player may not volley a ball twice in succession.

3. Any ball touching the ground does not count and ends the count.

Teaching Suggestions: Players should be responsible for calling illegal returns on themselves and thus interrupting the consecutive volley count. The balls used should be of equal quality, so that one team cannot claim a disadvantage. Groups should be taught to count the volleys out loud, so that their progress is known.

Mini-Volleyball

Playing Area: Gymnasium or badminton court

Players: Three on each team

Supplies: A volleyball or trainer volleyball

Skills: Most volleyball skills

Mini-Volleyball is a modified activity designed to offer opportunities for successful volleyball experiences to children between the ages of 9 and 12. The playing area is 15 feet wide and 40 feet long. The spiking line is 10 feet from the centerline. Many gymnasiums are marked for badminton courts that are 20 by 44 feet with a spiking line 6.5 feet from the center. This is an acceptable substitute court.

The modified rules used in Mini-Volleyball are as follows.

1. A team consists of three players. Two substitutions may be made per game.

2. Players are positioned for the serve so that there are two front-line players and one back-line player. After the ball is served, the back-line player may not spike the ball from the attack area or hit the ball into the attack area unless the ball is below the height of the net.

3. The height of the net is 6 feet, 10 inches.

4. Players rotate positions when they receive the ball for serving. The right front-line player becomes the back-line player, and the left front-line player becomes the right front-line player.

5. A team wins a game when it scores 15 points and has a 2-point advantage over the opponent. A team wins the match when it wins two out of three games.

The back-line player cannot spike and thus serves a useful function by allowing the front players to receive the serves while moving to the net to set up for the spikers.

Teaching Suggestion: This game can be modified to suit the needs of participants. Sponge training balls work well in the learning stages of Mini-Volleyball.

Rotation Mini-Volleyball

Playing Area: Basketball or volleyball court

Players: Three on each team

Supplies: A volleyball

Skills: All volleyball skills

Three games, involving 18 active players, can be played at the same time crosswise, on a regular basketball court. The remaining children, organized in teams of three, wait on the sideline with teams designated in a particular order. Whenever a team is guilty of a "side out," it vacates its place on the floor and the next team in line moves in. Each team keeps its own running score. If, during a single side in, 10 points are scored against a team, that team vacates its place. Teams in this arrangement move from one court to another and play different opponents. The one or two extra players left over from team selection by threes can be substitutes and should be rotated into play on a regular basis.

Regulation Volleyball

Playing Area: Volleyball court

Players: Six on each team

Supplies: A volleyball

Skills: All volleyball skills

Regulation volleyball should be played with one possible rule change: In early experiences, it is suggested that the server be allowed a second chance when failing to get the first attempt over the net and into play. This should apply only to the initial serve. Some instructors like to shorten the serving distance during the introductory phases of the game. It is important for the serving to be done well enough to keep the game moving.

A referee should supervise the game. There are generally three calls.

1. *"Side out."* The serving team fails to serve the ball successfully to the other court, fails to make a good return of a volley, or makes a rule violation.

2. *"Point."* The receiving team fails to make a legal return or is guilty of a rule violation.

3. *"Double foul."* Fouls are made by both teams on the same play, in which case the point is replayed. No score or side out results.

Teaching Suggestion: There should be some emphasis on team play. Back court players should be encouraged to pass to front court players rather than merely batting the ball back and forth across the net.

Variation: The receiver in the back court is allowed to catch the serve, toss it, and propel it to a teammate. The catch should be limited to the serve, and the pass must go to a teammate, not over the net. This counteracts the problem of children in the back court being unable to handle the serve to keep the ball in play if the served ball is spinning, curving, or approaching with such force that it is difficult to control.

Three-and-Over Volleyball

Playing Area: Volleyball court
Players: Six on each team
Supplies: A volleyball
Skills: All volleyball skills

The game Three and Over emphasizes the basic offensive strategy of volleyball. The game follows regular volleyball rules with the exception that the ball must be played three times before going over the net. The team loses the serve or the point if the ball is not played three times.

Rotation Volleyball

Playing Area: Volleyball court
Players: Variable

Supplies: A volleyball
Skills: All volleyball skills

If four teams are playing in two contests at the same time, a system of rotation can be set up during any one class period. Divide the available class time roughly into three parts, less the time allotted for logistics. Each team plays the other three teams on a timed basis. At the end of a predetermined time period, whichever team is ahead wins the game. A team may win, lose, or tie during any time period, with the score determined at the end of the respective time period. The best win-loss record wins the overall contest.

Four-Square Volleyball

Playing Area: Volleyball court
Players: Two to four on each team
Supplies: A volleyball
Skills: All volleyball skills

A second net is placed at right angles to the first net, dividing the playing area into four equal courts. The courts are numbered as in Figure 31.9. There are four teams playing, and an extra team can be waiting to rotate to court number 4. The object of the game is to force one of the teams to commit an error. Whenever a team makes an error, it moves down to court 4 or off the courts if a team is waiting. A team errs by not returning the ball to another court within the prescribed three volleys or by causing the ball to go out of bounds.

The ball is always put in play with a serve by a player from team number 1, the serve being made from any point behind the end line of that team. Players must rotate for each serve. The serve is made into court 3 or 4. Play proceeds as in regular volleyball, but the ball may be volleyed into any of the other three courts. No score is kept. The object of the game is for team 1 to retain its position.

Teaching Suggestion: The game seems to work best with five or more teams. With four teams, the

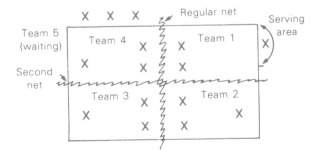

Figure 31.9 Four-square volleyball courts

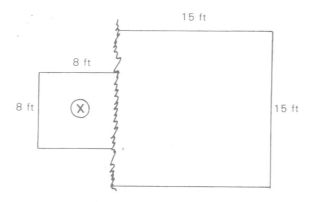

Figure 31.10   Court for Wheelchair Volleyball

team occupying court 4 is not penalized for an error, because it is already in the lowest spot.

Wheelchair Volleyball

Children in wheelchairs can participate successfully in some phases of volleyball. For example, a child confined to a wheelchair can compete against another student on a one-on-one basis when courts are laid out as illustrated in Figure 31.10. The difference in size of the playing areas equalizes the mobility factor. The net should be about 6 feet in height. Serving by the able child is done from behind the back line and by the disabled child with the wheels on the back line. Rules should be adjusted as necessary.

VOLLEYBALL SKILL TESTS

Serving and volleying are the skills to be tested in volleyball. Serving is tested in two ways: (a) with a simple serve and (b) with an accuracy score.

Simplified Serving

In the simplified serving test, the child to be tested stands in normal serving position behind the end line on the right side and is given a specific number of trials in which to serve. The score is the number of successful serves out of ten trials. The serve must clear the net without touching and must land in the opponent's court. A ball touching a boundary line is counted as good.

Serving for Accuracy

To test serving for accuracy, a line is drawn parallel to the net through the middle of one of the courts. Each half is further subdivided into three equal areas by lines drawn parallel to the sidelines. This makes a total of six areas, which correspond to the positions of the members of a volleyball team. The areas are numbered from 1 to 6 (Figure 31.11).

Each child is allowed one attempt to serve the ball into each of the six areas in turn. Two points are scored for serving into the designated court area. One point is scored for missing the designated area but landing in an adjacent area. No points are scored otherwise.

Wall Volleying

For the wall volleying test, the player stands behind a restraining line 4 feet away from a wall. A line, representing the height of the net, is drawn on the wall parallel to the floor and 6.5 feet up. A player is allowed 30 seconds to make as many volleys as possible above the line while staying behind the restraining line. A counter is assigned to each testing station to count the successive volleys. To start, the child makes a short toss to self for the first volley. If time permits, more than one 30-second period can be allowed, with the best count being taken as the score. A mat can mark the restraining line. Stepping on top of the mat makes that volley illegal.

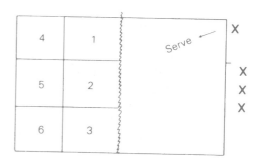

Figure 31.11   Layout of court for service testing

Limited Space Activities and Subject Matter Integration

This chapter is divided into two major parts: The first half deals with limited space activities while the latter part shows how to integrate physical education with other subject matter. Subject matter integration can make an important contribution to learning because some academic concepts and skills are learned best through activity.

The basic premise of physical education is that it demands space and room for activity. At times, however, the need arises to conduct physical education in the classroom because of inclement weather. When the weather is good, little need exists, because more than one class can use playground facilities. Adverse weather, however, creates facility problems when indoor (gymnasium) space is inadequate for a daily program or is nonexistent. The choice is then between conducting physical education in the classroom, with its inherent limitations, or having the children forgo their activity experiences for the day.

Providing an instructional physical education program in the classroom setting involves the careful selection and teaching of appropriate activities in a challenging environment. Children should make progress toward physical fitness and skill development through the classroom presentations. Merely entertaining the students with a variety of classroom games is much less demanding but is not instructional. Games can be part of the offerings but should not be the only emphasis.

LIMITED SPACE ACTIVITY

When an activity area is unavailable, teaching physical education in the classroom becomes necessary. Even though the effectiveness of the program is seriously hampered, it remains important that some physical activity be available to children. It is important that the sessions make a significant contribution to the fitness objective. In addition, sequenced skill presentations should be offered so that children have the opportunity to learn and enhance motor skills.

The Noise Problem

Children must recognize that activity is a privilege and that their cooperation is essential. They need to keep exuberance under control so that their activity does not interfere with other classes. (This can be a significant problem if one classroom is directly above another.) If possible, an entire section of the school should have physical education periods at the same time. When all classes in the same part of the building are playing simultaneously, they will not disturb each other.

Preparing Facilities

When classroom desks and chairs are movable, a variety of activities are possible. Furniture can be pushed together to permit circle activities and rhythmic activities. Chairs and desks can be pushed to one side to form an open space. If mats, balance beams, or benches are to be used, several wider aisles can be made by pushing adjacent rows together. Rotating station groups offers excellent possibilities.

Instruction should be given in how to prepare desks for moving. All personal items must be put away, desktops cleared, and books and other objects stacked underneath in such a way that they will not fall out when the desks are moved. Projecting items that might cause tripping should be placed in safe positions. Windows should be opened and the room temperature lowered. Cleanliness can be a problem and may limit or eliminate activities in which children are on the floor. Individual mats or carpet squares can be a partial solution. Sweeping or vacuuming takes time and is disruptive.

If desks and chairs are fixed, space is more limited. Established aisles should be used, and as much space as possible cleared. Halls have a low priority for use. The noise permeates the entire building, and activity interferes with other students' passing.

Equipment and Supplies

If there is to be an appreciable amount of classroom physical education, a set of equipment and supplies separate from that used in the regular physical education program is needed. Having a supply cart that contains the items most used is an efficient system. The cart can be rolled directly into the classroom and saves sending monitors to a central point to carry items back to the classroom. Equipment carts that contain portable balance beams, light folding mats, balance boards, individual mats, and other equipment are also time-savers.

Each classroom should have a special collection of games, targets, manipulative objects, and other items for indoor play. Many of the items can be constructed by the children. Only supplies that will not damage the classroom should be used. Small sacks stuffed with excelsior, fleece balls, beanbags, yarn balls, rolled-up socks sewn together, balloons, and other articles of this nature can be used with little danger.

Conducting Activities

The teacher must plan judiciously to extract as much activity as possible from the experiences. As many children as possible should engage in activity at one time. Taking turns sometimes may be necessary, but standing around and waiting should be minimized. Safety must be a concern. Children should keep their feet well under their desks to avoid tripping players who are using the aisles.

Classrooms differ relative to the amount of usable space and the movable furniture, making it difficult to present a program that will fit most situations. Circuit training (pp. 300–303) can be adapted for skill teaching. Each station should have a poster giving directions and cues for optimal performance. Another possibility is to combine circuit training with instruction. One-half of the class is assigned to stations while the other half receives directed instruction from the instructor.

FITNESS DEVELOPMENT

Fitness activities can be adapted to classroom work. A fitness corner permanently installed in the classroom can be used to supplement circuit training. This usually consists of a support beam mounted high on a wall or on the ceiling from which a variety of equipment—rings, hoops, trapezes, climbing poles and ladders, and climbing ropes—is hung. Several types are available from commercial sources. Equipment should be compact yet able to accommodate six or more children. Rubber bands made from inner tubes cut into two widths (1- and 2-inch) are useful for resistance exercises. A chart describing different resistance exercises can be posted. Some means of storage must be devised or the articles will be scattered around the classroom.

Aerobic Activities

Many of the fitness activities in Chapter 13 can be adapted for the classroom. For example, aerobic dancing can be performed alongside the youngsters' desks. Continuity drills can be performed by substituting running in place for jump roping. Astronaut drills can be performed up and down the aisles of the classroom. Circuit training can be effective in the classroom if there is enough room around the perimeter to create stations. The circuit could consist entirely of fitness activities or could combine fitness activities and other movement tasks. Fitness should not be eliminated from the program when youngsters have to enter the classroom. A little ingenuity will allow the teacher to assure that fitness continues despite facility limitations.

Isometric Conditioning Exercises for Classroom Use

Isometric exercises are characterized by having virtually no movement of the body part, but a high degree of muscular tension. The muscles undergo a holding contraction of 8 to 12 slow counts. To prevent movement, the pulling, pushing, or twisting action is usually braced against some external force. This can be a desk, chair, wall, door frame, the floor, or a special isometric apparatus. Alternatively, one set of muscles can be worked against another, either individually or with a partner.

In the regular classroom, where narrow confines and furniture limit activity, isometrics have special value because they involve no movement. Many exercises can be done by children seated at their desks, with the desks used as braces.

Maximum or near-maximum tension of the muscle group must be reached and held for approximately 8 seconds. Repetition of an exercise at any one session is not needed, because maximum development is gained from one contraction at an exercise session. Contractions should be performed at different joint angles to ensure strength development throughout the full range of movement.

Isometric exercises are presented in five categories: (a) abdominals, (b) arms, chest, and shoulders, (c) back, (d) legs, and (e) neck. In each case, the arms provide the stabilizing force for the specified development, so in a sense, all of the exercises benefit the arms and shoulders.

Abdominals

1. Sit straight against a backrest. Hold the edges of the chair with the hands. Pull the stomach in hard against the backrest.

2. Sit with hands (palms down, fingers extended) on the lower portion of the top of the thighs. Press down with the hands and up with the legs. (This exercise can also be done by placing the hands on the knees and lifting the straightened legs.)

3. Stand about 4 feet behind a chair. Bend forward at the waist until the hands can be put on the back of the chair. (The elbows are straight.) With a strong downward pull from the abdominal wall and the arms, pull down against the chair.

Arms, Chest, and Shoulders

1. Stand or sit. Clasp the fingers together in front of the chest with forearms held parallel to the floor (elbows out). Pull against the fingers to force the elbows out. Be sure to keep the chest up, the shoulders back, and the head erect.

2. Stand or sit. Using a grip with the palms together and the fingers interlocked (knuckles upward), push the palms together. Be sure the elbows are up and out.

3. Sit. Drop the hands, straight down, to the sides. Curl the fingers under the seat. Pull up with the shoulders, keeping the body erect.

4. Sit. Rest the thumb and near part of the hands on top of the chair seat. Push to raise the seat completely off the chair. Hold.

5. Stand or sit. With the left palm up and the right palm down, clasp the hands in front of the body, chest high. Press down with the right hand, resisting with the left. Reverse.

6. Sit. Grasp two books (with a total thickness of about an inch) in an opposed thumb grip. Squeeze hard with both hands.

7. Sit or stand. Put both hands on top of the head. Slide the hands toward the elbows so that each grasps an elbow. Raise the arms high and

attempt to pull them apart while resisting with the hands on the elbows.

Back

1. Sit, bent forward and grasping the toes. Pull upward with the back while holding the toes.
2. Sit. Slide the hands forward to grasp the knees. From a slightly forward bend, pull back against the knee pressure. This exercise can also be done by placing the hands under the thighs near the knees.
3. Sit. Grasp the right hand under the chair. Apply pressure by leaning to the left. Reverse direction.

Legs

1. Sit with legs outstretched, the right ankle over the left. Press down with the right leg. Reverse position. Bend the knees and repeat right and left.
2. Sit, leaning forward. Cup the right hand around the outside of the left knee and vice versa. Force the knees outward against the inward pressure of the hands.
3. Sit, leaning forward. Place the cupped right hand against the inside of the left knee and vice versa. Force the knees together against the outward arm pressure.

Neck

1. Stand or sit. Clasp the hands behind the back of the head. Keeping the elbows well out, force the head back against the pressure of the hands.
2. Sit or stand. Place both hands flat against the forehead. Move the head forward against the pressure.
3. Sit or stand. Place the heel of the right hand against the head above the ear. Force the head to the right against the arm pressure. Repeat on the left side.

Isometric exercises using wands can be adapted for the classroom (see p. 430). Instead of using a 1-meter wand, consider the lummi stick or a 12-inch section of broom handle.

LESSON FOCUS ACTIVITIES

Rhythmics

Rhythmics are easily adapted to classroom activity, particularly when circle space can be arranged by moving the furniture to the center of the room.

Rhythmic activities done in place are ideal, because children can be scattered in the available space. Selections featuring identification of body parts and individual movement are excellent for younger children. Lummi stick rhythms should be considered. If enough pathways in and around the furnishings can be arranged, fundamental movements guided by a drum or recorded music provide controlled activity. Chapter 16, on rhythmic activities, contains additional ideas.

Manipulative Activities

Selected manipulative activities can be used in the classroom. The major restriction is that many of the throwing, catching, kicking, rebounding, and batting activities do not suit the classroom situation.

Prevention of facility damage is an overriding factor. Manipulative articles that cannot damage the facilities—balloons, yarn balls, paper balls, beanbags, and 8½-inch foam rubber balls—are preferable. Target games in which the article is tossed or rolled at a target are recommended.

Balloons, particularly for younger children, provide excellent challenges. A group of five or six children can be assigned two balloons. They try to keep the balloons aloft for a stipulated time period, while remaining glued to their chairs or the floor. A balloon that touches the floor is out of play.

Individual activities in which a child handles an object are implemented easily. Children can balance beanbags on various body parts or toss and handle beanbags individually in a controlled situation. Juggling with scarves or small juggling balls is within the scope of classroom activities.

Depending on room size, a small (12-to-16-foot) parachute might be used. Wands for isometric exercises and ropes placed on the floor can stimulate a wide range of activity.

Stunts and Tumbling

If there is room for six mats, a full-fledged tumbling program is feasible. With room for only one or two mats, tumbling is best used as a station teaching circuit. Individual stunt activities that demand little movement, especially in-place balance stunts, are examples of suitable activity.

Apparatus Activities

The apparatus available in the fitness corner can be used in an apparatus program. The difficulty of moving apparatus to the classroom, setting it up, and returning it is a serious limitation. Low, portable balance beams have value because these can be set up in aisles. A workable idea is to have apparatus set up at one or two stations. Balance boards, bounding boards, bongo boards, jumping boxes, and magic ropes are possible apparatus items for the stations.

Movement Experiences

Movement experiences in which children remain in personal space, either seated or standing, can take a number of directions. For younger children, reinforcing the concept of laterality is excellent activity. Commands that stimulate laterality are as follows:

"Point to the right, to the left, in front of you, behind you."

"Can you point your thumbs up, down, toward each other, away from each other? In the same direction to the right, to the left?"

"Put your arms out wide, forward, up high, down low."

"Turn your toes in, out. To the right, left."

"See if you can bend down, bend backward, to the right, to the left."

Identifying different body parts by touching provides similar experiences. Children can be asked to touch various body parts with the right hand, the left hand, and with both hands. Mirroring the movements of the teacher aids in visual recognition. The teacher makes various movements with the arms, and children mirror the movements. Later, they can try to copy the movements instead of mirroring them.

The Haida War Canoe Paddle is an interesting activity. (The Haidas were Indians who lived along the coast of British Columbia and traveled great distances in large canoes.) Each child uses a ruler as a paddle. The youngster at the head of the row is the bow paddler. All keep time with the bow paddler on the same side of the row. When the bow paddler shifts to the other side, all paddlers follow suit.

Other ideas, such as the following, can generate creative activity. Children can pretend to reel in a fish, catch fireflies, pound a hammer, pump up a tire, and so on. Poems also can elicit movement, particularly poems with specific movement commands. Two examples are provided. The first one starts with the children seated.

Two Little Hands

Two little hands go clap, clap, clap.
Two little feet go tap, tap, tap.

Two little knuckles go rap, rap, rap.
A quick jump from the chair,
Two little arms high in the air,
Two little fists grasp the hair.
Two little feet go jump, jump, jump.
Two little fists go thump, thump, thump.
Two little arms go pump, pump, pump.
One little body turns round and round,
One makes a face just like a clown,
One little body sits quietly down.

Exercise Time

I put my hands up high,
I put them way down low.
I put them way out wide,
And turn them up just so.
I jump with two feet fast,
I jump with two feet slow.
I turn round and round like a top,
Then I hold my head just so.
I move my hands like wings,
And then I try to swim.
I quickly sit way down
And look around with a grin.

GAMES AND RELAYS

Games and relays selected for this section focus on activity for all children. Relays should be revolving in nature, where all team members are active throughout the activity.

Target Games

Target games can serve as one station in circuit training. They are high-interest activities and can offer challenge and variety to a fitness circuit.

Basketball Bounce

Formation: Individual or by teams

Players: Two to six for each basket

Supplies: A basketball, volleyball, or other rubber ball; a wastepaper basket

Each player in turn stands behind a line that is 5 to 10 feet from a wastepaper basket. Five chances are allowed to bounce the ball on the floor and into the basket. Five points are scored for each successful basket.

Beanbag Pitch

Formation: File—by rows

Players: Two to six for each target

Supplies: Beanbags, a small box for each team

A target box is placed at the head of each row. A pitch line is drawn 10 to 15 feet in front of the target. From behind the line, each player takes a specified number of pitches at the box. Scores are recorded for each player, and the team with the highest score wins. Many other targets are possible. The children can design them.

Bowling

Formation: File—by rows

Players: Two to six for each target

Supplies: A bowling pin or pins; balls for rolling

Many bowling games are possible in the classroom, with the aisles used as the alleys. Various kinds of balls can be rolled. The target can be a single pin or a group of pins, and competition can be between individuals in a row or between rows. Children can design their own bowling games.

Chair Quoits

Formation: File

Players: Two to six for each target

Supplies: A chair for each group; five deck tennis rings or rope rings

A line is established about 10 feet from a chair turned over so that the legs point toward the thrower. Each player throws the five rings. A ringer on the back legs scores 10 points, and one on the front legs scores 5 points. Score should be kept for several rounds.

Variation: Fruit jar rings can be used with the chair or with other targets. Special peg targets can be constructed (see p. 765).

Tic-Tac-Toe

Formation: None

Players: Two to four for each target

Supplies: A tic-tac-toe target board, six beanbags or yarn balls of one color and six of another

The tic-tac-toe target is constructed from 1-by-4-inch boards standing on end to make a throwing target a little less than 4 inches deep, with each of nine squares separated by a 1-inch wide

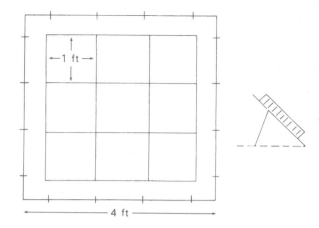

Figure 32.1 Tic-tac-toe target

border. The spaces themselves are 1 foot square. The target is mounted on a 4-by-4-foot piece of sturdy plywood. A prop should be placed behind the board so that it is tilted at about a 45-degree angle (Figure 32.1).

The object of the game is to get three squares covered in a line in any direction. Only one beanbag is permitted in a square. If a second beanbag lands inside a square, it is removed. The game can be played one against one or partners against partners. Alternate sides toss at the target.

Games with Limited Movement

Animals Move

Formation: Standing in the aisles between desks or scattered

Players: Entire class

Supplies: None

The player who is it stands at the front of the room and calls out the name of a mammal, bird, fish, or reptile, and a movement. For instance, the leader might call out, "Horses fly. Birds crawl. Salmon swim." When the leader states a correct relationship, the class must move accordingly. In the latter case, they would make a swimming movement. When an incorrect relationship is given, the children should not move. Those who move at the wrong time can sit down and wait until a new leader is selected. Games should be kept short so that all children have a chance to lead and no one has to sit out too long.

Teaching Suggestion: As the children become skilled at the game, the teacher should stress quality movement. The children can be encouraged to improve their hopping, flying, or jumping.

Bicycle Race

Formation: Rows

Players: Half the class

Supplies: Desks

The children stand in the aisle between two rows of desks. Alternate rows perform at a time. Children place one hand on their own desk and one on the desk next to them. On the signal "Go," the children, supported by their hands, imitate a bicycling motion with their legs. The child who rides the longest without touching the floor with the feet is the winner for the row. Winners can compete later for bicycle riding champion of the room.

Do This, Do That

Formation: Scattered

Players: Entire class

Supplies: None

One child is the leader and performs various movements, accompanied by commands of "Do this" or "Do that." All players execute the movements accompanied by "Do this." If the directions are "Do that," no one is to move. Those who move at the wrong time are eliminated and sit down in place. The game continues until some of the children have been eliminated. The game is then re-formed with another leader, who is selected from the children who were not caught.

Imitation

Formation: Scattered

Players: Entire class

Supplies: Record player, records

A leader stands in front of the class and performs for a musical phrase (eight counts) with any desired movement. For the next eight counts, the children imitate the same movements in the same sequence. The leader sets another round of movements, and the children again imitate. After a time, the leader selects another child to be the new leader.

O'Grady Says

Formation: Scattered

Players: Entire class

Supplies: None

A leader stands in front and calls out various military commands, such as "Right face," "Left face," "About face," "Attention," and "At ease."

The players are to follow only when the command is preceded by the words *O'Grady says.* Anyone moving at the wrong time is eliminated and must sit down. Additional commands involving other movements can be used. To be effective, the commands must be given rapidly.

Put Hands

Formation: Scattered—standing or seated

Players: Entire class

Supplies: None

One child is the leader and stands in front of the class. The leader gives certain directions verbally and then tries to confuse the class by doing something else. He might say, "Put your hands on top of your head" and put his own hands on top of his shoulders. Those who follow his actions instead of his words have a point scored against them. Possible directions are the following.

"Put your hands on your shoulders [toes, knees, head, chest]."

"Reach out to the side [to the front, to the back, up high]."

"Put your right [left] hand on your shoulder [behind your back]."

After a short time, the leader should be changed.

Variation: Other movements can be introduced, such as "Right hand point west," "Left hand forward, right hand to the sky," and "Head right, jump left."

Shuffle Foot

Formation: Scattered—by pairs

Players: Two

Supplies: None

One person is the "same"; the other is the "different." The two children stand facing each other about 3 feet apart. They clap three times, and on the third clap each puts a foot forward. If the feet are the same (right, right; left, left), the student designated the same wins. If the feet are different, the other child wins. The game goes on to a set number of points.

Simon Says

Formation: Scattered—standing or seated

Players: Entire class

Supplies: None

One player is selected to be Simon and stands in front of the class. Simon gives a variety of commands, such as "Stand up," "Clap your hands," "Turn around," and others, and may or may not precede a command with the words *Simon says*. No one is to move unless the command is preceded by these words. Those who move at the wrong time are eliminated and must sit out the game. The leader gives commands rapidly, changing to different movements. Simon tries to confuse the class by doing all of the movements.

Snap

Formation: Seated in a circle

Players: 10 to 15

Supplies: None

The game involves a three-count rhythm. The children must practice the rhythm well before the game can be successful. On count 1, the children slap their knees; on count 2, they clap their hands; and on count 3, they snap their fingers.

Each child in the circle has a number. The leader calls a number on the third count. The player whose number was called then calls another number when snapping the fingers. The object of the game is to maintain a precise rhythm, calling the numbers back and forth across the circle.

The following are errors.

1. Breaking the rhythm
2. Not calling another number after yours has been called
3. Calling when your number has not been called
4. Calling the number of a player who has been eliminated

Sticky Hands

Formation: Small circle

Players: 6 to 12

Supplies: None

Children stand close together in a circle. They extend their hands, which are "sticky like glue." A child who grasps a hand cannot let go. The children reach into the mass of hands and across the circle to find two hands (belonging to different people), which they grasp. The grips must not be released. By stepping over and around, twisting under and through, the group tries to unscramble itself.

Who's Leading?

Formation: Circle—either sitting at desks or on the floor

Players: Entire class

Supplies: None

One child is it and steps away from the circle and covers the eyes. The teacher points to a child in the circle, who becomes the leader. The leader starts any desired motion with the hands, the feet, or any other body part. All of the children follow the movements. The child who is it uncovers her eyes and watches the group, as they change from one motion to another, to try to determine who is leading. Players should cover up for the leader, who also tries to confuse the guesser by looking at other players. The child who is it gets three guesses. If not successful, she chooses another child to be it. If she does guess correctly, she gets another turn, but a limit of three turns should be imposed.

Teaching Suggestion: The game seems to work best when the guesser is positioned in the center of the circle, because she cannot then observe all of the children at once. The children can also be standing, but this gets tiring.

Games with Locomotor Movement

Around the Row

Formation: Rows

Players: As many as are in a row

Supplies: None

The game is played by rows, with an extra player for each row. On the command "March," children walk around the row. On signal, they stop marching and attempt to get a seat. One player is left out. The game continues to the next row, using the player left out as the extra. Walking only (no running) is permitted. Roughness should not be tolerated.

Balloon Football

Formation: Two lines facing each other 4 to 6 feet apart

Players: Entire class

Supplies: Balloon or light beach ball

The class is divided into two teams. Players sit in their chairs and keep one hand on the back of the chair throughout the game. The balloon or beach ball is tossed between the two teams. Both teams try to bat it over the heads of their opponents so that the ball touches the floor behind the opposing team. Each touchdown scores a point. A student should be placed behind each team to serve as scorekeeper and ball retriever. The balloon should be put into play at different places along the two lines to prevent action from being concentrated among a few players.

Balloon Volleyball

Formation: Standing, sitting on the floor, or seated at desks

Players: Entire class

Supplies: Two balloons and a rope

Children are positioned on both sides of a rope stretched just above their reach. They try to bat a balloon back and forth across the rope. The balloon can be batted as often as necessary. Two balloons used at once provide good action. A system of rotation should be set up, so that all players have a chance to occupy a position near the rope. Scoring is accomplished when one side fails to control a balloon and allows it to touch the floor or a wall.

Variation: A small marble or button placed inside the balloon causes it to take an erratic path, which adds interest to the game.

Classroom Mousetrap

Formation: Circle

Players: Entire class

Supplies: None

Several pairs of children form arches around the circle. The arches remain up until the teacher says "Snap"; then they are brought down. The other children (the mice) scurry through the arches and try to avoid being caught. Anyone caught forms additional arches.

Colors

Formation: Scattered—standing or seated

Players: Entire class

Supplies: A set of flash cards of different colors

The teacher flashes a color card. All children touch five different objects of that color and return to position. There is no scoring, just activity.

Variation: Shapes can be the focus. The teacher holds up a shape (triangle, circle, square), and the children seek five articles of that same shape to touch.

Hide the Beanbag

Formation: Scattered

Players: 15 to 20

Supplies: A small beanbag

One child, the searcher, stands to the side with eyes covered. The other children sit cross-legged. One child is given the beanbag and must hide it by sitting on it.

The searcher moves among the children, trying to locate the beanbag, as the children clap softly. They clap louder when the searcher nears the child with the beanbag. The searcher tries to identify the one with the beanbag. If the guess is correct, another child is selected to be the searcher. If the identification fails, the searcher tries again (up to three guesses), and then another child becomes the searcher.

Teaching Suggestion: The teacher should choose the child to hide the beanbag. This is an opportunity to involve shy or less popular children in the game.

Hunter, Gun, Rabbit

Formation: Two lines facing each other

Players: Entire class

Supplies: None

The children are divided into two teams, which line up facing each other. They can sit or stand. Each team has a captain. The teams decide privately on one of the following three imitations.

1. *Hunter*—bring the hands up to the eyes and pretend to be looking through binoculars.
2. *Gun*—bring the hands and arms up to a shooting position and pretend to shoot.
3. *Rabbit*—put the hands in back of the head with fingers pointed up, and move the fingers back and forth like moving rabbit ears.

A signal is given, and each team pantomimes its choice. In scoring, the following priorities hold.

1. If one side is the hunter and the other the gun, the hunter wins because the hunter shoots the gun.
2. If one team selects the gun and the other imitates a rabbit, the gun wins because the gun can overcome the rabbit.
3. If one side is the rabbit and the other the hunter, the rabbit wins because it can outrun the hunter.

4. If both teams have the same selection, no point is scored.

The first team to score 10 points wins.

Teaching Suggestion: The teacher should keep the game moving. One way to do this is to have the child on the right of each line go down the line and whisper the choice to the team members. The child then stands on the left, and a new child is at the right of each line, ready to select the next imitation.

Orienteering

Formation: Standing

Players: Entire class

Supplies: Chart of a compass face (optional)

Students stand to the right of their desks. Either the teacher or a chosen student stands facing the class. This person calls out various directions: north, southwest, and so on. The rest of the class must quickly face in the proper direction. When students turn in the wrong direction, they can either sit down or have a point scored against them.

Variations:

1. To introduce children to a compass and to simple orienteering skills, a chart with the face and directional needle of a compass can be used. The leader turns away from the class, places the needle in a certain direction, and then shows the compass to the class. The class responds by turning toward the proper direction.

2. Regular orienteering can be done on a modified basis by setting up a course with the path to be followed described in terms of numbers of steps in a given compass direction. Inside some buildings, however, compasses are not accurate.

Ten, Ten, Double Ten

Formation: None

Players: Entire class

Supplies: A small object

All of the children except one leave the classroom. The child left in the room places the object in a spot that is visible but not too easily found. The children return to the room. As soon as a child sees the object, he pretends to search for another moment, so that he does not give away the position. He then calls out, "Ten, 10, double 10, 45, 15, buckskin 6," and sits down. The other children

continue to search. The child who found the object first gets to place it for the next game.

Who Am I?

Formation: Small circle or scattered

Players: 8 to 16

Supplies: None

The children recite this verse in unison:

This morning as I walked down the street
Whom do you think I chanced to meet?

One child is the demonstrator and proceeds to pantomime an action (e.g., firefighter, police officer, banker, baseball player). The children try to guess what the action represents. A successful guesser becomes the new demonstrator. If no one guesses, the present demonstrator gets another turn, after which another child takes over.

Zoo

Formation: Seated

Players: Entire class

Supplies: None

Children are in their regular seats. Seven children are chosen to stand in front of the class, and one of them is selected as the leader. The leader directs each of the other six children to choose a favorite animal and then places them in a line, saying the animal name as she does so.

On signal, the six children, performing in the order in which they were just announced by the leader, imitate the animal that they have chosen. (Ten to 15 seconds should be allowed for this.) On a second signal, the rest of the children stand, wave their arms, and jump or hop in place (turning around if they wish). They then sit down, close their eyes, cover them with their hands, and put their head down on the desk.

The leader then arranges the six animals in a different order. When this has been done, the seated children raise their heads. Another signal is given, and the animals perform once again for a short period. Once this has been accomplished, any seated child can volunteer to place the six children in their original positions, naming the animal in each case. If the child succeeds in placing the animals in their original standing position and in calling them by their chosen animal name, he becomes an animal in the zoo and chooses a name for himself. The child then takes his place among the animals, and the game continues until 12 children (or some other designated number) are in the zoo. Other categories, such as flowers, Mother Goose characters, play characters, and so on, can be used.

Relays

Relays can be used occasionally in the classroom program. Most of the appropriate relays involve object handling or a task. Few classrooms have sufficient space for a variety of relays. Some relays can use the regular seating arrangement, but others may require special formations. Relays using the blackboard for spelling, word formation, and arithmetic can be of value, but not as scheduled physical education activities.

Flag Chase

Formation: Hollow square—seated in chairs

Players: Entire class

Supplies: Four flags (or beanbags), chairs for all competitors, a marker centered 3 feet in front of each team

The class is divided into four even teams, facing center and seated on the sides of the square, with a marker in front of each team. The player on the left end of her team has a flag. On signal, this player runs to the marker, goes around it from the right (counterclockwise), and then runs to the seat on the right of the team. In the meantime, all players have moved one place to the left, vacating the right seat. The runner sits in the vacant chair, and the flag is passed down the line to the left. The player now in the leftmost seat becomes the new runner and runs the same course as the previous runner. The race ends when the flag has been returned to the lead-off runner in the original position in the left seat.

Variations:

1. An under-the-leg pass can be used, with the stipulation that the flag must go under all legs during transit.
2. The run around the marker can be omitted, with the runner going directly from the left to the right seat.

Overhead Relay

Formation: File—by rows

Players: Entire class

Supplies: A beanbag, eraser, or similar object for each team

Each row forms a team. The first person in each row has in front of her the object that is to be passed to the desk behind. At the signal to pass, this child claps her hands, picks up the object, and passes it overhead to the child behind. The next child places the object on his desk, claps the hands, and then passes the object overhead. When the last child in the row receives the object, she runs forward to the head of the row, using the aisle to the right. After she has passed by, each child, using the same aisle, moves back one seat. The child who has come to the front then sits down in the first seat, places the object on the desk, claps the hands, and passes the object overhead. This continues until the children are back in their original seats and the object is on the front desk. The first row finished wins.

SUBJECT MATTER INTEGRATION

Some evidence supports the theory that selected academic skills and concepts can be better learned through activity. Whether this premise is accepted or not, there is little doubt that learning to apply academic concepts in a different setting is an important practice. Physical education offers many opportunities for integrating subject matter and activity. Integrating physical education activities with other subject matter areas is limited only by the ingenuity of the teacher and the interests of youngsters. Classroom teachers play an important role in this process and can supplement efforts of the physical education specialist. Integrating physical education experiences with other areas of the curriculum not only demonstrates to children that the teacher values the program but also makes physical activity more meaningful to them. The following discussion examines various subject matter areas and gives specific ideas for enhancing academic skills and concepts through physical activity.

Art

Posters, decorations, and costumes bring together art and physical education. Some ideas for integrating art and physical education follow:

1. Illustrate features of various games, such as ball toss targets, shuffleboard courts, and hopscotch, and four-square playing areas.
2. Make bulletin boards and other displays for classroom, halls, and gymnasiums. Some themes might be proper diet, activity and physical fitness, examples of great athletes at work, lifetime sports and leisure activity, and basic skills needed for specific sports.

3. Select a skill (such as throwing) and illustrate the various phases of a successful throw. Illustrate and analyze the rules of opposition, proper arm position, body rotation, and the follow-through.

4. Watch another class participating in a sport and create some action figures that capture the flavor of the sport. Analyze basic movements in various sports and games for their similarities and differences.

5. Develop costumes for a mock Olympiad. Study insignias of various countries and place them on the uniforms.

6. Carry out a contest to develop a school insignia and slogan. Posters could be painted and entered in the competition. The winning insignia could be silk-screened onto T-shirts for school teams.

7. Design charts of athletic fields or game areas, and illustrate where players should be placed for various game strategies.

8. Draw athletic fields and game areas to scale. Visit a ball park and attempt to draw the entire facility to scale, including bleachers, dugouts, dressing rooms, and showers.

9. Make programs for upcoming pageants, gymkhanas, and physical education demonstrations. The programs could be illustrated or contain a map of the school's location. Provide a description of the evening's program.

10. Posters of encouragement could be painted and put up to show support for intramural teams, classroom competitions, and after-school sports programs.

11. Make progress charts for activities such as jogging, push-ups, and curl-ups. High achievers could be given an award for achievement, and other students could be rewarded for participating. Students could design and paint these awards.

12. Study sculpture, paintings, and other art forms that illustrate early physical activities. Greek friezes and Egyptian art are excellent sources for the study of sport, dance, and gymnastics.

13. Design a playground that is both artistic and functional. Discuss how the artistic design and function must be integrated for a successful playspace.

Geography

Because the origins of physical education materials are diverse, geographical associations provide the classroom teacher with another source of learning experiences. It is possible to find clues about the play and sports habits of people in their location, terrain, and other geographical factors. Some areas of study could be the following:

1. Study the climate in different areas of the United States to ascertain how climate affects play habits. Factors such as altitude and weather could be studied.

2. Play and study games of different countries. Cultural factors such as dress, folklore, mores, and industries might be related to the games in which people participate.

3. During a rhythmic unit in which folk dances are being taught, discuss the origin of the dance and the characteristics of the country and its people. Make costumes to make the dances more authentic.

4. Have students from other countries visit the class to explain their play habits and games.

5. Study the Olympics to see which countries dominate certain sports in the competition. This would give a clue to the emphasis certain countries place on various sports and might be traced to the type of physical education found in the schools.

6. Study geographical and climatic factors of various areas to see how they affect athletic performance. For instance, discuss how altitude at the Mexico Olympic Games in 1968 seriously affected long-distance runners but aided long jumpers.

7. Language barriers during international competition often cause problems for officials and referees. Discuss attempts to remedy this problem.

Health, Safety, and Wellness

It is difficult to separate health, safety, and wellness from physical education. Physical education should be carried on in a healthful and safe atmosphere. Many opportunities for cooperative teaching of related concepts arise between classroom teachers and various subject matter specialists. Safety considerations for each activity are important in the planning. Many more ideas can be found for integrating the area of wellness in Chapter 11.

1. Discuss physical fitness concepts. The basic steps in developing physical fitness and their relationship to the general health of the individual should be clearly understood.

2. Consider the importance of exercise in promoting physical and mental wellness. Carry out research to see what specific effects exercise has on the human body and mind. The effects of drugs, tobacco, and alcohol should be explored and discussed as a function of human wellness.

3. Declare a safety week for the school. Students could develop a list of safety standards for the school and make posters that illustrate proper safety techniques.

4. Relate activities and skills learned in physical education to leisure and recreation. Students should realize the value of learning skills at an early age so that they will be able to use the skills in lifetime activity.

5. When physical examinations are given to classes, discuss the reasons for periodic examinations. Cover congenital as well as acquired defects, conditions caused by disease, and the problems of contagious disease.

6. Discuss the value of exercise in promoting healing and improving certain conditions. Students with asthma, if their situation is faced openly, can learn to gauge how much activity they can handle. If a child's limb is broken, discuss the problem of muscle atrophy to demonstrate the need for exercise and use of muscles.

7. Conduct a posture checkup day. Discuss the mechanics of posture, with emphasis on methods of improving posture among the class.

8. Analyze nutrition, rest, and body care to see the role they play in daily living and maintaining a healthy body.

9. Take a period to inspect equipment and facilities for safety. After the inspection, discuss existing conditions and new standards.

10. Develop simple experiments to show the immediate effects of exercise on the body. Try measuring pulse rate or breathing rate before and after exercise. Or, collect air exhaled at rest and after exercise in plastic bags. Consider reasons for the body adaptations demonstrated.

11. Explore the crucial balance between caloric intake and exercise. Children must understand that obesity is controlled through a combination of proper diet and adequate exercise.

12. Plan a daily and weekly schedule for work, rest, and play, and then compare the plan with recommended time allotments and with other students' schedules.

13. Prepare a unit on first aid to gain a basic understanding of proper procedures for treating injury.

14. Do a class project dealing with various physical and mental handicaps. This can foster a sensitivity to youngsters possessing handicaps in a physical education setting.

History

Physical education is rich in historical background. Many present-day activities are based in tradition. The historical aspects of physical education should be developed. An appreciation of physical education could be furthered if children understood the background of an activity.

1. Study the origin of various activities. Events such as the discus throw, the shot put, and the pole vault are performed now only because of tradition.

2. Explore the origin and adaptation of present-day sports such as baseball, basketball, and American football. Analyze the relationship between rule changes and the higher athletic achievements of modern athletes.

3. The history and development of sports equipment and facilities are often interesting and revealing to students. For example, compare the Roman Colosseum with present-day stadiums, or compare levels of performance with different types of poles used for vaulting.

4. Study a particular sport to bring out the records and achievements of outstanding players. Examples of questions to guide discussion might be the following: Who were big names and pioneers in sports? Who were the outstanding individuals who set records, and what were these records? What individuals achieved outstanding performances on an international level, including the Olympic performances? A sports quiz could be made up to include items from each of the categories. Be sure to include achievements of women and men.

5. Study the ethnic background, historical context, and meaning of dances to make them more interesting.

6. Compare the fitness of different peoples. The ancient Greek, Persian, and Roman civilizations placed much emphasis on fitness, as do modern-day countries.

7. Study the fascinating history of the Olympics. The evolution from the ancient games to the

present-day Olympics offers many insights into the values of different societies.

8. Study medieval knights and their jousting tournaments.

Language Arts

Physical education materials make useful subjects for written and oral expression. The world of sports and games provides many examples of outstanding individuals who can serve as topics for presentations. Additional suggestions follow:

1. To increase motivation for reading, make use of game descriptions, rules of various sports, autobiographies of sports heroes, newspaper reports of game scores, and books oriented toward improvement in a given sport.

2. Use writing activities such as the following. Write a summary of a game program your school has conducted. Go to an intramural contest and report the results for the school newspaper. Find out as much as possible about your sports hero, and write a short story about that individual.

3. Practice oral expression by giving demonstrations and describing various points of performance, explaining rules of various activities to other students, reporting the results of a school contest to students who were unable to attend, or working in small groups to evaluate each other's performances.

4. To add some interest to spelling, learn words that will occur in the coming physical education lesson. A few different sports terms could be added to the weekly spelling list, and a spelling bee using only terms and words found in sports and physical education could be conducted.

5. Try writing plays about famous sports heroes, about the origin and development of games, or about imaginary athletes. Pantomime various sports and games activities, and let other members of the class attempt to guess the activity being pantomimed.

6. Study the origin of terminology used in physical education. Words such as *gymnasium, calisthenics,* and *exercise* have special origins.

7. When playdays or demonstrations are to be organized, have the class write the script to be used by the announcers. Cover the basics of public speaking and the use of the public address system.

8. Dramatize stories about athletes, important people in the history of sports, and famous referees and officials. Work in small groups and then give presentations to the rest of the class.

9. Conduct choral readings of well-known poems about sports, such as "Casey at the Bat."

10. Listen to short story or poem and then act it out.

11. Write about physical activity done outside of school. To stimulate writing, have students write about their favorite activity, how they learned to swim, and so on.

Music

Rhythm is an integral part of physical education, and much of the program features both music and rhythm. Musical training should not be isolated from physical education. The two areas overlap and should blend in the children's experiences. Ideas for combining musical and physical education include the following:

1. Learn the characteristics of music and rhythm and interpret the rhythm through movement.

2. When action songs are presented, divide the learning of the song and the movement patterns between the music teacher and the physical education teacher.

3. To understand more about music, learn the names of different musical selections and become familiar with the heritage of music.

4. Create rope-jumping and ball-bouncing routines to a selected piece of music.

5. Do exercises to music to understand the different tempos found in music as well as learning to move to the tempo.

6. Use the tom-tom often in introductory activities. Learn the fundamental locomotor movements and do them to the beat of the drum.

7. In an activity such as European Rhythmic Running (p. 252), make your own rhythm by chanting, clapping the hands, and stamping the feet.

8. Make tapes for exercise to music.

Number Concepts (Mathematics)

Number concepts can be strengthened through physical education. Practical applications of the processes of addition, subtraction, division, multiplication, percentage computation, and measurement can be demonstrated through selected procedures. The following ideas can enhance numerical concepts:

1. Measure your own and other students' performances. Learn to read a tape measure and a stopwatch to evaluate performances in terms of distance, time, and height.

2. After a self-test or standardized fitness test, work out the class averages.

3. Learn percentages by working out batting averages, team standings, and field goal accuracy. This is an especially good task for the student who cannot participate because of an injury or illness.

4. For a study of geometric principles, analyze the layout of fields and game areas. Rectangles, diamonds, and circles are used often as playing areas.

5. To understand the metric system better, compare European and American performances. Measurements at a track meet might be made with the metric system.

6. Enhance basic arithmetic skills by using equations instead of numbers as signals in games. For example, instead of calling out "Eight," say, "Thirty-six divided by three minus four."

7. Play number hopscotch to develop number recognition and memory. A large square containing 16 to 25 smaller squares is drawn on the playground and a number is placed in each of the smaller squares. A leader calls out a sequence of numbers and a player hops into each of the squares containing the numbers called.

8. Measure and lay out a playing field. Laying out a track and areas for field events could be a class project.

Projects

Class projects in physical education and related areas form excellent educational opportunities. The teacher and children should plan together. Many ideas can be found for these projects. Playdays are an excellent one. A playday could be organized with one or more classes in the same school, with a class in another school, or among the children of the class itself. Demonstrations and exhibitions for parents are fruitful projects. A convocation program or demonstration in the gymnasium before other children merits consideration.

A foreign country day can be planned, involving all specialists and teachers in the school. The physical education specialist could be responsible for preparing a show of games played in a certain country, the art teacher might assist in the preparation of native costumes, and the music teacher could teach a class to sing songs unique to the country. It might also be possible to cook a lunch that resembles food eaten in the selected country, and the foreign language teacher might help prepare a short play or skit in a foreign language.

Another suggestion is to invite another class to a rhythmic party. The program can be planned, invitations written, committees formed, and all the necessary details arranged. The enterprising teacher will think of many other project ideas. Projects could be done each season or once a year.

Facilities, Equipment, and Supplies

*T*he facilities for physical education can be classified in two categories: outdoor and indoor. Climatic conditions should determine which type of facility is more important for the school. Usually, outdoor space provides enough room for several classes to work simultaneously. Where weather conditions require frequent use of indoor space, a minimum of one indoor teaching station for every eight classrooms is needed. In addition, to meet the needs of disabled youngsters (as required by Public Law 94-142), another indoor play area, separate from but close to the regular indoor facility, is needed.

Physical education facilities should be planned in terms of maximum projected enrollment. Too often, planning is done in terms of the present situation. Later, when classrooms are added to the school, they are added without change in the physical education areas. What was previously an adequate arrangement now becomes a scheduling problem. Adding physical education facilities is difficult because of generally escalating costs and the relatively high cost of physical education facilities in comparison with the cost of adding regular classroom space.

OUTDOOR FACILITIES

The standards for outdoor play areas call for a minimum of 10 acres for the school, with an additional acre for each 100 pupils in the maximum projected enrollment. Parking areas, cycle racks, and entry roads are in addition to these standards. The outdoor areas should include field space for games, a track, hard-surfaced areas, apparatus areas, play courts, age-group-specific play areas, covered play space, and a jogging trail.

Fields should be leveled, drained, and turfed, because grass is the most usable field surface. An automatic sprinkler system is desirable, but the sprinkler heads must not protrude to become safety hazards. Automatic installations permit sprinkling during the evening and night, so that the fields are not too soggy for play the next day.

A hard-top area should be marked for a variety of games, such as tetherball, volleyball, and basketball courts. Four-square courts, hopscotch layouts, and circles for games are examples of other markings that can be put on these surfaces. Simple movement pattern courses can also be marked.

Some administrators prefer a hard surface for the entire play area, because this eliminates the mud problem and the need for sprinkling, and in general lowers maintenance costs. Hard surfaces usually are used when play space is limited and when the number of students makes keeping a good turf surface difficult.

An official track (440 yards or 400 meters) may be installed when the interest in track and field is high. As a minimum, space should be provided for a smaller track (220 yards or 200 meters), and it should be placed in an area where it will not interfere with other activities. For schools where a permanent installation is not practical, a temporary track can be laid out each spring (see p. 711).

Separate play spaces for different age groups should be included in the planning. Such areas should contain apparatus designed for each age group. The play area for primary-level children should be well away from areas where footballs and softballs are used.

Small, hard-surfaced play courts can be located strategically near the edges of the outdoor area, thus spreading out the play groups. These courts, approximately 40 by 60 feet, can be equipped for basketball or volleyball or for both. A covered shed can be divided for use by different age groups. Climatic conditions would dictate the need for such facilities.

A jogging trail can stimulate interest in jogging. Small signs indicating the distances covered and markers outlining the trail are all that are needed. Stations with exercise tasks can be placed at intervals. For example, a station could have directions to accomplish a specified number of Pull-Ups or to do a Flexed-Arm Hang for a specified number of seconds. Such a circuit is popularly called a *parcourse*.

An area set aside as a developmental playground is an important part of the total play space. The area should contain equipment and apparatus and should be landscaped to have small hills, valleys, and tunnels for children. A recommended approach is to divide the playground into various developmental areas so that children must use different body parts in different areas of the play space. For example, one area might contain a great deal of climbing equipment to reinforce arm-shoulder girdle development, and another area might challenge the leg and trunk regions. Equipment and apparatus should be abstract in nature; creation and imagination are left to the children. Apparatus can be manipulated and changed to suit the needs and desires of the youngsters.

SAFETY ON THE PLAYGROUND

Physical education teachers should assume the responsibility for proper and safe use of various pieces of apparatus on the playground. Rules for conduct should be posted on a bulletin board in the activity area. Playground supervisors should understand the rules and enforce them.

Studies by the U.S. Consumer Product Safety Commission (1986a, b) show that the majority of injuries (60 to 70%) are caused when children fall from apparatus and strike the underlying surface. The type of surface under equipment is a major factor affecting the severity of injuries associated with falls from apparatus. Injuries range from minor bruises to skull fractures, concussions, brain damage, and death. Falls onto paved surfaces resulted in a disproportionately high number of severe injuries.

Slides offer a high potential for accidents. The greatest number of injuries occur from falls over the side, from the platform, and from the ladder. Roughhousing, improper usage, and slipping are the most prominent causes of accidents. Rules should be established so that only one person is on the platform, with the next user waiting at the base of the ladder.

Concrete, asphalt, and other paved surfaces placed under apparatus require little or no maintenance, which is often the basis for their use. However, hard surfaces do not provide injury protection from accidental fall impacts and therefore are unsuitable for use. Organic materials such as pine bark nuggets, pine bark mulch, shredded hardwood bark, and cocoa shell mulch are suggested. Other materials are wood chips, shredded tires, and sand. If hard surfaces are already in place, outdoor interlocking tiles or dense synthetic turf may be placed over the existing base.

If loose, organic materials are used, a 6-inch level of material to cushion the impact of falling should be a minimum. Frequent leveling, grading, and replacement of the material is necessary, as children will move the material away from the impact areas. The material should be screened to eliminate insects, animal excrement, and concealed sharp objects. Unfortunately, organic materials decompose, become pulverized and dusty, and mix with dirt, which cause a loss of their cushioning properties. In rainy or humid weather, they can absorb moisture and pack down, resulting in a loss of resiliency. Finally, materials must be selected that will not become firm during freezing temperatures.

The choice of materials needs to be based on local conditions and the availability of necessary funds. As important as selection of the proper material is continuous and correct maintenance. Allied to proper maintenance is the need for a checklist of proper procedures to be followed. This form should be filled out and dated on a regular basis.

OUTDOOR APPARATUS AND EQUIPMENT

The continued emphasis on physical fitness should dictate the selection of outdoor equipment. Equipment that offers "sit and ride" experiences (swings, merry-go-rounds, and teeter-totters) does not meet this criterion. A second criterion is that of safety. Each piece of equipment should minimize the potential for injury. As a general rule, if equipment has moving parts, its potential for injury is increased. Suggestions for equipment are offered below based on their potential to develop various components of fitness. The categories can be useful if teachers want to develop a challenge course that develops all parts of the body. Outdoor equipment should stimulate children's creative drives and their desire to move.

Upper Body Development

Most children do not receive enough activity that develops upper body strength. In order to develop arm-shoulder girdle strength on the playground, youngsters must have the opportunity to climb, swing, and elevate their body. Climbing is important for physical development and to help children learn to overcome the fear of new situations. The following are examples of equipment that could be used to development arm-shoulder girdle strength:

Large telephone cable spools that are fastened securely so they will not move or tip over. Youngsters can climb on and jump off the spools.

Climbing poles placed next to platforms that children can reach by climbing the poles.

Logs and clean railroad ties, positioned vertically, with handholds or handles placed in strategic locations for climbing.

Climbing ropes attached to tracks (tracks can be locked up in a storage area when school is not in session).

Tires attached to telephone poles or logs for climbing through and around.

Jungle gyms that are attached securely.

Horizontal ladders in a variety of combinations and forms. Arched ladders are quite popular and allow children to reach the rungs easily. Uniladders, consisting of a single beam with pegs on each side, offer a different ladder challenge to children.

Logs anchored vertically with handholds provided for climbing.

Horizontal and Turning Bars

A set of three horizontal bars of different heights is a valuable piece of apparatus. Turning bars made from 3-inch galvanized pipe offer exciting possibilities for children. The bars can be 6 to 10 feet in length and 30 to 36 inches above the ground.

Lower Body Development

Equipment and apparatus for enhancing lower body development should encourage youngsters to use locomotor movements throughout space. Allow enough distance and area to ensure movement. Suggestions for lower body development are the following:

Large spaces, which encourage free movement and running games.

Railroad ties anchored vertically at varying heights and distances, which encourage children to walk, run, hop, and jump from one to the other.

Used automobile tires fastened on the ground in different patterns to stimulate moving in and out, around and over the tires using different movements.

Stairways and platforms for climbing on and jumping off.

Stepping stones to encourage movement patterns. Stones can be placed so they encourage oppositional patterning while moving.

Miniature challenge courses that contain tires to move over and through, sand pits to run or jump into, and poles or cones arranged for moving around and dodging.

Development of Balance

Balance is improved through regular practice. A number of pieces of equipment can be used to challenge youngsters' balance skills. Youngsters should be encouraged to move under control while practicing balance. The following are suggestions for offering balance challenges:

Balance beams made of 4-by-4-inch beams can be permanent installations. They can be arranged in various patterns but should not be more than 12 to 18 inches above the floor surface.

Logs, anchored securely, and used as balance beams.

Balance beams which start with a wide width (6 inches) and progress in difficulty to (1.5 inch).

Wooden ladders secured 6 inches above the ground offer opportunities to walk on the rungs and rails.

Development of Sport Skills

Basketball Goals

Outdoor basketball goals may or may not be combined with a court. Youngsters play a lot of one-goal basketball, and a regulation court is not needed for this game. The goals should be in a surfaced area, however. Outdoor baskets for elementary school use should be 8 to 9 feet above the ground. The lowered height sometimes poses a problem, because children can jump up and grasp the front of the rim, which may damage or tear the basket loose. Strong construction that withstands such abuse is one solution. Some schools have reverted to the 10-foot-high basket, thus putting it out of reach of most children.

Volleyball Standards

Volleyball standards should have flexible height adjustments, including a low height of 30 inches for use in paddleball.

Softball Backstops

Softball backstops can be either fixed or portable.

Tetherball Courts

Tetherball courts should have fastening devices for the cord and ball so that they can be removed from the post for safekeeping. The immediate playing area should be surfaced.

Track and Field Equipment

Jumping standards, bars, and pits should be available. These must be maintained properly.

INDOOR FACILITIES

The gymnasium must be well planned for maximum use. The combination gymnasium-auditorium-cafeteria facility leaves much to be desired and creates more problems than it solves. Although it may be labeled a "multipurpose room," a better description is probably "multiuseless." The cafeteria poses a particular problem. The gymnasium must be vacated before the lunch hour so that chairs and tables can be set up, and the facility is not available again for physical education activities until it has been cleaned, which usually involves mopping. This eliminates noonhour recreational use, thus leaving little play area for the children during inclement weather. In extreme cases, a lack of help postpones gymnasium use for the early part of the afternoon, until the custodian has completed cleaning chores. Special programs, movies, and other events necessitating chairs and the use of the area also complicate the situation.

The gymnasium should be located in a separate wing connected to the classrooms by a covered corridor. It should provide ready access to play areas. Isolating the gym from the rest of the school minimizes the noise problem and allows afterschool and community groups to use the facilities without access to other parts of the school.

The indoor facility should be planned in such a way that athletic contests can be scheduled there at times, but the primary purpose of the gymnasium is not as an athletic facility. Consideration for spectators should not be a major planning concern. Only after basic physical education needs have been met should the needs of spectators be considered.

In the gymnasium, markings and boundaries should be put on the floor to outline convenient areas for the more common activities. The markings should be painted on the floor after the first or second sealer coat has been applied. A finish coat should then be applied on top of the line markings. Figure 33.1 is an example of how floor markings can maximize the usefulness of a facility.

Temporary lines needed occasionally during the year can be applied with pressure-sensitive tape. These tapes are, however, difficult to remove completely and are likely to take off the finish when removed. A hardwood (preferably maple) floor is recommended for the gymnasium. Other surfaces limit community use and create both safety and maintenance problems.

For safety reasons and for rebound practice, walls should have a smooth surface for a distance of 8 to 10 feet up from the floor. Walls and ceilings should have acoustical treatment. In original construction, a recess for each set of ropes on tracks is an excellent feature. Insulation should conform to modern health standards, and older buildings should be scrutinized for unacceptable insulation materials, such as asbestos fibers and certain formaldehyde-based plastics.

The lighting should be of sufficient intensity and fixtures should be recessed to prevent damage. Lights should be arranged so that they can be serviced from the floor. Exposed beams should be available for attaching apparatus, and all walls should have electrical outlets. A permanent overhead public address system is desirable, permitting permanent installation of a record, tape, or CD player for easy and quick access. In original construction, the player can be recessed.

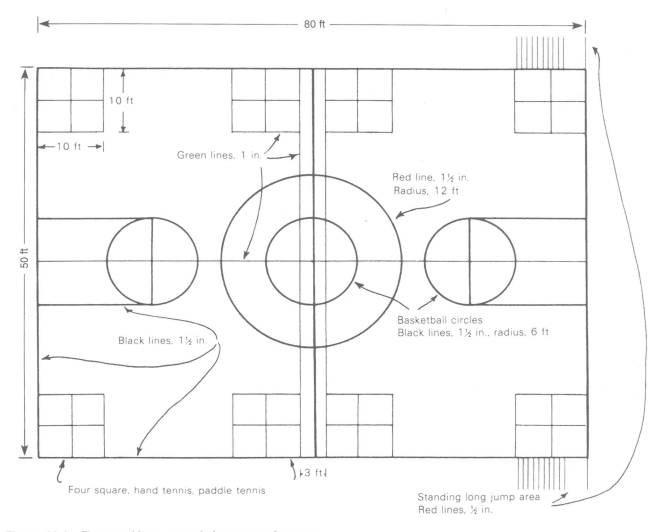

Figure 33.1 Floor markings to maximize gymnasium use

Windows should be placed high on the long sides of the gymnasium. Protection from glare and direct sun should be provided.

If baskets and backboards need to be raised and lowered often, a motor-driven system eliminates laborious hand cranking. The system switch should be activated with a key.

Adequate storage space must be given careful thought. The storage space needed for the equipment and instructional supplies used in present-day physical education is considerable, and the area should be designed so that the materials are readily available.

One problem frequently associated with a combination auditorium-gymnasium facility is the use of the physical education storeroom for storage of bulky auditorium equipment such as portable chairs on chair trucks, portable stages, and lighting fixtures and other paraphernalia for dramatic productions. Unless the storage facility is quite large—and most are not—an unworkable and cluttered facility is the result. The best solution is two separate storerooms for the dual-purpose facility, or at least one very large storeroom.

A separate storage area of cabinets is essential for outside groups that use the facility. These groups should not have access to the regular physical education supply room. If they are permitted to use school equipment, the equipment should be checked out to the group and later checked in again.

Many storage areas in European schools have doors on tracks, similar to American overhead garage doors. This design has a number of advantages, the main one being that the overhead opening makes the handling of large apparatus much easier.

Most architects are unaware of the storage needs of a modern physical education program. Teachers can only hope that the architects designing new schools will be persuaded to allow for sufficient storage. For the physical education specialist, an office-dressing room is desirable. The office should contain a toilet and a shower.

If contract or task approaches are important in the instructional process, an area to house instructional materials is also desirable. This should be a place where the children can go to search through materials and view loop films and videotapes as they complete their learning packets.

EQUIPMENT AND SUPPLIES

Equipment refers to items of a more or less fixed nature. *Supplies* are those nondurable items that have a limited period of use. To illustrate the difference, a softball is listed under supplies, but the longer-lasting softball backstop comes under the category of equipment. Equipment needs periodic replacement, and budget planning must consider the lifespan of each piece of equipment. Supplies generally are purchased on a yearly basis. It is important to have adequate financing for equipment and supplies and to expend funds wisely.

If the objectives of the physical education program are to be fulfilled, instructional materials must be available in sufficient quantity. Enough equipment should be present so that the children do not waste practice time waiting for turns.

Policies covering the purchase, storage, issuance, care, maintenance, and inventory of supplies are necessary if maximum return on the allotted budget is to be realized. Program features should be decided first, and a purchasing plan should then be implemented based on these features. Having a minimal operational list of instructional supplies stabilizes the teaching process.

Equipment constructed by the school staff and homemade equipment should be considered. Quality must not, however, be sacrificed. Articles from home (e.g., empty plastic jugs, milk cartons, old tires, and the like) should be regarded as supplementary materials. Care must be taken that the administration does not look for the cheap, no-cost route to securing supplies and thus sacrifice valuable learning experiences when the program needs require an appreciable investment.

Some articles can be constructed adequately at the school or in the home, and these merit consideration for the sake of economy. Such items as yarn balls, hoops, lummi sticks, balance beams, bounding boards, and others can be made satisfactorily by school staff, by parents, and in some instances by students. For other articles, the administration must be reminded that constructed equipment is usually a temporary solution only, undertaken in the early phases of a program when equipment costs are high and cannot all be met immediately.

PURCHASING POLICIES

The purchase of supplies and equipment involves careful study of need, price, quality, and material. The safety of the children who will use the equipment is of vital concern.

Quantity buying by pooling the needs of an entire school district generally results in better use of the tax dollar. However, cooperative purchasing may require compromises on equipment type and brand to satisfy different users in the system. If bids are requested, careful specifications are necessary. Bids should be asked for only on specified items, and "just as good" merchandise should not be accepted as a substitute.

One individual within a school should be made responsible for the physical education supplies and for keeping records of equipment, supplies, and purchasing. Needs will vary from school to school, and it is practical for school district authorities to deal with a single individual at each school. Prompt attention to repair and replacement of supplies is possible under this system. The individual designated should also be responsible for testing various competing products to determine which will give the best service over time. Some kind of labeling or marking of materials is needed if this is to be accomplished.

An accurate inventory of equipment should be undertaken at the start and end of each school year. Through a sound inventory system, the durability of equipment and supplies and an accounting of supplies lost or misplaced can be established.

The ordering of supplies and equipment should be done by the end of the school year or earlier, if possible. A delivery date in August should be specified so that orders can be checked and any necessary adjustments made before the school year begins.

Most equipment of good quality will last from 7 to 10 years, thus keeping replacement costs to a minimum. The policy of some purchasing agents of selecting low-cost items with little regard for quality is financially unsound.

Budgetary practices should include an allotment for the yearly purchase of instructional supplies as well as major replacement and procurement costs for large items, which are usually staggered over a number of years. Once sufficient equipment and supplies have been procured, the budget considerations are for replacement and repair only.

INDOOR EQUIPMENT

Several principles should govern the choice of indoor equipment. First, a reasonable variety and amount of equipment should be available to keep children active. Included should be items to facilitate arm-shoulder girdle development (i.e., climbing ropes, climbing frames, ladders, and similar apparatus). A criterion for selection is that most, if not all, indoor equipment should be of the type that the children themselves can carry, assemble, and disassemble. A regular trampoline, for example, would not meet this criterion.

Mats for Tumbling and Safety

Mats are basic to any physical education program. Enough mats must be available to provide a safe floor for climbing apparatus. At least eight should be present. The light, folding mats are preferable because they are easy to handle and store. They stack well and can be moved on carts. Mats should have fasteners so that two or more can be joined (Figure 33.2). The covers should be plastic for easy cleaning. (The one objection to plastic covers is that they are not as soft as the type of mat cover used for wrestling.) Mats should be 4 feet wide and 7 or 8 feet long. Heavy hand-me-down mats from the high school program, some with canvas covers, may prove counterproductive, because they are difficult to handle and bulky to store.

Other mats that might be considered are thick, soft mats (somewhat similar to mattresses) and inclined mats. Soft mats are generally 4 inches or more thick and may entice the timid to try activi-

Figure 33.2 Tumbling mats stored on walls with Velcro® fasteners

ties that they otherwise would avoid. Inclined mats are wedge-shaped and provide downhill momentum for rolls.

Individual Mats

Strong consideration should be given to obtaining a supply of 30 to 35 individual mats to be used mostly for the primary-level program. The mats, which can be 20 by 40 inches or 24 by 48 inches, are useful for practicing many interesting movement experiences and introductory tumbling activities. Expense is, however, a key factor. The initial outlay, including a carrying cart, is quite high, but the mats do last indefinitely with care and add much to the program.

Tape Recorder, Record Player, and/or CD Player

A tape recorder and record player with a variable speed are a necessity. Pause control is also helpful. The advantage of the tape recorder is that it can easily be transported outdoors. In addition, tape recorders are much more durable and are less apt to be damaged from out-of-control children and equipment. A programmable compact disc (CD) player is also a desirable addition. A portable combination tape and CD player may be the most affordable and versatile choice.

Balance-Beam Benches

Balance-beam benches have double use. They can serve as regular benches for many types of bench activity, and when turned over, they can be used for balance-beam activities. Wooden horses or their supports can serve as inclined benches. Six benches are a minimum for class activity.

Balance Beams

A wide beam (4 inches) is recommended for kindergarten and 1st grade. Otherwise, a 2-inch beam should be used. Balance beams with alternate surfaces (2 and 4 inches) can be constructed from common building materials.

Chinning Bar

The chinning bar is especially useful for physical fitness testing and in body support activities. The portable chinning bar installed in the gymnasium doorway is an acceptable substitute.

Climbing Ropes

Climbing ropes are essential to the program. At least eight should be present, but more than eight allows better group instruction. Climbing rope sets on tracks are most efficient to handle (Figure 33.3). With little effort or loss of time, the ropes are ready for activity. Ropes on tracks are available in a variety of materials, but good-quality manila hemp seems to be the most practical. Ropes should be either 1¼ or 1½ inches in diameter.

Quality climbing ropes made of synthetic fibers are appearing on the market. The best are olefin fiber ropes, which are nonallergenic and have nonslip qualities, thus forestalling the problem of slickness, a characteristic of plastic ropes and even of older cotton ropes. Climbing ropes on tracks and other large apparatus can be purchased from the Robert Widen Company, P.O. Box 2075, Prescott, AZ 86302.

Figure 33.3 Climbing ropes on tracks

Volleyball Standards

Volleyball standards should adjust to various heights for different grade levels and games.

Supply Cart

A cart to hold supplies is desirable. Other carts can be used for the record player and for regular and individual mats.

Jumping Boxes

Small boxes used for jumping and for allied loco-motor movements extend the opportunities to work on basic movement skills. Boxes should be 8 and 16 inches high (Figure 33.4). If the boxes are made about 16 by 16 inches with a rubber skid-proof surface on the bottom, they will be stable. Holes drilled through the sides provide fingerholds for ease of handling. Eight boxes, four of each size, are a minimum number for the average-sized class.

Horizontal Ladder Sets

Horizontal ladders that fold against the wall make an excellent indoor equipment addition. The ladder may be combined with other pieces of apparatus in a folding set.

Other Indoor Items

A portable chalkboard is desirable, as is a wall screen for viewing visual aids. A large bulletin board and a wall chalkboard should be located near the main entrance to the gym. The wall chalkboard permits quick announcements or notes. An audiovisual

Figure 33.4 First graders using 16-in. jumping boxes

cart or stand for projectors is helpful. It should contain sufficient electrical cord to reach wall outlets.

Rebound nets for throwing and kicking have excellent utility. They do, however, pose storage problems. Substitute goals for basketball and related games can be designed. One suggested goal is 4 feet square, with the rim 5 feet above the ground. Beginners can find success with this goal design. The frame can be made of 1-inch pipe or plastic (PVC) tubing.

SUPPLIES FOR PHYSICAL EDUCATION

A basic list and an optional list of supplies should be established for each program. The basic list stipulates the instructional materials that should be available for teaching. In addition, extra basic-list items should be held in storage for replacement during the year. Optional supplies depend on personal preferences and available funds.

It is difficult to find equipment that offers the most quality for the money spent. Typically, manufacturers change specifications and reduce the quality of equipment, often for the purpose of saving money. The Robert Widen Company is recommended as a source because they stay informed on the current state of technology in equipment. They evaluate equipment from many sources and warranty all equipment for one year. For information write the Robert Widen Company, P.O. Box 2075, Prescott, AZ 86302 or call 1-800-862-0761.

Basic Supply List

Ball inflator with gauge (1)

Balloons, rubber (1 for each child and extras in reserve)

Balls

Beach balls, 12 to 16 inch (2 to 6)

Cageballs, 24 inch (2 with an extra bladder in reserve)

Playground balls, rubber, mostly 8½ inch (1 for each child)

Small balls, sponge or tennis, in assorted colors (50)

Sport balls (for primary) in a variety of sponge or plastic forms, such as footballs, soccer balls, volleyballs, and basketballs (8 of each type)

Sport balls (junior-sized), football, basketball, soccer ball, volleyball (8 of each)

Yarn or fleece balls (1 for each child)

Basketball nets (6 in reserve)

Batting tees for softball (4 to 6)

Beanbags, in assorted colors (2 for each child)

Cones, rubber, for boundary markers (24)

Eyeglass protectors (4 or more)

Gym scooters (4 for relays or 1 for every two children for games)

Hockey sets (2)

Hoops, 36 or 42 inch (1 for each child with extras in reserve)

Clubs or bowling pins (16 or more)

Individual mats (1 for each child)

Jump ropes, individual, in a variety of lengths (1 for each child)

Jump ropes, long (8)

Jump-the-shot ropes (3)

Lummi sticks (32 pairs)

Magic (stretch) ropes (8)

Measuring tape, 50 foot or longer (1)

Paddles, wooden (1 for each child)

Parachute, 24 or 28 foot (1)

Pinnies or other team markers (1 for every two children)

Records, a sufficient supply

Scoops, bottle (1 for each child)

Softball equipment—balls, gloves, masks, bases, bats, protector

Stopwatches, ⅕ or ⅒ second (3)

Tambourine (1)

Tetherball sets as needed

Tinikling pole sets, 10-foot poles (6)

Tom-tom or dance drum (1)

Tote bags for balls (12 or more)

Track and field equipment—batons (8), jump boards, hurdles, crossbars or ropes, starter, jump standards

Tug-of-war ropes, individual (1 for every two children)

Volleyball nets (2)

Wands (1 for each child)

Whistles (8)

Wire baskets for holding items (6 or more)

Optional Supply List

Bongo boards (8)

Broom handles (8)

Deck tennis rings (16)

Footsteps, tiles, or rubber footprints (40)

Frisbees (16)

Fun balls, in a variety of forms (36)

Hockey sticks, 12-inch size for scooter or hand hockey (2 sets)

Lime for marking fields

Liner, dry, for marking fields

Microphone for record player (1)

Parachute, 10 or 12 foot (1)

Pitching targets (2)

Pogo sticks (8)

Repair kit for balls (1)

Shuffleboard equipment

Stilts, regular (6 pair)

Stilts, tin can (6 pair)

Table tennis equipment

Tape, colored, for temporary marking of gymnasium floor

Tires, auto

Tires, bicycle

Tool chest—saw, hammer, pliers, and so on

Tubes, auto, oversized and inflatable (6)

Tug-of-war rope, 60 foot or more (1)

Wooden blocks, 1 by 1 inch for relays (24)

Other miscellaneous items purchased commercially or made at home

STORAGE PLANS

When a class goes to the gymnasium for physical education, the teacher has a right to expect sufficient supplies to be available to conduct the class. A master list stipulating the kinds and quantities of supplies in storage should be established. A reasonable turnover is to be expected, and supply procedures should reflect this. Supplies in the storage facility should be available for physical education classes and for organized after-school activities. The supplies should not be used for games played during recess or for free play periods; each classroom should have its own supplies for such purposes. A system should be established for the storage of equipment and supplies. "A place for everything and everything in its place" is the key to good housekeeping. Bins, shelves, and other assigned areas where supplies and equipment are to be kept should be labeled.

Figure 33.5 Portable ball cart

Both teachers and students must accept responsibility for maintaining order in the storage facility. Squad leaders or student aides can assume major responsibility. At the end of the week, the teacher in charge of the storage area can assign older children to help tidy the area, put any stray items back in place, and repair or replace articles as needed. A principal will be more favorably inclined toward purchase requests when obvious care is taken of instructional materials.

Some schools use small supply carts of the type pictured in Figure 33.5. The carts hold those articles used most frequently. They take up some additional space but do save time in accessing needed items. The carts can be built inexpensively to meet specific needs, or commercially manufactured equipment carriers can be purchased. A cart that holds the record player and carts that store and move mats and balls are helpful.

An off-season storage area, where articles not in present use can be kept, should be established. Equipment not in current use should be kept in this separate area, perhaps under lock and key.

CARE, REPAIR, AND MARKING

A definite system should be developed for repairing supplies and equipment. A quick decision must be made about whether to repair an item locally or to send it out of the area for repair. If the repair process is lengthy and not cost efficient, using the article until it can no longer be salvaged may be preferable to being deprived of its use. An area should be established for equipment needing repair, so that all articles to be repaired are evident at a glance.

Balls must be inflated to proper pressures. This means using an accurate gauge and checking the pressures periodically. The inflation needle should be moistened before insertion into the valve. Children should kick only those balls made specifically for kicking (i.e., soccer balls, footballs, and playground balls).

Softball bats and wooden paddles should not be used to hit rocks, stones, or other hard materials. Neither should bats be knocked against fences, posts, or other objects that might cause damage. Broken bats should be discarded; they are unsafe, even when taped around the break. Children should learn to keep the trademark up when batting. Bats should be taped to prevent slippage.

Cuts, abrasions, and breaks in rubber balls should be repaired immediately. In some cases, repairs can be made with a vulcanized patch, such as those used for repair of tire tubes. In other cases, a hard-setting rubber preparation is of value. In some instances, repair may be beyond the scope of the school, and the ball should be sent away for repair.

For off-season storage, balls should be deflated somewhat, leaving just enough air in them to retain the shape. Leather balls should be cleaned with an approved conditioner.

Mats are expensive, and proper care is needed if they are to last. A place where they can be stacked properly must be provided, or if the mats have handles, they should be hung from those. A mat truck is another storage solution if there is space for storing the truck. The newer plastic or plastic-covered mats should be cleaned periodically with a damp, soapy cloth.

For small items, clean plastic ice-cream bucket containers make adequate storage receptacles. Most school cafeterias have these and other containers that can be used in the storage room to keep order. Small wire baskets also make good storage containers.

All equipment and supplies should be marked. This is particularly important for equipment issued to different classrooms. Marking can be done with indelible pencil, paint, or stencil ink. Few marking systems are permanent, however, and re-marking at regular intervals is necessary. Sporting goods establishments have marking sets. An electric burning pencil works well but must be used with caution so as not to damage the equipment being marked.

Rubber playground balls come in different colors, and assignment to classrooms can be made on the basis of color. A code scheme with different-colored paints can be used also. It is possible to devise a color system by which the year of issue is designated. This offers opportunity for documentation of equipment usage and care.

CONSTRUCTING EQUIPMENT AND SUPPLIES

This section is divided into two parts. In the first part, recommendations for sources and materials needed to construct equipment and supplies are offered. In the second part, diagrams and specifications for building equipment in an economical manner are listed. If the recommended equipment can be described adequately without an illustration, it is included in the first part. For simplicity, measurement units are abbreviated throughout this section.

Recommendations for Constructing Equipment and Supplies

The supply of balls can be augmented with tennis balls or sponge balls. Discarded tennis balls from the high school tennis team are useful. Holes can be poked in the tennis balls if they are too lively for young children to handle. Sponge balls are inexpensive and with care last indefinitely.

A good supply of ropes for jumping is essential. We are partial to the newer, plastic-link jump ropes, because these have good weight, come in attractive colors, can be shortened easily (by removing links), and can be purchased with color-coded handles. The handles provide good leverage for turning. However, ropes can also be made from cord. Heavy sash cord or hard-weave polyethylene rope is suitable. The ends should be whipped, heated, or dipped into some type of hardening solution to prevent unraveling. The lengths can be color coded with dye or stain. Kindergarten through grade 2 use mostly 7-ft ropes, with a few 6- and 8-ft lengths. Grades 3 through 6 use mostly 8-ft ropes, with a few 7- and 9-ft lengths. Instructors will require 9- or 10-ft ropes.

Enough ropes should be available in the suggested lengths to provide each child with a rope of the correct length. The supply of ropes should include eight to ten long ropes (14 or 16 ft) for long-rope jumping activities. A jump-the-shot rope can be made by tying an old, completely deflated volleyball on one end of a rope.

Beanbags are made easily. Good-quality, bright-colored muslin is suitable as a covering. Some teachers have asked parents to save the lower legs of worn-out denim jeans; this material wears ex-

tremely well and is free. Some instructors prefer a beanbag with an outer liner that snaps in place to allow for washing. Another idea is to sew three sides of the beanbag permanently. The fourth side is used for filling and has an independent stitch. The beans can be removed through this side when the bag is washed. Beanbags should be about 4 by 4 in. and 6 by 6 in. and can be filled with dried beans or peas, wheat, rice, or even building sand.

For games requiring boundary markers, pieces of rubber matting can be used; or small sticks or boards, painted white, are excellent. A board 1 by 2 in. across and 3 or 4 ft in length makes a satisfactory marker.

Tetherballs should have a snap-on fastener for easy removal.

Old tires, even those from bicycles, can be used. Chapter 19 contains many ideas for tire use.

Schools near ski areas may be able to get discarded tow ropes. These make excellent tug-of-war ropes.

Bowling pins or clubs can be turned in the school shop, or suitable substitutes can be made. For example, pieces of 2-by-2-in. lumber cut short (6 to 10 in.) stand satisfactorily. Lumber companies usually have dowels 1 to 1½ in. in diameter. Sections of these make a reasonable substitute for clubs. Broken bats also can be made into good substitute clubs.

White shoe polish has numerous marking uses and can be removed from the floor with a little scrubbing.

Three-pound coffee cans can be used as targets. Empty half-gallon milk cartons also have a variety of uses.

Inner tubes can be cut in strips and used as resistance exercise equipment. The tube should be cut crossways in 1½-in.-wide strips.

Old bowling pins can be obtained from most bowling alleys free of charge. Because the standard pins are too large for the children to handle easily, cutting 2 to 4 in. off the bottom is recommended. Parallel cuts through the body of the pin provide hockey pucks and shuffleboard disks. Another way to trim bowling pins is described on page 758.

For kindergarten and first-grade children, improvised balls can be made from crumpled newspaper bound with cellophane tape. Papier-mâché balls are also useful. Light foam rubber cubes can be trimmed to make interesting objects for throwing and catching.

Bamboo for making tinikling poles can sometimes be procured from carpet stores, which use the poles to give support to the center of a carpet roll. Plastic tinikling sticks are available commercially.

Good savings on rubber traffic cones can be realized if these are purchased from a highway department supply source, where they are usually less expensive than cones purchased from physical education equipment supply firms. Plastic jugs, half filled with sand, can be used in place of traffic cones.

Diagrams and Specifications for Constructing Equipment and Supplies

Safety standards should apply to all school-constructed equipment; the construction and the materials used should not create any safety hazards. The design must be educationally sound and utilitarian.

Balance Beam

The balance beam is used for many kinds of activity. Two types of stand for a 2-by-4-in. beam are shown in Figure 33.6. The beam can be placed with the wide or the narrow side up, depending on the skill of the performer. If the beam is longer than 8 ft, a third stand should be placed in the middle. Care must be taken to sand and apply multiple coats of finish to the beam to prevent splintering and cracking.

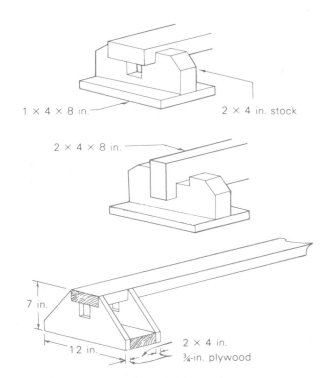

Figure 33.6 Balance beam with stand

Balance-Beam Bench

The balance-beam bench is a versatile piece of equipment. Its dimensions can be modified depending on the age of the users (Figure 33.7). It should be made of hardwood or hardwood plywood and should be well finished. Hooks can be fastened to the underside of the bench to provide even more uses for this important piece of apparatus.

Balance Boards

Many styles of balance board can be constructed, depending on the materials available and individual needs (Figure 33.8). Glue a piece of rubber matting to the top of the board to prevent slipping and place it on an individual mat or on a piece of heavy rubber matting. A square board is easier to balance than a round one, for its corners touch the floor and give more stability.

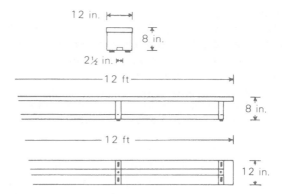

Figure 33.7 Balance-beam bench

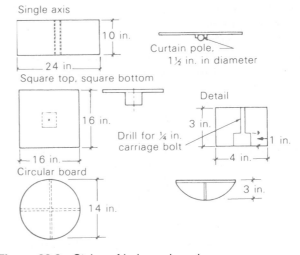

Figure 33.8 Styles of balance board

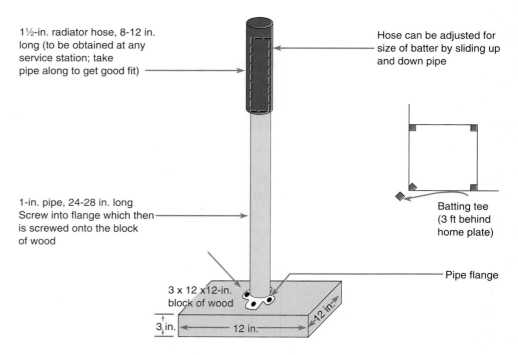

Figure 33.9 Batting tee construction

1½-in. radiator hose, 8-12 in. long (to be obtained at any service station; take pipe along to get good fit)

Hose can be adjusted for size of batter by sliding up and down pipe

1-in. pipe, 24-28 in. long Screw into flange which then is screwed onto the block of wood

Batting tee (3 ft behind home plate)

Pipe flange

3 x 12 x12-in. block of wood

3 in.

12 in.

12 in.

Batting Tee

Ideally, the batting tee should be adjustable to accommodate batters of various heights (Figure 33.9). Constructing an adjustable tee takes time, however, and the results are not always satisfactory. An alternative is to make several nonadjustable tees of different heights.

Materials:

One piece of 1-in. pipe, 24 to 28 in. long

One piece of radiator hose, 8 to 12 in. long, with an inside diameter of 1½ in.

One block of wood, 3 by 12 by 12 in.

One pipe flange for 1-in. pipe, to be mounted on the block

Screws and hose cement

Directions: Mount the flange on the block and screw the pipe into the flange. Place the radiator hose on the pipe. Paint as desired. To secure a good fit for the radiator hose, take the pipe to the supply source. If the hose is to remain fixed, then secure it with hose cement.

An alternative method is to drill a hole in the block and to mount the pipe directly in the hole with mastic or good-quality glue. Note that 1-in. pipe has an outside diameter of approximately 1 in., allowing the hose to fit properly over it.

Blocks and Cones

Blocks with grooves on the top and on one of the sides are excellent for forming hurdles with wands.

A 4-by-4-in. board, cut in lengths of 6, 12, and 18 in., yields a variety of hurdle sizes. Cones can be notched and used in place of the blocks (Figure 33.10).

Bowling Pins

Bowling alleys give away old tenpins, which can be used for many purposes. Some suggested uses are as field and gymnasium markers, for bowling

Blocks 4 x 4 x 12 in. or 4 x 4 x 18 in.

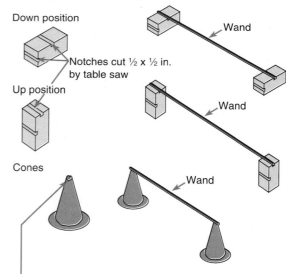

Down position

Notches cut ½ x ½ in. by table saw

Up position

Cones

Wand

Wand

Wand

Cut a ½-in. notch on each side of top lip of cone

Figure 33.10 Notching blocks and cones to make hurdles

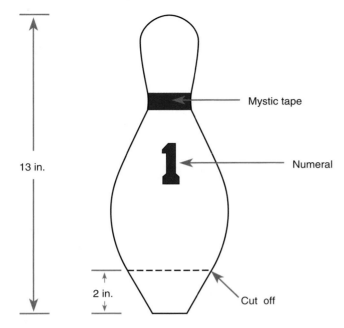

Figure 33.11 Bowling pin

games, and for relays. The bottom 2 in. of the pin should be cut off, and the base sanded smooth (Figure 33.11). Pins can be numbered and decorated with decals, colored tape, or paint.

Conduit Hurdles

Conduit hurdles are lightweight and easy to store. Because they are not weighted and fall over easily, children have little fear about hitting them. The elastic bands can be moved up and down to create different heights and different challenges. Conduit can be purchased at most electrical supply houses.

Materials:

> One piece of ½-in. electrical conduit pipe, 10 ft long
>
> One piece of 1-in. stretch elastic tape
>
> Wood doweling, ½ in. in diameter

Directions: Bend the piece of conduit to the following dimensions: Uprights should be 30 in. high, the base should be 30 in. wide, and the sides of the base should be 15 in. long. A special tool for bending the conduit usually can be purchased from the supply house where the conduit was bought. Sew loops on each end of the elastic tape, so that the tape will slide over the ends of the hurdles with a slight amount of tension. If necessary, short pieces of doweling can be put in the ends of the conduit to raise the height of the hurdle (Figure 33.12).

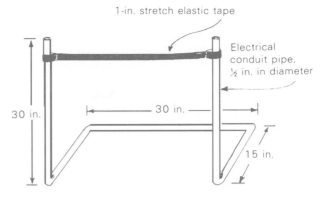

Figure 33.12 Conduit hurdle construction

Footsies

Footsies can be made economically by the children. They provide an excellent movement challenge. The activity requires coordination of both feet to keep the footsie rotating properly.

Materials:

> Plastic bleach bottle, half-gallon size
>
> One piece of ⅛-in. clothesline-type rope
>
> Old tennis ball
>
> Large fishing swivel, preferably with ball bearings

Directions: Cut a circular strip about 2 in. wide out of the bottom of a bleach bottle. Cut two holes in the strip about 1 in. apart. Thread a 3-ft piece of clothesline through the holes, and tie a knot on the outside of the strip. Cut the clothesline in half and tie the swivel to each end of the cut cord. The swivel prevents the rope from becoming twisted.

Puncture the tennis ball with an ice pick, making two holes directly across from each other. Thread the line through the holes with a piece of wire or a large crochet hook. Tie a large knot near the outer hole so that the line cannot slip back through (Figure 33.13).

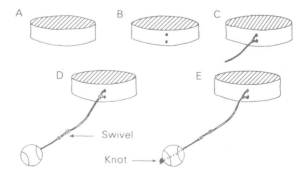

Figure 33.13 Footsie construction

Gym Scooters

Scooters are easily constructed from readily available materials and can be made in many sizes and shapes. The casters should be checked to make sure that they do not mark the floor. Scooters have many activity applications, as described previously, and can also be used to move heavy equipment.

Materials:

> One piece of 2-in. yellow pine board, 12 by 12 in.
>
> Four ball-bearing casters with 2-in. wheels of hard rubber
>
> Protective rubber stripping, 4 ft in length, and cement
>
> Screws and paint

Directions: Actual dimensions of the board are around 1⅝ by 11⅝ in. Two pieces of ¾-in. plywood glued together can be substituted. Cut and round the corners, smoothing them with a power sander. Sand all edges by hand, and apply two coats of paint. Fasten the four casters approximately 1½ in. diagonally in from the corners. A rubber strip fixed around the edges with staples and cement (Figure 33.14) will cushion the impact of the scooter on other objects.

Hoops

Hoops can be constructed from ½-in. plastic water pipe (PVC), which unfortunately is available in

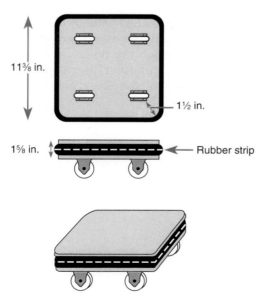

Figure 33.14 Gym scooter construction

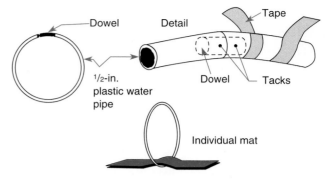

Figure 33.15 Hoop construction

drab colors only. The cost savings of using the pipe are, however, great. Hoops can be constructed in different sizes. A short piece of doweling, fixed with a power stapler or tacks, can be used to join the ends together (Figure 33.15). An alternative joining method is to use special pipe connectors. Weather-stripping cement helps make a more permanent joint.

Hurdle and High-Jump Rope

The weighted hurdle and high-jump rope is ideal for beginning hurdlers and high jumpers who may fear hitting the bar. The rope can be hung over the pins of the high-jump standards; the weights keep the rope fairly taut.

Materials:

> One piece of ⅜-in. rope, 10 ft long
>
> Two rubber crutch tips (no. 19)
>
> Tacks (no. 14) and penny shingle nails
>
> Lead (This can be purchased at plumbing outlets.)

Directions: Drive a carpet tack through the rope approximately ¾ in. from each end. Drive three nails into the bottom of each of the two rubber crutch tips. Place the rope ends inside the crutch tips and fill the tips with hot lead (Figure 33.16).

Individual Mats

Individual mats can be made from indoor-outdoor carpeting that has a rubber backing. This prevents the mat from sliding on the floor and offers some cushion. The mats also can be washed easily when they become soiled. Mats of different colors are preferable, because they can be used for games, for color tag, and for easy division of the class according to mat color. Carpet stores often have small pieces and remnants that they will sell cheaply or give away.

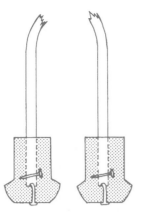

Figure 33.16 Weighted hurdle and high-jump rope construction

Figure 33.17 Folding individual mat

Another type of individual mat is designed to fold (Figure 33.17). These mats are useful for aerobic dance classes because they are lighter and easier to handle than the carpet mats. The major drawback is that the folding mats are more expensive.

Jumping Boxes

Jumping boxes are used to develop a wide variety of body management skills. The dimensions can be varied to satisfy individual needs but 8 and 16 in. boxes seem to be the most useful.

Materials:

¾-in. marine plywood

Wood screws, paint, and glue

Carpet pad remnants

Naugahyde or similar material to cover box top

Upholstery tacks

Directions: Cut the four sides to similar dimensions and then sand them together to make sure they are exactly the same size. Use a countersink and drill the screw holes, apply glue at the joints, and screw the sides together. When the box is assembled, sand all edges to remove any sharpness. Paint the boxes, preferably with a latex-based paint, because it does not chip as easily as oil-based enamel. If handholds are desired, drill holes and then cut them out with a saber saw (Figure 33.18). Covering is optional; if desired, cut a carpet pad remnant to match the size of the top of the box, and cover with a piece of Naugahyde. The Naugahyde should overlap about 4 in. on each side of the box so that it can be folded under a double thickness and then tacked down.

Jumping Standards

Jumping standards are useful for hurdling, jumping, and over-and-under activities. Many shapes and sizes are possible (Figure 33.19).

Materials:

Two pieces of ¾-in. plywood 25 in. long, cut as shown

Two blocks of wood, 2 by 4 by 6 in.

Glue and paint

Broomstick, 48 in. long

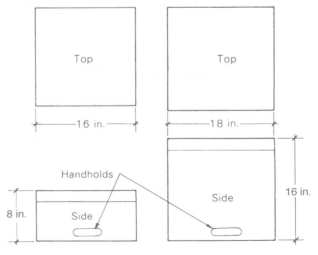

Figure 33.18 Jumping box construction

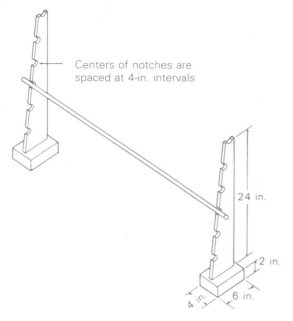

Figure 33.19 Jumping standard construction

Directions: The wood blocks should be mortised lengthwise, about 1 in. deep. After the uprights have been cut to form, set them with glue into the blocks—making sure that the uprights are plumb. Paint as desired. Small circles of various colors can be placed at each of the corresponding notches of the uprights for quick positioning of the crosspiece.

Ladder

A ladder laid on the floor or on a mat provides a floor apparatus for varied movement experiences and has value in remedial programs and programs for exceptional children. Sizes may vary (Figure 33.20).

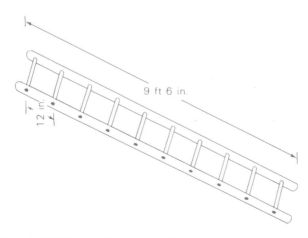

Figure 33.20 Ladder construction

Materials:

Two straight-grained 2-by-4-in. timbers, 9½ ft long

Ten 1¼-in. or 1½-in. dowels, 20 in. long

Glue

Paint or varnish

Directions: Round the ends and sand the edges of the timbers. Center holes for the ladder rungs 12 in. apart, beginning 3 in. from one end. Cut the holes for the rungs ¹⁄₁₆ in. smaller than the diameter of the rungs. Put glue in all the holes on one timber, and drive in all the rungs. Next, glue the other timber in place. Varnish or paint the ladder.

Lummi Sticks

Lummi sticks are excellent tools for developing rhythmic skills. The sticks can also be used as relay batons.

Materials:

1-in. doweling, in 12-in. lengths

Paint and varnish

Directions: Notches and different colors are optional, but these decorations do make the sticks more attractive. If desired, use a table saw to cut notches ⅛ in. wide and ⅛ in. deep. Round off the ends and sand the entire stick. Paint and varnish the stick as shown in Figure 33.21.

Magic Ropes

Magic or stretch ropes can be made by stringing together 25 to 30 large rubber bands. Common

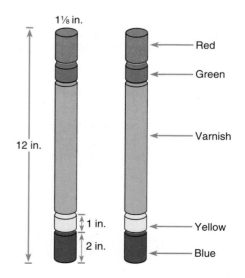

Figure 33.21 Lummi stick construction and decoration

clothing elastic also can be used to make the ropes (Figure 33.22). Some teachers have had success with shock cord, which usually can be purchased at a boating marina or hardware store. Bungee cord of the proper length may also be used. Similar to shock cord, it may be purchased at many sports equipment outlets.

Outdoor Bases

There are many satisfactory methods for constructing bases. They can be made from heavy canvas by folding the canvas over three or four times and stitching it together. Heavy rubber matting can be cut to size. More permanent bases can be made from outdoor plywood and painted (Figure 33.23).

Materials:

Exterior ¾-in. plywood

One ½-in. carriage bolt, 14 in. long

Paint

Directions: Cut the plywood into 12-by-12-in. squares. Bevel and sand the top edges. Drill a ½-in. hole in the center of the base and then paint the base. When the paint has dried, place the carriage bolt in the center hole and drive it into the ground. More holes can be used to make the base more secure. Large spikes can be substituted for the carriage bolt.

Use ⅜-in. stretch elastic tape

Wrist loops

15 ft

Figure 33.22 Magic rope construction

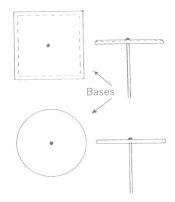

Bases

Figure 33.23 Outdoor base construction

Paddles

Paddles can be made in many sizes and with different thicknesses of plywood (Figure 33.24). Usually, ¼-in. plywood is recommended for kindergarten through grade 2, and ⅜-in. plywood for grades 3 through 6. Paddles can be painted or varnished, and the handles taped to give a better grip. Holes can be drilled in the paddle area to make it lighter and to decrease air resistance. Good-quality plywood, perhaps marine plywood, is essential.

For hitting a foam rubber ball or a newspaper ball, nylon-stocking paddles can substitute quite effectively for wooden paddles. Because of their light weight, they do not cause injuries. They are therefore excellent for primary-age children. A badminton bird can be used with the paddle for various activities, such as hitting over a net, and for many individual stunts.

Materials:

Old nylon stocking

Wire coat hanger

Masking tape or athletic tape

String or wire

Directions: Bend the hanger into a diamond shape. Bend the hook into a loop, which becomes the handle of the paddle (Figure 33.25). Pull the stocking over the hanger, beginning at the corner farthest from the handle, until the toe of the nylon is as tight as possible against the corner point of the hanger. Hold the nylon at the neck of the hanger and stretch it as tight as possible.

Tie the nylon securely with a piece of heavy string or light wire. Wrap the rest of the nylon around the handle to make a smooth, contoured surface. Complete the paddle by wrapping tape around the entire handle to prevent loosening.

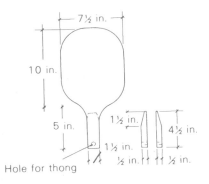

7½ in.

10 in.

5 in.   1½ in.   4½ in.

1½ in.   ½ in.   ½ in.

Hole for thong

Figure 33.24 Paddle construction

Figure 33.25 Frame for nylon-stocking paddle

Paddle Tennis Net Supports

The advantage of paddle tennis net supports is that they stand by themselves on the floor and still provide proper net tension. The stands come apart easily and quickly and can be stored in a small space. For lengths up to 8 ft or so, a single center board, with holes on each end, can be used, thus eliminating the need for bolting two pieces together (Figure 33.26).

Materials:

> Two broomsticks or ¾-in. dowels, 2 ft long
>
> Two 1-by-4-in. boards, 2 ft long
>
> One or more additional 1-by-4-in. boards
>
> Glue

Directions: For the upright supports, drill a hole ¾ in. in diameter in the center of each 1 by 4. Drive the dowel into the hole, fixing it with glue. The dowels can be notched at intervals for different net heights.

The length of the crosspiece depends on how much court width is to be covered. If a single crosspiece is to be used, holes should be bored in each end. The holes should be big enough (⅞ in.)

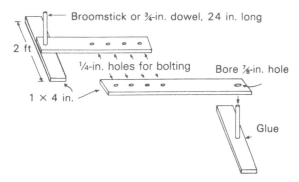

Figure 33.26 Paddle tennis net support construction

so that the dowel slides through easily. If the crosspiece is in two halves, ¼-in. bolts are needed to bolt the halves together, as indicated in the diagram.

Partner Tug-of-War Ropes

Partner tug-of-war ropes can be made from garden hose and ropes (Figure 33.27). The cheaper, plastic garden hose (⅝ in. in diameter) works much better than the more expensive rubber hose. The plastic hose does not crease as easily and gives the hands more protection. The white, soft, braided nylon rope (⅜ in. in diameter) offers adequate strength and is much easier to handle than other types of rope. A bowline knot should be used, because it does not slip and tighten around the hands. The ends of the nylon rope should be melted over a flame to prevent them from unraveling.

Plastic Markers and Scoops

One-gallon plastic jugs filled halfway with sand and recapped make fine boundary markers. The markers can be painted different colors to signify goals, boundaries, and division lines. The jugs also can be numbered and used to designate different teaching stations. Plastic bottles can be cut down to make

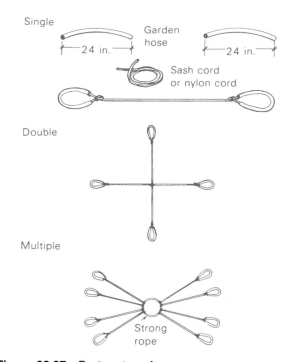

Figure 33.27 Partner tug-of-war ropes

scoops (Figure 33.28), which have many activity possibilities.

Rings, Deck Tennis (Quoits)

Deck tennis is a popular recreational net game that requires only a ring as basic equipment. The rings can be made easily by the students and are useful for playing catch and for target throwing. They can be fashioned from heavy rope by braiding the ends together, but the construction method illustrated in Figure 33.29 is easier. Weather-stripping cement helps strengthen the joints.

Ring Toss Target

Many ring toss targets can be made from 1-by-4-in. lumber and old broom or mop handles. They can be made to hang on the wall or to lie flat on the ground. The quoits constructed from garden hose are excellent for throwing at the targets. The target

pegs can be painted different colors to signify different point values.

Materials:

> Two 1-by-4-in. boards, 18 to 20 in. long
>
> Five pegs, 6 in. long (old broom handles)
>
> Screws and paint

Directions: Glue and screw the 1-by-4-in. boards together, as shown in Figure 33.30. Bore the proper-sized holes in the boards with a brace and bit, and glue or screw the pegs into the holes. Note that two blocks must be screwed on the ends of the board placed on top so that the target stands level. Paint the base and the sticks, and if desired, number the sticks according to point value.

Sit-and-Reach Box

Sit-and-reach boxes are used for measuring flexibility in the Fitnessgram test. The basic sit-and-reach box is a 12-in. cube with a top that is 21 in. long. Sit-and-reach boxes for the Fitnessgram test require that the top of the box be calibrated in inches. The 9-in. mark is lined up with the side of the box where the feet are placed. Figure 33.31 shows a sit-and-reach box that is calibrated in both inches and centimeters. It is available from the Robert Widen Company, P.O. Box 2075, Prescott, AZ 86302.

Tire Stands

Tire stands keep tires in an upright position (Figure 33.32). The upright tires can be used for movement problems, over-and-through relays, and vaulting activities, and as targets. Tires are much cleaner and more attractive when they are painted both inside and out.

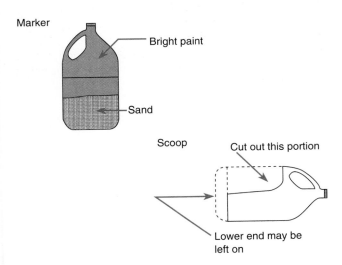

Figure 33.28 Plastic marker and scoop

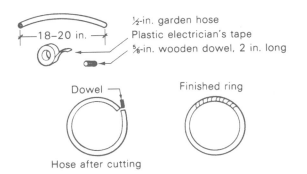

Figure 33.29 Ring construction

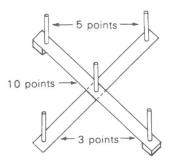

Figure 33.30 Ring toss target construction

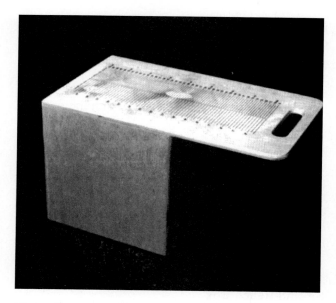

Figure 33.31 Sit and reach box with centimeters and inches scale

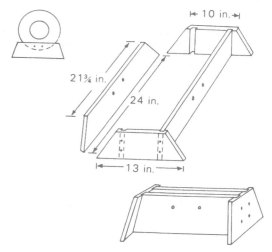

Figure 33.32 Tire stand construction

Materials:

Two 1-by-6-in. boards, 24 in. long, for side pieces

Two 1-by-6-in. boards, 13 in. long, for end pieces

Four ⅜-in. carriage bolts, 2 in. long

Glue, screws, and paint

One used tire

Directions: Cut the ends of the side boards at a 70-degree angle. Dado each end piece with two grooves ¾ in. wide and ¼ in. deep. The distance between the grooves is determined by the width of the tire. Round off the corners and sand the edges. Glue and screw the stand together. Install the tire in the frame by drilling two ⅜-in. holes in each side of the frame and in the tire. Secure the tire inside the frame with the bolts. Paint both the tire and the frame a bright color. Note that the frame dimensions will vary according to the size of the tire, making it necessary to adjust the frame dimensions to the tire.

Track Starter

The track starter simulates a gun report. If many starters are made, the children can start their own races.

Materials:

Two 2-by-4-in. boards, 11 in. long

Two small strap hinges

Two small cabinet handles

Directions: Cut the boards to size, and sand off any rough edges. Place the two blocks together, and apply the two hinges with screws. Add the two handles on the outside of the boards. Open the boards and then slam them together quickly to obtain a loud bang (Figure 33.33).

Wands

Handles from old brooms or mops make excellent wands (Figure 33.34). The handles may have dif-

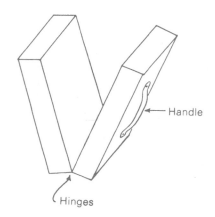

Figure 33.33 Track starter

⅝-in. or ¾-in. doweling

Lengths: grades K–1 = 30 in., 2–3 = 36 in., 4–6 = 42 in. or 1 m

Figure 33.34 Wand dimensions

ferent diameters, but this is not an important factor. The ends can be sanded and the wands painted different colors. If noise is a concern, rubber crutch tips can be placed on the wand ends.

Yarn Balls

Yarn balls can be used to enhance throwing and catching skills and for many games. They have an advantage over balls in that they do not hurt when they hit a child, and they can be used in the classroom or in other areas of limited space. Yarn balls can be made by the older children or by the PTA. Two construction methods are offered here; both work well. When possible, wool or cotton yarns should be used, because the balls will then shrink and become tight when soaked in hot water or steamed. Nylon and other synthetic yarns are impervious to water and so do not shrink and bond.

Materials for Method One:

One skein of yarn per ball

One piece of box cardboard, 5 in. wide and about 10 in. long

Strong, light cord for binding

Directions for Method One: Wrap the yarn 20 to 25 times around the 5-in.-wide dimension of the cardboard. Slide the yarn off the cardboard, and bind it in the middle with the cord to form a tied loop of yarn. Continue this procedure until all of the yarn is used up and tied in looped bunches. Next, take two of the tied loops and tie them together at the center, using several turns of the cord. This forms a bundle of two tied loops, as illustrated in Figure 33.35. Continue tying the bundles together until all are used. Now cut the loops and trim the formed ball. The cutting should be done carefully so that the yarn lengths are reasonably even, or considerable trimming will be needed.

Materials for Method Two:

Two skeins of yarn per ball

Two cardboard doughnuts, 5 or 6 in. in diameter

Strong, light cord for tying

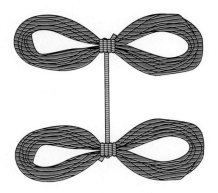

Figure 33.35 Yarn ball, method one

Directions for Method Two: Make a slit in the doughnuts so that the yarn can be wrapped around the cardboard. Holding strands from both skeins, wrap the yarn around both doughnuts until the center hole is almost completely filled with yarn (Figure 33.36). Lay the doughnut of wrapped yarn on a flat surface, insert a pair of scissors between the two doughnuts, and cut around the entire outer edge. Carefully insert a double strand of the light cord between the two doughnuts and catch all of the individual yarn strands around the middle with the cord. Tie the cord as tightly as possible with a double knot. Remove the doughnuts and trim the ball if necessary.

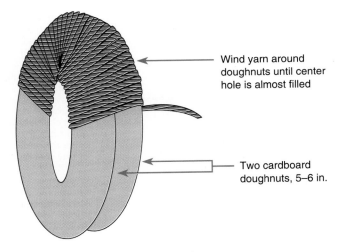

Wind yarn around doughnuts until center hole is almost filled

Two cardboard doughnuts, 5–6 in.

Figure 33.36 Yarn ball, method two

REFERENCES AND SUGGESTED READINGS

U.S. Consumer Product Safety Commission. (1986a). *A handbook for public playground safety, Vol. I.* Washington, DC: Author.

U.S. Consumer Product Safety Commission. (1986b). *A handbook for public playground safety, Vol. II.* Washington, DC: Author.

General Index _____

Activities Index ⎯⎯⎯⎯⎯⎯⎯